MEXICO

This thirteenth edition updated by
Robert Savage

Based on original text by
Stephen Keeling, Shafik Meghji, Robert Savage and Daniel Stables

Contents

RUINS OF THE ANCIENT MAYAN CITY OF CALAKMUL, CAMPECHE

Introduction to **Mexico**

The home of tacos, Aztecs, sombreros and tequila, not to mention Pancho Villa, Salma Hayek and Frida Kahlo: almost everyone on the planet knows something about Mexico. Yet there's far more to this country than the stereotypes. One of the world's great civilizations, Mexico offers a tantalizing blend of Mesoamerican cultures, Spanish traditions and contemporary arts. Its landscapes range from the shimmering blue coastline of Baja California and the iconic cactus-strewn deserts of the north, to the Maya villages and gorgeous palm-smothered beaches of the south. You can climb volcanoes, watch whales, sunbathe on golden beaches and tour agave farms. And sprinkled throughout you'll find richly adorned colonial churches, giant pyramids and some of the tastiest food in the world.

The 130 million people of Mexico reflect this variety, too. Indigenous communities represent around ten percent of the population, with the Nahua, Maya, Zapotec, Mixtec, Otomí and Totonac the largest groups. There are also a few Mexicans of predominantly **Spanish** or European descent, invariably forming the ranks of the mega-rich, even if billionaire Carlos Slim (see page 8) actually has Lebanese ancestry. The great majority of the population (over eighty percent), though, is **mestizo**, with a mix of European, African, Middle Eastern, Asian and Indigenous heritage. Add in a multitude of distinct regional identities, from the cowboy culture of the northern deserts to the Mesoamerican traditions of the south, and you have a thrilling, constantly surprising place to travel.

Despite the inevitable influence of the US, looming to the north, and close links with the rest of the Spanish-speaking world (an avid audience for Mexican pop and soap operas), the country remains resolutely individual. The music that fills the plazas in the evenings, the buildings that circle around them, even the smells emanating from a row of taco carts: they all leave you without any doubt about where you are.

DAY OF THE DEAD CELEBRATIONS IN VERACRUZ

Mexico has a fairly robust economy, the world's twelfth largest, a remarkably thorough and efficient internal transport system and a vibrant contemporary arts and music scene. Indeed, in the past thirty years or so Mexico has largely become a **middle-class society**, perhaps the country's greatest achievement since Independence. Mexico has the highest GDP in Latin America after Brazil, but huge inequalities of wealth remain and it is far from all suburbs and SUVs.

Adventure in Mexico can be found through happening upon a **village fiesta**, complete with rowdy singing and dancing, or hopping on a rural bus, packed with farmers all carrying machetes half their height and curious about how you've wound up going their way. It's also true that Mexico is not always an easy place to travel around. The power may go off, the water may not be drinkable and occasionally it can seem that there's incessant, inescapable noise and dirt. Although the *mañana* mentality is largely an outsiders' myth, rural Mexico is still a land where timetables are not always to be entirely trusted, where anything that can break down will break down (often when it's most needed) and where any attempt to do things in a hurry is liable to be frustrated.

More deeply disturbing are the extremes of wealth and poverty that still exist, most poignantly in the big cities, where unemployment is high and living conditions beyond crowded, as well as the ongoing **drug wars** that provide a seemingly non-stop stream of sensational, often gruesome, headlines. While the

USA

San Diego
Tijuana
Mexicali
Ensenada
Phoenix
Tucson
Sonoita
Nogales
Agua Prieta
El Paso
Ciudad Juárez
HWY 1
HWY 45
Río Bravo
Río Grande
Hermosillo
Guerrero Negro
Guaymas
Ciudad Obregón
Alamos
Creel
Barranca del Cobre
Chihuahua
Santa Rosalía
Hidalgo del Parral
Jiménez
Sea of Cortez
Los Mochis
Torreón
HWY 40
Culiacán
Tropic of Cancer
La Paz
Durango
Cabo San Lucas
SanJosé delCabo
Mazatlán
Zacatecas
Aguascalientes
San Blas
Tepic
León
Guadalajara
Guanajuato
Puerto Vallarta
Lagunade Chapala
Morelia
Pátzcuaro
HWY 200
Uruapan
Barra de Navidad
Colima
Manzanillo
Lázaro Cárdenas
Ixtapa
Zihuatanejo

PACIFIC OCEAN

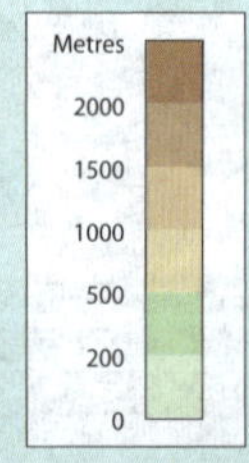

MEXICO
Fort Worth
Dallas
20
35
Austin
New Orleans
Houston
Ciudad Acuña
Del Rio
San Antonio
Eagle Pass
Piedras Negras
Nuevo Laredo
Laredo
Río Grande
HWY 85
McAllen
Río Bravo
Brownsville
Reynosa
Matamoros
Saltillo
Monterrey
Real de Catorce
Ciudad Victoria
Tropic of Cancer
GULF OF MEXICO
Tampico
San Luis Potosí
HWY 180
San Miguel de Allende
Querétaro
Tuxpán
Tula
Pachuca
El Tajín
Teotihuacán
Xalapa
MEXICO CITY
Veracruz
Toluca
Cuernavaca
Puebla
Córdoba
HWY 135
Bahía de Campeche
Coatzacoalcos
Villahermosa
Oaxaca
Monte Albán
Mitla
Acapulco
HWY 200
Puerto Escondido
Puerto Ángel
Huatulco
Tehuantepec
Golfo de Tehuantepec
Tuxtla Gutiérrez
San Cristóbal de las Casas
Palenque
Yaxchilán
HWY 190
Tapachula
GUATEMALA
BELIZE
HONDURAS
EL SALVADOR
Calakmul
Chetumal
HWY 186
Campeche
HWY 180
Uxmal
Mérida
Progreso
Chichén Itzá
Valladolid
Cobá
Tulum
HWY 307
Cancún
Cozumel
0
200
kilometres

FACT FILE

- The world's **richest person** in the 2010–2013 period was Mexican: Carlos Slim Helú is thought to be worth around US$82 billion thanks to his holdings in companies such as Telmex and América Móvil.
- Because it is built on an ancient lake bed, **Mexico City is sinking** at a rate of 15–20cm per year.
- Mexico is the **home of chocolate** (from the Náhuatl "xocolatl"), chiles and maize (corn), though it exports more tomatoes than any other crop (also derived from the Náhuatl word "tomatl").
- The Chihuahua is officially the **world's smallest breed of dog** and really is named after the Mexican state of Chihuahua.
- Bugs have been **culinary delicacies** in Mexico since Aztec times, with some of the most popular *cocopaches* (a type of cockroach), *chicatanas* (flying ants) and *escamoles* (ant larvae and pupae).
- Some 66 million years ago the Chicxulub asteroid crashed into the Yucatán Peninsula, dramatically disrupting the climate around the world and triggering the extinction of the dinosaurs.

violence is very real in some parts of the country and it pays to be vigilant, the danger for tourists is generally minimal – for the most part, you'll find this is a friendly, varied and enormously enjoyable place in which to travel. Mexico is a country that draws you back again and again.

Where to go

Mexico City, though a nightmare of urban sprawl, is totally fascinating, and in every way – artistic, political, cultural – the capital of the nation. Around the city lie the chief relics of the pre-Hispanic cultures of central Mexico: the massive pyramids of **Teotihuacán** and the main Toltec site at **Tula. Guadalajara**, to the west, is a city on a more human scale, capital of the state of **Jalisco** and in easy reach of **Michoacán**: between them, these states share some of the most gently scenic country in Mexico, where the thickly forested hills are studded with lakes and ancient villages.

South of the capital, the states of Oaxaca and Chiapas, home to some of the largest populations of pure Indigenous groups, are mountainous and beautiful, too, but in a far wilder way. The city of **Oaxaca** is especially enticing, with an extraordinary mix of colonial and Indigenous life, superb markets and fascinating archeological sites. Likewise, the strength of Indigenous traditions in and around the market city of **San Cristóbal de las Casas** in Chiapas continues to make it a big travellers' centre. It's typically the stop before the picturesque Maya ruins of **Palenque**. East into the **Yucatán** there is also traditional Indigenous life, side by side with a tourist industry based around truly magnificent Maya cities – **Chichén Itzá** and **Uxmal** above all – and the burgeoning Caribbean resorts that stretch down the coast, most notably **Cancún and Playa del Carmen**.

On the Pacific coast, where the surf is wilder and the scenery more rugged than in the Caribbean, **Acapulco** is the best known of the beach destinations. Along the ocean to the north, hundreds of kilometres of relatively empty sand are broken up only by resort cities like **Mazatlán** and **Puerto Vallarta**. Relatively few tourists venture over to the Gulf coast, despite the attractions of **Veracruz** and its mysterious

VIBRANTLY PAINTED HOUSES IN GUANAJUATO'S HISTORIC OLD TOWN

MEXICO'S MAGNIFICENT MARKETS

The colour and bustle of Mexico's **markets** is hard to beat. Even if you have no intention of buying, half an hour is always well spent meandering through narrow aisles surrounded by heaps of perfectly ripe fruit and stacks of *nopal* cactus leaves (though stay away from the meat sections if you're at all squeamish). In small villages, like those around Oaxaca (see page 587), inhabitants still recognize one day of the week as the traditional market day.

Towns of any size will have a market, usually daily, an important centre of local life and source of cheap eats (San Cristóbal de las Casas and Papantla are good examples), while in the cities, each *barrio* has its own vibrant mercado: among the best are Mexico City's **La Merced** (see page 135) and the arts and crafts-oriented Ciudadela (see page 134). Markets in San Miguel Allende are also better known for arts and crafts (see page 324), as are Oaxaca's city **mercados** (see page 574). Toluca (see page 189) is the mother of them all, Mexico's largest market held every Friday.

ruins. A pity, as for music and general bonhomie, the city's central plaza is one of the country's finest destinations.

Coming through the **Bajío**, the heart of the country, you'll pass the beautiful silver-mining towns of **Zacatecas** and **Guanajuato**, the historic centres of **San Miguel de Allende** and **Querétaro**, and many smaller places with a legacy of superb colonial architecture. Between here and the US border lie vast deserts and mountain ranges, home to the **Copper Canyon**, with its spectacular rail journey, the mysterious ruins at **Paquimé** and the dynamic industrial city of **Monterrey**. **Baja California** in the far

MEXICO'S BEST BEACHES

Mexico boasts a mesmerizing **coastline** of around 9330km, with millions of tourists coming here solely for the country's exceptional **beaches**. The following have been selected as much for the scene – whether backpacker or spring-breaker – as for sand quality, water and scenery.

Playa Cacaluta Wonderfully isolated Huatulco beach, accessible only by boat. See page 614

Mahahual A real castaway, end-of-the-world beach. See page 768

Playa La Audiencia, **Manzanillo Bay** Perfect cove of honey-coloured sands. See page 220

Playa de Balandra, **La Paz** Family-friendly, shallow lagoons of crystal-clear water. See page 543

Playa Maruata, **Michoacán** Long, wild and mostly empty, save for nesting green turtles at certain times of the year. See page 217

Playa El Requesón Gorgeous spit of sand jutting into the Sea of Cortez and surrounded by cactus-spiked mountains. See page 537

Playa La Ropa, Zihuatanejo Classic Pacific resort beach, hemmed in by palm trees. See page 210

Tulum Maya ruins, pristine Caribbean waters and silky sands. See page 758

Yelapa, **Puerto Vallarta** Another beach only accessible by boat, lined with fun bars and palapa restaurants. See page 240

Zipolite This laid-back beach is a great place just to chill out. See page 609 northwest of Mexico is a major destination in its own right, with world-class whale watching, untrammelled beaches and crumbling Spanish ruins.

When to go

Summer, from June to October, is in theory the **rainy season** in Mexico, but just how wet it is varies wildly from place to place. In the heart of the country you can expect a heavy but short-lived downpour virtually every afternoon; in the north hardly any rain falls, ever. Chiapas is the wettest state, with many minor roads washed out in the autumn, and in the south and low-lying coastal areas summer is stickily humid too. Along the beaches, September to mid-November is **hurricane season** – you'll usually get wet weather, choppy seas and mosquitoes, if not a full-on tropical storm. Late **winter** is the traditional tourist season, and in the big resorts like Acapulco and Cancún, the months from December through to April are the busiest. Mountain areas, though, can get very cold then; in fact, nights in the mountains can be extremely cold at any time of year.

Visitors come all year round – sticking on the whole to the highlands in summer and the coasts in winter. November is probably the ideal time to visit, with the rains over, the land still fresh and the peak season not yet begun.

CLIMATE

	Jan	Mar	May	Jul	Sep	Nov
ACAPULCO						
Max/Min (°C)	31/22	31/22	32/25	33/25	32/25	32/24
Max/Min (F)	88/72	88/72	90/77	91/77	90/77	90/75
Rainfall (mm)	13	5	0	203	279	15
MÉRIDA						
Max/Min (°C)	28/18	32/20	34/21	33/23	32/23	29/19
Max/Min (F)	22/64	90/68	93/70	91/73	90/73	84/66
Rainfall (mm)	25	13	76	127	178	25
MEXICO CITY						
Max/Min (°C)	22/6	27/10	27/13	24/13	23/13	23/9
Max/Min (F)	72/43	81/50	81/55	75/55	73/55	73/48
Rainfall (mm)	13	13	76	152	127	13
OAXACA						
Max/Min (°C)	28/8C	32/12	32/15	28/15	27/15	28/10
Max/Min (F)	82/46	90/54	90/59	82/59	81/59	82/50
Rainfall (mm)	51	25	127	203	279	51
TIJUANA						
Max/Min (°C)	20/6	21/8	23/12	27/16	27/16	23/10
Max/Min (F)	268/43	70/46	73/54	81/61	81/61	73/50F
Rainfall (mm)	51	25	5	2	13	25

Author picks

Surviving 42-degree desert heat, tramping hurricane-battered Pacific beaches and scaling lofty volcanoes, our hard-travelling authors have visited every corner of this vast, magnificent country – from the ancient caves of Baja California to the dense rainforest of the Lacandón Jungle. Here are a few of their favourite things:

Dawn by kayak Paddling through the glassy, desert-backed waters of Bahía Concepción as the sun rises, surrounded by marine life, is an otherworldly experience (see page 537).

Hit the Road Driving Hwy-1, from the US border to the southern tip of Baja California, through deserts, isolated mountain ranges and tropical beach towns, rates as one of the world's greatest road journeys (see page 511).

Death-defying cliff divers A dazzling display of skill and courage takes place four times a day in Acapulco (see page 207), when the resident *clavadistas* throw themselves from the rocky cliffs of La Quebrada – with a somersault or two thrown in for good measure.

Subterranean swimming The *cenotes* of northern Yucatán are magical places for a refreshing dip; X'keken and Samula are two of the best (see page 726).

A window onto the Aztec world Rent a boat and soak up the carnival atmosphere, flowers and traditional floating gardens at the Mexico City suburb of Xochimilco (see page 113).

Go syncretic The Iglesia de San Juan Bautista (see page 647), in the village of San Juan Chamula, Chiapas, is an incredibly vibrant blend of Catholicism and animist tradition, with the local Maya praying on a floor of pine needles.

Best underground club You can't get more underground than *La Mina Club* (see page 363) in Zacatecas – it's inside the old El Edén mine shafts.

Microbreweries Baja California's expanding craft-beer scene can be sampled at *Plaza Fiesta* (see page 517), *Cervecería Wendlandt* (see page 523) in Ensenada and *Baja Brewing Co* in San José del Cabo (see page 555).

Our author recommendations don't end here. We've flagged up our favourite places – a perfectly sited hotel, an atmospheric café, a special restaurant – throughout the Guide, highlighted with the ★ symbol.

LA PAZ BEACH, BAJA CALIFORNIA SUR

IGLESIA DE SAN JUAN BAUTISTA, SAN JUAN CHAMULA

30 things not to miss

It's not possible to see everything Mexico has to offer in one trip – and we don't suggest you try. What follows, in no particular order, is a selective taste of the country's highlights: ancient ruins, vibrant cities and spectacular landscapes. All highlights are colour-coded by chapter and have a page reference to take you straight into the Guide, where you can find out more.

1 GUANAJUATO

See page 334

This gorgeous colonial town, sandwiched into a narrow ravine, is home to one of the country's finest Baroque churches, a thriving student scene and a relaxed café and bar culture.

2 SILVER JEWELLERY FROM TAXCO

See page 182

The town of Taxco, an interesting place in itself, offers the most exquisite silver products in the country.

3 SIAN KA'AN BIOSPHERE RESERVE

See page 765

A huge, stunning coastal nature reserve with ecosystems ranging from tropical forest through fresh- and saltwater marshes to barrier reef. Wildlife of every sort lives here, but it's especially good for bird watching.

4 TEQUILA

See page 268

Visit the town that gave birth to Mexico's favourite tipple, surrounded by fields of blue agave, and enjoy tours of local distilleries.

5 THE BONAMPAK MURALS

See page 666

The ancient temples at Bonampak, in the far south of Mexico, depict vivid scenes of Maya life.

6 BAJA BEACHES

See page 537

Tour the Sea of Cortez beaches along Bahía Concepción, whose pristine azure waters contrast with desert-fringed mountains.

7 EL TAJÍN

See page 406

Once the most important city on the Gulf coast but only rediscovered in 1785.

8 DIVING OFF COZUMEL

See page 755

Mexico has fantastic diving opportunities: the coral reefs off Isla Cozumel provide some of the best.

9 BAJA WHALE WATCHING

See pages 531 and 533

Between December and April, thousands of grey whales come to mate in the lagoons of Guerrero Negro and San Ignacio.

10 REAL DE CATORCE

See page 372

This extraordinary ghost-town once thrived on the wealth of its silver mines.

9

11 THE ZÓCALO, MEXICO CITY

See page 71

The eternal heart of the city, the capital's main plaza is surrounded by its cathedral and the ruins of Aztec Tenochtitlán.

12 VOLADORES DE PAPANTLA

See page 405

An ancient religious ritual, this gravity-defying dance is still mesmerizing.

13 CALAKMUL

See page 776

Deep in the heart of the jungle, this is the largest-known archeological zone in Mesoamerica.

14 TULUM

See page 758

This fashionable town boasts a picturesque Maya site overlooking a spectacular beach, plus an array of great places to stay, eat and drink.

15 CENOTES, VALLADOLID

See page 726

Take a refreshing dip in crystal-clear sinkholes, one with the roots of a huge alamo tree stretching down into it.

13

16

16 MUSEO FRIDA KAHLO

See page 106

Politics, art and national identity combine at the home of Frida Kahlo and Diego Rivera.

17 MARIACHI

See page 134

You'll find mariachi played the length and breadth of the country but most notably in Mexico City's Plaza Garibaldi.

18 PALENQUE

See page 657

This Maya site is remarkable for its distinctive architectural style and its setting in jungle-smothered hills.

19 CHICHÉN ITZÁ

See page 719

The most famous of the Maya cities. See the sprawling ruins and complex carvings over a couple of days.

20 THE RIVERA MURALS

See page 76

Diego Rivera's murals at the Palacio Nacional in Mexico City.

17

18

19

20

21

22

23

21 MUSEO NACIONAL DE ANTROPOLOGÍA

See page 97

An enormous collection of artefacts from all the major pre-Hispanic cultures.

22 NIGHTLIFE IN PLAYA DEL CARMEN

See page 750

Dance on the sand or in super-hip small clubs alongside stylish Mexico City weekenders and European expats in this Caribbean boomtown.

23 XOCHIMILCO

See page 113

Take in the carnival atmosphere and colours while being punted around the canals and serenaded by mariachi bands.

24 PYRAMID OF THE SUN, TEOTIHUACÁN

See page 145

The granddaddy of all ancient Mesoamerican pyramids, built in 100 AD and some 70m high.

25 LAGO DE PÁTZCUARO

See page 286

Most famous for its Day of the Dead celebrations, this enchanting lake is a worthy destination year-round.

26
27
28

26 OAXACA MARKETS

See page 574

Any market in Mexico is a feast for the senses, but Oaxaca's are especially vibrant, with everything from fresh produce to some of the country's most imaginative textiles.

27 MÉRIDA

See page 697

The capital of Yucatán state, nicknamed the "White City", has a gorgeous historic centre filled with architectural gems, plus a lively cultural scene.

28 ZACATECAS

See page 355

Ancient silver mines, thrilling ziplines and one of Mexico's most opulent cathedrals.

29 CHARREADA

See page 54

The ultimate *charro* (cowboy) event, traditional *charreadas* (rodeos) make a brilliant spectator sport.

30 THE COPPER CANYON

See page 482

Whether you take the awe-inspiring train ride or hike along the canyon floor, a visit to this vast system of chasms is a definite highlight.

29

30

Itineraries

The following itineraries span the entire length of this incredibly diverse country, from the deserts and jaw-dropping canyons of the north to the grand colonial cities of the centre and the Maya ruins, beaches and jungles of the south. Given the vast distances involved, you may not be able to cover everything, but even picking a few highlights will give you a deeper insight into Mexico's natural and historic wonders. The trips below give a flavour of what the country has to offer and what we can plan and book for you at http://roughguides.com/trips.

CLASSIC MEXICO

This three-week tour focuses on the southern and central parts of the country, traditionally the most popular targets for independent travellers.

❶ **Mexico City** Soak up the museums, murals and markets of the nation's crazy, high-octane capital, leaving a couple of days for Cholula and Teotihuacán. See page 66

❷ **Oaxaca** Head to Mexico's most enticing state, its capital the best place to sample *mole*, mescal and Indigenous crafts. See page 564

❸ **Zapotec and Mixtec heartland** After the obligatory visit to Monte Albán, spend two to three days exploring the Indigenous markets and ruins around Oaxaca. See page 584

❹ **Palenque** Heading north, these are some of the grandest jungle-smothered Maya ruins in the country, all easily accessible from the town of the same name. See page 657

❺ **Yaxchilan and Bonampak** From Palenque you can strike out into the Lacandón Maya heartland and these more isolated, romantic ruins. See pages 668 and 664

❻ **Tulum** Back on the Yucatán mainland enjoy the stunning beach, enigmatic ruins and top eating and drinking options at the hippest spot on the Riviera Maya. See page 758

❼ **Chichén Itzá and cenotes** End your trip by soaking up Mexico's most magical Maya ruins followed by a dip in a giant limestone sinkhole. See pages 719 and 726

THE GREAT OUTDOORS

Mexico is home to exceptionally varied landscapes and ecosystems, but you can get a decent taster in two to three weeks.

❶ **Whale watching in Baja** Witness the annual grey whale migration from the central Baja towns of Guerrero Negro and San Ignacio. See pages 531 and 533

❷ **Bahía Concepción** South of Mulegé lie the finest beaches in Baja, perfect for kayaking or just lounging on the sands. See page 537

❸ **Isla Espíritu Santo** Take a day trip from La Paz to see sea lions, dolphins, manta rays and whale sharks. See page 541

❹ **Copper Canyon Railway** Take the ferry from La Paz to Los Mochis and the terminus for this train ride into the mountains. See page 482

❺ **Hiking in the Sierra Tarahumara** Jump off the Copper Canyon railway to explore remote trailsand Rarámuri settlements. See page 490

❻ **Costalegre** Continue south along the Pacific to the wildest, least-developed stretch of Mexican coast. See page 225

❼ **Climbing volcanoes** Head inland to conquer the majestic peak of the Nevado de Colima, or check out volcanic activity at Popocatépetl. See pages 224 and 170

❽ **Rafting at Jalcomulco** End up on Mexico's Gulf coast near Xalapa for whitewater rafting, climbing and canyoning. See page 387

RUTA DE LA PLATA (THE SILVER ROUTE)

Spanish Mexico was fuelled by silver, leaving a rich architectural and cultural legacy in the heart of the country. Take at least two weeks to travel this route between Mexico City and Monterrey.

❶ **Taxco** Start by loading up on jewellery at Mexico's silver capital, just south of Mexico City, a confection of cobbled alleys and colonial, whitewashed homes. See page 180

❷ **Real del Monte, Hidalgo** Head north of Mexico City to this charming mountain retreat, an old mining town with a curious Cornish connection. See page 155

❸ **Guanajuato** Continue into the Bajío to enjoy the cafés, bars, restored mining shafts and creepy nineteenth-century mummies of this grand colonial silver town. See page 334

❹ **San Miguel Allende** Take the short bus ride to the most beautifully preserved and cosmopolitan town in the Bajío, crammed with art galleries and craft stalls. See page 321

❺ **Pozos** This crumbling mining community is a less developed, more romantic version of San Miguel, home to vast, abandoned mine workings. See page 333

❻ **San Luis Potosí** Dynamic city with elegant Baroque buildings and museums dedicated to sculptor Federico Silva. See page 366

❼ **Zacatecas** The capital of the northern Bajío is rich in silver history, with the restored El Edén mine, silversmith school and spectacular art collections. See page 355

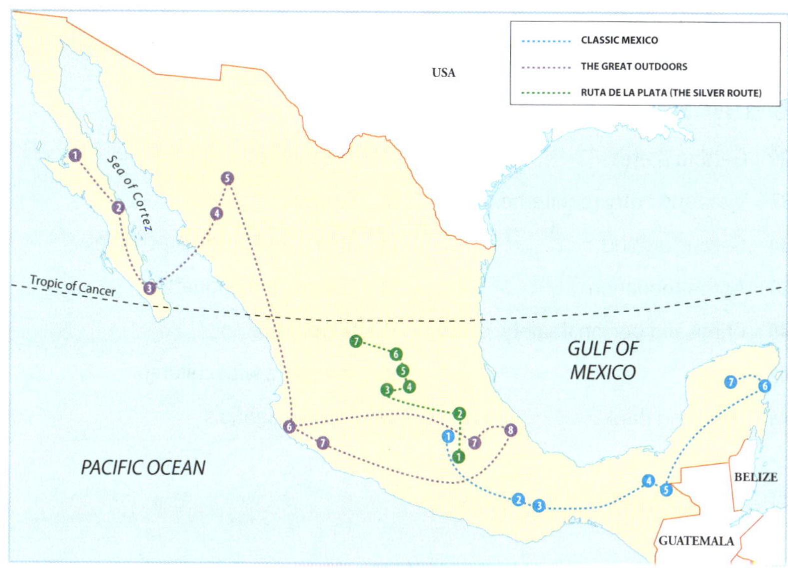

THE ARCH (EL ARCO) OF CABO SAN LUCAS

Basics

Getting there

The quickest and easiest way to get to Mexico is to fly. If you're willing to have your journey take a little longer, it is also possible to travel overland from the US via train, bus or car, or by water – several cruise lines stop along the country's Pacific and (to a lesser extent) Caribbean coasts.

To some extent, airfares to Mexico depend on the **season**. Ticket prices to Mexico City and other non-resort destinations show little, if any, fluctuation. Some fares though, especially to resort areas, do vary; they tend to be highest around Easter, from early June to mid-September and at Christmras and New Year. Prices may drop during the "shoulder" seasons – mid-September to early November and late April to early June – and the best deals are usually available during the low season (November to March, excluding Christmas and New Year). Flying at weekends can also sometimes add to round-trip fares, however if you book far enough in advance you can often avoid paying more. At the time of writing, schedules were still being affected by the Covid-19 pandemic, making prices even more unpredictable.

Flights from the US and Canada

From most places in North America, flying is the most convenient way to reach Mexico. There are **flights** from just about every major **US** city, with the least expensive and most frequent leaving from "gateway" cities in the south and west, especially Dallas, Houston, Los Angeles, Miami and Orlando. If you live close to the border, it's usually cheaper to cross into Mexico and take an **internal flight**. If it's a resort that you want, you may well find that one of the airlines offers an attractive deal including a few nights' accommodation.

Aeroméxico (http://aeromexico.com/en) flies direct to dozens of destinations in Mexico, and can make connections to many others. The bigger US airlines – especially American Airlines (http://aa.com), Delta (http://delta.com) and United (http://united.com) – have connections to Mexico City and the more popular resorts from all over the US. Budget Mexican airlines, such as Viva Aerobus (http://vivaaerobus.com) and Volaris (http://volaris.mx), also run flights into Mexico from a handful of American cities.

For the lowest-priced round trip to Mexico City or Cancún in high season, travelling from the US, try to fly out of Dallas, Miami, Houston, New York or LA. There are direct flights to many parts of Mexico from numerous other US airports, but adding a feeder flight from any US or Canadian city to one of the main gateways should be straightforward. The Delta hub in Atlanta is also a good origin point if you're looking for the best deal in high season.

There are fewer direct scheduled flights from **Canada** to Mexico, although Air Canada (http://aircanada.com) flies to Mexico City from Montréal, Toronto and Vancouver, and Aeroméxico flies there from Montréal. Air Canada also serves Cancún from Toronto and Montréal. However, the biggest choice of direct flights is offered by WestJet (http://westjet.com), which does not serve Mexico City, but does have flights to Cancún and several other beach resorts from a number of Canadian airports, supplemented in some cases by Sunwing (http://flysunwing.com), Air Transat (http://airtransat.ca), and winter charter flights. Flying via the US expands your options further.

To bag the lowest high-season round-trip fares to Mexico City or Cancún try to fly out of Toronto, Montreal or Vancouver and reserve your tickets as far in advance as possible.

Flights from the UK and Ireland

BA (http://britishairways.com) has direct scheduled flights from London to Mexico City and Cancún; Virgin (http://virgin-atlantic.com) has direct flights to Cancún. There are also (generally cheaper) charter flights to Cancún from Gatwick, Birmingham and Manchester with TUI (http://tui.co.uk) and Thomas Cook (http://thomascook.com). Flying from anywhere else in the UK or Ireland, or to any other destination in Mexico, you will have to change planes somewhere.

A BETTER KIND OF TRAVEL

At Rough Guides we are passionately committed to travel. We believe it helps us understand the world we live in and the people we share it with – and of course tourism is vital to many developing economies. But the scale of modern tourism has also damaged some places irreparably, and climate change is accelerated by most forms of transport, especially flying. We encourage all our authors to consider the carbon footprint of the journeys they make in the course of researching our guides.

ROUGH GUIDES ONLINE

Find everything you need to plan your next trip at http://roughguides.com. Read in-depth information on destinations worldwide, make use of our unique trip-planner, book transport and accommodation, check out other travellers' recommendations and share your own experiences.

Even from London, although a direct flight is easiest, it can be cheaper to take an indirect flight with a European or US carrier. From other British and Irish airports, you can either fly via London with BA, or use a European or North American airline, changing planes at their hub cities (Air Europa, for example, codeshares with Aeroméxico via Madrid; http://aireuropa.com). Another possibility is to fly via the US and either continue overland or buy an onward flight once in the country. LA and Houston are logical points from which to set off overland, and, along with Miami, have reasonably priced onward flights to several Mexican destinations. **Prices** for scheduled return flights from London to Mexico City are lowest in the winter off-season, but peak in price during the month of August. Charter flights to Cancún are also at their most affordable in the low season, cost the most in August, and your stay will probably be limited to one or two weeks.

From Australia, New Zealand and South Africa

The **high season** for flights to Mexico from the southern hemisphere is mid-June to mid-July and mid-December to mid-January, though prices do not vary vastly between seasons. There are no direct flights to Mexico from Australia, New Zealand or South Africa, so you will have to change planes somewhere en route.

From **Australia**, your widest choice of airlines is out of Sydney, where there are flights to Mexico with Delta (http://delta.com) via LA or Houston, with United (http://united.com) via LA, with Air Canada (http://aircanada.com) via Vancouver, or with Latam Airlines (http:// latamairlines.com) via Santiago de Chile. United also serve Melbourne. Otherwise, you can fly with Qantas (http://qantas.com.au) from almost any Australian airport to LA, continuing to Mexico with an American or Mexican airline.

From **New Zealand**, your choice is very similar: Air Canada via Vancouver, an American airline via LA or Auckland to LA with Air New Zealand (http://airnewzealand.com), continuing with a Mexican or American airline. From other New Zealand airports, you will probably need to change planes additionally at Auckland or Sydney. Prices vary however the best deals can be booked up to a year in advance.

From **South Africa**, your most direct route is with Delta or United from Johannesburg via the US, or on SAA (http://flysaa.com) in combination with an American or Mexican airline. You can also fly with a European airline such as KLM (http://klm.com), Lufthansa (http://lufthansa.com) or British Airways (http://britishairways.com) via their hubs in Europe. From other South African airports, you'll usually have to fly via Johannesburg. Fares will vary according to the season.

Trains

US passenger **train** services reach the border at El Paso, on the LA–Dallas line. El Paso is served by Amtrak's *Sunset Limited* service three times weekly from New Orleans, Houston, Tucson and LA. The *Sunset Limited* also picks up Amtrak's *Texas Eagle* (from Chicago, St Louis, Little Rock and Dallas) overnight at San Antonio. The journey takes just over sixteen hours from LA, nineteen and a half from Houston, or – including an eight-hour layover in San Antonio – 26.5 hours from Dallas and 48.5 hours from Chicago.

Arrivals on these services (around 8am from LA, 4.15pm from Chicago and New Orleans) give you time to cross the border, have something to eat in Ciudad Juárez and catch a bus on to Mexico City.

Check current timetables with Amtrak (1 800 872 7245, http://amtrak.com).

Buses

US **bus** travel is pretty grim compared to the relative comfort of Amtrak, but you have a wider range of US border posts to choose from. Count on at least 52 hours' journey time from New York to El Paso or twelve hours from San Francisco to Tijuana – and at least a further day's travel from either point to Mexico City.

Greyhound (1 800 231 2222 or 1 214 849 8100, http://greyhound.com) runs regularly to all the major border crossings. Some of their buses will also take you over the frontier to a Mexican bus station, which saves a lot of hassle. Greyhound agents abroad should be able to reserve your through tickets with their Mexican counterparts, which is even more convenient but involves pre-planning. Additionally, many Mexican bus companies cross the border into the US, so that you can pick up a bus to Mexico City as far north as Houston or LA.

More countercultural, and arguably better value, are overland tours from San Francisco with Green Tortoise Adventure Travel (http://greentortoise.com). Converted school buses provide reasonably comfortable transport and sleeping space for up to 35 people; the clientele comes from all over the world, and communal alfresco cooking is the rule.

Driving

Taking your own **car** into Mexico will obviously give you a great deal more freedom, but it's an option fraught with complications. Aside from border formalities, you'll also have to contend with the state of the roads, the style of driving and the quality of the fuel.

Licences and permits

Driving licences from the US, Canada, the UK, Ireland, Australia, New Zealand and most European countries are valid in Mexico, but it's a good idea to arm yourself with an **International Driving Licence** – available from motoring organizations such as the AAA in the US, the CAA in Canada or the AA in Britain. If you fall foul of a Mexican traffic cop for any reason, show that first; if they abscond with it you at least still have your own licence.

As a rule, you can drive in Baja California, western Sonora and the Zona Libre (the border area extending roughly 25km into Mexico) without any special formalities. To drive elsewhere in Mexico, however, you must obtain a temporary **importation permit** (for a fee) at the border, or online at http://www.banjercito.com.mx/registrovehiculos.

To make sure you don't sell the car in Mexico or a neighbouring country, you'll also be required to post a cash bond, the amount of which will depend on the make and age of your vehicle, though it will be around US$500 for a car less than five years old. This can be done in cash (US dollars only), or with the credit or debit card of the owner of the vehicle (who must be present), at Banjército, the Mexican army bank, which has offices at border posts specifically for the purpose. You'll need to show registration and title documents for the car, plus your driver's licence and passport, and you'll probably be asked to supply two photocopies of these as well as your tourist card.

The permits are good for 180 days, during which time you can drive your car out of Mexico and return, but there are penalties in force if you exceed the limit, including forfeiture of your vehicle, and you must be sure to have your importation permit terminated

BORDER CROSSINGS

There are some forty **frontier posts** along the US–Mexico border. Many of them are only open during the day, and are more or less inaccessible without your own transport. For a full list, see http://bwt.cbp.gov. The main ones, open 24 hours a day, seven days a week, are, from west to east:

San Diego, California (San Ysidro)–**Tijuana**, Baja California.
Calexico, California–**Mexicali**, Baja California.
Nogales, Arizona–**Nogales**, Sonora.
Douglas, Arizona–**Agua Prieta**, Sonora.
El Paso, Texas–**Ciudad Juárez**, Chihuahua.
Laredo, Texas–**Nuevo Laredo**, Tamaulipas.
Brownsville, Texas–**Matamoros**, Tamaulipas.

BORDER PRACTICALITIES

When crossing the border (especially on foot) it's easy to go straight past the immigration and customs checks. There's a **free zone** south of the frontier, and you can cross at will and stay for up to three days. If, as likely, you're heading further south, however, be sure to stop at the Mexican immigration office, pay the entry fee (*derecho de no inmigrante*), pick up a **tourist card (FMM)**, and get it stamped and your bags checked. Otherwise, you'll be stopped after some 20km and sent back to complete the formalities. See "Entry requirements", see page 32, for more information.

TROUBLED AREAS

The area bordering the US, particularly **Ciudad Juárez**, and also Tijuana, are some of the biggest hot spots in Mexico's **drugs war** (see page 41). Extra caution should be exercised when crossing this area, especially by car.

TOP 5 ARCHEOLOGICAL SITES

Chichén Itzá. See page 719.
Teotihuacán. See page 142.
Palenque. See page 660.
Calakmul See page 776.
Monte Albán. See page 581.

when you finally do leave, or the authorities may assume your vehicle is still in the country; if you write it off while you are in Mexico, you need to inform Mexican customs and obtain permission to leave without it.

Insurance

US and Canadian **auto insurance** policies don't cover Mexico, so you will need to take out a Mexican policy, available from numerous agencies on either side of every border post. Rates depend on the value of the vehicle and what kind of coverage you want, but be sure to set aside a daily budget for basic liability on a short trip. To arrange a policy before leaving the US, contact Instant Mexico Insurance Services (http://instant-mex-auto-insur.com), Oscar Padilla Mexican Insurance (http://mexicaninsurance.com), or the acknowledged leader in the field, Sanborn's Insurance (http://sanborns.com).

To get discounts on insurance, it might be worth joining a travel club, such as Discover Baja Travel Club (http://discoverbaja.com) or Sanborn's Sombrero Club (1 800 222 0158). These clubs typically also offer discounts on accommodation and free travel advice.

The American and Canadian AAs produce road maps and route planners for travel to Mexico, and members may qualify for discounted insurance at affiliated border agencies, but their emergency/breakdown services do not cover you once you are inside Mexico.

Boats

If you want to **sail** to Mexico in your own boat, similar conditions apply to those in effect for motor vehicles (see page 31).

Alternatively, you could take a **cruise**. Several lines offer cruises on the Pacific coast, most popularly between LA and Acapulco, stopping at Los Cabos, Mazatlán, Puerto Vallarta and Zihuatanejo. Others ply the Caribbean side out of Miami, taking in Cozumel, Playa del Carmen and other Mexican destinations. Prices per person (not including drinks) for a week-long cruise, plus airfare are lowest when booked up to a year in advance and go (way) up from there the closer you get to the day of departure. Agencies specializing in cruises include those listed below.

AGENTS AND OPERATORS

Journey Latin America http://journeylatinamerica.co.uk. Well-established Latin America specialists offering a range of itineraries throughout the country, including ones focusing on the country's Maya and Aztec heritage.

My Mexico Tours http://mymexicotours.com. A range of interesting small-group tours, on and off the beaten track, with an emphasis on getting to know the country.

North South Travel http://northsouthtravel.co.uk. Friendly, competitive travel agency, offering discounted fares. Profits are used to support projects in the developing world, especially promoting sustainable tourism.

Red Tag https://redtag.ca/. Canadian youth and student travel firm.

Trailfinders http://trailfinders.com. One of the best-informed and most efficient agents for independent travellers.

USIT http://usit.ie. Ireland's main youth and student travel specialists.

CRUISE LINE CONTACTS

Carnival Cruise Lines http://carnival.com. One of the world's largest and most well connected cruise ship operators.

Holland America http://hollandamerica.com. US based cruise and vacation company with a good range of itineraries for most budgets.

Royal Caribbean Cruises http://royalcaribbean.com. One of the world's largest cruise line operators based out of Miami, Florida.

Visas and entry requirements

Citizens of the US, Canada, the UK, Ireland, Australia, New Zealand, Japan and most EU countries do not need **visas** to enter Mexico as tourists for less than 180 days. Other Europeans can stay for ninety days. Non-US citizens travelling via the US, however, may need a US visa (see page 33).

Visas, obtainable only through a consulate (in person or by mail), are required by nationals of South Africa and many developing countries, as well as by anyone entering Mexico to work, to study or for stays longer than six months. Business visitors usually need a Business Authorization Card available from consulates, but nationals of countries exempt from a tourist visa can enter on business for up to thirty days on a tourist card (see below). For more detailed information on who needs a visa, visit the website of the Instituto Nacional de Migración at inm.gob.mx/spublic/portal/inmex.html.

Tourist cards and the derecho do no inmigrante

All visitors, regardless of nationality, need a valid **passport** and a **tourist card** (or FMM – *Forma Migratoria Múltiple*). The only exception applies to visits of less than three days to the 20km, duty-free strip adjoining the US border, into which you can come and go more or less as you please (though you still need a passport or photo ID). Visitors entering by land and passing beyond this Zona Libre (you'll be sent back at a checkpoint if you haven't been through customs and immigration) are also required to pay a *derecho de no inmigrante* entry fee, payable at a bank. Some land crossings have a bank at the border post, otherwise you'll need to go to a bank to pay it before you leave Mexico.

Tourist cards are otherwise free, and if you're flying direct, you should get one on the plane or from the airline before leaving. A good travel agent should be able to arrange one for you, too, and they're also issued by Mexican consulates (every major US city and most border towns have one), in person or by post. Finally, failing all these options, you should be able to get tourist cards at airports or border crossings on arrival. However, if they've run out, you'll have to twiddle your thumbs until the next batch comes in, and if your passport is not issued by a rich Western country, you may encounter difficulty in persuading border officials to give you a card at all; it's therefore preferable to get one in advance. Entering from Belize or Guatemala, it's not unknown for border posts to run out of tourist cards, or for officials to (illegally) demand a fee for issuing them. To find the address of an embassy or consulate not listed below, see under "Representaciones" at http://sre.gob.mx.

Most people officially need a **passport** to pick up their tourist card, but for US and Canadian citizens entering by land, all that's required is proof of citizenship (an original birth certificate or notarized copy, for instance, or naturalization papers), along with some form of photo ID (such as a driver's licence). Passports are still best, however.

A tourist card is valid for a **single entry** only, so if you intend to enter and leave Mexico more than once you should pick up two or three. On the card, you are asked how long you intend to stay. Always apply for longer than you need, since getting an extension is a frustrating and time-consuming business. You don't always get the time you've asked for, and at land borders with Belize and Guatemala they sometimes only give fifteen or thirty days (though they may give you more if you specifically ask). Immigration officers sometimes ask to see bank statements or other proof of sufficient funds for your stay, especially if they judge that you do not look sufficiently wealthy (or are from a developing country).

Don't lose the tourist card stub that is given back to you after immigration inspection. You are legally required to carry it at all times, and if you have to show your papers, it's more important than your passport. It also has to be handed in on leaving the country – without it, you may encounter problems and delays. Note that, contrary to what crooked border officials may tell you, there is no exit fee when leaving Mexico.

Should you lose your tourist card, or need to have it renewed, head for the nearest **immigration department office** (Departamento de Migración); there are branches in the biggest cities. In the case of renewal, it's far simpler to cross any of Mexico's borders (or even fly to Cuba or Jamaica) for a day and get a new card on re-entry than to apply for an extension; if you do apply to the immigration department, it's wise to do so a couple of weeks in advance, though you may be told to come back nearer the actual expiration date. Whatever else you may be told, branches of SECTUR (the tourist office) cannot renew expired tourist cards or replace lost ones – they will only direct you to the nearest immigration office.

US VISAS

Non-US citizens travelling via the US may need a **US visa**, even if they will only be in the country in transit. Citizens of the UK, Ireland, Australia, New Zealand and most Western European countries can enter under the Visa Waiver Program. Apply well in advance at http://esta.cbp.dhs.gov/esta. South African citizens need to obtain a visa. Visit the website of the US embassy in your country of residence for further details.

MEXICAN CONSULATES AND EMBASSIES ABROAD

Australia 14 Perth Ave, Yarralumla, Canberra, ACT 2600; 02 6273 3947, http://embamex.sre.gob.mx/australia.

Belize Corner of Wilson St and Newtown Barracks, Belize City; 223 0193, http://embamex.sre.gob.mx/belice.

Canada 45 O'Connor St, Suite 1000, Ottawa, ON K1P 1A4; 1 613 233 8988, http://embamex.sre.gob.mx/canada; 2055 Peel, Suite 1000, Montreal, PQ H3A 1V4; 1 514 288 2502, http://consulmex.sre.gob.mx/montreal; 11 King St W, Suite 350, Commerce Court W, Toronto, ON M5H 4C7; 1 416 368 2875, http://consulmex.sre.gob.mx/toronto; 1177 W Hastings St, Suite 411, Vancouver, BC V6E 2K3; 1 604 684 3547, http://consulmex.sre.gob.mx/vancouver; 833 4th Ave SW, Suite 1100, Calgary, AL; 2P 3T5, 1 403 264 4819, http://consulmex.sre.gob.mx/calgary.

Cuba 518 C 12 (at the corner of Ave 7ma), Reparto Miramar, Municipio Playa, Havana; 53 21 41433, http://embamex.sre.gob.mx/cuba.

Guatemala 7–57 2ª Av, Zona 10, Apartado Postal 01010, Guatemala City; 2420 3400, http://embamex.sre.gob.mx/guatemala; 5 C 17–24, Zona 3, Quetzaltenango; 7767 5542 to 4, http://consulmex.sre.gob.mx/quetzaltenango; 3-A Av 4-74, Zona 1, Tecún Umán, 7776 8114, http://consulmex.sre.gob.mx/tecunuman.

Ireland 19 Raglan Rd, Ballsbridge, Dublin 4; 01 667 3105, http://embamex.sre.gob.mx/irlanda.

New Zealand 185–187 Featherston St, Level 2 (AMP Chambers), Wellington; 04 472 0555, http://embamex.sre.gob.mx/nuevazelandia.

South Africa Parkdev Building, Brooklyn Bridge, 570 Fehrsen St, Brooklyn, Pretoria 0181; 012 460 1004, http://embamex.sre.gob.mx/sudafrica.

UK 16 St George St, London W1S 1FD; 020 7499 8586, http://embamex.sre.gob.mx/reinounido.

USA 1911 Pennsylvania Ave NW, Washington, DC 20006; 1 202 728 1600, http://embamex.sre.gob.mx/eua; and in nearly fifty other US towns and cities, including these near the border:

Arizona 1201 F Ave, Douglas, AZ 85607; 1 520 364 3107, http://consulmex.sre.gob.mx/douglas; 135 W Cardwell St, Nogales, AZ 85621; 1 602 287 2521; http://consulmex.sre.gob.mx/nogales.

California 408 Heber Ave, Calexico, CA 92231–2811; 1 760 357 3863, http://consulmex.sre.gob.mx/calexico; 1549 India St, San Diego, CA 92101; 1 619 231 8414, http://consulmex.sre.gob.mx/sandiego.

Texas 301 Mexico Bvd, Suite F-2, Brownsville, TX 78520; 1 956 542 4431, http://consulmex.sre.gob.mx/brownsville; 2398 Texas Spur 239, Del Rio, TX 78840–8980; 1 830 775 2352 or 1 866 701 7777, http://consulmex.sre.gob.mx/delrio; 2252 E Garrison St, Eagle Pass, TX 78852; 1 830 773 9255 or 6, http://consulmex.sre.gob.mx/eaglepass; 910 E San Antonio Ave, El Paso, TX 79901; 1 915 549 0003, http://consulmex.sre.gob.mx/elpaso; 1612 Farragut St, Laredo, TX 78040; 1 956 723 6369, http://consulmex.sre.gob.mx/laredo; 600 S Broadway St, McAllen, TX 78501; 1 956 686 0243, http://consulmex.sre.gob.mx/mcallen; 127 Navarro St, San Antonio, TX 78205; 1210 227 9145 or 6, http://consulmex.sre.gob.mx/sanantonio.

Customs

Duty-free allowances into Mexico include: 20 packets of cigarettes, 25 cigars or 300g of tobacco; three litres of alcoholic drinks or six litres of wine; two cameras; one laptop; and three mobile phones. If you are carrying more than US$10,000 with you, you must declare it. For full details, see https://sat.gob.mx/home/home. Leaving Mexico, note that it is illegal to take antiquities (including Aztec and Maya artefacts) out of the country, and penalties are extremely serious.

Getting around

Distances in Mexico can be huge, and if you're intending to travel on public transport, you should be prepared for some very long journeys. Getting from Tijuana to Mexico City, for example, can take nearly two days nonstop by bus. Although public transport at ground level is frequent and reasonably efficient everywhere, taking an internal flight at least once may be worthwhile for the time it saves.

By bus

Within Mexico, **buses** (long-distance buses are called *camiones* rather than *autobuses* in Mexican Spanish) are by far the most common and efficient form of public transport. The legendary craziness of Mexican bus drivers is largely a thing of the past, and many bus companies have installed warning lights and buzzers to indicate when the driver is exceeding the speed limit (though these are often ignored by the driver). In recent years the government has been trying to improve the safety record through regular mechanical checks and also with random alcohol and drug tests on the drivers.

Classes

There are basically two **classes** of bus, first (*primera*) and second (*segunda*), though on major long-distance routes there's often little to differentiate them. First-class vehicles have reserved seats, videos and air-conditioning (which can be fierce – you may want a jumper), though an increasing number of second-class lines have the same comforts. The main differences will be in the number of stops – second-class buses call at more places, and consequently take longer to get where they're going – and the fare, which is about ten percent higher on first-class services (sometimes a lot more, check before you ride). On important routes there are also **deluxe**, or **pullman**, buses, with names like *Primera Plus* or *Turistar Plus* and fares around thirty percent higher than those of the first-class buses.

Stations

Most towns of any size have a modern **bus station**, known as the **Central Camionera** or **Central de Autobuses**. Don't let the word "central" fool you, as they are usually located a long way from the town centre. Where there is no unified terminus you may find separate first- and second-class terminals, or

BANDITRY: A WARNING

You should be aware when driving in Mexico, especially in a foreign vehicle, of the danger of **bandits**. Robberies and even more serious assaults on motorists do occur, above all in the northwest and especially in the state of Sinaloa. This was something tragically highlighted in late 2015 when two Australian travellers driving through Sinaloa were stopped, robbed and shot dead by a gang. Robbers may try to make you stop by indicating that there is something wrong with your vehicle; they've also been known to pose as policemen, hitchhikers and motorists in distress, so think twice about offering a lift or a helping hand. On the other hand, there are plenty of legitimate police checkpoints along the main roads, where you must stop, and increased security (to combat the drug cartels) has very much reduced hold-ups of buses. Robbers mainly target cargo trucks rather than private cars, but it is nonetheless best to avoid driving at night, particularly in the north of the country, but also in Michoacán and Guerrero, on Hwy-200 along the Pacific coast from Jalisco to Oaxaca, and on Hwy-57 (Mexico City–San Luis Potosí–Matahuela). It's always safer to use a toll (*cuota*) highway than a free one. The US State Department currently advises its citizens to avoid travelling at night on highways anywhere in the country.

individual ones for each company, sometimes little more than bus stops at the side of the road. There is some form of baggage deposit (left luggage) office in most bus stations – usually known as a guardería, *consigna* or simply *equipaje*. Before leaving anything, make sure that the place will be open when you come to collect your bags. If there's no formal facility, staff at the bus companies' baggage dispatching offices can often be persuaded to look after your things for a short while.

Tickets

Always check your route and arrival time, and whenever possible buy **tickets** from the bus station in advance to get the best (or any) seats. Alternatively, try the operator's website or an agent such as Miescape (https://miescape.mx). Prices are reasonable: a first-class ticket on the Cancún–Mérida route can be enjoyed on most travel budgets, for example. While there are very rarely problems getting a place on a bus from its point of origin or from really big towns, in smaller, mid-route places, you may have to wait for the bus to arrive (or at least to leave the previous stop) before discovering if there are any seats – the increased prevalence of computerized ticketing is easing the problem.

Timetables

Terms to look out for on the timetable, besides *local* and *de paso* (buses that originate in another destination), include *vía corta* (by the short route) and *directo* or *expreso* (direct/nonstop – in theory at least). *Salida* is departure, *llegada* arrival. A decent road map will be extremely helpful in working out which buses are going to pass through your destination. http://miescape.mx/miescape is a useful site for checking schedules.

By air

There are more than fifty airports in Mexico with regular passenger **flights** run by local airlines, plus several smaller airports with feeder services. The big company – formerly state-owned and with international as well as domestic flights – is Aeroméxico (http://aeromexico.com), which connects most places to Mexico City, usually several times a day. There are numerous other smaller and no-frills airlines such as Aeromar (http://aeromar.com.mx), Volaris (http://volaris.com), Viva Aerobus (http://vivaaerobus.com) and AeroServicio Guerrero (http://asg.com.mx), which also cover most major destinations. Competition between the companies keeps prices steady and relatively low: one-way tickets are generally the most affordable however they are also nonrefundable.

Internal **airfares** reflect the popularity of the route: the more popular the trip, the lower the price. Thus the flight from Tijuana to Mexico City costs much the same as the much shorter but less popular flight from Tijuana to Chihuahua, but even the more expensive routes can be worthwhile for the time they save. While the smaller airlines might be cheaper, there are few discounts and the price of a ticket on a particular flight doesn't normally vary from agent to agent.

By rail

Since Mexico's railways were privatized in 1995, all passenger services have been withdrawn bar one suburban service out of Mexico City and a couple of tourist lines: the **Copper Canyon railway** in Chihuahua, an amazing scenic journey and one of the country's top tourist attractions (see page 482), and the **Tequila Express** from Guadalajara (see page 270).

By boat

Ferries connect Baja California with a trio of ports on the Pacific mainland: Santa Rosalía to Guaymas, and La Paz to Mazatlán and Topolobampo (for Los Mochis). For information on schedules and fares see http://mexbound.com/mexico-ferry.php. There are also smaller boats to islands off the Caribbean and Gulf coasts: from Chiquilá to Isla Holbox, from Cancún to Isla Mujeres and from Playa del Carmen to Cozumel. Though more expensive than they once were, all these services are still pretty reasonable.

By car

Driving in Mexico requires care and concentration, and almost inevitably involves at least one brush with bureaucracy or the law (for details on licences and insurance, see page 57). Hitchhiking is possible, but due to safety concerns, the scarcity of lifts and the vast distances involved, it's not recommended.

Car rental

Renting a car in Mexico is often an extremely good way of quickly seeing a small area that would take days to explore using public transport. Always check **rates** carefully to make sure they include insurance, tax and the mileage you need. Daily rates with unlimited mileage start vary according to the season; weekly rates usually cost around the same as six days. In some resorts **mopeds**, **motorbikes** and even **golf carts** are also available for short distances, but most of the large, international companies don't deal with them because of the high frequency of accidents amongst tourists and locals..

Fuel

The government oil company, PEMEX, has a monopoly and sells two types of **petrol**: Magna Sin (regular unleaded), and Premium (high-octane unleaded). Both of these cost slightly more than regular unleaded north of the border.

DISTANCE CHART (IN KM)

	Acapulco	Aguas-calientes	Cancún	Chihuahua	Ciudad Juárez	Durango	Guadalajara	Matamoros
Acapulco	–	889	1951	1732	2109	1281	859	1361
Aguascalientes	889	–	2144	979	1356	417	250	819
Cancún	1951	2144	–	3086	3463	2524	2174	2331
Chihuahua	1732	979	3086	–	377	632	1188	1097
Ciudad Juárez	2109	1356	3463	377	–	1009	1565	1474
Durango	1281	417	2524	632	1009	–	556	880
Guadalajara	859	250	2174	1188	1565	556	–	995
Matamoros	1361	819	2331	1097	1474	880	995	–
Mérida	1647	1840	304	2782	3159	2220	1870	2027
Mexico City	390	514	1630	1456	1833	894	544	971
Monterrey	1341	582	2349	790	1167	573	771	307
Nogales	2572	1748	3855	769	635	1508	1698	2050
Oaxaca	653	984	1702	1938	2315	1376	1026	1368
San Luis Potosí	800	168	2043	1043	1420	481	344	651
Tampico	863	575	1833	1307	1684	888	751	498
Tijuana	3151	2504	4597	1532	1294	2087	2777	2629
Tuxtla Gutiérrez	967	1389	1155	2331	2708	1769	1419	1764
Veracruz	711	898	1332	1808	2185	1279	929	999
Villahermosa	1090	1283	861	2225	2602	1663	1313	1470

Roads and traffic

Traffic circulates on the right, and the normal speed limit is 40km/h (25mph) in built-up areas, 70km/h (43mph) in open country and 110km/h (68mph) on the freeway. Some of the new highways are excellent, and the toll (*cuota*) superhighways are better still, though extremely expensive (check prices online at http://sct.gob.mx, clicking on "Tarifas vigentes de carreteras"). Away from the major population centres, however, roads are often narrow, winding and potholed, with livestock wandering across at unexpected moments. Get out of the way of Mexican bus and truck drivers – if you signal left to them on a stretch of open road, it means it's clear for them to overtake.

Every town and village limits the speed of through traffic with a series of *topes* (speed bumps) across the road. Look out for the warning signs and take them seriously; the bumps are often huge. It's wise to avoid driving at night, not only for road safety reasons, but also because of the threat of hold-ups (see page 35). Any good road map should provide details of the more common symbols used on Mexican **road signs**. One convention of note: the first driver to flash their lights at a junction, or where only one vehicle can pass, has the right of way – you're not being invited to go first.

Most large towns have extensive **one-way systems**. Traffic direction is often poorly marked (look for small arrows affixed to lampposts), though this is less of a problem than it sounds: simply note the direction in which the parked cars, if not the moving cars, are facing.

Parking

Parking restrictions are complicated and foreigners are easy pickings for traffic police, who usually remove one or both plates in lieu of a ticket (retrieving them can be an expensive and time-consuming business). Since **theft** is also a real threat, you should use a hotel with secure parking. In Mexico City, residents' cars are banned from driving on one day of every week, determined by their licence number: the ban also applies to foreign cars, but rented vehicles are exempt.

Breakdowns and accidents

Unless your car is a basic-model VW, Ford or Dodge (all manufactured in Mexico), **spare parts** are expensive

Mérida City	Mexico	Monterrey	Nogales	Oaxaca	San Luis Potosí	Tampico	Tijuana	Tuxtla Gutiérrez	Veracruz	Villa-hermosa
1647	390	1341	2572	653	800	863	3151	967	711	1090
1840	514	582	1748	984	168	575	2504	1389	898	1283
304	1630	2349	3855	1702	2043	1833	4597	1155	1332	861
2782	1456	790	769	1938	1043	1307	1532	2331	1808	2225
3159	1833	1167	635	2315	1420	1684	1294	2708	2185	2602
2220	894	573	1508	1376	481	888	2087	1769	1279	1663
1870	544	771	1698	1026	344	751	2777	1419	929	1313
2027	971	307	2050	1368	651	498	2629	1764	999	1470
–	1326	2046	3551	1398	1739	1529	4293	851	1028	557
1326	–	954	2242	482	413	473	2821	875	385	769
2046	954	–	1743	1387	541	517	2322	1783	1018	1489
3551	2242	1743	–	2707	1812	2076	817	3100	2577	2994
1398	482	1387	2707	–	895	870	3303	547	369	841
1739	413	541	1812	895	–	407	2568	1288	798	1182
1529	473	517	2076	870	407	–	2839	1266	501	972
4293	2821	2322	817	3303	2568	2839	–	1070	305	776
851	875	1783	3100	547	1288	1266	1070	–	765	294
1028	385	1018	2577	369	798	501	305	765	–	471
557	769	1489	2994	841	1182	972	776	294	471	–

ADDRESSES

In Mexico **addresses** are frequently written with just the street name and number (thus: Madero 125), which can lead to confusion as many streets are known only as numbers (C 17). Calle (C) means "street"; Avenida (Av), Bulevar (Blv), Calzada and Paseo are other common terms – most are named after historical figures or dates. An address such as Hidalgo 39 8° 120, means Hidalgo no. 39, 8th floor, room 120 (a ground-floor address would be denoted PB for *planta baja*). Many towns have all their streets laid out in a **numbered grid** fanning out from a central point – often with odd-numbered streets running east–west, even ones north–south. In such places a suffix – Ote (for *Oriente*, East), Pte (for *Poniente*, West), Nte (for *Norte*, North) or Sur (South) – may be added to the street number to tell you which side of the two central dividing streets it is.

Note that "s/n" is used in an address to indicate "sin número", meaning that the building in question does not have a street number.

and hard to come by – bring a basic spares kit. Tyres in particular suffer on burning-hot Mexican roads, so you should carry at least one good spare. Roadside *vulcanizadoras* and *llanteros* can do temporary repairs; new tyres are expensive, but remoulds aren't a good idea on hot roads at high speed. If you have a breakdown on any highway between 8am and 8pm, there is a free mechanic service known as the **Ángeles Verdes** (Green Angels; https://gob.mx/sectur/angelesverdes). As well as patrolling major routes looking for beleaguered motorists, they can be reached by phone on 078 or on local state hotlines, or by email at angelesverdes@sectur.gob.mx, and they speak English.

Should you have a minor **accident**, try to come to some arrangement with the other party – involving the police will only make matters worse, and Mexican drivers will be just as anxious to avoid doing so. If you witness an accident, you may want to consider the gravity of the situation before getting involved. Witnesses can be locked up along with those directly implicated to prevent them from leaving before the case comes up – so consider if your involvement is necessary to serve justice. In a serious incident, contact your consulate and your Mexican insurance company as soon as possible.

By bike

You wouldn't expect Mexico to be big on **cycling**, with its vast size and the heavy and inconsiderate traffic in big cities. However, it has improved over the years with better access to bicycle lanes and an increasingly popular bicycle sharing programme, EcoBici, in Mexico City. The Yucatán Peninsula, being quite flat, lends itself to cycling, and bicycles can be rented in Campeche, Isla Mujeres, Playa del Carmen, Isla Cozumel and Tulum (see pages 693, 737, 748, 755 and 761). So does the area around Oaxaca, where you can also rent bikes (see page 576). Bicycle tour firms in Mexico include Bicicletas Pedro Martinez (http://bicicletaspedromartinez.com), Backroads (http://backroads.com) and Mexico Bike Tours (https://mexicobiketour.com.mx).

Local transport

Public transport within Mexican towns and cities is always plentiful and inexpensive, though crowded and not particularly user-friendly. Mexico City has an excellent **metro** system and there are smaller metros in both Guadalajara and Monterrey. Elsewhere, however, you'll be reliant on buses (often a flat fare, though this varies from place to place). Wherever possible we've indicated which bus to take and where to catch it, but often only local people will fully understand the intricacies of the system and you may well have to ask: the main destinations of the bus are usually marked on the windscreen, which helps.

In bigger places *combis* or **colectivos** offer a faster and perhaps less crowded alternative for only a little more money. These are minibuses, vans or large sport utility vehicles that run along fixed routes to set destinations; they'll pick you up and drop you off wherever you like along the way, and you simply pay the driver for the distance travelled. In Mexico City, *combis* are known as **peseros**.

Taxis

Regular **taxis** can also be good value, but be aware of rip-offs – unless you're confident that the meter is working, fix a price before you get in. In the big cities, there are often tables of fixed prices posted at prominent spots. At almost every airport and at some of the biggest bus stations you'll find a booth selling vouchers for taxis into town at a fixed price depending on the part of town you want to go to – sometimes there's a choice of paying more for a private car or less to share. This will invariably cost less than just hailing a cab outside the terminal, and will certainly offer extra security. In every case you should know the name of a hotel to head for, or they'll take you to the one that pays the biggest commission. Never accept a ride in any kind of unofficial or unmarked taxi, and in Mexico City be especially cautious (see page 118).

ACCOMMODATION ALTERNATIVES

Useful websites that provide alternatives to standard hotel and hostel accommodation:
Airbnb http://airbnb.com.
CouchSurfing http://couchsurfing.org.
Homestay http://homestay.com.
Tripping http://tripping.com.
Vacation Rentals by Owner http://vrbo.com.

Accommodation

Finding a room is rarely difficult – in areas that are not overly touristy the inexpensive places to stay are usually concentrated around the main plaza (the zócalo), with others near the market, train station or bus station (or where the bus station used to be, before it moved to the outskirts of town). In bigger cities, there's usually a relatively small area in which you'll find the bulk of the less expensive possibilities. The more modern and expensive places often lie on the outskirts of towns, accessible only by car or taxi. The only times you're likely to have big problems finding somewhere to stay are in coastal resorts over the peak Christmas season, at Easter, on Mexican holidays and almost anywhere during a local fiesta, when it's well worth trying to reserve ahead.

Hotels

Mexican hotels may describe themselves as anything from *paradores*, *posadas* and *casas de huéspedes* to plain *hoteles*, all terms that are used more or less interchangeably. A *parador* is totally unrelated to its top-end Spanish namesake, for example, and although in theory a *casa de huéspedes* means a small cheap place like a guesthouse, you won't necessarily find this to be the case.

All rooms should have an official **price** displayed. A room with one double bed (*cama matrimonial*) is almost always cheaper than a room with two singles (*doble* or *con dos camas*), and most hotels have large "family" rooms with several beds, which are tremendous value for groups. In the big resorts, there are lots of apartments that sleep six or more and include cooking facilities, for yet more savings. A little gentle haggling rarely goes amiss, and many places will have some rooms that cost less, so just ask (*"Tiene un cuarto mas barato?"*).

A/c (*aire acondicionado*) is a feature that inflates prices – it is frequently optional. Unless it's very hot and humid, a room with a simple ceiling fan (*ventilador*) is generally fine. In winter, especially at altitude or in the desert, it will of course be **heating** rather than cooling that you want – if there isn't any, make sure there's enough bedding and ask for extra blankets if necessary.

When looking at a room, you should always check its **insect proofing**. Cockroaches and ants are common, and there's not much you can do about them, but decent netting over the bed will keep mosquitoes out.

ACCOMMODATION PRICE CODES

The hotel prices quoted in this book are for the least expensive room for two people in high season, not including breakfast. Other options are usually available, including rooms with two beds, single rooms, dormitory accommodation in hostels and so on. The following key has been outlined based on these criteria. It has been applied throughout the guide to all accommodation listings and all prices are in Mexican pesos.
M$ = M$500-700
M$$ = M$700-1300
M$$$ = M$1300-2600
M$$$$ = M$2600-4500+

TOP 5 PLACES TO STAY

Luz en Yucatán Mérida. See page 703.
Tribu Isla Holbox. See page 731.
Playa Frambes Lighthouse Resort Mulegé. See page 537.
Las Golondrinas Oaxaca. See page 578.
Quinta Chanabnal Palenque. See page 659.

Campsites, hammocks and cabañas

Camping is easy enough if you are hiking in the backcountry, or happy simply to crash on a beach, but **robberies** are common, especially in places with a lot of tourists. There are very few organized campsites, and those that do exist are first and foremost trailer parks, not particularly pleasant to pitch tents in. Of course, if you have a van or **RV** you can use these or park just about anywhere else – there are a good number of facilities in the well-travelled areas, especially down the Pacific coast and Baja.

If you're planning to do a lot of camping, an **international camping card** is a good investment, serving as useful ID and getting you discounts at member sites. A range is available online.

In a lot of less official campsites, you will be able to rent a hammock and a place to sling it for the same price as pitching a tent, maybe less, especially if you're packing your own hammock (Mexico is a good place to buy these, especially in and around Mérida in the Yucatán).

Beach huts, or **cabañas**, are found at the more rustic, backpacker-oriented beach resorts, and sometimes inland. Usually just a wooden or palm-frond shack with a hammock slung up inside (or a place to sling your own), they are frequently without electricity, though as a resort gets more popular, they tend to transform into sturdier beach bungalows with modern conveniences and higher prices. At backwaters and beaches too untouristed even for cabañas, you should still be able to sling a hammock somewhere (probably the local bar or restaurant, where the palapa serves as shelter and shade).

Hostels

There are numerous hostels in Mexico, mainly concentrated in the more touristy areas. Some eighteen are affiliated to Hostelling International (http://hihostels.com); an HI card gets you a small discount, but is not essential. HI-affiliated hostels, however, are not necessarily better than non-affiliated ones, of which there are many.

Crime and personal safety

Despite soaring crime rates and dismal-sounding statistics, you are unlikely to run into trouble in Mexico if you stick to well-travelled paths. Even in Mexico City, which has a dangerous reputation, the threat is not that much greater than in many large North American and European cities. Obviously there are areas in cities where you wander alone, or at night, at your peril; but the best precaution is common sense. The narco war (see page 41) and the still-simmering conflict in Chiapas do not generally affect tourists.

Avoiding theft

Petty theft and **pickpockets** are your biggest worry in Mexico, so don't wave money around, try not to look too obviously affluent, don't leave cash or cameras in hotel rooms, and deposit your valuables in your hotel's safe if it has one (make a note of what you've deposited and ask the hotelier to sign it if you're worried). Crowds, especially on public city transport, are obvious hot spots: thieves tend to work in groups and target tourists. Distracting your attention, especially by pretending to look for something (always be suspicious of anyone who appears to be searching for something near you), or having one or two people pin you down while another goes through your pockets, are common ploys. Razoring of bags and pockets is another gambit, as is the more brutish grabbing of handbags, or anything left unattended even for a split second. **Mugging** is less common than pickpocketing, but you should steer clear of obvious danger spots, such as deserted pedestrian underpasses in big cities – indeed, avoid all deserted areas in big cities. Use ATMs in shopping malls or enclosed premises, and only in daylight when there are plenty of people around.

Robbery and sexual assault on tourists by cab drivers are not unknown, and it is not a good idea to hail a cab in the street in Mexico City (see page 118). Instead, phone for a radio cab or, failing that, take the next best option and get a cab from an official *sitio*. At night the beaches in tourist areas are also potentially dangerous.

When travelling, keep an eye on your bags (which are safe enough in the luggage compartments underneath most buses). Hold-ups of buses happen from time to time, and you may well be frisked on boarding to check for firearms, since the bandits are most often passengers on the bus.

Drivers are likely to encounter problems if they leave anything in their car. The **vehicle** itself is less likely to be stolen than broken into for the valuables inside. To avoid the worst, always park legally (and preferably off the street) and never leave anything visible inside the car.

Police

Mexican **police** are poorly paid and **graft** is an accepted part of the job, though often difficult for foreign visitors to accept. If a policeman accuses you of some violation (this is almost bound to happen to drivers at some stage), explain that you're a tourist, not used to the ways of the country – you may get off scot-free, but more likely the subject of a "**fine**" will come up. Such on-the-spot fines are open to negotiation, but only if you're confident you've done nothing seriously wrong and have a reasonable command of Spanish. Otherwise pay up and get out.

These small bribes, known as *mordidas* (bites), may also be extracted by border officials or bureaucrats (in which case, you could get out of paying by asking for a receipt, but it won't make life easier). In general, it is always wise to back off from any sort of confrontation with the police and to be extremely polite to them at all times.

Far more common than the *mordida* is the **propina**, or tip, a payment made entirely on your initiative. There's no need to do this, but it's remarkable how often a few pesos complete paperwork that would otherwise take weeks, open firmly locked doors or even find a seat on a previously full bus. All such transactions are quite open, and it's up to you literally to put your money on the table.

Should a crime be committed against you – in particular if you're robbed – your relationship with the police will obviously be different, although even

THE DRUGS WAR

Mexico is a major staging post on the **cocaine-smuggling** route from South America to the US, and use of cocaine is widespread and growing, with **crack** a blight in parts of the capital and some northern cities. Also growing is the use of **methamphetamine** ("hielo"), which is manufactured in Mexico, especially in areas close to the US border. **Heroin** is also manufactured in some northern states. In this ever-growing and increasingly lucrative trade, powerful, well-connected cocaine- and methamphetamine-smuggling cartels, known as "**narcos**" have long fought over territory, with each gang having its own pet politicians and police in the states it controls.

The situation changed radically in 2007 when President Felipe Calderón declared war on the *narcos*, who turned their guns on the police and army as well as each other. Innocent civilians often got caught in the crossfire, and thousands of people a year were killed in incidents related to the drugs war, with the biggest hot spots in areas bordering the US, and in major drug-producing states such as Sinaloa, though nowhere was safe.

Calderón's successor, **Enrique Peña Nieto**, initially changed tack, setting up a national police force, the *gendarmerie*, to tackle the problem. However, a surge in violence in Michoacán soon forced him to send in the army again.

Civicus, an international civil society NGO, stated in 2015: "Successive Mexican governments have ramped up the rhetoric about getting tough on drug trafficking. The result has been an egregious and sustained assault on human rights: it is estimated that 100,000 people have been killed in the drug war, and a further 25,000 'disappeared'.

THE DRUGS WAR AND TOURISM

Tourists are not usually affected, but June 2009 saw tourist hotels hurriedly evacuated as a two-hour gun battle engulfed a section of Acapulco. Drug-related violence continues to be a particular problem in the northern states of Sonora, Chihuahua, Coahuila, Nuevo Leon, Tamaulipas, Sinaloa and Durango, and also in Guerrero, Jalisco, Michoacán and Nayarit. Armed clashes between security forces and drug groups may break out without warning, and you should exercise extreme caution outside of tourist areas in all of these states.

in this eventuality it's worth considering whether the lengthy hassles you'll go through make it worth reporting. Some insurance companies will insist on a police report if you're to get any refund – in which case you may practically have to dictate it to the officer and can expect little action. Other firms may be prepared to accept that you were robbed and the theft was not reported to the police, but they are quite within their rights to demand that you do report it, and you will need to check with them. The department you need in order to *presentar una denuncia* (report the theft officially) is the Procuradoría General de Justicia.

The Mexican **legal system** is based on the Napoleonic code, which assumes your guilt until you can prove otherwise. Should you be jailed, your one phone call should be to your **consulate** – if nothing else, they'll arrange an English-speaking lawyer. You can be held for up to 72 hours on suspicion before charges have to be brought. Mexican jails are grim, although lots of money and friends on the outside can ameliorate matters slightly.

Drugs

Drug offences are the most common cause of serious trouble between tourists and the authorities. Under heavy pressure from the US to clamp down on the trade, local authorities are particularly happy to throw the book at foreign offenders. While the law has decriminalized small quantities of cannabis (up to 5g), cocaine (up to 0.5g) and heroin (up to 0.05g), if you're caught with quantities reckoned to be for distribution you can wave goodbye to daylight for a long time, and don't expect much help or sympathy from your consulate.

Other naturally occurring drugs – Mexico has more species of psychoactive plants than anywhere else in the world – still form an important part of many Indigenous rituals, most notably the **peyote cactus** (used primarily by the Huichols in the northern deserts). Though the authorities turn a blind eye to Indigenous use, use by non-Indigenous Mexicans and tourists is as strongly prohibited as that of any other illegal drug, and heavily penalized. Expect searches and even occasionally hotel raids by police if staying in areas known for peyote.

Health

Most travellers visit Mexico without catching anything more serious than a dose of "Montezuma's Revenge". You will still want the security of health insurance (see page 57), but the important thing is to keep your resistance high and to be aware of the health risks linked to poor hygiene, untreated water, mosquito bites, and undressed open cuts.

Lack of sanitation in Mexico is much exaggerated, but a degree of caution is wise. Avoid food that looks like it has been on display for a while or not freshly cooked, and always peel fruit before eating it. Avoid raw shellfish, and don't eat anywhere that is obviously dirty (easily spotted, since most Mexican restaurants are scrupulously clean). Salads are healthy, but think twice before eating them if you have a sensitive stomach. In general, keep an eye out for cleanliness of street stalls – beware of food that has been left out to breed germs rather than food that has been freshly cooked. For advice on water, see page 43.

There are no required vaccinations for Mexico, but it's worth visiting your doctor at least four weeks before you leave to check that you are up to date with **tetanus**, **typhoid** and **hepatitis A** shots, as well as a **rabies** shot and **anti-malarial** pills if you're going to be in areas where they are recommended (see page 43).

For comprehensive coverage of the sort of health problems encountered by travellers, try the *Rough Guide to Travel Health* by Dr Nick Jones – unfortunately now out of print, but still obtainable from some suppliers.

Diarrhoea

Diarrhoea (Montezuma's Revenge, or simply *turista* as it's also known in Mexico) is the medical problem you're most likely to encounter, and no one, however cautious, seems to avoid it altogether. If you go down with a mild dose unaccompanied by other symptoms, it may simply be due to your body being unfamiliar with the local bacteria, but if your diarrhoea is accompanied by cramps and vomiting, it could be **food poisoning** of some sort. Either way, it will probably pass of its own accord in 24 to 48 hours without treatment. In the meantime, it's essential to replace the fluid and salts you're losing, so drink lots of water. If you have severe diarrhoea, and whenever young children have it, add **oral rehydration salts** – *suero oral* (brand names: Dioralyte, Electrosol, Rehidrat). If you can't get these, dissolve half a teaspoon of salt and three of sugar in a litre of water.

Avoid greasy food, heavy spices, caffeine and most fruit and dairy products; some say bananas, papayas, guavas and prickly pears (*tunas*) help, while plain yogurt or a broth made from yeast extract (such as

WHAT ABOUT THE WATER?

In a hot climate and at high altitudes, it's essential to increase **water** intake to prevent dehydration. Most travellers, and most Mexicans if they can, stay off the tap water. A lot of the time it is in fact drinkable, and in practice it may be impossible to avoid completely: ice made with it, unasked for, may appear in drinks, utensils are washed in it, and so on.

Most restaurants and *licuaderías* use **purified water** (*agua purificada*), but always check; most hotels have a supply and will often provide bottles of water in your room. Bottled water (generally purified with ozone or ultraviolet) is widely available, but stick with known brands, and always check that the seal on the bottle is intact since refilling empties with tap water for resale is common (carbonated water is generally a safer bet in that respect).

There are various methods of **treating water** while you are travelling, whether your source is from a tap or a river or stream. Boiling it for a minimum of five minutes is the time-honoured method, but it is not always practical, will not remove unpleasant tastes and is a lot less effective at higher altitudes – including much of central Mexico – where you have to boil it for much longer.

STERILIZATION AND PURIFICATION

Chemical sterilization, using either chlorine or iodine tablets or a tincture of iodine liquid, is more convenient, but leaves a nasty aftertaste (which can to some extent be masked with lime juice). Chlorine kills bacteria but, unlike iodine, is not effective against amoebic dysentery and giardiasis. Pregnant women or people with thyroid problems should consult their doctor before using iodine sterilizing tablets or iodine-based purifiers. Too many iodine tablets can cause gastrointestinal discomfort. Inexpensive iodine removal filters are available and are recommended if treated water is being used continuously for more than a month or is being given to babies.

Purification, involving both filtration and sterilization, gives the most complete treatment. Portable water purifiers range in size from units weighing as little as 60g, which can be slipped into a pocket, up to 800g for carrying in a backpack.

Another user-friendly alternative is a handheld ultraviolet (UV) water purifier such as Steripen (http://steripen.com).

Marmite or Vegemite, if you happen to have some with you) can be easily absorbed by your body when you have diarrhoea. Drugs like Lomotil or Imodium plug you up – and thus undermine the body's efforts to rid itself of infection – but they can be a temporary stop-gap if you have to travel. If symptoms persist for more than three days, or if you have a fever or blood in your stool, seek medical advice (see "Getting medical help", page 45).

Malaria and dengue fever

Malaria, caused by a parasite that lives in the saliva of female *Anopheles* mosquitoes, is endemic in some parts of Mexico. Areas above 1000m (such as the capital) are malaria-free, as are Cancún, Cozumel, Isla Mujeres and all the beach resorts of the Baja and the Pacific coasts. Daytime visits to archeological sites are risk-free, too, but low-lying inland areas can be risky, especially at night. According to the US-based Centers for Disease Control and Prevention (CDC) the main risk areas are Chihuahua, Chiapas, Durango, Nayarit and Sinaloa, with rare cases in Campeche, Jalisco, Oaxaca, Sonora, Tabasco and the municipality of Othón P. Blanco in the southern part of Quintana Roo, bordering Belize. Chloroquine (brand names: Nivaquin, Resochin, Avloclor, Aralen) is the recommended malaria prophylactic for travellers to Mexico; you need to start taking the pills one week before you arrive and continue for one month after you depart. Chloroquine is unsuitable for sufferers from various complaints such as epilepsy and psoriasis but daily proguanil (brand name Paludrine) can be used in its place. Consult a physician before beginning any course of medication; see http://www.nc.cdc.gov/travel for more information on malaria in Mexico.

If you go down with malaria, you'll probably know. The fever, shivering and headaches are like severe flu and come in waves, usually beginning in the early evening. Malaria is not infectious, but can be dangerous and sometimes even fatal if not treated quickly, so you should seek medical help immediately.

The most important thing, obviously, is to avoid **mosquito** bites altogether. Though active from dusk till dawn, female *Anopheles* mosquitoes prefer to bite in the evening. Wear long sleeves, skirts or trousers, avoid dark colours, which attract mosquitoes, and put **repellent** on all exposed skin, especially feet and ankles, which are their favourite targets. Plenty of good brands are sold locally, though health departments recommend carrying high-DEET brands available from travel clinics at home. An alternative is to burn coils of **pyrethrum** incense such as Raidolitos (these are readily available and burn all night if whole, but break easily). Sleep under a **net** if you can – one that hangs from a single point is best if you're going to buy one (you can usually find a way to tie a string across your room to hang it from). Special mosquito nets for hammocks are available in Mexico.

Another illness spread by mosquito bites is **dengue fever**, whose symptoms are similar to those of malaria, plus a headache and aching bones. Dengue-carrying mosquitoes are particularly prevalent in urban areas during the rainy season and fly during the day, so wear insect repellent in the daytime if mosquitoes are around. The only treatment is complete rest, with drugs to assuage the fever – and take note that a second infection can be fatal.

Other bites and stings

Other biting insects can also be a nuisance. These include bed bugs, sometimes found in cheap (and, occasionally, in not so cheap) hotels – look for squashed ones around the bed. Sandflies, often present on beaches, are quite small, but their bites, usually on feet and ankles, itch like hell and last for days. Head or body lice can be picked up from people or bedding, and are best treated with medicated soap or shampoo.

Scorpions are mostly nocturnal and hide during the day under rocks and in crevices, so poking around in such places when in the countryside is generally ill-advised. If sleeping in a place where they might enter (such as a beach cabaña), shake your shoes out before putting them on in the morning, and try not to wander round barefoot. Some scorpion stings are dangerous and medical treatment should always be sought – cold-pack the sting in the meantime. **Snakes** are unlikely to bite unless accidentally disturbed – walk heavily and they will usually slither away. A fifth or so of Mexico's snake species are venomous, the most dangerous being rattlesnakes (cascabel, found in the north), coral snakes (coralillo, found particularly in Guerrero, Oaxaca, Veracruz and Chiapas) and the nauyacas (found mainly in the south and the Yucatán). If you do get bitten or stung, remember what the snake or scorpion looked like (kill it if you can do so without receiving more bites), try not to move the affected part (tourniquets are not recommended due to dangerous risk of gangrene – if you do use one, it is vital to relieve it for at least ninety seconds every fifteen minutes), and seek medical help: antivenins are available in most hospitals. Black widow spiders also exist in Mexico; tarantulas are more fearsome-looking, but a lot less dangerous.

Altitude and heat problems

Two other common causes of health problems in Mexico are altitude and the sun. The solution in both cases is to take it easy. Arriving in Mexico City (2240m), in particular, you may find any activity strenuous, and the thin air is made worse by the high concentration of pollutants. Allow yourself time to acclimatize. If going to higher altitudes (mountain climbing, for example), you may develop symptoms of **Acute Mountain Sickness (AMS)**, such as breathlessness, headaches, dizziness, nausea and appetite loss. More extreme cases may include vomiting, disorientation, loss of balance and coughing up of pink frothy phlegm. A slow descent almost always brings immediate recovery.

Tolerance to the sun, too, takes a while to build up: use a strong **sunscreen** and, if you're walking during the day, wear a hat or keep to the shade. Be sure to avoid dehydration by drinking enough (water or fruit juice rather than beer or coffee, and aim to drink at least three litres a day), and don't exert yourself for long periods in the hot sun. Be aware that overheating can cause **heatstroke**, which is potentially fatal. Signs are a very high body temperature without a feeling of fever, accompanied by headaches, disorientation and even irrational behaviour. Lowering body temperature (a tepid shower, for example) is the first step in treatment.

Less serious is **prickly heat**, an itchy rash that is in fact an infection of the sweat ducts caused by excessive perspiration that doesn't dry off. A cool shower, zinc oxide powder and loose cotton clothes should help.

Hepatitis

Hepatitis A is transmitted through contaminated food and water, or through saliva, and thrives in conditions of poor hygiene. It can lay a victim low for several months with exhaustion, fever and diarrhoea, and can even cause liver damage. The Havrix vaccine has been shown to be extremely effective; with a booster after six months, protection lasts for ten years.

Hepatitis symptoms include a yellowing of the whites of the eyes, general malaise, orange urine (though dehydration can also cause this) and light-coloured stools. If you think you have it and are unable immediately to see a doctor, it is important to get lots of rest, avoid alcohol and do your best not to spread the disease. If medical insurance coverage is an issue, you can go to a pathology lab (most towns have them) to get blood tests before paying a greater amount to see a doctor.

More serious is **hepatitis B**, which is passed through blood or sexual contact, in the same way as HIV, but more easily. A hepatitis B jab is recommended if you will be in contact with those with weaker immune systems, for example, working around medical patients or with children. Ideally three doses are given over six months, but, if time is short, there are other options that take one to two months, with a booster given after a year.

Other diseases

Typhoid and cholera are spread in the same way as hepatitis A. **Typhoid** produces a persistent high fever with malaise, headaches and abdominal pains, followed by diarrhoea. Vaccination can be by injection or orally, though the oral alternative is less effective, more expensive and only lasts a year, as opposed to three for a shot in the arm. **Cholera** appears in epidemics rather than isolated cases – if it's about, you will probably hear about it. Cholera is characterized by sudden attacks of watery diarrhoea with severe cramps and debilitation.

Immunizations against **mumps**, **measles**, **TB** and **rubella** are a good idea for anyone who wasn't vaccinated as a child and hasn't had the diseases, and it's worth making sure you are covered for **tetanus**. You don't need a shot for **yellow fever** unless you're coming from a country where it's endemic (in which case you need to carry your vaccination certificate).

Rabies exists in Mexico and the rabies vaccine is advised for anyone who will be more than 24 hours away from medical help, for example if going trekking in remote areas. The best advice is simply to give dogs a wide berth, and not to play with animals at all, no matter how cuddly they may look. A bite, a scratch or even a lick from an infected animal could spread the disease – rabies can be fatal, so if you are bitten, assume the worst and get medical help as quickly as possible. While waiting, wash any such wound immediately but gently with soap or detergent and apply alcohol or iodine if possible. If you decide to get the vaccination, you'll need three shots spread over a four-week period prior to travel.

Getting medical help

For minor medical problems, head for a **farmacia** – look for a green cross and the *Farmacia* sign. Pharmacists are knowledgeable and helpful, and many speak some English. One word of warning, however: in many Mexican pharmacies you can still buy drugs such as Entero-Vioform and Mexaform (both used to treat diarrhoea), which can cause optic nerve damage and have been banned elsewhere; it is not a good idea, therefore, to use local brands unless you know what they are. Note that the purchase of prescription drugs without a Mexican prescription is illegal; a US prescription will not suffice.

For more serious complaints you can get a list of English-speaking **doctors** from your government's nearest consulate. Big hotels and tourist offices may also be able to recommend medical services. Every Mexican border town has hundreds of doctors (dentists, too) experienced in treating gringos, since they charge less than their colleagues across the border. Every reasonably sized town should also have a state- or Red Cross-run **health centre** (*centro de salud*), where treatment is free. Treatment at health centres should be adequate for minor problems, but for anything involving an overnight stay, go to a private hospital (for which your travel insurance should cover you).

MEDICAL RESOURCES

Canadian Association for Global Health 613 241 5785, https://cagh-acsm.org. Has an extensive list of travel health centres.

CDC 1 800 232 4636, http://cdc.gov/travel. Official US government travel health site.

International Society for Travel Medicine US; 1 404 373 8282, http://istm.org. Has a full list of travel health clinics.

Hospital for Tropical Diseases Travel Clinic UK; 020 3456 7890, https://www.uclh.nhs.uk/our-services/our-hospitals/Hospital-of-Tropical-Diseases.

MASTA (Medical Advisory Service for Travellers Abroad) UK; 0330 100 4200, http://masta-travel-health.com for the nearest clinic.

Tropical Medical Bureau Ireland; 353 1 2715 200, http://tmb.ie.

The Travel Doctor Aus; 1 300 658 844, http://traveldoctor.com.au. Lists travel clinics in Australia, New Zealand and South Africa.

Food and drink

Whatever your preconceptions about Mexican food, if you've never eaten in Mexico, they will almost certainly be wrong. Food here bears very little resemblance to the concoctions served in

"Mexican" restaurants or fast-food joints in other parts of the world – you certainly won't find chile con carne outside the tourist spots. Nor, as a rule, is it especially spicy.

Where to eat

Basic meals are served at **restaurantes**, but you can get breakfast, snacks and often full meals at cafés too; there are **takeaway** and **fast-food** places serving sandwiches, tortas (filled rolls) and tacos (tortillas folded over with a filling), as well as more international-style food; there are establishments called **jugerías** (look for signs saying "Jugos y Licuados") serving nothing but wonderful *jugos* (juices), *licuados* (fruit blended with water or milk) and fruit salads; and there are **street stalls** dishing out everything from tacos to orange juice to ready-made vegetable salads sprinkled with chile-salt and lime. Just about every **market** in the country has a cooked-food section, too, and these are invariably the cheapest places to eat, if not always the most enticing surroundings. Big cities and resorts have international restaurants – **pizza**, **burgers** and **Chinese** food are ubiquitous, and **Argentine** restaurants are the places to go for well-cooked, quality steaks.

On buses (especially second-class ones), people clamber on at stops with home-made foods, local specialities, cold drinks or coffee. You'll find wonderful things this way that you won't come across in restaurants, but they should be treated with caution, and with an eye to hygiene.

What to eat

The basic Mexican diet is essentially one of **corn** (*maíz* as a crop, *elote* when eaten), supplemented by **beans** and **chiles**. These three things appear in an almost infinite variety of guises.

> ### EATING PRICE CODES
> The restaurant prices quoted in this book are for a two-course meal for one including a glass of wine. The following key has been applied throughout the guide based on these criteria and all prices are in Mexican pesos.
> **M$** = M$50-75
> **M$$** = M$75-150
> **M$$$** = M$150-300
> **M$$$$** = M$300-600+

Beans and vegetables

Beans (*frijoles*), an invariable accompaniment to egg dishes – and pretty much everything else too – are usually of the pinto or kidney variety and are almost always served **refritos**, ie boiled up, mashed and "refried" (though actually it is the first time they're fried). They're even better if you can get them whole in some kind of country-style soup or stew, often with pork or bacon, as in **frijoles charros**. You'll find **corn** in soups and stews such as **pozole** (with meat), or roasted on the cob at street stalls. Mexican **vegetables** include the green tomatillo (*tomate*, as opposed to *jitomate*, which is an ordinary tomato), *nopales*, which are prickly pear fronds (the fruit being a *tuna*), and *huitlacoche*, a fungus that grows on corn. You may also get to eat courgette flowers (*flor de calabaza*), which are especially popular in quesadillas.

Tortillas and tamales

As well as being eaten as a vegetable in its own right, corn is ground into flour for **tortillas**, basically flat maize pancakes (tortillas made of wheat flour, or *de harina*, are rare except in the north). The ground maize is combined with salt and water in a paste (*masa)* which is pressed or patted flat by hand, then heated on a *comal*, a flat steel sheet. While smarter restaurants serve bread rolls (*bolillos*), a stack of tortillas is a common accompaniment in cheaper places, and they also form the basis of most **antojitos** (appetizers or light courses). Simplest of these are **tacos**, tortillas filled with almost anything, from beef and chicken to green vegetables, and then fried (they're usually still soft, not at all like the baked taco shells you may have had at home). With cheese, either alone or in addition to other fillings, they are called **quesadillas**. **Enchiladas** are rolled, filled tortillas covered in salsa and baked; **enchiladas suizas** are filled with chicken and have sour cream over them. **Tostadas** are flat tortillas toasted crisp and piled with ingredients – usually meat, salad vegetables and cheese (smaller bite-size versions are known as *sopes*). Tortillas torn up and cooked together with meat and (usually hot) sauce are called **chilaquiles**; this is a traditional way of using up leftovers. In the north, especially, you'll also come across **burritos** (large wheat-flour tortillas, stuffed with anything, but usually beef and potatoes or beans) and **gorditas** (delicious fat corn tortillas, sliced open, stuffed and baked or fried). Also short and fat are **tlacoyos**, tortillas made with a stuffing of mashed beans, often using blue-corn flour, which gives them a rather bizarre colour.

Corn flour, too, is the basis of **tamales** – found predominantly in central and southern Mexico – which are a sort of cornmeal pudding, stuffed,

SALSA

Most Mexican food is not in itself terribly spicy – the fire comes from the red and green salsa supplied as condiments on the table, and the salsa can be a good guide to the quality of a restaurant. A place with a superior salsa on the table will probably serve up some decent food, whereas a place that takes no pride in its salsa is likely to treat its food in the same manner. To a certain extent you can tell from the presentation: a place that has grubby, rarely changed salsa dishes probably just refills them from a supermarket-bought can, and will not take the same pride in its food as a *casero* (home-cooking) restaurant that proudly puts its own salsa on the table in a nice bowl. Usually you get a red salsa and a green one, and sometimes bottled hot-sauce condiments too.

Nowadays, the red bowl may contain a **raw**, California-style salsa: tomato, onion, chile and coriander (cilantro) finely chopped together. More common, though, are the traditional **cooked** salsas: either green or red, and relatively mild (though start eating with caution, just in case). The recipes are – of course – closely guarded secrets, but the basic ingredients are tomato (the verdant Mexican tomatillo in green versions), onion and one or more of the hundreds of varieties of chile.

flavoured and steamed in corn or banana leaves. They can be either savoury, with additions like shrimp or corn kernels, or sweet when made with something like coconut.

Meat, seafood and eggs

Except in the north, **meat** is not especially good – beef in particular is usually thin and tough; pork, goat and occasionally lamb are better. If the menu doesn't specify what kind of meat it is, it's usually pork – even steak (*bistec*) can be pork unless it specifies *bistec de res*. For thick American-style steaks, look for a sign saying "Carnes Hereford" or for a "New York Cut" description (only in expensive places or in the north or at fancier resorts). **Seafood** is almost always fresh and delicious, especially the spicy shrimp or octopus cocktails which you find in most coastal areas (**coctél/campechana de camarón** or **pulpo**), but beware of eating uncooked shellfish, even *ceviche* (though the lime juice it is marinated in does kill off most of the nasties). **Eggs** in country areas are genuinely free range and flavoursome. They feature on every menu as the most basic of meals, and at some time you must try the classic Mexican combinations of **huevos rancheros** (fried eggs on a tortilla with red salsa) or **huevos a la mexicana** (scrambled with onion, tomato and chile).

Vegetarian and vegan food

Vegetarians and **vegans** can eat well in Mexico, although it does take caution to avoid meat altogether. Many Mexican dishes are naturally meat-free and there are always fabulous fruits and vegetables available. Most restaurants serve vegetable soups and rice, and items like quesadillas, *chiles rellenos* and even tacos and enchiladas often come with non-meat fillings. Another possibility for vegetarians is **queso fundido**, simply (and literally) melted cheese, served with tortillas and salsa. Eggs, too, are served anywhere at any time, and many *jugerías* serve huge mixed **salads** to which grains and nuts can be added.

However, vegetarianism, though growing, is not particularly common, and a simple cheese and chile dish may have some meat added to "improve" it. Worse, most of the fat used for frying is animal fat (usually lard), so that even something as unadorned as refried beans may not be strictly vegetarian (especially as a bone or some stock may have been added to the water the beans were originally boiled in). Even "vegetarian" restaurants, which can be found in all the big cities, often include chicken on the menu. You may well have better luck in pizza places and Chinese or other ethnic restaurants.

Meals

Traditionally, Mexicans eat a light breakfast very early, a snack of tacos or eggs in mid-morning, lunch (the main meal of the day) around 2pm or later – in theory followed by a siesta, but decreasingly so, it seems – and a late, light supper. Eating a large meal at lunch time can be a great way to save money – almost every restaurant serves a cut-price **comida corrida** (a set meal, changing daily).

Breakfast (*desayuno*) in Mexico can consist simply of coffee (see page 49) and *pan dulce* – sweet rolls and pastries that usually come in a basket; you pay for as many as you eat. More substantial breakfasts consist of eggs in any number of forms (many set breakfasts

REGIONAL CUISINE

It's easy to think of Mexican food as one cuisine. In reality, while there are common themes, each region has its own excellent specialities. Here are a few regional highlights.

BAJA CALIFORNIA

In Baja, the sea is all around, so it makes sense that *mariscos* (seafood) and *pescado* (fish) dominate menus – the fish taco is an eternal favourite. Northern Baja is home to Mexico's wine industry, and drinking wine with your meal is far more common here than elsewhere in the country.

THE NORTH

Dining in the north, where the land is too dry to grow produce, tends to revolve around grilled meat: the *asado* (barbecue) is king. *Cabrito asado* (roast kid) is the classic dish, often served in gargantuan portions and accompanied only by tortillas and salsa. These basic ingredients combine into burritos and fajitas, dishes that have travelled north of the border to become what most of the world thinks of as "Mexican food".

CENTRAL MEXICO

With fertile valleys and highlands that receive enough rain to sustain agriculture, central Mexico has the widest range of local ingredients. This is the land of the avocado (and therefore guacamole) and the birthplace of tequila. Mexico's second city, Guadalajara, excels with its *birria*, a soupy stew, while coastal towns dish up tasty *camarones* (prawns). Further south, Oaxaca claims the country's finest tamales, stuffed cornmeal dough cooked in banana leaves.

THE YUCATÁN

Influenced by the flavours of the Caribbean, an abundance of tropical fruits and the all-powerful burn of the *habanero chile*, Yucatecan cuisine is a world apart from that of central Mexico. The most celebrated dish is *cochinita pibil*, pork marinated in a *recado* made from garlic, chiles, black pepper, cumin, cinnamon, oregano and vinegar, then wrapped in plantain leaves and grilled. For more on Yucatecan cuisine, see page 702.

include *huevos al gusto*: eggs any way you like them), and at fruit-juice places you can have a simple *licuado* (see page 49) fortified with raw egg (*blanquillo*). Freshly squeezed orange juice (*jugo de naranja*) is always available from street stalls in the early morning.

Snacks mostly consist of some variation on the taco/enchilada theme (stalls selling them are called *taquerías*), but tortas – rolls heavily filled with meat or cheese or both, garnished with avocado and chile and toasted on request – are also wonderful, and you'll see takeout torta stands everywhere. Failing that, you can of course always make your own snacks with bread or tortillas, along with fillings such as avocado or cheese, from shops or markets.

At **lunch time** (around 1–5pm) many restaurants serve a comida corrida (known in smarter places as the *menu del día* or *menu turístico*), usually consisting of three or four courses – always reasonably priced. A typical *comida* will consist of "wet" soup, probably vegetable, followed by "dry" soup – most commonly *sopa de arroz* (rice seasoned with tomato or chile), or perhaps a plate of vegetables, pasta, beans or guacamole (avocado mashed with onion, and maybe tomato, lime juice and chile). Then comes the main course (usually meat or fish), followed by pudding, usually fruit, *flan* or *pudin* (crème caramel-like concoctions), or rice pudding. Other Mexican desserts worth looking out for include meringue made with *pulque* (see page 50), and *capirotada* (bread pudding, especially popular during Lent).

Some restaurants also offer set meals in the evening, but this is rare, and on the whole going out to **eat at night** is more expensive.

Drinks

The basic drinks to accompany food are water or beer. If you're drinking **water**, stick to bottled stuff (*agua mineral* or *agua de Tehuacán*) – it comes either plain (*sin gas*) or carbonated (*con gas*).

Jugos, licuados and refrescos

Soft drinks (*refrescos*) – including Coke, Pepsi, Squirt (fun to pronounce in Spanish), and Mexican brands like apple-flavoured Sidral (which are usually extremely sweet) – are on sale everywhere. Far more tempting are the real **fruit juices** and *licuados* sold at shops and stalls displaying the "Jugos y Licuados" sign and known as *jugerías* or *licuaderías*. Juices (**jugos**) can be squeezed from anything that will go through the extractor. Orange (naranja) and carrot (zanahoria) are the staples, but you should also experiment with some of the more obscure tropical fruits such as soursop or mamey. *Licuados* are made of fruit mixed with water (**licuado de agua** or simply **agua de**...) or milk (**licuado de leche**) in a blender, usually with sugar added, and are always fantastic.

Limonada (fresh lemonade) is also sold in many of these places, as are **aguas frescas** – flavoured cold drinks, of which the most common are **horchata** (rice milk flavoured with cinnamon) and **agua de arroz** (like an iced rice-pudding drink – delicious), **de jamaica** (hibiscus) or **de tamarindo** (tamarind). These are also often served in restaurants or sold in the streets from great glass jars. Make sure that any water and ice used is purified – street stalls are especially suspect in this regard. Juices and *licuados* are also sold at many ice-cream parlours – *neverías* or *paleterías*.

The ice cream, more like Italian *gelato* than the heavy-cream US varieties, can also be fabulous and comes in a huge array of flavours, with fruit flavoured being some of the best.

Coffee and tea

A great deal of **coffee** is produced in Mexico, and in the growing areas, especially the state of Veracruz, as well as in the traditional coffeehouses in the capital, you will be served superb coffee. In its basic form, **café solo** or **negro**, it is strong, black, often sweet (ask for it *sin azúcar* for no sugar), and comes in small cups. For weaker black coffee ask for **café americano**, though this may mean instant (if you do want instant, ask for "Nescafé"). White is **café cortado** or **con un pocito de leche**; **café con leche** can be delicious, made with all milk and no water (ask if it's "hecho de leche" – made of milk). **Espresso** and **cappuccino** are often available too, or you may be offered **café de olla** – stewed in the pot for hours with cinnamon and sugar, it's thick, sweet and tasty. Outside traditional coffee areas like Chiapas, however, the coffee is often terrible, with instant common.

Tea (té) is often available too, and you may well be offered a cup at the end of a *comida*. You may also be offered herb teas such as **manzanillo** (camomile) or **yerbabuena** (mint). If you get the chance to try traditional **hot chocolate** ("the drink of the Aztecs"), then do so – it's an extraordinary, spicy, semi-bitter concoction, quite unlike the milky bedtime drink of your childhood. Artisan chocolate shops sell the chocolate for this (you just add boiling water), and occasionally sell it as a drink too.

Alcohol

You'll normally be drinking in **bars**, the least heavy atmosphere among which is in **hotel bars**, tourist

SOME LIKE IT NOT SO HOT: THE MEXICAN CHILE

Mexican cooks use at least a hundred different types of **chiles**, fresh or dried, in colours ranging from pale green to almost black, and all sorts of different sizes (large, mild ones are often stuffed with meat or cheese and rice to make **chiles rellenos**). Each has a distinct flavour and by no means all are hot (which is why we don't use the English term "chilli" for them), although the most common, **chiles jalapeños** – which can be green or red, and are traditionally grown around the city of Xalapa – certainly are. The hottest is the **habanero**, 25 times hotter than the **jalapeño**. Far less intimidating is the **chile poblano**, a large, mild chile used in dishes such as **chiles rellenos** and **chiles en nogada**, a seasonal dish of stuffed poblano chiles in a white sauce made of walnuts and cream cheese or sour cream, topped with red pomegranate: the colours of the national flag.

MOLE

Chile is also the basic ingredient of more complex cooked sauces, notably **mole**, which is Mexico's version of a curry, traditionally served with turkey or chicken, but also sometimes with enchiladas (rolled, filled tortillas). There are several types of *mole*, the two most common being the rather bland *mole verde*, and the far richer and more exciting **mole poblano**, a speciality of Puebla. Half of the fifty or so ingredients in this extraordinary mixture are different types of chile, but the most notable ingredient is chocolate.

CHOCOLATE

The Olmecs of the Gulf coast began mixing cacao beans into a bitter **chocolate** drink around three thousand years ago. By the time Cortés and the conquistadors reached New Spain in the early sixteenth century, the use of cacao had spread to the Aztecs, who consumed *chocoatl* cold and mixed with spices – this "drink of the gods" was said to be a favourite of Aztec emperor Moctezuma. Chocolate remains a popular drink in Mexico today (now with lots of added sugar), but its most distinctive use is in **mole poblano**, a thick sauce of chocolate and chiles that accompanies otherwise savoury dishes – particularly chicken. Though found all over the country, *mole* remains a speciality of Puebla in central Mexico, where the dish originated in the colonial era.

areas or anything that describes itself as a "ladies' bar". **Cantinas** are for serious drinking, traditionally macho places that were closed to women (they typically had a sign above the door prohibiting entry to "women, members of the armed forces and anyone in uniform"). Especially in big cities they are now more liberal, but in small, conservative places they remain exclusively male preserves with an atmosphere of drunken bonhomie and an undercurrent of readiness for a fight, where women may not be welcome and are sometimes still even banned.

If you don't feel comfortable in bars, you can buy alcohol from most shops, supermarkets and, cheapest of all, *agencias*, which are normally agents for just one brand. For bottles you pay a deposit: to get it back, keep your receipt and return your bottles to the same store. Bigger, 940ml bottles are known as *caguamas* (turtles), or in the case of Pacífico, *ballenas* (whales).

Beer and wine

Mexican beer (*cerveza*) is mostly light lager (*cerveza clara*) – usually light in flavour as well as colour. Sol, Tecate and Dos Equis are typical brands; if you want something more flavoursome try Modelo, Bohémia or Corona, or a dark (*oscura*) beer, of which the best are Negra Modelo, Indio and Bohémia Obscura. Microbreweries are increasingly springing up. Try a *michelada*, a beer cocktail made by adding ice, lime and Worcestershire and Tabasco sauces to dark beer and rimming the glass with salt. The milder *chelada* is a light beer mixed with plenty of lime and salt, and both are refreshing on a sunny day.

Wine (*vino* – *tinto* is red, *blanco* is white) is not seen a great deal, although Mexico does produce a fair number of perfectly good vintages. You're safest sticking to brand names like Hidalgo or Domecq, although it may also be worth experimenting with some of the new labels, especially those from Baja California, such as L. A. Cetto, which are attempting to emulate the success of their neighbours across the border and in many cases have borrowed American techniques and wine-makers.

TOP 5 PLACES TO EAT

Cetli Tulum. See page 763.
Ceviche de Guerrerense Ensenada. See page 516.
Taquería Hermanos González La Paz. See page 545.
Oaxaca's markets Oaxaca. See page 574.
La Viña de Bacco San Cristóbal de las Casas. See page 646.

Tequila, mescal and pulque

Tequila, distilled from the cactus-like agave plant and produced mainly in the state of Jalisco, is the most famous Mexican spirit, usually taken with lime and salt, or a chile and tomato chaser called *sangrita*, but *añejo* or *reposado* tequila (aged in the vat) should be sipped straight, and not wasted in cocktails such as margarita (tequila, lime juice and triple sec – considered a ladies´ drink). Mexican law allows up to 49 percent cane or corn to be added to the agave from which tequila is made, so unless the label says "100% de agave", it won't be. The proprietary brands, José Cuervo and Sauza, make bog-standard white tequilas as well as smoother, aged versions (Cuervo Tradicional and Sauza Hornitos), but connoisseurs prefer posher makes such as 1921, Herradura or Don Julio. "Gold" tequila contains extraneous colourings and is worth avoiding. For more on tequila, see page 271.

Mescal (often spelled mezcal) is basically the same thing as tequila, but is made from a slightly different variety of plant, the maguey, and is younger and less refined. In fact, tequila was originally just a variety of mescal. The spurious belief that the worm in the mescal bottle is hallucinogenic is based on confusion between the drink and the peyote cactus, which is also called mescal, but by the time you've got down as far as the worm, you'll be too far gone to notice anyway.

Pulque, a mildly alcoholic milky beer made from the same maguey cactus, is the traditional drink of the poor and sold in special bars called *pulquerías*. The best comes from the State of Mexico, and is thick and viscous – it's a little like palm wine, and definitely an acquired taste. Unfermented *pulque*, called *aguamiel*, is sweet and non-alcoholic.

Other spirits and cocktails

Drinking other spirits, you should always ask for **nacional**, as anything imported is fabulously expensive. **Rum** (*ron*), **gin** (*ginebra*) and **vodka** are made in Mexico, as are some very palatable **brandies** (brandy or coñac – try San Marcos or Presidente). Most of the **cocktails** for which Mexico is known – margaritas, piñas coladas and so on – are available only in tourist areas or hotel bars, and are generally pretty strong.

The media

The Mexican media can be very sensationalist, and news is mostly local, and often heavily slanted towards the government, but for Spanish-speakers there is an independent press, as well as some interesting programmes on TV.

Newspapers

Few domestic **newspapers** carry much foreign news, and the majority of international coverage does not extend beyond Latin America. Most papers are lurid scandal sheets, brimming with violent crime depicted in full colour. Each state has its own press, however, and they do vary: while most are little more than government mouthpieces, others are surprisingly independent.

If you read Spanish you could try *Reforma* (http://reforma.com), which has a good reputation for independence and political objectivity, while the more left-wing *La Jornada* (http://jornada.com.mx) is quite daringly critical of government and organized crime, and its journalists regularly face death threats as a result. The press has gradually been asserting its independence since the mid-1990s, tackling such subjects as human rights, corruption and drug trafficking, though journalists still face danger if they speak out, not only from shady government groups but also from drug traffickers. Reporting on links between the two is particularly dangerous. At least 150 journalists have been killed in Mexico since 2009, according to press freedom NGO Reporters Without Borders, which rates it as one of the most dangerous countries in the world for journalists.

Television

You can usually pick up a dozen channels in Mexico without cable or satellite. Four are run by the main **TV** company, Televisa, and another couple by TV Azteca. Canal 22 tends to show cultural programmes, though they are often rather dry. Canal Once is the most original and independent channel, and frequently has something quite interesting on, especially late in the evening. **Cable** and **satellite** are widespread, and even quite budget hotels offer numerous channels, many of them American.

THE SODA TAX

Mexicans have dangerously sweet teeth: more than thirty percent of the population is obese, many more are overweight, and diseases like diabetes are rife. **Sugary drinks** are one of the key causes: each Mexican drinks the equivalent of 163 litres of Coca-Cola a year – the highest rate in the world.

In an attempt to tackle this expanding problem, the Mexican government introduced a ten percent "**soda tax**" in January 2014, plus additional taxes on high-calorie snacks like crisps and biscuits. Six months later these policies were followed by wide-ranging restrictions on TV and cinema advertising of sugary soft drinks and high calorie foods.

Early signs suggested that these steps have had a positive impact: sugary drink purchases had fallen six percent by the end of 2014, and the "soda tax" had raised more than M$18 billion in revenue. Inevitably, however, there has been a **backlash**. In late 2015, following fierce lobbying from multinational fizzy drinks manufacturers, the government agreed to halve the tax for sweetened drinks with a "lower sugar content".

Campaigners and public health experts, by contrast, are urging the government to go further and instead increase the tax, abolish VAT on bottled water to make it cheaper than sugary drinks, and to provide free drinking water in schools, among other measures.

DÍA DE LOS MUERTOS

If visitors know just one Mexican holiday, it's probably the **Day of the Dead**, when families honour and remember those who have died. Actually taking place over two days, November 1 and 2, it's an Indigenous tradition unique to Mexico. With a few exceptions (such as the beautiful torch-lighting ceremony and festive dances around Lago de Pátzcuaro), it's usually a private rite. In every home, and in many businesses, people set up *ofrendas* (altars) for the deceased: the centrepiece is always a photograph, lit by candles. In addition to the photo, the person's favourite foods are also placed on the altar, as a way of luring the soul back to this world. For the same reason, strong-scented, bright orange marigolds are often laid in a path leading to the altar, and resinous *copal* incense is lit.

On the streets, market stalls brim with eggy, orange-scented *pan de muertos* and colourfully iced sugar skulls. Families usually gather to eat dinner on the night of November 1, then visit gravesites, which are also cleaned and decorated. Far from being a sad time, the Day of the Dead is an occasion for telling funny stories, bonding with family and generally celebrating life.

On Mexican TV you can watch any number of US shows dubbed into Spanish, but far and away the most popular programmes are the *telenovelas* – soap operas that dominate the screens from 6pm to 10pm and pull in millions of viewers. Each episode takes melodrama to new heights, with nonstop action and emotions hammed up to the maximum for riveted fans. Plot lines make national news, and *telenovela* stars are major celebrities, despite their ludicrously over-the-top acting styles.

Radio

Radio stations in the capital and Guadalajara (among others) have programmes in English for a couple of hours each day, and in many places US broadcasts can also be picked up. Reactor (in Mexico City on 105.7MHz FM, and online at http://imer.mx/reactor) plays a mix of music including modern Mexican sounds, and from México state, Radio Chapingo (1610kHz AM, http://onlineradiobox.com/mx/radiochapingo) plays the traditional music of Indigenous ethnic groups as well as modern Mexican music of various genres. If you have a short-wave radio, you can get the Voice of America (http://voanews.com) and, at certain times, Radio Canada (http://ici.radio-canada.ca).

Festivals

Stumbling, perhaps accidentally, onto some Mexican village fiesta may prove to be the highlight of your travels. Everywhere, from the remotest Indigenous village to the most sophisticated city suburb, devotes at least one day annually to partying. Usually it's in honour of the local saint's day, but many fiestas have pre-Christian origins, and any excuse – from harvest celebrations to the coming of the rains – will do.

Even the tiniest village in Mexico has an annual fiesta. They usually last at least a couple of days and often involve some blend of rodeos, bullfights, dancing, fried snacks, carnival rides, fireworks and processions around the church. They offer a great opportunity to see Indigenous dances – such as the **Danza de los Viejitos** (Dance of the Little Old Men) in Michoacán, or the feather-bedecked **quetzales** in Cuetzalan, Puebla. Details of the most important local fiestas can be found at the end of each chapter, while the most important nationwide are listed below.

In addition to these, there are plenty of lesser local festivals, as well as certain major festivals celebrated throughout the country. Traditional dances and music form an essential part of almost every fiesta, and most include a procession behind some revered holy image or a more celebratory secular parade with fireworks. No two fiestas will be quite the same. The Catholic saints' calendar provides countless opportunities for celebrating, with many of the biggest events observed with a combination of religious fervour and all-out partying.

A festival calendar

JANUARY

New Year Jan 1. Still largely an occasion to spend with family, the actual hour being celebrated with the eating of grapes.

Twelfth Night (Epiphany, Reyes) Jan 6. Presents are traditionally given on this, the last day of Christmas, when the biblical Magi are believed to have arrived bearing gifts. Nowadays, things are shifting into line with American custom, and more and more people are exchanging gifts on December 25 instead.

Ortiz Tirado Music Festival late Jan. A festival of classical music held annually in Alamos, Sonora, in honour of opera singer Alfonso Ortiz Tirado (who died in 1960), draws leading classical musicians and singers from across the world.

FEBRUARY

Carnaval moveable. The last week of taking one's pleasures before the forty-day abstinence of Lent, celebrated throughout the Roman Catholic world, but is at its most exuberant in Latin America. Like Easter, its date is not fixed, but generally falls in February or early March, celebrated with costumes, parades, eating and dancing, most spectacularly in Veracruz and Mazatlán, working its way up to a climax on the last day, Mardi Gras (Shrove Tues). Carnaval is celebrated most vigorously in the coastal cities, including Veracruz and San Miguel on Cozumel. The city of Mazatlán claims to have the world's third-largest Mardi Gras party, after Rio and New Orleans.

MARCH

Festival Internacional de Guitarra late March or early April. A celebration of guitar music held annually in Morelia, and attended by musicians from around the world.

APRIL

Semana Santa (Holy Week) moveable. The country's biggest holiday, beginning on Palm Sunday and finishing a week later on Easter Sunday. Still a deeply religious festival in Mexico, it celebrates the resurrection of Christ, and is also an occasion to venerate the Virgin Mary, with processions bearing her image now a hallmark of the celebrations. Pilgrims converge on churches, and people re-enact the Passion of Christ. The most famous staging is in Iztapalapa, outside Mexico City, where the event involves a cast of thousands, buckets of fake blood and more than a million spectators. Transport is disrupted everywhere as virtually the whole country is on the move, and you will definitely need to plan ahead if travelling. Many places close for the whole of Holy Week, and certainly from Thursday to Sunday.

MAY

Cinco de Mayo May 5. Commemorating the 1862 Battle of Puebla, it's a public holiday in Mexico, but is actually celebrated more enthusiastically in the US, where many Gringos (who see the date as a chance to have a theme party involving sombreros, nachos and tequila) have come to believe that it's Mexico's equivalent of the US's July 4. In Mexico it's not such a big deal, except in Puebla, where it is celebrated with an exuberant fiesta.

JUNE

Día de San Juan (St John's Day) June 24. Celebrating the birth of the biblical St John the Baptist, but also handily close to the summer solstice, this is celebrated with bonfires, fairs, *charreadas* (rodeos) and sometimes water throwing in towns and villages nationwide.

JULY

Día de Santiago (St James's Day) July 25. An opportunity for a fiesta in many parts of the country, most notably in Chiapas, where big celebrations are held at San Cristóbal de las Casas.

AUGUST

Día de la Asunción (Assumption Day) Aug 15. This is the day when the Virgin Mary is believed to have ascended to heaven, and although it isn't a public holiday, it's celebrated around the country, most notably at Oxkutzcab and Izamal in Yucatán, and Cholula in Puebla State.

SEPTEMBER

Independence Day Sept 16. While Easter and Carnaval are popular, this one is more official, marking the historic day in 1810 when Manuel Hidalgo y Costilla issued the Grito (Cry of Independence) from his parish church in Dolores, now Dolores Hidalgo, Guanajuato, which is still the centre of commemoration. You'll also find the day marked in the capital with mass recitation of the Grito in the Zócalo, followed by fireworks, music and dancing. Nevertheless, in some ways it's more solemn than the religious festivals.

Festival Internacional de Santa Lucía end of Sept and beginning of Oct. Formerly the Festival Cultural of Monterrey's Barrio Antiguo, showcasing local rock bands and other eclectic musicians, this festival has been reborn, having outgrown the confines of the Barrio Antiguo to become a citywide event. It's now Mexico's third-biggest music festival after Guanajuato's Festival Cervantino and Alamos' Festival Ortiz Tirado.

OCTOBER

Festival Internacional Cervantino mid-Oct. Guanajuato's big, two-and-a-half-week music fest, dating back to the 1970s. Every October, it brings together Mexican marimba legends, French jazz artists, choral music from England and international dance troupes. For more details, see page 344.

NOVEMBER

The Day of the Dead (All Saints'/Souls' Day, and its eve) Nov 1–2. Offerings are made to ancestors' souls, frequently with picnics and all-night vigils at their graves, and people build shrines in their homes to honour their departed relatives. Sweetmeats and papier-mâché statues of dressed-up skeletons give proceedings a rather gothic air. Head for cemeteries to see the really spectacular stuff, or to Pátzcuaro (see page 281). For more details, see page 288.

DECEMBER

Día de la Virgen de Guadalupe Dec 12. Celebrations everywhere, and a huge day for pilgrims at the Basílica de Nuestra Señora de Guadalupe in Mexico City, home of Mexico's most important Virgin (a manifestation, that is, of the biblical Virgin Mary), who appeared on this day in 1551 (see page 117).

Christmas Dec 25. A major holiday, with loads of people on the move and transport booked solid for weeks ahead. Gringo influence is heavy nowadays, with Santa Claus and Christmas trees, but the Mexican festival remains distinct in many ways, with a much stronger religious element (virtually every home has a Nativity crib). One of the more bizarre Christmas events takes place in Oaxaca, where there is a public display of Nativity cribs and other sculptures made of radishes.

Sports and outdoor activities

You'll find facilities for golf, tennis, sailing, surfing, scuba diving and deep-sea fishing – even horseriding and hunting – at all the big resorts.

Sport fishing is enormously popular in Baja California and the big Pacific coast resorts, while freshwater bass fishing is growing in popularity too, especially behind the large dams in the north of the country. **Diving** and **snorkelling** are big on the Caribbean coast, with world-famous dive sites at Cozumel and on the reefs further south. The Pacific coast has become something of a centre for **surfing**, with few facilities as yet (though you can rent surfboards in major tourist centres such as Acapulco and Mazatlán) but with plenty of Californian surfers who follow the weather south over the winter. The most popular places are in Baja California and on the Oaxaca coast, but the biggest waves are to be found around Lázaro Cárdenas in Michoacán. A more minority-interest activity for which Mexico has become a major centre is **caving**. With a third of the country built on limestone, there are caverns in most states that can be explored by experienced potholers or spelunkers.

The Ministry of Tourism publishes a leaflet on participatory sports in Mexico, and can also advise on licences and seasons.

Spectator sports

Mexico's chief spectator sport is soccer (*fútbol*; see page 157). Mexican teams have not been consistently successful on the international stage, but going to a game can still be a thrilling experience. The capital and Guadalajara are the best places to see a match, and the biggest game in the domestic league, "El Clásico", between Chivas from Guadalajara and América from Mexico City, fills the city's 150,000-seater Aztec stadium to capacity. **Baseball** (*béisbol*) is also popular, as is **American football** (especially on TV). **Jai alai** (also known as **frontón**, or **pelota vasca**) is Basque handball, common in big cities and played at a very high speed with a small hard ball and curved scoop attached to the hand; it's a big gambling game.

Mexican rodeos (*charreadas*), mainly seen in the north of the country, are as spectacular for their style and costume as they are for the events, while **bullfights** remain an obsession: every city has a bullring – Mexico City's Plaza México is the world's largest – and the country's *toreros* are said to be the world's most reckless, much in demand in Spain. Another popular blood sport, usually at village level, is **cock fighting**, still legal in Mexico and mainly attended for the opportunity to bet on the outcome.

Masked **wrestling** (*lucha libre*) is very popular in Mexico, too, with the participants, Batman-like, out of the game for good should their mask be removed and their secret identity revealed. Nor does the resemblance to comic-book superheroes end in the ring: certain masked wrestlers have become popular social campaigners out of the ring, always ready to turn up just in the nick of time to rescue the beleaguered poor from eviction by various landlords or persecution by corrupt politicians. For more on wrestling, see page 136.

Culture and etiquette

Mexicans are generally very courteous, and in some ways quite formal. It is common, for example, to address people as señor or señora, while being too brusque can give quite a bad impression.

Most Mexicans are also quite religious, and about three-quarters are **Roman Catholic**; you will often see little altars by the roadside, and many people cross themselves whenever they pass a church. It is wise to avoid open disrespect for religion unless you are sure of your company. While male travellers will find the country very easy-going, women may encounter a few difficulties arising from traditional Latin machismo.

Sexual harassment and discrimination

Machismo is engrained in the Mexican mentality and, although it's softened to some extent by the gentler mores of Indigenous culture, most women will find that a degree of harassment is inevitable.

On the whole, most hassles will be limited to **comments** (*piropos*, supposedly compliments) in the street, but situations that might be quite routine at home can seem threatening without a clear understanding of the nuances of Mexican Spanish. Avoid eye contact – wearing sunglasses helps. Any provocation is best ignored – Mexican women are rarely slow with a stream of retaliatory abuse, but it's a dangerous strategy unless you're very sure of your ground, and coming from a foreigner, it may be taken as racism.

Public transport can be one of the worst places for harassment, especially groping in crowded situations. On the Mexico City Metro, there are separate women's carriages and passages during rush hours.

Problems are aggravated in the big tourist spots, where legendarily "easy" tourists attract droves of would-be gigolos. Away from resorts and big cities, though, and especially in Indigenous areas, there is rarely any problem – you may as an outsider be treated as an object of curiosity, and usually such curiosity can also extend to friendliness and hospitality. On the whole, the further from the US border you get, the easier things will become.

The restrictions imposed on drinking are without a doubt irksome: women can now drink in cantinas, but even in so-called "ladies' bars", "unescorted" women may be looked at with suspicion. Even in the roughest places, you are unlikely to be refused service nowadays, but whether or not you would feel comfortable drinking there is a different matter.

Tipping

At expensive restaurants in tourist resorts, waiters and waitresses are used to American tipping levels (15–20 percent), but elsewhere levels are more like those in Europe (10–15 percent). In mid-range and upmarket hotels, you will be expected to tip chambermaids (a few dollars, depending on the standard of the hotel and the length of your stay) and porters (10–20 pesos or a dollar is fine). It is not usual to tip taxi drivers, but small tips are expected by petrol-station and car-park attendants and the bagboys at supermarkets (all of these will be happy with a few pesos of small change).

Shopping

The craft tradition of Mexico, much of it descended directly from arts practised long before the Spanish arrived, is still extremely strong. Regional and highly localized specialities survive, with villages throughout the republic jealously guarding their reputations – especially in the states of Michoacán, Oaxaca and Chiapas, as well as the Yucatán Peninsula. There's a considerable amount of Guatemalan textiles and embroidery about, too.

Crafts

To buy crafts, there is no need to visit the place of origin – **shops** in Mexico City and all the big resorts gather the best and most popular items from around the country. On the other hand, it's a great deal more enjoyable to see where the articles come from, and certainly the only way to get any real bargains. The good stuff is rarely inexpensive wherever you buy it, however, and there is an enormous amount of dross produced specifically for tourists.

FONART shops, in major centres throughout Mexico, are run by a government agency (https://www.gob.mx/fonart) devoted to the promotion and preservation of crafts; their wares are always excellent, if expensive, and the shops should be visited to get an idea of what is available. Where no such store exists, you can get a similar idea by looking at the best of the tourist shops.

Among the most popular items are: **silver**, the best of which is wrought in Taxco, although rarely mined there; **pottery**, made almost everywhere, with different techniques, designs and patterns in each region; **woollen goods**, especially blankets, which are again made everywhere, and *sarapes* from Oaxaca – always check the fibres and go for more expensive natural dyes; **leather**, especially tyre-tread-soled *huaraches* (sandals), sold cheaply wherever you go; **glass** from Jalisco; **lacquerware**, particularly from Uruapán; and **hammocks**, the best of which are sold in Mérida.

It is illegal to buy or sell antiquities, and even more criminal to try taking them out of the country (moreover, many items sold as valuable antiquities are little more than worthless fakes) – best just to look.

Markets

For bargain hunters, the **mercado** (market) is the place to head. There's one in every Mexican town which, on the traditional market day, will be at its busiest with villagers from the surrounding area bringing their produce for sale or barter. Mercados are mainly dedicated to food and everyday necessities, but most have a section devoted to crafts, and in larger towns you may find a separate crafts bazaar.

Unless you're completely hopeless at bargaining, prices will always be lower in the market than in shops, but shops do have a couple of advantages. First, they exercise a degree of quality control, whereas any old junk can be sold in the market; and second, many established shops will be able to ship purchases home for you, which saves an enormous amount of frustrating bureaucracy.

Bargaining and haggling are very much a matter of personal style, highly dependent on your command of Spanish, aggressiveness and, to some extent, experience. The old tricks (never showing the least sign of interest – let alone enthusiasm – and walking away will always cut the price dramatically) do still hold true; but make sure you know what you want, its approximate value and how much you are prepared to pay. Never start to haggle for something you definitely don't intend to buy – it'll end in bad feelings on both sides. In shops there's little chance of significantly altering the official price unless you're buying in bulk, and even in markets most food and simple household goods have a set price (though it may be doubled at the sight of an approaching gringo).

Travelling with children

Children under the age of 18 can enter the country either with their own passport or on the passport of a parent with whom they are travelling, but if they are not accompanied by both parents, they will need written consent from whichever parent is not with them (or from both if they are on their own).

Travelling with younger kids is not uncommon – most Mexicans dote on children and they often help to break the ice with strangers. The main problem, especially with small children, is their extra vulnerability. They need protecting from the sun, unsafe drinking water, heat and unfamiliar food. Chile peppers in particular may be a problem for kids who are not used to them. Diarrhoea can also be dangerous for younger children: rehydration salts (see page 42) are vital. Ensure that your child is aware of the dangers of rabies and other animal-borne illnesses; keep children away from all animals and consider a rabies shot.

For touring, hiking or walking, child-carrier backpacks are ideal: they can weigh less than 2kg. If the child is small enough, a fold-up buggy is also well worth packing – especially if they will sleep in it while you have a meal or a drink.

Travel essentials

Accessible travel

An estimated five percent of Mexicans have some kind of significant disability, and Mexico has made massive advances in accessibility in recent years, although problems still remain. Ramps and wheelchair accessibility are now the norm in public buildings, and braille is increasingly common on public notices too. The real scandal so far as people with disabilities are concerned is the continued abuse of those confined to residential institutions or living on the street.

Hotels vary, but, especially at the top end of the market, it shouldn't be too difficult to find accommodation and tour operators who can cater for your particular needs. If you stick to **beach resorts** – Cancún and Acapulco in particular – and top-end hotels, you should be able to find places that are wheelchair-friendly and used to disabled guests. US chains are very good for this, with Choice, Days Inn, Holiday Inn, Leading Hotels of the World, Marriott, Radisson, Ramada, Sheraton and Westin claiming to have the necessary facilities for at least some disabilities in some of their hotels. Check in advance with tour companies, hotels and airlines that they can accommodate you specifically.

Unless you have your own **transport**, the best way to travel in Mexico may be by air; buses still rarely cater for disabled people and wheelchairs. Kerb ramps are increasingly common, especially in big cities, but less so in smaller places, where streets and pavements may not be in great nick, and people are not especially more likely to volunteer help than at home. Depending on your disability, you may want to find an able-bodied helper to accompany you.

RESOURCES

Disabled Holidays UK 0161 260 2281, http://disabledholidays.com. UK travel agency specializing in holidays for people with disabilities. Their website has a page on Mexico, with information on accessible hotels across the country.

Mexico Accesible Mexico 322 225 0989; US 1 866 519 6165; Canada 1 877 839 3484; http://accesiblemexico.com. A Puerto Vallarta firm offering a range of services, from mobility equipment to wheelchair-friendly timeshares.

Costs

The developed tourist resorts and big cities are invariably more expensive than more remote towns, and certain other areas also have noticeably higher prices – among them the industrialized north. Prices can also be affected by **season** and many hotels raise

ROUGH GUIDES TRAVEL INSURANCE

Looking for travel insurance? Rough Guides partners with top providers worldwide to offer you the best coverage. Policies are available to residents of anywhere in the world, with a range of options whether you are looking for single-trip, multi-country or long-stay insurance. There's coverage for a wide range of adventure sports, 24-hour emergency assistance, high levels of medical and evacuation cover and a stream of travel safety information. Even better, roughguides.com users can take advantage of these policies online 24/7, from anywhere in the world – even if you're already travelling. To make the most of your travels and ensure a smoother experience, it's always good to be prepared for when things don't go according to plan. For more information go to www.roughguides.com/bookings/insurance.

their prices during busy times of the year. Summer, Christmas and Easter are the peak times for Mexican tourists, and areas like Acapulco and Cancún, which attract large numbers of overseas visitors, put their prices up during the high season. Special events are also likely to be marked by price hikes.

As always, if you're **travelling alone** you'll end up spending more – sharing rooms and food saves a substantial amount. In the larger resorts, you can get apartments for up to six people for even greater savings. If you have an **International Student** or **Youth Card**, you might find the occasional reduction on a museum admission price, but don't go out of your way to obtain one, since most concessions are, at least in theory, only for Mexican students. Cards available include the ISIC card for full-time students and the International Youth Travel Card (IYTC) for under-31s, both of which are available from youth travel firms. A university or college photo ID card might even work in some places.

Most restaurant bills come with fifteen **percent IVA** (Impuesto de Valor Añadido, or Valued Added Sales Tax) added; this may not always be included in prices quoted on the menu. **Service** is sometimes added to bills; if not, the amount you tip is entirely up to you – in cheap places, it's typically 10–15 percent, but more like 15–20 percent in smarter venues. See page 55 for more on tipping.

Electricity

Theoretically 110 volts AC, with simple two-flat-pin rectangular plugs – most North American appliances can be used as they are. Travellers from the UK, Ireland, Europe, Australasia and South Africa should bring along a converter and a plug adaptor. Cuts in service and fluctuations in current sometimes occur.

Insurance

There are no reciprocal health arrangements between Mexico and any other country, so travel **insurance** is essential. Credit cards (particularly American Express) often have certain levels of medical or other insurance included, and travel insurance may also be included if you use a major credit card to pay for your trip. Some package tours, too, may include insurance.

Before paying for a new policy, it's worth checking whether you are already covered: some all-risks home insurance policies may cover your possessions when overseas, and many private medical schemes include cover when abroad. In Canada, provincial health plans usually provide partial cover for medical mishaps overseas, while holders of official student/teacher/youth cards in Canada and the US are entitled to meagre accident coverage and hospital in-patient benefits. Students in Canada and the US will often find that their health insurance policies extend over the holidays and for one term beyond the date of last enrolment.

After exhausting the possibilities above, you might want to contact a specialist travel insurance company, or consider the travel insurance deal offered by Rough Guides (see page 57). A typical travel insurance policy usually provides cover for the loss of baggage, tickets and – up to a certain limit – cash or cheques, as well as cancellation or curtailment of your journey. Most of them exclude so-called **dangerous sports** unless an extra premium is paid: in Mexico this can mean scuba diving, whitewater rafting, windsurfing and trekking, though probably not kayaking or jeep safaris. Many policies can be chopped and changed to exclude coverage you don't need – for example, sickness and accident benefits can often be excluded or included at will. If you do take medical coverage, ascertain whether benefits will be paid as treatment proceeds or only after your return home, and whether there is a 24-hour medical emergency number. When securing **baggage cover**, make sure that the per-article limit will cover your most valuable possession. If you need to make a claim, you should keep receipts for medicines and medical treatment, and in the event you have anything stolen, you must make an

USEFUL WEBSITES

Latin America Bureau http://lab.org.uk. Website of this well-respected UK-based charity with the latest news, analysis and information from across the region, including Mexico.

Mexico Cooks! http://mexicocooks.typepad.com. This culinary blog will get your mouth watering with restaurant reviews, recipes and foodie news.

The News http://thenews.mx. Handy English-language website with news, features and sports updates from across Mexico.

The Yucatan Times http://theyucatantimes.com. English-language news site focusing on the touristy peninsula.

Visit Mexico http://visitmexico.com. The country's official tourist website is worth a visit.

official statement to the police and obtain a copy of the declaration (*copia de la declaración*) for your insurance company.

Internet

Internet cafés are easy to find in all the larger cities and resort destinations, and the level of service is usually excellent. One or two offer cheap VOIP phone calls too. In smaller towns and villages, such facilities are still rare. Depending on where you are, internet access can cost can vary to extreme amounts. Major tourist resorts can be the most expensive places, and in these areas it's best to look for cheaper internet cafés around the town centre and avoid those in the luxury hotel zones. Internet facilities in large cities are usually open from early morning until late at night, but in smaller towns they have shorter opening hours and may not open on Sundays. Wi-fi (generally free) is widespread in hotels, hostels, restaurants, cafés and even town plazas.

Laundry

Lavanderías (laundries) are ubiquitous in Mexico, as the majority of households don't own a washing machine. Most *lavanderías* charge by the kilo, and for a few dollars you'll get your clothes back clean, pressed and perfectly folded in less than 24 hours. Many hotels also offer laundry services that, although convenient, tend to charge by the item, adding up to a considerably greater cost.

LGBTQ+ travellers

There are no federal laws governing **homosexuality** in Mexico, and hence it's **legal**. There are, however, laws enforcing "public morality", which, although they are supposed only to apply to prostitution, are often used against gay people. 1997 saw the election of Mexico's first "out" congresswoman, the left-wing PRD's Patria Jiménez, and in 2003 the federal parliament passed a law against discrimination on various grounds including sexual preference. In 2005, however, a gay man from Tampico successfully claimed political asylum in the US after demonstrating the extent of persecution he faced in his hometown. There have been more positive moves recently, though: in June 2015 the Supreme Court issued a "jurisprudential thesis" that changed the legal definition of marriage to include same-sex couples.

There are a large number of **LGBTQ+ groups** and **publications** in Mexico. The **lesbian** scene is not as visible or as large as the gay scene for men, but it's there and growing. There are gay bars and clubs in the major resorts and US border towns, and in large cities such as the capital, and also Monterrey, Guadalajara, Veracruz and Oaxaca; elsewhere, private parties are where it all happens, and you'll need a contact to find them.

As far as popular **attitudes** are concerned, religion and machismo are the order of the day, and prejudice is rife, but attitudes are changing. Soft-core porn magazines for gay men are sold openly on street stalls and, while you should be careful to avoid upsetting macho sensibilities, you should have few problems if you are discreet. In Juchitán, Oaxaca, on the other hand, gay transgender males, known as *muxes*, are accepted as a kind of third sex, and the town has a transgender basketball team.

You can check the latest LGBTQ+ rights situation in Mexico on the International Gay and Lesbian Human Rights Commission website at http://iglhrc.org, and information on the male gay scene in Mexico (gay bars, meeting places and cruising spots) can be found in the annual *Spartacus Gay Guide*, available in specialist bookshops at home, or online at http://spartacusworld.com.

Living in Mexico

There's virtually no chance of finding temporary **work** in Mexico unless you have some very specialized skill and have arranged the position beforehand. Work **permits** are almost impossible to obtain. The few foreigners who manage to find work do so mostly in language schools. It may be possible, though not legal, to earn money as a private English tutor by advertising in a local newspaper or at a university.

The best way to extend your time in Mexico is on a **study programme** or **volunteer project**. A US organization called AmeriSpan selects language schools in countries worldwide, including Mexico, to match the needs and requirements of students, and provides advice and support. For further information, call (US or Canada) 1 800 511 0179 or see http://amerispan.com.

Volunteers need to apply for a voluntary work visa (FM3), for which you will need to present a letter of invitation from the organization for which you are volunteering.

STUDY AND WORK PROGRAMMES

AFS Intercultural Programs http://afs.org, http://afsusa.org, http://afscanada.org, http://afs.org.au, http://afs.org.nz, http://afs.org.za; international enquiries; +1 212 807 8686. Intercultural exchange organization with programmes in over fifty countries, including Mexico (but there's no branch in the UK).

Council on International Educational Exchange (CIEE) http://ciee.org. Leading NGO offering study programmes around the world, including Mexico.

Earthwatch Institute http://earthwatch.org. Matches volunteers with scientists working on particular projects, sometimes in Mexico, but it's not cheap: volunteers must raise a minimum contribution to the cost of research for each one-to two-week stint.

Go Abroad http://goabroad.com. With almost 17,000 verified study-abroad opportunities across the globe, this organization has a good selection of the best programmes throughout Mexico.

Studyabroad.com http://studyabroad.com. Language programmes, semester-long and year-long courses and internships in Guadalajara, Cuernavaca, Puebla and Mexico City.

Volunteer South America http://volunteersouthamerica.net. A useful site with links to free and low-cost volunteering opportunities across Latin America, including Mexico.

Mail

Mexican **postal services** (*correos*) can be quite slow and unreliable. Airmail to the capital should arrive within a few days, but it may take a couple of weeks to get anywhere at all remote. Packages frequently go astray. **Post offices** (generally open Mon–Fri 8am–4.30pm, Sat 8am–noon, sometimes longer at the central office in big cities) usually offer a **poste restante/general delivery** service: letters should be addressed to "Lista de Correos". Mail is held for two weeks, though you may get around that by sending it to "Poste Restante" with "Favor de retener hasta la llegada" (please hold until arrival) on the envelope. Letters are often filed incorrectly, so you should have staff check under all your initials. To collect, you will need your passport or some other official ID with a photograph. There is no fee.

For personal mail, Mexican **addresses** begin with the street and house number. The number goes after the street name (Juárez 123 rather than 123 Juárez), and is followed if appropriate by the floor or apartment number (*planta baja* means ground floor). After that comes the *cólonia* (the immediate neighbourhood), then the town, then finally the zip code and the state (on one line in that order – in the case of Mexico City, "México DF" is the equivalent of the state).

Sending letters and cards home is also easy enough, if slow. Anything sent **abroad** by air should have an airmail (*por avión*) stamp on it or it is liable to go by surface mail. Letters should take around a week to North America, two to Europe or Australasia, but can take much longer (postcards in particular are likely to be slow). Anything at all important should be taken to the post office and preferably registered rather than dropped in a mailbox, although the dedicated airmail boxes in resorts and big cities are supposed to be more reliable than ordinary ones. Postcards or letters up to 20g cost a few dollars to North America or the Caribbean and a little more to the British Isles, Europe or South America. Australasia, Asia, Africa or the Pacific rank among the more expensive places to send a postcard.

The process of sending **packages** out of the country is drowned in bureaucracy. Regulations about the thickness of brown paper wrapping and the amount of string used vary from state to state, but any package must be checked by customs and have its paperwork stamped by at least three other departments. Take your package (unsealed) to any post office and they'll set you on your way. Many stores will send your purchases home for you, which is much easier. Within the country, you can send a package by bus if there is someone to collect it at the other end.

Maps

Reliable options available outside of Mexico include Mexico road maps published by Globetrotter (1:3,500,000), GeoCenter (1:2,500,000), Hallwag (1:2,500,000) and Freytag & Berndt (1:2,000,000). In Mexico itself, the best maps are those produced by Guía Roji, who also publish a Mexican road atlas and a Mexico City street guide. Guía Roji maps are widely available – try branches of Sanborn's or large Pemex stations – and can also be ordered online at http://guiaroji.com.mx.

More detailed, large-scale maps – for hiking or climbing – are harder to come by. The most detailed, easily available area maps are produced by International Travel Map Productions (http://itmb.ca), whose Travellers' Reference Map series covers various regions of the country. INEGI, the Mexican office of statistics, also produce very good topographic maps on various scales. They have an office in every state capital (addresses on their website at http://inegi.org.mx – via their interactive map). Unfortunately, stocks can run rather low, so don't count on being able to buy the ones that you want.

Money

The Mexican **peso**, usually written $, is made up of 100 centavos (¢, like a US cent). Bills come in denominations of $20, $50, $100, $200, $500 and $1000, with coins of 10¢, 20¢, 50¢, $1, $2, $5 and $10. The use of the dollar symbol for the peso is occasionally confusing; the initials MN (*moneda nacional* or national coin) are occasionally used to indicate that it's Mexican, not American, money that is being referred to. Prices in this book are generally quoted in Mexican pesos (M$). Note, however, that these will be affected by factors such as inflation and exchange rates. Check an online currency converter such as XE (http://xe.com) or OANDA (http://oanda.com) for up-to-date rates. Some tour operators and large hotels quote prices in US dollars, and accept payment in that currency.

ATMs

The easiest way to access your money in Mexico is in the form of **plastic**, though it's a good idea to also have some cash back-up. Using a Visa, MasterCard, Plus or Cirrus card, you can withdraw cash from **ATMs** in most towns and tourist resorts. By using these you get trade exchange rates, which are somewhat better than those charged by banks for changing cash, though your card issuer may well add a foreign transaction fee, and these can be as much as five percent, so check with your issuer before leaving home. Local ATM providers may also charge a transaction fee; generally speaking, rates and fees make it cheaper to use an ATM for more than around US$100, but to change cash in a *casa de cambio* (see below) for anything much less than that. If you use a credit card rather than a debit card, note all cash advances and ATM withdrawals obtained are treated as loans, with interest accruing daily from the date of withdrawal. Travellers' cheques are increasingly difficult to change in Mexico, but it is possible to get a **prepaid card**, like a form of travellers' cheques in plastic, which you charge up with funds at home and then use to withdraw money from ATMs – MasterCard, Visa and American Express all issue them. Some ATMs in big city centres and resorts can issue US dollars as well as – or instead of – pesos.

USEFUL AND EMERGENCY NUMBERS

General emergency number 066
Police 060
Fire 068
Ambulance 065
Green Angels (tourist highway breakdown) 078
National operator 020
International operator 090
Directory enquiries 040
Tourist information 078

Banks and exchange

Banks are generally open Monday to Friday from 9.30am to 5pm, often with shorter hours for **exchange**. Commission on currency exchange varies but the exchange rate is fixed daily by the government. Not all banks can change money, and only larger branches of the big banks, plus some in tourist resorts, will change currencies other than dollars – and even then at worse rates than you would get for the dollar equivalent.

Casas de cambio (*forex bureaux* aka *bureaux de change*) have varying exchange rates and commission charges, and tend to have shorter queues, less bureaucratic procedures and longer opening hours. The exchange rates are generally better than at banks, but always worth checking, especially for travellers' cheques. Some *casas de cambio* will change only US dollars, but others take euros, Canadian dollars, pounds sterling and other currencies. $100 bills usually attract a better rate than small bills. Again, it's worth shopping around, especially if you intend to change a large sum. Even in a *casa de cambio*, you'll need your passport to change money.

Guatemalan quetzales and Belizean dollars are best got rid of before entering Mexico; otherwise, your best bet for changing them is with tourists heading the other way. It is a good idea to change other currencies into US dollars at home before coming to Mexico, since the difference in the exchange rate more than outweighs the amount you lose in changing your money twice. In some touristy places, such as Acapulco and Tijuana, US dollar bills are almost as easy to spend as pesos. If you're desperate, hotels, shops and restaurants that are used to tourists may change dollars or accept them as payment, but rates will be very low.

Opening hours

It's almost impossible to generalize about **opening hours** in Mexico; even when times are posted at museums, tourist offices and shops, they're not always adhered to.

The **siesta** is still around, and many places will close for a couple of hours in the early afternoon, usually from 1pm to 3pm. Where it's hot – especially on the Gulf coast and in the Yucatán – everything may close for up to four hours in the middle of the day, and then reopen until 8pm or 9pm. In central Mexico, the industrial north and highland areas, hours are more like the standard nine-to-five, and shops do not close for lunch.

Shops tend to keep long hours, say from 9am to 8pm. Museums and galleries open from about 9am or 10am to 5pm or 6pm. Many have reduced entry fees – or are free – on Sunday, and most are closed on Monday. Some museums close for lunch, but archeological sites are open all day. For opening of post offices see page 59; for banks see page 60.

Phones

Local **phone** calls in Mexico are cheap, and some hotels will let you call locally for free. Coin-operated **public phones** exist, but internal long-distance calls are best made with a **phonecard** (sold at newsstands and usable in public phones on almost every street corner). Slightly more expensive, but often more convenient, are *casetas de teléfono* (phone offices), mainly found at bus stations and airports. Calling abroad with a phonecard or from a *caseta* is expensive. Some internet offices offer **VOIP international calls**, which may be cheaper, but the line will not be as good. Skype is generally the best option.

It is also possible to **call collect** (*por cobrar*). In theory, you should be able to make an international collect call from any public phone, by dialling the international operator (090). If you have a calling card from your home phone company, you can use the company's toll-free number and have the call billed to you at home.

Calling Mexico from abroad, dial the international access code (011 from the US or Canada, 00 from Britain, Ireland or New Zealand, 0011 from Australia, 09 from South Africa), followed by the **country code** for Mexico, which is 52. Mexican **numbers** are ten-digits including the area code (*lada*), which is usually three digits, although Mexico City (55), Guadalajara (33) and Monterrey (81) have two-digit area codes. The number itself is usually seven digits, again excepting Mexico City, Guadalajara and Monterrey, where phone numbers have eight digits. If dialling from abroad, you dial the area code immediately after the 52 for Mexico. If dialling long-distance within Mexico, or from a mobile, you need to dial 01, then the area code and the number. If dialling from a landline with the same area code, you omit it. The area code for toll-free numbers is 800, always preceded by the 01.

DIALLING CODES

Mexico long-distance 01 + area code + number
US & Canada 001 + area code + number
UK 00 44 + area code (minus initial zero) + number
Ireland 00 353 + area code (minus initial zero) + number
Australia 00 61 + area code (minus initial zero) + number
New Zealand 00 64 + area code (minus initial zero) + number
South Africa 00 27 + area code (minus initial zero) + number

Mobile phones

To use a **mobile phone** in Mexico is expensive if you simply take your own phone and use it under a roaming agreement. If you are there for any length of time, buy a prepaid phone. You can buy a Mexican SIM-card to get a Mexican number for your own handset, but this involves registering your identity (so you'll need a passport, and you may need to go to the phone company's main office), something that doesn't always work for a foreigner, so make sure your mobile works before you leave the store. Your phone charger will not work in Mexico if it is designed for a 220–240v electricity supply. Calls from mobiles are pricey, and with a SIM-card from abroad you pay to receive as well as make international calls.

Like landlines, Mexican mobile phones have ten-digit numbers, of which the first two or three are the area code. Generally speaking, to call a mobile from a landline, first dial 044 if it has the same area code, 045 if not, or the international access code plus 52-1 if calling from abroad, and then the ten-digit number; note, however, that some mobile numbers work in the same way as dialling landline numbers – unfortunately, you cannot tell from the number alone how it will work.

Photography

It's easy enough to get prints made from a **USB** stick in Mexico. **Film** is also manufactured in the country and, if you buy it from a chain store like Sanborn's rather than at a tourist store, costs no more than at home. Slide film is hard to come by, and any sort of camera hardware will be expensive.

Senior travellers

Mexico is not a country that offers any special difficulties – or any special advantages – to **older travellers**, but the same considerations apply here as to anywhere else in the world. If choosing a package tour, consider one run by firms such as Road Scholar (http://roadscholar.org) or Saga (http://saga.co.uk), which specialize in holidays for the over-50s.

Do remember that Mexico's high altitude, desert heat and tropical humidity can tire you out a lot faster than you might otherwise expect. As far as comfort is concerned, first-class buses are generally pretty pleasant, with plenty of legroom. Second-class buses can be rather more boneshaking, and you may not want to take them for too long a journey.

Senior citizens are often entitled to **discounts** at tourist sights, and on occasion for accommodation and transport, something which it's always worth asking about.

Time

Five **time zones** exist in Mexico. Most of the country is on GMT–6 in winter, GMT–5 in summer (first Sun in April till last Sun in Oct), the same as US Central Time. Baja California Sur, Sinaloa, Nayarit and Chihuahua are on GMT–7 in winter, GMT–6 in summer (the same as US Mountain Time). Baja California is on GMT–8 in winter, GMT–7 in summer, the same as the US West Coast (Pacific Time); and finally, Sonora is on GMT–7 all year round, and does not observe daylight saving time. The state of Quintana Roo changed time zones in early 2015, moving to GMT–5 in winter and GMT–4 in summer, bringing it into line with Eastern Standard Time.

Toilets

Public toilets in Mexico are usually decent enough, but in bars or hole-in-the-wall restaurants, they can be quite basic, and may not have paper. It's therefore wise to carry toilet paper with you. In bus stations, you usually have to pay to use them. Paper should usually be placed in a bin after use, rather than flushed, as it may otherwise block the plumbing.

Toilets are usually known as *baños* (literally bathrooms) or as *excusados* or *sanitarios*. The most common signs are "Damas" (Ladies) and "Caballeros" (Gentlemen), though you may find the more confusing "Señoras" (Women) and "Señores" (Men) or even symbols of the moon (women) and sun (men).

Tourist information

The first place to head for **information**, and for free maps of the country and many towns, is the Mexican Government Ministry of Tourism (**Secretaría de Turismo**, abbreviated to **SECTUR**; http://www.gob.mx/sectur, with travel information at http://visitmexico.com), which has offices throughout Mexico and abroad.

Once you're in Mexico, you'll find tourist offices (sometimes called *turismos*) in most towns. Each state capital will have one run by SECTUR, but most are run by state and municipal authorities; sometimes there'll be two or three rival ones in the same town. Many tourist offices are extremely friendly and helpful, with informed staff and free information and leaflets by the cart-load, but others are barely capable of answering the simplest enquiry. We have listed the most useful ones in the relevant city and regional sections throughout the Guide. You can also call SECTUR toll-free round the clock in Mexico at 078 or 553 002 6300, or toll-free from the US or Canada on 1 866 640 0597, or from the UK 00 800 1111 2266.

Zika virus

The general consensus among reputable international health organizations is that, at the time of writing, Mexico has a moderate risk of mosquito-acquired Zika virus infection; the risk increasing further still in regions that are less than 2000 metres above sea level. By that rule, the only regions of Mexico that are 2000 metres above sea level – and therefore in the lower-risk category – are Mexico City and Puebla. It you're pregnant and thinking about a trip to Mexico, consider postponing non-essential travel until after you've had your baby. Women should also avoid becoming pregnant while travelling in Mexico, and for eight weeks after leaving any area with active Zika virus cases. For the most up-to-date and expert advice about the Zika virus, consult your country's foreign office or state department.

GOVERNMENT TRAVEL ADVICE

Australian Department of Foreign Affairs http://smartraveller.gov.au.

British Foreign & Commonwealth Office http://gov.uk/government/organisations/foreign-commonwealth-office.

Canadian Department of Foreign Affairs http://voyage.gc.ca.

US State Department http://travel.state.gov.

PALACIO DE BELLAS ARTES

Mexico City

PALACIO DE BELLAS ARTES

1 Mexico City

One of the world's mega-cities, with more than 25 million people occupying a shallow mountain bowl at over 2400m above sea level, Mexico City has to be seen to be believed. Spreading out beyond the federal district (Distrito Federal) which is supposed to contain it, the city has a vibe which is at once both edgy and yet laid-back and cosmopolitan at the same time. Despite its terrible pollution (see page 74), the capital is a fun place to be, and nowhere near as intimidating as you might expect. It's also very easy to find your way around, with an efficient metro system, and generally easy-to-navigate grid of streets.

On arrival you may brace yourself for the city's hard edge, but be prepared to be lulled by it. Mexico's capital may initially seem to lack the colour and charm of some of the country's smaller towns, but it can be pretty too, and there's certainly no denying its dynamism. The city centre still retains its colonial feel, its streets bustling with the comings and goings of daily commerce. The fact that different products are sold in specific areas – stationery here, electrical fittings there – sometimes makes it seem like a giant market. To the west, steel and glass take over from brick and stone as tradition gives way to modernity, but in the suburbs, in laid-back *barrios* like San Ángel and Coyoacán, there's as much charm as in any small Mexican town, and a surprising number of little squares overlooked by old churches amid leafy residential backstreets. For many Mexicans, in fact, the city's most important site is the **Basilica de Guadalupe**, sited in the suburbs to the north of town. To the southwest, meanwhile, is Chapultepec Park and some of the biggest attractions you'll want to see, notably the outstanding **Museo Nacional de Antropología.** Even in the centre, around the garden known as the **Alameda** in particular, there's music, art (**Diego Rivera** and **Frida Kahlo**, as well as their contemporaries) and colour enough to seduce you, and the hustle and bustle only seem to amplify it. While the outer edges of the city are largely shantytowns, built piecemeal by migrants from elsewhere in the country, hidden among them are a number of gems, such as the **pyramids** of Tenayuca, Santa Cecilia Acatitlán and Cuicuilco, and the canals of **Xochimilco**.

As much the heart of the modern capital as it was of the Aztec civilization that once thrived here, the **Zócalo**, or main square, is the place to get your bearings. Immediately to its west, in the streets between the Zócalo and the Alameda, is the main **commercial area**. Beyond that, the city stretches northward and southward, its urban area now extending beyond the political boundaries of the **Distrito Federal** which is supposed to contain it (in the same way that the DC is supposed to contain the city of Washington). It's crisscrossed by a series of axes (*ejes* in Spanish), of which the north–south *eje central* (central axis, aka Lázaro Cárdenas) is plied by a very useful trolleybus linking the northern and southern bus terminals. Roughly parallel with it, 1km or so over to the west, **Avenida de los Insurgentes** also bisects the city more or less from north to south, and is said to be the longest continuous city street in the world, linking the centre to **San Ángel** and **Coyoacán**, and the **University City**, all at the southern end of town. Even more important from a tourist perspective is **Paseo de la Reforma**, which runs diagonally across the city, northeast to southwest, connecting the centre with **Bosque de Chapultepec Park**.

Brief history

The Aztecs (or, to use their own name, the Mexica), an ambitious and flourishing culture, founded their capital of Tenochtitlán in 1325 on an island in the middle of a lake, at a spot where their god Huitzilopochtli told them they would find an eagle

MARIACHI IN PLAZA GARIBALDI

Highlights

❶ **The Zócalo** Mexico City's huge central square, surrounded by the cathedral, Aztec ruins and the Palacio Nacional. See page 71

❷ **Palacio de Bellas Artes** Not only an architectural masterpiece in its own right, it's also home to some of the city's most impressive murals. See page 85

❸ **Museo Mural Diego Rivera** Rivera's most Mexican mural, depicting just about everybody from Mexican history. See page 88

❹ **Museo Nacional de Antropología** The country's finest museum, with displays on all of Mexico's major pre-Columbian cultures. See page 97

❺ **Coyoacán** Visit the houses where Frida Kahlo and León Trotsky lived, spend an evening checking out the local bars, then come back for the colourful Sunday market. See page 105

❻ **Museo Dolores Olmedo Patiño** A huge collection of works by Diego Rivera and Frida Kahlo. See page 112

❼ **Xochimilco** Ride the ancient waterways on flower-festooned boats. See page 113

❽ **Plaza Garibaldi** The frenetic site of massed mariachi bands. See page 134

❾ **La Merced** Explore Mexico City's largest and most vibrant market. See page 135

HIGHLIGHTS ARE MARKED ON THE MAPS ON PAGES 68 AND 72

1

MEXICO CITY

HIGHLIGHTS

4 Museo Nacional de Antropología

5 Coyoacán

6 Museo Dolores Olmedo Patiño

7 Xochimilco

ACCOMMODATION

Brasilia	1
Cartagena	2
Fiesta Inn	4
Hilton Mexico City Airport	3
NH Aeropuerto	6
We Hotel Aeropuerto	5

Freight Only

0 2 kilometres

Tula (97km) & Querétaro (216km)
Tula (97km) & Querétaro (216km)
Pachuca (24km) & Teotihuacán (48km)
Toluca
Toluca (64km)
Puebla (140km)
Puebla (140km)
Cuernavaca (93km)

San Rafael
Santa Cecilia Acatitlán
Tenayuca
Tlanepantla
Fortuna
Calz Vallejo
Av M A Camacho
Anillo Periférico
Indios Verdes
Terminal del Norte (Bus Station)
Basílica de Nuestra Señora de Guadalupe
Guadalupe
Calz de Guadalupe
Calz Cuitlahuac
La Raza
Bosque de Aragón
Tacuba
Buenavista
Av Rio Consulado
Plaza de las Tres Culturas
Calz San Joaquin
See "Central Mexico City" Map
Instituto de Migración
See "Chapultepec & Polanco" Map
Hipódromo de las Américas
Alameda
Cathedral
Zócalo
Polanco
Mocampo
Paseo de la Reforma
TAPO (Bus Station)
Blvd Puerto Aereo
Airport
Museo Nacional de Antropología
Palacio National
Deportiva Venustiano Carranza
Chapultepec
Chapultepec Park
Insurgentes
Lazaro Cardenas
Calz San Antonio Abad
Calz Zaragoza
See "Zona Rosa, Roma & Condesa" Map
Ciudad Deportiva Magdalena Mixhuca
World Trade Center
Ciudad Deportiva
Av Constituyentes
ABC Hospital
Polyforum Siqueiros
Calz de Tlalpan
Terminal Poniente (Bus Station)
Estacho Azul
Plaza México
Rio Churubusco
Museo Frida Kahlo
Teatro de los Insurgentes
Av Universidad
Museo Nacional de las Intervenciones
San Ángel
Coyoacán
División del Norte
Central de Autobuses del Sur (Bus Station)
El Pedregal
See "Coyoacán & San Ángel" Map
Ciudad Universitaria
Anillo Periférico
Anillo Periférico
Estadio Olímpico
University Library
Museo Diego River Anahuacalli
Estadio Azteca
Calz de Tlalpan
Cuicuilco
Tlalpan
Museo Dolores Olmedo Patiño
Xochimilco
N

FINDING YOUR STREET

Many **street names** are repeated over and over in different parts of Mexico City – there must be dozens of thoroughfares called Morelos, Juárez or Hidalgo, and a good score of 5 de Mayos. If you're taking a cab, or looking at a map, be clear which area you are talking about – it's fairly obvious in the centre, but searching out an address in the suburbs can lead to a series of false starts unless you know the name of the official **colonia**, or urban district (abbreviated "Col" in addresses outside the centre), that you're looking for. If you're going to be spending much time in the city, and are likely to be visiting places out of the centre, consider investing in Guia Roji's *Ciudad de México* street atlas, which is available at bookshops and street stalls all over town, and covers every street of the city and its suburbs, with an index.

devouring a snake atop a nopal cactus. It was from here that their empire grew to cover the whole of central Mexico. This empire was already firmly established when Hernán Cortés and his troops arrived in November 1519. The Aztec emperor, **Moctezuma II** (Montezuma), a broodingly religious man, apparently believed Cortés to be a reincarnation of the pale-skinned, bearded god Quetzalcoatl. Accordingly, he admitted him to the city – fearfully, but with a show of ceremonious welcome. The Spanish repaid this hospitality by taking Moctezuma prisoner. They then attacked the great Aztec temples, killing priests and placing Christian chapels alongside their altars.

Growing unrest in the city at the emperor's passivity, and at the rapacious behaviour of his guests, led to **rebellion**. In June 1520, Moctezuma was killed – according to the Spanish, stoned to death by his own people while trying to quell a riot – and the Spaniards fled the city with heavy losses on what they called **Noche Triste** (Sad Night; see page 786). Cortés and his surviving followers escaped to Tlaxcala to regroup. In May 1521, with numbers swelled by Indigenous allies, and ships built in secret to attack by water, the Spaniards laid **siege** to Tenochtitlán, landing on the south of the island and fighting their way north through the city, street by bloody street. The Aztec emperor **Cuauhtémoc** was finally captured on August 13, 1521, and subsequently tortured to try to find out where his supposed treasure was hidden. He was finally executed four years later in Honduras.

Spanish and post-colonial Mexico City

The Spanish systematically smashed every visible aspect of Aztec culture, as often as not using the very stones of the old city to construct the new. The **new city** developed slowly in its early years. It spread far wider, however, as the lake was drained, filled and built over. Pestilent from the earliest days, the inadequately drained waters harboured fevers, and the native population was constantly swept by epidemics of European diseases. Many of the buildings, too, simply began to sink into the soft lakebed, a process probably accelerated by regular earthquakes.

By the third quarter of the nineteenth century, the city comprised little more than the area around the Zócalo and Alameda. Chapultepec Castle, Coyoacán, San Ángel and the Basilica of Guadalupe were still surrounded by fields and the last of the basin's former lakes. From late 1870 through to 1911, however, the dictator Porfirio Díaz presided over an unprecedented, and self-aggrandizing, **building programme** that saw the installation of trams, the expansion of public transport and the draining of some of the last sections of the Lago de Texcoco, which had previously hemmed the city in. These all fuelled further growth, and by the outbreak of the Revolution in 1910, Mexico City's residents numbered over four hundred thousand, regaining for the first time in four centuries the population level it had held before the Conquest.

The modern city

During the Revolution, thousands fled to rapidly industrializing Mexico City in search of jobs and a better life. Between 1910 and the mid-1940s the city's population

TENOCHTITLÁN – THE CITY THAT WALKED ON WATER

And when we saw all those cities and villages built in the water, and other great towns on dry land, and that straight and level causeway leading to Mexico, we were astounded. These great towns and cities and buildings rising from the water, all made of stone, seemed like an enchanted vision from the tales of Amadis. Indeed, some of our soldiers asked whether it was not all a dream.

Bernal Díaz, The Conquest of New Spain

The Aztec capital of **Tenochtitlán** was built on an island in the middle of a lake traversed by great causeways, a beautiful, strictly regulated, stone-built city of 300,000 residents. The Aztecs had arrived at the lake around 1325, after years of wandering and living off what they could scavenge or pillage from settled communities. According to legend, their patron god Huitzilopochtli had ordered them to build a city where they found an eagle perched on a nopal cactus, devouring a snake. It is this legend that is the basis of the nopal, eagle and snake motif that forms the centrepiece of the modern Mexican flag.

The lake proved an ideal site: Well stocked with fish, it was also fertile, once the Aztecs had constructed **chinampas**, or floating gardens of reeds. These enabled them to grow crops on the lake, as a result of which they were self-sufficient in food. The lake also made the city virtually impregnable: the **causeways**, when they were completed, could be flooded and the bridges raised to thwart attacks (or escape, as the Spanish found on the Noche Triste; see page 786).

The island city eventually grew to cover an area of some thirteen square kilometres, much of it reclaimed from the lake, and from this base the Aztecs were able to begin their programme of **expansion**: initially dominating the valley by a series of strategic alliances, war and treachery, and finally, in a period of less than a hundred years before the brutal Spanish Conquest of 1521, establishing an empire that demanded tribute from, and traded with, the most distant parts of the country. Yet almost nothing of this amazing city survived the Conquest. "All that I saw then," Bernal Díaz later wrote of his account of Tenochtitlán, "is overthrown and destroyed; nothing is left standing." It is only relatively recently – particularly during construction of the Metro, and with the 1978 discovery of remains of the Templo Mayor beneath the colonial Zócalo – that a few remains of Tenochtitlán have been brought to light.

The city's defeat, moreover, is still a harsh memory: Cortés himself is hardly revered, but the natives who assisted him, in particular La Malinche, the Veracruz woman who acted as Cortés' interpreter, are non-people. Tributes to Moctezuma are rare, though **Cuauhtémoc**, his successor who led the fierce resistance, is commemorated everywhere; Malinche is represented, acidly, in some of Diego Rivera's more outspoken murals.

quadrupled and the cracks in the infrastructure quickly became gaping holes. Houses couldn't be built quickly enough to cope with the seven-percent annual growth, and many people couldn't afford them anyway, so **shantytowns** of scrap metal and cardboard sprang up. Most neighbourhoods had little or no water supply and sanitation was an afterthought. Gradually, civic leaders tried to address the lot of citizens by improving the services and housing in shantytowns, but even as they worked, a new ring of slums mushroomed just a little further out. This expansion badly strained the transport system, necessitating the construction of a **Metro** system in the late 1960s.

Urban growth continues today: some statisticians estimate that there are a thousand new arrivals each day, mainly from high-unemployment rural areas, and the urban area now extends beyond the limits of the Distrito Federal and into the surrounding states. Despite the spread, Mexico City remains one of the world's most densely and heavily populated cities, with an unenviable list of major social and physical problems, including an extreme vulnerability to earthquakes – the last big one, in 1985, killed over nine thousand people, made 100,000 homeless and left many of the city's buildings decidedly skewed.

Central Mexico City

The heart of Mexico City is the **Zócalo**, built by the Spanish right over the devastated ceremonial centre of the Aztec city of Tenochtitlán. Extraordinary uncovered ruins – chief of which is the **Templo Mayor** – provide the Zócalo's most compelling attraction, but there's also a wealth of great colonial buildings, among them the huge **cathedral** and the **Palacio Nacional** with its striking **Diego Rivera murals**. You could easily spend a couple of days in the tightly packed blocks hereabouts, investigating their dense concentration of museums and galleries, especially notable for works by Rivera and his "Big Three" companions, David Siqueiros and José Clemente Orozco.

West of the Zócalo the *centro histórico* stretches through the main commercial district past the **Museo Nacional de Arte** to the sky-scraping **Torre Latinoamericana** and the **Palacio de Bellas Artes** with its gorgeous Art Deco interior. Both overlook the formal parkland of the **Alameda**, next to which you'll find a number of museums, including **Museo de Tequila y Mezcal**, which tells the story of Mexico's best-known liquors, and the **Museo Mural Diego Rivera**, with the artist's famed *Sueño de una Tarde Dominical en la Alameda*. Further west, the **Monumento a la Revolución** heralds the more upmarket central suburbs, chiefly the **Zona Rosa**, long known as the spot for plush shops and restaurants, though that title has largely been usurped by swanky **Polanco** and hipper **Condesa**.

The Zócalo

Metro Zócalo

The vast paved open space of the **Zócalo** – properly known as the Plaza de la Constitución – was once the heart of **Aztec Tenochtitlán**, and is today one of the largest city squares in the world after Beijing's Tiananmen Square and Moscow's Red Square. The city's political and religious centre, it takes its name from part of a monument to Independence that was planned in the 1840s for the square by General Santa Anna. Like most of his other plans, this went astray, and only the statue's base (now gone) was ever erected: *el zócalo* literally means "the plinth". By extension, every other town square in Mexico has adopted the same name. It's constantly animated, with pre-Hispanic revivalist groups dancing and pounding drums throughout the day and street stalls and buskers in the evening. Stages are set up here for major national holidays, and, of course, this is the place to hold demonstrations. Over 100,000 people massed here in March 2001 to support the Zapatistas after their march from Chiapas in support of Indigenous people's rights; in July 2006 the square proved too small to contain the millions of demonstrators who gathered to challenge the result of that year's presidential election, a contest widely believed – especially in the left-leaning DF – to have been fixed. Spreading out from the Zócalo, the crowds reached as far as Paseo de la Reforma.

MÉXICO, MEXICO CITY AND EL DF

For clarity, we've referred to Mexico's capital as **Mexico City** throughout this Guide, though Mexicans frequently refer to it simply as **México**, in the same way that Americans refer to New York City as New York. It's a source of infinite confusion to visitors, but the country took its name from the city, so "México" can mean either, and in conversation it most often means the latter. The capital is also referred to as **El DF** ("El Day Effay"), short for "Distrito Federal". The title **Ciudad de México** is used much less commonly, usually in an official context. The country as a whole is generally called 'La República', while any area that lies outside Mexico City and Mexico State that envelops it can be referred to as "La Provincia" (The Province), although this is not a term which is appreciated by those who live there.

Though you're not guaranteed to see any protests, among the Zócalo's more certain entertainments is the ceremonial **lowering of the national flag** from its giant pole in the centre of the plaza each evening at sundown (typically 6pm). A troop of presidential guards march out from the palace, strike the enormous flag and perform a complex routine, at the end of which the flag is left, neatly folded, in the hands of one of their number. With far less pomp, the flag is quietly raised again around half an hour later.

You get a great view of this, and of everything else happening in the Zócalo, from the rooftop terrace restaurants (see page 124) in the *Hotel Majestic* and *Gran Hotel Ciudad de México* on the west side of the square.

Weekends in the Zócalo see a small tourist market on the west side of the cathedral, offering the same knick-knacks you'll see at most tourist sites around the country. Witch doctors also patrol the area offering pre-Hispanic cleansing rituals. During

the week tradesmen offering freelance work occupy this bit of pavement; they don't appreciate having their photos taken.

Catedral Metropolitana

North side of Zócalo • Discretion is required during services; guided tours hourly • Free; tours charge • https://catedralmetropolitana.mx • Metro Zócalo

Mexico City's cathedral holds the distinction of being the largest church in Latin America. Like so many of the city's older, weightier structures, it has settled over the years into the soft, wet ground beneath – the tilt is quite plain to see, despite extensive work to stabilize the building. The first church on this site was constructed only a couple of years after the Conquest, using stones torn from the Temple of Huitzilopochtli, but the present structure was begun in 1573 to provide Mexico City with a cathedral more suited to its wealth and status as the jewel of the Spanish empire. The towers weren't completed until 1813, though, and the building incorporates a plethora of architectural styles. Even the frontage demonstrates this: relatively austere at the bottom where work began soon after the Conquest, it flowers into full Baroque as you look up, and is topped by Neoclassical cornices and a clock tower. If you want to climb the clock tower, join one of the guided tours that start from the information desk to the right as you enter.

COUGHS AND ROBBERS – SELF-PRESERVATION IN MEXICO CITY

Mexico City comes with an unenviable reputation for overcrowding, grime and crime, and to some extent this is deserved. Certainly there is **pollution**. The whole urban area sits in a low mountain bowl that deflects smog-clearing winds away from the city, allowing a thick blanket of haze to build up throughout the day. Conditions are particularly bad in winter, when there is no rain, and pollution levels (reported daily in the English-language newspaper, *The News*, http://thenews.mx) tend to peak in the early afternoon. In response, the **Hoy No Circula** ("Don't drive today") law prohibits car use from 5am to 10pm for one day in the working week for vehicles over six years old, the day depending on the car's number plate. Nonetheless, those prone to **respiratory problems** may have some difficulty on arrival, due to the city's air quality and altitude.

The capital is where the Mexican extremes of **wealth** and **poverty** are most apparent, with shiny, valet-parked SUVs vying for space with pavement vendors and beggars. Such financial disparity fuels **theft**, but just take the same precautions you would in any large city; there is no need to feel particularly paranoid. Keep your valuables – especially credit or debit cards – in the hotel safe (even cheap hotels often have somewhere secure; muggers who catch you with an ATM card may keep hold of you till they have extracted enough cash with it), don't flash large wads of money around and keep an eye on your camera and other valuables in busy market areas. At night, avoid the *barrio* known as **Doctores** (around the Metro station of the same name, so-called because the streets are named after doctors), and the area around Lagunilla market, both centres of the street drug trade, and therefore opportunist crime. Note that mugging is not the only danger – abduction for ransom is increasingly common too.

Taxis have a bad reputation and, though drivers are mostly helpful and courteous, there are reports of people being robbed or abducted (often in stolen taxis). If possible, get your hotel to call you a cab (more expensive), or call one yourself, for example from one of the firms mentioned on page 118. If you do have to hail a cab in the street, always take one whose registration, on both the number plate and the side of the vehicle, begins with an L (for "libre" – to be hailed while driving around), and which has the driver's identification prominently displayed. Better still, find a taxi rank and take a *sitio* taxi that can be traced to that rank (with a number beginning in R, S or T, and again with the driver's ID prominently displayed). Do not take taxis from the airport or bus terminals other than prepaid ones, and avoid taking those waiting outside tourist spots.

Inside, although the size of the cathedral is striking, the chief impression is that it's a rather gloomy space, with rows of dimly lit side chapels. It is enlivened mostly by the **Altar de los Reyes**, a vast gilt *reredos* built of wood between 1718 and 1737. It's located behind a main altar that features effigies of European kings and queens as well as two early eighteenth-century oil paintings, the *Asunción de la Virgen* and *Adoración de los Reyes* by Juan Rodríguez Juárez. Fans of ornate handiwork will also appreciate the detailed work in gold and wood on the central *coro* (choir).

Sagrario

Next door to the cathedral • No entry wearing caps, shorts, miniskirts or dark glasses • Free

The **Sagrario**, despite its heavy, grey Baroque facade and squat, bell-topped towers, feels both lighter and richer inside, with exuberant churrigueresque decoration and liberal use of gold paint. It was originally built as the parish church, and performs most of the day-to-day functions of a local church, such as baptisms and marriages.

Templo Mayor

Seminario 8 • Charge; video tour; charge • http://inah.gob.mx • Metro Zócalo

Just off the Zócalo, down beside the cathedral, lies the entrance to the site where the **Templo Mayor** has been excavated. Although it had been worked out by the beginning of the twentieth century that Tenochtitlán's ceremonial area lay under this part of the city, it was generally believed that the chief temple, or Teocalli, lay directly beneath the cathedral. Archeological work only began in earnest in 1978 after workmen uncovered a huge stone disc, weighing over eight tonnes, which depicted the fall of **Coyolxauhqui**, goddess of the moon. The disc's symbolism (see page 76) indicated that it must have lain at the foot of the city's Teocalli, which would have been topped by a double shrine, dedicated to the sun god **Huitzilopochtli** and the rain god **Tlaloc**. The nineteenth- and twentieth-century buildings on the site were therefore cleared away, and excavation began.

The temple remains

Entering the site, you'll be able to see the bare ruins of the foundations of the great temple and one or two buildings immediately around it. The excavations are highly confusing since, as was normal practice, a new temple was built over the old at the end of every 52-year calendar cycle (and apparently even more frequently here), resulting in a whole series of temples stacked inside each other like Russian dolls – there are seven here. Look at the models and maps in the museum first (see opposite) and it all makes more sense.

Of the seven reconstructions of the temple, layers as far down as the second have been uncovered, though you can only see the top of the structure as the bottom is now well below the water table. Confusing as it is trying to work out what's what, it's a fascinating site, scattered with odd sculptures, including some great serpents, and traces of its original bright paintwork in red, blue and yellow. Seeing it here, at the heart of the modern city, brings the ceremonies and sacrifices that took place rather close to home. It's also worth walking past here in the evening when the **floodlit pyramid ruins** can be seen from the surrounding streets.

Museo del Templo Mayor

The **museum** of the Templo Mayor, entered through the site on the same ticket, helps set the temples in context, with some welcome reconstructions and models of how Tenochtitlán would have looked at its height. There are some wonderful pieces retrieved from the site, especially the replica **tzompantli** (wall of skulls) as you enter, the eagle in Room 1 with a cavity in its back for the hearts of sacrificial victims, a particularly beautiful *pulque* god statue and, of course, the huge **Coyolxauhqui stone** (see page 75), displayed so as to be visible from points throughout the museum. The museum's design is meant to simulate the temple, so you climb through it to reach two rooms at the top, one devoted to Huitzilopochtli, the other to Tlaloc, in the same way that the temple was originally topped by two shrines, one for each god.

The best items are towards the top of the museum, including some superb stone masks such as the one from Teotihuacán, black with inset eyes and a huge earring, typical of the objects paid in tribute by subject peoples from all over the country. On the highest level are two magnificent, full-size terracotta eagle warriors and numerous large stone pieces from the site. The descent back to the ground level concentrates on everyday life in Aztec times – with some rather mangy stuffed animals to demonstrate the species known to the Aztecs – along with a jumble of later items found while the site was being excavated. There are some good pieces here: look for the superb turquoise mosaic, little more than a handspan across, but intricately set with tiny pieces forming seven god-like figures; and the two large ceramic sculptures of **Mictlantecihtli**, the god of death, unearthed in 1994 from tunnels excavated below the nearby Casa de las Águilas.

Palacio Nacional

East side of Zócalo, but public entrance from Moneda • Free, but ID required to enter; locker for bags; charge • https://www.gob.mx/palacionacional • Metro Zócalo

The east side of the Zócalo is entirely taken up by the more than 200m-long facade of the **Palacio Nacional**. The so-called New Palace of Moctezuma stood here and Cortés made it his first residence. From 1562 the building was the official residence of the Spanish viceroy, and later of presidents of the republic. The present building, for all its apparent unity, is the result of centuries of agglomeration and rebuilding – the most recent addition was the third storey, in 1927. It still holds the office of the president, who makes his most important pronouncements from the balcony – especially on September 15, when the **Grito de la Independencia** (see page 138) signals the start of the country's Independence celebrations.

Diego Rivera's murals

The chief attraction in the Palacio Nacional is the series of **Diego Rivera murals** that decorates the stairwell and middle storey of the main courtyard. Begun in 1929, the murals are classic Rivera, ranking with the best of his work. The great panorama of Mexican history, *México a Través de los Siglos*, around the **main staircase**, combines an unbelievable wealth of detail with savage imagery and a masterly use of space. On the right-hand wall Quetzalcoatl sits in majesty amid the golden age of the Valley of México, surrounded by an idealized vision of life in Teotihuacán, Tula and Tenochtitlán. The main section depicts the Conquest, oppression, war, Inquisition, invasion, Independence and eventually Revolution. Almost every major personage and event of Mexican history is here, from the grotesquely twisted features of the conquistadors to the national heroes: balding, white-haired Hidalgo with the banner of

COYOLXAUHQUI AND HUITZILOPOCHTLI

Coyolxauhqui was the daughter of Coatlicue, the mother goddess who controlled life and death; on discovering that her mother was miraculously pregnant, Coyolxauhqui vowed to wipe out the dishonour by killing her. Before she could do so, however, **Huitzilopochtli** sprang fully armed from Coatlicue's womb, and proceeded to decapitate and dismember his sister (who is therefore always portrayed with her head and limbs cut off) and threw her body down a mountain. He then drove off the four hundred other brothers who had gathered to help her: they scattered to become the stars. The human sacrifices carried out in the temple – meant to feed Huitzilopochtli, the sun god, with the blood he needed to win his nightly battle against darkness – were in part a re-enactment of this, with the victims being thrown down the steps afterwards.

Independence; squat, dark Benito Juárez with his Constitution and laws for the reform of the Church; Zapata, with a placard proclaiming his cry of "*Tierra y Libertad*"; and Pancho Villa, moustachioed and swaggering. On the left are post-Revolutionary Mexico and the future (as Rivera envisaged it), with Karl Marx pointing the way to adoring workers. Businessmen stand clustered over their tickertape in front of a somewhat ironic depiction of the metropolis with its skyscrapers and grim industrial wastes. Rivera's wife, the artist Frida Kahlo, is depicted, too, behind her sister Cristina (with whom Rivera was having an affair at the time) in a red blouse with an open copy of the Communist Manifesto.

A series of smaller panels was intended to go all the way round the upper (now middle) storey, an over-ambitious and unfinished project. The uncoloured first panel lists the products that the world owes to Mexico, including maize, beans, chocolate, tobacco, cotton, tomatoes, peanuts, prickly pears and *chicle* (the source of chewing gum). The remainder of the completed paintings reach halfway around and mostly depict the idyll of aspects of life before the Conquest – market day, dyeing cloth, hunting scenes and so on. The last (completed in 1951) shows the arrival of the Spanish, complete with an image of La Malinche (the Maya woman widely perceived to have betrayed native Mexicans by shacking up with Cortés) bearing Cortés' blue-eyed baby – the first Mexican *mestizo*.

Other attractions

Also on the Palacio's middle storey is the chamber used by the Mexican Legislature from 1845 to 1872, when it was presided over by Benito Juárez, who lived in the palace until his death. The room houses the original copy of the 1857 Constitution, which was drawn up there, but is frequently closed for renovations.

Before leaving the building, it's worth taking a moment to wander around some of the other **courtyards** (there are fourteen in all), and through the small floral and cactus **gardens**.

Gran Hotel Ciudad de México

16 de Septiembre 82 • http://granhoteldelaciudaddemexico.com.mx • Metro Zócalo

Located at the southwest corner of the Zócalo, the **Gran Hotel Ciudad de México** (see page 124) is well worth a visit to admire the opulent lobby with its intricate ironwork, cage-lifts and wonderful Tiffany stained-glass dome. Indeed, it's worth going up to the third and fourth floors for a closer look at the ceiling. Like the *Majestic* (see page 124) in the same block, the *Gran Hotel* has a terrace restaurant with great views over the Zócalo.

Nacional Monte de Piedad

Monte de Piedad 1, at corner of the Zócalo and 5 de Mayo • Free • Metro Zócalo

On the west side of the Zócalo, arcades shelter a series of shops, almost all of which sell hats or jewellery. For an unusual shopping experience, though, you can't beat the **Nacional Monte de Piedad**, just to the north. This huge building, supposedly on the site of the palace in which Cortés and his followers stayed as guests of Moctezuma, is now the National Pawn Shop, an institution founded as far back as 1775. Much of what is pawned here is jewellery, but there's also a wide variety of fine art and sculptures, and just about anything that will command a reasonable price. From time to time, they hold major auctions to clear the place out, but it's worth coming here just to take in the atmosphere and watch the milling crowds.

North of the Zócalo

Just a couple of blocks north of the centre the vast openness of the Zócalo gives way to a much more intimate section of small colonial plazas and mostly eighteenth-century buildings. It is still an active commercial area, and is packed with a variety of interesting sights, including ornate churches, small museums and some very fine Rivera and Siqueiros **murals**, all of which can be seen in a few hours.

Plaza Santo Domingo

Metro Zócalo

Beside the cathedral, Calle Monte de Piedad runs three blocks north (becoming República de Brasil) to the little colonial plaza of **Santo Domingo**. In the middle of the square, a small fountain plays on a statue honouring La Corregidora, a heroine of Mexico's Independence struggle (see page 309). Eighteenth-century mansions line the sides of the plaza along with the fine Baroque church of Santo Domingo, built on the site of the country's first Dominican monastery. Under the arcades you'll still find clerks sitting at little desks with ageing electric typewriters, as you will in most large

DIEGO RIVERA

Diego Rivera (c.1886–1957), husband of **Frida Kahlo** (see page 110), was the greatest of *Los Tres Grandes*, the "Big Three" Mexican artists – the other two being **José Clemente Orozco** and **David Siqueiros** – who interpreted the Revolution and Mexican history through the medium of enormous murals, and put the nation's art onto an international footing in the first half of the twentieth century. His works remain among the country's most striking sights.

Rivera studied from the age of 10 at the **San Carlos Academy** in the capital, immediately showing immense ability. He later moved to Paris, where he flirted with many of the new artistic trends, in particular Cubism. More importantly, though, he and Siqueiros planned, in exile, a popular, native art to express the new society in Mexico. In 1921 Rivera returned from Europe to the aftermath of the Revolution, and right away began work for the Ministry of Education at the behest of the socialist Education Minister, poet and presidential hopeful José Vasconcelos. Informed by his own Communist beliefs, and encouraged by the leftist sympathies of the times, Rivera embarked on the first of his massive, consciousness-raising **murals**, whose themes – Mexican history, the oppression of the natives, post-Revolutionary resurgence – were initially more important than their techniques. Many of his early murals are deceptively simple, naive even, but in fact Rivera's style remained close to major trends and, following the lead of Siqueiros, he took a scientific approach to his work, looking to industrial advances for new techniques, better materials and fresh inspiration. The view of industrial growth as a panacea (particularly in the earlier works of both Rivera and Siqueiros) may have been simplistic, but the artists' use of technology and experimentation with new methods and original approaches often had startling results.

RIVERA AND TROTSKY

Communism continued to be a major source of motivation and inspiration for Rivera, who was a long-standing member of the Mexican Communist Party. When ideological differences caused a rift in Soviet politics, he came down on the side of **Leon Trotsky**'s "revolutionary internationalism". In 1936, with Trotsky running out of countries that would accept him after seven years on the run from Stalin's henchmen, Rivera used his influence over Mexican President Lázaro Cárdenas to get permission for Trotsky and his wife Natalia to enter the country. They stayed with Diego and Frida rent-free at their Coyoacán house before Trotsky moved down the road to what is now the **Museo Casa de León Trotsky**. The passionate and often violent differences between orthodox Stalinists and Trotskyites spilled over into the art world, creating a great rift between Rivera and ardent Stalinist Siqueiros, who was later jailed for his involvement in an assassination attempt on Trotsky (see page 112). Though Rivera later broke with Trotsky and was eventually readmitted to the Communist Party, Trotsky continued to admire Rivera's murals, finding them "not simply a 'painting', an object of passive contemplation, but a living part of the class struggle".

Mexican cities – carrying on the ancient tradition of public scribes, their main function is to translate simple messages into the flowery, sycophantic language essential for any business letter in Spanish, but they'll type anything from student theses to love letters. Alongside them are street printers working with antiquated hand presses, churning out business cards, forged documents and invitations on the spot.

Museo de la Medicina

Brasil 33, on northeast corner of Plaza Santo Domingo • Free • 55 5623 3123 • Metro Zócalo

The **Museo de la Medicina** occupies grand rooms around a courtyard that was once the headquarters of the Inquisition in New Spain. It was here that heretics were punished, and although the cruelty of the Inquisition is often exaggerated, it was undoubtedly the site of some gruesome scenes. The extensive museum kicks off with interesting displays on Indigenous medicine, religion and herbalism, often with reference to infirmity,

FOLLOWING THE RIVERA TRAIL

There is a huge amount of Rivera's work accessible to the public, much of it in Mexico City, but also elsewhere around the country. The following is a rundown of the major Rivera sites, approximately ordered in accordance with their importance within each area.

NEAR THE ZÓCALO, THE ALAMEDA AND CHAPULTEPEC

Palacio National (see page 76). Major murals right in the heart of the capital.
SEP (see page 80). There are many of Rivera's early murals around the courtyards of the Ministry of Education.
Palacio de Bellas Artes (see page 85). Rivera's monumental *El Hombre en Control del Universo* (and others), as well as murals by his contemporaries.
Museo Mural Diego Rivera (see page 88). One of Rivera's most famous murals, *Sueño de una Tarde Dominical en la Alameda*, is on display here.
Museo de Arte Moderno (see page 100). Several quality canvases by Rivera and his contemporaries.
Antiguo Colegio de San Ildefonso (ENP) (see page 80). One relatively minor Rivera mural.
Museo Nacional de Arte (see page 86). A handful of minor canvases.

THE SUBURBS

Cárcomo de Dolores (see page 102). Two murals on water-related subjects by a lake in the Bosque de Chapultepec.
Estadio Olímpico (see page 111). Mosaic relief depicting the relationship between sport and the family.
Museo Dolores Olmedo Patiño (see page 112). A massive collection of Rivera works from almost every artistic period.
Museo Frida Kahlo (see page 106). Just a couple of Diego's works displayed in the house where he and Frida spent some of their married life.
Museo Casa Estudio Diego Rivera y Frida Kahlo (see page 104). Diego's and Frida's pair of houses designed by Juan O'Gorman.
Museo Diego Rivera Anahuacalli (see page 111). Large Maya-style house built by Rivera and housing his collection of pre-Columbian sculpture.
Teatro de los Insurgentes (see page 104). Mosaic depicting the history of Mexican theatre.

OUTSIDE THE CAPITAL

Palacio de Cortés, Cuernavaca (see page 171). Early murals on a grand scale.
Museo Robert Brady, Cuernavaca (see page 173). A few paintings by both Frida and Diego.
Museo Casa Diego Rivera, Guanajuato (see page 340). Relatively minor works and sketches in the house where Diego was born.

in sculpture. It is surprising how often skin diseases, humped backs and malformed limbs crop up in pre-Columbian art: note the terracotta sculpture bent double from osteoporosis. The progress of Western medicine from colonial times to the present is also well covered, with an intact nineteenth-century pharmacy, a complete radiology room from 1939 and an obstetrics and gynaecology room filled with human embryos in bottles. A "wax room" upstairs shows full-colour casts of various skin ailments, injuries and infections – the diseased genitalia are always a hit with local schoolkids. As you leave, don't forget the "exhibit of the week" room by the entrance.

SEP

Brasil 31 (with another entrance at Argentina 28) • Free • Metro Zócalo

From the Plaza de Santo Domingo, República de Cuba runs a block east to the **Secretaría de Educación Pública (SEP)**, the Ministry of Education building, where, in 1923 and 1924, Rivera painted his first **murals** on returning from Paris. Don't be put off by the tight security – simply proclaim the word "murales" and you'll be shown straight through.

The driving force behind the murals was **José Vasconcelos**, a revolutionary Minister of Public Education in the 1920s but better known as a poet and philosopher, who promoted educational art as a means of instilling a sense of history and cultural pride in a widely illiterate population. He is the man most directly responsible for the murals in public buildings throughout the country. Here, three floors of an enormous double patio are entirely covered with frescoes, as are many of the stairwells and almost any other flat surface. Compared with what he later achieved, Rivera's work is very simple, but the style is already recognizable: panels crowded with figures, drawing inspiration mainly from rural Mexico, though also from an idealized view of science and industry.

The most famous panel on the ground floor is the relatively apolitical *Día de los Muertos*, which is rather hidden away in a dark corner at the back. Continuing clockwise, there are equally striking images: *Quema de Judas* and *La Asamblea Primero de Mayo*, for example, and the lovely *El Canal de Santa Anita*. On the first floor the work is quite plain, mostly in tones of grey – here you'll find the shields of the states of Mexico and such general educational themes as *Chemistry* or *Physics*, mostly the work of Rivera's assistants. On the second floor are heroic themes from the Revolution. At the back, clockwise from the left-hand side, the triumphant progress of the Revolution is traced, culminating in the happy scenes of a Mexico ruled by its workers and peasants.

Museo de la Caricatura

Donceles 99 • Charge • 55 5521 2447 • Metro Zócalo

The **Museo de la Caricatura** is a museum of Mexican cartoons and caricatures. Located in a particularly fine example of an eighteenth-century nobleman's dwelling, complete with central courtyard, it exhibits a selection of work from Mexico's most famous caricaturists, but without a strong sense of Mexican history and a comprehensive grasp of Spanish much of the impact is lost. It's still worth nipping in to see a small selection of bizarre nineteenth-century prints of skeletal mariachis by **José Guadalupe Posada**, a great influence on the later Muralist movement, and to take a break in the museum coffee shop in the central patio.

ENP (Antiguo Colegio de San Ildefonso)

Justo Serra 16 • Charge, free Tues & 5–9pm last Wed of the month • https://www.sanildefonso.org.mx • Metro Zócalo

As in the SEP (see above), José Vasconcelos was largely responsible for the murals which adorn the interior of the eighteenth-century **Antiguo Colegio de San Ildefonso** (also called the Escuela Nacional Preparatoria, or **ENP**), a building also notable for its imposing colonial facade on Justo Serra, facing the north side of the Templo Mayor. Many artists are represented here, including Rivera and Siqueiros, but the most famous works are those of **José Clemente Orozco**, which you'll find on the main staircase and around the first floor of the main patio. If you can, visit on the last Wednesday of the month to enjoy a range of free performances, from live music to book readings, within extended opening hours (5–9pm).

Museo de la Luz

San Ildelfonso 43 • Charge • http://museodelaluz.unam.mx • Metro Zócalo

Housed in part of the northern wing of the Antiguo Colegio de San Ildefonso, with its entrance on San Ildelfonso, the **Museo de la Luz** is a kind of hands-on celebration of all facets of reflection, refraction, iridescence and luminescence, spread over three floors. Good Spanish is essential if you want to learn anything, but it's fun just playing with the optical tricks and effects, and exploring the use of light in art.

Museo de las Constituciones

San Ildelfonso (cnr Aztecas), almost diagonally opposite the Museo de la Luz • Free • http://museodelasconstituciones.unam.mx • Metro Zócalo

The former Templo de San Pedro y San Pablo, built for the Company of Jesus between 1576 and 1603, was later used as a library, military college and correctional school, and was eventually taken over by the university. The interior decoration – plain white, with the arches and pilasters painted in floral designs by Jorge Enciso and Roberto Montenegro – was, like those in SEP (see opposite) and the ENP (see opposite), influenced by Vasconcelos. The church has since been turned into the **Museo de las Constituciones**, with exhibits and explanations in Spanish on the string of constitutions which Mexico has had since Independence, but the murals will be of far more interest to most visitors, particularly Montenegro's almost pre-Raphaelite 1922 *Tree of Life*, at the far end of the building as you enter.

Plaza de Loreto and around

Three blocks northeast of the Zócalo • Metro Zócalo

The **Plaza de Loreto** feels a world apart. It is a truly elegant old square, entirely unmodernized and flanked by a couple of churches. On one side is the **Templo de Loreto**, with its huge dome leaning at a crazy angle: inside, you'll find yourself staggering across the tilted floor. **Santa Teresa**, across the plaza, has a bizarre cave-like chapel at the back, entirely artificial. North of the Templo Loreto is a large and not especially exciting covered market, the **Mercado Presidente Abelardo Rodriguez**, inside most entrances of which is a series of large murals dating from the 1930s by an assortment of artists including Antonio Pujol and Pablo O'Higgins.

East of the Zócalo: along Calle Moneda

Calle Moneda, running east from the centre, is one of the oldest streets in the city, and it's fascinating to wander up here and see the rapid change as you leave the immediate environs of the Zócalo. The buildings remain almost wholly colonial, prim and refurbished around the museums, then gradually become shabbier and shabbier. Within four or five blocks you're into a very depressed residential area, with street stalls spreading up from the giant market of La Merced, to the south.

Museo de la SHCP

Moneda 4 • Free • 55 3688 1100 • Metro Zócalo

Just a few steps from the Zócalo, the **Museo de la SHCP** occupies the former archbishop's palace and presents Mexican fine art from the last three centuries in rooms surrounding two lovely open courtyards. The building was constructed over part of Tenochtitlán's ceremonial centre, the Teocalli, and excavations have revealed a few foundation sections for the Templo de Tezcatlipoca pyramid that once stood here. Notice the short flight of stairs, a jaguar carved in high relief and a series of anthropomorphic sculptures.

Casa de la Primera Imprenta

Licenciado Primo Verdad 10 (at Moneda) • Free • https://casaleonoracarrington.uam.mx • Metro Zócalo

The **Casa de la Primera Imprenta** occupies the house where the first printing press in the Americas was set up in 1535, though the only indication of this is the model of the press that sits close to the entrance. Archeological finds unearthed during restoration work are displayed in one room; other rooms house temporary exhibits.

Centro Cultural Ex-Teresa Arte

Licenciado Primo Verdad 8 • Free • https://exteresa.inba.gob.mx • Metro Zócalo

You'll feel as if you aren't on solid ground the moment you step into the **Centro Cultural Ex-Teresa Arte**, one of the city's most subsided buildings which exhibits art and photography inside a Spanish imperial stone church. The exhibitions are put on by a non-profit organization funded by the National Institute of Fine Arts, which are usually interesting but make rather poor use of the dizzying space.

Museo Nacional de las Culturas

Moneda 13 • Free • http://museodelasculturas.mx • Metro Zócalo

The **Museo Nacional de las Culturas** occupies the sixteenth-century Casa de la Moneda, the official mint until 1848 and later the National Museum, where the best of the Aztec artefacts were displayed until the construction of the Museo Nacional de Antropología (see page 97). Now immaculately restored, it houses a collection devoted to the archeology and anthropology of other countries. With rooms of exhibits set around a quiet patio, it is more interesting than you might guess, though still somewhat overshadowed by so many other high-class museums in the city.

Santa Inés

Moneda 26 • Free • Metro Zócalo

The eye-catching blue and gold **dome** of the church of **Santa Inés** is the church's only striking feature, and there's little else to admire apart from the delicately carved wooden doors. Painters Miguel Cabrera and José Ibarra are both buried somewhere inside, but neither is commemorated in any way.

Museo José Luis Cuevas

Academia 13 • Charge • http://museojoseluiscuevas.com.mx • Metro Zócalo

The church of Santa Inés' former convent buildings have been transformed into the **Museo José Luis Cuevas**, an art gallery with changing displays centred on the 8m-high bronze, *La Giganta*, designed by Cuevas. The only permanent collection is one room full of erotica ranging from pre-Hispanic sculpture to line drawings, some by Cuevas – this one isn't for the easily shocked.

Academia de San Carlos

Academia 22, on the corner of Moneda and Academia • Free • https://academiasancarlos.unam.mx • Metro Zócalo

The **Academia de San Carlos** still operates as an art school, though on a considerably reduced scale from its nineteenth-century heyday; inside are galleries for temporary exhibitions and, in the patio, copies of classical sculptures.

Templo de la Santísima Trinidad

Santísima 12 • Free • Metro Zócalo

The **Templo de la Santísima Trinidad**, from which the street takes its name, boasts one of the city's finest Baroque facades, floridly decorated with saints and cherubs. As with many old colonial churches in the city centre, its soft footing has caused it to slump, and its sideways list has become so serious that it was closed for many years for strengthening work. After being remodelled by architect Manuel Tolsá, it was reopened to the public in 2016 and today features a number of regularly updated, local art exhibits.

South of the Zócalo

South of the Zócalo, Pino Suárez leads down to meet Izázaga, which marks the southern edge of the city centre proper. The area to the east of Pino Suárez is largely a market area, and leads over to the wonderful **La Merced** market, while both Pino Suárez and Izázaga have a couple of sights that are worth a brief foray.

Suprema Corte de Justicia

On the corner of the Zócalo • Free, but ID required to enter • https://www.scjn.gob.mx • Metro Zócalo

A colonial-style modern building houses the **Suprema Corte de Justicia**. Inside are three superb, bitter murals by Orozco named *Luchas Proletarias* (*Proletarian Struggles*), *Las Riquezas Nacionales* (*The Nation's Riches*) and *La Justicia* (*Justice*). The last, depicting Justice slumped asleep on her pedestal while bandits rob the people of their rights, was, not surprisingly, unpopular with the judges and powers that be, and Orozco never completed his commission here.

Museo de la Ciudad de México

Pino Suárez 30 • Charge, free Wed • https://mexicocity.cdmx.gob.mx/venues/museum-of-the-city-of-mexico • Metro Zócalo

A couple of blocks south of the Zócalo, the **Museo de la Ciudad de México** is housed in the colonial palace of the Condes de Santiago de Calimaya. This is a fabulous building, with carved stone cannons thrusting out from the cornice, magnificent heavy wooden doors and, on the far side, a hefty plumed serpent obviously dragged from the ruins of some Aztec temple to be employed as a cornerstone. The rooms are mostly given over to temporary exhibits on all manner of themes, but on the top storey is the preserved studio of the landscape artist **Joaquín Clausell**, its walls plastered with portraits and little sketches that he scribbled between working on his paintings.

The church and hospital of Jesús Nazareno

On the west side of Pino Suárez • Free • Metro Pino Suárez

A memorial marking the spot where, according to legend, Cortés first met Moctezuma, is where you'll find the church and hospital of **Jesús Nazareno**. The **hospital**, still in use, was founded by Cortés in 1528. As such, it's one of the oldest buildings in the city, and exemplifies the severe, fortress-like construction of the immediate post-Conquest years. The **church**, which contains the remains of Cortés and a bronze plaque to the left of the altar with the simple inscription "H.C. (1485–1547)", has been substantially remodelled over the years, its vaulting decorated with a fresco of the Apocalypse by Orozco.

Pino Suárez and Zócalo Metro stations

More or less opposite Jesús Nazareno (see above) is a small open space and an entrance to a bookshop-lined subterranean walkway, the **Tunel del Libro**, between Zócalo and Pino Suárez Metro stations, where there's a café and a space for silent reading. **Zócalo station** has models of the Zócalo at different times in the past in its main concourse, and old pictures of the famous square reproduced on its platforms. **Pino Suárez station**, meanwhile, has a whole **Aztec shrine** in the middle of it. Uncovered during the station's construction, it has been preserved as an integral part of the concourse, and you'll pass right by it if changing lines here. Dating from around the end of the fourteenth century, the shrine was dedicated to Quetzalcoatl in his guise of Ehecatl, god of the wind.

Claustro de la Merced

Uruguay 168 • Metro Merced or Pino Suárez

Heading east from Pino Suárez along Salvador or Uruguay takes you to the giant **market** area of La Merced (see page 135). If you walk on Uruguay you'll pass a beautiful cloister (claustro), all that remains of the seventeenth-century **Convento de la Merced**, the subject of extensive recent restoration work.

Museo de la Charrería

Isabel la Católica 108 • Free • 55 5709 4823 • Metro Isabel la Católica

On the south side of Izázaga, at Isabel la Católica, a handsome colonial building holds the **Museo de la Charrería**, dedicated to all things cowboy, with a collection that includes old photographs, some of them inevitably rather camp, as well as sketches, watercolours, costumes, spurs and brands.

West to the Alameda

The streets that lead down from the Zócalo towards the Alameda – **Tacuba**, **5 de Mayo**, **Madero**, **16 de Septiembre** and the lanes that cross them – are the most elegant and least affected by modern development in the city, lined with ancient buildings, traditional cafés, and shops and mansions converted into offices, banks or restaurants. At the end of Madero, you come to the outer edge of the colonial city centre, and should find yourself, by contrast, standing between two of the most striking modern buildings in the capital: the **Torre Latinoamericana** and the **Palacio de Bellas Artes**. Though it seems incredible when you compare them, they were completed within barely 25 years of each other.

Along Madero

On **Madero** you'll pass several former aristocratic palaces now given over to a variety of uses. At no. 27 stands a slightly dilapidated mansion built in 1775 by mining magnate José de la Borda (see page 180) for his wife and presided over, on the corner of Bolivar, by a statue of the Virgin of Guadalupe. Still further down Madero, at no. 17, you'll find the **Palacio de Iturbide** (Metro Allende), currently occupied by Banamex and thoroughly restored. Originally the home of the Condes de Valparaíso in the eighteenth century, it was, from 1821 to 1823, the residence of the ill-fated "emperor" Agustín de Iturbide. Nowadays it periodically houses free art exhibitions laid on by the bank. In the next block, the last before you emerge at Bellas Artes and the Alameda, the churrigueresque church of **San Francisco** (Metro Bellas Artes) stands on the site of the first Franciscan mission to Mexico.

Casa de los Azulejos

Madero 4 • Metro Bellas Artes

The sixteenth-century **Casa de los Azulejos** (House of Tiles), now a branch of the Sanborns department store chain, is so-called for its exterior, swathed entirely in blue and white tiles from Puebla that were added during remodelling in 1737. The building survived a gas explosion in 1994 – though there was quite a bit of structural damage, luckily no one was hurt, and one of the most famous features of the building, the giant Orozco mural on the staircase, suffered few ill effects. Inside you'll find a restaurant (see page 128) in the glassed-over patio, as well as all the usual shopping (see page 134).

Torre Latinoamericana

Lázaro Cárdenas 2 • Charge • http://torrelatino.com • Metro Bellas Artes

The distinctly dated steel-and-glass skyscraper of the **Torre Latinoamericana** was completed in 1956 and, until a few years ago, was the tallest building in Mexico and, indeed, the whole of Latin America. It has now been outdone by the World

Trade Center (formerly the *Hotel de México*, on Insurgentes) and doubtless by others in South America, but it remains the city's outstanding landmark and a point of reference no matter where you are. By world standards it is not especially tall, but on a clear day the views from the 139m observation deck are outstanding; if it's smoggy you're better off going up around dusk, catching the city as the sun sets, then watching as the lights delineate it far more clearly. Having paid the fee, you're whisked up to the 36th floor where another lift takes you to "El Mirador", a glassed-in **observation area** with coin-operated telescopes on the 42nd and 43rd floors, and an outdoor terrace on the 44th floor.

Palacio de Bellas Artes

Av Juárez (at Lázaro Cárdenas) • Museum charge, free Sun or when there is no special exhibition on; main theatre tours free; charge to take photos, even with a phone • http://palacio.inba.gob.mx • Metro Bellas Artes

Facing the Torre Latinoamericano across Avenida Juárez, there's an equally impressive and substantially more beautiful engineering achievement in the form of the **Palacio de Bellas Artes**. It was designed in 1901, at the height of the Díaz dictatorship, by the Italian architect Adamo Boari and built, in a grandiose Art Nouveau style, of white marble imported from Italy. The construction wasn't actually completed, however, until 1934, with the Revolution and several new planners come and gone. Some find the whole exterior overblown, but whatever your initial impressions, nothing will prepare you for the magnificent interior – an Art Deco extravaganza incorporating spectacular lighting, chevron friezes and stylized masks of the rain god, Tlaloc.

Much of the interior splendour can be seen any time by wandering into the amazing Art Deco **foyer** (free) and simply gazing around the lower floor, where there is a good arts bookshop and the *Café del Palacio* restaurant (see page 127). Some of the finest interior decor in the building is generally hidden from view in the **main theatre**, an important venue for classical music, opera and dance, but it can be seen, without attending a concert, if you join a tour, on which you'll be shown the amazing Tiffany glass curtain depicting the Valley of México and volcanoes, as well as the detailed proscenium mosaic and stained-glass ceiling. Visitors wanting to join the main theatre tours can do so for a fee, Monday to Friday at 1pm and 1.30pm.

Museo del Palacio de Bellas Artes

If you want to see more of the building, you might consider visiting the art museum on the middle two floors, the **Museo del Palacio de Bellas Artes**. In the galleries here you'll find a series of exhibitions, permanent displays of Mexican art and temporary shows of anything from local art-school graduates' work to that of major international names. Of constant and abiding interest, however, are the great murals surrounding the museum's central space. On the first floor are *Nacimiento de la Nacionalidad* (*Birth of Our Nationality*) and *México de Hoy* (*Mexico Today*) – dreamy, almost abstract works by **Rufino Tamayo**. Going up a level you're confronted by the unique sight of murals by **Rivera**, **Orozco** and **Siqueiros** gathered in the same place. Rivera's *El Hombre en Control del Universo* (*Man in Control of the Universe*), celebrating the liberating power of technology, was originally painted for Rockefeller Center in New York City, but destroyed for being too leftist – arch-capitalist Nelson Rockefeller objected to Rivera's inclusion of Karl Marx, even though he was well aware of Rivera's views when he commissioned the work. This is Rivera's own copy, painted in 1934, just a year after the original. It's worth studying the explanatory panel, which reveals some of the theory behind this complex work.

Several smaller panels by Rivera are also displayed; these, too, were intended to be seen elsewhere (in this case on the walls of the *Hotel Reforma*, downtown) but for years were covered up, presumably because of their unflattering depiction of tourists. The works include *México Folklórico y Turístico*, *La Dictadura*, *La Danza de los Huichilobos* and, perhaps the best of them, *Agustín Lorenzo*, a portrayal of a guerrilla fighter against the French. None of them was designed to be seen so close up, and you'll find yourself wanting to step back to get the big picture. *Catarsis*, a huge, vicious work by Orozco, occupies almost an entire wall, and there are also some particularly fine examples of Siqueiros' work: three powerful and original panels on the theme of *Democracía* and a bloody depiction of the torture of Cuauhtémoc in *El Tormento de Cuauhtémoc*, and of the same Aztec ruler's heroism in *Apoteosis de Cuauhtémoc* (*Cuauhtémoc Reborn*). The uppermost floor is devoted to the **Museo de la Arquitectura** (same ticket and hours), which has no permanent collection, but frequently has interesting exhibits.

Correo Central

Corner of Tacuba and Lázaro Cárdenas • Free • 55 5510 2999 • Metro Bellas Artes

The **Correo Central** is the city's main post office. Completed in 1908, it was, like the Palacio de Bellas Artes, designed by Adamo Boari, but in a style much more consistent with the buildings around it. Look closely and you'll find a wealth of intricate detail on the facade, while inside it's full of richly carved wood.

Museum of Naval History

On the fourth floor of the Correo Central • Free • Explanations in Spanish only

Naval buffs will enjoy the **Museum of Naval History**, featuring models of old ships, a reconstruction in miniature of Cortés' waterborne battle against the Aztecs on the Lake of Texcoco, plus photos and artefacts of the 1914 US occupation of Veracruz.

Palacio de Minería

Tacuba 5 • Museo Manuel Tolsá • Charge • http://filmineria.unam.mx

The **Palacio de Minería** is a Neoclassical building which was built right at the end of the eighteenth century. It was designed by Spanish-born Manuel Tolsá, who is the subject of the devotional **Museo Manuel Tolsá** (accessed from a door to the east of the main entrance) – a couple of rooms of paintings and architectural drawings, strictly for fans only. The exterior of the palacio makes an interesting contrast with the post office and with the Museo Nacional de Arte directly opposite (see below), and the main entrance has some impressively large meteorites on display.

Museo del Ejército y Fuerza

Filomeno Mata 6 • Free • 55 5512 3215

The Convento de las Betlemitas, a small seventeenth-century convent, now houses the **Museo del Ejército y Fuerza** (Army Museum). Its exhibits are a mix of vintage weapons, flags, uniforms and paintings (plus a few photos) of battles and patriotic heroes, notably the Niños Héroes (see page 94). Aside from diehard Mexican patriots, the museum will mostly appeal to weapons buffs.

Torture and Capital Punishment Exhibition

Tacuba 15 • Charge • Metro Bellas Artes

The macabre **Exposición de Instrumentos de Tortura y Pena Capital** exhibits instruments of torture and execution from the time of the Inquisition onwards. Kicking off with instruments of public humiliation, such as an old pillory, it swiftly moves on to fiendish implements of torture, methods of applying the death penalty and instruments used specifically on women. Skeletons and dummies of the victims add to the gruesomeness.

Museo Nacional de Arte

Tacuba 8 • Charge, free Sun, photo permit charge, video permit charge • http://munal.mx • Metro Bellas Artes

The **Museo Nacional de Arte** is set back from the street on a tiny plaza in which stands one of the city's most famous sculptures, **El Caballito**, portraying Carlos IV of Spain. This enormous bronze, the work of Manuel Tolsá, was originally erected in the Zócalo in 1803. In the intervening years it has graced a variety of sites and, despite the unpopularity of the Spanish monarchy (and of the effete Carlos IV in particular), is still regarded affectionately. The latest setting is appropriate, since Tolsá also designed the nearby Palacio de Minería (see page 86). The open plaza around the sculpture is now often the scene of intense pre-Columbian drumming and dancing, which usually draws an appreciative crowd.

Though the museum is the foremost showcase of Mexican art from the 1550s to the 1950s, with a collection of over a thousand pieces, its interest is mainly historical. Most of the major Mexican artists are represented, but with essentially mediocre examples spiced only occasionally with a more striking work. It's worth coming here to see something of the dress and landscape of old Mexico, and also some of the curiosities, but don't expect masterpieces.

Temporary displays take up the ground floor (along with a good bookshop and café), leaving the two floors above for the permanent collection.

The top floor

To follow the displays in chronological order, start on the **top floor**, where rooms 1 to 14 cover **pre-Independence art**, the earliest works indistinguishable from those of Inquisition Spain – lots of saints, virgins and gory martyrdoms. José de Mora's 1719 *Señor de Chalma* in room 10 – a crucifixion scene apparently copied from a painting in Chalma that was later destroyed by fire – seems to give the first hint of an emerging Mexican style. **Nineteenth-century art** starts in rooms 15 to 19 – **José Maria Obregón**'s depiction of the medieval Italian painters Giotto and Cimabue in room 17 may interest art historians – and continues on the middle floor.

The middle floor

As the nineteenth century progresses, Mexican themes take hold, with paintings like Obregón's *El Descubrimiento del Pulque* (*The Discovery of Pulque*) and *La Fundación de México* in room 20. **José Maria Velasco**'s landscapes of the Valley of México in room 22 abandon the history in favour of contemporary Mexico, and in the same room, an illustration of the Zócalo in the early nineteenth century by the British artist and traveller John Phillips is interesting more for historical than artistic reasons.

Room 27 heralds the **twentieth century**, with paintings like the macabre 1914 *Paisaje de Zacatecas con Ahorcados II* (*Zacatecas Landscape with Hanged Men II*) by Francisco Goitia. That room, and the next, also have a handful of minor works by **Diego Rivera**, but the cubist works by him in room 31 are a lot more interesting. Indeed, room 31 marks the climax of the collection, with strking works by Rivera's fellow muralists **David Siqueiros** (such as *Accidente en la Mina*), **José Clemente Orozco** (*Cabeza Flechada* or *Head Shot Through with Arrows*) and a self-portrait by **Juan O'Gorman**, as well as Rivera's excellent portrait of Adolfo Best Maugard. Siqueiros' full-length portrait of art patron Maria Asúnsolo coming downstairs, in room 30, is also not to be missed.

The Alameda and beyond

From behind Bellas Artes, Lázaro Cárdenas runs north towards the **Plaza Garibaldi** (see page 134) through an area crowded with seedy cantinas and eating places, theatres and burlesque shows. West of the Palacio de Bellas Artes lies the **Alameda**, first laid out as a park in 1592, and taking its name from the *alamos* (poplars) then planted. The Alameda had originally been an Aztec market and later became the site where the Inquisition burned its victims at the stake. Most of what you see now – formally laid-out paths and flowerbeds, ornamental statuary and fountains – dates from the nineteenth century, when it was the fashionable place to stroll. It's still popular, always full of people, particularly at weekends, but it's mostly a transient population – office workers taking lunch, shoppers resting their feet, messengers taking a short cut and street vendors selling T-shirts.

Museo de Tequila y Mezcal

Plaza Garibaldi • Charge • http://mutemgaribaldi.mx • Metro Garibaldi or Bellas Artes

The Museum of Tequila and Mezcal (MUTEM) tells the story of Mexico's best-known liquors, as well as that of Plaza Garibaldi and its mariachis. Explanations are in Spanish and English, with lots of old photos. It's one of those museums that would be equally good as a book – there aren't any exhibits as such, apart from a large variety of agave plants – and the very limited free samples aren't worth getting excited about either, although the rooftop bar is good. It nevertheless makes for a fun half-hour's worth of information, and if you come here on a Friday or Saturday night, you can spill out into the square afterwards to sample the liquors in question to the sound of mariachi musicians.

Museo de la Estampa

Hidalgo 39 • Charge, free Sun • https://munae.inba.gob.mx • Metro Bellas Artes

On the north side of the Alameda, Avenida Hidalgo traces the line of an ancient thoroughfare, starting from the Teatro Hidalgo, right opposite Bellas Artes. To the west, a little sunken square by the church of Santa Vera Cruz, the **Museo de la Estampa**, is dedicated to engraving, an art form taken seriously in Mexico, where the legacy of José Guadalupe Posada (see page 351) is still revered. There is no permanent collection, but you may expect anything from engravings and printing plates from pre-Columbian times to the modern age, including works by Posada.

Laboratorio Arte Alameda

Dr Mora 7 • Charge, free Sun • http://inba.gob.mx/recinto/32 • Metro Hidalgo

The **Laboratorio Arte Alameda** is an art museum built into the glorious seventeenth-century monastery of San Diego. The cool, white interior is filled with temporary exhibitions of challenging contemporary art. They're all superbly displayed around the church, chapel and cloister of the old monastery.

Museo Mural Diego Rivera

Corner of Balderas and Colón • Charge, free Sun; photo permit charge • http://inba.gob.mx/recinto/46/museo-mural-diego-rivera • Metro Hidalgo

One of the buildings worst hit by the 1985 earthquake was the *Hotel del Prado*, which contained the Rivera mural *Sueño de una Tarde Dominical en la Alameda* (*Dream of a Sunday Afternoon in the Alameda*). The mural survived the quake, and was subsequently picked up in its entirety and transported around the Alameda – it can now be seen in the **Museo Mural Diego Rivera**, at the western end of the park. It's an impressive work – showing almost every famous Mexican character out for a stroll – but one suspects that its popularity with tour groups is as much to do with its relatively apolitical nature as with any superiority to Rivera's other works. Originally it included a placard with the words "God does not exist", which caused a huge furore, and Rivera was forced to paint it out before the mural was first displayed to the public.

Panels at the back of the sala housing the mural (Spanish on one side, English on the other), and also a leaflet available at the entrance (for a small charge), explain every character in the scene: Cortés is depicted with his hands stained red with blood; José Guadalupe Posada stands bowler-hatted next to his trademark skeleton, *La Calavera Catrina*, who holds the hand of Rivera himself, portrayed as a 9-year-old boy; Frida Kahlo stands in motherly fashion, just behind him.

Paseo de la Reforma and around

Paseo de la Reforma is the most impressive street in Mexico City, lined by tall, modern buildings. It was originally laid out in the 1860s by Emperor Maximilian to provide the city with a boulevard to rival the great European capitals, and doubled as a ceremonial drive from his palace in Chapultepec to the centre. It also provided a new impetus, and direction, for the growing metropolis. The original length of the broad avenue ran simply from the Bosque de Chapultepec to the junction of Juárez – at 5km a very long walk, but there are plenty of buses and *peseros* – and although it has been extended in both directions, this stretch is still what everyone thinks of as Reforma.

"**Reforma Norte**", as the extension towards Guadalupe is known, is just as wide (and the traffic just as dense), but is almost a term of disparagement. **Real Reforma**, however, remains imposing – ten lanes of traffic, lines of trees, grand statues at every intersection and perhaps three or four of the original French-style, nineteenth-century houses still surviving. Twenty or thirty years ago it was the dynamic heart of the growing city, with even relatively new buildings being torn down to make way for yet newer, taller, more prestigious towers of steel and glass. The pulse has since moved elsewhere, and the fancy shops have relocated, leaving an avenue now mostly lined with airline offices, car rental agencies and banks, and somewhat diminishing the pleasure of a stroll.

Church of San Hipólito

Corner of Reforma and Puente de Alvarado • Free • 55 5510 4796 • Metro Hidalgo

The church of **San Hipólito** was founded by the Spanish soon after their eventual victory, both as a celebration and to commemorate the events of the Noche Triste (see page 786). The present building dates from 1602, though over the years it has been damaged by earthquakes and rebuilt. It now lists very visibly to one side.

Panteón de San Fernando

Plaza San Fernando • Free • 55 5518 4736 • Metro Hidalgo

The Baroque eighteenth-century church of **San Fernando**, by the plaza of the same name, was once one of the richest churches in the city. Stripped over the years, it is now mostly of interest for its *panteón* (graveyard), last resting place of **Benito Juárez** and many of his colleagues in the reform movement, whose names will be familiar from the streets which now bear them: Ignacio Zaragoza, Guillermo Prieto, Miguel Lerdo de Tejada, Melchor Ocampo, Ignacio Comonfort.

Museo Nacional de San Carlos

Puente de Alvarado 50 • Charge, free Sun • http://mnsancarlos.inba.gob.mx • Metro Revolución

Where Puente de Alvarado meets Ramos Ariza, the **Museo Nacional de San Carlos** houses the country's oldest art collection, begun in 1783 by Carlos III of Spain, and comprising largely European work of the seventeenth and eighteenth centuries with some notable earlier and later additions. Major names are largely absent, but look for the delicate *San Pedro, San Andrés y San Mateo* by fifteenth-century Spanish painter Maestro de Palaquinos, portraits by Reynolds, Rubens and Hals and a luminous canvas of Breton women by the sea (*Mujeres Bretones a la Orilla del Mar*) by another Spaniard, Manuel Benedito y Vives. Travelling exhibitions are also frequently based here.

Monumento a la Revolución

Plaza de la República; mirador entrance from west side • Charge, free Wed • http://mrm.mx • Metro Revolución

The vast **Monumento a la Revolución** was originally intended to be the central dome of a new home for the Cortes (parliament), though its construction was interrupted by the Revolution and never resumed – in the end they buried a few heroes of the Revolution under the mighty columns (including Pancho Villa and presidents Madero, Carranza and Cárdenas) and turned the whole thing into a memorial. An **elevator** has now been added to take you up to the **mirador** at the top. The views aren't as good as from the Torre Latinoamericano (see page 84), but you can see out to the edge of the city, especially to the north and west.

1

PUENTE DE ALVARADO

West of Reforma, Calle Hidalgo becomes the **Puente de Alvarado**. This was once one of the main causeways leading out of Tenochtitlán, across the lake which surrounded it, and was the route by which the Spanish attempted to flee the city on **Noche Triste** (Sad Night), July 10, 1520. Following the death of Moctezuma, and with his men virtually under siege in their quarters, Cortés decided to escape the city under cover of darkness. It was a disaster: the Aztecs cut the bridges and, attacking the bogged-down invaders from their canoes, killed all but 440 of the 1300 Spanish soldiers who set out, and more than half their native allies. **Greed**, as much as anything, cost the Spanish troops their lives, for in trying to take their gold booty with them they were, in the words of Bernal Díaz, "so weighed down by the stuff that they could neither run nor swim".

The street takes its name from **Pedro de Alvarado**, one of the last conquistadors to escape, crossing the broken bridge "in great peril after their horses had been killed, treading on the dead men, horses and boxes". In 1976, a **gold bar** like those made by Cortés from melted-down Aztec treasures was dug up in Calle Tacuba. It's now in the Museo Nacional de Antropología (see page 97). Without doubt, it was part of the treasure being carried by one of the conquistadors attempting to flee the city – a treasure which, as in all good treasure stories, ended up putting a curse on its robbers.

Museo Nacional de la Revolución

Charge, free Sun • https://www.cultura.cdmx.gob.mx/recintos/mnr

Underneath the monument, the **Museo Nacional de la Revolución** tells the history of the Revolution through archive pictures, old newspapers, films and life-size tableaux. Part of the museum is devoted to the construction of the monument itself. Other sections cover the Porfirio Díaz dictatorship, the various stages of the revolution, and how it broke down into civil war, resulting in the emergence of a new constitution and republic.

Zona Rosa

To the south of Reforma lies the **Zona Rosa** (Metro Insurgentes), a triangular area bordered by Reforma, Avenida Chapultepec and, to the west, Chapultepec Park. You'll know you're there as the streets are all named after famous cities. Packed into this tiny area are hundreds of bars, restaurants, hotels and shops, all teeming with a vast number of tourists and a cross section of Mexico City's aspiring middle classes. Until the 1980s this was the city's swankiest commercial neighbourhood, but the classiest shops have moved to Polanco (see page 93) and many of the big international chains have relocated to the out-of-town shopping centres that have sprung up around the Periférico. Though there's no shortage of good shops, and the selection of restaurants, cafés, clubs and bars in the Zona Rosa is respectable (see pages 129, 127 and 132), it has lost its exclusive feel. It does however claim to have an *ambiente joven* (young vibe), and it's certainly popular with young people, as well as hosting Mexico City's gay village, which is located around the northern end of Amberes. Otherwise, there isn't much you'd come here especially to see. One historical figure who stayed here was **Pancho Villa**, quartered, when his troops were in town, at Liverpool 76.

El Ángel

Paseo de la Reforma at Florencia and Rio Tiber • Elevator available • Free, but ID needed for the lift • Metro Insurgentes or Sevilla

The column of **El Ángel**, officially known as the **Monumento a la Independencia**, was built in 1910. In its base you can visit a room containing the skulls of Independence heroes Hidalgo, Aldama, Allende and Jiménez, and at weekends you can take a lift to the top of the monument, but it's a popular ride, so expect queues (the line snakes

1

around from the door in the plinth). You can go up on weekdays, but you'll need to request permission from the *delegacion's* offices beforehand: a tedious exercise that requires around an hour and your passport.

Museo de Cera and ¡Aunque Ud. No lo Crea!

Londres 6 • One museum charge, discounted joint ticket for two museums • Metro Cuauhtémoc

The Zona Rosa's only real attraction is the **Museo de Cera** (Wax Museum), located on its eastern fringes. Thoroughly tacky, with a basement chamber of horrors that includes Aztec human sacrifices, it shares its site with the Mexican branch of **Ripley's Believe It or Not Museum** (called in Spanish "¡Aunque Ud. No lo Crea!"), which displays such marvels as flea costumes and hair sculpture.

Colonia Cuauhtémoc

The northern side of Reforma, where the streets are named after rivers (Tiber, Danubio and the like), is a much quieter, posh residential area officially known as **Colonia Cuauhtémoc**, though it's usually just bundled in with the Zona Rosa. Here you'll find some of the older embassies, notably the US embassy, on Reforma, bristling with razor wire and security cameras.

Museo Venustiano Carranza

Río Lerma 35 • Charge, free Sun, video permit charge • 55 4664 9455 • Metro Insurgentes

Near the British embassy in Cuauhtémoc is the **Museo Venustiano Carranza.** Carranza was a Revolutionary leader and president of the Republic who was shot in 1920. The building was his home in Mexico City and contains exhibits relating to his life and to the Revolution.

Parque Sullivan

Just north of the junction of Reforma and Insurgentes

Parque Sullivan hosts free open-air exhibitions and sales of paintings, ceramics and other works of art every Sunday (roughly 10am–4pm); some of them are very good, and a pleasant holiday atmosphere prevails.

Roma and Condesa

South of the Zona Rosa lie the residential districts of **Roma** and **Condesa**, full of quiet leafy streets once you get away from the main avenues that cut through. Both suburbs were developed in the 1930s and 1940s, but as the city expanded they became unfashionable and run-down. That all changed in the 1990s when artists and the bohemian fringe were drawn here by low rents, decent housing and proximity to the centre of the city. Small-time galleries sprang up and the first of the bars and cafés opened.

Condesa, in particular, is now one of the best areas for good eating in the city, and definitely the place to come for lounging in pavement cafés or dining in bistro-style **restaurants** (see page 129). The greatest concentration is around the junction of

GLORIETAS

The length of Reforma is punctuated by **glorietas** – roundabouts at the major intersections – each with a distinctive statue, providing easy landmarks along the way. The first, if heading southwest from the Alameda, is the **Glorieta Colón**, with a statue of Christopher Columbus. Around the base of the plinth are carved various friars and monks who assisted Columbus in his enterprise or brought the Catholic faith to the Mexicans.

The Plaza de la República is just off to the north. Next comes the crossing of Insurgentes, nodal point of all the city's traffic, with **Cuauhtémoc**, last emperor of the Aztecs and leader of their resistance, poised aloof above it all in a plumed robe, clutching his spear, surrounded by warriors. Bas-relief engravings on the pedestal depict his torture and execution at the hands of the Spanish, desperate to discover where the Aztec treasures lay hidden. **El Ángel**, a golden winged victory atop a 40m column (see page 90), is the third to look out for, and the place to alight for the centre of the Zona Rosa.

Michoacán, and Tamaulipas, but establishments spread out into the surrounding streets, where you'll often find quiet neighbourhood places with tables spilling out onto the pavement. Sights in the usual sense are virtually nonexistent, but you can pass a few hours just walking the streets keeping an eye out for interesting art galleries, which seem to spring up all the time. The leafy thoroughfare of Nuevo Leon bisects the *colonia*, with the leafy Parque México to the east, which is a popular haven from the raucous city outside the limits of the circular Avenida Amsterdam, where jogging and café culture are the main order of business.

Parque México and around

Parque México, officially Parque San Martín, is a large green space virtually in the heart of Condesa that was set aside when the owners of the horse track sold it to developers back in 1924. The streets around the park, especially Avenida México, are rich in 1930s architecture, showcasing Mexico's own distinctive version of Art Deco.

GETTING TO ROMA AND CONDESA

By Metro The Metro system gives Condesa a wide berth, with line 1 skirting the north and west while line 9 runs along the south side. For more direct access to Condesa's main restaurant district take line 1 to Juanacatlán, and cross the Circuito Interior using the nearby footbridge. This brings you onto Francisco Marquez, which leads to the restaurants – a 10min walk in all. Alternatively, take line 9 to Chilpancingo.

By Metrobús Take line 1 to Sonora or Campeche.

On foot It is easy enough to walk to Condesa south from the Zona Rosa (Metro Insurgentes, Sevilla or Chapultepec).

Polanco

High-priced high-rise hotels line the northern edge of Chapultepec Park, casting their shadow over the smart suburb of **Colonia Polanco**. Along the *colonia's* main drag, **Presidente Masaryk**, the beautiful people drive by in their Porsches and Lexus SUVs on their way to the Fendi or Ferragamo stores, and Polanco also has great dining, but otherwise, unless you've got brand-name shopping in mind or need to visit one of the district's embassies, there's not much reason to come out this way. In recent years something of a culinary renaissance has occurred to the north of **Parque Lincoln**, where three blocks of restaurants serve up varying qualities of world cuisine to a predominantly expat community.

Sala de Arte Público David Siqueiros

Tres Picos 29 • Charge, free Sun • 55 8647 5340 • Metro Polanco

The only tourist sight in Polanco is the **Sala de Arte Público David Siqueiros**, a small but interesting collection of the great muralist's later work, including sketches he made for the Polyforum murals (see page 103). They're all displayed in his former residence and studio, donated (along with everything in it) to the people of Mexico just 25 days before his death in 1973.

If it is not already playing, ask to see the hour-long **video** (in English) on his life and work made just before his death, and watch it surrounded by his murals, which cover just about every piece of wall space.

Bosque de Chapultepec

The **Bosque de Chapultepec** (http://chapultepec.org.mx) is a vast green area, about a thousand acres in all, dotted with trees, museums, boating lakes, gardens, playing fields and a zoo. It provides an escape from the pressures of the city for seemingly millions of Mexicans, with the result that the most visited areas get a heavy pounding and some areas are occasionally fenced off to allow the plants to recover.

Most of the Bosque is taken up by **Chapultepec Park**, which is divided into three sections: the easternmost **Primera Sección**, or First Section, is home to the points of greatest interest, including the zoo; the **Segunda Sección**, or Second Section, is mostly aimed at kids, with an amusement park, technology museum and natural history museum; and the **Tercera Sección**, or Third Section, is a massive forest in the making, with hundreds of tree saplings planted here each year.

Brief history

The rocky outcrop of **Chapultepec** (Náhuatl for "hill of the locust"), from which the entire area has taken its name, is mentioned in **Toltec** mythology, but first gained historical significance in the thirteenth century when it was no more than an anonymous island among the lakes and salt marshes of the valley. Here the **Aztecs**, still a wandering, tribal group, made their very first home, though it proved to be only temporary when they were subsequenty defeated and driven off by neighbouring cities.

Once **Tenochtitlán**'s power was established they returned here, channelling water from the springs into the city, and turning Chapultepec into a summer resort for the emperor, with plentiful hunting and fishing around a fortified palace. Several Aztec rulers had their portraits carved into the rock of the hill, though most of these images were destroyed by the Spaniards soon after the Conquest.

ESSENTIALS — **BOSQUE DE CHAPULTEPEC**

OPENING HOURS

Chapultepec is a big place with a lot to do. You could easily spend a couple of days here and still not see everything, but if you are selective you can cover the best of it in one tiring day. It can be tempting to visit on Sun, when some of the museums are free, and the park is at its vibrant best. However, if you want to be able to move freely it's worth coming during the week.

The Primera Sección The Primera Sección and its museums are only open during the daytime, and are closed on Mon. The Museo de Arte Moderno and Rufino Tamayo museums are free on Sun; the Museo Nacional de Antropología used to be, but no longer is. The entrances to these museums are grouped together along Paseo de la Reforma, less than a 15min walk from Chapultepec Metro station, but you may prefer to catch a *pesero* ("Auditorio", "Reforma km 13" and others) along Reforma.

The Segunda and Tercera Secciónes These secciónes – though not the attractions inside them – are open all the time.

ACCESS

How you approach the Bosque depends on what you want to see first.

The Primera Sección The easiest access to the First Section of the park is via the Metro Chapultepec station, from where you follow the crowds over a bridge across the Circuito Interior (inner ring road). Straight ahead you'll see the Niños Héroes monument and the castle containing the Museo Nacional de Historia. What you may be more interested in taking in along with Section One are the Museo Nacional de Antropología, the Museo de Arte Moderno and the Museo Rufino Tamayo, all officially outside of the Primera Sección yet still surrounded by parkland. You're unlikley, however, to fit all of these into one day.

The Segunda Sección Visitors with kids may want to head straight for the Second Section, either picking up a *pesero* along Constituyentes (routes 2, 24 and others) from Metro Chapultepec, or going direct to Metro Constituyentes and walking from there.

Primera Sección and around

Free • Metro Chapultepec

The **First Section** of the park is dominated by **Chapultepec Hill**, crowned by Emperor Maximilian's very peaceful-looking "castle". Also in the First Section is the **zoo** and the nearby **boating lake**, all week, but especially on Sundays, the area around these attractions is full of vendors selling souvenirs, snacks and sweets.

Monumento a los Niños Héroes

Directly opposite the park's main entrance, coming in from Chapultepec metro station

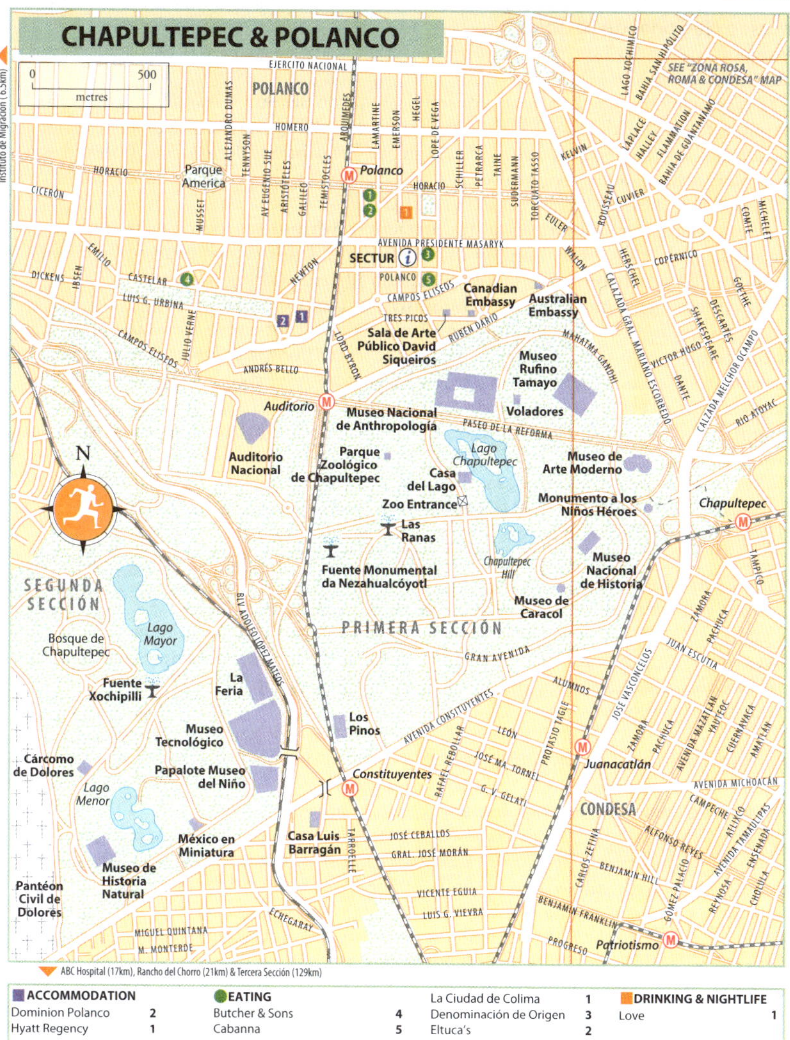

This strange, six-columned monument is dedicated to the **Niños Héroes**: cadets who attempted to defend the castle (then a military academy) against American invaders in 1847. According to the story, probably apocryphal, the last six flung themselves off the cliff wrapped in Mexican flags rather than surrender.

Museo de Caracol

Near the top of Chapultepec Hill • Charge, free Sun • http://caracol.inah.gob.mx

The modern **Museo de Caracol** is devoted to "the Mexican people's struggle for Liberty". Its full name is the Museo Galería de la Lucha del Pueblo Mexicano por su Libertad, but it's colloquially known as the "shell museum" for the snail-like spiralling route through the displays. These trace the history of the constant wars that have beset the country – from Independence, through the American and French interventions to the Revolution.

1 Museo Nacional de Historia

At the top of Chapultepec Hill • Charge • http://mnh.inah.gob.mx • Land trains from the bottom of the hill run every 15min, with a small charge for the round trip

The castle which today houses the **Museo Nacional de Historia** was built in 1785 as a summer retreat for the Spanish viceroy. Until then it had been the site of a hermitage established on the departure of the Aztec rulers. Following Independence it served as a military school, but the present design was dictated by Emperor Maximilian, who remodelled it in the image of his Italian villa.

The setting is very much part of the attraction, with many rooms retaining the opulent furnishings left behind by Maximilian and Carlota, or by later inhabitants with equally expensive tastes, notably Porfirio Díaz. Rivalling the decor is a small group of carriages, including the fabulously pompous Cinderella-goes-to-the-ball state coaches favoured by Maximilian. A collection of furniture, glassware and medals leads on to the main attraction of the lower floor, a series of ornate rooms viewed from a black-and-white tiled terrace that affords fabulous views over the park and city. Peer into Maximilian's ornate office, games room and drawing room, all gilt and dark wood, then move on to Carlota's bedroom and a gorgeous tiled bathroom.

There are several murals here as well, including a number of works by **Orozco** and **Siqueiros**, but the ones by **Juan O'Gorman** most directly attract attention for their single-minded political message.

Lago Chapultepec

On the south side of Reforma, opposite the Museo de Antropología • Hourly charge for boat rentals of various sizes

If you like messing about in **boats**, you'll probably enjoy **Lago Chapultepec**, a boating lake where you can rent vessels of various sizes and while away a leisurely afternoon. A smaller lake, just across the path from the Monument to the Niños Héroes, is used for radio-controlled boats.

Parque Zoológico de Chapultepec

At the western side of Lago Chapultepec • Free • http://data.sedema.cdmx.gob.mx

The **Parque Zoológico de Chapultepec** occupies a large area in the centre of the park and is divided up into climatic zones (desert, tropical, temperate forests, etc), some of which work better than others. Enclosures are mostly open air and tolerably large, though the animals still look bored and confined, and you wonder about their sanity on a Sunday afternoon when half of Mexico City's children seem to be vying for their attention. Probably the most satisfying sections are the most archetypally Mexican: the desert zone, and the enclosure of **xoloitzcuintles**, the hairless dogs that represent the last surviving of four pre-Columbian breeds.

All the big beasts make an appearance, too: tigers, bears, lions, bison, camels, giraffes, hippos, elephants and the ever-popular **giant pandas**. The zoo is inordinately proud of these, evidenced by the posters around town that advertise new baby bears when they are born – in fact, this was the first place in the world to breed giant pandas in captivity.

Los Pinos and around

The street which heads south from Metro Auditorio, Calzada Chivatito, changes its name about halfway to Molino del Rey, after the major battle fought here during the Mexican–American War. Near its southern end is **Los Pinos**, the president's official residence, which is strictly off-limits. A couple of footbridges lead across the *periférico* (Blv López Mateos) to the park's Second Section.

Casa Luis Barragán

Francisco Ramírez 14 • Appointment only Sun–Thurs 11am–5pm • Charge • http://casaluisbarragan.org • Metro Constituyentes

Outside the park limits, south of Avenida Constituyentes, the **Casa Luis Barragán** is a 1948 modernist house designed by Mexican architect Luis Barragán, all whitewash and right angles. Nowadays, it's used for modern art exhibitions.

Museo Nacional de Antropología

Charge, video charge • www.mna.inah.gob.mx

The park's outstanding attraction – for many people the main justification for visiting the city at all – is the **Museo Nacional de Antropología**, one of the world's great museums, not only for its collection, which is vast, rich and diverse, but also for the originality and practicality of its design. Opened in 1964, the exhibition halls surround a patio with a small pond and a vast, square concrete umbrella supported by a single slender pillar around which splashes an artificial cascade. The halls are ringed by gardens, many of which contain outdoor exhibits.

The entrance from Reforma is marked by a colossal statue of the rain god Tlaloc – the story goes that its move here from its original home in the east of the city was accompanied by furious downpours in the midst of a drought. Just east of the museum is a large open plaza, at one end of which is a small clearing pierced by a 20m pole from which **voladores** "fly". This Totonac ceremony (see page 405) is performed several times a day, and loses a lot of its appeal through its commercial nature – an assistant canvasses the crowd for donations as they perform – but it is still an impressive spectacle.

Pre-Classic

The **Pre-Classic** room covers the development of the first cultures in the Valley of México and surrounding highlands – pottery and clay figurines from these early agricultural communities predominate. Notice especially the **small female figures** dated 1700–1300 BC from Tlatilco (a site in the suburbs), which are probably related to some form of fertility or harvest rites. The influence of the growing Olmec culture begins to be seen in later artefacts, including the amazing **acrobat** vase, also from Tlatilco. With the development of more formal religion, recognizable images of gods also appear: several of these, from Cuicuilco in the south of the city, depict **Huehueteotl**, the old god or god of fire, as an old man with flames on his back.

Teotihuacán

The next hall is devoted to **Teotihuacán** (see page 142), the first great city in the Valley of México. A growing sophistication is immediately apparent in the more elaborate nature of the pottery vessels and the use of new materials, shells, stone and jewels. There's a full-scale reproduction of part of the **Temple of Quetzalcoatl** at Teotihuacán, brightly polychromatic as it would originally have been. It contains the remains of nine sacrificial victims dressed as warriors, complete with their funerary necklaces: a relatively recent confirmation of human sacrifice and militarism at Teotihuacán. Nearby is a reconstruction of the inside courtyard and central temple of an apartment complex bedecked in vibrant murals representing ritual life in the city, including *El Paraíso de Tlaloc*, a depiction of the heaven reserved for warriors and ball-players who died in action.

Toltec

The **Toltec** room begins with reproductions of vibrant red and blue murals from Cacaxtla near Tlaxcala (see page 158) and then objects from Xochicalco, a city near modern Cuernavaca (see page 171), which flourished between the fall of Teotihuacán and the heyday of Tula. The large stone carvings and pottery show a distinct Maya influence: particularly lovely is the stylized stone **head of a macaw**, similar to ones found on Maya ball-courts in Honduras. Highlights of the section devoted to Tula are the weighty stone carvings, including one of the Atlantean columns from the main temple there, representing a warrior. Also of note are the **Chac-mool**, a reclining figure with a receptacle on his stomach in which sacrificial offerings were placed, and high up, above a large frieze, the **standard bearer**, a small human figure that acted as a flagpole when a standard was inserted into the hole between its clasped hands. Overlooking some human remains, there's an exquisite little mother-of-pearl-encrusted sculpture of a **coyote's head** with teeth made of bone and a bearded man (possibly a warrior in a headdress) emerging from its mouth.

Mexica (Aztec)

Next comes the biggest and richest room of all, the **Mexica Gallery**, characterized by massive yet intricate stone sculpture, but also displaying pottery, small stone objects, even wooden musical instruments. Facing you as you enter is the **Ocelotl-Cuauhxicalli**, a jaguar with a hollow in its back in which the hearts of human sacrifices were placed (it may have been the companion of the eagle in the Templo Mayor Museum; the two were found very close to each other, though over eighty years apart). Among the hundreds of other powerful pieces – most of the vast Aztec pantheon is represented – snakes, eagles and human hearts and skulls are prominent. Among the statues is a vast image of **Coatlicue**, goddess of the earth, life and death, and mother of the gods. She is shown with two serpents above her shoulders, representing the flow of blood; her necklace of hands and hearts and pendant of a skull represent life and death respectively; her dress is made of snakes; her feet are eagles' claws. As a counterpoint to the viciousness of most of this, be sure to notice **Xochipilli**, the god of love, flowers, dance and poetry. You'll come across him, wearing a mask and sitting cross-legged on a throne strewn with flowers and butterflies, in the section to the left of the entrance as you come in. Also impressive is a reconstructed version of **Moctezuma's headdress**, resplendent in bright blue quetzal feathers, and a **gold bar** lost by one of Cortés' troops during their attempted escape on "Noche Triste" (see page 786).

Piedra del Sol

The room's undoubted highlight, directly opposite the entrance, is the enormous 24-tonne **Piedra del Sol**, the Stone of the Sun or Aztec Calendar Stone. The latter, popular name is not strictly accurate, for this is much more a vision of the Aztec cosmos, completed under Moctezuma only a few years before the Spanish arrived. The stone was found by early colonists, and deliberately reburied for fear that it would spread unrest among the population. After being dug up again in the Zócalo in 1790, it spent years propped up against the walls of the cathedral. In the centre is the sun god and personification of the fifth sun, Tonatiuh, with a tongue in the form of a sacrificial knife and claws holding human hearts on each side, representing the need for human sacrifice to nourish the sun; around him are symbols for the four previous incarnations of the sun – a jaguar, wind, water and fiery rain; this whole central conglomeration forms the sign for the date on which the fifth world would end (as indeed, with the Spanish Conquest, it fairly accurately did). Encircling all this are hieroglyphs representing the twenty days of the Aztec month and other symbols of cosmic importance, and the whole thing is surrounded by two serpents.

Oaxaca

Moving round to the third side of the museum, you reach the halls devoted to cultures based away from the highlands, starting, in the corner of the museum, with the **Zapotec** and **Mixtec** people of **Oaxaca**. Although the two cultures evolved side by side, the Zapotecs flourished earlier (from around 900 BC to 800 AD) as accomplished architects with an advanced scientific knowledge, and also as makers of magnificent pottery with a pronounced Olmec influence. From around 800 AD many of their sites were taken over by the Mixtecs, whose overriding talents were as craftsmen and artists,

NAVIGATING THE MUSEO NACIONAL DE ANTROPOLOGÍA

The museum's rooms, each devoted to a separate period or culture, are arranged chronologically in an anticlockwise pattern around the central courtyard. As you come into the **entrance hall** there's a small circular space with temporary exhibitions, usually very interesting and devoted to the latest developments in archeology; here too is the small **Sala de Orientación**, which presents an audio-visual overview of the major ancient cultures. Off to the left you'll find the **library** and a **shop** selling postcards, souvenirs, books in several languages on Mexican culture, archeology and history, and **guidebooks** (two sizes, in Spanish, English, French or German; prices vary according to size), which provide photographs and descriptions of most of the important pieces. **The ticket office**, and the **entrance** to the museum proper, is by the huge glass doors to the right, where you can also rent headsets, which effectively take you on a **tour** of the museum's highlights in Spanish, English or French for a charge (and you have to deposit a piece of ID as security); they're very cursory, but you do get around the whole museum with some form of explanation. Labelling of individual items is mostly in Spanish, though the general introduction to each room is accompanied by an English translation.

THE COLLECTION

A complete tour of the museum starts on the right-hand side with three **introductory rooms** giving an overview of Indigenous culture, an introduction to anthropology and a history of the peopling of the Americas. These rooms are followed on the right-hand side by halls devoted to the **Pre-Classic**, **Teotihuacán** and **Toltec** cultures. At the far end is the vast **Mexica** (Aztec) room, followed around the left wing by **Oaxaca** (Mixtec and Zapotec), **Gulf of Mexico** (Olmec), **Maya** and the cultures of the **north** and **west**. Every hall has at least one outstanding feature, but if you have limited time, the Aztec and the Maya rooms are the **highlights**; what else you see might depends on what area of the country you plan to head on to. The upper floor is given over to **ethnography collections**, which are devoted to the life and culture of the various Indigenous groups today; stairs lead up from each side. Downstairs, behind the hall given over to the cultures of the north and west, is a very welcome **restaurant**.

working in metal, precious stone and clay. The best site in the country for both these cultures is Monte Albán (see page 581).

The Zapotec collection demonstrates a fine sense of movement in the human figures: a reproduction of part of the carved facade of the Temple of the Dancers at Monte Albán; a model of a temple with a parrot sitting in it (in the "Monte Albán II" section); vases and urns in the form of various gods; and a superb jade mask representing the bat god Piquete Ziña.

Gulf of Mexico

Next is the **Gulf of Mexico** room, in which are displayed some of the treasures of **Olmec** art as well as objects produced in this region during the Classic period. The Olmec civilization is considered the mother culture of Mexico for its advanced development as early as 1500 BC, which provided much of the basis for the later Teotihuacán and Maya cultures. Olmec figures are delightful, but have many puzzling aspects, in particular their apparently African features, nowhere better displayed than in some of the famed **colossal heads** dating from 1200–200 BC, long before Africa is supposed to have had any connection with the Americas. Many of the smaller pieces show evidence of deliberate deformation of the skull and teeth. The statue known as "the wrestler" (though labelled in Spanish only as "*hombre barbado*"), with arms akimbo as if at the point of starting a bout, and the many tiny objects in jade and other polished stones are all outstanding. The later cultures are substantially represented, with fine figures and excellent pottery above all. The two most celebrated pieces are a statue of **Huehueteotl** (though labelled only as a "*dios viejo*") looking thoroughly grouchy with a brazier perched on his head, and the so-called **Huastec Adolescent**, a young Huastec priest of Quetzalcoatl (perhaps the god himself) with an elaborately decorated naked body and a child on his back.

Maya

The hall devoted to the **Maya** is the most varied, reflecting the longest-lived and widest-spread of the Mesoamerican cultures. In some ways it's a disappointment, since their greatest achievements were in architecture and in the decoration of their temples – many of which, unlike those of the Aztecs, are still standing – so that the objects here seem relatively unimpressive. Nevertheless, there are reproductions of several buildings, or parts of them, friezes and columns taken from them and extensive collections of jewellery, pottery and minor sculpture. Steps lead down into a section devoted to burial practices, including a reproduction of the Royal Tomb at **Palenque** (see page 657) with many of the objects found there – notably the prince's jade death mask.

Temple of Paintings

Outside, a trio of small temples from relatively obscure sites is reproduced, the Temple of Paintings from **Bonampak** (see page 664) among them. The three rooms of the temple are entirely covered in frescoes representing the coronation of a new prince, a great battle and the subsequent punishments and celebrations. They are much easier to visit than the originals and in far better condition.

Northern and western societies

As a finale to the archeological collections on the ground floor, there's a large room devoted to the north and the west of the country. **Northern** societies on the whole developed few large centres, remaining isolated nomadic or agricultural communities. The small quantities of pottery, weapons and jewellery that have survived show a close affinity with native peoples of the southwestern USA. The **west** was far more developed, but it, too, has left relatively few traces, and many of the best examples of **Tarascan culture** (see page 289) remain in Guadalajara. Among the highlights here are some delightful small human and animal figurines in stone and clay, a Tarascan Chac-mool, a jade mask of Malinaltepec inlaid with a turquoise and red-shell mosaic, and a two-storey reconstruction of the houses at Paquimé in the Chihuahua desert.

The Ethnography Section

The **Ethnography Section** is on the upper floor. You must cross the courtyard back towards the beginning of the museum before climbing the stairs – otherwise you'll go round in reverse order. The rooms relate as closely as possible to those below them, showing the lifestyle of surviving Indigenous groups today through photographs, models, maps and examples of local crafts. Regional dress and reproductions of various types of huts and cabins form a major part of this inevitably rather sanitized look at the poorest (and most oppressed) people in Mexico, and there are also objects relating to their more important cults and ceremonies.

Museo de Arte Moderno

Paseo de la Reforma, some 300m east of the Museo Nacional de Antropología • Charge, free Sun • https://mam.inah.gob.mx

The **Museo de Arte Moderno** consists of two low circular buildings dedicated to twentieth-century Mexican and Latin American art. The majority of the galleries, along with a separate gallery reached through the **sculpture garden**, are devoted to temporary and touring exhibitions, which are usually well worth inspection.

Permanent collection

The **permanent collection** is exhibited only in Sala D, which does not hold all of it, so the works are rotated regularly. Among them, all the major Mexican artists of the twentieth century are represented. Of works by Siqueiros, the most powerful is *Madre Campesina*, in which a peasant woman carries her child barefoot through an unforgiving desert of cacti. Diego Rivera's portrait of his second wife, Lupe Marín, was painted in 1938, long after their divorce. The eponymous fruit-seller in Olga Costa's *Vendedora de Frutas* is surrounded by bananas, sugar cane, watermelons, pumpkins, pawpaws, soursops and *mameyes*, all painted in vibrant reds and yellows – about as Mexican a subject as you could want.

Las Dos Fridas

The museum's star attraction must be Frida Kahlo's *Las Dos Fridas*, which stands out even among the museum's fine representative selection of haunting and disturbing canvases by Kahlo. One of her earliest full-scale paintings, it depicts her on the left in a white traditional dress, her heart torn and wounded, and her hand being held by a stronger Frida on the right, dressed in modern clothes and holding a locket with a picture of her husband Diego Rivera as a boy. As the works are rotated, not all of these will necessarily be on display at any one time.

Museo Rufino Tamayo

Paseo de la Reforma • Charge, free Sun • http://museotamayo.org

Hidden among trees across the street from the Museum of Modern Art is the **Museo Rufino Tamayo**, another fine collection of modern art – this one with an international focus. The modernist structure was built by the artist Rufino Tamayo, whose work in murals and on smaller projects was far more abstract and less political than the Big Three, though he was their approximate contemporary and enjoys a reasonable amount of international fame. There is much of his own work here, and exhibits of his techniques and theories, but also a fairly impressive collection of European and American twentieth-century art – most of it from Tamayo's private collection. Artists represented may include Picasso, Miró, Magritte, Francis Bacon and Henry Moore, though not all of these are on permanent display. First-rate contemporary international exhibits usually find their way here and sometimes take over the space of parts of the permanent collection.

Segunda and Tercera secciónes and around

Over the years, new sections of parkland have been added to the west of the original Bosque de Chapultepec. These are occasionally still referred to as the **Nuevo Bosque de Chapultepec**, but are more commonly known as the **Segunda Sección** and **Tercera Sección**. With very few places to cross the *periférico*, it is difficult to reach the newer parts of the park from the old. It is far better to make a separate visit to these sections, especially if you've got kids.

Segunda Sección

There are few compelling reasons to visit either section for adults, though the Second Section is an enjoyable area to stroll about, and a good deal quieter than the main section of the park. Approaching the Second Section from Metro Constituyentes, follow Avenida Constituyentes west for a few metres and then cross it on a footbridge.

Mexico en Miniatura

Just inside the Segunda Sección's main entrance on Constituyentes • Charge

All that's now left of the rather tacky Mexico Magic fun park is **Mexico en Miniatura**, a collection of 150 models of "the most emblematic monuments of the republic" created by artist Pedro Ramírez Vásquez. Sights represented here include all the famous pre-Hispanic ruins, plus colonial and modern attractions from around the country, including Mexico City's Zócalo, the Palacio de Bellas Artes and archeological sites from Teotihuacán to Chitchén Itzá.

Papalote Museo del Niño

Constituyentes 268 • Museum charge; cinema charge; music-and-visuals dome charge; discount for museum and cinema combination tickets, and museum, cinema and music-and-visuals dome combination tickets • http://papalote.org.mx

If you turn right after coming in through the Segunda Sección's main entrance on Constituyentes, you'll come to the **Papalote Museo del Niño**, a kind of cross between an adventure playground and a science experiment, with loads of fascinating hands-on experiments, plus an IMAX cinema and a music-and-visuals dome. Adults may feel as if they have entered some sort of psychotic kindergarten, but if you have kids, it will keep them entertained.

La Feria

Charge; all packages include some, but not all, rides • https://www.laferia.com.mx

La Feria is the city's premier fun park. Here you'll find assorted rides and sideshows, easily the best of which is the old-fashioned wooden roller coaster (*montaña rusa*). For adrenaline-fiends, there's also a newer and more exciting roller coaster, right by the entrance. The cheaper entry packages mostly include children's rides (with 1.40m height restrictions), but fewer adult ones. Recent additions include rescued reptile and dolphin enclosures.

Museo de Historia Natural and Cárcomo de Dolores

Charge, free Tues; charge to bring in a camera

The **Museo de Historia Natural** consists of ten interconnecting domes filled with displays on nature and conservation, biology and geology, including rundowns on Mexico's mineral wealth, flora and fauna. Modern and well presented – and with the obligatory dinosaurs – it is again particularly popular with children, but the educational value of the explanations will be lost if you don't speak Spanish.

The ticket for the Museo de Historia Natural also entitles you to visit the **Cárcomo de Dolores**, near the Lago Menor lake, a gazebo containing two murals by Diego Rivera: *El Agua, Origen de la Vida* and *El Fuente de Tlaloc*.

Panteón Civil de Dolores

On Constituyentes, between the second and third sections of Chapultepec Park • Daily 6am–6pm • Free • Pesero (route #24 to "Panteón Dolores") from Metro Chapultepec or along Av Constituyentes

The **Panteón Civil de Dolores** is a huge cemetery, Mexico City's answer to Père Lachaise or Highgate. Among those buried here are Diego Rivera, José Clemente Orozco and other illustrious Mexicans. There's an information office at the main gate (closed at weekends) where you can ask for directions to specific graves.

Tercera Sección

The **Tercera Sección** of Chapultepec Park lies 1km west of the Second Section, beyond the Panteón Civil de Dolores cemetery. It formerly hosted a number of weekend amusement park-type attractions, but those are all now closed, and the space is now a climate-change PR project, with supposedly the most ambitious inner-city forest-planting plan on the planet, if you believe the hype (very few specific details have actually been released, such as the number of saplings planted or how extensive the project will be). It is, however, a top spot for sunset pictures, among leafy green surrounds.

South of the centre

Mexico City spreads itself furthest to the south, where a series of old villages has been swallowed up by the urban sprawl. These harbour some of the most enticing destinations outside the centre, including the colonial suburbs of **Coyoacán** and **San Ángel**, the archeological site of **Cuicuilco** and the canals of **Xochimilco**.

GETTING TO THE SOUTHERN SUBURBS

It's not at all difficult to get out to any of the sights outside the city centre on public transport, but getting from one to the other can be tricky if you're cutting across the main north–south routes. In fact, there is easily enough to see out this way to justify a couple of separate trips, thereby avoiding the slightly complicated matter of traversing the area. And while none of the connections you have to make is impossible, it's worth taking a few short taxi rides between them, from San Ángel to Coyoacán, for example, or from Coyoacán to Rivera's Anahuacalli Museum. If you want to see as much as possible in a day or even an afternoon, you might consider hiring a taxi to take you round the lot; if you bargain, this may not be as expensive as it sounds.

To San Ángel and the University City The best approach is along Insurgentes Sur, plied by the Metrobús (see page 121). There are also plenty of *peseros* from the bus stands by Metro Chapultepec or Tasqueña for services along the Calzada de Tlalpan and to the southwest of the city, above all to Xochimilco. If you'd rather stick to the Metro, take line 3 to Miguel Ángel de Quevedo, between San Ángel and Coyoacán.

To Coyoacán If you don't fancy walking from San Ángel (see page 105), buses head down Altavista by the *San Ángel Inn*; from the centre, buses leave from Metros Chapultepec, Insurgentes or Cuauhtémoc. In each case look for "Coyoacán" or "Colonia del Valle/Coyoacán". There's also a trolleybus which runs in both directions along Lázaro Cárdenas. Metro line 3, too, passes close by, though note that Viveros station is considerably closer to the action than Coyoacán station: from Viveros, walk south on Av Universidad, then turn left (east) to reach the centre. If you're coming straight from the centre of town down Cuauhtémoc or Lázaro Cárdenas, it makes sense to visit the Kahlo and Trotsky museums (see pages 106 and 108) first, in which case you'll want to get off the bus immediately after passing under Av Río Churubusco. The Metro stops are slightly more distant, but a good approach is to take line 2 to General Anaya and walk west past the Museo de las Intervenciones and the Trotsky and Frida Kahlo houses.

Insurgentes

Insurgentes, the most direct approach to the suburbs, is interesting in its own right: leaving behind the Glorieta de Insurgentes (the roundabout at Insurgentes Metro station), it runs almost perfectly straight all the way out to the university, lined the whole way with huge department stores and malls, cinemas, restaurants and office buildings. A little under halfway to San Ángel, you pass on the right the enormous **World Trade Center**, crowned by *Bellini*, an expensive revolving restaurant (see page 129).

Polyforum Siqueiros

Insurgentes Sur 701 (cnr Filadelfia) • Charge • 55 5536 4520 • Metrobús Poliforum

The exterior of the garish **Polyforum Siqueiros** is plastered in brash paintings by David Siqueiros and some thirty other artists. Inside, it contains what is allegedly the world's largest mural (about 4500 square metres), painted by Siqueiros alone, entitled *La Marcha de la Humanidad en la Tierra y hacia el Cosmos* (*The March of Humanity on Earth and Towards the Cosmos*). For the full impact of the changing perspectives and use of sculptural techniques, try to see the **sound-and-light show** with taped narration (in Spanish) by Siqueiros (Saturdays and Sundays, at noon and 2pm). Elsewhere, the building houses visiting art exhibitions and a sizeable display of expensive crafts for sale.

Plaza México and around

Off Insurgentes to the west • Metro San Antonio or Metrobús Ciudad de los Deportes

Plaza México is the largest bullring in the world, with a capacity of 48,000. You can't actually see it from Insurgentes, but it's only a ten-minute walk along San Antonio. Hard by is the Estadio Azul, a 65,000-seat football stadium that is Cruz Azul's home ground.

Teatro de los Insurgentes

Just before San Ángel • Metrobús Teatro Insurgentes

The facade of **Teatro de los Insurgentes** is covered in a huge mosaic designed by Diego Rivera depicting the history of Mexican theatre, and assorted historical figures. At the top are the insurgents (*los Insurgentes*) of Mexico's War of Independence: Hidalgo, Morelos and Benito Juárez on the left, and Zapata on the right.

San Ángel

The upmarket colonial suburb of **San Ángel** lies 12km southwest of central Mexico City, clustered around the point where Insurgentes Sur and Revolución almost meet, linked by the 200m-long Avenida La Paz. With its markets, ancient mansions and high-priced shops – Cartier, Italian designer furniture and the like – around flower-draped patios, San Ángel is a very exclusive place to live. It also makes an inviting place to visit, packed with little restaurants and cafés where you can sit outside and watch the crowds go by. Whether you choose to visit on Saturday (market day – see page 135) or one of the quieter days of the week, consider sticking around until evening to blow an appreciable wad of cash on some of the finest dining in the city (see page 130).

Plaza San Jacinto

San Ángel is especially appealing on Saturdays when the delightful **Plaza San Jacinto** is taken over by Bazar Sábado, a lively outdoor art market. Initially, the Saturday market was based in one of the mansions on the square, which still opens every weekend selling upmarket crafts and artworks, but nowadays there are stalls in all the surrounding streets, complete with fairground rides.

Casa del Risco

Plaza San Jacinto 15 • Free • http://museocasadelrisco.org.mx • Metrobús Dr Galvez

Plaza San Jacinto is surrounded by San Ángel's oldest mansions, notably the eighteenth-century **Casa del Risco**, housing a collection of mostly European antique furniture and paintings put together by twentieth-century diplomat Isidro Fabela. There's an extraordinary fountain in the central patio made from seashells and old porcelain plates and cups, broken and whole.

Museo del Carmen

On Revolución just south of its junction with La Paz • Charge, free Sun • https://lugares.inah.gob.mx/es/museos-inah/museo/404-museo-de-el-carmen • Metrobús Dr Galvez

San Ángel takes its name from the former Carmelite Convent of San Angelo Mártir, which is now run as the **Museo del Carmen**. Its three brightly coloured, tiled domes preside over this part of town and add the final touch of grace to what is a lovely example of early seventeenth-century architecture. The church is still used but the rest of the convent has become a museum where just walking through the maze of monks' cells, rooms and courtyards is pleasurable enough, though there's also an extensive collection of colonial religious paintings and furniture. Just about everyone wants to make their way to the crypt to see the dozen **mummies**, found here by troops during the Revolution and thought to be eighteenth-century nuns and monks, now displayed behind glass. Elsewhere, check out the extensive displays on daily life in New Spain and a collection of eighteenth-century oils by Cristóbal de Vallalpando.

Museo Casa Estudio Diego Rivera y Frida Kahlo and the San Ángel Inn

Diego Rivera 2 • Charge, free Sun • http://inba.gob.mx/recinto/51

From central San Ángel, it's just over half a kilometre along Altavista to the **Museo Casa Estudio Diego Rivera y Frida Kahlo**, a pair of modernist houses built for Diego Rivera

A WALK FROM SAN ÁNGEL TO COYOACÁN

The most enjoyable way to take in San Ángel and Coyoacán on the same day is to put an hour or so aside and **walk** between the two. The most pleasant route (see map, page 107), through quiet streets past some of the city's prime real estate, starts at the main junction in the centre of San Ángel where Revolución passes the Museo del Carmen (see above). From here, follow La Paz northeast and cross Insurgentes to reach the **Jardín de la Bombilla**, a small park centred on a blockish concrete **monument** to General Alvaro Obregón, who was assassinated here in 1928, soon after being re-elected as president. Revolutionary workers (holding a corn cob, oak leaves, a hammer and a sickle) flank the monument, and you can duck inside to see the bronze statue of Obregón.

On the east side of the park, cross Chimalistac and walk through the tiny Plaza Frederico Gamboa, overlooked by the sixteenth-century **Capilla de San Sebastián Martir**, with a statue of the Virgin of Guadalupe above the door. When you reach the other side of the square, take a left (you're now headed north) and cross Miguel Ángel de Quevedo, passing **Parque Tagle** on your left, then turn right into Arenal. This leads you across Universidad to the **Capilla de San Antonio de Padua**, a little red chapel sited attractively next to a small stone bridge – a prime spot for photo opportunities.

Continue east on the peaceful, cobbled Francisco Sosa, one of the most beautiful streets in the city, and also one of the oldest. Peer over the high walls lining the street to catch a glimpse of some gorgeous residences – the only way to get any closer to these houses is to visit the **Museo Nacional de la Acuarela**, Salvador Novo 88 (free; http://acuarela.org.mx), a small museum inside one. Devoted to watercolour painting, the collection includes some architectural and graphic art as well. Look for work by early twentieth-century painter Saturnino Herrán, and don't miss the temporary exhibits in a separate gallery reached through a small sculpture garden.

Ten minutes' walk further along Francisco Sosa brings you to the **Plaza Santa Catarina**, a tranquil square overlooked by a mustard-yellow church and with a couple of restaurants. From here it is a short walk to Coyoacán's Plaza Central, reached through a twin-arched gateway.

If you're still in a walking mood, you could continue along Avenida Hidalgo to the Museo Nacional de las Intervenciones (see page 111) and General Anaya metro station.

and Frida Kahlo in 1931–32 by the leading contemporary architect, Juan O'Gorman. Tucked behind an organ cactus fence opposite the prestigious *San Ángel Inn* restaurant (see page 131) sits a small compound with a large maroon-coloured house (Diego's) and a much smaller blue abode (Frida's), connected by a rooftop causeway. From 1933 to 1941 they both stayed here, living and working apart yet still near enough to visit each other and for Frida to deliver Diego's meals. In both buildings the walls are concrete, the floors are wooden and many of the windows go from floor to ceiling – very advanced for the early 1930s and especially for Mexico. Indeed, the whole set-up is in such contrast to the Blue House in Coyoacán (see page 106) that it is hard to imagine that the houses were inhabited by the same people.

Diego's studio contains some of his painting materials, along with personal items, reproductions of some of his work and some large papier-mâché skeletons. Temporary exhibits take up much of Frida's house, though there are a couple of fine portraits of her taken by photographer Nikolas Muray, with whom Frida had an affair in the late 1930s, and some of Frida's own *ex voto* paintings of her debilitating accident.

Coyoacán

Around 6km east of San Ángel lies **COYOACÁN**, another colonial township that has been absorbed by the city. Even before the Conquest it was a sizeable place.

1

Originally the capital of a small lakeshore kingdom, it was subjugated by the Aztecs in the mid-fifteenth century. Cortés based himself in Coyoacán during the siege of Tenochtitlán, and continued to live here while the old city was torn down and construction began on the capital of Nueva España. The focus of the area is the spacious **Plaza Central**, but no visit to Coyoacán is complete without strolling out to the northern reaches of the suburb to the two main sights, the **Frida Kahlo** and **Leon Trotsky museums**.

Plaza Central

Coyoacán's **Plaza Central** is one of the city's main stomping grounds for artists, artisans and musicians. It is actually made up of two adjoining plazas – **Plaza Hidalgo** and the **Jardín del Centenario**. Bars and cafés ring the plaza, and on the south side of Plaza Hidalgo is the sixteenth-century **Church of San Juan**. On Sunday, there's a market in the Plaza Central, and the area is taken up by stalls and various rock, folk and reggae bands. It's far and away the most fun place in the city to buy your souvenirs (T-shirts make good buys here, some of them hand-painted), though a lot of things can be found cheaper elsewhere.

Palacio Municipal

On the north side of Plaza Hidalgo • Tourist office: 55 5658 0221

The small **Palacio Municipal** (also known as the Casa de Cortés) is said to have been commissioned by Hernán Cortés himself. Inside the *palacio* are two **murals** by pupils of Rivera's – one by Aurora Reyes depicting the Conquest, and one by Diego Rosales showing the torture of Cuauhtémoc. The latter is particularly apposite since it was in Coyoacán that the Aztec leader was tortured and finally killed. The murals aren't usually open to the public, but if you ask at the **tourist office** in the same building they might let you take a peek at Reyes's mural, in the Sala de Cabildos, a municipal office. The other mural is in the *capilla* (registry office), which is generally only open if there's a wedding on – should you stumble upon one you can discreetly put your head round the door for a quick look.

Plaza la Conchita

Southeast of Coyoacán's main square, Calle Higuera leads down to the small but pretty Plaza la Conchita. On the east side of the plaza, the **Capilla de la Concepción** still has traces of the original red paint on its facade, and has undergone much-needed restoration work over the years. Overlooking the square from the other side, on the corner with Higuera, the distinctive red **Casa de la Malinche** at Vallarta 47 (not open to the public) is the house in which Hernán Cortés installed his Maya mistress – and where he allegedly later murdered his wife shortly after her arrival from Spain.

Museo de Culturas Populares and around

Av Hidalgo 289, just off Plaza Hidalgo • Charge, free Sun • https://mncp.cultura.gob.mx

The **Museo de Culturas Populares** has colourful displays on popular cultural forms, mostly dolls, masks and costumes. Avenida Hidalgo also leads to the Museo Nacional de las Intervenciones (see page 111)– to find it, continue down Avenida Hidalgo for about 300m, and bear left down General Anaya, which leads directly to the museum (crossing División del Norte on the way), a fifteen- to twenty-minute walk.

Museo Frida Kahlo

Londres 247, at Allende • Charge; ticket also valid for Museo Anahuacalli (see page 111); audio guide charge • http://museofridakahlo.org.mx • Metro Coyoacán

The **Museo Frida Kahlo** is just a few minutes' walk from the centre of Coyoacán. The appropriately named Blue House was the Kahlos' family home and this is where Frida

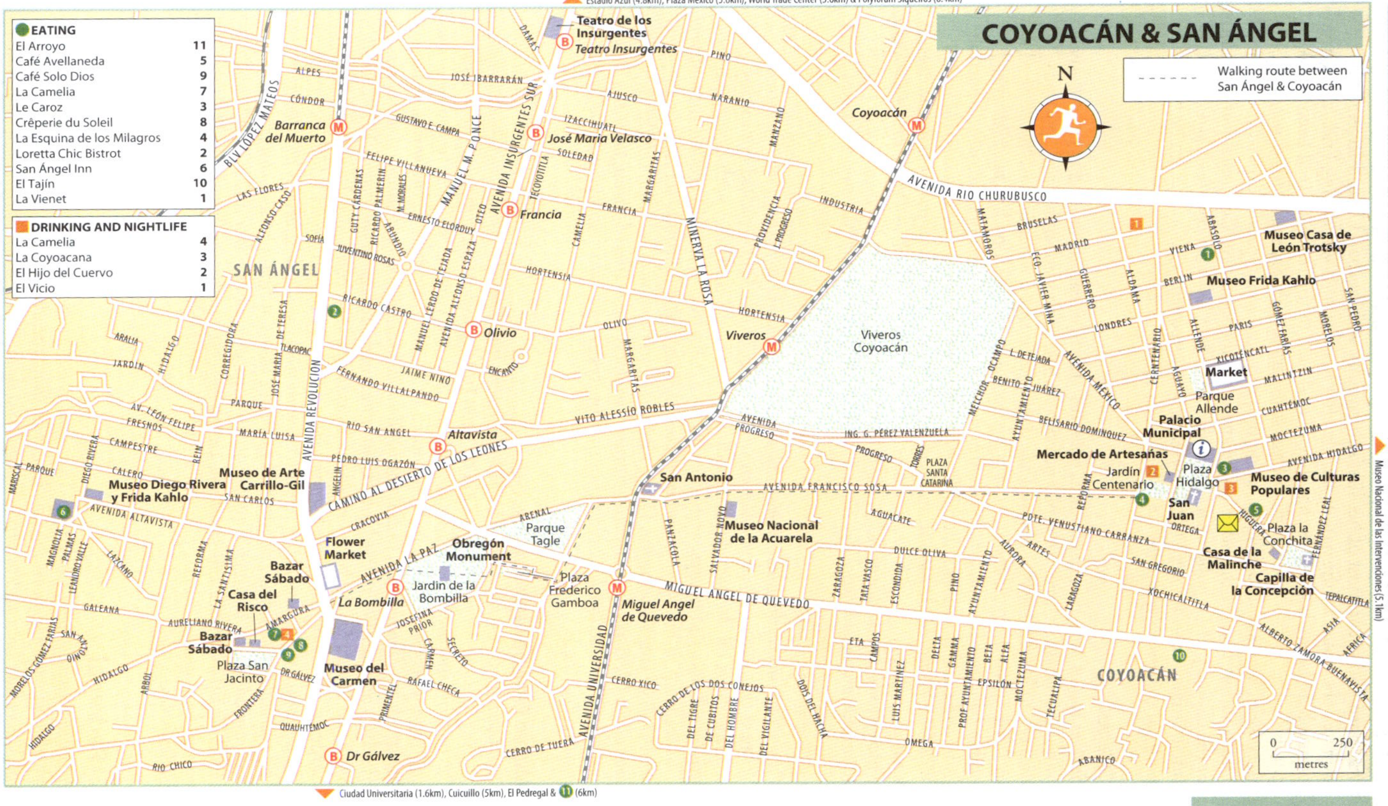

1

was born and spent most of her life, sporadically with husband Diego Rivera, who donated the house to the nation shortly after her death. It was during Frida and Diego's tenure here in the late 1930s that they played host to the newly arrived **Leon Trotsky** and his wife. Trotsky, ever fearful of assassins, apparently expressed his concern about the ease of access from a neighbouring property, and in a typically expansive gesture Diego simply bought the other house and combined the two. Continually at the centre of the capital's leftist bohemian life, Diego and Frida hosted a coterie of artists and intellectuals at this house; D.H. Lawrence was a frequent visitor, though he had little political or artistic sympathy with Kahlo, let alone Trotsky.

Galleries

Several rooms have been set aside as **galleries**. The first features around twenty relatively minor (and less tortured) examples of Frida's work, from some of her early portraits through to her final work, *Viva la Vida*, a still life of sliced watermelons. She painted it in 1954, when the pain and trauma of her recent leg amputation had taken their toll on her painterly control, if not her spirit. Look too for a beautiful charcoal self-portrait from 1932 and the more political *El Marxismo Dará la Salud a los Enfermos* (*Marxism Will Give Health to the Sick*) from 1954. A room full of Frida's signature **tehuana dresses** leads to more paintings, including over a dozen by Rivera, such as *Paisaje de la Quebrada*, which shows a rock face at Acapulco into which Diego painted his own face in purple. Alongside are several works by Velasco and Orozco, as well as a Klee and a Tanguy.

Interior and artefacts

Other sections of the house faithfully show the artesanía style that Frida favoured. Witness the blue and yellow kitchen with "Diego" and "Frida" picked out in tiny ceramic mugs on the wall. Its extraordinary decoration continues with bizarre papier-mâché animals and figures, and an impressive collection of *retablos* around the stairway. This leads up to Frida's airy studio where her wheelchair is artfully set next to an easel and, of course, a mirror. Diego's influence in the house is seen more through his interest in Mexico's pre-Hispanic culture. Artefacts are scattered throughout the house and a small collection is displayed in the courtyard on a two-step pyramid he had constructed there.

Museo Casa de León Trotsky

Río Churabasco 410 • Charge; camera charge • http://museotrotsky.org.mx • Metro Coyoacán

Trotsky's House, or the **Museo Casa de León Trotsky**, where the genius of the Russian Revolution and organizer of the Red Army lived and worked, is about four blocks away and represents virtually the only memorial to Trotsky anywhere in the world. After Lenin's death, Trotsky was forced into exile and condemned to death, and as increasing numbers of countries refused him asylum he sought refuge in Mexico in 1937, aided by Diego Rivera (at the time an ardent Trotskyite), who petitioned President Lázaro Cárdenas on his behalf. Here Stalin's long arm finally caught up with him (see page 112), despite the house being reinforced with steel gates and shutters, high walls and watchtowers. Today the fortified building seems at first a little incongruous, surrounded by the bourgeois homes of a prosperous suburb, but inside it's a human place, set up as he left it, if rather dustier: books on the shelves, his glasses smashed on the desk and all the trappings of a fairly comfortable ordinary life – except for the bullet holes.

El Pedregal

Around 2km south of San Ángel, Insurgentes enters the great lava field of **El Pedregal**, which gets its name from the vast lava flow that spreads south of San Ángel through the University City and beyond. Craggy and dramatic, it was regarded as a completely useless stretch of land, the haunt of bandits and brigands, until the early 1950s, when architect Luis Barragán began to build extraordinarily imaginative houses here, using the uneven lava as a feature. Now it's filled with an amazing collection of luxury homes, though you'll unfortunately be able to see little of what is behind the high walls and security fences even if you drive around. El Pedregal is also home to the **university campus**, the **Olympic Stadium** (Estadio Olímpico) and **Cuicuilco**, the oldest pyramid in central Mexico.

GETTING TO EL PEDREGAL

By bus/pesero/Metrobús Getting to the Pedregal area is easy, as it's reached from San Ángel by just about any bus or *pesero* heading south along Insurgentes. All stop outside the Olympic Stadium, right opposite the university library, and many (try those marked "Villa Olímpica", "Cuicuilco" and "Tlalpan") continue on to the pyramid at Cuicuilco, visible on the left just after you pass under the *periférico*. Metrobús line 1 also plies the same route.

By Metro The university can also be reached on Metro line 3, but note that Copilco is the most convenient station, Universidad much less so as it brings you out at the back of the campus, from where you have to walk all the way through – past the *frontón* courts and medical faculty – to reach the library.

University City

To the east of Insurgentes is the **University City** (Ciudad Universitaria). After over fifty years of use, the campus is beginning to show its age, and while it's no longer the avant-garde sensation it was when it opened, it remains a remarkable architectural achievement. The whole thing was built in just five years (1950–55) during the presidency of Miguel Alemán, and is now one of the largest universities in the world, with some three hundred thousand students and staff. It's also the oldest on the American continent: granted a charter by Philip II in 1551, the University of Mexico occupied a succession of sites in the city centre (including the Hospital de Jesús Nazareno and what is now the Escuela Nacional Preparatoria), was closed down several times in the nineteenth century and was finally awarded its status as the Universidad Nacional Autónoma de México (UNAM) in 1929.

The Library

Ciudad Universitaria • Metro Copilco (south down Cerro del Agua from the station, bearing right after the campus entrance gate, and it's over to the left after 500m)

The campus is dominated by the astonishing, rectangular twelve-storey university **library**, each face of which is covered in a mosaic designed by **Juan O'Gorman** – mostly natural stone with a few tiles or glass to supply colours that would otherwise have been unavailable. Representing the artist's vision of the country's progression through history, the focus of the larger north and south faces is on pre-Hispanic and colonial Mexico; on the west wall are the present and the university coat of arms; on the east, the future is ranged around a giant atom. It's remarkable how these have been incorporated as an essential feature of the building – at first it appears that there are no windows at all, but look closely and you'll see that in fact they're an integral part of the design, appearing as eyes, mouths or as windows of the buildings in the mosaic.

The rest of the campus

More or less opposite the library are the long, low **administration buildings** (*rectoría*), with a **giant mural** in high relief by Siqueiros (or a "sculptural painting", as he called it), intended to provide a changing perspective as you walk past. At the front of the *rectoría* are the university theatre and the **Museo Universitario de Ciencias y Artes** (MUCA; free), the latter a wide-ranging general collection, with interactive scientific exhibits, plus displays on contemporary art and culture. Behind them spread out the enormous grounds of the main campus, starting with a large esplanade known as the Plaza Mayor, with sculptural groups dotted around a shallow artificial pond. Towards the back of the *rectoría* are more murals, adorning the **Faculties of Science and Medicine**; continue past

1

FRIDA KAHLO

Since the 1970s, **Frida Kahlo** (1907–54) has been considered Mexico's most internationally renowned artist, outshining even her husband, Diego Rivera (see page 78), who recognized her as "the first woman in the history of art to treat, with absolute and uncompromising honesty, one might even say with impassive cruelty, those general and specific themes which exclusively affect women". Julie Taymor's 2002 biopic *Frida*, starring Salma Hayek, further consolidated her role as a **feminist icon**. Her work is deeply personal, centred on her insecurities and her relations with her family, her country and her politics. "I paint myself," she said, "because I am so often alone, and because I am the subject I know best." Her relatively short painting career was never prolific and the largest collection of her work is at the **Museo Dolores Olmedo Patiño** (see page 112).

The daughter of a *mestizo* Mexican mother and Hungarian Jewish father, Frida was born in the Blue House in Coyoacán (now the **Museo Frida Kahlo**, see page 106). When she was 6, she battled a bout of polio that left her right leg withered. She rebounded and, as a precocious 14-year-old at Mexico City's top school, first met **Diego Rivera** (twenty years her senior) who was painting a mural there. She shocked her friends by declaring that she wished to conceive his child "just as soon as I convince him to cooperate", but they didn't meet again for many years.

At 18, and already breaking free of the roles then ordained for women in Mexico, Frida had begun to pursue a career in medicine when she suffered a gruesome **accident**. The bus she was riding in was struck by a tram, leaving her with multiple fractures and a pelvis skewered by a steel handrail. It was during the months she spent bedridden, recovering, that she first took up a paintbrush. Later in life, she reflected "I had two accidents in my life. One was the bus, the other Diego." After her recovery she fell in with a left-leaning bunch of artists, free-thinkers and Communists where she again met Rivera. Within a year they were married: she a striking woman of 21; he a massively overweight man twice her age with a frog-like face and an unparalleled reputation for womanizing. Diego went about his affairs quite publicly (including briefly with Frida's sister, Cristina). He was furious when Frida took up with other men, but her several affairs with women seemed to delight him. After her death he wrote, "Too late now, I realized that the most wonderful part of my life had been my love for Frida."

Encouraged by Diego, Frida pursued her **painting** career. Over half of her canvases are **self-portraits**: imbued with personal symbolism, with themes of abortion, broken bones and betrayed love explored through the body set in an unlikely juxtaposition of elements.

In 1932 Frida miscarried and was hospitalized in Detroit where she painted *Henry Ford Hospital*. This disturbing depiction of her grief shows her naked body lying on a bed in an industrial wasteland, surrounded by a foetus, pelvic bones and surgical implements all umbilically tied back to her. After returning to Mexico, her circle of friends expanded to include Trotsky (with whom she had a brief affair), Cuban Communist Julio Antonio Mella and muralist David Siqueiros (later implicated in an attempt to kill Trotsky, see page 112). By now Frida and Diego were living in paired houses in San Ángel (see page 104), which allowed them to maintain relatively separate lives. In 1939 they **divorced**, a devastating event Frida recorded in *Autoretrato con el Pelo Cortado* (*Self-Portrait with Cropped Hair*), in which her trademark long tresses and Indigenous *tehuana* dresses (both much loved by Diego) are replaced by Diego's oversized suit and cropped hair. They **remarried** a year later, with Frida insisting on financial independence and a celibate relationship.

The injuries from her accident dogged her throughout her life, and as her physical condition worsened she found solace in her work (as well as in drink and painkilling drugs), painting *La Columna Rota* (*The Broken Column*) in 1944, with her crushed spine depicted as an Ionic column. Despite increasing commercial and critical success, Frida had only one **solo exhibition** of her work during her lifetime, in Mexico City just a year before she died. In her later years she was wheelchair-bound, but continued the **political activism** she had always pursued, and died after defying medical advice and taking part in a demonstration against American intervention in Guatemala while she was convalescing from pneumonia in July 1954. By this stage, she knew she was dying; defiantly, on her last work, she daubed the words "Viva la Vida" – "Long Live Life".

these to reach another grassy area with the **Botanical Gardens** and several large walls against which the students play *frontón*.

Estadio Olímpico

Directly across Insurgentes from the university library

The sculptured oval of the one-hundred-thousand-seat **Estadio Olímpico** was built in 1952. Its main facade is decorated with a mosaic relief by Diego Rivera designed to represent the development of human potential through sport. Most taxi drivers will tell you that the stadium was deliberately designed to look like a giant sombrero, but this, sadly, is not the case; it's undeniably odd, though, half sunk into the ground as if dropped here from a great height and slightly warped in the process.

Calzada de Tlalpan

Along with Insurgentes, the other main approach to the south is the **Calzada de Tlalpan**, which runs south from the Zócalo more or less in parallel with Metro line 2 (initially underground, then running down the middle of the road) and subsequently the Tren Ligero, almost all the way to Xochimilco.

The two train lines provide the easiest access to some fine museums – including Diego Rivera's Anahuacalli and the wonderful Museo Dolores Olmedo Patiño. The Tren Ligero passes the giant **Estadio Azteca** football stadium on its way to the canals of Xochimilco, and Metro line 2 also provides alternative access to the eastern end of Coyoacán.

Museo Nacional de las Intervenciones

20 de Agosto and General Anaya • Charge, free Sun • https://www.intervenciones.inah.gob.mx • Metro General Anaya (exit to the west of the Calzada de Tlalpan and 5min walk along 20 de Agosto); for the Trotsky and Frida Kahlo museums (see pages 108 and 106), take General Anaya, cross División del Norte and go straight ahead for about 500m, by which time Anaya has merged into Hidalgo; for central Coyoacán, continue straight on (see map, page 107); for the Trotsky Museum, take a right down Morelos (not signposted) opposite Hidalgo 62

The **Museo Nacional de las Intervenciones** occupies the old Franciscan **Convento de Churubusco**, which owes its present incarnation to the 1847 battle in which the invading Americans, led by General Winfield Scott, defeated a Mexican force under General Anaya – another heroic Mexican effort in which the outnumbered defenders fought to their last bullet.

The building itself is a stunner, especially if you arrive at the darkening of day as the lights are coming on in the gardens. The exhibits, all on the upper floor, may not mean a great deal unless you have a reasonable grasp of Mexican history. They're labelled only in Spanish – and not very fully at that – and are dedicated to the history of foreign military adventures in Mexico: skeletons in the cupboards of Britain, Spain, France and the US are all rattled loudly. One section is devoted largely to the Mexican–American wars – with a very different perspective from that of the Alamo. Much of what's on show, however, comprises paintings of generals and flags, and unless you're a history buff you might better spend your time in the pleasant surrounding gardens. Apart from the Metro, the museum is also accessible by *pesero* ("Gral Anaya") from Coyoacán: pick it up by the market at the junction of Allende and Xicoténcatl.

Museo Diego Rivera Anahuacalli

Museo 150 • Charge or free with ticket from Museo Frida Kahlo (see page 106) • http://museoanahuacalli.org.mx • Tren Ligero Xotepingo; from the station, follow the signs to the Calle Museo exit, double back at the bottom of the steps and take the first left down Museo; after 100m, cross División del Norte, and it's about 500m ahead on your right

It's a ten-minute walk from the Tren Ligero station at Xotepingo to the bizarre **Museo Diego Rivera Anahuacalli**, designed and commissioned by Diego Rivera to house his huge collection of pre-Hispanic artefacts. It's an extraordinary blockish structure,

1

THE ASSASSINATION OF TROTSKY

The first attempt on Trotsky's life, in his house at Coyoacán (see page 108), left more than seventy scars in the plaster of the bedroom walls. At 4am on May 24, 1940, a heavily armed group led by painter David Siqueiros (who had been a commander in the Spanish Civil War and was working under the orders of the Stalinist Mexican Communist Party) overcame the guards and pumped more than two hundred shots into the house. Trotsky, his wife and son survived only by hiding under their beds. After this, the house, already heavily guarded, was further fortified. Unknown to all, though, the eventual assassin had already inveigled his way into the household, posing as a businessman being converted to the cause. Although he was never fully trusted, his arrival at the house on the afternoon of **August 20**, with an article that he wanted Trotsky to look over, seemed innocuous enough. Trotsky invited him into the study and moments later the notorious **ice pick** (the blunt end), which had been concealed under the killer's coat, smashed into Trotsky's skull. He died some 24 hours later, in the hospital after an operation failed to save his life. The killer, who called himself Frank Jackson and claimed to be Belgian, served twenty years in jail, though he never explained his actions or even confessed to his true identity, **Jaime Ramón Mercader del Río**.

started in 1933 and worked on sporadically until Rivera's death, then finished off by Juan O'Gorman and opened in 1963. Inspired by Maya and Aztec architecture, this sombre mass of black volcanic stone is approached through a courtyard reminiscent of a Maya ball-court. The exquisite objects in the collection form part of a thoroughly imaginative exhibit: one small chamber contains nothing but a series of **Huehueteotls**, all squatting grumpily under the weight of their braziers, and the studio has ball-player and animal displays.

The **ground floor** is devoted to objects from the main cultures of the Valley of México – Teotihuacán, Toltec and Aztec – which provided Rivera with an important part of his inspiration. On the **middle floor**, rooms devoted to the west of Mexico (arguably the best such collection in the country) surround the huge airy space that Rivera planned to use as a studio. It's been fitted out with portraits and sketches, including preliminary studies for *El Hombre en Control del Universo*, his massive mural in the Palacio de Bellas Artes (see page 85). On the **top floor** are more Aztec objects, along with pottery and small figures from Oaxaca and the Gulf coast. Up here you can also get out onto the **rooftop terrace**, from where there are magical views of Popocatépetl and Ixtaccíhuatl, both of which seem really close here, their snowy peaks glistening on less smoggy days.

Walking through the dark recesses of the museum, note the ceilings, each with individual mosaic designs, and even the floor of the rooftop terrace, which is inlaid with snake, dog and frog forms, distinct but barely noticeable if you're not looking for them. As you leave the main museum, you'll see a low building diagonally to the left, which houses temporary exhibitions and is worth a visit if only to get a sense of the underlying volcanic rock – part of El Pedregal (see page 108)– which was hewn away to provide building materials for the museum. The museum offers guided tours only, every 30 minutes until 4.30pm, except on Fridays, when the last is at 4.15pm.

Museo Dolores Olmedo Patiño

Av México 5843 • Charge, free Tues • http://museodoloresolmedo.org.mx • Tren Ligero La Noria; from the station, go straight ahead from the exit and take the first left – the museum is a 2min walk on your left

Just round the corner from La Noria Tren Ligero station, the **Museo Dolores Olmedo Patiño** sits amid peaceful and beautifully tended grounds where peacocks strut, oblivious of the busy streets outside, and houses the largest private collection of Diego Rivera's work. It's built into a seventeenth-century mansion, donated in 1994 by the elderly Dolores Olmedo, a wealthy collector and longtime friend and patron of

Rivera's. Over the years she amassed over 130 of his works, all of which are on display here. They span his career, from his Cubist period in the early twentieth century through self-portraits (exhibiting varying degrees of flattery) to 25 sunsets painted in Acapulco from the balcony of his patron's house. The collection is immensely varied, making this perhaps the best place to get a true sense of just how versatile a master he was. Look particularly for three large and striking nudes from the early 1940s, and sketches for his famous paintings of calla lilies.

Rivera's work is reason enough to come here, but the museum also has an outstanding collection of two dozen paintings by **Frida Kahlo**. With the works arranged in approximate chronological order, it is easy to see her development as an artist, from the Riveraesque approach of early works such as 1929's *The Bus*, to her infinitely more powerful self-portraits. Many of her finest works are here, including *Henry Ford Hospital*, *A Few Small Pricks*, *La Columna Rota* and *Autorretrato con Mono* (Self-Portrait with Monkey), the latter featuring Mexico's most distinctive canine breed, the grey-skinned Xoloitzcuintle, of which Kahlo kept several as pets. To see these hairless pre-Columbian dogs in the flesh, wander out into the garden where a few are still kept. There's also a portrait of Kahlo by Rivera elsewhere in the museum, in a pastiche of her own style.

Though easily overshadowed by the Rivera and Kahlo pieces, there is also a worthwhile collection of wood-block prints done by **Angelina Beloff**, Diego's first wife, featuring scenes from Mexico and her native Russia.

Xochimilco

Tren Ligero Xochimilco

The **floating gardens** adjoining the suburb of **Xochimilco** offer an intense carnival atmos-phere every weekend and are likely to be one of your most memorable experiences of the city. Considerable effort has been expended in recent years to clean up the canals and maintain the water levels that had been dropping here, so Xochimilco ("place of the flower fields" in Náhuatl) looks set to remain the most popular Sunday outing for thousands of Mexicans. It's also the one place where you get some feel for the ancient city and its water-borne commerce, thriving markets and dazzling colour – or at least an idealized view of it. Rent any of the colourful boats and you'll be ferried around many kilometres of canals, continually harangued by women selling flowers, fruit and hot food from tiny canoes, or even by larger vessels bearing marimba players and entire mariachi bands who, for a small fee, will grapple alongside you and blast out a couple of numbers. The floating gardens themselves are no more floating than the *Titanic*: following the old Aztec methods of making the lake fertile, these *chinampas* are formed by a raft of mud and reeds, firmly rooted to the bottom by the plants. The scene now appears like a series of canals cut through dry land, but the area is still a very important gardening and flower-producing centre for the city. If you wander the streets of Xochimilco town you'll find garden centres everywhere, with wonderful flowers and fruit in the **market** that enlivens the town centre for much of Saturday (though whether it's healthy to eat food raised on these dirty waters is open to question).

Off the huge central plaza is the lovely sixteenth-century church of **San Bernardino**, full on Sundays with a succession of people paying homage and leaving offerings at one of its many chapels; in the plaza itself there are usually bands playing or mime artists entertaining the crowds.

ESSENTIALS **XOCHIMILCO**

GETTING THERE

For the easiest approach to Xochimilco, take the Metro to Tasqueña station (line 2) and the Tren Ligero (light rail, identifiable by a separate icon) from there to Xochimilco (end

1

of the line); there are also buses and *peseros* from Tasqueña as well as buses direct from the city centre, down Insurgentes and around the *periférico* or straight down the Calzada de Tlalpan. On Sun many extra services are laid on. To get a boat, go straight ahead from the Tren Ligero station exit and follow the "embarcaderos" signs (about a 10min walk).

BOAT HIRE

CostLanchas (launches) can be hired for up to twenty people – the official price should be posted up at the *embarcadero* (dock), and it's probably best to avoid *embarcaderos* where it isn't. There's a long tradition of milking tourists here, so be certain of what you've agreed on before parting with any money. Remember that there are likely to be sundry extras, including the cold beers thoughtfully provided by the boatman, and any flowers, food or music you find yourself accepting on your way.

Trips You'll be encouraged to go for two hours, but try to avoid paying upfront or you're likely to get only an hour and a half, which will include a visit to the garden centre of their choice. The boatman won't like it, but you can always take your business elsewhere. Also, be clear which boat you are getting or you are liable to be shuffled to an inferior and less attractive model.

When to go You can rent a boat on any weekday for a little less-crowded cruising, but Sun is by far the most popular and animated day; Sat is lively, too, partly because of the produce market.

North of the centre

Compared to the southern suburbs, the area north of the city centre has less to offer, but two sites of compelling interest – the emotive **Plaza de las Tres Culturas** and the great **Basílica de Guadalupe** – are worth an afternoon of your attention. Further out, and harder to get to, you'll find the pyramids of **Tenayuca** and **Santa Cecilia Acatitlán**, the city's two most dramatically preserved remains of Aztec architecture (though strictly speaking outside of the Distrito Federal).

Plaza de las Tres Culturas

Eje Central trolleybus (get off at Flores Magón), or Metro Garibaldi (cross Reforma then 400m north up Lázaro Cárdenas), or take a northbound bus or *pesero* along Reforma Norte to Glorieta Cuitlahuac

The **Plaza de las Tres Culturas** is the site of the ancient city of Tlatelolco, located to the north of Tenochtitlán. Today, a lovely **colonial church** rises in the midst of the city's **excavated ruins**, exemplifying the second of the three cultures from which the plaza takes its name. The **modern buildings** that surround it – mostly a rather ugly 1960s housing project but including the Ministry of Foreign Affairs – represent the third culture. The area's most striking modern building, 1km west of the plaza at the junction of Flores Magón with Insurgentes Norte, is the triangular **Torre Insignia**, which dates from 1962.

The ruins of Tlatelolco

Free • 55 5583 0295

The ancient ruins of **Tlatelolco** were once the core of a city considerably more ancient than Tenochtitlán, based on a separate but nearby island in the lake. For a long time, its people existed under independent rule in close alliance with the Aztecs of Tenochtitlán, but it was by far the most important commercial and market centre in the valley; even after its annexation to the Aztec empire in 1473, Tlatelolco retained this role. When **Cortés** and his troops arrived, they marvelled at the size and order of the Tlatelolco market. Cortés himself estimated that some sixty thousand people – buyers and sellers – came and went each day, and Bernal Díaz wrote:

We were astounded at the great number of people and the quantities of merchandise, and at the orderliness and good arrangements that prevailed…every kind of goods was kept separate and had its fixed place marked for it… Some of the soldiers among us who had been in many parts of the world, in Constantinople, in Rome, and all over Italy, said that they had never seen a market so well laid out, so large, so orderly, and so full of people.

In 1521 the besieged **Aztecs** made their final stand here, and a plaque in the middle of the plaza recalls that struggle: "On the 13th of August 1521", it reads, "defended by the heroic Cuauhtémoc, Tlatelolco fell under the power of Hernan Cortés. It was neither a triumph nor a defeat, but the painful birth of the mixed race that is the Mexico of today." The ruins are a pale reflection of the ancient city – the original temples, whose scale can be inferred from the size of the bases, rivalled those in Tenochtitlán. The chief temple, for example, had reached its eleventh rebuilding by the time of the Conquest – what you see now corresponds to the second stage, and by the time nine more had been superimposed it would certainly have risen much higher than the church that was built from its stones. On top was likely a double sanctuary similar to that on the Templo Mayor of Tenochtitlán. The smaller structures include a square **tzompantli**, or wall of skulls, near which nearly two hundred human skulls were discovered, all with holes through the temples – presumably the result of having been displayed side by side on long poles around the sides of the building. Guided tours are available in English, Monday to Friday 9am–2pm, but must be arranged in advance.

Church of Santiago Tlatelolco

Adjacent to the Tlatelolco ruins – though still in use and not considered part of them – is the **Church of Santiago Tlatelolco**. Erected in 1609, it replaced an earlier Franciscan monastery, parts of which survive, arranged about the cloister. In the early years after the Conquest, the friars established a college at which they instructed the sons of the Aztec nobility in European ways, teaching them Spanish, Latin and Christianity. Bernardino de Sahagún was one of the teachers, and it was here that he wrote down many of the customs and traditions of the natives, compiling the most important existing record of daily Aztec life in his famous *Historia General de las Cosas de Nueva España*.

Basílica de Nuestra Señora de Guadalupe

Half a kilometre east of Insurgentes on the Eje 5 Norte • Charge • Metro La Villa Basilica; also accessible by bus or *pesero* north along Reforma, or by trolleybus along Reforma from Metro Hidalgo (direction "Indios Verdes")

The **Basílica de Nuestra Señora de Guadalupe** is in fact a whole series of churches, chapels and shrines set around an enormous stone-flagged **plaza** and climbing up the rocky hillock where the miracles that led to its foundation occurred. It is Mexico's most important religious site, and is visited by millions of pilgrims from all across Latin America every year. Indeed, its religious significance predates the arrival of Christianity, as it was previously a shrine to the Aztec mother goddess Tonantzin. The first church here was built in 1533, but the large (and massively subsided) Baroque basilica you see straight ahead of you as you come through the main entrance to the plaza was completely reconstructed in the eighteenth century and again remodelled in the nineteenth and twentieth.

Around the site, there swirls a stream of humanity – pilgrims, sightseers, priests and salesmen offering candles, souvenirs, pictures of the Virgin, snacks and any number of mementos. On **December 12**, the anniversary of the second apparition, their numbers swell to hundreds of thousands (newspaper reports claim millions). You'll see the pilgrims on the approach roads to the capital for several days beforehand, many covering the last kilometres on their knees in an act of penance or devotion. For others, though, the day is more of a vast fiesta, with dancing, singing and drinking.

The main church

To the left of the great plaza as you come in from Calzada de Guadalupe is the modern home of Juan Diego's cloak with the image of the Virgin on it. This huge, round modern **church** was built in 1976, with space inside for ten thousand worshippers and for around four times that when the great doors all round are thrown open to the crowds, as they are pretty much every Sunday. You'll find it crowded whenever you visit, and there seems to be a service permanently in progress. The famous **cloak**, framed in gold and silver, hangs above the main altar. To prevent anyone lingering too long at the spot right underneath, you must board a travelling walkway and admire the image as you glide respectfully by.

The church museum

Around the back of the Baroque basilica, the **Museo de la Basílica de Guadalupe** contains a large collection of *ex voto* offerings, and some of the church's religious art treasures, including a series of slightly insipid early eighteenth-century canvases by José de Ibarra and more powerful oils by Miguel Cabrera and Cristóbal de Villalpando.

Capillas on the hill

From the plaza you can walk round to the right and up the hill past a series of little chapels associated with the Virgin's appearance. Loveliest is the **Capilla del Pocito**, in which there is a well said to have sprung forth during one of the apparitions. Built in the eighteenth century, it consists of two linked elliptical chapels, one smaller and one larger, both with colourful tiled domes and magnificently decorated interiors. On the very top of the hill, the **Capilla de las Rosas** marks the spot where the miraculous roses grew.

Museo de los Ferrocarrileros

Alberto Herrera • Free • https://cultura.cdmx.gob.mx/recintos/mf • Metro La Villa Basilica

If heading to the Basilica from La Villa Basilica Metro station, train buffs will want to stop off first at the **Museo de los Ferrocarrileros**, a small railway museum in the former train station of La Villa, just outside the Metro station to the east of Calzada de Guadalupe. Inside are exhibits in Spanish on the trade in *pulque* (the station was on the Mexico City–Veracruz railway, an important route for transporting it), but of most interest are the old locomotives standing outside, which enthusiasts will definitely want to see, although you can't climb onto them.

Tenayuca

Just off Av de los Cien Metros • Charge, video permit required • "Ruta 88" *pesero* northbound from Metro Deportivo 18 de Marzo (5 blocks west of the Basílica de Nuestra Señora de Guadalupe) or La Raza (40min, but not all go to the *pirámide* of Tenayuca, so check first) or "Tenayuca" *pesero* northbound from Lázaro Cárdenas; some bus tours visit Tenayuca and Santa Cecilia on their way to Tula and Tepotzotlán

THE TLATELOLCO MASSACRE

The Mexican state showed its most brutal side in the Plaza de las Tres Culturas on October 2, 1968, when troops and tanks were **ordered to fire** on an almost 250,000-strong **student demonstration**. It was the culmination of several months of student protests over the government's social and educational policies, which the authorities were determined to subdue, with only ten days left before the Olympic Games opened in the city. Records of the death toll vary from an official figure at the time of thirty to student estimates of more than five hundred, but it seems clear today that hundreds is more accurate than tens. Mexican philosopher Octavio Paz saw the violence as part of the cycle of history – a ritual slaughter to recall the Aztec sacrifices here – but it's perhaps better seen as an example of at least one thread of continuity between all Mexico's civilizations: the cheapness of life and the harsh brutality of their rulers. Paco Ignacio Taibo II's book, *68*, which is available in English translation, analyzes the incident in detail.

THE VIRGIN OF GUADALUPE

The **Virgin of Guadalupe**, Mexico's first Indigenous saint, is still the nation's most popular – you'll see her image in churches throughout the country. The Virgin's banner has been fought under by both sides of almost every conflict the nation has ever seen, most famously when Hidalgo seized on it as the flag of Mexican Independence. According to the legend, an Aztec Christian convert, **Juan Diego**, was walking over the hill here (formerly dedicated to the Aztec earth goddess Tonantzin) on his way to the monastery at Tlatelolco one morning in December 1531, when he was stopped by a brilliant vision of the Virgin, who ordered him, in Náhuatl, to go to the bishop and tell him to build a church on the hill. Bishop Juan de Zumarraga was unimpressed until, on December 12, the Virgin reappeared, ordering Diego to gather roses from the top of the hill and take them to the bishop. Doing so, he bundled the flowers in his **cloak**, and when he opened it before the bishop he found the image of the dark-skinned Virgin imprinted into the cloth. Today Diego's cloak hangs above the altar in the gigantic modern basilica, which takes its name from the celebrated (and equally swarthy) Virgin in the monastery of Guadalupe in Spain.

The 20m-high pyramid in the main square at **Tenayuca**, a suburb just outside the city limits, is another site that predates Tenochtitlán by a long chalk. Indeed, there are those who claim it was the capital of the tribe that destroyed Tula. In this, its history closely mirrors almost all other valley settlements: a barbarian tribe from the north invades, conquers all before it, settles in a city and becomes civilized, borrowing much of its culture from its predecessors, before being overcome by the next wave of migrants. There's little evidence that Tenayuca ever controlled a large empire, but it was a powerful city and provides one of the most concrete links between the Toltecs and the Aztecs.

The site

The pyramid that survives dates from the period of Aztec dominance and is an almost perfect miniature replica of the great temples of Tlatelolco and Tenochtitlán. Here the structure and the monumental double stairway are intact – only the twin sanctuaries at the top and the brightly painted decorations would be needed for it to open for sacrifices again tomorrow. This is the sixth superimposition; five earlier pyramids (the first dating from the early thirteenth century) are contained within it and are revealed in places by excavations which took place in the 1920s. Originally there was a seventh layer built on top, of which some traces remain.

The most unusual and striking feature of Tenayuca's pyramid is the border of interlocking stone **snakes** that must originally have surrounded the entire building – well over a hundred of them survive. Notice also the two coiled snakes (one a little way up the north face, the other at the foot of the south face) known as the "turquoise serpents". Their crests are crowned with stars and aligned with the sun's position at the solstice.

Santa Cecilia Acatitlán

Charge, video permit required • inah.gob.mx/zonas/136-zona-arqueologica-santa-cecilia-acatitlan • *Pesero* route #88 (see page 122), and also #79, continues from Tenayuca to Santa Cecilia Acatitlán; alternatively, it's a 20min walk, or short taxi ride, from Tenayuca, or a short ride on feeder bus #R10 from San Rafael station on the suburban train line from Buenavista; to return to the city, catch a *pesero* to Metro Deportivo 18 de Marzo (lines 3 & 6)

The pyramid at **Santa Cecilia Acatitlán** is much smaller and simpler than that at Tenayuca, but it's been wholly restored and is remarkably beautiful with its clean lines. When first encountered by the Spanish, this was a temple with a double staircase very similar to the others, but the outer structure was stripped away during

1

AUTHORIZED TAXIS

The airport and all four bus terminals have a system of **authorized taxis** which **guarantee the clients' safety**, and all have booths selling rides inside the terminal buildings. The authorized system is the same wherever it operates from – you'll find a large map of the city marked out in zones, with a standard, set fare for each; you pick where you're going, buy a ticket at the booth, then walk outside and present the ticket to one of the waiting cabs. One ticket is good for up to four people to one destination. The driver may drop you a block or two from your hotel rather than take a major detour through the one-way systems (best to accept this unless it's very late at night), and may occasionally demand a large tip, which you're in no way obliged to pay.

excavation to reveal an earlier, well-preserved building inside. It's a very plain structure, rising in four steps to a single-roofed shrine approached by a ramped stairway. The studded decorations around the roof represent either skulls or stars. You approach the pyramid through a small museum in a colonial house, whose displays of finds from the site and elsewhere include an Aztec incense burner and a reconstructed nineteenth-century kitchen; in the garden just outside, you are greeted by a large, inanely grinning stone skull.

ARRIVAL AND DEPARTURE — MEXICO CITY

Being dropped unprepared into the vastness of Mexico City may seem daunting, but it's not hard to get into the centre, or to a hotel, from any of the major points of arrival. The only problem is likely to be hauling large items of luggage through the invariable crowds – take a cab if you are at all heavily laden, but make sure it's a prepaid "authorized" taxi (see box below).

BY PLANE

Mexico City's airport (http://aicm.com.mx) is surprisingly central, just 6km east of the Zócalo (if you're sitting on the left-hand side of the plane the views as you come in to land are amazing). Most hotels are used to late arrivals, so don't be overly concerned if your flight gets in late at night, though it is wise to have somewhere booked in advance for your first night. There are two terminals, on opposite sides of the airport, and quite a long way from each other by land; most airlines use Terminal 1, which is rather more convenient than the new Terminal 2.

Facilities Wherever you come in, you'll find several ATMs and numerous *casas de cambio*, open 24hr and with reasonable rates for US dollars (rates vary, so shop around), though not always such good rates for travellers' cheques or other currencies (they'll usually take Canadian dollars, pounds sterling, euros, and sometimes Swiss francs, Japanese yen and some Latin American currencies). There are also plenty of pricey restaurants and snack bars, car rental agencies (see page 123), a post office, internet cafés and 24hr left luggage lockers.

Information There are several airport enquiry desks dotted around, and tourist information kiosks in Terminal 1, Sala A (55 5786 9002), and Terminal 2 near exit gate 2 (55 2598 3532), which are helpful but have a limited range of information, and only cover Mexico City.

Transfers between terminals To get from one terminal to the other, there's a monorail service called Aerotrén (upstairs from Sala D in Terminal 1, upstairs in Sala M in Terminal 2), but only passengers with boarding passes are allowed to use this. Otherwise there are red buses (daily 4am–1am; charge) from exit gate 6 (Sala D) in Terminal 1 and exit gate 4 in Terminal 2.

Taxis The only way to get into town is by prepaid authorized taxi, and there are desks for these in both terminals. Prices vary slightly from firm to firm, so it's worth comparing rates before choosing. The authorized airport taxis have a monopoly on arrivals and it's illegal for regular taxi drivers to pick up passengers at the airport, so don't bother trying to flag one down. Getting from town back to the airport is simpler. Any taxi driver will make the trip, and you can expect to pay a flat fee.

Metro Metro Terminal Aérea, line 5, calls at Terminal 1. Come out of the doors at the end of Sala A, then follow the covered walkway for 200m. Note that large bags are banned on the Metro (see page 121). From Terminal 2 (but not in the other direction), the inter-terminal bus (see below) stops at Hangares metro station, but in fact the nearest metro station is Pantitlan (out of the airport precincts and then take a left along the main road for 500m, or hop on a *pesero*), far more convenient than Hangares because it is on four different lines, but not a good area to be with your baggage at night.

Metrobús Line 4 of the Metrobús, which takes two east–west routes through the city centre to TAPO (see page 121), serves both airport terminals. There is a small charge for the journey and there are no baggage restrictions. At the airport you can pick it up from exit gate 6 (Sala D) in Terminal 1 and exit gate 4 in Terminal 2.

Pesero The main road outside Terminal 2 can be reached by *peseros* bound for Pantitlan from Rayón at Reforma (Metro Garibaldi, lines B & 8). From the terminal, head out to the main road to pick up a *pesero* to Metro Garibaldi.

Intercity buses If you don't want to stop in Mexico City, there are first-class buses from the airport straight to Cuernavaca, Pachuca, Puebla, Toluca and Querétaro. The bus stops are upstairs from Sala E1 in Terminal 1 and at exit gate 4 in Terminal 2.

Car rental Desks are located in zones E1 and E2 of Terminal 1, and on the main concourse of Terminal 2. The cheapest deals are with local firm Gold Car Rental (located in Terminal 1, zone E1, 55 2599 0090, intgold@avantel.net). International franchise chains represented at the airport include Avis (55 5762 3688 or 01 800 288 8888, http://avis.com.mx), Budget (01 800 002 8343, http://budget.com.mx), Europcar (800 436 0310 or 800 201 2084, http://europcar.com.mx), Hertz (01 800 709 5000, http://hertz.com), National (800 627 6276 or 01 800 716 6625, http://nationalcar.com.mx) and Sixt (55 5784 3011, http://sixt.com.mx). Rental cars are exempt from the Hoy No Circula one-day-a-week driving restriction (see page 74). For cheaper rentals head to Av Baja California, where Eclipse (Baja California 111, 55 7583 9562, http://eclipserent.com) has more competitive deals than the international companies.

Airlines Aeroméxico, Juárez 76, 55 5512 4000 or 01 800 021 4000; Air Canada, Manuel Avila Camacho 1 8°, Lomas de Chapultepec 55 9138 0280 or 800 719 2827; Delta, Masaryk 513, Polanco 55 5279 0909; Iberia, Ejercito Nacional 436 9°, Polanco 55 1101 1515; Lufthansa, Paseo de las Palmas 239, Lomas de Chapultepec 55 4738 6561; United, Andres Bello 45, Polanco 55 5283 5500 or 01 800 900 5000; VivaAerobus, Mesones 47 and other locations including Central de Autobuses del Norte 55 4777 5050.

Destinations The further the destination is from Mexico City, the more sense it makes to fly there; you won't gain much flying to cities that are only a few hours away by road, and much more expensive by air, but if you're heading to places like Tijuana or Cancún, the plane will not only be faster, but much cheaper too. Flights are likely to be cheapest if you can book them a few weeks ahead. The following domestic airports are served by direct flights from Mexico City: Acapulco (6–10 daily; 55min); Aguascalientes (5–9 daily; 1hr 5min); Bajío/León (6–8 daily; 55min); Cabo San Lucas (4–7 daily; 2hr); Campeche (3–4 daily; 1hr 40min); Cancún (30–37 daily; 1hr 30min–2hr 10min); Chetumal (1–2 daily; 1hr 50min); Chihuahua (6–8 daily; 2hr 10min); Ciudad Carmen (3–6 daily; 1hr 30min); Ciudad Juárez (3–6 daily; 2hr 20min); Ciudad Obregón (2–3 daily; 2hr 25min); Ciudad Victoria (3–5 daily; 1hr 30min); Colima (2–5 daily; 1hr 25min); Cozumel (4 weekly; 2hr); Culiacán (10 daily; 2hr); Durango (3–4 daily; 1hr 40min); Guadalajara (26–33 daily; 1hr 10min); Hermosillo (7–9 daily; 2hr 40min); Huatulco (3–7 daily; 1hr 10min); Ixtapa/Zihuatanejo (4–7 daily; 1hr); La Paz, Baja California Sur (4 daily; 2hr 20min); Lázaro Cárdenas (1–2 daily; 1hr 15min); Los Mochis (1–2 daily; 2hr 15min); Manzanillo (4–6 daily; 1hr 40min); Matamoros (1–2 daily; 1hr 25min); Mazatlán (3–4 daily; 1hr 40min); Mérida (12–14 daily; 1hr 40min); Mexicali (2–3 daily; 3hr 35min); Monterrey (23–37 daily; 1hr 30min); Morelia (4–6 daily; 50min); Nuevo Laredo (1–3 daily; 1hr 40min); Oaxaca (7–10 daily; 1hr); Puerto Escondido (1–2 daily; 1hr 30min); Puerto Vallarta (6–10 daily; 1hr 30min); Reynosa (4–6 daily; 1hr 35min); Saltillo (2–7 daily; 2hr); San Luis Potosí (5–9 daily; 1hr 10min); Tampico (5–9 daily; 1hr); Tapachula (3 daily; 1hr 40min); Tepic (1–2 daily; 1hr 25min); Tijuana (12–15 daily; 3hr 35min); Torreón (4–5 daily; 1hr 40min); Tuxtla Gutiérrez (8–11 daily; 1hr 25min); Veracruz (6–12 daily; 50min); Villahermosa (5–12 daily; 1hr 20min); Zacatecas (3–4 daily; 1hr 20min).

BY BUS

There are four principal long-distance bus stations in Mexico City, one for each point of the compass, though in practice the northbound terminal handles far more than its share, while the westbound one is tiny. All have Metro stations pretty much right outside, as well as authorized taxis (see page 118).

Destinations The list opposite indicates which destination is served from which station, but if you're uncertain which bus station you should be leaving from, any taxi driver should know which terminal to take you to. The further a destination is from Mexico City, the more likely it is that the long and arduous bus ride will cost you more than the plane fare, so it's worth checking the price of a flight before you book that *camión*.

Facilities The terminals have guarderías (left luggage offices, often expensive, especially at TAPO and Taxqueña), post and telephone offices, ATMs and a tourist information kiosk.

Tickets It's rare not to be able to get onto a bus at short notice, but it can be worth booking in advance for long-distance journeys or for express services to popular destinations at busy times – that way you'll have a choice of seat and be sure of getting the fastest service. Mi Escape (55 5784 4642, http://miescape.com.mx) – with offices at TAPO bus station (Tunnel 1), Isabel la Católica 83 in the centre, Hamburgo 254 (at Sevilla) in the Zona Rosa and Masaryk with Hegel in Polanco, among other places – can book tickets for a small fee with many but not all bus lines.

TERMINAL DEL NORTE

From anywhere north of Mexico City, you'll probably arrive at the Terminal del Norte, Av de los Cien Metros 4907. The

1

largest of the city's four stations, it handles direct routes to and from the US border, and services to every major city north of Mexico City, including the fastest services to Guadalajara and Morelia. There's a Metro station right outside the entrance (Metro Autobuses del Norte; line 5), and trolleybuses just outside, which head down the Eje Central (Lázaro Cárdenas) to Bellas Artes and on to the Central de Autobuses del Sur. Alternatively, if you head four blocks east, you come to Insurgentes, where you can catch the Metrobús Line 1 (see page 121). If you want to get a taxi, go to the kiosk selling tickets for authorized taxis (see page 118), which will take you to popular destinations such as the Zócalo and Alameda, the Zona Rosa and Polanco, all for a fair price (plus a surcharge between 10.30pm and 6.30am). If you arrive late at night and don't want to search for a hotel in town, there are places nearby (see page 124).

TERMINAL DE AUTOBUSES DE PASAJEROS DE ORIENTE (TAPO)

Buses from points east (including a number of places that you may think of as south, such as Chiapas or the Yucatán), will usually drop you at the Terminal de Autobuses de Pasajeros de Oriente, known as TAPO, which is located on Av Ignacio Zaragoza. It has a Metro station (Metro San Lázaro; lines 1 and B) just down a connecting tunnel, which also leads you to the stops for city buses and *colectivos* plying Zaragoza towards the Zócalo and the Alameda, as well as Metrobús line 4 (see page 121). In the same tunnel, opposite the Metro entrance, is a sales desk for the authorized taxis (see page 118), which run to the Zócalo and Alameda, Zona Rosa and Polanco (all charge extra 10.30pm–6.30am).

CENTRAL DE AUTOBUSES DEL SUR (TAXQUEÑA)

Buses from the Pacific coast (Cuernavaca, Taxco and Acapulco in particular) generally arrive at the Central de Autobuses del Sur (Tasqueña or Taxqeña), Av Tasqueña 1320, outside which is a big terminus for local buses and *peseros* (*combis*) to the centre and points south of town, and a Metro station (Metro Tasqueña; line 2). To find the Metro, head right as you leave the terminal, and you'll see the sign. Alternatively, to your left, on Av Tasqueña, trolleybuses head up the Eje Central (Lázaro Cárdenas) to Bellas Artes, and on to the Terminal del Norte. Authorized taxis (see page 118) are metered from here to the Zócalo, Alameda or Zona Rosa, and to Polanco.

TERMINAL PONIENTE (OBSERVATORIO)

Buses from places west of Mexico City, especially services passing through Toluca, but also Jalisco, Michoacán and the western part of the State of Mexico, terminate at the Terminal Poniente (Observatorio), at the junction of calles Sur and Tacubaya. To get the Metro (Metro Observatorio; line 1), leave from the exit in the middle of the terminal, where it makes a bend (next to the authorized taxi kiosk), and the entrance is straight ahead, hidden behind the market stalls. Authorized taxis (see page 118) also run from here to Polanco, the Zona Rosa, the Alameda and Zócalo (with a surcharge between 9pm and 6am). Buses (signed "Metro Observatorio") head south on Reforma to the terminal, or pick up from the stands by the entrance to Chapultepec Park.

OTHER STOPS

Apart from the major terminals listed above, there are large open-air bus stops at the end of all the Metro lines such as Indios Verdes (line 3) or El Rosario (lines 6 and 7), with slow services to places up to an hour or so outside the city limits. For destinations in the capital's hinterland it can sometimes be quicker to leave from these. Obviously, the best way into town from these places is by Metro.

DESTINATIONS

(N = Terminal del Norte; S = Central de Autobuses del Sur/Taxqueña; E = TAPO; W = Terminal Pte/Observatorio) Acapulco (S, 55 daily; 6hr); Aguascalientes (N, 29 daily; 6hr); Amecameca (E, every 15min; 1hr 15min); Campeche (E, 7 daily; 17hr); Cancún (E, 7 daily; 24hr); Chalma (W, every 20min; 2hr 30min); Chetumal (E, 2 daily; 18hr); Chihuahua (N, 22 daily; 18hr); Chilpancingo (S, 28 daily; 3hr 30min); Ciudad Juárez (N, 16 daily; 24hr); Ciudad Obregón (N, at least hourly; 26hr); Colima (N, 6 daily; 11hr); Córdoba (E, at least hourly, more at weekends; 4hr); Cuautla (S, every 10min; 2hr; E, every 10min; 3hr); Cuernavaca (S, every 15min; 1hr 30min); Dolores Hidalgo (N, every 40min; 4hr); Durango (N, 9 daily; 12hr); Guadalajara (N, hourly; 6hr; W, 14 daily; 7hr); Guanajuato (N, 11 daily; 5hr); Guaymas (N, 12 daily; 27hr); Hermosillo (N, hourly; 32hr); Ixtapa (S, 5 daily; 10hr); Ixtapan de la Sal (W, hourly; 2hr); León (N, 1–2 hourly; 5hr); Los Mochis (N, at least hourly; 21hr); Malinalco (W, 2 daily 10am & 3pm; 2hr 30min, or via Chalma); Manzanillo (N, 4 daily; 12hr); Matamoros (N, 10 daily; 14hr); Matehuala (N, 13 daily; 7hr); Mazatlán (N, hourly; 15hr); Mérida (E, 5 daily; 28hr); Mexicali (N, 22 daily; 30hr); Monterrey (N, 17 daily; 12hr); Morelia (W, every 30min; N, hourly; 4hr 30min); Nuevo Laredo (N, hourly; 15hr); Oaxaca (E, 22 daily; 6hr); Orizaba (E, at least hourly, more at weekends; 4hr); Pachuca (N, every 10min; 2hr); Palenque (E, 1 daily; 13hr); Pátzcuaro (W, 10 daily; N, 8 daily; 7hr); Playa del Carmen (E, 4 daily; 22hr); Puebla (E, every 20min; N, hourly; 2hr); Puerto Escondido (S, 6 daily; E, 1 daily; 15hr); Puerto Vallarta (N, 7 daily; 12hr); Querétaro (N, every 15min; 2hr 40min); Saltillo (N, 10 daily; 10hr); San Cristóbal de las Casas (E, 8 daily; 17hr); San Luis Potosí (N, hourly; 5hr); San Miguel Allende (N, every 40min; 4hr); Taxco (S, 13 daily; 2hr 30min); Tehuacán (E, hourly; 4hr); Tehuantepec (E, 6 daily; 10hr); Teotihuácan (N, every 15min; 1hr); Tepic (N, hourly; 12hr); Tepoztlán (S, every 40min; 1hr 15min); Tijuana (N, hourly;

42hr); Tlaxcala (E, every 20min; 1hr 40min); Toluca (W, every 5min; 1hr 30min); Tula (N, every 40min; 1hr 30min); Tuxpan (N, hourly; 4hr); Tuxtla Gutiérrez (E, 14 daily; 14hr); Uruapan (W, 16 daily; N, 8 daily; 6hr 30min); Valle de Bravo (W, every 20min; 3hr); Veracruz (E, at least hourly, more at weekends; 7hr); Villahermosa (E, 20 daily; 11hr); Xalapa (E, at least hourly; 5hr); Zacatecas (N, 14 daily; 8hr).

BY TRAIN

Following privatization, intercity passenger train services ceased to run, and the only service now running out of Buenavista station (on Mosqueta by Insurgentes Nte; metro or metrobús Buenavista) is a suburban train (https://factura.fsuburbanos.mx/CFDI) to Cuautitlán in México state.

GETTING AROUND

For all its size and frantic pace, once you're used to the city, it is surprisingly easy to get around, with an efficient and very cheap public transport system as well as reasonably priced taxis. You'll probably want to **walk** around the cramped streets of the centre, but remember the altitude – walking gets tiring quickly, especially for the first day or so. If you're heading for Chapultepec or the Zona Rosa, you're better off taking the **bus** or **Metro** – it's an interesting walk all the way down Reforma, but a very long one. As for the outer suburbs, you've got no choice but to rely on public transport. You'll save a lot of hassle if you avoid travelling during **rush hour** (about 7–9am & 5–8pm).

BY METRO

Mexico City's Metro system (http://metro.cdmx.gob.mx) is French-built, fast, quiet and efficient, though in some respects not tremendously well designed: interchanges can be very long, and the system seems to be configured so that journeys often require two legs. It can also get pretty crowded, and at peak hours stations designate separate entries for women and children (look for the "Mujeres" signs), who have exclusive use of the front two cars.

Tickets Tickets are inexpensive and are sold individually. There's no discount for bulk purchases, though to save time queuing and messing about with tiny quantities of change it makes sense to buy several at a time.

Luggage In theory you're not allowed luggage of any size on the Metro (the official limit is 80cm x 50cm x 30cm), but in practice you can get away with carrying a big bag if you board at a quiet station at a calm time, and these days even a backpack seems to be tolerated at busy times. The first train leaves from each end of the line at 5am on weekdays (6am Sat and 7am Sun), with the last train at midnight.

Orientation There aren't always maps of the system on platforms, and certainly not on the trains, where you'll just find pictographic representations of the line you are on, along with the stations where you can transfer to other lines. The map opposite details the system, but it's wise to work out before you set off which way you'll be travelling on each line, and where to change. Direction is indicated by the last station at either end of the line (thus on line 2 you'll want either "Dirección Cuatro Caminos" or "Dirección Tasqueña"). To find your connection at interchange stations, follow the "Correspondencia" signs.

BY TREN LIGERO

Tren Ligero (light rail) runs south from Tasqueña (the southern terminus of line 2) as far as Xochimilco, entirely above ground. It requires a different ticket from the Metro system – when you change at Tasqueña you'll need to buy a Tren Ligero top-up rail card (there's a flat fee for the initial purchase) from the ticket window or the machines on the concourse and then pay an additional fare per journey.

BY BUS

Buses in Mexico City are very efficient, if you know where you're going. Fares are a flat rate and government-subsidized, so you won't pay much per journey. Destinations are displayed in the front window, which is somewhat more helpful than looking for route numbers, since the latter are not posted up and rarely used, and some buses terminate before the end of the route. One of the most useful routes is along Reforma, and the area just by Chapultepec Metro station at the entrance to the park is also a major bus terminus, from where you can get to almost any part of the city. Note that during rush hour it can be almost impossible to get a bus: once they're full, they simply don't stop to let passengers on. In 2008, the city government introduced pink buses for women only, mostly to tackle the problem of groping on public transport; the women-only buses are easily recognizable from their colour, and say "Servicio Exclusivo Mujeres" on the front, but most women of course just take whatever bus turns up first.

BY TROLLEYBUS

There are also trolleybuses running in both directions along Lázaro Cárdenas (the "Eje Central", or Central Axis) between Terminal del Norte and Central del Sur (Tasqueña), as well as on some other major routes. There are a range of fares and they don't give change.

BY METROBÚS

On four routes, there is a service called Metrobús (http://metrobus.cdmx.gob.mx), an articulated bus with its own dedicated lane, and fancy bus stops that look more like stations. The most useful route is line 1, which plies Insurgentes from pretty much one end to the other. Also useful is line 4, which runs east–west and serves the airport. Except for the airport service (which costs more), there's a flat fare, but in order to use the metrobús, you have

to buy a card (for a flat fee which includes one journey) from a machine at one of the stations on lines 1, 2 or 3. You charge up the card with credit at the same machines. Stations on line 4 don't have machines, but there should be attendants on hand who will sell you a card. You can also obtain and charge cards in branches of 7-Eleven or the similar chain Extra. The system is rather inconvenient if you just want to take the odd journey (especially as the machines don't give change, like rejecting coins and often have a queue, and credit has been known to mysteriously vanish from the cards), but there's no other way to pay the fare.

BY PESERO

Running down the major through routes, especially on Reforma and Insurgentes, you'll find *peseros* (*colectivos*), which are smaller and faster but charge more than the bus (if less than a regular taxi) and will let you on and off anywhere along their set route. They're mostly thirty-seater buses or VW vans, usually green with a white roof, and with their destination displayed on the windscreen – drivers of the smaller vehicles may sometimes hold up a number of fingers to indicate how many free seats they have. Like buses, *peseros* have route numbers, but routes often have branches, and a vehicle may start or finish in the middle of a route rather than at the end, so again it's more helpful to check the destination in the window. One of the most useful routes runs from Chapultepec Park via Av Chapultepec to the Zócalo.

BY TAXI

Ordinary taxis (usually red and gold) come in a variety of forms (some are still VW beetles, though these are fast disappearing) and there have been robberies at the hands of the drivers (see page 74), so you should think twice before taking one, especially if you are on your own. If you do decide to, it's best to take one from a taxi rank (*sitio*) rather than hail one in the street. From the airport or bus terminals, always use a prepaid authorized taxi, and never go with a driver who accosts you on arrival with the offer of a cab. Legitimate taxis other than authorized prepaid ones should have a meter – make sure it's switched on. Red-and-white radio taxis, which you have to call by phone, charge slightly more, but in general work the same way. *Taxis de turismo* lie in wait outside hotels and charge rates at least triple those of ordinary taxis; in the normal course of events you should avoid them, but they do have a couple of advantages, namely that the drivers know the tourist sights, and should speak English – they can be worth it if, for example, you want to go on a tour for a few hours, in which case, with some ferocious haggling, you might even get a bargain. If you need to phone a taxi, try Servitaxis (55 5272 1123) or Taxi-Mex (55 5634 9912) or, to the airport, one of the firms listed on page 118. It can be difficult to get a taxi in the rush hour.

BY CAR

Rental cars (see page 119) are available from the airport and elsewhere, but it is generally better to wait until you are ready to leave the city before renting. There are thousands of agencies throughout the city, and the small local operations are often cheaper than the big chains. Either way, renting a car isn't going to be cheap, and a car can be a liability while you're in the city. Expect to pay a moderate amount a day for the cheapest car with tax, insurance and unlimited mileage, more in July and Aug; the usual deal for a week is that you pay for six days and get the seventh free. The major operators have offices at the airport and in the Zona Rosa, and some of the smaller companies do too.

If you already have a car, choose a hotel with secure parking and leave it there for the duration of your stay, except possibly to do a tour of the south of the city. Driving in the city is a nightmare, compounded by confusing one-way and through-route systems and by the near-impossibility of finding anywhere to park. Also note that the "Green Angels" who operate on highways (see page 38) do not operate within Mexico City.

BY BICYCLE

On Sun mornings, many streets in the city centre are closed to motorized traffic so that cyclists have exclusive use of the roadways.

INFORMATION AND TOURS

TOURIST OFFICES

Mexico City tourist office The DF government's tourist authority maintains a useful website (http://www.turismo.cdmx.gob.mx), in Spanish and English, with excellent background information, advice, tips and patchy listings, and you can call them on 55 5286 7097, or toll-free from outside the city on 800 008 9090. They also maintain tourist information booths at the airport (see page 118), at all four bus terminals, and dotted around town. None have much printed material to take away, but the staff are usually very helpful and well versed in the ways of the city. The most central is in the Zócalo between the cathedral and Monte de Piedad (daily 9am–6pm; 55 5518 1003; Metro Zócalo).

SECTUR The Mexico City branch of SECTUR (Mexican federal government's tourist office) is at Presidente Mazaryk 172, Polanco (Mon–Fri 8am–6pm; call 24hr on 55 3002 6300 or 078; Metro Polanco). It's flush with handouts about Mexico City and the country as a whole, but inconveniently sited a long way from where you're likely to be spending your time.

CITY TOURS

Sightseeing tours that take in the city and often include the surrounding area are available from most of the more expensive hotels, while the DF government runs an hour-long city-centre tour on buses in the style of old trams leaving from Juárez by Bellas Artes (Mon–Sat 10am–5pm, Sun 2–5pm), though the commentary is in Spanish only.

Turibus 55 5133 2444, http://turibus.com.mx. One of the best tour operators, running open-top double-deckers on two routes: a northern route taking in the city centre, and a southern route that heads down Insurgentes Sur to Coyoacán and the University. You can get on and off the bus at any stage en route; stops for the northern route include the Zócalo (República de Brasil, on the west side of the cathedral), the Benito Juárez Monument on the south side of the Alameda and El Ángel on Reforma; at Las Cibeles (Plaza Madrid) in Roma, you can change from the northern to the southern route. Both run daily (every 30–40min, 9am–9pm) and tickets costs vary between weekdays when they are slightly more affordable, and weekends (there are also discounts available for a two-day ticket). Each circuit takes around 3hr, and the commentary comes in a choice of languages including English.

1

ACCOMMODATION

Accommodation in Mexico City ranges from budget **hostels** to some of the swankiest **hotels** in the country, but the best-value places can fill up quickly, so **booking ahead** is always a good idea. Most places have 24hr reception desks and are geared for late arrivals and early departures, and, with reasonably cheap taxi fares into the Zócalo or Zona Rosa, it seldom makes financial sense to stay near the bus stations or airport. However, if you arrive especially late or are just in transit and need a place to rest up for a while, there are places to stay that are very handy for the **airport** and **Terminal del Norte**.

HOTELS

AROUND THE ZÓCALO, SEE MAP PAGE 72

Azores Brasil 25; http://hotelazores.com; Metro Allende or ZócaloWell-situated modern hotel with small but clean and comfy rooms around a central atrium, each en suite and with TV, though only one room on each floor has an outside window. M$$

Catedral Donceles 95; http://hotelcatedral.com; Metro Zócalo. Very presentable mid-range place. All rooms have TV and telephone, and some even have a jacuzzi. Internet access is available, and there's a good restaurant and a terrace overlooking the cathedral. M$$$

★ **Gillow** Isabel la Católica 17; http://hotelgillow.com; Metro Allende. Friendly and good-value mid-priced hotel with carpeted rooms, in-house travel agency and leather sofas in the public areas. Cable TV, wi-fi and the expected amenities in rooms (it's worth paying a little extra for a larger room with a small patio or seating area). Ten percent discount for cash payment. M$$$

Gran Hotel Ciudad de México 16 de Septiembre 82; http://granhoteldelaciudaddemexico.com.mx; Metro Zócalo. The city's most famous hotel, situated right on the Zócalo with sumptuous public areas (see page 77), and a selection of rooms and suites, some of which are gorgeously deluxe. Breakfast included and does significant discounts if you book in advance, particularly via the website. M$$$$

Hampton Inn & Suites Uruguay 24; http://hilton.com; Metro Zócalo. Good-value option with a free breakfast included. Quiet and comfortable with a peacful inner courtyard, complete with a stained-glass ceiling. M$$$

Hotel Canada Callejón de 5 de Mayo 47 2; https://hotelcanada.com.mx; Metro Allende or Zócalo. Quiet, friendly place that's moder, clean and realtively affordable. Standards are high considering the price, with light, airy, spotless rooms, good firm beds and decent sheets. M$$

Isabel Isabel la Católica 63; http://hotel-isabel.com.mx; Metro Isabel la Católica. Good-value hotel offering services such as taxis and laundry, plus a restaurant and bar. Rooms (with or without bathroom, the latter on the roof), though a little bit sombre, are quite spacious with TV and safe. Rooms at the back are quieter. It's worth booking a few days ahead. M$

Majestic Madero 73; http://hotelmajestic.com.mx; Metro Zócalo. This luxury Best Western hotel on the Zócalo is rather stately and has bags of character. It's considerably cheaper than many of the places in the Zona Rosa and has many of the same facilities. Some rooms have Zócalo views, as does the *La Terraza* restaurant on the top floor (see page 128). Breakfast included. M$$$

República Cuba 57; 55 5512 9517; Metro Allende. Old and fairly dingy but also very cheap hotel (especially for two people sharing a double bed) on a quiet street. All rooms are en suite, and some have TV. M$

Washington 5 de Mayo 54; 55 5512 3502; Metro Allende or Zócalo. Good-value hotel very near the Zócalo. The cheapest rooms are pretty poky, and windows can be a luxury, but they're all decent, and come with a nicely tiled bathroom, cable TV, phone and wi-fi. It's worth asking for a corner room, which is bigger and better, with outside windows, for only a small amount more. M$$$

Zamora 5 de Mayo 50; 55 5512 8245, hotelzamora1@gmail.com; Metro Allende or Zócalo. One of the more basic downtown hotels. The low prices, excellent location, free wi-fi and friendly management make the occasional noise, threadbare towels and variable cleanliness acceptable. You'll pay extra for a private bathroom. It's very popular so you may have to book ahead at busy times. M$

AROUND THE ALAMEDA, SEE MAP PAGE 72

Fleming Revillagigedo 35; http://hotelfleming.com.mx; Metro Juárez. A charcoal-grey cube on the outside, with salmon-pink, carpeted rooms on the inside: the decor at this business-style hotel is a little bit stuck in the 1980s, with floral patterns absolutely everywhere, but it's comfortable enough and there's room service, wi-fi and a bar and restaurant. M$$$

★ **Hilton Mexico City Reforma** Av Juarez 70; http://hilton.com; Metro Hidalgo. By far one of the ritziest hotels in this neighbourhood, this Hilton bucks the corporate chain design trend, with mid-century furnishings throughout, and a rather nice rooftop pool. If you want a hotel with all the trimmings, this is a good pick. M$$$$

Managua Plaza de San Fernando 11; 55 5512 1312; Metro Hidalgo. Good-value, if functional, place with a cafeteria that does room service, and rooms with TV, bathroom and free bottled water, all in a quiet location facing the Jardín de San Fernando. M$$

Pánuco Ayuntamiento 148; 55 5521 2916; Metro Juárez. Clean and good value. Located in a drab part of town a little distance from the most popular tourist areas, though tolerably close to the Zona Rosa. The carpeted rooms each have a writing desk and TV – and a lot of fake marble. Parking and a restaurant on site. Often full Fri and Sat. M$

AROUND THE REVOLUTION MONUMENT, SEE MAP PAGE 72

Casa Blanca Lafragua 7; http://hotel-casablanca.com.mx; Metro Revolución. Attractive but rather impersonal modern high-rise hotel, with perfectly decent rooms at prices a good deal lower than a lot of the Zona Rosa places. There's even a rooftop pool, a gym, business facilities and a restaurant. Wheelchair-friendly with an adapted room. Breakfast included. M$$$

THE ZONA ROSA, ROMA AND CONDESA, SEE MAP PAGE 91

★**La Casona** Durango 280, at Cozumel; https://casonaroma.com; Metro Sevilla. In an early twentieth-century building at the northern end of Condesa, *La Casona* has an understated, if slightly quirky, European-style elegance, with polished wooden floors, antique furniture, a piano in its lounge and quite a collection of art – including masks, original cartoons and paintings. The rooms are all different, with an aesthete's attention to detail, and it has a good restaurant. Breakfast included. M$$$

Geneve Londres 130; http://hotelgeneve.com.mx; Metro Insurgentes. A large, century-old, but thoroughly modern, hotel right in the heart of the Zona Rosa with an understated, elegant feel. Rooms are comfortable, if unspectacular, with cable TV and minibars, but the facilities are excellent, and include the lovely Salon Jardín with its stained glass and iron roof, a restaurant, gym, spa and on-site *Sanborns* restaurant. The lobby has interesting exhibits on the hotel's history and past clients, who have included Marlon Brando, William Randolph Hearst and Charles Lindbergh. Breakfast included. M$$$

Hotel Del Principado Londres 42; http://hoteldelprincipado.com.mx; Metro Insurgentes. The double rooms (with two double beds) are rather more spacious and get rather more light than the one-bed rooms (in which it's worth asking for a king-size bed, as these cost no extra), but all have a TV and phone, and there's free wi-fi, parking facilities and a laundry service. Breakfast included. M$$

Manalba Antonio Caso 23; https://hotelmanalba.com.mx; Metro Revolución. Squat and ugly from outside, but tastefully decorated within. Good-value rooms all come with cable TV and purified water, though you might want to spend extra for a more spacious double (with the standard two double beds) or for twin beds and a jacuzzi. M$$

★**Maria Cristina** Rio Lerma 31, Cuauhtémoc; http://hotelmariacristina.com.mx; Metro Insurgentes. A lovely little colonial-style hotel near the Museo Venustiano Carranza. Popular with European visitors, the rooms are bright and quiet, though without the wood panelling and blue tiles of the public areas. Standard rooms have fans, deluxe rooms have a/c. M$$

Posada Viena Marsella 28, at Dinamarca; https://soylocal.co; Metro Cuauhtémoc or Insurgentes. Lovely fresh and bright rooms decorated in rustic Mexican style, with ceiling fans though no a/c, at this comfortable but unpretentious four-star. The room price is the same for double, king-size or twin beds. M$$

Roosevelt Insurgentes Sur 287; http://hotelroosevelt.mx; Metro Insurgentes. The 1938 Art Deco exterior of this mid-range hotel on the edge of Condesa has been spruced up, and the interior and rooms have been intelligently and stylishly modernized with tasteful use of grey, pink and brick-red. There's also satellite TV, wi-fi and a decent downstairs restaurant. M$$$

Segovia Regency Chapultepec 328; http://hotelsegovia.com.mx; Metro Insurgentes. Reliable high-rise hotel with parking facilities. The carpeted rooms aren't huge, though they're certainly not spartan either, and all have a/c and wi-fi. It's often fully booked with business regulars, so reserve ahead, especially during the week. M$$$

POLANCO, SEE MAP PAGE 95

Dominion Polanco Aristóteles 21; http://dominionpolanco.com; Metro Polanco. Very chic hotel a short walk away from Mexico City's hottest shopping district. Offering everything from master suites to two bedroom furnished apartments, the Dominion Polanco also serves up some envy inducing views over Lincoln Park, however you'll pay extra for this. There's also an above average hotel pool and spa on site. M$$$$

Hyatt Regency Campos Elisos 204; http://mexicocity.regency.hyatt.com; Metro Polanco. Not the most expensive high-rise business hotel in the city but as luxurious as you could want, with an indoor pool, rooftop tennis courts, gym and acres of glass and marble. M$$$$

THE AIRPORT AND AROUND, SEE MAP PAGE 68

Fiesta Inn Blvd. Puerto Aéreo 502; http://fiestainn.com; Metro Terminal Aérea. Just ten minutes from the airport in a taxi or via transfer shuttle, this little hotel had soundproofing in all the right places so you barely hear the constant roar of planes overhead. As a stopover hotel before or after a long flight, the Fiesta Inn ticks all the right boxes: big beds, clean rooms, free wi-fi, powerful showers and efficient terminal transfers in the painfully early hours. M$$

Hilton Mexico City Airport Airport Terminal 1; http://hilton.com; Metro Terminal Aérea. An elevator from Sala G (upstairs from Sala E3) takes you up to this efficient upmarket hotel which occupies much of the terminal's third floor with its restaurants, bars, gym and well-appointed, though not especially large, rooms (some with runway views). The multichannel TV even has in-house movies and flight information screens. The rack rate may apply when demand is high, but rates are usually substantially lower (sometimes by as much as half) at weekends in particular. M$$$$

NH Aeropuerto Airport Terminal 2; http://nh-hotels.com.mx; Metro Hangares. A very sleek, modern hotel,

1

with extremely spacious public areas. The large rooms are equipped with either a king-size bed or two double beds, and the five-star facilities include a pool, gym and fitness centre. An elevator takes you from the ground floor of the terminal to the sixth floor, where the hotel is located. M$$$

We Hotel Aeropuerto Blv de Puerto Aéreo 380; https://wehotelsgroup.com.mx; Metro Terminal Aérea. The cheapest of the hotels near the airport, with well-maintained rooms (some with runway views); all have TV and phone, plus there's room service from the on-site restaurant. The hotel is a taxi ride from Terminal 2, but just a short walk from Terminal 1 (follow signs from Sala A to the Metro, and cross the busy road using the footbridge). M$$$

TERMINAL DEL NORTE AND AROUND, SEE MAP PAGE 68

Brasilia Av de los Cien Metros 4823; https://hotelbrasilia.com.mx; Metro Autobuses del Norte. Good-value business-style hotel (though sometimes a bit snooty towards backpackers) just 150m southeast of the bus station (turn left as you exit and it's straight ahead of you), where you can get a peaceful sleep in comfortable, carpeted rooms with cable TV and phone. There's a decent, if slightly pricey, restaurant on site, parking facilities and even room service. You'll pay extra for a/c. M$$

Cartagena Av de los Cien Metros; 55 5368 3527; Metro Autobuses del Norte. A hotel/motel a block from the terminal, this option is a secure and comfortable building which takes reservations a week in advance and offers discounts if you pay in cash. M$$

HOSTELS

AROUND THE ZÓCALO, SEE MAP PAGE 72

Hostal Amigo Isabel la Católica 61; https://www.hostelamigo.com; Metro Isabel la Católica. Backpackers' hangout with eight- to ten-bed dorms, some with outside windows, but there are lockers (bring your own padlock), several private rooms (not cheap), free internet, a luggage deposit, a bar, a kitchen and communal areas. The hostel also runs tours, some of which are free to guests. Breakfast and dinner included. Dorms M$, doubles M$$

Hostal Moneda Moneda 8; 55 5522 5803; Metro Zócalo. Convivial hostel with eight-bed dorms, a couple of lounges (one with TV), a decent kitchen, a bar and a panoramic rooftop terrace where the buffet breakfast is served. Private rooms are also available, but pricey. Make a reservation if you are to arrive after 11pm. Half board included in price. Dorms M$, doubles M$$

Hostel Catedral Guatemala 4; https://mundojovenhostels.com; Metro Zócalo. Large, secure and efficiently run modern place behind the cathedral. Open 24hr, it has spotless six-bunk rooms, most with private bathroom, and some private rooms. There's an on-site travel agency, internet access, a café and bar, free coffee all day, Spanish classes available and a rooftop terrace with fabulous views. The only drawbacks are the small kitchen, limited communal areas and noise. Bring your own lock for the lockers, and consider bringing earplugs too. Discount with HI card. Breakfast included. Dorms M$, doubles M$$

Mexico City Hostel Brasil 8; http://mexicocityhostel.com; Metro Zócalo. Great location and decent enough eight- or twelve-bed dorms, as well as wi-fi and free internet access, but the small, dark, private rooms are seriously overpriced, and you may have to go up or down a floor to find a bathroom. Breakfast included. Dorms M$, doubles M$$

AROUND THE REVOLUTION MONUMENT, SEE MAP PAGE 72

★ **Casa de los Amigos** Ignacio Mariscal 132; http://casadelosamigos.org; Metro Revolución. The community-oriented, Quaker-run *Casa*, on a quiet street in the house where José Clemente Orozco spent the last decade of his life, pitches itself as a guesthouse, though it still has eight- and four-bed dorms as well as a few singles and doubles. Clean and comfortable with a good kitchen (breakfast available), a meditation room/library and occasional film screenings, it's popular with long-stay guests (minimum two-night stay). No alcohol and no smoking. Dorms M$, doubles M$$

ROMA & CONDESA, SEE MAP PAGE 91

Hostel Home Tabasco 303, Roma; 55 4932 8645; Metro Sevilla. This small twenty-bunk hostel in a quiet street is called "*Home*" because it was originally a family house. It's a little distant from the main sights, but has, as it advertises, a "chilled atmosphere", a kitchen and free internet, and is open 24hr. As well as the six- and eight-bunk dorms there's a sunny lounge and a small kitchen. Breakfast included. Dorms M$, doubles M$$

Puerta Roja Condesa Juan Escutia 125, Condesa; https://puertaroja.com.mx; Metro Chapultepec. This multistorey building around a sunken courtyard is a good catch-all budget option for those wanting to stay close to the action in Condesa. Decor is modern and the rooms are simple and elegant. Also has a lively bar at the entrance which doubles up as a reception during the day. M$$

EATING

There are reasonably priced restaurants, cafés, *taquerías* and juice stands on every block. The choice of where to eat ranges from traditional coffeehouses to fast-food lunch counters, taking in expensive **international** and rock-bottom **Mexican** cooking along the way, as well as food stalls in **markets** throughout the city: Merced is the biggest, but not a terribly pleasant place to eat. At the back of Plaza Garibaldi, there's a whole market hall given over to nothing but food stands, each vociferously competing with its neighbours. Mexico City also abounds in **rosticerías**, roast chicken shops, serving tasty set meals and crispy chicken with beer in a jolly atmosphere. More so than anywhere else in the country, Mexico City is flooded with **chain restaurants**, both American franchises and slightly classier Mexican chains such as *Sanborns* and *VIPS*; on the whole, you're much better off with a comida corrida. Top-class restaurants are mostly concentrated in **Polanco**.

CAFÉS, CHEAP EATS AND SNACKS

AROUND THE ZÓCALO, SEE MAP PAGE 72

Café Emir Uruguay 45; https://www.emircafe.mx; Metro Zócalo. Modernized café that's been operating since 1936 and serves good espresso, empanadas, cakes and even a range of baklava (*dulce árabe*). M$

Café el Popular 5 de Mayo; 55 5518 6081; Metro Allende. A cheap place with an old-fashioned feel, serving simple food round the clock. It's almost always crowded, and the turnover is pretty fast, with great breakfasts, coffee and snacks. Meal deals include beef with fries, *refritos*, scrambled egg, coffee and a roll. M$

★ **Café de Tacuba** Tacuba 28; https://cafedetacuba.mx; Metro Allende. There's good coffee and excellent food at moderate prices (popular dishes include *pollo al mole* and chiles stuffed with cheese) at this famous cantina-style restaurant a world apart from the city life outside. The locals have been packing it out since 1912, often bringing in mariachi bands off the street that will play continuously if paid enough. M$$$$

Dulcería de Celaya 5 de Mayo 39; http://dulceriadecelaya.com; Metro Allende. Founded in 1874, this is wonderland for sweet-lovers, with real old-school fruit-based confectionery, including candied fruit, *dulce de membrillo* (quince jelly), *camotes* (sweet-potato candy), and limes stuffed with coconut. M$$$

Jugos Canada 5 de Mayo 49; 55 5518 3717; Metro Allende. Very good torta and juice bar with decent prices, despite its central location. A *vampiro* (blood-like combination of orange, celery and beetroot juice) is always a good bet; *licuados* are a bargain. M$$

Pastelería Ideal Uruguay 74; http://pasteleriaideal.com.mx; Metro San Juan de Letrán. A cavernous bakery (made to look even larger by mirrors), with a huge range of cakes, biscuits and moulded gelatine confections, not to mention luscious chocolate cherries. M$$

La Vasconia Tacuba 73; https://lavasconia.com.mx; Metro Allende. One of the best bread and cake shops in the centre, founded in 1870, with a huge range of rolls, biscuits, pastries and even lemon meringue *"pay"*. There's also an eating area where they serve breakfasts, snacks and main courses (a quarter of a roast chicken, for example). M$$

TOP 5 PLACES TO EAT TRADITIONAL MEXICAN FOOD

Los Girasoles See page 128
Restaurant Bar Chon See page 128
El Arroyo See page 130
Fonda Garufa See page 129
San Ángel Inn See page 131

AROUND THE ALAMEDA, SEE MAP PAGE 72

Cafe Epico Luis Moya 75; 55 5510 2856; Metro Balderas. The food's good here, including standard Mexican mains, burgers and tortas big enough to share. This is also a popular breakfast spot. M$

Café del Palacio inside Bellas Artes; 55 5512 2593; Metro Bellas Artes. An elegant café-restaurant in Art Deco surroundings. Enjoy limited views of Tamayo's murals as you eat amid business lunchers and pre-theatre diners. The list of what's available isn't huge, but they change it fortnightly. Typical dishes include *huachinango a la veracruzana* (snapper in red chile sauce), or roast beef in balsamic sauce. There's also a two-course *menu del Palacio*. M$$$$

ZONA ROSA, SEE MAP PAGE 91

La Casa del Toño Londres 144; https://sucursales.lacasadetono.mx; Metro Sevilla. The spot for *pozole*, an Aztec pork stew that many see as the ultimate hangover cure. This 24hr branch of the city-wide chain serves up piping-hot bowls of the delicious stuff along with tacos and other staples. A very popular place for food following a party in the Zona Rosa. M$$

Cocina Mexicana La Güera Londres 154; 55 8107 6845; Metro Insurgentes. A traditional Mexican kitchen with no thrills, lots of flavour and low prices. This is a good option if you're sticking to a slightly tighter travel budget. M$

El Lugarcito Londres 210; 55 6891 4627; Metro Insurgentes. A small and peaceful café a little away from the main bustle of the Zona, serving coffee, breakfasts and meals at prices that are modest for the area. M$$

El Trompito Londres 119-A; 55 5511 1015; Metro Insurgentes. If you're looking for a cheap snack amid the Zona's tourist traps, this modest little *taquería* could be the oasis you need, with tacos, tortas and *alambres* at reasonable prices in clean surroundings. M$

CONDESA, SEE MAP PAGE 91

Neve Gelato Cuernavaca 124 (at Michoacán); 55 5211 4983; Metro Patriotismo or Juanacatlán. They do crêpes and cakes here, but what draws the crowds is the luscious ice cream in flavours fruity (soursop, black cherry, *mamey*) or nutty (toasted almond, amaretto, hazelnut, tiramisú). M$$

Nevería Roxy Tamaulipas at Alfonso Reyes; http://neveriaroxy.com.mx, Metro Patriotismo. Located on a pretty corner, this classic of the Condesa has been serving up delicious ice

1

cream and sorbet since 1946. Two scoops served in a cone, waffle cup or bowl is a delight on a hot day. Also serves up big sundaes and banana splits. M$$

POLANCO, SEE MAP PAGE 95

La Ciudad de Colima Horacio 522, at Lamartine; 55 5545 2719; Metro Polanco. Good but overpriced *jugería* with some unusual *jugos* such as (depending on the season) starfruit (*carambola*), kiwi, sapodilla (*chicu*) and *mamey*. M$$$

SAN ÁNGEL AND SOUTH, SEE MAP PAGE 107

Café Solo Dios Plaza San Jacinto 2; 55 6325 4897; Metrobús Dr Gálvez. This popular hole-in-the-wall café and takeaway spot does great espressos, frappés and all the usual variations, all made from organic Chiapas beans. M$

Crêperie du Soleil Madero 4-C; 55 5616 6768; Metrobús Dr Gálvez. Small and peaceful café that's good for an espresso, cakes and, of course, crêpes, both sweet (for example three berries, with blackberries, raspberries and strawberries) and savoury (try popeye, with creamed spinach and cheese). M$$

COYOACÁN, SEE MAP PAGE 107

Café Avellaneda Higuera 40-A; 55 6553 3441. This intimate coffee shop and café is a welcome reprieve from the busy city throb of the neighbourhood. Expect standard sandwich fare, plus a range of more unusual sweet treats such as pink pepper and cranberry cookies. This is also one of the rare spots in the city where you can ask for non-dairy milk. M$$

Le Caroz Allende 5, on Plaza Hidalgo; http://lecaroz.com. Coyoacán's excellent local bakery supplies a wide range of breads, luscious cakes, wobbly multicoloured jellies and a few savouries. Their speciality is *pan dulce*. M$$

La Vienet Viena 112, at Abasolo; 55 5554 4523. A good place for refreshments in between visits to the Kahlo and Trotsky houses, this small daytime café serves great coffee and cakes as well as breakfasts (until noon) and lunch-time menus with single dishes such as *quesadillas sincronizadas* too. M$$$

RESTAURANTS

AROUND THE ZÓCALO, SEE MAP PAGE 72

Casa de los Azulejos Madero 4; 55 5512 1331; Metro Bellas Artes. Flagship *Sanborns* restaurant in a wonderful sixteenth-century building (see page 134), with prime seating around a fountain in an enclosed three-storey courtyard. The food is *Sanborns* stock in trade of well-prepared Mexican staples, though a little overpriced. The breakfasts, chicken fajitas and chicken tacos are among the popular menu items here. M$$$

El Cuatro 20 Isabel la Catolica 10; 55 5518 1226; Metro Allende. This cash-only spot is popular with locals, so you'll definitely receive above-average service if you attempt to order, and banter, in Spanish. Mexican fare is front and centre on the menu, portions are generous, and price tags inexpensive. Don't leave without trying the salsa verde or something from the stupendously extensive taco selection. M$$

★ **Danubio** Uruguay 3; http://danubio.com; Metro San Juan de Letrán. Established restaurant that's specialized in seafood since 1936. A hearty *bacalao a la Vizcaina* (Basque-style saltfish, in red pepper and tomato sauce) is a firm favourite here, or there's succulent seabass fillet stuffed with seafood. M$$$$$

★ **Los Girasoles** Tacuba 8-A (at Plaza Manuel Tolsá); 55 5510 0630; Metro Allende. One of the most appealing restaurants in the centre, with Mediterranean decor, a casual atmosphere and great food served at moderate prices, including burritos of *pibil* pork, which you might follow with chicken in *mole poblano*. M$$$

Kam Ling Cerrada de 5 de Mayo 14; 55 5521 5661; Metro Allende. Straightforward Chinese food in seriously large proportions to eat in or take away. There's a buffet, set menus or individual dishes such as Cantonese-style squid with green pepper in black bean sauce, or chow mein of chicken, beef or pork, all washed down with huge pots of jasmine tea. M$$$

Pausa Café Belisario Dominguez 518; 55 5789 0574; Metro Allende. Full of character, this moderately priced café and restaurant is decked out with rustic décor. Patrons come for the coffee and the hearty (albeit carb heavy) menu options. Popular dishes here incude an ecletctic mix of pancakes, pasta and spicy cheese melts. M$$

Restaurant Bar Chon Regina 160; 55 5542 0873; Metro Merced. A veritable eating adventure, specializing in pre-Hispanic dishes, with starters such as *mescal* worms, *escamoles* (ant eggs) or *chapulines* (grasshoppers), served with or without guacamole. If you prefer a main course from outside the insect kingdom, there's frogs' legs, or crocodile steak in *mole verde*. M$$$$

Restaurante Food Design Mumedi Madero 74; https://mumedi.mx; Metro Zócalo. This sunny and spacious spot is more than just a restaurant. It's also a hotel, store and museum with a focus on design and creativity above all else. This ethos is reflected on the menu, with dishes from around the world and prices that might make you look twice. M$$$$

La Terraza 4th floor of Majestic; 55 5521 8600; Metro Zócalo. Restaurant with a terrace overlooking the Zócalo, although the view deteriorates significantly once you're seated. The buffet breakfast is good, and in the evening there's à-la-carte dining with well-prepared Mexican standards such as chicken with a choice of *moles*. M$$$$

Terraza 7th floor of Gran Hotel Ciudad de México; 55 1083 7700, http://granhoteldelaciudaddemexico.com.mx/en/terraza; Metro Zócalo. High-class eating and unbeatable views over the Zócalo at this top-notch renovated rooftop restaurant bar, and on the way up you can even snatch a peek at the *Gran Hotel*'s amazing Tiffany glass ceiling. You could just pop up for one of their enormous cocktails (the house speciality is a gargantuan strawberry margarita), but then you'd be missing out on dishes like snapper steak in garlic with veg of the day or *pollo en mole poblano*. Alternatively, drop by any time before 6pm at the weekend for a gluttonous buffet brunch. M$$$$

AROUND THE ALAMEDA, SEE MAP PAGE 72

La Cocinita de San Juan Ernesto Pugibet 21; http://lacocinadesanjuan.com.mx; Metro Pino Suarez. If you're after proper pre-Hispanic cuisine, including such delights as ant eggs (*escamoles*), spiders, wild boar or crocodile (a real treat), this place beside the exotic meats market gets them all in fresh daily. You can have your meat a number of different ways (tacos, tortas, myriad sauces), or opt for more traditional options like hamburgers or *mole*, but the truly adventurous will go for the "mixed insects". Reservations are essential. M$$$$

Oriental Dolores 27; 55 5521 3093; Metro Bellas Artes. A reasonable choice among the chop-suey houses in Mexico City's mini-Chinatown, serving the usual standards (apart from chow mein, which is inexplicably absent from the menu), as well as its own specialities such as chicken Canton or steamed fish with ginger. M$$$

ZONA ROSA, SEE MAP PAGE 91

Don Asado Rio Lerma 210, Cuauhtémoc; http://donasado.mx; Metro Sevilla. Uruguayan steak house serving wonderful chargrilled steaks, perfectly done to whatever turn you so desire. A *tira de asado* (a typical Uruguayan cut) is always a good choice, or you can opt for a mixed grill for two. M$$$$

La Lanterna Reforma 458, at Toledo; https://lalanterna.mx; Metro Insurgentes. Long-standing and convivial trattoria with an intimate and suitably Italian feel, enhanced by pasta freshly made in-house and combined with a choice of delicious sauces. The *segundi piatti* are equally wonderful, with *osso buco alla milanese* (braised veal shanks) or *saltimbocca alla romana* (prosciutto-wrapped veal). M$$$

O'Mandu Estocolmo 18; 55 5207 4554; Metro Insurgentes. Reputed to be the best Korean restaurant in the city, and with good reason, O'Mandu serves up top-notch Korean barbecue in a casual atmosphere. A nice surprise here is the variety of Korean breads on offer. You can eat like a king here without breaking the bank, but do yourself a favour and steer clear of the pre-mixed cocktails. M$$$$

Restaurante Vegetariano Yug Varsovia 3; http://lovegetariano.com; Metro Insurgentes. A worthy contact point for vegetarians and vegans, with breakfasts, salads and *antojitos* in bright cheery surroundings. There's a particularly good buffet lunch upstairs. M$$

CONDESA, SEE MAP PAGE 91

For serious dining, especially in the mid-range, head to Condesa, about 20min walk south of the Zona Rosa. We've mentioned a few options in this area, but they are really just starting points, and the real pleasure is in simply wandering around and seeing what takes your fancy. The two principal streets for hungry visitors are Tamaulipas and Michoacán on the west side of Nuevo León, and Amsterdam to the east, the circular road that runs around Parque México.

Agapi Mu Alfonso Reyes 96; https://agapimu.rest; Metro Juanacatlán or Patriotismo. The best Greek restaurant in the city, but very low-key and affordable as long as you don't go too mad on the *retsina* and Hungarian wines. It's especially fun from Thurs to Sat, when there's live music and Greek dancing. Moussaka inevitably heads the list of main courses, followed by less well-known but equally delicious dishes such as *psári costas* (fish wrapped in vine leaves in an egg and lemon sauce). M$$$

Bellini 45th floor, World Trade Center, Av de las Naciones; http://bellini.com.mx; Metrobús Poliforum. A posh revolving restaurant atop one of the city's tallest buildings, where business people come to impress their clients, and the romantically inclined enjoy candlelit dinners. Dishes from an international menu are prepared to the highest standards and service is impeccable. It's obviously not the cheapest place in town, but not stupidly expensive either: even at the top end of the menu, you can start with smoked salmon, caviar and avocado, followed by red snapper in lobster sauce without emptying your wallet. M$$$$

Café la Gloria Vicente Suarez 43; 55 5211 4185; Metro Patriotismo or Juanacatlán. Pleasant little bistro serving pasta dishes, salads or the likes of chicken with mushrooms, spinach and cream of *elote* (corn), or *filet mignon*. Desserts include profiteroles, chocolate mousse or blueberry cheesecake. M$$$$

Daikoku Michoacán 25; http://daikoku.mx; Metrobús Sonora. The best sushi in Condesa, and possibly the city as a whole, Daikoku also serves up good ramen, sashimi, tempura and Japanese desserts for fair prices. Also has a cookery school upstairs where you can spend anywhere from an afternoon to three months learning the mind-bogglingly precise art of sushi. M$$$$

Don Keso Amsterdam 73; 55 5553 3827; Metro Juanacatlán. An eclectic yet relaxed spot with a simple menu that's done well. The pizza is especially good and there's often a combo drink-meal deal to be had. If you eat here, ask for a table on the patio to add in some excellent people watching between courses. M$$$

Fonda Garufa Michoacán 93; http://garufa.com; Metro Patriotismo or Juanacatlán. The original eatery of the colonia; the loyal regulars will tell it you was here before Condesa was cool, and it's no wonder it has such longevity. Top-quality cuisine as well as pastries and excellent coffee. Grab a street-side table or head for the balony upstairs and

1

watch peaceful Condesa life go by as you tuck into excellent steaks or dishes such as salmon mayonnaise. M$$$

El Jamil Amsterdam 306 (at Celaya); 55 5564 9486; Metro Sevilla. A good Lebanese restaurant with *mezze* such as hummus or *babaghanouj* (aka *moutabel* – eggplant and tahini dip), and mains such as *shish tawouk* (charcoal-grilled chicken kebab). You can round it off with coffee and baklava, or sit outside and smoke a *sheesha* (water-pipe). M$$

Kitchen 6 Teotihuacan 14 at Amsterdam; 55 5264 1748; Metrobús Sonora. Build your own burger with the best ingredients, choosing everything from the bread onwards, at this stylish (although rather dark) restaurant with street-side tables and an extensive selection of craft beer. The six-sauce fries are also a good sharing option as well as sandwiches and salads for those looking for something different. M$$

★ **Mercado Roma** Queretaro 225; http://mercadoroma.com; Metrobús Sonora. A big food hall with a collection of gourmet world cuisines ranging from fantastic shawarma to delectable tapas, with a friendly and attractive seating area at the back, ringed by various bars serving up craft beer, wines and the country's best mescal and tequila. There's a mezzanine offering desserts and a rooftop bar with microbrewed beers and signature cocktails. A very popular spot for the trendy crowd at weekends. M$$$$

Tandoor Amsterdam 72 (at Parras); https://tandoor.com.mx; Metro Juanacatlán. The best curry in the area, thanks largely to the fact they use a real *tandoor* oven, is served up in this maharaja-style building with a pretty rooftop (the second-generation management have their roots in Pakistan). The spices are authentic and you can expect to eat well. This spot also does takeaway. M$$$$

Tristán Campeche 398; 55 9044 7435; Metro Juanacatlán. Serving a mix of internationally inspired fusion food, this is a fun spot for everything from curry mussels to lamb burgers. M$$$

Vitalica Sonora 221; 55 1342 0234; Metrobús Sonora. A grill restaurant with a kitchen offering some of the best steaks around Parque México, this relaxing spot is something of an oasis from the busier street a few metres beyond. M$$$$

El Zorzal Cnr of Alfonso Reyes and Tamaulipas; 55 5273 6023; Metro Patriotismo. Argentine steakhouse serving up juicy slices of steer (a 300g churrasco, for example), and *alfajor* pastries or crêpes filled with *dulce de leche* for dessert. There's also a famous torta stand that operates on the same corner (look for the multicoloured umbrella and long queue) that serves up *chilaquiles* and chicken sandwiches. M$$$$

POLANCO, SEE MAP PAGE 95

★ **Butcher & Sons** Virgilio 8, at Parque Lincoln; http://butcherandsons.com; Metro Auditorio. This chain, which also has a stand in Mercado Roma (see above), cooks up the best burgers in Mexico City, with fresh-baked buns, delicious patties and ingredient combinations named after rock stars. It's worth waiting for a street-side table since the interior gets a little cramped. M$$$

Cabanna Av. Pdte. Masaryk 134; http://cabanna.com.mx; Metro Polanco. A good, reliable option for fresh and well-seasoned seafood; here you can tuck into a great plate of salmon for a fair price, with the same being said for a pound of prawns. A mix of regularly rotated DJs and mood lighting makes the place almost painfully hip. M$$$$

Denominación de Origen Hegel 406, at Presidente Masaryk; 55 5255 0612; Metro Polanco. Classy modern Spanish restaurant with a long bar, lots of whole hams and dishes like *bacalao a la vizcaína* (saltfish Basque-style, in sweet pepper sauce), or a superb Andalusian *gazpacho*. M$$$

Eltuca's Newton 116, at Lamartine; 55 5545 8388 or 9; Metro Polanco. Forget the rubbish they sell at the international junk-food chains: what you get here are proper burgers, made from sirloin steak and grilled over charcoal. You don't get them flipped in an instant, but they're worth the wait. A straight burger is a firm favourite here, and for non-carnivores there are salads, salmon burgers and veggie burgers. Home delivery is also available within Polanco. M$$

SAN ÁNGEL AND SOUTH, SEE MAP PAGE 107

The southern suburbs of San Ángel and Coyoacán are good hunting grounds and it is worth sticking around for your evening meal after a day's sightseeing.

El Arroyo Insurgentes Sur 4003, Tlalpan, 6km south of San Ángel; http://arroyorestaurante.mx; Metrobús Fuentes Brotantes. Well off the beaten path, but worth the journey, this unusual restaurant has a small bullring (used by novice bullfighters in bloodless *corridas* April–Oct) and almost a dozen dining areas that can jointly seat over 2500. There's always a lively atmosphere, helped along by mariachis and other entertainment starting weekdays at 4pm, weekends at 5pm. The Mexican food is good too – barbecued meats are the speciality, ordered by the portion or by the kilo (a kilo of pork barbecued in maguey leaves for example, is around four portions) – and they usually keep at least four types of flavoured *pulque*. M$$$$

La Camelia Madero 3 (by Plaza San Jacinto), San Ángel; 55 7158 0167; Metrobús Dr Gálvez. If karaoke peppered in between plates of hearty Mexican cuisine is your thing, then look no further than *La Camelia*. If, however, you prefer peace and quiet with your main course, you might want to keep walking. The more offbeat items on the menu include a colourful seafood soup and octopus cake, a savoury black sponge baked in squid ink and filled with cream cheese. M$$$

Loretta Chic Bistrot Revolución 1426; 55 9130 1675; Metro Barranca del Muerto. A fun little spot and especially

PULQUE AND PULQUERÍAS

Pulque is the fermented sap of the maguey cactus, a species of agave that grows in the countryside north and east of Mexico City. A pre-Hispanic concoction traditionally considered to be a poor man's drink, *pulque* had its heyday in the first half of the twentieth century – but as beer, wine and spirits became more affordable, *pulque*'s stock went down. At one time there were over 1400 **pulquerías** in the capital, but today owners estimate that there are only around a hundred or so left. It's possible, however, that Mexico City's *pulquerías* may yet see a revival, as the drink has seen a rise in popularity of late among young Mexicans, particularly students interested in their cultural roots. Regardless of demand, production continues much as it has done for centuries, with barrels being shipped daily to the capital.

Unless you are looking for them, *pulquerías* are hard to spot; they're concentrated in less salubrious areas of town mostly unvisited by tourists and often have no sign, just a pair of swinging doors guarding a dark interior. Like cantinas, they are traditionally macho territory, and women are more likely to receive a respectful welcome when accompanied by male friends.

These places are not set up for anything much more sophisticated than knocking back glasses of the slightly astringent, viscous green-white beverage, usually ladled out of barrels behind the bar. The emphasis is as much on socializing as drinking, which is a good thing since most *pulque* is only two to four percent alcohol and getting drunk requires considerable commitment, particularly since the thick liquid is extremely bloating. The task is made easier when *pulque* is blended with fresh fruit juices – pineapple, oats, guava and many others – *pulque* flavoured in this manner is known as *curado*. The most popular hunting ground is the **Plaza Garibaldi**, although there's a chance to try it on a night out in Condesa (see *Wichitos* below).

Los Duellistas Aranda 30; 55 1394 0958; Metro Sam Juan Letrán; see map page 72. During the day you're best off exploring the district south of Bellas Artes, where choices include this place which attracts a young clientele. M$$

Restaurante Los Tonos Plaza Garibaldi; 55 3571 2038; Metro Garibaldi; see map page 72. Catering to visitors and locals alike, this café is a reliable, inexpensive option if you're in a hurry and need something to grab and go. M$$$

Wichitos Tamaulipas 104; 55 5211 7098; Metro Juanacatlán; see map page 91. The only Condesa *pulquería*, serving up pure or *curado* flavours including pineapple, oats and guava by the quarter, half and whole litre. You can also try a sampler of three different *pulques*. Gets very lively at the weekends when crowds come for the regular drinks they also serve. Has a good food menu that tries to pack in the whole of Mexican rustic cuisine. M$$$

convenient if you have tickets for a show at the nearby Teatro Helenico. With dishes from around the world, the menu does pack a wow factor, although the portions tend to be on the smaller side. The restaurant also offers valet parking and good city views from the terrace. M$$$$

San Ángel Inn Diego Rivera 50, at Altavista; http://sanangelinn.com; Metrobús Dr Gálvez. Popular with visiting dignitaries and tourists, this late seventeenth-century former Carmelite monastery has been an elegant restaurant with a sumptuous garden setting since 1915. The menu has European overtones, but is mainly Mexican, featuring starters such as *huitlacoche* crêpes, and mains such as chiles stuffed with meat and cheese, plus fine wine or margaritas to accompany it. Reservations required. M$$$$

COYOACÁN, SEE MAP PAGE 107

La Esquina de los Milagros Plaza Jardín del Centenario 18-B; http://laesquina.com.mx. Elegant indoor dining with white tablecloths, or outdoors on decking on the main square, with dishes such as stuffed *chile poblano* or fish cooked in a banana leaf. There's a lunch-time menu, and live jazz music most evenings. M$$$

El Tajín Centro Veracruzano, Miguel Ángel de Quevedo 687; http://eltajin.com.mx. Veracruz specialities at medium to high prices; the fish dishes, such as *huachinango a la Veracruzana* (snapper in tomato, olive and caper sauce), and octopus in green herbs, are exquisite. M$$$$

DRINKING AND NIGHTLIFE

Club-oriented nightlife starts late, with live acts often hitting the stage after 11pm and few places really getting going before midnight. Cuban music is particularly popular, and with Cuba just a short flight away, Mexico City provides a local but international proving ground for the island's talent.

BARS

Bars range from dirt-cheap *pulquerías* and cantinas to

1

upscale lounges and hotel bars. As elsewhere in the country, cantinas and *pulquerías* are still largely a male preserve. More civilized bars, where you might sit around and chat, are relatively thin on the ground.

AROUND THE ZÓCALO AND THE ALAMEDA, SEE MAP PAGE 72

La Ópera 5 de Mayo 10, near Bellas Artes; http://laoperabar.com. Metro Bellas Artes. The best watering hole downtown, in the grand tradition of upmarket cantinas with magnificent *fin-de-siècle* decor – ornate mahogany panelling, a brass-railed bar, gilt-framed mirrors in the booths – and a bullet hole in the ceiling reputedly put there by Pancho Villa. You also can dine here, but most people come for a fairly pricey beer, tequila or cocktails in the booths or at the bar.

Tio Pepe Independencia 26, at Dolores; 55 8044 5884; Metro Bellas Artes. A cantina with moulded ceilings and wooden bar. Minstrels frequently drop in to bash out a few numbers, and women are nowadays welcome, but may feel more comfortable in the saloon (*La Mascota*) next door.

ZONA ROSA, ROMA AND CONDESA, SEE MAP PAGE 91

Wallace Tamaulipas 45, Condesa; https://wallacebar.mx; Metro Chilpancingo. A stylish whisky bar on a street with a number of cool options. The island bar here has over 100 brands of whisky and can make just about any cocktail you request. There's a chilled-out lounge upstairs, but reserve a street-side table ahead of time if you want to make the most of the street's party atmosphere. DJs Thurs–Sat.

SAN ÁNGEL AND COYOACÁN, SEE MAP PAGE 107

La Camelia Madero 3 (by Plaza San Jacinto), San Ángel; 55 7158 0167; Metrobús Dr Gálvez. Early-evening boozing to recent US and Latin pop hits, either inside or out on the street, at this vintage cantina dating from 1931. There's decent food and a traditional, if never raucous, cantina atmosphere.

La Coyoacana Higuera 14; 55 5658 5337. This classic cantina serves up both chilled nights and raucous get togethers, where shots and letting your hair down are the order of the day.

El Hijo del Cuervo Jardín Centenario 17, Coyoacán; http://elhijodelcuervo.com.mx. Dark and hip bar with seats overlooking the square and music that ranges from Latin rap to rock. There's no cover charge, and a lively evening atmosphere.

LIVE MUSIC VENUES

The live music scene has broadened appreciably over the years in Mexico City, and there are venues for all kinds of bands, offering anything from old-fashioned romantic ballads to cutting-edge alternative rock bands.

AROUND THE ZÓCALO AND THE ALAMEDA, SEE MAP PAGE 72

Zinco Jazz Club Motolina 20, at 5 de Mayo; http://zincojazz.com; Metro Allende. Small but congenial venue, really just a bar-restaurant with entertainment by local jazz bands, tucked away in the vaults beneath the Art Deco splendour of the Banco de México building. Entry fees vary depending on what's on.

ZONA ROSA, ROMA AND CONDESA, SEE MAP PAGE 91

Cantina Bicentenario Vicente Suarez 42, Condesa; 55 5553 5451; Metro Juanacatlán. The most authentic cantina in trendy Condesa, this is the place to come for a real Mexican drinking experience. Mariachi bands, micheladas and botanas are served up here with relish, no matter how messy you get.

Multiforo Alicia Cuauhtémoc 91, between Colima and Durango, Roma; https://multiforoalicia.com.mx; Metro Cuauhtémoc. "Who hasn't been to Alicia doesn't know rock music", they claim, which may be an exaggeration, but this is still the place to catch Mexico's latest rock *ondas*. Most of the action is on Fri & Sat night. Expect to pay a modest entry fee, depending who's on.

TOQUES: SUPERCHARGED NIGHTLIFE

When out drinking in Mexico City, it's not unusual to witness Mexicans electrocuting themselves for fun. The traditional drinking game **Toques** sees individuals or groups forming a human chain, undergoing increasingly strong electrical currents until they can take no more. The aim is to withstand the current as high up the voltage meter as possible before **shouting for mercy**, or "Ya!" in Spanish. The voltage starts at 20 and reaches a rare maximum of 120. The difficult leap is from 95 volts to 110. The men who offer this bizarre game patrol a route around the popular drinking areas (particularly the centre, Condesa, Roma, Zona Rosa) and identify themselves by clicking together the metal handles of their apparatus. A game costs around a small amount to enter and ends when you cry for mercy. Groups play by linking hands (or touching any other bare bit of skin) to form a chain which can be broken by releasing any link. Despite the screams it may elicit, the game is safe, although it should be avoided by anyone with a heart pacemaker.

Ruta 61 Baja California 281, Condesa; 55 5211 7602; Metro Chilpancingo. This cosy little blues club has jam sessions on Wed (free), and live music Thurs–Sat (expect to pay an entry fee), with tables to sit at while listening (reservation advised).

Tequilería La Perla d Occidente Tamaulipas 47, Condesa; 55 5904 7554; Metro Patriotismo or Sevilla. Tequila bar with an impressive selection and live music, with DJs at the weekend.

CLUBS

Entry can be expensive, more so for for men (women often get in for much less or sometimes for free), though any entry fee is likely to include a drink, or even *bar libre*, where your drinks are free for at least part of the evening. Be aware that dress restrictions are still very much the order of the day here, and a lot of clubs won't let you in wearing jeans or trainers.

Love Masaryk 169, Polanco; http://lovepolanco.club; Metro Polanco; see map page 95. A discotheque, like they used to make them, complete with dress-to-impress wardrobe rules, chic decor and lots of pretty young patrons shaking their booties to pop hits old and new, but unless you're a VIP, you'll need to reserve in advance (by phone or online) in order to get in. There is an entry fee for men, but it's free for women.

Mama Rumba Querétaro 230, at Medellin, Roma; 55 5264 7823; Metro Insurgentes; see map page 91. Reservations are advised for this dance bar. The Hispano-Afro-Caribbean rhythms pumped out by the Cuban house band get the small dancefloor packed, so come prepared to move your feet even if you don't know the steps. Bands come on at 11pm. Wheelchair access.

El Vicio (formerly El Hábito) Madrid 13, Coyoacán; http://elvicio.com.mx; Metro Coyoacán (800m); see map page 107. Small and quirky fringe theatre and music club, with plays and live jazz. Also on site are *Novo's* restaurant and the Teatro la Capilla.

LGBTQ+ BARS

The Zona Rosa (pink zone) is Mexico City's LGBTQ+ zone, and in particular the northernmost section of Amberes between Hamburgo and Reforma, where you'll find a slew of gay and lesbian bars. The listings magazine *Tiempo Libre* also has a section on gay and lesbian events and locales.

Bb Amberes 18; 55 5207 7626; Metro Insurgentes; see map page 91. Pumping house music, black lights and a generally garish ambience make this pretty loud all round for such a small venue. Lesbians supposedly have their own smoochy pink section called the *Pussy Bar*, although gay and straight couples can also be found there.

Marrakech Salon Generalito Filomeno Mata 18-H; 55 2522 5315; Metro Allende; see map page 72. One of the city centre's most popular gay spots away from the Zona Rosa, although straight people are also welcome. There's a sweaty dancehall at the back, and lively karaoke on Sun. Also does decent food until around 7pm.

Papi Amberes 18 at Estrasburgo; 55 4022 0542; Metro Insurgentes; see map page 91. Billing itself as "the original fun bar", this is a place for kitsch pop music, drag acts, beer, cocktails and general hedonism.

Touch Amberes 11 at Reforma; 56 2214 9854; Metro Insurgentes; see map page 91. A multi-level club offering raucous karaoke on the ground floor, a disco playing classic hits in the middle and full-on rave/electro higher up. There's a quieter terrace for smoking and chat on the top.

ENTERTAINMENT

Mainstream Hollywood **movies** make it to Mexico just a few weeks after their release in the US and often before they get a British or European release. One of the largest concentrations of cinemas is along Insurgentes, where half a dozen multiplexes total around fifty screens in all. While Mexican **theatre** tends to be rather turgid, there are often excellent **classical music** concerts and **opera** or **ballet** performances by touring companies. The Palacio de Bellas Artes (see page 85) and the Auditorio Nacional are the main venues, but other downtown theatres, as well as the Polyforum (see page 103) and the Teatro de los Insurgentes (see page 104), may have interesting shows. For listings, see http://mexicocity.com/v/theatre-and-dance.

Casa del Lago Bosque de Chapultepec (by the lake, near entrance on Reforma); http://www.casadellago.unam.mx; Metro Auditorio. Music, dance and film all feature among the cultural activities organized by the University (UNAM) at this beautiful lakeside mansion in Chapultepec Park, but the most popular events are the Sat afternoon classical concerts, which are listed on the website, and almost always free.

SHOPPING AND MARKETS

SEE MAP PAGE 72

The big advantage of **shopping** in the capital is that you can get goods from all over the country and, if you are flying out of here, you don't have to lug them around Mexico, though they will usually be more expensive than at the source. An odd hangover from Aztec times is the practice of devoting a whole street to one particular trade, which occurs to some extent throughout the city. There are blocks where you can buy nothing but stationery, while other areas are packed exclusively with shoe shops and still others only sell musical instruments. Every area of the city has its own **market** selling food and essentials, and many others set up stalls for just one day a week along a suburban street. Replica Mexican football shirts can be found in the *tianguis* (street markets) on San Juan Letrán between Bellas Artes and Salto del Agua, or those in the streets north and east of the Zócalo.

1

DEPARTMENT STORES

Liverpool Carranza 92 (across 20 de Noviembre from El Palacio de Hierro); http://liverpool.com.mx; Metro El Sagrario. The original branch of a nationwide chain founded in the nineteenth century, which originally imported much of its stock from the English port from which it takes its name.

El Palacio de Hierro 20 de Noviembre 3 (just south of the Zócalo); http://elpalaciodehierro.com; Metro El Sagrario. A department store whose original branch, established in 1891, is actually in colonia Roma (at Durango 230). It's generally considered the most upmarket of Mexico City's department stores.

Sanborns Madero 4 (near the main post office); http://sanborns.com.mx; Metro Bellas Artes. Sells books, maps and quantities of tacky souvenirs, and also has a sizeable pharmacy, as well as a good restaurant (see page 128), all housed in the beautiful Casa de los Azulejos (see page 84).

CRAFTS

Centro Artesanal Buenavista Aldama 187, just east of the former train station; Metro Buenavista. Handicrafts from around the country in what is claimed to be Mexico's largest shop. Rather pricey compared to the Ciudadela, and less characterful.

Centro Artesanal de San Juan (Mercado de Curiosidades Mexicanas) About five blocks south of the Alameda along Dolores; Metro San Juan de Letrán.Modern tourist-oriented complex that's possibly the least appealing of the major artesanía markets, though there are still deals to be had (particularly in silver), provided you haggle.

Ciudadela cnr of Balderas and Emilio Donde; Metro Balderas. The best place in the capital to buy regional crafts and souvenirs from every part of the country. If you forgot to pick up a hammock in the Yucatán or some Olinalá lacquerwork in Guerrero, fear not: you can buy them here for not a great deal more. Bargaining has limited rewards.

FONART Juárez 89 (at Balderas); 55 5093 6000; Metro Hidalgo. FONART is a government agency that promotes crafts and helps the artisans with marketing and materials. The fixed prices are usually higher than elsewhere, but it is worth visiting to check price and quality before venturing to the markets. FONART also has outlets at Reforma 116 (at Milán; Metro Cuauhtémoc) and the airport (Terminal 2).

MARKETS

Bazar Sábado Plaza San Jacinto, San Ángel; Metrobús Dr Gálvez. Very popular open-air art and sculpture market that operates on Sat only, although pretty much the same market moves lock, stock and barrel the next day (Sun) to Parque Sullivan, just north of the Zona Rosa (see page 92).

Coyoacán markets Metro Viveros. There are two interesting markets in Coyoacán: the daily market, three blocks up from Plaza Hidalgo, on Allende between Malintzin/Xicoténcatl and Plaza Hidalgo, is mostly given over to food, although it also sells crafts, clothing and other

MARIACHI IN PLAZA GARIBALDI

Plaza Garibaldi (Metros Bellas Artes and Garibaldi) is the traditional final call on a long night around the capital's bars, and as the night wears on and the drinking continues, it can get pretty rowdy. The plaza is on Lázaro Cárdenas, five blocks north of Bellas Artes in a thoroughly sleazy area of cheap bars, grimy hotels and several brightly lit theatres offering burlesque and strip shows. Despite a high-profile police presence, **pickpockets** are always a threat and it's best to avoid coming laden down with expensive camera equipment or an obviously bulging wallet.

Hundreds of competing **mariachi** bands gather here in the evenings, all in their tight, silver-spangled *charro* finery and vast sombreros, to play for anyone who'll pay them. A typical group consists of two or four violins, a brass section of three trumpeters standing some way back so as not to drown out the others, three or four men on guitars of varying sizes and a vocalist, though a truly macho man will rent the band and do the serenading himself. Mariachis take their name, supposedly, from the French *mariage*, it being traditional during the nineteenth-century French intervention to rent a group to play at weddings. You may also come across *norteño* bands from the border areas with their Tex-Mex brand of country music, or the softer sounds of **marimba** musicians from the south. Simply wander round the square and you'll get your fill – should you want to be individually serenaded, pick out a group and negotiate your price.

At the back of the square is a huge market hall in which a whole series of stalls serve simple food and vie furiously for customers. Alternatively, there is at least one prominent *pulquería* on the square (see page131), and a number of fairly pricey restaurant/bars, which try to drown out the mariachi bands with their own canned music, and tempt customers with their no-cover entry. The last Metro leaves at midnight.

BALLET FOLKLÓRICO

The **Ballet Folklórico** (http://balletfolkloricodemexico.com.mx) is a long-running, internationally famed compilation of traditional dances from all over the country, elaborately choreographed and designed, and interspersed with Mexican music and singing. Despite the billing, it isn't really very traditional – although it does include several of the more famous native dances, they are very jazzed up and incorporated into what is, in effect, a regular musical that wouldn't be out of place on Broadway.

The Ballet Folklórico perform in the **Palacio de Bellas Artes** (see page 85), where the theatre is an attraction in itself. Performances are on Sundays and Wednesdays. You should try to book at least a couple of days in advance – **tickets** are available either from the Palacio de Bellas Artes box office direct or through Ticketmaster (http://ticketmaster.com.mx) – or arrange to go with an organized tour, for which you'll pay a considerable premium.

things; the Mercado de Artesanías, at Carrillo Puerto 25, is a covered market for crafts and street fashion formerly held on Sun in the main square.

La Lagunilla Spreading along Rayon, a couple of blocks north of the Plaza Garibaldi; buses ("La Villa") heading north on Reforma, or Metro Garibaldi. Comes closest to rivalling La Merced in size and variety, but is best visited on a Sun when the *tianguis* expands into the surrounding streets, with more stalls selling stones, used books, crafts and bric-a-brac.

Mercado de Sonora Three blocks south of La Merced on Fray Servando Teresa de Mier; Metro La Merced. This market is famous for its sale of herbal medicines, medicinal and magical plants, and the *curanderos* (Indigenous herbalists) who go there. Nowadays you'll find anything from conjuring tricks and novelties to statues of underground religious figures such as La Santa Muerte and Jesús Malverde.

La Merced Corner of Izazaga San Pablo and Eje 1 Ote; Metro La Merced. The city's largest market, a collection of huge modern buildings, which still can't contain the vast number of traders who want to set up here. Almost anything you could conceive of finding in a Mexican market (and much more) is sold here, though fruit, vegetables and other foods dominate. Even if you're not buying you could easily spend half a day browsing metre-diameter columns of *nopal* leaves as high as a man, stacks of dried chiles and all manner of hardware from juice presses to volcanic-stone mortars known as *molcajetes*. The Metro takes you right into the heart of things.

Palacio de las Flores Corner of Luis Moya and Ernesto Pugibet; Metro Salto de Agua or Balderas. A small market selling nothing but flowers – loose, in vast arrangements and wreaths, growing in pots, even paper and plastic. Similar markets can be found in San Ángel and Xochimilco.

ENGLISH-LANGUAGE BOOKS AND NEWSPAPERS

International weeklies are available downtown from newspaper stands (especially along 5 de Mayo). Sanborns, dotted all over town, usually have a modest supply of English-language material, much of it business-oriented. Terminal 1 at the airport has numerous small shops partly stocked with English-language magazines and airport novels, plus a few foreign newspapers.

American Book Store Bolivar 23, Centro Histórico; http://americanbookstore.com.mx; Metro Allende. Despite the name, their stock of books in English is limited and mostly business or computer-oriented. OK for a few paperbacks, magazines and newspapers.

La Torre del Papel Callejón de Betlemitas 6a, beside the Museo del Ejército y Fuerza, near the central post office; Metro Bellas Artes. Stocks up-to-date newspapers from all over Mexico and Latin America as well as a good showing of US, British, Spanish and Italian newspapers, plus magazines such as *National Geographic*, *The Economist*, *Entertainment Weekly* and *Paris Match*.

SPORT

Sport is probably the city's biggest obsession, and while **football**, **wrestling** and **bullfighting** are the three

THE DEMISE OF HAGGLING

Haggling for a bargain is no longer the thrilling (or daunting) prospect it once was in Mexico City. The nation's increasing prosperity and sophistication means that most things have fixed prices. As a tourist (and especially if your Spanish is poor) you can expect people to try to bump up the price occasionally, but on the whole what you see is what you pay.

leading lights, the sporting calendar doesn't stop there. One sport that's missing is **Frontón** (see page 54), which used to be played at Frontón México, on Plaza de la República, but it closed when the players went on strike in 1993, and has never reopened.

HORSE RACING AND RODEO

Hipodromo de las Americas Industria Militar, Lomas de Sotelo; http://hipodromo.com.mx; Metro Cuatro Caminos. Horse racing throughout the year, particularly Sat afternoons; buses and *peseros* heading west on Reforma will take you there – look for "Hipodromo".

Rancho del Charro Constituyentes 500 (near the Third Section of Chapultepec Park); https://eventoslienzoscharros.com.mx; pesero (routes #2, #24 and others) along Constituyentes from Metro Chapultepec. More exciting horse action in the *charreadas*, or rodeos, put on here by amateur but highly skilled aficionados most weekends (often free); call or check their website to find out what's going on.

FOOTBALL

Fútbol (football, meaning soccer) is undoubtedly Mexico's most popular sport. There are usually at least two games every Sun afternoon (Jan–June & Aug–Nov; check local papers for fixture details) and you can almost always get a ticket at the gate. The exceptions are the big games such as major local derbies, and "El Clásico", when América host Chivas from Guadalajara, the biggest team from the country's second-largest city; if you want to be sure of a ticket, they can be bought in advance from Ticketmaster (http://ticketmaster.com.mx).

Estadio Azteca Tren Ligero or Ruta #26 ("Xochimilco") colectivo, both from Metro Tasqueña. The big games are held at the 114,000-seat Estadio Azteca, which hosted the World Cup finals in 1970 and 1986, and is home to América (Las Águilas, or The Eagles), the nation's most popular and consistently successful club side. Mexico City's other major team, Atlante (Los Potros, "the Colts"), shares the stadium with América.

Estadio Azul Metro San Antonio or from Metrobús station Ciudad de los Desportes on Insurgentes. Cruz Azul (known as Los Cementeros for having been started and still owned by a cement company to the north of the city) pack out Estadio Azul right by the city's main bullring (see page 103).

LA LUCHA LIBRE

Though its popularity has waned in recent years, **lucha libre**, or wrestling, remains one of Mexico's most avidly followed spectator sports. Over a dozen venues in the capital alone host fights several nights a week for a fanatical public. Widely available magazines, comics, photonovels and films recount the real and imagined lives of the rings' heroes and villains, though the nightly telecasts are now a thing of the past.

Mexican wrestling is generally faster, with more complex moves, and more combatants in the ring at any one time than you would normally see in an American or British bout. This can make the action hard to follow for the uninitiated. More important, however, is the maintenance of stage personas, most of whom, heroes or villains, wear **masks**. The *rudos* tend to use brute force or indulge in sneaky, underhanded tactics to foil the opposition, while the *técnicos* use wit and guile to compensate for lack of brawn. This faux battle, not at all unlike WWE on-screen antics, requires a massive suspension of disbelief – crucial if you want to join in the fun.

One of the most bizarre features of wrestling was the emergence of wrestlers as political figures – typically still in costume. The most famous of these, **Superbarrio**, arose from the struggle of Mexico City's tenant associations for fair rents and decent housing (after the 1985 earthquake), to become part of mainstream political opposition, even challenging government officials to step into the ring with him, and acting as a sort of unofficial cheerleader at opposition rallies.

The most famous wrestler of all time, however, was without doubt **El Santo** ("the Saint"). Immortalized in more than twenty movies, with titles such as *El Santo vs the Vampire Women*, he would fight, eat, drink and play the romantic lead without ever removing his mask, and until after his retirement, he never revealed his identity. His reputation as a gentleman in and out of the ring was legendary, and his death in 1984 widely mourned. His funeral was allegedly the second best-attended in Mexican history after that of President Obregón.

In Mexico City, fights can usually be seen on Tuesdays at the **Arena Coliseo**, Peru 77 (Metro Allende), and on Fridays at the **Arena México**, Dr Lucio 197 at Dr Lavista, Colonia Doctores (two blocks south and one east of Metro Balderas, but not a good area to be in at night). Tickets are sold on the door.

BULLFIGHTING

Soccer and wrestling may be more popular, but there is no event more quintessentially Mexican than the **bullfight**. Rooted in Spanish machismo and imbued with multiple layers of symbolism and interpretation, it transcends a mere battle of man against animal. If you don't mind the inherent cruelty of the spectacle (essentially you're watching an animal being artfully tortured to death), it's worth attending a *corrida de toros* to see this integral part of the Mexican experience. It is a sport that transcends class barriers; every Sunday afternoon during the winter season men and women from all walks of Mexican society file into the stadium – though some admittedly end up in plush *sombra* (shade) seats while the masses occupy concrete *sol* (sun) terraces.

Each **fight** is divided into three *suertes* (acts) or *tercios* (thirds), each announced by a trumpet blast. During the first *tercio*, several *toreros* with large capes tire the bull in preparation for the *picadores* who, from their mounts atop heavily padded and blindfolded horses, attempt to force a lance between the bull's shoulder blades to further weaken him. The *toreros* then return for the second *tercio*, in which one of their number (and sometimes the matador himself) will try to stab six metal-tipped spikes (known as *bandilleras*) into the bull in as clean and elegant a manner as possible.

Exhausted and frustrated, but by no means docile, the bull is now considered ready for the third and final *tercio*, the *suerte de muleta*. The matador continues to tire the bull while pulling off as many graceful and daring moves as possible. By now the crowd will have sensed the bravery and finesse of the matador and the spirit of the bull he is up against, and shouts of "¡Olé!" will reverberate around the stadium with every pass. Eventually the matador will entice the bull to challenge him head-on, standing there with its hooves together. As it charges he will thrust his sword between its shoulder blades and, if it is well executed, the bull will crumple to the sand. However barbaric you might think it is, no one likes to see the bull suffer and even the finest performance will garner the matador little praise without a clean kill.

It may well be that the future of the bullfight in Mexico City is extremely limited. There have been numerous protests against the cruelty of the sport by those living in the capital. Mexico City's hallowed Plaza Mexico has rarely been full in recent years, and at the time of writing new legislation to recognize the sentience of animals and the cruelty of blood sports was gaining unequivocal cross-party support.

Estadio Olímpico "Tlalpan" bus from Metro Chilpancingo. Elsewhere in the city, the university side, UNAM (Las Pumas), have a strong following at the Estadio Olímpico across the road from the university (see page 111).

BULLFIGHTING

Plaza México Ciudad de los Deportes; https://laplazamexico.com; Metrobús down Insurgentes to Ciudad de los Deportes, or walk 10min east from Metro San Antonio. This giant 48,000-seat arena is the largest bullring in the world, with elaborate posters around town and most major newspapers advertising upcoming events. Look out too for the weekly coverage of the scene in the press during the season. Tickets can be bought at the gate and you won't pay much for general admission to the sunny concrete benches far from the action. For a little more and you'll have the luxury of some shade, and from there prices rise rapidly the closer you get to the ring; the most expensive spots are the front-row seats in the shade.

DIRECTORY

Banks and exchange ATMs are widespread. If using a bank, note that many will only change money in the morning, and may not change currencies other than US dollars; Banamex is generally your best bet. Most large hotels and shops will change dollar travellers' cheques and cash dollars, but the quickest and easiest places to change money are *casas de cambio*, scattered all over town. In the *centro histórico* try CI Banco, Madero 27, at Bolivar, or Cambios Exchange, at Madero 13, near Gante. You'll find several in the Zona Rosa, especially on Amberes, Londres and Liverpool, and a couple on the south side of Reforma, just south of the Monumento a la Revolución.

Courier services DHL, Madero 70-C, Centro Histórico https://dhlproductosyservicios.com; FedEx, Reforma 308, Zona Rosa, and other locations (800 900 1100, http://fedex.com/mx_english).

1

FIESTAS IN MEXICO CITY

Día de los Santos Reyes (Jan 6). Celebrations include a fiesta with dancing at Nativitas, a suburb near Xochimilco.

Bendicíon de los Animales (Jan 17). Children's pets and peasants' farm animals are taken to the cathedral to be blessed.

Día de San Pedro (June 29). Marked by traditional dancing in San Pedro Actopan, on the southern outskirts of the DF.

Día de Santa Marta (July 25). Celebrated in Milpa Alta, near Xochimilco, with Aztec dances and mock fights between Moors and Christians.

Independence Day (Sept 15). The president of the republic proclaims the famous Grito at 11pm in the Zócalo, followed by the ringing of the Campana de Dolores and a huge firework display.

Día de Santa Cecilia (Nov 22). Santa Cecilia is the patron saint of musicians, and her fiesta attracts orchestras and mariachi bands from all over to Santa Cecilia Tepetlapa, near Xochimilco.

Día de la Señora de Guadalupe (Dec 12). The saint's day of Mexico's favourite Virgin heralds a massive pilgrimage to the Basilica of Guadalupe (see page 115), running for several days, with a more secular celebration of music and dancing.

Cultural institutes Several countries maintain cultural institutes and libraries for their nationals within Mexico City, often allowing short-term visitors to use some of their facilities. They can also be useful places for contacts, and if you're looking for work, long-term accommodation or travelling companions, their notice boards are good places to start. The US has the Biblioteca Benjamín Franklin, Liverpool 31, at Berlin; Metro Cuauhtémoc); the UK has the British Council, Lope de Vega 316, Chapultepec; Metro Polanco).

Embassies and consulates Australia, Rubén Darío 55, Polanco (55 1101 2200, http://mexico.embassy.gov.au; Metro Auditorio); Belize, Bernardo de Gálves 215, Lomas de Chapultepec (55 5520 1274, embelize@prodigy.net.mx); Canada, Schiller 529, Polanco (55 5724 7900, toll-free emergency number for Canadians 001 800 514 0129, http:// international.gc.ca/country-pays/mexico-mexique; Metro Polanco); Guatemala, Explanada 1025, Lomas de Chapultepec (55 5540 7520); Ireland, Manuel Avila Camacho 76 3°, Lomas de Chapultepec (55 5520 5803, http://dfa.ie/irish-embassy/mexico; Metro Polanco or Auditorio); New Zealand, Jaime Balmes 8 4°, Polanco (55 5283 9460, https://www.mfat.govt.nz/en/countries-and-regions/americas/mexico; Metro Polanco); South Africa, Andrés Bello 10 9°, Polanco (55 1100 4970, safrica@prodigy.net.mx; Metro Polanco); UK, Río Lerma 71, consular section at Rio Usumacinta 30, Cuauhtémoc (55 1670 3200, https://www.gov.uk/world/organisations/british-embassy-mexico-city; Metro Insurgentes); US, Reforma 305 at Danubio, Zona Rosa (55 5080 2000, Metro Insurgentes).

Emergencies All emergency services (police, fire, ambulance) 080; police 060; fire department 068; Red Cross ambulance 065; Locatel, which gives information on missing persons and vehicles, medical emergencies, emotional crises and public services 55 5658 1111, locatel.df.gob.mx; tourist helpline 55 5250 0123 or 55 5250 0151.

Hospitals The American-British Cowdray Hospital (ABC) is at the junction of Observatorio and Sur 136, Col Las Américas (55 5277 6060; Metro Observatorio). Embassies should be able to provide a list of multilingual doctors if necessary. As for pharmacies, Sanborns offers a wide range of products at most branches, as well as dispensing some prescription drugs. Other options include El Fénix, Madero 41 (at Motolinia; 55 5527 0060), and Isabel la Católica 15 (at 5 de Mayo; 55 5527 0060). There are homeopathic pharmacies at Mesones 111-B (at 20 Noviembre; 55 5542 2755) and República Guatemala 16 (behind the cathedral; 55 5512 3527).

Internet Cybercafés generally charge by the hour. Those in the suburbs (there are several in Xochimilco, for example) tend to be slightly cheaper than those in town. In the centre, most places are closed at weekends; options include: Internet Express, ground floor, Centro Comercial Bialos, Donceles 87, on the corner of Brasil (Metro Zócalo or Allende); Lafoel Internet Service, Donceles 80, at Brasil (Metro Zócalo or Allende); Alegro, Tacuba 849 (Metro Allende). In the Zona Rosa, there are several inside the roundabout at Glorieta Insurgentes.

Laundry Self-service launderettes are surprisingly rare in Mexico City, but most hotels should be able to point one out. Options include: La Maquina, 2nd floor, Centro Comercial Bialos, Donceles 87, on the corner of Brasil; and Lavandería Automática Edison, Edison 91, at Arriaga, near the Plaza de la República (Metro Revolución).

Left luggage Most hotels will hold your bags for the rest of the day after you've checked out, and some will allow you to leave excess luggage for several days, sometimes for a small charge. All four main bus terminals and both airport terminals have left-luggage facilities, though prices vary vastly (the Central del Norte is the cheapest).

Photographic supplies For specialist needs, head to C Donceles, between Republica de Argentina and Allende, or Foto Regis at Juárez 80, on the south side of the Alameda (http://fotoregis.com).

Post office The main post office is on Lázaro Cárdenas at Tacuba, across the street from Bellas Artes. Branch offices can be found at Ponciano Arriaga 11, near the Revolution Monument, and Higuera 23 in Coyoacán, among other places. For speedier and more reliable delivery (though a lot more expensive, of course), see "Courier services" (see page 137).

Spanish courses There are many Spanish courses in the city, though most people prefer to study in such places as Cuernavaca, San Miguel de Allende and Guanajuato. For those who prefer the metropolis, the most prestigious language school in town is the Universidad Autonomo's Centro de Enseñanza para Extranjeros, located at Universidad 3002 in the Ciudad Universitaria (http://cepe.unam.mx). Also worth checking out is http://planeta.com/mexico.html, which has good links to Mexican language schools.

Telephones Local, domestic long-distance and international phone calls can be made from any public phone with a phonecard. Cheaper international calls can be made via the internet, though very few internet locales offer this service – those which do include a couple inside the roundabout at Glorieta Insurgentes. Otherwise, a number of shops have public phones (for international services look for the blue "Larga Distancia" signs). You can dial direct from most big hotels, but it will cost much more. *Casetas de larga distancia* are closing down in the face of widespread use of cardphones.

Travel agencies A particularly good firm for youth and student fares is Mundo Joven (http://mundojoven.com), with offices at Guatemala 4 behind the cathedral (55 5482 8282), Eugenio Sue 342, at Homero in Polanco (55 5250 7191), and Terminal 1, Sala E2 in the airport (55 2599 0155).

Visas and tourist cards Should you lose your tourist card, or want an extension, apply, when your original length of stay is almost finished, to the Instituto de Migración, Ejército National 862, at the western end of Polanco (800 004 6264; *peseros* from Chapultepec to Toreo run along Ejército Nacional). Extensions are pretty much routine if the period is two weeks or less, and should take around half an hour; go to desk D23 – "Ampliación de Estancia". Longer extensions will require copies, form filling and possibly an onward ticket or proof of sufficient funds.

Around Mexico City

PIRÁMIDE DEL SOL, TEOTIHUACÁN

Around Mexico City

2

Striking out from Mexico City, there are places worth visiting in every direction. Those covered in this chapter can all be taken in on day trips from the capital, but many are worth a longer stay. The heart of this region is the Valley of México, a mountain-ringed basin dominated by the vast snowcapped peaks of Popocatépetl and Ixtaccíhuatl. Since long before the Mexican nation existed, it has been the country's centre of gravity. Even in the days of the Aztecs, cities such as Texcoco (now in the State of México) and Tlaxcala (now capital of its own little state) vied with Tenochtitlán (Mexico City) for domination.

Much of the region around Mexico City belongs to the **State of México**, whose capital is **Toluca**, to the west, but the state actually reaches all the way round the northern edge of Mexico City and covers its eastern side as well. Also encrusted around the capital are the small states of **Hidalgo** (to the north), **Morelos** (to the south) and **Tlaxcala** (to the east). The city of Puebla, though its state sprawls eastward towards Veracruz, is tucked in tidily next to Tlaxcala, just as **Taxco** is next to Morelos, though actually it belongs to Guerrero, the same state as Acapulco. All around the region, but particularly to the north of Mexico City, you'll be able to see impressive pre-Hispanic sites.

North of Mexico City

The day trip that almost everyone takes from Mexico City is to the pyramids of **Teotihuacán**, about 75km northeast, easily the largest of Mexico's archeological sites, with enough to see to occupy a full day. Also among the destinations accessible as day trips from Mexico City's Terminal del Norte is **Tula**, the centre that succeeded Teotihuacán as the valley's great power. On the way you can stop at **Tepotzotlán**, which holds some of the finest Baroque and colonial art in the country. To the east, **Pachuca** is home to the national photography museum, and nearby is **Real del Monte**, where Cornish miners introduced soccer to Mexico in the nineteenth century.

Teotihuacán

Charge for Ruins & Museo del Sitio, video permit fee

Most visitors to Mexico City head out at some stage to the pre-Columbian pyramids at **Teotihuacán**: there's a constant stream of tours, buses and cars heading this way, and the ruins can get quite busy, especially on a Sunday. As it's an extensive site that can easily take up most of a day, it's best, if possible, to head out here as early as you can manage and do most of your exploration in the cool of the morning, before the crowds arrive.

The ruins reveal a city planned and built on a massive scale, the great **pyramids** so huge that before their refurbishment one would have passed them by as hills without a second look. At its height this must have been the most imposing city in pre-Hispanic America, with a population thought to have been around 150,000 (though estimates vary), spread over an area of some 23 square kilometres (as opposed to the four square kilometres of the ceremonial centre). Back then, every building – grey hulks now – would have been covered in bright polychrome murals.

THE CHURCH OF SANTA PRISCA, TAXCO

Highlights

❶ **Teotihuacán** The largest pre-Hispanic site in the country, dominated by the huge Pirámide del Sol and only slightly less huge Pirámide de la Luna. See page 142

❷ **Real del Monte** A lovely mountain town with fresh air, and an unexpected Cornish influence dating from the nineteenth century. See page 155

❸ **Puebla** Marvellous Spanish architecture and wonderful cuisine in the original home of *mole poblano*. See page 161

❹ **Cuernavaca** Charming colonial city that's a favourite place to study Spanish. See page 171

❺ **Taxco** Once a silver-mining centre, now a silver-buying centre, this whitewashed hillside town makes a welcome stop on the road to Acapulco. See page 180

❻ **Malinalco** This charmingly picturesque little village is overlooked by a small but breathtakingly scenic archeological site. See page 185

❼ **Valle de Bravo** A peaceful lake surrounded by lush green hills, this popular escape from Mexico City is a blissful world apart and perfect for a few days in the sun. See page 191

HIGHLIGHTS ARE MARKED ON THE MAP ON PAGE 144

2

Calzada de los Muertos

The main entrance, by Puerta 1, is at the southern end of the 2km-long **Calzada de los Muertos** (Causeway of the Dead), which originally extended 1.5km further south, and formed the axis around which the city developed. A broad roadway some 40m wide and linking all the most significant buildings, it was built to impress, with the low buildings that flank most of its length serving to heighten the impact of the two great pyramid temples at the northern end. Other streets, leading off to the rest of the city, originally intersected it at right angles, and even the Río San Juan was canalized so as not to disturb the symmetry (the bridge that then crossed it would have extended the full width of the street).

Its name is somewhat misleading, as it's more a series of open plazas linked by staircases than a simple street. Neither is it in any way linked with the dead, although the Aztecs believed the buildings that lined it, then little more than earth-covered mounds, to be the burial places of kings. They are not, and although the exact function of most remains unclear, all obviously had some sacred significance. The design, seen in the many reconstructions, is fairly uniform: low three- or four-storey platforms consisting of vertical panels (*tableros*) supported by sloping walls. In many cases several are built on top of each other – clearly demonstrated in the **Edificios Superpuestos** (superimposed buildings) on the left-hand side shortly

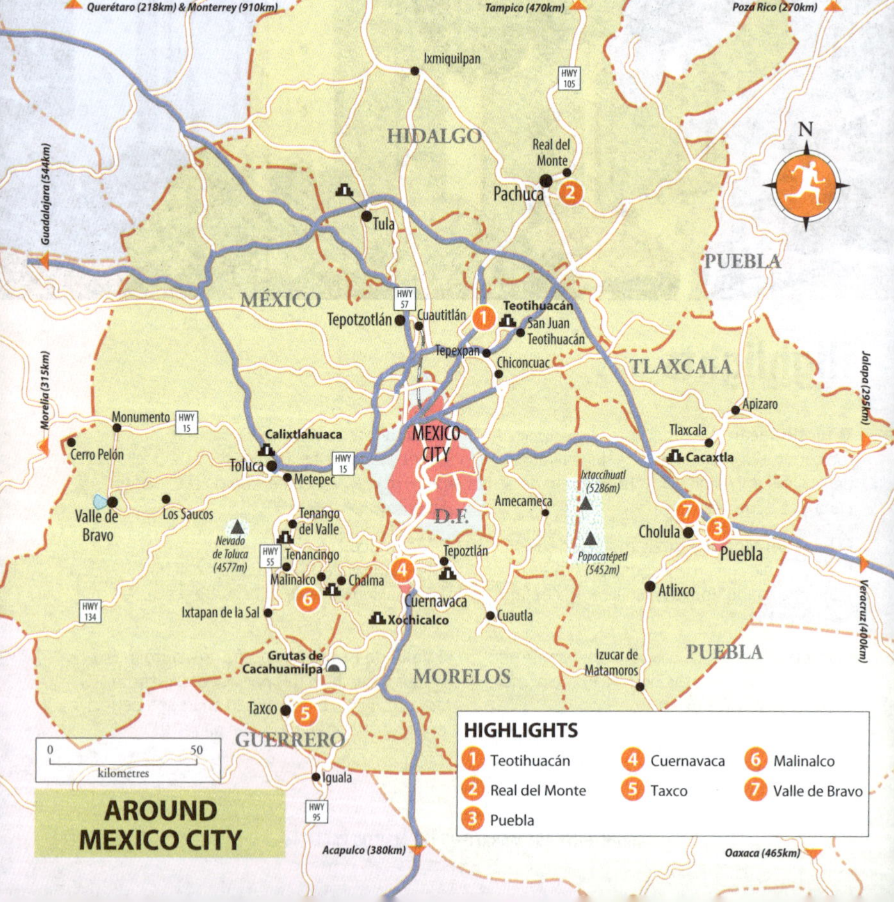

THE RISE AND FALL OF TEOTIHUACÁN

The rise and fall of **Teotihuacán** is almost exactly contemporary with imperial Rome. There is evidence of small agricultural communities in the vicinity dating to around 600 BC; by 200 BC a township had been established on the present site. From then until 1 AD (the period known as the **Patlachique** phase) the population increased, and the city assumed its most important characteristics: the great pyramids of the Sun and Moon were built, and the Calzada de los Muertos laid out. Development continued through the **Tzacualli** and **Miccaotli** phases (1–250 AD) with more construction and the blossoming of artistic expression. Then through the **Tlamimilolpa** phase (250–450 AD) there is evidence of the city's influence (in architecture, sculpture and pottery) occurring at sites throughout modern Mexico and into Guatemala and Honduras. From 450 to around 650 AD (**Xolalpan** phase) it reached its peak in both population and power, with much new building and addition to earlier structures.

By the end of this period, however, there were already signs of decline, and the final phase, the **Metepec**, lasted, at most, a century before the city was sacked, burnt and virtually abandoned. This may have been the result of invasion or internal strife, but the underlying reasons could have been as much ecological as military. Vast forests were cut down to build the city (for use in columns, roof supports and door lintels) and huge quantities of wood burnt to make the lime plaster that coated the buildings. The result was severe soil erosion that left the hillsides as barren as they appear today. In addition, the agricultural effort needed to feed so many people (with no form of artificial fertilizer or knowledge of crop rotation) gradually sapped what land remained of its ability to grow more.

Whatever the precise causes, the city was left, eventually, to a ruination that was advanced even by the time of the Aztecs. To them it represented a holy place from a previous age, and they gave it its present name, which translates as "the place where men became gods". Although Teotihuacán features frequently in Aztec mythology, there are no written records – what we know of the city is derived entirely from archeological and artistic evidence, so that even the original name remains unknown.

beyond the river. Here, excavated structures underneath the present level may have been the living quarters of Teotihuacán's priests.

La Ciudadela

Directly opposite the entrance at Puerta 1 lies **La Ciudadela**, the Citadel. This enormous sunken square, surrounded by stepped platforms and with a low square altar in the centre, was the city's administrative heart, with the houses of its chief priests and nobles arranged around a vast meeting place. Across the open space stands a tall pyramid construction inside which, during excavations, was found the **Temple of Quetzalcoatl**. With the back of the newer pyramid demolished, the elaborate (Miccaotli phase) temple structure stands revealed. Pyramids aside, this is one of the most impressive sections of the whole site, rising in four steps (of an original six), each sculpted in relief and punctuated at intervals by the stylized heads of Quetzalcoatl, the plumed serpent, and **Tlaloc**, the rain god. Traces of the original paint can be seen in places.

Pirámide del Sol

The great **Pirámide del Sol** (Pyramid of the Sun) is Teotihuacán's outstanding landmark, a massive structure 70m high and, of Mexico's ancient buildings, second in size only to Cholula (itself a total ruin). Its base is almost exactly the same size as that of the great Pyramid of Cheops in Egypt, but the lower-angled sides and its stepped nature make it very much lower. There are wonderful views from the top nonetheless, and the bulk is all the more remarkable when you consider the accuracy of its alignment: on two days a year (May 19 and July 25), the sun is directly over the pyramid at noon, and the main west facade faces the point at which the sun

sets on these days. This alignment just off the cardinal points determined the line of the Calzada de los Muertos and of the entire city. Equally remarkable is the fact that the 2.5 million tonnes of stone and earth used in its construction were brought here without benefit of the wheel or any beast of burden, and shaped without the use of metal tools. The pyramid you see was reconstructed by **Leopoldo Batres** in 1908, in a thoroughly cavalier fashion. He blasted, with dynamite, a structure that originally abutted the south face, and stripped much of the surface in a search for a more complete building under the present one. In fact, the Pirámide del Sol, almost uniquely, was built in one go at a very early stage of the city's development (about 100 AD), and there is only a very small older temple right at its heart.

The cave

You approach the pyramid by a short staircase leading to the right off the Calzada de los Muertos onto a broad esplanade, where stand the ruins of several small temples and priests' dwellings. The main structure consists of five sloping layers of wall divided by terraces – the large flat area at the top would originally have been surmounted by a sanctuary, long disappeared. Evidence of why this massive structure came to be raised here emerged in 1971 when archeologists stumbled on a tunnel (closed to the public) leading to a clover-leaf-shaped **cave** directly under the centre of the pyramid.

This, clearly, had been some kind of inner sanctuary, a holy of holies, and may even have been the reason for Teotihuacán's foundation and the basis of its influence. Theories abound as to its exact nature, and many fit remarkably with legends handed down through the Aztecs. It's most likely that the cave was formed by a subterranean spring, and came to be associated with Tlaloc, god of rain but also a bringer of fertility, as a sort of fountain of life. Alternatively, it could be associated with the legendary "seven grottoes", a symbol of creation from which all later Mexican peoples claimed to have emerged, or to have been the site of an oracle, or associated with a cult of sacrifice – in Aztec times the flayed skins of victims of Xipe Totec were stored in a cave under a pyramid.

Pirámide de la Luna

At the end of the Calzada de los Muertos rises the **Pirámide de la Luna** (Pyramid of the Moon), a smaller structure built slightly later (but still during the Tzacualli phase), whose top, thanks to the high ground on which it's built, is virtually on a level with that of the Pirámide del Sol. The structure is very similar, with four sloping levels approached by a monumental stairway, but for some reason this seems a very much more elegant building: perhaps because of the smaller scale, or perhaps as a result of the approach, through the formally laid-out **Plaza de la Luna**. The top of the pyramid offers the best overview of the site's layout, looking straight back down the length of the central thoroughfare. It is perfect for sunset, though as it is then close to closing time the guards will soon chase you down.

Palacio de Quetzalpapálotl

The **Palacio de Quetzalpapálotl** (Palace of the Quetzal-butterfly) lies to the left of the Plaza de la Luna, behind the low temples that surround it. Wholly restored, it's virtually the only example of a pre-Hispanic roofed building in central Mexico and preserves a unique view of how the elite lived at Teotihuacán. The rooms are arranged around a patio whose elaborately carved pillars give the palace its name – their stylized designs represent birds (the brightly coloured quetzals, though some may be owls) and butterflies. In the galleries around the patio several frescoes survive, all very formalized and symbolic. **Mural art** was clearly very important in Teotihuacán, and almost every building has some decoration, though much has been removed for restoration.

Palacio de los Jaguares and Templo de los Caracoles Emplumados

Two earlier buildings, half-buried under the palace, still have substantial remains. In the **Palacio de los Jaguares**, jaguars in feathered headdresses blow conch shells from which emerge curls of music, or perhaps speech or prayers to Tlaloc (who appears along the top of the mural); in the **Templo de los Caracoles Emplumados** (Temple of the Plumed Snail Shells), you see a motif of feathers and seashells along with bright green parrots. Other murals, of which only traces remain, were found in the temples along the Calzada de los Muertos between the two pyramids.

Tepantitla, Tetitla and Atetelco

Mural art was not reserved for the priests' quarters – indeed, some of the finest frescoes have been found in outlying apartment buildings. The famous *Paradise of Tlaloc* mural, reproduced in the Museo Nacional de Antropología (see page 97), was discovered at **Tepantitla**, a residential quarter of the old city across the road from the back of the Pirámide del Sol. Only a part of it survives here, but there are others in the complex depicting a procession of priests and a ball-game. All have great vitality and an almost comic-strip quality, with speech bubbles emerging from the figures' mouths, but their themes always have a religious rather than a purely decorative intent. More can be seen at **Tetitla**, to the west of the main site, and **Atetelco**, a little further west, just off the map on page 144.

Museo del Sitio

Plan to spend at least some of your time in Teotihuacán's excellent **Museo del Sitio**, situated behind the Pirámide del Sol and surrounded by a lovely sculpture and botanical garden. In the **first room**, artefacts from the site are well laid out and effectively lit to highlight the key features of each item in the cool interior. There's just about everything you would expect of a ritual site and living city, from sharp-edged obsidian tools and everyday ceramics to some fine polychrome vessels decorated with animal and plant designs, and a series of five ceremonial braziers or censers ornamented with appliqué flowers, butterflies and shields.

Vast windows framing the Pirámide del Sol take up one entire wall of the **second room**, where you walk across a glass floor over a relief model of the entire city as it might once have been. The glass floor leads you to the **third room**, where burials from under the Temple of Quetzalcoatl have been relocated, along with statues of gods (often bottom-lit to accentuate the gruesome features), including a trio of braziers carried by the sun god Huitzilopochtli.

ARRIVAL AND DEPARTURE — TEOTIHUACÁN

By bus Buses leave (every 15min, 6am–9pm; 1hr) from Mexico City's Terminal del Norte (see page 119). Go to the second-class (left-hand) side of the bus station and look for the Autobuses Teotihuacán stand in Sala 8 (55 5781 1812); be aware that these buses have, from time to time, been targeted by bandits, so don't bring a lot of cash or your passport; carry a photocopy instead. A slightly quicker alternative is to catch the Metro to Indios Verdes (line 3) and head to the northern end of the parking area outside, from where buses leave frequently for "Las Pirámides". A road, the Carretera de Circunvalación, provides access to the main structures through one of six gates (each with parking and lines of souvenir stalls): buses might arrive at any *puerta* (gate), though Puerta 1 and Puerta 2 are the most common. These are also the best places to wait for buses back to Mexico City (the last at 9pm), but late in the day most return buses visit all the gates before departing the site.

EATING — SEE MAP PAGE 146

Cinco Estrellas Outside Puerta 2; 594 956 2555. This is one of a little group of cheap eateries just outside Puerta 2 – all remarkably good value – whose representatives will be on your case as soon as you set foot outside the gate (you can leave the site and re-enter, so long as you hold on to your ticket). A comida corrida here will set you back a modest amount, and it includes a free glass of tequila or *pulque*, or you can get a portion of quesadillas, and they also do breakfasts. M$$

La Gruta 200m west of Puerta 5; http://lagruta.mx. A fancy and very impressive-looking restaurant, set deep in an open-sided cave, with white-jacketed waiters. The setting is wonderful, but the food and service don't always match the price, with offerings such as chicken with red and green *mole* or Tampico-style tenderloin with Mexican trimmings. M$$$$

Las Pirámides main entrance, Puerta 1; 594 956 8877. The main restaurant and bar on the site itself offers a three-course tourist menu and some basic à la carte dishes such as chicken in red or green *mole*. Prices are high considering the quality of the food, but the view of the site from the top-floor restaurant is great. M$$$$

Tepotzotlán

TEPOTZOTLÁN lies en route from the capital to Tula, and it's possible to visit the two on one long day from the metropolis. Tepotzotlán is also close enough to the city to be a morning's excursion, though once you're there, you may find the town's slow pace and colonial charm seduce you into staying longer. On Saturdays, with loads of Mexican visitors, the festive atmosphere is particularly enjoyable, while on Sundays a crafts market draws large crowds. In the week before Christmas, Tepotzotlán's renowned *pastorelas*, or **Nativity plays**, are staged here (with accommodation booked up far in advance). At other times of the year, you may catch a concert in the church or cloisters.

Museo Nacional del Virreinato

Beside the cathedral on the main plaza • Charge, video permit fee) • http://virreinato.inah.gob.mx

Atmosphere apart, the reason most people come to Tepotzotlán is to see the magnificent Baroque **Church of San Francisco Javier** and the adjacent **Colegio**, now together forming the **Museo Nacional del Virreinato** (Viceroyalty Museum). The entire museum is in Spanish, but English-speaking guides can be found for hire at the museum's entrance. The church was founded by the Jesuits, who arrived in 1580 on a mission to convert the Otomí locals. Most of the huge complex you see today was established during the following century but constantly embellished right up to the expulsion of the Jesuits in 1767. The **facade** of the church – which looks onto the main square and is considered one of the finest examples of churrigueresque architecture in the country – was completed barely five years before. The wealth and scale of it all gives some idea of the power of the Jesuits prior to their ousting; after they left, it became a seminary for the training of regular priests until the late nineteenth century, when the Jesuits were briefly readmitted. The Revolution led to its final abandonment in 1914.

Iglesia de San Francisco Javier

The main entrance to the Colegio de San Francisco Javier leads into the **Claustro de los Aljibes**, with a well at the centre and pictures of the life of Ignatius Loyola (founder of the Jesuits) around the walls. Off the cloister is the entrance to the church, the **Iglesia de San Francisco Javier**. If the facade is spectacular, it's still barely preparation for the dazzling interior. Dripping with gold, and profusely carved with a bewilderment of saints and cherubim, it strikes you at first as some mystical cave of treasures. The main body of the church and its chapels house five huge gilded cedar-wood altarpieces, stretching from ceiling to floor and beautifully lit to bring out the fascinating detail from both the alabaster around the windows and discreetly placed lamps. Much of the painting on the main altar (dedicated to the church's patron saint) is attributed to **Miguel Cabrera**, sometimes considered to be Mexico's Michelangelo, whose talents are also on display towards the main church door, which is framed by two large oils, one depicting worshippers bathing in the blood from Jesus's crucifixion wounds.

Camarín and Capilla of the Virgen de Loreto

All this is still only the start, for hidden to one side is arguably the greatest achievement of Mexican Baroque, the octagonal **Camarín de la Virgen**. It's not a large room, but every centimetre is elaborately decorated and the hand of the native craftsmen is clearly evident in the exuberant carving – fruit and flowers, shells and abstract patterns crammed in between the angels. There's a mirror angled to allow visitors to appreciate the detail of the ceiling without straining their necks. The Camarín is reached through the **Capilla de la Virgen de Loreto**, inside which is a "house" tiled with eighteenth-century *azulejos* – supposedly a replica of Mary's house at Nazareth, in which Jesus grew up.

Around the central cloister

Directly off the **central cloister** of the Colegio are rooms packed with a treasure of beautiful silver reliquaries and crucifixes, censers, custodia, vestments and even a pair of silver sandals; notice, too, the painted panel depicting the spiritual conquest of New Spain and showing the relative influence of the Franciscans, Augustinians and Dominicans in the sixteenth century, and above it the diagram of churches liberally dotted among the lakes of the Valley of México.

The **upper storey** around the cloister contains more religious paintings than anyone could take in on one visit, including portraits of the Society of Jesus and others of beatific eighteenth- and nineteenth-century nuns. Here too is the **Cristo del Árbol**, a crucifix carved towards the end of the seventeenth century from a single piece of wood.

Claustro de los Naranjos and Huerta

2

Stairs descend to the **Claustro de los Naranjos**, planted with orange and lemon trees and with a fountain in the middle. Around it are displays of wooden religious statuary – Balthazar and Caspar, two of the three Magi, are particularly fine. Other rooms contain more colonial miscellany – lacquerwork, furniture (notably an inlaid wooden desk) and clothes – and some temporary exhibition space. Outside extends the walled **Huerta**, or garden, some seven acres of lawns, shady trees and floral displays, as well as vegetables and medicinal herbs cultivated as they would have been by the monks. It is not as well tended as it could be, but makes a break from the museum and has a few architectural pieces and large sculptures dotted around, including, at the far end, the original eighteenth-century **Salto del Agua** that stood at the end of the aqueduct carrying water from Chapultepec into Mexico City (a replica of the fountain stands in the capital now, near Metro Salto del Agua).

The Botica and Capilla Doméstica

Returning to the main cloister, you find a mixed bag, with pre-Hispanic statuary leading on to details of Spanish exploration, suits of armour, exquisite marquetry boxes and a sequence of rooms, one filled with ivory statues, another laid out for Spanish nobles to dine, and then the **Botica**, or pharmacy, with bottles, jars, pestles and mortars, and all the other equipment of an eighteenth-century healer. The **Capilla Doméstica** also opens off the cloister, a whirl of painted and gilded Rococo excess, with a magnificent gilded *retablo* full of mirrors and little figures.

ARRIVAL AND DEPARTURE — TEPOTZOTLÁN

By bus Buses to Tepotzotlán from Metro Cuatro Caminos or Metro Rosario in Mexico City are slow, rattling their way round the suburbs for what feels like hours (though the total journey is actually little over 1hr) before finally leaving the city. Alternatively, take an indirect ("via Refinario") Tula bus or a second-class Querétaro bus from the Terminal del Norte to the Caseta de Tepotzotlán, a road junction about 200m before the first motorway tollbooths. From there it's about a 15min walk (or 5min by local bus or taxi) west along Av Insurgentes into the centre of Tepotzotlán. The same road junction by the tollbooths is also the place to pick up buses on to Tula or back to Mexico City. Local buses and *peseros* serve Cautitlán and Lechería stations on the suburban train line to Buenavista in Mexico City (but not all those going to Cautitlán serve the station).

ACCOMMODATION

Hotel Posada Los Angeles Av Insurgentes 10; 55 5876 8399. One of four pleasant hotels occupying a cul-de-sac at the southeast corner of the cathedral complex, this is well located, being a short stroll from the busier centre, and with various eating options nearby. All rooms are en suite and tastefully decorated. M$$

Hotel Principal Calle Eva Samano 17 (a block north of the plaza); 56 4374 5249. An inexpensive and very central option which offers significant discounts on weeknights, as well as for those who pay with cash. Two tiers of eighteen basic rooms, all en suite and clean, look out over a slim courtyard with a café above the entrance. M$

Posada San José Plaza Virreinal 13; 55 5876 0835. Beside *Pepe's* on the central plaza (see page 151) is Tepotzotlán's best sleeping option for price, location and all-round convenience. The most recent renovations solved a glut of problems, and the rooms are now airy, bright and decked out with mod cons to suit all travellers. M$$

EATING

Hostería del Convento Plaza Virreinal (east side); http://hosteriadelconvento.mx. Quite pricey but set beautifully in the grounds of the seminary, and serving excellent Mexican and international food (steak with chipotle, filet mignon with fries and salad). They also do a reasonably priced buffet. M$$$

Municipal market On the west side of the plaza. Has multiple stands offering classic Mexican dishes such as *birria*, *pozole* and *huarache* in a classic Mexican setting. Pull up a stool at any of the informal eateries and enjoy the lively atmosphere. You'll be pestered by the stand owners for custom when you walk in, but the stands with the

TULA AND THE TOLTECS

In legend at least, the mantle of Teotihuacán fell on Tollan, or **Tula**, as the next great power to dominate Mexico. The **Aztecs** regarded the city they constructed as the successor to Tula and hence embellished its reputation – the streets, they said, had been paved with gold and the buildings constructed from precious metals and stones, while the **Toltecs**, who founded Tula, were regarded as the inventors of every science and art. In reality, it seems unlikely that Tula was ever as large or as powerful a city as Teotihuacán had been – or as Tenochtitlán was to become – and its period of dominance (about 950–1150 AD) was relatively short. Yet all sorts of **puzzles** remain about the Toltec era, and in particular their apparent connection with the Yucatán – much of the architecture at **Chichén Itzá**, for example, appears to have been influenced by the Toltecs. Few people believe that the Toltecs actually had an empire that stretched so far: however warlike (and the artistic evidence is that Tula was a grimly militaristic society, heavily into human sacrifice), they would have lacked the manpower, resources or any logical justification for such expansion.

One possible answer lies in the legends of **Quetzalcoatl**. Adopted from Teotihuacán, the plumed serpent attained far more importance here in Tula, where he is depicted everywhere. At some stage Tula apparently had a ruler identified with Quetzalcoatl who was driven from the city by the machinations of the evil god Texcatlipoca, and the theory goes that this ruler, defeated in factional struggles within Tula, fled with his followers, eventually reaching Maya territory, where they established a new Toltec regime at Chichén Itzá. Though popular for a long time, this hypothesis has now fallen out of fashion following finds at Chichén Itzá that seem to undermine it (see page 719).

most customers are usually the safest bets, so don't let the hollering influence your decision, nor should you expect it to continue once you plump for a set stand. M$$

Pepe's Plaza Virreinal 13; 55 5876 0520. The *Hotel Posada San José's* restaurant, with a terrace directly opposite the Church of San Francisco Javier, which you can gaze at while enjoying their speciality, *cabrito Pepe* (slow-roasted goat). If you want to get pre-Hispanic, you can precede it with a plate of *escamoles* (ant eggs) as a starter. M$$$$

Los Virreyes Plaza Virreinal 32; http://restaurantelosvirreyes.com. This relaxing and well-run restaurant on the north side of the square offers gourmet dining on its airy terrace overlooking the square and the smog you've just emerged from further to the south. Don't allow the waiters to lead you up here if you're only after a few drinks and a snack, though, as much of the local fare is available for less in the downstairs bar, including Mexican classics such as mescal worms and rabbit *al pastor* (in an *adobe* of dried chiles). At weekends they do a buffet and on Sun the dishes available in the buffet include paella. M$$$

Tula

The modern city of **Tula de Allende** lies on the edge of the Valley of México, 90km north of Mexico City. A pleasant enough regional centre with an impressive, if fortress-like, mid-sixteenth-century **cathedral and Franciscan monastery**, Tula is most notable for its wonderful pre-Hispanic pyramid site.

Tula's archeological site

2km north of Tula's town centre • Charge, free Sun, video permit fee • From the bus station (a 30min walk), turn right up Xicohténcatl to the main road (Ocampo), then turn right again, over the river and left before the train tracks (by the *Hotel Sharon*), following signs to "Zona Arqueológica" (or the pyramid symbol); on buses into town, ask to be dropped off beside the train tracks by the *Hotel Sharon;* a taxi from town is affordable on most travel budgets

Only a small part of Tula's **archeological site** itself is of interest: though the city spreads over some considerable area only some of it has been excavated, and the outlying digs are holes in the ground, meaningful only to the archeologists who created them. The ceremonial centre, however, has been partly restored. The significance of the site is made much clearer if your Spanish is up to translating all the information presented in the **museum** (same hours) by the entrance, and filled with fragments of Atlantes, Chac-mools and basalt heads, along with assorted bits of sculpture and frieze.

Templo de Tlahuizcalpantecuhtli and Atlantes

2

The site's centrepiece is the low, five-stepped pyramid of the **Templo de Tlahuizcalpantecuhtli** (Temple of the Morning Star, or Pyramid B), atop which stand the **Atlantes** – giant, 5m-tall basalt figures that originally supported the roof of the sanctuary and represent Quetzalcoatl in his guise as the morning star, dressed as a Toltec warrior. The figures wear elaborately embroidered loincloths, sandals and feathered helmets, and sport ornaments around their necks and legs – for protection, each bears a sun-shaped shield on his back and a chest piece in the form of a stylized butterfly. Each also carries an *atlatl*, or spear-thrower, in his right hand and arrows or javelins in his left.

Other pillars are carved with more warriors and gods. Reliefs such as these are a recurrent theme in Tula: the entire temple was originally faced in sculpted stone, and although it was pillaged long ago you can still see some remnants – prowling jaguars and eagles, symbols of the two great warrior groups, devouring human hearts. In front of the temple is a great L-shaped colonnade, where the partly reconstructed pillars originally supported a huge roof under which, perhaps, the priests and nobles would review their troops or take part in ceremonies in the shade. Part of a long bench survives, with its relief decoration of a procession of warriors and priests. More such benches survive in the **Palacio Quemado** (Burnt Palace – it was destroyed by fire), next to the temple on the western side. Its three rooms, each a square, were once covered with a small central patio to let light in. The middle one is the best preserved, still with much of its original paint and two Chac-mools.

The ball-courts and the Coatepantli

The main square of the city stood in front (south) of the temple and palace, with a low altar platform in the centre and the now ruinous pyramid of the Templo Mayor on the eastern side. The larger of two **ball-courts** in the central area is on the western side of the square: although also largely ruined, this marks one of the closest links between Tula and Chichén Itzá, as it is of identical shape and orientation to the great ball-court there. To the north of the temple stands the **Coatepantli** (Serpent Wall), elaborately carved in relief with images of human skeletons being eaten by giant snakes; beyond this, across an open space, there's a second ball-court, smaller but in better order.

Sala Histórica Quetzalcoatl

C Zaragoza, just off the main square • Free • 77 3732 1183

In Tula itself, a small local museum, the **Sala Histórica Quetzalcoatl**, hosts art exhibitions on the ground floor, and upstairs has a small display of archeological finds, including a mammoth tusk and some Toltec artefacts, which won't take you more than ten minutes to check out.

ARRIVAL AND DEPARTURE — TULA

By bus The bus station is on Xicohténcatl, close to the town centre. For the town centre, turn right as you leave, take the first left (Rojo del Rio) to the end, where a right turn into Hidalgo brings you to the cathedral and main square (Plaza de la Constitución). If you're coming from Mexico City's Terminal del Norte, note that tickets to Tula are sold by Autobuses del Valle de Mezquital – the desk furthest to your left when you enter the terminal. The second-class service can set you down at the Caseta de Tepozotlán (see page 150; 1hr).

Destinations Mexico City Nte (direct every hour; 1hr 30min, second class "via Refinario" every 20min; 2hr); Pachuca (every 40min; 1hr 15min); Querétaro (9 daily; 2hr 30min).

ACCOMMODATION

Casablanca Pasaje Hidalgo 11 (off C Hidalgo by no. 129); http://casablancatula.com. Friendly staff and sparkling rooms – all en suite – around a brightly painted tangerine and orange courtyard (with parking) make this a good choice. Windows face into the courtyard, so rooms at the top get the most light. M$$

Cuéllar 5 de Mayo 23, opposite the cathedral; 773 732 2920 A modern hotel with cool, shaded rooms, a sunny courtyard, small pool and outdoor jacuzzi, plus parking space and wi-fi. M$$$

Real Catedral Zaragoza 106, next to the museum; www.hotelrealcatedral.com. A charming old colonial building on the outside, but less so within, especially in the cheapest rooms, which are small and dark with low ceilings. All stays include breakfast and they'll usually do you a deal on the price, especially if you're staying more than one night. M$$

2

EATING

Casablanca Hidalgo 114; 773 732 2274. A large, slightly old-fashioned hall where they serve breakfasts and, from 1.30pm onwards, buffets with salad bar, and comidas corridas. M$$$

Crepería D'Pilli North side of Plaza de la Constitución; 222 536 1240. A small café and crêperie on the main square serving crêpes both sweet and savoury (ham and cream cheese). M$$

Hooke Wings & Beer Southeast corner of the plaza; 773 733 6525. A rooftop spot serving up exactly what the name suggests, this is one of the town's few bars and a good place to people-watch as the sun sets over the archeological site in the distance. Prepares a good *michelada*, and also offers more filling meals from its extensive menu. M$$

El Rey Juanelo Hidalgo at Morelos (at the back of a shopping arcade); 771 443 5632. If you're venturing no further into Hidalgo state, then this is the place to try out the region's famous pastes, Mexicanized Cornish Pasties brought here by English miners in the nineteenth century. Savoury and sweet fillings are various, although be warned that they are a lot spicier than their European ancestors. M$

Pachuca

In recent years, **Pachuca**, the capital of Hidalgo state, has burst out of the ring of hills that once hemmed it in, its expansion fuelled by the need to move industry away from Mexico City. It remains a fairly small city by Mexican standards, although the uncontrolled expansion is obvious on the hills surrounding its centre, which is easily walkable and full of colonial mansions built on the profits of the rich silver-mining country all about. If you have the time, it is worth venturing to nearby towns where the mining heritage is more apparent and the clean mountain air is refreshing.

The zócalo and around

Pachuca's centre boasts two main squares: **Plaza de la Constitución**, where *colectivos* from the bus station will drop you, and a block to its southeast (south down Hidalgo then east along Ocampo), the **zócalo**. The zócalo, all rather prim and proper, is dominated by the **Reloj Monumental**, a 40m Neoclassical clock tower whose construction was funded by the Cornish-born local mining magnate Francis Rule in 1910 to mark a hundred years of Mexican independence. There's further evidence of Pachuca's Cornish connection just a block north of the zócalo (or east of Plaza de la Constitución) at Allende 102, where the **Methodist Church** (daily 6.30am–7pm) was originally built for Cornish miners at the beginning of the twentieth century. For more on Pachuca's Cornish heritage, see page 155.

Museo de la Fotografía

Inside the Centro Cultural Hidalgo on Casasola (at Hidalgo), reached by walking three blocks south along Matamoros, then left for 300m along Revolución (which becomes Arista) • Free • 771 714 3653

The late sixteenth-century ex-Convento de San Francisco now operates as the **Centro Cultural Hidalgo**, and contains Pachuca's most compelling museum, the **Museo de la Fotografía**. Drawing on over a million photographic works stored here as part of the national archive, the museum does a great job of showcasing both Mexican and foreign photographers. Early photographic techniques are illustrated before you move on to the gallery space, where displays change constantly but almost always include images from the Casasola Archive. The pre-eminent Mexican photojournalist of his day, **Agustín Casasola** chronicled both the Revolution and everyday life in its wake, forming an invaluable record of one of Mexico's more turbulent periods.

Museo de Minería

Mina 110, one block south and two blocks east of the zócalo • Charge • https://archivohistoricoymuseodemineria.org

Pachuca's **Museo de Minería** is of historical importance because it houses the state's mining archives, but from a visitor's point of view, unless you have a particular interest in the history of mining, its exhibition of mineral samples and old mining equipment (picks, helmets, lamps and the odd ore cart) is only mildly diverting.

ARRIVAL AND INFORMATION — PACHUCA

By bus The bus station is about 5km south of the centre. *Colectivos* outside run frequently to Plaza de la Constitución in the town centre.

Destinations Mexico City Nte (every 10min; 2hr); Mexico City airport (13 daily; 2hr); Puebla (20 daily; 2hr); Tula (second class every 15–30min; 2hr 30min; direct every 30–60min; 1hr 15min).

By colectivo *Colectivos* to the bus station ("Centro-Central"; 10min) depart from the northwest corner of Plaza de la Constitución. To Real del Monte (20min) and Mineral del Chico (45min), they depart from one block north of Plaza de la Constitución, at La Raza with Carranza. Note that there is no direct transport between Real del Monte and Mineral del Chico, so you have to come back to Pachuca to get from one to the other, and the last *colectivos* back to Pachuca from both of them leave at around 7pm.

Tourist information There's a small tourist office (daily 8am–6pm; 800 718 2600) in the base of the Reloj Monumental clock tower on the zócalo. The state tourist office has a website at http://hidalgo.travel/wordpress.

ACCOMMODATION

América Victoria 203, a block south of the zocalo; https://hotelamericaweb.com.ar. A very basic option, but not bad for the price and its fairly central location, with rooms arranged around a very orange patio, with bath, TV and some with king-size beds. M$

Ciro's Plaza de Independencia 100, north side of the zocalo; http://hotelciros.com. A very centrally located three-star with a bright orange facade, offering a slightly higher standard of comfort than most Pachuca hotels, but less character. Pleasantly furnished rooms have phone and TV; and those at the front have views over the zócalo. There are often promotional discounts available, and a junior suite doesn't cost much more than a standard room. Breakfast included. M$$

Emily Plaza de Independencia, south side of the zocalo; http://hotelemily.com.mx. This four-star is run by the same firm as *Ciro's* across the zócalo, with the same orange facade, though it's slightly posher, with a restaurant. A junior suite here costs the same as a standard room, and also the same as a junior suite at *Ciro's*, and there are master suites as well. Breakfast included. M$$

Gran Hotel Independencia Plaza Independencia 116, west side of zocalo; 771 715 0515. Grand it ain't, but it is the cheapest option on the plaza, with clean and comfortable rooms, all en suite, as well as a colourful cantina-style bar in the downstairs courtyard. Staff can help with arranging trips in the surrounding area. M$$

★ **Hotel de los Baños** Matamoros 205, east side of the zocalo; http://hoteldelosbanos.com.mx. The most characterful place in town, just off the zócalo, with carpeted rooms, each with TV and bathroom, around a central, enclosed courtyard. For very little more than the standard room prices, you can opt for type "A" doubles with attractively carved wooden furniture, or type "B" where the craftsmanship is decidedly over the top. M$

EATING

Pachuca is known in Mexico for **pastes**, which originated with the Cornish pasties once made by miners working in nearby Real del Monte (see opposite). They still come *tradicional* (or *tipo Inglés*), filled with ground meat, onion, potato and *jalapeños* (for that Mexican twist), as well as with fillings such as chicken *mole* or *refritos*. Though they differ in shape, they're closely related to typical Mexican empanadas, which are usually sold in the same shops and are stuffed with tuna, pineapple or even rice pudding. You'll find bakeries selling *pastes* all over the region.

Alex Steak Glorieta Revolución 102, about 500m south of the zocalo; 771 713 0056. Enormous and beautifully prepared steaks are the speciality here, with most cuts available. The house steak comes with mushroom sauce, and they do a barbecue brunch on Sun in summer. M$$$$

La Gran Titania Guerrero 1000; 771 202 2879. On the northeast corner of the food market where more delights can be found, this rustically styled eatery offers good *carnitas* (non-traditional meats) such as tongue, ribs and *surtido* to get your Mexican juices flowing. Hailed

HIDALGO'S CORNISH CONNECTION

In 1824, a British firm took over the old **silver mines** in Real del Monte, which had first been opened by the Spanish in the mid-sixteenth century. Needing some mining expertise, the British brought over some 350 **Cornish tin miners** to help run the pits, but pulled out in 1848, to be replaced by a Mexican successor firm. Most of the tin miners stayed on, however, and their legacy in Pachuca and Real del Monte lives on too, in the form of some surprisingly authentic **Cornish pasties**, and the introduction of **fútbol** (soccer), which was played for the first time on Mexican soil in Real del Monte. A plaque in the car park at the southern end of Hidalgo marks the spot where that first game was played, and it was this same Cornish community who went on to found Pachuca football club and the Mexican football league (see page 157).

throughout the town as a good hangover-cure spot. M$

Mi Antiguo Café Matamoros 115, east side of the zocalo; 771 107 1837. Good for espressos, croissants, burgers and *antojitos* (such as chicken *fajitas*), with set breakfasts and a lunch-time menu. M$$$

Pastes el Billar Ocampo 100, just off the east side of the zocalo; 771 715 6060. This firm claims to have been the first to sell Cornish pasties in Mexico, and they still do Cornish-style meat and potato *pastes*, as well as chicken *pastes* with red or green *mole*, and rice pudding versions for afters. M$

Presto Pizza e Piú Gómez Pérez 104; https://prestopizza.com.mx. Close to Plaza Juarez, this casual pizzeria serves up authentic Italian flavours, with optional Mexican spice selections on every table. A standard pepperoni pizza is always a safe bet here. M$$

Reforma Matamoros 111, east side of the zócalo. An informal place on the plaza, offering a lunch-time menu and *antojitos* including enchiladas and *chilaquiles* (both with red or green sauce). M$$

Real del Monte

Seventeen kilometres north of Pachuca, draped across pine-clad hills, sits **REAL DEL MONTE** (aka Mineral del Monte), a once very wealthy silver-mining town, and, at over 2700m, a nice retreat from Mexico City. It's a quietly appealing place where you can wander around the well-tended streets, and carefully explore mining relics in the surrounding hills. The town's architecture is largely Spanish colonial, but is given an odd twist by the almost exclusive use of red corrugated-iron roofing, and the existence of Cornish-style cottages with their double-pitched rooflines.

Paste Museum

Av Juarez 114, at the town entrance • Charge • 771 797 1548

Not content with selling the town's signature delicacy at every possible outlet, Real del Monte now boasts the world's only museum dedicated to *pastes*. The highlight of the tour is the making and subsequent consumption of your own creation, filled with either meat and potato, or refried beans for those of a Mexican persuasion. All explanations are in Spanish, including the baffling fifteen-minute video documenting the pasty's exodus from Cornwall to the mountains of central Mexico and the wider world. There's an interesting collection of ovens used to make the baked turnover through the ages. Don't miss the awkward photos of Prince Charles' visit during its 2012 inauguration. The museum is open daily (except Tues), with the last tour at 5.15pm.

The British cemetery

On the edge of town

Many of Real del Monte's original Cornish tin miners (see box below), who were Methodist rather than Catholic, now rest in the British cemetery (**Panteón Inglés**), the visiting of which entails a bit of a climb. You'll need to find the caretaker to open it up, but he should, with luck, be somewhere nearby (and will appreciate a tip for his trouble).

Mina de Acosta

Guerrero, at the northeastern end of town • Charge, photo and video permit fees • https://www.rutadelaplata.org

This old silver mine, now converted into a museum, was in use from 1727 until 1985. The chimney and elevator date from the nineteenth century. Not only can you see all the workings and ore bogeys, but you can even go inside one of the original mining tunnels, with a free guided tour.

ARRIVAL AND INFORMATION — REAL DEL MONTE

By colectivos *Colectivos* from Pachuca will drop you on Hidalgo, which leads down to the main square in the centre of town. The last one back to Pachuca leaves around 7pm from the southern end of Hidalgo.

Tourist office Located in the town hall (Palacio Municipal) just off the main square on Licona Ruiz (771 206 6123), and at weekends there's a stall in the main square. Online information can be found at https://www.gob.mx/sectur/articulos/real-de-monte-hidalgo.

ACCOMMODATION

Los Portales Licona Ruiz 2, on the main square; 771 797 0423. Polished wooden floorboards and wooden furniture add character to the rooms in this wonderful old mansion dating from 1855. The cheapest rooms have views over the main square, and Emperor Maximilan and Empress Carlota are supposed to have stayed here when they visited in 1865. M$$

Real del Monte Iturbide 5, off the main square, behind the church; https://www.realdelmontehotel.mx. A small hotel with old-fashioned rooms, all different, but all with wooden floors, antique-style furniture and heaters to ward off the chilly nights. Some have views over the rooftops on the hillside below. Extra charges Fri & Sat. M$$

EATING AND DRINKING

Bar La Especial Plaza Hidalgo; 771 797 0322. Founded in 1967, this is one of the oldest bars in town, with a history you'll feel the second you stroll through the swinging saloon doors, a friendly cantina with a brass-topped bar and more tequila than you can wave a mescal worm at. Serves up lots of free snacks alongside the drinks and they stay open until the last client stumbles out of the door.

Real de Plateros Hidalgo 56; 771 291 7509. This chain, which you'll see throughout town and in other parts of Hidalgo state, is popular for a reason, producing the best *pastes* (meat and potato), as well as empanadas including cheese and chorizo, and sweet ones such as pineapple, blackcurrant jam or rice pudding. M$$

Restaurante Real del Monte Av Hidalgo 55; http://restauranterealdelmonte.com. One of the few places in town where you can escape the *paste* fever, this friendly and expansive restaurant has a balcony with fantastic views over the town and valley beneath. Does Mexican classics as well as traditional local food. The speciality Is the Molcajete Minero, a mix of steak, sausage, fried cheese and salsa verde served up in a bubbling mortar. Also has an extensive selection of tequilas. M$$$

Mineral del Chico

The scenic village of **Mineral del Chico** is the main base for exploring the **Parque Nacional El Chico** (http://planeta.com/el-chico), which is known for its excellent hiking among beautiful pine forests and rugged rock formations, as well as wildlife including armadillos, grey foxes, eagles, falcons and rattlesnakes. Although there are campsites in the park, most people prefer to stay in the village, which is small (as its name suggests) and picturesque, spreading uphill from its church and main square.

ACCOMMODATION AND EATING — MINERAL DEL CHICO

Gran Compaña Alfonso Corona del Rosal; 771 715 4421. Mineral del Chico's main eating option, doubling up as a bar when the tourists are in town. New York strip is among the various steak options on offer, along with chicken and fish dishes. M$$$

El Paraíso 1km from the village centre on the road to Pachuca; https://www.hotelelparaiso.mx. A beautiful location among verdant woodland, surrounded by mountains with well-kept gardens and fresh, modern rooms in chalet-style buildings. Expect to pay extra on Fri & Sat. M$$$

Posada del Amanencer Morelos 7; http://www.posadadelamanecer.com. Welcoming accommodation in the centre of the village. All rooms are carpeted and come with big TVs, fireplaces and wi-fi. There's also a good restaurant. M$$

FOOTBALL IN MEXICO

As in much of Latin America, **fútbol** in Mexico is a national addiction, if not an obsession. Turn on the TV and often as not you'll find a match. If you can get to see a live game, it's a different experience entirely. For **up-to-date information** on Mexican league teams, fixtures and tables, visit http://futbolmexicano.com.

ORIGINS

Football was introduced to Mexico in the nineteenth century by Cornish miners in Real del Monte, Hidalgo (see page 155), and it was in that state, by descendants of those same Cornishmen, that Mexico's first football club, Pachuca, was founded in 1901. The football **league** was created six years later.

THE LEAGUE TABLE

Mexico's football league follows a complicated ladder system: the first division is divided into three tables of six teams each, which are decided by the previous season's placings, with the league champions placed first in table one, second placed top of table two and so on. The top two teams of each table compete in a play-off for the league championship.

There are two **seasons** a year: Apertura (Aug–Nov) and Clausura (Jan–June). At the end of the Clausura season, the two seasons' winners (if they are different) compete to decide that year's champion of champions.

Relegation to a lower division is decided over a two-season (yearly) loss average, so it is, in fact, technically possible to come first in the league and be relegated in the same season. However, relegation need not be the disaster that it might seem. Take, for example, Puebla C.F., who, when relegated in 1999, simply bought the team promoted from Primera B (Curtodores), changed their name to Puebla and relocated them, which is perfectly legal under Mexican financial regulations. Similarly, there are no regulations preventing anyone from owning more than one team, which can lead to a clash of interests that are never more than speculated upon; suspicion of corruption is rife but rarely, if ever, investigated.

WATCHING A GAME

Matches are always exciting and enjoyed by even the most diehard "anti-futbolistas". Music, dancing and, of course, the ubiquitous **Mexican Wave** make for a carnival atmosphere, enhanced by spectators dressing up and wearing face paint. They're usually very much family affairs, with official salespeople bringing soft drinks, beer and various types of food at fixed prices to your seat. **Stadiums** tend to be mostly concrete, with sitting room only, and can sometimes be dangerously overcrowded, though accidents are thankfully rare.

The bigger clubs are those of Mexico City (América, Cruz Azul, Pumas – the national university side – Necaxa and Atlante) and Guadalajara (Chivas, Atlas and Tecos), and the games between any of these can draw crowds of up to eighty thousand, while smaller clubs like those of Puebla, Irapuato and Celaya may get no more than ten thousand or fifteen thousand spectators per game. The vast distances between clubs make travelling to away games impossible for many fans, one reason why smaller, more out-of-the-way clubs don't get as much support. Opposing fans aren't generally separated, but an atmosphere of self-policing prevails – making it an ideal family occasion. The greatest risk is often to the referee, who is frequently escorted from the pitch by armed riot police.

For **national games** the whole country is united, and football has many times been shown to rise above partisan politics. In 1999, despite being outlawed by the government, the EZLN football squad even played an exhibition match against the national side in Mexico City's Estadio Azteca.

★ **La Trucha Grilla** Alfonso Corona del Rosal; 771 7123 4394. The enormous metal trout suspended over the entrance and the fantastic smells coming out of the open kitchen as you walk in shouldn't leave you in much doubt as to what the house speciality is here. The fresh local fish are prepared a number of different ways, all using local herbs and spices. Also does steak, chicken and vegetarian options. The owners actually head up the local tourism board and are on hand with ready advice. M$$

East of Mexico City

East of Mexico City, and among the destinations reached from its TAPO bus terminal, is the region's second-largest city, the thriving and ultra-colonial **Puebla**. This city not only warrants a couple of days of your time in its own right, but makes an excellent base for forays north to more tranquil **Tlaxcala**, and west to **Cholula** with its enormous ruined pyramid. Both were important tributary states of the Aztecs when Cortés marched this way from the coast to pillage and conquer in the name of European civilization. Puebla and Cholula also offer excellent views of central Mexico's twin volcanoes, **Popocatépetl** and **Ixtaccíhuatl**, although the former is continually off-limits due to the continuing threat of eruption.

Tlaxcala

Allied to Cortés in his struggle against the Aztecs, as well as with colonial Spain in the War of Independence, **TLAXCALA**, the capital of a tiny state of the same name, has become a byword for treachery. Because of its alliance with Cortés, the town suffered a very different fate from that of nearby Cholula, which aligned itself with the Aztecs (see page 168), and in the long run this has led to the disappearance of its ancient culture. The Spaniards founded a colonial town here – now restored and very beautiful in much of its original colonial glory, but whether because of its traitorous reputation or simply its isolation, development in Tlaxcala has been limited.

The town lies 125km east of Mexico City and 40km north of Puebla in the middle of a fertile, prosperous-looking upland plain surrounded by rather bare mountains. It's an exceptionally pretty and much rehabilitated colonial town, comfortable enough but also fairly dull. Most of the interest lies very close to the zócalo, with its cluster of banks, post office and central bandstand, where the terracotta and ochre tones of the buildings lend the city its tag of "Ciudad Roja", the Red City.

Palacio de Gobierno

North side of the zócalo • Free • https://www.tlaxcala.gob.mx

The entire north side of the zócalo is taken up by the **Palacio de Gobierno**, whose patterned brick facade is broken by ornate windows and doorways. The building

incorporates parts of a much earlier structure, erected soon after the Conquest, and inside boasts a series of brilliantly coloured **murals** by local artist Desiderio Hernandez Xochitiotzin, who took nearly fifty years to complete them. The panels depict the history of the Tlaxcalan people from their migration from the north to their alliance with Cortés. The two most spectacular are one on the stairs depicting the Spanish Conquest and another at the bottom showing the Great Market. Visitors should enter via the easternmost door.

Parroquia de San José

1 de Mayo 4 • Free

The tiled facade of the **Parroquia de San José** dominates a small square off the side of the zócalo. It's an attractive building, but except for two fonts beside the door depicting Camaxtli, the Tlaxcalan god of hunting and war, the inside is a disappointment. Note the seventeenth-century painting beside the altar that depicts the baptism of a Tlaxcalan chief, as overseen by Cortés and his mistress, La Malinche.

Museo de Artes y Tradiciones Populares

Sanchez 1 at cnr 1 de Mayo, three blocks west of the zócalo • Charge • 246 462 5704

Tlaxcala's third museum is the **Museo de Artes y Tradiciones Populares**. It focuses on traditional crafts and customs, with sections on bell making (including an example cast on the site) and a fascinating room on the manufacture and consumption of *pulque*.

Museo de la Memoria

Independencia 3 (on Plaza Xicohténcatl) • Charge • 246 466 0792

Directly south of the zócalo is a smaller square, Plaza Xicohténcatl, where you'll find the **Museo de la Memoria**, a modern museum devoted to the cultural history of the region. Its imaginative displays (some interactive) – illustrating pre-Hispanic *tianguis* (markets), Franciscan life under the Spaniards and the ruling hierarchy in Tlaxcala before and after Cortés – make up for the fact that it's light on artefacts.

Museo Regional de Tlaxcala

Calzada ex-Convento San Francisco • Charge • 246 462 0262

At the southeastern corner of Plaza Xicohténcatl, a broad, tree-lined path leads up to a triple set of arches. Beyond them, an open area overlooking the city's pretty nineteenth-century bullring is flanked on one side by the ex-Convento de San Francisco, started in 1537. Wrapped around the convent's cloister, the **Museo Regional de Tlaxcala** covers local life from prehistoric times to the present day – an unexceptional collection, but well displayed, in a series of whitewashed rooms.

Catedral de Nuestra Señora de la Asunción

Calzada ex-Convento San Francisco, next door to the Museo Regional • Free • 246 462 1511

The **Catedral de Nuestra Señora de la Asunción** is relatively plain, though it has a beautiful vaulted wooden ceiling decorated in Mudéjar style, with a strong Moorish influence, as was then common in southern Spain. The Moors were expelled from Spain in 1492, and though their influence continued for some decades, it is only apparent in Mexican churches started immediately after the Conquest. One large chapel, more richly decorated than the rest, contains the font in which Xicohténcatl and other Tlaxcalan leaders were baptized in the presence of Hernán Cortés in 1520.

The open chapel

At the end of Calle Capilla Abierta (a continuation of Guerrero) • Open access

Opposite Museo Regional and the Catedral de Nuestra Señora de la Asunción, steps lead down to the **open chapel** (*capilla abierta*). Open chapels – in the open air, that is, rather than inside a church – are a particularly Mexican religious structure, typical of the very early colonial period, and this one, built in 1537, is no exception. Like most open chapels, it has three arches, but the ones here are unusual for being pointed. The lower walls bear traces of ancient frescoes.

Santuario de Ocotlán

Hidalgo 1, Ocotlán, 1km east of the zócalo, walking one block north on Juárez, then right onto Guridi y Alcocer until it forks, bearing left onto the very steep Calzada de Agua Santa, past the Pocito chapel • Free

The twin wedding-cake towers of the **Santuario de Ocotlán** overlook the town from a hill to the east, which gives great views over the surrounding countryside. The church's facade is a riot of churrigueresque excess that ranks it alongside those at Tepotzotlán and Taxco, and it's no less florid inside. The huge Baroque *retablo* seems to spread seamlessly to the dome and along the transept in a frenzy of gilt woodwork, an exuberance justified by the miraculous work of the church's Virgin.

According to legend, she appeared to a poor Indigenous person in 1541 with instructions to cure an epidemic with waters from a stream that had miraculously sprung forth. Naturally everyone recovered. Then the Virgin asked the person to bring the local Franciscan monks to a forest. Once they were there, fire suddenly burst forth, but though the flames were fierce, they didn't burn the trees. The next day the monks returned, to find that one pine tree (*ocotlán*) contained a wooden image of the Virgin. Now installed on the altar, it is carved and painted very much in the style of the times. The life of Our Lady of Ocotlán is portrayed around the eight walls of the ornate **Camarín de la Virgen** (the Virgin's Dressing Room) behind the altar. In May, the church and surrounding streets host the procession of the Virgin, attended by thousands of pilgrims.

ARRIVAL AND DEPARTURE — TLAXCALA

By bus The bus station is southwest of the centre on Josefa Castelar. *Colectivos* parked outside the bus station run to nearby villages and the zócalo, though it's only a 10min walk: exit the bus station and turn right downhill to the next main junction, then take a right down Guerrero for five blocks and left down Juárez. To return to the bus station, go back the way you came, or, for a short cut, climb the stairs at the southern end of Mariano Sanchez (Escalinata de los Héroes), or take a *colectivo* from 20 Noviembre at Lardizábal. At the same spot, you'll also find frequent but slow second-class buses to Puebla (1hr).

Destinations Mexico City TAPO (every 30min; 1hr 45min); Pachuca (14 daily; 3hr); Puebla (every 20min; 40min).

INFORMATION

Banks Banorte, on the zócalo at Plaza de la Constitución 10, is the most central bank with exchange facilities and an ATM, but there are others along Independencia.

Internet Lorena, Porfirio Díaz 13 (Mon–Sat 8am–9pm, Sun 10am–6pm; charge).

Post office Plaza de la Constitución 20, east side of the zócalo (Mon–Fri 8am–7pm, Sat 8am–3pm).

Tourist office Juárez and Lardizábal, behind the Palacio de Gobierno (Mon–Fri 8.30am–7pm, Sat & Sun 10am–7pm; 246 462 0109). The state tourist office's website is at http://turismotlaxcala.com.

ACCOMMODATION

SEE MAP PAGE 158

Hotel Alifer Morelos 11, near the junction with Xicohténcatl; http://hotelalifer.com.mx. This is the nearest you'll get to low-cost accommodation in Tlaxcala, and it's pretty good value. The rooms are all carpeted, with TV, and there's parking, wi-fi and a bar-restaurant. M$$

Hotel Misión San Francisco Plaza de la Constitución 17, southern side of the zocalo; https://www.bookonline.com/hotel/hotel-san-francisco-tlaxcala. A beautiful sixteenth-century building, with some original features, though largely rebuilt in the nineteenth century. The rooms are all modern, but if you want one with period features in the oldest part of the hotel, ask for one in the *zona antigua*. The lobby has an amazing stained-glass ceiling, and a cosy little bar just off it. Breakfast included. M$$$

Posada la Casona de Cortés Lardizábal 6; http://lacasonadecortes.com.mx. A beautiful and very good-value little hotel, with a variety of rooms of different shapes and sizes around a pretty patio garden. M$$

EATING

SEE MAP PAGE 158

Casa de los Magueyes Plaza Xicohtencatl 7; 246 462 7309. A cosy restaurant with outdoor seating, serving all varieties of coffee, cheesecake, a good spread at breakfast pastry and a vast menu for lunch and dinner. M$$

Indomable Café Plaza de la Constitución 8, east side of the zocalo; 246 498 1143. Top notch coffee, and also freshly baked goods, with muffins, pastries and more. Be sure to ask the server what the coffee of the day is for the best deal. M$

Los Portales Plaza de la Constitución 8, east side of the zocalo; 246 462 5419. A broad range of *antojitos*, burgers, salads, pasta dishes and the delicious *sopa tlaxcalteca*, made from black beans, tortilla chips, cheese, avocado and *chicharrón* (pork crackling). M$$

Restaurante La Casona de Tlaxcala Jose de Morelos and Priv. Morelos; 246 462 9673. A pleasant eating space, with tiled floor and polished wooden tables, offering breakfasts (till noon) and good-value set menus. M$$

DRINKING AND NIGHTLIFE

SEE MAP PAGE 158

Liverpub Plaza de la Constitución 11, on the west side of Plaza Xicohténcatl; 246 144 5622. A convivial gastropub where you can sink a few *chelas* (beers) while playing pool and watching the game.

Pulquería la Tia Yola Plaza Xicohténcatl, southeast corner; 246 462 7309. This jolly little *pulquería* was opened with the specific aim of reviving the art of *pulque*-making (not to mention *pulque*-drinking), and claims to have the state's best, available in several fruit flavours.

Revolución Plaza de la Constitución 9 (upstairs); 246 466 1637. Overlooking the zócalo above *Los Portales*, this low-ceilinged, stone-walled music bar gets quite lively after 8pm, when there are live bands performing most nights.

Cacaxtla, Xochitécatl and Tizatlán

Some 23km southwest of Tlaxcala **Cacaxtla and Xochitécatl** • Charge • 246 462 9375 **Tizatlán** • Charge • Cacaxtla can be reached by frequent *colectivo* ("San Miguel del Milagro") from Mariano Sanchez and Lardizábal in Tlaxcala (40min); from Puebla, buses serve the village of Nativitas, 5km away

A particularly fine series of murals depicting battle scenes was discovered in 1975 at the ancient site of **Cacaxtla.** They are clearly Maya in style, which would seem to indicate trade or perhaps even a Maya settlement here. Two kilometres west of Cacaxtla, the ruins of **Xochitécatl** have three impressive pyramids and monolithic stones, but it isn't served by public transport. The rather less impressive archeological site of **Tizatlán**, 4km north of town, can be reached by *colectivo* from Lardizábal and 20 de Noviembre.

Puebla

The elegant colonial city of **PUEBLA**, the republic's fifth-largest city (after Mexico City, Guadalajara, Monterrey and Tijuana), is an easy forty-minute trip from Tlaxcala, or a couple of hours by bus from Mexico City – with glorious views of the snowy heights of Popocatépetl and Ixtaccíhuatl on the way. Known for its fine cuisine, Puebla has a remarkable concentration of sights – a fabulous **cathedral**, a "hidden" **convent**, museums and colonial **mansions** – while the mountainous surrounding country is in

CINCO DE MAYO

Military defeat seems to play a larger part in Puebla's history than it does in most of Mexico – the city fell to the Americans in 1847 and to the French in 1863 – but that isn't what's remembered. Rather, what's remembered and commemorated here is the greatest victory in the country's history, at the **Battle of Puebla** in 1862, when a force of some two thousand Mexicans defeated a French army three times its size. The French were trying to make the Austrian prince Maximilian emperor of Mexico, but when they tried to occupy Puebla, Mexican troops based in the two forts on the Cerro de Guadalupe (the Fuerte de Loreto and the Fuerte de Guadalupe; see pages 165 and 166) beat them off, forcing them to withdraw back towards their base at Veracruz and putting a serious dent into French plans. To this day, Puebla commemorates May 5 (**Cinco de Mayo**) with a massive fiesta, and there's a public holiday throughout the country.

places startlingly beautiful. The city centre and Cerro de Guadalupe, where all these sights are to be found, form quite a compact area, easy to get around, and you can see the best of the city and nearby **Cholula** in a couple of leisurely days, or even – at a brisk trot – in one packed day.

Brief history

The city was founded by the Spaniards in 1531, preferring it to the ancient sites of Cholula and Tlaxcala possibly because the memories of Indigenous power there remained too strong. It rapidly assumed great importance as a staging point on the journey from the capital to the port at Veracruz and for the shipment of goods from Spain's Far Eastern colonies, which were delivered to Acapulco and transported across Mexico from there. Wealth was brought, too, by the reputation of Puebla's ceramics, particularly its tiles. This industry – still very much in evidence – was helped by an abundance of good clays in the region, and by settlers from Talavera in Spain, who brought traditional ceramic skills with them. The city did well out of colonial rule, and, perhaps not surprisingly, it took the wrong side in the War of Independence. As a result, it preserves a reputation for conservatism and traditional values, not dispelled even by the fact that the start of the Revolution is generally dated from the assassination of Aquiles Serdán in his Puebla home.

The zócalo

Puebla's **zócalo** is one of the country's prettiest, with trees, grass, benches and a large fountain, lined on three sides with arcades, the perfect spot to imbibe a dose of fine caffeine while watching the comings and goings in the square. Beautiful colonial

buildings, such as the **Palacio Municipal** (town hall) on the north side, give the square a lovely Baroque feel. The zócalo is also the centre for the numbering system of Puebla's ancient grid of streets, the lowest numbers indicating streets nearest to the square.

The cathedral

South side of zócalo • Free

The zócalo's south side is dominated by the great looming **cathedral**, the second largest in the republic. Built between 1562 and the middle of the following century, the exterior is ugly and grey, but the inside improves considerably, with amazing ornamentation in onyx, marble and gilt, and a wonderful altar designed by Manuel Tolsá in 1797. The cathedral, and particularly the tower, was partly funded by Bishop Juan de Palafox y Mendoza, an illegitimate son of a Spanish nobleman who grew up with his poor mother but inherited his father's fortune.

The Archbishop's Palace

5 Oriente 5, behind the cathedral • **Biblioteca Palafoxiana** • Charge • **Casa de la Cultura** • Free • 222 246 6922

The old **Archbishop's Palace** was converted to a library in the seventeenth century – the Biblioteca Palafoxiana, reputed to be the oldest library in the Americas – and houses the original collection of ancient books and manuscripts on its upper floor. Downstairs there's the **Casa de la Cultura**, which hosts regular exhibitions of local arts and crafts.

Museo Amparo

2 Sur 708 at 9 Ote • Charge, free Mon • http://museoamparo.com

The undoubted star in Puebla's museum firmament is the modern **Museo Amparo**, which concentrates on art from pre-Hispanic Mesoamerica, with additional material from the colonial and more recent eras. Set in a pair of modernized colonial buildings with peaceful courtyards and piped classical music, the collection is the legacy of philanthropist Manuel Espinosa Iglesias, who set up the Amparo Foundation in honour of his wife. Everything in the museum is thoroughly documented at strategically located computer consoles.

The historical significance of the pieces isn't glossed over, but the focus is firmly on aesthetics, with well-presented cases displaying artefacts to their best advantage. To set the tone, the entrance features an impressive glass replica of a **tzompantli skull-wall** with alternating Olmec and Totonac heads in each of the glass blocks. A room decorated with reproduction **cave paintings** from Altamira in Spain, Arnhemland in Australia, Utah, Norway and Baja California puts Mexico's cultural development into some sort of context.

The main collection

Though far smaller than that in Mexico City's anthropology museum, the main collection is well chosen and a good deal more manageable. It is particularly strong on the Olmecs, a people who greatly influenced life around Puebla and left behind some strikingly beautiful pieces such as the half-metre-wide stone head on display here. Elsewhere notice the exquisite Colima jaguar, the beautiful carved conch shell from the Gulf coast and the sculpture of a kneeling woman from Nayarit with her distinctive face and body painting. The museum is open daily except Tuesday with guided tours (Spanish only) available on Sundays.

La Estrella de Puebla

Osa Mayor 2520 • Charge (extra for VIP booth) • 222 223 6430

One of North America's largest Ferris wheels is also one of Puebla's most modern attractions, and particularly worth the ride on clear days when the enormous masses of Popcatépetl and Iztacchíhuatl are visible at the fringes of the city. The ride lasts around twenty minutes and takes you up to altitudes of 80m. For those less keen on heights the area is surrounded by various restaurants, bars and a brand-new shopping mall with original Botero artwork throughout.

Museo Regional de la Revolución Mexicana

6 Ote 206 • Charge, free Tues • 222 242 1076

2

The devotional **Museo Regional de la Revolución Mexicana** records the struggles for Liberalism of the Serdán family against the dictatorship of Porfirio Díaz. The assassination of Aquiles Serdán in this house was one of the most important steps in the fall of Díaz: the date of Serdán's death, November 18, 1910, is – in the absence of any firmer indicators – generally recognized as marking the start of the Revolution. The bullet holes in the house have been lovingly preserved, and a huge smashed mirror still hangs on the wall where it appears in contemporary photos of the carnage. Revolution buffs will also enjoy the biographies of key figures in the struggle, photos of the ragtag bands of wide-hatted revolutionaries with their bandoleers, and the trap door in the floor under which Serdán spent several fruitless hours trying to avoid his eventual end.

Mercado Victoria and around

3 Nte between 4 and 8 Pte

The impressive glass-and-iron **Mercado Victoria** was once Puebla's main market, but is now a rather sanitized shopping centre. East of the market, candy stores along 6 Oriente sell **camotes**, gooey fingers of sweet potato and sugar flavoured with various fruits, which are a local speciality. If you're thinking of buying any to take home, however, note that they only last a couple of weeks.

Church of Santo Domingo

5 de Mayo between 4 and 8 Pte, and opposite 6 Ote • Free

Head north from the zócalo along 5 de Mayo and you'll reach the church of **Santo Domingo**, which is directly to the east of the Mercado Victoria. The church's main chapel, the **Capilla del Rosario**, is – even in comparison with the cathedral – a quite unbelievably lavish orgy of gold leaf and Baroque excess; a constant hushed, shuffling stream of devotees lights candles and prays to the image of the Virgin.

Museo José Luis Bello y Zetina

5 de Mayo 408, three doors north of the church of Santo Domingo • Free • http://museobello.org

The **Museo José Luis Bello y Zetina** displays the paintings and furniture of the wealthy Bello family, who lived here during the nineteenth century – you'll see everything from seventeenth-century Flemish masters to a Napoleonic bedroom suite. It somehow seems too comfortless to be a home yet not formal enough for a museum, though the enthusiasm of your personal guide (whose services are free but not compulsory) may rub off.

Taller Uriarte

4 Pte 911 at 9 Nte • Tours every 30min, Mon–Fri • Free entry; charge for tours • http://uriartetalavera.com.mx

The **Taller Uriarte** is about the best known of Puebla's pottery factories. It's a small-scale affair shoehorned into what appears to be just another urban house, but it's well set up for visitors. You can see every stage of the pottery-making process, from forming the plates and bowls to painting the intricate designs in paints whose colours are completely transformed during firing into distinctive blues and yellows. And of course you can buy examples of the pottery afterwards.

Ex-Convento de Santa Rosa

3 Nte 1203 • Free • 222 232 7792

The **ex-Convento de Santa Rosa's** main claim to fame is that the great *mole poblano* was invented here in its wonderful yellow-tiled kitchens. The kitchens are the highlight of a guided tour that includes rooms full of crafts from around the state of Puebla.

Museo Religioso Santa Mónica

18 Pte 103 at 5 de Mayo, nine blocks north of the zócalo • 222 232 0178

The city's remarkable convent now operates as the **Museo Religioso Santa Mónica**. Here, from the suppression of the church in 1857 until their discovery in 1934, several generations of nuns lived hidden from the public gaze behind a smokescreen of secret doors and concealed passages. Just how secret they were is a matter of some debate – many claim that the authorities simply turned a blind eye – and certainly several lay families were actively supportive, providing supplies and new recruits. But it makes a good story, embellished by the conversion of the building into a museum that preserves the secret entrances along with many religious artworks and a beautiful seventeenth-century cloister. Several simple cells are also in evidence, and from the hidden chapel you can look down through a screen at the still-operating church next door.

Cerro de Guadalupe

2km northwest of the city centre • *Colectivo* #72 (sometimes marked "Centro Cívico") from Héroes del 5 de Mayo, three blocks east of the zócalo

Crowning the **Cerro de Guadalupe**, the site of numerous nineteenth-century battles and sieges, is the **Centro Cívico 5 de Mayo**, a collection of museums. Neither of the two forts nor any of the museums here is a match for sights downtown, but they are a decent place to spend a couple of hours away from the fumes and the noise of the centre.

Fuerte de Loreto

Charge, free Sun

Your first stop on the Cerro de Guadalupe should be the **Fuerte de Loreto**, a fort whose moat and high walls protect a large empty parade ground and a small church containing the **Museo de la No Intervención**. This focuses on the events surrounding the 1862 Battle of Puebla, celebrated on 5 May (Cinco de Mayo; see page 161), and records 150 years of the defence of the republic through replicated battle scenes. The views of Popo and Ixta from the battlements are some of the best in Puebla.

Museo Regional de Puebla

Charge, free Sun

The best of the rest of the sights on the Cerro de Guadalupe is the modern **Museo Regional de Puebla**, largely devoted to the state's archeology and ethnology. There's some exquisite Olmec jade sculpture and sculptural pieces along with a 4m-high polychrome statue of San Cristóbal from the seventeenth century and sections of wider relevance, such as a detailed explanation of native migration from east Asia through Alaska.

Museo Interactivo Imagina

Charge, extra for some exhibits

Across the way from the Museo Regional, the modern **Museo Interactivo Imagina** is a collection of educational interactive games and exhibits aimed largely at children, its main theme being a scientific understanding of the world. It kicks off with a look at the human body and its place in evolution, followed by technology (with lots of machines to play with), the physical world, art and finally a taxidermic exhibition of animals from different parts of the world. Unfortunately, all explanations are in Spanish.

Planetarium

Charge

Next door to the Museo Interactivo, Puebla's **planetarium** is state-of-the-art, with an IMAX screen and impressive explanatory films about the cosmos, with digital projection and three shows a day. Commentary is in Spanish, but that won't stop you being gobsmacked by the photography and special effects.

Fuerte de Guadalupe

Charge, free Sun

The highest point on the hill is occupied by the **Fuerte de Guadalupe**, the meagre but well-tended remains of a nineteenth-century fort. Along with the Fuerte de Loreto, to which it was connected by a trench, the fort played a crucial part in the 5 May 1862 Battle of Puebla (see page 161). For all the sense of history, however, all that remains of the fort now are just a few arches and roofless rooms.

ARRIVAL AND DEPARTURE — PUEBLA

By plane Puebla's airport (officially Aeropuerto Hermanos Serdán, though of course nobody really calls it that) is near the village of Huejotzingo, 25km northwest of Puebla and 7km northwest of Cholula (227 102 5080). Buses, minibuses and authorized taxis connect it to CAPU and central Puebla and Cholula.

Destinations Cancún (1 daily; 2hr 5min); Guadalajara (4 weekly; 1hr 10min); Monterrey (6 weekly; 1hr 25min); Tijuana (1 daily; 3hr 55min).

By bus Puebla's bus station, known by the acronym CAPU (Central de Autobuses de Puebla 222 249 7211, http://capu.com.mx), is 5km northwest of the city centre. Buses into town run from outside the station; going the other way they can be picked up on 9 Sur or Nte. There are also authorized taxis to the centre (these cost extra between 10pm and 6am). CAPU has a guardería (baggage deposit), ATMs and a bureau de change. Tlaxcala is also served, more conveniently by buses from the Flecha Azul terminal on 10 Pte between 11 Nte and 13 Nte, by the railway museum (every 5–10min; 1hr).

Destinations Cholula (every 15–25min; 20min); Cuernavaca (hourly; 3hr 30min); Mexico City TAPO (12–16 hourly; 2hr); Mexico City Nte (hourly; 2hr), Mexico City airport (hourly; 3hr); Oaxaca (18 daily; 4hr 30min); Pachuca (20 daily; 2hr); Tlaxcala (every 15min; 1hr); Veracruz (28 daily; 4hr 30min).

By combi Cholula is served by frequent *combis* from 14 Pte at 11 Nte, saving you the need to trek out to CAPU.

INFORMATION AND TOURS

Municipal tourist office Palafox y Mendoza 14, on the north side of the zócalo (daily 9am–8pm; 222 309 4300, https://www.visitpuebla.mx/es). Has free maps and information about the city and runs a tourist information kiosk on the south side of the square (Mon–Fri 10am–5.30pm).

State tourist office 5 Ote 3, near the corner of 16 de Septiembre (Mon–Sat 8am–8pm, Sun 9am–2pm; 222 777 1519, toll-free from outside the state 01 800 326 8656), with information about Puebla and the region.

City tours Túribus (222 226 7289) runs a 90min sightseeing tour (hourly 10am–6pm; charge) from the west side of the zócalo.

ACCOMMODATION — SEE MAP PAGE 162

Colonial de Puebla 4 Sur 105; http://colonial.com.mx. Luxurious lodgings in a beautiful colonial building next to the Autonomous University of Puebla. All rooms have TV and phone, and many have beautifully tiled bathrooms. There's also a fine restaurant on site. M$$$

Hostal de Santo Domingo 4 Pte 312; 55 8920 2780. More like a budget hotel than a hostel, but still backpacker-oriented and very friendly. The ten-bed dorms (including one for women only, for M$20 extra) each have their own bathrooms, and the private rooms are spacious and mostly en suite. Breakfast included. Dorms and doubles available. M$

Hotel Aristos Puebla Reforma 533; https://hotelesaristos.com. Good value and one of the best mid-market options – this small hotel has a small pool and dated (but clean) decor. M$$

Palace 2 Ote 13; http://hotelpalacepuebla.com. Good-value, modern three-star hotel just one block off the zócalo. The lobby area and restaurant are pretty busy, and the rooms aren't huge, but they're clean and fresh, with TV, fan and good bathrooms. M$$

Reforma 2000 4 Pte 916, corner of 11 Nte; http://hotelreforma2000.com. Handy for the bars in the Zona Esmeralda, as well as for transport to CAPU, Cholula and Tlaxcala, this well-priced little hotel has spacious, carpeted rooms with TV and phone, its own lively bar and restaurant, and parking facilities. M$$

Regio 5 Mayo 1004; 222 232 4774. Rock-bottom prices, and basic, yes, but very far from being the worst accommodation in town. The staff aren't always close to the phone so reserving ahead can be a hassle, although they nearly always have space for walk-ins. It's friendly, decent, housed in a nice old colonial building, and has its own slightly shabby charm. It's worth paying M$40 extra for en suite. M$

★ **Sacristía de la Compañía** 6 Sur 304; http://mesones-sacristia.com. Gorgeous hotel in a two-hundred-year-old house with just nine spacious junior and master suites, each one different, but all with wooden beams and elegantly decorated with antiques. The restaurant is excellent (see below), and they even offer cookery classes. Breakfast included. Junior suites and master suites available. M$$$$

EATING

SEE MAP PAGE 162

2

While in town you should definitely check out the **local specialities**, particularly **mole poblano**, an extraordinary sauce made from chocolate, chiles and any number of herbs and spices. Typically served over chicken, turkey or enchiladas, Puebla's is the original, where it was supposedly invented in colonial times for the viceroy's visit to the Convento de Santa Rosa. Another taste sensation is **chiles en nogada**, a dish reputedly concocted in 1821 to celebrate Mexican Independence and made to resemble the colours of the Mexican flag; it's usually served July–Sept.

CAFÉS AND CHEAP EATS

Café Aguirre 5 de Mayo 4; 222 956 2771. Predictable and reliable café-restaurant that's a long-standing local favourite and is always popular with businesspeople. Their speciality is *chilaquiles*, but they also do a good-value lunch-time menu. M$$

Caldos Angelita 9 Nte 607 and cnr 6 Pte; https://caldosangelita.com. A popular no-nonsense diner doling out hearty bowlfuls of wonderful chicken broth and excellent *mole poblano*, but be warned that the food often runs out before closing time. M$

Italian Coffee Company Reforma 121; http://italiancoffee.com. Teas, infusions, flavoured espresso coffees and cakes in convivial surroundings. Other branches around town include one at 4 Ote 202, one at 16 Septiembre opposite the cathedral and two more in the zócalo – in fact, they now have branches nationwide, and in the US too, but they started here in Puebla. M$

La Mexicana Av 3 Pte 316; 221 357 3042. Basic but reliable restaurant serving a wide range of traditional Mexican dishes. Cheap and pricier menus are available at lunch time. M$$

La Zanahoria 5 Ote 206; http://lazanahoria.mx. A bustling vegetarian café and restaurant in Mexican style, with a vast array of wholesome herbivorous choices. Soya burgers and salads are good value, though no match for the buffet (cheaper at weekends), or the *menu del día*. M$$

RESTAURANTS

Fonda de Santa Clara 3 Pte 307, a couple of blocks northwest of the zocalo; http://fondadesantaclara.com. Best-known – and most touristy – restaurant in town, serving local food with an upmarket twist (*pollo al mole poblano*, enchiladas in three different *mole* sauces) in a pretty room decorated with Mexican art, but service is often slow, and the food can be hit or miss. There's a second branch at 3 Pte 920. M$$$

Sacristía de la Compañía 6 Sur 304; http://mesones-sacristia.com. Come here for fine dining in this superb hotel's lovely enclosed courtyard. Efficient, friendly service and a good wine list make this one of Puebla's best dining experiences. Try the house *mole*, preceded by their special soup made with fried tortilla chips, *chicharrón*, cheese and chipotle. This spot also has a great bar at the back for a pre- or post-dinner drink. M$$$

DRINKING AND NIGHTLIFE

SEE MAP PAGE 162

Central Puebla is mostly quiet at night and to find any **bars** you'll have to head a few blocks south to the **Plazuela de los Sapos**, beside the enormous Estrella de Puebla Ferris wheel (see page 163) near 6 Sur and 5 Pte, where several lively drinking holes face each other across a small square. On Thurs, Fri and Sat nights in particular, you might also head around six long blocks west of the zócalo to the Zona Esmeralda, where there's a string of bars and clubs to keep you going. Otherwise, many people head out to **Cholula** to join the lively, student-heavy crowd there, though you'll have to be prepared for a fairly expensive taxi ride back: buses stop running at around 11pm, just when the clubs start warming up.

La Boveda 6 Sur 503; 222 246 7555. The most happening among a handful of bars on the Plazuela de los Sapos that pump out Latin and US pop hits. It has live music most nights from 8pm.

Breve Espacio Puebla Calle 7 Nte. 8; 222 480 9536. One part bar, one part performance space and several parts tequila, this venue makes for an odd but fun evening out. Just don't make the mistake of calling this place a theatre or nightclub to anyone who works there.

Kabana Juárez 1305; 222 162 4891. Lively bar and grill west of the town centre in the Zona Esmeralda (Juárez is a continuation of 7 Pte west of the Paseo Bravo) with friendly staff, super attentive service and no cover charge when there's live music.

Paulaner Keller Av. Juarez 1501 A; 222 232 3496. If you were to fuse a German beer hall with a salsa dance studio, the result would be *Paulaner Keller*. It's near impossible not to have a good time here; just don't take your surroundings too seriously.

DIRECTORY

Banks and exchange Banamex, at Reforma 135 (between 3 Nte and 5 de Mayo), is among the banks near the zócalo which change money and have ATMs. There's a *casa de cambio* in the arcade between the north side of the zócalo and 2 Ote, and one at CAPU.

Internet CyberByte, 2 Sur 505 (daily 9am–midnight; charge); Cyber Space, 2 Sur 701 (Mon–Sat 9am–9.30pm, Sun 10am–8.30pm; charge).

Post office The main post office, at 16 de Septiembre and 5 Ote, has an efficient Lista de Correos; there's also a branch office at 2 Ote 411.

2

Cholula

Puebla's expansion in recent years has made **Cholula**, 15km to the west, virtually a suburb. Nonetheless, it retains its small-town charm and has one abiding reason to visit: the **ruins of Cholula**. A rival of Teotihuacán at its height, and the most powerful city in the country between the fall of Teotihuacán and the rise of Tula, Cholula was, at the time of the Conquest, a vast city of some four hundred temples, famed as a shrine to Quetzalcoatl and for the excellence of its pottery (a trade dominated by immigrant Mixtecs). But it paid dearly for an attempt, inspired by its Aztec allies, to ambush Cortés on his march to Tenochtitlán: the chieftains were slaughtered, their temples destroyed and churches built in their place. The Spaniards claimed to have constructed 365 churches here, one for each day of the year. Although there are a lot of churches, the true figure certainly doesn't live up to the claim. There may well be 365 chapels within the churches, though, which is already a few hundred more than the village population could reasonably need.

Pirámide Tepanapa

Between San Andrés, 6 Sur, 6 Pte and 5 Nte • Charge (including museum)

Arriving in Cholula, you can't miss the **Nuestra Señora de los Remedios**, picturesquely sited atop a hill with Popocatépetl in the background. If you climb up to it, you can buy snacks such as *chapulines* (fried grasshoppers) on the way. What's not immediately apparent is that the hill is in fact the remains of the **Great Pyramid of Cholula** – the Pirámide Tepanapa – the largest pyramid ever constructed, though it's now ruined, overgrown and really not much to look at. At 66m, it is lower than the largest of the Egyptian pyramids, but with each side measuring 350m it is also squatter and bulkier. As at other sites, the outer shell was built over a series of nested pyramids, constructed between 200 BC and 800 AD.

The archeological site

The **archeological site** around and underneath the pyramid is usually accessed from an entrance on San Andrés through a 400m-long series of tunnels dug by archeologists. Though undoubtedly fascinating, the ruins are a good deal less impressive than some of the more famed sites around the Valley of México. The ring of superimposed structures around the **Patio de los Altares** is certainly worth a look, and there are some fine **murals**, but these can be better appreciated in the site **museum** where replicas are kept.

The tunnels

Even when you can go inside, the section open to the public is just a fraction of the 8km of exploratory tunnels which honeycomb the pyramid. They're well lit and capacious enough for most people to walk upright, but there's still a palpable sense of adventure as you spur off down side tunnels, which reveal elements of earlier temples and steep ceremonial stairways that appear to go on forever into the gloom. Emerging at the end of one tunnel, you'll find an area of open-air excavations, where part of the great pyramid has been exposed alongside various lesser shrines with explanations in English of their importance.

The zócalo

Capilla Real • Free

One side of Cholula's large zócalo – the Plaza de la Concordia – is taken up by the ecclesiastical buildings of the **Convento de San Gabriel**, built from 1529 on the site of the temple of Quetzalcoatl. The Gothic main church is of little interest, but behind it is the great mustard-yellow **Capilla Real**, topped by 49 tiled cupolas. Moorish in conception, the interior comes with a forest of columns supporting semicircular arches and immediately recalls the Mezquita in Córdoba, Spain.

ARRIVAL AND DEPARTURE — CHOLULA

By bus Buses for TAPO in Mexico City serve the Estrella Roja terminal at 12 Pte 108 (8 daily; 3hr). Buses for CAPU in Puebla can be picked up across the street at the corner of 3 Nte (every 15min until around 9pm; 30min). From the Estrella Roja terminal, head down 5 de Mayo to get to the zócalo; from there, follow Morelos past the old train tracks to reach the pyramid.

By colectivo There's a constant stream of *colectivos* from Puebla (14 Pte, between 9 and 11 Nte) that run from around 5am to 10pm, most of which run right by the archeological site. To get back to Puebla you can pick them up on 5 Pte.

ACCOMMODATION

Reforma 4 Sur 101 at Morelos; 222 247 0149. Small rooms with tiny bathrooms, all round the ground-floor car park. Its relatively central location and low rates are the only thing that make this place stand out. M$

Suites San Juan 5 Sur 103 at Hidalgo; 222 178 0398. It looks like a car park but there are Tardis-like rooms tucked away in the corner, a lot bigger on the inside than they look on the outside. Some are even bigger than others, and as they're all the same price, it's worth asking for a large room. There's also a restaurant, where breakfast is included in the weekend price, but not in the weekday price. M$

Trailer Park Las Américas 6 Nte at 30 Ote; 222 413 7373. You may have a job finding anyone in attendance at this slightly ramshackle site, where you can camp or park an RV, so it's wise to call in advance. M$

Villas Arqueológicas 2 Pte 601; https://www.villascholula.com. Fresh rooms with tiled floors set around a pool. The rooms aren't huge, but they're cool and relaxing, and "spa" services (massage, in other words) are available to help you relax even more. Prices rise at weekends. M$$

EATING

Enamorada Portal Guerrero 1, west side of zocalo; 222 188 7131. Eternally popular with coffee lovers, diners and those here to drink while listening to the occasional band (most nights from 8pm), this place also does a good Sun morning buffet brunch. Starters include *huitlacoche* (corn fungus), with mains such as steak in mustard sauce. M$$

Güero's Hidalgo 102, south side of zocalo; 222 247 2188. A bright, modern restaurant where they'll do you a good set breakfast till noon, and solid Mexican food thereafter, including *tampiqueña* (sliced beef served with chile, relish, cheese, *refritos* and guacamole) and *pozole* (soup with meat and corn). M$$$

Los Jarrones Portal Guerrero 7, west side of zocalo; 222 308 4361. Students swarm to this rustic-style café, which does a good comida corrida, as well as dishes such as roast *cecina* (cured beef), or sirloin steak in roquefort sauce. M$$

NIGHTLIFE

Cholula is generally regarded as the **nightlife** capital of the Puebla region, but aside from a few bars in town, most of the action has moved about 3km out to the Recta A Cholula, the main Cholula–Puebla highway, which is thoroughly inconvenient and makes taxi rides essential. Establishments also tend to be far apart from each other. The best bet is to ask locally for the current hot spot and commit yourself to just one place for the night – not a bad idea when entry can cost a fair amount.

Around Cholula

Churches Variable opening hours; if closed just knock for access • "Chipilo" buses from the corner of 3 Nte and 6 Pte run to Acatepec and Tonatzintla

If you want to explore some of the churches around Cholula, head for **ACATEPEC**, easily reached by local bus. The spectacular village church here, San Francisco, has a superb Baroque facade entirely covered in glazed bricks and *azulejos* of local manufacture. It's not particularly large but it is beautifully proportioned and quite unexpected in this setting.

THE LEGEND OF "POPO" AND "IXTA"

The full names of Mexico's ever-smoking **volcanoes** come from an **Aztec Romeo-and-Juliet-style legend**. Popocatépetl (Smoking Mountain) was a warrior, Ixtaccíhuatl (White Lady) his lover, the beautiful daughter of the emperor. Believing Popocatépetl killed in battle, "Ixta" died from grief, and when he returned alive he laid her body down on the mountain, where he eternally stands sentinel, holding a burning torch. From the west, Ixta does somewhat resemble a reclining female form and the various parts of the mountain are named accordingly – the feet, the knees, the belly, the breast and so on.

In the village of **TONATZINTLA**, a 1km walk to the northwest, the plain facade of the church of Santa María conceals a remarkably elaborate Baroque treasury. Here local craftsmen covered every available centimetre in ornament, interspersing bird, plant and native life with the more usual Christian elements.

Popocatépetl and Ixtaccíhuatl

"Popo" and "Ixta", as the snow-clad volcanic peaks of **Popocatépetl** (5452m) and **Ixtaccíhuatl** (5285m) are affectionately known, are the nation's second- and third-highest peaks (after the 5700m Pico de Orizaba). You get excellent views of them from almost anywhere west of the capital, and viewing from afar is all most people do these days. "Popo" has been rumbling and fuming away since September 1994, and for much of the time since then the region has been on Yellow Alert, with evacuation procedures posted throughout surrounding towns. Activity was renewed in December 2000, culminating in the largest eruption on record. Though there were no devastating lava flows, the crater spat out hot rocks, dust fell on the capital and, on several occasions, Mexico City's airport (over 60km away) was closed for a few hours. Local villagers, evacuated for weeks during the eruption, were forced to stand idly by while their livestock trampled their fields. Between 2012 and 2018, renewed activity, including the expulsion of volcanic ash, led the authorities to step up the level of alert to "**Yellow Phase 3**", which means among other things that no access is allowed within 12km of the volcano until further notice.

Parque Nacional de Volcanes

Charge per day when operating; to enter the park you'll need to fill out and submit a formal request at the park office in Amecameca at Plaza de la Constitución 9 (597 978 3829)

Given the unpredictable and intermittent explosions of Popocatépetl and Ixtaccíhuatl (particularly the former), much of the **Parque Nacional de Volcanes** and its 12km radius is often off limits to the public. A small section of the **park remains open**, where the **Cultural Conservation Centre** at the top opens from time to time and offers talks (all in Spanish) on the geography of the area and the cultural history of the peaks. For details on the latest situation, contact the park office.

A good option if you're after an eyeful of the huge peaks is the town of **Amecameca** (often just "Ameca"), an hour east of Mexico City, where dramatic views of the volcanoes can be enjoyed from the comfort of the palm-lined zócalo. From here you can drive, hitch or get a taxi (there are no buses), when the situation allows, to the Paso de Cortés, a 3800m-high pass between the volcanoes. It makes for a memorable experience, with the two giants rising high above you on either side. **Climbs** up Ixta also begin in Ameca; this is a challenging trek for serious mountaineers only, involving a night or two at very high altitude, and a technical 3km-long ridge traverse (often requiring ropes) to reach the summit.

ARRIVAL AND DEPARTURE — PARQUE NACIONAL DE VOLCANES

By bus The bus station in Amecameca, served by "Servicio Volcánes" (AV) buses from TAPO in Mexico City (every

20min, 5am–9pm; 1hr 30min;) and in the other direction from Cuautla, is on 20 de Noviembre, just off the zócalo's northwest corner.

ACCOMMODATION

El Marques 20 de Noviembre, at the beginning of town, three blocks northwest of bus station, Ameca; 597 978 1192. Shades of jolly orange and sunny yellow deck out the bright, spacious rooms, where you can park your car right outside. Good views of the sierra from the front. M$

San Carlos Constitución 10, southeast corner of the zócalo, by the church, Ameca; 597 978 0746. An absolute bargain: the rooms are fresh and clean, all with bathrooms, and the place is as central as you could want. You do, however, pay extra to have a telly in your room. M$

2

South of Mexico City

Heading south from Mexico City, you climb over the mountains and descend to **Cuernavaca**, which brims with colonial mansions and gardens, and draws visitors on account of its proximity to several important archeological sites, notably the hilltop pyramid sites of **Tepoztlán** and **Xochicalco**. An hour further south the silver town of **Taxco** straggles picturesquely up a hillside, making it one of the most appealing destinations hereabouts. From Mexico City, all of these places can be reached via the Central de Autobuses del Sur at Taxqueña.

Cuernavaca

With its refreshing spring-like climate, **CUERNAVACA** has always provided a place of escape from Mexico City, but it isn't always as refreshing as it claims to be. The state capital of Morelos is rapidly becoming industrialized, and the streets in the centre are permanently clogged with traffic and fumes. The gardens and villas that shelter the rich are almost all hidden away or in districts far from the centre, and many of them belong to narco-barons, whose rivalries brought a spate of **violence** in 2010. The spring of that year saw disco-theques attacked and castrated corpses hung from bridges as deputies of a local kingpin fought for succession in the wake of his assassination by Mexican marines. The ensuing conflict left some fifty people dead, although the situation has calmed down somewhat since then.

Brief history

The Aztecs called the city Cuauhnahuac ("place by the woods"), and it became a favourite resort and hunting ground for their rulers; the Spaniards corrupted the name to Cuernavaca ("cow horn") simply because they couldn't pronounce Cuauhnahuac. Hernán Cortés seized and destroyed the city during the siege of Tenochtitlán, then built himself a palace here. The palace-building trend has continued over the centuries: Emperor Maximilian and the deposed Shah of Iran both had houses here, and the inner suburbs are packed with the high-walled mansions of wealthy Mexicans and expats.

The zócalo

Cuernavaca's **zócalo** has two parts: the Plaza de Armas and, to its northwest, the smaller Jardín Juárez, with its bandstand. Around the twin plazas you'll find a series of cafés where you can sit outdoors under the watchful eye of a huge, black, volcanic-rock **statue of Morelos** that faces the Palacio de Gobierno, across the plaza.

Museo Regional Cuauhnahuac

Eastern end of the Plaza de Armas • Charge • 777 312 8171

Located behind the Plaza's statue of Morelos, the **Museo Regional Cuauhnahuac** is housed in the sixteenth-century **Palacio de Cortés**. Work on this building began as

CUERNAVACA

0 — 100 metres

DRINKING & NIGHTLIFE

Barecito	2
El Garage	3
Samanna	1
Tumbao	4

EATING

Los Arcos	7
Casa Hidalgo	8
La India Bonita	2
La Maga Café	3
Las Mañanitas	1
Marco Polo	5
Pollo y Más	6
Vienes	4

ACCOMMODATION

América	4
Casa Colonial	7
Colonial	5
Hostería del Sol	6
Las Mañanitas	1
Roma	2
Royal	3

Mexico City (87km)
Salto de San Antón (99km)
1, Pyramid of Tepanzolco (1km) & Cuautla (50km)
Pyramid of Tepanzolco (1km)
Acapulco (291km)

Linares
Cuaglia
Guerrero
Estrella Blanca bus terminal
Pullman de Morelos Casino de la Selva bus terminal
Avenida del Parque
Arista
Matamoros
Avenida Obregón
Degullado
No Reelección
Market
López Mateos
Aragón y León
Laundry
Morrow
Arteaga
Market bus terminal
Gándara
Jardín Borda
Morelos
Lerdo de Tejeda
Rayón
Comonfort
Jardín Juárez
Catedral de la Asunción
Hidalgo
Plaza de Armas
Gutenberg
Plazaela del Zacate
Museo Robert Brady
Museo Regional Cuauhnahuac
Netzhualcoyotl
Casas
Bulevar Juárez
Francisco Leyva
Cuauhtémoc
Abasolo
Atlacon
Pullman de Morelos downtown terminal
Galeana
Motolinia
N
Cuauhtémotzin
Estrella Roja bus terminal
Bocanegra
Humboldt
Avenida Morelos
Francisco Leyva
Himno Nacional
Estrella de Oro bus terminal
Rufino Tamayo
Jardín Etnobotánico

early as 1522, when, although Tenochtitlán had fallen, much of the country had yet to come under Spanish control – the fortress-like aspect of the palace's older parts reflects this period. Over the centuries, though, it's been added to and modified substantially – first by Cortés himself and later by the state authorities to whom it passed – so that what you see today is every bit a palace. The museum is a good one, spacious and well laid out with a substantial section covering local archeology, including some fine examples of steles and a lovely seated figure from Xochicalco. In fact, the building is partly constructed over the ruins of a small pyramid, which can be seen in the courtyard and elsewhere. There's also a substantial collection of colonial art, weaponry and everyday artefacts – look for the sixteenth-century clock mechanism from the cathedral and a reproduction of a *cuexcomate*, a kind of thatched granary still found around the state.

Diego Rivera murals

The museum's highlight, though, is a series of **murals** around the gallery, painted by Diego Rivera in 1929 and 1930. Depicting Mexican history from the Conquest to the Revolution, they concentrate in particular on the atrocities committed by Cortés, and on the revolutionary Emiliano Zapata, who was born in the state of Morelos, raised most of his army from among its peasant farmers and remains a local hero. From the balcony, there are wonderful, though sometimes hazy, views to the east with Popocatépetl in the far distance.

The cathedral

Cnr of Morelos and Hidalgo • Free • https://www.facebook.com/CatedralCuer

The **Catedral de la Asunción** is three blocks west of the zócalo on the south side of a grassy tree-shaded compound that also contains a couple of other small churches. Founded by Cortés in 1529, the cathedral looks bulky and threatening from the outside (at one stage there were even cannons mounted along the battlemented roof line), but it has been tastefully refurbished within and stripped almost bare, a modernist approach which can be an enormous relief if you've grown tired of the churrigueresque and Baroque flamboyance elsewhere. Most of the decor is understated, but traces of murals discovered during the redecoration have been uncovered in places – they have a remarkably East Asian look and are believed to have been painted by a Christian Chinese or Filipino artist in the days when the cathedral was the centre for missions to the Far East. At one time, the main Spanish trade route came through here, with goods brought across the Pacific to Acapulco, overland through central Mexico and on from Veracruz to Spain. If, after viewing the interior of the cathedral, you need your fix of golden exuberance, pop into the **Capilla del Santísimo**, where there's a small gilt *retablo* and Stations of the Cross in charcoal on paper.

Museo Robert Brady

Netzahualcoyotl 4 at cnr 20 de Noviembre • Charge • https://museorobertbrady.com

The **Museo Robert Brady** occupies a former sixteenth-century convent and holds the Iowa-born artist's private collection. Brady moved to Cuernavaca in the 1960s, and lived here until his death in 1986. Filled with art from around the world and decorated in an intensely colourful artesanía style, the museum is a fabulous place, with rooms arranged aesthetically, and without regard to history, geography or classification of artistic styles. As a result, what you see is more like a beautiful home than a typical museum, and is well worth a visit.

The rooms, arranged around a couple of outside patios complete with sculptures and a delightful pool, are filled with works by most of the greats of twentieth-century **Mexican art**. Even the bathrooms contain works by Diego Rivera and Rufino Tamayo, and there are also pieces by Frida Kahlo, Graham Sutherland, and some particularly

THE MARIACHI MASS

Until his death in 2000, Cuernavaca's bishop was **Luis Cervantes**, one of the country's most liberal and outspoken clergymen. Apart from doing up his cathedral (see above), he was renowned for instituting the "Mariachi Mass", which has been continued by his disciples. Every Sunday, this service is conducted to the accompaniment of traditional Mexican music and usually attracts large crowds.

good works by Rafael Coronel, including a portrait of Peggy Guggenheim. Everything is labelled in English.

Jardín Borda

Morelos 271, immediately west of the cathedral • Charge • 777 318 1050

A large formal garden adjacent to the mansion of Taxco mining magnate José de la Borda (see page 180), the **Jardín Borda** falls short of the grandeur Borda dreamed of when he commissioned the garden in the eighteenth century, yet both the garden and the mansion are a delightfully tranquil reminder of the haven Cuernavaca once was. Emperor Maximilian and Empress Carlota later adopted Borda's mansion as their weekend home.

Salto de San Antón

Bajada del Salto, Barrio de San Antón • Free

About twenty minutes' walk into the suburbs beyond the Jardín Borda is the **Salto de San Antón**, a beautiful 36m cascade surrounded by vegetation and natural columns of crystallized basalt. Unfortunately, the site has been overdeveloped and is marred by concrete walkways, litter and a faint stench from the polluted water, but it's still pretty, and the road to the falls passes a number of flower shops and restaurants.

Jardín Etnobotánico

Matamoros 200, Col. Acapantzingo, 2km southeast of the centre • Free • 777 244 2023

The pretty grounds and collection of medicinal plants at the **Jardín Etnobotánico** are just about worth taking a taxi (or a long walk) to see. As well as the labelled specimens – coffee, guavas, roses and medicinal herbs – there is a small museum of traditional medicine. This latter is housed in the **Casa de la India Bonita**, a retreat commissioned in 1866 by Emperor Maximilian for himself and the local girl he took for a mistress, who is known to history only as "La India Bonita".

Pyramid of Teopanzolco

Rio Balsas, 2km northeast of the city centre • Charge • 777 314 1284 • City bus #4 or #10 from Degollado, but check with the driver because not all buses go as far as the pyramid

The **Pyramid of Teopanzolco** is the area's sole significant reminder of the pre-colonial period. So effectively buried was this site that it took an artillery bombardment during the Revolution to uncover it. Located to the northeast of the centre beyond the old train station (which is what the gunners were aiming at), it's a small temple containing two pyramids, one built over the other.

ARRIVAL AND DEPARTURE — CUERNAVACA

By bus Cuernavaca doesn't have a single main bus station. Instead, bus companies have their own depots in different parts of town. Pullman de Morelos operate very frequent buses from Mexico City's Central del Sur to their city-centre terminal on Netzahualcoyotl at Abalolo, but they also have a second, less convenient terminal at Casino de Selva, so when buying Pullman de Morelos tickets from Mexico City, take a bus to "Centro" rather than "Casino" if you want to end up downtown. Estrella Blanca's terminal is easy to find, on Morelos, just north of the centre, with services to and from Guerrero (Taxco and Acapulco) and the west of Mexico state (Ixtapan de la Sal and Toluca). Estrella Roja

(Puebla and Cuautla) have a terminal three blocks south of the zócalo at Cuauhtémotzin and Galeana, and Estrella de Oro's terminal (the best for Acapulco) is even further south, on Morelos near its junction with Galeana. Finally, there's a terminal for second-class services within the state of Morelos (notably Tepoztlán and Cuautla) by the market. From Puebla, although a few services use the Estrella Roja terminal, you'll more likely be dumped at the Autobuses Oro terminal, which is way out on Blv Cuauhnahuac, 7km southeast of the centre, from where you'll need to take a local bus or taxi into town.

Destinations Acapulco (Estrella de Oro terminal, 12–15 daily; Estrella Blanca terminal, 3 daily; 5hr from both); Cuautla (Estrella Roja terminal, every 20–30min; 1hr 20min; market terminal, every 30min; 1hr 40min); Ixtapan de la Sal (Estrella Blanca terminal, hourly; 2hr 45min); Mexico City (Pullman de Morelos terminal, every 15min; Casino terminal every 10min; roughly 1hr 50min from both); Mexico City airport (Casino terminal, hourly; 1hr 40min); Puebla (Estrella Roja terminal, 4 daily; Autobuses Oro terminal, hourly; 3hr 15min from both); Taxco (Estrella Blanca terminal, hourly; 1hr 40min); Tepoztlán (market terminal, every 30min; 1hr); Toluca (Estrella Blanca terminal, every 30min; 2hr 30min).

2

INFORMATION

Tourist office The state tourist office, near the Estrella de Oro terminal, at Morelos 187 Sur (Mon–Fri 9am–6pm; 777 314 3709, http://turismoycultura.morelos.gob.mx), is generally helpful, with information on buses and excursions, but their branch office at Hidalgo 5 in the city centre (daily 9am–6pm; 777 314 3920) tends to be better informed about local tourist sights.

ACCOMMODATION

SEE MAP PAGE 172

Cuernavaca has a reasonable range of **hotels** close to the centre but little that is particularly appealing in budget categories: many of the cheaper options are just north of the centre on Matamoros and the streets that connect it with Morelos. Visitors looking for mid-range and top-end places are well served, with some establishments occupying grand old mansions in the centre and others spread around pools and lush gardens in the suburbs. The tourist office has a list of contact addresses for families offering **private rooms**, a service aimed at students attending local language schools – the schools themselves and their notice boards are also good sources for such accommodation.

América Aragón y León 14; 777 318 6127. A simple but clean and respectable place in a street mostly full of dives; all rooms have bath, but only those at the front have outside windows (the others have windows onto the inner courtyard). M$

Casa Colonial Netzahualcoyotl 37; http://hotelcasacolonialcuernavaca.com. Gorgeous rooms in a delightful eighteenth-century mansion close to the Museo Robert Brady (see page 173). With attractive colonial public areas and a pool, this is one of the most appealing places in the centre, and the price includes breakfast. TV on request, but no phones. Prices rise by some on Fri & Sat. M$$

Colonial Aragón y León 19; http://hotelcolonialcuerna.wixsite.com/hotelcolonial. This is the most comfortable hotel on Aragón y León. Its rooms all have ceiling fans, bathroom and TV, and are arranged around a pleasant little patio garden. M$

Hostería del Sol Callejón de la Bolsa del Diabolo, by Hidalgo 3; 777 318 3241. This well-kept little place has some quite charming rooms, nicely decorated with pretty tiles and paintwork. En-suite rooms cost extra. M$

★ **Las Mañanitas** Linares 107; http://lasmananitas.com.mx. Beautiful luxury hotel, just a 10min walk from the zócalo. The streetfront entrance gives little clue of the oasis within, where peacocks, flamingoes and African cranes strut around a pool and lush gardens. The tiled-floor rooms come with heavy wooden furniture and all the fittings, and there's a superb restaurant on site (see below). Breakfast included. Prices rise to on Fri & Sat. M$$$$

Roma Matamoros 17; 777 318 8777. This little hotel has rooms set around a small atrium, all with bathroom, TV and overhead fans, plus suites with a/c. There's a small swimming pool and bar as well as a café-restaurant, wi-fi and parking facilities. Rates include breakfast for one person, and rise on Fri & Sat. M$$

Royal Matamoros 11; http://hotelesroyal.com.mx. The rooms here are arranged around a tangerine-coloured central patio with parking space, and the ones on the top floor are the cheapest, though they're otherwise exactly the same as the rest. There's wi-fi throughout. M$$

EATING

SEE MAP PAGE 172

CAFÉS, CHEAP EATS & SNACKS

★ **La Maga Café** Morrow 9; 777 310 3871. You don't get much more local than this farm-to-table café, complete with self-serve sinks to wash the vegetables you buy, should you choose to eat them there and then. A good choice for vegetarians and beer fans alike. All prices negotiable. M$

Pollo y Más Galeana 4; 734 343 1711. This cheap snack-bar opposite the zócalo churns out decent roast chicken, burgers, enchiladas, comida corridas and *antojitos*; set menus, and set breakfasts offer the best value for money. M$$

Vienes Lerdo de Tejada 302; http://vienes.com.mx. Austro-Hungarian café, bar, patisserie and restaurant (set menu available), just a block from the zócalo; a great spot for continental-style coffee and pastries. The name is a pun on *vienés*, meaning "Viennese", and *vienes*, meaning "you come". M$$

2

RESTAURANTS

Los Arcos Jardín de los Héroes 4; 777 312 4486. Ever-popular restaurant and bar on the south side of the zócalo serving espresso coffee and a wide range of dishes, from Cuernavaca-style enchiladas (stuffed with chorizo) to steak in mustard sauce. There's also a set menu. In the evening most people are here to drink and listen to the live music, which comes in a variety of styles and abilities. M$$

Casa Hidalgo Jardín de los Héroes 6; http://casahidalgo.com. Next door to *Los Arcos* but rather posher, with white table linen, an outside terrace, a roof terrace and various balconies with views over the zócalo. Dishes include stuffed chiles (prices vary depending on the filling), or fish with mango and green coriander. M$$$

La India Bonita Morrow 15-B, just off Morelos; http://laindiabonita.com.mx. This lovely restaurant with a pleasant outdoor patio has excellent food and impeccable service. Firm favourites on the menu include the House *mole*, the grilled rib-eye and the set breakfast costs. There's live music most evenings, which on Sat takes the form of a folk ballet. M$$$

Las Mañanitas Ricardo Linares 107; 777 312 5021. People drive hours to visit this well-known restaurant which serves fine Mexican and international cuisine in the sumptuous grounds of the hotel of the same name (see above). Traditional Mexican starters include red maguey worms, followed by mains such as rock-lobster tails thermidor or entrecôte bourguignonne. M$$$$

Marco Polo Hidalgo 30; http://marco-polo.com.mx. Superior Italian restaurant serving up its own home-made pasta, or you can attempt to get through one of their huge pizzas. M$$$$

DRINKING AND NIGHTLIFE

SEE MAP PAGE 172

There are two main centres of evening activity in Cuernavaca: in the centre, Plazuela del Zacate, south of the zócalo, is a lively square full of bars, while 2km to the east, in Lomas del Mirador, a block of Av Plan de Ayala just east of Av Tepanzolco has the city's biggest concentration of clubs. For something more sedate, there are free concerts from the bandstand in the Jardín Juárez every Thurs evening at 6pm, and live music at 8pm in *Los Arcos* and *La India Bonita* (see above). Be aware that when tensions between the narco-barons are high, nightspots are a prime target for violence, so keep your ear to the ground, and maybe avoid going out during times of trouble.

Barecito Comonfort 17; 777 565 1107. This place is a bit café-like for a nightlife bar, but it's lesbian-owned and LGBTQ+-friendly, as well as being a generally laid-back venue, which is handy if you just want to hang out with a quiet drink rather than go for it on the dancefloor.

El Garage Casas 5; 777 240 0820. There's live music every night, with an eclectic mix of bands, at this bustling bar on the Plazuela del Zacate, which also does good cocktails, as well as *chelas* (beers) and shorts (largely mescal and tequila).

Samanna Plan de Ayala 708, Lomas del Mirador; 735 274 9138. The city's longest-standing discotheque starts off the evening as a bar, often with live bands later on, and it's even been known to host the odd salsa festival. It's fun rather than sophisticated, and quite popular with local rich-kids, but not exclusively so.

Tumbao Casas 11. With fluorescent tropical decor, and DJs mixing everything from salsa to techno, this is the liveliest of the bars on Plazuela del Zacate, and definitely the one to go for if you want to give your booty a good old shake.

DIRECTORY

Banks and exchange *Casas de cambio* include Gesta on the cnr of Galeana and Lerdo de Tejada, plus more at Morrow 9, Matamoros 10 and Hidalgo 7.

Internet All hotels have wi-fi, although internet cafés abound if you need a computer. Try Cyber Gasso, Hidalgo 22–D (Mon–Fri 8am–9pm, Sat & Sun 10am–9pm; charge).

Laundry Try the laundrette opposite *Hotel América* (Mon–Fri 8am–8pm, Sat 9am–7pm).

Pharmacy The handiest pharmacy is the 24hr Farmacia del Ahorro at the cnr of Hidalgo and Galeana, just south of the zócalo.

Post office At the southwest cnr of the zócalo (Mon–Fri 8am–7.30pm, Sat 9am–12.30pm).

Spanish courses The state tourist office website has a page on schools offering Spanish language courses in Cuernavaca. Find more information about this, and other local community outreach projects, at http://cilacfreire.mx).

Tepoztlán

An interesting side trip from Cuernavaca is to **TEPOZTLÁN**, just 27km to the northeast and dramatically sited in a narrow valley spectacularly ringed by volcanic mountains. Until recently this was an isolated agrarian community inhabited by

Nahuatl-speaking people whose lives had changed little between the time of the Conquest and the beginning of the twentieth century. Given its history as an important stronghold of the original Zapatista movement, it was on Tepoztlán that anthropologist Oscar Lewis based his classic study *Life in a Mexican Village*, in which he traced the effects of the Revolution. In recent years, though, new roads and a couple of luxury hotels have begun to change things – Tepoztlán has become a popular weekend retreat from the capital, with its good selection of restaurants and quality arts and crafts shops, though midweek it is still a peaceful spot. For now, at least, the stunning setting also survives, as does a reputation for joyously boisterous **fiestas** (especially Sept 8, celebrating the conversion of the local ruler to Christianity in 1538). Note that accommodation is expensive in Tepoztlán, so you may decide to visit on a day trip.

Ex-Convento Dominico de la Natividad

Eastern side of the zócalo • Charge for museum

On Sundays and Wednesdays a **market** is held in the zócalo, where you'll also find the massive **ex-Convento Dominico de la Natividad**. It was a fortress for a while during the Revolution, but is now in a rather beautiful state of disrepair with some attractive murals still surviving in the cloister. Around the back and accessed off Gonzales, part of the church has been given over to the **Museo de Arte Prehispánico**, which holds a remarkably good archeological collection.

Santuario del Cerro Tepozteco

Charge, free Sun

Several pre-Hispanic temples have been found on the hilltops in the area, and you can see one to the north, perched high up in impossibly steep-looking terrain. This is the **Santuario del Cerro Tepozteco**, reached from the northern end of Tepozteco after an exhausting 5km walk of an hour or so up what is little more than an upgraded dry stream bed at times. If you're fit, the hike is worth it for the views from this artificially flattened hilltop, and for the chance to inspect the site at close quarters. The small, three-stepped, lime-washed pyramid here was dedicated to Tepoztecatl, a god of *pulque* and of fertility, represented by carvings of rabbits. There were so many *pulque* gods that they were known as the four hundred rabbits: the drink was supposedly discovered by rabbits nibbling at the agave plants from which it is made. This one gained particular kudos when the Spaniards flung the idol off the cliffs, only for his adherents to find that it had landed unharmed – the big September fiesta is in his honour. Follow the example of Mexicans and reward your efforts with a picnic lunch (water and soft drinks are available at a price), but do buck the litter-dropping trend and take your empty containers away with you.

ARRIVAL AND INFORMATION — TEPOZTLÁN

By bus Second-class bus services from Cuernavaca's market terminal (every 15min; 45min) use a terminal in Tepoztlán on the old Cuernavaca road, a continuation of 5 de Mayo about 0.5km south of the zócalo. The other bus terminal, used by Cristobal Colón's services between Cuautla (every 30min; 40min) and Mexico City Sur (every 30min; 1hr 15min), is by a *gasolinera* about 300m further out along the same road. Estrella Roja services (roughly every 30min) stop just round the corner. Some of the more frequent Mexico City–Cuautla *directo* services (every 10min) may set you down at the *caseta* on the *autopista* west of town (accessed from the western end of 22 de Febrero, which runs off 5 de Mayo a block south of the zócalo), but don't count on being able to board buses here.

ACCOMMODATION

Posada Ali Netzahualcoyotl 2, off Tepozteco three blocks north of the zocalo; 739 395 1971. Out towards the ruins, this little hotel keeps its lower-cost rooms tucked under the eaves. Larger rooms have sunflower-carved headboards on the beds and wood-beamed ceilings, and everyone has access to the small pool and *frontón* court. Prices may be open to negotiation, especially midweek. M$$$

★ **Posada del Tepozteco** Paraíso 3, parallel with 5 de

Mayo, a block west of the zocalo; http://posadadeltepozteco.com.mx. If your budget can manage it, *the* place to stay in Tepoztlán is this elegant but unpretentious *posada*, wonderfully sited above most of the town, with lovely views of the mountains from the terraces and outdoor pool. The rooms and suites are simple but well equipped, though you pay slightly more for a balcony and mountain view. For a weekend reservation there's a 2-night minimum, although discounts are always available midweek. Breakfast included. M$$$$

EATING

2

El Chinelo Tepozteco 15, half a block north of the zocalo; 739 395 1112. Solid Mexican cuisine in simple surrounds with no messing about. Dishes on offer include enchiladas *suizas*, chicken *mole* or chile stuffed with cheese. M$$$

Los Colorines Tepozteco 13 (half a block north of the zócalo, next door to El Chinelo); 739 395 0198. As colourful as its name suggests, this jolly restaurant does a good line in superior Mexican cuisine, and is an excellent place to try *cecina de Yecapixtla*, Yecapixtla being a town near Cuautla which is known nationwide for its cured beef (*cecina*). And should you fancy a tasty Mexican vegetable for your starter, they'll do you a plate of *huauzontles* (the flowering heads of a quinoa-like plant, not dissimilar to broccoli). M$$$

Teposnieves 5 de Mayo 21, half a block north of the zocalo; 739 395 4839. The original branch of what is now a chain has ice creams and sorbets in more flavours than you can count; fig and mescal is a favourite, but if you want something more unusual, there's chile and onion, rose petal or beetroot sorbet. They do tasters to help you decide what you want and there are several smaller branches around town too. M$

Cuautla

Some 50km southeast of Cuernavaca, and an hour and a half by bus, lies **Cuautla**, a pleasant if unexciting little town, where Independence leader and local boy **José María Morelos** was besieged by a royalist army in 1812, and where the great revolutionary leader **Emiliano Zapata** is buried, a block south of the zócalo in the Plazuela de la Revolución del Sur. Born in the adjoining village of Anenecuilco, he now lies under a huge bronze statue depicting him in heroic pose – moustached, with a broad-brimmed sombrero on his head and a bandoleer across his shoulder; in one hand he clutches a rifle, and in the other a proclamation demanding "Tierra y Libertad" ("land and freedom").

Casa de Morelos

West side of zócalo • Free • 555 839 5864

The **Casa de Morelos** is a beautiful colonial mansion with gardens that was, for three months in 1812, home to José María Morelos (see below), and contains archeological finds and items of local historical interest, some of which were only discovered when the place was being done up in 1992, as well as information (in Spanish) on local history, Indigenous peoples and local heroes, including Morelos, of course, and also Zapata.

Museo José María Morelos y Pavón

Batalla 19 de Febrero de 1812 (continuation of Galeana) • Free • 735 352 4808

Cuautla's former train station is now home to the **Museo José María Morelos y Pavón**, which mainly traces the life and times of Morelos and the Independence movement of the state that bears his name. For train buffs, the 1904 **steam locomotive** and carriages once used by the town's other great native son, Emiliano Zapata, may be of interest. From time to time, you can take a very short (800m) ride on it for a small fee, but the days on which it operates are sporadic.

Agua Hedionda

Av Progreso, Col. Otilio Montaño, 2km east of the town centre • Charge • https://aguahedionda.mx • Yellow-and-white #11 *combi* from Plazuela de la Revolución (15min)

Cuautla has something of a reputation for its thermal **spas**, and there are several large complexes a little way out from the centre, though the emphasis is more on swimming than luxuriating. The most renowned of the spas is **Agua Hedionda**, known for the high concentration of therapeutic minerals in its waters. It has a big pool for splashing about in at a warm 27°C, as well as private pools, jacuzzis and hydromassage services, and you could easily spend half a day luxuriating there, especially if you happen to have a skin condition that responds well to hot, sulphurous mineral waters (or any other excuse really).

ARRIVAL AND INFORMATION — CUAUTLA

By bus Cuautla has three bus stations, all close to each other a couple of blocks east of the zócalo, on or off 2 de Mayo.

Destinations Amecameca (Cristobal Colón terminal, every 10min; 1hr 45min); Cuernavaca (Estrella Roja terminal, every 30min; 1hr 30min); Mexico City Sur (Cristobal Colón terminal, every 10min; 2hr); Mexico City TAPO (Cristobal Colón terminal, every 10min; 3hr); Tepoztlán (Cristobal Colón and Estrella Roja terminals, every 30min from each; 50min).

Tourist office There's a small and very helpful tourist office at the old train station, four blocks north of the zócalo on Galeana (daily 8am–8pm; 735 352 5221), but not all the staff speak English.

ACCOMMODATION

Colón South side of zócalo at corner of Guerrero; 735 352 2990. How good this hotel is depends on what room you get: the front rooms are bright and spacious, with panoramic views of the zócalo, and are an outstanding bargain, especially if you're coming here from tourist traps like Cuernavaca or Tepoztlán. The interior rooms, on the other hand, which cost exactly the same, are small and stuffy with no outside windows (though still very cheap). It's first come, first served, so early birds stand the best chance of catching the worm. There is an extra charge for a kingsize bed. M$

Defensa del Agua Defensa del Agua 34, three blocks north and two east of the zocalo; 735 352 1679. Spacious modern rooms with ceiling fans surround a patio shared between a small pool and a car park. There's also wi-fi and a branch of the *Italian Coffee Company* (see page 167) on the premises. Rooms cost extra at weekends. M$$

España 2 de Mayo 22, one block south and half a block east of the zocalo; 735 352 2186. A good budget bargain, very handy for the zócalo and the bus terminals, with rooms done out in cool peppermint green and white, and equipped with a TV and fan. M$

EATING

Las Golondrinas Nicolás Catalán 19–A, one block north of the zocalo; 735 117 7038. This restaurant may not be as elegant as it evidently once was, but the fountains still splash as you sink back in comfy chairs and tuck into corn and *cuitlacoche* soup, a fish *brochette* in *ranchera* sauce or regional specialities such as barbecued rabbit *molcajete*. M$$$

Restaurante Casa Morelos Southwest corner of zocalo; 735 308 0098. An unassuming little bar-café with outside seating, bargain breakfasts and decent mains. M$$

Xochicalco

Some 38km southwest of Cuernavaca • Charge

While not much is known of the site's history, or the people who inhabited it, the impressive hilltop ruins of **Xochicalco** are regarded by archeologists as one of the most significant in central Mexico because of the connections it shows to both the ancient culture of Teotihuacán and the later Toltec peoples. Xochicalco flourished from around 700 to 900 AD – thus overlapping with both Teotihuacán and Tula – and also displays clear parallels with Maya and Zapotec sites of the era.

The setting, high on a bare mountaintop, is reminiscent of Monte Albán (see page 581), the great Zapotec site near Oaxaca. Like Monte Albán and the great Maya sites (but unlike Tula or Teotihuacán), Xochicalco was an exclusively religious and ceremonial centre rather than a true city. The style of many of the carvings, too, recalls Zapotec and Maya art. Their subjects, however, and the architecture of the temples, seem to form a transition between Teotihuacán and Tula. The appearance of **Quetzalcoatl** as a human is especially noteworthy, as he was to turn up in this form at Tula and almost every subsequent site, rather than simply as the feathered serpent of Teotihuacán.

The museum

Arriving at the site, your first stop is at the **museum**, on a neighbouring hilltop from the ruins themselves, where you can take a look at some of the more portable pieces unearthed here. A carved stele that once graced one of the lower courtyards (and has now been replaced by a concrete pillar) takes pride of place in the first room, and is followed by numerous slabs of carved stone, a delicate alabaster bowl and some fine jade masks. From here it is a ten-minute walk to the ruins themselves.

Pirámide de Quetzalcoatl

Much the most important surviving monument here is the **Pirámide de Quetzalcoatl**, on the highest part of the site. Around its base are carved extremely elaborate plumed serpents, coiling around various seated figures and symbols with astronomical significance – all clearly Maya in inspiration. On top, part of the wall of the sanctuary remains standing, though it now surrounds a large hole. In 1993 the centre of the pyramid was excavated to reveal the remains of an earlier pyramid inside.

The Solar Observatory

The other main point of interest is the **Solar Observatory**, located to the northwest of the main pyramid and down the hill a little, accessed through the northern ball-court. Here you'll find the entrance to some subterranean passages, a couple of natural **caves** augmented by steps and tunnels, one of which features a shaft in the roof that is oriented so as to allow the sun to shine directly in. At astronomical midday (midway between sunrise and sunset) for around five weeks either side of the summer solstice – May 14/15 to July 28/29 – the shaft casts a hexagonal patch of light onto the cave floor. At any time, the custodian should point out the remains of frescoes on the walls.

ARRIVAL AND DEPARTURE — XOCHICALCO

By bus There's a very slow and circuitous second-class bus from Cuernavaca's market bus station (every 30min; 1hr). The alternative is to take the half-hourly Miacatlán bus from Cuernavaca's Pullman de Morelos terminal (every 30min; 30min), which will take you to the Crucero de Xochicalco, 4km from the site. There's often a taxi waiting here to run you to the site for about M$60; otherwise you'll either have to walk (uphill) or else wait for the second-class bus to come by.

By car If you're driving, or if you go with a tour, you can continue another thirty-odd kilometres down the road beyond Xochicalco to the caves of Cacahuamilpa (see page 184), from where Taxco (see below) is only a short distance.

Taxco

Silver has been mined in **TAXCO** since before the Conquest. Supplies of the metal have long been depleted, but it is still the basis of the town's fame, as well as its livelihood, in the form of jewellery, which is made in hundreds of workshops here, and sold in an array of shops (*platerías*) catering mainly to tourists. The city is an attractive place, like some Mexican version of a Tuscan village, with a mass of terracotta-tiled, whitewashed houses lining narrow, cobbled alleys that straggle steeply uphill. At intervals the pattern is broken by a larger mansion, or by a courtyard filled with flowers or by the tower of a church rearing up; the twin spires of **Santa Prisca**, a Baroque wedding cake of a church in the centre of town, stand out above all.

Brief history

Though it might seem a prosperous place now, Taxco's development has not been entirely straightforward – indeed, on more than one occasion the town has been all but abandoned. The Spaniards came running at the rumours of mineral wealth here (Cortés himself sent an expedition in 1522), but their success was short-lived, and it wasn't until the eighteenth century that French immigrant **José de la Borda** struck it fabulously rich by discovering the San Ignacio vein. It was during Borda's short lifetime that most of what you see originated – he spent an enormous sum on building the church of Santa Prisca, and more on other buildings and a royal lifestyle here and in Cuernavaca; by his death in 1778 the boom was already over. In 1929 however, the silver trade saw a revival, sparked by the arrival of American architect and writer **William Spratling**, who set up a jewellery workshop in Taxco, drawing on local traditional skills and pre-Hispanic designs. With the completion of a new road around the same time, a massive influx of tourists was inevitable – the town has handled it all fairly well, becoming rich at the expense of just a little charm.

The church of Santa Prisca

Plaza Borda • Free • 762 622 0183

The heart of town is the diminutive **Plaza Borda** (zócalo), ringed by recently restored colonial buildings and dominated by Taxco's one outstanding sight, the church of

Santa Prisca. Towering over the zócalo, its hyper-elaborate facade was built in a single stint between 1751 and 1759, and displays a rare unity. Inside there's a riot of gilded churrigueresque altarpieces and other treasures, including paintings by Miguel Cabrera, a Zapotec who became one of Mexico's greatest colonial religious artists.

Casa Borda

Plaza Borda 1 • Free • 762 622 6617

It's worth popping in for a quick look at José de la Borda's house, the **Casa Borda**, in the northeast corner of the zócalo. Built to order in 1759, it had two sets of quarters, one for Borda himself, and another for his son, who was the priest at Santa Prisca. Nowadays it's used as a cultural centre, with theatrical workshops and the occasional exhibition, but it's open to the public and offers good views over the town from many of its windows. There are two storeys at the front, but four at the back.

Museo Guillermo Spratling

Porfirio Delgado 1 • Charge • 762 622 1660

William Spratling's personal collection of antiquities is contained in the **Museo Guillermo Spratling**, right behind Santa Prisca and reached down Calle del Arco at the right-hand side of the church. There are several good pieces, but overall it's disappointing, especially if you've already been to the Museo Nacional de Antropología in Mexico City (see page 97).

Museo de Arte Virreinal

Juan Ruíz de Alarcón 6 • Charge • 762 627 4258

Taxco's most interesting museum, the **Museo de Arte Virreinal** is housed in the beautiful colonial Casa Humboldt, an old staging inn named after a German explorer-baron who spent just one night here in 1803. Labels in Spanish and English provide detailed and diverting background on the town, its religious art and history, partly focusing on Taxco's importance on the Spanish trade routes between Acapulco and Veracruz.

The silver shops

Beyond the few sights, the way to enjoy Taxco is simply to wander the streets, nosing about in *platerías* and stopping occasionally for a drink. If you're in the market for **silver** you can be fairly sure that the stuff here is the real thing (check for the mark: ".925" or "sterling"), but prices are much the same as they would be anywhere and quality and workmanship can vary enormously: there's everything from mass-produced belt buckles and cheap rings to designer jewellery that will set you back thousands of dollars. The shops off the main streets will be cheaper and more open to bargaining. A section in the **market**, down the steps beside the zócalo, dedicated to silver-hawkers, is a good place to start. But the bulk of the market seems to specialize in tacky tourist goods.

The teleférico

At the northern edge of town • Charge

There is little of interest in the immediate vicinity of Taxco, but to while away an afternoon you could catch the **teleférico** (cable car) to the hilltop *Hotel Monte Taxco*, where you'll be rewarded with great views. The stroll up to the *teleférico* is a pleasant one anyway: follow Benito Juárez to Plazuela el Minero, a small square with a statue of a miner, and then head left up Avenida de los Plateros to the northern end of town (around 2km), where the remains of the Los Arcos aqueduct cross the road. If you don't fancy the walk, take a "Los Arcos" *combi* from the zócalo.

ARRIVAL AND DEPARTURE

TAXCO

BY BUS

Taxco has two bus stations, about 1km apart on Av de los Plateros (formerly Av Kennedy), the main road that contours around the side of the valley at the bottom of town. Estrella Blanca has the most frequent services to Cuernavaca (17 daily; 1hr 40min); Mexico City Sur (9 daily; 2hr 15min); Ixtapan de la Sal (every 40min; 1hr 20min); Toluca (every 40min; 3hr 30min) and most other destinations, but for buses to destinations within Guerrero, you're better off heading for the Estrella de Oro terminal, where you'll find more buses to places like Acapulco (12 daily; 5hr) and Chilpancingo (20 daily; 3hr).

Getting to/from town From either terminal it's a very steep 10min walk, a *combi* or taxi ride to Plaza Borda (the zócalo). Ignore offers of a free taxi to a "silver mine" – in fact just a small tunnel (not a mine) with a tacky souvenir shop. To get into town on foot from the Estrella Blanca terminal, cross the road and turn right up the hill and then left to climb even more steeply past the church of Santa Veracruz to the centre. From Estrella de Oro, head straight up Calle de Pilita, the steep alley directly across from you, until you come to the Plazuela de San Juan, on your right; from there go down Cuauhtémoc to the zócalo.

2

INFORMATION

Tourist office Av de los Plateros, opposite Plazuela el Minero, at the northern end of Juárez (daily 9am–5pm; 762 622 0798). A more conveniently located kiosk on the west side of the zócalo (daily 9am–5pm) dispenses much the same information.

ACCOMMODATION

SEE MAP PAGE 181

Taxco has some excellent **hotels**, and when the day-trippers have left, the place settles into a calmer mode. There are inexpensive places near the zócalo, and at the higher end of the scale you're swamped with choices. Particularly nice are some lovely restored colonial buildings that now serve as comfortable hotels.

Agua Escondida Plaza Borda 4, north side of zocalo; https://www.aguaescondida.com. The deceptively small frontage gives little clue to the actual size of this rambling hotel. There are several cheaper, older rooms hidden away at the back (where there's also a pool), or slightly newer ones – some with good views – nearer the reception, but they aren't worth the price difference. Those at the front can be noisy at night. Up to fifty percent discounts if you book over the phone a few days in advance. M$$

★ **Los Arcos** Juan Ruíz de Alarcón 2; http://hotellosarcosdetaxco.com. A couple of blocks east of the zócalo, this beautiful hotel has wonderfully cool, large rooms in a seventeenth-century colonial building set around a lovely brick and stone courtyard with a big tree growing through it, as well as an excellent (and not particularly expensive) restaurant. Book ahead, particularly at weekends when the price goes up. M$$$

Casa de Huéspedes Arellano Pajaritos 23; 762 622 0215. A good-value budget hotel right in the market, with three sun terraces. The higher up you get, the cheaper the rooms, though some only have shared bathroom facilities. M$$

Casa Grande Plazuela de San Juan 7; 762 622 0969. A fun place to stay, friendly, with a slightly run-down charm, and cheerful rooms, some of which are en suite (for an extra charge). Those on the top floor have direct access to the scenic rooftop terrace. M$$

Emilia Castillo Juan Ruíz de Alarcón 7; 762 622 1396. Beyond a glass mosaic sunsplash in reception and a big mural in the lounge area, this bright hotel in a colonial mansion near the zócalo has homely if smallish rooms with tiled floors and warm colours. Rooms cost more on Fri and Sat. M$$

Posada San Javier Estacadas 32; http://hotelposadasanjaviertaxco.net. Spacious hotel on a steep hill, with a pool and attractive gardens. Rooms are large and simply but tastefully decorated (and some have good views). Rate includes continental breakfast. M$$

Santa Prisca Cena Obscuras 1, just off Plazuela de San Juan; 762 622 0080. Attractive converted colonial building just off the zócalo, with a pleasant flower-filled patio with banana trees and bougainvillea, and a variety of rooms. Don't get too excited about the "balconies" on offer with some rooms, however: the views are great and the rooms themselves are larger, but the "balconies" aren't big enough to sit out on (and cost extra). M$$

EATING

SEE MAP PAGE 181

Finding somewhere to **eat** in Taxco is no problem: there are several enticing places around the zócalo that are wonderful for watching the world go by. They do tend to be expensive, though, and by sacrificing a little atmosphere you'll do better along some of the streets that lead away from the centre. All except the cheapest of the hotels have their own dining rooms, and, for rock-bottom prices, the market has a section of food stalls, which are better than they look.

El Adobe Plazuela de San Juan 13; http://eladoberestaurante.info. Homely restaurant where excellent Mexican food is served for moderate prices either in the cosy interior or on a balcony overlooking the square. Try the house steak, with chile and *epazote* (a Mexican herb with a distinctive flavour). M$$$

2

La Hamburguesa Plazuela de San Juan 5; 762 622 0941. A cosy little eatery, just off the nearby plaza. Here you can feast on hearty, homestyle burgers for breakfast, lunch or dinner. Better yet, there's nothing on the menu here that'll break the bank. M$$

Restaurant Bar Acerto Plaza Borda 12; 762 622 0064. Directly opposite Santa Prisca and with excellent views, especially if you can get one of the prized window seats. Formerly known as *Bar Paco*, it has been the place to come since 1937 and remains a nice spot for sipping a beer or dining on well-prepared dishes, including Mexican classics such as *pollo al mole*. M$$$

Santa Fe Hidalgo 2; 762 622 1170. Amid walls decked with photos of past patrons and old-time Taxco, this popular local restaurant has been serving up good, solid grub since 1954. If it's breakfast you're after, you can get one here, and if not, they'll do you anything from a *pozole* to a T-bone. M$$$

DRINKING AND NIGHTLIFE

SEE MAP PAGE 181

In the evening everyone gathers around the zócalo to see and be seen, to stroll or to sit outdoors with a coffee or a drink at one of the **bars**.

Bar Berta Plaza Borda 9; 762 107 5590. Traditional meeting place almost next to the church, and one of several places in Mexico claiming to be the original home of the margarita, though their version of it is unique: a mix of tequila, lime, mineral water and honey, known as a "Berta", invented by the bar's original *dueña* (the eponymous Berta) back in the 1930s.

La Concha Nostra Upstairs at Plazuela de San Juan 7 (same building as the Casa Grande hotel); 762 622 7944. A lively bar overlooking Plazuela de San Juan, with live music weekends, but also serving pasta, pizza and *antojitos*, especially during the day (the spaghetti with octopus and mushroom quesadillas are also good here). M$$

DIRECTORY

Banks and exchange There are several banks with ATMs on the streets surrounding the zócalo. *Casas de cambio* include Balsas, just off Plazuela de San Juan at Carlos Nibbi 2 (Mon–Fri 9.30am–3pm & 4.30–5.30pm, Sat & Sun 8am–3.30pm).

Internet Cyber Click, Hidalgo 8 (daily 10am–9pm; charge); unnamed internet station, Cuauhtémoc 14 (Mon–Sat 10am–9.30pm, Sun 4–9.30pm; charge).

Grutas de Cacahuamilpa

Charge • Buses between Taxco (Estrella Blanca terminal) and Ixtapan de la Sal pass within 1km of the entrance (ask to be dropped off at the junction and walk down the hill for 15min); there are also *combis* to the Grutas every hour or so from opposite Taxco's Estrella Blanca bus terminal

Just 20km north of Taxco on the highway to Ixtapan de la Sal and Toluca, you pass close to the vast complex of caves known as the **Grutas de Cacahuamilpa**. This network of caverns, hollowed out by two rivers, extends for some 70km. The ninety-minute obligatory tour (in Spanish only) obviously takes in only a fraction of these, passing evocative rock formations, all illuminated to better illustrate their names: "the hunchback", "the bottle of champagne" and others. Among the graffiti you're shown a rather prim note from the wife of Maximilian: "María Carlota reached this point". Alongside, Lerdo de Tejada, who became president in 1872, five years after Maximilian's execution, has scrawled "Sebastian Lerdo de Tejada went further". There's a restaurant and several food stalls by the entrance.

West of Mexico City

The southwest of the State of Mexico is dominated by the state capital, **Toluca**, which is served by extremely frequent buses from Mexico City's Terminal Poniente. The main artery through the region is Hwy-55, superseded in places by a modern *autopista* but still used by most of the buses to the small towns. Coming up from Acapulco or Taxco, Hwy-55 passes through the spa town of Ixtapan de la Sal on its way to Toluca, but you'll need to take a detour to see the charming – and increasingly upmarket – village of Malinalco, with its hilltop temple, and the nearby market town of Tenancingo. West of Toluca, on the way out to Michoacán, the main attraction is the beautiful lakeside town of Valle de Bravo, which is also a good base for visiting parts of the Monarch Butterfly Sanctuary.

2

Tenancingo

If you're heading north from Ixtapan de la Sal towards Toluca, the next town of any size along Hwy-55 is **TENANCINGO**. Although it's a friendly place with a bustling market, most tourists only come here to pick up a vehicle to or from Malinalco (see opposite). Tenancingo is worth at least a brief stop in its own right, however. The town's tiny zócalo stands at the top (northern, uphill end) of Juárez, its central street running past the **market** (four blocks south of the zócalo), which is at its height on Thursdays and Sundays, when you can hardly move in the surrounding streets. Liqueurs made from the fruits that grow in abundance on the plain surrounding the village and finely woven traditional *rebozos* (shawls) are sold here, many of them produced at the lovely monastery of **El Santo Desierto**. This is also a big flower-growing region, and as you pass through you'll see whole fields devoted to one bloom – such as roses and chrysanthemums – and acres of land protected by plastic greenhouses.

ARRIVAL AND DEPARTURE — TENANCINGO

By bus Many people will only be here to change buses, but this may involve a walk across the town centre. Buses between Toluca and Ixtapan de la Sal (every 20min; 45min to Ixtapan, 1hr to Toluca) run along Paseo de los Insurgentes (Hwy-55), which skirts the eastern edge of the town centre, and will drop you off at the junction with Hidalgo or Madero (follow these for five blocks west to reach Victoria). Some buses to Ixtapan may also run along Hidalgo, however, stopping typically at Farmacia Morelos, near the junction with Victoria. On Thurs and Sun in particular, however, you will have to to pick them up at Insurgentes with Hidalgo or Madero. *Combis* and shared taxis for Malinalco (frequent; 30min) run from Victoria with Juárez (six blocks south of the zócalo). For Chalma (frequent; 45min), they run from a terminal at the southern end of Victoria (near its junction with Insurgentes).

ACCOMMODATION AND EATING

Hotel Lazo Victoria 100, two and a half blocks south of the zocalo; 714 142 0083. Rooms are plain and functional, but they all have bathrooms with constant hot water, and they're set around a verdant courtyard with caged birds and lots of foliage. Several small cafés nearby serve cheap Mexican staples. M$

Malinalco

The village of **Malinalco**, 20km east of Tenancingo, is a lovely little place nestled in a fertile, alluvial valley at 1800m and surrounded by rich villas – many of them, complete with swimming pools, the weekend homes of the capital's privileged few. The fact that it is noticeably warmer than most of the towns hereabouts makes it a popular retreat in winter. While the village centres on the huge Augustinian church of **Santa Mónica** and has a vibrant Wednesday morning **market**, the real reason to come here is to see the exemplary **Aztec ruins**.

The Malinalco archeological site

Guerrero • Charge

The Aztec **site of Malinalco** sits high on a hill to the west of town (follow Guerrero west from the zócalo) and can be reached after a twenty- to thirty-minute walk up a very steep, stepped path. Having only been started in 1501, it was still incomplete at the time of the Conquest but it is undeniably one of the most evocative sites of its kind, carved in part from the raw rock hillside of the Cerro de los Idolos. Looking back over the village and valley, the ruins may be small, but they are undeniably impressive, the main structures and the stairways up to them partly cut out of the rock and partly constructed from great stone blocks.

The main temple

The most remarkable aspect is the circular inner sanctuary of the main temple or **Cuauhcalli** (House of the Eagle), hewn entirely from the face of the mountain. You approach up a broad staircase, on either side of which sit stone jaguars – in the centre an all but worn-away human statue would have held a flag. This was the setting for the sacred **initiation ceremonies** in which Aztec youths became members of the warrior elite, and there are images of warriors throughout: to one side of the entrance, a broken eagle warrior sits atop Quetzalcoatl, the feathered serpent; guarding the other side are the remains of a jaguar warrior, representative of the second Aztec warrior class.

The rest of the site

Other structures at the site include a small circular **platform** by the entrance, unfinished at the time of the Conquest, and a low **pyramid** directly in front of the main temple. Beyond this lie two larger temples. The first, **Edificio III**, again has a circular chamber at the centre, and it is believed that here Aztec warriors killed in battle were cremated, their souls rising to the heavens to become stars. **Edificio IV** was originally a temple of the sun; much of it was used to construct the church in the village. Below the pyramids, visible from about halfway up the steps to the ruins, you can see another **pre-Hispanic building** nestling among the mountains. It's still used by local residents as a place of pilgrimage each September 29: formerly a shrine to an Aztec altar-goddess, it is now dedicated to San Miguel.

Museo Universitario Schneider

Guerrero • Charge • 714 147 1288

On the way from the town centre to the archeological site, the **Museo Universitario Schneider** is a well-laid-out little museum of archeological finds from the area, many donated by local residents who unearthed them while gardening or working on their homes. There's also a suit of conquistador armour, and a reconstruction of the shrine of Cuauhcalli from the site.

ARRIVAL AND INFORMATION — MALINALCO

By bus or shared taxi The easiest way to reach Malinalco is by bus or shared taxi from Tenancingo (see page 185). Most buses arrive in the zócalo in front of the church of Santa Mónica, but those through to Chalma sometimes hurtle straight down Morelos, which bypasses the centre: ask to be dropped at the end of Hidalgo, which runs 200m to the zócalo. From Mexico City Pte, there are two direct daily buses to Malinalco (10am & 3pm but it's advisable to be there 30min early just in case; 2hr 30min), though there are departures every 20min for Chalma, from where there are frequent local services.

Tourist office There's a tourist office in the town hall at the uphill end of the zócalo (Mon–Fri 9am–5pm, Sat 9am–3pm; 714 147 0111), with a kiosk under the bandstand at the lower end of the zócalo (daily 9am–3pm).

ACCOMMODATION

Casa Limón Rio Lerma 103, 1km south of the zocalo; http://casalimon.com. If only the most exclusive place in town will do, this super-chic boutique hotel will fit the bill, though it isn't very conveniently located. With its elegant stone decor, modern, spacious rooms, a bar, restaurant and pool, it's very classy indeed, but – except by special arrangement (which you may be able to arrange) – it's only open for business Thurs–Sun, and lovely though it undeniably is, it isn't worth six times the price of the *Marmil* or *Santa Mónica*, which is what it will cost you. Breakfast included. M$$$$

Marmil Progreso 67; www.hotelmarmil.com. It's a steep 10min walk uphill from the zócalo to this pretty little hacienda-style hotel. With country-style rooms, off-street parking, ceiling fans, a pool and cable TV, it's very popular and is almost always full at weekends, so reserve ahead if you can. If coming by bus from Tenancingo, ask to be dropped near the hotel. M$$

Santa Mónica Hidalgo 109, near the zócalo on the way to the archeological site; http://hotelsantamonicamalinalco.weebly.com. A very homely, rustic, family-run little place. Its rooms, set around a pretty little garden, are small but have everything you'll need (bathroom, wi-fi, TV). Rooms cost extra Fri & Sat. M$

EATING

Come in the middle of the week and you'll find some of the **restaurants** closed, but at weekends there are at least half a dozen places catering to the weekly influx from the capital and Cuernavaca. Everything is close by so you can walk around and take your pick. Cheap food stalls are found at the top end of Juárez, in the southeast corner of the main plaza. One thing that's really good to eat in Malinalco is trout, fresh from a local trout farm, and widely available in local restaurants.

Ehecatl Hidalgo 210, a block east of the main square; 714 366 1297. A magical garden setting, done out in pretty colours but still very rustic, makes the perfect spot to lunch or dine on anything from a trout fillet to a T-bone steak. M$$$

Má-Li Hidalgo 22, by a bridge over a stream on the way from the zócalo to the archeological site; 714 147 0129. This wine bar, which also specializes in fondue and *pepitos* (steak sandwiches), signals just how upmarket tourism in Malinalco has become. For such a little village, it's mighty posh, but tasteful too, with a play area for kids, for example, and a little library, including some books in English. A fondue for two here will set you back a fair penny, or try a trout stuffed with ham and wrapped in bacon for a real treat. M$$$$

Los Placeres Plaza Principal 6-B, west side of zocalo; https://losplaceresmalinalco.wordpress.com. The best of the bar-restaurants on the zócalo, with a great ambience and excellent food including vegetarian dishes, lots of healthy salads and delicious breakfasts. It's only open a few days a week, however. M$$

2

DIRECTORY

Banks There are ATMs by the town hall and just off the zócalo at Hidalgo 203.

Internet Cyber Mali, Hidalgo 207 (just off the zócalo; daily 9am–8pm; charge).

Chalma

10km east of Malinalco • *Colectivos* (every few min) and shared taxis from Malinalco's zócalo, buses from Mexico City Pte (every 20min; 2hr 30min), and *colectivos* from Tenancingo

Nestled among impressive craggy peaks, **Chalma** is an important place of pilgrimage, although the town itself is a complete dump. Its filthy, muddy streets are lined with stalls offering tacky souvenirs to the pilgrims who converge here every Sunday and at times of special religious significance (especially the first Fri in Lent, Semana Santa and Sept 29), camping out for many kilometres around. In fact, so many people come here that it's impossible to get anywhere near the church.

The Sanctuario

The pilgrims flock here to take part in rituals that are a fascinating blend of Christian and more ancient pagan rites. Originally, the deity Oztocteotl, god of caves, was venerated here in a natural cave. When the first missionaries arrived, he was "miraculously" replaced by a statue of Christ, which was moved in the seventeenth century to a new church, the **Sanctuario de Chalma**. It is this church that is now the focus of pilgrimage and the site of miraculous appearances by a Christ-like figure.

The sacred ahuehuete tree

There's another heavily visited wet shrine on the way into town (buses, taxis and *combis* will set you down on request), at Ocuilán de Arteaga, 6km to the north, where a miraculous spring issues from the roots of a huge old **ahuehuete tree**. Many people stop here first, and then proceed the last few kilometres to the Sanctuario on foot.

Teotenango

Accessible from Tenango del Valle, 30km north of Tenancingo • Free • Regular combis to Tenango del Valle from Tenancingo (30min), and buses from Toluca (every 10min; 30min)

From **TENANGO DEL VALLE**, you can visit the nearby remains of the large fortified Malatzinca township of **Teotenango**. From Tenango, it's a fifteen-minute walk to the entrance, then a steep ten-minute hike up to the site: to get there from the centre of the village, head north along Porfirio Díaz Norte, then take a left up Roman Piña Chan Norte. There's a small museum on site.

Metepec

Some 18km north of Tenango de la Valle, and 10km south of Toluca • From Toluca, take a local bus from 5 de Mayo (off Inés de la Cruz a block east of Hotel San Francisco)

The village of **METEPEC** is famed as a **pottery**-making centre. Brightly coloured wares can be found at craft shops throughout the country; supposedly, the figures that characterize these pots were originally inspired by the saints on the facade of Metepec's sixteenth-century monastery, and in the twentieth century Diego Rivera taught the villagers new techniques of colouring and design. There's a market here on Mondays.

Toluca

The capital of the state of México, **TOLUCA DE LERDO** is today a large and modern industrial centre, sprawling across a wide plain. At an altitude of nearly 2700m, it is the highest city in the country, and is surrounded by beautiful mountain scenery, dominated by the white-capped **Nevado de Toluca**. It is probably not a place you'll want to linger, but on Fridays it is the site of what is allegedly the largest single **market** in the country.

Unusually for a Mexican city, Toluca's centre is marked not by an open plaza, but by a central block surrounded on three sides by the nation's longest series of arcades, built in the 1830s and known as **portales**, lined with shops, restaurants and cafés: Portal Madero is to the south along Hidalgo; Portal 20 de Noviembre is to the east along Allende; and Portal Reforma is to the west along Bravo. The fourth side is taken up by the nineteenth-century **cathedral** and, to its east, the mustard-yellow church of **Santa Cruz**. Most of the central sights are clustered north of the *portales* and the cathedral, close to the two massive open plazas: **Plaza de los Mártires**, north of the cathedral, which is dominated on its north side by the Palacio del Gobierno, and to its east, **Plaza Garibay**, which is rather prettier, with shrubbery and fountains.

Jardín Botánico Cosmovitral

Plaza Garibay (east side) • Charge • 722 214 6785

The **Jardín Botánico Cosmovitral** is Toluca's botanical garden. It's housed in an enormous, 100m-long Art Nouveau greenhouse, which was built in 1909 and served as the main market until 1975. With predominantly semi-tropical displays, small pools and even a well-tended Japanese corner, the Jardín Botánico is extremely attractive in itself, but the highlight is undoubtedly the building's amazing Mexican-muralist-style stained-glass panels by local artist Leopoldo Flores. Come early or late to catch the low sun giving a coloured cast to the plants.

Museo de Bellas Artes

Santos Degollado 102, on northwestern corner of Plaza Garibay • Charge, free Wed & Sun • http://patrimonioyserviciosc.edomex.gob.mx/bellas_artes

The **Museo de Bellas Artes** typically shows off some of the best fine arts in the state. The building it's located in – a Carmelite convent dating from 1697 – is no less interesting than the exhibits, which are mainly religious images, both paintings and sculptures, dating from the sixteenth to the twentieth centuries.

Museo José Maria Velasco

Lerdo de Tejada 400, at Nicolás Bravo • Charge, free Wed & Sun • 722 213 2814

The **Museo José Maria Velasco** occupies two floors of a colonial house and displays a good collection of nineteenth-century paintings, much of it by Velasco, who was born in the State of México in 1840, though he spent much of his life in Mexico City. There's a re-creation of his studio, along with busts, portraits and some delightful landscapes, including a delicate rendering of the volcanoes and the Valley of México.

Museo Felipe Santiago Gutiérrez and Museo Taller Nishizawa

Museo Felipe Santiago Gutiérrez Nicolás Bravo 303 • Charge, free Wed & Sun • 722 213 2647 • **Museo Taller Nishizawa** Nicolás Bravo 305 • Charge, free Wed & Sun • 722 215 7465

The State of México makes a point of honouring its artistic sons, and adjoining the Velasco museum (entrance round the corner on Nicolás Bravo) are two more museums dedicated to local painters. The **Museo Felipe Santiago Gutiérrez** fills a colonial mansion with sketches, oils and portraits of prominent nineteenth-century Mexicans; but there is more interest next door at the **Museo Taller Nishizawa**, where large abstract landscape canvases by Japanese-Mexican artist Luis Nishizawa take pride of place alongside pen-and-ink drawings and some of his more recent portraiture.

The market

On and around Paseo Tollocan, 3km southeast of the centre, just east of the bus station • Every Fri (and to a lesser extent throughout the week)

For many people, the market constitutes the overriding reason to visit Toluca. It certainly attracts hordes of visitors from the capital, but is so vast that there can be no question of its being overwhelmed by tourists; quite the opposite, many outsiders find themselves overwhelmed by the scale of the place, lost among the thousands of stalls and crowds from the state's outlying villages. Though increasingly dominated by cheap imported goods and clothing, there is still a substantial selection of **local crafts** – woven goods and pottery above all. Many visitors stop over on a Thursday night (book accommodation in advance), or make an early start from Mexico City on Friday morning.

Centro Cultural Mexiquense

Some 8km west of the city centre at Bvd Jesús Reyes Hercoles 302, Delegación San Buenaventura • Charge, free Wed & Sun • 722 274 1222

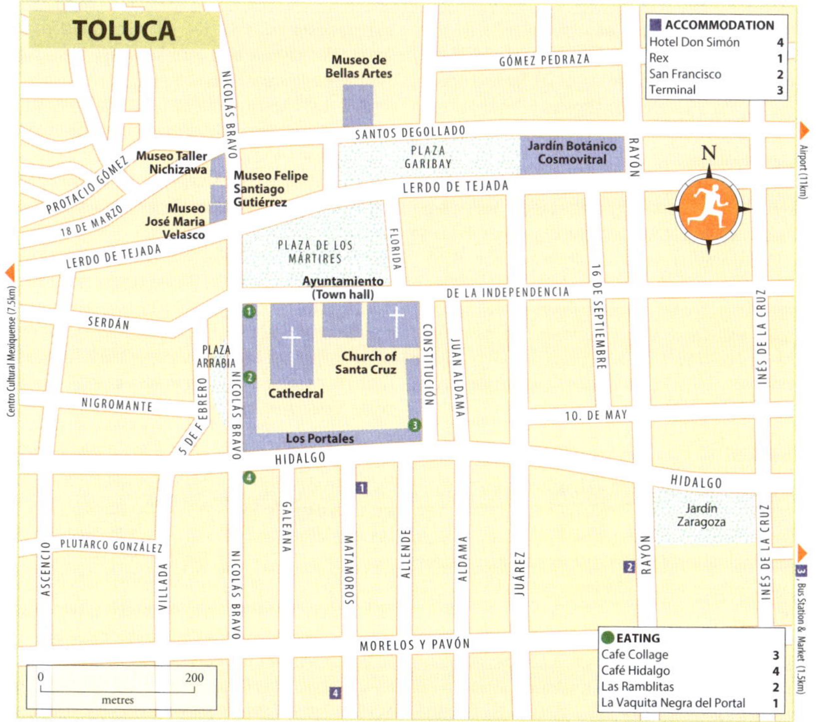

The **Centro Cultural Mexiquense** harbours several museums scattered in park-like grounds. Among them are the **Museo Regional**, devoted to the archeology and history of the state, a small **Museo de Arte Moderno** and, perhaps the most interesting, the **Museo de Artes Populares**, a collection of local crafts, ancient and modern, in a restored hacienda. Although local buses run out there (look for buses marked "Centro Cultural Las Palomas" running along Lerdo de Tejada), you really need your own transport to explore the place fully.

ARRIVAL AND DEPARTURE — TOLUCA

By plane The airport, 11km northwest of town, off Hwy-134, is connected to the city centre by taxi and local bus (picked up in town on Santos Degollado). There are also direct buses from the airport to Mexico City's Terminal Poniente (Observatorio) bus station.

Destinations Acapulco (1–2 daily; 50min); Cancún (3–4 daily; 2hr 45min); Cabo San Lucas (1 daily; 2hr 15min); Guadalajara (1 daily; 1hr 10min); Ixtapa/Zihuatanejo (1 daily; 50min); Monterrey (1–2 daily; 1hr 25min); Puerto Vallarta (1 daily; 1hr 15min).

By bus Toluca's modern bus station (usually referred to as *la terminal* rather than *la central*) is right by the market, 3km southeast of the centre. To pick up a local bus to the centre, exit the bus station and head left down Felipe Berriázabal (the street in front of the terminal) to the junction with Paseo Tollocan; buses into the centre run along Rayón, and you should get off at Hidalgo. Coming back, pick up your bus (marked "Terminal") on Juárez (parallel with Rayón, one block to the west). Note that local buses stop running around 9pm and that *de paso* services from Zitácuaro (see page 298) and Valle de Bravo (see page 191) to Mexico City usually stop on the bypass (Av las Torres, with pylons running down the middle), 500m south of the bus station.

Destinations Cuernavaca (every 30min; 2hr 30min); Ixtapan de la Sal (every 30min; 1hr); Mexico City Pte (every 10min; 1hr 30min); Morelia (hourly; 4hr); Querétaro (hourly; 3hr 30min); Taxco (every 1hr; 3hr); Tenancingo (every 10min; 1hr); Tenango del Valle (every 10min; 30min); Valle de Bravo (every 20min; 2hr).

ACCOMMODATION — SEE MAP PAGE 189

In general, Toluca's **hotels** are at the low end of the scale, with very few places in the centre, and a number of fairly grotty ones clustered around the market. The ones near the market tend to fill up by Thurs nights when finding a room can be difficult, even in the city centre, so it's worth booking ahead then if possible.

Hotel Don Simón Matamoros 202; www.hoteldonsimon.com. One of the better city-centre options, with a super modern feel and artwork everywhere you look. The large lobby bar is well known for its coffee and cocktails. M$$$

Rex Matamoros 101, opposite Portal Madero; https://hotelrex.mx. A clean and relatively low-priced city-centre hotel, with simple but well-maintained rooms, all with bathroom and TV. You pay a bit more to have a carpeted room than for one with a wooden floor (otherwise there's no difference). M$$

San Francisco Rayón Sur 104; http://hotelsanfrancisco.com.mx. This was once quite a plush business hotel – but it's become rather worn around the edges over the years, although it still has an atrium with a panoramic elevator, and some quite impressive paintings on the walls. The rooms are spacious and comfortable, even if the carpet's getting a bit threadbare in places. It's still the most upmarket city-centre choice, and they usually offer a discount of about a third on the rack rate. M$$

Terminal Felipe Berriázabal 101; http://terminaltoluca.com.mx/hotel.html. Right by the bus station, with direct access from the terminal, and as functional as you'd expect a bus terminal hotel to be, but it's clean and decent, the rooms are large and have a bathroom, 24hr hot water and TV, and those on the fifth floor upwards are carpeted (with slightly higher rates). M$

EATING — SEE MAP PAGE 189

Cafe Collage Constitución 112, on the east side of the portales; 722 167 4750. Serving up a decent mix of sweet and savoury, this café-diner is usually abuzz with shoppers from the mall next door. Be sure to try the stacked pancakes with blueberry syrup or the bacon burger if you stop in. M$$$

Café Hidalgo Hidalgo 233 at Nicolás Bravo, opposite the southwest corner of the portales; http://restaurantehidalgo.mx. A great spot for coffee or breakfast in pleasantly old-fashioned surroundings, or for a comida corrida, or a steak. The house speciality is *platillo Hidalgo*, which is basically just a mixed grill. M$$$

Las Ramblitas Portal Reforma 108, on the west side of the portales; 722 215 5488. This cheap and cheerful diner is a good place for a budget city-centre meal, serving tasty set breakfasts, as well as *pozole*, dishes such as enchiladas or *mole poblano* and a fixed price lunch-time menu. M$$

La Vaquita Negra del Portal Portal Reforma 124, at the northeast corner of the portales; 722 167 1377. An excellent deli and *tortería*, selling cheeses and cold cuts by weight or in tortas, which you can eat seated at the counter with big plates of chile pickles to spice them up. A torta *toluqueña* ("Tolucan torta") contains local white cheese and chorizo. M$

Calixtlahuaca

12km north of Toluca • Charge • From Toluca either by taxi or by circuitous local bus (roughly every 15min; 30min) from the stop on Santos Degollado, one block north of the main square at its junction with Nicolás Bravo

While in Toluca, put a couple of hours aside to visit the archeological site of **Calixtlahuaca**, located on a hillside just outside the village of Calixtlahuaca. This was the township of the Matlazinca people, inhabited from prehistoric times and later subjugated by the Aztecs, who established a garrison here in the fifteenth century. Calixtlahuaca was not a willing subject, and there were constant rebellions; after one, in 1475, the Aztecs allegedly sacrificed over eleven thousand Matlazinca prisoners on the **Temple of Quetzalcoatl**. This, several times built over, is the most important structure on the site. Dedicated to the god in his role as Ehecatl, god of wind, its circular design is typical, allowing the breezes to blow freely around the shrine.

2

Nevado de Toluca

If you've got your own vehicle – and a sturdy model at that – one trip you should make is to the crater of the extinct **Nevado de Toluca** (Xinantécatl; 4690m), which rises high enough above the surrounding plain for it to rank as Mexico's fourth-highest peak. A rough dirt road – impractical during the rainy season or midwinter – leads all the way to the crater rim, from where there are numerous trails leading down to the sandy crater floor and two small lakes, the **Lagos del Sol** and **de la Luna**, right in its heart. From its jagged lip the views are breathtaking: below you the lakes; eastwards a fabulous vista across the valleys of Toluca and México; and to the west a series of lower, greener hills ranging towards the peaks of the Sierra Madre Occidental. If you do hike down into the crater, remember to take it easy in this thin, high-altitude air.

Valle de Bravo

West from Toluca, the road towards Morelia and the state of Michoacán is truly spectacular. Much of this wooded, mountainous area – as far as Zitácuaro – is given over to villas inhabited at weekends by wealthy refugees from the capital, and nowhere more so than at the small lakeside town of **VALLE DE BRAVO**. Set in a deep, pine-clad valley, the town sits on the eastern shore of an artificial lake, **Lago Avandaro**. With terracotta-tiled roofs, iron balconies affixed to many of the older buildings and a mass of whitewashed houses all huddled together, it is an immediately appealing place, something that has drawn a coterie of artistic refugees from the big city. They

BUTTERFLY SANCTUARIES IN THE STATE OF MEXICO

Valle de Bravo is a good base for visiting the **Monarch Butterfly Sanctuary** areas in the State of Mexico. The price and season are exactly the same as they are over the state line in Michoacán (see page 298; mid-Nov to end of March, daily 9am–4pm, charge including compulsory guide), but the sanctuary areas here receive fewer visitors and are more unspoilt, if less scenic. The easiest sanctuary area to visit from Valle de Bravo is at **Los Saucos**, whose gate is right on a main road and served by hourly buses between Valle de Bravo and Mexico City – make sure you get on a "por Saucos" bus. There are also organized tours every day in season, which can be booked through the tourist office or the tourist information kiosks in Valle de Bravo. **Cerro Pelón**, which is considered by many to be the prettiest of all the butterfly sanctuary areas, is slightly more remote, but can be reached on hourly Tepascelptepec-bound buses from Valle de Bravo.

2

FIESTAS AROUND MEXICO CITY

Bendicíon de los Animales (Jan 17). Children's pets and peasants' farm animals are taken to church to be blessed – a particularly bizarre sight at the cathedral in Taxco (see page 180), where it coincides with the fiestas of Santa Prisca (Jan 18) and San Sebastián (Jan 20).

Carnaval (the week before Lent, variable Feb–March). Especially lively in Cuernavaca (see page 171) and nearby Tepoztlán; also in Chiconcuac on the way to Teotihuacán.

Palm Sunday (the Sun before Easter Sun). A procession with palms in Taxco (see page 180), where representations of the Passion continue through Holy Week.

Semana Santa (Holy Week). Observed everywhere. There are very famous Passion plays in the suburb of Itzapalapa, culminating on the Friday with a mock Crucifixion on the Cerro de la Estrella, and similar celebrations at Chalma and nearby Malinalco (see page 185).

May Day (May 1). In Cuautla marked by a fiesta commemorating an Independence battle.

Día de la Santa Cruz (May 3). Celebrated with fiestas and traditional dancing, in Xochimilco (see page 113), Tepotzotlán (see page 148) and Valle de Bravo (see page 191).

Cinco de Mayo (May 5). Public holiday for the Battle of Puebla – celebrated in Puebla (see page 161) itself with a grand procession and re-enactment of the fighting.

Día de San Isidro (May 15). Religious processions and fireworks in Tenancingo (see page 185), and a procession of farm animals through Cuernavaca (see page 171), on their way to be blessed at the church.

Religious festival in Tlaxcala (see page 158; third Mon in May). An image of the Virgin is processed around the town, followed by hundreds of pilgrims.

Día de Santiago (July 25). Particularly celebrated in Chalco, near Amecameca. The following Sunday sees a market and regional dances at the Plaza de las Tres Culturas (see page 114) and dances, too, in Xochimilco (see page 113).

Día de Santa Marta (July 29). In Milpa Alta, near Xochimilco, celebrated with Aztec dances and mock fights between Moors and Christians.

Día de la Asunción (Assumption; Aug 15). Honoured with pilgrimages from Cholula (see page 168) to a nearby village, and ancient dances in Milpa Alta.

Día de San Miguel (Sept 29). Provokes huge pilgrimages to both Taxco (see page 180) and Chalma.

Día de San Francisco (Oct 4). A *feria* in Tenancingo (see page 185), with much traditional music-making, and also celebrated in San Francisco Tecoxpa, a village on the southern fringes of the capital.

Fiesta del Santuario de la Defensa (Oct 12). A street party that centres around an ancient church just outside Tlaxcala (see page 158).

Día de Santa Cecilia (Nov 22). St Cecilia is the patron saint of musicians, and her fiesta attracts orchestras and mariachi bands from all over to Santa Cecilia Tepetlapa, not far from Xochimilco.

Feria de la Plata (Dec 1). The great silver fair in Taxco (see page 180) lasts about ten days from this date.

Christmas (Dec 25). In the week leading up to Christmas, Nativity plays – also known as *posadas* – can be seen in many places. Among the most famous are those at Taxco (see page 180) and Tepotzotlán (see page 148).

mostly keep to themselves, leaving the water's edge for weekenders who descend for upmarket relaxation: boat trips, sailing, swimming, waterskiing, riding, paragliding, hiking and golf.

The zócalo, ringed with restaurants and centred on a twin-towered church, sits on a rise a fifteen-minute walk from the waterfront, where most of the action is centred, and sees spectacular sunsets. Here there's a wharf (*embarcadero*) from which you can take boat rides to the parts of the lake inaccessible by road: either rent one by the hour, or join a *lancha colectiva* for a fee.

VALLE DE BRAVO

ARRIVAL AND INFORMATION

By bus Second-class buses to Valle de Bravo run from Toluca (every 30min; 2hr) and Mexico City Pte (every 20min; 3hr). To travel to or from Morelia or Zitácuaro, you'll have to change at a junction called "Monumento", which has hourly buses to Valle, but don't leave it too late as buses won't stop there after dark. The bus station is on 16 de Septiembre (no guardería). Head downhill and take a right at the end (Juárez) to get to the centre.

Tourist office Auditorio Municipal on Porfirio Díaz, off Juárez between 16 de Septiembre and Independencia (Mon–Fri 9am–5pm, Sat 10am–3pm; 726 269 6200). There's also a tourist information kiosk by the *embarcadero* (daily 9am–5pm), and, at weekends, one in the zócalo too (Fri–Sun 9am–3pm).

ACCOMMODATION

Posada Casa Vieja Juárez 101; 726 262 0318. A hacienda with iron gates, behind which a central patio (with fountain) doubles as a car park, and is surrounded by a sunny veranda with a variety of rooms. Some are bigger than others (so it may be worth checking a few), but all are cool and attractive. M$$

Posada los Girasoles Plaza Independencia 1; 726 262 2967. Right on the main square, this charming little hotel has big, fresh rooms with red-tiled floors and firm beds, though some of them are a bit dark. Rooms cost extra Fri and Sat. M$

Puesta del Sol Santa Maria 119, just east of the lakefront plaza; https://hotelpuestadelsol.mx. A charming, modern hotel with stunning views across the lake and just a stone's throw from the jetty. The prices rise at the weekends, but during the week they're often willing to negotiate a discount, particularly if you book ahead. With restaurant, massage, spa and jacuzzi on site, you may not feel the need to leave. M$$$

EATING

The four boat-like restaurants close to the jetty are some of the best places to watch the town's spectacular sunsets, although patrons should avoid *La Balsa*, where both service and product are shoddy.

El Portal Plaza Independencia 101; 726 262 0623. A good upmarket choice, right on the zócalo, where you can get salads, pizzas or *antojitos*, followed by dishes such as trout, steak or a mixed grill for two. M$$$$

La Ranchita 16 de Septiembre 400. Low-priced eats on the way to the bus station. Firm favourites here include the comida corrida, or a slice of beef, pork or chicken with *refritos*. M$

Restaurante Paraíso C Atardecer at Plaza Estrella; 726 262 4731. Grab the table at the very edge of this building as it tapers off to a point over the waterfront plaza and watch the action below. Serves up lots of different cuts of steak as well as good seafood. The perfect spot to watch day turn into night in this pretty little plaza. M$$$

Restaurante Las Truchas C Atardecer, 100m up from plaza; 726 262 6428. The menu is diverse but fun with a focus on seafood. The freshly caught trout and ceviche are popular here. A safe bet for eating well in a town overrun with establishments serving up tourist slop. M$$$

Acapulco and the Pacific beaches

ACAPULCO BAY AT SUNSET

Acapulco and the Pacific beaches

The journey north from Acapulco to Puerto Vallarta, some 900km along the Pacific coast, is defined by languid, tropical beach life at its finest. There's history here, to be sure, but it's the buttery sands studded with palms, the makeshift bars on the beach, lagoons and torpid villages that dominate, topped off with heart-melting sunsets and a rich array of seafood. Separating these stretches of wild, untouched coastline – and in stark contrast – are some of the most popular, brash and enjoyable resorts in Mexico.

Acapulco – the original, the biggest and, for many, the best of these resorts – hugs a steep-sided, tightly curving bay that, for all its excesses of high-rise development, remains breathtakingly beautiful. While tourists swarm the congested beaches, the city retains a local feel, with the coarse characteristics of a working port. Further north, **Zihuatanejo** is an attractive, gentle resort where magnificent villas have popped up on the slopes overlooking inviting swathes of palm-dotted beach, while the handsome towns of **Colima** and **Comala** provide colonial allure (and dramatic volcanic scenery) inland. Further along the Pacific, the **Costalegre** contains some of the wildest and most beautiful stretches of coast anywhere, anchored by **Barra de Navidad** and its glorious sweep of sand surrounded by flatlands and lagoons. At the northern end of Jalisco state, international **Puerto Vallarta** feels altogether more manageable than Acapulco, with cobbled streets fanning out from a colonial plaza overlooking an oceanfront boulevard. With its party ambience and unbridled commercialism it's certainly a resort, but if you travel far enough from the downtown beaches you can still find cove after isolated cove backed by forested mountains.

Acapulco

Most people – even if they've not the remotest idea where it is – have heard of **ACAPULCO**. It's been the *grande dame* of the Mexican tourist industry since the 1950s, and today Mexico City-by-the-sea is a crazy, tropical party town where the rich and poor of the capital come to play; the swankiest clubs and restaurants nestle in the hills, while the masses pack the beaches, fiesta-style. But what makes Acapulco really special is its stunning **bay**: a sweeping scythe-stroke of yellow sand backed by the white towers of the high-rise hotels and, behind them, the jungly green foothills of the sierra. Even though the city itself has a population of over half a million and hundreds of thousands of visitors come through each year, it rarely seems overcrowded. There's certainly always space to lie along the beach, partly because of its sheer size, and partly because of the number of rival attractions – everything from hotel pools to parasailing to romantic cruises. If you only do one thing in Acapulco, though, make sure you see its most celebrated spectacle, the leap of the daredevil **high divers** (see page 207). In recent years, drug violence has escalated in Acapulco, leading to a slew of harrowing headlines. The statistics are scary, but the violence is largely confined to warring drug gangs, and you'd be very unlucky to be caught up in it as a tourist. For more information on staying safe in Acapulco, see page 202.

Centro Histórico

Acapulco's scrappy **Centro Histórico** wraps around the western end of the bay, with Plaza Álvarez, better known simply as the **zócalo,** at its centre, a shady, languid square

COMALA

Highlights

❶ **Acapulco** The king of Mexican resorts is a brash, exhilarating city with romantic dining, serious partying and death-defying cliff divers. See page 196

❷ **Barra de Potosí** An untouched beach where you can eat fresh fish and row through a mangrove lagoon. See page 210

❸ **The Michoacán coast** Explore one of the wildest sections of the Pacific coast, anchored by the gorgeous beaches at Playa Maruata. See page 216

❹ **Nevado de Colima** Hike the pine-smothered slopes of this awe-inspiring volcano. See page 224

❺ **Comala** Captivating colonial town, where you can sip a beer and feast on free snacks while mariachis compete for your attention in the plaza. See page 225

❻ **Costalegre** A tantalizing stretch of coastline punctuated by small, low-key resorts. See page 225

❼ **Puerto Vallarta** Luxury resorts, stylish B&Bs and a languid colonial centre, with the beaches of the Bahía de Banderas nearby; humpback whales frolic offshore from December to April. See page 230

HIGHLIGHTS ARE MARKED ON THE MAP ON PAGE 198

with kioscos and fountains. The plaza is packed with cheap gift stalls on Sundays, and is surrounded by budget places to eat and drink, but there's not much to see. The **Catedral de Nuestra Señora de la Soledad** is a modern construction completed in 1950, with a striking blue dome that resembles a Russian Orthodox church. Walk down to the malecón for boat trips around the bay, fishing trips and the incongruous strip of sand known as **Playa de Tlacopanocha**, usually packed out on holidays, though it's a poor place to swim.

Museo Histórico de Acapulco

Hornitos s/n • Charge • 744 482 1114

About the only place in Acapulco that gives even the slightest sense of the historic role the city played in Mexico's past is the excellent **Museo Histórico de Acapulco**, a short walk away from the zócalo inside the **Fuerte de San Diego**. Soon after it was founded by the Spanish in the 1520s, the **shipping route** between the city and the Spanish colony of the Philippines, on the other side of the Pacific, became the most prized and preyed
3 upon in the world. From Acapulco, goods were transported overland to Veracruz and then shipped onwards to Spain.

Galleries inside cover the history of the fort and the Acapulco region, beginning with the pre-Hispanic **Yopes** and **Tepozteco** cultures. The most interesting rooms chronicle Spain's exploration of the Pacific from Acapulco, beginning in the 1500s, with special focus on the Manila/Asian trade; the Philippines and Mexico still share much in

WHEN TO VISIT ACAPULCO

Like many of Mexico's top resorts, Acapulco now experiences two **high seasons**: late November or early December through to the end of April (when *norteamericanos* flock south), and the hurricane season of July and August, when Mexican families take their summer vacations. Indeed, unlike Cancún, Los Cabos and Puerto Vallarta, 75 percent of Acapulco's visitors are domestic tourists. If you can, it's best to avoid Christmas and Semana Santa (Easter) altogether, and remember that any US or Mexican public holiday will likely bring the crowds. Thursday to Sunday tends to be busy year-round. Low season in Acapulco is May and June (when the weather is still good), and September and October (when it's usually rainy).

common, from the Catholic Church and food and drink, to a love of telenovelas. **Pirates** are covered (Brits beware, Sir Francis Drake is definitely one of the pirates here), as is the role of **José María Morelos** in the fight for independence.

La Casa de los Vientos

Inalámbrica 6, Cerro de la Pinzona (off La Quebrada) • Interior closed to the public

The only other cultural diversion in the *centro histórico* is **La Casa de los Vientos** (aka "Exekatlkalli" or "House of the Winds"), the house where **Diego Rivera** spent the last two years of his life with his former model and partner, Dolores Olmedo Patiño. Rivera spent eighteen months working on five grand **murals** here between 1955 and 1957, several preserved in his studio on the grounds; sadly, the house has remained in private hands since Olmedo's death in 2002 and is off-limits. Instead, art fans traipse up here to see the stunning murals that cover the entire outside wall of the house, made of seashells and coloured tiles; the 20m snake on the right depicts **Tlaloc**, the Aztec god of rain, fertility and lightning, while the 12.7m feathered serpent on the left is **Quetzalcoatl**, another important Aztec god but worshipped by many Mesoamerican civilizations.

Playas Caleta and Caletilla

Playas Caleta and **Caletilla** (take any "Caleta" bus from Costera) have a quite different atmosphere from those in the main part of the bay. Both have almost legendary status in Mexico, but it's the party families come for, not tranquillity. The beaches are actually very small, divided by a small rocky outcrop – they tend to be jam-packed at weekends, with a boisterous, carnival-like atmosphere and every centimetre of sand covered with beach umbrellas and towels. You wouldn't come here for seclusion, but it's loads of fun, the water is almost always calm and the beach is reasonably clean. From here you can take a water taxi across to Isla La Roqueta (see below), hang out at super-cool *Boca Chica* (see page 205), or rent kayaks.

Isla La Roqueta

Water taxis to the island (every 30min) cost a small fee (return) for a direct launch or there are detours past the submerged bronze statue of the Virgin of Guadalupe in glass-bottomed boats • Fondo de Cristal 744 410 9707

From the entrance to Mágico Mundo Marino between the two beaches, small boats ply the channel to the **Isla La Roqueta**, where there is another small but cleaner beach with a palapa restaurant. From the beach you can hike up to the small **lighthouse** on top of the island for views of the city, or take another water taxi to the famous *Palao Island Club* restaurant (see page 206), further along the island shore. The other side of the island is prime scuba-diving and snorkelling territory (see page 207). If you take the glass-bottomed boat out here you'll see the underwater bronze statue of the **Virgen de Guadalupe**, said to have been created by local fishermen in 1956. The story goes that the metal was collected from locals donating old keys.

Palma Sola (1.7km) & Cerro El Veladero (4.3km)

DRINKING & NIGHTLIFE	
Baby'O	4
Believe	6
Dinsmoor	5
Dubai Acapulco Bar	2
Palladium	7
Paradise	3
Papitos Picante Disco	1

1 (8km), 1, 2, 3 & Pie la Cuesta (10km)

3

AV PUEBLO NUEVA
RIO BALSAS
NIÑOS HÉROES
AV BAJA CALIFORNIA
AV RUIZ CORTINES
AV BAJA CALIFORNIA
AV JOSE FCO RUIZ
11 DE MARZO
INSURGENTES
AV VICENTE GUERRERO
AV MEXICO
AV ACAPULCO
C 14
C 13
C 10
AV SANTA CRUZ
EMILIANO ZAPATA
AV BAJA CALIFORNIA
Unidad Deportiva (Guerreros Acapulco)
BERNAL DIAZ DEL CASTILLO
AV CONSTITUYENTES
AV EJIDO
Central Ejido Bus Terminal
CAMPECHE
DURANGO
NUEVO LEÓN
NIÑOS HÉROES
SONORA
Papagayo Bus Terminal
Parque Papagayo
DEL MERCADO
MALPASO
RIO GRANDE
CHIHUAHUA
18 DE MARZO
SONORA
AV CUAUHTEMOC
Papagayo Adventure
JUAN N. ALVAREZ
RIO COLORADO
DIEGO H. MENDOZA
VASCO NÚÑEZ DE B.
AV COSTERA MIGUEL ALEMÁN
Playa Papagayo
CALZ. PIE DE LA CUESTA
IMSS
AV CUAUHTÉMOC
AV CONSTITUYENTES
VALDEZ ARÉVALO
Playa Hornos
Playa Tamarindos
N
Cliff Divers
AV ADOLFO LOPEZ MATEOS
La Casa de los Vientos
SEE "OLD TOWN ACAPULCO" MAP
Playa Angosta
Playa Tlacopanocha
AV LAS PLAYAS
AV COSTERA MIGUEL ALEMAN
AV GRAN VIA TROPICAL
AV ADOLFO LOPEZ MATEOS
AV COSTA GRANDE
AV LA SUIZA
AV AGUADA
OASIS
AV GRAN VIA TROPICAL
AV ADOLFO LOPEZ MATEOS
Mundo Magico Marino
Playa Caleta
Playa Caletilla
Roqueta Beach
Isla La Roqueta
0 500
metres

3

ADDRESSES ALONG COSTERA

Finding places along Costera can be tricky, as the numbering system is completely meaningless: 50 could be followed by 2010, which is next door to 403. The best **landmarks**, apart from the big hotels, are (moving east from the zócalo): **Parque Papagayo**, the roundabout with the **Diana Glorieta statue** and **El Rollo Waterpark**.

Zona Dorada

The **beaches** around **Acapulco Bay**, despite their various names – Tamarindo, Hornos, Hornitos, El Morro, Condesa and Icacos – are in effect a single sweep of sand along what's known as the **Zona Dorada** (roughly from where the old town ends at the big Mexican flag to the end of the bay).

From Caleta, a single seafront drive, the **Costera Miguel Alemán** – usually just "Costera" – stretches from the old town around the bay for 10km, linking almost everything of interest. For authentic Mexican seaside atmosphere it's hard to beat the stretch of Costera between the **Diana Glorieta statue** (traffic circle) and the **Fiesta Americana** hotel, lined with restaurants, bars blaring music and the **Paradise Bungy**. Stroll along the malecón to soak it all up. The beaches around here are also the place to come if you want to indulge in such frolics as being towed around the bay on the end of a parachute, water-skiing or sailing. Outfits offering all of these are dotted at regular intervals along the beach.

Diamante

Beyond Acapulco Bay, across the hills to the south, lies another major resort zone known as **Diamante**, with deluxe hotels lining the coast all the way to the airport and the former village of **Barra Vieja**. On the way you'll pass some of the fanciest hotels and villas in Acapulco, as well as some mesmerizing views of the city. **Puerto Marqués** (buses marked "Puerto Marqués") is the first of the beaches, a sheltered, deeply indented cove with restaurants and beach chairs right down to the water's edge. Nearby, the **Punta Diamante** is home to the most expensive hotel in Acapulco – the *Banyan Tree Cabo Marqués* – but you can continue by road to **Playa Revolcadero** (though only an occasional bus comes this far). This beach, a long, exposed stretch of sand, is beautiful but frequently lashed by heavy surf that makes swimming impossible.

Pie de la Cuesta

The public bus from Acapulco (marked "Pie de la Cuesta") runs every 10min or so down Escobeda then along Costera east of the zócalo; the last bus back leaves around 8pm

Around 15km north along the coast from central Acapulco, **PIE DE LA CUESTA** is far more serene than the city and a good place to watch the sun sink into the Pacific, enjoy

STAYING SAFE IN ACAPULCO

At the time of writing, available statistics put Acapulco at number ten in world cities for homicide rates per capita (behind Caracas, Venezuela, at number two and Mexico's Los Cabos at number one). Locals attribute this to the so-called "media war on Mexico" and it's true that it's extremely rare for tourists to be affected by the drug violence. Since 2011 the streets (and skies) have been patrolled by federal police, making things safer, particularly in the tourist areas, but it pays to be vigilant. Like any big city, Acapulco suffers some petty crime and the usual rules apply: avoid empty backstreets at night, don't flash expensive equipment and only take official taxis. Check the latest FCO advice before you travel at http://www.gov.uk/foreign-travel-advice/mexico/safety-and-security

a day out at the **Laguna de Coyuca**, or to ride horseback along the shore where the thunderous waves are a multi-sensual spectacle. The sand extends for many kilometres up the coast, but at the Acapulco end, where the bus drops you, there are several rickety bars and some tranquil **places to stay** (see page 206).

Laguna de Coyuca

Behind the beach, and only separated from the ocean by the hundred-metre-wide sandbar on which Pie de la Cuesta is built, lies the **Laguna de Coyuca**, a vast freshwater lake said to be three times the size of Acapulco Bay. Fringed with palms and rich in bird and animal life, the lagoon is big enough to accommodate both the ubiquitous noisy jet skiers and the more sedate **boat trips** that visit the three lagoon islands (see page 205).

ARRIVAL AND DEPARTURE — ACAPULCO

By plane Acapulco is connected to the US and Canada by numerous seasonal flights (typically Nov–April), but domestic choices are far smaller, and flying elsewhere in Mexico usually involves a change in Toluca, Guadalajara (Aeromar, TAR) or Mexico City. Arriving at Acapulco's General Juan N. Álvarez International Airport (744 435 2060), 23km southeast of the city, you'll find a couple of ATMs, Alamo, Europcar, Hertz and Thrifty car rental counters and basic information on the city. Transport prices are set according to an expensive zone system (buy tickets before you leave the baggage claim area): the cheapest option is a shared minibus ride, which will take you anywhere in the city – you need to reserve this service in advance to get back (allow at least 40min for the journey (744 462 1095). You can also take taxis (which cost an exorbitant amount to most destinations in the city) or hire a whole van for a similar fee. Hotel taxis charge less for the return journey, but you can get cheaper rates from taxis in the street (see page 204).

Destinations Mexico City (frequent; 1hr 10min); Monterrey (3 weekly; 1hr 55min); Tijuana (seasonal, 6 weekly; 3hr 50min); Toluca (3 daily; 1hr).

By bus Most long-distance buses arrive at one of three

THE MYSTERIES OF PALMA SOLA

High above the city, on the slopes of the Cerro El Veladero, lies Acapulco's most unexpected (and under-visited) sight: ancient carvings and enigmatic petroglyphs dating back to 800 BC. Protected within the **Zona Arqueológica de Palma Sola** (free), the site is thought to have been a ceremonial and pilgrimage centre, though little else is known about who created the other-worldly images. You can wander the eighteen most important granite rocks (via some steep paths) and visit the small exhibition hall on site, but it can be awkward to find (it's at the end of Av Palma Sola, along a pedestrian-only lane called La Mona, in the colonia of Independencia) – taxis will charge around a reasonable amount (ask the driver to wait). Be prepared for jaw-dropping views across the city.

terminals: the two main ones are the Estrella de Oro group terminal ("EDO"), 3km east of the zócalo at Cuauhtémoc 1490 (at the northeast corner of Parque Papagayo), connected to the centre by "Caleta" city buses (cross over Cuauhtémoc), or to the hotels along Costera by "Río/Base" buses; and the Papagayo (Central de Lujo) terminal, further west at Cuauhtémoc 1605 at Caminos, facing Parque Papagayo (Estrella Blanca, Futura, Pacifico, Chihuahuenses, Costa Line and Turistar use this). To get to the zócalo, take a "Zócalo" bus. The Central Ejido terminal, at Ejido 47, 2km north of the zócalo, mostly serves buses along the coast. Buses marked "Centro" or "Caleta" go to the zócalo. Taxis are always available at all terminals: from the EDO, Papagayo or Central Ejido to the zocalo, Caleta or Costera.

Destinations EDO Terminal: Chilpancingo (every 30min; 2hr); Lázaro Cárdenas (frequent); Mexico City (hourly; 5–6hr); Taxco (4 daily; 5hr); Zihuatanejo (6 daily; Económica at least hourly; 4–5hr).

Destinations Papagayo (Central de Lujo): Guadalajara (5 daily; Económica frequent; 14hr); Mexico City every terminal served (frequent; 5–6hr); Puerto Escondido (8 daily; 7hr); Puerto Vallarta (2 daily; 18–19hr); Tijuana (2 daily; 49hr).

Destinations Central Ejido: Manzanillo (1 daily; 11hr); Mazatlán (3 daily; 20hr 30min); Taxco (1 daily; 4–5hr).

INFORMATION

Tourist office The Fideicomiso de Promoción Turística de Acapulco (Mon–Fri 9am–6pm, Sat 9am–2pm; 744 484 7232, http://visitacapulco.travel) is based at Costera 2408, in Plaza Comercial Arrecife (Fracc Club Deportivo), but you'll get more information from the booths (usually daily 8am–2pm & 3–9pm) set along the waterfront: at Caleta Beach, at the pier in front of the zócalo, at the big Mexican flag in front of Papagayo Park and at the Diana Glorieta circle. For support relating to tourist security, including a 24-hour phone hotline, try CAPTA Tourist Assistance and Protection at Costera 38A (daily 9am–9pm; 744 484 9800, http://acapulco.gob.mx/capta).

GETTING AROUND

By bus You can reach everywhere near the zócalo on foot, but to get further afield, you'll need to take taxis or one of the frequent buses (look for "Caleta/Base", "Zócalo" or "Hornos") that run all the way along Costera. From the east, "C Río" buses travel past the big hotels, then turn inland onto Cuauhtémoc, where they pass the Estrella de Oro bus station and the market before rejoining Costera just before the zócalo. "Caleta" buses continue round to Playa Caleta – note that in bad traffic (which is most of the time), it can take almost an hour to ride the length of Costera. Buses are affordable (there's a small additional charge for those with a/c); be prepared for blaring techno or Latino pop at all hours of the day.

By taxi Taxis are plentiful all over the city; at all the bus stations and major hotels, they operate on a zone system, which is more or less the same wherever you are (though some hotel taxis charge a little more), with rates usually displayed on boards. Between *centro histórico* and the bus stations it's inexpensive, Caleta is a little more, while locations along Costera vary in price. You'll save money by flagging down the cheaper VW Beetle taxis on the street, but even here you'll have to negotiate pretty hard to pay local rates, as these drivers are well aware of the tourist "zone" system; these taxis should charge fifty percent less (locals save a good deal more for the first few km), but you'll likely only get a small discount on zone rates.

ACCOMMODATION

SEE MAPS PAGES 200 AND 203

IN THE CENTRE

Acapulco Amor José Azueta 12; http://hotelacapulcoamor.com. Beneath the glass box of an exterior, this comfortable, friendly hotel features basic, modern rooms with a soothing

ACAPULCO BOAT TRIPS AND THEME PARKS

Acapulco Bay has a multitude of watersports activities and tours on offer. Touristy **cruises** depart from the docks along the malecón in front of the zócalo, while kiosks offer everything from banana boats and jet skis, to snorkelling and parasailing. Additionally, various outfits along the hotel strip in Pie de la Cuesta offer tours to Laguna de Coyuca (see page 203) – prices are set per person – but it's worth checking what's on offer and how long the cruise is, as times tend to differ. Most boats stop on one island for lunch (not included in the price) and swimming. You can also get picked up from Acapulco: contact Aca Tours (744 110 4324), which charges varying amounts, depending on where your hotel is (includes pick-ups, tour in English, open bar and buffet).

Acarey Costera 100 (near zócalo); 744 482 6646, https://www.facebook.com/YateAcarey. The best of the tour boats charges around a moderate set fee (children below 140cm tall go free) for 2.5 hours around the bay (sunset cruises Oct–April 4.30–7pm (daily), 7.30–10pm (Sat only); May–Sept 5.30–8pm; moonlight cruise year-round 10.30pm–1am).

Fish-R-Us Costera 100; 744 483 8383, http://fish-r-us.mx. This professional outfit runs sea-fishing and scuba-diving tours as well as cruises around the bay. Night-time excursions (typical catch are sailfish, dorado and red snapper) are particularly appealing, illuminated by the lights of the town shining out from all around the coast.

AMUSEMENT PARKS

Parque Papagayo Manuel Gómez Morín 1, at Costera, 744 277 9652. This fifty-acre public park at the edge of the *centro histórico* attracts picnicking families and joggers with its green spaces, swimming pool, aviary, roller-skating rink, boating lake and fairground rides (free).

Papagayo Adventure (744 485 6591) is a pay to enter (children under 3 go free) attraction, featuring a ropeway, climbing wall and various activities for kids.

3

marine colour scheme and pine furniture. There's wi-fi, TV and a/c, and decent breakfasts. M$$

Angelita Calzada La Quebrada 37; 744 483 5734. One of Acapulco's cheapest options, with spartan but sizeable rooms with private bath and fan leading off a courtyard. The eccentric management of Doña Angelita keeps life interesting. M$

Asturias Calzada La Quebrada 45; 744 483 6548. A welcoming budget option with clean, passable rooms around a courtyard. Its small pool makes it marginally better value than the competition in this price bracket. M$

El Mirador Acapulco Plazoleta La Quebrada 74; http://miradoracapulco.com. The location of this classic 1930s hotel – right above La Quebrada (see page 207) – couldn't be better. Lodging is in clean, rather characterless, rooms with tiled stone floors and balconies overlooking the ocean. There are three pools and a bar-restaurant on site, where guests can watch the cliff divers for free. M$$$

CALETA AND CALETILLA

★ **Boca Chica** Playa de Caletilla s/n; http://bocachicahotelacapulco.com-hotel.com. Stylishly appointed resort carved into the cliff-face at the end of Playa Caletilla, with all-white rooms featuring retro showers, flatscreen TVs and free wi-fi – Mexican artist Claudia Fernández has decorated the 1950s interior, with a luxurious spa, gym, massage cabañas, pool terrace and special sushi takeout menu adding to the allure. M$$$

Los Flamingos López Mateos s/n; http://hotelflamingosacapulco.com. An Acapulco retro classic, this landmark 1930s hotel was once owned by a Hollywood gang that included Tarzan (Johnny Weissmuller), Cary Grant and John Wayne. The Coco Loco cocktail was apparently invented here in 1935, and the lush gardens and sublime sunset views from Acapulco's highest cliffs are a perfect accompaniment. The rooms have seen better days but are still spacious, characterful and comfortable. M$$

Playa Linda Costera 1; 744 482 0814. Modern mid-range hotel with sparsely decorated rooms, some with sea-view balconies, a short walk from the beaches. All rooms (sleeping up to four) have a/c and TV, and many have fully equipped kitchenettes. M$$$

ZONA DORADA

★ **Las Brisas** Carretera Escénica 5255; http://lasbrisashotels.com.mx. Overlooking the eastern end of the bay, high above the ocean amid blossom-smothered gardens, this luxury resort – established in 1957 with a unique all-pink-and-white colour scheme – is the most exclusive in the city. More like a small village, its individual villas offer private swimming pools, jacuzzis and delivered breakfasts, and they also rent out pink jeeps to any occupant. You access the water via the La Concha beach club below, and every room has a sea-view terrace with mesmerizing vistas. The hotel was immortalized in a Ringo Starr song, and famous guests have left hand prints in pink plaster (Sophia Loren, Neil Armstrong, JFK, Denzel Washington and Morgan Freeman among them). M$$$$

Gran Plaza Costera 123; 744 440 5555. Certainly, the most memorable building on the beach, shaped like a curved pyramid, with clean, modern rooms (if a little gaudy – gold features prominently) with cable TV and an attractive pool. Free wi-fi. M$$$

Elcano Costera 75 (at Del Parque and Las Palmas); 744 434 1500. This renovated 1950s monolith, with an all-pervasive nautical theme, has spic-and-span blue-and-white rooms with tiled floors, cable TV, comfortable beds and well-proportioned bathrooms, though the a/c can be weak. The best rooms have terraces overlooking the ocean, but all rooms have ocean views. There's a beachside pool, four jacuzzis, a beachfront restaurant and two bars. M$$$

Pacific Paradise Punta Bruja 1, near Playa Condesa; https://pacific-paradise-suites.allacapulcohotels.com. Mediterranean-style budget resort with spotless, if not exactly stylish, rooms across three floors. Situated a few blocks back from Costera, so nights are quieter and it's better value than many of the beachside establishments. M$$$

3

Del Valle Manuel Gómez Morín 150, opposite the eastern entrance to Parque Papagayo; 744 485 8336. *Del Valle* has a convenient location, spacious, well-maintained rooms (some with a/c), a pool and private kitchens (outside the rooms) that can be rented for a daily fee. M$$$

DIAMANTE

★ **Bambuddha** Carretera Barra Vieja km 37; http://bambuddha.com.mx. This gorgeous Asian-themed boutique hotel, with bamboo palapas right on the beach, is a wonderfully languid retreat, specializing in yoga, meditation and detox programmes. Minimum two-night stay at weekends; three nights during the week. M$$$$

Banyan Tree Cabo Marqués Cabo Marqués, Lote 1, Col Punta Diamente; http://banyantree.com. This resort is the gold standard in Acapulco luxury, though if you stay here you may not leave; it's a self-contained, all-inclusive resort with villas set into the cliffs. The jaw-dropping infinity pool comes with a stunning view of the Pacific, but all the facilities are first class (spa, restaurant, bar). Travelling into the city can be time-consuming and expensive from here – most guests hire drivers. M$$$$

PIE DE LA CUESTA

Acapulco Trailer Park 744 460 0010. Some 15km north of central Acapulco lies the only place with official year-round camping, with sixty full hook-ups and spaces for tents as well as RVs; it's relatively pricey but includes free wi-fi and water. M$$

Baxar Hotel Fuerza Aérea Militar 356 http://baxar.com.mx. Rustic chic epitomized, this intimate beachside enclave has colourful, breezy rooms with tiled private bath and mosquito nets (some have a/c). The restaurant serves great fresh fish and there's a pool and guaranteed relaxation. Significant discounts are available if you book online. M$$$

★ **Villa Nirvana** Fuerza Aerea 302; 744 460 1631. American expats Pamela and Daniel built this wonderful expansive villa right on the beach, with chilled-out pool, wi-fi and hammocks slung throughout, as well as a fridge full of ice-cold beer. Thunderous breaking waves on one of the area's wildest stretches of coastline make for a wonderful backdrop. Ask for room 16. M$$$

EATING

SEE MAPS PAGES 200 AND 203

To eat cheaply in Acapulco you're confined to the area around the **zócalo,** where no-frills joints serve unmemorable but filling comidas corridas. Eating by the **beach** – where there's more choice – is more expensive, and increasingly so as you head east. Throughout the tourist zone, especially along Costera, you'll find Mexican chains such as *Texas Ribs* and *Harry's Prime Steakhouse*. Heading into the hills of **Diamante**, the Avenida Escénica has world-class restaurants where delectable food, flawless service and goose-bump-inducing views are likely to be the highlight of your stay. Prices are on a par with upscale New York and London, but well worth the splurge. *Ceviche Acapulco* is the city's signature dish, served in numerous restaurants; the other local speciality, *pescado a la talla* (whole, charred-grilled red snapper), is best experienced in Barra Vieja.

CENTRO HISTÓRICO

El Amigo Miguel Juárez 31; 744 483 6981. The original of an Acapulco chain (the most popular is on the malecón), open since 1970, serving good soups, *antojitos* and seafood – sea bass, garlic shrimp and grilled Pacific lobster – at reasonable prices in clean, if functional, surroundings with a pleasant second-floor dining room. M$$$

Mariscos Nacho's Azueta 7; 744 330 9904. Multistorey seafood place with fresh daily produce from the local markets. Does a good pasta marinera and shrimp done however you like. M$$

Mi Piaci Plaza Alvarez 6 (zócalo); http://mipiaci.com.mx. Probably the most modern place on the plaza, a respectable Italian restaurant serving all the usual pizzas, pastas and calzones for reasonable prices. M$$$

Tortas Ricardo's Juarez 9; 744 482 1140. Huge variety of generously stuffed tortas (rolls) for small prices, just off the zócalo, with some seating in the no-frills but clean interior. M$

ISLA DE LA ROQUETA

Palao Island Club Isla de la Roqueta; 55 1409 3380. Fun place to spend the afternoon, with a small beach, walking trails over the island and heaps of seafood and cold beers. The buffet lunch is a set price for as much as you'd like (with floor show and boat ride). Ferries depart daily from Muelle Palao, Costera 100 (11am & 1pm; return 3.30 & 5.30pm). M$$

ZONA DORADA AND DIAMANTE

100% Natural Costera 200 (plus several other branches);

http://100natural.com. One of a chain of healthy-eating places which serves classic Mexican breakfast dishes alongside fruit shakes, good salads and burgers. M$$

★ **Bellavista** Inside Hotel Las Brisas, Carretera Escénica 5255; http://lasbrisashotels.com.mx. Try to visit this stunning resort for a drink or meal even if you're not staying here – the views are utterly mind-blowing. Right on the top of the cliff, the efficient staff serve breakfast and dinner, while *Sunset Bar* mixes up their house margaritas to enjoy over the stunning sunsets. M$$$$

Carmenere Costera, next to Oceanic 2000; 744 201 3031. Mediterranean cuisine in a small, beautiful space just off Costera; the romantic ambience enhances the subtle flavours, al dente pastas and delectable mains such as nut-coated Pacific sea bass, or rib-eye steaks. M$$$$

★ **Chile, Maiz y Frijol** Costera 116; 744 481 0300; www.facebook.com/chimafri. This tiny gem of a restaurant, overlooking the Costera, serves up classic Mexican dishes in a homely environment, with food cooked behind the counter. Gargantuan quesadillas and spicy enchiladas come recommended, as do the breaded and garlic prawns. M$$$

El Nono Costera 179; 744 485 1672. This no-frills, open-air restaurant is the perfect place to soak up the Costera beach scene while staying close to the old town, with fresh seafood and, as the staff are keen to tell you, the coldest beer on the beach. M$$$

★ **Sirocco** Escénica 120; http://sirocco.com.mx. Classic Spanish restaurant, with especially good paellas, seafood and tapas. The views over Puerto Marqués add to the wow factor, especially after a few mojitos. Reservations essential. M$$$$

★ **Tacos Tumbras** Costera, 62 opposite Oceanic 2000; http://tacostumbras.mx. Cheap local chain with a couple of outdoor restaurants on Costera, with plastic furniture, and meat roasted at the counter. The clubbers' and taxi drivers' late-night favourite for its very succulent tacos *carne asada*. M$$

★ **Zibu** Escénica s/n; http://zibu.mx. High above Puerto Marqués, the views from this Mex-Thai fusion restaurant are phenomenal (with hummingbirds flitting between flowers), but the food is the real star. Asian and Mexican flavours are delicately balanced; jalapeño sauces replace wasabi on tuna sashimi, and prawns come with sweet tamarind and mango dressing. Owner Eduardo Wichtendahl is the son of celebrity Mexican chef Susanna Palazuelos. M$$$$

3

BARRA VIEJA

★ **Esmirna del Mar** Carretera Barra Vieja 1; http://esmirna.restaurantwebexperts.com. Chilled-out beach restaurant lauded for its interpretation of the local speciality, *pescado a la talla*. Fresh fish is served with adobo or garlic seasoning, rice, salads, *pico de gallo* and corn tortillas. M$$

PIE DE LA CUESTA

Ricarda Yopes Seafront, 100m west of Villa Nirvana (look for large yellow sign); 744 222 6012. Friendly Ricarda serves up filling breakfasts and delicious dinners of fresh fish and shrimp from the local market; grab a table on the sand and enjoy the thunderous waves as you eat. She also has a great michelada mix, and offers tours of the lagoon behind the town for a small fee. M$$$

ACAPULCO'S DIVERS

Acapulco's famed **clavadistas** (cliff divers) have been plunging some 35m from the heights of La Quebrada into a rocky channel since the early 1920s (organized officially since 1934), timing their leap to coincide with an incoming wave. Mistimed, there's not enough water to stop them hitting the bottom, though the chief danger these experts seem to face is getting back out of the water without being dashed against the rocks. It could easily be corny, but it's undeniably impressive, especially when floodlit at night. The **dive times** – 1pm, 7.30pm, 8.30pm, 9.30pm and 10.30pm – are rigidly adhered to. A typical display involves several exponents, most taking the lower (25m) platform with some diving simultaneously, and a final dive from the upper level after first asking for the Virgin's intervention at the clifftop shrine. The final diver at the 10.30pm show leaps into the darkness (they turn off the floodlights) with two flaming torches. From the road you can see the spectacle for nothing (get there early), but you'll get a much better view if you go down the steps from the Plazuela de Quebrada to a **viewing platform** (there's a small fee) more or less opposite the divers. Get here early for a good position. Alternatively, you can sit in the lobby bar at *El Mirador Acapulco* hotel (the cover here includes two drinks); watching from their overpriced *La Perla* restaurant is not worth it, however. To get there, simply climb the Calzada La Quebrada from the town centre, about fifteen minutes' walk from the zócalo. Heading back, hotel taxis will take you into the centre, to the bus terminals and along Costera.

DRINKING AND NIGHTLIFE

SEE MAP PAGE 200

When it comes to nightlife, Acapulco firmly adheres to the Madrid school of partying; many people don't even think about eating dinner until 10pm, and clubs won't get going till long after midnight. You could spend several weeks in Acapulco simply trawling its scores of **bars and nightclubs** – there are people who claim never to have seen the town during daylight hours. Anywhere with music or dancing will demand a hefty **cover charge** – in high season more so for men than women.

Baby'O Costera 22, east of El Rollo Waterpark; http://babyo.com.mx. Set in an imitation cave, this is one of the more consistently popular clubs as well as one of the oldest, opening in 1976; past patrons include Elizabeth Taylor, Tony Curtis and Sly Stallone. It's also one of the most expensive (with a hefty cover charge) – drinks are not included. The well-dressed, well-heeled crowd is usually high on attitude if they have managed to get in – *Baby'O* tries to maintain a spurious exclusivity by turning people away at the door (it can only accommodate 250). All in all a mainstream affair, with cheesy 1980s music mixed with house and Latin.

Believe Escénica 22; 744 446 7109. Boasting magnificent views over Acapulco Bay, this local favourite is always a safe bet of a weekend, with a varied roster of DJs throwing out a crowd-pleasing selection of English- and Spanish-language floor-fillers. Cover charges are standard, but be aware that the 'free bar' (until 4am) does not preclude the expectation of some pretty hefty tips. Smart-casual dress code.

Dinsmoor Escnénica s/n; 755 6868 7771. The new kid on Acapulco's nightlife scene, *Dinsmoor* is the fresh incarnation of former favourite *Mandara*. The psychedelic artwork outside invokes Sinatra and other vintage Acapulco figures, but there's nothing backward-looking about the club itself, with its huge dancefloor hosting a never-ending stream of resident and visiting DJs.

Dubai Acapulco Bar Acapulco Costera 39690; 744 186 1200. The resident live band is excellent and the cover charge here is cheaper than most spots. Visitors should brace themselves for the especially strong drinks.

★ **Palladium** Escénica, Playa Guitarrón; http://palladium.com.mx. It's all about the glorious bay views at this justifiably hyped club with the best music selection – techno, house and hip-hop – in the city. A slightly older and dressier crowd adds to the friendly, gregarious atmosphere. Considered the best club in the city, and long queues testify to its kudos. There is a cover charge, but that comes with an open bar.

Paradise Costera 107; http://restauranteparadise.com.mx. Popular restaurant-bar just off Condesa beach, near the bungee tower and on the busiest section of Costera – a good place to start your evening. The restaurant section fades away as the evening wears on, replaced by a boisterous club-like atmosphere replete with local entertainers, wet T-shirt contests and plenty of cheap booze.

Papitos Picante Disco Piedra Picuna s/n, opposite El Presidente hotel; 744 326 1354. While not as LGBTQ+-friendly as Puerto Vallarta, Acapulco does have a thriving gay scene: this is one of the more reliable clubs – small and a little claustrophobic, but featuring strippers and other live shows.

DIRECTORY

Banks Banks (particularly Banamex) and *casas de cambio* (slightly poorer rates) are numerous along Costera. Bancomer is on the zócalo; HSBC is not far away at Carranza 7.

Consulates Canada, Pasaje Diana, Costera 121, Fracc Magallanes 744 484 1305 (Mon–Fri 9.30am–12.30pm); US, Pasaje Diana (next to *Hotel Continental Emporio*), Costera 121, Office 14, Fracc Magallanes 800 681 9374 (Mon–Fri 10am–2pm).

Emergencies 911.

Hospital Cruz Roja 065 or 744 481 2691; IMSS Hospital, Adolfo Ruiz Cortinez 744 445 5371.

Laundry Lavandería Lava Chip, La Paz, at José Maria Iglesias (charge/kg; 744 217 7283).

Pharmacy Plenty of 24hr places in the hotel zone along Costera, and Botica Acapulco near the zócalo at Carranza 3 (also 24hr).

Post office At Costera 315, three blocks east of the zócalo (Mon–Fri 8am–7pm, Sat 9am–2pm).

Tourist police 744 485 0490; CAPTA tourist information 744 481 1854 or 744 484 9800.

Zihuatanejo

Around 250km along the coast from Acapulco, **ZIHUATANEJO** ("zee-watt-a-NEH-ho"), for all its growth in recent years, has retained something of the look and feel of the traditional fishing village it once was. In stark contrast to neighbour Ixtapa, what building there has been is small-scale, low-key and low-rise, and the town looks over an attractive bay, ringed by broad, sandy beaches excellent for swimming and snorkelling. This said, it is definitely a **resort**: taxi drivers are forever advertising for customers, trinket and tacky T-shirt shops are abundant and as likely as not there'll be a cruise ship moored out in the bay. Despite the proliferation of luxury hotels, though, there are at least a fair number of small, reasonably priced places to stay as well as some inexpensive restaurants. For some, Zihuatanejo is the ideal compromise – quiet by night, yet with the more commercial excitements of Ixtapa nearby.

Museo Arqueológico de la Costa Grande

Paseo del Pescador 7, at Plaza Olof Palme • Entry by donation • 755 554 7552

The pedestrianized Paseo del Pescador (or just malecón) runs behind the beach, and at the southern end you'll find the **Museo Arqueológico de la Costa Grande**, a small and straightforward look at the early history of the region. Inside you'll find pre-Columbian archeological finds such as pottery, tools, simple jewellery and rock engravings from important sites such as Cerro de la Madera and Tierras Prietas, with exhibits beginning with the first settlements in the region and ending with the arrival of the Spaniards. Most labelling is Spanish only.

3

Playa La Madera

Four main beaches surround the Bahía de Zihuatanejo, but the **Playa Principal**, the main town beach, is best avoided – with muddy water, brown sand and persistent hawkers, it is an interesting place to people-watch, but with the port nearby it's a bad idea to swim here. Instead follow the footpath east from the end of the beach across the normally dry outlet of a drainage canal, then around a rocky point to the calm waters of **Playa La Madera**, a broad, moderately clean 400m strand of sand that shelves softly

THE VIRGIN OF THE TREE

The car park at Playa La Ropa might seem an unlikely place for a miracle, but according to locals, on November 27, 2006 an image of the **Virgin of Guadalupe** – Mexico's patron saint and most revered apparition of Mary – suddenly appeared carved into the trunk of a plum tree right here. The image was quickly deemed a miracle, and though officially unsanctioned by the Church, it is now a mini-pilgrimage site, with candles, offerings and bright flowers enveloping the tree.

into the ocean, making it a good option for kids. There's a handful of restaurants and hotels on the hill behind, as well as some expensive condos.

Playa La Ropa

3

A kilometre or so over the headland from Playa La Madera, past the *mirador* with great views across the bay, lies **Playa La Ropa** (reachable by bus), which takes its name – "Clothes Beach" – from silks washed up here when one of the *nao de China* (trading ships from China) was wrecked offshore. This is Zihuatanejo's finest road-accessible beach, perfect for swimming and palm-fringed for more than a kilometre, with a variety of beachfront restaurants and hotels.

Playa Las Gatas

You can walk fifteen minutes beyond the end of Playa La Ropa to gorgeous **Playa Las Gatas**, named after the nurse sharks that used to populate the waters, but the path is difficult to follow: as there are no roads, most people take boats from the main pier in Zihuatanejo (daily 8am–5pm, last return 5.30pm; 10min). Las Gatas is the last of the bay's beaches, its crystalline blue water hemmed in by jungle-smothered hills and surrounded by a reef, giving it the enclosed feel of a South Pacific swimming pool. It's safe for kids, though the sea bottom is mostly rocky and tough on feet. The clear waters are great for **snorkelling** – you can rent gear (by the day) from vendors among the rather pricey palapa restaurants.

Barra de Potosí

For absolute peace and quiet, the best thing you can do is to take a day trip out of Zihuatanejo to **Barra de Potosí**, a tiny community situated at the southern end of the expansive, postcard-perfect, golden sandy beaches of Playa Larga and Playa Blanca, which curve steeply round the bay and keep going as far as the eye can see. There are plenty of *enramadas* (beach restaurants) here that sell delicious seafood for half the price of the restaurants in town, and boat trips into the **Laguna de Potosí**, a large mangrove estuary teeming with birdlife. It's possible to travel to Barra de Potosí by public transport (see below).

ARRIVAL AND DEPARTURE — ZIHUATANEJO

ZIHUATANEJO

By plane From the Ixtapa-Zihuatanejo International Airport, 20km south of the centre (only 2km off the highway to Acapulco), ignore the crowds of time-share sellers offering lifts and buy transport tickets from the official counters: *colectivo* (shared) taxis charge less, while regular taxis will be a fair amount more. Almost all the flights here are from the US and Canada (seasonal); Aeroméxico, Aeromar and VivaAerobus fly around five times daily to Mexico City, where you must change for all other domestic destinations with the exception of Santiago de Querétaro (4 weekly).

By bus Buses arrive at Zihuatanejo's Central de Autobuses (and the adjacent Estrella de Oro terminal), about 2km and a 25min walk from the centre of town on the road to Acapulco (Hwy-200). There are plenty of taxis outside the station, and if you cross Hwy-200 via the overpass, you can pick up passing "Zihuatanejo" buses (10min), which will generally drop you off at the top of Juárez (heading back, catch "La Correa" buses).

Destinations Acapulco (hourly; 4–5hr); Ixtapa (continuously; 15min); Lázaro Cárdenas (hourly; 2hr); Manzanillo (1 daily; 7–8hr); Mexico City (frequently; 9hr); Morelia (3 daily; 5–7hr); Puerto Vallarta (1 daily; 10–11hr); Tijuana (2 daily; 43–45hr).

BARRA DE POTOSÍ

By bus/truck To get to Barra de Potosí, board a Petatlán-bound bus from the main bus station or bus stop on Las Palmas and Cocos in downtown Zihuatanejo and ask the driver to drop you off at the village of Los Achotes. From here, pick-up trucks (*colectivos*) leave when full to run the final bone-rattling 20min to the beach.

GETTING AROUND

By bus Once in town, local "microbuses" are among the most affordable ways to get around, depending on the destination. Pick them up on Juárez.

By taxi Taxis charge according to a schedule of fixed fares; rides between downtown Zihuatanejo and Ixtapa cost the most; Zihuatanejo to Playa La Ropa cost less; to Playa Madera is the cheapest fare. Trips within downtown (including the bus station) are equally affordable but the price increases again when you start heading out to destinations like Playa Larga and Playa Linda. Add forty percent between midnight and 5am.

3

INFORMATION

Tourist office The municipal tourist office (Mon–Fri 8am–4pm; 755 555 0700,) is inconveniently located about 1km north of town in the Palacio Municipal, Paseo Zihuatanejo 21, near the Fuente del Sol fountain. There is a smaller office on Paseo de la Bahía s/n, close to Playa La Ropa, and, in high season only, a tourist booth in the centre at Álvarez s/n.

State tourism office The helpful state tourism office is at Galo 3, near Plaza Kioto (Mon–Fri 8am–3.30pm & 5–7pm, Sat 8am–1pm; 755 544 8361). Useful websites include http://ixtapa-zihuatanejo.com and http://zihuatanejo.net.

ACTIVITIES

Zihuatanejo offers various activities to distract you from lounging on the beach. Quite apart from jet skiing, parasailing and getting dragged around on a huge inflatable banana, you could arrange to go **fishing** for dorado, yellowtail, bonito or big game; numerous fishermen offer this service along the main beach and around the pier. Options are small game along the coast (think bonito and dorado) and big game further out in open ocean (sailfish, mahi-mahi and marlin). Prices vary, but expect to pay anywhere a fairly substantial amount for a day's charter, which will also include lunch, drinks and snorkelling. **Diving** is also popular in the area.

Carlo Scuba Playa Las Gatas; http://carloscuba.com. Carlo's runs PADI-certified dives from its base at Playa Las Gatas (all trips include transport from Zihuatanejo pier). Other options include Discover Scuba Dive and the PADI Open Water Course.

Ixtapa Sportfishing Charters US; http://ixtapasportfishing.com. Zihuatanejo is a sailfish angling paradise. Trips start in a small super-*panga*.

Zihuatanejo Dive Center Paseo Las Salinas, beside the footbridge; 131 0998, http://scubazihuatanejo.com. Poto, as he likes to be called, offers PADI-certified dives to forty locations around the coast, including the particularly rewarding Morros de Potosi. Trip options include a day's diving or for snorkelling. The center also offers whale-watching trips between December and April for and surf lessons.

ACCOMMODATION

Zihuatanejo's **high season** is fairly long, from around mid-Nov to the end of April. Outside those times some of the marginally more expensive hotels drop their **rates** to those of the budget places – which tend to vary their prices less. **Playa La Madera**, while part of Zihuatanejo, has a different feel, slightly removed and a touch exclusive – though not necessarily more expensive. **Playa La Ropa**, more than 1km from the centre, feels a world apart and is home to the most luxurious options.

CENTRAL ZIHUATANEJO, SEE MAP PAGE 209

Casa Elvira Juan N. Álvarez 29; 755 101 2700. The oldest hotel in town has been a favourite budget option since 1956, with a friendly owner who is probably the oldest man in town. There's a communal kitchen and very good restaurant on site. The six rooms with shared bath (no hot water) are unadorned but perfectly adequate (there's an extra charge for a/c). M$

Hostel Rincón del Viajero Paseo Las Salinas 50, La Noria; 755 103 4566, http://hostelworld.com. The town's only hostel is not the cleanest or quietest place, but it's an amiable enough spot, with hippy art gracing the walls and hammocks hanging in a shaded garden. Dorms and doubles are available. M$

R3 Marias Colonia La Noria; http://hotelr3mariasnoria.com.mx. A friendly family are the bedrock of this hotel at the town's lagoon inlet, with stunning views over the bay beyond (ask for room "Zihua"). Good strong a/c, a chilled-out vibe and a 2min stroll from the action make this one of the most appealing options in town. M$$

Zihuatanejo Centro Ramírez 2; http://zihuacentro.com. One of the most comfortable options in the centre, a couple of blocks from the waterfront. Its a/c rooms are equipped with decent cable TV, and there's access to a small pool and bar. M$$

PLAYA LA MADERA, SEE MAP PAGE 209

Aura del Mar López Mateos, Playa La Madera; http://hotelauradelmar.com. This charming hotel has comfortable, rustic-chic suites with rugged adobe walls and wooden furnishings. Large private terraces have hammocks from which to enjoy the sea views. Other facilities include a swimming pool, a games room with ping-pong, air hockey and table football, an internet café, and a fitness centre with sauna, steam room and massage rooms. M$$$

3

Bungalows Adelamar Adelita 40, Playa La Madera; http://thebest100hotels.com/bungalows-adelamar. Eight immaculately clean, modern apartments (holding up to four people) in a tranquil location close to the beach, all with well-equipped kitchens and some with small gardens. There's also an excellent communal pool. M$$$

Bungalows Sotelo López Mateos, Playa La Madera; https://www.sotelozihua.mx. Comfortable, cheerfully decorated apartments with a/c, internet, satellite TV, balconies, kitchens and great sea views. The most luxurious rooms have jacuzzis on the balcony. M$$$

Casa Sun & Moon Calle Adelita 10; http://casasunandmoon.com. On a gentle hill overlooking Playa Madera, this pleasant whitewashed hotel offers comfortable rooms with sunny yellow walls, opening onto a communal terrace with access to a kitchen and living area. The more expensive suites feature beds on a mezzanine and private kitchen/living areas. M$$$$

PLAYA LA ROPA, SEE MAP PAGE 214

★ **La Casa Que Canta** Camino Escéncio, Playa La Ropa; http://lacasaquecanta.com. Guests rave about this beautifully designed, thatched-roof hotel draped over the hillside. The breezy rooms are luxuriously decorated with traditional artesanía, and the secluded, romantic gardens are composed of labyrinthine pathways that lead to intimate hideaways. There's also a stellar restaurant and a spa and fitness centre. M$$$$

Catalina Beach Resort Playa la Ropa s/n; http://catalina-beach-resort.com. A good-value beachfront option, *Catalina* is one of the oldest and friendliest hotels in town with great facilities for the price. The rooms do vary – some are showing their age – but the large terraces with hammocks and glorious views are the attraction here. Tropical gardens, a pool and an oceanfront restaurant are perfect for relaxing. M$$$

Gran Pacifica Resort Playa las Gatas 40880, Playa La Ropa s/n; https://www.pacifica.com.mx. *The* place to splurge, and one of the most opulent hotels on the coast, this hotel is a justly popular romantic getaway, with jaw-dropping views at every turn and impeccable service. M$$$$

Tentaciones Hotel & Lounge Pool Camino Escéncio, Playa La Ropa; http://hoteltentaciones.com. Another gorgeous luxury hideaway, hidden among lush cliffs and ponds above the beach, and consisting of four one-bedroom palapa suites with verandas overlooking the bay. All come with satellite TV, marble-clad bathrooms and the usual plush amenities. Rates include American breakfast. M$$$$

La Villa Luz Escénica la Ropa 97; http://lavillaluz.com. A lovely palapa-style boutique, a couple of minutes' walk from the beach, combining a boho look with an intimate atmosphere across just seven rooms. Breezy linens hang over the beds from robust wooden frames and shutters open to reveal ocean or garden views; some suites feature furnished terraces, and all have a/c. Winding paths lead through a lovely garden to a kidney-shaped pool shaded by palm trees. M$$$$

PLAYA LARGA, SEE MAP PAGE 209

Casa Kau-Kan Domicilio Conocido s/n, Playa Larga; 755 115 7847. The epitome of good taste and discretion, this small, beachside boutique has spacious, artful suites with separate living areas and plush bathrooms. Gourmet food, a tranquil pool and gorgeous gardens create an aura of refined pampering in an isolated natural setting with many kilometres of deserted beach (no phones or TVs). M$$$

BARRA DE POTOSÍ, SEE MAP PAGE 214

★ **La Casa del Encanto** Javier Rodriguez s/n; 755 125 1680. There are just six lovely guestrooms at this homely B&B, each decked out in a different style, but all featuring a cheerful colour palette, traditional patterned textiles and pleasingly weathered-looking furnishings. Rooms open onto shaded terraces with seats and hammocks, while hearty breakfasts are served each morning in the lush garden. M$$$

EATING

CENTRAL ZIHUATANEJO, SEE MAP PAGE 209

Cenaduría Antelia Nicolás Bravo 14; 755 554 3091. Open since 1975, this snug old-time joint is a great spot to eat unadulterated Mexican staples for a bargain price – tacos, enchiladas and the like – until midnight. M$

Coconuts Pasaje Agustín Ramírez 1; http://coconutszih.com. Set in a charming old house (the remains of a coconut factory built in 1865) with a stunning patio. The food is good, with a varied menu featuring healthy fish, fresh poultry and creative vegetarian dishes. The overall ambience is quite romantic, especially with low-key jazz in the evenings. M$$$$

Doña Licha Los Cocos 8; 755 554 3933. A wide menu of excellent and inexpensive comidas corridas (ribs, tripe and pork chops), served with mountains of rice and beans, has earned this place a loyal following. With a lackadaisical, raw atmosphere, complete with blasting TV and erratic service, the copious platters of food are undoubtedly the main attraction. M$$

El Mediterráneo 5 de Mayo 4; 755 554 1202. This Greek-themed Mexican/Mediterranean fusion restaurant is especially lauded for its pastas and fresh tuna – sit in the garden at the back to soak up the relaxed ambience. M$$$

La Papa Loca Colegio Militar at Palapas (all taxi drivers know it); 755 554 8016. A local institution serving up baked potatoes, smashed open and covered with all sorts of delights including cheese, carne al pastor, cream and sauce. Indeed the "Crazy Potato", their signature dish, features all of them. Also does tacos, fish and big juices for cheap. The street-level tables and atmosphere make this unmissable. M$$

La Sirena Gorda Paseo del Pescador 90; 755 554 2687. Fairly expensive but well sited, so you can soak up the bustle of the town centre as you dine on succulent tuna steaks and seafood cocktails, as well as a selection of American dishes, in the balmy night air. Creatively decorated with paintings of the eponymous chunky mermaid. M$$$

Tamales y Atoles Any Guerrero 38, at Ejido. No prizes for guessing what is on the menu at this good-value, bustling, beach joint that packs in locals and tourists looking for its sixteen different kinds of tamales, which range from chicken and chile to cheese and squash blossom. The signature dish is *pozole* (pork stew, traditionally eaten on Thurs); there are also good tacos. Mexican breakfasts served daily. M$$

PLAYA LA ROPA, SEE MAP PAGE 214

Panaderia y Pasteleria La Peque Nicolás Bravo 15; 755 130 5780. This no-frills street bakery serves up some seriously tasty cakes and some equally mouth-watering breads. With a heavenly smell detectable blocks away, this is a good spot to grab a sandwich for lunch or a sweet snack, covered in icing. The bakery often sells out by mid-afternoon so plan your trip accordingly. M$

3

DRINKING AND NIGHTLIFE

SEE MAP PAGE 209

Kokomo Bar Ejido 3; 755 558 2990. Lively joint smothered in naff wood-effect wallpaper, with a packed bar and tables further back. Very popular with the locals and a sure-fire bet for a rowdy drink or two. Daily happy hour.

DIRECTORY

Emergencies 911; Cruz Roja (Red Cross) 065.

Money and exchange Banamex, on Ejido at Guerrero (24hr ATM), and Banorte, Ejido 8 at Juárez.

Pharmacy Farmacia del Ahorro, Benito Juarez (Daily 7am–11pm).

Police Tourist police 060 or 755 554 2207.

Post office Edificio SCT, between Telegrafistas and Palmar.

Ixtapa

Just 7km north of Zihuatanejo, **IXTAPA** could hardly be more different. Ixtapa is a computer-planned "paradise" resort, established by state tourism body Fonatur in the 1970s, and, even today, a fairly soulless place. Its single coastal drive (**Paseo Ixtapa**) runs past a series of concrete boxes of varying heights, making Zihuatanejo far more appealing.

The beaches

Hotels and condos completely cordon off Ixtapa's lovely 2.5km stretch of beach – **Playa de Palmar** – from the road, forcing those who can't afford the hotels' inflated prices to squeeze through a couple of access points or use the hotels' facilities for pretty reasonable day rates. The beach is fine for volleyball or long walks, but often too rough for easy swimming, and plagued by jet skis.

Playa Quieta

Powered watersports are also in evidence at the inappropriately named **Playa Quieta**, some 5km north of Ixtapa, which is dominated by *Club Med* and seemingly perpetual clans of inebriated spring-breakers. The water here is wonderfully clear and the surrounding vegetation magnificent, but with the exception of a solitary seafood restaurant you won't get anything to eat or drink unless you pay handsomely to enter the confines of the three luxury resorts that dominate the beach.

IXTAPA AND ZIHUATANEJO AREA
Lázaro Cárdenas (90km)
Airport (11km), Barra de Potosí (20km), 2 & Acapulco (253km)
PACIFIC OCEAN
Zihuatanejo
Ixtapa
Ixtapa Bus Station
Central de Auto Buses
SEE "ZIHUATANEJO" MAP
HWY 200
PETATLÁN - ZIHUATANEJO
CIUDAD LÁZARO CÁRDENAS - ZIHUATANEJO
PASEO DE LOS PELICANOS
PASEO IXTAPA
PASEO DE CANTIL
BLVD PLAYA LINDA
BLVD IXTAPA
Parque Aventura Ixtapa
Mundo Mágico Acuaparque
Delfiniti Ixtapa
Club Med
Playa de Palmar
Playa Linda
Playa Quieta
Isla Ixtapa
PLAYA LA ROPA
Playa la Ropa
Bahía de Zihuatanejo
Playa Las Gatas
PLAYA LAS GATAS
N
EATING
Panaderia y Pasteleria La Peque 3
Ruben's Hamburgers 2
El Tiburón de la Costa 1
DRINKING & NIGHTLIFE
El Camino 2
The General's Sports Bar 1
ACCOMMODATION
La Casa del Encanto 2
La Casa Que Canta 4
Catalina Beach Resort 5
Golondrinas 57 1
Gran Pacifica Resort 7
Tentaciones Hotel & Lounge Pool 3
La Villa Luz 6
0 2
kilometres

Playa Linda

Playa Linda is a huge sweep of greyish sand, with a cluster of *enramadas* at the pier end where the local bus from the centre of town drops you off. As well as the usual trinket vendors, you can hire horses or rent jet skis and surfboards at the shacks along the beach. To find all the space you need, keep walking away from the crowded pier end: the restaurants are supplanted by coconut groves, which in turn give way to small cliffs and an estuary with birdlife and reptiles.

Isla Ixtapa

Boats leave from the pier at Playa Linda for **Isla Ixtapa**, a small island a couple of kilometres offshore with two fine swimming beaches, a spot reserved for snorkelling (you can rent gear) and diving (you can easily walk between the three locations) and a few restaurants, but nowhere to stay.

ARRIVAL AND DEPARTURE — IXTAPA

By plane Transport from the Ixtapa-Zihuatanejo International Airport (see page 210) is the usual overpriced monopoly: *colectivo* taxis charge around a modest amount per person, while taxis will be considerably more; in the other direction the fare is just half the price.

By bus Some long-distance buses now serve Ixtapa directly via the bus terminal at Plaza Ixpamar, in the commercial area behind the seafront (Paseo Ixtapa), but otherwise you'll have to change at Zihuatanejo's Central de Autobuses (see page 210); you can catch a local bus (every 15min, 6am–11pm) along the seafront to Ixtapa across Hwy-200 from the bus station or from the top of Juárez at Morelos in downtown Zihua.

Tourist office For information, try online travel agencies such as http://ixtapa-zihuatanejo.com, or visit the Oficina de Convenciones y Visitantes, inside the Edificio Plaza Zocalo, Local 8 Altos, Andador Cerro La Puerta, Manzanza 2, Lote 16 (Mon–Fri 8am–4pm; 755 553 1270).

GETTING AROUND

By bus Local "microbuses" (Ixtapa to Zihuatanejo).

By taxi Taxis charge fixed fares; rides between downtown Zihuatanejo and Ixtapa; Ixtapa to Playa La Ropa; to Playa La Madera; within downtown; to Playa Larga; to Playa Linda. Add forty percent midnight–5am.

ISLA IXTAPA

By boat Boats depart when full from Playa Linda (usually every 30min, 9am–5pm; 20min). You can also get there on a daily launch from Zihuatanejo, which leaves at 11am and returns at 5pm (1hr).

ACCOMMODATION AND EATING — SEE MAP PAGE 214

Golondrinas 57 Paseo de Las Golondrinas (next to the Palma de Real golf course); 755 557 1675. Independent travellers usually skip Ixtapa's resort hotels in favour of Zihuatanejo, but one appealing alternative here is this quirky little hotel, full to the brim with character. There's no luxury here but it has everything you need to hand and it's budget friendly too. M$$

Ruben's Hamburgers Centro Comercial Flamboyant, Andador Punta San Esteban; http://rubenshamburgers.com. For something tasty and quick in town, head to *Ruben's* for juicy sirloin, cheese and chicken chargrilled burgers, and huge baskets of fries. M$$

El Tiburón de la Costa Calle Prinicipal s/n; 755 553 0074. Perennially popular, informal joint serving the best seafood in town. Take a plastic seat (beneath the watchful gaze of a giant artificial shark) and take your pick of the fresh catch of the day, with the succulent prawns and lobster both particular specialities. M$$$

DRINKING AND NIGHTLIFE — SEE MAP PAGE 214

El Camino Plaza Ixpamar; 755 121 5683. A relaxed spot to kick off a night out, with all the usual beers on offer and a

IXTAPA FOR KIDS

Golfito Ixtapa Paseo de la Garzas; 755 553 1395. Every kid loves mini golf, and though this one's somewhat dated, it's cheap and serves up plenty of challenges.

Parque Aventura Ixtapa Carretera Zihuatanejo-Lázaro Cárdenas (Hwy-200) km 4.8; 755 115 1733. Rope ladders, Himalayan rope bridges and eleven zip lines (some 250m long and 30m high) provide the thrills at this popular theme park, though it's fairly tame by international zip standards.

good selection of tequila.

The General's Sports Bar Plaza Kiosko; 755 139 4999. Popular with tourists, expats and locals alike, with the coldest beer in town, TV screens for live events and excellent bar food – all presided over by the inimitable "general" himself.

The Michoacán coast

North of Ixtapa, Hwy-200 follows the coast for 100km or so before crossing the Guerrero border into **Michoacán** state and the industrial city of **Lázaro Cárdenas**. From here the highway continues for another 260km through a wilder, virtually uninhabited area: there are fabulous beaches, but for the most part the mountains of the **Sierra de Coalcomán** drop straight into the ocean – it's the most spectacular, best preserved and least developed section of the Pacific coast. You'll make the most of this region if you have your own transport, though experienced hikers often camp and walk large sections of the coast. If you do travel by bus, sit at the front and prepare for some severe hairpin bends. If at all possible, avoid travel at night.

3

Playa Azul

Once a small-time, slow-moving beach surrounded by lagoons, **PLAYA AZUL** has been rather overrun by the growth of Lázaro Cárdenas, 24km away. However, there are still several reasonably priced hotels and a wide, often deserted strip of silky sand, backed by scores of palapa restaurants.

ARRIVAL AND DEPARTURE — PLAYA AZUL

By bus Long-distance buses don't pass directly through Playa Azul, so ask to be dropped off at La Mira, the nearest town on Hwy-200 – from here *colectivos* run the remaining 7km down to Playa Azul (for a small charge).

By colectivo *Colectivos* (40min) run back and forth to Lázaro Cárdenas bus station from the centre, and you can also take taxis. The road into town runs parallel to the beach down to the vast plaza at the southern end.

ACCOMMODATION AND EATING

Bungalows Delfin Venustiano Carranza; 753 536 0006. Reliable budget option, offering drab but clean and comfortable rooms and bungalows with tiled en-suite bathrooms, wall-mounted TVs and decent wi-fi, as well as a pleasant outdoor double pool. The beach is a few minutes' walk away. A/c rooms cost more. M$$

Hotel Delfin Venustiano Carranza; 753 536 0007. Better value than *Bungalows Delfin* down the road, this eye-catching white-and-orange hotel offers slightly poky, old-fashioned but perfectly comfortable rooms and a large outdoor pool. There are no dining facilities, but plenty of options nearby. M$$

María Isabel Madero s/n; 753 104 7160, www.facebook.com/HotelMIPA. For somewhere cheap, try the basic but comfortable *María Isabel*, on the far side of the plaza, which has spotless motel-like rooms, very friendly staff and a pool of its own. You'll pay extra for a/c. M$$

María Teresa Independencia 626 (on the plaza); 753 536 0005, https://facebook.com/HotelMariaTeresaPlayaAzul. The best accommodation in town is *Hotel María Teresa*, on the plaza, which features attractive rooms, a lovely palm-fringed pool and a garden bar-restaurant serving breakfast only. M$$

Caleta de Campos

As you move deeper into Michoacán, **CALETA DE CAMPOS**, some 56km from Playa Azul, is in many ways the best place to stop. A small village that acts as a service centre for the area, it's friendly and unassuming, with two lovely beaches and impressive ocean views. There is something of a Wild West feel to the place: the streets are unpaved, and horses stand tied to hitching posts alongside the camper vans of North American surfers and the fancy new cars belonging to visitors from the city. For much of the year the place is virtually deserted, but in winter, when Californian beach boys come down in pursuit of sun and surf (the waves are perfect for beginners), and at weekends, when families from Lázaro Cárdenas pile in, it can get crowded.

ARRIVAL AND DEPARTURE — CALETA DE CAMPOS

By bus Buses stop on Hwy-200 or at the small station on the plaza. It should be possible to pick up long-distance buses to Manzanillo (north) or Lázaro Cárdenas (south), but you won't be able to reserve seats. Minibuses (hourly) also connect Caleta de Campos with Lázaro (1hr 20min), where you can more easily change to long-distance services.

ACCOMMODATION AND EATING

You'll find plenty of budget accommodation in Caleta, much of it close to the beach, and numerous places to grab a meal; there is a string of bars and restaurants down at the beach and a plethora of taco stands and mini-markets along the main street.

Partour Caleta Carretera 200, north end of town; 443 108 0177. Cliff-top complex at the northern extremity of town that offers everything from basic rooms with kingsize beds right up to entire villas with kitchens, decks and jacuzzis rentable by the night. All options have a/c. Doubles and villas available. M$$$

Yuritzi Corregidora 10; http://hotelyuritzi.mx. A modern, well-managed establishment that has its own generator and water supply. All rooms come with TV, but it's extra for a/c. M$

3

Playa Maruata and Colola

Just over 100km from Caleta de Campos, **PLAYA MARUATA** is by far the most enticing beach on the coast, and the best one for camping. Once an isolated **Nahua** fishing village, it has developed into a laid-back backpacker and surfer resort, with locals providing cheap eats and accommodation, as well as leading the effort to protect the turtles that frequent their beaches.

The main beach is a 3km stretch of sand perfect for swimming and snorkelling, while the more intriguing middle section is riddled with boulders and caves, including an enigmatic finger of rock known as the **Dedo de Dios** ("God's finger"). The third section is known as Playa de los Muertos, dogged by dangerous currents and waves. From Maruata it's another 80km to the Colima border at Boca de Apiza – there are numerous surfer hangouts along the way (Playa La Ticla and San Juan de Alima among them).

A further 8km up the coast from Playa Maruata is Colola, another long stretch of sand much favoured by wildlife spotters, as it's far less known and tends to attracts more turtles than Maruata. During October and November especially, vast numbers of both leatherback and green turtles make their way up the sandbar to lay their eggs, and hotel owners organize beach walks to see them.

ARRIVAL AND DEPARTURE — PLAYA MARUATA AND COLOLA

By bus To get to Playa Maruata by bus you'll need to take a Tecomán/Lázaro Cárdenas–Manzanillo bus and tell the driver you want to go to Maruata or Colola: he'll drop you on Hwy-200 where it's a 1.5km walk down to the beach and the main village. Heading back you'll just have to flag buses down (no reservations).

ACCOMMODATION

Cabañas Colola Colola Beach; 555 137 5943. A number of three-bedroom structures (given their balconies, the best rooms are the upstairs lofts) overlook the beach where the turtles appear around dusk. Rooms are spartan but have mosquito nets. There's a restaurant, which operates in the Aug–Jan high season (outside of which prices drop), as well as a swimming pool, which operates all year round. M$$

Centro Ecoturistico Ayult 443 115 0311. These simple thatched cabañas, which rise strikingly from the beach on a steeply winding path, come with showers and bathrooms, though you can also sleep in a hammock beneath their shelter on the sand. You'll find them at the western end of the beaches. It can be hard to book in advance, but as long as it's not Easter or Christmas, you can be fairly sure of space. Cabañas and camping options are available. M$

The Colima coast

The relatively tiny state of **Colima** has just 139km of coastline, stretching from the Boca de Apiza to the Cerro de San Francisco in Jalisco, but there's plenty to tempt you off Hwy 200. The southern section boasts several laid-back villages worth exploring, from the surf magnet of **Boca de Pascuales** to **Cuyutlán**, with a long beach lined with palapa restaurants. In stark contrast, **Manzanillo** is a major resort and another Mexican fishing port claiming the title "sailfish capital of the world".

Boca de Pascuales

BOCA DE PASCUALES, 13km from the workday town of **Tecomán**, is little more than a bunch of palapa restaurants, but its beach is renowned for huge waves and challenging **surf**; this is a river-mouth beach break with some of the nastiest and fastest tubes in Mexico (breaking right and left) – it's definitely not for the inexperienced. Even swimming can be dangerous, but otherwise it's a fine place to hang out for a few days.

ARRIVAL AND DEPARTURE — BOCA DE PASCUALES

By bus To reach Boca de Pascuales, you'll first need to take a bus to Tecomán, 50km south of the city of Colima and 30km from the Michoacán border. Buses run to Tecomán from Colima, Lázaro Cárdenas and Manzanillo. Minibuses run to Boca from Tecomán's bus station (hourly, 7am–8pm; 20min).

By taxi Taxis run from Tecomán to Boca.

3

ACCOMMODATION AND EATING

★ **Las Hamacas del Mayor** http://lashamacasdelmayor.mx. The best restaurant in town has been serving top-notch seafood since 1953 and still draws a large crowd, in spite of its remote location. Mains include lobster dishes. M$$$

Hotel Real de Pascuales Playa de Pascuales s/n; 313 102 3501. A pleasant hotel right on the beach, with a thatched-roof reception and clean and comfortable – if unremarkable – rooms, set around a dusty courtyard. There's a small outdoor pool and direct access to the beach; surfboards are available to buy or rent. Camping is also available for a nightly fee. M$$

Cuyutlán

Some 25km west of Tecomán on Hwy-200, **CUYUTLÁN** is the most appealing of a series of tiny resorts that adorn the shoreline between the Michoacán border and Manzanillo, backed by an immense coconut grove that stretches along a narrow peninsula almost as far as the port city. Popular with Mexican holidaymakers, the old town around the main plaza is sleepy, its inhabitants idling away the day on wooden verandas under terracotta roofs. In spring, the **coast** both here and further south is subject to the **Ola Verde**: vast, dark-green waves up to 10m high that crash down on the fine grey sand. Theories to explain their green hue vary widely – though most experts think it is phosphorescence created by microscopic phytoplankton – but whatever the reason, the Ola Verde has been a part of Cuyutlán lore ever since a huge tsunami destroyed the town in 1932. At other times of the year the surf is impressive but easier to handle and it's OK to swim; surfers usually head south to **Paraíso** and Boca de Pascuales (see page 218).

Centro Ecológico de Cuyutlán "el Tortugario"

Around 4km on the road to Paraíso • Charge, discount for children aged 3–10 • http://tortugariocuyutlan.com

It's worth taking a trip out to the **Centro Ecológico de Cuyutlán "el Tortugario"** – catch a cab from the plaza or stroll south down the beach for about 45 minutes. From July to December, three **turtle** species (the olive ridley, the black and the leatherback) visit the local beaches to lay their eggs, and a team from the centre goes out every night to collect them before they end up as someone's dinner. The newly hatched turtles are then kept in tanks for a couple of days before being released back into the sea (usually Aug–Dec Sat 3pm). Out of the egg-laying season, there's a resident turtle population, crocodiles, iguanas and lots of information on hand. The sanctuary also organizes 45-minute boat **tours** (charge; discount for children aged 3–10; 10am–4pm) through the mangrove tunnels of the idyllic, jungly **Estero Palo Verde**, part of the **Laguna Cuyutlán** and well known for its birdlife.

Museo de la Sal

Juárez, at Progreso, two blocks east of the plaza • Donation suggested • 313 326 4014

Cuyutlán was once an important salt-producing centre under the Spanish, but salt was being made here way back in pre-Columbian times. This long history is celebrated at the **Museo de la Sal**, housed in an original, wooden salt *bodega*. If you're interested, the retired salt-workers who run the place will talk you through the compound's long history.

ARRIVAL AND DEPARTURE — CUYUTLÁN

By bus To get to Cuyutlán from Manzanillo, you must first catch to the inland market town of Armería (40km southeast of Manzanillo, 20km west of Tecomán), which has a bank, a post office and a long-distance bus stop on the main street (Hwy-200). Here, walk two blocks north from the long-distance bus stop, then one block east to the market, where there are regular buses (every 30min, 6am–7.30pm; 20min). From Tecomán local buses run regularly to Cuyutlán.

ACCOMMODATION AND EATING

Concierge Plaza San Rafael Veracruz 46; http://conciergecuyutlan.com. Lovely rooms, some facing the beach, all with fans, hot water and access to an outdoor pool. Also boasts a lovely thatched-roof restaurant on site. M$$

Fénix Hidalgo 201; 314 121 1594. The *grande dame* of the town since 1933, featuring some great old-fashioned rooms opening onto spacious communal verandas. The rooms on the second floor are bigger, and all go for half the price for solo travellers. Free wi-fi, satellite TV and restaurant/bar on site, and they'll also let you use the kitchen if you clean up after yourself. M$$

Mariscos Playa Cuyutlan Adolfo Lopéz Mateos 175; 313 322 5962. Basic place on the beach serving huge platters of ocean-fresh seafood, rice and salad, accompanied by cold beer. M$$

Morelos Hidalgo 185; 313 326 4013. With clean, basic rooms (the renovated ones are the most comfortable), fans, hot water and the area's best swimming pool, this is one of the best deals in town. There's a good restaurant on site too, serving basic meals in a lovely dining room with vines hanging from white columns. M$

3

Manzanillo

Colima state's second city and the busiest cargo port in Mexico, **MANZANILLO** is clearly a working town: tourism – although highly developed – very definitely takes second place to trade. Downtown, crisscrossed by railway tracks, rumbles with heavy traffic and is surrounded by a bewildering array of inner harbours and shallow lagoons that seem to cut the city off from the land. It's this genuine, workaday character that makes Manzanillo stand out on this stretch of coast, its **centro histórico** making a pleasant contrast with the great scythe of beaches and resorts along Manzanillo and Santiago bays.

Centro histórico

Much of Manzanillo's old town, or **centro histórico**, has been spruced up in recent years, centring on its main plaza, the **Jardín Alvaro Obregón**, right on the harbour and embellished with rose gardens and exuberant topiary. The long **boardwalk**, dominated by a 25m-tall **sailfish memorial** and local favourite the **Fuentes Danzarinas** (dancing fountains), is best ambled along at sunset. That said, few tourists spend time in the centre – most head to the hotels and club resorts of the **Península de Santiago** around Manzanillo Bay to the northwest – even though old Manzanillo is a lot more interesting than this sanitized resort area, and cheaper, too.

Playa Las Brisas

While locals might go **swimming** from the tiny harbour beach of **Playa San Pedrito** and in the Laguna de Cuyutlán behind the town, both are polluted. You're far better off heading for the **beaches** further along Manzanillo Bay, along the Zona Hotelera. The nearest of these, at **Playa Las Brisas**, is closer to town than you would think – just across the entrance to the inner harbour – though it seems further away due to convoluted routes around the Laguna de San Pedrito. Frequent **buses** (20min) from the centre (from Juárez near the plaza and marked "Las Brisas") run all the way along the single

seafront drive. The 6km beach (which is known as **Playa Azul** at the top end) shelves steeply to the ocean, causing the tide to crash upon the shore; consequently, the beach is not as conducive to swimming as those further around the bay.

Playa La Audiencia

Better and more sheltered swimming can be found along the coast 11km from downtown, where Manzanillo Bay is divided from Santiago Bay by the rocky **Península de Santiago**. If you're prepared to walk a little way, you can reach the calm and tranquil waters of the beautiful cove of **Playa La Audiencia**, on the west side of the Santiago peninsula (facing Santiago Bay). The current can be strong here, so take it easy – regardless of your swimming ability.

Santiago Bay beaches

Santiago Bay stretches for around 8km beyond the Península de Santiago, with "Miramar" **buses** running all the way to the far side and passing a string of beaches. The main four, from east to west, are: Playa Santiago; Playa Olas Altas; Playa Miramar 3km further on, the best beach for **surfing** (shops rent boards on the beach); and Playa La Boquita, another 3km and a bit harder to reach, via Club Santiago.

ARRIVAL AND DEPARTURE — MANZANILLO

By plane The Aeropuerto Internacional Playa de Oro is 30km north of Manzanillo's Zona Hotelera (Hwy-200 km 42). There are no buses to the airport, so you have to take a fixed-price *colectivo* or taxi, with rates set according to a zone system. Alamo (314 334 0124), Budget (314 334 2270), Hertz (1 800 709 5000) and Thrifty (314 334 3282) have car-rental desks at the airport. The airport ATM is temperamental, so make sure you have pesos on arrival. Flights primarily connect Manzanillo with cities in the US and Canada: for domestic destinations you'll have to change in Mexico City via Aeroméxico.

By bus The Terminal de Autobuses is several km northeast of the centre, just off Hwy-200 near Playa Las Brisas. Buses to the main plaza (marked "Jardín" or "Centro") and the beaches (marked "Santiago") leave from the station entrance. Taxis run to the centre and to Península de Santiago, but fix the price first. The ETN bus station is off Hwy-200 at km 13.5.

Destinations Acapulco (1 daily; 7–8hr); Barra de Navidad (frequently; 1hr 30min); Colima (frequently; 1hr 30min); Guadalajara (frequently; 5–6hr); Lázaro Cárdenas (8 daily; 6–7hr); Mexico City (4 daily; 12hr); Puerto Vallarta (hourly; 5–7hr); Tecomán (frequent; 1hr); Tijuana (2 daily; 35hr).

INFORMATION AND TOURS

Tourist office The helpful Oficina de Convenciones y Visitantes is north of Playa Azul several km out of town, at Miguel de la Madrid 14540 (Mon–Fri 9am–2pm & 4–7pm; 314 333 1380).

Tours Given the steady flow of North American cruise and package tourists visiting Manzanillo, it's no surprise that local travel agents have developed a wide range of day trips taking in everything from tours of Colima, the volcanoes and Cuyutlán, to zip lines, iguana farms and ATV expeditions. Try Tlaloc Tours (http://tlaloctours.com) or Go Manzanillo (http://gomanzanillo.com).

ACCOMMODATION

SEE MAP PAGE 220

3

Finding a **place to stay** is no problem in Manzanillo, with most of the budget options close to the plaza in the **centro histórico**, and a host of mid-range and luxury resorts stretching north around the bay in the **Zona Hotelera**; as the original seaside strip, **Las Brisas** offers a number of dated, monolithic hotels which tend to be cheaper than elsewhere, except when the area is flooded by holidaymakers from Guadalajara, while the rocky **Península de Santiago**, further north, is smothered in luxury resorts. **Prices** at all but the cheapest hotels drop by about 25 percent outside the high season (roughly Dec–May) and Semana Santa.

CENTRO HISTÓRICO

Colonial Bocanegra 28, at México; http://hotelcolonialmzo.com. This 1940s gem drips with faded colonial grandeur: heavy wooden furnishings and an Andalucian mosaic-tiled courtyard with a fountain add to its allure. The clean, spacious rooms, with a/c and cable TV, are perfectly comfortable. M$$

Zar Manzanillo Azueta 3; http://hoteleszar.com/manzanillo. If you want to be by the sea, but still within walking distance of the main plaza, try this professionally run resort, set around a pool backing onto Playa San Pedrito about 1km east of the centre (a 20min walk from the plaza along the waterfront). The red-and-white rooms come with flatscreen TVs and free wi-fi. M$$

ZONA HOTELERA AND BEYOND

Las Hadas Golf Resort & Marina Av de los Riscos and Vista Hermosa, Península de Santiago; http://lasbrisashotels.com.mx. This amazingly flashy wedding-cake-style hotel complex is where Dudley Moore and Bo Derek frolicked in the film *10*, with a vast range of amenities and Moorish-themed architecture; rooms are all white, with marble floors and bay views. M$$$$

★ **Pepe's Hideaway** Camino Don Diego 67, Península de Santiago; 213 261 6821, http://trivago.com. Beachside resort of luxury palapas with mesmerizing views and sunsets, handmade chairs and tables, tiled bathrooms and ceiling fans; it feels very remote and tranquil, right on the tip of the peninsula. M$$$

La Posada Cárdenas 201, Playa Las Brisas; 314 333 1899, http://facebook.com/pinkposada. Bright, pink-washed B&B right on the beach, with tranquil gardens, a pool and rooms fitted with folksy Mexican rugs and blankets (some with a/c and kitchenette) exuding a retro 1950s vibe. There are excellent made-to-order breakfasts, internet access, and an honour bar included in the price. M$$$

EATING

SEE MAP PAGE 220

Rather like the hotels, the cheapest **places to eat** are concentrated around Jardín Alvaro Obregón in Centro, while you'll find modern chains and posher places spread out along the bay on Hwy-200. If you head down México, Centro's main commercial and shopping street, you'll find a whole series of *taquerías*, while there are several very cheap places – grimy and raucous on the whole – in the market area three blocks down México and at the bottom end of Juárez by the railway tracks.

CENTRO HISTÓRICO

Chantilly Juárez at Madero; 314 333 7182, http://grupochantilly.com.mx. This locally famous and bustling restaurant, open since 1950, makes a substantial comida corrida, good *antojitos* and the best ice cream in town. M$$$

Dolphy Morelos, at Jardín Alvaro Obregón; http://dolphy.com.mx. Tempting ice-cream shop, strategically located on the main plaza (there are several branches dotted around the city). Try the "sundae yogurt" flavour, topped with chocolate sauce and gummy bears. M$

ZONA HOTELERA AND BEYOND

Blueberry Bistro Café Audiencia 37; 314 168 6773. It's

easy to while away a good few hours in this modern café-restaurant, with great coffee and tea and a wide range of breakfasts and sandwiches to match. In the evening, you'll find one of the best collections of craft beers and imported spirits in Manzanillo. M$$

Café Costeño Cárdenas 1613, Playa Las Brisas; http://cafecosteno.com.mx. Excellent, relaxing place for a coffee – or a frozen cappuccino – inside or on a shady patio. Does tasty oversized American breakfasts or all the classic Mexican dishes (cash only). M$

La Carnita Asada Restaurante Division del Nte 801; 552 929 6846. Serves a hearty menu of grilled meats for reasonable prices. The fruity sangria pitchers are the perfect accompaniment to the mesquite-grilled steaks. M$$$

Juanito's Miguel de la Madrid km 14, Playa Santiago; http://juanitos.com. Fun family restaurant specializing in breakfasts, burgers, *chilaquiles*, tacos and refreshing drinks (fresh-fruit smoothies) since 1976. M$$

★ La Sonrisa Miguel de la Madrid, Playa Azul; 314 117 8604. The best tacos in the city, especially famous for their giant chorizo and *carne asada* quesadillas. Some tables inside and on the street. Any taxi driver will know it. M$

DRINKING AND NIGHTLIFE

SEE MAP PAGE 220

Sunset Lounge Miguel de la Madrid; 332 187 1981. Music led bar adorned with electronica and pop memorabilia. There are live DJs here more often than not and the food menu, albeit limited, is really rather good. The cocktails are nothing to write home about but the atmosphere here more than makes up for that.

3

DIRECTORY

Banks HSBC (at Bocanegra) and Bancomer (no. 122), with ATMs, are both on México.

Post office The post office is at Vicent de Guerrero 182, in the *centro histórico* (Mon–Fri 9am–5pm, Sat 9am–1pm).

Colima and around

COLIMA, capital of the state and 98km inland from Manzanillo, is a distinctly colonial city, and a very beautiful one too, overlooked by the perfectly conical **Volcán de Colima** and, in the distance, the Nevado de Colima. With a handful of sights inside the city limits and interesting excursions nearby, it's a pleasant place to stop over for a night or two. Colima's Old World ambience, favourable climate – cooler than the coast, but never as cold as in the high mountains – and several good-value hotels and restaurants add to its appeal.

The city's prettiest features are its chain of shady formal **plazas** or jardíns – Colima is known as the "City of Palms" – and a number of attractive **courtyards**, many of which are now used as restaurants and cafés and make wonderfully cool places to relax. The central **Plaza Principal** (known as Jardín Libertad) is where you'll find the government offices and the unimpressive Neoclassical cathedral, which dates from 1941.

Museo Regional de Historia

Portal Morelos 1, at Reforma • Charge, free Sun 5–8pm • http://bit.ly/MuseoRegional

The **Museo Regional de Historia** stands across the street from the Palacio de Gobierno in a lovely nineteenth-century building that also houses the university art gallery. Displays on **local crafts** include animal and diabolical masks used in traditional dances, while the later rooms are chock-full of **pre-Hispanic ceramics**: gorgeous figurines with superbly expressive faces, fat Izcuintli dogs and people working on mundane, everyday tasks. Many of these were found in local *tumbas de tiro* – well-like tombs up to 16m deep, more commonly found in South America and the Pacific Islands. Labelling in Spanish only.

Museo Universitario de Artes Populares

Gabino Barreda and Manuel Gallardo Zamora, Universidad de Colima • Charge • 312 316 1126

If you've more time to spare, wander eight blocks north of the plaza to the **Museo Universitario de Artes Populares**, which has an eclectic but poorly explained collection of folk art, including masks, traditional textiles and costumes modelled by enormous papier-mâché figures, and a small musical instrument collection – look for the violin made from scrap wood and a Modelo beer can.

La Campana

Av Periférico Norte, between Tecnológico de Colima and Arroyo Pereira, 3km northwest of the centre; head north out of town along Gabino Barreda and take a left onto Tecnológico • Charge • 312 313 4945 or 312 313 4946

The source of some of the Museo Regional de Historia's treasures is the ruined Early Classic city at **La Campana**, which dates back to around 300 BC and is believed to have reached its zenith between 100 and 600 AD. Excavations have revealed some small pyramids, temple remains and one shaft tomb indicative of the Tehuchitlán tradition.

ARRIVAL AND DEPARTURE

COLIMA AND AROUND

By plane The Aeropuerto Nacional de Colima (312 314 4160) is 22km northeast of the centre of Colima, with daily flights from Mexico City on Aeromar and Volaris, and flights to Tijuana via Volaris. Taxis run into the centre of Colima and to Manzanillo.

By bus Some 4km east of the centre, Colima's main bus station, the Terminal Foránea (or Central de Autobuses), handles frequent first and second-class buses from Guadalajara and Manzanillo. Taxis and city buses #2, #4 and #5 run towards the central plaza from the station. Many second-class Manzanillo buses and all local services, including the one to Comala, operate from the Terminal Rojos, 7km west of the centre of town. If you arrive here, a #4 or #6 bus will take you to the centre of town; from the centre, take a #2 or buses marked "Rojos" from Madero, at Revolucíon, to get back.

3

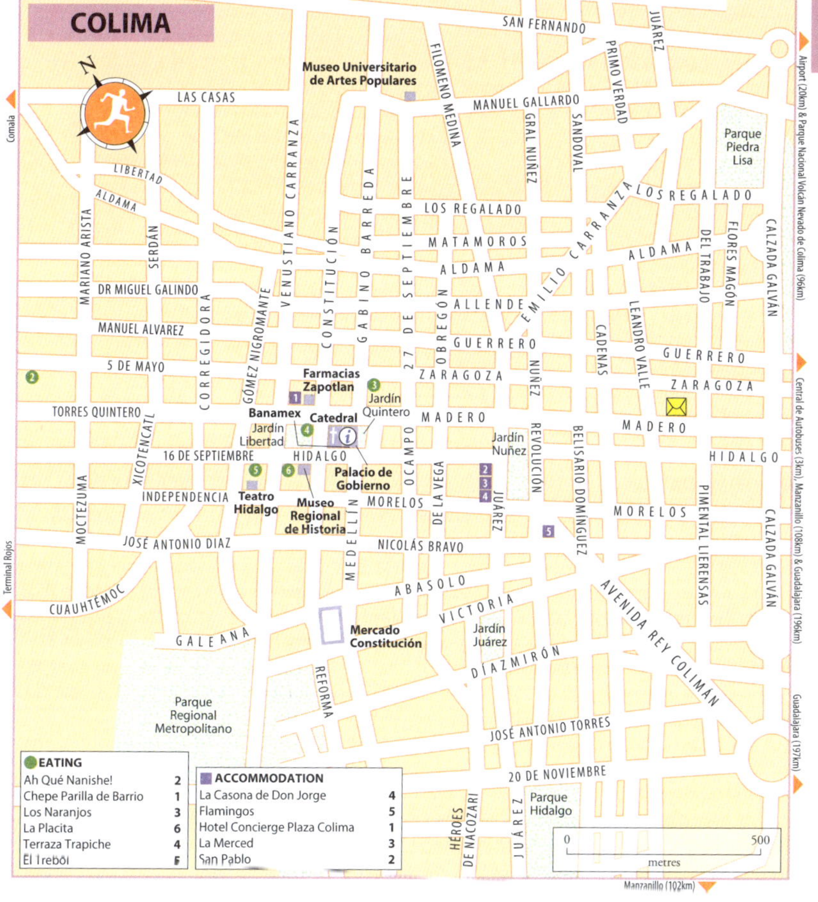

3

CLIMBING THE NEVADO DE COLIMA

The **Parque Nacional Volcán Nevado de Colima** comprises two spellbinding volcanoes rising north of Colima. The **Volcán de Colima** (3860m), also known as Volcán de Fuego, is officially still active and erupts from time to time, most recently in January 2017. It is far less frequently climbed than its larger and more passive brother, the **Nevado de Colima** (4330m), which, with its pine- and oak-forested slopes, is popular with local mountaineers during the clear, dry winter months. Unless there's a lot of snow – in December and January crampons and an ice axe are essential – and provided you are fit and can get transport high enough, it's a relatively easy **hike** up to the summit. Joining an **organized tour** is the hassle-free alternative and recommended for less experienced hikers: Admire Mexico Tours (312 314 5454, http://admiremexicotours.com) offers half-day and day trips from Colima and Comala.

Independently, you'll need to set three days aside for the climb, take a sleeping bag and waterproofs, pack enough food and water for the trip, and walk from the village of El Fresnito. First, take a bus from Terminal Foránea in Colima to Ciudad Guzmán (about 1hr 30min) and from there catch a bus to **El Fresnito** (25 minutes), where there are very limited supplies. Ask for the road to La Joya – on foot now, take this road and keep right until the route becomes obvious. This rough service road for the radio antennae leads up through cow pastures and goes right past the cabin at La Joya (3500m), about six to eight hours' walking (35km). You pay the **entry fee** and can tank up from the supply of running water here, but don't expect to stay in the hut, which is often locked, and even if open may be full, as it only sleeps six – bring camping equipment. The usual route from here is via a steep climb to the radio antennae ("Las Antenas"), from where it's another stiff but non-technical walk to the summit. Plan on a day from La Joya to the summit and back, then another to get back to Colima, though a very fit walker starting before dawn could make the trip back to Colima, or at least Ciudad Guzmán, in a day. Note that **hitching** isn't likely to be an option as the logging roads up here are rough, requiring high clearance or 4WD vehicles, and see very little traffic. Needless to say, only fit and experienced walkers who are confident in their ability and aware of the risks should even think about attempting the climb.

Destinations Comala (frequent; 20min); Guadalajara (at least hourly; 3hr); Lázaro Cárdenas (4 daily; 6–7hr); Manzanillo (frequent; 1hr 30min–2hr); Mexico City (8 daily; 10–11hr); Puerto Vallarta (8 daily; 8hr); Tecomán (at least hourly; 45min); Tijuana (2 daily; 38hr).

INFORMATION

Tourist office Colima's extremely helpful tourist office, inside the Palacio de Gobierno, on Reforma and Hidalgo at the Plaza Principal (Mon–Fri 9am–5pm; 312 308 0520), has a variety of maps and pamphlets.

ACCOMMODATION

SEE MAP PAGE 223

★ **La Casona de Don Jorge** Juárez 88; 312 330 7289. Lovely mid-range option in a nineteenth-century mansion overlooking the Jardín Nuñez. Rooms are homely and modern, beds are either wrought iron or carved from beautiful dark wood, and fast wi-fi, satellite TV and pleasant tiled bathrooms come as standard. The adjoining, blue-hued Café Casona is a great spot for breakfast or coffee. M$$

Flamingos Rey Colimán 18; 312 312 2525. One of the better budget options. The rooms are a little gloomy, but have nice wooden beds, private bathrooms, balconies and TVs. M$

★ **Hotel Concierge Plaza Colima** Medellín 12; http://conciergeplazacolima.com. In a prime location, right on the Jardín Libertad, this hotel exudes Old World colonial grandeur (dating from 1880, it once housed the state governors). While all have a/c, rooms vary enormously; the best are the light and airy deluxe ones (worth the extra charge) with hand-painted furniture, French windows and wrought-iron balconies. There's a great café next door. M$$$

La Merced Juárez 82; http://hotellamerced.com.mx. Characterful old hotel housing passable fan-ventilated rooms with bath around a central patio and some less attractive, newer rooms – the best rooms are at the back. All have Sky TV, and there's parking. M$$

San Pablo Juárez 80; http://hotelsanpablo.com.mx. Very pleasant, professionally run mid-range property, with welcoming rooms featuring huge wooden beds, wall-mounted TVs, a/c and stylish en-suite bathrooms. No restaurant, but there's a little café where you'll find tea, coffee, juice and biscuits. M$$

EATING

SEE MAP PAGE 223

Ah Qué Nanishe! 5 de Mayo 267, west of Mariano Arista; http://menu.nanishe.com. The name of this surprisingly inexpensive courtyard restaurant appropriately means "how delicious" in Zapotec. It specializes in dishes from the owner's native Oaxaca: *mole*, *chapulines* (baked grasshoppers) and *tlyaduas* (large flour tortillas). Well worth the walk from the centre. M$$

Chepe Parilla de Barrio Amado Nervo 726, north of the city centre; http://menu.chepeparrilla.com. One of the city's very finest restaurants, this Argentinean-style steakhouse is well worth venturing out from the city centre (a ten-minute taxi ride) for a treat. Alongside juicy steaks you'll find fantastic raw seafood dishes like tuna carpaccio and salmon tartare as well as good pastas, accompanied by an extensive menu of spirits, wine and beer. M$$$$

★ **Los Naranjos** Gabino Barreda 34, north of Madero; 312 312 8390. Friendly dual restaurant, with one informal side serving up a comida corrida, while the other offers a buffet that includes *chilaquiles*, quesadillas, eggs, fruit, tea and coffee, as well as à la carte options. M$$$

La Placita South side of main square; 312 313 2910. One of a series of places housed under the colonnades and arches of the main square, where an antique a/c system is a rumbling background accompaniment to the lunch specials and cheap beers. M$$

★ **Terraza Trapiche** Hotel Ceballos; 312 244 8380. Fashionable spot on the roof terrace of *Hotel Ceballos*, ever popular with a hip young crowd and a great place to look out over the Jardín la Libertad as you try out a few craft beers, courtesy of local brewery Cervecería de Colima. There's great food on offer too, from tacos and *ceviche* to more substantial hamburgers and pork belly. M$$$

El Trébol Degollado 59, at 16 de Septiembre; 312 312 2990. Comfortable, cosy and inexpensive place just off the plaza for egg dishes, snacks and light meals. M$

3

DIRECTORY

Banks and exchange There's a Banamex with an ATM on Hidalgo, a few doors down from the tourist office, and several *casas de cambio* on Juárez, along the western side of Jardín Nuñez.

Pharmacy Farmacias Zapotlan, Francisco Madero at main plaza (daily 9am–7pm).

Post office The post office is at Francisco Madero 475.

Comala

You can get a closer look at the regal volcanoes north of Colima by spending an afternoon at **COMALA**, a tidy, picture-perfect Pueblo Mágico 10km north of the state capital. Here, in the central plaza or **Jardín Principal**, admire the church of **San Miguel del Espíritu Santo**, completed in 1832, or just sip a beer or margarita while enjoying a stellar view of the mountains and listening to mariachi bands. Friday and Saturday are the liveliest times, when you can mingle with day-tripping, predominantly middle-class Mexicans from Guadalajara; on Sundays and Mondays there are craft markets in the square.

ARRIVAL AND DEPARTURE

COMALA

By bus Buses run frequently to Comala from Colima's Terminal Rojos (every 15min; 20min).

EATING

Piccolo Suizo Miguel Hidalgo 2; 312 690 5937. There are numerous homogenous restaurants huddled together around the Jardín Principal offering *botanas* – plates of snacks, dips and tacos – free with drinks from noon until about 6pm. For something different, head east to the other side of the church to find the unexpected: a Swiss restaurant in Comala. In truth it's a pretty international affair, with good pizzas, pastas and paellas alongside classic Swiss cheese fondue. There's also an extensive wine list. Everything is artfully presented in a gourmet style, but it needn't be prohibitively expensive by any means. M$$$$

The Costalegre

Most of the Jalisco coast, between Manzanillo and Puerto Vallarta, has been dubbed the **Costalegre** (the "happy coast"; http://costalegre.com), the wildest, most undeveloped stretch of Mexico's Pacific shore. Beyond the low-key resorts of Melaque and Barra de Navidad, Hwy-200 snakes north for around 225km past lonely beaches, small villages and vast swathes of jungle-smothered mountains.

Barra de Navidad

Some 60km north of Manzanillo, just across the border in Jalisco, the **Bahía de Navidad** is edged by fine, honey-coloured sands anchored by the twin towns of **San Patricio-Melaque** and **BARRA DE NAVIDAD** at the southern end of the bay – here the beach runs out into a sandbar, forming a lagoon behind the town.

The beaches

Barra de Navidad is a small, sleepy town, where the main activities revolve around **beaches**. A continuous arc of golden sand joins Barra with Melaque, running along the bay for some 8km – at Barra it's known as **Playa de Navidad**, a fairly narrow and steep section that is often washed away during hurricanes.

If you have time, it's worth taking a **panga** across the Laguna de Navidad to check out one of the bars or restaurants in the *Grand Isla Navidad Resort* (see page 227) on the **Isla Navidad**, back in Colima state, or **Colimilla**, a small village a bit further along the lagoon. Colimilla is popular chiefly for its seafood restaurants (see page 227), and as a base for the 2–3km walk over to the rough Pacific beach of **Playa de los Cocos**.

ARRIVAL AND DEPARTURE — BARRA DE NAVIDAD

By plane The nearest airport is at Manzanillo (see page 220), just a 20min drive away. Taxis run to Barra (*colectivos* are a more budget friendly option).

By bus Buses arrive at the town's main terminals, which are on Veracruz, Barra's main drag: ETN is at Veracruz 269, Primera Plus is at Veracruz 228. The services you are likely to need – post office, phones and hotels – are all close by; in any case, it only takes 20min to walk around the whole town.

Destinations Colima (hourly; 3hr); Guadalajara (hourly; 6hr); Manzanillo (every 30min; 1hr 30min); Mexico Nte (1 daily; 13hr); Mexico Pte (1 daily; 13hr).

GETTING AROUND

By bus Minibuses run along Veracruz (local buses stop by the Primera Plus station) and on to Melaque via Hwy-200 every 15min.

By taxi Taxis line up at Veracruz and Michoacán, with prices to most places fixed: Melaque, Manzanillo airport, Manzanillo, Playa de los Cocos and Tenacatita.

By boat *Pangas* depart from the jetty at the end of Veracruz to Isla Navidad and the *Grand Bay Hotel*, and also to Colimilla (every 30min, 6am–6pm; by shared *panga* or by private *lancha*).

INFORMATION AND TOURS

Tourist office The office at Veracruz 98 (Mon–Fri 10am–6pm; 315 355 5100, http://costalegre.com) serves both Barra de Navidad and San Patricio-Melaque.

ACCOMMODATION — SEE MAP PAGE 226

Barra de Navidad Legazpi 250; www.hotelbarradenavidad.com. For unrivalled beach access, this is a good-value choice – it's right on the sand. Rooms are simple but comfortable, with big-screen TVs and a/c; the best have wonderful sea views. There's also a pool on site and a huge breakfast included. M$$$

Cabo Blanco Armada and Puerto de la Navidad; http://hotelcaboblanco.com. Set in quiet palm-dotted grounds a 15min walk east of the main strip, with large, comfortable rooms with balconies overlooking the outdoor pool. Mexican and international food – and occasional live music – at the in-house buffet restaurant. M$$$

Delfin Morelos 23; http://hoteldelfinmx.com. Bright, arcaded hotel 5min from the beach. Clean, very spacious rooms with fan lead off an attractive balcony with views of the bay, while two larger apartments offer lagoon views and kitchenettes. There's also a great pool with sun deck, a restaurant where breakfast is served, and two roof terraces. M$$

Grand Isla Navidad Resort Circuitos de los Marinos, Isla Navidad (across the bay); http://islanavidad.com.mx. Luxurious resort with a mountain backdrop, an idyllic location on the bay and a complete range of facilities for golfers and watersports enthusiasts as well as those in need of serious pampering. Rooms are the epitome of taste and style, dripping with marble and exotic woods, and with all the luxuries you'd expect. M$$$$

Sarabi Veracruz 196; http://hotelsarabi.com. Cheap and centrally located hotel with bland but perfectly acceptable a/c rooms. Communal areas are kitted out with low-slung wicker chairs and collections of books for guests to borrow; there's also a small double swimming pool. M$$

EATING — SEE MAP PAGE 226

Norma's Pasteles Veracruz and Legazpi. This popular stall (manned by the indomitable Norma Torres) sells irresistible slices of home-made cakes and desserts. Try the *pastel de tres leches* (sweet milk pudding). M$

Pancho's Legazpi 53; 315 355 5176. This earthy restaurant is one of Barra's original palapas, now managed by Pancho's son and serving great fresh seafood: specials include the shrimp "a la diabla" (spicy devilled shrimp) and zesty marlin *ceviche*. M$$

★ **Ramón** Legazpi 260, opposite Hotel Barra de Navidad (see above); 315 355 6435. Open all day and with an extensive range of Mexican and international food, including some excellent fish and chips, and *chiles rellenos*, especially good with shrimp. Lots of free salsa and tortilla chips to start. M$$$

Restaurant Paty Jalisco 52, at Veracruz; 315 355 8387. The best of a number of similar budget places, serving decent *ceviche*, fresh fish, *carne asada* and fantastic barbecue chicken, as well as all the Mexican staples. M$$

3

PLAYA DE LOS COCOS

Fortino's Southern end of main drag; 314 337 9075. Family favourite since 1967, priding itself on serving only the freshest seafood. Bring insect repellent if dining after dark. M$$

Restaurante Colimilla 50m south of Fortino's; https://colimilla.com. Large beachside restaurant whose palapa extends into the lagoon. Huge range of fish and seafood, and as a plus you can pay by credit card (most restaurants here are cash only). M$$

DRINKING AND NIGHTLIFE

SEE MAP PAGE 226

★ **Marlena's Bar** Veracruz 167; 315 355 8645. Set on a cosy courtyard off the strip, this popular joint is buzzing throughout the week, with live music most nights and a homely atmosphere courtesy of the eponymous Marlena, a friendly German lady. Happy hour 5–8pm.

★ **Seamaster** Legazpi 146; 315 355 8296. Also, a popular restaurant serving seafood, steaks and chicken dishes, this perennial favourite is a great place to stop by for a beer or a margarita as the sun goes down.

DIRECTORY

3

Banks and exchange The town now has Bancomer and Banamex ATM machines on Veracruz (these often malfunction), but no actual bank branches.

Post office The post office is at Veracruz 179.

San Patricio-Melaque

Perched at the northern end of the Bahía de Navidad, **SAN PATRICIO-MELAQUE** seems much more typically Mexican than Barra de Navidad (5km south), with a central plaza, church and largish market. Though it remains popular with Mexican families and budget travellers, Melaque is also much scruffier than Barra, more commercial and has a more transitory feel – the main highlight, unsurprisingly, is its pristine beach, **Playa Melaque**, with a smattering of rustic palapa restaurants at the west end. There's no tourist office; the office in Barra de Navidad serves both towns (see page 227).

ARRIVAL AND DEPARTURE

SAN PATRICIO-MELAQUE

By bus The two long-distance bus stations (Primera Plus and Elite) face each other at the junction of Carranza and Gómez Farías and have frequent connections to Barra de Navidad (every 15min; 10min).

Destinations Guadalajara (hourly; 6hr); Manzanillo (hourly; 1hr 30min); Puerto Vallarta (4 daily; 4–5hr).

By taxi Taxis to Barra are inexpensive.

ACCOMMODATION

Accommodation in Melaque is generally very cheap, especially during the low season (Aug–Nov) when prices are negotiable down to a third of their cost, though little is open at this time.

Bahía Legazpi 5; 315 355 6894, http://facebook.com/melaquehotelbahia. The friendly Moreno family run this little hotel, a short walk from the beach and one of the best deals in town. Its 23 compact rooms enclose a tranquil inner patio and a pool, and come with cable TV, wi-fi and a/c; some have a kitchenette, or there's a communal kitchen for guests to use. M$$

La Paloma Ocean Front Retreat Las Cabañas 13; http://lapalomamexico.com. Luxurious resort right on the beach, hosted by an amicable bunch of Canadians and featuring spacious studios with kitchen, sun deck, ocean views and clean, cheerful decor. The on-site Paloma Art Center runs week-long workshops in watercolour painting. Nov–Mar is adults-only, while in May, Sept and Oct the hotel tends to close for renovations. M$$$

Posada las Gaviotas Hidalgo 1; http://posadalasgaviotas.com. Friendly budget option right in the heart of things, close to the bus stations, beach and main square. Rooms are painted in cheerful primary colours and feature cable TV and wi-fi; most are fan-cooled. M$$

Posada Pablo de Tarso Gómez Farías 408; http://posadapablodetarso.com. Lovely rooms with wooden ceiling beams, terracotta-tiled floors, TVs, fans and a/c, set around a verdant colonial courtyard. There's also a good pool overlooking the sea. Significant discounts are available online. M$$$

★ **Villas Camino del Mar** Francisco Villa 6, corner Abel Salgado Velazco; http://villascaminodelmar.com.mx. Wonderful hideaway on the south side of town hosted by the lovely Gloria, and offering a range of apartments in a large whitewashed villa around an inviting pool overlooking the beach; all come with kitchenettes, wi-fi and fans, and some have a/c. Discounts sometimes on offer in the older building next door (mainly during low season). M$$

EATING

Some of the best **eating** in Melaque can be had from street stalls around the central plaza, or enjoying the sunset from numerous identical palapa joints along the beachfront. During the quieter months many restaurants and stalls will be closed.

★ **La Taza Negra** Vicente Guerrero 112; 315 355 7080. Fantastic modern coffee shop serving up hot and cold lattes, cappuccinos, macchiatos and the rest, with beans roasted in-house. There's a range of *pan dulce*, sandwiches and light bites too, and regular live music in the courtyard. M$

Tacos Guerrero Alvaro Obregón 29, north of main square; 315 355 6191. A very popular place, *Tacos Guerrero* serves up margaritas and cheap, tasty Mexican food. M$$

Taco Surf Juarez 16; 322 175 4037. A popular street-level taco kitchen serving *gringas de camarón* and plates of five fish tacos. All very delicious and served with a smile. M$$

Vainilla Pimienta Cabañas 14; 314 110 3550. The fanciest restaurant in Melaque is an eclectic kind of place, with a vaguely Mediterranean menu spanning delicious grilled meat and seafood, decent pasta dishes and the odd Middle Eastern *kofta* and kebab. Everything is beautifully presented in a gourmet style, and there's an extensive wine menu. M$$$$

DIRECTORY AND TOURS

Banks and exchange Opposite the bus station, in the Pasaje Comercial, you'll find the *casa de cambio* Melaque (which changes travellers' cheques). Opposite on Gómez Farías is Banamex bank, with a 24hr ATM; you can also exchange travellers' cheques here.

Post office The post office is at Orozco 13, around the corner from *Hotel San Patricio*.

The Only Tours A charming couple (American expat Ray and his Mexican wife Eva) offer trips on land and sea, from snorkelling at Tenacatita and boogie boarding at Boca de Iguana to ATV tours of the ranches, rivers and unspoilt countryside near Melaque (315 355 6777, raytoursmelaque@yahoo.com).

Playa Tenacatita

Some 27km north of Barra de Navidad and Melaque, a signed, paved road off Hwy-200 leads 9km to **PLAYA TENACATITA**, a gorgeous curve of bone-white sand on a coral-strewn cove, with the added attractions of a mangrove lagoon that teems with birdlife and still, clear waters perfect for snorkelling.

Costa Careyes

Another 30km north of Tenacatita (at Hwy-200 km 52) lies **Costa Careyes** (the "turtle coast"), another series of fine beaches with Playa Careyes itself gate-guarded and ringed by expensive villas, nestled in the hills. It's possible to visit for the day; just explain you want access to the beach and the guards will open the gates for you. On nearby protected **Playa Teopa**, endangered **olive ridley turtles** lay their eggs (Aug–Oct); biologists have established a conservation programme to make sure the turtles' eggs are collected before they fall victim to predators (the babies are released after the eggs hatch in a laboratory).

Bahía de Chamela

A further 20km north from Careyes on Hwy-200, the **Bahía de Chamela** comprises a huge, sweeping arc of superb beaches and nine islands, which are popular dive spots. Although large hotels are cropping up here with alarming frequency, you'll still find long sections of untouched beach where you can pitch a tent.

The focal point of the area is the junction known as "**El Super**" at Hwy-200 km 72, while the village of **Chamela** itself is at km 63; tragically, much of the village was destroyed by Hurricane Patricia in 2015. From El Super there's an unpaved road that leads to the honey-coloured sands of **Playa Chamela**, while **Playa Pérula**, at the northern end of the bay, is a 1km walk or drive down a dusty track from Hwy-200 km 76. Note that since 2010 beaches along the bay have been facing **legal disputes**, meaning that beach access has been limited in places – check before you go.

ARRIVAL AND DEPARTURE **BAHÍA DE CHAMELA**

By bus Take a second-class bus from Barra de Navidad (see page 227) towards Vallarta, ask to get off at km 72 (El Super) and walk 1km down to the beach.

By car The easiest way to explore this section of the coast is by car (you can rent cars relatively easily in Puerto Vallarta; see page 234).

ACCOMMODATION AND EATING

Bungalows Mayar Chamela Hwy-200 km 72, Playa Chamela; 315 333 9711. These eighteen basic but spacious cabañas have plain but perfectly pleasant rooms with fan, kitchen and an on-site pool. Quality varies, so take a look first before accepting a room. M$$

Casa Punta Pérula Libertad 41 (Hwy-200 km 76), Playa Pérula; https://www.casapuntaperula.com. Homely bed and breakfast with pink-washed adobe walls, close to the main square and sitting right on the beach. Rooms are not the biggest, but are very comfortable and all have a/c and satellite TV. Some feature balconies overlooking the garden or the ocean. M$$$

Villa Polinesia Hwy-200 km 72, Playa Chamela; 331 857 8382. Attractive oceanfront Polynesian-style cabañas ("Villas Tahitianas") surrounded by palm trees, with bathroom (hot water), fan and terrace (no TV). Larger cabins can accommodate groups. M$$$

3

Puerto Vallarta and around

Thanks to its mesmerizing sunsets, kilometres of sandy beaches and a laid-back, colonial centre, **PUERTO VALLARTA** is a small city dependent almost entirely on tourism; it attracts a mixed bag of North American retirees, Mexican families, spring-breakers, cruise-ship day-trippers and LGBTQ+ visitors taking advantage of its emergence as one of the **gay** centres of Mexico. If you're looking for traditional Mexico you might find this wholly unappealing, but while it's true that PV (as it's known) can be more expensive and certainly more touristy than the average Mexican town, it can also be lots of fun. It's smaller and more relaxed than Cancún and Acapulco, and its location, surrounded by lofty mountains, is spectacular. Behind the beaches there's a vibrant Mexican city, largely undisturbed by the flow of visitors, which means that the choice of tasty, cheap **street food** – especially tacos – is some of the best on the coast, and in between the souvenir shops and chichi boutiques are some exceptionally good **art galleries**. The beach remains the primary attraction, however, with the less crowded resorts and villages of the **Bahía de Banderas** fringed by endless stretches of sand and backed by the jungle-covered slopes of the Sierra Madre.

Brief history

The town was officially founded in the 1850s (when it was known as Las Peñas – it was renamed in 1918, after Ignacio L. Vallarta, former governor of Jalisco), but there had been a small fishing and smuggling village located where the Río Cuale spills out into the bay for years. Initially developed by the Union en Cuale mining company, it remained a sleepy place until the 1950s, when Mexican airlines started promoting the town as a resort (the first hotel opened in 1948). Their efforts received a shot in the arm in 1963, when **John Huston** chose Mismaloya, 10km south, as the setting for his film of Tennessee Williams' play *The Night of the Iguana*, starring Richard Burton. In recent decades, frantic development has mostly overwhelmed the tropical-village atmosphere, though the historic town centre at least retains its charming cobbled streets and white-walled, terracotta-roofed houses.

Centro Histórico

The **Plaza Principal**, official buildings, market and the bulk of the shops and upscale restaurants lie on the north side of the **Río Cuale**, Vallarta's busy downtown or **Centro Histórico**. The plaza lies at the heart of the old town, with its pleasant cobbled streets, colonial-style houses and breezy oceanfront boulevard. Here, families gather in the evenings among the balloon sellers and hot-dog stands, while tourists explore the city's restaurants, bars and clubs.

Templo de Nuestra Señora de Guadalupe

Hidalgo 370, between Zaragoza and Iturbide • Free • http://parroquiadeguadalupevallarta.com

The Plaza Principal is backed by the most memorable building in PV, the vaguely Art Nouveau **Templo de Nuestra Señora de Guadalupe**. Building started in 1918, with the famous crown that makes it so special completed in 1963; this collapsed in the earthquake of 1995, and what you see today is a giant fibreglass tiara replacement ("La Corona de Nuestra Señora") modelled on one that Emperor Maximilian's wife, Carlota, wore in the 1860s. The image of the Virgin of Guadalupe inside is said to have been painted by famed San Miguel Allende artist **Ignacio Ramírez** (aka "El Nigromante").

The malecón

Puerto Vallarta's wide **malecón** skirts the beaches in front of the old town, a pleasant promenade to admire the bay and those heavenly sunsets. The malecón meets the main plaza at the tiny **Plaza Aquiles Serdán**, with a strange little amphitheatre and **Los Arcos**,

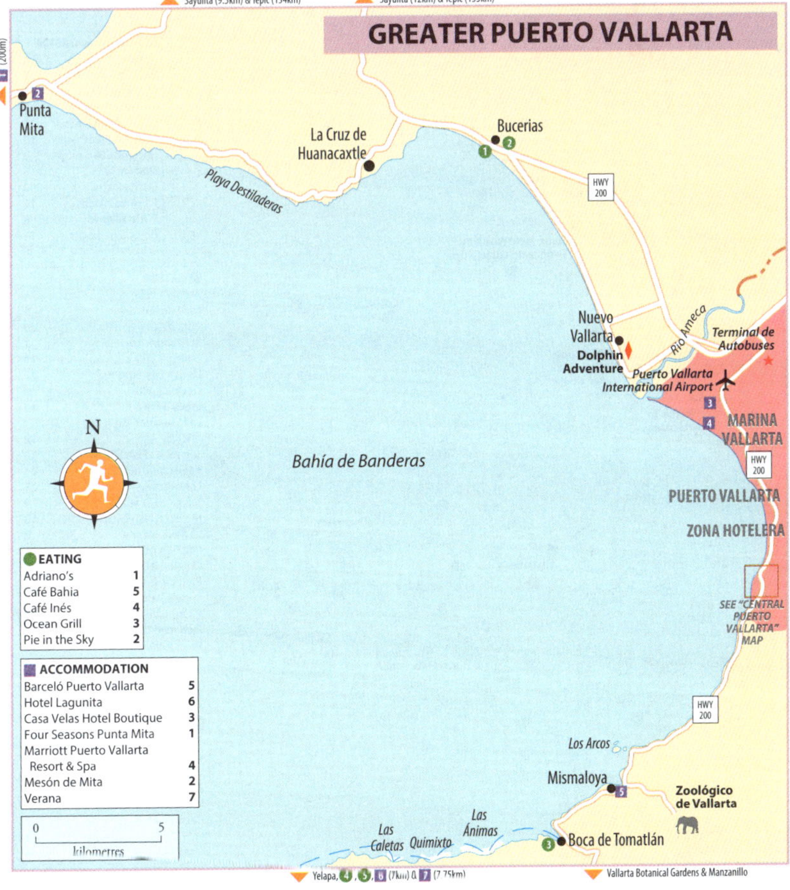

3

3

four arches looking out over the sea like a lost fragment of the Roman empire; with hawkers, mimes, musicians and food stands, it is one of the best places for people-watching in the city. The malecón goes north as far as 31 de Octubre and *Hotel Rosita* on the edge of downtown; to the south it crosses the Río Cuale to run along the town beach and the cheaper hotels in what's optimistically labelled the **Zona Romántica**.

Museo Histórico Naval

Zaragoza 4, just off Plaza Principal and the malecón • Charge, children under 6 free • 322 223 5357

The rather stuffy **Museo Histórico Naval** provides a fairly detailed history of the town and region from a nautical perspective, starting with the Spanish Conquest and ending with Mexico's modern navy. Some interesting episodes are covered with dioramas, paintings and photos, and there's extensive English labelling. The staff, fully suited and booted in naval uniform, are very informative too.

Mercado Municipal Río Cuale

Rodríguez, at Insurgentes and the river • Free • 322 152 6584

Near the river, the two-storey **Mercado Municipal Río Cuale**, aka the Flea Market, dates back to the 1960s, and was extended in 1979. The market is crammed with local jewellery, papier-mâché, clothes and souvenir stalls, but remember never to accept the first price – bargain for everything.

3

Isla Río Cuale

The **Isla Río Cuale**, in the middle of the river that splits the old town and the Zona Romántica, is a lush, garden-like pedestrian-only space, containing a museum (see below), a clutch of souvenir shops and some good restaurants. On the north side, at Serdán 437, there is the **Centro Cultural Cuale** (322 223 0095), which holds all sort of arts classes and shows local art exhibits; on the way you'll pass **John Huston's statue** (with a rather odd quote, eulogizing Humphrey Bogart).

Museo del Cuale

Isla Río Cuale • Free, video fee • 322 135 0762

At the seaward end of the island, the **Museo del Cuale** is a small but worthy attempt to document the pre-Columbian history of the region with plenty of rare artefacts and captions in English. Highlights include the symmetrical patterned ceramics of the **Chupícuaro** culture (400 BC–200 AD), shaft tombs dating from 0–500 AD and the sophisticated pottery of **Aztatlán** culture (900–1200 AD). Ceramic female images figure prominently, emphasizing the importance of women to West Mexico cultures.

The beaches

Puerto Vallarta's **beaches** vary in nature as you move round the bay: to the north, Vallarta's busy downtown eventually morphs into an area of good beaches and fancy hotels imaginatively dubbed **Zona Hotelera** by the local authorities. This ends at the upscale **Marina Vallarta** development and the airport. Further north, beyond the Río Ameca, lies **Nuevo Vallarta** (see page 240).

PV ARTWALK

Vallarta's art scene has boomed since the 1990s, with contemporary artists such as Xaime Ximénez, Michael Whitlow and Rodo Padilla among many with studios in the city. Get a taster on the weekly ArtWalk evenings (late Oct to April; http://puertovallartaartwalk.com), when the best thirteen galleries downtown open their doors every Wednesday 6–10pm.

Playa de los Muertos

The main (and most fun) town beach lies in the Zona Romántica, south of the plaza and the river. **Playa de los Muertos** (Beach of the Dead), or "Playa del Sol" as the local tourist office would prefer it known, is not very large, and features coarse, brown sand and reasonably calm surf, despite facing apparently open water. It's also the most crowded of the city's beaches – locals, Mexican holidaymakers and foreign tourists are packed in cheek by jowl during the high season. With the omnipresent hawkers selling everything from fresh fruit and tacos to handicrafts and fake jade masks, it can be a far from relaxing experience, but it's always entertaining. The **gay** section of this beach is at its southern end, opposite the *Blue Chairs Resort* (see page 235) – look out for the blue chairs. Further south is a series of steep-sided coves, sheltering tiny, calm enclaves (see page 238).

ARRIVAL AND DEPARTURE — PUERTO VALLARTA

3

BY PLANE

Arrival Puerto Vallarta's airport (officially Aeropuerto Internacional Gustavo Diaz Ordaz; 322 221 1298) lies 10km north of the centre on the coastal highway (Hwy-200), with numerous flights connecting Puerto Vallarta with the US and Canada. Useful domestic links include Aéreo Calafia's daily service to Mazatlán (and on to Los Cabos). Pay for taxis at the booth before leaving the terminal: rates are tied to an expensive zone system which spans Marina Vallarta, downtown and the Zona Romántica or Nuevo Vallarta. *Colectivos* run to downtown and the Zona Romántica, but only go when full and when enough people are heading in the same direction. In all cases, ignore the hordes of time-share sellers. If luggage is not a problem, a far cheaper option is to walk out of the terminal onto the main road and catch a city bus (marked "Olas Altas" or "Centro"). Regular taxis also run from here into downtown (see below). All the major car-rental firms (see page 234) have desks at the airport, and you'll find a few ATMs and places to change money.

Destinations Aguascalientes (2 daily; 1hr 15min); Guadalajara (4 daily; 50min); Mexico City (frequent; 1hr 30min); Monterrey (2 daily; 1hr 35min); Puebla (1 daily; 3hr 20min); Tijuana (3 weekly; 2h 50min); Toluca (4 daily; 1hr 30min).

BY BUS

The Terminal de Autobuses is around 12km north of the city centre (beyond the airport), one long block off the main highway (Hwy-200). Local buses pass along the road outside – buses heading south are usually marked "Olas Altas" or "Centro", while those in the other direction are marked "Hoteles", "Ixtapa" or "Juntas"; be sure to ask the driver if the bus is going to the city centre, just in case. Taxis should follow a fixed-rate system (rates displayed at the exit) to: *Centro Histórico,* Zona Romántica, Marina, Mismaloya, Nuevo Vallarta, Bucerías, Punta Mita and Sayulita. Expect to pay the same coming back, but make sure you agree the fare before you set off.

Destinations Acapulco (3 daily; 19hr); Barra de Navidad (4 daily; 3hr 30min); Guadalajara (frequent; 5hr 30min); Los Mochis (2 daily; 8hr); Manzanillo (6 daily; 5hr 30min); Mazatlán (4 daily2; 6–8hr); Mexico City (9 daily; 13hr); Tepic (frequently; 3hr 30min–4hr).

GETTING AROUND

By bus Destinations are marked on the front of public buses (daily 5am–11.30pm): downtown buses are marked "Centro" ("Tunel" means the bus bypasses the *Centro Histórico* and goes straight to the Zona Romántica). To get to the Terminal de Autobuses catch the Las Juntas or Ixtapa bus with "Central Camionera" on the front.

By taxi Always fix the price before you get in a taxi (no meters). Most drivers charge according to a vaguely set fixed-rate system (for foreigners at least): hops around the *Centro Histórico* and Zona Romántica will be budget friendly, but you'll pay more for trips up to the airport, the Marina area and Bucerías. Taxis to Punta Mita are a lot more and fares to Mismaloya vary.

Car rental Alamo, Francisco Medina Ascencio 4600b, 322 221 3030 or the airport 322 221 1228; Avis, at the airport 322 221 0783 and *Secrets hotel*, David Alfaro Siqueros 164 322 224 4859; and Hertz, at the airport 800 709 5000 and at Paradise Plaza, Paseo de los Cocoteros 85, Nuevo Vallarta 800 709 5000.

INFORMATION AND ACTIVITIES

Tourist office The Dirección de Turismo office (Mon–Sat 8am–7pm, Sun 10am–4pm; 322 222 0923, http://visitpuertovallarta.com) is on the corner of Independencia and Juárez, just off the Plaza Principal.

Newspapers For up-to-date, if somewhat promotional, information on what's going on in town, pick up the free English-language daily *Vallarta Today* (http://vallartatoday.com), available in gringo hangouts.

Websites Puerto Vallarta is also well represented on various websites such as http://puertovallarta.net, http://

vallartalifestyles.com and http://vallartadaily.com.

Chico's Dive Shop Díaz Ordaz 772; 322 222 1895, http://chicos-diveshop.com. Runs diving and snorkelling trips to nearby sites daily at 10am and 3pm. The best time to see manta rays is July–Nov. Also offers dive classes, from refresher lessons to four-day PADI courses.

Vallarta Undersea Edificio Marina del Rey, Marina Vallarta; 322 209 0025, https://vallartaundersea.com/tours.htm. Runs daily dive trips at 9am to Los Arcos and Las Islas Marietas, and also rents snorkelling and scuba gear. Snorkellers can join the dive trips for an additional fee.

ACCOMMODATION

Staying in Puerto Vallarta means opting for one of the resorts along the coast, or a hotel downtown, within easy walking distance of Playa de los Muertos and the Plaza Principal. Many **resorts** offer all-inclusive packages, and, with a few exceptions, are quite similar (and often pricey). The more affordable options mainly lie south of the Río Cuale in the Zona Romántica, close to the old town. **Camping** on any of the more popular beaches around the middle of the bay is prohibited, but if you're reasonably well equipped and protected against mosquitoes, you could try **Punta de Mita** at the northern end of the bay or **Boca de Tomatlán** to the south (where the main road turns inland), each of which from time to time sees small communities established on the sand.

CENTRO HISTÓRICO, SEE MAP PAGE 232

El Chanclas Hostel Juaréz 793; 322 104 3451. Friendly hostel one block back from the beach, whose name – 'the flip flop' – pretty much says it all. Beachy and relaxed, there's a choice of mixed or female-only dorms, good breakfasts, and beer pong on the terrace. Reception open 8am–10pm only; call ahead if you're going to be late. M$

Los Cuatro Vientos Matamoros 520; http://cuatrovientos.com. A PV institution, with many return guests. Artistic touches and local handicrafts give the spotless rooms a homely feel. There is a small pool and the terrace has wonderful views. Owner Gloria is a good resource when planning tours or dining out in the area. M$$$

★ **Hacienda San Angel** Miramar 336; http://haciendasanangel.com. Hotel histories don't come much more romantic than that of *Hacienda San Angel*, which was bestowed by Richard Burton on his wife Susan as a Valentine's gift in 1977. Suites retain all the hacienda's historic charm, with carved furniture sourced from European cathedrals, nineteenth-century religious artworks on the walls and beautiful Mexican rugs on the tiled floors. A spectacular place if you're looking to splurge. M$$$$

Porto Allegro Hidalgo 119; http://hotelportoallegro.com. Lovely four-star in the heart of downtown, a stone's throw from both Isla Río Cuale and Playa de los Muertos. Rooms are tasteful and traditional, and have a/c, fans and flatscreen TVs. Hearty breakfasts are served each morning, it's dog friendly, and there's a gym on site. M$$$

ZONA ROMÁNTICA, SEE MAP PAGE 232

Azteca Madero 473, at Jacarandas; 322 222 2750. A long-standing, reliable choice with simple, surgically clean rooms with fans, hot water and free wi-fi overlooking a peaceful courtyard full of flourishing plants. There's no bell, so you may have to shout. Panoramic views from the rooftop terrace. M$

Belmar Insurgentes 161; http://belmarvallarta.com. Well located and economical, this snug, friendly hotel has clean, pleasant rooms with TV, wi-fi, fans and tiny bathrooms – it's extra for a kitchenette. Request a room with a balcony on the top floor. M$$

Blue Chairs Resort Malecón and Almendro 4, at Playa de los Muertos; https://www.bluechairs.com. LGBTQ+ visitors, even if not staying here, will inevitably gravitate to this gay-owned and operated landmark on the town beach. The resort has suites with or without kitchens and ocean views, as well as a rooftop bar and pool. Straight guests are also welcome. M$$$

★ **Hacienda Alemana** Basilio Badillo 378; http://haciendaalemana.com. Top B&B run by a Mexican-German family, with ten crisp, stylish rooms with flatscreen TVs and *sauerbraten*, *bratwurst* and German beer in *steins* – they even celebrate Oktoberfest here. Free wi-fi and gourmet breakfast included, all a short walk from the beach. M$$$$

Hortencia Madero 336, at Insurgentes; http://hotelhortencia.com. A variety of terracotta-hued, spacious rooms, all with a/c, cable TV, free wi-fi and fan in a convenient location. M$$

Oasis Hostel Libramiento 222; http://oasishostel.com. Clean and sociable hostel a 15min walk from the city centre. Dorm beds come with breakfast and internet access included, and there are also two en-suite doubles, as well as a TV room with cable and DVDs. Options include dorms and private doubles. M$

Playa Los Arcos Olas Altas 380, at Diéguez; http://playalosarcos.com. The best-equipped and most spacious of the beachfront hotels, with a lively social scene centred around the large pool and adjacent palapa restaurant, with live sport on the TV. Well-appointed rooms with a/c, TV and safe, though they can smell very musty in the rainy season. M$$$

Posada de Roger Basilio Badillo 237; http://hotelposadaderoger.com. Some of the sombre rooms here have seen better days, but they all have a/c, cable TV, safe and fan, and overlook a spacious, shady courtyard. The on-site *El Tucan* restaurant is considered one of the best breakfast spots in town. Only a couple of blocks from the beach, and with a small rooftop pool. M$$$

3

Villa del Mar Madero 440, at Jacarandas; http://hvilladelmar.com. Relaxed, long-time favourite of budget travellers. All motel-style rooms have bathrooms; the larger, more expensive "suites" also have small balconies, a/c, TV and kitchenettes. M$$

MARINA VALLARTA, SEE MAP PAGE 231

★ **Casa Velas Hotel Boutique** Pelícanos 311; http://hotelcasavelas.com. Pick of the elegant modern resorts along Vallarta's northern coast, ideal for some serious pampering (and spending). Ultra-stylish suites blend Mexican and contemporary decor, and there's golf, swimming pools and a spa – the private beach club is a 15min walk (or free shuttle ride) away. If you ever decide to venture off the premises, remember it's quite a hike to the old town. M$$$$

★ **Marriott Puerto Vallarta Resort & Spa** Paseo La Marina Norte 435; http://marriott.com. Resort featuring luxurious rooms with huge flatscreen TVs, balconies and gasp-inducing views. Lounge at the huge pool, sample the best spa in town (see box, page 236) and dine in one of several excellent restaurants on site. The cute chile garden, kids' club and Huichol art throughout are nice touches. A day pass to the pool includes a credit for food and drink. This spot also has one of the best buffet breakfasts in the city and visitors can buy 24hr internet passes. M$$$$

EATING

SEE MAP PAGE 232

3

CENTRO HISTÓRICO

★ **Café des Artistes** G. Sanchez 740; http://cafedesartistes.com. The epitome of Pacific coast gourmet dining. The quality of chef Thierry Blouet's French cuisine matches the sophisticated surroundings – the intriguing menu features suckling lamb with eggplant cloud and grilled octopus with bean sauce and decadent desserts. Eat in the garden or dining room decorated with vivid artwork. Live piano and flute music add to the refined atmosphere. M$$$$

La Dolce Vita Díaz Ordaz 674, at Dominguez; http://dolcevita.com.mx. Pizzas, pasta and other dishes, such as beef carpaccio and chicken *cacciatore*, at reasonable prices. Live jazz Thurs–Sun. M$$$

La Michoacana Plaza Principal, at Morelos and Zaragoza; 322 294 8524. This place has been dishing up heavenly ice cream and fruity ice popsicles (think coconut, *mamey* and lemon pie) since 1957, and remains a firm favourite with the crowds milling around the plaza. M$

Pepe's Taco Honduras 173, between Peru and México; 322 223 1703. This no-frills restaurant (plenty of seating) has been serving mouthwatering *tacos carne asada* since 1987. M$

Planeta Vegetariano Iturbide 270, at Hidalgo; 322 222 3073, https://facebook.com/PlanetaVegetarianoPV. Large menu and all-you-can-eat vegetarian buffet with a choice of main courses, salads, soup, dessert and a soft drink. The walls are painted with fantastic frescoes, and the food is cheap and deliciously spiced. M$$

River Café Isla Río Cuale 4; http://rivercafe.com.mx. High-quality dining in the middle of leafy Isla Río Cuale, with creations such as *chipotle* mussels, baked brie wheels and baked lamb lasagne. Great vegetarian, vegan and gluten-free options too. Pricey, but a nice treat. M$$$$

Trio Guerrero 264; http://triopv.com. An elegant townhouse filled with original art and hanging plants provides the setting for Mediterranean-fusion cuisine prepared by a German-Swedish chef with Michelin credentials. In addition to dishes like over-roasted rabbit with garlic sauce and slow-roasted buffalo stew, there are home-made pastas, Lebanese salads, sautéed calamari and an imaginatively prepared selection of seafood dishes. It's a fabulous treat, if you fancy splurging. M$$$$

ZONA ROMÁNTICA

Archie's Wok Rodríguez 130; http://archieswok.com. State-of-the-art Asian cooking served in a stylish setting, with an emphasis on seafood in Filipino, Thai and Chinese sauces – think Thai garlic shrimps, almond chicken and sizzling fish in banana leaves. A little pricey, but touted as one of the best Asian restaurants on the Pacific coast. Live music at the weekend. No reservations. M$$$

Café de Olla Basilio Badillo 168, between Olas Altas and Pino Suárez; 322 223 1626, http://bit.ly/CaféDeOlla. Good traditional Mexican food – enchiladas, *carne asado*, *chile relleno* – served in a lively dining room adorned with local artwork, and delivered by cheerful, attentive waiters. M$$$

SPA THERAPY

If the heat, crowds and traffic are getting you down, make for the *Marriott Puerto Vallarta Resort*'s **Ohtli Spa** (see page 236), the most luxurious and soothing in town. The place has a modern, minimalist feel, with single-sex plunge pools, steam rooms, saunas, an aqua therapy pool and themed treatment rooms, from Thai massage beds to a romantic couples/group room with jacuzzi. Guests pay a lesser fee for the pools and steam rooms, non-guests pay more – and treatments are extra.

TACO TOUR

Numerous **tacos** stalls occupy the streets of Puerto Vallarta at night, offering a tasty introduction to this essential street food. The following tour starts a few blocks east of the malecón in the Zona Romántica and roughly heads north through downtown, though you'd have to be extremely hungry to visit every stall in one night.

La Hormiga Feliz ("The Happy Ant") Madero, at Vallarta; see map page 232. This stall has been knocking out delicious *bírria*, tacos and quesadillas since the 1970s. M$

Tacos Memo Grill Badillo, at Aguacate; see map page 232. Sumptuous *tacos asada, quesadillas con carne, hamburguesas* and burritos. M$

Marisma Fish Taco Naranjo 320, at Carranza; 322 222 1395, https://facebook.com/marismafishtaco; see map page 232. The best fish and shrimp tacos in town. There's another branch in Marina Vallarta. M$

Rico Mac Taco México 1139; 332 222 4204; see map page 232. Though this congenial sit-down place attracts a fair share of tourists, the tacos are excellent, there are lots of bars nearby, and it (officially at least) never shuts, making it perfect for after-hours eats. M$$$

Mariscos El Jefe México and Chile; see map page 232. Not strictly a taco place, but beloved for its fresh, local seafood, delicious *ceviche* and prawn cocktails since 1970. M$$$

El Carboncito Honduras 127, across from Pepe's; see map page 232. End up at the connoisseurs' favourite – a small (usually unmarked) stall known for serving the finest *tacos el pastor* you'll find in the city. The secret: mesquite-infused charcoal and superb, tongue-singeing salsa. M$

3

Daíquiri Dick's Olas Altas 314; http://daiquiridicks.com. Informal beachside dining (perfect for sunset drinks) and a varied menu of generous dishes draw a big gringo crowd. The signature dish, *pescado Vallarta* – a whole grilled, seasoned fish served on a stick – is worth the 30min wait. Other crowd pleasers, including lobster tacos and chicken in masala sauce, are equally good. Closed Sept. M$$$$

Derby City Burgers Rodolfo Gómez 131; 322 223 3323. Perhaps not the "tastiest burgers in Mexico", but close; gourmet beef burgers ranging from the classic House Burger to Bluegrass BBQ Burgers and the "Mex-Cali" (pepper jack cheese, *jalapeños*, avocado and sour cream). Cash only. M$$

Fredy's Tucán Basilio Badillo 245, at Vallarta; 322 223 0778; https://facebook.com/fredystucanpuertovallarta. Bright, airy and with tropical decor, this is one of the best venues for Mexican, continental and American breakfasts, including omelettes, pancakes, French toast, granola, yogurt, and fresh-baked bread. European football matches are screened in the hotel bar on evenings and at weekends. M$$

★ **Joe Jack's Fish Shack** Basilio Badillo 212; http://joejackspv.com. Fabulous seafood, but best known for its fish and chips and chowders, renowned as the tastiest in town; the "Tasty" burger is also excellent. Sit at the bar downstairs, or enjoy the views from the rooftop dining area. "Burger Wednesdays" offers any burger with fries for a special deal. Free wi-fi. M$$

Kaiser Maximilian Olas Altas 380-B, next to Playa Los Arcos hotel (see page 235); http://kaisermaximilian.com. Upscale, expensive restaurant with an old-European slant: traditional Austrian dishes like lamb with rosemary and sautéed squid, as well as more traditional Mexican and international offerings. The pavement patio is a nice spot for a gourmet coffee and an exceedingly rich pastry. M$$$$

Langostinos Diéguez 109 at Playa Los Muertos; 322 222 0894. Phenomenal sunset views from seats right on the sand, excellent lime margaritas and tasty surf and turf combos – the menu includes everything from burgers and snacks to fresh fish and lobster. Happy hour daily; bring cash as they'll charge three percent extra on your card. M$$$

★ **Los Muertos Brewing** Constitucion Lazaro Cardenas; http://losmuertosbrewing.com. For those who like craft and artisanal beer, this relaxed spot pours a range of seven different house brews, ranging from pilsner and blonde ale to stout and occasional seasonal specials. Happy hour sees pints sold for a bargain. Also serves good, hearty food – try the burgers and pizzas (by the slice and build your own. M$$

El Palomar de los González Aguacate 425; http://elpalomardelosgonzalez.com. Perfect for a romantic candlelit dinner, this elegant mansion, carved into the hillside south of the centre, has stunning views from its rooftop patio. The seafood dishes are the highlight of the menu, but the Mexican specialities are also well executed. A good wine list and exotic desserts ensure a long, indulgent evening. M$$$$

★ **Panadería y Pastelería Yarita** Basilio Badillo 244; 322 113 0344. Best traditional bakery in the city, with irresistible empanadas, banana bread, pastries, cake and mini custard éclairs. M$

Las Tres Huastecas Olas Altas 444, at Rodríguez; 322 222 3017. No-frills, cantina-style restaurant since 1965, a block from Playa de los Muertos, that specializes in classic Mexican dishes such as chicken in *mole* sauce and a creative ensemble of fish tacos and enchiladas. One of the cheapest places in this part of town M$$

DRINKING AND NIGHTLIFE

SEE MAP PAGE 232

The **malecón** (Paseo Díaz Ordaz) is the centre of Puerto Vallarta's night-time activity, lined with ornate, hangar-size places that specialize in creating a high-energy party atmosphere – pop, techno and 1980s rock compete for the airwaves with salsa, jazz and the more gentle strumming of marauding mariachis. Check http://visitpuertovallarta.com for the latest events and listings. The Zona Romántica also has its share of clubs, which are generally less pretentious and more varied in character. This is where you'll find most of the **LGBTQ+ nightlife** (see http://gayguidevallarta.com).

CENTRO HISTÓRICO

La Bodeguita del Medio Paseo Díaz Ordaz 858 (malecón); http://labodeguitadelmedio.com.mx. Write your name on the wall if you can find the space in this Cuban chain made famous by the original Hemingway Havana haunt. The *mojitos* are the signature tipple (ask for Havana Club seven-year-old rum), and the live salsa goes from open 'til close.

★ **Cheeky Monkey** Paseo Díaz Ordaz 556 (malecón), at Corona; 322 222 8938. Difficult to turn down another dollar-margarita, especially when they're as potent as these. This bar above the malecón is the perfect place to get your evening started – three levels, balcony views of the bay and stunning sunsets. The food isn't bad either.

Mandala Paseo Díaz Ordaz 640 (malecón), at Abasolo; 998 883 3333. Huge, warehouse-like *discoteca* and video bar, attracting tourists and upscale locals with its Asian-themed interior (think *Buddha Bar*) and Latino pop and dance music. Cover charge.

Morelos Morelos 589, one block back from the malecón; 322 270 4103, http://facebook.com/BarMorelosPuertoVallarta. Try a variety of mescals at this darkly stylish bar, where exposed brick walls are lit by lavish chandeliers and adorned with bronze skulls. There's also a decent range of craft beers, and a soundtrack of live rock music.

★ **The Zoo** Paseo Díaz Ordaz 630 (malecón); http://zoodancebar.com. Leopard- and zebra-skin chairs and plastic gorillas swinging from the rafters (not to mention staff in animal costumes) lend a kitsch element to this wildly popular club, where DJs play the latest dance tunes for a hip young clientele. No cover.

ZONA ROMÁNTICA

Apaches Olas Altas 439; 322 141 6752, https://facebook.com/apachespuertovallarta. Popular and welcoming lesbian-owned, gay-friendly joint where groups gather for martinis and cocktails at happy hour, filling the cosy, indoor bar and pavement tables.

Paco's Ranch Vallarta 237; http://pacosranchpv.com. This is the largest and most popular gay club in town, but it also draws a straight contingent. It's a multifaceted venue with DJs playing the latest in techno, hip-hop and pop on the ground floor; Mexican music, a cantina and pool table on the first floor (open from 1pm); a rooftop bar on the second; and strippers in a smaller space connected to the main club by a passageway. There are nightly drag shows and happy hours.

El Solar Paraguay 1294, at Nicaragua; 322 222 4034. If the cheesy dance music and cheap shots of the malecón aren't your thing, then try this lovely beachfront bar overlooking Playa Camarones. It does great cocktails – try the jalapeño *mezcalita* – and good seafood, ribs and steak, all accompanied by a perfect Vallarta sunset.

DIRECTORY

Banks and exchange Banamex, on the Plaza Principal has an ATM. There are branches of Banorte downtown, at Díaz Ordaz 690, and in Zona Hotelera, at Francisco Medina Ascensio 500 (same hours). Other ATMs are plentiful. You can change money at the numerous *casas de cambio* on the streets surrounding the plaza: rates vary, so shop around.

Consulates Canada, Plaza Peninsula, Francisco Medina Ascencio 2485, Zona Hotelera Norte 322 293 0098 (Mon–Fri 9am–1pm); US, Paseo de los Cocoteros 85 Sur, Paradise Plaza, Interior Local L-7, Nuevo Vallarta 334 624 2102 (Mon–Thurs 8.30am–12.30pm; closed every second Wed and US and Mexican holidays) – in emergencies call US Consulate General in Guadalajara (555 080 2000, ext. 0).

Emergencies Police 060, 911 or 322 178 8999.

Hospitals English-speaking medics at CMQ Hospital, Basilio Badillo 365, between Insurgentes and Aguacate 322 223 1919; and Cruz Roja, Río Balsas and Río Plata 322 222 1533.

Laundry There are facilities scattered throughout town, all charging around per load – try Lavandería El Jabon, Cardenas 258, or Lavandería Paola, Guerrero 317.

Pharmacy CMQ, Basilio Badillo 367; 322 222 2941, next to CMQ Clinic, is open 24hr; or try Farmacia Guadalajara at Zapata 232 (322 222 0101), also 24hr.

Post office The main post office is at Colombia 1014, at Argentina, north of the old town.

Bahía de Banderas

Puerto Vallarta lies at the centre of the **Bahía de Banderas**, prime beach territory easily explored via rental car, or, with more time, public bus and water taxi. Indeed, for the more peaceful and scenic **beaches** further south – **Playa Las Animas** and **Yelapa** are the most appealing – a boat is the only means of access.

LOS ARCOS

From the beach at Mismaloya boats are on hand to take you snorkelling at **Los Arcos**, a magical underwater park around a group of offshore islands, some creating the eponymous arched geological formations. A superb array of brightly coloured fish – parrot, angel, pencil, croaker and scores of others – negotiates the deep rock walls and the boulder-strewn ocean floor. Operators usually charge a modest amount for basic snorkelling trips.

To the north, over the state line in Nayarit, the bay arcs out to **Punta de Mita**, some 30km away. A summer preserve for Guadalajarans and a winter retreat for motorhome vacationers from the north, these gorgeous beaches offer facilities in just a few spots – **Nuevo Vallarta**, **Bucerías** and **Punta de Mita** – leaving many kilometres of secluded sand for camping and some excellent surf breaks.

3

Mismaloya

Some 10km south of Puerto Vallarta, the best-known and most accessible beach is **Mismaloya**. Here John Huston filmed *The Night of the Iguana*, building his set at the mouth of what was once a pristine, jungle-choked gorge on the southern side of the gorgeous bay; it's been endowed with a romantic mystique ever since. The beach itself remains pretty but quite small, with a handful of palapa restaurants and enthusiastic vendors, selling everything from coconuts to sarongs, crammed into the southern end. Boats depart the beach for **Los Arcos** (see page 239). Public access is via the Paseo del Rio along the river, just to the south of the hotel entrance; you can use the hotel facilities for a daily fee (includes buffet lunch).

Boca de Tomatlán

If you're after peace and quiet, your best option is to continue along the highway for another 4km past Mismaloya until you reach the village of **Boca de Tomatlán**, the departure point for the *lanchas* that shuttle passengers to and from the southern beaches (see below); there's not much in Boca itself. The bus from Vallarta terminates at the top of the hill – it's a short walk down to the beach and *embarcadero* from here to catch a **water taxi** (see page 241). Look out for dolphins and rays as the boat speeds south.

Vallarta Botanical Gardens

Hwy-200 km 24 • Charge • http://vbgardens.org • Take the El Tuito bus from Carranza and Aguacate in the Zona Romántica (every 20min)

In the hills high above Boca de Tomatlán lies the 20-acre **Vallarta Botanical Gardens**, a lush, tropical interlude from the beaches below. In addition to admiring the blossoms, Mexican orchids, blue agave and exotic plants, you can enjoy jungle river-swimming, visit the Hacienda de Oro Visitor Centre and eat at the restaurant.

Las Ánimas

Usually the first stop on the water-taxi route, around ten minutes from Boca, **Las Ánimas** is a large bay with a long, sandy beach. There are plenty of beach restaurants here, and watersports – jet skiing, banana boats and parasailing – so it tends to be the busiest stop, especially in the afternoons.

Quimixto and Las Caletas

Quimixto is the second stop on the water-taxi route, though it's become less popular in recent years and therefore much less crowded. The beach is similar to Las Ánimas, but with no activities and far fewer places to eat – there's also a small village at the southern end. The other main attraction is the hike or horse ride to the local waterfall, a 30m cascade that plunges into a lagoon safe for swimming. A bit further south, the small cove and beach known as **Las Caletas** (John Huston's former home) has become a private watersports centre for Vallarta Adventures (http://vallarta-adventures.com), but water taxis will also stop here.

Yelapa

The old hippy hangout of **Yelapa** remains the most enticing target along this stretch of coast, some thirty minutes from Boca and the final water-taxi stop. Beautifully located on a gorgeous bay, hemmed in by tropical hills and coconut palms, it has managed to retain a rustic, laid-back vibe, despite the arrival of day-trippers, electricity and satellite dishes; locals still hook octopus and surgeonfish right off the pier, frigate birds glide over the water and turkey vultures skulk in the trees.

Boats pull up first at **La Playa**, the white-sand beach lined with palapa restaurants, before heading across the bay to **El Pueblo**, the "town", a cluster of houses clinging to the cliffs (with a church and a few small shops).

The Falls

From the beach you can walk up the Rio del Tuito to the **Upper Cascadas** (aka "Cascada Catedral"), through the languid village of El Paso, past fields of maize, mango trees and sleepy dogs and cattle (around 1.5hr hike). Check directions before you go, as it's a bit tricky at the end. From El Pueblo, another cobblestone path leads up to the much closer and slightly more impressive lacy falls of **La Cascada Cola de Caballo**, where there's a small pool and drink stall. Horses and guides can be hired at the beach to take you up to either falls, but you shouldn't get lost walking – the friendly locals will point you in the right direction.

Nuevo Vallarta

Just across the Nayarit state border, **NUEVO VALLARTA**, 12km north of PV airport, is a mega-resort, an ever-expanding cluster of astronomically expensive hotels. Although the creamy-white beach here is spectacular, it's backed by modern towers.

Bucerías

For a more local beach experience, you're better off pushing on to laid-back **BUCERÍAS**, the last stop along the northern side of the bay before Hwy-200 cuts inland, which has wonderful views across the water to Puerto Vallarta from its seafront **restaurants** (see page 242). The village is a bit shabby, but the flea-market stalls make for good shopping, and the popular beach is a long swathe of chalk-white sand.

Punta de Mita

PUNTA DE MITA is more developed than Bucerías (21km away), with most of the bars, cafés and seafood restaurants along the handsome beach attached to hotels and resorts in the area known as **Playa Anclote**. The beach here is a wide, kilometre-long curve of silky coral sand, and the water is shallow with long wave breaks, making it perfect

BAHÍA DE BANDERAS ZIP LINES

The region boasts two zip lines (aka "canopy tours") competing for your pesos. The oldest is **Los Veranos Canopy Tour** (1.5hr–2hr; http://canopytours-vallarta.com), in the small village of Las Juntas y Los Veranos, above Boca de Tomatlán. This is a series of fourteen exhilarating zip lines along cables up to 60m high and 335m long over the Río Orquídeas, whizzing past coffee trees, vanilla vines and agave plants. You can also meet monkeys, iguanas and toucans at an animal sanctuary, before winding down with a tequila tasting (both included). Competition is supplied by **Canopy River** (http://canopyriver.com), with twelve higher zip lines (200m), a small river beach in the jungle and hotel pick-up and transportation to the site – including a 15-minute mule ride.

ZONA PACÍFICO TIME

If you travel north of Puerto Vallarta you need to put your watch back one hour: Nuevo Vallarta, Bucerías, Punta de Mita and Sayulita officially lie within the Zona Pacífico (Pacific Zone), the equivalent of Canadian and US Mountain Time, which starts at the Jalisco/Nayarit state border, just north of Puerto Vallarta's airport. However, because Nuevo Vallarta, Bucerías and Punta de Mita are so close to PV, most businesses work on Zona Central (US Central) times; Sayulita officially changed to Central time in 2011. If you are given a time followed by the word Jalisco, it means Zona Central; if followed by Nayarit, it is Zona Pacífico time.

for beginner surfers. On the highway, you can continue north to **Sayulita** from here without backtracking to Vallarta.

ARRIVAL AND DEPARTURE — BAHÍA DE BANDERAS

By bus (north side) To get to the beaches north of Puerto Vallarta, catch any northbound Autotransportes Medina "Punta de Mita" bus (every 10min to; Bucerías and Nuevo Vallarta; Destiladeras; Punta de Mita). These buses originate in downtown Vallarta at 1410 Brasil, between Guatemala and Brasilia. Taxi vans will whisk you to Sayulita from Punta Mita (20min); alternatively, take the bus back to Bucerías, and catch the local bus from Vallarta to Sayulita from there.

By bus (south side) Buses to Mismaloya (20–25min) and Boca de Tomátlan (another 10min) every 10–15min. Water taxis depart from Boca (see below). Buses to El Tuito (via the Botanical Gardens) depart Carranza and Aguacate in the Zona Romántica every 20–30min.

By taxi Taxis run from downtown to Nuevo Vallarta; other popular routes include Bucerías and Punta Mita; you can also get taxis to Mismaloya and Boca de Tomátlan, though you might save some pesos starting in the Zona Romántica. From Bucerías, Nuevo Vallarta is a small fare away, Punta de Mita and Sayulita cost more. Taxis within each area charge a flat fee for short rides.

By water taxi From Playa de los Muertos in the Zona Romántica, water taxis depart 10am, 11am, 1pm, 3pm and 5pm (usually hourly, 9am–6pm in high season, Nov–March) for Las Ánimas, Quimixto and Yelapa (25–45min). The last boat back departs 4pm. Water taxis from Boca de Tomátlan also run to Las Ánimas (10min), Quimixto and Yelapa (30min), but always check current schedules at the dock: boats usually run every 90min or so from 7am, with the last boat back usually 4pm. If you get stuck, a private boat ride from Yelapa back to Boca will cost a princely sum.

TOURS AND ACTIVITIES

Boat tours If you'd rather take an organized boat tour or "booze cruise" to the southern beaches, visit http://puertovallartatours.net or http://vallarta-adventures.com. Most day cruises run to Los Arcos, Las Ánimas and Quimixto (Yelapa is pricier), usually with food, soft drinks and snorkelling included.

Whale-watching tours Alternatively, book an organized whale-watching tour from Puerto Vallarta with an operator such as Vallarta Whales, departing from Los Peines Pier (http://vallartawhales.com). Humpback whales appear in the bay from around Dec–April.

ACCOMMODATION — SEE MAP PAGE 231

MISMALOYA

Barceló Puerto Vallarta Hwy-200 km 11.5; http://barcelo.com. This huge luxury hotel dominates the beach at Mismaloya, a full-scale all-inclusive resort with four pools, top restaurants and activities. Each suite comes with at least partial views of the sea, and living room with sofa and two TVs. M$$$$

YELAPA

Accommodation here is primarily provided by rental apartments; just arriving on the beach and enquiring will usually get you a place (see http://yelapa.info).

Hotel Lagunita At the far end of Yelapa beach; 449 498 9313. Beautiful thatched cabañas (holding up to six people) on a beach with its own pier. There are also yoga classes, a pool and a beachfront restaurant serving Mexican and international food. M$$$

Verana In the hills west of Yelapa; accessed by private boat from Boca de Tomatlán; http://verana.com. This ultra-luxe hillside hideaway is the brainchild of a former film-set designer, and it shows: these picture-perfect houses and bungalows, backing onto thick jungle, are Hollywood-worthy. Open-air bathrooms are hewn from the stone of the cliffs, private terraces overlook the bay, and Indigenous masks and artworks adorn the walls. There's superb Mexican food at the restaurant, and daily yoga sessions. Open November–June. M$$$$

PUNTA DE MITA

Four Seasons Punta Mita At the western end of the headland; http://fourseasons.com/puntamita. Punta Mita's original luxury resort is still one of its best, with spacious *casita*-style accommodation with beachfront or ocean views, gourmet restaurants, two Jack Nicklaus-designed golf courses, three pools and tennis courts. M$$$$

Mesón de Mita Anclote 200; http://hotelmesondemita.com. Staying in Punta de Mita doesn't have to break the bank; this lovely hotel faces the ocean with sixteen cosy rooms equipped with TVs, a/c and wi-fi. M$$$

EATING

SEE MAP PAGE 231

PLAYA COLOMITOS (BOCA DE TOMATLÁN)

★ **Ocean Grill** https://oceangrill.mx. The most spectacular place to eat on the bay overlooks Playa Colomitos, a short boat ride (or free restaurant shuttle) from Boca de Tomatlán. Pick the catch of the day, lobster, octopus or luscious shrimp smothered in a choice of six sauces (try the lemon ginger butter). Cash only. No children or pets. M$$$$

3

BUCERÍAS

Adriano's Del Pacifico 11; 322 117 8115. With bright orange walls and an extensive range of fresh fish, this is the best but also one of the pricier restaurants on the strip, with superbly executed international (filet mignon with creamy mushroom sauce) and Mexican classics. M$$$

Pie in the Sky Héroe de Nacozari 202; 329 298 0838, https://facebook.com/pieinthesky.mx. For a teatime treat, visit the locally renowned *Pie in the Sky* bakery for heavenly molten fudge chocolate brownies (*beso*), Belgian chocolate mousse, bagels and exotic cheesecakes. Free wi-fi. M$$

YELAPA

Yelapa's beach palapas offer a similar range of beers, cocktails and seafood such as lobster, shrimp and fish tacos – fresh, but not especially cheap. You'll get cheaper food in El Pueblo's cafés.

★ **Café Bahia** 322 182 6806. This friendly restaurant acts as a de facto information centre, just off the water-taxi pier, selling excellent hand-drawn maps along with superb home-cooked food – everything from full American breakfasts to baked goods, Mexican classics, veggie dishes and some mean cocktails. Cash only. M$$

Café Inés Marlin 1 (main path between the beach and

PACIFIC COAST FIESTAS

Día de la Candelaria (Feb 2). Celebrated in Colima with dances, processions and fireworks.

Fiesta Brava (Feb 5). A day of bullfights and horse races in Colima.

Carnaval (the week before Lent; variable Feb–March). Acapulco and Manzanillo are both famous for the exuberance of their celebrations; rooms can be hard to find.

Semana Santa (Holy Week). Widely observed: the Palm Sunday celebrations in Petatlán, just south of Zihuatanejo, are particularly fervent.

Cinco de Mayo (May 5). Celebrations in commemoration of the victorious battle of Cinco de Mayo, especially in Acapulco.

Festival de las Lluvias (May 8). Celebrated in Mochitlán, near Chilpancingo, the festival has pre-Christian roots: pilgrims, peasants and local dance groups climb a nearby volcano at night, arriving at the summit at dawn to pray for rain.

Founder's Day (May 8). The city of Manzanillo celebrates the day it was founded.

Día de San Isidro (May 15). A week-long festival in Acapulco to celebrate St Isidore the Labourer, the patron saint of farmers, with dances and cockfights.

Día de la Marina (Navy Day; June 1). Celebrated in the ports, particularly Puerto Vallarta, Manzanillo and Acapulco.

Día de Santiago (July 25). Celebrated in several villages immediately around Acapulco.

Feria (first week of Nov). Colima's major festival runs from the last days of October until November 11.

Día de los Muertos (Day of the Dead; Nov 2). Widely observed, with picturesque traditions in Atoyac de Alvarez, just off the Acapulco–Zihuatanejo road.

Día de la Virgen de Guadalupe (Dec 12). In honour of the patroness of Mexico. Acapulco has fervent celebrations, while in Manzanillo the celebrations start at the beginning of the month. In Puerto Vallarta they continue until the end of it.

town areas); 322 138 0612. The affable Inés serves up delicious and generously-portioned offerings, and some of the best coffee in town. M$$$

Sayulita

On the other side of the Punta de Mita, 22km north of Bucerías on Hwy-200, languorous **SAYULITA** is another popular gringo outpost with an enchanting, jungle-fringed beach, famous seafood and some inviting places to stay.

Other than lounging on the beach, the main activity here is **surfing**: there's a main right break, and a faster left break north of the river mouth (near the campsite). The waves are medium–sized, meaning there's something here for a wide range of ability levels.

ARRIVAL AND DEPARTURE — SAYULITA

By bus Regular "Compestela" buses (usually white and green) connect Puerto Vallarta bus station with Sayulita every 30min (last bus 7pm; 1.5hr); these also stop at Bucerías and pass by Puerto Vallarta airport on Hwy-200 (make sure it says "Sayulita" on the front). Buses to and from Puerto Vallarta terminate at Sayulita outside the Salud Clinic, located on the main road into town. The last bus back to PV usually leaves around 8.40pm. Vallarta Plus (http://vallartaplus.com) operates first-class buses between Sayulita and Guadalajara (departing Guadalajara at 7.35am and 9.05am and Sayulita at 1pm & 3pm; 4hr 25min).

By taxi Taxis from downtown Vallarta vary in price, depending on the group size and your negotiation skills (airport taxis are the most expensive but you can flag one down for a little less just outside the airport on Hwy-200). Nearby destinations from here include Punta de Mita and Bucerías.

INFORMATION AND ACTIVITIES

Tourist information There's no tourist office; check http://sayulita.com or http://sayulitalife.com for the latest information.

Banks and exchange There are several ATMs in town.

Lunazul Surf School http://lunazulsurfing.com. Rents boards by the day and offers lessons.

ACCOMMODATION

Amazing Hostel Sayulita Pelicanos 102; http://theamazinghostelsayulita.com. Living up to its name, this hostel, two blocks from the beach, with its own pool, climbing wall, surfboards, kayaks and bikes, is the best place to stay in town. The mixed and female-only dorms are clean and come with lots of ceiling fans. There's also a good range of private rooms, communal kitchen, laundry and free wi-fi. M$$

Petit Hotel Hafa Revolución 55; 322 779 3573. For a more boutique experience try this exceptionally stylish hotel, an artsy North African-themed gem two blocks from the beach. Free wi-fi and tranquil roof deck, but a/c is extra per night. M$$$

Playa Escondida Playa Escondida 1; http://playa-escondida.com. This luxurious, resort, with four-to-eight-person cabañas either facing a secluded stretch of beach or tucked away in jungle and palms, is the most enticing place to stay in town. There's a minimum two-night stay and most rooms come with canopy beds, ocean views and free wi-fi. M$$$$

EATING

Sayulita is well known for its **fish and shrimp tacos**, which come with optional pickled cabbage and the other regular accompaniments. They're found all over town, but you'll do well to avoid the rip-off merchants in the town centre, who can be very aggressive.

Aaleyah's Nachos & Wings Revolución 60; 322 157 5417, https://facebook.com/AaleyahsNachosandWing. Everything from tacos to addictive nachos, burgers, tortas and salads, as well as knockout margaritas (often 2 for 1 during happy hour). M$$

ChocoBanana Plaza Mayor; http://chocobanana.restaurantsnapshot.com. Open-fronted and friendly, this bustling café serves up great breakfasts all day. Don't leave without trying the eponymous "chocobanana", a chilled banana dipped in molten chocolate and then rolled in granola. M$$

Don Pedro's Marlin 2; http://donpedros.com. This huge beachfront palapa restaurant knocks out dependable Mexican-Mediterranean cuisine, wood-fired pizzas and tasty dishes such as beer-battered shrimp and *mahi-mahi ceviche*. M$$$

Latitude 20 Sayulita Manuel N. Navarrete 79; http://latitude20mex.com. Part restaurant, part sports bar, *Latitude 20* is a margarita fuelled friendly spot — just one block from the beach. Between the BBQ food and the matches playing on the big screens here, there's always a decent sized crowd in attendance. It can get lively, too. The portions here certainly cater to those with a healthy appetite. M$$$

3

Inland Jalisco and Michoacán

WATERFALL AT URUAPAN

Inland Jalisco and Michoacán

Separated from the country's colonial heartland by the craggy peaks of the Sierra Madre, the stretch of land from Guadalajara to Mexico City through the semitropical states of Jalisco and Michoacán has an unhurried ease that marks it out from the rest of the country. Comprising a complex landscape of lofty plains and rugged sierras, the area is blessed with supremely fertile farms, fresh pine woods, cool pastures and lush tropical forest.

Something of a backwater until well into the eighteenth century, the high valleys of Michoacán and Jalisco were left to develop their own strong regional traditions and solid farming economy. Wherever you go, you'll find a wealth of local commercial goods, both agricultural and traditionally manufactured items, from avocados to tequila, glassware to guitars. Relative isolation has also made the region a bastion of conservatism – in the years following the Revolution, the Catholic *Cristero* counter-revolutionary guerrilla movement enjoyed its strongest support here.

Easy-going **Guadalajara**, Mexico's second city, is packed with elegant buildings and surrounded by scenic countryside. Outside the city, the land is spectacularly green and mountainous, studded with volcanoes and lakes, most famously **Laguna de Chapala**. There are also some superb colonial relics, especially in the forms of **Morelia** and **Pátzcuaro**, although it's the latter's majestic setting and well-preserved Indigenous tradition that first call your attention.

The region has not been unaffected by the country's **drug wars**, however, as was gruesomely illustrated during Independence Day celebrations in 2008, when gangsters threw grenades into the crowd in Morelia's main square, killing eight people. The drug lords aren't interested in law-abiding tourists, so there's no cause for undue alarm, but you'll notice an increased presence of heavily armed soldiers and federal police, especially in smaller towns. What you won't see is the number of Michoacán's villages which are now under the control of armed gangs, whether drug producers or local vigilantes, but at any rate no force belonging to the state. Unless you go looking for trouble in the cities, you should be fine. If travelling along the state's byways, do so during the hours of daylight.

Guadalajara

The second city of the Mexican Republic and capital of the state of Jalisco, **GUADALAJARA** is considered the most "Mexican" of the country's big cities. Being less frenetic than the capital, however, doesn't make it peaceful, and Guadalajara is huge and sprawling. Its conversion to a sleek metropolis has resulted in a hike in prices and some sacrifice of Mexican mellowness in favour of a US-style business ethic, but it's still an enjoyable place to visit, with the edge on Mexico's other big cities for trees, flowers, cleanliness and friendliness. Parks, little squares and open spaces are numerous, while downtown, around the cathedral, is a series of plazas unchanged since the days of the Spanish colonization. This small colonial heart of Guadalajara can still, especially at weekends, recall an old-world atmosphere and provincial elegance. The centre is further brightened by the **Plaza Tapatía**, which opens out the city's historical core to pedestrians, mariachi bands and street theatre.

Guadalajara's rapid expansion has swallowed up numerous communities: once-distinct villages are now barely distinguishable from the city all around. Heading **west**,

HERRADURA TEQUILA DISTILLERY, JALISCO

Highlights

1. **Guadalajara** Experience the drama of mariachi music in Mexico's second-largest city, the capital of Jalisco. See page 246

2. **Tequila** Visit a tequila distillery and, of course, sample the legendary spirit in a café on the town's plaza. See page 268

3. **Uruapan** Take in the cascading waterfalls and lush surroundings of the Parque Nacional Eduardo Ruíz. See page 276

4. **Paricutín** Hike through an unearthly landscape of lava fields to climb up this still-active volcano. See page 279

5. **Lago de Pátzcuaro** One of the best places in Mexico for seeing the spectacular and moving Day of the Dead celebrations on a stunning volcanic lake. See page 286

6. **Morelia** Enjoy *pan dulces*, wine and classical music in one of the cafés overlooking the central plaza of this wonderful old colonial city. See page 290

7. **Monarch Butterfly Sanctuary** See the millions of brightly coloured migratory butterflies which in winter blanket the fir trees around Angangueo. See page 298

HIGHLIGHTS ARE MARKED ON THE MAP ON PAGE 248

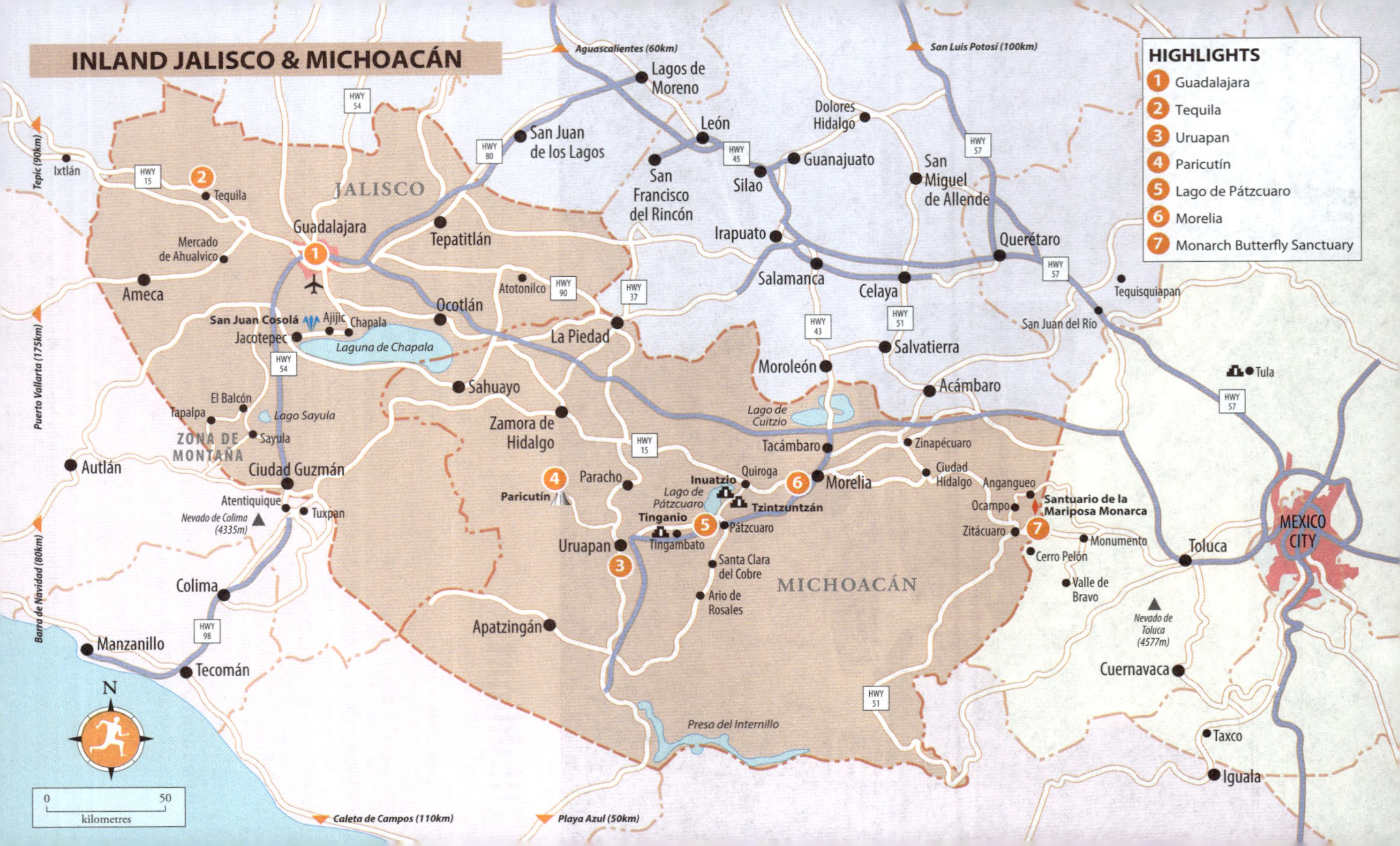
INLAND JALISCO & MICHOACÁN
HIGHLIGHTS
1 Guadalajara
2 Tequila
3 Uruapan
4 Paricutín
5 Lago de Pátzcuaro
6 Morelia
7 Monarch Butterfly Sanctuary
JALISCO
MICHOACÁN
Aguascalientes (60km)
San Luis Potosí (100km)
Tepic (90km)
Puerto Vallarta (175km)
Barra de Navidad (80km)
Caleta de Campos (110km)
Playa Azul (50km)
Lagos de Moreno
León
Dolores Hidalgo
San Juan de los Lagos
San Francisco del Rincón
Guanajuato
Silao
San Miguel de Allende
Irapuato
Querétaro
Salamanca
Celaya
Tequisquiapan
San Juan del Río
Salvatierra
Moroleón
Acámbaro
Tula
Lago de Cuitzio
Tacámbaro
Zinapécuaro
Ciudad Hidalgo
Angangueo
Ocampo
Santuario de la Mariposa Monarca
Zitácuaro
Monumento
Cerro Pelón
Valle de Bravo
Toluca
MEXICO CITY
Nevado de Toluca (4577m)
Cuernavaca
Taxco
Iguala
Ixtlán
Tequila
Guadalajara
Mercado de Ahualvico
Ameca
Tepatitlán
Atotonilco
Ocotlán
La Piedad
San Juan Cosolá
Ajijic
Chapala
Jacotepec
Laguna de Chapala
Sahuayo
El Balcón
Tapalpa
Lago Sayula
Sayula
ZONA DE MONTAÑA
Zamora de Hidalgo
Autlán
Ciudad Guzmán
Paracho
Paricutín
Quiroga
Inuatzio
Lago de Pátzcuaro
Tzintzuntzán
Morelia
Tinganio
Pátzcuaro
Tingambato
Uruapan
Santa Clara del Cobre
Ario de Rosales
Atentiquique
Tuxpan
Nevado de Colima (4335m)
Colima
Apatzingán
Manzanillo
Tecomán
Presa del Internillo
HWY 54
HWY 80
HWY 15
HWY 45
HWY 57
HWY 90
HWY 37
HWY 43
HWY 51
HWY 98
N
0
50
kilometres

the university area blends into chic suburbs and some of the city's most expensive real estate. **East**, Tlaquepaque and Tonalá are the source of some of the area's finest handicrafts. And finally to the **north**, Zapopan has a huge, much revered church and a museum of Indigenous traditions, while the Barranca de Oblatos offers stunning canyon views and weekend picnic spots.

Brief history

Guadalajara was founded in 1532, one of the fruits of the vicious campaign of **Nuño de Guzmán** at the time of the Conquest – his cruelty and corruption were such that he appalled even the Spanish authorities, who threw him into prison in Madrid, where he died. The city (named after Guzmán's birthplace) thrived, was officially recognized by Charles V in 1542 and rapidly became one of the colony's most Spanish cities – in part because so much of the Indigenous population had been killed or had fled during the Conquest. Isolated from the great mining industry of the Bajío, Guadalajara evolved into a regional centre for trade and agriculture. The tight reins of colonial rule restrained the city's development, and it wasn't until the end of the eighteenth century, as the colonial monopolies began to crumble, that things really took off. Between 1760 and 1803 the city's population tripled, reaching some 35,000; a new university was established; and the city became famous for the export of wheat, hides, cotton and wool.

When Spain's colonial empire finally fell apart, Guadalajara supported Hidalgo's independence movement and briefly served as the capital of the nation. By the beginning of the twentieth century it was already the second-largest city in the Republic, and in the 1920s the completion of the rail link with California provided a further spur for development. More recently, the exodus from Mexico City and attempts at industrial decentralization have continued to swell the urban area's population, which now tops four and a half million.

The centre of the old city is a relatively compact **grid** around the junction of Morelos and 16 de Septiembre. East of here Morelos leads to the Plaza Tapatía and the Mercado Libertad, while to the west are busy shopping streets. Juárez, a couple of blocks south, is actually the main east–west **thoroughfare** in the centre, heading out to the west past the university, where it becomes Vallarta. The main north–south arteries in the centre are the Calzada del Federalismo, along which the Tren Ligero, the city's metro, runs, and Calzada Independencia, off which Revolución leads southeast, to Tlaquepaque, the new bus station and Tonalá.

Plaza Guadalajara and around

Plaza Guadalajara, formerly known as the Plaza de los Laureles for its topiaried laurel trees, faces the main west entrance of the **cathedral**, which is where any tour of the city inevitably starts. The porticoed building on Plaza Guadalajara's north side, the **Presidencia Municipal**, was only built in 1952, though you wouldn't know it. In common with the other nearby plazas, crowds of people are entertained by an array of street performers and wandering musicians at weekends and on warm evenings; there are frequently bands playing during the day, too.

The cathedral

Alcalde (between Hidalgo and Morelos) • Free

With the Sagrario, or sacristy, next door, the cathedral takes up an entire block at the very heart of the city's colonial centre, bordered by a further three plazas to form the shape of a Latin cross. With its pointed, tiled twin towers, the cathedral is a bizarre but successful mixture of styles. Building work began in 1561 and didn't finish for over a century – since then, extensive modifications, which effectively disguise the fact that there was probably never a plan behind the original design, have included

4

a Neoclassical facade and new twin yellow-tiled towers (the originals collapsed in an 1818 earthquake). The richly decorated interior is best seen in the evening, when they turn on the lights. One of the cathedral's stranger points of interest is the mummified remains of a girl (the face has been remodelled in wax), known as Santa Inocencia, said to have been murdered by her own father for her Christian beliefs in the eighteenth century. Today people pray to her for blessings and miracles, particularly in relation to children. The picture of the Virgin in the sacristy is attributed to the Spanish Baroque artist Bartolomé Esteban **Murillo**.

Rotonda de los Jaliscienses Ilustres

On the north side of the cathedral

The **Rotonda de los Jaliscienses Ilustres** is a Neoclassical circle of seventeen Doric columns, the latest architectural expression of Jaliscan pride, and one which commemorates the state's heroes, 26 of whom surround it in the form of statues, although only a few occupy any of the 98 niches set aside for their ashes.

Plaza de la Liberación

The largest of the four squares surrounding the cathedral is the **Plaza de la Liberación**, to its east. The square is surrounded by interesting buildings (see below), including the Museo Regional, the Palacio de Gobierno, the Teatro Degollado and the church of San Agustín.

Museo Regional

Liceo 60, east side of Rotonda de los Jaliscienses Ilustres and north side of the cathedral • Charge, free Sun; camera or video permit fee • 333 613 2703

Housed in an eighteenth-century colonial mansion, the **Museo Regional** has, over time, been a religious seminary, a barracks and a school; it's now a supremely elegant setting for an extensive and diverse collection. Downstairs, exhibits start with a section devoted to regional **archeology** and range from stone tools and the skeleton of a mammoth to the finest achievements of western Mexican pottery and metalworking. The peoples of the west developed quite separately from those in southern and central Mexico, and there is considerable evidence that they had more contact with South and Central American cultures than with those who would now be regarded as their compatriots. The deep **shaft tombs** displayed here are unique in Mexico, but were common down the Pacific coast in Peru and Ecuador.

Upstairs, along with rooms devoted to the state's **modern history** and ethnography, is a sizeable gallery of colonial and modern art. Most remarkable here is the large collection of **nineteenth-century portraiture**, a local tradition that captures relatively ordinary Mexicans in a charmingly naive style.

Teatro Degollado

Degollado 53 (east side of Plaza de la Liberación) • Free

The **Teatro Degollado** was modelled on La Scala in Milan. Built in the mid-nineteenth century and inaugurated in 1866 during the brief reign of Emperor Maximilian (see page 791), it's an imposing, domed Neoclassical building with a Corinthian portico; look on the portico's pediment for a frieze depicting the Greek Muses. A programme of drama and concerts is still staged here, mostly in October during the fiesta, though also sporadically throughout the rest of the year. The impressively restored **interior** is notable for its frescoed ceiling, which illustrates scenes from the fourth canto of Dante's *Divine Comedy*. The theatre is open Tues–Sun, 10am–2pm — except when the stage is in use.

The churches of Santa María and San Agustín

On either side of the theatre, at Hidalgo 158 and Degollado 33 respectively

Two small churches, **Santa María** and **San Agustín**, are the only remains of a monastery that once stood here. San Agustín has a fine Baroque facade; relatively plain Santa María is one of the oldest churches in the city, built in the seventeenth century on the site of Guadalajara's first cathedral.

Plaza de Armas

Plaza de Armas, on the south side of the cathedral, is flanked by the Palacio de Gobierno and centres on an elaborate *belle époque* **rotunda**, which was a present from the people of France. With a canopy held up by topless Art Nouveau maidens bearing musical instruments, it's still in use as a bandstand, with music (often the state band) in the evenings.

Palacio de Gobierno

Plaza de Armas • **Palacio** Free • **Museum** Free

Dominating the eastern side of the Plaza de Armas, the **Palacio de Gobierno** is recognizable by its Baroque facade with a clock surrounded by elements from the Aztec calendar. It was here that Padre Miguel Hidalgo y Costilla (the "father of Mexican Independence") proclaimed the abolition of slavery in 1810, and, in 1858, Benito Juárez was saved from the firing squad by the cry of "*Los valientes no asesinan*" – "the brave don't murder". But the overwhelming reason to enter the arcaded courtyard is to see the first of the great **Orozco murals**.

The main mural dates from 1937 and is typical of Orozco's work (see page 253) – Hidalgo blasts triumphantly through the middle, brandishing his sword against a background of red flags and the fires of battle. Curving around the sides of the staircase, scenes depict the Mexican struggle for liberty, from a pre-Conquest Eden to post-Revolutionary emancipation. Upstairs in the domed Congress Hall a smaller Orozco mural (painted just before his death in 1949) also depicts Hidalgo, this time as *El Cura de Dolores* (the priest from Dolores), legislator and liberator of slaves.

The Museum

The Palacio also contains a **museum**, covering the history of the city, the history of the Palacio de Gobierno itself and the manufacture of tequila. Aside from the guided tours, which are in Spanish and English, the explanations are in Spanish only. The most interesting thing in the museum is the chance to enter one of the Palacio's corner bastions to see how the round loopholes allowed soldiers to shoot directly along the sides of the building and down the adjoining streets.

Plaza Tapatía

Spanning Independencia, which passes underneath it, **Plaza Tapatía** is not so much a square as a very long and elegant pedestrian precinct. Though it looks thoroughly modern, the plaza was constructed in the late nineteenth century, demolishing some of the city's oldest neighbourhoods in the process. It takes its name from *tapatío* – an adjective used to describe anything typical of Guadalajara, supposedly derived

ACCOMMODATION

Ana-Isabel	5
Chapala	4
Don Quijote Plaza	12
Fénix	7
Francés	2
Hospedarte (Hostel Guadalajara)	3
Hotel Cervantes	9
Hotel de Mendoza	1
León	13
Maya	6
Posada Regis	8
The Roof Backpackers	11
Santiago de Compostela	10

SHOPPING

Librería Gonvill	1

EATING

Birriería el Compadre	14
Birrieria Las Nueve Esquinas	13
Café la Flor de Córdoba Portales	2
Café Madoka	3
Café Madrid	5
Chai	6
La Chata	9
Chong Wah	7/8
La Gorda	11
El Mexicano	1
Pastelería Luvier	10
El Tacazo	4
Taquería Los Faroles	12

DRINKING & NIGHTLIFE

La Condesa	6
La Fuente	1
Green Light Eco-Bar	3
Hotel Francés	2
La Prisciliana/Club Ye*Ye	5
La Mutualista	4

JOSÉ CLEMENTE OROZCO

José Clemente Orozco (1883–1949) was a member, along with Diego Rivera and David Siqueiros, of the triumvirate of brilliant artists who emerged from the Revolution and transformed Mexican painting into an enormously powerful and populist political statement, especially through the medium of the **giant mural**. Their chief patron was the state – hence the predominance of their work in official buildings and educational establishments – and their aim was to create a national art that drew on native traditions. Almost all their work is consciously educational, rewriting – or, perhaps better, rediscovering – Mexican history in the light of the Revolution, casting the imperialists as villains and drawing heavily on pre-Hispanic themes. Orozco, a native of Jalisco (he was born in Zapotlan, now Ciudad Guzmán), was perhaps the least overtly political of the three; certainly, his later work, the greatest of which is here in Guadalajara, concentrates on his nuanced style.

As a child he moved to Guadalajara and then to Mexico City, where he was influenced by renowned engraver **José Guadalupe Posada** (see page 351) and where he painted murals from 1922 to 1927. His best works from this period are the series including *The Destruction of the Old Order* which he painted at the Antiguo Colegio de San Ildefonso in Mexico City (see page 80). Then followed seven years in the US, where works included his mammoth *The Epic of American Civilization* at Dartmouth College in Hanover, New Hampshire, where it's now displayed. It was in the years following his return, however, in the late 1930s and 1940s, that his powers as an artist reached their peak, above all in his works at Guadalajara's Hospicio Cabañas and the University of Guadalajara (see page 255).

from the capes worn by Spanish grandees; Guadalajarans themselves are often referred to as *Tapatíos*.

At its eastern end, the plaza opens out to a broad paved area full of wacky anthropomorphic **bronze sculptures**, the work of Guadalajara native **Alejandro Colunga**. Stretched, squashed and generally distorted human figures form chairs, their patinas rubbed shiny by thousands of tired shoppers and tourists.

Instituto Cultural–Hospicio Cabañas

Plaza Tapatía (eastern end) • Charge, student discount, free Tues, children under 12 always free; charge to bring in a camera or a video camera

Overlooking the eastern end of Plaza Tapatía, the **Instituto Cultural–Hospicio Cabañas** was founded as an orphanage by Bishop Juan Cabañas y Crespo in 1805 and took nearly fifty years to complete. Designed by Spanish architect Manuel Tolsá, the Hospicio is a huge, beautiful and tranquil building, with 23 separate patios surrounded by schools of art, music and dance; an art cinema/theatre; various government offices; and a small cafeteria. The chapel, the **Capilla Tolsá**, is a plain and ancient-looking structure in the form of a cross, situated in the central patio right at the heart of the building.

The Orozco murals

The Instituto also houses various Orozco **murals** which, in keeping with their setting, have a more religious theme than those in the government palace: the conquistadors are depicted as the Horsemen of the Apocalypse, trampling the native population beneath them. The Man of Fire – who leads the people from their dehumanizing, mechanized oppression – has a symbolic role as liberator, which is clearly the same as that of Hidalgo in the palace murals. In this case, he is a strange synthesis of Christian and Mexican deities, a Christ-Quetzalcoatl figure. There are benches on which you can lie back to appreciate the murals, and also a small museum dedicated to Orozco, with sketches, cartoons and details of the artist's life.

Mercado Libertad

Javier Mina

The vast **Mercado Libertad** is known locally as **Mercado San Juan de Dios**. Guadalajarans claim it's the largest indoor market in the world. Although the building is modern, much of what's inside is thoroughly traditional, and it's one of the few places in the city where you can still haggle over prices. Beyond the touristy souvenir stalls, you'll find *curanderas* offering herbal remedies, dried iguanas (for witches' brews) and the renowned Paracho guitars. There are also countless stalls selling regional food and colourful fruit, vegetables, chocolate, spices and traditional leather goods from saddles to clumpy working boots. The market is chaotic and engrossing, but before you buy crafts here, pay a visit to the **Instituto de la Artesanía** by the Parque Agua Azul (see page 254), or to the expensive boutiques in Tlaquepaque (see page 267), to get some idea of quality and value.

Immediately southwest of the Mercado is the **Plaza de los Mariachis**, a place to return after dark to hear Guadalajara's finest musicians (see page 267).

The churches of San Francisco and Nuestra Señora de Aranzazu

16 de Septiembre • Free

The churches of **San Francisco** and **Nuestra Señora de Aranzazu** face each other at the southern end of the city centre. San Francisco lies on the site of what was probably Guadalajara's first religious foundation, a Franciscan monastery established in the years just after the Conquest. The present church was begun in 1684 and has a beautiful Baroque facade. Aranzazu, by contrast, is entirely plain on the outside, but conceals a fabulously elaborate interior, with three wildly exuberant, heavily carved and gilded churrigueresque retables. The **Jardín de San Francisco**, which would be pleasantly peaceful were it not for the number of local buses rattling by, lies across from the two churches.

Parque Agua Azul

Independencia (entrance just south of the junction with Calzado González Gallo) • Free • Buses ("Parque Agua Azul") from Jardín de San Francisco; *macrobús* Niños Héroes

Though it's an important area of green in the bustling city, you couldn't really describe **Parque Agua Azul** as peaceful: there's always some kind of activity going on and the green areas are permanently packed with kids enjoying the zoo and playgrounds. An outdoor concert stage, *la concha* (the shell), hosts popular free performances on Sundays, and weekends see football games and crowds. Nonetheless, by Guadalajara standards, it's a haven of calm, especially during the week, and the park includes attractions such as a dome full of butterflies; exotic caged birds, including magnificent toucans; a palm house, also full of tropical birds; and a strange, glass-pyramid orchid house.

Instituto de la Artesanía Jalisciense

Calzado González Gallo 20, just north of the entrance to the Parque Agua Azul • Free • http://info.jalisco.gob.mx

The **Instituto de la Artesanía Jalisciense** is a showcase for regional crafts that is as much a museum as a shop. Its collection is ambitious, with examples of all sorts of local crafts – furniture, ceramics, toys, glassware, clothing – of the highest quality. Many of the items are expensive, but are worth it considering the fine quality of workmanship.

Biblioteca IberoAmericana Octavio Paz

Calle Pedro Morena, some four blocks north of San Francisco, and just west of the Plaza de Armas at the junction with Colón • Free

The "Ex-Templo de la Compañía", or the **Biblioteca IberoAmericana Octavio Paz**, was originally a church and later became a university lecture hall, during which time the nineteenth-century Neoclassical facade was added and it was decorated with **murals** by **David Siqueiros** and **Amado de la Cueva**. Currently a library, it has dramatic crimson-hued murals depicting workers, peasants and miners in a heroic-socialist style; they are open to visitors and make an interesting contrast to Orozco's work. Outside there's an attractive little plaza, and the pedestrianized streets make a pleasant escape from the traffic, if not the crowds.

The churches of Santa Monica, San Felípe and Las Capuchinas

Some six blocks north of the Biblioteca IberoAmericana Octavio Paz and very close to the junction of San Felipe and González Ortega • Free

Among these three good examples of the beautiful, little-known Baroque churches that stud Guadalajara, the oldest is the **Templo de Santa Monica**, on Santa Monica between San Felípe and Reforma, with fabulously rich doorways and an elegant stone interior. The nearby **Templo de San Felípe Neri**, on San Felípe at Contreras Medellin, is a few years younger – dating from the second half of the eighteenth century – and more sumptuously decorated, with a superb facade and lovely tower. Both of these churches have extravagant rainspouts, which take the form of dragons on San Felípe. A block along González Ortega, at the corner of Garibaldi, the **Templo de las Capuchinas** is, conversely, plain and fortress-like; inside, though, it's more interesting, with paintings and a lovely vaulted brick roof.

4

Museo de la Ciudad

Independencia 684 • Charge, free Sun

The **Museo de la Ciudad**, housed in a former convent, showcases the city's history through photos and artefacts, with explanations in Spanish. The downstairs rooms illustrate the city's history from the sixteenth to the nineteenth centuries, with torture items such as a barbed scourging chain, and some unusual statuettes of Jesus – one of him post-crucifixion, lying on his father's lap, and another of him as a child, maybe 7 or 8 years old, complete with stigmata, holding up a chalice.

Ex-Convento del Carmen

Juárez 638 (at 8 de Julio) • Entry to exhibitions is free; entry to film showings, classes & workshops chargeable; costs vary

Four blocks south of the Museo de la Ciudad, the **Ex-Convento del Carmen** was one of the city's richest monasteries, but its wealth has largely been stripped, leaving an austere, white building of elegant simplicity. Modern art exhibitions, dance events and concerts are regularly staged here, and a programme of forthcoming events is posted outside the entrance.

Universidad de Guadalajara

The Parque Revolución, on Federalismo (and the north–south Tren Ligero line), west of the Ex-Convento del Carmen, marks the eastern end of the campus of the **Universidad de Guadalajara**. A fifteen-minute walk west along Juárez from the centre, the university area is quieter, the streets broader and there's also a younger atmosphere, with plenty of good restaurants and cafés.

Museo de las Artes Universidad de Guadalajara (MUSA)

Juarez 975 • Free

The impressive **Museo de las Artes Universidad de Guadalajara (MUSA)** contains some of José Clemente Orozco's most important murals, which were among the first he

CENTRAL GUADALAJARA
DRINKING & NIGHTLIFE
The Black Sheep 3
El Callejón de los Rumberos 4
Casa Bariachi 1
La Moresca 2
ACCOMMODATION
Isabel 3
Misión Carlton 4
Quinta Real 1
Villa Ganz 2
EATING
Ahogadas Beto's 1
Alta Fibra 7
Chan 9
La China Poblana 4
Goa 5
La Fonda de la Noche 2
Pierrot 3
Pizza del Perro Negro 6
La Trattoria 8
SHOPPING
Librería Gandhi 1
(600m)
SEE "GUADALAJARA: CENTRO HISTÓRICO" MAP
Alameda
San Juan de Dios
Plaza Universidad
Bicentenario
La Paz
Juárez
El Refugio
Mexicaltingo
Teatro Diana
Niños Heroes
Instituto de la Artesanía Jalisciense
Parque Agua Azul
Agua Azul
Central Vieja (Old Bus Station)
Licenzo Charro
University of Guadalajara
Templo Expiatorio
Museo de las Artes Universidad de Guadalajara (MUSA)
ICMNJ
Alianza Francesa
Washington
Train Station for Tequilla Express
Ciprés
Héroe de Nacozari
Santa Filomena
Unidad Deportiva
ZONA MINERVA
Monumento Los Arcos
Centro Magno (Shopping Mall)
CECM (Language School)
Canadian Consulate
MINERVA CIRCLE
PLAZA DEL SOL
AVENIDA CHAPULTEPEC
CIRCUNVALACION SANTA EDUWIGES
CIRCUNVALACION AGUSTIN YAÑEZ
AVENIDA MARIANO OTERO
CALZ LAZARO CÁRDENAS
AVENIDA LÓPEZ MATEOS SUR
LÓPEZ MATEOS
AVENIDA HIDALGO
AVENIDA VALLARTA
AVENIDA MEXICO
NIÑOS HÉROES
CALZADA DEL FEDERALISMO
16 DE SEPTIEMBRE
INDEPENDENCIA SUR
AVENIDA DE LA PAZ
AVENIDA INGLA TERRA
AVENIDA NIÑOS HÉROES
CIRCUITO WASHINGTON
0 1 kilometre
N

painted in Guadalajara. To see them, head for the main hall (*paraninfo*) and check out the frescoed dome and front wall. As so often with Orozco, the theme of the works fits the setting: the dome shows the glories and benefits of learning, while the wall shows the oppressed masses crying out for books and education, which are being denied them by fat capitalists and the military. The museum also houses temporary exhibitions, mainly of modern art, and usually worth popping in to see. Immediately south of the museum is the **Templo Expiatorio**, a modern neo-Gothic church modelled on Orvieto Cathedral in Italy and featuring some innovative stained glass and an attractive altarpiece.

San Pedro Tlaquepaque

5km southeast of the centre • #275 or TUR bus from the centre (16 de Septiembre) to Niños Héroes with Independencia (just after a brick pedestrian bridge and traffic circle), then walk down Independencia to El Parian

TLAQUEPAQUE (officially San Pedro Tlaquepaque) is famous for its artesanías and its **mariachi** bands. Once a separate town, it has long since been absorbed by urban sprawl, and most of its traditional crafts taken over by chichi designer-furniture and jewellery stores, but you can still find crafts such as ceramics, glass, jewellery and textiles. Prices are high, but so are standards, and there are usually some moderately priced ceramics and glassware.

Tlaquepaque centres around a pleasantly laid-back main square complete with bandstand, on whose north side is the blockish church of **San Pedro**. To the west of the square, the three-domed **Nuestra Virgen de la Soledad** is an almost equally distinctive landmark. To the east there's a small local Mercado Municipal; its entrance is on the north side of El Parian (see below). Nearby, several banks have ATMs in case you've been carried away by the shopping experience.

4

El Parian

At the plaza's southeast corner

El Parian, ostensibly an enclosed plaza, is, in effect, the biggest bar that you've ever seen – actually a dozen or so separate establishments, but since everyone sits outside, with the tables tending to overlap and strolling serenaders wandering around at random, it all feels like one enormous place. Food, drink and prices are good, but check the bill for added service charges.

At the weekend, particularly Sunday afternoons, you'll see mariachi at its best here, and locals add their own vocal renditions to the musicians' backing. On weekdays it can be disappointingly quiet (or pleasantly peaceful, depending on your fondness for mariachi).

Museo Pantaleón Panduro

Princiliano Sánchez 191, at Flórida • Charge

For an insight into just how wonderful the local ceramics can be, visit the **Museo Pantaleón Panduro**, which was named after the father of Jaliscan ceramicists. Here you can see exemplary prizewinning pieces from the museum's annual ceramics competition (held each June).

Museo Regional de la Cerámica

Independencia 237 • Free • 333 860 1177

To learn something of the techniques used in making ceramics, visit the small **Museo Regional de la Cerámica**, which has displays of pottery not only from Tlaquepaque but from all over the state, especially Tonalá (see below). Beyond the individual works of some of the finest craftsmen, there's a traditional kitchen on display, complete with all its plates, pots and pans, and the building is a fine old mansion in its own right. Of course, there is also a shop.

4

The shops

Tlaquepaque's fancier **shops** and galleries lie near the Museo Regional, many in lovely colonial-era houses along Independencia, itself closed to traffic and so a pleasant street along which to window-shop. The parallel Juárez is a little less exclusive and may be a better hunting ground for more moderately priced goods. For full details of all the area's recommended shops, see page 267.

Tonalá

8km southeast of Tlaquepaque • #275 or TUR bus southbound from 16 de Septiembre to Av Tonalá at Tonaltecas Sur

TONALÁ is a ceramics manufacturing centre, and, like Tlaquepaque, it was once an autonomous village, but that's where the similarities end. There's more of a workaday feel to Tonalá, with no pedestrian streets, and fewer designer home-furnishing stores. Here, the emphasis is more on the crafts themselves. Goods are cheaper, too, especially if you go (as you should) for the animated **street markets** (Thurs & Sun roughly 8am–4pm), when Tonaltecas Sur is clogged with stalls selling all sorts of ceramic goods, glassware and handicrafts. Some are pretty good value, some are factory seconds and others are just junk. Mostly, Tonalá is about strolling and browsing, but if you've more than a passing interest in ceramics, see page 268 for some specific **shops**.

Museo Nacional de la Cerámica

Constitución 104 • Free • 333 683 2519

Specific sights are limited in Tonalá, but those with an interest in Mexican ceramics might like to visit the **Museo Nacional de la Cerámica**. The museum has examples from every Mexican state, with both contemporary and antique pots to demonstrate the different styles.

Zapopan

7km northwest of the city centre • #275 and TUR buses from Tlaquepaque and northbound on 16 de Septiembre

ZAPOPAN is the site of the **Basílica de la Virgen de Zapopan**, one of the most important churches in the city, much revered by the Huichol people. Pope John Paul II gave a Mass in the giant **Plaza de las Américas** in front of the church during a visit to Mexico in 1979, and a statue commemorates the event. The Baroque temple houses a miraculous image of the Virgin: the 25cm-high figure was dedicated to the local Indigenous people by a Franciscan missionary, Antonio de Segovia, after he had intervened in a battle between them and the conquistadors. Since then, it has been constantly venerated and is still the object of pilgrimages, especially on October 12, when several hundred thousand people gather early in the morning to march the Virgin back to the Basílica after an annual six-month tour of all the churches in Guadalajara.

Museo Huichol Wixarica de Zapopan

Eva Briseño 152 (Plaza de las Américas, north side) • Charge, discount for children • 333 636 4430

Beside the church, the small **Museo Huichol Wixarica de Zapopan**, an ethnographic museum, exhibits clothes and objects relating to Huichol traditions, as well as a photographic display of their modern way of life. They also sell Huichol crafts, including psychedelic yarn paintings (*cuadros de estambre*) and beadwork.

Museo de Arte de Zapopan

Andador 20 de Noviembre 166 • Free • http://maz.zapopan.gob.mx

Just south of the Plaza de las Américas, the **Museo de Arte de Zapopan** is Guadalajara's best contemporary art gallery. Changing exhibitions cherry-pick the best talent from Mexico and abroad – painting, sculpture, photography, video installations, you name it.

Parque Mirador Independencia

About 8km north of the city, at the end of Calzada Independencia • Free • *Macrobús* stop Mirador

The **Barranca de Oblatos** is a magnificent 600m-deep canyon, along the edge of which a series of parks offers superb views and a welcome break from the city. The **Parque Mirador Independencia**, a popular family spot with picnic areas, is located by the northern terminal of the Independencia *macrobús* route. Concrete paths wind down to the brink of the canyon, where you can gaze down past vegetated bluffs and cliffs to the river far below. Several good cafés and restaurants near the entrance to the Parque Mirador cater to student budgets.

SHOPPING
La Casa de Salvador Vásquez Carmona 1
Galeria José Bernabe 2
Mis Amores 3

4

ARRIVAL AND DEPARTURE GUADALAJARA

BY PLANE

Guadalajara's airport is some 17km southeast of the city on the road to Chapala, and has flights to US and Canadian as well as Mexican destinations. Airport facilities include money exchange and car rental, and there's also the usual system of fixed-price taxis and vans to take you downtown, with vouchers sold inside the terminal (cars with up to four people; 45min–1hr). The cheap way of getting into town is to head out of the terminal and right, continue for about 200m to the next junction, and take a bus (every 20min, 5am–9pm) from the stop in front of the PEMEX station to the Central Vieja. City bus #176 to the city centre also passes here, but does not usually stop to pick up passengers.

Destinations Cabo San Lucas (2–3 daily; 1hr 30min); Cancún (3–4 daily; 2hr 45min); Chihuahua (2–4 daily; 1hr 45min); Ciudad Juárez (1–3 daily; 2hr 10min); Cuidad Obregón (1–2 daily; 2hr); Hermosillo (1–4 daily; 2hr 5min); La Paz, Baja California Sur (1–3 daily; 1hr 40min); Mérida (1–2 daily; 2hr 25min); Mexicali (1–2 daily; 2hr 50min); Mexico City (24–32 daily; 1hr 30min); Monterrey (8daily; 1hr 20min); Puerto Vallarta (1–3 daily; 50min); Tijuana (8–10 daily; 3hr); Torreón (6–7 weekly; 1hr 20min); Tuxtla Gutierrez (5 weekly; 2hr); Veracruz (2–3 daily; 1hr 30min); Villahermosa (6 weekly; 2hr).

Airlines Aeromexico, Vallarta 2440 (333 630 3271); American, Vallarta 2440 (01 800 904 6000); Delta, Air France and KLM, via Mexjal López Cotilla 1701 (333 630 3130); United, Astral Plaza, Moctezuma 3515 (5283 5500); VivaAerobus, Vallarta 1088 (334 777 0770).

BY TRAIN

The train station, 2km south of the centre at the bottom of Calzada Independencia, is used by both the Tequila Express and José Cuervo Express (see page 270), which can only be taken as part of a pre-booked tour.

BY BUS

Central Nueva Long-distance first-class buses use the Central Nueva (or Camionera Nueva), out in suburbia 10km southeast of the city centre (map page 250). It consists of seven buildings strung out in a wide arc, plus shops and two half-decent hotels (see page 263). The buildings are organized by bus company rather than route, so there are buses to Mexico City from just about every building, for example, but staff are usually happy to tell you which company, and therefore which building, suits your needs. In general, *salas* 1 and 2 serve destinations in Jalisco, Colima and Michoacán, and many of the premium services to Mexico City, Morelia and many towns in the Bajío. *Salas* 3 and 4 have buses to the north and northwest, with services to Puerta Vallarta, the US border and up the Pacific coast, plus points en route. *Sala* 5 is for eastbound services towards San Luis Potosí and Tampico, as well as some more local services. *Sala* 6 serves the Bajío, the northeast and many local second-class buses. *Sala* 7 serves the north and northeast again, as well as Mexico City.

Transport into town #616 ("Centro") and the slightly dearer (but faster) turquoise TUR bus stop outside each *sala*, while #644B or #275 go from Av Revolución, the main road behind *sala* 1 (which takes a more direct route than #616); all these take you to Av 16 de Septiembre. The last city buses between the terminal and the centre leave at around 10pm. An authorized taxi downtown costs a flat fee. Going the other way, take #616, #644B, #275, the faster TUR bus, or anything marked "Central Nueva" heading south along 16 de Septiembre. Note that the Central Neuva is connected to the Central Vieja by the #616 city bus.

Destinations Aguascalientes (25 daily; 3hr); Colima (1 hourly; 3hr); Guanajuato (10 daily; 4hr); Lagos de Moreno (2 hourly; 2hr 35min); Manzanillo (2 hourly; 5hr); Mazatlán (2–3 hourly; 6–7hr); Mexico City (every 20–30min, plus numerous overnight; 7hr); Morelia (48 daily; 3–5hr); Pátzcuaro (2 daily; 5hr); Puerto Vallarta (2–3 hourly; 5–6hr); Querétaro (2 hourly; 4–5hr); San Juan de los Lagos (20 daily; 2hr); San Luis Potosí (hourly; 5hr); Tepic (1 hourly; 2hr); Tijuana (24 daily; 35hr); Toluca (6 daily; 6hr); Uruapan (hourly; 4–5hr).

Central Vieja Second-class services for destinations within about 150km of Guadalajara use the Central Vieja (old bus station) between Los Angeles and 5 de Febrero, an easy walk from the city centre (map page 250). Alternatively, you can take a cab, but the bus is the most budget friendly option — take either #616 bus from 16 de Septiembre, or *macrobús* to Niños Héroes. There are two *salas*, each with a charge to enter.

Destinations Ajijic (*Sala* A; every 30min; 1hr 15min); Chapala (*Sala* A; every 30min; 1hr); Guadalajara airport (*Sala* A; every 20min, 5am–9pm; 20min); Jocotepec (*Sala* A; hourly; 1hr 15min); Tapalpa (*Sala* B; 13 daily; 3hr); Tequila (*Salas* A & B; every 20min from each; 2hr).

GETTING AROUND

Getting around town is not too difficult once you've got the hang of the transport system, but the best way to get around is usually **on foot** – Guadalajara's streets are even more pleasant if you appreciate them slowly, and most city-centre attractions are within walking distance of each other.

By bus Almost all buses are funnelled through the centre on a few main roads, with destinations on the windscreen. The sheer number of buses and the speed at which they move can make things slightly more difficult, however, especially at peak hours when you may have to fight to get

USEFUL BUS ROUTES IN GUADALAJARA

All of these also run in the opposite direction: the #600 numbers are minibuses.
#62 Calzada Independencia–soccer stadium and bullring–Central Vieja
#176 Centro (Ramón Corona at Degollado)–airport
#275 Tonalá–Central Nueva–Tlaquepaque–Centro (16 Septiembre)–Zapopan
#616 Centro (Jardín de San Francisco)–Central Vieja–Central Nueva
#629 Centro–Morelos (westbound)/Pedro Moreno (eastbound)–Minerva Circle
#702 TUR Tonalá–Central Nueva –Tlaquepaque–Centro (16 de Septiembre)–Zapopan

on; if possible, get a local to show you exactly where your bus stops. Most bus rides cost a small fee, but the turquoise, a/c TUR express buses cost a little more. For the most useful routes, see page 261. Along Calzada Independencia, the *macrobús*, with its own dedicated lanes, and stations with platforms, costs a set fee in exact coins only (no change is given). If using the *macrobús* a lot, it may be more convenient to buy a card from a machine at any stop, which you can charge up with credit at the same machine, thus saving the need for exact change.

By metro The Tren Ligero (metro system), with one north–south and one east–west line, is designed for local commuters. You may not use it at all, though it can be handy for quick east–west travel across the centre. To ride, pay the exact coins into a machine on the platform or, as with *macrobús* (see above), buy a chargeable card from a machine in the station.

By taxi Taxis are reliable if you're in a hurry, and for a group they aren't usually too expensive as long as you establish a price at the outset; many downtown taxi ranks post a list of fixed prices. From the centre to the Plaza del Sol, Central Nueva or Zapopan should cost the same amount; it'll be a little less to Tlaquepaque and more to the airport. Fares are generally 25 percent higher between 10pm and 6am.

Car rental Agents can be found at the airport, and there's a slew on Niños Héroes at Manzano (just west of 16 de Septiembre); downtown offices include Alamo, Vallarta 1285 (333 613 5551); Avis, Avenida de las Americas 1169 (333 817 5226); Budget, Mariano Otero 1288 (333 613 0027); Europcar, Lázaro Cárdenas 2838 (333 122 6979); and Quick, Niños Héroes 954 (333 614 6052).

4

INFORMATION AND TOURS

Tourist office There's a very helpful office at Libertad 1725 (Mon–Thurs 9am–6pm, Fri 9am–3pm)), and tourist information booths (opening times vary slightly, but all approximately Mon–Fri 9am–2pm & 3–7pm, Sat & Sun 9am–3pm) at the airport, Plaza de Guadalajara, Plaza de la Liberación, Morelos with Independencia, Plaza Tapatía and Jardín de San Francisco. Finally, there's also a booth at the corner of Juárez and Progresso, by El Parian in Tlaquepaque (Mon–Fri 10am–8pm, Sat & Sun 10am–7pm). Alternatively, you can call the state tourism office on 333 668 1600, or toll free from elsewhere in the country on 01 800 363 2200. Guadalajara's city council has a very good tourist information website, http://guadalajara.gob.mx.

Listings The best source of listings information is the *Ocio* magazine section that comes with the Friday edition of Guadalajara's main newspaper, *Milenio*. The cooler cafés often have a copy lying around, and tourist information booths sometimes keep one. In English, the weekly *Guadalajara Reporter* (http://theguadalajarareporter.net) reflects the concerns of the expat community in town and around Laguna de Chapala.

City bus tours Tapatío Tour (333 613 0887, http://tapatiotour.com.mx) run an hourly hop-on, hop-off bus tour on two central routes, and every 2hr on two outer routes (daily 9.30am–8pm), with tickets valid on all four routes during one day (children and students get a discount). Tickets can be bought on board or at major stops, online or from their central stop on the south side of Rotonda de los Jaliscenses Ilustres.

Calandria tours A more leisurely alternative is by *calandria*, an elegant horse-drawn covered carriage. These can be picked up from Plaza Guadalajara (north side), Mercado de San Juan de Dios, or Jardín de San Francisco. Most drivers are knowledgeable (and entertaining) city guides and charge a set amount (for 1–5 people) for a 35min tour, or slightly more for a longer (1hr) tour.

ACCOMMODATION

With a range of **hotels** to suit all budgets (as well as a couple of **hostels**) right in the *centro histórico*, there is little reason to stay elsewhere in the city. In this area you'll be able to walk to everything in the centre and have easy access to buses for the outlying suburbs. If you're looking for a budget option and the central places are all full, consider some of the **cheap hotels** around the old bus station or in the streets south of the Mercado Libertad. Both areas are noisy and none too appealing, though the hotels we've listed are fine. Most of the more **expensive** business hotels

HACIENDA RETREATS

For a completely different perspective on Jalisco, consider staying at one of the numerous well-preserved **haciendas** within an hour's drive of Guadalajara. They are easy, if somewhat pricey, overnight escapes which offer a change of pace from the bustling city. Haciendas are ideal for those on shorter trips who want quickly and comfortably to experience a bit of the countryside, and learn a little about a different side of *Tapatío* lifestyle. Jalisco's state tourist office (333 668 1600 or 01 800 363 2200, http://visitjalisco.com.mx) can provide information on these and other rural homes and relaxing retreats. You can also go directly to http://haciendasycasonas.com, which has links to more than twenty such places.

tend to be a long way out to the west of the city, though you're almost certainly better off in the **luxury B&B-style places** downtown or in Tlaquepaque. There's also Av López Mateos, 2km to the west of the centre, which is Guadalajara's **motel** row.

HOTELS AND B&BS

CENTRO HISTÓRICO, SEE MAP PAGE 252

Ana-Isabel Javier Mina 164; http://hotelanaisabel.com.mx. Simple but clean tiled rooms with TVs and parking nearby. Apart from one room, windows face inward, which can make them rather dark (those on the top floor less so). Go for the quieter rooms at the back if possible. M$

Chapala José María Mercado 84; 333 617 7159. Overlooking the market, but entered down a side street, this place doesn't look very inviting at first glance, but the rooms, though small, are neat and equipped with a TV and ceiling fan (though not wi-fi). M$

Don Quijote Plaza Héroes 91; http://hoteldonquijoteplaza.com.mx. This small, friendly hotel has a rather dark, colonial-style courtyard, with fish and turtles in its central fountain, but the rooms are fresh and modern, and it has a bit more character than most of the hotels in this price bracket. M$$

Fénix Corona 160; www.hotelfenixguadalajara.com. Large, modern, four-star hotel with impeccable rooms right in the centre. Go for one on the upper floors with views of the cathedral. Promotional rates are usually available. Wheelchair-accessible. Breakfast included. M$$$

Francés Maestranza 35 (just off the plaza behind the cathedral); www.hotelfrances.com. Guadalajara's most appealing upmarket hotel, in a beautiful colonial building, founded as an inn in 1610 (its elevator is said to be the second ever installed in the city). Rooms are pleasant and traditionally styled. Even if you're not staying, it's worth dropping in for a superbly mixed margarita in the lobby bar. M$$

Hotel Cervantes Calle Prisciliano Sánchez 442; www.hotelcervantes.com.mx/. The rooms at this hotel are simple but clean, albeit overly orange. Cable TV is included although the wi-fi can be patchy. M$$

Hotel de Mendoza Carranza 16 (at Hidalgo); http://demendoza.com.mx. Attractive establishment in a refurbished colonial convent – the great location makes it an ideal base for sightseeing. Rooms come with all amenities (including a safe) and access to the nicest pool in the centre. Breakfast included. M$$$

Maya López Cotilla 39; 333 614 5454. Verging on the kitsch, with a model of a Maya temple in the lobby, this place offers vibrant pink decor in the public areas, and lilac and yellow in the rooms, which all have TVs, but don't all have fans. Rooms with fans cost no extra, so you may as well ask for one, and rooms on the top floors are brighter and quieter. The area's a bit noisy given its proximity to the Mercado Libertad, but it's close to the centre. M$

Posada Regis Corona 171; 333 614 8633. Run by the same people as the *Posada San Pablo* (see below), this appealing old building, smack-bang in the centre of town, has high-ceilinged rooms around a peaceful, covered courtyard with great murals. Of the downstairs rooms, only #8, #9 and #10 have outside windows, but they also have small economy rooms on the roof that are ideal for one person but acceptable for two. M$

The Roof Backpackers Miguel Blanco 1115; http://theroof.mex.tl/gallery.html. One of Guadalajara's newer backpacker-focused options, this modern hostel features functional but clean and comfortable mixed and single-sex dorms, and privates with either en-suite or shared bathrooms. It's a sociable sort of place, with a communal kitchen and a lounge with a TV, and board games. M$

Santiago de Compostela Colón 272; http://hotelsantiagodecompostelagdl.com. Attractive hotel set around an enclosed courtyard decorated with Turkish rugs. Rooms are well appointed with a/c, carpets and cable TV, though the streetside ones can be noisy. All have a deep tiled bath, but you may just prefer to use the lovely rooftop pool. M$$

AROUND THE CENTRAL VIEJA, SEE MAPS PAGES 252 AND 256

León Independencia 557 Sur; 333 619 6141. This place is very cheap and basic, but perfectly serviceable if you don't mind just the bare-bones essentials. Rooms have bathrooms and (just about tepid) "hot" water, with towels and soap provided, but no TV or wi-fi. Even so, it's still a budgeteer's bargain. M$

Misión Carlton Niños Héroes; http://hotelesmision.com.mx. A more pleasant option than most in the vicinity of the Central Vieja, offering plain but decent-sized (if a little scruffy) rooms with pine furniture and flatscreen TVs. Massages are available at a basic spa, while the usual basic Mexican fare is on offer at the restaurant. M$$

WEST OF THE CENTRE, SEE MAP PAGE 256

Isabel José Guadalupe Montenegro 1572; http://hotelisabel.com. Great-value, friendly hotel with homely, traditional rooms (TV, wi-fi, a/c) looking out onto a quiet garden – there's even an outdoor swimming pool. Traditional Mexican breakfasts are served each morning in the on-site café. M$$

Quinta Real México 2727; http://quintareal.com. Gorgeous luxury hotel that's also well set up for business guests. The grounds are spacious and immaculately tended, with a pool, and the suites (there are no plain rooms) come with neo-colonial styling and every amenity. M$$$$$

Villa Ganz López Cotilla 1739; http://villaganz.com. A gorgeous boutique hotel in a 1930s mansion, with nine impeccably decorated suites and most luxuries on hand; no pool, but free use of a nearby gym. Common areas are so delightful you'll never want to step outside, though it is only a short walk to some great bars and restaurants. Promotional rates are often available. M$$$$$

TLAQUEPAQUE AND CENTRAL NUEVA, SEE MAPS PAGES 250 AND 258

Casa Campos Miranda 30; http://casacampos.mx. One of the most charming places in town to lay your head, this beautifully remodelled colonial house comes with modern fittings, an understated elegance and an unbeatable location for artesanía shopping. Downstairs rooms have ceiling fans, upstairs rooms have a/c. Reserve well ahead, especially in winter. Breakfast included. M$$$

★ **La Casa del Retoño** Matamoros 182; http://lacasadelretono.com.mx. Neatly set away from the commercial bustle of Tlaquepaque, this lovely little red-and-yellow B&B has eight beautiful, artesanía-decorated rooms, a sunny terrace so full of plants it's almost a bit of jungle, and a garden where you can eat breakfast or just hang out. Breakfast included. M$$$

Donde el Indio Duerme Independencia 74; 333 535 2189. Much more basic than everything else hereabouts; simple, reasonably clean rooms at good prices. Rooms are noisy, and the wi-fi doesn't work, but some rooms do at least have a TV. M$

La Villa del Ensueño Florida 305; http://villadelensueno.com. This "Villa of Dreams" is a delightful boutique hotel with spacious rooms all tastefully decorated and with lovely tiled bathrooms. A pool and quiet little spaces to hang out in make it a great place to come back to between shopping forays. Breakfast included. M$$$$

Vista Junior Revolución, beside Sala 1; http://vistahoteles.com. Conveniently located by the Central Nueva, this hotel is modern and soulless, and not the cleanest place in town, but has two pools, a restaurant and 24hr room service, and the rooms are reasonably quiet. M$

HOSTELS

CENTRO HISTÓRICO, SEE MAP PAGE 252

★ **Hospedarte (Hostel Guadalajara)** Maestranza 147; http://hospedartehostels.com. Very central and modern hostel housed in an old building and still popularly known by its previous incarnation as *Hostel Guadalajara*. This place is full of backpackers and language students, with internet access, laundry and cooking facilities, free bicycle rental, private lockers and friendly staff who regularly organize nights out to interesting bars. A light breakfast is included and various packages including multi-day stays and tours are available. There's a discount available for card-carrying Hostelling International members. There's another branch to the west, in Chapultepec. Standard dorms and doubles available. M$

4

EATING

Tapatíos take their food seriously. Guadalajara boasts hundreds of **places to eat**, ranging from elegant restaurants to unpretentious cafés, and from *loncherías* (cafés with an emphasis on short orders) to *neverías* (with ice cream and fresh-fruit drinks). Don't pass up the **street vendors** either – their fresh tacos and bags of spiced fruit are delicious and make a cheap, healthy snack. For basic meals, the mezzanine of the **Mercado Libertad** has seemingly hundreds of little stands, each displaying their own specialities. There's a more limited, if handier, selection at the **Mercado Corona**. In the centre, your best choice is west of the cathedral, where traditional cafés and restaurants line **Juárez**. The town's signature dish is the torta ahogada (drowned sandwich) – a pork roll with *pozole* broth poured all over it. Eaten with a spoon, accompanied by chopped onions and lime juice, it's absolutely delicious when done well.

CAFÉS

CENTRO HISTÓRICO AND AROUND, SEE MAP PAGE 252

Café la Flor de Córdoba Portales Pedro Moreno 398; http://cafelaflordecordoba.com. Caffeinating *Tapatíos* for more than 80 years, this little place is a beloved local favourite, and now has several other branches across the city. Hot and iced coffees on offer alongside a tempting selection of tarts and pastries. M$

Café Madoka Gonzalez Martínez 76; 333 613 0649. Big, traditional café, operating since 1959 and serving tasty breakfasts (especially the *chilaquiles al pollo* with juice and coffee), soups and *antojitos* (*enchiladas suizas*). You can also just play dominoes and sip a coffee; try the "Café Madoka Especial", served with a dollop of vanilla ice cream. M$$

Café Madrid Juárez 264 near Corona; 333 614 9504. A smallish 1950s-style diner and coffee bar, good for moderately priced breakfasts, *comidas corridas* sandwiches and snacks such as chicken or beef *fajitas*. M$$

Chai Juárez 200, at Maestranza; http://chai.com.mx. A bright, trendy café serving, as its name suggests, Indian-style tea, as well as coffees, snacks, panini, deli-style sandwiches and even pizzas, not to mention weekend buffet brunches. It's also a popular spot for an evening beer for the city's trendy crowd. M$$

TLAQUEPAQUE, SEE MAP PAGE 258

Café San Pedro Juárez 85; 333 639 0616. Tlaquepaque's best coffee, though a bit pricey, with seating under the *portales* and a great range of teas and cakes. Their speciality is a frappuccino. M$

4

CHEAP EATS AND SNACKS

CENTRO HISTÓRICO AND AROUND, SEE MAPS PAGES 252 AND 256

Birriería el Compadre C. Leandro Valle 895; 333 614 5550. A nice little restaurant serving up traditional Mexican dishes, with a smattering of international cuisine to boot. The menu is especially meat-heavy and most single orders will serve two people. M$$

Chan Los Ángeles 131; 333 619 9446. A handy cheap diner by the Central Vieja, offering fish and meat dishes, and reasonable *comidas corridas* (noon–6pm). They also offer breakfasts for a good price (7am–noon), but the coffee is instant only. M$$

Pastelería Luvier Colón 182; http://luvier.mx. One of the best of many *panaderías* and *pastelerias* in the centre, with lots of sweet breads, cakes, pastries and tarts, but not too much in the savoury department bar plain bread rolls. M$$

El Tacazo Juárez 246; 333 636 3636. A little hole-in-the-wall place serving fast, flavourful tacos, popular and cheap. Choices include *tacos arabe* (with pork in *chimole* sauce), or, for the more adventurous, tacos with *lengua de res* (ox tongue) or *cabeza de res* (ox head). M$

Taquería Los Faroles Ramón Corona 250; 331 514 5369. This popular taco and torta joint isn't the nicest environment, with its garish plastic tables and chairs in need of a revamp, but it serves a wide range of tacos, and is a decent place to have your first taste of torta ahogada (or tacos dorados), washed down with *horchata*. M$

TOP 5 GUADALAJARA EATING PLACES

Birrieria las Nueve Esquinas see page 264
La Gorda see page 264
Ahogadas Beto's see page 264
Pierrot see page 265
La Trattoria see page 265

RESTAURANTS

CENTRO HISTÓRICO AND AROUND, SEE MAPS PAGES 252 AND 256

Birrieria Las Nueve Esquinas Colón 384; www.las9esquinas.com. Peacefully set on a quiet plaza, this little restaurant serves up traditional Mexican mutton dishes and does excellent *birria de chivo* (goat stew). M$$

La Chata Corona 126; http://lachata.com.mx. Excellent medium-priced Mexican dishes, including chicken *mole* and *platillo jalisciense* (chicken with side snacks). Hugely popular with local families since 1942, so expect to queue, especially at mealtimes. Extensive breakfasts go for a reasonable price daily. M$$

Chong Wah Juárez 558; 333 613 9950. Moderately priced Cantonese food to eat in or take away. Though there are now a fair few Chinese restaurants around town, this remains the best, and their buffet lunch (small/large) is also one of the best. There's another branch literally just round the corner at Gonzalez Martínez 77. M$$

★ **La Fonda de la Noche** Calle Jesús 251; 333 825 4275. Acclaimed restaurant set in a lovely turn-of-the-century house, atmospherically lit by hanging lanterns. Open for dinner only, the restaurant offers an artful take on classic Mexican cuisine with *sopas*, tostadas and *chiles en nogada* prepared and presented beautifully. M$$

★ **La Gorda** Corona 181; http://lagorda.com.mx. A Guadalajara institution "The Fat Girl" serves up exactly what made its patron so rotund: large helpings of classic Mexican *antojitos* such as enchiladas and *sopa azteca* at relatively cheap prices. Great traditional breakfasts, too. There are various locations around town but this is the original. It's very popular with the locals, so be prepared to queue. M$$

El Mexicano Morelos 83; www.grupoelmexicano.com. In a retro chic setting, this moderately expensive restaurant serves traditional Mexican fare, set against giant murals, vaulted ceilings and on an evening, live music too. You should be warned that the top shelf tequila here is dangerously affordable. M$$$$

WEST OF THE CENTRE, SEE MAP PAGE 256

★ **Ahogadas Beto's** Buzeta 757; https://www.ahogadasbetosguadalajara.com.Guadalajara's best torta ahogada by popular consent, this neighbourhood joint serves up their

GASTRONOMÍA JALISCIENSE: TAPATÍO SPECIALITIES

While in Guadalajara, you shouldn't miss out on some of Jalisco's culinary specialities. The most celebrated is **birria**, stewed beef or mutton in a spicy, but not particularly hot, sauce, and served with tortillas or in tacos from street stalls, bars and in markets. **Roast goat** is another favourite, often seen in the markets along with a goat's skull (just in case you don't know what *chivo* means). **Pozole**, a stew of pork and hominy (ground maize), is also popular, and typically found as a restaurant special on Thursdays. Rarely seen much beyond the city limits, there's also **torta ahogada** (literally "drowned sandwich"), a bread roll stuffed with a filling of your choice (traditionally pork) then drenched with a thin, spicy salsa that soaks right through the bread. It's a bit messy, but extremely delicious. And then, of course, there's **tequila**, discussed more fully on page 271.

delicious drowned sandwiches from both the to-go stand out front and their simple restaurant inside. This hidden gem is a bit of a mission to get to (a taxi from the centre is the best way to get here) but well worth the effort for the original scoff. M$

Alta Fibra Niños Héroes 2840-A; 331 057 9383. Very popular with *Tapatío* (Guadalajara native) families, *Alta Fibra* specializes in high-fibre foods; the menu isn't vegetarian, but it is low fat, with lots of salads. Excellent-value comidas corridas are popular here, and there's a wholemeal bakery next door. M$$

La China Poblana Juárez 887; 338 825 6632. This little place opens only very briefly in the afternoon for traditional Puebla dishes at reasonable prices, including favourites such as chicken *mole* and *chiles en nogada*. M$$

Goa López Cotilla 1520; http://goa.com.mx. One of only a handful of Indian restaurants in Guadalajara, intimately lit and with Bollywood on the screen. Serves a range of excellent dishes, several straight out of the tandoor. Dishes include tamarind chicken and fish vindaloo. You can also order a shisha pipe with fruit-flavoured tobacco. M$$

★ **Pierrot** Justo Sierra 2355; http://restaurantpierrot.com. The city's finest French restaurant, in gracious surroundings and with attentive but never intrusive service. The filet mignon in mushroom sauce and the chocolate mousse are both spectacular. M$$$$

Pizza del Perro Negro De la Paz 1985, just off Chapultepec Sur; http://muertealapizzafalsa.com. Their self-appointed tagline of 'the best pizza in the world' might be a bit of a stretch, but it's certainly up there with the best you'll find in Guadalajara – doughy, thick crust topped with a dizzying array of ingredients, including Mexican classics like *cochinita pibil* (slow-roasted pork). M$$

La Trattoria Niños Héroes 3051; http://latrattoria.com.mx. This spacious and lively Italian restaurant is one of Guadalajara's best. *Segundi piatti* include *pollo alla marsala* and devilled prawns. Evening reservations recommended. M$$

TLAQUEPAQUE, SEE MAPS PAGES 250 AND 258

★ **Mariscos el Social** Calzada Delicias 117 (1km south to the end of Herrera y Cairo, then 400m east); 333 838 5754. Locally – and deservedly – renowned seafood diner, where a big cup of juicy king prawns and octopus is helped down by zingy, fresh, raw *habanero* salsa and ice-cold beer – or excellent tequilas accompanied by their own *sangrita*. They also do wonderful grilled snapper, *ceviche* and seafood soup with a whole crab and a pair of nutcrackers. M$$

Restaurante Cielito Lindo Independencia 208; 333 659 2680. Pleasant courtyard restaurant with endless lanterns hanging overhead. The soups are a work of art in their own right, as are the perfectly presented oysters. Fair warning – the cocktails here cost almost as much as some of the dishes. M$$$

DRINKING AND NIGHTLIFE — SEE MAPS PAGES 252 AND 256

Traditionally the centre of town hasn't been that lively, but things are picking up, particularly southwest of the cathedral (along López Cotilla, Madero and Sanchez) and in the **Nueve Esquinas** quarter, three blocks further south, where Colon and Galeana meet. The best of the town's nightlife is concentrated along Av Chapultepec, a north–south thoroughfare 2km west of the centre, where you'll find everything from chilled-out bars to electro clubs. Take time to stroll through the pedestrianized walkway in the middle where street performers and dancercise go until the early hours. **López Mateos** has a number of trendy pubs with live music and a younger crowd. Some have open bars on certain nights of the week with a pricey cover charge for men, but it's normally less for women.

BARS

The Black Sheep Libertad 1872; 333 825 7000. Lively multistorey bar in what looks like a haunted mansion, but is actually a former brothel (and actually the club-like extension of the original business three doors down the road, under the same management, but which caters to a rockier crowd). Offers strong and cheap cocktails as well as a range of imported beers.

El Callejón de los Rumberos Chapultepec Sur 287, at Lerdó de Tejeda; 332 931 9748, www.facebook.com/ElCallejonDeLosRumberos. Cuban-style dance bar featuring salsa and other Latin sounds. They even have dance classes, but shorts and T-shirts are banned (though the bar features plenty of photos of visiting musicians wearing the latter).

Casa Bariachi Vallarta 2221; http://casa-bariachi.com. Loud and colourful restaurant-bar decorated with giant *piñatas*, where the entertainment includes 2hr cabaret sessions featuring traditional dance and mariachi bands in the afternoons and evenings.

La Condesa Colón 349, at Libertad. A lively cantina, where there's music and dancing from 6pm nightly. The dancefloor isn't huge, but it's just the right size to keep this a cantina with dancing rather than a dance club with a bar.

★ **La Fuente** Pino Suarez 78, www.facebook.com/cantinalafuentemx. A bare-bones piano bar and cantina that looks like it's been around longer than Guadalajara itself. It's nevertheless the most authentic watering hole you'll find in the city, with cheap beers and a lively atmosphere. Look out for the old bicycle in a niche and to the right above the bar. It was left by a client in the 50s who drank his weight in beer before announcing he had no money to pay his bill. He left his bike in lieu of payment, promising to return the following day with the money. He never came back, and his legacy has become the bar's symbol, as well as the fact that clients have to pay for each round immediately.

Green Light Eco-Bar Madero 494, at González Martínez; 333 156 6191. It isn't clear what exactly is ecological about this trendy bar-café, but the alfresco roof terrace, shaded with parasols, is a top place to relax with a beer, a coffee or a snack of an afternoon or evening. It's something of a LGBTQ+ hangout, but certainly not exclusively so. The downstairs area is a music video bar.

Hotel Francés Maestranza 35; www.hotelfrances.com. Piano-bar-style establishment in the courtyard of one of the centre's grander hotels. Come in the early evening for 2x1 happy-hour drinks (the margaritas are good). On Fri evenings there are mariachis, folk dancers and a *charreo* lassooist.

La Moresca López Cotilla 1835, at De Cervantes Savedra; http://lamoresca.com. An elegant restaurant downstairs, with an upmarket wine bar upstairs that makes a good spot for a bottle of house red (or white) and a bruschetta.

LIVE MUSIC VENUE

La Mutualista Madero 553; 333 452 6466. On Thurs, Fri and Sat nights from 8pm this cavernous venue (ordinarily just a large and friendly cantina) gets taken over by a band (usually Cuban, sometimes rock) and everyone hits the dancefloor. Ceiling fans and wide-open windows give a suitably Cuban dancehall feel.

4

ENTERTAINMENT

There's an impressive range of traditional Mexican and classical concerts, contemporary gigs, classic and modern film, theatre and opera performances and art exhibitions in town – you can see some kind of performance most nights of the week. Anyone on a tight budget should check out the **Plaza de Armas**, where there's usually something free happening. One thing no visitor to Guadalajara should miss is hearing mariachi in its hometown, specifically at the **Plaza de los Mariachis**. Going to the **cinema** in Guadalajara is not particularly convenient, as suburban multiplexes have killed downtown movies. The big shopping centres such as Centro Magno and Plaza del Sol have the latest blockbusters, and we've also listed a couple of more convenient alternatives.

LIVE MUSIC AND THEATRE

Instituto Cultural Mexicano Norteamericano de Jalisco (ICMNJ) Enrique Díaz de León 300; http://institutocultural.com.mx. This is a language school, offering lessons in English for locals and Spanish for foreigners, but it also puts on free cultural events, including, from time to time, classical music concerts and recitals.

Plaza de Armas There are regular free performances of

GUADALAJARA FIESTAS

Several entertaining **fiestas** take place throughout the year, including the highly animated Día de San Pedro in Tlaquepaque (June 29), with mariachi, dancing and processions; and the Día de la Virgen de Zapopan (Oct 12), an all-night fiesta capped with a massive early morning procession that starts before dawn at the cathedral and finishes in Zapopan. Crowds and assorted food vendors start arriving the evening before, with all sorts of music and the *portales* choked with people bedding down for the 4am start. In the autumn, everything cranks up to fever pitch for the Fiestas de Octubre (http://fiestasdeoctubre.com.mx), a month-long celebration when downtown Guadalajara comes alive with all manner of outdoor performances and bands, often free. Daily events include *charreadas* (rodeos), processions and fireworks, as well as all kinds of free entertainment – modern Mexican music performances are put on from noon in the fairgrounds of the Benito Juárez auditorium.

Jaliscan music in the rotunda just south of the cathedral, often featuring the State Band of Jalisco or Guadalajara's own Municipal Band.

Plaza de los Mariachis Guadalajara is the home of mariachi, and you shouldn't leave town without experiencing it. It all happens in the Plaza de los Mariachis, a short pedestrianized street by the Mercado Libertad and the church of San Juan de Dios, where mariachi bands stroll between bars, playing to anyone prepared to cough up for a song. Musicians start arriving in the late afternoon, but it's best after dark, when there are usually several bands. Unless they play for you personally – in which case you'll have to negotiate a price before they start – you needn't spend anything at all. This area is notorious for pickpockets, so keep your wits about you. You'll also find mariachi bands in Tlaquepaque.

Teatro Degollado Degollado 53; 333 030 1391. This magnificent theatre in central Guadalajara (see page 251) hosts a regular programme of theatre and dance. Pick up details of events from the tourist office or from Ticketmaster (ticket desk in Fabricas de Francia department store at Juárez 272).

Teatro Diana 16 de Septiembre 710; http://teatrodiana.com. This large, modern theatre puts on everything from serious plays, opera and ballet to classical and folk music concerts and children's matinees, but all the performances are of course in Spanish.

CINEMA

Cineclub Alianza Alianza Francesa López Cotilla 1199; https://alianzafrancesagdl.mx. Attached to Guadalajara's French cultural institute, this cinema shows French films every Tuesday and Friday at 8pm, usually with Spanish subtitles.

Cinépolis Centro Magno Vallarta 2425; http://cinepolis.com. A large chain multiplex in an upmarket shopping mall, around 3km west of downtown. Movies here are the latest Hollywood offerings, dubbed into Spanish.

Ex-Convento del Carmen Juárez 638; 333 030 1355. This arthouse cinema attached to the former convent shows alternative and classic movies, and holds the occasional film festival. Foreign films are usually shown in their original language with Spanish subtitles.

LGBTQ+ GUADALAJARA

SEE MAP PAGE 252

Guadalajara has a reputation for being one of Mexico's most LGTBQ+-friendly cities, and while that doesn't mean public displays of affection are widely accepted, there's greater freedom in the dozen or so bars and clubs that advertise their orientation with rainbow flags. Guadalajara's **gay quarter** is centred on the junction of Ocampo and Sanchez, about five blocks southwest of the cathedral. Spanish-speakers can check out what's going on at http://gaygdl.mx.

La Prisciliana Sanchez 396; 333 613 6041. Dark and chilled-out upstairs gay bar (though straight people are welcome too) with casual drinking to Latin dance beats. *Club Ye*Ye* downstairs, with minimal grey and black decor and big video screens, is also very popular with both lesbians and gay men (and heterosexuals).

4

SHOPPING AND MARKETS

The giant Mercado Libertad (see page 254) may be the biggest of Guadalajara's markets, but every city *barrio* has its own. They include the very touristy Mercado Corona near the cathedral, and craft markets and upscale boutiques in Tlaquepaque and Tonalá. The flea market El Baratillo (Sun) is vast, sometimes stretching a kilometre or more along Javier Mina, starting a dozen blocks east of the Mercado Libertad.

BOOKS

Librería Gandhi López Cotilla 1567; http://gandhi.com.mx; see map page 256. A vast multi-level bookshop (one of a nationwide chain), with books in Spanish and English as well as Italian, French, German and more. Also has large collections of DVDs and music.

Librería Gonvill López Cotilla 501, at Donato Guerra; http://gonvill.com.mx; see map page 252. A good city-centre bookshop, with a wide selection of books in Spanish, as well as a small section of books in English, mostly novels.

CRAFTS

Agustín Parra Independencia 154–158; 333 657 8350, www.facebook.com/GaleriaAgustinParra; see map page 258. Don't miss this fabulous showcase of the work of Agustín Parra Echauri, a nationally famous local artisan whose works on display here include Baroque-style furniture, doors and religious icons, some of them enormous. Two popes have visited the shop, as shown in photos above the counter.

Antigua de México Independencia 255; 333 635 3402, http://antiguademexico.com; see map page 258. Comprises two lovely colonial houses that sell upmarket fabrics, furniture and antiques to a mainly Mexican clientele.

La Casa de Salvador Vázquez Carmona López Cotilla 328; 333 683 2896; see map page 259. You may need to knock on the door to gain access – the place looks like a simple private residence, and gives no indication of being a shop or workshop. However, around the rear patio, Carmona shapes pots and bowls, hand-fires them, then paints the finished article. He'll show you his gallery complete with finished pots that have graced the covers of magazines and design glossies.

Galeria José Bernabe Hidalgo 29; 333 683 0040; see map page 259. Close to Tonalá's central plaza, this is the place to come for superb and highly regarded *petatillo*, an intricate ceramic form with painted animals and flowers on a cross-hatched background.

Galeria Sergio Bustamante Independencia 238; http://coleccionsergiobustamante.com.mx; see map page 258. The showcase for world-famous painter and sculptor Bustamente's works – the gallery is full of his fantastical figures in papier-mâché, resin and bronze. They are worth looking at even if the price and size are such that you won't be buying. Don't miss the toilet, which has more sculpture in its own enclosed courtyard.

Gallery Rodo Padilla Calle Independencia 139; https://rodopadilla.com; see map page 258. Considerably cheaper than most of the galleries in the neighbourhood, stocking charming little clay figurines, handcrafted onsite.

Mis Amores Tonaltecas Sur 80; 331 721 1443; see map page 259. A shop full of skeletons – not real ones of course, but it has all sorts of ceramics, papier-mâché and sheet-metal ones, including designs based on the works of Posada (see page 351), such as *La Catrina*, his famous skeleton woman with a huge floral hat.

SPECTATOR SPORTS

Bullfighting Bullfights are considered to be a sport for connoisseurs, and the cognoscenti watch the *corrida* at the city's largest bullring, the Plaza de Toros Nuevo Progreso (http://plazanuevoprogreso.com.mx), almost 4km northeast of the centre along Calzada Independencia. Fights occur several times in Oct, then on irregular Sundays until March (4.30pm). Ticket office open Mon–Sat 11.30am–6pm.

Football Guadalajara's biggest team, FC Guadalajara (Las Chivas; http://chivasdecorazon.com.mx), play their home matches at the flying-saucer-like Estadio Akron, on the western edge of town near where Vallarta meets the Pereferico (bus #649 from Juárez with Federación). Matches are usually on Sat night or Sun afternoon. Tickets vary a good deal in price and can usually be bought at the gate, or in advance from Boliti Movil (https://boletomovil.com/chivas). The enormous Estadio Jalisco, almost opposite the bullring (*macrobús* to Monumental), is home to FC Atlas (http://atlasfc.com.mx) – the City to Chivas' United. The stadium, formerly used by Chivas too, was a venue for matches at both the 1970 and 1986 World Cups. Tickets here are cheaper than elsewhere. Second-tier club Tecos (officially, Estudiantes de la Universidad Autónoma de Guadalajara) have their stadium (Estadio Tres de Marzo) in Zapopan.

Rodeos Jaliscans pride themselves on their equestrian skills, notably in the regular *charreadas* (rodeos) held every Sun (from noon) at the Lienzo Charro de Jalisco, Dr Michel 577, near the Parque Agua Azul. For details call 333 619 0315 or just turn up; tickets are usually reasonably priced.

DIRECTORY

Banks and exchange There are numerous banks with ATMs throughout the centre, including around Corona and Juárez. Virtually identical rates, faster service and longer hours are available in the *casas de cambio* around the corner of Maestranza and López Cotilla. After hours, bigger hotels will usually change money at a considerably worse rate.

Consulates Canada, World Trade Center (Torre Pacifico, 8th floor), Mariano Otero 1249 (331 818 4200); Guatemala, Mango 1440, Colonía del Fresno (333 811 1503); South Africa, Mexicaltinzgo 1665 2nd floor, Colonia Moderna (333 825 7570); US, Progreso 175, Colonía Americana (333 268 2100).

Emergencies The general emergency number is 911.

Laundry The closest laundry to the centre is at Aldama 129, off Independencia in a slightly rough area a few blocks south of the Mercado Libertad.

Pharmacy Farmacia Guadalajara, with several locations in the centre, including Moreno 170 near Plaza Tapatía and López Cotilla 423 at Galeana (both daily 7am–10pm).

Post office Venustiano Carranza 16 at the junction with Independencia; also at Alcalde 500.

Spanish courses Guadalajara is a decent place to learn Spanish, with several schools sited close to the historic centre. One of the most popular is IMAC, Donata Guerra 180 at Madero (333 614 1414, http://spanish-school.com.mx/guadalajara) with a schedule allowing short or long courses as well as classes in ceramics, guitar and flamenco, and homestay opportunities. Others worth considering are Guadalajara University's CECM, Tomás V. Gómez 125 (333 616 4399, https://cecm.proulex.com/2021/index.php), and the Instituto Cultural Mexicano Norteamericano de Jalisco (ICMNJ), Díaz de León Sur 300 (333 825 5838, http://institutocultural.com.mx).

Travel agent Mundo Joven Vallarta 2440 (333 630 9186, http://mundojoven.com; Mon–Fri 10am–7pm, Sat 10am–2pm).

Tequila

The approach to **TEQUILA**, some 70km northwest of Guadalajara, is through great fields of spiky, cactus-like blue agave. It's from these rugged plants that the quintessentially Mexican liquor has been produced since the sixteenth century, with the *indígenas* fermenting its precursor for at least 1500 years before that, a legacy which earned Tequila and its surroundings UNESCO World Heritage status in 2006. The town itself is a pretty enough little place, with its fine church and smattering of bourgeois mansions, but most tourists come to visit the distilleries.

Visiting Tequila is particularly fun during one of its **fiestas**: the town celebrates the **Día de la Santa Cruz** (May 3) with mariachi and plenty of imbibing; and **La Señora de la Salud** (Dec 8) with rodeos, cockfights, fireworks and more drinking. **World Tequila Day** (May 27) is celebrated with parades and drinking, but in Amatitán rather than Tequila itself (arguably, Amatitán was the original centre of "mescal wine" production before the arrival of the railway made Tequila its distribution centre and gave the liquor its modern name).

José Cuervo distillery

José Cuervo 35 (cnr Ramón Corona), north of the main square • Basic tour (45min–1hr) Charge; extended tours (90min–4hr); other experiences cost extra • http://mundocuervo.com

Of all the distillery tours, the slickest is run by José Cuervo in their La Rojeña factory, parts of which date back to 1758. The basic tour makes a quick turn through the factory, where you can taste the surprisingly sweet baked agave and the fiery raw distillate (ABV 55%) which it produces, then continues to the barrel storage area, where you can try a little of the finished product. Extended tours take in all this, give you a chance to sit down and learn how to appreciate the qualities of the various tequilas and include a margarita and a visit to the old storage cellars – it's worth the few extra pesos. At the weekend there are even more extended "VIP" tours, which include chocolate tasting, cellar tours, and tequila blending. Tours in English are run daily but are subject to change dependent on group size (min 5 people required) so check in advance.

Casa Sauza

Luis Navarro 80 • Charge (student discount) • http://casasauza.com

Cuervo's rival proprietary firm, Sauza, offer hour-long tours at their **La Perseverancia** distillery which are a little less stage-managed than Mundo Cuervo but still informative. More expensive tours are also on offer, which take in visits to the botanical garden and agave fields, extra tastings (some including meals) and cellar tours. Casa Sauza is easy to find: just one block south of the Museo Nacional del Tequila and across the road.

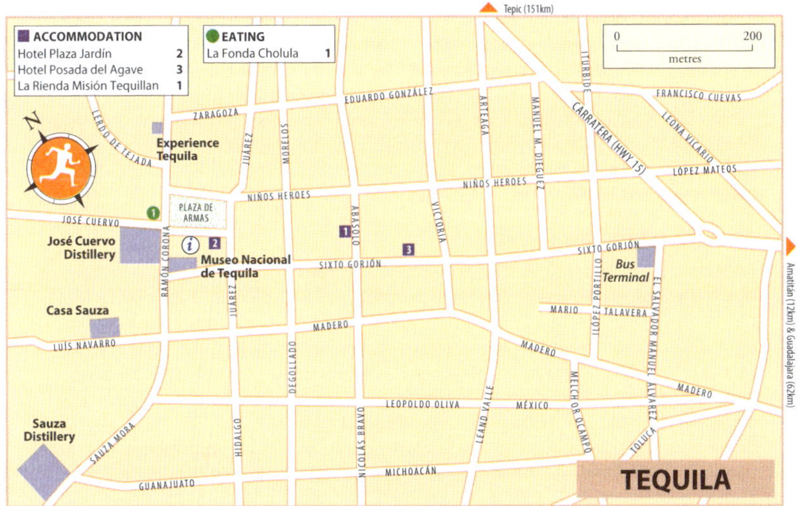

Museo Nacional del Tequila

Ramón Corona 34 • Charge, discount for children • https://tequilajalisco.gob.mx

The small but proud **Museo Nacional del Tequila** is where you can learn about the history of the popular drink and its crucial role in the town's development. The museum has a fine collection of tequila bottles (both ornate and primitive; the two Guinness World Record-holding largest-ever bottles are particularly impressive), old distillery paraphernalia and agave art.

Herradura distillery

Hacienda San José del Refugio, Amatitán, 15km southeast of Tequila on the main road from Guadalajara • Charge • http://herradura.com

For connoisseurs, the serene **Herradura distillery**, in the small town of **Amatitán**, deserves a stop. Buses between Guadalajara and Tequila will set down and pick up on the road 300m from the hacienda. Tour groups here tend to be smaller than at the proprietary distilleries in town (you may even be alone), and you get to see a distillery which uses strictly traditional methods – all of Herradura's tequilas are one hundred percent agave, and their product is considered to be among the best (the real ale of tequilas, if you like). It's also possible to tour the distillery and agave fields in style on the luxury train, *Herradura Express* (departs 10am from Ferromex in Guadalajara).

ARRIVAL AND INFORMATION — TEQUILA

By bus Regular buses run from Guadalajara's Central Vieja (see page 260), and can also be picked up outside the Periférico Sur station, the southern terminus of Guadalajara's Tren Ligero line 1. The bus terminal in Tequila

4

THE TEQUILA EXPRESS AND OTHER TOURS

One of the best ways to experience the Tequila region is to travel there from Guadalajara by train. This is one of only three train rides left in Mexico (the others being the longer Copper Canyon run – see page 482 – and a suburban line in Mexico City – see page 121). You have to travel as part of a tour package and it's obviously touristy, but it gives you a chance to learn something of the process and see how the agave is harvested, and includes a meal and samples.

There are two tours: the **Tequila Express** (http://tequilaexpress.mx) doesn't actually take you to the town of Tequila but travels at a stately pace through blue agave fields and stops at Amatitán, home of Herradura's Hacienda San José del Refugio (see page 270), a tour of which is included. It runs at weekends and holidays. Tickets should be bought, at least a few days in advance, online or in Guadalajara from the Chamber of Commerce cashier department, Vallarta 4095 at Niño Obrero (333 880 9099; Mon–Fri 9am–6pm).

Alternatively, José Cuervo run their own José Cuervo Express during the day at weekends, or on Friday nights. This takes you to Tequila itself, with a tour of the Cuervo distillery (see page 269), and can also be booked in Guadalajara at *Hotel Camino Real*, Vallarta 5005 (http://mundocuervo.com). Most tours can be arranged by your hotel.

SMALLER DISTILLERY TOURS

Aside from the main Tequila distilleries (see page 269), **tours** are also available to smaller, less well-known operations, at prices that vary depending on what's included and how far afield they go. These trips can be a bit hit-or-miss, but when they're good, they can be wonderful experiences with far fewer people and a more personal touch. In Tequila itself, Experience Tequila offers a variety of tours (Ramon Corona 109; 01 503 922 1774 or 155 3060 8242, http://experiencetequila.com). You can also go on an organized trip from Guadalajara such as the Tequila Grand Tour, bookable at their office on López Cotilla 212 (333 952 1774, www.facebook.com/tequila.g.tour). The tour leaves the city daily at 9.15am from Morelos 223 (hotel transfers included) and visits three haciendas: Cuervo, Tres Mujeres and La Cofradia.

MAKING TEQUILA

Visitors to Tequila are often surprised to learn that the town's eponymous spirit is more complex than its reputation lets on. As with alcoholic beverages considered more sophisticated, like champagne, **tequila** is subject to strictly enforced appellation rules: true tequila must be made from at least 51 percent **Weber blue agave** grown in the *Zona Protegida por la Denominación de Origen* – essentially all of Jalisco plus parts of Nayarit, Michoacán, Guanajuato and Tamaulipas. The balance can be made up with alcohol from sugar or corn, but a good tequila will be one hundred percent agave, which gives more intense and flamboyant flavours, and will be stated on the label.

The agave takes seven to ten years to reach an economically harvestable size. The plant is then killed and the spiky leaves cut off, leaving the heart, known as the **piña** for its resemblance to an oversized pineapple. On distillery tours you can see the hearts as they're unloaded from trucks and shoved into ovens, where they're baked for a day or so. On emerging from the ovens, the warm and slightly caramelized *piñas* are crushed and the sweet juice fermented, then distilled.

Tequila isn't a drink that takes well to extended **ageing**, but some time in a barrel definitely benefits the flavour and smoothness. The simplest style of tequila, known as *blanco* or *plata* (white or silver), is clear, and sits just fifteen days in stainless-steel tanks. The *reposado* (rested) spends at least two months in toasted, new white-oak barrels. The degree to which the barrels are **toasted** greatly affects the resulting flavours; a light toast gives spicy notes; a medium toast brings out vanilla and honey flavours; and a deep charring gives chocolate, smoke and roast almond overtones. If left for over a year the tequila becomes *añejo* (old), and typically takes on a darker colour. A fourth style, *joven* (young), is a mix of *blanco* with either *reposado* or *añejo*. While the nuances of tequila are slowly being explored by a select few, the benefits of oak ageing aren't appreciated by all – many still prefer the supple vegetative freshness of a good *blanco*.

is at the eastern end of Sixto Gorjón, along which it's a 750m walk to the Plaza de Armas in the centre of town. Autotransportes Quick buses (from *Sala* B in Guadalajara's Central Vieja) go into the terminal; TequilaPlus buses (from *Sala* A) stop just outside it.

Tourist office In the Presidencia Municipal, José Cuervo 25 on the Plaza de Armas (zócalo) in the centre of town (daily 9am–3.30pm; 374 742 0012).

ACCOMMODATION AND EATING

SEE MAP PAGE 269

La Fonda Cholula Ramón Corona 55, southwest corner of Plaza de Armas; http://conelsazondelagave.com.mx/cholularestaurante. A bright, colourful place to eat right opposite Mundo Cuervo, and indeed run by José Cuervo. They have nice shady rooftop seating and serve respectable *chiles en nogada*. M$$$

Hotel Plaza Jardín José Cuervo 13 (Plaza de Armas, south side); http://hotelplazajardin.com. Right on the main square, this lovely old hotel has a/c rooms, a nice rooftop terrace and its own restaurant and bar. Some of the inside rooms can be a little bit gloomy, however, and only some of the double rooms have views over the plaza. M$$$

Hotel Posada del Agave Sixto Gorjón 83; 374 742 0774. Vibrant orange and lime-green decor make this quite a jolly place, though interior windows mean some of the rooms are a bit dark. All are equipped with ceiling fans and TV. M$$

La Rienda Misión Tequillan Abasolo 47; 374 742 3232. In a quiet spot a couple of blocks back from the noise of Plaza de Armas, this friendly hotel offers simple but charming rooms with old-fashioned decor and terracotta floors, along with TVs, fans and a/c. Tours are available, and there's a little shop on site. M$$

Laguna de Chapala

At around 16km wide and 77km long, **Laguna de Chapala**, just over 50km south of Guadalajara, is the largest lake in Mexico. Its northern shore has long been a favourite retreat for *Tapatíos*, especially since the early years of the twentieth century when dictator Porfirio Díaz regularly spent his holidays here. Expats from north of the border, particularly Canadians, have also been appreciative of the lake scenery and even year-round temperatures. It is said that there are now around thirty thousand such people living in and around Guadalajara, a sizeable proportion of whom have settled on the lakeside – particularly in **Chapala** and in the smaller village of **Ajijic**. The same firm who run the Tequila Grand Tour (see page 270) also operate a day trip to Chapala and Ajijic from Guadalajara. **Peak season** is November to April, which coincides with the arrival of seasonal snowbirds.

Chapala

CHAPALA, on the northern shore of the lake, is a sleepy community with a quiet charm and relaxed pace, but it becomes positively festive on sunny weekends, when thousands come to eat, swim or take a boat ride out to one of the lake's islands. Shoreline restaurants all offer the local speciality, *pescado blanco*, famous despite its almost total lack of flavour and lake-bottom origins. Head to the left along the promenade, past streets of shuttered nineteenth-century villas, and you'll find a small **crafts market**. There's even a flat *ciclopista* (cycle path) running along the lakeside between Chapala and Ajijic for easy cycling and walking, with nice views of the lake; on a hot day it beats taking the bus.

If you're in the mood for a longer walk, you might consider heading up to the cross on the top of the hill overlooking the town: there's a path starting on López Cotilla between no. 316 and no. 318, across the street from *Hotel Candilejas*.

ARRIVAL AND DEPARTURE — CHAPALA

By bus The bus station is on Madero at Miguel Martinez. Turn left at the exit and from here, the main street, Madero, stretches six blocks down to the lakeside, where Ramón Corona leads off to the left. The main square is halfway down Madero, where López Cotillo crosses it (take a left here to reach Juárez and then Zaragoza, both parallel with Madero). Hidalgo, the road to Ajijic, branches off Madero to the right just beyond the main square. Coming from Guadalajara's Central Vieja (*Sala* A), it's best to take a *directo* service (every 30–45min, 6am–9pm; 45min) rather than the second-class bus (every 20min; 1hr 30min), which stops at every little village along the way. The last *directo* bus back to Guadalajara leaves Chapala at 7.30pm. Buses to Ajijic (15min) and San Juan Cosalá (25min) leave from the bus station every 20min, and can also be picked up along Hidalgo, as can slower local buses to the same destinations.

ACCOMMODATION

Hotel Montecarlo Hidalgo 296 (1km west of Madero); https://hotelmontecarlo.hotelesudg.com. A modern resort hotel by the lakeside (though fenced off from it), which offers tennis courts, a pool, lake views and airy rooms amid grounds with grass and trees. M$$$

★ **Quinta Quetzalcoatl** Zaragoza 307; https://villaqqhotel.com. The nicest option in town, where D.H. Lawrence wrote *The Plumed Serpent*. There's a wide assortment of gorgeous rooms, each with its own private terrace, set in a lovely garden with a small pool; children are not allowed, and in winter particularly, you should book well ahead. M$$$

Villa Samary Morelos 199; 376 765 3960. A cheerful little yellow-and-blue guesthouse, with homely, if dated, rooms set around a small, leafy courtyard. Owner Maria is very accommodating, which makes up for the spotty wi-fi and lack of a/c – rooms have small, old TVs. M$

LAGUNA DE CHAPALA ENVIRONMENTAL PROBLEMS

The Laguna de Chapala averages only 8m deep, and during the 1980s and 1990s the **water level** dropped when the government used its feeder rivers as a freshwater supply for Guadalajara and Mexico City; the lake receded so far that shoreline property was 2km from the water's edge. Levels have now improved thanks to heavier rainfall and the work of the twenty thousand-strong group Amigos del Lago de Chapalabut agricultural runoff has raised **nitrate pollution** to unsustainable levels and encouraged the growth of choking water hyacinth. The *charales*, the fish for which the lake was once famed, are virtually gone.

EATING

Café Paris Madero 421; 376 765 5353. A central café with outside tables, very popular among American expats and locals alike for good breakfasts and reasonably priced *comidas*, as well as great booths for people-watching. M$$

Cazadores Ramon Corona 18, at the lakeside end of Madero; 376 765 2162. *Cazadores* has been serving hearty surf-and-turf dinners amid the faded elegance of a grand mansion since 1956. A *filete Malinche* (steak with onion and *chile poblano* sauce) won't set you back too much, and a fish fillet with all the trimmings is even more affordable. M$$

Chapala's Fonda Paseo de los Ausentes 621, under the portales of the main square; 376 765 4380. A good old no-nonsense Mexican diner dishing out big portions of tasty *chilaquiles* (a bargain with just beans, but a little more when you add chicken), breakfasts, soups and *antojitos*. M$

DIRECTORY

Banks and exchange A gaggle of banks with ATMs gathers around the junction of Madero and Hidalgo, and there's a money changer at Madero 423-A.

Laundry Zaragoza 341, on the corner of López Cotilla.

Post office Degollado 323, near the corner with Guerrero.

Telephones Caseta telefónica at Encarnacion Rosas 10, just off the main square.

Ajijic

With its narrow cobbled streets, **AJIJIC**, 11km west of Chapala, is smaller, quieter and more self-consciously arty. It may be a wonderful place to paint or retire, with a thriving expat social and cultural life, but as a visitor you're likely to exhaust its charms in a couple of hours – long enough to wander by the lake, visit the art galleries, have a meal and perhaps check out the **Casa de Cultura**, on the north side of the plaza, which hosts musical performances and art exhibitions. The large expat community also means there are apartments and houses to rent for longer stays; check out the notice boards in shops and galleries.

4

ARRIVAL AND DEPARTURE — AJIJIC

By bus Slow local buses from Chapala (every 30min) will drop you in the centre, whereas larger buses (every 20min) will leave you on the Carretera Chapala, from where Colón runs six blocks southward to the lake, with the main square halfway along it.

ACCOMMODATION

Hotel Italo Guadalipe Victoria 8, two blocks east of the main square; 376 766 2221. Not tremendously welcoming, but a decent bet for the price, with a good Italian restaurant (see below), although the bells of the church next door ring every hour – light sleepers will want to try elsewhere. M$

Mis Amores Hidalgo 22, one block west of the main square; 376 766 4642. One of the best picks in town, and Ajijic's answer to a contemporary boutique hotel, with tasteful decor, individual terraces shaded by banana trees and a warm proprietor; advance booking is advisable. Continental breakfast included. Rooms are extra on Fri & Sat, and it's advisable to book well ahead for weekend stays. M$$

La Nueva Posada Donato Guerra 9, by the lake, four blocks east of Colón; http://hotelnuevaposada.com. An eclectically decorated, welcoming place that feels like a grand hotel, with large rooms, lovely gardens, an excellent restaurant (see below), small pool and distant water views. Ten percent discount if you pay cash (pesos or dollars). Breakfast included. M$$$

EATING

If you're **eating** on a tight budget, head for the makeshift family-run *sopes* stands around the plaza, where you can dine heartily. Food on offer will include **hearty soups** with freshly chopped onions and cilantro, as well as *antojitos* of various sorts, and the usual hot or cold drinks.

La Casa del Cafe Colón, a block before the lake; 376 766 2876. A delightful coffee house where you can select your own beans from a variety of Latin American origin, before kicking back in their big comfortable chairs and watching the locals and tourists stroll by on the cobbles outside. *Chilaquiles* for breakfast are particularly good, especially the chipotle variety. M$$

Hotel Italo Guadalipe Victoria 8; 376 766 2221. The restaurant here serves up a variety of authentic pizzas and pasta dishes, and claims to use "original Italian ingredients". The daily specials are usually good. M$$

La Nueva Posada Donato Guerra 9; http://hotelnueva posada.com. A lovely restaurant with lake views, where you can sit down to *sopa azteca* followed by pork chops with port and cranberry sauce, or grilled salmon with Grand Marnier and balsamic glaze, all done to perfection. M$$

South towards the coast

Some of the most delightful subalpine scenery in Mexico lies southwest of Laguna de Chapala, on the road to Colima. You'll miss much of it if you stick to the speedy toll road (Hwy-54), though even that has its exciting moments as it passes the Zona de Montaña: the following places are all reached from the far slower, far more attractive, if bumpier, old road plied by second-class buses.

Tapalpa

The town of **TAPALPA**, 120km southwest of Guadalajara, makes an ideal base for a few days of relaxation amid upland pastures and pine forests. It is reached via a steep, winding road off the old highway, which climbs continuously until it crests a 2300m ridge at **El Balcón**. If you're driving, stop here to check out the view back down the valley (on a bus, it's on the left if coming up to Tapalpa) and to feel the near-constant steady breeze, a phenomenon that drew World Cup paragliding events in 2002 and 2004.

Pretty little Tapalpa, 10km further on, lies amid magnificent surroundings – ranch country and tree-clad hills that are often covered in a gentle mist. With a population of only around sixteen thousand, there's a village feel to it, especially around the plaza. Here you'll find eighteenth-century wooden-balconied houses, encircling *portales* and two impressive **churches** – the larger with an unusually plain brick interior. On the outskirts, clusters of cabañas dot the woods luring upwardly mobile *Tapatíos*, and a fair bit of desirable real estate has sprung up in recent years.

Tapalpa is on the Guadalajara weekender circuit, so try to visit midweek when its old-world charm is little affected (although hotels remain pricey). The town centres around a stunningly picturesque main square, where several old buildings have been refurbished as restaurants and hotels. The place gets very cold in winter, and even summer nights can become chilly, but people brew their own mescal, which may help warm you up.

ARRIVAL AND INFORMATION — TAPALPA

By bus Buses to and from Guadalajara, Ciudad Guzman and Sayula, among other destinations, stop at the modern Autobuses Sur de Jalisco at Juan Gil Preciado 11, a 10min walk north of the main square along the main road.

Destinations Ciudad Guzmán (2 daily; 2hr 50min); Guadalajara's Central Vieja (12 daily; 3hr); Sayula (2 daily; 1hr).

Tourist information Tourist office, Morelos 10, on the north side of the main square (daily 9am–3pm; 343 432 0650 ext. 125,). For more information see http://visitmexico.com/en/jalisco/tapalpa.

Banks and exchange There's a Banorte with ATM at Matamoros 1 in the southeast corner of the main plaza.

ACCOMMODATION

Tapalpa's general shortage of **accommodation** isn't usually a problem during the week, when there shouldn't be too many visitors, but all rooms are often taken at weekends and around the **fiesta** for the Día de la Virgen de Guadalupe (Dec 12), when the town attracts pilgrims from far and wide.

La Casa de Maty Matamoros 69, south side of main square; http://lacasadematy.com.mx. This is the pick of the pricier places to stay in town; its comfortable, rustic rooms, each with a fireplace, are set around a beautiful plant-filled courtyard with a fountain. M$$$

Real Carretero Agustin Yáñez 12 (half a block east of the main square); http://realcahotel.com. Lovely rooms in an old nineteenth-century colonial building, which combine modern amenities (flatscreen TV, modern tiled bathrooms) with period features like lovely ceiling beams, wooden shutters and exposed brickwork. M$$

Villa de San José Cerrada Ignacio López 91, one block

WALKS AROUND TAPALPA

There's good **walking** in almost any direction from Tapalpa, with plenty of wildlife, especially birds, to spot; black vultures (urubu birds) are often seen soaring on the thermals. You can also hire horses (look for the signs) for the popular ride to the local waterfall. One especially pleasant hike is to **Las Piedrotas** (5km; around 1hr each way), which follows a decent but little-used road towards Chiquilistlán (marked as you enter Tapalpa). It passes the romantic ruins of an old water-driven paper mill, and climbs towards a gorgeous valley of pasturelands, studded with wild flowers and huge boulders. If you don't fancy walking both ways, get a taxi to drop you off (from opposite the bus office on Ignacio López), and walk back.

southeast of the main square; 343 432 0451. A pretty little hotel with lots of country-style charm, and rooms with warm wooden floors. M$$

EATING

Numerous **restaurants** around the main plaza serve plain country food. Look out for places selling *ponche de granada*, a local wine made from pomegranates (you can usually find it in the *mercado artesanal* west of the main square). Tapalpa is also a good place to try *queso fundido*, as the farms hereabouts produce good cheese.

Los Girasoles Obregón 110, off the southwest corner of the main square; 343 432 0086. A good restaurant for treats such as chile stuffed with cheese and plantains in green coriander and *chipotle* sauce, or breast of chicken with mushrooms and brown rice. They also do their own charcuterie. M$$

Paulinos Morelos 8, north side of the main square; 343 432 0109. With its balcony overlooking the main square, this is a nice spot to watch the town come awake over *huevos rancheros*, or to tuck into a T-bone. M$$

La Villa Raúl Quintero 93, southeast corner of the main square; 343 432 1428. Open since 1950, this bar-restaurant with a lazy terrace on the square is an excellent place to enjoy a sundowner, but they also do food such as *sabanitas al gratin* (a slice of beef, ham and cheese), or *huevos rancheros*. M$$

4

Ciudad Guzmán

The birthplace of José Clemente Orozco, **CIUDAD GUZMÁN** is a busy little town thoroughly steeped in local culture, with attractive colonnaded streets in the centre. The centre of the main plaza is a bandstand with a replica of Orozco's *Man of Fire* mural from Guadalajara (see page 253). As ever, almost everything of interest is on or around the plaza, where you'll find banks, phones and places to stay.

Museo Arqueológico de Ciudad Guzmán

Ángel Gonzalez 21, off Reforma, a block west of the main plaza • Charge, free Sun • 341 124 7395

The pleasant and well laid-out little town museum, the **Museo Arqueológico de Ciudad Guzmán** is really just one room, but there are some lovely clay figures and animals in the collection of local archeology.

ARRIVAL AND DEPARTURE — CIUDAD GUZMÁN

By bus Central de Autobuses is 2km west of town. Local buses (#6b and, less directly, #5a) run from outside to Reforma and the main plaza; to get back to the Central pick them up on the west side of the plaza by Portal Morelos 85 (Plaza Anita).

Destinations Colima (10 daily; 1hr); Guadalajara's Central Nueva (24 daily; 2hr); Guadalajara's Central Vieja (13 daily; 3hr 30min); Manzanillo (8 daily; 3hr); Mexico City (2 overnight; 8–9hr); Tapalpa (4 daily; 1hr 30min).

ACCOMMODATION

Hotel Flamingos Federico del Toro 133, a block north of the main plaza; http://hotelflamingos.com.mx. A concrete block with large, functional, starkly lit rooms all with TVs; perfectly fine, if in need of a revamp. M$

Hotel Zapotlán Federico del Toro 34, west side of the main plaza; https://hotelzapotlan.mx. Stylish old hotel set around a beautiful glasshouse-like covered courtyard with palms, creepers and three tiers of cast-iron landings.

Rooms at the top get more light, so they cost a little bit more, and the ceiling fans are quite low in some rooms, so watch your head. In the new block, behind the pool and outdoor jacuzzi, are some larger, more deluxe and considerably more expensive executive rooms, with a/c and private jacuzzis. M$$

EATING AND DRINKING

You can have an inexpensive and healthy **breakfast** with cereal and fresh juice at the stands behind the church in the main square, where you can also get soups and other simple meals. The salty local cheeses are a treat and can be bought at the daily market near the stalls.

Juanito Federico del Toro 61-B, west side of the main plaza; 341 412 0039. The main dishes in this large diner aren't great bargains (steak *tampiqueña* for example), but the set menu is, featuring dishes like *sopa de arroz* and *bistec a la Mexicana*, and it's also a good place for breakfast. M$$

Los Portales Refugio Barragán del Toscano 32, one block south of the main plaza; 341 412 4073. Delicious, reasonably priced breakfasts and Mexican main dishes in a Moorish-style courtyard alive with plants and set around a central fountain. Fish fillet Colima (stuffed with prawn and octopus) is a top pick here, as is the steak *tampiqueña*. M$$

Tacos Valente Federico del Toro 31-A, west side of the main plaza; 341 410 6627. A slightly clinical environment is more than made up for by the best tacos in town, with beef, pork or bean varieties going for a bargain. You can also enjoy these in the form of a torta instead. M$

Northwestern Michoacán

4

From Guadalajara, the most direct route to Mexico City heads through the major junction of La Piedad and continues east towards Irapuato. If you can afford to dawdle a while, though, it's infinitely more rewarding to follow the slower, southern road through Zamora and Morelia, spending a couple of days in Uruapan and Pátzcuaro. From Uruapan, Hwy-37 slices south through the mountains to the Pacific coast at Lázaro Cárdenas (see page 216).

Uruapan

URUAPAN, they say, means "the place where flowers bloom" in the Tarascan language, though *Appleton's Guide* for 1884 tells a different story: "The word Uruapan comes from *Urani*, which means in the Tarasc language 'a chocolate cup', because the Indigenous people in this region devote themselves to manufacture and painting of these objects." Demand for chocolate cups, presumably, has fallen since then, but whatever the truth, the modern version is certainly appropriate: Uruapan, lower (at around 1600m) and warmer than most of its neighbours, enjoys a steamy subtropical climate and is surrounded by thick forests and lush parks.

Plaza Morelos

The animated **Plaza Morelos**, a long strip of tree-shaded open space, is in every sense the heart of Uruapan. It's surrounded by everything of importance: shops, market, banks, principal churches and many of the hotels. This is the place to head first, either to find somewhere to stay or simply to get a feel for the town. The **Casa de la Cultura**, in the northwest of the plaza, was renovated in 2016 and hosts regular cultural events, exhibitions, concerts and dance performances, as well as summer schools for local children.

Museo Indígena Huatapera

Plaza Morelos • Free • 452 524 3434

The town's only overt tourist attraction is **La Huatapera**, one of the oldest surviving buildings in Uruapan, which has been exquisitely restored to house the **Museo Indígena Huatapera**, a small display of arts and crafts from the state's four Indigenous peoples: the Purépecha, the Nahua, the Otomí and the Mazahua. Look out for particularly fine Purépecha lacquerware gourds, and a Nahua harp with its lute-like acoustic box, as well as beaten copperware from Santa Clara del Cobre (see page 290).

The small courtyard and adjoining chapel were built by Juan de San Miguel, the Franciscan friar who founded the town itself, and were later adopted by Bishop Quiroga as a hospital and training centre. The carvings around the windows bear a marked Arab influence, as they were crafted by Christianized Moorish artisans from Spain (Mudéjares).

MICHOACÁN INFORMATION

The Michoacán state tourism department's website is https://visitmichoacan.com.mx. This chapter covers the whole of Michoacán except for the coastal region, which is covered in Chapter 8 (see page 462).

Mercado de Antojitos

Half a block north of the plaza, on the west side of the Museo de las Cuatro Pueblos Indígenas, and accessible via an alley

The **Mercado de Antojitos** is a large open **market** section, where women serve up meals for stallholders and visitors alike at a series of long, open-air tables. Here you'll find the cheapest, and very often the freshest and best, food in town – this is a great place to sample the salty regional cheese, *adobada*. The rest of the market, with herb and fruit stalls but mostly clothes, shoes and CDs, sprawls along Corregidora and Constitución.

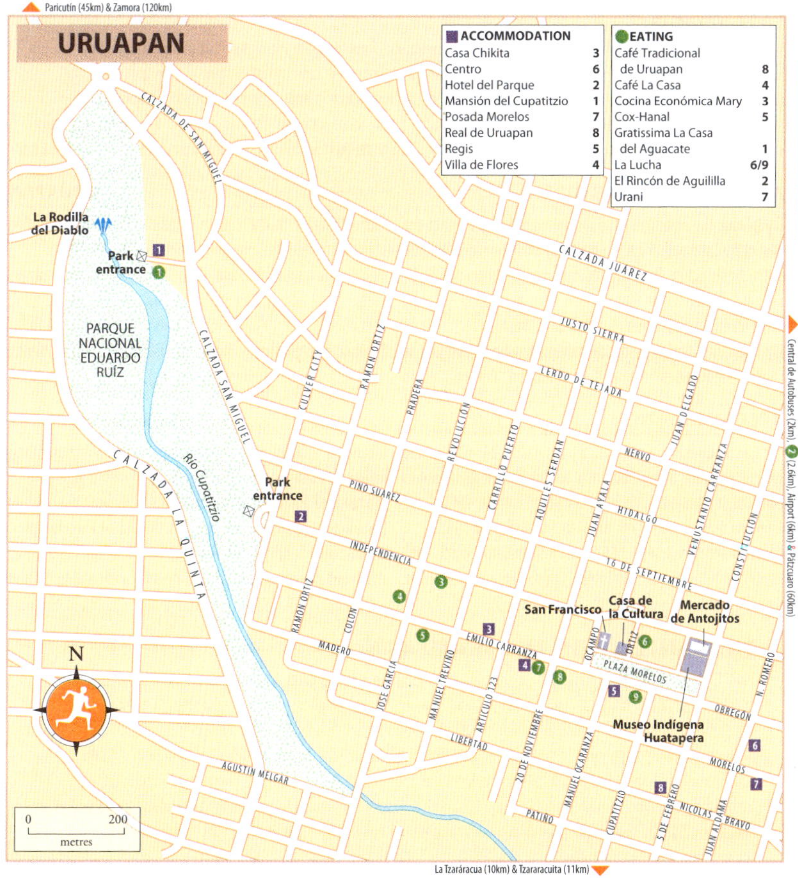

4

Parque Nacional Eduardo Ruíz

Calzada de San Miguel, 1km from the plaza on the northwestern edge of downtown • Charge, discount for children aged 3–9

Comprising just fifty acres, the **Parque Nacional Eduardo Ruíz** (or Parque Nacional Barranca Cupatitzio) is far more compact than national parks you may be used to elsewhere. As much (luxuriant and tropical) city park as national, it remains one of Uruapan's proudest assets. The Río Cupatitzio flows through in a little gorge, via a series of man-made cascades and fountains. The river springs from a rock known as *La Rodilla del Diablo* ("the Devil's knee"); according to legend, water gushed forth after the Devil knelt here in submission before the unswerving Christian faith of the drought-ridden population. Alternatively, it is said that the Devil met the Virgin Mary while out strolling in the park, and dropped to his knees in respect. *Cupatitzio* means "where the waters meet", though it's invariably translated as "the river that sings" – another appropriate, if not entirely accurate, tag.

Locals come here to stroll the cobbled footpaths betweens stands of banana plants, gaze at the cascades (particularly good during or just after rain), catch trout and eat at assorted restaurants and taco stands. There are two entrances, one at the end of Independencia (take a bus along here if you don't feel like walking), and one up by the *Mansión del Cupatitzio* hotel, with a string of crafts stalls along Calzada de San Miguel between them.

La Tzarárracua

12km to the south of central Uruapan • Open access • Bus ("Tzarárracua") from the south side of the plaza at Cupatitzio (hourly)

4

The river crashes over the waterfall of **La Tzarárracua**, an impressive 25m plunge amid beautiful forest scenery. This is also a popular outing with locals, especially at weekends, so if you don't fancy taking the bus, you could share a taxi. If it seems too crowded here, make for the smaller falls, **Tzararacuita**, about 1km further downstream.

ARRIVAL AND DEPARTURE URUAPAN

By plane The airport is 4km southeast of the centre, at the end of Av Latinoamericana, served by bus #66 from Hidalgo with Constitución. The only destinations currently served by scheduled passenger flights from here are Los Angeles (1 weekly; 4hr) and Tijuana (1 daily; 3hr 20min).

By bus The Central de Autobuses is 3km northeast of the centre; local buses from outside (marked "Centro") go to Plaza Morelos in the centre of town. Taxis from the bus station operate on a prepaid system to the *centro*.

Destinations Guadalajara (frequent; 4hr 30min); Lázaro Cárdenas (2 hourly; 3hr 30min); Leon (1 daily; 5hr 30min); Mexico City Pte (9 daily; 6hr); Mexico City Nte (10 daily; 5–6hr); Morelia (every 15min; 2hr); Paracho (every 20min; 45min); Pátzcuaro (every 15min; 1hr).

ACCOMMODATION SEE MAP PAGE 277

★ **Casa Chikita** Carranza 32-A; 452 524 4174. This welcoming B&B in a nineteenth-century house done out in colonial style has lovely, high-ceilinged rooms, set around an open central courtyard. Breakfast included. M$$$

Centro Aldama 3; 452 144 0800. A family-run place with simple but clean rooms, all with bathrooms and hot water, arranged around two sunny courtyards; nothing fancy, rather spartan in fact – but friendly and cheap. M$

Hotel del Parque Independencia 124, near the Parque Nacional; 452 524 3845. This is the best of the cheapies: clean and friendly, with large en-suite rooms (those at the front are nicest but can be noisy), wi-fi, cable TV and

THE DANCE OF THE LITTLE OLD MEN

The **Danza de los Viejitos**, or the **Dance of the Little Old Men**, is the most famous of Michoacán's traditional dances. It is also one of its most picturesque, with the performers (usually children), dressed in baggy white cotton and masked as old men, alternating between parodying the tottering steps of the *viejitos* they represent and breaking into complex routines. Naturally enough, there's a lot of music, too. You'll see the dance performed at festive occasions all over Michoacán, but the finest expression is at the guitar-making town of Paracho, 50km south of Zamora.

URUAPAN FIESTAS

The most exciting and interesting local fiestas are: Año Nuevo (Jan 1), when the Danza de los Viejitos (see page 278) is performed; Palm Sunday (the week before Easter), the culmination of a week's celebration when the *indígenas* collect palms from the hills and make ornaments from the leaves; Día de María Magdalena (July 22), when there's a procession of animals through the streets; Día de San Francisco (Oct 4), one of the year's biggest saint's day celebrations; and the Feria del Aguacate (Nov/Dec), a three-week avocado fair with agricultural exhibits and artesanía displays.

parking facilities. M$$

Mansión del Cupatitzio Calzada Rodilla del Diablo 20, at the northern end of the Parque Nacional Eduardo Ruíz; http://hotelmansiondelcupatitzio.com. Uruapan's finest hotel, with superb service, a pool, terrace restaurant and beautiful grounds full of plants and flowers. The hotel is conveniently adjacent to the entrance to the national park. Wheelchair accessible with an adapted room. M$$$

Posada Morelos Morelos 30; 452 523 2302. This secure, family-run hotel set around a pleasant courtyard has single rooms with shared bathroom facilities for those on a budget, and slightly pricier en-suite options. Rooms adjoining the street can be noisy. M$

Real de Uruapan Nicolas Bravo 110; http://hotelrealdeuruapan.com. Nine-storey international-style hotel with carpeted rooms, each with TV and phone. The top floor is occupied by the restaurant (see below), with the standard rooms on the lower floors, superior rooms (with queen-size beds and better views, but otherwise the same) on the next few floors, and junior suites on the eighth floor. M$$$

Regis Portal Carillo 12; http://hotelregis.com.mx. Friendly place in a central location featuring characterful rooms with the accompaniment of twittering caged birds. Parking is available and some rooms overlook the plaza (though that can make them noisy). M$$

★ **Villa de Flores** Emilio Carranza 15; 452 523 5620. Set in a lovely colonial villa, this friendly hotel offers atmospheric rooms gathered around two shaded courtyards. The high ceilings and stone floors can make things a little chilly at night, but the traditional wrought-iron lanterns and carved wood furniture more than make up for it. Good value, too. M$

4

EATING

SEE MAP PAGE 277

★ **Café Tradicional de Uruapan** Carranza 5; 452 523 5680. This Uruapan institution serves great breakfasts, superb local coffee, ice cream, cakes, *antojitos*, *pozole* and a decent range of herbal and fruit teas, including an intriguing take on the piña colada. The window seating's bright and airy, the interior a bit darker. M$$

★ **Café La Casa** Revolución 3; 452 524 3611. Charming courtyard café-cum-cocktail lounge that's good for a coffee during the day or a tequila in the evening, when it becomes a bit of a hangout. Food includes cheesesteak baguettes and delicious wood-oven pizzas. M$$$$

Cocina Económica Mary Independencia 63; 452 519 4869. A good, low-priced restaurant offering wholesome home-style cooking at low prices. They do good breakfasts, and their *comidas corridas* usually have a decent choice of *guisados* (main courses), but their coffee isn't great. M$$

Cox-Hanal Carranza 31-A; 452 524 6152. Yucatán-style *antojitos* (M$12 tacos include *cochinita pibil* and chicken *chimole*), plus ice-cold beers, all at low prices and in clean surroundings, generally getting livelier as the evening wears on. M$$

Gratissima La Casa del Aguacate Rodilla del Diablo 13; http://gratissima.mx. A cosy, if somewhat gloomy, café-restaurant overlooking the lush foliage and waterfalls of the Parque Nacional, which serves up healthy breakfasts, smoothies and salads alongside heartier hamburgers, rib-eye steaks and trout dishes. Often to a soundtrack of live guitar music. M$$$

La Lucha Garcia Ortiz 22; 452 688 2688, www.facebook.com/cafelaluchaoficial. A small café that's been going since the Revolution, La Lucha now has several branches in town but this spot is the original; still serving up great local coffee and home-made cakes the traditional way. M$

El Rincón de Aguilila Chiapas 367; http://elrincondeaguililla.com. The finest restaurant in Uruapan serves hearty, reasonable breakfasts (try the delicious *barbacoa de res*) and a huge menu of comidas which includes superb seafood and, in particular, steak. M$$$

Urani Juárez 116; http://heladosurani.com. Local branch of the nationwide coffee shop-restaurant, which offers a wide-ranging menu throughout the day, with crêpes, paninis and other light bites on offer alongside decent coffee and ice cream. There are a couple of other branches around town. M$$

DIRECTORY

Banks and exchange Numerous banks with ATMs lie along Cupatitzio, a block or so south of the plaza, and there are *casas de cambio* (for US dollars only) at Portal Degollado 15 in the northeast corner of the plaza and at Carranza 14-D, just west of Juan Ayala.

Telephones There's a *caseta telefónica* at Manuel Ocaranza 3, just south of the plaza, plus one on the west side of Plaza Morelos.

Paricutín

An ideal day trip from Uruapan, the "new" **volcano of Paricutín**, about 40km northwest of town, gives you an unusual taste of the surrounding countryside. On February 20, 1943, a Purépecha peasant working in his fields noticed the earth rumble and then smoke. The ground soon cracked and lava began to flow to the surface. Over a period of several years, it engulfed the village of Paricutín and several other hamlets, forcing the evacuation of some seven thousand inhabitants. The volcano was active for eight years, producing a cone some 400m high and devastating an area of around twenty square kilometres. Now there are vast fields of lava (mostly cooled, though there are still a few hot spots), black and powdery, cracked into harsh jags, along with the dead cone and crater. Most bizarrely, a church tower – all that remains of the buried hamlet of San Juan Parangaricutiro – pokes its head through the surface. The volcano wasn't all bad news, though: during its active life the eruptions spread a fine layer of dust – effectively a fertilizer – on the fields that escaped the full lava flow, and drew tourists from around the world. It is still popular, especially on Sundays, when adventurous souls from Uruapan come out to explore the atmospheric slopes of the volcano and the ruined church.

4

To see much of Paricutín you really need to set aside a day. You'll want to leave Uruapan early (say 7am or 8am) so you get as much of the hiking as possible done in the cool of the day and catch the ruined church in the morning light. It's also a good idea to take food and drink as there is very little available in Angahuan.

Angahuan

The volcano of Paricutín is visited from the small and very traditional Purépecha village of **Angahuan**, where the women still wear heavily pleated satin skirts with an embroidered apron and a shawl.

The church

On the **plaza**, the **church** warrants a second glance. Built in the sixteenth century, its doorway was carved in the largely Arab Mudéjar style by Andalusian artisans. The cross in the courtyard, on the other hand, is most definitely Mexican, complete with serpents, a skull and other pre-Hispanic motifs. In the street to the right of the church (as you look at it), across from the side gate of the courtyard, a door lintel has been turned into a kind of lava frieze of the volcano and church tower.

The Centro Turistico

Camino al Volcan Paricutín, Col Angahuan – from the plaza, head down Juárez (opposite the church) for about 200m to an ornately carved wooden house on the left (opposite no. 16); veer left here (not signposted) and head straight on for 1km • Charge

The **Centro Turístico de Angahuan** offers superb views of the volcano from its mirador, has a small museum on the creation of the volcano and local Purépecha culture, and includes a decent restaurant.

ARRIVAL AND DEPARTURE — PARICUTÍN

By bus Buses leave from the Central de Autobuses in Uruapan (every 30min, 5am–8pm; 40min). They drop you on the highway by Angahuan, a 10min walk from the village's main plaza.

By car Take the main road from Uruapan to Los Reyes; the turn-off for Angahuan is well signposted.

ACCOMMODATION

Centro Turístico Camino al Volcan Paricutín, Col Angahuan; www.volcanparicutin.com.mx. In a beautiful

PARICUTÍN BY HORSE

Getting off the bus in Angahuan, and in the village, and on the way to the Centro Turístico, you'll meet people offering to guide you or take you on **horseback**; it's not a bad idea to hire a **guide**, as the paths through the lava are numerous and can be difficult to follow. Prices fluctuate with demand, but you can probably expect to pay a reasonable amount for a guide for the day, plus another fee for each horse (one for the guide plus one for each tourist). A return trip to the cone of the volcano will take about eight hours, either on foot or on horseback. If you just want to see the ruined church, a couple of hours will suffice (and rates for guides and horses will be rather cheaper). The horse trail is easier than the walking trail, though it finishes at the base of the main cone, leaving you to tackle the final steep climb on your own.

location among aromatic pine trees, the Centro Turístico offers concrete cabins for four or six people, each with a bathroom and open fire, or rooms for up to three people, again with bathrooms. There's also camping. Doubles, 6-bed cabins and 4-bed cabins are available. M$$

Tinganio (Tingambato)

Charge • Buses between Uruapan and Pátzcuaro (every 15min in each direction) pass right by the site; by car take the *cuota* highway from Uruapan towards Pátzcuaro then the Zirahuén exit and follow the *libre* road past Ajuno to Tingambato – it lies approximately 40km west of Pátzcuaro

4

The small but pretty and well-restored pre-Hispanic ruin of **TINGANIO** is roughly halfway between Uruapan and Pátzcuaro, in a town that is now called **Tingambato**. First inhabited around 450–600 AD, the site grew massively between 650 and 900 AD. Teotihuacán's influence is evident in the architecture, especially in the pyramid dominating the religious area, which overlooks a plaza with a cruciform altar. The adjacent ball-court, on the other hand, betrays Toltec influence in its design. Beyond it, a grove of avocado trees hides an unexcavated pyramid. In the residential area just to the north, a sunken plaza with two altars and five stairways, each to a separate residence, is very much in the style of Teotihuacán, but the tomb under the largest residence (which the caretaker will open on request) has a false dome suggestive of Maya influence. Surrounded by beautiful countryside, the site is best appreciated from atop the pyramid. Except on Sundays, you won't see many other visitors here.

Pátzcuaro

PÁTZCUARO is almost exactly halfway between Uruapan and Morelia, some 60km from both, yet strikingly different from either, boasting both fine colonial architecture and a rich Indigenous culture. Sitting on **Lago de Pátzcuaro** (see page 286), Mexico's most beautiful lake, it hosts spectacular Day of the Dead celebrations (see page 288). Although the outskirts of Pátzcuaro straggle about 3km or so down to the lakeshore, the centre of town is very small, focusing on the two main squares, Plaza Vasco de Quiroga (or Plaza Grande) and Plaza Gertrudis Bocanegra (Plaza Chica).

More than anywhere else in the state, Pátzcuaro owes its position to **Bishop Vasco de Quiroga** (see page 283), whose affection for the area's Indigenous peoples led him to settle in the Purépechan heartland on the shores of Lago de Pátzcuaro. It was he who decided, in the face of considerable opposition from the Spaniards in Morelia (then known as Valladolid), to build the cathedral here, where it would be centrally located. Although subsequent bishops moved the seat of power back to Morelia, the foundation had been laid for the community's continued success. Pátzcuaro enjoyed a building boom in the sixteenth century and has been of secondary industrial and political importance ever since. Throughout the centre are old mansions with balconies and coats of arms, barely touched since those early years. Today, quaint Pátzcuaro has developed into an upmarket and artistically inclined town with numerous boutiques. You can spend hours wandering around the beautiful – and expensive – arts, crafts and antique shops, aimed mainly at visitors from Mexico City and abroad.

Plaza Gertrudis Bocanegra and Plaza Vasco de Quiroga

Nothing much worth seeing in Pátzcuaro lies more than a few minutes' walk from **Plaza Gertrudis Bocanegra**, named after a local Independence heroine, and **Plaza**

VASCO DE QUIROGA – THE NOBLE CONQUISTADOR

When the Spaniards arrived in Michoacán in 1519, they found the region dominated by the **Purépechan** people – whom they named **Tarascans** – whose chief town, Tzintzuntzán, lay on the shores of Lago de Pátzcuaro. The Tarascan civilization, a serious rival to the Aztecs before the Conquest, had a widespread reputation for excellence in the arts, especially metalworking and feathered ornaments. Though the Tarascans submitted peaceably to the Spaniards in 1522 and their leader converted to Christianity, they did not avoid the massacres and mass torture that **Nuño de Guzmán** meted out in his attempts to fully pacify the region. Guzmán's methods were overly brutal, even by colonial standards, and an elderly Spanish nobleman-turned-priest, **Vasco de Quiroga**, was appointed bishop to the area in an attempt to restore harmony. He succeeded beyond all expectations, securing his reputation as a champion of the native peoples – a reputation that persists today. He coaxed the native population down from the mountains to which they had fled, established self-sufficient agricultural settlements and set up missions to teach practical skills as well as religion. The effects of his actions have survived in a very visible way for, despite some blurring in objects produced for the tourist trade, each village still has its own craft speciality: lacquerware in Uruapan, guitars in Paracho, copper goods in Santa Clara del Cobre, to name but a few.

Vasco de Quiroga. The finest of Pátzcuaro's mansions are on the latter, especially the seventeenth-century **Casa del Gigante**, with its hefty pillars and crudely carved figures. Another nearby mansion is said to have been inhabited by Prince Huitzimengari, son of the last Tarascan king. Both are privately owned, however, and not open to visitors.

4

Biblioteca

Plaza Bocanegra • Free

There are more luxurious houses on the Plaza Bocanegra, but the most striking building is the **Biblioteca**, with its rough-hewn wooden barrel ceiling. The former sixteenth-century church of San Agustín, it has been converted into a library and decorated with **murals** by **Juan O'Gorman** depicting the history of Michoacán, notably Nuño de Guzmán burning alive the leader of the Tarascans. O'Gorman (1905–82) possessed a prodigious talent, and is one of the muralists who inherited the mantle of Rivera and Orozco: his best-known work is the decoration of the interior of Chapultepec Castle in Mexico City (see page 96).

Basílica de Nuestra Señora de la Salud

Plazuela de la Basilica • Free • 434 342 0055

East of the Plaza Bocanegra, Quiroga's cathedral – the **Basílica de Nuestra Señora de la Salud**, or **Colegiata** – was intended to be Pátzcuaro's masterpiece, with space for thirty thousand worshippers. A massive structure for such a small town, it was never completed, and the existing basilica, finished in the nineteenth century, is only the nave of the original design. Even so, it is often full, for local people continue to revere Quiroga: the first chapel on the left as you walk in the main entrance is the **Mausoleo de Don Vasco**, the doors typically closed and adorned with notes of thanks for his miraculous interventions. The church also possesses a miraculous healing image of the Virgin, crafted in a traditional Tarascan method out of *pasta de caña*, a gum-like modelling paste made principally from maize. Services here are extraordinary, especially for the town's patron saint, the Virgin de la Salud, on December 8.

Museo de Artes y Oficios and around

Cnr of Alcantarilla and Enseñanza • Charge

The **Museo de Artes y Oficios**, south of the basilica, occupies the ancient Colegio de San Nicolas. Founded by Quiroga in 1540, the college is now devoted to a superb collection of regional handicrafts: local lacquerware and pottery; copperware from Santa Clara del Cobre; and traditional masks and religious objects made from *pasta de caña*, which, apart from being easy to work with, is also very light, and hence easily carried in processions. Some of the objects on display are ancient, others the best examples of modern work, and all are set in a very beautiful building. Almost opposite, the church of **La Compañía** was built by Quiroga in 1546 and later taken over by the Jesuits.

Casa de los Once Patios

Between Dr Coss and Lerin

The **Casa de los Once Patios** is an eighteenth-century convent converted into a crafts showhouse, full of workshops and moderate to expensive boutiques. As its name suggests, the complex is set around a series of tiny courtyards, and it's a fascinating place to stroll through even if you can't afford the goods. You can watch restored treadle looms at work, admire the intricacy with which the best lacquerware is created and wander at liberty through the warren of rooms and corridors.

El Humilladero

Nueva del Cristo, 1km from centre along Serrato

El Humilladero ("the place of humbling") is probably the oldest church in Pátzcuaro, standing on the site where the last Tarascan king, Tanganxoan II, accepted Spanish authority – hence the humbling name. Such a tag may seem appropriate with hindsight, though a more charitable view suggests that Tanganxoan was simply hoping to save his people from the slaughter that had accompanied resistance to the Spaniards elsewhere. The church itself, while pretty enough, is often closed, so there's little to see.

ARRIVAL AND INFORMATION — PÁTZCUARO

By bus to Central de Autobuses Some buses terminating in Pátzcuaro may stop at Estación (see below), but all will take you to the main Central de Autobuses, 2km south of town, and a 15min walk from the centre (cross the main road, head right and turn left down Federico Tena) or a brief bus ride (take services marked "Centro" or "Col Popular"). Buses back to the Central, can be picked up in Plaza Bocanegra or along Federico Tena. Buses for Santa Clara del Cobre start at the central but are best picked up from the main road opposite the top of Federico Tena.

Destinations Guadalajara (2 daily; 4–5hr); Mexico City Pte (6 daily; 6–8hr); Mexico City Nte (8 daily; 5–7hr); Morelia (2 hourly; 1hr); Quiroga (every 15min; 30min); Uruapan (every 30min; 1hr); Santa Clara del Cobre (every 5min; 20min).

By bus to Estación Through buses between Uruapan and Morelia stop at "Estación" (the old train station) by the harbour (handy for *Villa Pátzcuaro*), from where you can get a bus to the centre. Leaving town, this is also the best place to pick up buses to Uruapan and Morelia, since, in addition to the through services (every 15min), those originating at the Central also stop here.

Tourist information The tourist office is on the west side of Plaza Quiroga at Hidalgo 1 (daily 9am–8pm; 434 342 0216 ext.106; http://patzcuaro.gob.mx).

ACCOMMODATION — SEE MAP PAGE 282

Pátzcuaro offers an excellent range of places to stay; prices are a little higher than elsewhere in the state, but if you are prepared to pay a bit more you'll get a lot more elegance. Most establishments are on one or other of the plazas, with the ritzier ones surrounding Plaza Vasco de Quiroga and a selection of simpler places around the Plaza Bocanegra.

PÁTZCUARO FIESTAS

Aside from the Day of the Dead (see page 288), Pátzcuaro's main fiestas are New Year (Jan 1), when the Danza de los Viejitos (Dance of the Little Old Men; see page 278) is performed, and La Señora de la Salud (Dec 8), a saint's day event attended by many Tarascan pilgrims. On La Señora de la Salud, you'll see worshippers in an intense, almost hypnotic fervour; the scrubby park outside the basilica becomes a fairground and there is all manner of Tarascan dances.

LAKE WITH A VIEW

The best views of **Lago de Pátzcuaro** are found west along the road to the Cerro del Estribo: head out along Terán past the Templo San Francisco. It is about 1km from here to the Cerro del Calvario, a tiny hill topped by the little chapel of El Calvario. You won't be able to see much from the chapel, so take the road to the right just before you reach it and continue on along a cobbled, cypress-lined avenue. Over the subsequent 3km, you'll climb more than 200m to a viewpoint with great vistas over Lago de Pátzcuaro and Janitzio. You can get a taxi out here from town, or if you're walking and don't fancy the road, look out for a parallel horse trail on the right. From the viewpoint, 417 steps lead straight up to the summit of Cerro del Estribo (Stirrup Hill), though the views aren't especially better.

Prices generally spike at Christmas/New Year, Semana Santa and Easter. The same is true around the **Day of the Dead** (first two days of Nov), when you'll need to book at least a couple of months ahead (more like six to twelve months for some of the posher places).

Casa del Sol Michoacán 43, Col San Lazarao; 434 342 0975. Home-stay in a workaday *barrio* very near the bus station (instead of turning left down Federico Tena, take the next left to the top of a rise, and it's almost opposite you), where you can either rent rooms in the house, or dorm beds in a shack in the garden. It's only 10min from the centre, very friendly and by far the cheapest deal in town, especially for single travellers. Rooms with shared bathrooms cost a little less. M$

★ **La Casa Encantada** Dr Coss 15; http://hotelcasaencantada.com. Gorgeous and intimate American-owned B&B in the heart of town. All the rooms are different (there are even two self-catering suites), and the whole place is beautifully decorated with lovely little touches everywhere. Includes a hearty Mexican breakfast. M$$$

Los Escudos Plaza Hidalgo 73; 434 342 1290. Beautiful colonial building with good-value rooms around two flower-filled courtyards; all are carpeted and have TV, and some have fireplaces too. Ask for a room in the original hotel and not the extension next door. M$$

Gran Hotel Plaza Bocanegra 6; https://granhotelpatzcuaro.mx. Friendly hotel right on the plaza, with smallish but very homely rooms, each with a coffee maker, TV, phone and wi-fi. It's worth asking for a room with an outside window. Deals are negotiable out of season. M$$

Hotel Misión Pátzcuaro Lázaro Cárdenas 321; http://hotelesmision.com.mx. A beautiful pink-hued hotel in an old colonial building, with comfortable rooms appointed in a suitably traditional style. Heavy carved wooden doors lead out onto a leafy covered courtyard, where you can enjoy coffee and traditional Mexican breakfasts. Despite the traditional look, all rooms have all the mod cons you'd expect, including wi-fi and cable TV. M$$

Hotel Posada la Basílica Árciga 6, opposite the basilica; https://hotelposadalabasilica.com. Delightful rooms, some with fireplaces, all decked out in a traditional style with beautiful carved wooden furniture, in an eighteenth-century building with superb views of the town and a great restaurant (see page 286). Rooms have all the expected amenities, including cable TV, phones and wi-fi. Breakfast included. M$$$

Hotel Posada Camelinas Efrén Urincho 17; http://patzcuaro.com/hoteles/posada_camelinas. It doesn't look like much from its position on a scruffy dead-end street, but inside this hotel is lovely, with a sunny yellow paint job and large, homely rooms with carved wooden furniture. It's popular with pilgrims who have come to visit the nearby basilica, which adds to the peaceful atmosphere. M$

Hotel Posada de la Salud Serrato 9; http://posadadelasalud.mxhotel.site. Behind the basilica, and a short walk from the centre, this beautiful little hotel, peaceful and spotless, is in a house dating from the early nineteenth century. Some rooms have fireplaces, and there's a small garden. M$$

★ **Mansión Iturbe** Portal de Morelos 59; http://mansioniturbe.com. Once a muleteer's house, dating from 1790, this small luxury inn and architectural jewel is run by a mother–daughter team. There's a library, superb dining and attractive bedrooms with soaring ceilings and down duvets. Throughout, the hotel is decorated by artworks from Michoacáno artists and artisans. Breakfast included. M$$$

EATING

SEE MAP PAGE 282

For cheap eats try the food stalls in the **market**, which is at its most colourful and animated on Fridays. Most evenings you can also get basic food from the stalls in the Plaza Bocanegra. One feature of virtually all menus in town is *pescado blanco*, a rather flabby white fish from the lake (though usually nowadays from other lakes), and *sopa tarasca* – a tomato-based soup with chile and bits of tortilla. At the lake itself, a line of restaurants faces the landing jetty, serving *pescado blanco*, or whitebait-like *charales*.

SNACKS

La Pacanda Portal Hidalgo s/n, Plaza Quiroga. Just a

couple of wooden carts with metal tubs on ice serving superb ice cream and sorbets since 1905. Try interesting flavours like tequila (which is amazingly good), mandarin and tamarind. M$

RESTAURANTS

★ **Don Rafa** Mendoza 30; http://restaurantedonrafa.com.mx. A pleasant room decorated with old photos of Pátzcuaro makes a comfortable setting for enjoying classic Mexican dishes like enchiladas *de mole, bistec a la Mexicana* or traditional breakfasts, with delicious fresh salsa on every table and attentive service. M$$

★ **Doña Paca** Portal de Morelos 59, attached to the Mansión Iturbe hotel (see page 288); http://donapaca.com. Come here for comfortable and elegant dining and a menu of reasonably priced regional dishes, including creative salads with local ingredients, and some local delicacies which are pricier but worth splashing out for, including *mole Michoacano and chile relleno Uruapan.* M$$$

Lupita Plaza Quiroga 3; 434 345 0659. Particularly acclaimed for its delicious steaks, this smart restaurant also serves fantastic fish, soups, salads and classic Mexican dishes, either in the wood-panelled, colonial-style dining room or on a patio outside. M$$$

4

El Patio Plaza Quiroga 19; 434 342 0484. Good coffee, reasonably priced breakfasts, *antojitos* (including local ones such as *corundas* and *huchepos*,), steaks, salads and sandwiches. You may be either reassured or put off by their statement (in English) that "Our menu is not too hot or spicy". M$$$

La Pérgola Inside the Gran Hotel (see page 285); http://lapergolanj.com. Relaxed, high-ceilinged restaurant, where the menu changes with the seasons. It's one of the best spots in town for a hearty breakfast, though you can also have lunch or supper here, dining on such dishes as rainbow trout or *carne asada*. M$$

★ **La Surtidora** Portal Hidalgo 71, Plaza Quiroga; 434 342 2835. Doubling as a liquor store (bottles of spirits line the wood-panelled walls from ceiling to floor), this evocative restaurant (open since 1916) does an excellent line in breakfast, lunch and dinner, serving up well-presented dishes such as *sopa tarasca* and breast of chicken stuffed with *huitlacoche* and nuts in *chile poblano* sauce. M$$

Tekare Arciga 6, inside the Hotel Posada La Basílica (see page 285); 434 342 1108. The house speciality is *kurucha urapiti* (lake fish, though not actually from Lago de Pátzcuaro nowadays), or try the chicken in peanut sauce – a change from *mole*, though that's available too. The restaurant has great views of the town and beyond to the lake. M$$$

DRINKING

SEE MAP PAGE 282

El Campanario Plaza Quiroga 12; 434 342 1313. Reasonably lively bar, often with a DJ or a couple of musicians playing in the corner. The decor's a bit strange, but in a pleasing kind of way, and there's even a model of a *torero* (bullfighter) with a bull's face in a glass case on the wall.

DIRECTORY

Banks and exchange There are several ATMs along Portal de Morelos and La Paz, which run parallel to one another in the middle of town. At the corner of Buena Vista and Ahumada there's a *casa de cambio*.

Laundry Try the laundrette in front of the Templo San Francisco.

Post office Obregón 13.

Spanish courses The Centro de Lenguas y Ecoturismo de Pátzcuaro, Navarette 50 (434 342 4764) offers well-regarded language classes and homestays.

Telephones You can phone and fax from *casetas* on the east side of Plaza Bocanegra.

Lago de Pátzcuaro and around

Apart from the beautiful town itself, Pátzcuaro's other great attraction is **Lago de Pátzcuaro.** The lake was once a major thoroughfare, but that role has declined since the completion of roads linking the lakeside villages a few years back. Most locals now take the bus rather than paddle around the water in canoes, but there is still a fair amount of traffic and regular trips out to the closest island, **Janitzio.**

The lake's other draw is the chance to see and photograph the famous **butterfly nets** wielded by Indigenous fishermen in tiny dugout canoes. It is a long time since this was considered a viable means of gaining food, but a handful of nets are maintained to catch tourists. Occasionally a group of locals lurking in readiness on the far side of Janitzio will paddle into camera range when a sufficiently large collection of money has been taken.

Finally, no visit to Pátzcuaro is complete without an excursion to the small lakeside villages, which, thanks to Vasco de Quiroga, each specialize in different **artesanía.**

The islands

From a distance, the island of **Janitzio** looks quaint, but as you get closer it appears almost squalid. With fishing becoming ever less viable and with no land flat enough for agriculture, the conical, car-free island has found itself relying increasingly on the tourism industry – you'll be besieged by souvenir hawkers from the moment you arrive. Still, it is worth the journey if only for the opportunity to spend some time on the lake and for the expansive views from the top of the island. From the dock, head straight up one of the many alleys that climb steeply between assorted **fish restaurants** (generally better away from the dock) and tacky souvenir stalls to the summit, which is crowned by an ugly 40m **statue of José María Morelos** (see page 294). Ascend the spiral staircase inside (daily 8am–7pm; charge), past murals depicting Morelos' life and the struggle for Independence, to the viewpoint right by an image of his upraised, clenched fist. If heights make you queasy, there's a pleasant path that encircles the island running around the lakeshore. It takes about thirty minutes to make a full circuit.

There isn't a great deal to see or do on the other islands in the lake, with the exception of **Isla Yunuén**, where it's possible to stay (see page 288). The island is much greener

THE DAY OF THE DEAD AROUND LAGO DE PÁTZCUARO

The **Day of the Dead** (Nov 1, and through the night into the next day) is celebrated in spectacular fashion throughout Mexico, but nowhere more so than on Lago de Pátzcuaro, particularly the island of **Janitzio**. On this night, the locals conduct what is an essentially private meditation, carrying offerings of fruit and flowers to the cemetery and maintaining a vigil over the graves of their ancestors until dawn, chanting by candlelight. Death is considered a continuation of life, and this is the time when the souls of *muertitos* (deceased loved ones) return to the land of the living. It's a spectacular and moving sight, especially early in the evening as Indigenous people from the surrounding area converge on the island in their canoes, with a single candle burning in each bow.

Impressive and solemn though the occasion is, over the years it has become somewhat marred by its sheer press of **spectators**, both Mexican and foreign. Thousands head over to tiny Janitzio, and from around 10pm on November 1 until around 3am the following morning you can hardly move, especially in the cemetery where the vigil takes place amid a riot of marigolds and candles. If you can manage it, stay up all night and return to the cemetery around 5am when it is quiet and the first hint of dawn lightens the eastern sky. Alternatively, head to one of the other lakeside communities marking the Day of the Dead – Tzurumutaro, Ihuatzio, Cucuchucho or Tzintzuntzán. There's no guarantee of a quiet and respectful vigil, but crowds will be smaller and the cemeteries no less amazing.

4

and more laid-back than Janitzio, with traditional Purepécha architecture, and there isn't a whole lot to do here, which is, after all, really the point of coming. The island's name means "half moon", in reference to its shape.

ARRIVAL AND DEPARTURE — LAGO DE PÁTZCUARO

LAGO DE PÁTZCUARO

By bus/minibus Buses and minibuses leave from Plaza Bocanegra in Pátzcuaro. Those marked "Lago" drop you right by the boats, otherwise it's a 4km (less than 1hr) walk down to the jetty; follow the "*embarcadero*" signs.

THE ISLANDS

Janitzio Fares to the island from Pátzcuaro's Muelle General (main dock area) are fixed (get your ticket from the office on the quay before you board). Seventy-seat *lanchas* make the stately, if noisy, half-hour crossing when full (daily 7am–7pm, roughly every 20–30min). The last boat back leaves Janitzio at around 7.30–8pm.

Isla Yunuén You can get a boat from the Muelle General (main dock area) in Pátzcuaro with a minimum of three people. Failing that, it'll cost you more. The journey takes 1hr 40min, stopping at Janitzio. If you're staying in Yunuén, you'll have to negotiate a pick-up for your return to Pátzcuaro.

ACCOMMODATION — SEE MAP PAGE 287

Cabañas de Yunuén Isla Yunuén; 434 342 4473. Beautifully rustic and absolutely immaculate wooden cabins, each with a small kitchen and TV, on a little island in the middle of the lake; very idyllic. If you want to stay here on the Day of the Dead, you'll need to book months ahead. M$$$

Hacienda Patzcuaro 3.5 km Carretera Pátzcuaro–Santa Clara del Cobre; 443 333 0762. This comfortable, upscale oasis, south of town off the Santa Clara del Cobre road, offers pony treks, ecotours and superb cuisine in serene wooded surroundings. Rooms have lovely wooden ceiling beams, wrought iron beds and Indigenous carvings adorning the walls. Breakfast included. M$$$

Villa Pátzcuaro Lázaro Cárdenas, 2km north of town; http://villapatzcuaro.com. Great little hotel and RV park in spacious grounds with a small pool. Rustic-style rooms (breakfast included) are tasteful, very clean and decorated in a stylish but traditional way; there are also a couple of self-contained houses for longer stays. Tent and RV campers have access to a kitchen. Frequent buses from Plaza Bocanegra pass right outside. Double M$$, house M$$$, camping/person M$

Ihuatzio

12km north of Pátzcuaro, around 4km off the Pátzcuaro–Quiroga road • Charge

While they're no match for the ruins at Tzintzuntzán (see below), further around Lago Pátzcuaro, the older, pre-Tarascan ruins of **IHUATZIO** are interesting in their own right and worth a peek if you have the time. Located on a remote track that traverses a cow pasture, Ihuatzio was strategically located near the shores of Lago de Pátzcuaro and used for water defence and enemy lookout. The ruins are essentially divided into two sections, one older than the other: the first (900–1200 AD) is thought to have been constructed by the Náhuatl, and the second dates from 1200–1530 AD, during the Tarascan occupation. Two 15m-high **squared-off pyramids**, once considered a sort of Plaza de Armas, are the main features of the site open to the public.

ARRIVAL AND DEPARTURE — IHUATZIO

By bus Buses to Ihuatzio leave from Plaza Bocanegra in Pátzcuaro every few minutes during the site's opening hours. You'll be dropped at the end of a cobblestone road and will have to walk 1500m to the site's entrance. On the walk, look for three vegetated hummocks which are the unexcavated ruins of *yácatas* (see below). To continue to Tzintzuntzán, hop on one of the frequent Quiroga-bound buses or *colectivos* from the road where you were dropped off.

Tzintzuntzán

15km north of Pátzcuaro on the road to Quiroga • Charge

TZINTZUNTZÁN, ancient capital of the Tarascans (aka Purépechas), was established around the end of the fourteenth century, when the capital was moved from Pátzcuaro, and by the time of the Conquest the Spaniards estimated that there were as many as forty thousand people living here, with dominion over all of what is now Michoacán and large parts of the modern states of Jalisco and Colima. Homes and markets, as well as the palaces of the rulers, lay around the raised **ceremonial centre**, but all that can be seen today is the artificial terrace that supported the great religious buildings (*yácatas*), and the partly restored ruins of these temples.

Even if you do no more than pass by on the road, you can't fail to be struck by the scale of these buildings and by their semicircular design, a startling contrast to the rigid, right-angled formality adhered to by almost every other major pre-Hispanic culture in Mexico. Climb up to the terrace and you'll find five *yácatas*, of which four have been partly rebuilt. Each was originally some 15m high, tapering in steps from a broad base to a walkway along the top less than 2m wide. Devoid of any ornamentation, the *yácatas* are in fact piles of flat rocks, held in by retaining walls and then faced in smooth, close-fitting volcanic stone. The terrace, which was originally approached up a broad ceremonial ramp or stairway on the side furthest from the water, affords magnificent views across the lake and the present-day village of Tzintzuntzán. Tzintzuntzán means "place of the hummingbirds"; you're unlikely to see one nowadays, but the theory is that there were plenty of them around until the Tarascans – who used the feathers to make ornaments – hunted them to the point of extinction. The ruins are around 1km from the village and are signposted "Zona Arqueológica" up a side road.

TZINTZUNTZÁN FIESTAS

Tzintzuntzán has several good **fiestas**. Carnaval here takes the form of a week-long party called La Fiesta del Señor del Rescate, celebrating a miracle in which, during a nineteenth-century measles epidemic, the sexton of the church discovered an old painting of Christ hidden away in the crypt, and made a vow that if prayers to this image would rescue the town, he would pay for a huge party in celebration; the prayers duly worked, and the party is held every year to this day. Unfortunately the miraculous image itself was destroyed by fire in 1944. Also big here is Semana Santa (the week before Easter Sunday), when the Thursday sees the ceremony of Washing the Apostles' Feet, followed on Good Friday by further scenes from Christ's Passion acted out around town.

4

The village

Down in the **village**, which has a reputation for producing and selling some of the region's best ceramics, you'll find what's left of the enormous **Franciscan Monastery** founded around 1530 to convert the Tarascans. Much of this has been demolished, and the rest substantially rebuilt, but there remains a fine Baroque **Templo de San Francisco** and a huge atrium where the Indigenous people would gather for sermons. Vasco de Quiroga originally intended to base his diocese here, but eventually decided that Pátzcuaro had the better location and a more constant supply of water. He did leave one unusual legacy, though: the **olive trees** planted around the monastery are probably the oldest in Mexico, since settlers were banned from cultivating olives in order to protect the farmers back in Spain. The broad, veined trunks certainly look their age, and several have just a few living branches sprouting from what look like dead trees.

ARRIVAL AND DEPARTURE — TZINTZUNTZÁN

By bus Buses to Tzintzuntzán leave from Pátzcuaro's Central de Autobuses (every 10min; 15min), but can also be picked up on the highway close to the *embarcadero*.

By colectivo You can also take a *colectivo* from Plaza Bocanegra to Ihuatzio (15min), and another from there to Tzintzuntzán (15min).

Santa Clara del Cobre

Approximately 25km south of Pátzcuaro, via a country road over a pine-draped pass, lies **Santa Clara del Cobre**, long celebrated for the **copper crafts** on which it continues to thrive. There are no fewer than two hundred family-run studios (*talleres*) and shops, many of which line the quaint town's arcades and side streets selling everything from cheap bracelets and thimbles to hammered sinks and sparkling *carnitas* cauldrons.

Museo Nacional del Cobre

Morelos 263 at Pino Suárez • Charge

A large amount of copper is on display at the town's **Museo del Cobre**, which exhibits a small but impressive collection of decorative and utilitarian copper crafts. Sadly, only a handful of these intricate old designs are still being incorporated into the production of modern goods.

ARRIVAL AND INFORMATION — SANTA CLARA DEL COBRE

By bus and combi Buses and *combis* to Santa Clara from Pátzcuaro (every 5min; 20min) leave from the main road opposite the top of Federico Tena. They return to Pátzcuaro from the southwest corner of the main plaza. A taxi between Pátzcuaro and Santa Clara costs a set fee.

By car Driving from Pátzcuaro, follow signs for Opopeo.

Festivals The annual Feria Nacional del Cobre (Copper Fair), combined with the Fiesta de la Virgen del Sagrario, is held in Santa Clara del Cobre for ten days in July or August. Festivities include exhibits and sales of handworked copper, as well as music and dance.

ACCOMMODATION AND EATING

Hotel Oasis Portal Allende 144, north side of main plaza; 434 343 0040. Serviceable hotel, centrally located, with carpeted rooms, some with views over the main plaza. Rooms with mountain views are larger and cost a little bit more (though they'll take more people – up to four. M$$

El Portal Portal Matamoros 18, east side of main plaza. Serves good breakfasts and *comidas corridas* along with fish dishes such as lake fish done various ways, or fish soup. M$

Morelia

The state capital, **MORELIA**, is in many ways unrepresentative of Michoacán. It looks Spanish and, despite a large Indigenous population, it feels Spanish – with its broad streets lined with seventeenth-century mansions and outdoor cafés sheltered by arcaded plazas, you might easily be in Salamanca or Valladolid. Indeed, the city's name was

Valladolid until 1828, when it was changed to honour local-born Independence hero José María Morelos.

City ordinances decree that all new construction must perfectly match the old, such that it preserves a remarkable unity of style. Nearly everything is built of the same faintly pinkish-grey stone (trachyte), which, being soft, is not only easily carved and embellished but weathers quickly, giving even relatively recent constructions a battered, ancient look. Best of all are the plazas dotted with little cafés where you can while away an hour or two.

Brief history

Morelia has always been a city of Spaniards. It was one of the first they founded after the Conquest – two Franciscan friars, Juan de San Miguel and Antonio de Lisboa, settled here among the native inhabitants in 1530. Ten years later, they were visited by the first viceroy of New Spain, **Antonio de Mendoza**, who was so taken by the site that he ordered a town to be built, naming it after his birthplace – Valladolid in Castile – and sending fifty Spanish families to settle it. From the beginning, there was fierce rivalry between the colonists and the older culture's town of Pátzcuaro. During the lifetime of **Vasco de Quiroga**, Pátzcuaro had the upper hand, but later the bishopric was moved here, a university founded, and by the end of the sixteenth century there was no doubt that Valladolid was predominant.

Plaza de Armas

4

Flanking the cathedral, the **Plaza de Armas** (or de los Martíres) is the place to sit around and revel in the city's leisurely pace – relax with a coffee and a morning paper (you can buy a few international newspapers from the stands here) in the cafés under its elegant arcaded *portales*. There are band concerts here on Sundays.

The cathedral

Madero Pte 2 • Free

At the heart of the city, Morelia's massive **cathedral** boasts two soaring towers that are said to be the tallest in Mexico; they can certainly be seen from all over the city and beyond. It's an important social hub for the city's residents who are extremely proud of the beautiful building. Begun in 1640 in the relatively plain Herrerian style, the towers and dome were not completed for some hundred years, by which time the Baroque had arrived with a vengeance; nevertheless, the parts harmonize remarkably, and for all the cathedral's size and richness of decoration, perfect proportions prevent it from becoming overpowering. The interior, refitted towards the end of the nineteenth century after most of its silver ornamentation had been removed to pay for the wars, is restrained compared to its counterpart in Guadalajara, but is very beautiful, with its subtle stained glass and rose gold-coloured arches. A few early colonial religious paintings are preserved in the choir and the sacristy, and organ recitals are still held from time to time.

Museo Michoacano

On the southwestern edge of Plaza de Armas, at the corner of Allende and Abasolo • Charge • 443 312 0407

The **Museo Michoacano** occupies a palatial eighteenth-century mansion. Emperor Maximilian lodged here on his visits to Morelia, and it now houses a collection that reflects the state's diversity and rich history: the rooms devoted to archeology are, of course, dominated by the **Tarascan culture**, including pottery and small sculptures from Tzintzuntzán, but also display much earlier objects, notably some obsidian figurines. Out in the patio are two magnificent old carriages, while upstairs the colonial epoch is represented in a large group of religious paintings and sculptures and a collection of old books and manuscripts

MORELIA
EATING
Cafe del Ajedrecista 3
Café Galeria Teatro Ocampo 4
Calle Real 8
El Comalito 7
La Copa de Oro 2
Del Olmo 5
Gaspachos la Cerrada 11
Los Mirasoles 6
Rico Pay 9
San Miguelito 12
Super Cocina Las Rosas 1
El Tragadero 10
ACCOMMODATION
Casino 4
Catedral 5
Holiday Inn Express 11
Hostel Allende 7
Hostal San Fransiskuni 10
Hotel el Carmen 1
Hotel Historia 8
Hotel de la Soledad 3
Hotel Posada Don Vasco 9
Señorial 2
Virrey de Mendoza 6
0 150 metres
(2km)
Central Camionera (5km)
Casa de la Cultura
Entrance
Conservatorio de las Rosas
Santa Rosa
Museo de Arte Colonial
Plaza del Carmen
Jardín de las Rosas
Museo del Estado
Palacio Clavijero
Mercado de Dulces y Artesanías
Centro de Atención al Turista
Palacio de Gobierno
La Compañía (Public Library)
Colegio de San Nicolas
Zócalo
Plaza de Armas
Plaza Melchor Ocampo
Catedral
Museo Michoacano
Plaza San Agustin
Casa Natal de Morelos
Iglesia de San Agustín
Museo Casa de Morelos
Templo de las Monjas
Palacio Federal
Plaza Valladolid
San Francisco
Casa de las Artesanías
Plaza Capuchinas
Mercado Independencia
Plaza Revolución
Plaza Villalongin
Fuente de las Tarascas
Acueducto
Sanctuario de Guadalupe
Plaza Morelos
Museo de Arte Contemporaneo
Bosque Cuauhtémoc
Madero Poniente
Madero Oriente
Morelos Norte
Morelos Sur
Virrey de Mendoza
Hermenegildo Galeana
Heroes de Nocupetaro
Gen. Garcia Pueblita
Eduardo Ruiz
Carlos Salazar
Lerdo de Tejada
Guadalupe Victoria
Romero
Leon Guzman
Santiago
Tapia
Valentin Gomez Farias
Nigromante
Guillermo Prieto
Ignacio Zaragoza
Benito Juarez
Melchor Ocampo
Emiliano Zapata
Trabajo
Nacozari
Pino Suarez
Alvaro Obregón
Belisario Dominguez
20 de Noviembre
Aquiles Serdan
Serapio Rendon
Dr Miguel de Silva
Plan de Ayala
Amado Nervo
Revolución
1 de Mayo
Luis Moya
Callejón de Romance
Allende
Valladolid
Corregidora
Hidalgo
Matamoros
Granaditas
Andres Quintana Roo
Ignacio Lopez Rayon
Aldama
Soto y Saldaña
Antonio Alzate
Bartolome de las Casas
Humboldt
Clavijero
Cabrera
Margil
Mariano Elizaga
Cordoba
Padre Lloreda
V. de Leon
Vicente Santa Maria
Miguel
Torre
Juan Jose Lejarza
Sanchez de Tagle
Diego Jose Abad
Isidro Huarte
Sor Juana Ines de la Cruz
Samuel Ramos
Gertrudis Bocanegra
Justo Mendoza
Fray Antonio de San Miguel
Revillagigedo
Motolinia
Tata Vasco
Nicolas Bravo
Vicente Guerrero
Abasolo
Fuente de los Remedios
Manuel Muniz
Leona Vicario
Garcia Obeso
Benedicto López
Vasco de Quiroga
Andres del Rio
Lázaro Cárdenas
Juan Ruiz de Alarcon
Ana Maria Gallega
M. Cervantes Saavedra
Rafael Carrillo
Rio Amatlan
Ventura Puente
M. Monterde

Plaza Melchor Ocampo

A smaller square, the **Plaza Melchor Ocampo**, flanks the cathedral on the other side. Facing it, the **Palacio de Gobierno** was formerly a seminary – Independence hero Morelos and his nemesis Agustín Iturbide studied here, as did Ocampo, a nineteenth-century liberal supporter of Benito Juárez. It's of interest now for Alfredo Zalce's **murals** adorning the stairway and upper level of the patio: practically the whole of Mexican history, and each of its heroes, is depicted.

Immediately east of the square on Madero are several **banks** that are among the most remarkable examples of active conservation you'll see anywhere: old mansions that have been refurbished in traditional style, and somehow manage to combine reasonably efficient operation with an ambience that is wholly in keeping with the setting.

Calle Nigromante and around

One block west of the Plaza de Armas, the **Colegio de San Nicolas** is part of the University of Michoacán. Founded at Pátzcuaro in 1540 by Vasco de Quiroga, and moved here in 1580, the college is the second oldest in Mexico and hence in all the Americas – it now houses administrative offices and various technical faculties, while cultural performances (often free) are also held here regularly. To the side, across Nigromante in what was originally the Jesuit church of **La Compañía**, is the public library, while next to this is the beautiful **Palacio Clavijero**, now converted into government offices.

Alongside the Palacio, down Gomez Farias, enclosed *portales* are home to the **Mercado de Dulces y Artesanías**, groaning with the sweets for which the city is famed, along with stalls selling leather jackets, guitars and other handicrafts, though little of much quality. At the north end of Nigromante, on another charming little plaza – the Jardín de las Rosas – you'll come across the Baroque church of **Santa Rosa** and, beside it, the **Conservatorio de las Rosas**, a music academy founded in the eighteenth century. From time to time it hosts concerts of classical music – the tourist office should have details, as does http://conservatoriodelasrosas.edu.mx.

4

Museo del Estado

Guillermo Prieto 176, near the corner of Santiago Tapia • Free • 443 304 5772

Inside an eighteenth-century former home, the complete furniture and fittings of a traditional *farmacia* have been reconstructed as part of the **Museo del Estado**. Somewhat incongruously, there are also prehistory and archeology collections. This is mostly minor stuff, though there are some intriguing ceramic figurines and some fine, unusual Tarascan jewellery, including gold and turquoise pieces, and necklaces strung with tiny crystal skulls. Upstairs, there's one room of colonial history and various ethnological exhibits illustrating traditional local dress and lifestyles – a butterfly fishing net from Pátzcuaro plus displays on copper working and guitar manufacture.

Casa de la Cultura and around

Casa de la Cultura, Morelos Nte 485 • Free • http://lacasadelacultura.org

On the north side of Plaza del Carmen, entered from Morelos, the beautiful old Convento del Carmen now houses the **Casa de la Cultura**. It's an enormous complex, worth exploring in its own right, with a theatre, café, space for temporary exhibitions and classes scattered around the former monastic buildings. International films are sometimes screened here. The collection of colonial art at the nearby **Museo de Arte Colonial**, Juárez 240 (free), is almost entirely regional, and not of great interest, though there is an expansive display of rather gory crucifixes.

Museo Casa de Morelos and around

Museo Casa de Morelos, Morelos Sur 323 • Charge • 443 313 2651

JOSÉ MARÍA MORELOS Y PAVÓN

A student of Hidalgo, **José María Morelos** took over the leadership of the **Independence movement** after its instigators had been executed in 1811. While the cry of Independence had initially been taken up by the Mexican (Creole) bourgeoisie, smarting under the trading restrictions imposed on them by Spain, it quickly became a mass movement. Unlike the original leaders, Morelos (a *mestizo* priest born into relative poverty) was a populist and genuine reformer. Even more unlike them, he was also a political and military tactician of considerable skill, invoking the spirit of the French Revolution and calling for universal suffrage, racial equality and the break-up of the hacienda system, under which workers were tied to agricultural servitude. He was defeated and executed by Royalist armies under Agustín de Iturbide in 1815 after waging years of guerrilla warfare, a period during which Morelos had come close to taking the capital and controlling the entire country. When Independence was finally gained – by Iturbide, who had changed sides and later briefly served as emperor – it was no longer a force for change, rather a reaction to the fact that by 1820 liberal reforms were sweeping Spain itself. The causes espoused by Morelos were, however, taken up to some extent by Benito Juárez and later, with a vengeance, in the Revolution – almost a hundred years after his death.

Around Michoacán you'll see Morelos' image everywhere – notably the massive **statue** atop Isla de Janitzio (see page 287) – invariably depicted with a kind of bandana over his head. He's also pictured on the **fifty-peso note**, which features the butterfly-net fishers of Pátzcuaro, monarch butterflies and masks for the Danza de los Viejitos.

Two blocks southeast of the cathedral, the **Museo Casa de Morelos** is the relatively modest eighteenth-century house in which Independence hero José María Morelos y Pavón lived from 1801 (see page 294). It's now a museum devoted to his life and the War of Independence. You can see the house where the man was born, the **Casa Natal de Morelos**, nearby at Corregidora 105, on the corner of García Obeso (free). It now houses a library and a few desultory domestic objects.

Templo y Convento de San Agustín

Garcia Obeso 162 • Free

Southwest of the cathedral is the centre's functioning church for daily worship. The interior is equally as splendid as its larger neighbour, and it holds Mass a minimum of four times a day, and every hour on the hour on Sundays. Look out for the black Jesus on the left-hand side and the tasteful array of souvenirs beside the east entrance.

Casa de las Artesanías

Plaza Vallladolid • Free (includes tour) • http://artesanias-michoacan.com

Plaza Valladolid is dominated on its east side by the sixteenth-century church of **San Francisco**. The church's former monastery, which stands next door to it, has been turned into the **Casa de las Artesanías**, possibly the most comprehensive collection of Michoacán's crafts anywhere. Almost all of them are for sale. The best and most obviously commercial items are downstairs, while on the upper floor is a series of rooms devoted to the products of particular villages, often with craftspeople demonstrating their techniques (these are staffed by villagers and hence not always open), and a collection of historic items which you can't buy.

The aqueduct and around

One of the most attractive parts of town to while away a few hours lies about fifteen minutes' walk east along Madero from the cathedral, some five blocks beyond the

Baroque facade of the **Templo de las Monjas** and the adjacent Palacio Federal, to where the old **aqueduct** leads southeastward from **Plaza Villalongin**. Built on a winding course between 1785 and 1789, the aqueduct's 253 arches brought water into the city from springs in the nearby hills.

Callejón del Romance

Several roads meet just south of Plaza Villalongin at the **Fuente Las Tarascas**, which features three bare-breasted Tarascan women holding up a vast basket of fruit. East of the fountain, Madero bears slightly left and, off to its north, just past the aqueduct, the **Callejón del Romance** (Romance Lane) is a pretty, bougainvillea-draped alley of nineteenth-century homes, which has a couple more fountains at its northern end.

Calzada Fray Antonio de San Miguel

Leading between east and southeast from Plaza Villalongin, the **Calzada Fray Antonio de San Miguel** (named for the bishop who built the aqueduct) is a broad and leafy pedestrianized walkway that leads down to the wildly overdecorated **Sanctuario de Guadalupe**, where market stalls, selling above all the sticky local *dulces*, set up at weekends and during fiestas.

Avenida Acueducto

The last of the three roads east of Plaza Villalongin is Avenida Acueducto, which leads southeast, following the aqueduct. On its southern side, the **Bosque Cuauhtémoc** is a pleasant park with some beautifully laid-out flower displays, where young lovers while away the sunny afternoons together.

Museo de Arte Contemporáneo Alfredo Zalce (MACAZ)

Av Acueducto 18 • Free • 443 312 4544

Avenida Acueducto passes the small **Museo de Arte Contemporáneo Alfredo Zalce (MACAZ)**, where the only permanent works on display are by local sculptor Alfredo Zalce, who died in 2003. There are always temporary exhibitions on, however, featuring modern artists from Mexico and around the world.

ARRIVAL AND DEPARTURE — MORELIA

By plane Morelia's airport, 27km northeast of town on the Zinapecuaro road (Hwy-120), has flights to a handful of US airports, as well as to Mexico City (1–3 daily; 1hr) and Tijuana (2 daily; 3hr 15min).

By bus Morelia's modern bus station, the Central Camionera, is around 3km northwest of the centre on the city's ring road. Of the three terminal halls, *Sala* A is mostly for first-class intercity services, *Sala* B for first-class intercity and local services and *Sala* C for second-class services. To get into town, you can catch a cab (fixed-price tickets sold inside the terminal) or walk out onto the main road and wait for a Roja 1 *colectivo* (look for a white minibus with a red band) which will take you into town along Madero. To get back to the bus station, catch the same from along Ocampo.

Destinations Aguascalientes (6 daily; 5–7hr); Guadalajara (frequent; 3hr 30min–7hr); Guanajuato (3 daily; 3hr 30min); León (hourly; 3hr 30min); Mexico City Nte (at least 1 hourly; 3hr–4hr 30min); Mexico City Pte (at least 2 hourly;

MORELIA FESTIVALS

Try to get here for the Festival Internacional de Guitarra (dates vary; held in September in 2018, but previously in March/April), a fantastic gathering of musicians from around the world; Expo Fiesta (dates vary in April/May), the Michoacán Expo Fair celebrating the arts and industry of the region; Morelos' birthday (Sept 30), celebrated with civic events, fairs, dances and fireworks; or the Festival Internacional de Música (second and third week in Nov, http://festivalmorelia.mx), an international festival with concerts, recitals, operas and conferences.

4–5hr); Pátzcuaro (frequent; 1hr); Querétaro (30 daily; 2hr 30min–4hr); Uruapan (1 hourly; 2hr); Zitácuaro (every 30min; 3hr).

INFORMATION

Tourist information For information about Morelia specifically, there's a Centro de Atención al Turista at Portal Hidalgo 245, on the north side of Plaza de Armas, (Mon–Fri 9am–9pm; 443 312 0414, https://visitmichoacan.com.mx). The state tourist office, for information about Michoacán more generally, is east of the centre at Tata Vasco 80 (Mon–Fri 9am–6pm, and sometimes weekends too; 443 317 8054 or 443 317 8032, https://visitmichoacan.com.mx).

ACCOMMODATION

SEE MAP PAGE 292

HOTELS

Casino Portal Hidalgo 229; http://hotelcasino.com.mx. Beautiful hotel on the Plaza de Armas set around a covered courtyard. It's in an old colonial building, and there's a great painting of the hotel around 1900 behind the reception desk; rooms are rather more generic than the exterior suggests, but have lovely carved wooden shutters and furniture and the occasional glimpse of rugged, original stonework. They're equipped with most of the amenities you'd want, including a gym, though not a/c. Breakfast included. M$$$

Catedral Ignacio Zaragoza 37; http://hotelesmision.com.mx. Light, airy rooms with king-size beds and ceiling fans around a restaurant in a covered colonial courtyard; the property doubles as the Spanish consulate. Rooms with a cathedral view cost slightly more than those without. M$$

Holiday Inn Express Portal Hidalgo 245, on the Plaza de Armas; https://www.ihg.com. Great position under the colonial arches; inside it's very modern, if rather soulless. There's a/c, free wi-fi and a gym, but only eight of its sixty rooms have outside windows. Breakfast included. M$$$

Hotel el Carmen Eduardo Ruíz 63; http://hotelelcarmenmorelia.com.mx. Friendly hotel on a pretty square, with clean rooms, mostly with TV and bathroom. The cheapest rooms are tiny and cell-like, overlooking the Plaza del Carmen. Breakfast included. M$

★ **Hotel de la Soledad** Ignacio Zaragoza 90; http://hoteldelasoledad.com. This spectacular colonial building is the city's oldest inn and an absolutely gorgeous upmarket hotel. Breezy rooms, all with king-size beds, are set around a beautiful open courtyard at the front, while those round the less attractive back courtyard have been modernized (all have a/c), but have lost some of their character in the process. The junior suites, on the other hand, combine the best of both worlds, with all mod cons, beautiful decor and lashings of period charm. M$$$$

★ **Hotel Historia** Ignacio Allende 329; http://hotelhistoria.com.mx. Housed in a grand colonial mansion in the heart of the *centro histórico*, this professional hotel combines an Old World atmosphere with very comfortable, good-value accommodation. Rooms have high, wooden ceilings, iron chandeliers and balconies which offer a glimpse of the cathedral poking above the rooftops. M$$$

Hotel Posada Don Vasco Vasco de Quiroga 232; 443 312 1484. Far and away the best deal in this price range, in a great old colonial building, with a variety of rooms – some atmospheric, with period architecture, but others dull and modern, or small and stuffy – so it's worth having a look round before deciding. Services include cable TV, free wi-fi and free phone calls to Mexican landlines. M$

Señorial Santiago Tapía 543; 443 274 3928. This shabby hotel in a run-down old colonial building is not the most salubrious place in town, but in a city where low-price accommodation is hard to find, it's perfect for hardcore budgeteers who need a really cheap place to sleep and aren't otherwise too fussy. It's worth paying extra for a private bathroom. M$

Virrey de Mendoza Madero 310 Pte; http://hotelvirrey.com. Fantastic colonial grandeur: even if you can't afford to stay, it's worth dropping by to take a look or have a drink in the courtyard. The rooms aren't as impressive as the lobby, but it is a lovely spot just the same for its history, majestic public spaces and fine service. M$$$

HOSTELS

Hostel Allende Allende 843; http://hotelallende.com.mx. Slightly institutional hotel/hostel with rooms around a leafy courtyard that's good for relaxing. Single-sex dorms are vastly outnumbered by cubicle-like private rooms, all with bathrooms. There's a small kitchen, free wi-fi and 24hr check-in. Breakfast included. Dorms M$, doubles M$$

Hostal San Fransiskuni Alzate 302; http://hostalsanfransiskuni.com. A small, informal hostel in an old colonial house, equipped with pleasant four- and five-bed dorms, each with a bathroom, and a handful of private rooms with shared bathroom facilities. There's free wi-fi, and they speak English. Prices include breakfast, although you'll still find yourself hungry after the meagre offerings (get there early if you can). M$

EATING

SEE MAP PAGE 292

On a fine day it's hard to resist the temptation of the cafés and restaurants in the *portales* around the Plaza de Armas:

fairly expensive for a full meal, but good for snacks or for a breakfast of coffee and *pan dulce*. As ever, the cheapest eating is at the **food market** in Plaza Capuchinas, but Morelia's big Mercado Independencia, just to its south, is on the whole a disappointment, certainly not as large or varied as you'd expect. Chief among Morelia's specialities are its **dulces**, sweets made of candied fruit or evaporated milk – cloyingly sweet to most non-Mexican tastes, they're very popular here. You can see a wide selection at the **Mercado de Dulces y Artesanías** (see page 293). Morelians also get through a lot of *rompope* (a drink that you'll find to a lesser extent all over Mexico) – again, it's very sweet, an egg concoction based on rum, milk and egg, with vanilla, cinnamon or almond flavouring.

CAFÉS

Cafe del Ajedrecista C. de Melchor Ocampo 322; 443 328 3851. A peaceful place to enjoy a drink or a snack near the pretty Jardín de las Rosas. They also host the local chess club and invite visitors to get involved. M$$

★ **Café Galeria Teatro Ocampo** upstairs in the Teatro Ocampo, on Ocampo and Prieto; 443 317 3777. Overlooking Ocampo, a lush, almost baronial, interior makes this one of the most popular spots in town for good coffee and people-watching. With a good number of breakfast options and sweet or savoury crêpes, it's not as expensive as you might expect. Try to get a table overlooking the street. M$$

Calle Real Madero Ote 440; http://callereal.mx. Magnificent old-fashioned candy store with a café serving decadent coffees with drizzles of *cajeta*, and a wide selection of interesting confectionery prepared in traditional copper pots, including sugarless fruit sweets. There's a small Museo del Dulce upstairs on the 4th floor. M$

Del Olmo Juárez 95; 443 275 7460. Sophisticated but relaxed café-bar, set around a pretty interior courtyard, with good coffee. They do breakfast deals until 1pm and a *comida corrida* from then on. There's also free wi-fi. M$$$

★ **El Tragadero** Hidalgo 63; 443 313 0092. Old monochrome photos of Morelia line the walls of this relaxed café-restaurant, a good place for breakfast, inexpensive lunch and classic Mexican creole side-dishes like pork trotters in vinegar. Favourite dishes include *filete de pescado con papas* (aka fish and chips). M$$

CHEAP EATS AND SNACKS

La Copa de Oro Juárez 194-B at Santiago Tapia; 443 313 1049. An excellent place for a delicious selection of fresh *jugos*, and they also do salads, tortas and comidas corrida. M$$

Gaspachos la Cerrada Hidalgo 67; 443 457 2202. Nothing like a Spanish *gazpacho*, a Morelian *gaspacho* is a finely chopped fruit salad, topped – if you like – with grated cheese and chile powder. Plenty of places around town sell it, but this is the most renowned. A cup of *gaspacho* here won't set you back much. M$

Rico Pay Allende 329-A; 443 147 5251. With one of the best selections of sweet and savory pies in these parts, Rico Pay is a budget friendly and little-known gem with a reassuringly calm vibe. If you're feeling particularly famished, try a slice or two of the corn pie. M$$

Super Cocina Las Rosas Santiago Tapia 270, at Prieto. A row of pots bubbling on the stove contain the day's dishes, which might include meatballs, or chicken breast stuffed with cheese, all for a similar price. They also do pretty good breakfasts, but only with instant coffee. Note that they may close earlier if the food runs out so it's best to get here early. M$$

RESTAURANTS

El Comalito Madero 533 Pte; 443 313 9739. Tarascan and Mexican dishes in a relaxed and comfortable setting. Expect the likes of *pechuga azteca* (chicken breast stuffed with cheese) and salmon *a la plancha* cooked with fresh tarragon. M$$

★ **Los Mirasoles** Madero 549 Pte; 443 317 5775. Contemporary Mexican cuisine in a plush conversion of a seventeenth-century mansion – the courtyard is enchanting. There's a full range of delicious Michoacán specialities, including tacos *chamorro* (leg of pork) and *arrachera* fillet in walnut sauce. There's also a premium tasting menu. M$$$$

San Miguelito Av Camelinas, Fraccionamiento La Loma (at the southern end of Ventura Puente, opposite the Centro de Convenciones, 2km southeast of the centre); 443 324 2300. Superb, unpretentious Mexican dishes such as fish cooked in a banana leaf, and you can start with a *plato mescalero* of snacks to go with mescal (prices include two shots). The bar is a re-created bullring. Be sure to sit in the room filled with three hundred effigies of St Anthony and say a prayer for a good spouse. M$$$

4

DIRECTORY

Banks and exchange There are plenty of very grand banks with ATMs along Madero Ote, plus a *casa de cambio* at Prieto 48 near the Plaza de Armas, and one at Morelos Nte 51.

Pharmacy Farmacias del Ahorro, Madero Pte 33, opposite the cathedral (daily 24hr), several others along Madero and Morelos Sur.

Post office Madero Ote 369.

Telephones There are a number of *casetas* dotted around town, of which the most central is at Portal Galeana 103, on Madero opposite the cathedral.

The Monarch Butterfly Sanctuary and around

120km east of Morelia • Charge, discount for children • Pick-ups from Angangueo (see page 264) in season direct to the sanctuary entrance at El Rosario (40min), and also to the highway 2km from the entrance for Sierra Chincua; if no direct transport to El Rosario, you can go via the nearby village of Ocampo, 9km down the road; in season there are also direct buses from Mexico City Pte (Autobuses Zincantepec)

Each winter more than 150 million monarch **butterflies** migrate from the northeastern US and Canada to the Oyamel fir forests in the lush mountains of Michoacán in order to reproduce. It's an amazing sight at any time, but especially in January and February when numbers peak: whole trees are smothered in monarchs, branches sagging under the weight. In the cool of the morning, they dry their wings, turning the entire landscape a rich, velvety orange, while later in the day they take to the air, millions of fluttering butterflies making more noise than you'd ever think possible. As the afternoon humidity forces them to the ground, they form a thick carpet of blazing colour. The place to see the monarchs is in the **Santuario de la Mariposa Monarca** about 120km east of Morelia, with entrances at El Rosario and Sierra Chincua, near the village of Angangueo. While the Sierra Chincua entrance is, on the face of it, less convenient, with public transport dropping you 2km short, the hike inside the sanctuary is actually less strenuous from here. There are also sections of the sanctuary across the state line in the State of Mexico, which are most easily visited from Valle de Bravo (see page 191), but can also be accessed from Zitácuaro.

Visiting the monarchs is possible on day trips from Morelia and Mexico City, but it is more satisfying to stay locally (probably in Angangueo) and visit at a more leisurely pace. It is best to go early in the morning (and preferably on weekdays, to avoid the crowds), when the butterflies are just waking up and before they fly off into the surrounding woodlands. The walk to the best of the monarch-laden trees is about 2km, mostly uphill at an altitude of almost 3000m: take it easy if you're not acclimatized.

Tour guides, who are on hand at all the various park entrances and whose services are included in the entry fee, show you around the sanctuary and give a short explanation of the butterflies' life cycle and breeding habits. For a couple of weeks on either side of the main season, those same guides run the place unofficially, still charging the entry price and offering their services for a tip. There are fewer butterflies but it is still worth the journey any time from early November to early April, although the best time is in January or February. The sanctuary is open each year from mid-November to the end of March.

Zitácuaro

Most people approaching the butterfly sanctuary change buses at **Zitácuaro**, a small town prettily scattered over low hills at around 1900m. Being a little warmer than Angangueo makes it a potential base for visiting the Butterfly Sanctuary, even though it is further away from the most popular park areas at El Rosario and Sierra Chincua. It is however closer to the less frequented, and prettier, park area at **Cerro Pelón** in the State of Mexico (see page 191), though you will need to arrange your own transport (for example through the *Hotel Rancho San Cayetano*) to go there as it is not served by public transport from Michoacán.

Zitácuaro's epicentre is the junction of Hidalgo and Revolución, around which you'll find half a dozen hotels, restaurants, cinemas, and *casetas*. The main square, Plaza Juárez, a block south on Revolución and then a block west on Ocampo, is dominated by a statue of Benito Juárez, facing the town hall. The nearest thing to a tourist attraction here is the sixteenth-century church in the neighbouring village of **San Francisco** (known locally as **San Pancho**). The village has minor movie fame as the scene of the *dénouement* in John Huston's 1948 film classic, *The Treasure of the Sierra Madre*, starring Humphrey Bogart (see page 819).

LIFE CYCLE AND HABITAT OF THE MONARCH BUTTERFLY

The sheer size of the congregation of monarch butterflies in the hills of Michoacán is astonishing, but not as impressive as their 4500km **migration**. In the autumn, when the weather starts to turn cold in the Great Lakes region of the US and Canada, the butterflies head south, taking just four to five weeks to make it to Michoacán. The cool temperatures allow them to conserve energy, the trees provide shelter from wind and precipitation and the fog-laden air prevents them from drying out. Monarchs typically have a **life cycle** of around two to five weeks, but when they fly south they go into a phase known as "reproductive diapause", and end up living for seven months in all. The same butterflies remain in Michoacán all winter, then breed in spring in time for their caterpillars to dine on the newly emergent milkweed plants – their only food source – before returning to the US and Canada.

Around ten percent of all migrating monarchs get eaten by black-headed grosbeaks and black-backed orioles, but that offers no danger to species survival. The real threat is loss of this crucial mountain **habitat**. This was recognized as far back as 1986, when several key overwintering sites were protected from logging, but the local peasant families need the wood and they were never fully compensated for the loss of this resource. The Mexican government more than tripled the size of the reserves in 2000, but logging continued to a large enough extent that in early 2007 new president Felipe Calderón declared a "zero tolerance" policy against it, and increased policing. To learn more, check out the Monarch Watch website at http://monarchwatch.org.

4

ARRIVAL AND DEPARTURE — ZITÁCUARO

By bus The bus station is about 1km east of the centre, and is served by regular *combis* from right outside. Alternatively, you can walk to the centre, turning left along Pueblita, and then right down Hidalgo after two blocks.

Destinations Angangueo (frequent; 1hr); Mexico City Pte (1 hourly; 3hr); Morelia (frequent; 3hr); Ocampo (frequent; 45min); Toluca (2 hourly; 1hr 30min).

ACCOMMODATION

El Arco Hidalgo Ote 69, at Mora del Cañonazo Nte; 715 132 3425. Behind a boxy steel-and-glass exterior lies a simple hotel, with perfectly comfortable but no-frills rooms with wall-mounted TVs and a/c, and free coffee in the foyer. M$

México Revolución Sur 22; 715 153 2811. A block and a half south of Revolución with Hidalgo, this reasonably modern hotel is one of the better choices around that junction, with en-suite rooms, wi-fi and a downstairs restaurant. M$

Rancho San Cayetano Carretera a Huetamo km2.3 (2km south of town); www.ranchosancayetano.com. A wonderful place, set in private woodland, with lovely scenery, attractive rooms, a pool and a good restaurant. In season, they can also advise on visits to different butterfly locations. M$$$

EATING

Mimaki Jose Maria Coss Pte 12; 715 153 9257. This modern restaurant offers a menu which is ostensibly Japanese but really pan-Asian and beyond, with California rolls and other international sushi favourites on offer alongside spicy meat and noodle dishes, and creative takes on fajitas, tacos and other Mexican favourites. M$$

La Trucha Alegre Pueblita Sur 31; 715 113 4962. In this cavernous dining room, half a block north of Revolución with Nicolás Guillén, they serve trout in 35 different guises, including stuffed or bathed in all kinds of sauces; a simple trout *a la plancha* with *salsa verde* is a favourite here. It's a fun place to stick around of an evening too, with regular live music and occasional theme nights. M$$

Angangueo

Most butterfly visitors stay at **Angangueo**, 29km north of Zitácuaro, a former mining town wedged into a valley at almost 2600m: it can be cool in the evenings. The name is Purépechas for "entrance to the cave", presumably an early reference to its mineral extraction potential. The mines have now closed, but with its terracotta-tiled roofs,

JALISCO AND MICHOACÁN FIESTAS

Both Jalisco and Michoacán preserve strong native traditions and are particularly rich in fiestas: the list below is by no means exhaustive, and local tourist offices will have further details.

New Year's Day (Jan 1). Celebrated in Pátzcuaro (see page 281) and Uruapan (see page 276) with the Danza de los Viejitos (Dance of the Little Old Men; see page 278).

Día de los Santos Reyes (Jan 6). Twelfth Night is celebrated with many small ceremonies and dances such as Los Sonajeros (rattles), Las Pastoras (the shepherdesses) and El Baile de la Conquista (conquest). Particularly good at Los Reyes (west of Uruapan) and Cajititlán (30km south of Guadalajara).

Día de San Sebastian (Jan 20). Traditional dances in Tuxpan (30km southeast of Ciudad Guzmán).

Día de Nuestro Señor del Rescate (Feb 1). In Tzintzuntzán (see page 289), the start of a week-long fiesta founded in the sixteenth century by Vasco de Quiroga.

Carnaval (the week before Lent, variable Feb–March). Celebrated everywhere.

Palm Sunday (the Sun before Easter Sun). Palm ornament market in Uruapan (see page 276).

Semana Santa (Holy Week). Observed everywhere, but especially in Tzintzuntzán (see page 289).

Día de la Santa Cruz (May 3). Native dances in Angangueo (see page 299); mariachis and tequila in Tequila (see page 268).

Día del Señor de la Misericordia (last Sun in May). Fiesta and dances in Tuxpan (southeast of Ciudad Guzmán).

Corpus Christi (Thurs after Trinity, variable late May to early June). Traditional dances in Paracho (50km south of Zamora).

Día de San Pedro (June 29). Mariachi and dance festival in Tlaquepaque, Guadalajara (see page 246).

Día de la Preciosa Sangre de Cristo (first Sun in July). Torch-lit religious processions in Quiroga (25km northeast of Pátzcuaro).

Día de María Magdalena (July 22). Fiesta in Uruapan (see page 276) featuring a procession of animals.

Día de Santiago Apóstol (July 25). Lively celebrations and fireworks in Tuxpan (southeast of Ciudad Guzmán) and Uruapan (see page 276).

Fiesta tradicional (Aug 8). Ancient pre-Columbian fiesta in Paracho (65km south of Zamora).

Feria Nacional del Cobre (ten days in July or August). National Copper Fair in Santa Clara del Cobre (see page 290), near Pátzcuaro.

Fiestas de Octubre (all month). Massive cultural festival in Guadalajara (see page 246).

Día de San Francisco (Oct 4). Saint's day celebrations in Uruapan (see page 276).

Día de la Virgen de Zapopan (Oct 12). Massive pilgrimage in Guadalajara (see page 246).

Festival de Coros y Danzas (Oct 24–26). Singing and dancing competitions in Uruapan (see page 276).

Día de los Muertos (Day of the Dead; Nov 2). Celebrated everywhere, but especially around Pátzcuaro (see page 288). Also picturesque in Zitácuaro.

Arrival of the monarch butterfly (second week of Nov). *Las monarcas* start arriving in Michoacán in big numbers around now.

Festival Internacional de Música (second and third week of Nov). International Music Festival in Morelia (see page 290).

Día de la Inmaculada Concepción (Dec 8). Celebrated in Sayula (32km north of Ciudad Guzmán on the Tapalpa road).

La Señora de la Salud (Dec 8). Pilgrimage and dances in Pátzcuaro (see page 281) and Tequila (see page 268).

Día de la Virgen de Guadalupe (Dec 12). Large celebrations in Tapalpa (see page 274).

Pastoral plays (Dec 24). Performed in Tuxpan (southeast of Ciudad Guzmán).

winding streets and houses stacked up the hillside, it is an attractive enough place and offers the best selection of hotels and restaurants around – certainly better than Ocampo. Angangueo celebrates the Día de la Santa Cruz (May 3) with traditional dances. Most things happen on Morelos, which becomes Nacional at the point where the minor road Matamoros heads off up to the butterfly sanctuary. If you're feeling energetic, note that it's possible to walk back to Angangueo (around 2hr) downhill from the butterfly sanctuary entrance at El Rosario.

ARRIVAL AND DEPARTURE — ANGANGUEO

By bus Buses drop off at the top of the town, and then head down to the junction of Nacional and Matamoros.

Destinations Mexico City Pte (4 daily; 4hr); Ocampo (frequent; 25min); Zitácuaro (frequent; 1hr).

ACCOMMODATION

Don Bruno Morelos 92, 1km south of the town centre; 715 156 0026. The best place to stay in Angangueo by far: large, carpeted rooms (all featuring religious images) surround a lovely garden, with a good restaurant and free wi-fi. It's a bit of a climb to the bus stop, but otherwise couldn't be more convenient. M$$

Juárez Nacional 15, in the town centre; 715 156 0023. A friendly place with reasonable en-suite rooms set around a flower-filled courtyard. The stationery shop next door doubles as the hotel reception. M$

Plaza Don Gabino Morelos 147; 715 156 0322. Friendly hotel in a traditional villa backing onto the forest on the main road southwest of the town centre. Low-ceilinged rooms are basic but homely, though there's no heating and they can get chilly in the mornings and evenings. The restaurant is well regarded and serves traditional regional dishes. M$$

Rancho Cumbra Monarca El Rosario, 2km down the hill from the sanctuary entrance; http://ranchocumbremonarca.com. Also known locally as *Rancho Givali*, this is the closest accommodation to the butterfly sanctuary, right there in the woods, offering comfortable, traditional rooms and a good restaurant. Rooms have tiled floors and crucifixes on the walls, and TVs with DVD players. If you want to take the chill off those winter evenings, it's worth asking for one with a fireplace. M$$$

Real Monarca Nacional 16-A, in the town centre; http://hotelrealmonarca.wixsite.com/hotelrealmonarca. Rosa Ramirez runs this very cosy posada on the main hotel street, and includes a continental breakfast with her rates. Rooms are spotless and they can organize tours of other regional sights out of season. M$$

4

EATING

Restaurant Los Arcos Plaza de la Constitucion 5-A; 715 150 0512. The best eating place in the town centre, where you'll pay very reasonable prices for good, home-style Mexican dishes (chicken *mole*, for example). The range is limited, but the food is always good, and they do great breakfasts and *comidas corridas*. M$$

The Bajío

SCULPTURE AT LAS POZAS

The Bajío

North of Mexico City, the fertile valleys of the Bajío ("Lowlands") are sprinkled with wealthy colonial towns and rugged, dust-blown hills. This has long been the most heavily populated part of the country, providing much of the silver and grain that supported Mexico throughout the years of Spanish rule. Indeed, the legacy of Spanish architecture remains at its most impressive here, in meticulously crafted towns that – at their cores at least – have changed little over the centuries.

The Bajío grew rich on just one thing – **silver** – but in time the region also grew restive under the heavy-handed rule of Spain. The wealthy Creole (Spanish-blooded but Mexican-born) bourgeoisie were free to exploit the land and its people, but didn't control their own destinies; lucrative government posts and high positions in the Church were reserved exclusively for those actually born in Spain, while the Indigenous peoples and poor *mestizos* were condemned either to landless poverty or to near-fatal labour. Unsurprisingly, then, the Bajío was ripe for revolution. This land is *La Cuna de la Independencia* (the **Cradle of Independence**), where every town seems to claim a role in the break with Spain. **Dolores Hidalgo**, in particular, is a point of pilgrimage for anyone with the least interest in Mexico's independence movement, as is, to a lesser extent, **Querétaro**, a large and booming modern city that preserves an underrated colonial quarter at its heart. Querétaro also serves as a good base for exploring the **Sierra Gorda**, particularly the concrete fantasy sculptures of **Las Pozas** near Xilitla. **Guanajuato**, quite simply one of the country's most scenic colonial towns, is close to **San Miguel de Allende**, which also has its advocates, as much for its wonderful setting as for the comforts of home, ensured by a large population of foreign artists, gringo retirees and language students. Heading north, the less-visited city of **Aguascalientes** is a real pleasure, with an appealing roster of colonial relics, art from José Posada and fabulous food. The north of the region is dominated by the colonial cities of **Zacatecas** and **San Luis Potosí** – both eponymous state capitals and oases of culture and sophistication, built largely with the bounty of the silver mines that riddle the landscape hereabouts. Approaching the Bajío from the US border, you cross several hundred kilometres of desert landscape punctuated only by the occasional ranch, or defunct mining towns, such as the wonderfully strange semi-ghost-town of **Real de Catorce**, where decades of abandonment are gradually being reversed.

Querétaro and around

Of all the colonial cities in the Bajío, **QUERÉTARO** is perhaps the most surprising, with a tranquil historical core that boasts magnificent mansions and some of the country's finest ecclesiastical architecture. Little more than two hours from Mexico City, it's also a wealthy and booming city of over eight hundred thousand people, one of the fastest growing in the republic. Querétaro's colonial centre is particularly magical at the weekends, when festive crowds and markets throng the streets, and church bells echo across plazas linked by narrow alleys lined with restaurants and bars.

There are points of interest, too, in the surrounding hills of the Sierra Gorda, notably the small towns of **Bernal** and **Tequisquiapan**, and the much more distant charms of Edward James's jungle "sculpture garden" at **Xilitla**.

Highlights

❶ **Peña de Bernal** Hike up the slopes of this stunning tower of rock, one of the world's tallest monoliths, easily accessible from the colonial city of Querétaro. See page 316

❷ **Las Pozas** Visit the surreal creation of English eccentric Edward James, a fantasy of concrete statues and structures surrounded by lush jungle. See page 320

❸ **San Miguel de Allende** Gorgeous colonial town with boutique hotels and highly regarded Spanish language schools. See page 321

❹ **Guanajuato** Captivating university town set dramatically over the steep slopes of a ravine. See page 334

❺ **Posada pilgrimage** José Posada's macabre work is the pride of Aguascalientes, shown in the Museo José Guadalupe Posada and the Museo de la Muerte. See page 351

❻ **Mercado de la Bírria** The aromatic birrierías at Aguascalientes' Mercado de la Bírriaare eye-popping, but slow-roasted goat is the real star. See page 354

❼ **Zacatecas** Handsome former silver-mining town located high up in the northern deserts. See page 355

❽ **Real de Catorce** Artfully restored colonial hotels, fine Italian meals and haunting desert scenery in a semi-ghost town. See page 372

HIGHLIGHTS ARE MARKED ON THE MAP ON PAGE 306

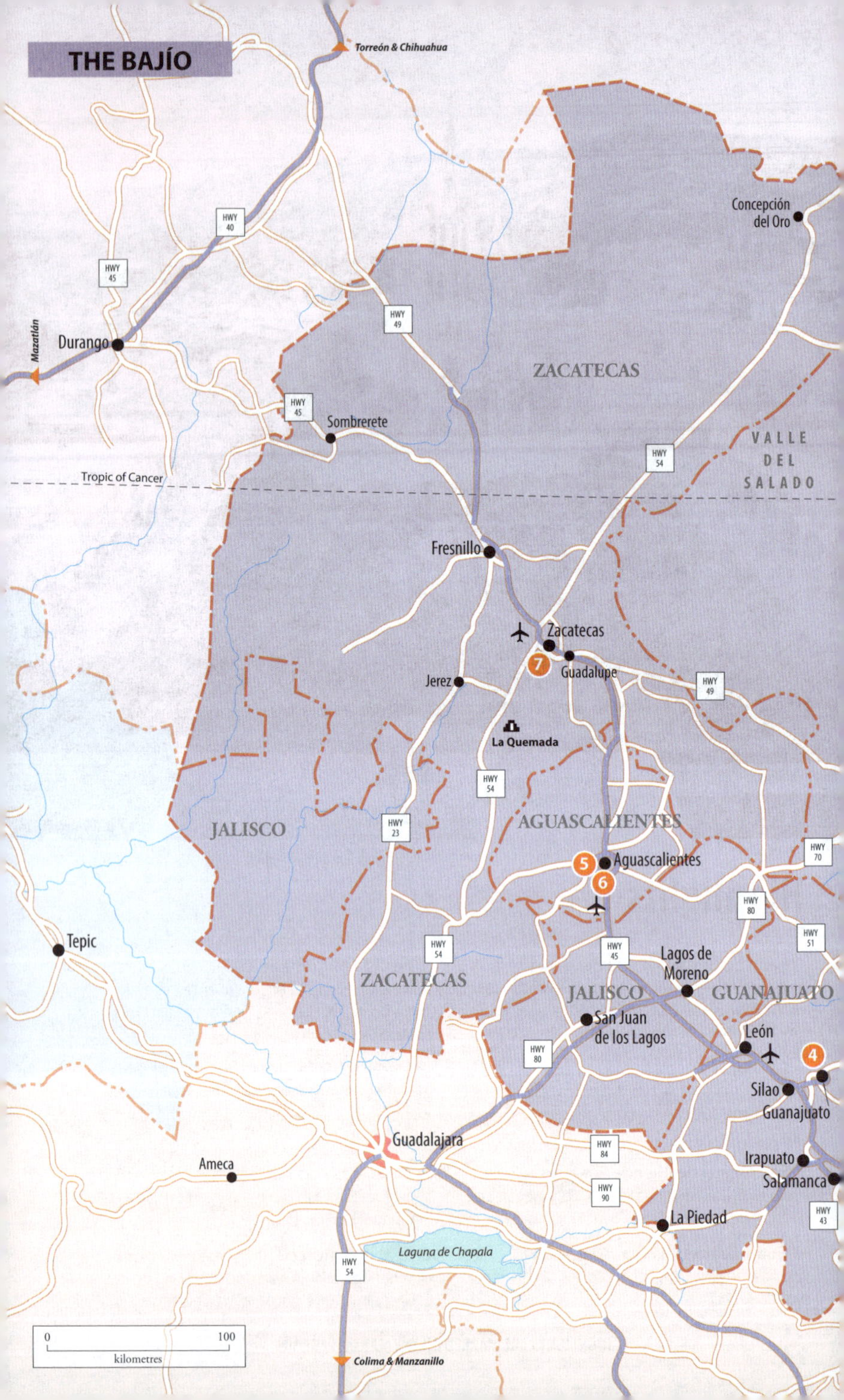
THE BAJÍO
Torreón & Chihuahua
Mazatlán
Durango
HWY 40
HWY 45
HWY 49
HWY 45
Sombrerete
Tropic of Cancer
Concepción del Oro
ZACATECAS
VALLE DEL SALADO
HWY 54
Fresnillo
Zacatecas
7
Guadalupe
Jerez
HWY 49
La Quemada
HWY 54
HWY 23
JALISCO
AGUASCALIENTES
5
Aguascalientes
6
HWY 70
HWY 80
HWY 51
Tepic
HWY 54
HWY 45
Lagos de Moreno
ZACATECAS
JALISCO
GUANAJUATO
San Juan de los Lagos
León
4
HWY 80
Silao
Guanajuato
Guadalajara
HWY 84
Irapuato
Ameca
Salamanca
HWY 90
HWY 43
La Piedad
Laguna de Chapala
HWY 54
0
100
kilometres
Colima & Manzanillo

HIGHLIGHTS
1 Peña de Bernal
2 Las Pozas
3 San Miguel de Allende
4 Guanajuato
5 Posada pilgrimage
6 Mercado de la Bírria
7 Zacatecas
8 Real de Catorce
Saltillo
Saltillo & Monterrey
Matamoros
HWY 54
HWY 85
HWY 57
HWY 31
HWY 101
Río Corona
Presa de Las Adjuntas
Ciudad Victoria
HWY 85
HWY 70
Estación Catorce
Real de Catorce
Matehuala
Wadley
HWY 57
SAN LUIS POTOSÍ
GULF OF MEXICO
HWY 57
HWY 101
HWY 80
Ciudad Mante
San Luis Potosí
Tampico
HWY 70
Río Verde
HWY 70
Ciudad Valles
HWY 105
HWY 85
LA RESERVA DE LA BIOSFERA SIERRA GORDA
Xilitla
Dolores Hidalgo
HWY 57
San Luis de la Paz
Santuario de Atotoncilo
Pozos
Jalpan
Landa de Matamoros
Escondido
La Gruta
San José Iturbide
San Miguel de Allende
QUERÉTARO
HWY 85
HWY 105
HWY 120
Cañada de la Virgen
Bernal
Ezequiel Montes
HWY 45
Querétaro
Celaya
Tequisquiapan
San Juan del Río
HWY 85
HWY 51
HWY 57
Acámbaro
Pachuca
Tula
HWY 130
Morelia
Toluca
Mexico City

5

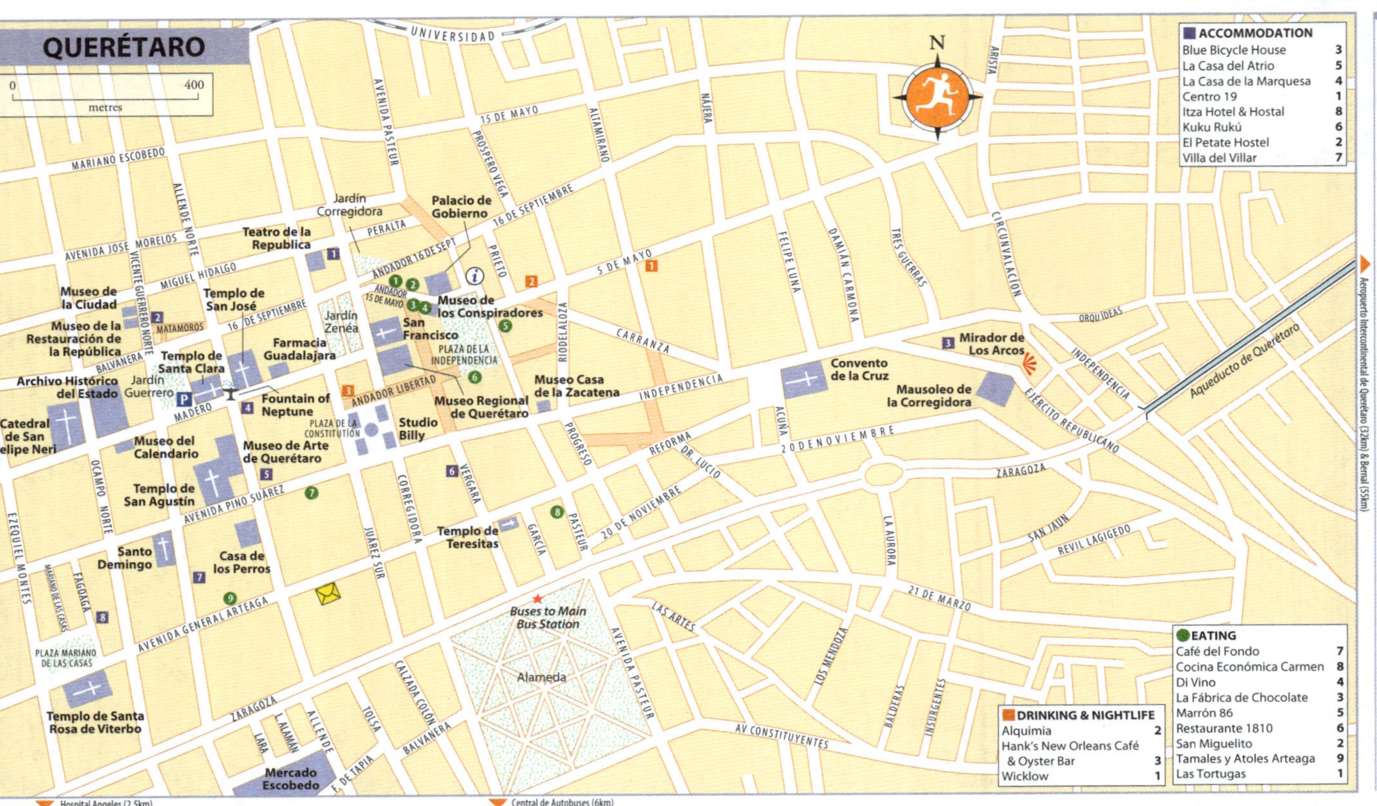

Jardín Zenéa and around

Querétaro's main plaza is the elegant **Jardín Zenéa**, with its typical triumvirate of bandstand, clipped trees and bootshines. To the west lies the commercial centre with the bulk of the chain stores, but you'll probably spend much of your time to the east among the gift shops, restaurants and bars leading to the **Plaza de la Independencia** (see page 310), or one block south to the **Plaza de la Constitución**. Formerly a market square, the latter has been transformed into an attractive modern plaza with a central fountain that mimics the domed roof of the building on its south side. Just to the north of Jardín Zenéa lies the shady **Jardín Corregidora**, with an imposing statue of La Corregidora (see page 309) and several restaurants and bars where you can sit outside.

Templo de San Francisco

Jardín Zenéa • Free

The **Templo de San Francisco**, dominating the Jardín Zenéa, was one of the earliest churches founded in the city. Its eye-popping facade incorporates a dome covered in *azulejos* – coloured tiles imported from Spain around 1540 – but for the most part San Francisco was rebuilt in the seventeenth and eighteenth centuries. Take a look at the similarly opulent interior for an introduction to the city's remarkable treasure trove of religious art.

Museo de los Conspiradores

Andador 15 de Mayo no. 18 • Free • 442 214 5423

One of the city's newer museums is the small but illuminating **Museo de los Conspiradores**. The museum marks Querétaro's importance as home of the nation's Independence conspirators by charting the emergence of popular revolutions against absolutist monarchy in the late eighteenth century onwards (thus "conspirators"). Galleries provide special emphasis on risings in the US, France, Peru and Haiti, and the ideas they generated.

Museo Regional de Querétaro

Corregidora 3 (Jardín Zenéa) • Charge • 442 212 4888

Adjoining the Templo de San Francisco, in what used to be the Convento de San Francisco, is the **Museo Regional de Querétaro**. The building alone is reason enough to visit, though the displays inside are well worth an hour or two. Built around two large tangerine-coloured cloisters, the museum charts the history of Querétaro state, beginning with a large section on prehistoric culture and the region's Indigenous tribes. Displays upstairs focus on the spiritual history of the region under the Spanish missionaries. The final series of galleries tackles the revolutionary period, beginning with the stirrings of nationalism in the 1760s through to 1917, with artefacts, documents and detailed commentary. Precious items include the key and keyhole through which **La Corregidora** passed on her news in 1810 (see page 309), and the

LA CORREGIDORA

It was in Querétaro, meeting under the guise of literary associations, that the Mexican Independence conspirators (or "reformers") laid their earliest plans. In 1810 one of their number, María Josefa Ortiz de Domínguez, wife of the town's Corregidor (or governor – she is known as "**La Corregidora**"), was locked in her room while her husband was ordered to seek out the conspirators (though he was also sympathetic to their cause) – she managed to get a message out to Ignacio Pérez, who carried it to Independence movement leaders Allende and Hidalgo in the towns of San Miguel and Dolores, thus precipitating an unexpectedly early start to the independence struggle.

incredibly ornate table on which the **Treaty of Guadalupe Hidalgo** was signed in 1848 (ending the Mexican–American War by handing over almost half of Mexico's territory to the US). The corridor outside is lined with fifteen **Miguel Cabrera** paintings. As impressive as the museum is, you really need to read Spanish to make the most of it (no English labels).

Teatro de la República

Juárez and Ángela Peralta • Free • 442 212 0339

There's more to see a couple of blocks north of the Jardín Zenéa at the **Teatro de la República**. Opened in 1852, this grand theatre has played a vital role in Mexican history: a court met here to decide the fate of Emperor Maximilian in 1867, and in 1917 the Mexican Constitution was agreed upon inside. A small exhibition celebrates the latter event upstairs (above the lobby), though the main reason to walk up here is to take a peek at the theatre itself, a magnificent space with four levels of enclosed balcony seating. Today the theatre is home to the Querétaro Philharmonic Orchestra and hosts several concerts through the year – call or ask at the tourist office for the latest programme.

Plaza de la Independencia

One block east of Plaza de la Constitución and Jardín Zenéa lies the **Plaza de la Independencia**, aka Plaza de Armas, a very refined, arcaded open space and the most appealing place to eat and drink alfresco in the city (see page 314). In the middle of the plaza stands a statue of Don Juan Antonio de Urrutia y Arana, the man who built Querétaro's all-important aqueduct (see page 313), providing the city with drinking water.

Palacio de Gobierno

Plaza de la Independencia • Free

On the north side of Plaza de la Independencia is the Casa de la Corregidora, now the **Palacio de Gobierno**, office of the Governor of Querétaro state. It was here, on September 14, 1810, that La Corregidora was locked up (see page 309). Free guided tours are usually available on demand to see busts of La Corregidora and her husband, plus some of the elegant interiors and a series of striking historical murals by Víctor Cauduro created 2012–2015.

Museo Casa de la Zacatecana

Independencia 59 • Charge • http://museolazacatecana.com

One of the best museums in the city lies a block south of the Plaza de la Independencia. The **Museo Casa de la Zacatecana** is an expertly preserved eighteenth-century mansion, incredibly evocative of the period and enhanced with English videos and English labels throughout. The rooms are filled with over six hundred pieces of art and furniture, but the real draw (for Mexican tourists, at least) is the grisly

THE LEGEND OF THE ZACATECANA

Visit the **Museo Casa de la Zacatecana** (see page 310) and you'll be introduced to the ghoulish legend of the woman who lived here in the seventeenth century. The story goes that the original owner – from Zacatecas – was murdered by his wife (she was rumoured to have had lovers). Soon after this the evil *zacatecana* was also stabbed to death mysteriously. Years later, human bones were dug up in the back of the house – but there were two skeletons, not one, prompting some to believe the wife had also murdered the killer she had hired to murder her husband; ghosts have been seen here ever since.

legend associated with the house (see page 310). Less macabre highlights include the fascinating "universal history" parchment (1882) in Sala 1, with global cultures displayed like branches of a tree, and the Salon de los Cristos upstairs, containing 54 crucifixes and a Miguel Cabrera painting of the cross (1746). The Salon de los Rejoles overflows with 39 antique clocks – an interesting way to present what would otherwise be fairly dry exhibits.

Jardín Guerrero and around

Two blocks west of Jardín Zenéa, **Jardín Guerrero** is a far more relaxed place, with food vendors dozing peacefully under trees and families enjoying the delicious sweet snacks on offer.

Fountain of Neptune

Heading along Madero from Jardín Zenéa towards Jardín Guerrero you'll pass the famous **Fountain of Neptune** at Allende, designed by **Francisco Tresguerras** in 1797. Tresguerras (1765–1833) is rightly regarded as one of Mexico's greatest architects – he was also a sculptor, painter and poet – and was almost single-handedly responsible for developing a native Mexican architectural style diverging from (though still close to) its Spanish roots.

Templo de Santa Clara

Madero 42 • Free, donation suggested • 442 212 1777

Beside the Fountain of Neptune and backing on to the Jardín Guerrero is the deceptively simple church of **Templo de Santa Clara**, once attached to one of the country's richest monasteries, dating back to 1633. Inside it's a riot of Baroque excess, with gilded cherubs and angels swarming all over the profusely decorated *retablos* (gold-painted wooden altarpieces), created in the 1770s, virtually lining the length of the nave.

Museo del Calendario

Madero 91 • Charge • http://mucal.mx

Carry on west down Madero beyond Jardín Guerrero and you get to the **Museo del Calendario**, an unusual museum created by local company Calendarios Landin that celebrates the art of calendar making. Galleries occupy a wonderfully restored eighteenth-century mansion and chart the history of calendars in Mexico with displays of over 400 originals. Spanish labels only.

Catedral de San Felipe Neri

Madero, at Ocampo • Free, donation suggested

Just beyond the Museo del Calendario on Madero lies **Catedral de San Felipe Neri**, which was completed in 1805 but only given cathedral status in 1931. The facade is a wonderful blend of pink sandstone and soaring Corinthian columns looking like carrot tops, but by Querétaro's standards, the interior is relatively plain.

Museo de la Restauración de la República

Guerrero 23 • Free • 442 224 3004

Aficionados of Mexican history should make time for the **Museo de la Restauración de la República**, one block north of Jardín Guerrero. An ex-Capuchin monastery founded in 1721 (though most of what you see was added in the nineteenth century), its small and well-presented series of rooms and courtyards is dedicated to the history of the **French Intervention** (1863–67) and the restoration of the Republic under Benito Juárez, highlighted with period weaponry, old prints, scale models and other bits and pieces. A room is also dedicated to French-backed

Emperor Maximilian himself, who was imprisoned here in 1867 before being shot – again, though, you need to read Spanish to get the most out of the museum.

Museo de la Ciudad

Guerrero 27 • Charge • 442 212 4702

Occupying the same ex-convent premises as the Museo de la Restauración de la República, the **Museo de la Ciudad** fills a warren of rooms and galleries with temporary exhibitions, mainly contemporary installation art, painting, sculpture and photography.

Museo de Arte de Querétaro

Allende 14 • Charge, free Tues • https://museodeartedequeretaro.com.mx

A block south of the Jardín Guerrero lies the **Museo de Arte de Querétaro**, occupying the former Palacio Federal next to the church of **San Agustín** (another example of Baroque splendour – check out the gargoyles with water spouts on the roof). Originally an Augustinian monastery completed in 1728, the museum is one the most ornate buildings in town. In the cloister, every surface of the two storeys of portals is carved with grotesque figures, no two quite alike, and with abstract designs. The sculptures, often attributed to Tresguerras though almost certainly not by him, are full of religious symbolism, which you should try to get someone to explain to you. The large figures supporting the arches, for example, all hold their fingers in different positions: three held up to represent the Trinity, four for the Evangelists and so on. The main galleries are devoted to mediocre seventeenth-century European painting (mostly anonymous artists but some by **Miguel Cabrera**) and nineteenth-century Mexican art downstairs, along with temporary exhibition spaces usually featuring much better contemporary work.

Templo de Santa Rosa de Viterbo

Arteaga, at Montes • Free • 442 214 1691

The **Templo de Santa Rosa de Viterbo**, completed in 1752, sits a few blocks southwest of the Jardín Guerrero, but is well worth the short walk. Its magnificent interior rivals Santa Clara for richness of decoration, plastered with artwork, murals and vast gold churrigueresque *retablos*, but here there is no false modesty on the outside either. Two enormous painted flying buttresses support the octagonal cupola (remodelled by Tresguerras) and a blue-and-white-tiled dome. The tower, too, is Tresguerras' work, holding what is said to be the first four-sided public clock erected on the American continent. Inside, note the Mudéjar-style ivory pulpit and, in the sacristy, portraits of José Velázquez de Lore (who funded the church) and Sor Ana María de San Francisco y Neve (by an anonymous artist), one of the most admired religious paintings in Mexico.

Convento de la Cruz

Ejército Republicano, at Felipe Luna • Charge

A short walk east from the centre lies the **Convento de la Cruz**, built on the site of the battle between the Spaniards and the Otomí and Chichimecas in 1531. According to legend, the fighting was cut short by the miraculous appearance of Spanish patron saint St James ("Santiago" in Spanish – the city's full name is Santiago de Querétaro – who coincidentally was also claimed to have helped vanquish the Moors), and a dazzling cross in the sky, which persuaded the Otomí and Chichimecas to accept defeat and become Christians.

The **Capilla del Calvarito**, next door to the monastery entrance, marks the spot where the first Mass was celebrated after the battle. The monastery itself was founded in 1683 by the Franciscans as a college (Colegio Apostólico de

Propaganda Fide) and grew over the years into an important centre for the training of missionaries, with a massive library and rich collection of relics. Because of its hilltop position and hefty construction, the monastery was also frequently used as a fortress. Functioning as one of the last Spanish redoubts in the War of Independence, it was also Maximilian's headquarters for the last few weeks of his reign and he was subsequently imprisoned here to await execution (before being moved to the monastery on Guerrero; see page 311).

The monastery's greatest source of pride is the **Árbol de la Cruz**, a tree in the garden whose thorns sprout in the shape of little crosses. The tree grew, so the story goes, from a walking stick left behind by a mysterious saintly traveller who slept here one night. It certainly does produce thorns in the form of crosses, and the monks, who appear very excited by the phenomenon, point out that an additional five percent of the thorns grow with extra spikes to mark the spots where nails were driven through Christ's hands and feet; look for the framed collection in the entrance foyer. Half-hour guided tours in English are available on request.

Mausoleo de la Corregidora

Ejército Republicano • Free

Come up to the Convento de la Cruz in the late afternoon, then wander 200m further east along Ejército Republicano to the **Mausoleo de la Corregidora**, where the heroine's remains (see page 309), along with those of her husband, are surrounded by statues of other illustrious Querétanos. Across the road the **Mirador de los Arcos** provides a spellbinding sunset view of the city's 1.3km-long **aqueduct** (Acueducto de Querétaro), a graceful series of 74 arches up to 23m high, built between 1726 and 1738 to bring water into the city from springs nearly 9km away.

Cerro de las Campañas

Tecnológico, at Hidalgo • Charge • 442 215 9031

One kilometre west of the centre via Morelos or Hidalgo, the gentle eminence of the **Cerro de las Campañas** ("Hill of Bells") commands wide, if less than scenic, views over Querétaro and its industrial outskirts. Maximilian and his two generals, Miguel Miramón and Tomás Mejía, faced the firing squad here (a small chapel, built in 1900 by Porfirio Díaz near the entrance, marks the spot). The hill is dominated by a vast stone statue of the victor of that particular war, Benito Juárez, glaring down over the town.

Museo La Magia del Pasado

Cerro de la Campanas • Charge, free for kids under 15 • 442 224 0498

Beyond the statue of Benito Juárez on the Cerro de las Campañas is the mildly entertaining **Museo La Magia del Pasado**, with lots of interactive exhibits on Querétaro's history targeted primarily at kids; the main focus is the Republican attack of 1867 that led to Maximilian's capture.

ARRIVAL AND INFORMATION — QUERÉTARO

By plane Aeropuerto Intercontinental de Querétaro (442 192 5500, http://aiq.com.mx) is 32km northeast of the centre on Hwy-200 to Tequisquiapan. Aeroméxico runs daily flights from Monterrey, which is much quicker than the bus, but can be expensive. There are also direct flights from Atlanta, Chicago, Dallas and Houston in the US, and other destinations in Mexico via TAR Aerolineas, Viva and Volaris. Taxis charge a moderate amount for the trip into town. Hertz and Budget have rental counters at the airport.

By bus Querétaro's massive Central de Autobuses (with internet café and a 24hr left luggage (guardería)) lies 6km south of town and is one of the busiest in this part of Mexico, with three separate terminals: A for long-distance and first-class companies, and B and C for shorter runs and second-class companies (don't confuse these for salas A, B, C and D inside Terminal A). Fixed-price taxis (buy a ticket from the kiosk) run from outside all terminals (downtown is zone C), and an endless shuttle of local buses runs to the centre from the end of Terminal B. Buses generally don't enter the historic centre, so get off at Zaragoza, by the Alameda, and

5

walk from there. This is also the spot to pick up services back to the bus station (#19, #25 or #36).

Note that there are hourly first-class buses (ETN) to San Miguel de Allende beginning at 8.50am, and at least three to Guanajuato.

Destinations Aguascalientes (6 daily; 5hr); Bernal (hourly; 1hr); Dolores Hidalgo (every 40min; 2hr); Guadalajara (every 30min; 4–5hr); Guanajuato (73 daily; 2hr 30min–3hr); Jalpan (hourly; 5hr); Mexico City and Mexico City Airport (every 30min; 3–4hr); Morelia (every 30–60min; 3–4hr); San Juan del Río (every 20min 6am–10pm; 45min); San Luis Potosí (hourly; 2hr 30min); San Miguel de Allende (every 40min; 1hr 15min); Tequisquiapan (every 30min; 1hr); Xilitla (1 first-class daily at noon; 5–7hr; 3–4 second-class daily; 7–8hr);

Tourist office The tourist office, Pasteur Nte 4 (daily 9am–7pm; 442 238 5067, http://queretaro.travel), offers free maps and basic advice.

GETTING AROUND

By bus All city buses are the same fee (cash) or slightly less with a prepaid card, but if the bus is part of the flashy new Qrobús system you'll need a prepaid card with a minimum amount already loaded to board (buy them at the Casa de la Cultura or the Antigua Presidencia Municipal).

By taxi The city has been battling to introduce taxi meters for years, but until this is implemented make sure you agree the price with the driver in advance – the bus station should be the cheapest fare from downtown. The city is home to ride-sharing services Cabify (http://cabify.com) and Uber (http://uber.com) – use of smartphones and the usual precautions apply.

ACCOMMODATION

SEE MAP PAGE 308

As with most Bajío cities, there are plenty of good-value **motel** chains on the outskirts of Querétaro, but unless you are just passing through by car, or don't mind taking a lot of taxis, opt for the far more convenient options in the *centro histórico*. Querétaro now has numerous **boutique**-type places, usually conversions of old mansions. There are also several budget options and **hostels**, with dorm beds. All accommodation has free wi-fi unless otherwise mentioned.

★ **La Casa del Atrio** Allende Sur 15; http://lacasadelatrio.com. This posh B&B has garnered a loyal following, combining first-class hospitality with an art gallery; the six cosy rooms are adorned with art, rugs and murals by Claudia Ramos, with views of San Agustín church and two arches from the city aqueduct in the garden. M$$$$

La Casa de la Marquesa Madero 41; 442 227 0500. Enchanting hotel housed in a 1756 mansion with a gorgeous Moorish courtyard. The antique-furnished Imperial suites are magnificent, though they also have slightly less luxurious rooms in a separate building across the road. Breakfast included. M$$$

Centro 19 Corregidora 19, at Ángela Peralta; 442 212 1234. Considering the quality, location and price, this is a great option; no wonder its rooms – modern, simple but stylish – are almost always booked solid. Free parking and cable TV. M$$

★ **Kuku Rukú** Vergara 12; http://kukuruku.mx. This hotel offers stylish double rooms and posher suites decked out with contemporary art, all including breakfast. The hotel describes itself as eco-friendly thanks to its use of solar power, collected rainwater and its own vegetable garden. M$$

★ **Villa del Villar** Vicente Guerrero Sur 33, between Pino Suárez and Arteaga; 442 223 2270. One of the best deals in town, with ten modern, well-equipped rooms within an enchanting sixteenth-century mansion – each one is named after a different town in Querétaro state, and features the traditional arts or crafts of that locale. M$$$

HOSTELS

Blue Bicycle House Ejército Republicano 15, La Pastora; 442 527 1766, https://www.facebook.com/bluebicyclehouse. Excellent hostel with modern mixed and women's dorm plus simple but stylish doubles with cable TV and shared bathrooms. Dorms (mixed) are the cheapest; doubles are about twice the price. M$

Itza Hotel & Hostal Francisco Fagoaga 17, between Arteaga and Pino Suárez; 442 212 4223. Solid budget option arranged around a tranquil interior patio, with cheap doubles available (some with private bathrooms). Breakfast and parking are extra but the use of free bikes is included. M$

★ **El Petate Hostel** Matamoros 20, just off Vicente Guerrero; http://elpetatehostel.com. Extremely well-designed hostel in a fabulous location, with 12-person dorms decorated with cool murals and modern, comfy bunks. Also offers a variety of private rooms with single and double beds. Free computer use, plus bright patio with shared TV and kitchen. M$

EATING

SEE MAP PAGE 308

There's plenty of good food in Querétaro, but try to sample a couple of **local specialities**; the hearty lentil soup (pork-broth based) laced with chunks of dried fruit (usually just called "sopa regional"), and the *enchiladas Queretanas*, tortillas fried in a chile sauce and stuffed with onions and cheese. If you want to get together something of your own, head for the **Mercado Escobedo**, sprawled across several blocks just off Calzada Zaragoza, not far from the Alameda.

CAFÉS AND SNACKS

Café del Fondo Pino Suárez 9; 442 212 0170. This airy multi-roomed café serves bargain breakfasts: fresh juice, good coffee (with a big coffee grinder wafting aromas over the tables), and a plate of eggs, enchiladas or hotcakes for a good price. There are also more substantial dishes available throughout the day. One room is often devoted to boardgames, most frequently chess, and mariachis occasionally wander in to serenade diners. M$$

★ **La Fábrica de Chocolate** Andador 5 de Mayo 10; 442 212 6606. Best place in the city for Oaxacan chocolate and churros (the cornerstone of a healthy breakfast), plus chocolate ice cream and lots of chocolate-themed gifts (like shampoo and soap). M$$

★ **Tamales y Atoles Arteaga** Arteaga 48; 442 224 2265. This local secret, on a stretch of street with several tamale specialists, knocks out steaming-hot tamales as you wait: choose from regular (*salsa verde con carne* or *rajas con queso*) or *Tamales Oaxaqueños* (like *mole con pollo*). M$

Las Tortugas Andador 5 de Mayo 27; 442 753 6992. This venerable snack stop, decorated in bullfighting memorabilia (the original founder was a fan), has been knocking out tasty tortas since 1956. Crusty baps are filled with ham, cheese, chicken or mince, and enhanced by spicy salsas. M$

RESTAURANTS

★ **Cocina Económica Carmen** Pasteur Sur 50; 442 224 3086. This no frills Mexican spot has garnered rave reviews for its fresh and budget friendly fare. M$$

Di Vino Andador 5 de Mayo 12; http://divino.com.mx. Quality Italian restaurant and wine bar, a great place to splurge, with superb pastas and especially fresh seafood (with over two hundred Italian wines). Top-class service and a classy atmosphere. M$$$$

Marrón 86 Pasteur 9, Plaza de la Independencia; 442 214 3994. Prime real estate under the colonnades on the Plaza de Armas or in the tiny courtyard at the back. The pasta dishes, stuffed baguettes and salads are so-so, and their coffee is really the highlight. Free wi-fi. M$

Restaurante 1810 Andador Libertad 62 (Plaza de la Independencia); http://restaurante1810.com. Outstanding sidewalk restaurant that does regional specialities with a French twist. You'll have to take your chances with the live entertainment – sometimes relaxing jazz, though often cheesy crooners. M$$

★ **San Miguelito** Andador 5 de Mayo 39; https://www.sanmiguelitoqro.com.mx. This unique spot has a justly earned reputation as one of the city's best restaurants, and you're guaranteed an impressive selection of delicious regional, national and international dishes in eclectic surroundings – it's set inside the courtyard of the *Casona de los Cincos Patios*. Try the chicken in chipotle sauce or one of their fine steaks. M$$$$

DRINKING AND NIGHTLIFE

SEE MAP PAGE 308

Evening **entertainment** tends to involve a couple of beers in one of the restaurants or an hour or two lingering in one of the cafés on the plazas – during holidays it's especially lively on Plaza de la Independencia and Jardín Zenéa, with street performers and buskers with guitars and violins, and families enjoying ice creams. For a livelier bar scene, trawl along 5 de Mayo and see where the night takes you. The bigger **clubs** are all out in the suburbs and fashions change rapidly, so ask around and follow the crowd (probably by taxi). Many have some sort of live music at weekends and a cover charge to get in.

Alquimia 5 de Mayo 71; 442 384 0666. Sophisticated, dimly lit bodega with bottles racked up behind the bar and the doors thrown open to the street. Perfect for a quiet beer or one of their delicious cocktails.

Hank's New Orleans Café & Oyster Bar Juárez Sur 7; http://hanksmexico.com. The former *Harry's* bar has one of the most sought-after terraces in the city, overlooking Plaza de la Constitución (it also serves fresh seafood, Cajun and creole dishes), with a decent wine and cocktail list.

Wicklow 5 de Mayo 86; 442 212 0947. Every aspiring international city seems to have at least one Irish pub, and Querétaro is no exception, *Wicklow*'s green-washed exterior hinting at all the usual themes inside – Guinness, stews and plenty of good craic.

DIRECTORY

Banks and exchange There are several banks around the Jardín Zenéa that will change currency, and a couple of *casas de cambio* south along Juárez.

Books and newspapers Querétaro has plenty of bookshops, but you'll be lucky to find anything in English. International weeklies can usually be found at the newspaper stands around the Jardín Zenéa and the Plaza de la Independencia. Beyond that, Sanborn's, at Constituyentes 172, 2km southeast of the centre, has a wide range of magazines.

Emergencies For general emergencies call 066; Cruz Roja 442 229 0505.

Hospital Hospital Angeles (442 192 3000, http://hospitalesangeles.com/queretaro), Bernardino del Razo 21, Ensueño, is the best private hospital in the region, with English-speaking staff and 24hr facilities.

Pharmacy There are dozens of pharmacies around the centre, including the large Farmacia Guadalajara at Madero 32, just west of the Jardín Zenéa.

Post office Arteaga 5.

5

Around Querétaro

It's worth spending a few days exploring the towns and villages of Querétaro State close to the capital, particularly the great peak at **Bernal** and the historic enclaves of **Tequisquiapan** and **San Juan del Río**.

Bernal

The pretty village of **BERNAL**, 60km east of Querétaro, hunkers under the skirts of the soaring **Peña de Bernal**, a 350m-high chunk of volcanic rock that towers over the plains. By wandering towards the peak (mototaxis are also on hand to drive you to the base) you'll soon pick up a rough but clearly marked path about two-thirds of the way to the top (the ascent takes up to an hour, half that to get down), where there's a small shrine and long views stretching out below. Only appropriately equipped rock climbers should continue up the metal rungs to the summit, passing a memorial plaque to an earlier adventurer along the way.

At weekends, half of Querétaro seems to come out here, gorging on the locally celebrated gorditas and making for a festive atmosphere, but midweek it is an altogether more peaceful place: the mountain is likely to be deserted and you'll be just about the only thing disturbing the serenity of the plaza with its charming little church (**Templo de San Sebastián**) and terracotta-washed buildings, sumptuous in the afternoon light. Be forewarned, however, that many businesses are only open at the weekends and many more shut in May.

ARRIVAL AND INFORMATION — BERNAL

By bus Flecha Amarilla provides buses every 2hr from Querétaro's bus terminal B (6.35am–7.25pm; 45min) which drop you on the highway a 5min walk from Bernal centre; the last bus back passes at around 5pm (just flag them down).

Tourist office Try the small tourist office on Hidalgo (usually open Thurs–Tues 10am–5pm; 441 296 4126), which runs west from the plaza, though there isn't much they can tell you that you can't discover for yourself in 10min.

ACCOMMODATION AND EATING

Mesón de la Roca Hidalgo 5; http://larocca.mx. One of the best places to eat, in a shaded courtyard, serving moderately priced and well-presented Mexican dishes and, for the daring, Oaxaca grasshopper tacos. M$$$

Parador Vernal Lázaro Cárdenas 1; http://paradorvernal.com.mx. If you get stuck, or just fancy a night here (not a bad thing), there are tantalizing views of the rock from the comfy rooms at *Parador Vernal*, on the eastern edge of town. M$$$

Tequisquiapan

Some 57km east of Querétaro, along a road lined with factories and workshops, **TEQUISQUIAPAN** ("Tequis" to locals) is a former Otomí village that developed in the Spanish colonial period primarily on account of its warm springs. Exclusive villas, all with beautifully tended walled gardens, are set around the central **Plaza Miguel Hidalgo**, itself ringed by arched *portales* on three sides and the pretty pink church of **Santa María de la Asunción** on the fourth. It is very popular with wealthy *chilangos* (residents of Mexico City) up from the capital, but has never really caught on with foreign tourists. Although perfect as a weekend escape from the city, there's little to do other than bathe in your hotel pool, dine in one of many restaurants around the plaza and nose around the boutiques, some of which are cheap, many expensive and almost all of the highest standard. Like San Juan del Río, further south, Tequisquiapan has a big **crafts market** (Mercados de Artesanías) – especially active on Sundays – one block from the main plaza.

ARRIVAL AND INFORMATION — TEQUISQUIAPAN

By bus Flecha Azul buses from Querétaro (Terminal B, every 30min; 6.30am–9pm; 1hr 15min) run direct to Tequisquiapan, and there's also buses from San Juan del Río, 20km south. From the bus station, 2km from the centre, take a local bus or walk (20min) to Plaza Miguel Hidalgo.

Destinations Mexico City (8 daily; 3hr); Querétaro (every

FESTIVALS IN TEQUIS

It is worth timing a visit to Tequisquiapan with one of the town's many **festivals**, including the **Feria del Toro de Lidia** (middle week of March), which features bullfights, and the **Feria Internacional del Queso y del Vino** (late May and early June), a major wine and cheese festival. There's plenty of free food and drink and no shortage of other entertainment, including music and dancing.

30min; 1hr); San Juan del Río (every 20min; 30min).

Tourist office Free town maps are available from the tourist office (Mon–Fri 9am–7pm, Sat & Sun 10am–8pm; 414 273 0295, http://larutadelquesoyvino.com.mx or http://tequisquiapan.com.mx) on the main square (Plaza Miguel Hidalgo).

ACCOMMODATION

Hotel La Plaza Juárez 10 (Plaza Santa María); http://hotelplazatequis.com. Relaxed mid-range option, with its own pool and some very attractive suites, all decked out in a vaguely Spanish colonial style. M$$

Hotel Rio Niños Héroes 33; 414 273 0015, http://booking.com. One of the best hotels in town, right in the centre, with cable TV, free wi-fi, spacious gardens, palapa bar and an enticing pool. Rooms come in "classic" style (wood furniture, tapestries) or with a sleek, contemporary design. M$$$

EATING

Fortaleza Nicolás Bravo 8; 414 273 3111. This weekend-only restaurant and bar, a short walk from the plaza, has garnered a loyal following with artfully prepared Mexican classics, seafood and a decent array of vegetarian dishes. M$$$

K'puchinos Restaurant y La Luna Bar Andador Independencia 7; http://kpuchinos.com.mx. This local stalwart, right by the church, offers a tasty introduction to typical Querétaro dishes, including Tequis-style *pollo en mole* and *pozoles*, enchiladas Queretanas and some local artisanal cheese plates. Free wi-fi. Sister bar *La Luna* opens upstairs in the evening. M$$$

San Juan del Río

Though **SAN JUAN DEL RÍO**, 50km southeast of Querétaro, looks insignificant from the highway, it is in fact a major market centre and the second-largest city in the state, a popular weekend outing from both Querétaro and Mexico City. Among the goods sold here are **gemstones** – mostly local opals, but also imported jewels, which are polished and set in town – as well as baskets, wine and cheese. If you're going to buy gems, be very careful: it's easy to get ripped off. Other purchases are safer, though not particularly cheap on the whole. The best-known local wine is Hidalgo, a brand sold all over the country and usually reliable. The **Mercado Reforma** and the twin central squares of the Plaza Independencia and Plaza de los Fundadores (aka Jardín Madero) are a couple of long blocks north of **Avenida Juárez**, up Hidalgo from the bus station.

Museo de la Muerte

2 de Abril 42 • Free • 427 272 4215

There is more of interest a couple of blocks south of Juárez at the **Museo de la Muerte**, housed in the Neoclassical Panteón de la Santa Veracruz (used as a cemetery until 1866) on a hill overlooking town, which conveys the different ways Mexicans express their connectedness with the dead.

ARRIVAL AND INFORMATION — SAN JUAN DEL RÍO

By bus Direct buses from Querétaro (Amealcenses from Terminal B; every 20min) take 40min to get to San Juan del Río's bus station, a couple of km south of town. A local bus will run you up Hidalgo and drop you on a broad section of Av Juárez, where there's a central fountain, manicured trees and an attractive arcade on one side.

Destinations Mexico City (every 15min; 2hr); Querétaro (every 20min 5am–11pm; 45min); Tequisquiapan (every 20min; 30min).

Tourist information Visit http://turismo.sanjuandelrio.gob.mx for current information.

ACCOMMODATION

Layseca Juárez Ote 9; http://hotellayseca.com.mx. The best-value hotel downtown occupies an eighteenth-century colonial house with rooms decorated in period style with antiques but modern bathrooms, set around an appealing open courtyard. M$$

Portal de Reyes Juárez Pte 9; http://hotelportaldereyes.com. Another great downtown option, a short walk from the plazas, offering a bit more comfort than the *Layseca*, with satellite TV, spacious modern rooms and a decent pool. M$$$

EATING

Café La Parroquia Plaza de los Fundadores 3; 427 272 4740. Colonial-style café with great coffee, good service and perfectly located right on the main plaza. Also serves standard Mexican dishes, including especially tasty enchiladas. M$$

Viva La Vida Plaza Independencia 65; 427 272 7000. Perched on the main plaza, this congenial place offers a wide-ranging menu of Mexican breakfasts, enchiladas, burgers, crêpes, pastas and pizzas. M$$

The Sierra Gorda and Xilitla

The hill country to the northeast of Querétaro is the **Sierra Gorda**, a remote and mountainous region where roads are winding and travel slow. Much of the area was incorporated within the **Reserva de la Biosfera Sierra Gorda** in 1997, a designation that affords its natural and historic attractions a limited amount of government protection.

Apart from the wonderful tropical fantasy world of **Las Pozas** at Xilitla, the area's main attractions are the **Sierra Gorda missions**. These five communities (each with an ornate church) were founded by Spanish Franciscan **Fray Junípero Serra** (1713–84), who spent nine years in the Sierra Gorda during the 1750s and 1760s, working with, and gaining the trust of, the Indigenous people (mainly the **Pame**). Serra was canonized by Pope Francis in 2015 (becoming St Junípero Serra).

There are bus services to most places and several companies run tours, but this is an ideal region to explore by car, motorbike or even bicycle (though you'll need to be fit for the latter).

Jalpan

The main road from Querétaro towards Xilitla is Hwy-120, picked up at the small town of Ezequiel Montes. From there it twists its way through the mountains, with the only major town on route **JALPAN**, in the heart of the Sierra Gorda, 120km northeast

RUTA DE LAS MISIONES (MISSION ROUTE)

Beyond Jalpan, the other four Sierra Gorda missions are harder to visit without your own transport, but given their architectural beauty, isolation and unspoiled natural settings, well worth the effort:

San Miguel Concá On Hwy-69 to San Ciro de Acosta, 40km north of Jalpan. The smallest of the missions, completed around 1754. Concá is a Pame word that means "with me".

Santa María de la Purísima Concepción del Agua Built between 1760 and 1768 in Landa de Matamoros, 22km east of Jalpan on Hwy-120 towards Xilitla. The last of the missions to be built.

San Francisco de Asís de Tilaco Best-preserved church, with a florid Baroque facade and soaring, multi-tiered tower (completed between 1754 and 1762), some 27km beyond Landa (15km east on Hwy-120, then 12km south of La Lagunita).

Nuestra Señora de la Luz de Tancoyol (22km east of Landa along Hwy-120, then another 22km north on the signposted road to Tancoyol). The most ornate of the five missions with an incredibly intricate facade, constructed during the 1760s.

THE SURREAL WORLD OF EDWARD JAMES

Born in 1907 to a second-rank British aristocratic mother and American railroad millionaire father, **Edward James** may well also have been an illegitimate descendant of King Edward VII. He grew up cosseted by an Eton and Oxford education, and with no lack of money set about a life as a poet and artist. Meeting with only limited success, he turned his attentions to becoming a patron of the arts, partly in an attempt to prolong his waning marriage to a Hungarian dancer, Tilly Losch. Despite his bankrolling ballets that served as vehicles for her talent (notably those by George Balanchine's first company), she eventually left him, whereupon he retreated from London society to Europe. Here he befriended Salvador Dalí, and agreed to buy his entire output for the whole of 1938. As James increasingly aligned himself with the Surrealists, Picasso and Magritte also benefited from his patronage. Indeed, Picasso is reputed to have described James as "crazier than all the Surrealists put together. They pretend, but he is the real thing." During World War II, James moved to the US, where he partly funded LA's Watts Towers and made his first visit south of the border. After falling in love with Xilitla, he moved here in the late 1940s and experimented with growing orchids (which all died in a freak snowstorm in 1962) and running a small zoo. In his later years he was often seen with a parrot or two in tow as he went about building his concrete fantasy world. Aided by local collaborator and long-time companion **Plutarco Gastelum Esquer** and up to 150 workers, James fashioned **Las Pozas**, continually revising and developing, but never really finishing anything. By the time he died in 1984, he had created 36 sculptures, spread over more than 20 acres of jungle. He left his estate to the Gastelum family, though without making any provision for the upkeep of his work.

of Querétaro. Now the largest of the mission towns and a Pueblo Mágico since 2010, it is an attractive colonial place centred on its church, **Santiago de Jalpan**. This was Serra's first mission in the area, built between 1751 and 1758, and its elaborate "Mestizo Baroque" facade became a template for the others to follow. On either side of its central stucco panel are the Virgins of Pilar and Guadalupe, the patrons of Spain and Mexico.

Museo Histórico de la Sierra Gorda

Fray Junípero Serra 1 • Charge • 441 296 0165

For more background on the missions and the Pame craftsmen who built them, visit the **Museo Histórico de la Sierra Gorda** in the late sixteenth-century colonial building on the plaza (previously used as military barracks and prison), with exhibits of prints, antiques and model replicas of all the missions.

ARRIVAL AND DEPARTURE — JALPAN

By bus Jalpan bus station is 1km northeast of the centre. Primera Plus runs three first-class buses from Querétaro daily (3hr 30min), at 8.10am, noon and 3.10pm. Buses return at 5am, 2pm and 5pm. The noon departure from Querétaro continues on to Xilitla (5–6hr total), returning at 3pm. From Jalpan, second-class services run on to Xilitla (2hr) every hour or so from 7am–5pm.

ACCOMMODATION

Hotel María del Carmen Independencia 8; https://www.hotelmariadelcarmen.com.mx. Modern hotel right on the plaza, with rooms decked out in a simple rustic style with wood-frame beds, clean tiled floors and a small pool. M$$$

Hotel Misión Jalpán Fray Junípero Serra s/n; http://hotelesmision.com.mx. Next door to the museum (facing the plaza) is this inviting member of the Misión chain, a gorgeous colonial property with spectacular views of the mission church and a pool. Rooms are simple but very cosy. M$$$

Xilitla

Travelling through the Sierra Gorda is a joy in itself, but really doesn't prepare you for the picturesque small town of **XILITLA** (pronounced Hee-leet-la), sprawled over

5

the eastern foothills some 320km northeast of Querétaro and 55km beyond Jalpan. Hemmed in by limestone cliffs, it's set in a dramatic location, and at just 600m, it's warmer than the rest of the Bajío, with a lusher feel. There are tremendous views over the surrounding temperate rainforest, which is thick with waterfalls, birdlife and flowers, particularly wild orchids. It is a lovely place to relax, though you might devote a few minutes to admiring the beautifully preserved interior of the sixteenth-century **Ex-Convento de San Agustín**, which overlooks the central plaza, Jardín Hidalgo. The real justification for the lengthy journey to Xilitla, however, is to visit **Las Pozas**, some 2.5km east of town along a dirt road.

Las Pozas

Camino a Las Pozas • Charge • http://laspozasxilitla.org.mx • Head down Ocampo on the north side of the plaza, turn left and follow the signs (20min walk). It is a pleasant walk downhill (40min on the way back), or you can grab a taxi

Having lived in Xilitla since 1947, English eccentric **Edward James** (see page 319) spent the 1960s and 1970s creating the surreal jungle fantasy of **Las Pozas**, full of outlandish concrete statues and structures. Sprouting beside nine pools ("pozas") of a cascading jungle river, you'll find a spiral staircase that winds up until it disappears to nothing, stone hands almost 2m high, thick columns with no purpose, a mosaic snake and buildings such as the "House With Three Stories That Might be Five" and "The House Destined To Be a Cinema". Only one is in any sense liveable, a hideaway apartment four storeys up where James spent much of his time. With so little complete, there are all sorts of unprotected precipices: take care. In 2007, the Fundación Pedro y Elena Hernández bought the site for US$2.2 million (then M$24 million), with the aim of turning it into a world-class attraction.

For now at least you can see everything in a few hours, but plan to spend the better part of a day here bathing in the pools and just chilling out; the restaurant is usually open Wednesday to Sunday. You can also request a **guided tour for a fee** (in English, if guide available; 1hr 15min), which can be a good way to get to grips with what's on display.

ARRIVAL AND DEPARTURE — XILITLA

By bus Getting to Xilitla by bus can be time-consuming – if you suffer from travel/motion sickness stock up on medication. Six twisting hours through the Sierra Gorda from Querétaro via Jalpan it's more easily accessed by second-class bus from the unexciting but sizeable town of Ciudad Valles, on the highway between San Luis Potosí and Tampico, some 80km north. There are also direct services from Tampico and San Luis Potosí. Flecha Roja, Flecha Amarilla (Jalpan and Querétaro) and Vencedor (Jalpan, Ciudad Valles and Tampico) have adjacent terminals just off the main highway on Niños Heroes – all a short walk from Jardín Hidalgo.

Destinations Ciudad Valles (hourly; 2–3hr); Jalpan (hourly; 2hr); Querétaro (1 daily; 5–6hr); San Luis Potosí (2 daily; 5–6hr); Tampico (4–5 daily; 5–6hr).

ACCOMMODATION AND EATING

Hotel Dolores Matamoros 211; www.hoteldoloresxilitla.mx. Modern and very clean budget hotel featuring elegant rooms with TV and fan, some also with a/c and fine mountain views. To get there, follow Hidalgo east from the main square for one long block, head straight across the road and down a long flight of stairs. At the bottom of the steps turn left. M$

Hotel Hostal del Café Niños Heroes 116; 489 365 0018. Cosy option, with bright, clean rooms with rustic theme, free but slow wi-fi and a rich breakfast included. TV available in public lounge, but you'll spend more time in the lush garden or on the terrace. M$$

★ **Posada El Castillo** Ocampo 105; http://elcastilloxilitla.com. The place to stay in Xilitla is *Posada El Castillo* (built by Plutarco Gastelum and now managed by his granddaughters), in the house where James lived when he wasn't ensconced in his hut or apartment at Las Pozas. His spirit still inhabits the eight highly individual guestrooms, harmoniously blending Mexican, English and Moorish styles (fans only, no a/c). There's a lovely pool, meals are served and the hosts not only speak English but also have produced a documentary on James's life and work, which they screen for guests. No credit cards. M$$$

Restaurante Cayo's Miguel Álvarez Acosta 117; 489 365 0044. One of several serviceable restaurants, with good basic Mexican food (try the cheese-filled *enchiladas huastecas*; or seafood soup, a speciality) and superb views across the palms. M$$

San Miguel de Allende

Set on a steep hillside overlooking the Río Laja and dominated by red rooftops and domed churches, **SAN MIGUEL DE ALLENDE** is the most hauntingly beautiful town in the Bajío. The colonial centre remains wonderfully preserved, and still serves as the spiritual centre of the Mexican community – seen at dawn, its cobbled, hilly streets are quite unlike anything else in the region. There are few major sights, but the whole town (which has been a national monument since 1926, hence no new buildings, no flashing signs and no traffic lights) is crowded with old seigniorial mansions and graceful churches.

Unsurprisingly, San Miguel's appeal has not gone unnoticed. Today it serves as a picture-perfect version of Mexico for hundreds of artists and writers, as well as flocks of foreign students drawn to the town's several language and arts schools. More visibly, it has attracted a large population of US and Canadian **expats** (mostly retirees), and property prices here are on a par with San Francisco (a *Starbucks* even graces the plaza). Though the connection goes back to the 1940s, the latest influx can in part be attributed to Tony Cohan's popular book *On Mexican Time* (published in 2000), which tells the story of a writer and his artist wife who abandon smog-ridden Los Angeles for a quieter life in San Miguel, where they restore an old house, learn the local lifestyle and are slowly seduced by the colonial city's unique charm. Now something like ten percent of the population are foreigners, some ten thousand of whom live in the vicinity more or less permanently, generally in peaceful co-existence with the locals.

For all its popularity, the town is a pleasant place to rest up in comfort for a while – assuming you have plenty of cash. The country hereabouts is still ranching territory, though even this is increasingly being taken over by tourist activities: attractions include hot springs, a nearby golf course, horseriding at a couple of dude ranches and mountain biking.

El Jardín Principal

Everything in San Miguel revolves around **El Jardín Principal**, the main plaza, which is within walking distance of almost everything you'll want to see – on Sundays traditional Mexican bands play live music throughout the afternoon. The plaza is dominated by its distinctive church (see below), while on the north side is a block containing the former **Presidencia Municipal**, completed in 1736, and the **Galería San Miguel** (see page 323). The east and west sides of the square are lined with covered *portales*, under whose arches vendors of drinks and trinkets shelter from the sun, with a row of shops behind them. Just off the plaza at Umarán 3 is the Casa del Insurgente, former home of revolutionary hero Juan de Mafuele, but better known as the **Casa de los Perros**, for its central balcony supported by little stone dogs.

La Parroquia de San Miguel Arcángel

El Jardín Principal • Free, donation suggested

The most famous of the city's landmarks, **La Parroquia de San Miguel Arcángel** – the parish church – takes up the south side of the Jardín Principal. This gloriously over-the-top structure, with a towering pseudo-Gothic facade bristling with turrets and spires, was built in 1880 by Zeferino Gutiérrez, a self-taught Indigenous stonemason. Gutiérrez supposedly learned about architecture by studying postcards of great French cathedrals and then drew diagrams in the dust to explain to his workers what he wanted, and the church does seem to reflect the French penchant for neo-Gothic architecture at that time. Inside, the patterned tilework of the floor, the *azulejos* along the walls and the pure semicircular vaulting along the nave exhibit distinct Moorish influences. Look out for the *Cristo de la Conquista* in a side

5

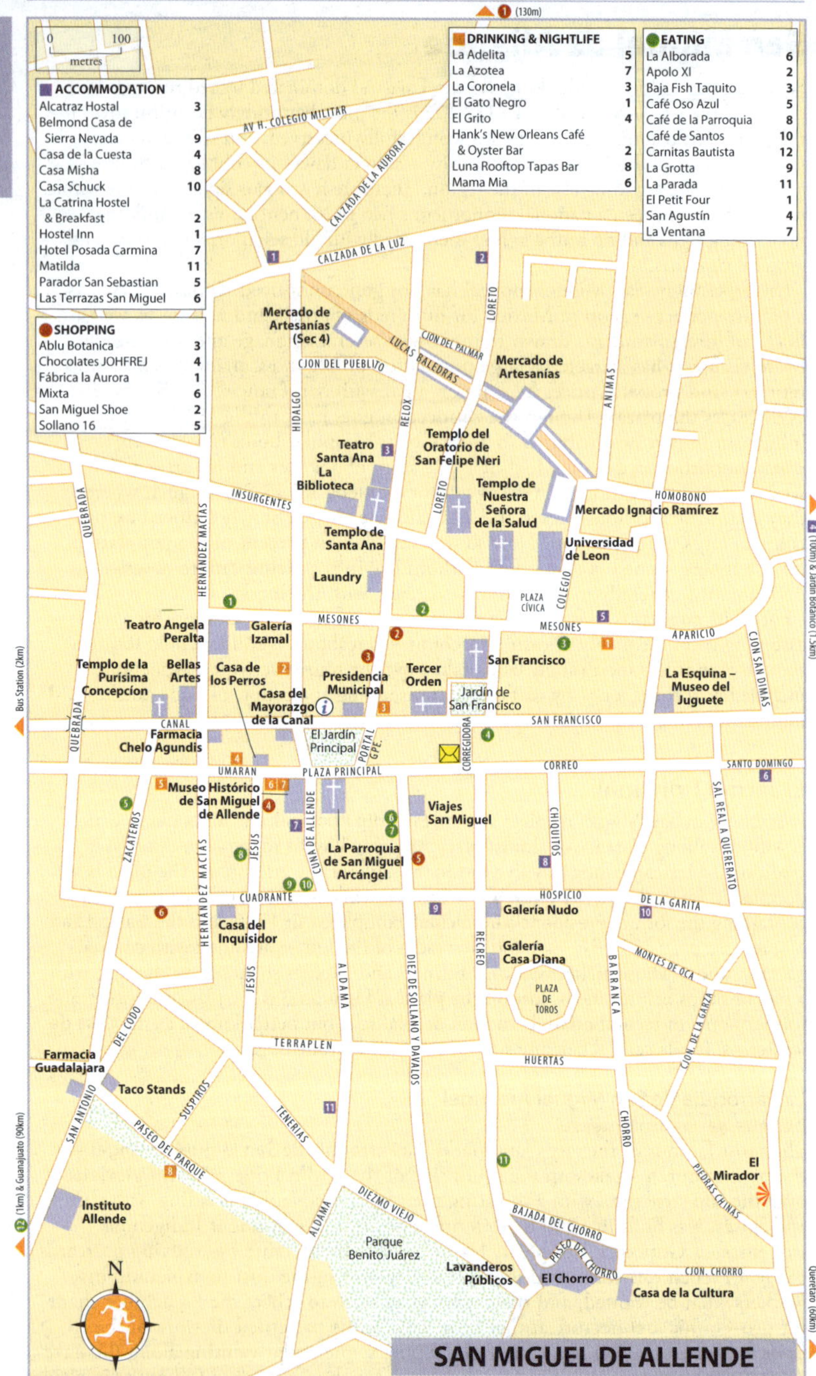

SAN MIGUEL'S TOP ART GALLERIES

San Miguel has been attracting artists since the 1930s – you'll find many of them in the Fábrica la Aurora (see page 329). Other galleries worth checking out include:

La Calaca Mesones 93; 415 152 3954. Features the lesser-known but worthwhile up and comers on the local art scene. Exhibits change frequently.

Galería Arte Contemporáneo SMA Sollano 13; http://arte-contemporaneo.com.mx. Current and emerging Mexican talent such as abstract painter Jordi Boldó, Luis Granda and Gabriel Vergara.

Galería Casa Diana Recreo 48; http://galeriacasadiana.com. Primarily home for the work of Italian-born artist Pedro Friedeberg (his wife Diana is the gallery sub-director), including his iconic "hand chair".

Galería Nudo Recreo 36 & 10-B; http://galerianudo.com. Has shown the work of Oaxacan artist Alejandro Santiago, Nestor Quiñones and others.

Photographic Gallery SMA Mesones 57; https://www.photogallerysma.com. The town's premier photo gallery, with some of the best touring exhibits in Mexico.

chapel to the left of the altar, a revered sixteenth-century image of Christ framed by two giant, faded murals.

Near here is the **Capilla del Santisimo**, smothered in bold, Modernist murals. Note also the small statue and shrine to San Judas Tadeo on the right side of the nave, littered with photos and votive offerings. Ex-president Anastasio Bustamante (1780–1853) spent his last days in San Miguel, and is buried in the crypt, designed by famed architect Francisco Tresguerras (usually open on Nov 2 only).

Museo Histórico de San Miguel de Allende

Allende 1 • Charge • 415 152 2499

The Casa de Don Ignacio de Allende, at the southwest corner of the Jardín, was the birthplace of the Independence hero Miguel Allende in 1769: a plaque notes *Hic natus ubique notus* – "here was born he who is famous everywhere". The house now operates as the **Museo Histórico de San Miguel de Allende**, with artfully designed galleries chronicling the history of the town with some lovely artefacts and old documents, all with English labels. The lower floor covers the early colonial period through to the beginning of the independence movement and the arrival of Allende on the scene, following his military career from 1801. There's also a preserved *botica* (apothecary) from 1919 down here, and a reproduction of a *pulpería* (small store). Upstairs the Allende connection is explored further, with galleries dedicated to his role in the events of 1810–11, his illegitimate children, disagreements with Hidalgo and his ultimate capture and execution. The unequivocal message seems to be that Hidalgo's role in Mexican independence has been exaggerated: Allende was actually "the first to disturb America's calm".

Other rooms have been restored in period style, to reflect the lives of wealthy townsfolk in the eighteenth century, with an oratory, kitchen and various living rooms.

Casa del Mayorazgo de la Canal (Casa de Cultura Banamex)

Canal 4 • Free • http://fomentoculturalbanamex.org

Just off the plaza, the lavish **Casa del Mayorazgo de la Canal** was built for the wealthy and influential De la Canal family in the eighteenth century. Now owned by Banamex, a few rooms are open to the public for temporary art exhibitions with a Mexican theme, and there's a decent bookshop and video room. You won't see much of the interior beyond the impressive courtyard, its multi-tiered arches only hinting at the opulence further inside.

Jardín de San Francisco

A block east along San Francisco from the Jardín Principal, the quieter space of **Jardín de San Francisco** is dominated by two colonial churches. The elaborate churrigueresque facade of the **Templo de San Francisco** contrasts sharply with its Neoclassical tower (added in 1799 by Francisco Tresguerras), tiled dome and plain, but light and airy, Neoclassical interior, and overshadows the modest simplicity of its smaller neighbour, seventeenth-century **Tercer Orden**.

Plaza Cívica and around

Behind and to the north of Jardín de San Francisco, San Miguel's old market area has been refurbished to create the **Plaza Cívica**, complete with a huge equestrian statue of Allende – you'll usually see clumps of students near here, outside the Ex-Colegio de San Francisco de Salas (once a highly regarded Jesuit school), now part of the **Universidad de León**.

Templo de Nuestra Señora de la Salud

Plaza Cívica, Insurgentes s/n • Free

Next door to the university building, the **Templo de Nuestra Señora de la Salud**, with its unusual concave churrigueresque facade topped by a scallop-shell pediment, was completed in the eighteenth century as the college chapel.

Templo del Oratorio de San Felipe Neri

Insurgentes s/n • Free

Completed in 1712, the ornate crimson Baroque facade of the **Templo del Oratorio de San Felipe Neri** shows signs of native influence – presumably the legacy of Indigenous labourers. The main interest lies inside with a series of oil paintings in the pinkish interior, among them a group of 33 around the altar and dome depicting the life of St Philip Neri, and an image to the right of the altar of the Virgen de Guadalupe attributed to Miguel Cabrera. The main altar itself is another creation of Zeferino Gutiérrez. One of the chapels inside, the gold-smothered **Santa Casa de Loreto**, is a copy of the Santa Casa di Loreto in Italy (known as the "Holy House", thought to be the actual home of Mary – miraculously transported from Nazareth), and was put up by the Conde Manuel de la Canal in 1735.

Mercado Ignacio Ramirez

Colegio • Free

The **Mercado Ignacio Ramirez** (town market) has managed to remain almost entirely traditional, with fruit, vegetables, medicinal herbs, pots and pans all on display, and little exists specifically for tourists among the cramped tables with their low canvas awnings.

Mercado de Artesanías

Balderas • Free

Behind the regular market along Andador Lucas Balderas lies the **Mercado de Artesanías**, crammed with the sort of handicrafts you see all over Mexico (folk art, pottery, colourful textiles, cut glass, papier-mâché and silver jewellery), though little of what's here seems especially good value. You'll find much more exciting goods in the many crafts shops around town.

La Biblioteca

Insurgentes 25 • Free • Tour charge, cash only • http://bibliotecasma.com

From the Oratorio de San Felipe Neri you can head west along Insurgentes to **La Biblioteca**, a library that lends a substantial collection of books in English (see "Directory", page 330, for more details). Inside the library, the *Café Santa Ana* offers a quiet space to sit down and read, while on Sundays you can join the popular two-hour **House and Garden Tour**, which takes you inside two or three historic private homes

SAN MIGUEL'S MURAL MASTERPIECE

Don't leave San Miguel without visiting the mesmerizing **Sala Quetzal** inside La Biblioteca (see page 324), all four walls smothered with exuberant murals by artist David Leonardo (born in Mexico City in 1963). Inspired by Mesoamerican art, the swirling images are a barrage of colours, peoples and symbols, depicting aspects of Mexican history. The room is open during library hours, but no photos are allowed.

each week. You should also enquire here (or check the website) about the programme at the library's **Teatro Santa Ana**, which shows movies and plays. Tours of the house and garden area available on Sundays, 10am–noon.

La Esquina – Museo del Juguete Popular Mexicano

Núñez 40 • Charge • http://museolaesquina.org.mx

San Miguel's quirkiest museum is a short walk east of the Jardín, an unusual collection dedicated to traditional Mexican toys dubbed **La Esquina – Museo del Juguete Popular Mexicano**. The three rooms contain a variety of dolls, masks, toy instruments and rocking horses.

Bellas Artes

Hernández Macías 75 • Free • 415 152 0289, http://facebook.com/BellasArtesSMA

The Centro Cultural Ignacio Ramírez "El Nigromante", more simply known as **Bellas Artes**, is just one block downhill from the Jardín. Housed in the romantic cloistered courtyard of the 1765 **Convento de la Concepción**, it's an arts institute run by the state fine-arts organization (replacing the original school established by Felipe Cossio del Pomar here in 1938), concentrating on music and dance, but to a lesser extent teaching visual arts, too. Mexicans can take courses here for virtually nothing; foreigners pay rather more (prices vary).

Around the courtyard there are various exhibitions, and several murals, including an entire room covered in vivid, abstract designs by **Davíd Alfaro Siqueiros** from the 1940s. Dedicated to the life of Ignacio Allende, the mural was left unfinished after Siqueiros fell out with the school's owner. The **Templo de la Purísima Concepción**, part of the complex, is notable mainly for its tall pink-and-yellow dome raised on a drum, said to be the work of the untrained Zeferino Gutiérrez in 1891, this time modelled on Les Invalides in Paris.

Instituto Allende

San Antonio 22 • Free • http://instituto-allende.edu.mx

In 1938 Peruvian artist Felipe Cossio del Pomar founded the Escuela Universitaria de Bellas Artes in San Miguel, an arts foundation that enjoyed an enormous boost after World War II, when returning American GIs found that their education grants could be stretched much further in Mexico; Pomar relocated the school in 1950 as today's well-respected **Instituto Allende**. A steep but pleasant walk south of the old centre, it's housed in a former 1730s hacienda of the Condes de la Canal and offers courses in all kinds of arts, from painting to sculpture to photography, in crafts like silverwork and weaving, and Spanish-language instruction at every level (see page 327), all within verdant, park-like grounds. There are craft shops and a café down here too, and an office dealing with long-term accommodation.

El Chorro

Ten minutes' walk south of the Jardín, shaded **Parque Benito Juárez** was created out of the fruit orchards that belonged to many of the city's old families. The homes round about are still some of the fanciest in town. From here it's an uphill stroll to **El Chorro**, the little hill whose springs supply the city with water, and the site of the settlement originally founded by Franciscan friar Juan de San Miguel in 1542. At the foot of the hill you'll find the **Lavaderos Públicos**, a series of twenty old-fashioned crimson stone tubs – some locals still occasionally do washing here.

Casa de la Cultura and El Mirador

Bajada del Chorro 4 • 415 154 5670

From the *lavaderos* the cobbled Paseo del Chorro winds uphill past egrets nesting in trees to the old water storage building, which now serves as the **Casa de la Cultura**, another popular location for classes, events and shows. To get the best views over town, make for **El Mirador** (climb the steps behind the Casa, walk along Callejón de Chorro and turn left along Salida Real de Querétaro), the viewing point on the road to Querétaro, where there's a little belvedere, a small café and San Miguel spread out below, with the broad plain and a ridge of mountains behind.

Jardín Botánico

Paloma • Charge • http://elcharco.org.mx • Follow Homobono east from the market, and continue along Cuesta de San José and Antiguo Camino a Querétaro; after 10min or so you reach signs to one of the pedestrian entrances on Paloma. Free bus Tues, Thurs, Sat & Sun 9.30am from Calle de Mesones, at Plaza Cívica (return at 1pm)

When you've had your fill of swanky cafés and artesanía shopping, consider spending a few hours at the **Jardín Botánico**, 1.5km northeast of town. Officially known as **El Charco del Ingenio**, it sprawls over the hill just behind a suburb of some of San Miguel's finest new homes. The garden itself resembles almost any patch of northern Mexico desert (it is meant to), but comes heavily planted with various types of cactus, which has made it incomparably richer botanically than the surrounding desert. Around 10km of grassy paths wind through its 220 acres, some accessible by mountain bike. If you're here around a full moon, check the website for details of the *temazcales*, ritual herb steam baths built within the garden, and open to the public (reservations required; 415 154 8838).

ARRIVAL AND DEPARTURE — SAN MIGUEL DE ALLENDE

By plane San Miguel's closest major airports are at Querétaro (see page 313; 1hr 30min) or near León (see page 346; 1hr 30min–2hr), from where English-speaking Viajes San Miguel, Sollano 4 (Mon–Fri 9am–2.30pm & 4.30–7pm, Sat 10am–2pm; 415 152 2537, http://viajessanmiguel.com), runs a shuttle van (reserve in advance) meeting most flights at either airport. BajioGo also runs a shuttle to León or Querétaro airport; Mexico City airport is is also an option.

By bus San Miguel has frequent services to Guanajuato and Querétaro. Omnibus runs some first-class services to points north and the US border, while Primera Plus and ETN run to Mexico City. The Central de Autobuses is about 2km west of the centre at Calzada de Estación 90, from where there are taxis into the centre (fix the price first as there are no meters), and regular local buses (marked "Centro–Central") that run into town along Canal.

Destinations Dolores Hidalgo (every 40min; 1hr); Guanajuato (14 daily; 1hr–1hr 30min); Mexico City (8 daily; 4hr); Querétaro (every 40min; 1hr 30min)

INFORMATION

Tourist office San Miguel's helpful tourist office (Mon–Fri 9am–8pm, Sat 10am–8pm, Sun 10am–6pm; 415 152 0900) is on the north corner of El Jardín at no. 10. As well as the usual racks of leaflets and maps, it can provide details of local art and language courses.

Newspapers and websites For more information, pick up one of the free ad-driven booklets scattered around town, the weekly gringo newspaper *Atención San Miguel* (out Fri; http://atencionsanmiguel.org), or visit http://visitsanmiguel.travel.

TOURS AND ACTIVITIES

The tourist office can also supply lists of local guides and tour operators. Most offer walking tours of the town for a fee, and day trips to Dolores and Atotonilco (around 6hr) and the ancient pyramids of Cañada de la Virgen (3–4hr), with a minimum three people. Try BajioGo at Jesús 11 (daily 8am–8pm; 415 152 1999, http://bajiogo.com) or Viajes

San Miguel (see above). For the House and Garden Tour see page 324.

Bici-Burro Hospicio 1; 415 152 1526, http://bici-burro.com. A range of van, hiking and bike tours, most frequently to the Santuario de Atotonilco (38km; 4hr), or to Pozos (20km; 7hr).

Coyote Canyon Horseback Adventures 415 154 4193, http://coyotecanyonadventures.com. Group and private riding trips, lessons and even moonlit excursions at a variety of levels at their ranch 16km southwest of town. All trips give a great introduction into *charro* life; they run half-day outings as well as full-day and overnight excursions. Other activities include hot-air ballooning and ziplining.

★ **Patronato Pro Niños Walking Tour** 415 152 7796, http://patronatoproninos.org. Meet in the Jardín across from the Parroquia for a gentle stroll around town (2hr 30min) and a good deal of local history. All the proceeds go towards medical care for underprivileged children. Private tours at any time are a set fee (1–4 people) and you pay extra for each additional person after that.

ACCOMMODATION

SEE MAP PAGE 322

Belmond Casa de Sierra Nevada Hospicio 42; http://belmond.com. Luxury hotel complex with fifteen spacious rooms set in Casa del Parque, the main building, around a soothing colonial courtyard built in 1580 and lush with greenery, and four other colonial mansions. All guests have access to the hotel's refreshing pool and classy restaurant, *Andanza*. M$$$$

★ **Casa de la Cuesta** Cuesta de San José 32; http://casadelacuesta.com. Mexican folk-art, crafts and antiques adorn this gorgeous colonial home, renovated as a boutique B&B. With just six rooms, all with fireplace and outdoor terrace, attention is personal and relaxed, and breakfast is served on the lush patio. Check out the exclusive Other Face of Mexico Gallery on site. M$$$$

★ **Casa Misha** Callejón de Chiquitos 15; www.casamisha.com. Another luxury boutique hotel awash with tasteful French and Mexican colonial antiques; the seven rooms come with smart TVs, wi-fi and patios that spill out onto lush gardens, but the real highlight is breakfast on the roof terrace, with sleepy San Miguel sprawled out below. M$$$$

Casa Schuck Bajada de la Garita 3; http://casaschuck.com. Splendidly styled and colourful hotel with antiques, ten amply sized rooms, a small but beautiful pool, leafy nooks and personal touches. Welcoming owners make this one of San Miguel's best bets. M$$$$

Hotel Posada Carmina Cuna de Allende 7, a few metres south of the Jardín; http://posadacarmina.com. Large rooms with brick floors, high ceilings and white walls are set amid yet more colonial splendour around a congenial restaurant (*La Felguera*, open till 5pm); there are cheaper, but still very comfy, remodelled rooms in an adjacent wing – all come with flatscreen satellite TVs. You can't beat its location, one block from the Jardín, and the staff are friendly and very helpful. M$$$

★ **Matilda** Aldama 53; http://hotelmatilda.com. A slice of modern luxury amid all those colonial options in San Miguel, this flashy boutique hotel offers stylish rooms with LCD TV and large bathrooms with double sinks, decorated with the photographs of Eduardo Zaylan. Lounge at the spa or try the gourmet restaurant, *Moxi*. M$$$$

Parador San Sebastian Mesones 7; www.hotelparador

LEARNING SPANISH IN SAN MIGUEL

For many people, the reason to come to San Miguel is to learn Spanish. Notice boards around town advertise private lessons, but most people end up taking one of the courses run by the main **language schools**, each of which offers a range of courses taught by professional Mexican teachers. Instruction is almost entirely in Spanish, with the focus on practical usage rather than academic theory. The best known is the Instituto Allende, though the others compete admirably on both price and quality. Students usually stay with a local family to consolidate the instruction.

Academia Hispano Americana Mesones 4; 415 152 0349, http://ahaspeakspanish.com. Respected school running four-week Spanish immersion sessions (6hr/day) and more relaxed semi-intensive programmes (4hr/day), plus extension courses in Mexican history, literature and folklore.

Instituto Allende Ancha de San Antonio 20; 415 152 0190, http://instituto-allende.edu.mx. The most prestigious of the schools, the Instituto conducts university-credited four-week courses (starting the first Mon of each month), offering everything from 50min to four hours a day throughout the year at all levels. There are also intensive one-to-one classes, less demanding monthly courses and special subject courses in topics such as Mexican history, ceramics, paper-making and photography, among others.

Instituto Habla Hispana Calzada de la Luz 25; 415 152 1535, http://mexicospanish.com. Runs month-long courses with around twenty contact hours per week; alternatively, you can just do a week long course. They'll also organize homestays with prices that vary, based on the selection of a shared double or your own private room.

5

sansebastian.com. Cool and tranquil, with simple, clean rooms around a colonial courtyard. Ask for one of the larger rooms at no extra cost – a huge bargain. Breakfast not included, and free wi-fi in public areas only. M$$

Las Terrazas San Miguel Santo Domingo 3; http://terrazassanmiguel.com. These five luxurious units on the hillside, four blocks from the plaza, come with kitchen, cable TV, bathrooms and private terraces; breakfast included. Fabulous option for families or groups. M$$$

HOSTELS

Alcatraz Hostal Relox 54; 415 121 3984. Friendly centrally-located hostel with cosy four- and six-bunk dorms (two mixed and one female-only), with fans and balconies, a big kitchen and free purified water. Excellent breakfast included. M$

La Catrina Hostel & Breakfast Loreto 80; http://lacatrinahostel.com. Justly popular (reserve ahead) option with a choice of comfy dorms and doubles, some with private bathrooms, all with a/c and cable TV. Free use of computers, common room and basic breakfast included (it's extra for a fuller cooked breakfast). M$

Hostel Inn Calzada de la Luz 31-A; https://hostel-inn.san-miguel-de-allendehotels.com. Excellent budget option a few blocks from the Jardín, with shared kitchen, garden and luggage storage; choose from four-to six-person dorms, budget doubles with shared bathroom and en-suite doubles. M$

EATING

SEE MAP PAGE 322

Eating in San Miguel can be an expensive business; even local staples such as coffee and margaritas are likely to cost half as much again as they would in, say, Querétaro, and to find a decent supermarket or grocery store you'll have to take a taxi or bus to the outskirts. The **mercado** (see page 324) has the usual budget choices (tortas, tacos, *menudo*, *jugos* and the like), but nothing special (look for the "*fonda*" section, which has seating). Still, San Miguel's **restaurants** can be a tremendous relief for long-term travellers, with flavours you may not have tasted for weeks and a surprising array of **vegetarian** options.

Baja Fish Taquito Mesones 11; http://bajafishtaquito.com. Small, unassuming diner with a few tables and bar stools serving authentic Ensenada-style fish (marlin) and shrimp tacos, plus tostadas, quesadillas and seafood *coctéles*. M$

Café Oso Azul Zacateros 17; 415 121 7402. Contender for best coffee in town, an attractive courtyard café that roasts its own beans every few days, supplied by one of the owner's organic coffee plantations in Veracruz. Delicious, beautifully presented breakfasts are the winner here. M$$

Café de la Parroquia Jesús 11; 415 152 3161, www.facebook.com/cafedelaparroquiasma. A great little place with seats inside or in the courtyard, justly popular with expats for breakfasts of hotcakes or yogurt and fruit. Good Mexican food served as well – tamales, *chilaquiles* and the like – and coffee all day long. M$$$

Café de Santos Cuna de Allende 21; 415 101 5148, www.facebook.com/cafedesantossma. Small café with some prime real estate for people watching over delicious sandwiches. There's a good selection of tasty Mexican staples served here too and it's a popular spot with expats. M$$

La Grotta Cuadrante 5; http://lagrotta.com.mx. Terrific pasta and pizza joint. Cosy room with red-washed walls and with kitchen pans hanging from the ceiling. The home-made pasta dishes are tasty but no match for the crispy pizza and calzone. Also, fresh salads and a small selection of main dishes like trout and garlic prawns. M$$$

★ **La Parada** Recreo 94; 415 152 0473, www.facebook.com/laparadasma. This superb Peruvian restaurant has become a local institution in San Miguel, with a creative menu divided into seafood (lots of *ceviche*), soups and salads and "flavours of Peru" (slow-cooked pork sandwich, stir-fried chicken livers) sections, plus a massive pisco sour cocktail list. M$$$

El Petit Four Mesones 99; 415 154 4010. Delightful little French patisserie with a few tables where you can tuck into a pain au chocolat or a slice of *tarte aux pommes* with your espresso. Superb raspberry tarts. M$$

STREET FOOD OF SAN MIGUEL

Looking to save money in San Miguel? Try these tasty snack options – cash only.

La Alborada Sollano 11; 415 154 9982. All types of *caldos* and *pozoles* (stews; chicken and pork, "red or green" style) in a small courtyard. M$

Apolo XI Mesones 43; 415 111 8889. Small shop selling cheap *carnitas* (sold by the kilo) or tacos and tortas to take away or munch on an open-air terrace upstairs. The hot and vinegary house pickles will curl your toes. M$

★ **Carnitas Bautista** Guadiana 2 (off Ancha de San Antonio); 415 168 2315. Be prepared for long waits at this legendary joint, where every part of the pig is roasted and served in tortillas or gorditas with fresh salsas. M$

Taco stands Ancha de San Antonio and Nemesio Díez. Try the cluster of nameless stalls here for fabulous tacos (try the roasted lamb or *chicharrón* in salsa), from around 7am till early afternoon, and *barbacoa* (lunch only). M$

★ **San Agustín** San Francisco 21; 415 152 5795. Owned by retired Argentine *telenovela* star Margarita Gralia, this tempting café is especially known for its sugary, fried *churros* eaten with hot chocolate – either sweet Spanish, semi-sweet French, or Mexican, flavoured with cinnamon. If you can, get the table with a view of Templo de San Francisco – go early to avoid disappointment. M$$

La Ventana Sollano 11 (enter through Alborada restaurant); 415 154 7728. Your best bet in town for a caffeine fix, this quiet coffee shop features dark organic roasts from Chiapas and all manner of java concoctions. Drinks also available to go from a street-front window (*ventana*). Cash only. M$

DRINKING AND NIGHTLIFE

SEE MAP PAGE 322

BARS

La Adelita Umarán 30; 415v101 9892. A small but charming dive bar with good prices and an even better ambiance. Reputed to have the cheapest beer in town, this spot also crams in live music and the occasional games night.

La Azotea Umarán 6; 415 152 8265. San Miguel's hippest rooftop bar and lounge, adorned with contemporary art, drapes and comfy sofas. Pricey but exquisite margaritas and justly hyped "tacos de Jícama" to snack on.

La Coronela San Francisco 2; 415 152 5032. Dependable upmarket cantina decorated with old Mexican cinema posters, featuring two-for-one beers on Mon and Fri.

El Gato Negro Mesones 12; 415 152 6544. Tiny and hip swinging-door cantina dating back to 1921, plastered in photos of Marilyn Monroe – plus a couple of Jim Morrison and John Lennon. The drinks are cheap, and there's no entry fee; though it looks old-fashioned, women are welcome. There's also an old-fashioned *pissoire*.

Hank's New Orleans Café & Oyster Bar Hidalgo 12; http://hanksmexico.com. This local mini-chain restaurant has one of the most stylish bars in San Miguel (it also serves fresh seafood, Cajun and creole dishes), with a decent wine list.

★ **Luna Rooftop Tapas Bar** (Rosewood Hotel) Nemesio Díez 11; http://rosewoodhotels.com. Enjoy fine Mexican and Spanish tapas while soaking up the most magical views of San Miguel. Great sofas and canopies to keep out the sun during the day.

Mama Mia Umarán 8; http://mamamia.com.mx. Probably the most happening nightspot in town, with restaurant (great pizza and pasta), sensational terrace bar with enthralling views over the rooftops and the adjacent after-hours *Mama's Bar*. You can count on good DJs, live bands (everything from jazz and Cuban to traditional Mexican) and live salsa on Fri and Sat nights.

CLUBS

El Grito Umarán 15; 415 120 0156. Top club in town since 1998, and still the place to be seen for fashionable locals, if they're willing to pay the entry fee. The cavernous interior is decked out with colonial chandeliers, stonework and sculpture, while DJs spin the usual mix of house and Latino sounds.

SHOPPING

SEE MAP PAGE 322

Ablu Botanica Relox 18; http://ablubotanica.com. Locally produced scented candles, bath, beauty and bodycare products.

Chocolates JOHFREJ Jesús 2A; http://johfrej.com. San Miguel's artisan chocolatier since 1920. Also does scrumptious hot chocolate and home-made ice cream.

★ **Fábrica la Aurora** Calzada de la Aurora, via Hidalgo; http://fabricalaaurora.com. This former cotton mill contains numerous art studios, restaurants, and shops selling home furnishings, jewellery and antiques.

Mixta Pila Seca 3; http://mixtasanmiguel.com. Popular store selling an eclectic mix of local, Mexican and international products: jewellery, furniture, clothing, greeting cards and home decor.

★ **San Miguel Shoe** Mesones 48; 415 154 4702. The town's most famous shoe shops, selling a vast range of extra-comfy handmade Mexican footwear fondly known as "combat cocktail sandals". Local cobbler Santiago Gallardo Muñiz was allegedly inspired by San Miguel's unsteady cobblestones.

Sollano 16 Sollano 16; 415 154 8872. Fashionable design store selling home furnishings, jewellery, antiques and stylish accessories.

DIRECTORY

Banks and exchange Banamex, at the northwest corner of El Jardín at Canal 4; Banorte, half a block east of Banamex at San Francisco 17; and HSBC at San Francisco 31. Most banks have ATMs.

Books The best bookshop is the US-expat-owned Garrison & Garrison at Hidalgo 26, Plaza Artesanal Bicentenaria (415 109 7387); it sells a thoughtful range of new and secondhand English-language books.

Consulates US, Plaza La Luciernaga, Libramiento José Manuel Zavala 165, Colonia La Luciernaga (Mon–Thurs 9am–1pm; 415 152 2357).

Emergencies General emergencies 066; Cruz Roja 415 152

5

SAN MIGUEL'S CULTURAL CALENDAR

Like most of Mexico, Easter (Semana Santa) is the biggest celebration in San Miguel, but September is a more interesting month for visitors: on **Independence Day** (Sept 16) crowds gather to celebrate with fireworks, dances, bullfights and a rodeo. The most important town fiesta is of **San Miguel Arcángel**, two days of processions, concerts, traditional dancing, bullfights and ceremonies around September 29, St Michael's traditional feast day. The other major saint's day is the **Fiesta de San Antonio de Padua** (June 13), with a colourful parade for one of the town's patron saints, St Antony of Padua, involving a procession of garishly dressed revellers known as "Los Locos" (the Crazies).

Film and music **festivals** also pepper the year in San Miguel, kicking off with the **Guanajuato International Film Festival** (third week of July; http://giff.mx), a week-long short-film festival hosted jointly by San Miguel and Guanajuato. The quarter-century-old **Festival Internacional de Música de Cámara** (Chamber Music Festival; first two weeks in Aug; http://festivalsanmiguel.com) features a range of performances by internationally acclaimed musicians. The **Festival Internacional de Jazz & Blues** (last week of Nov/ first week Dec; http://sanmigueljazz.com.mx) includes two shows nightly by international performers at various locations in town. At other times, check out the programme at the **Teatro Ángela Peralta** at Mesones 82 (415 152 2200), which typically hosts ballet, theatre and occasional performances of classical music throughout the year.

2545; police 415 152 2890.

Internet The Jardín and Biblioteca are wi-fi hot spots.

Laundry Lavandería El Reloj at Relox 34-A.

Library La Biblioteca, Insurgentes 25, allows visitors to borrow books after obtaining a library card (two passport photocopies and a fee required; check out 4 books for 15 days) and leaving a deposit.

Pharmacy Farmacia Chelo Agundis, Canal 26 (daily 10am–midnight; 415 152 1198). English spoken. Farmacia Guadalajara, at Ancha de San Antonio 13, is open 24hr.

Post office and couriers Correo 16. There are numerous express postal services, including DHL, at Correo 21 and opposite the post office.

Around San Miguel

One of the easiest and most enjoyable outings from San Miguel is to spend a good part of the day at one of the local **hot springs**, where the warm thermal waters are ideal for soaking your bones. There are numerous hotels and mini-resorts with geothermal pools all around the area, but the best and easiest to reach are clustered around ten minutes' drive northwest of town on the road to Dolores Hidalgo. The **Santuario de Jesús Nazareno de Atotonilco** and enigmatic **Cañada de la Virgen** are equally enticing cultural attractions, while the intriguing half-deserted settlement of **Mineral de Pozos** and historic towns of **Dolores Hidalgo** and **San José Iturbide** make easy and absorbing excursions.

La Gruta and Escondido Place

Carr San Miguel–Dolores Hidalgo, km 10 (Hwy-51) • **La Gruta,** charge (the locker deposit is refundable) • 415 185 2162 • **Escondido Place**, charge • http://escondidoplace.com

The most popular hot spring in the San Miguel area is **La Gruta**, right by the Dolores highway, with a series of outdoor mineral pools at different temperatures all surrounded by lawns and banana trees. There's even a little grotto you can swim into, with an artificial waterfall, and a small and reasonably priced restaurant on site with snacks and fajitas. Best in the early morning – try to avoid the weekends altogether, when the pools get packed.

Around 500m before La Gruta, a side road leads just over a kilometre to **Escondido Place**, an equally appealing proposition, with small lily-filled lakes all around, outdoor pools and a series of small indoor ones linked by little tunnels and cascades. It can be quiet here midweek, but comes alive at weekends. Remember to bring towels.

ARRIVAL AND DEPARTURE — LA GRUTA AND ESCONDIDO PLACE

By bus Second-class buses to Dolores Hidalgo from San Miguel's bus station will drop off on the highway near both sets of pools; you can also take a "Santuario" (Atotonilco) bus from Calzada de la Luz and Relox (every hr from 7am). To get back, just flag down any bus you see.

By taxi Taxis will normally charge you a flat fee each way, though locals pay half that (the spa will call a taxi for you to return).

Santuario de Jesús Nazareno de Atotonilco

C Principal, Atotonilco • Free (charge for the side chapel) • http://santuariodeatotonilco.org

A day at the hot springs can be conveniently combined with a worthwhile outing to the "Sistine Chapel of Mexico", the **Santuario de Jesús Nazareno de Atotonilco** (easily confused with the larger Atotonilco el Grande in Jalisco state), 5km further in the same direction, then 2km down a side road. This is a dusty, rural Indigenous community whose church has come to be a centre of pilgrimage for two reasons – it was founded by **Padre Felipe Neri** (constructed between 1740 and 1776), who was later canonized, and it was from here that Padre Hidalgo, marching from Dolores to San Miguel, took the banner of the Virgin of Guadalupe that became the flag of the Mexicans in the War of Independence. His comrade-in-arms Allende was married here in 1802. The seven chapels of the church, liberally plastered with paintings by Baroque master **Juan Rodríguez Juárez** and murals by local artist **Miguel Antonio Martínez de Pocasangre**, are freely interspersed with poems, biblical passages and painted statues demonstrating every kind of Mexican popular art, from the naive to the highly sophisticated. The shrine was declared a UNESCO World Heritage Site in 2008.

ARRIVAL AND DEPARTURE — SANTUARIO DE ATOTONILCO

By bus Direct buses ("Santuario" or "Atotonilco") leave every hour from Calzada de la Luz in San Miguel (45min) and spend ten to fifteen minutes in Atotonilco, giving you just enough time for a quick look before the run back, when you can get dropped off at the hot springs (same bus).

By taxi Taxis will charge at a flat fee one-way and double for the return (ask the driver to wait), from San Miguel de Allende.

Cañada de la Virgen

Off Hwy-67 • Charge (no bags allowed inside the site) • 415 109 2466

The impressive ancient Mesoamerican pyramids of **Cañada de la Virgen** were opened to the public in 2011 after years of archeological excavations. Around 30km southwest of San Miguel, the intriguing site comprises seven enormous pyramidal structures associated with the Otomi of the Toltec-Chichimec culture and constructed between 540 and 1050 AD. Note that you must walk around 1.5km between the entrance and the actual site (after taking a free shuttle bus from the visitor centre). By far the easiest way to visit the pyramids is via an organized tour from San Miguel (see page 326) or with **Albert Coffee Archaeotours**, led by one of the original archeologists at the site (4.5hr; http://albertcoffeetours.com; charge, includes all transport).

Dolores Hidalgo

Fifty kilometres or so from both Guanajuato and San Miguel de Allende, **DOLORES HIDALGO** is as ancient and as historically rich as either of its southern neighbours. This was Father Hidalgo's parish, and it was from the church in the main plaza here that the historic **Grito de la Independencia** ("Cry of Independence") was first issued in 1810 (see page 788). The town celebrates the event annually with the **Fiestas de Septiembre**, ten days of cultural and sporting events, music and fireworks, culminating with the *Grito* around dawn on the sixteenth.

Perhaps because of its less spectacular location or maybe because there is no university or major language school, Dolores hasn't seen a fraction of the tourist development that has overtaken other places in the Bajío (despite being named yet another Pueblo

Mágico in 2002). It's a good bet, though, for a one-night stopover, and if you can't find accommodation in Guanajuato or San Miguel, this is certainly the place to head; you'll get a better room here for appreciably less. True, there is less to see, but it's an elegant little town and thoroughly Mexican.

Museo Histórico Curato de Dolores

Morelos 1, at Hidalgo • Charge • 418 182 0171

Just a couple of blocks from the bus station as you walk along Hidalgo towards the central Plaza Principal, the **Museo Histórico Curato de Dolores**, Father Hidalgo's home between 1804 and 1810, was rebuilt after the Spanish destroyed it and has been converted into a museum devoted to his life, very much a point of pilgrimage for Mexicans on day trips. It's a bit heavy on written tributes from various groups to the "Father of Independence" and on copies of other correspondence he either sent or received – but it's edifying nonetheless and includes a few highlights such as his letter of excommunication from the Inquisition less than a month after the *Grito*.

Parroquia de Nuestra Señora de los Dolores

Plaza Principal

The beautifully laid-out Plaza Principal at the heart of Dolores is dominated by the exuberant churrigueresque facade of the **Parroquia de Nuestra Señora de los Dolores**, the illustrious church where Don Miguel Hidalgo issued the *Grito* (this is where a representative of the president repeats the *Grito* every Sept 15). The church was completed in 1778, with Hidalgo assuming the position of parish priest in 1803.

Museo del Bicentenario

Plaza Principal • Charge • 418 182 7731

Next door to the church is the **Presidencia Municipal**, birthplace and former home of revolutionary hero Mariano Abasolo and now the **Museo del Bicentenario**. The museum chronicles the history of Dolores, primarily from the Porfirio Díaz era, with rare jewellery, old weapons, portraits and black-and-white photographs – there's even a recording of Díaz, made by Thomas Edison in 1909.

Museo de la Independencia Nacional

Zacatecas 6 • Charge, free Sun • 418 182 8277

Just off the Plaza Principal is the **Museo de la Independencia Nacional**, which served as the town jail until 1959 – Hidalgo famously freed the prison inmates here in 1810. Today, the vibrant, graphic murals inside depict significant scenes from Mexican history from the Aztec perception of the world through to the many Indigenous rebellions against Spain and the life of Hidalgo.

Casa Museo José Alfredo Jiménez

Guanajuato 13 at Nuevo León • Charge • http://museojosealfredojimenez.com.mx

Don't leave town without paying homage to the greatest *ranchera* singer of all time at the **Casa Museo José Alfredo Jiménez**, containing a small but wonderfully presented collection of personal effects, record sleeves and biographical information. Jiménez (1926–73) was born in Dolores and is buried here, his colourful **tomb** (inside the Panteón Municipal, heading out of town on Hwy-110 to Guanajuato) topped with a giant *sarape* and sombrero.

ARRIVAL AND INFORMATION — DOLORES HIDALGO

By bus Dolores is connected to both San Miguel de Allende and Guanajuato by regular, rapid second-class buses to and from the Flecha Amarilla terminal, at Hidalgo 26 beside the river.

Destinations Guanajuato (every 30min; 1hr 30min); Mexico City (every 40min; 5–6hr); Querétaro (every 40min; 2hr); San Luis de la Paz (every 30min; 1hr 10min); San Luis Potosí (14 daily; 2hr 30min); San Miguel de Allende (every

40min; 1hr).

Tourist office There's little need to visit Dolores' small tourist office (Mon–Fri 9am–5pm, Sat 10am–2pm; 418 182 1164, http://dolores-hidalgo.com), Plaza Principal 11, by the church, but they can give advice on where to buy the town's famous ceramics.

ACCOMMODATION

Hotel Hidalgo Hidalgo 15; http://hotelposadahidalgo.com. Comfy modern hotel located one block north of the bus station and two blocks south of the Plaza Principal, with laundry and a gym on site. M$$

Posada Cocomacán Plaza Principal 4; https://hotelposadacocomacan.com. Lovely colonial property dating from the 1720s, with a cool interior, cable TV and some rooms overlooking the plaza. M$$

EATING

Dolores Hidalgo is home to the country's most unusual **ice cream** flavours: Mexicans come in droves to the Plaza Principal to lick scoops of creamy alfalfa, *mole*, *cerveza*, shrimp and avocado (fortunately most vendors let you sample before you commit to a full cone). Try popular stalls *Helados Aguilar* or *Helados Josué*.

★ **Carnitas Vicente** Norte (Mariano Balleza) 65; 418 182 1390. This has been a Dolores tradition since 1980, a restaurant dedicated to the finest *carnitas* (spicy shredded Mexican-style pork) in the region, stuffed into gorditas or piled onto plates and served by the kilo. M$$$

★ **DaMonica** Hidalgo 12; 418 182 4587. This top-quality Italian restaurant offers excellent service and tasty pastas (spaghetti with mussels and shrimp, gnocchi with gorgonzola), pizzas and home-made soups and breads – the owner (Monica Dimitri) hails from Milan, and it shows. M$$$

El Fruty Hidalgo 2 (just off Plaza Principal); http://elfruty.com.mx. Set in a beautiful colonial house with a quiet courtyard (shaded by orange trees), this popular spot does all the classic Mexican dishes as well as regional specialties, beginning with good-value breakfasts. M$$

Mineral de Pozos

San Miguel de Allende eighty years ago? That may be pushing things a bit, but **MINERAL DE POZOS** is certainly far quieter and less developed than its popular neighbour (see page 321). Once a rich and flourishing mining community, since the 1950s it's been referred to as a ghost-town, though in reality it is far from dead, having experienced a revival in the last ten years. Indeed, a San Miguel-like transformation is well under way, with foreigners buying up property, and several restaurants, attractive hotels, absorbing art galleries, shops and numerous North American artists (many of whom are part-timers) setting up shop. Around 3500 people live in the streets clustered around the white dome of **Parroquia San Pedro** and the **Jardín Principal** – in 2012 Pozos became another Pueblo Mágico, cementing its tourist potential.

Yet crumbling ruins still outnumber the development – for now at least – and the town's edges, fringed with desert, mine workings and abandoned haciendas, remain an enchanting, if potentially dangerous, place. Many tunnels are unmarked, and if you're hiking take extra care. Highlights include the ruins of the **Hacienda de Cinco Señores**, a vast abandoned mine complex, and the three distinctive sixteenth-century Jesuit smelters (*hornos*) of **Santa Brígida**. Note that Pozos lies at around 2300m above sea level, and it can get quite cold on winter nights.

ARRIVAL AND INFORMATION — MINERAL DE POZOS

By bus Travelling by bus to Pozos means changing several times, usually via Dolores Hidalgo and San Luis de la Paz; from Guanajuato it's faster to take a bus to Dolores and change there for San Luis de la Paz (1hr 10min), rather than a direct bus to the latter. From San Miguel de Allende you'll also have to take a bus to Dolores (every 40min) and change there for San Luis de la Paz, or take an organized tour or a taxi (see below). Once in San Luis de la Paz; take a local bus marked "Pozos" or take a taxi (15min). From Querétaro take a bus to San José Iturbide (55min) and change there.

Destinations San José Iturbide (every 30min; 40min); San Luis de la Paz (every 30min; 20min).

Cars and taxis Many travellers choose to rent cars and drive to Pozos (it's just 45min from San Miguel de Allende). Alternatively, San Miguel de Allende taxis will charge a flat fee for a round trip (up to six people); from Querétaro it'll cost you more.

Tourist information Visit www.facebook.com/Quehacerenmineraldepozos for the latest information.

5

ACCOMMODATION

★ **Casa Mexicana** Juárez 2 on the Jardín Principal; 462 170 1833. This five-bedroom B&B boasts exquisite and individual rooms set around a blossom-filled garden, and with an on-site art gallery. Expertly prepared meals are also served to non-guests, or you could just drop in for a margarita. M$$$

Posada de la Minas Manuel Doblado 1; 442 293 0213. A fabulous colonial mansion one block from the plaza, with six inviting rooms featuring everything from Mexican folk art to Victorian themes; laundry available. M$$$

El Secreto de Pozos Jardín Principal 4; 442 620 6032, www.facebook.com/ElSecretoPozos. Tranquil B&B with three rooms just off the plaza, all beautifully designed and blending traditional and contemporary styles; there are wood-burning fireplaces. M$$$

EATING

La Pila Seca Aldama 8; 442 293 0020. Cheap and popular Mexican classics served in an art-smothered dining room close to the Jardín. *Enchiladas Potosinas*, *arrachera* and big breakfasts. Free wi-fi. M$$

Posada de las Minas Manuel Doblado 1; 442 293 0213. Atmospheric restaurant in the grand colonial hotel of the same name (see above), with tables in the elegant courtyard and a menu of Mexican and American standards. M$$$

San José Iturbide

Some 30km south of Mineral de Pozos and 55km north of Querétaro, **SAN JOSÉ ITURBIDE** is an immaculate colonial town centred on its tidy **Plaza Principal**. It's chiefly distinguished by a behemoth Neoclassical church, **Parroquia de San José**, dedicated to Agustín de Iturbide (1783–1824), an opportunist from Michoacán who started the War of Independence as a general loyal to Spain – inflicting major defeats on Morelos – only to change sides later. Having helped secure Mexico's independence without any concomitant reform, he briefly declared himself emperor in 1822 (he was executed two years later).

ARRIVAL AND DEPARTURE — SAN JOSÉ ITURBIDE

Only one first-class bus goes to/from Querétaro and Mexico City per day; the Central de Autobuses is at Domínguez 38, between Otoño and Gómez Pedraza, three blocks west of the Plaza Principal.

Destinations Mexico City (1 daily 6am; 4hr 25min); Pozos (every 30min; 40min); Querétaro (first class 1 daily 6am, 1hr 30min; second class every 15min, 2hr); San Luis de la Paz (7 daily; 1hr).

ACCOMMODATION

Hotel Boutique Nautilus Plaza Echegaray; 419 181 3496. There's little reason to stay in San José, but if you just fancy a night in a small Mexican town, then try this excellent boutique hotel. M$$$

Hotel Posada Unión Callejón Olivera 10; 419 198 0071. One of the cheapest options in the centre is this convenient, comfortable but basic hotel, two blocks along Allende. M$

EATING

El Diezmo Nicolás Campa 16, at Plutarco Elías calles; http://eldiezmohotel.com.mx. A swish hotel with a great restaurant serving a range of international dishes (pizzas, pastas, tacos and the like), and wonderful views of the church. M$$$

Mariscos La Palapa Plutarco Elías Calles 12; 419 139 0281. This seafood restaurant, knocks out creative dishes, paired with an excellent selection of wines. M$$

Guanajuato and around

Shoehorned into a narrow ravine, **GUANAJUATO** was for centuries the wealthiest city in Mexico, its mines pouring out silver and gold in prodigious quantities. Today it presents an astonishing sight: upon emerging from the surrounding hills you come on the city quite suddenly, a riot of colonial architecture, tumbling down hills so steep that at times it seems the roof of one building is suspended from the floor of the last. Declared a UNESCO World Heritage Site in 1988, Guanajuato is protective of its image: there are no traffic lights or neon signs here, and the topography ensures that there's no room for new buildings. The town's pristine reputation was cemented in

2012, when **Pope Benedict XVI** chose Guanajuato (and neighbouring León) as the only stops on his Mexican visit.

Today the city of around 170,000 has plenty of life in its narrow streets, many outstanding places to eat and drink, and lots to see: churches, theatres, museums, battlefields, mines and mummified corpses, to name but a few of the city's attractions. There's an old-fashioned, backwater feel to the place, reinforced by the local students' habit of going serenading in black capes, the brass bands playing in the plazas and the city's general refusal to make any special effort to accommodate the flood of (mostly domestic) tourists.

Guanajuato's main thoroughfare is Juárez, but below this passes an underground roadway: the **Subterráneo Miguel Hidalgo**. It was built as a tunnel to take the river under the city, but the river now runs deeper below ground, and its former course, with the addition of a few exits and entrances, has proved very handy in preventing traffic from clogging up the centre entirely; more tunnels have since been added to keep the traffic flowing.

Mercado Hidalgo

Juárez, at Mendizábal

Approaching the centre of Guanajuato from the west side, heading east up Juárez, the first building of note is the **Mercado Hidalgo**, a huge iron-framed construction of 1910 reminiscent of British Victorian train stations and crammed with every imaginable sort of goods (from Mexican chocolate and fresh fruit to local dolls and T-shirts). It's also a fun, cheap place to eat (see page 344).

Plaza San Roque

East of the Mercado Hidalgo, to the left and through the **Jardín de la Reforma**, with its fountain and arch, you get to the lovely, serene **Plaza San Roque**. A small, irregular, flagged space, the plaza has a distinctly medieval feel, heightened by the raised facade of the crumbling **Templo de San Roque** that towers above. It's a perfect setting for the city's annual **Festival Internacional Cervantino** (see page 344). The Callejón de los Olleros leads back down to Juárez, or you can cut straight through to the livelier **Plazuela San Fernando**, with its stalls and restaurants.

Callejón del Beso

Halfway along Juárez the **Plazuela de los Angeles** is little more than a slight broadening of the street, but from here steps lead up to some of Guanajuato's steepest, narrowest alleys. Just off the plazuela is the **Callejón del Beso** (20m up Callejón del Patrimonio and turn left), so-called because at only 69cm wide, it is slim enough for residents to lean out of the upper-storey balconies and exchange kisses across the street – naturally enough, there's a legend of star-crossed lovers associated with it (see page 335).

LEGEND OF THE KISS

The legend of the Callejón del Beso is classic Romeo and Juliet: two young lovers – in this case Doña Ana and her suitor, Don Carlos – separated by mean, feuding parents. The story has a fittingly tragic ending; in a desperate bid to see his love, Don Carlos bought the house opposite Doña Ana's, across an alley so close they could hold hands. When Ana's father caught them, he was so incensed he stabbed his daughter to death at the window – poor Carlos was left kissing her lifeless hand. Today it is said that couples who kiss while standing on the third step of the Callejón del Beso are guaranteed seven years of happiness.

5

Plaza de la Paz

The **Plaza de la Paz** is the civic heart of Guanajuato, boasting some of its finest **colonial buildings**, notably the late eighteenth-century **Casa del Conde Rul y Valenciana** (built by the owners of the richest mine in the country; Don Diego Rul was killed fighting rebels in 1814). It was designed by Eduardo Tresguerras, undoubtedly the finest Mexican architect of his time, and played host briefly to Baron Alexander von Humboldt in 1803, the German naturalist and writer, an event commemorated by a plaque. Today it serves as the regional courthouse. Next door the lavish **Palacio Legislativo** was completed in 1903 and remained in use until 2017, when it became the **Museo Palacio de los Poderes** (Tues–Sun 9am–5pm; free; guided tours 1pm; charge). Today you can peruse its beautifully preserved rooms, ornate decor and original wooden furniture. The **Casa de Gobierno** (closed to the public), a short way down towards the Jardín de la Unión, is another fine mansion, this time with a plaque recording that Benito Juárez lived here in 1858, when Guanajuato was briefly his provisional capital.

Basílica de Nuestra Señora de Guanajuato

Plaza de la Paz • Free • **Galería Mariana,** charge • 473 732 0314

On the eastern side of the Plaza de la Paz stands the honey-coloured **Basílica de Nuestra Señora de Guanajuato**, a Baroque parish church that was completed in 1796 in honour of an ancient image of the Virgin, patroness of the city (aka Nuestra Señora de Guanajuato). The statue arrived in Guanajuato in 1557, a gift from Charles V and his successor Philip II, in gratitude for the wealth that was pouring

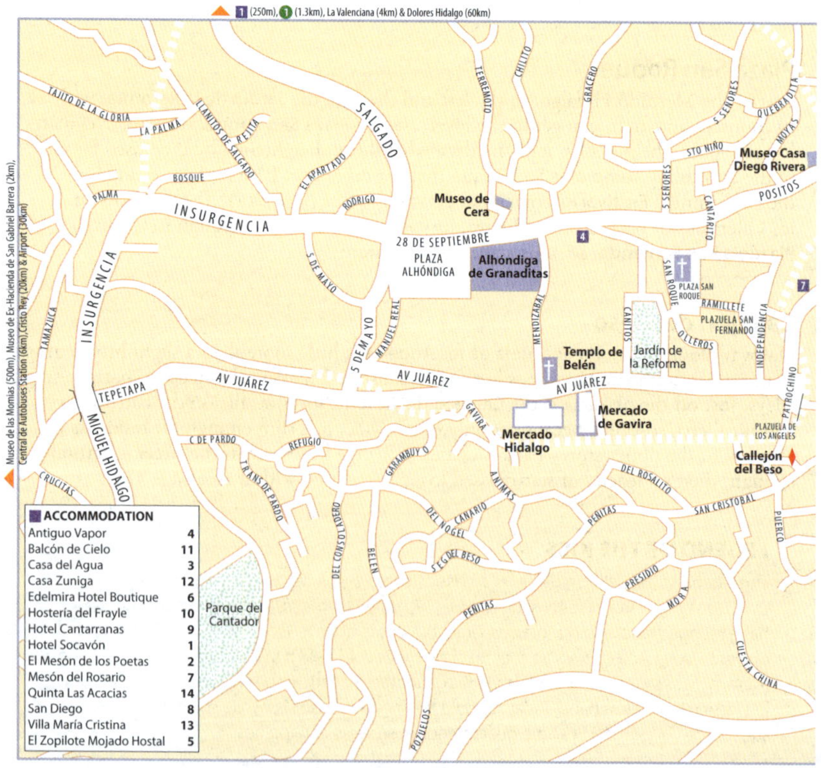

from here into Spanish royal coffers. The wooden statue sits on a silver pedestal in the middle amid several paintings by Miguel Cabrera in the old baptistery, now **Galería Mariana**, with a separate entrance on the far side of the basilica (Ponciano Aguilar 7).

Jardín de la Unión

Just a short distance further east from Plaza de la Paz on the main street (Juárez has become Obregón at this point) is the **Jardín de la Unión**, Guanajuato's main plaza. Created in the 1860s on land once owned by the church, it's a delightful little square – or rather triangle – shaded with trees, surrounded by cafés and with a bandstand in the centre from which the town band regularly plays (usually Thurs at 6pm, Sun at noon & 7pm). This is the best time to sit and linger over a drink, enjoying the passing spectacle of the evening *paseo*.

Templo de San Diego

Sopeña, at Jardín de la Unión • Free

Facing the Jardín de la Unión across Obregón stands the **Templo de San Diego**, inside which are several eighteenth-century oil paintings and intriguing chapels. One altar in particular (just to the left as you enter) is dedicated to the infant Jesus (Niño de la Caridad) and mawkishly filled with toys and children's tiny shoes left as offerings. The church was reconstructed around 1784 for the Franciscans in the churrigueresque style so popular at the time.

Museo Ex-Convento de Dieguino

Sopeña, at Jardín de la Unión • Charge • 473 732 5296

On the north side of Templo de San Diego a separate entrance leads down to the **Museo Ex-Convento Dieguino**, an art gallery space among the stone foundations of the church – the small display of archeological finds here, and the renovated crypt space itself, are interesting, but unless an exhibition is on show, there's not much else to see.

Teatro Juárez

Sopeña, at Jardín de la Unión • Charge, extra fee for cameras

Next door to the church of San Diego is the imposing Neoclassical frontage of the **Teatro Juárez**, all Doric columns and allegorical statuary. Built at the end of the nineteenth century, it was opened in 1903 by the dictator Porfirio Díaz himself. The interior of the theatre is fabulously plush, decked out in red velvet and gilt, with chandeliers and an opulent Moorish theme throughout (the proscenium is supposed to show a panorama of Constantinople). Upstairs you can also visit the Neoclassical **Salón Tocador** (powder room, used by wealthy ladies).

Museo Iconográfico del Quijote

Manuel Doblado 1 • Charge, free Tues • http://museoiconografico.guanajuato.gob.mx

Beyond the Jardín, Obregón becomes Sopeña, lined with fancy boutiques, restaurants and bars as far as the pretty pink church of San Francisco, which marks the **Plaza San Francisco**. Here, too, is the **Museo Iconográfico del Quijote**, an extraordinary little collection devoted entirely to Don Quixote, testament to the influence of **Miguel de Cervantes**' seminal novel on subsequent generations of artists. The museum contains mainly paintings of the don – including some by Pedro and Rafael Coronel – but also a Dalí print, a Posada engraving of the hero as a *calavera*, an imposing sculpture by Federico Silva, murals, tapestries, sculptures, busts, miniatures, medals, plates, glassware, chess sets, playing cards, pipes and cutlery – you name it, it's here. There's also a mural-smothered shrine to the maestro himself, containing a statue of Cervantes.

Museo Olga Costa-José Chávez Morado

Pastita 158, Torre del Arco • Charge • 473 731 0977

The seventeenth-century Hacienda de Guadalupe is where Mexican muralist **José Chávez Morado** (1909–2002) and his German painter wife (**Olga Costa**) spent much of their married life. Morado moved out and donated the building to the city of Guanajuato on his wife's death in 1993, and today it exists as the **Museo Olga Costa-José Chávez Morado**. The house has been left largely as it was when the couple lived here, an eclectic mix of objects explained (in Spanish) by the guide:

LEARNING SPANISH IN GUANAJUATO

Guanajuato has become a popular place to spend a couple of weeks learning Spanish – you can opt to **stay with a local family** (typically charged by the week), sharing meals with them and getting plenty of opportunity to try out your new language skills; most schools can arrange this. Classes with up to five students usually **cost** more, but it does get cheaper the more hours you clock per day. One-to-one tuition is the most expensive option.

Don Quijote Guanajuato Pastita 76; 473 731 3056, http://donquijote.org. This Spanish school chain (it's based in Salamanca) has a popular operation in Guanajuato, with "super intensive" courses.

Escuela Mexicana Potrero 12; 473 732 5005, http://escuelamexicana.com. School in the heart of town offering everything from one-week beginners' courses to extensive advanced classes and an array of specialist courses in such subjects as culture, literature, politics and Mexican cooking. Their intensive "Spanish for Travellers" requires four hours of coursework a day and one or two weeks' commitment.

EL PÍPILA

In 1810, Father Hidalgo approached Guanajuato at the head of his insurgent force – mostly peons armed with nothing more than staves and sickles. The Spanish, outnumbered but well supplied with firearms, shut themselves up in the **Alhóndiga**. The almost certainly apocryphal story goes that Hidalgo's troops could make no impact until a young miner, nicknamed **El Pípila** ("the Turkeycock"), volunteered to set fire to the wooden doors – with a slab of stone tied to his back as a shield, he managed to crawl to the gates and start them burning, dying in the effort. The rebels, their path cleared, broke in and massacred the defenders wholesale. It was a short-lived victory – Hidalgo, later forced to abandon Guanajuato, was eventually tracked down by the royalists and executed. His head and the heads of his three chief co-conspirators, Allende, Aldama and Jiménez, were suspended from the four corners of the Alhóndiga as a warning to anyone tempted to follow their example, and there they stayed for over ten years, until Mexico finally did become independent.

eighteenth-century majolica ceramics, seventeenth-century French chairs, Dutch porcelain, Persian wall hangings and a fine collection of ex votos. There's little of their work on show, but notice Morado's blue-and-white lamp, and his stained-glass windows – all blotches in red, yellow, blue and black – on the way up to the studio, now given over to temporary exhibitions. The museum is less than thirty minutes' walk from the Jardín de la Unión, or you can flag down any bus marked "Pastita" at the eastern end of town.

Pípila

Mirador del Cerro de San Miguel Funicular • **Funicular or bus** charge each way

The **Monumento al Pípila**, a bulky statue on the hillside almost directly above the Jardín de la Unión, honours local miner **Juán José Martínez**, aka "El Pípila" (see page 339). Built in 1939, the statue affords staggering views of Guanajuato; from the viewpoint at its base you seem to be standing directly on top of the church of San Diego, with red, blue and yellow houses spilling down the otherwise bare hills. It's an especially magical spot for the 45 minutes or so during which the sun sets behind the hills and the electric lights start to come on in town. Around you'll always find crowds of Mexican tourists trawling the food stalls here for snacks to munch while enjoying the views.

The steep climb up the hill takes about twenty minutes and ten minutes coming down. There are several possible routes up through the alleys – look for signs saying "al Pípila" – including up the Callejón del Calvario, to the right off Sopeña just beyond the Teatro Juárez; from the Plazuela San Francisco; or climbing to the left from the Callejón del Beso. The signs run out, but if you keep climbing as steeply as possible you're unlikely to get lost and the paved trail is fairly easy to follow. There's also a bus ("Pípila") that takes you round the scenic Carretera Panorámica, or the **funicular**, a cliff railway that whisks you up the steep valley side from behind the church of San Diego.

Templo de La Compañía

Lascuráin de Retana, at Del Sol • Free • **Pinacoteca Virreinal** charge

The **Templo de La Compañía**, a highly decorated monumental churrigueresque church, is just about all that's left of a Jesuit seminary founded in 1734; step inside to admire the unusually light interior afforded by the clear glass in the dome, added in 1884 and inspired by St Peter's in Rome. Behind the altar is a gallery or **Pinacoteca Virreinal** with a few seventeenth- to nineteenth-century religious oil paintings, mostly anonymous but including four small portraits of saints by Miguel Cabrera, and a Virgin by José de Ibarra. The Jesuit seminary was an educational establishment that eventually metamorphosed into the **Universidad Guanajuato**, now one of the most prestigious in Mexico. The current university building next door to the church is in fact quite modern – only finished in 1955 – but was designed to blend in with the town, which, for its size, it does surprisingly effectively.

Museo del Pueblo de Guanajuato

Positos 7 • Charge • 473 732 2990

Next door to the Universidad Guanajuato, the **Museo del Pueblo de Guanajuato** is a collection of local art and sundry oddities, housed in the eighteenth-century home of the Marqués de San Juan de Rayas. It's an arresting building with a delightful little Baroque chapel (added in 1776), where much of the decoration has been replaced by modern murals painted by one of the standard-bearers of the Mexican muralist tradition, **José Chávez Morado** (see page 338). Look out also for paintings by **Hermenegildo Bustos** (1832–1907), one of the most influential Mexican artists of the nineteenth century.

Museo de Arte Contemporáneo "Primer Depósito"

Positos 25 • Charge • 473 732 1125

The small but enchanting **Museo de Arte Contemporáneo "Primer Depósito"** was established by local artist Javier de Jesús Hernández Capelo, with the permanent collection comprising bronze sculptures by the likes of the English-born Mexican surrealist Leonora Carrington, along with José Luis Cuevas, Sergio Hernández and Gabriel Macotela. There is also a collection of works by local contemporary artist **Jazzamoart** (aka Francisco Estupiñán), whose painting is mostly connected to jazz.

Museo Casa Diego Rivera

Positos 47 • Charge • 473 732 1197

Guanajuato's most famous son was born here in 1886, his old home now preserved as the absorbing **Museo Casa Diego Rivera**. For most of his life Rivera, an ardent revolutionary sympathizer and Marxist (see page 78), went unrecognized by his conservative home town, but with international recognition of his work came this museum, in the house where he was raised until he was 6. Initially the Rivera family only occupied the lower floor, which is now furnished in nineteenth-century style, though only the beds and a cot actually belonged to them. The place is far bigger than it looks from the outside, and the extensive upper floors contain many of Rivera's works, especially early ones, in a huge variety of styles – Cubist, Pointillist, Impressionist – showing the influences he absorbed during his years in France and Spain. Although there are no major works on display, the many sketches and small paintings are well worth a look, particularly those showing his fascination with all things pre-Columbian.

Museo Regional de Guanajuato (Alhóndiga de Granaditas)

Mendizábal 6 • Charge, extra fee with cameras • 473 732 1112

The Museo Regional de Guanajuato or **Alhóndiga de Granaditas**, the most important of all Guanajuato's monuments, lies west of the Museo Casa Diego Rivera, more or less above the market. Originally a granary completed in 1809, and later a prison, this was the scene of the first real battle and some of the bloodiest butchery in the War of Independence (see page 339).

Inside, there's a memorial hall devoted to the Martyrs of Independence and the **museum** itself, upstairs. On the staircases are **murals** by local artist José Chávez Morado (see page 338) depicting scenes from the War of Independence and the Revolution, as well as native folklore and traditions. The museum's exhibits, mostly labelled in Spanish, span local history from pre-Hispanic times to the Revolution:

the most interesting sections cover the Independence battle and everyday life in the colonial period. One of the iron cages in which the rebels' heads were displayed is present, as are lots of weapons and flags and a study of Guanajuato's mining industry in the 1890s, the city's last golden age. There's also plenty of art, including a wonderful series of portraits by Hermenegildo Bustos, the celebrated artist born near León.

Museo de las Momias

Explanada del Panteón Municipal Charge, student discount (extra fee with cameras) • 473 732 0639 • Catch buses marked "Panteón" or "Momias" anywhere along Alonso or Juárez, or walk about 500m west of the Mercado Hidalgo, along Juárez and Tepetapa, then left onto Calzada del Panteón

Tucked away in the hills west of the Alhóndiga, the ghoulish **Museo de las Momias** contains more than a hundred mummified human corpses in glass cases, exhumed from the local public cemetery. All the bodies were originally laid out in crypts, but if after five years relatives were unable or unwilling to make the perpetuity payment, the remains were usually removed. Over time many were found to have been naturally preserved, and for years the cemetery became an unofficial tourist attraction. The damage done to the site prompted the government to step in, and now the "interesting" bodies are on display here – others, not properly mummified or too dull for public titillation, have been burned or transferred to a common grave. Some of the wasted, leathery bodies are more than a century old (including a smartly dressed mummy from the 1860s said to have been a French doctor), while others are relatively recent fatalities. The burial clothes hang off the corpses almost indecently – some are completely naked – and the labels (in English) delight in pointing out their most horrendous features: one twisted mummy, its mouth opened in a silent scream, is the "woman who was buried alive"; another, a woman who died in childbirth, is displayed beside "the smallest mummy in the world". Some of the labelling is written in the first person, adding another disturbing twist. It's all absolutely grotesque, but not without a degree of macabre fascination. At the end of the main exhibit you can exit or continue into the **Salón del Culto a la Muerte**, a house-of-horrors-style extension, with an array of holographic images, jangly motorized skeletons, a rusty old chastity belt and yet more mummies. Fans of kitsch will be delighted with the hawkers outside selling mummy models and mummy-shaped shards of rock.

Museo Ex-Hacienda de San Gabriel de Barrera

Carr Guanajuato-Marfil, km 2.5 • Charge, extra fee with cameras • https://museoexhaciendasangabrieldebarrera.com.mx • Take any bus going to Marfil, and ask to be dropped at Hotel Misión Guanajuato

If the crush of Guanajuato gets too much for you, head 2km west to the **Museo Ex-Hacienda de San Gabriel de Barrera**, once the colonial home of the wealthy Barrera family, now transformed into an alluring little museum. The seventeen beautifully restored **gardens** of the hacienda range through an eclectic selection of international styles – including English, Italian, Roman, Arabic and Mexican – and make a wonderful setting for the house, which has been renovated with a colonial look. Dimly lit rooms evoke daily life among the wealthy silver barons of nineteenth-century Guanajuato and include numerous oil paintings and fine pieces of furniture dating back several centuries: simple and almost medieval on the ground floor, opulent and rich in domestic detail upstairs. It's an enlightening place to wander at your leisure and brings home the sheer wealth of colonial Guanajuato.

La Valenciana

From close by the Alhóndiga, buses labelled "Valenciana" (they can be infrequent so a taxi might be more reliable) wind their way 4km uphill to the old silver mine shafts and stupendous church in the village of **La Valenciana**, a slice of colonial Mexico barely changed since the eighteenth century.

Templo de San Cayetano de Valenciana

Carr Guanajuato-Dolores Hidalgo, km 1.5 • Free • 473 732 3596

Overlooking Guanajuato and dominating the village of La Valenciana with its elaborate facade and one completed tower is the extraordinarily sumptuous **Templo de San Cayetano de Valenciana**. Built between 1765 and 1788, it's the ultimate expression of Mexico's churrigueresque style, with a profusion of intricate adornment covering every surface – even the mortar, they say, is mixed with silver ore. Inside, notice the enormous gilded *retablos* around the main altar and in the transepts, and the delicate filigree of the roof vaulting, especially around the dome.

The church was constructed for its sponsor, the Conde de Rul y Valenciana, who also owned La Valenciana **silver mine** – for hundreds of years the richest in Mexico, tapping Guanajuato's celebrated **Veta Madre** (Mother Lode). Silver and gold are still mined around here, and exploitation continues apace with a clutch of ways to lure tourists to the associated silver shops, rock-sellers and restaurants.

Bocamina San Cayetano

Carr Guanajuato-Dolores Hidalgo • Daily 10am–7pm • Charge

Behind the Templo de San Cayetano de Valenciana, the original Mina de la Valenciana entrance now operates as the **Bocamina San Cayetano**, one of 23 interconnecting pits in the region and named after the patron saint of miners. Donning a hard hat lends some credibility to a thirty-minute tour of the upper tunnels (a steep climb 70m down), which end at a shrine to the mine's patron.

Bocamina San Ramón

Callejón de San Ramón 10 • Charge • 473 732 3551

Another Valenciana mine entrance has become the **Bocamina San Ramón**, just beyond the Templo de San Cayetano de Valenciana on the main road, which has a small museum in a lavish hacienda (once owned by one of the mine foremen), and another tour into the first section of an ancillary mine shaft (48m deep and 50m long), part of which has been converted into a bar and restaurant.

Cerro de Cubilete and the statue of Cristo Rey

The easiest way to get up here is on one of the tours advertised all around Guanajuato, though you can do the same for less than half the price by nipping out to the Central de Autobuses and picking up one of ten daily Autobuses Vasallo de Cristo, which run up there in around thirty minutes (every 1–2hr; daily 6am–6pm) – you can also pick up buses in Valenciana. The bus goes right to the top, waits for an hour, then returns

If you approached Guanajuato from León, you'll already have seen the huge statue of **Cristo Rey** crowning the 2661m **Cerro de Cubilete**, 20km west of the city. Variously claimed to occupy the geographical centre of the republic or just the state of Guanajuato, it seems a neat coincidence that it should be on the highest hill for many kilometres. Nevertheless, the complex of chapels and pilgrims' dormitories is without question magnificently sited, with long views across the plains. At its heart is a 20m bronze statue – erected in 1950 and ranking as the world's second-largest image of Christ, just behind Rio de Janeiro's – standing on a golden globe flanked by cherubs, one holding a crown of thorns, the other the golden crown of the "King of Kings".

ARRIVAL AND DEPARTURE GUANAJUATO

By plane The Aeropuerto Internacional de Guanajuato (472 748 2120; sometimes referred to as Del Bajío International Airport, or even León airport) is actually 30km west of Guanajuato at Carr Silao-León, km 5.5 (closer to León; see page 346). Taxis operate on an expensive fixed-rate scale of fares: direct to central Guanajuato (35–40min). Taxis to central León are a little less expansive. To save money from the airport you could take a taxi to Silao (10min), and take a bus from there to Guanajuato (45min). In the other direction taxis from Silao to the airport should charge much less.

VivaAerobus offers a useful no-frills service from Monterrey, while Volaris flies budget from Tijuana; Aeroméxico provides a link with Mexico City for other domestic destinations, but in all cases remember to factor in the cost of the airport taxi. Flights to various locations in the US are offered by Aeroméxico, American Airlines, United and Volaris.

Destinations Chicago (2 daily; 5hr); Dallas (3 daily; 2hr); Houston (4 daily; 2hr); Los Angeles (1–2 daily; 3hr); Mexico City (9 daily; 1hr); Monterrey (3–4 daily; 1hr 10min); Tijuana (2–3 daily; 2hr 30min).

By bus The Central de Autobuses lies 6km west of the city centre. Regular local buses ("Centro–Central") shuttle into town in about 15min, usually stopping outside the Mercado Hidalgo and the Jardín de la Reforma. Taxis charge a roughly average fee (meters are not used).

There are relatively few first-class buses from Guanajuato direct to San Miguel de Allende (ETN runs 4 daily; 1hr 30min), but there are plenty of second-class departures; if you have problems getting anywhere else, head for León, which is on the main north–south highway and has much more frequent services. For Dolores Hidalgo, you can go to the bus terminal or go straight to the stop known as "Dos Ríos", a few blocks up the hill from the Alhóndiga in the direction of San Javier (locals should know it).

Destinations Dolores Hidalgo (every 30min; 1hr 30min); Guadalajara (hourly; 4hr); Lagos de Moreno (2 daily; 1hr 45min); León (hourly; 1hr); Mexico City (hourly; 5hr); Querétaro (8 daily; 2hr 30min); San Luis Potosí (10 daily; 3hr); San Miguel de Allende (16 daily; 1hr 30min–2hr).

INFORMATION

Tourist information There's a basic information booth on Jardín Union (Mon–Fri 10am–7.30pm, Sat 10am–5pm, Sun 10am–2pm; 473 109 2104), where you'll find maps but not much else; there are also lots of private information booths throughout town (at Plazuela de los Angeles and Plazuela San Fernando, for example), but these primarily offer tours and hotel reservations.

ACCOMMODATION

SEE MAP PAGE 336

NEAR THE MERCADO HIDALGO

Antiguo Vapor Galarza 5; http://hotelavapor.com. Set in a beautifully converted eighteenth-century house, this elegant hotel has a boutique feel, combining modern luxury with exposed brick, wrought iron and wood furniture; breakfast included. M$$$

Hotel Socavón Alhóndiga 41-A; http://hotelsocavon.com.mx. A dark tunnel opens into the sunny courtyard of this small, friendly place that's well cared for. Attractive brick-ceilinged rooms all come with TVs, and breakfast is included. A short walk from the centre but worth it – there's a decent Mexican restaurant (*La Fonda del Minero*) and parking on site. M$$

Mesón del Rosario Juárez 31; http://hotelmesondelrosario.com. Great location in the heart of town (midway between the mercado and jardín), set in a colonial mansion built in 1784 with small but clean rooms decked out in period style, tile-clad bathrooms and cable TV – good-value deals online. M$$$

JARDÍN DE LA UNIÓN AND AROUND

Balcón de Cielo Carr Panorámica Pípila; http://travelbymexico.com/guan/balcondelcielo. Truly spectacular location next to Pípila, high above the jardín (right next to the funicular station). Features a lovely terrace and smallish but clean and comfy rooms. You'll need to take taxis after 9.30pm. M$$$

Casa del Agua Plazuela de la Compañía 4; 473 734 1974. Elegant seventeenth-century building converted into a chic hotel on contemporary lines. There are just fifteen light and airy rooms, all very nicely appointed with spa bath and cable TV, with breakfast included. M$$$

★ **Casa Zuniga** Callejón de Pochote 38; www.casazunigabnb.com. Welcoming modern B&B on the slopes right next to the funicular and near the Pípila, with eight cosy, colonial-style rooms, friendly hosts Rick and Carmen Zuniga, lip-smacking steak and eggs for breakfast and fabulous views from the terrace. M$$$

★ **Edelmira Hotel Boutique** Allende 7; http://edelmirahotel.com. Beautiful colonial-style property with stylish indoor pool, hot tub and spectacular rooftop terrace. Rooms feature contemporary decor with a/c, parquet floors, stone walls and flatscreen TVs. M$$$$

Hostería del Frayle Sopeña 3; https://hotelhosteriadelfrayle.com. This is the best option near the jardín, located in a lovely colonial-style building right in the heart of things with bougainvillea-draped courtyards, spacious common areas and rooms that feature artfully tiled en-suite bathrooms. Room quality varies, so look at a few first. Can be noisy, of course. M$$$

Hotel Cantarranas Cantarranas 50; 473 732 5144. Comfortable hotel with spacious rooms, free tea and coffee, smart TVs and a charming roof top terrace. M$$$

El Mesón de los Poetas Positos 35; http://mesondelospoetas.com. Very comfortable rooms (with cable TV), all painted in blues, yellows and reds, and lined with

5

decorative tiles. Shady interior patios provide respite from the heat and noise of the city. Prices rise substantially from Jan to mid-March. Breakfast is extra. M$$$

San Diego Jardín de la Unión 1; http://hotelsandiegogto.com.mx. Fine colonial warren of a place in the very centre with tiled public areas and a variety of rooms, all with local TV only (and no a/c) – some are much bigger than others so take a look before you pay. There are great plaza views from its front rooms, but overall this hotel is showing its age, and the location is its best selling point. M$$$

El Zopilote Mojado Hostal Mexiamora 51; http://elzopilotemojado.com. Colourful guesthouse doubling as café and arts hub, offering simple, cosy rooms with balconies and shared living room with terrace. Breakfast is extra. M$$$

OUTSIDE THE CENTRE

Quinta Las Acacias Paseo de la Presa 168; http://www.quintalasacacias.com. Justly popular hotel, just outside the centre near the Presa de la Olla (lake) overlooking a shady park. Rooms feature a blend of Mexican and continental styles; four-poster beds, tiled floors and rich warm colours – the suites have jacuzzis. M$$$$

Villa María Cristina Paseo de la Presa de la Olla 76; http://vmchotel.com. This opulent gem is the most luxurious (and most expensive) hotel in town (southeast of the centre on the Carr Panorámica), with just thirteen enchanting suites, featuring whirlpool tubs or steam baths and Bang & Olufsen sound systems, set in a converted colonial hacienda. The buffet breakfast is extra. M$$$$

EATING

SEE MAP PAGE 336

For a cheap meal try the **Mercado Hidalgo** and its modern annexe, the **Mercado de Gavira**, where there is tempting *birria* (goat or mutton stew), tacos and tortas – *Carnitas Latlán* is a local favourite. You'll only pay a small amount for a filling meal, or even less for a plate of tacos.

Café Tal Temezcuitate 4; http://cafe-tal.com.mx. Enticing if tiny café (all indoors), which roasts its own beans and consequently has some of the best coffee in town. They also have fresh fruit and yogurt breakfasts, a variety of teas and free wi-fi. M$

Casa Mercedes Arriba 6, San Javier; http://casamercedes.com.mx. One of the city's most popular restaurants is the best place for a splurge, with just six candle-lit tables in a homely dining room and a creative menu of gourmet Mexican food from chef Jesús Cárdenas. It's a little over-hyped, but with prickly-pear margaritas, *mole verde* with pistachio, duck tacos and spectacular *chile rellenos* it's certainly an experience. Reservations essential. M$$$$

El Gallo Pitagórico Constancia 10; http://elgallopitagorico.com. One of Guanajuato's most popular restaurants, with a predominantly Italian menu, eclectic decor and a fabulous location high on the valley slopes right behind the San Diego church (it's a steep walk). Dine on prosciutto and melon followed by a tasty *putanesca* as the sounds of the Jardín de la Unión waft up through the open windows. M$$

El Tapatío Lascuráin de Retana 20; 473 732 3291. This student taverna, opposite the university and always bristling with students and teachers, offers bargain *menu del día* (3 courses), decent cocktails and some of the best *arrachera* (steak) in town. M$$

Tasca de la Paz Plaza de la Paz 28; 473 734 2225. Smart Spanish restaurant with outdoor tables, serving European delights such as paella, chicken in white wine and *jamón*

FESTIVE GUANAJUATO

Guanajuato's two-and-a-half-week **Festival Internacional Cervantino** (early to mid-Oct; 473 731 1150, http://festivalcervantino.gob.mx) is the city's top fiesta, a celebration of sixteenth-century Spanish author **Miguel de Cervantes** and his most famous character, the hapless romantic, Don Quixote. The festival features performances by international and Mexican musicians, dancers, theatre groups and street-performers, and each year a different region or country is picked to be the focus. The festival has its foundations in the 1950s, when students performed **entremeses** – swashbuckling one-act plays from classical Spanish theatre – outdoors in places such as Plaza San Roque. These still take place here, and you don't need good Spanish to work out what's going on, as they're highly visual and very entertaining; some performances are free, but most are ticketed (http://ticketmaster.com.mx). Guanajuato actually plays host to several boisterous **festivals**, including the **Fiestas de San Juan y Presa de la Olla** (June 24), when fireworks, fairground rides and the crowning of the "Reina de las Fiestas" (Queen of the Festivals) take place on the saint's day at the Presa de la Olla, and the **Apertura de la Presa de la Olla** (first Mon in July), the traditional opening of the dam's floodgates to sluice out and clean the city's riverbed (celebrated by local dances and serenading).

CALLEJÓNEADAS

An excellent way to start the evening off in Guanajuato is to follow one of the organized **callejóneadas** – walking tours that wind through the side streets and back alleys following a student minstrel group known as *estudiantinas*. *Callejóneadas* are aimed primarily at Mexicans, so without fluent Spanish and some local knowledge you'll miss most of the jokes and risqué tales, but they're great fun all the same. It is possible to buy your own beer or wine and just tag along, but for the full experience you'll need a ticket. These can be bought (for a modest amount) from any of the information booths along Juárez, or from the *estudiantinas* who hang around the Jardín de la Unión from around 6.30pm. They entitle you to a *porrón* (a kind of ceramic drinking vessel), which is topped up as you promenade. In high season, there's something happening most nights of the week, but at other times of the year Tuesday, Thursday, Friday and Saturday are your best bets, and the event usually kicks off around 8.30pm.

serrano. M$$

Truco 7 Truco 7; 473 732 8374. Beautiful little old-school café with a young, convivial atmosphere, comfy chairs and art covering the walls. Great, moderately priced breakfasts, *comidas*, salads, steaks and wonderful garlic soup with an egg poached in it – there's even boiled eggs and cornflakes. Ask for your cappuccino *sin miel* to avoid getting a dollop of corn syrup in it. Cash only. M$$

★ **La Vie en Rose** Cantarranas 18; 473 737 4506. Enticing French bakery with excellent coffee and a range of tasty pastries from almond croissants to rum chocolate cake and macarons, with views of the Jardín from the balcony. M$$

DRINKING AND NIGHTLIFE

SEE MAP PAGE 336

BARS

Antik Café Ayuntamiento 11 (entrance on Truco); http://antik.laespiraldesign.com. Cool café with red drapes, comfy sofas and a vaguely Baroque theme; becomes a hip lounge bar at night, with live music on Fridays and a decent menu of comfort food. Cash only.

Bar Fly Sóstenes Rocha 30 (on the corner); 473 119 4501. Tiny, sociable second-floor dive bar with folk, jazz or acoustic music most nights, and seldom any entry fees; usually reverts to reggae/ska dance club later on.

Los Lobos Manuel Doblado 2; 473 732 7040. Dim and often crowded bar that resounds nightly to thumping rock classics, with pool table in the back. Cheap-ish Mexican beer. Cash only.

Luna Danae Constancia 9; 473 432 5393. A terrace bar with great views and decent cocktails, but the price tags definitely reflect the prime real estate.

★ **One Bar & Lounge** (Hotel Boutique 1850) Jardín de la Unión 7; 473 732 2795. Treat yourself to a night atop one of the city's poshest hotels, with a stylish lounge bar overlooking the main plaza and hills beyond.

★ **Santo Café** Campanero 4; https://www.santocafegto.com. Reached by a small bridge over a pedestrian alley, this quiet restaurant, café and bar is a favourite of students looking to wax philosophical over a drink; there's also free wi-fi.

CLUBS

★ **La Dama de las Camelias** Sopeña 32, opposite Museo Iconográfico; 473 732 7587. Great bar imaginatively decorated with evening dresses, high-heeled shoes and smashed mirror fragments. *La Dama* usually gets going around midnight, offers dancing most nights and great salsa late on Fri. Entry fee.

Guanajuato Grill Alonso 4; 473 597 8771. Guanajuato's most popular club tends to be packed with local youth dancing to hardcore house and techno; it's especially crammed Fri and Sat.

DIRECTORY

Banks and exchange Banks can be found along Juárez: Bancomer at no. 9, Banamex on Plazuela de San Fernando and a convenient branch of Banorte between Plaza de la Paz and the Jardín de la Unión.

Emergencies Police 473 732 0266; Cruz Roja 473 732 0487.

Hospital For emergency medical attention visit Centro Médico la Presa (473 102 3100, www.centromedicolapresa.mx) at Paseo de la Presa 85.

Laundry Lavandería Positos, Positos 17 (473 732 3467; charge per kg for 5hr, add extra for express service).

Pharmacy Farmacia Santa Fe, Plaza de la Paz 52 (daily 9am–10pm).

Post office Ayuntamiento 25, opposite the Templo de la Compañía.

5

León and around

Travelling north from Querétaro, most express buses bypass Guanajuato and head straight for **LEÓN**, a teeming, industrial city of 1.6 million with a long history of excellence in **leatherwork**. This tradition is reflected in the scores of shoe factories and, in the centre, hundreds of shoe shops: it's a good place to buy hand-tooled cowboy boots, jackets, belts or just about anything else made of leather, but there's little else to see.

The Zona Piel

http://zonapiel.com

The area around the bus station, known as the **Zona Piel**, about 3km from the city centre, has the highest concentration of leather and shoe shops, most of which have very reasonable prices, although there are also some higher-class and more expensive boutiques. If you're changing buses in León, it's well worth taking an hour to wander round the station's immediate vicinity; walk south three blocks along Hilario Medina to Plaza Piel and Plaza del Zapato (http://plazadelzapato.com), opposite at López Mateos Ote 1601, two malls with the best concentration of stores.

Museo de Arte e Historia de Guanajuato

Calzada de los Heroes 908 • Free • 477 104 1100

Just to the south of the Zona Piel, León's modern cultural district contains the **Museo de Arte e Historia de Guanajuato**, a sprawling, eclectic museum with enlightening rooms on Guanajuato state history, Mexican art (with works from local artists such as Juan Nepomuceno Herrera, Hermenegildo Bustos, Diego Rivera and Olga Costa), and a whole floor dedicated to 33 reproductions of famous Ancient Greek and Roman sculptures. There are also high-quality travelling exhibitions. No English labels.

The Centro Histórico

If you have more time to explore the city, stash your bag at the bus station's guardería (daily charge) and head for the partly pedestrianized Centro Histórico. The linked **Plaza de los Fundadores** and **Plaza de los Martíres** are spacious, tranquil and elegant, with the stately **Catedral Basílica de Nuestra Madre de la Santísima de la Luz** consecrated in 1866 (Pope Benedict XVI visited in 2012), and a typically colonial Palacio Municipal. Little else survived a disastrous flood in 1883, but the plaza is surrounded by broad boulevards lined with shops, and there is a stunning church that deserves a look, the Templo Expiatorio del Sagrado Corazón de Jesús.

Templo Expiatorio del Sagrado Corazón de Jesús

Madero 721, between 13 de Septiembre and Juan Valle • **Crypt,** charge

The extraordinary **Templo Expiatorio**, 500m southeast of the main plazas, is a marble and granite neo-Gothic church started in 1920 and worked on ever since (it was officially completed in 2012 for Pope Benedict's visit). The Notre Dame-like facade is particularly impressive, with its high-relief bronze doors revealing a white interior illuminated by modern stained glass. You can also visit the atmospheric crypt or *criptas* (separate entrance at the rear), a series of underground chambers where families still pay "rent" for burial spaces (their use helps fund construction).

ARRIVAL AND DEPARTURE — LEÓN

By plane The Aeropuerto Internacional de Guanajuato (472 748 2120; sometimes referred to as Del Bajío International Airport, or even León Airport) is actually closer to León than Guanajuato city. Taxis operate on a very expensive fixed-rate scale of fares: direct to central León is a small fortune (see page 342 for more airport information).

By bus To get into town from the Central de Autobuses (Medina 303), walk left out of the station along Medina, pick up a local bus marked "Centro" headed to the right along López Mateos and get off at the "Centro Histórico" stop (heading back, take a bus marked "Central" along López Mateos).

Destinations Aguascalientes (hourly; 1hr 30min–2hr 30min); Guadalajara (10 daily; 3–4hr); Guanajuato (hourly; 45min); Mexico City (hourly; 5hr); Zacatecas (8 daily; 4hr).

ACCOMMODATION

Hotel Terranova Zona Piel Salina Cruz 112; http://hotelterranova.com. Best mid-range option, with simple but comfy rooms and tiled floors, decent range of English-language cable TV channels and ceiling fans (a/c in executive rooms only, for an extra charge). M$$

Hotsson Hotel López Mateos Ote 1102; http://hotsson.com. Best of the López Mateos hotels, and the closest to the old centre, with a contemporary Mexican theme, flatscreen TVs, outdoor pool and jacuzzi. M$$$

Ramada Plaza León Portal Bravo 14; www.wyndhamhotels.com. This hotel is all about the prime location overlooking the plaza in the heart of the old town; it also offers well priced four-star comforts, great views and cable TV. M$$$

EATING

Don't leave León without trying its famous *guacamayas* ("macaws" in English), "invented" here in the 1950s, essentially a roll stuffed with *chicharrón* (pork rinds) and seasoned with spicy *pico de gallo* salsa and a dash of lime.

Duros y Guacamayas "Don Diego" Ignacio Altamirano 307; 477 295 0979. The most famous *guacamayas* seller in León: Don Diego's tortas are crunchy, spicy and filling, served with fresh limes and ice-cold beer. M$

Guacamayas de José el Soñador Américas 602, at Roma; 477 199 7893. One of the best and most traditional street sellers of *chicharrón* and *guacamayas*, with a special spicy sauce that will knock your head off. M$

Panteón Taurino Calzada de los Héroes 404; http://panteontaurino.com.mx. Slightly kitsch but incredibly fun homage to bullfighters, housed in a "museum" of *toro* paraphernalia. The *parrilladas* (grills) are great value, but everything else – Mexican dishes to pasta – is good too. M$$$

Lagos de Moreno

Just 25km northwest of León, in Jalisco state, **LAGOS DE MORENO** lies at the intersection of the old road from Mexico City to Ciudad Juárez and Hwy-80 (which runs from Guadalajara to San Luis Potosí and the northeast). Though the town has always been a major staging post, few tourists stop here now, and despite the heavy traffic rumbling around its fringes, it's a quiet and rather graceful little town, with colonial streets climbing steeply from a small river to a hilltop monastery. Good bus connections make the town an absorbing day trip from Aguascalientes or even Guanajuato. Cross the bridge by the bus station and head to your left along the stream, away from the choking fumes of the main road, and it's hard to believe you're in the same place. Whether you plan to stay a couple of hours or a few days, you'll want to head for the central **Jardín de los Constituyentes.** In the streets around it is a smattering of colonial mansions and official buildings, including a forbidding-looking jail that's still in use.

Parroquia de la Asunción

Jardín de los Constituyentes • Free

The impressive pink stone towers of the **Parroquia de la Asunción**, completed in 1784, dominate the central square. The church is one of the finest examples of Mexican Baroque architecture, with a huge Neoclassical *retablo* and rare wooden pipe organ inside.

Museo de Arte Sacro

José Rosas Moreno s/n • Charge • 474 116 2490

At the back of the church, the **Museo de Arte Sacro** contains a surprisingly large collection of religious paintings, sculptures and liturgical ornaments from the

OUR LADY OF SAN JUAN DE LOS LAGOS

Some 45km southwest of Lagos de Moreno, on the road to Guadalajara, the old highway runs through **SAN JUAN DE LOS LAGOS**. From its outskirts, San Juan seems like any other dusty little town; in the centre, though, you'll find an enormous bus station surrounded by scores of hotels. This is thanks to **Nuestra Señora de San Juan de los Lagos**, a miraculous 38cm-tall **image of the Virgin Mary** contained in the town's vast eighteenth-century basilica, the second most important pilgrimage site in Mexico. Crafted in the early sixteenth century by the P'urhépecha of Michoacán, the statue is said to have performed its first miracle in 1623 (bringing a dead girl to life) and it's been venerated ever since. The town's busiest dates are February 2 (**Día de la Candelaria**) and December 8 (**Fiesta de la Inmaculada Concepción**), when the place is crammed with penitents, pilgrims, those seeking miraculous cures and others who are just there to enjoy the atmosphere. The celebrations build up for a couple of weeks beforehand, and spill over to several lesser events throughout the year, notably the first fortnight of August and the entire Christmas period. San Juan de los Lagos is around 122km and 1–2hr by first-class bus (hourly) from Guadalajara, and 1hr 30min from Aguascalientes (5 daily).

seventeenth to the nineteenth centuries, emphasizing the city's religious importance over the years.

Teatro José Rosas Moreno

José Rosas Moreno 320 • Free • 474 403 1084

The **Teatro José Rosas Moreno**, opposite the Museo de Arte Sacro, opened in 1907 to stage opera performances. It's worth a look for the beautiful mural on the dome depicting the Revolution and Independence, with local hero **José Rosas Moreno**, a famous writer of tales and fables, as the centrepiece.

Templo del Señor del Calvario

Constituyentes, at Escobedo • Free • 474 742 0364

Once you've seen the centre of Lagos, you might want to embark on the long climb up to the nineteenth-century **Templo del Señor del Calvario**, a hillside church ten blocks to the north designed as a mini version of St Peter's in Rome. Other than a fine sculpture, the *Señor del Calvario*, there's not much in the church itself, but it's worth the trek for the **view**, especially at sunset.

ARRIVAL AND DEPARTURE — LAGOS DE MORENO

By bus The Central de Autobuses is east of the centre at Padre Torres 380.

Destinations Aguascalientes (every 30min; 1hr 30min–2hr); Guanajuato (roughly hourly; 1hr 30min); León (2 first-class daily, frequent second-class; 1hr); Mexico City (4 first-class daily; 5–6hr); Zacatecas (hourly; 4hr).

Aguascalientes

The city of **AGUASCALIENTES**, 177km north of Guanajuato, is an important and booming provincial capital with some fine colonial monuments in among its newer buildings. Founded in 1575 by Spanish captain Juan de Montoro Rodríguez, Aguascalientes has mushroomed into a metropolitan area of almost one million today, with the newest development – malls, cinemas, luxury hotels – north of the centre along Hwy-45. Business travellers tend to stay up here, but if you've come to see the sights, make for the *centro histórico* instead, arranged around the **Plaza de la Patria**, with its grand cathedral, and the **Palacio de Gobierno**, with its impressive murals. A couple of engrossing **museums**, including tributes to artists José Posada and Saturnino Herrán, make the city an intriguing place to stop over for a day or two, especially when you take into account its tempting array of street **food**, particularly the sumptuous **bírria** (roast goat or mutton stew), and the city's reputation for some of the finest **fiestas** in Mexico – the **Feria de San Marcos** is the biggest, but rarely a week goes by without a celebration, or at least a band playing in one of the plazas at the weekend.

The Plaza de la Patria and around

Teatro Morelos • Free • 449 915 1941

The **Plaza de la Patria** is the traditional heart of Aguascalientes, an enormous area centred around the **Exedra**, an amphitheatre-shaped space for performances overlooked by a column erected in 1808. The column was supposed to honour King Charles IV of Spain, but in the 1980s it was topped with a Mexican eagle (which symbolizes the geographical centre of Mexico). On the south side of the cathedral is the **Teatro Morelos**, built in 1882 and notable as the location for the famous convention between Zapata, Villa and Carranza in 1914, commemorated with a large plaque on the cathedral wall opposite. Call or check the city website for the current theatre programme.

Palacio de Gobierno

Plaza de la Patria • Free

5

SAN MARCOS – "FESTIVAL DE MEXICO"

The nearly two-centuries-old **Feria de San Marcos** (https://feriasanmarcos.com) of Aguascalientes is famous throughout Mexico. Celebrated in the Jardín San Marcos from mid-April to mid-May, events include everything from bullfights and live music to film festivals and rides for kids (many of the events are free).

An entrancing Baroque mansion, the **Palacio de Gobierno** was constructed in 1665 as a private residence (it became the seat of the Aguascalientes state government in 1856 and remains so today). Built from reddish volcanic rock, it contains an arcaded courtyard with a grand central staircase, decorated with four marvellous **murals** featuring historically important *hidrocálidos* (citizens of Aguascalientes) by the Chilean artist Oswaldo Barra Cunningham, who learned his trade from Diego Rivera. The first of the murals, at the back on the ground floor, was painted in 1961, with others created in subsequent years: the most recent (from 1992) are at the front of the building.

Catedral Basílica de Nuestra Señora de la Asunción

Plaza de la Patria • 449 915 1052 • Free

On the other side of the plaza from the Palacio de Gobierno, the eighteenth-century **Catedral Basílica de Nuestra Señora de la Asunción** has been refurbished to reveal its full Baroque glory, in an ostentatious welter of gold, polished marble and several paintings by José de Alcíbar and Miguel Cabrera. The dome over the altar is particularly magnificent (the Virgen de la Asunción is patron of the city), but don't miss **La Capilla del Sagrario**, to the left of it, with a captivating all-turquoise interior. Look out also for the small plaque honouring Juan de Montoro Rodríguez, city founder, whose remains are said to be buried somewhere under the floor.

Casa de la Cultura

Carranza 101 • Free • 449 910 2010

Avenida Venustiano Carranza leads west from behind the cathedral to the **Casa de la Cultura**, a delightful seventeenth-century mansion given over to music and dance classes and the occasional exhibition in the **Galería de la Ciudad** at the entrance. The notice board here is an excellent place to find out what's on around town, and in the patio there's a small café – a perfect, tranquil spot to have a drink and watch the world go by.

Museo Regional de Historia

Carranza 118 • Charge • 449 916 5228

A little further down Carranza from the Casa de la Cultura, the **Museo Regional de Historia** chronicles local history (Spanish captions only) in an elegant mansion built in 1901; exhibits range from a fossilized mammoth tusk and prehistoric arrowheads to Spanish colonial artefacts. Highlights include some remarkable pieces of pre-Columbian pottery and jewellery; the white shell necklace is especially striking.

Jardín de San Marcos

Jardín de San Marcos • Free

Escape from the sun by heading west on Carranza to the shady **Jardín de San Marcos**, a lush, beautifully manicured park smothered with pink and violet bougainvillea. The park runs down to the **Templo de San Marcos**, completed in 1765 with another exuberant churrigueresque facade and dedicated to the Virgen del Carmen. In the sacristy there's a huge mural dubbed *Worshipping the Kings*, completed by Spanish artist José de Alcíbar in 1775.

Santuario Nuestra Señora de Guadalupe

Guadalupe Nájera 213 • 449 915 5033 • Free

Justly regarded as one of the most beautiful churches in Mexico, the **Santuario Nuestra Señora de Guadalupe** sports an incredibly ornate Baroque facade by master architect Felipe de Ureña, credited with bringing the Spanish churrigueresque style to Mexico. The church was completed in 1789, the interior a staggering confection of intricate carvings culminating in the pink sandstone *retablo* and magnificent dome (with a painting of the Virgin of Guadalupe created by José de Alcíbar in 1777). The church is a short walk north from the Jardín de San Marcos via Nicolás Bravo.

Museo José Guadalupe Posada and around

Jardín del Encino (Trujillo 222) • Charge • 449 915 4556 • To get to the Jardín del Encino, head east from the main plaza and take the first right, Díaz de León, south for about seven blocks

Though it only occupies a small building about 1km south of the centre, the **Museo José Guadalupe Posada** is one of the main reasons to visit Aguascalientes. Indeed, the town is almost a place of pilgrimage for devotees of this influential printmaker, who is best known for his political satire and criticism of the Catholic Church (see page 351). The permanent exhibit here contains a well-curated collection of Posada lithographs, along with the original plates and background information in Spanish.

Templo del Señor del Encino

Jardín del Encino • 449 915 9876 • Free

The Museo José Guadalupe Posada occupies the former priest's house of the adjacent **Templo del Señor del Encino**, another elegant eighteenth-century church of pinkish sandstone by Francisco Bruno de Ureña, the son of Felipe de Ureña. Beyond the churrigueresque facade lies a riotously gilded interior with vast paintings depicting the Stations of the Cross ("El Viacrucis"), completed by Andrés López and his brothers in

POSADA – THE ART OF THE MACABRE

The frequently macabre work of **José Guadalupe Posada** will be familiar even if his name is not: Diego Rivera was not so wrong when he described the prolific Posada as "so outstanding that one day even his name will be forgotten". He was born a baker's son in Aguascalientes in 1852, and was later apprenticed to a lithographer. In 1888 he moved to Mexico City, and started to create in earnest the thousands of prints for which he soon became known. He mainly worked for the editor and printer Vanegas Arroyo, and his images appeared on posters and in satirical broadsheets that flourished despite – or more likely because of – the censorship of the **Porfiriano era**. Some of Posada's work was political, attacking corrupt politicians, complacent clergy or foreign intervention, but much was simply recording the news (especially disasters, which so obsess the Mexican press to this day), lampooning popular figures or observing everyday life with a gleefully macabre eye. Later, the events and figures of the Revolution, grotesquely caricatured, came to dominate his work.

Technically, Posada moved on from lithography to **engraving** in type metal (producing the characteristic hatched effect seen in much of his work) and finally to zinc etching, an extremely rapid method involving drawing directly onto a zinc printing plate with acid-resistant ink, and then dipping it in acid until the untouched areas corrode. Although the *calaveras*, the often elegantly clad skeletons that inhabit much of his work, are his best-known creations, the Aguascalientes museum devoted to him covers the full range of his designs. They all bear a peculiar mix of Catholicism, pre-Columbian tradition, preoccupation with death and black humour that can only be Mexican – and that profoundly affected all later Mexican art. Rivera and Orozco are just two of the greats who publicly acknowledged their debt to Posada, who died in 1913.

5

MEXICO'S MOST MEXICAN ARTIST

A contemporary and friend of Diego Rivera, artist **Saturnino Herrán** (1887–1918) died young and never really achieved much recognition, though he has been dubbed "El más pintor de los mexicanos y más mexicano de los pintores" ("the greatest painter of the Mexicans, and the most Mexican of the painters"). Born and trained in Aguascalientes, it wasn't till his family moved to Mexico City in 1905 that he met Rivera. His breakthrough came in 1910 during the Centennial Anniversary of Mexico's Independence Day – Herrán organized an exhibition of work that incorporated Indigenous Mexican as opposed to European artistic traditions, a radical idea at the time. Herrán is best known today for his naturalistic and dignified paintings of Mexican indios, but he also designed stained-glass windows, book illustrations, and, near the end of his life, murals. Visit the Museo de Aguascalientes (see page 352) to sample his work.

1796. Also here is the miraculous and much-venerated "black Christ" of Encino – also depicted in stained glass above the main door – with strangely thick, long black hair.

Museo de Arte Contemporáneo No. 8

Primo Verdad, at Morelos • Charge, free Sun • 449 910 2010

A few blocks northeast of the Plaza de la Patria at the corner of Morelos and Primo Verdad, the **Museo de Arte Contemporáneo No. 8** is home to some of the most exciting and provocative art from the region, with exhibitions that change every two months. The core of the collection comprises prize-winning works from Mexico's prestigious National Student Contest for Visual Arts, between 1966 and 1980. There's also a permanent collection of work by **Enrique Guzmán**, the talented but troubled painter born here in 1952, who took his own life at the age of 34.

Museo Nacional de la Muerte

Jardín del Estudiante, Rivero y Gutiérrez • Charge, free Wed • http://museonacionaldelamuerte.uaa.mx

One block north along Morelos from the Museo de Arte Contemporáneo, in a graceful colonial monastery building next to **Templo de San Diego**, the **Museo Nacional de la Muerte** casts a morbid eye over Mexico's obsession with death rituals and images of death over the centuries, though it's not as grim as it sounds. The exhibits – donated by the engraver Octavio Bajonero Gil – start with Mesoamerican traditions, with plenty of ancient statuary and a massive collection of model skulls, though these are so colourfully painted, bejewelled and stylized they seem more like kids' toys than religious totems. Labels are in Spanish only, but this is really a visual experience. The museum ends with a stylish art gallery, all red-tinted, which houses an eclectic collection of death-related art from the nineteenth century on, including work by Posada and his predecessor, **Manuel Manilla**. Afterwards, raise your spirits in the tranquil courtyard café, in the shadow of San Diego's main dome.

Templo de San Antonio

Pedro Parga at Zaragoza • 449 915 2898 • Free

The fabulously ornate **Templo de San Antonio** was completed around 1906 by the architect Refugio Reyes; it's an Art Nouveau gem with elements of just about every architectural style, including Russian and Arabic. Inside, murals of the miracles of San Antonio by Candelario Rivas provide a blaze of colour.

Museo de Aguascalientes

Zaragoza 505 • Charge, Free Sun • 449 915 9043

Opposite the Templo de San Antonio is the imposing **Museo de Aguascalientes**, a bold Neoclassical palace constructed in 1903 by Refugio Reyes as a Catholic school (it was a teachers' college before it became the museum in 1975). This is essentially an art museum, with rooms dedicated to the block prints and paintings of **Gabriel Fernández Ledesma** (1900–83), and sculptor **Jesús F. Contreras** (1866–1902), whose sensual *Malgré Tout* (a copy of the original) and bronze friezes of Mesoamerican heroes adorn the courtyard. The main focus, however, is the naturalistic work of **Saturnino Herrán** (see page 352). Highlights include the baleful stare of *El Gallero*, the iconic beauty of *La Criolla del Manton*, the haunting *Vendedora de Ollas* and the vast *Labor*, with its contrasting images of motherhood and industrial workers. Herrán's large stained-glass panel, *El Hijo Prodigo*, stands in the courtyard.

Baños Termales de Ojocaliente

Tecnológico 102 • Charge • 449 970 0721, http://facebook.com/banostermalesdeojocaliente • To get there, take "Ruta 12" along López Mateos

You'll need to travel some 4km east of the centre to experience the **hot springs** that gave Aguascalientes its name – these first official baths were built in 1831, in a French-influenced Neoclassical style. Today the **Baños Termales de Ojocaliente** is really just an outdoor swimming pool complex, fed by the springs, on the road to San Luis Potosí – the private baths on site are much hotter and more atmospheric.

ARRIVAL AND INFORMATION — AGUASCALIENTES

By plane Jesús Terán Peredo International Airport (aka Aguascalientes International Airport; 449 918 2806) is 16km south of the city at Carretera Panamericana, km 22. You'll find all the major car rental firms and HSBC ATMs at the terminal. Taxis charge set fees into the centre (prices are fixed according to a zone system). Aeroméxico and Volaris have connections to Mexico City, while Volaris also flies to Tijuana and LA.

Destinations Dallas (2 daily; 1hr 45min); Houston (1 daily; 1hr 45min); Los Angeles (1 daily; 2hr 45min); Mexico City (8 daily; 1hr 15min); Tijuana (1 daily; 2hr 30min).

By bus The Central de Autobuses is around 2km south of the centre on the city's ring road (Av de la Convención), from where there's a frequent bus service into the Plaza de la Patria ("Centro"), at the heart of town. To get back to the bus station from the centre, catch a bus marked "Central" from along Galeana at Insurgentes, just opposite the Plaza Patria shopping mall. Taxis use meters in Aguascalientes; from the bus station to Plaza Patria should only be a small fee, though some drivers may optimistically try and set a higher price if they can – so insist on the meter.

Destinations Guadalajara (roughly hourly; 3hr); Guanajuato (2–3 daily; 3hr); León (every 30min; 2–3hr); Mexico City (hourly; 6hr); Querétaro (hourly; 6hr); San Luis Potosí (hourly; 3–4hr); Zacatecas (hourly; 2hr).

Tourist office On the ground floor of the Palacio de Gobierno (449 910 0051, http://vivaaguascalientes.com).

ACCOMMODATION — SEE MAP PAGE 349

As with the other Bajío cities, plenty of **motel** and **hotel** chains – *One Hotels*, *Fiesta* and *Marriott* among them – have arrived on the outskirts of Aguascalientes: they're a long way from anything of interest, but they can be good value. During the *ferias* (mid-April to mid-May and the week around Nov 1), rooms are almost impossible to obtain at short notice and cost at least fifty percent more.

Art Hotel Nieto 502; 449 917 9595. Bright, air-conditioned rooms with chic, contemporary decor and flatscreen TVs. The roof-top *Acapella Deck* bar and lounge is a great place to relax. M$$

Francia Aguascalientes Madero 113; http://hotelfrancia aguascalientes.com. This grand old dame was built in 1915 by the ubiquitous Refugio Reyes, but all its spacious, comfortable rooms have been modernized with plenty of amenities, including cable TV. M$$$

★ **El Giro Hostal** Allende 341; 449 917 9393. Located next to the Plaza de Toros San Marcos, the city's only hostel is a wise choice, with friendly owners and four clean mixed dorms for 5–7 persons. You also get hot water showers, tea and coffee and use of a kitchen and TV room. M$

Hotel Gya Boutique 5 de Mayo 568; 449 915 5973. Close to Plaza de los Mariachis, this modern business hotel features spacious rooms with polished stone floors and cable TV. M$$

Quality Inn Nieto 102, on Plaza de la Patria; http://choice hotelsmexico.com. The former *Hotel Río Grande* has become a standard business chain hotel, offering bags of comfort in a superb location. Some rooms have views over the plaza, and all have cable TV with lots of US channels. Breakfast included; this is the best mid-range choice in town. M$$$

Quinta Real Aguascalientes Aguascalientes Sur 601; www.caminoreal.com/quintareal. Though it could do with an update, this remains the most characterful hotel in the city, set in modern premises designed to look like a colonial monastery, with spacious suites and all the extras: pool,

5

BRANDY AND BURNING WATER

Hidrocálidos (citizens of Aguascalientes) love their booze. The state has been a **wine producer** since 1950, though the local brands are not always easy to find, except in the more expensive restaurants. The local **brandy** is commonly served, however: **San Marcos** is the best known, made here and sold all over the republic. You'll also come across **aguardientes** (literally "fiery waters") and **uvate**, a grape-based tipple mixed with lime juice and vodka.

lush gardens and terrace bar. It's on the southern edge of the city – it's around 15–20min to the centre by taxi. Wi-fi is extra. M$$$

EATING

SEE MAP PAGE 349

Bírria (slow-roasted barbecued lamb, shredded and served with a bowl of piquant broth, then eaten with a tortilla) and *lechón al horno* (roast suckling pig) are specialities in Aguascalientes, along with *atole* (sweet corn- and chocolate-based drink), and desserts with guava (*guayaba*). The city has three lively markets near the centre, all excellent places to eat (see below), though **Mercado Terán** is better known for fresh fruit, piles of chiles, meat and produce – you can also check out the fresh juice stalls here.

Cenaduría Farolito Moctezuma 105, at Victoria; 449 915 2404, http://farolitoags.wixsite.com/farolito. With a great location right on the plaza, an old-world feel (it was founded in 1922), wooden tables and decent Mexican food, this is a convenient option for lunch. M$$

Durería El Rey del Duro Matamoros Nte 207; 449 147 8140. "The King of Crackling" has been knocking out crispy pork rinds (*chicharrón* or "*duro*" here in Aguascalientes) with special sauce and tortillas since 1965. M$

Las Costillas de Sancho Av Aguascalientes Nte 402; http://lascostillasdesancho.com.mx. For a real treat, grab a taxi and head 4km north of the city centre to this exquisite restaurant, with a huge selection of fresh seafood, roasted meats, steaks and classic Mexican dishes. The ribs (*las costillas*) are a speciality. M$$$

Lechón Pascualito Jesús Díaz de León 101; 449 733 6284. This no-frills local shop has been knocking out *lechón* since 1956 – owners carefully roast, dice, then serve the meat in mouthwatering tacos or tortas. M$

★ **Mercado Juárez** aka Mercado de la Bírria, Victoria and Unión; 449 916 2030. If you love street food you're in for a treat here, as this market is effectively a whole alley of twenty cheap *bírrierias* (*bírria* stalls), with aromatic goat meat slow-roasted right in front of you. Pick the place with the most patrons. Big plates and small are both a bargain here. M$

Mercado Morelos Morelos and Obregón. Giant food court loaded with tempting snack stalls; the star here is *Taquería Ruben's*, where glorious *carne asada* and *bistek* are stuffed into tortillas as you sit at the counter and spoon on the salsa. M$

Mitla Restaurante Madero 222; 449 145 2041. Popular, old-fashioned Mexican restaurant that has been operating since 1938, with white-jacketed waiters serving a good selection of national and local dishes, including seafood and very reasonable comidas corridas. There's also an impressive breakfast buffet. M$$

★ **La Saturnina** Carranza 110; http://lasaturnina.com. Lovely and colourful courtyard café with a fountain (the house was designed by Refugio Reyes), great for breakfast (especially the Sunday buffet) or just coffee and cake; try the *café de olla* (cinnamon-infused coffee), a city speciality served black in a ceramic mug, the justly lauded *chilaquiles* and local-style tacos. The name is a tribute to painter Saturnino Herrán – copies of his *La criolla del mantón* adorn the walls. M$$

DRINKING

SEE MAP PAGE 349

Casa Corazón Carranza 124; http://facebook.com/CasaCorazonCentro. Bar and café in an old house dating from 1870 that opens for home-made desserts and coffee in the afternoon, but gets really busy in the evenings when it serves wine and beer.

Merendero Kiko's Andador Pani 132; 449 915 8129. Established in 1957 by Don Kiko himself and here since 1975, this is a multi-level sports bar with giant TV screens.

Pub Ummagumma Carranza 102; 449 101 7579. Great little bar that specializes in the unlikely combo of sushi and hamburgers; live music most Wed, Fri & Sat (entry fee). Cash only.

Pulquería Posada Nieto 443; www.facebook.com/lapulque. Friendly local bar, specializing in *pulque*, a milky, alcoholic tipple made from the fermented sap of the maguey plant.

DIRECTORY

Banks and exchange Banamex and Bancomer are on the north side of Plaza de la Patria, both with 24hr ATMs.

Laundry SLYT Super Lavandería, Elizondo 117 (charge per kg).

Pharmacy Plenty in the centre – try Farmacia Guadalajara (24hr), Madero 232, 1 block from Plaza de la Patria.

Post office The main post office is at Hospitalidad 108, a block north of the plaza and reached by following Morelos and then turning right.

Zacatecas

Almost 2500m above sea level and crammed into a narrow gully between two hills, the old silver town of **ZACATECAS** is overflowing with ornate colonial architecture and intriguing museums, ranking alongside Guanajuato as the Bajío's finest destinations – the obvious wealth projected by its fine stone buildings makes this another city that seems plucked straight out of classical Spain. Zacatecas is known for its high-quality art museums and subterranean tours of the old silver mine, **Mina El Edén**, but the main highlight is the ornate **cathedral**, from which all other main sights are within walking distance. Just a few paces from the market and from the important junction of Juárez and Hidalgo, the **Jardín Independencia** is in effect the city's main plaza, where people gather in the evenings, get their shoes shined and wait for buses. West of the Jardín Independencia is the **Alameda**, a thin strip of stone benches, splashing fountains and a bandstand that makes a cool retreat from the heat of the day.

Brief history

It didn't take the conquistadors long to discover the enormous lodes of silver in the hills of Mexico's central highlands, and, after some initial skirmishes with the Indigenous Zacateco, the city of Zacatecas was founded in 1546. For the next three centuries its mines disgorged fabulous wealth, enriching both the city and the Spanish Crown; in 1728 the mines here were producing one-fifth of all Mexico's silver. The end of the boom, when it came, was brought about more by the political uncertainties of the nineteenth century than by the exhaustion of the mines, some of which still operate today. Throughout nearly a century of war, Zacatecas itself became an important prize: there were major battles here in 1871, when Benito Juárez successfully put down local rebels, and in 1914 when Pancho Villa's División del Norte captured the city, completely annihilating its 12,000-strong garrison – known as the Toma de Zacatecas (Taking of Zacatecas), it was the bloodiest battle of the Revolution, with the military forces counting approximately 7,000 dead and many more civilian casualties. The loss of Zacatecas broke the back of the Huerta regime. Today Zacatecas is booming once

FIESTAS IN ZACATECAS

Zacatecas hosts several exuberant festivals – here are some of the best:

Festival Cultural Zacatecas (March/April). For two weeks around Semana Santa the city celebrates this enormous arts festival, with daily events all over town including everything from high-quality Mexican rock acts and even a few foreign bands to folkloric dance, opera and ballet. Most events are free.

Festival Zacatecas del Folclor International (late July–early Aug). Mexico's top international folk festival with around fifty nationalities represented, mostly performing in the plazas around the centre.

La Morisma de Bracho (weekend closest to Aug 27). Festival with up to ten thousand people engaging in mock battles between Moors and Christians, acted out on the Cerro de la Bufa.

Feria Nacional de Zacatecas (Sept, first two weeks). Zacatecas' principal fiesta features bullfights and plenty of traditional carousing. The activity happens at La Feria, 3km south towards Guadalupe.

5

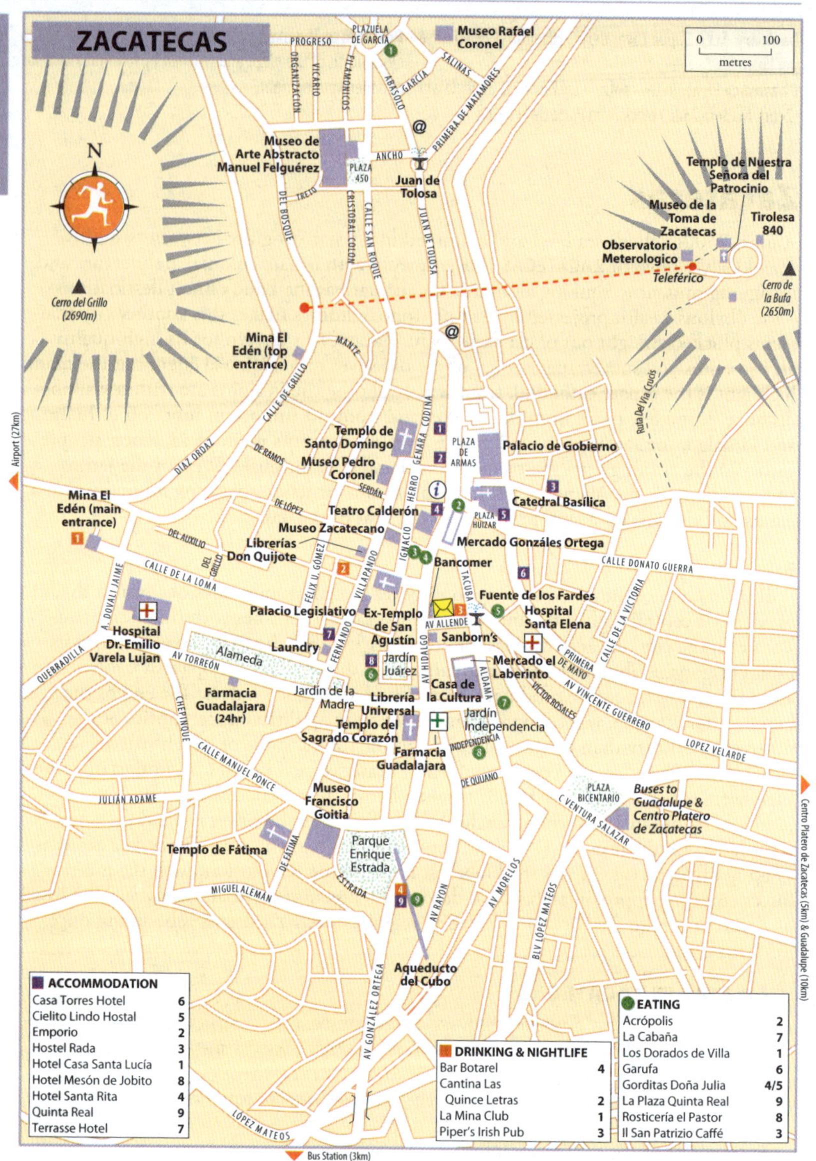

more, its business and light industry boosted by the increasing flow of traffic between Mexico and the US.

Catedral Basílica de Zacatecas

Hidalgo 617 • Free

Zacatecas's flamboyant **Catedral Basílica de Zacatecas** is the outstanding relic of the city's years of colonial glory: built in the pink sandstone typical of the region, it represents one of the latest, and arguably the finest, examples of Mexican Baroque architecture. It was completed in 1752, its facade carved with a wild exuberance unequalled anywhere in the country. The interior, they say, was once at least its equal – furnished in gold and silver, with rich wall hangings and a great collection of paintings – but as everywhere, it was despoiled or the riches removed for "safekeeping", first at the time of Juárez' reforms and later during the Revolution; only the structure itself, with its bulky Doric columns and airy vaulting, remains to be admired. Look out for the chapel on the left as you enter, dedicated to local priest and martyr **San Mateo Correa Magallanes** (1866–1927), murdered during the anti-Roman Catholic persecutions of the 1920s and canonized in 2001 – his bones lie in a special glass casket.

Palacio de Gobierno

Hidalgo 604, Plaza de Armas • Free • 492 923 9500

On the east side of Plaza de Armas, next to the cathedral, the **Palacio de Gobierno** was built as the residence of the Conde Santiago de la Laguna in 1727 and subsequently bought by the state government. In keeping with local fashion, a modernist mural – completed in 1970 by Antonio Pintor Rodríguez and depicting the city's history – embellishes the staircase of the interior courtyard.

Mercado González Ortega

Hidalgo & Tacuba • Free

On the south side of the cathedral, the **Mercado González Ortega** is a strikingly attractive market building, opened in 1889. It takes advantage of its sloping position to have two fronts: the upper level opening onto Hidalgo, the lower floor with entrances on Tacuba. Converted into a fancy little shopping mall, it's now filled with tourist shops and smart boutiques, as well as a superb wine store. At the southern end of the mercado, broad steps help turn the little **Plaza Goytia** into a popular place for street theatre.

Templo de Santo Domingo

Plazuela de Santo Domingo • Free

Climbing up from the west side of Plaza de Armas towards the Cerro del Grillo are streets lined with more mansions – some restored, some badly in need of work, but all deserted by the mining moguls who built them. The **Templo de Santo Domingo** stands raised on a platform above the plaza of the same name, just uphill from the Plaza de Armas – its hefty, buttressed walls a stern contrast to the lightness of the cathedral, though it was built at much the same time. The interior still gives a glimpse of the great wealth that funded its construction, with painted ceilings and ornate, gilded churrigueresque *retablos* in the side chapels.

Museo Pedro Coronel

Plazuela de Santo Domingo • Charge • 492 922 8021

Pedro Coronel (1923–85), older brother of Rafael Coronel (see page 359), was an artist in his own right, who managed to gather an art collection that reads like a *Who's Who* of modern but especially abstract and Catalan art. Today his collection forms the basis for the entertaining **Museo Pedro Coronel**, which occupies what was originally a seventeenth-century Jesuit monastery next to Santo Domingo church. Most of the work on display is relatively minor, but there are some real gems to look out for. You enter the complex through the nineteenth-century **library**, lined with faded tomes, and pass through a courtyard of orange trees before reaching the gallery proper on the second floor.

There are a few drawings by **Picasso** and a much larger ensemble from **Miró**, including his childlike but oddly compelling *Infancia de Ubu* series. Look out also for some typically abstract lithographs by Calder and Motherwell, and a tiny drawing by Henry

Moore. Kandinsky, Braque, Chagall, Dalí, Leger and Max Ernst are all represented, and don't overlook the dark scribbles of **Jean Cocteau**, created in the 1940s.

There's also a separate room of architectural drawings by Piranesi, and engravings by Hogarth (including his famous image *Gin Lane*). Some of the peripheral galleries are also interesting, in particular the large West African and Oriental collections, the latter featuring some intriguing Japanese painted screens dating from the nineteenth century.

Museo Zacatecano

Dr Hierro 307 • Charge • 492 922 6580

Heading south along Ignacio Hierro, you'll reach the old Casa de la Moneda, Zacatecas' mint in the days when every silver-producing town in Mexico struck its own coins. This has been restored and turned into the exhaustive **Museo Zacatecano**, its vaulted halls and courtyard an evocative showcase for the region's history. More murals by Antonio Pintor Rodríguez adorn the central staircase.

Visits begin with a video presentation giving the historic overview, but as with the rest of the museum you'll need to speak Spanish to make the most of this – there are no English labels. From here a series of beautifully presented galleries, containing artefacts, video screens, rare documents, dioramas of the silver mines and examples of silverwork, takes you through the history of Zacatecas from prehistoric times. Other rooms deal with the history of the building, completed in 1799 and operating as a mint until 1842 when it was sold to an English company – examples of coins made here are displayed.

Upstairs, art takes centre stage, with galleries devoted to muralist Rodríguez, composer Manuel Ponce (born in neighbouring Fresnillo) and the painted shells of Mario Arellano Zajur. Next are a couple of hundred wonderful hand-painted *retablos* (altarpieces), depicting just about every saint, martyr and apostle going. The final galleries display two hundred Huichol embroideries that incorporate an amazing range of geometric designs, as well as maize symbols, deer and butterflies, all executed in black, red and green (for death, life and prosperity respectively).

Ex-Templo de San Agustín

Plazuela Miguel Auza, at Callejón San Agustín • Free; admission varies for special exhibitions • 492 922 8063

The **Ex-Templo de San Agustín** has been under restoration, on and off, since the 1950s, and today its spacious, beautifully finished interior serves as an atmospheric gallery space for temporary art exhibitions, usually of a very high quality – local artists the Coronel brothers have both been featured in recent shows. The church dates back to the early sixteenth century, but after the Reform Laws it was converted into a casino and the adjoining monastery became a hotel. Don't miss the fabulously ornate Plateresque side door, a smaller version of the cathedral facade dating from the eighteenth century.

Museo de Arte Abstracto Manuel Felguérez

Colón, at Seminario • Charge • http://maamf.com.mx

North of the centre, the **Museo de Arte Abstracto Manuel Felguérez** is an extensive modern art gallery imaginatively converted from a prison and its associated church. In places the cells have been turned into mini-galleries where the intimacy of the space draws you into the works. Elsewhere several levels of cells have been ripped out to leave huge rooms with floor-to-ceiling paintings, sculptures and installations viewed from steel walkways that gradually take you higher.

Half of what's on show is by **Manuel Felguérez** (born 1928), a native of Zacatecas state and an approximate contemporary of the Coronel brothers (see page 357 and below). Within the field of abstract art he is almost as highly regarded, though it can take some effort to fully appreciate his work, particularly that of the early 1980s when he developed an obsession with male reproductive anatomy. He is perhaps most successful in his sculpture, notably the 1995 *El Arco del Día*, a huge bronze tripod that looks like it has just landed in a side chapel off the church. Nearby, his huge canvas entitled *Retablo de los Mártires* is also particularly striking. Elsewhere within the museum there is work by the Coronel brothers and several other of Felguérez' Mexican contemporaries, as well as an excellent art bookshop: almost everything is in Spanish.

Museo Rafael Coronel

Callejón de San Francisco • Charge • 492 924 2160 • If you don't fancy the 20-minute walk from the centre, several bus routes, including #5, #8 and #9, pass close by

Pedro Coronel may have amassed a spectacular art collection, but his brother Rafael (born 1931) has a far more beautiful museum, the centrepiece of which is a huge collection of traditional masks, possibly the finest in Mexico. The wonderful **Museo Rafael Coronel** occupies the Ex-Convento de San Francisco on the north side of town. Founded in 1593 as a Franciscan mission (the facade is said to be the oldest in the city), it was rebuilt in the seventeenth century, only to begin deteriorating after the Franciscans were expelled in 1857 and finally suffer destruction during Villa's assault. The building and gardens have now been partially but beautifully restored, and the museum brilliantly integrated with the ruins.

There are more than four thousand masks on display, which makes taking it all in a bit overwhelming. The masks trace the art's development in what is now Mexico from some very ancient, pre-Columbian examples to contemporary pieces: often there are twenty or more variations on the same theme, and one little room is entirely full of the visages of Moors and Christians from the La Morisma festival (see page 355). As well as the masks, you can see Coronel's impressive collections of ceramics and puppets, the town's original charter granted by Philip II in 1593 and sketches and drawings connected with Coronel's wife Ruth Rivera, architect and daughter of famed muralist Diego Rivera. There's also a bookshop and a cosy café.

Museo Francisco Goitia

Enrique Estrada 102 • Charge • 492 922 0211

At the back of the Parque Enrique Estrada, in the old governor's residence, stands another local artist's museum, the **Museo Francisco Goitia**. Goitia (1882–1960) was one of Mexico's leading painters early in the twentieth century, and this enjoyable little museum houses a permanent exhibition of his work and that of more modern local artists (including Pedro Coronel), as well as hit-or-miss temporary displays and travelling art shows.

Mina El Edén

Dovalí Jaime s/n • Charge; guided tour roughly every 15min, generally in Spanish, but ask if a bilingual guide is available • http://minaeleden.com. To reach the mine, take bus #7 from Hidalgo and Juárez to Hospital Dr Emilio Varela Lujan, or walk up Torreón, beyond the Alameda (follow the signs)

The **Mina El Edén**, or Eden Mine, is perhaps the most curious and unusual of all Zacatecas' attractions. This super-rich pit produced the silver that gave Zacatecas its immense wealth from 1586 to the 1960s. **Guided tours** (around 1hr) start at the main entrance, west of the centre, with a 500m small train ride through narrow, dark passages into the heart of the Cerro de Grillo. The first stop – where you get around fifteen minutes to wander around freely – is the well-presented **Museo de Rocas**, with displays of rocks and minerals from around the world (though mostly Mexico), including impressive geodes and fossilized ammonites and trilobites. Don't miss the stunning "Rosa del Desierto", a giant, prickly arrangement of gypsum and calcite deposits. You're then taken on a guided tour of the old mine workings – subterranean pools, chasms crossed on steel bridges and scattered machinery, all complete with colourfully lit mannequins dressed as miners and even a small shrine, the **Altar Santo Niño**.

5

Enthusiastic guides tell of the thousands of miners who died during the mine's four hundred years of operation. The high number of fatalities seems perfectly possible when you see level upon level of old galleries falling away for some 320m beneath you, inaccessible since the mine flooded when production stopped in 1966. The tour ends at a fountain near a lift that whisks you to the upper levels of the mine, where there's another stroll through 500m of tunnels to the upper entrance (about 200m from the cable car; see below). You can also return the way you came, or enter the mine from the upper entrance, though you may have a longer wait for a guide. It is also worth returning in the evening to *La Mina Club* (see page 363).

Cerro de la Bufa

Teleférico • Charge; services can be disrupted by strong winds

Zacatecas is dominated by the **Cerro de la Bufa** (2612m), with its extraordinary rock cockscomb crowning the ridge some 237m above the Plaza de Armas; at night it's illuminated, with a giant cross on top. A modern Swiss cable car connects the summit with the slopes of the **Cerro del Grillo** opposite – an exhilarating ride straight over the heart of the old town. The lower station of the **Teleférico** (cable car) is near the top entrance of Mina El Edén. It's a relatively easy climb up from the back of San Agustín (look for the signs up Callejon de Garcia Rojas, off Villalpando), or you can take bus #7 right to the door. Out from the station you pass right over the city centre – the views down on the houses are extraordinary. Most people come back the same way, but walking down the Cerro de la Bufa on the paved **Ruta del Via Crucis** is no great strain; the path ends at Altapalmira, which you can follow downhill until you see the red signs for the centre.

Templo de Nuestra Señora del Patrocinio

Explanada del Cerro de La Bufa • 492 922 1129

It's a brisk uphill walk to the Plaza de la Revolución and pristine **Templo de Nuestra Señora del Patrocinio**, a chapel dating back to 1795 with an image of the Virgin said to perform healing miracles. To get there, exit the Cerro de la Bufo *teleférico* station and turn right. The main viewpoints are behind here, offering a jaw-dropping panorama of Zacatecas and its surroundings.

Museo de la Toma de Zacatecas

Explanada del Cerro de la Bufa • Charge • 492 922 8066

Next to the chapel on the Plaza de la Revolución, the **Museo de la Toma de Zacatecas** honours Pancho Villa's spectacular victory here in 1914, completely annihilating its twelve thousand-strong garrison – it was the bloodiest battle of the Revolution, breaking the back of the Huerta regime (see page 448). The museum has been given a futuristic makeover, with interactive games and exhibits sure to enthral kids, holographic images, recordings, and rare photos – some showing harrowing scenes of piled-up dead bodies – and old weapons and uniforms. There is also an exhibit dedicated to Ángela Ramos aka "**Juana Gallo**" (immortalized in the eponymous 1961 Mexican movie; she is supposed to have joined the rebels at Zacatecas after her father and fiancé were murdered).

ZIP ZACATECAS

A more exhilarating attraction on the Cerro de la Bufa is just around the corner from Plaza de la Revolución, the museum and chapel: **Tirolesa 840**, a zip line that whips you across a gorge on the north side of the mountain (around 1km total). It's open daily 10am–6pm, with rides for a charge. Contact 812 747 7204 or visit http://facebook.com/Tirolesa840 for more information.

Behind the equestrian statue of Villa in the plaza outside, two paths skirt around the base of La Bufa to the **Mausoleo de los Hombres Ilustres**, where Zacatecanos who have made their mark on history have been buried since the 1940s, or at least have their memorials – unless you are a student of Mexican history, you're unlikely to have heard of any of them.

El Chico

The chapel and the museum do not sit on the actual summit of the Cerro de la Bufa: only one of the three peaks is accessible, **El Chico** (the smallest), topped by the **Observatorio Meteorologico**, another short walk uphill from behind the chapel. The observatory dates back to 1906, and though you can't go inside, the mesmerizing views are worth the climb. You might spot turkey vultures hanging out on the rocks near here.

ARRIVAL AND DEPARTURE — ZACATECAS

By plane The Aeropuerto Internacional de Zacatecas is 27km north of town; the only way to get into the centre is by taxi, which charge a fixed rate (ask your hotel to arrange one for the trip back). Volaris links the city with Tijuana, Los Angeles and Chicago, but for other destinations you'll need to take the Aeroméxico or VivaAerobus flight to Mexico City and transfer.

Destinations Chicago (1 daily; 4hr 25min); Los Angeles (3 weekly; 3hr); Mexico City (8 daily; 1hr 30min); Tijuana (1 daily; 2hr 30min).

By bus Zacatecas' modern Central de Autobuses is a hive of activity both day and night, 4km south of the centre. To get into town take "Ruta 8" bus (every few min 7am–9pm) or a taxi. If you take the bus, get off at the Jardín Independencia – it's within reasonable walking distance of most of the accommodation. To return to the bus terminal, take "Ruta 8" (marked "Central Camionera"), which runs frequently along Villalpando and then down González Ortega.

There are frequent long-distance bus services to all parts of northern Mexico, the Bajío and Mexico City, but if you're headed to Real de Catorce, you'll need to change at San Luis Potosí and then Matehuala: make an early start to be sure of getting there in a day. Autobuses Americanos runs daily buses direct to Laredo, El Paso and San Antonio, all in Texas.

Destinations Aguascalientes (hourly; 2–3hr); Chihuahua (hourly; 13hr); Ciudad Juárez (hourly; 18hr); Durango (hourly; 5hr); Guadalajara (hourly; 5–7hr); Jerez (hourly; 1hr); Mexico City (roughly hourly; 6–8hr); Monterrey (roughly hourly; 7–8hr); Querétaro (hourly; 6hr); San Luis Potosí (hourly; 3–4hr)

GETTING AROUND

Once in town you should be able to get around on foot, though taxis are easy to find at the Jardín Independencia – they don't use meters, so negotiate the price in advance.

INFORMATION AND TOURS

Tourist office The tourist kiosk at Hidalgo 613 (daily 9am–11pm; 800 712 4078, http://zacatecastravel.com) can provide a smattering of leaflets and informative, friendly advice in English.

Tours Several local agencies handle general travel requirements and offer tours of the city and to surrounding attractions: try Operadora Zacatecas, Hidalgo 630 (492 924 0050, http://operadorazacatecas.com.mx), opposite the *Hotel Casa Santa Lucía*. All the bigger hotels stock leaflets detailing daily tours around the city, to Guadalupe, Jerez and to La Quemada, among other destinations. Most tours require a minimum four persons.

ACCOMMODATION — SEE MAP PAGE 356

Casa Torres Hotel Primero de Mayo 325; http://hotelcasatorres.com. Quite unlike any other hotel in town, the rooms at this chic, modern place are tastefully decorated, with local artwork on the walls, flatscreen TVs and climate control. Standard rooms are fairly small so you may want to book a junior suite, or even a master suite with balcony and cathedral views. Breakfast (included) is served in the lovely top-floor restaurant/bar. M$$$

Cielito Lindo Hostal Aguascalientes 213; 492 921 1132. Beautiful old colonial property converted into a charming hotel (also known as "Cielito de María"), featuring comfy dorms with large wooden bunks, and doubles with shared and private bathrooms, tiled floors and TVs. Shared kitchen with a microwave and fridge only. Dorms M$, doubles M$$

Emporio Hidalgo 703; http://hotelesemporio.com. Hang with Mexico's rich and famous at the city's most luxurious, opulent hotel, set in a gorgeous Baroque mansion. Rack rates are expensive, but you should get an affordable rate on-line. The spacious rooms are decked out with modern amenities (flatscreens and decent cable TV), but with a few

5

PICASSO AT THE ACRÓPOLIS

You might not expect to find original artwork by Picasso, Dalí and Miró in a Mexican café, but the Acrópolis in Zacatecas is a special case. Opened in 1943, its owners have assembled a formidable art collection, displayed for the pleasure of their customers; many pieces, such as those by Oaxacan painter Rufino Tamayo and zacatecano Francisco Goitia, were donated by the artists themselves (some were created specially), others donated by wealthy patrons. While sipping your coffee, try to spot *The Princess and the Herd Boy*, one of several Japanese-inspired prints by Dalí, the much-reproduced *Tres Libres* by Miró and *Lord and Girl* by Picasso, a lithograph produced in 1959. See page 362 for the café review.

colonial touches. M$$$$

★ **Hostel Rada** De Nolasco 204; 492 206 8783, www.facebook.com/p/Hostal-RADA-100064874799714. A cheap and clean hostel located in the thick of it and enthusiastically run by Zacatecan locals. Dorms, double and twin rooms with shared bathrooms. Extras include internet access, cable TV, a book exchange and a sociable atmosphere. M$

Hotel Casa Santa Lucía Hidalgo 717; http://hotelcasasantalucia.com. Perhaps the best-value hotel, making attractive use of its beautiful ancient structure and providing comfortable rooms with high ceilings, big tiled bathrooms, exposed stonework and simple but tasteful decor. Breakfast is included, and there's a terrace with stellar views of the cathedral and La Bufa. M$$$

★ **Hotel Mesón de Jobito** Jardín Juárez 143; http://mesondejobito.com.mx. An entire alley off the city's most enchanting colonial square has been converted into this superb luxury hotel. Pretty, plush and private, all rooms come with a/c, and some with jacuzzis. There are two formal restaurants, and a bar with live music – just what you'd expect in a top hotel. M$$$

Hotel Santa Rita Hidalgo 507; http://hotelsantarita.com. Incredibly stylish (and expensive) hotel, featuring an intelligent refit of an old colonial house, replete with contemporary art; suites come with street or patio views and terraces, and polished wood floors. M$$$

★ **Quinta Real** Ignacio Rayón 434; www.caminoreal.com/quintareal. Gorgeous and outrageously luxurious hotel in the shadow of the colonial aqueduct that has beautifully incorporated what was once Zacatecas' bullring. Every comfort is taken to the extreme degree (there's even a "pillow menu"), and this is certainly a place worth saving up for, not to mention one of the most distinctive properties in the Americas. M$$$$

Terrasse Hotel Villalpando 209; http://hotelterrasse.com.mx. Señora Lupita runs this centrally located, top-value guesthouse, with simple but comfy modern rooms and continental breakfast included. Advance booking crucial. M$$

EATING

SEE MAP PAGE 356

For inexpensive tacos, tostadas and burgers, head away from the centre towards Ventura Sálazar, which is lined with places serving quick snacks. Other reliable hunting grounds are the compact **Mercado El Laberinto**, just north of the Jardín Independencia, and **Calle Aldama** in the mornings, for stalls selling tamales and *atoles*. While in Zacatecas, you should sample the local speciality, *asado de boda*, braised pork with chocolate and orange zest (once only served at weddings), and anything "zacatecano", usually meaning a dish smothered with poblano chiles and cream.

Acrópolis Hidalgo 325, at Plazuela Candelario Huizar; http://acropoliszacatecas.wixsite.com/restaurante. Established in 1943, this café serves up old-world ambience and appetizing Mexican breakfasts to well-heeled zacatecanos, as well as ice cream, fruit juices, good coffee and standard Mexican dishes. English menus are available. The art collection is amazing (see page 362). M$$

La Cabaña Independencia 251, at Juárez; 492 221 1410. Always alive with activity, this is one of the city's cheapest and most popular taco restaurants. Tasty meals served with a wide selection of salsas and beer at bargain prices in clean surroundings. Tacos are a bargain, and a full chicken dinner won't set you back much. Wonderfully fruity and thirst-quenching *aguas* are also sold to go. Try the sprightly *chía* flavour (a local herb). M$$

★ **Los Dorados de Villa** Plazuela de García 1314; 492 922 5722. Cosy little restaurant a short walk from the centre with lovely tiled walls and exotic birds. Look out for pictures of "Los Dorados", the young followers of Pancho Villa. The excellent traditional menu mostly comprises *moles* and enchiladas that keep people coming back for more. Reserve in advance. M$$

★ **Garufa** Jardín Juárez 135; 492 924 2910. Argentine restaurant chain specializing in gargantuan and super-succulent steaks imported from the pampas, along with cheaper salads and pasta dishes, all of which are served in attractive rustic surroundings. M$$$$

Gorditas Doña Julia Hidalgo 409; 492 922 7109. A one-trick pony, only serving gorditas stuffed with either various cuts of meat, refried beans, shredded nopal cactus in a hot salsa or *mole* and rice, either to go or to eat in this cheerfully bright, open-fronted restaurant. Second branch at Tacuba 72. M$

★ **La Plaza Quinta Real** Ignacio Rayón 434; www.caminoreal.com/quintareal. Pick of the bunch for an expensive, formal meal, if only for the setting overlooking the former bullring on a series of indoor terraces. Expect to spend a decent amount per person for a full meal of nopal stuffed with shrimp, chicken in a tamarind sauce, dessert, coffee and something from the wine list – which includes a decent selection from the Valle de Guadalupe. M$$$$

Rosticería el Pastor Independencia 214; 492 922 1635, www.facebook.com/ElPastorZacatecas. The scent of wood-roasted chicken wafts to the street from this inexpensive, family-friendly joint, housed in the old Colegio de Niñas, built in 1772. Here, you can get a full chicken dinner with all the fixings without breaking the bank. M$$

★ **Il San Patrizio Caffé** Hidalgo 403; 492 922 9838. The best (Illy) coffee in town, and only a little more expensive than places selling far inferior brews. The extra pesos are further justified by the peaceful courtyard setting, a choice of delicious cakes and a number of magazines to browse, some in English – blink and you'll miss the tiny sign, next to the tourist office. M$

DRINKING AND NIGHTLIFE

SEE MAP PAGE 356

Nightlife in Zacatecas, especially while the Universidad Autónoma de Zacatecas (UAZ) is in session, is a boisterous affair, with much of the early evening action happening on the streets – there always seems to be some procession or a band playing. On Fri and Sat evenings (and sometimes Thurs and even Sun) you may well encounter a **callejóneada** (see page 345) during which musicians – usually with several big drums and a brass section – promenade around the back alleys, often with a donkey bearing carafes of tequila. Ask your hotel about buying tickets, or head to the Plaza de Armas around 9pm to catch the start.

Bar Botarel Quinta Real, Ignacio Rayón 434; 492 922 9104. Stylish cellar bar built under the seating of what used to be the bullring. Arrive soon after 6pm to get one of the intimate booths, from where you can look out at the plaza and the rest of the hotel. Prices are almost twice what you pay in other places, but nowhere else has the same sense of romance. Live music Fri and Sat until midnight.

★ **Cantina Las Quince Letras** Mártires de Chicago 309; 492 922 0178. Most atmospheric bar in the city, a classic cantina with all sorts of bric-a-brac, antiques and paintings draped from the ceiling, cheap drinks and decent jukebox – live music some nights.

★ **La Mina Club** Dovalí Jaime s/n, inside Mina El Edén (see page 356); http://minaeleden.com.mx. Zacatecas' major club, right in the heart of the mountain and accessed on the same train used in the mine tour. From 11pm it is pumping with Latin sounds, US and European dance tunes, but mostly cheesy electronic techno music. If you don't enjoy being trapped in an enclosed space, *La Mina* is not for you. Entry charge on Sat.

Piper's Irish Pub Allende 117; 492 921 2829. Zacatecas has its very own Irish pub, serving genuine Guinness and microbrews, but also tasty bar food like chicken wings and showing all the big sports events on TVs.

DIRECTORY

Banks and exchange Plenty of banks are situated along Hidalgo between Juárez and Allende, all with 24hr ATMs and offering currency exchange.

Books and magazines The best source of English-language magazines is Sanborn's, Hidalgo 212. It's hard to find English-language books anywhere in Zacatecas, though there are plenty of Spanish bookshops: try Librerías Don Quijote at Villalpando 601, or Librería Universal at Hidalgo 109.

Emergencies For general emergencies call 066. Cruz Rojo (492 922 3005) handles medical emergencies.

Hospital Hospital Santa Elena (492 924 29 28) at Guerrero 143.

Laundry Fast Clean Lavandería, Villalpando 203, charges per kg.

Pharmacy Farmacia Guadalajara at Torreón 625 is 24hr; a more central branch is at Juárez 201, at Hidalgo (daily 7am–10pm). Farmacias de Similares (http://farmaciasdesimilares.com.mx) has branches at Hidalgo 131 and Tacuba 178.

Post office Allende 111.

MEZCAL DE ZACATECAS

Mescal is a distilled, smoky-tasting spirit made from the maguey plant (a form of agave), unique to Mexico. Though most mescal is made in Oaxaca (see page 580), Zacatecas produces its own line of highly lauded brands. Get a decent introduction at **Al Son Del Mezcal**, Hidalgo 411, where around twenty local mescals (including Huitzila, Antonio Aguilar, La Esclava, Hacienda de Robles and Teulito) are available to buy, taste or just drink.

5

Around Zacatecas

It's well worth basing yourself in Zacatecas to explore the immediate surroundings, not least the silverware at the **Centro Platero de Zacatecas**, the sumptuously decorated church in **Guadalupe**, the ruins of the great desert fortress at **Quemada** and the picturesque town of **Jerez**, a pleasant day trip anytime but essential for the enthralling cowboy festival on Easter Saturday. You can venture out to any of these places independently, though several travel agents in Zacatecas offer good quality tours (see page 361).

Centro Platero de Zacatecas

Ex-Hacienda de Bernardez, Fracc Lomas de Bernardez, Guadalupe • Free • http://centroplaterodezacatecas.com.mx • 5km south of central Zacatecas; "Ruta 11" from López Mateos runs to the nearest bus stop (40min), where you can ask directions and walk the last km; alternatively, take a taxi to the door (15min)

Galleries in Zacatecas sell stacks of jewellery, but prices are high. If you are serious about buying silver, or just want to see artisans at work, devote a couple of hours to visiting the **Centro Platero de Zacatecas.** Within this ex-hacienda, students and recent graduates of the on-site silversmith school maintain a series of small workshops where you can see them creating original designs, many influenced by pre-Columbian images, or iconography associated with Zacatecas. Everything is for sale, often at very reasonable prices.

Guadalupe

Just 7km southeast of Zacatecas' centre, **Guadalupe** is a virtual suburb of the state capital these days, but it's a large, historic place in its own right, founded in 1578. The heart of town is palm-fringed **Jardín Juárez**, where you'll find the **Convento de Nuestra Señora de Guadalupe** (once the largest Franciscan monastery in the world and still home to a gaggle of monks), the town's famous Templo de Guadalupe and the top-rate Museo de Guadalupe.

Templo de Guadalupe

Jardín Juárez Oriente • Free, donation suggested

You can't miss the enormous bulk of the **Templo de Guadalupe** at the heart of the Convento de Nuestra Señora de Guadalupe, with its dome and asymmetric twin towers (one Baroque, the other Moorish inspired). Inside, the central **Santuario de Nuestra Señora de Guadalupe** is a confection of gold and vibrant Neoclassical decoration, while the **Capilla Oscura** (Dark Chapel) houses a venerated image of Christ, El Cristo de Acuña. To the left of the entrance is the **Capilla de Nápoles**, completed in 1849, whose mesmerizing domed interior is coated in elaborately filigreed gold leaf – sadly, this chapel is only open on special occasions.

LEGENDS OF QUEMADA

Though we may never know for sure, **Huichol legend** seems to support the theory that **La Quemada** was built by a local ruling class. There was an evil priest, the story runs, who lived on a rock surrounded by walls and covered with buildings, with eagles and jaguars under his command to oppress the population. The people appealed to their gods, who destroyed the priest and his followers with "great heat", warning the people not to go near the rock again. Quemada was probably destroyed by fire around 1300 AD and was never reoccupied; even today, the Huichol, in their annual pilgrimage from the Sierra Madre to collect peyote around Real de Catorce to the east, take a long detour to bypass this area.

Museo de Guadalupe

Jardín Juárez Oriente • Charge, free Sun • 492 923 2089

A flagged, tree-studded convent courtyard provides access to both the church and the **Museo de Guadalupe**, housed in the Ex-Colegio Apostólico de Propaganda Fide, founded in 1707. It's a vast and confusing warren of a place, with seemingly endless rows of cells opening off courtyards, stairways leading nowhere and kilometre-long corridors lined with portraits of monks and vast tableaux from the life of St Francis. There are guided tours in Spanish, but it's more enjoyable to wander alone, at your own pace.

Oil paintings cover every wall of the gallery's 27 rooms of rough tiled floors and whitewashed walls, mostly with a religious theme: Cristóbal de Villalpando, Antonio de Torres, Gabriel José de Ovalle, Miguel Cabrera, Luis Juárez and José de Alcívar all feature. Look particularly for the *Virgin of the Apocalypse* by Cabrera, the mid-eighteenth-century *Passion of Christ* series of oils by Zacatecan artist de Ovalle, and *La Anunciación* by Villalpando, one of Mexico's most important painters of the early eighteenth century.

ARRIVAL AND DEPARTURE — GUADALUPE

Local buses (clearly marked) from Zacatecas run out to Guadalupe every few minutes from López Mateos (20min) – taxis should take you for a flat fee.

La Quemada

Carr Federal 54, km 56 • Charge, **Museo de La Quemada** • 492 922 5085

Surprisingly little is known about the enigmatic ruins of **LA QUEMADA**, some 52km south from Zacatecas on the road to Villanueva and Guadalajara. The scale of the complex isn't apparent until you're inside – from the road you can vaguely see signs of construction, but the whole thing, even the huge restored pyramid, blends so totally into the mountain behind as to be almost invisible. Most experts now think it developed between 400 and 1050 AD, most likely as a frontier post on the outskirts of some pre-Aztec sphere of domination – probably the **Toltecs** – charged with keeping at bay the southward depredations of the Chichimeca (over the years it has also been associated with the mythical Aztec city known as **Chicomóztoc**). Alternatively, it could simply be the work of a local ruling class, having exacted enough tribute to build themselves these palaces and needing the defences to keep their own subjects out.

In addition to the **Pirámide Votiva** (votive pyramid), you'll see the Salón de las Columnas, a large hall with eleven pillars still standing, the Juego de Pelota (ball-court), an extensive (if barely visible from the ground) system of roads heading out into the valley and many lesser, ruined structures all listed for eventual reconstruction. Much of the restoration work is based on drawings produced over the course of ten years from 1825 by a German mining engineer, Carlos de Berghes. Copies are on display in the superb **Museo de La Quemada**, at the site, which makes a masterful job of bringing the place alive with a select display of artefacts, a detailed area model and several explanatory videos (in Spanish only).

GETTING THERE — LA QUEMADA

By bus Getting to La Quemada is straightforward by public transport, with Villanueva-bound buses leaving every 30min or so from López Mateos in Zacatecas. They're usually happy to drop you at the start of the 2km access road (ask for "las ruinas"); the ride to this point takes about an hour, from where you've got a 30min walk to the entrance. To get back, hike to the highway and flag down the first bus you see.

By car/taxi Most visitors get to the site by car (it's a 30min drive along Hwy-54) or taxi. Organized tours charge a fee per person that's comparable to a one way taxi fare (see page 361).

Jerez

For an enjoyable day trip from Zacatecas consider **JEREZ**, another Pueblo Mágico 57km southwest of the city, best known for being the birthplace of lauded poet

THE JEREZ SPRING FESTIVAL

If you can, time your visit to Jerez to coincide with the annual ten-day **Feria de la Primavera** (spring festival), celebrated around Easter since 1824 with *charreadas* (rodeos), bullfights, bands and much tequila drinking. The climax is the Easter Saturday procession when an effigy of Judas is burned. Festivities around the **Día de la Virgen de la Soledad** (Sept 8–15) are also worthwhile, with an opportunity to catch the Chichimecan plumes of the Danzas de los Matlachines.

Ramón López Velarde (1888–1921, author of *La Suave Patria*), and its particularly lively **spring festival** (see page 366). At other times you can simply wander the pleasant colonial centre, visiting the poet's former home, now the **Museo Interactivo Casa Ramón López Velarde** (Tues–Sun 10am–5pm; charge), at Calle de la Parroquia 33, the Porfiriano-era **Teatro Hinojosa** (Mon–Fri 8am–7pm, Sat & Sun 11am–5pm; free) on Jardín Hidalgo, and the attractive eighteenth-century church of **Inmaculada Concepción** (at the junction of Flores and Reloj), just south of Jardín Páez, the main plaza.

ARRIVAL AND DEPARTURE — JEREZ

By bus Buses to Jerez leave hourly from Zacatecas' Central de Autobuses, and take about an hour to the bus station 1km from the centre.

San Luis Potosí

Situated to the north of the Bajío's fertile heartland, the sprawling industrial city of **SAN LUIS POTOSÍ** boasts a ravishing historic centre of colonial plazas and elegant stone buildings reminiscent of a classical Spanish town. Though a Franciscan mission was established in the area in the 1580s, San Luis was officially founded in 1592, as a supply town for the surrounding gold and silver mines discovered that year. Today San Luis Potosí is a prosperous place of over one million *potosinos* – most of the silver is gone, but there is a considerable manufacturing base. Tucked in among the splendour are some handsome churches, notably the **Templo del Carmen**, the garish masks of the **Museo Nacional de la Máscara** and the **Museo Federico Silva**, tribute to one of Mexico's greatest sculptors.

Plaza de Armas (Jardín Hidalgo)

The grand **Plaza de Armas**, or Jardín Hidalgo, is the traditional heart of San Luis Potosí, dominated by the **Palacio de Gobierno** and the impressive bulk of the **Catedral Metropolitana**, its twin towers soaring above the square like ornate candelabras. On the east side of the plaza lies the **Palacio Municipal**, still City Hall, while the elegant **Casa de la Virreina** on the north side was once home to the Spanish viceroys – dating to 1736, it's one of the oldest buildings in the city. These days the plaza seems to host a constant stream of anti-government protests, which can make access difficult, though rarely dangerous.

Catedral Metropolitana

Plaza de Armas • Free • 444 812 2439

Completed in 1730 and dedicated to Nuestra Señora de la Expectación, successive generations have ensured that little remains of the original **Catedral Metropolitana**. Even the Baroque towers, each a mass of twisted columns, are oddly mismatched; one tower is all grey, the other a sandy orange colour. Check out the opulent interior,

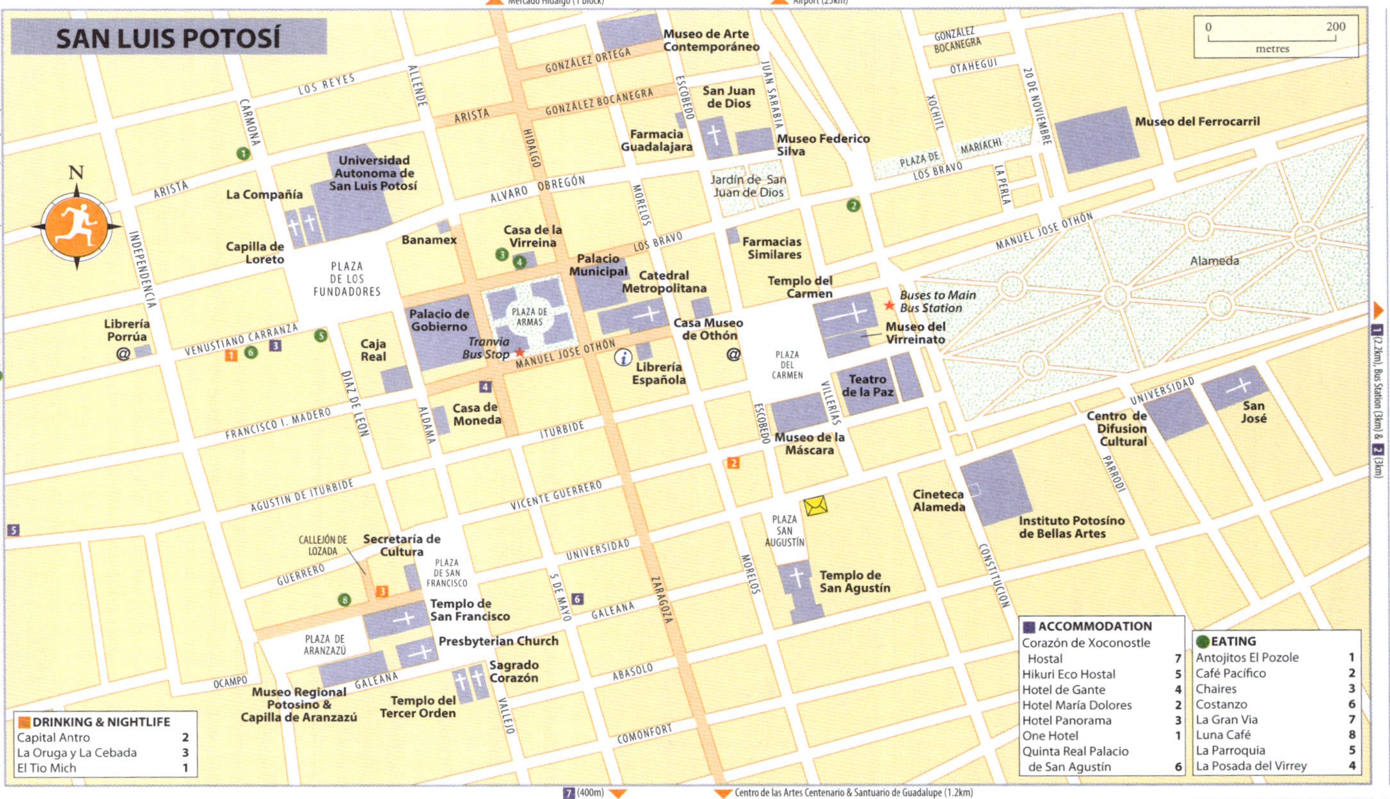
SAN LUIS POTOSÍ
0 200 metres
Mercado Hidalgo (1 block)
Airport (25km)
1 (2.2km), Bus Station (3km) & 2 (3km)
7 (400m)
Centro de las Artes Centenario & Santuario de Guadalupe (1.2km)
7 (200m), Zona Rosa (500m), La Bene Hospital (1km) & Parques Tangamanga (2km)
N
Museo de Arte Contemporáneo
San Juan de Dios
Farmacia Guadalajara
Museo Federico Silva
Jardín de San Juan de Dios
Museo del Ferrocarril
Universidad Autonoma de San Luis Potosí
La Compañía
Capilla de Loreto
Plaza de los Fundadores
Librería Porrúa
Caja Real
Banamex
Casa de la Virreina
Palacio Municipal
Catedral Metropolitana
Palacio de Gobierno
Plaza de Armas
Tranvía Bus Stop
Casa Museo de Othón
Librería Española
Farmacias Similares
Templo del Carmen
Buses to Main Bus Station
Museo del Virreinato
Plaza del Carmen
Teatro de la Paz
Alameda
Centro de Difusion Cultural
San José
Casa de Moneda
Museo de la Máscara
Cineteca Alameda
Instituto Potosíno de Bellas Artes
Plaza San Agustín
Templo de San Agustín
Callejón de Lozada
Secretaría de Cultura
Plaza de San Francisco
Templo de San Francisco
Presbyterian Church
Plaza de Aranzazú
Sagrado Corazón
Museo Regional Potosino & Capilla de Aranzazú
Templo del Tercer Orden
Los Reyes
Carmona
Arista
Independencia
Allende
González Ortega
González Bocanegra
Hidalgo
Alvaro Obregón
Escobedo
Juan Sarabia
Xochitl
Otahegui
González Bocanegra
20 de Noviembre
Plaza de Los Bravo
Mariachi
La Perla
Morelos
Los Bravo
Manuel José Othón
Venustiano Carranza
Díaz de León
Francisco I. Madero
Aldama
Iturbide
Villerías
Universidad
Parrodi
Agustín de Iturbide
Vicente Guerrero
Guerrero
Universidad
5 de Mayo
Galeana
Zaragoza
Constitución
Ocampo
Galeana
Vallejo
Abasolo
Comonfort
DRINKING & NIGHTLIFE
Capital Antro 2
La Oruga y La Cebada 3
El Tio Mich 1
ACCOMMODATION
Corazón de Xoconostle Hostal 7
Hikuri Eco Hostal 5
Hotel de Gante 4
Hotel María Dolores 2
Hotel Panorama 3
One Hotel 1
Quinta Real Palacio de San Agustín 6
EATING
Antojitos El Pozole 1
Café Pacífico 2
Chaires 3
Costanzo 6
La Gran Vía 7
Luna Café 8
La Parroquia 5
La Posada del Virrey 4

FESTIVE SAN LUIS

The most entertaining San Luis fiestas are the Día de la Asunción (Assumption; Aug 15), a religious festival with traditional dances outside the cathedral that coincides with the Feria de la Uva, the city's grape festival, and the Día de San Luis Rey (Aug 25), a huge fiesta enthusiastically enjoyed by virtually the whole town – a giant procession and fireworks follow.

decorated in the 1890s by celebrity Italian design duo Claudio Molina and Giuseppe Compiani.

Palacio de Gobierno

Plaza de Armas 11 • Free

Facing the cathedral across the Plaza de Armas is the long facade of the **Palacio de Gobierno**, with its balustraded roof. This, too, has been substantially refurbished since its completion in 1827, but at least alterations have preserved the harmony of its clean Neoclassical lines. Inside you can visit the **Sala Juárez**, a suite of rooms occupied by Benito Juárez when San Luis Potosí became his temporary capital in 1863 (head up either set of stairs and turn left). French troops supporting Emperor Maximilian soon drove him out, but Juárez returned in 1867, and in this building confirmed the death sentence passed on the hapless French puppet emperor.

Casa de Othón

Othón 225 • Charge • 444 812 7412

Just behind the cathedral lies the **Casa de Othón** (aka **Museo Othoniano**), a pretty and well-tended museum, though a rather lifeless tribute to Manuel José Othón, San Luis' most famous poet (who was born here in 1858), mainly comprising some of his manuscripts, belongings and period furniture. Othón's best-known poem is *Idilio Salvaje* ("Idyll of the Wild"), published in 1905, and hard to find in English translation.

Plaza del Carmen and around

East along Othón from Plaza de Armas lies the **Plaza del Carmen**, a much newer space created in 1973 but nevertheless ringed by historic buildings.

Templo del Carmen

Plaza del Carmen • Free

The **Templo del Carmen** is the most beautiful and harmonious of all San Luis' churches, dating from 1764. Exuberantly decorated with a multicoloured tiled dome and elaborate Baroque facade, it has an equally flashy interior: in particular, a fantastically intricate nineteenth-century *retablo* attributed to Francisco Tresguerras.

Museo del Virreinato

Plaza del Carmen, Villerías 115 • Charge • www.facebook.com/museodelvirreinato

Next door to the Templo de Carmen, housed in an eighteenth-century monastery, sits the moderately interesting **Museo del Virreinato**, a huge collection of artwork and artefacts from the Spanish colonial era. The eclectic displays include religious paintings (mostly minor work from the 1700s), ceramics, old books and heavy iron keys. There are even some creepy-looking mannequins, dressed in the various habits of the Catholic monastic orders.

Teatro de la Paz

Plaza del Carmen, Villerías 105 • Charge • 444 814 1075

The southeast corner of the Plaza del Carmen is dominated by the Roman-inspired bulk of the **Teatro de la Paz**, completed in 1894 under Porfirio Díaz and typical of the grandiose public buildings of that era, though its modern interior (open for performances only) fails to live up to the extravagance of the facade.

Museo Nacional de la Máscara

Plaza del Carmen, Villerías 2 • Charge, extra with camera • http://museonacionaldelamascaraslp.com.mx

At the southern end of Plaza del Carmen you'll find the absorbing **Museo Nacional de la Máscara**, dedicated to mask art and the city's best museum. It occupies the lavish former home of local landowner Ramón Martí. Completed in 1897, it was sold to the government just six years later. The mansion is finished off like a mini-palace, with exhibits on everything from pre-Hispanic masks and jade funerary pieces to Spanish-influenced demonic masks and costumes that are still worn for fiestas and traditional dances today. The upper level contains some expertly restored period rooms and **Sala XIX**, a small collection of the decorative pieces found in homes like this in the nineteenth century.

Templo de San Agustín

Plaza San Agustín (Abasolo 650) • Free • 444 812 5994

One block south of the Plaza del Carmen lies another magnificent Baroque church, the **Templo de San Agustín**, built around 1700 with an extravagantly carved tower. The handsome Neoclassical interior is adorned with murals completed in the 1890s by the Italians Molina and Compiani.

Museo Federico Silva

Jardín de San Juan de Dios, Obregón 80 • Charge, free Sun • www.museofedericosilva.org

Two blocks north of the Plaza del Carmen is the **Museo Federico Silva**, a tribute to one of Mexico's most exalted sculptors (born in Mexico City in 1923). The museum is housed in a Neoclassical school building completed in 1907, its open spaces a lovely synthesis of the classic and the contemporary, much like the works of Silva, who creates modern interpretations of Mexico's pre-Hispanic forms. His blockish volcanic stone and steel forms dominate the galleries: some are vaguely human and others geometric abstractions, but all are beautifully lit. Don't miss *Scriptum*, a huge block of stone (adorned with four simple carved circles) entirely filling a kind of crypt, below the ground floor, as if it were secreted deep within some Aztec pyramid.

Museo de Arte Contemporáneo

Morelos 235, at Ortega • Charge, free Sun • https://www.facebook.com/museomacslp

If the Museo Federico Silva whets your appetite for contemporary Mexican art, walk two blocks northwest to the **Museo de Arte Contemporáneo**, opened in 2010 in the handsome old post office (which dates from the 1860s). The temporary shows here feature up-and-coming local and national artists.

Plaza de los Fundadores and around

Immediately west of Plaza de Armas, the paved **Plaza de los Fundadores** is a much larger and more formal open space, commemorating the foundation of the city near this spot in 1592. The plaza is dominated by the enormous Neoclassical **Edificio Central de la Universidad**, the main state university building, and two small adjacent churches, the **Capilla de Loreto** (usually open on Sun only) and **La Compañía** (usually open daily). The fine portals of the **Ipiña Arcades** on the west side of the square continue around the corner into Avenida Venustiano Carranza.

There's more interest a block south along Aldama at Madero, where you can admire the peach-coloured Baroque facade of the **Caja Real**, the old mint dating from 1763

– one of the finest colonial mansions in San Luis. It is now owned by the university, which sometimes holds temporary exhibitions here.

Plaza and Ex-Convento de San Francisco

Templo de San Francisco • Free

Three blocks south of Plaza de los Fundadores is the tranquil **Plaza de San Francisco**, a lovely, shaded area redolent of the city's colonial history. It's named after the sprawling Franciscan monastic complex that once stood here – most of the religious institutions that remain were once part of it. Foremost are the ochre towers of the **Templo de San Francisco**, looming over the plaza's west side, with the interior featuring a magnificent crystal chandelier in the shape of a sailing ship, hanging over the nave.

At the southern end of the plaza are two more tiny and elaborate Franciscan remnants. The **Templo de Sagrado Corazón** (which dates from 1731) and the even older and far simpler **Templo del Tercera Orden** (established in 1698) stand side by side, while the small, neo-Gothic **Iglesia Nacional Presbiteriana** (National Presbyterian Church, a later addition from 1894), terribly incongruous amid all this Baroque grandeur, faces them across Galeana.

Museo Regional Potosino

Plaza de Aranzazú • Charge, free Sun • 444 812 0358

Another remnant of the Franciscan *convento* houses the **Museo Regional Potosino**, a collection of pre-Hispanic sculpture and other archeological finds, displays of local Indigenous culture and traditions and articles relating to the history of the state of San Luis Potosí. In addition to a fine cloister, there's access, upstairs, to the ornate Baroque chapel, **Capilla de Aranzazú** – said to be the only chapel in Latin America located on an upper floor – with exceedingly rich and enthusiastically restored churrigueresque decoration. You'll find the entrance to the museum behind the Templo de San Francisco at the **Plaza de Aranzazú**, another pleasant open space that hosts a small arts and crafts market on Saturdays.

Centro de las Artes and around

Calzada de Guadalupe 705 • Charge • www.ceartslp.gob.mx

At the heart of the ambitious **Centro de las Artes** complex is the former state prison, built in the 1890s and given a stylish contemporary makeover. Temporary exhibitions here showcase local and visiting artists – check the website in advance to see if a show is taking place, otherwise it can seem rather empty. Behind the main courtyard of galleries lies the old cell block, now the **Museo del Sitio** – the cell where **Madero** was held in 1910 is preserved shrine-like, occupied now with a bust of the great man. Beyond here a series of old prison buildings has been transformed into a theatre, library and various art spaces as well as open areas sprinkled with sculptures and gardens. One worthwhile stop is the **Museo Leonora Carrington San Luis Potosí** (http://leonoracarringtonmuseo.org; charge), dedicated to the English-born Mexican surrealist painter, containing sculptures, jewellery, engravings and personal objects.

The art centre is around 2km south of Plaza de Armas, a pleasant walk along pedestrianized Zaragoza and then the tree-lined walkway in the centre of the Calzada de Guadalupe. Just to the south lie the soaring 53m-high towers of **Basílica Menor del Santuario de Nuestra Señora de Guadalupe**; completed in 1800, this is the grandest church in the city.

ARRIVAL AND DEPARTURE — SAN LUIS POTOSÍ

By plane Arriving at the Aeropuerto Internacional Ponciano Arriaga (25km north of downtown), taxis run to the centre and back; Alamo (444 818 4400), Budget (444 822 2482) and Payless (444 816 7787) all have desks at the airport, and HSBC and Bancomer have ATMs on the lower level.

Destinations Dallas (2 daily; 1hr 45min); Houston (1 daily; 1hr 45min); Mexico City (8 daily; 1hr 10min); Tijuana (1 daily; 2hr 30min).

By bus Long-distance buses arrive at the main bus station (officially Terminal Terrestre Potosina or TTP), around 3km east of the centre on Hwy-57; for downtown and the Alameda, walk outside and board "Ruta 6". It appears to head out of town but doubles back: get off at the former train station (now the Museo de Ferrocarril) and walk from there. To return to the bus station, pick up Ruta 6 for "Central TTP" from the northwest corner of the Alameda on Constitución. Taxis work on a zone system from the bus station – buy a ticket before you exit the terminal. Rides into the city centre are slightly more expensive at night and taxis should use the meter.

Buses from San Luis cover every conceivable route, with departures for Mexico City and Monterrey every few minutes, and for the US border at least hourly. Flecha Amarilla has excellent second-class services to Dolores Hidalgo, San Miguel de Allende and Guanajuato – note that there is only one first-class service to Guanajuato (via Premier Plus), at 7am. Northbound, there are frequent services to Matehuala (2hr 30min), where you change for Real de Catorce.

Destinations Aguascalientes (hourly; 2hr 30min); Guadalajara (hourly; 4hr 45min–5hr); Guanajuato (1 daily; 3hr 5min); Matehuala (4 daily; 2hr 30min); Mexico City (hourly; 4hr 45min–6hr); Monterrey (5 daily; 6hr); Querétaro (hourly; 2hr 30min); San Miguel de Allende (3 daily; 4hr); Zacatecas (hourly; 2hr 30min–3hr).

GETTING AROUND

By bus Buses charge a flat fee per journey.

By taxi Taxis generally use meters that start at a set charge (9pm–6am) and go up every kilometre.

On foot Though surrounded by hills, San Luis is located on a pancake-flat plateau (1860m above sea level), and the centre is easy to explore on foot.

INFORMATION

Tourist office For general information, head for the helpful state tourist office, Othón 130, just off Plaza de Armas (Mon–Fri 9am–9pm, Sat 9am–3pm; 444 812 6769, http://visitasanluispotosi.com).

ACCOMMODATION

SEE MAP PAGE 367

The cheapest **rooms** in central San Luis are found in the slightly run-down area north of the **Alameda**, but you'll find all the modern motel chains – offering excellent value – out along Benito Juárez (Hwy-57). These generally attract drivers passing through and business travellers, but are worth considering if you don't mind taking taxis back and forth from the centre.

Corazón de Xoconostle Hostal 5 de Mayo 1040; http://corazondexoconostle.com. Excellent budget option downtown, with bright modern dorms and private doubles (with TVs), all with free use of computers, laundry room, shared kitchen, free coffee and basic breakfast. M$

★ **Hikuri Eco Hostal** Agustín de Iturbide 980, at Bolívar; http://hikurihostelslp.wixsite.com/hikurihostelslp. Hostel set over three floors of a beautiful old colonial building with plenty of recycled materials, a simple shared kitchen, rooftop patio and super-friendly Italian/Mexican owners. There are clean, modern dorms and two cosy doubles. M$

Hotel de Gante 5 de Mayo 140; 444 812 1493. Central, comfortable and spacious, with cable TV but little atmosphere; superb location though, and especially good value if you can get a room overlooking Plaza de Armas. M$$

Hotel María Dolores Benito Juárez (Hwy-57), opposite the Central de Autobuses; www.hotelmariadolores.com. Motel set around attractive gardens studded with palms and swimming pools. Restaurants, bars and nightclubs fill ancillary buildings, and rooms, all with cable TV and minibars, mostly have direct access to lawns. M$$$

Hotel Panorama Venustiano Carranza 315, just west of Plaza Fundadores; http://hotelpanorama.com.mx. Standard business hotel, though the rooms are fairly compact and a little overpriced; the floor-to-ceiling windows are great, but the bathrooms are tiny and some of the rooms are showing their age. You do get free transport to the airport, and it's the best hotel in the centre. M$$$

★ **One Hotel** Benito Juárez 140, opposite the Central de Autobuses; www.posadas.com. This modern chain offers superb value, with compact, minimalist rooms equipped with blond-wood furnishings, breakfast, flatscreen TVs and desks targeted at business travellers – cheap rates online and, mercifully, no smoking allowed anywhere in the hotel. M$$

Quinta Real Palacio de San Agustín Galeana 240 at 5 de Mayo; http://palaciodesanagustin.com. It's worth visiting this jaw-dropping colonial masterpiece for a drink even if you can't afford to stay; the ornate interior and lobby, once part of a monastery, hint at the gorgeous antique-filled suites inside. Facilities include a posh spa, access to a horse and carriage, chauffeur-driven cars and a golf course. M$$$$$

EATING

SEE MAP PAGE 367

San Luis specialities include deep-fried enchiladas and tacos or *enchiladas Potosinos* (or *Huastecas*), dripping with salsa

5

and cheese, and *cecina*, a thin cut of marinated and dried steak. The upper-level **Mercado Hidalgo** is home to food stalls that serve them, as well as a host of regular Mexican dishes – *Comedor Lucy* is a safe choice, but they're all pretty similar.

CENTRAL SAN LUIS

★Antojitos El Pozole Carmona 205, at Arista; 444 814 9900. Justly popular local chain established in 1985, famous for its *pozole* (thick stew of chunky bits of chicken, corn and spices): order *pozole rojo* or *blanco*. The *tacos rojos* and *quesadillas de papa* are also worth trying. This branch is most central, in what feels a bit like someone's house with several small rooms. M$$

Café Pacífico Constitución 220; 444 812 5414. Come here for a potent mix of gossip, action and basic Mexican food at moderate prices in a diner-like setting. This very popular old-fashioned café-restaurant even has a non-smoking section; the weekend brunch buffets are good value. M$$

Chaires Plaza de Armas 5; http://chaires.mx. Right on the plaza in part of the Casa de la Virreina, *Chaires* is alive with families, friends and canoodling couples sipping java and tucking into elaborate pastries. M$

Costanzo Carranza 325; http://chocolatescostanzo.com Lauded confection chain since 1935, with all manner of tempting chocolates and sweet things in shiny paper. Chocolates are priced per 100g, but even the most decadent selections won't set you back much here. M$

Luna Café Universidad 155; www.facebook.com/LunaCafemx. Slightly more upscale than *Los Frailes* next door, offering gourmet coffees and cocktails. M$

La Parroquia Carranza 303, at Plaza Fundadores; https://facebook.com/laparroquiapotosina. Comfortable middle-of-the-road diner featuring comfy booths, where crusty rolls replace the traditional stack of tortillas. Excellent breakfasts and comida corrida – a firm favourite with local office workers. M$$

La Posada del Virrey Plaza de Armas 3; 444 812 7150. Housed in old Casa de la Virreina right on the main plaza, this location can't be beaten – everything graces the menu, from spaghetti to *mole poblano*. M$$

LA AVENIDA

La Gran Via Carranza 560; http://lagranviaslp.com. Another San Luis institution, serving classic Spanish seafood and dishes such as *lechón asado* and *pollo al ajillo*. M$$$

DRINKING AND NIGHTLIFE

SEE MAP PAGE 367

San Luis has a vibrant **nightlife**, with numerous **clubs** staying open until the early hours at the weekend (note that most clubs and bars are cash only). The section of Carranza (affectionately known as **La Avenida**), starting half a kilometre west of Plaza Fundadores, has traditionally been the place to go, but the smaller and more central collection of bars along Universidad, north of the Templo de San Francisco, is also a good bet. For movies, check out the wonderfully restored **Cineteca Alameda**, facing the Alameda at Universidad 575, at Constitución (https://cinetecaalameda.com.mx).

Capital Antro Vicente Guerrero 380; 444 812 4479. This easily missed bar is the best place for a chilled out drink away from the crowds. Fair warning — the cocktails pack a punch.

La Oruga y La Cebada Callejón de Lozada 1; https://laorugaylacebada.com.mx. Excellent microbrew pub ("The Caterpillar and Barley"), serving tasty pale ales and snacks.

El Tio Mich Carranza 1255; 444 130 7862. San Luis' hottest nightspot and concert hall. The meat market begins after midnight – entry fee varies.

DIRECTORY

Banks and exchange There are banks with ATMs and several *casas de cambio* all around the main plazas, including Banamex at Allende and Obregón.

Books and newspapers The newsstands on Los Bravo, just off Plaza de Armas, usually have a few English-language publications, and it might be worth trying Librería Española at Manuel José Othón 170, and Librería Porrúa at Carranza 410.

Emergencies For general emergencies dial 066. For medical emergencies, the most convenient clinic is La Bene, Carranza 1090 (444 811 5694, http://labenesanluis.mx), or just call the Cruz Roja on 444 815 3635.

Pharmacy Farmacias Similares, Los Bravo 300, at Escobedo (daily 8am–11pm), and Farmacia Guadalajara, at Escobedo 605 (daily 7am–11pm; 444 812 1725).

Post office Universidad 526 (Mon–Fri 8am–6pm, Sat 9am–noon).

Real de Catorce

REAL DE CATORCE is an extraordinary place. Silver mines were founded in the surrounding hills in 1772, and at the height of its production in 1898 the town had forty thousand inhabitants. But by the turn of the twentieth century mining operations had slowed, and in 1905 they ceased entirely, leaving the population to drop to virtually zero over the next fifty-odd years. For a period, a few hundred inhabitants hung on in an enclave at the centre, surrounded by derelict, roofless mansions and, further out, crumbling foundations and the odd segment of wall. Legend has it that Real was "discovered" in the 1970s by an Italian hippy searching for peyote (which perhaps explains the town's curious Italian connection), and, particularly since the mid-1990s, an influx of artists, artesanía vendors, wealthy Mexicans and a few foreigners has given the town impetus to begin rebuilding.

The centre has been restored and reoccupied to the extent that the "ghost-town" tag is not entirely appropriate, though Real de Catorce certainly retains an air of desolation, especially in the outskirts; the occasional pick-up shoulders its way through the narrow cobbled streets, but most of the traffic is horses and donkeys. The population now stands at just under 1500, the foreign contingent coexisting amiably with locals who

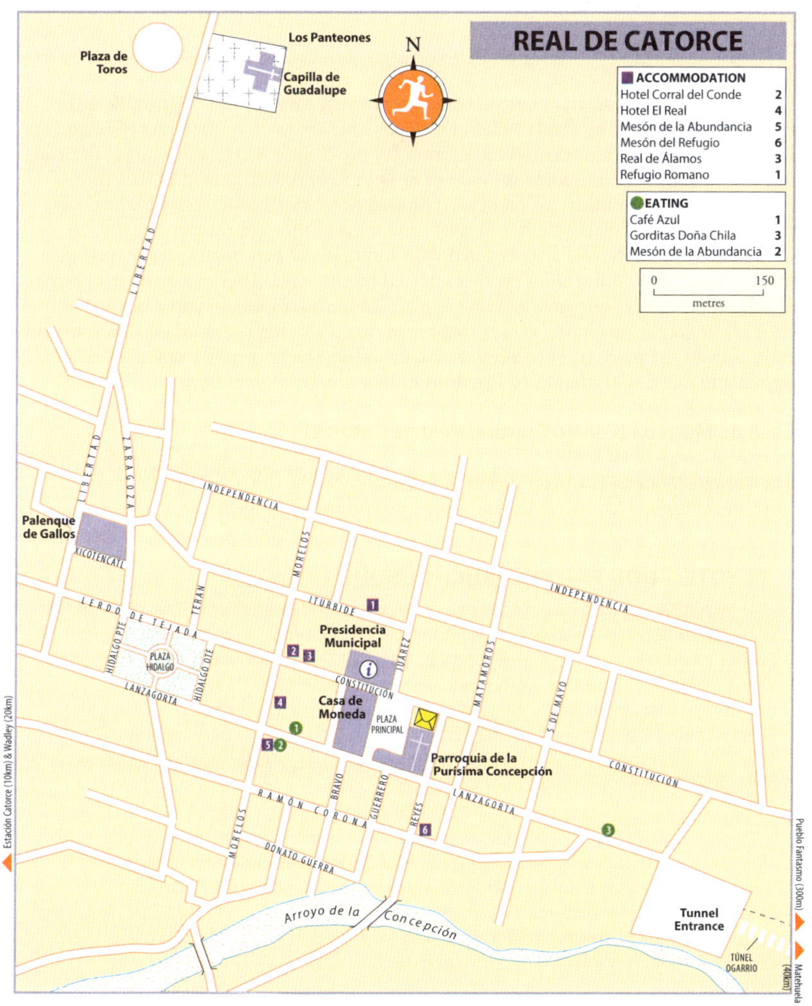

increasingly depend on the tourist industry (it was made a Pueblo Mágico in 2001). The town has also become another popular Hollywood location, featuring in movies such as *Bandidas* (2006) and *The Mexican* (2001), and allegedly providing Gore Verbinski with inspiration to make *Rango* in 2011. There's not much in the way of sights: simply wandering around, kicking up the dust and climbing into the hills are big and worthwhile pastimes here.

Túnel Ogarrio

Real de Catorce is built in a high mountain valley, at the end of a beautifully constructed 25km cobbled road through semi-desert dotted with agave and stunted Joshua trees. The final 2.3km is through the **Túnel Ogarrio**, opened in 1901, which is only broad enough for one vehicle at a time. As you drive through, the odd mineshaft leads off into the mountain to either side – by one there's a little shrine, the **Capilla de Nuestra Señora de los Dolores**, to miners who died at work and while building the tunnel.

Parroquia de la Purísima Concepción

Lanzagorta • Free

Real de Catorce's single main street, **Lanzagorta**, runs past the 1817 **Parroquia de la Purísima Concepción** on shaded Plaza Principal, and on down to the **Plaza Hidalgo** (aka Plaza de Armas), with its central bandstand. It's the church that attracts most Mexicans to Real, or rather the miraculous figure of St Francis of Assisi (known as Panchito, Pancho being a diminutive of Francisco) housed here. You'll soon spot the shrine by the penitents kneeling before it, but take time to head through the door to the left of the altar, where the walls are covered with hundreds of handmade *retablos* giving thanks for cures or miraculous escapes effected by the saint. They're a wonderful form of folk art, the older ones painted on tin plate, newer examples on paper or card or even photographs, depicting events that range from amazing to mundane – last-second rescues from the paths of oncoming trains, or simply the return of a stolen vehicle – all signed and dated with thanks to Panchito for his timely intervention.

Casa de Moneda (Centro Cultural Real de Catorce)

Plaza Principal • Charge • 488 887 5072

The **Casa de Moneda** is a magnificent old mansion on the other side of the plaza from the church, with two storeys on one side and three on the other, thanks to the

PEYOTE: FOOD FOR THE HUICHOL SOUL

The **Wirikuta**, the flat semi-desert at the foot of the Sierra Madre Occidental near Real de Catorce (and Wadley; see page 377), was a rich source of **peyote** long before the Spanish Conquest. The Huichol people (see page 465) traditionally make a month-long, 400km annual pilgrimage here (now often shortened by truck or car) from their homelands in northeastern Nayarit to gather the precious hallucinogenic cactus (it contains psychoactive alkaloids, particularly mescaline), which they regard as essential food for the soul. After the peyote "buttons" are collected, many are dried and taken away for later use, but some are carried fresh to their sacred site, Cerro Quemada (Burnt Hill), near Real de Catorce, for ceremonies.

Tales of achieving higher consciousness under the influence of peyote have long drawn foreigners, many of them converts of the books of **Carlos Castaneda** (who started writing about native Mexican shamanism in 1968). Indeed, Real de Catorce only made it onto the tourist itinerary after it became a waystation on the hippy-druggy trail in the 1970s. New Agers continue to visit, but the hills round about have been picked clean and there are fears that over-harvesting may threaten the continued Huichol tradition.

sloping site it was built on. This is where Real's silver was minted into coin, though Emperor Maximilian closed it just fourteen months after it was completed in 1865. After a meticulous restoration it now serves as an art gallery and cultural centre, with temporary exhibitions from all over Mexico and small permanent displays on the building's role as mint, plus old photographs of the town.

Palenque de Gallos and Los Panteones

Palenque de Gallos Xicotencatl • Free • **Los Panteones** Libertad • Free

Heading north out of town along Zaragoza, duck a few metres up Xicotencatl to the Roman-looking **Palenque de Gallos** of 1863, where cockfights were once held, then continue out along Zaragoza and Libertad to the ruinous Plaza de Toros, opposite **Los Panteones** where Real's dead lie covered by rough piles of dirt all around the decaying 1779 **Capilla de Guadalupe**. Peek inside the chapel to see its still-vibrant frescoes, which are going mouldy around the edges – just as they should be in a town like Real.

ARRIVAL AND INFORMATION — REAL DE CATORCE

By bus Most people arrive on buses from Matehuala, some 60km east. The bigger buses can't get through the Ogarrio tunnel, so you'll probably have to change buses at the eastern end for the run through (if driving, you have to wait in line and pay a toll (there's no toll coming back); you can park on the other side of the tunnel for a small fee during the day or it's more for overnight). These smaller buses (included) drop you at a dusty parking lot at the tunnel's western end, from where it is a short walk down Lanzagorta to the town centre. It always pays to ask about the latest bus timetables, but there are currently departures to Catorce from Matehuala (1hr 30min) at around 8am, noon, 2pm and 6pm (with buses returning at 7.40am, 11.40am, 3.40pm & 5.40pm).

Getting to Matehuala Matehuala is most easily accessible by frequent first-class buses from Monterrey and San Luis Potosí. The Central de Autobus is just off Hwy-57 on Heroes Potosionos, 2km south of the centre.

Destinations from Matehuala Mexico City (9 daily; 8hr); Monterrey (hourly; 3hr 15min); Real de Catorce (4 daily; 1hr 30min–2hr); San Luis Potosí (hourly; 2hr 30min–3hr)

Tourist office The tourist office (daily 10am–4pm; 488 887 5071) is in the Presidencia Municipal, Constitución 27, on Plaza Principal, but it is not always open.

ACCOMMODATION — SEE MAP PAGE 373

Day and overnight visitors from San Luis Potosí and Monterrey make the town much busier at weekends, Semana Santa and Christmas, when the better hotels put up their prices by around twenty percent. The town is also packed around the **Fiesta de San Francisco de Asís**, every weekend from the second Sat in Sept to the fourth Sun in Oct and for the entire week around Oct 4. At this time buses don't run through the tunnel and you either have to walk or ride one of the numerous horse-drawn carts for a few pesos. On arrival you may be approached by villagers eager to guide you to their favoured *casa de huéspedes*. You're not obliged to accept what they show you, but chances are you'll get a plain and small but clean **room**, which at least claims to have 24hr hot water: make sure there are plenty of blankets available as it can be very cold here at night. At the other end of the scale, Catorce is blessed with some wonderful hotels in converted **mansions**, often at very reasonable prices.

Hotel Corral del Conde Constitución 17; 488 887 5048. One of the best mid-range options. Rooms in the original part of the hotel have an elegantly rustic quality with stone walls, wooden beams and ageing furniture, while a newer section across the road has more modern but equally comfortable rooms. No wi-fi and cash only. **M$$**

Hotel El Real Morelos 20, behind the Casa de Moneda; 488 887 5058, https://facebook.com/hotelelreal. A charmingly converted old house with clean, airy rooms featuring native decoration, TVs (including videos and a video library), fireplaces and views galore. It's reputed to be haunted. **M$$$**

Mesón de la Abundancia Lanzagorta 11; http://mesondelaabundancia.com. Located on the corner of Morelos, this friendly hotel was rebuilt from the 1860s ruins of the old town Treasury, and is full of masks, huge stone-built rooms with beamed ceilings, rug-covered brick floors and ancient doors with their original hefty keys. Many rooms have small balconies, and the suites are very spacious. **M$$$**

★ **Mesón del Refugio** Lanzagorta 55; 488 887 5068. Tastefully restored eighteenth-century mansion, completely renovated in a chic, modern style with a glass-covered courtyard and cosy rooms with free (but weak) wi-fi, satellite TV, heating, telephone, and restaurant serving breakfast. **M$$$**

Real de Álamos Constitución 21; 488 887 5009. One of the better budget hostels, just west of the Palacio Municipal, with comfortable enough concrete-walled rooms, bathrooms with hot water and magical views from the roof. **M$**

HIKING AND RIDING CATORCE

Catorce's sights are soon exhausted, but you could spend days exploring the surrounding mountains, visiting ruins, or heading downhill to the *altiplano* (high plain) of the desert below. If you don't fancy the exercise, you'll see plenty of ageing US army jeeps, known here as "jeeps Willys", shuttling around the area. Negotiate the price before setting off.

HORSERIDING

One of the most relaxing ways to go is on **horseback**: horses are usually available around Plaza Hidalgo and in front of the *Mesón de la Abundancia*, from where **guides** will take you out across the hills, perhaps visiting the Huichol ceremonial site of Cerro Quemado, though this can seem unpleasantly voyeuristic if any Huichol are around. Midweek tours cost less; prices are higher at weekends.

SHORT HIKES

For **short hikes**, the best nearby destination is the **Pueblo Fantasmo** "Ghost Town," extensive mine ruins reached in an hour or so by following the winding track uphill, just to the left of the Ogarrio tunnel entrance as you face it.

LONG HIKES

The most rewarding unguided **longer hike** (12km one-way; 3hr down, 4hr return; 850m ascent on the way back) leads downhill on Allende from Plaza Hidalgo (with the stables on your left), then forks right after 50m and follows a 4WD track towards the trackside town of Estación Catorce. You'll soon find yourself walking among mine ruins – you'll pass a dam built to provide water and power for the mines, and the **Socavón de Purísima**, a tall chimney from one of the smelters. After about an hour you get to the small village of **Los Catorces**, and, beyond its cemetery, a second settlement known as **Santa Cruz de Carretas** (about 2hr from Real).

At this point, you've already experienced the best of the hike, but it is possible to continue to **Estación Catorce**, an hour further on. If the idea of hiking back seems too daunting, try flagging down the occasional vehicle, and be prepared to pay for your ride. Estación Catorce itself is not a place to linger, though if you get stuck, there are a couple of fleapit hotels and places to eat, located where **buses** depart, on the scruffy square by the rail tracks. Apart from local services to Wadley (at 10.30am, 4pm and perhaps a couple of others; 20min), most buses head to San Tiburcio where you can change for Saltillo and Zacatecas.

Refugio Romano Iturbide 38; http://refugioromano.net. High above the town with stellar views, a lovely garden and terrace, owners Lucio and Mayra run one of the friendliest places in town. Just three stylish rooms, enhanced by home-cooked meals featuring Lucio's Italian cooking (pizza, pastas, focaccia and the like). Free wi-fi in common areas. M$$$

EATING

SEE MAP PAGE 373

Café Azul Lanzagorta 27, next to Mesón de la Abundancia; 496 421 4400. Relaxed Swiss-run café serving the best espresso and cappuccino in town, home-made cakes and sweet and savoury crêpes. M$$

Gorditas Doña Chila Lanzagorta s/n; 488 887 5192. Authentic home-made gorditas in a variety of flavours (*chicharrón*, cheese and picadillo, ground beef with potatoes) with spicy salsa. Cash only. M$$

★ **Mesón de la Abundancia** Lanzagorta 11; http://mesondelaabundancia.com. The pick of the bunch. The Mexican and Italian food is superbly cooked and presented, and worth every peso: a full meal here includes a slice of torte and espresso. Credit cards accepted. M$$$$

DIRECTORY

Banks Real is slowly dragging itself into the modern world and now has a single Banorte ATM, in the Presidencia Municipal on Constitución, but bring lots of cash just in case.

Wadley

Around 10km south of Estación Catorce lies **WADLEY** (or Estación Wadley, named after American railroad builder William Wadley), a small, dusty village that at first acquaintance seems even less appealing than its northern neighbour. The 1922 railway station has long been abandoned (the railway carries freight only), but Wadley has still garnered a devoted following, chiefly for its proximity to a section of desert known to the Huichol as Wirikuta (see page 374), renowned for its abundant **peyote** (as explored in the 2008 experimental Indie flick *Wadley*).

Most people rent a room for a few days, usually with a kitchen as restaurants here are very limited: ask around and you should find somewhere for a relatively cheap amount per night, especially if you are staying a few days (most people end up with *Don Tomas*). Officially at least, "eating" peyote is illegal for anyone other than the Huichol, and there have been several police crackdowns in recent years.

ARRIVAL AND DEPARTURE — WADLEY

Most people visit Wadley with their own transport, or travel via Real de Catorce, usually with a local guide or jeep driver; *colectivo* jeeps Willys depart around 9–10am (45min) and return in the afternoon. Second-class buses usually run between Estación Catorce, Estación Wadley and Matehuala, but timetables often change so you must check in Real de Catorce before heading out.

Veracruz

CHURCH AND PICO DE ORIZABA VOLCANO

Veracruz

The central Gulf coast is among the least-visited yet most distinct areas of Mexico. From Mexico City, you descend through the southern fringes of the Sierra Madre Oriental, past the country's highest peaks, to a broad, hot and wet coastal plain. In this fertile tropical zone the earliest Mexican civilizations developed: Olmec culture dominated the southern half of the state from 1200 BC, while the civilization known as Classic Veracruz flourished between 250 and 900 AD at centres such as El Tajín. Today, Huastec and Totonac culture remains strong in the north. Cortés began his march on the Aztec capital from Veracruz, and the city remains, as it was throughout colonial history, one of the busiest ports in the country. Rich in agriculture – coffee, vanilla, tropical fruits and flowers grow everywhere – the Gulf coast is also endowed with large deposits of oil and natural gas.

The few non-Mexican tourists who find their way here are usually just passing through. In part, at least, this is because the area makes no particular effort to attract them; the **weather** can also be blamed – it rains more often and more heavily here than just about anywhere else in Mexico. Yet even in the rainy season the torrential downpours are short-lived, and within a couple of hours of the rain starting, you can be back on the streets in bright sunshine. Though there are long, windswept **beaches** all down the Atlantic coast, they are less beautiful than their Pacific or Caribbean counterparts, while the larger coastal towns are primarily commercial centres, of little interest to the visitor.

That said, domestic tourism to the area is on the rise, both to the beaches and, increasingly, for **adventure tourism** – whitewater rafting, kayaking, canyoning, climbing and more – around the eastern slopes of the **Sierra Madre** and the rivers that flow off it. **Veracruz** itself is one of the most welcoming of all Mexico's cities; too busy with its own affairs to create a separate life for visitors, the steamy tropical port draws you instead into the rhythms of its daily life, and its obsession with music. Less than an hour north lie **La Antigua** and **Villa Rica**, where Cortés established the first Spanish settlements on the American mainland, and **Cempoala**, ruined site of the first civilization he encountered. **El Tajín**, near the coast in the north of the state, is one of the most important archeological sites in the country, and **Filo Bobos**, only recently excavated, is also well worth a visit.

The colonial cities in the mountains are also delightful: **Xalapa**, seat of the Veracruz state government, is the finest, with its balmy climate, beautiful highland setting and superb anthropology museum. This area, and the high mountains around **Córdoba** and **Orizaba**, are the playground of the adrenaline tourist too. To the south, **Catemaco** is a spellbinding lake set in an extinct volcanic crater, where you can see the last remaining tract of Gulf coast **rainforest**. The area is renowned as a meeting place for native *brujos* and *curanderos*, witches and healers.

Veracruz

VILLA RICA DE LA VERACRUZ was the first town founded by the Spanish in Mexico, a few days after Cortés' arrival on Good Friday, 1519. Though today's city occupies the area of coast where he first came ashore, made camp and encountered Aztec emissaries, the earliest development – little more than a wooden stockade – was in fact established

COLOURFUL COSTUMES FOR CARNAVAL

Highlights

1 **Veracruz** Salsa with divas wearing outrageous costumes at the city's exuberant Carnaval. At any time of year, relax with an ice-cold mint julep and soak up the sounds of marimba in the zócalo, one of Mexico's most vibrant plazas. See page 380

2 **Xalapa** Enjoy the café culture in this university town surrounded by coffee plantations. The Museum of Anthropology here is second only to Mexico City's. See page 394

3 **Whitewater rafting** There are magnificent rafting opportunities, as well as other adrenaline sports, on the rivers that tumble down the tropical valleys of the Sierra Madre Oriental. Take a tour from one of the cities, or head directly to the riverside towns of Jalcomulco or Tlapacoyan. See page 400 and 401

4 **El Tajín** Explore the unique pyramids and ruins at this magnificent remnant of Classic Veracruz civilization; the awesome *voladores* perform their aerial dance here too. See page 406

5 **Catemaco** Take a boat trip across this enchanting lake, surrounded by one of the last remaining tracts of jungle in central Mexico, followed by a relaxing *temazcal*, a traditional sauna, or a session with a shaman. See page 412

HIGHLIGHTS ARE MARKED ON THE MAP ON PAGE 382

some way to the north (see page 402) before being moved to La Antigua (see page 402) and finally arriving at its present site in 1589. The modern city is very much the heir of the original; still the largest port on the Gulf coast, its history reflects every major event from the Conquest onwards. "Veracruz," states author Paul Theroux, "is known as the 'heroic city'. It is a poignant description: in Mexico a hero is nearly always a corpse."

Your first, and lasting, impression of Veracruz, however, will not be of its historical significance but of its present-day vitality. Its dynamic zócalo, pleasant waterfront location and relative absence of tourists make the city one of the most enjoyable places in the Republic in which to sit back and observe – or join – the daily round. This is especially true in the evenings, when the tables under the *portales* of the plaza fill up and the drinking and the marimba music begin, to go on late into the evening. **Marimba** – a distinctively Latin-Caribbean sound based around a giant wooden xylophone – is *the* local sound, but at peak times there are also mariachi and *norteño*

bands and individual crooners all striving to be heard over each other. When the municipal band strikes up from the middle of the square, confusion is total. Veracruz's riotous nine-day **Carnaval** celebrations (held in late February/early March) rival the best in the world, while the **Festival Internacional Afrocaribeño**, usually held in July or August, showcases dance, film, music and art from all over the Caribbean and Africa.

Brief history

Throughout the sixteenth and seventeenth centuries, Veracruz and the Spanish galleons that used the port were preyed on constantly by the English, Dutch and French. In the **War of Independence** the Spanish made their final stand here, holding the fortress of San Juan Ulúa for four years after the country had been lost. In **1838** the French occupied the city, in what was later dubbed "The Pastry War", demanding compensation for French property and citizens who had suffered in the years following Independence; in **1847** US troops took Veracruz, and from here marched on to capture the capital. In January **1862** the French, supported by Spanish and English forces that soon withdrew, invaded on the pretext of forcing Mexico to pay her foreign debt, but ended up staying five years and setting up the unfortunate Maximilian as emperor. Finally, in **1914**, US marines were back, occupying the city to protect American interests during the Revolution. These are the "Cuatro Veces Heroica" of the city's official title, and form the bulk of the history displayed in the museums here.

The zócalo

Fototeca de Veracruz • Free

The attractive **zócalo** is the heart of life in Veracruz in every sense – the place where everyone gathers, for morning coffee, lunch, afternoon strolls and at night. After dark, especially, it has an extraordinary energy, with tables set out under the *portales*, nonstop music and strolling crowds. The imposing **Catedral de Nuestra Señora de Asunción**, consecrated in 1721, dominates the square. Its most striking features are its solid, whitewashed exterior and tiled dome; inside, it's modest but attractive, with pinkish stone columns rising to a largely unadorned vaulted ceiling. On the plaza too is the elegant **Palacio Municipal**, one of the oldest in Mexico, originally built between 1609 and 1627, though it assumed its current form in the eighteenth century. The **Fototeca de Veracruz**, alongside, hosts beautifully presented photography exhibitions.

The malecón

The harbourfront promenade, the **malecón**, begins just a couple of blocks from the zócalo, past a stupendously tacky Mercado de Artesanías. This is a worthwhile stroll at any time of day or night – evenings are particularly animated as street vendors and entertainers compete for your attention, illuminated by the twinkling lights of the ships in the port and the spotlit "dancing" fountains outside the PEMEX building. *Tranvía* city tours start from here, and *lanchas* depart for harbour jaunts (see page 387).

Castillo de San Juan de Ulúa

Northern end of the harbour • Charge • At weekends and in high season, *lanchas* cross the harbour to the castle (additional charge); otherwise the easiest way to get here is to take a taxi – you may have to queue for a ride back

The **Castillo de San Juan de Ulúa** appears impregnable when viewed from across the harbour it repeatedly failed to protect. In most cases, this failure was hardly the fault of the fortress or its defenders: any sensible invader simply landed somewhere on the coast nearby, captured the city and, having cut San Juan off by land and sea, called for its surrender. Today the fortress, originally an island, now connected to the mainland by a causeway, is mostly an empty ruin of endless battlements and stairways. Apart from a small **museum**, the main attraction is the **prison** – many political prisoners died during

Toll Highway (22km), Xalapa (100km) & North

Castillo de San Juan de Ulúa (600m)

VERACRUZ AND BOCA DEL RÌO

0 1 kilometre

N

Toll Highway (24km), Xalapa (103km) & North

Airport (3km), Xalapa (113km) & Mexico City (400km)

Toll Highway (6.5km), Mexico City (415km) & South

FOR DETAIL SEE "CENTRAL VERACRUZ" MAP

Laundry

Aventura Extrema

Bus Stations

Acuario de Veracruz

Playa Villa Del Mar

GULF OF MEXICO

Isla Pajaros

Cancuncito

Isla de Sacrificios

Mundo Submarino

Laguna Real

Plaza Las Americas

Playa de Oro

Playa de Mocambo

GULF OF MEXICO

Reserva Natural Estatal Arroyo Moreno

BOCA DEL RÍO

Río Jamapa

CERVANTES Y PADILLA · YÁÑEZ · MONTESINOS · CONSTITUCIÓN · LANDERO Y COSS · INDEPENDENCIA · MIGUEL A DE QUEVEDO · MIGUEL ANGEL DE QUEVEDO · IGNACIO ALLENDE · HERNÁN CORTÉS · BOULEVARD MANUEL ÁVILA CAMACHO · DÍAZ ARAGÓN · SALVADOR DÍAZ MIRÓN · GENERAL PRIM · LAFRAGUA · ECHEVERRÍA · CALLE JUAN SOTO · VELAZQUEZ DE LA CADENA · GUADALUPE VICTORIA · JUAN DE DIOS PEZA · CALLE J B LOBOS · XALAPA · AV CONSTITUYENTES · AV MIGUEL ALEMÁN · DÍAZ MIRÓN · GENERAL MIGUEL NEGRETE · DOCTOR A IGLESIAS · DE LAS AMERICAS · NORTE · ADOLFO SUGAZTI SARMIENTO · CALZ COSTA VERDE · PASEO DE LAS FLORES · PASEO FRAMBOYANES · LUIS ECHEVERRÍA ÁLVAREZ · 3 O MARTE · NARANJO · C 8 O MAGNOLIAS · LÁZARO CÁRDENAS · AV URANO · RUIZ CORTINES · SALMÓN · DEL MAR · PASEO FLORESTA SUR · PASEO DE LOS JUNCOS · ANGOSTURA · MANTA RAYA · PROGRESO · FERNANDO LÓPEZ ARIAS · PASEO DE LOS ÉBANOS · AV MIGUEL ALEMÁN · DÍAZ MIRÓN · VERACRUZ - XALAPA · RÍO BRAVO · AV EJÉRCITO MEXICANO · CALLE DONATO CASAS · JOSÉ VASCONCELOS · RÍO NILO · LA NACIÓN · GRACIANO SÁNCHEZ · ART. 27 · CARRETERA FEDERAL · RÍO COTAXTLA · 8 O CÁNDIDO AGUILAR · EL TEJAR · LOS PINOS · PROGRESO · ÁVILA CAMACHO · PRIVADA DEL RASTRO · VÍA MUERTA · C DEL RASTRO · PASEO BOCA DEL RÍO · CAMINO REAL · CALLE INDEPENDENCIA

DRINKING & NIGHTLIFE

La Cervecería Del Puerto	1
El Muelle del Bule	1

ACCOMMODATION

Bello	1
Fiesta Americana	2
Hotel Indigo	3
Mocambo	4

EATING

El Cacharrito	1
Gran Café de la Parroquia	2
La Jarocha	4
El Recreo	3

the rule of Díaz in three dark, unpleasant cells known as El Purgatorio, La Gloria and El Infierno (Purgatory, Heaven and Hell).

Museo Histórico Naval

Arista 418 • 229 931 4078 • Charge • Labelling in Spanish only

Fans of naval history and of model ships will enjoy the **Museo Histórico Naval**, a romp through Mexican naval history from the Olmec period to the modern day, with plenty on the various heroic defenders of the city. There's a dramatic scale model of Cortés' battle with the Aztecs on Lago de Texcoco in 1521, and an entire room dedicated to the events of 1914, when US troops occupied Veracruz and Venustiano Carranza subsequently established his Constitutionalist government here.

Baluarte de Santiago

Francisco Canal between 16 de Septiembre & Gómez Farías • Museum charge (free on Sun), fortifications free

The blackened and threatening walls of the **Baluarte de Santiago** make a bizarre sight, stranded as they are four blocks from the sea, with the cannon threatening only the passing traffic. The sole survivor of what were originally nine forts along a 2650m-long wall, the Baluarte was built in 1635 to help fend off constant attacks by pirates and buccaneers; at the time, it stood at the water's edge. The small museum inside has a few pieces of exquisite pre-Columbian gold jewellery discovered in 1976 by a local octopus fisherman. By the time the authorities got wind of his find, most of it had been melted down and sold, but what little remains is lovely.

Museo de la Ciudad

Zaragoza 397 • 229 200 2236 • Free

Exhibits in the **Museo de la Ciudad**, which occupies a former nineteenth-century orphanage about five blocks south of the zócalo, cover local history and folklore from the city's earliest inhabitants to the 1950s. Inevitably, given the scope of material covered, it's a potted version, and many of the exhibits go completely unexplained, but there's some beautiful Olmec and Totonac sculpture, including one giant Olmec head; thought-provoking information on Mexico's African population, much of which was concentrated in this area after the slave trade; and enlightening sections on modern society.

Cultural centres

Instituto Veracruzano de Cultura • Free • **Las Atarazanas** J. S. Montero s/n • Free • **Casa Principal** Mario Molina 315 • Free

Veracruz's municipal government sponsors numerous cultural centres across the city, chief among them the **Instituto Veracruzano de Cultura**, occupying an old convent building on Francisco Canal, at the corner of Zaragoza. As well as regularly changing art exhibitions in its galleries, other rooms off the courtyard house classes and events, and you can also pick up information about cultural happenings across the city. Just a block away, **Las Atarazanas** were colonial warehouses that once backed onto the harbour; inside are more temporary exhibition spaces. More exhibits are generally held at the **Casa Principal**, a fine, converted eighteenth-century residence.

Acuario and the beaches

Acuario de Veracruz • Charge • http://acuariodeveracruz.com

You wouldn't make a special trip to Veracruz for its **beaches**, but for an afternoon's escape to the sea, they can be very enjoyable. Strips of sand hug the coast for some 12km southeast of the centre, linked together by Bulevar María Ávila Camacho, which runs all the way to Boca del Río. For the most part this is not attractive, with concrete strip development all the way, and a six-lane highway right behind the beach, but it is where much of the city's modern life is concentrated. About halfway to Boca, Avenida Ruíz Cortines cuts inland, taking a short cut away from the beach: here is some of

the city's most recent development, including vast shopping malls like the Plaza las Americas, and many of the biggest, newest hotels.

Swimmable beaches start a couple of kilometres from the centre, just beyond the Plaza Acuario shopping centre, home of the **Acuario de Veracruz**, a modern aquarium with some large ocean fish. This first section is the **Playa Villa del Mar**. The water here is not the cleanest, but it's popular with locals who frequent the many beachside palapa restaurants (for outrageously overpriced seafood), and there are boat trips to Cancuncito and the **Isla de Sacrificios**, more or less directly offshore. More attractive strands are further south, in particular in the area where Ávila Camacho and Ruíz Cortines join up again. Here **Playa Mocambo** is one of the best strips of sand, helped by the fact that the main road is for once not right alongside: there are plenty of beach bars, and a small water park with slides. It's also relatively easy to get to, as all the buses come past – get out at the *Hotel Mocambo*.

Boca del Río

Boca del Río lends its name to the whole southern half of this coast, but it's actually a small town in its own right, ten minutes or so beyond Mocambo by bus, located, as the name suggests, at the mouth of the Río Jamapa. There are more long, grey-sand beaches here, but the main attraction is the river. A string of small restaurants lines the riverfront in town, all offering seafood at competitive prices. You can also take trips upstream: a *lancha* costs about M$400 an hour, or at busy times you should be able to join a tour for around M$75 per person.

ARRIVAL AND DEPARTURE — VERACRUZ

BY PLANE

Veracruz International Airport is about 10km south of the city; there are ATMs and car-rental desks. Taxis between here and the centre cost a set fee; buy a ticket from the taxi desk in the terminal.

Destinations AeroMéxico (http://aeromexico.com) and Vivaaerobus (http://vivaaerobus.com) between them offer at least ten direct flights a day to Mexico City, and one or more a day to Cancún, Guadalajara, Mérida and Monterrey. International flights to Houston (daily) are operated by United (http://united.com).

BY BUS

The ADO first-class bus station is about 3km from the centre at Díaz Mirón 1698, with the AU second-class terminal right behind it facing Lafragua. To reach the centre, buy a ticket for a taxi from the booth on the south side of the first-class terminal (left as you exit). To take a local bus, walk to the stop on Díaz Mirón to the right as you exit, and take any – most will have "Díaz Mirón" or "Centro" on the windscreen. They mostly end up on Independencia as it runs past the zócalo. Tickets can be bought downtown at the Ticket Bus booth, at Aquiles Serdán 647, two blocks away from the *Gran Café del Portal*.

Destinations Cancún (4 first class daily; 20–22hr); Catemaco (10 first class daily, very frequent second; 3hr 30min–4hr); Coatzacoalcos (36 first class daily, very frequent second; 4hr 30min–6hr); Córdoba (very frequently, first & second; 1hr 45min); José Cardel (frequently, mainly second; 30min); Mexico City (very frequently, first & second class; 5hr 30min–7hr); Oaxaca (5 first class, 2 second daily; 7hr)–8hr 30min; Orizaba (very frequently, first & second; 2hr 30min); Papantla (9 first class daily, frequent second; 3–4hr); Puebla (15 first class daily, 15 second; 3hr 30min–5hr 30min); San Andrés Tuxtla (15 first class daily, very frequent second; 3hr); Tuxpán (22 first class daily, frequent second; 5hr 30min); Villahermosa (26 first class daily; 7hr); Xalapa (constantly first & second; 2hr).

INFORMATION AND TOURS

City tours mostly depart from the malecón, where you'll find traditional *tranvías* – buses done up to look like old trolley-cars – along with various rival tour buses. They leave every half-hour or so for a 45–60min tour of the old town; and it's especially fun at night, when the *tranvías* are lit up.

Bus and boat tours There are also bus tours down to Boca del Río (same price) and boat trips around the harbour (229 935 9417). All of these are more frequent at weekends and in high season, and busier in the late afternoon and evening.

Harbour tour There are plenty of other opportunities to take to the water in Veracruz. Asdic, which runs the harbour tours, also offers evening sailings in its disco catamaran; and from a base on the beach by the Acuario it sails around the Isla de los Sacrificios (now a nature reserve) to Cancuncito, a semi-submerged sandbar in the bay where you can disembark and swim in beautifully clear seas. Banana boats and jet-skis are also available here.

GETTING AROUND

By bus Although Veracruz is a large and rambling city, the *centro histórico* is relatively small and easy to navigate – anywhere further afield can be reached by local bus from somewhere very near the zócalo. All trips within the city (and as far as Boca del Río) are a flat fee, including the newer, a/c express buses, often (but not always) painted yellow. Buses for the beaches (marked "Boca del Río", "Playas" or "Mocambo") pass along Zaragoza close to the

WATERSPORTS

There's remarkably good **diving** at pretty good rates on a large number of little-visited reefs and beaches within the **Parque Nacional Sistema Arrecifal Veracruzano**. Try Dorado Buceo (http://doradobuceo.com); Mundo Submarino (http://mundosubmarino.com.mx), Ávila Camacho 3549; or Scubaver (http://scubaver.net), Hernandez y Hernandez 563.

For more adventurous tours further afield, above all **whitewater rafting** (mostly at Jalcomulco, see page 400), but also canyoning, rappelling and the like, try Amphibian (Insurgentes Veracruzanos 432, in the *Hotel Ruiz Milan* http://amphibianveracruz.com); Aventura Extrema (Sanchez Tagle 973; http://aventuraextrema.com.mx); or Mexico Verde (http://mexicoverde.com).

zócalo. Most take the quick route via Ruíz Cortines; for the scenic route along the coastal road take buses marked "Penacho" or join the open-air tour buses from the malecón (see page 383).

By taxi Taxis are easily found on the street, charge according to a zone system and are pretty honest – trips in the centre will cost you about the least, to the bus station it's a little more and then to Boca is more expensive. If your hotel calls for one it will be more expensive, though this is generally a safer option at night.

Car rental Europcar, Hertz and Dollar have offices at the airport and in the hotel zone; Kanguro is a local operator with airport and downtown branches (http://kangurorental.com.mx).

6

INFORMATION

Tourist information The tourist office, on the ground floor of the Palacio Municipal (daily 9am–9pm; 229 200 2000, https://facebook.com/DisfrutaVeracruzMX), has basic information and helpful staff on hand, though not always English-speakers.

ACCOMMODATION

There are **hotels** right next to the first-class bus station, and several very cheap and rather grim places around the back of the second-class terminal, but unless you've arrived late at night or face a very early departure, there's no point staying this far out. The other inexpensive places are mostly within a couple of blocks of the zócalo; they're nothing to write home about, and often noisy, but at least you should find a clean room with a fan. The best deals in the city are in the **mid-range**, and there are some decent hotels along the malecón within walking distance of the zócalo. If you want more luxury, head to the **beach**, where resort-style hotels form an ever-expanding hotel zone. Most of the year prices are very reasonable – and negotiable – but they double or triple for Carnaval and Semana Santa, and are also inflated at other Mexican holiday times, especially in August.

CITY CENTRE, SEE MAP PAGE 386

Emporio Paseo del Malecón 244; http://hotelesemporio.com/hoteles/emporio-veracruz. Classily modernized high-rise seafront hotel with elegant designer furnishings, three pools, gym, spa and good restaurants. Rooms ending in nine have uninterrupted sea vistas, and most have some view of the harbour. Big reductions out of season. M$$$

Gran Hotel Diligencias Independencia 1115; http://granhoteldiligencias.com-hotel.com. The most modern, and best, of the hotels on the zócalo, elegantly refurbished with cable TV and wi-fi in the rooms, plus most other facilities and a pool on a terrace overlooking the action in the square. M$$$

★ **Holiday Inn Centro Histórico** Morelos 225; http://ihg.com. Charming hotel built out of the renovated half of the nineteenth-century Faro Benito Juárez, with all the modern conveniences and a pretty pool enclosed by a courtyard embellished with elegant tiling. Look out for bargain deals online. M$$$

Hotel Sharida Av. Miguel Angel de Quevedo 3740; 229 178 0687. Ageing option near the zócalo, with a/c. Some rooms have been refurbished, including the priciest, which have flat screen TVs and satellite channels. M$$$

Imperial Miguel Lerdo 153; https://hotelimperial-losportales.com. If faded glory is your thing, you'll love the *Imperial*, an eighteenth-century building whose once magnificent public areas boast marble floors, a striking stained-glass ceiling and the first lift installed in Mexico (still going strong). At the time of writing, long-standing plans to elevate the space from a dusty old pile into a five-star resort remained – much like the building itself – frozen in time. M$$

Mallorca Aquiles Serdán 424; 229 475 8234. This drab budget hotel is pretty characterless, with staid, old-fashioned rooms, but that's to be expected at this price. It has a good location near both the zócalo and the malecón, and, crucially, has a/c. M$

Mar y Tierra Ávila Camacho at Figueroa; http://hotelmarytierra.com. Mid-priced seafront option, a 15–20min walk from the zócalo. A/c rooms in the old section are much smaller, so it's worth the extra for a newer room: both sections have many rooms with sea views at no extra cost. M$$

Meson del Mar Ávila Esteban Morales 543; 229 932 5043. Beautiful eighteenth-century colonial building with high ceilings and bright guestrooms. It's decorated with wonderfully carved wooden headboards and tiled blue birds in the bathroom. Each room is unique; ask to view one before you commit. M$$

Ruíz Milán Paseo del Malecón; http://ruizmilan.com.mx. Not quite as fancy as the exterior might lead you to believe, this is nonetheless a comfortable, business-style hotel in a great location. Three grades of room – the best are at the front – all with a/c and cable TV, plus a small indoor pool and hot tub, and a solid restaurant serving signature Veracruz dishes. M$$$

ACUARIO TO BOCA DEL RÍO, SEE MAP PAGE 384

Bello Ruíz Cortines 258; http://hotelbello.com. The ten-storey *Bello* is among the cheaper modern options in one of the busiest restaurant and nightlife areas, hence often fully booked. There's a courtyard pool, and rooms are business-like and comfortable: those on the upper floors at the back have views to the sea, a couple of blocks away. Big low-season reductions. M$$$

Fiesta Americana Ávila Camacho s/n; http://fiestainn.com. Dominating the Playa de Oro, this massive resort has a giant pool and spacious rooms and balconies, all with sea views. One of the longest-established in the hotel zone, but still among the best, with a great beachfront position. M$$$$

★ **Hotel Indigo** Ruíz Cortines 3533; https://hiltonhotels.com. Hip, colourful, contemporary hotel. Guestrooms have oversized all-white bedframes and furniture in shades of citrus. Updated amenities like complimentary wi-fi and iPod alarm clocks. M$$$

Mocambo Ruíz Cortines 4000 at Playa Mocambo; www.oyorooms.com/mx. Grand old beachside hotel complex built in 1932 with lots of dark wood and a nautical theme. Though rather faded, it's wonderfully atmospheric – you half expect Frank Sinatra to be wandering through the lobby – and facilities include large indoor and outdoor pools, a children's play area, wi-fi and several restaurants, among which is the well-regarded, formal *La Fragata*. M$$$

6

EATING

The zócalo is ringed by **bars** and **cafés**, but these are really places to drink, and, though most do serve food, it's generally an overpriced afterthought. There are a number of great places serving local **coffee**. Proper restaurants, though, are relatively scarce: the area around the old market building on Landero y Coss between Serdán and Mariano Arista has a whole series of small and cheap **fish restaurants** and cooked-food stalls, almost all of them lunch time only, but most of the places that are busy in the evening are down in the hotel zone, well south of the centre.

CITY CENTRE, SEE MAP PAGE 386

Bola de Oro Mario Molina 290; http://boladeoro.com.mx. A traditional coffee shop that has had a modern makeover. They still grind and roast their own local coffee and serve it as *café lechero* (see page 390), but they also have frappes, iced cappuccinos, fruit teas, waffles and *pan dulce*. M$

El Cochinito de Oro Zaragoza 190 at Serdán; 229 932 3677. This friendly, no-frills eatery has been around for 75 years, offering breakfast as well as a good selection of seafood dishes. The menu is translated into English and there are good-value *comidas*. M$$

La Fonda de las Gordas Zamora 138; 229 931 4300. Handy and inexpensive fast-food style place right on the zócalo; the speciality is *gorditas rellenas*, tortilla pockets with dozens of stuffings to choose from; *pollo pibil* is particularly good. Tortas, quesadillas and tamales are also available. M$

La Gaviota Trigueros 21; 229 931 8591. A useful address for nocturnal revellers, *La Gaviota* is open 24hr and offers a bit of everything on its extensive menu along with a well-stocked bar should you wish to keep the party going; the fish or prawn main dishes are ample, and the five-course lunch-time *comida* is more than filling. M$$$

Gran Café del Portal Independencia 1187 at Zamora, opposite the cathedral; http://grancafedelportal.com.mx. A local institution, serving great coffee (roasted on the premises) and pricey food. The cavernous interior has icily effective a/c and free wi-fi; don't expect a tranquil meal if you sit outside – you'll be serenaded by the house marimba band at any time of day, and will probably draw the attention of plenty of street vendors. M$$$

Nieves Guëro-Guëro Zamora 15 at Landero y Coss; https://facebook.com/nievesgueroguero. Fabulous, refreshing ice creams in tropical fruit and nut flavours; more similar to Italian *gelati* than to the creamy US variety. One of a city-wide chain, and three rival operators next door to each other here (don't be swayed by the sleeker, cleaner and confusingly named Guëro-Guëra, across the street), this little window boasts the richest flavours, served in styrofoam cups. M$$

Nutribionicos Centro Histórico Mario Molina 168;

COMIDA Y CERVEZA, A LA VERACRUZANA

Veracruz offers up some fabulous **food** – the state's coffee, fruit and vanilla are renowned, and the seafood is also superb. *Huachinango a la Veracruzana* (red snapper Veracruz-style) is served across the country, and is of course on every menu here; the Veracruzana sauce of tomato, chile, onions and olives can also spice up anything from steak to squid. Other local specialities include *pulpos a la marinera* (baby octopus), *arroz a la tumbada* (Veracruz-style rice, packed with seafood), *empanadas de camaron* (shrimp turnovers) and *jaiba*, a large local crab; look out too for anything made with *chile chipotle*, a hot, dark-brown chile with a smoky flavour – *chilpachole de jaiba* is a sort of crab chowder that combines the two. Sweet tamales, too, are a speciality, and to wash it all down, the brewery at Orizaba produces some of the best beers in the country. Stronger liquors include the mind-wiping *toritos*, made with fruits and blended with condensed milk and a tot of brandy.

http://nutribionicos.com.mx. If you're looking for some healthy menu options, try the extensive offerings at Nutribionicos Centro Histórico. You'll get a lot here for not very much and everything is super fresh. M$

Samborcito 16 de Septiembre 727; 229 283 5890. Large, no-nonsense local favourite with fans twirling under a palapa roof. A bit of a walk from the centre in an area that feels like a Caribbean shantytown, but worth it for the *picadas* (thick tortillas with cheese), tamales and other delicious Veracruz dishes. M$$

6

Sanborns Independencia 1069, at Miguel Lerdo; http://sanborns.com.mx. The Veracruz branch of the national department store and restaurant chain. Food ranges from Mexican snacks to filet mignon, served in an a/c dining room or the cosier adjoining café. Hearty breakfasts and good sized mains served here. M$$$

ACUARIO TO BOCA DEL RÍO, SEE MAP PAGE 384

El Cacharrito Privada Avila Camacho 71, next to Hotel Lois; http://elcacharrito.com.mx. Formal Argentine restaurant in the hotel zone, serving fabulous steaks and Argentine wines; the elegant first-floor dining room, with backlit bar and open kitchen behind glass, is an oasis of calm amid the traffic madness. With wine and three courses, it's easy to spend a lot per head. M$$$$$

★**Gran Café de la Parroquia** Gómez Farías 34 on the malecón and Ruíz Cortines 1815; http://laparroquia.com. A Veracruz institution that claims to have been going for two hundred years. *Café lechero* is the speciality – effectively a latte; you are brought a glass with black coffee, chink the glass with a spoon and another waiter arrives bearing a kettle of milk, which he adds from a great height. They serve breakfast and full meals too. M$$$

La Jarocha Oviedo 205; 229 334 3930. Close to the bridge and Palacio Municipal on the Boca del Río waterfront, *La Jarocha* serves excellent fish *comidas*, or the speciality *piña* or *coco relleno de mariscos* (pineapple or coconut stuffed with seafood). M$$

El Recreo Revolución 402, Boca del Río; http://sointec.wixsite.com/recreo. An excellent local restaurant on the plaza in Boca del Río. Inexpensive breakfasts, *café lechero*, handmade tortillas and gorditas, and fresh local seafood explain why this big place is always bustling. M$$

DRINKING AND NIGHTLIFE

An evening spent at an outdoor table under the *portales* on the **zócalo** is entertainment in itself, as mariachi, marimba and *norteño* bands compete for your attention with street vendors, fortune-tellers and, bizarrely, uniformed nurses offering to take your blood pressure. Most evenings around 7pm the municipal band or a folkloric dance troupe strikes up from the bandstand, and local couples dance *danzón* across the square, adding to the general madness. **Bars** and clubs are generally out of the centre, on the coast road or in the commercial strip along Ruíz Cortines; many of the bigger ones are close to the junction of Ruíz Cortines and Ávila Camacho.

CITY CENTRE, SEE MAP PAGE 386

Bar Palacio Miguel Lerdo on the zócalo. Along with its neighbours, *Flamingos* and *Prendes*, this is the place to take in the zócalo action over a beer or traditional mint julep, prepared with dark rum, dry sherry, vermouth, sugar and mint.

ACUARIO TO BOCA DEL RÍO, SEE MAP PAGE 384

La Cervecería Del Puerto Ávila Camacho 4294, on the waterfront; 229 283 3368, https://facebook.com/LaCerveceria. Most people come here for the waterfront views and the lack of a cover charge, but beyond that La Cervecería Del Puerto serves up a pretty impressive book of artisan beers; mostly local but with imports too.

El Muelle del Bule Ávila Camacho 9, on the waterfront; 229 921 5662. Tropical themed bar-restaurant with a palapa-covered terrace overlooking the Isla de Sacrificios, lively in the evenings and at weekends and a popular spot to watch football and other big-screen sports. Plenty of 2-for-1 promos in the early evening, and good food, too, with tacos, tostadas and seafood.

SHOPPING

SEE MAP PAGE 386

Coffee, vanilla and cigars are the souvenirs most Mexicans take home from Veracruz, and all of these (along with necklaces and lottery tickets) will be brought to you by a string of vendors if you sit down even for a minute anywhere around the zócalo.

Librería Educal Callejón Portal de Miranda 9, just off the zócalo beside the Fototeca; 229 932 6943. Classy bookshop that also sells a small selection of high-class artesanía and CDs of local and world music. Lots of glossy volumes on art and architecture (almost all in Spanish), plus a few guides and maps and a noticeboard of alternative events.

Mercado de Artesanías Landero y Coss, cnr Paseo del Malecón. Fabulously kitsch souvenirs, shells, cheap T-shirts and almost anything else you can think of on offer at dozens of stalls.

Popularte Upstairs at Mario Molina 23, cnr Landero y Coss, opposite the Mercado de Artesanías. State-run shop with high-quality (and high-priced) furniture, clothing, ceramics and jewellery. No sales pressure.

DIRECTORY

Banks and exchange Branches of all the main banks, where you can change travellers' cheques and find ATM machines, are around the junction of Independencia and Benito Juárez.

Hospitals The big hospitals are mainly south of the centre towards the bus station, including Hospital General ISSSTE on Díaz Mirón (229 937 0826); Hospital Español is more central at 16 de Septiembre 955 (229 262 2300, emergenices 229 931 4000). Call 911 for an ambulance.

Laundry Friendly, nameless lavandería at Francisco Canal 1684, two blocks west of Ignacio Allende (charge per kg).

Left luggage Guarderías can be found in both bus stations.

Pharmacies They're everywhere. Handiest is the Farmacía del Ahorro just off the zócalo by the *Gran Café del Portal* on Independencia at Mario Molina.

Police 229 938 0664 or emergency 911.

Post office On the Plaza de la República.

Sierra Madre Oriental

If you take the direct route **from Mexico City** to Veracruz – the scenic Hwy-150 – you'll bypass every major town en route; if you're driving yourself, note that the tolls along this stretch of road are extremely high. For those pressed for time, the fast highway is a blessing – Veracruz and the coast are very much the outstanding attractions – but the cities in the mountains merit a stop if you have room in your itinerary. Regardless of how fast you go or what form of transport you take, the journey over the **Sierra Madre Oriental** is one of the most beautiful in Mexico: as Ixtaccíhuatl gradually disappears behind you, the snow on the **Pico de Orizaba** comes into view, and the plains of corn and maguey in the west are supplanted on the eastern slopes by woods of pine and cypress, and by green fields dotted with contented cows out to pasture.

It's worth noting, however, that this is the rainiest area of the country, and while the damp brings bounties in terms of great coffee and a luxuriance of flowers, downpours can become a problem. Particularly irritating – especially in October and November – is what the locals call *chipichipi*, a persistent fine drizzle caused by warm airstreams from the Gulf hitting cooler air as they reach the eastern face of the sierra. Drivers should also watch out for the fog that frequently cloaks the higher sections of this road.

Orizaba

Midway between Puebla and Veracruz, **ORIZABA** is an industrial city and a major brewing centre: the giant Cervecería Cuauhtémoc Moctezuma produces some of the best **beer** in the republic, including globally famous brands Sol and Dos Equis – ask at the tourist office (see page 392) for details of tours. Despite the industry, the historic centre remains compact and attractive; because the old city was built up against a hill, development has spread in one direction only, so the *centro histórico* is right on the edge of town, with more modern development sprawling to the east and south. The **Parque Castillo**, with the imposing Catedral de San Miguel at Colón and Madero, marks the centre of the old town. There's not a great deal to see, but Orizaba makes an enjoyable short break or overnight stop; better yet, stay in Córdoba (see page 393), and make a day trip to see Orizaba's sights.

Palacio de Hierro

Madero Nte between Poniente 2 and 4 • Free

The **Palacio de Hierro**, on the main square opposite the cathedral, is an extraordinary nineteenth-century iron structure, prefabricated in Belgium. It houses not only the **tourist office**, but also no fewer than seven one- or two-room **museums** – all free – including the Museo de la Cerveza (beer museum), Museo del Fútbol (soccer) and, upstairs, the Museo Raíces de Orizaba, a small collection of local archeology.

6

Cerro del Borrego

Cable-car entrance: on the riverside walk, between Poniente 5 and Colón Poniente • Charge • http://orizaba.travel

Colón Poniente heads west from the plaza towards the looming **Cerro del Borrego**, atop which a vast Mexican flag flies and from where, if you brave the stiff climb, there are fabulous views of the city, as well as a small restaurant, tower and museum. Alternatively, you can zip up in a six-minute cable car; tickets allot you two hours at the top. Along the way, Colón crosses the **Río Orizaba**, where an attractive riverside walk winds beneath the city's many bridges, and continues past the **Palacio Municipal** before ending at the **Alameda**, a shady park beneath the Cerro.

Museo de Arte del Estado

Av Oriente 4 at C 23 Sur • Charge • 272 724 3200

The 37 works by Diego Rivera housed in Orizaba's **Museo de Arte** constitute one of Mexico's finest collections of this iconic artist. Housed alongside other local art from colonial to contemporary – including many fascinating nineteenth-century portraits and local landscapes – they make this the most worthwhile visit in the city. The restored eighteenth-century Oratorio de San Felipe Neri, which houses the museum, is also an attraction in itself: unfortunately it's a long way out – over a dozen blocks east of the centre.

ARRIVAL AND INFORMATION — ORIZABA

By bus The ADO is on Av Oriente 6 near Sur 11; most second-class services also stop here or nearby. Oriente 6 is Orizaba's main commercial street, and you'll find big business hotels and numerous restaurants here: head five blocks west and three north for the Parque Castillo at the heart of the old town.

Destinations Córdoba (very frequently; 50min); Mexico City (very frequently; 4hr–$hr 30min); Oaxaca (4 daily; 4hr 30min–6hr); Puebla (very frequently; 2hr 20min); Veracruz (40 daily; 2hr 50min); Villahermosa (10 daily; 7–9hr); Xalapa (7 daily; 3–4hr).

Tourist information The helpful tourist office is on the ground floor of the Palacio de Hierro (daily 9am–7pm; 272 728 9136, http://orizaba.travel).

ACCOMMODATION

Hoteles Haus Express Av Oriente 6 505, cnr Sur 11; https://hoteleshausexpress.com.mx. A good-value option right next to the ADO terminal, with well-soundproofed modern rooms, all with a/c, flatscreen TV and wi-fi. M$$

Misión Hotel Av Oriente 6 464, just up from the ADO on the opposite side of the street; http://hotelesmision.com.mx. Pleasant low-rise property that combines the amenities of a modern business hotel with a more traditional character in the rooms, which are set around a tiled courtyard. Facilities include a small pool and wi-fi. Smart and comfortable. M$$$

Plaza Palacio Poniente 2 no. 2; 272 725 9933. Facing the Palacio de Hierro and cathedral across a pedestrianized street, this could hardly have a better location. Rooms are simple, with fan and cable TV, but comfy and quiet. M$$

Posada del Viajero Madero Norte 242; 272 726 3320. Decent budget choice with clean but tiny rooms (narrow, though high ceilings), with hot water but patchy wi-fi, around an internal courtyard. Just half a block from the Palacio de Hierro facing the market. M$

EATING

There are plenty of **taco stands** in the historic centre and in the market, but the bulk of the restaurants are out on Av Oriente 6 and in the more modern areas of town east of the centre. There are some great **cafés** in the centre, though. The daily Mercado Melchor Ocampo is on Madero Norte just off Parque Castillo.

La Braza Av Oriente 6 94300 by the ADO; 272 724 2627. Fast-food style grill that's always busy, day and night; grilled meats the speciality, but there's also a wide menu including breakfast, tacos and a good-value *comida*. M$$

Cafeteria Dauzon Colón Poniente 8, cnr Sur 5; http://pasteleriasdauzon.com. A great café and cake shop that also serves a very good-value lunch-time *comida* and sandwiches, to eat in or take away. M$

Gran Cafe de Orizaba Madero Norte, cnr Poniente 2, in the Palacio de Hierro; 272 728 8349. Wonderful, old-fashioned café with original fittings and a terrace facing the cathedral. Great coffee, and a modest selection of sandwiches, cakes and other light bites. M$

Mellado Colón Poniente 89, cnr Norte 3; 272 725 5526. Seemingly stuck in a time warp, this old-time wood-panelled café serves cheap, delicious tortas, above all, but also drinks, ice creams and other light meals. M$

6

PICO DE ORIZABA

Orizaba is situated close to the foot of the loftiest peak in Mexico, the **Pico de Orizaba** (Citlaltépetl), a perfectly formed, snow-capped volcano. There is a fair amount of disagreement over its exact height – 5636m seems the most widely accepted, though locals often claim more – but there's no disputing that it's a beautiful sight and a seriously challenging climb, for experienced mountaineers only. Numerous local companies offer guides and facilities, mostly based in the village of **Tlachichuca**, which at 2600m is where the main trails begin. To get there, take a second-class bus to the small town of Serdán (2hr), where you change for Tlachichuca itself (1hr); there are also occasional buses direct from Puebla. Details of the climb (Oct–May only) can be found in R.J. Secor's *Mexico's Volcanoes*. Reliable operators include Summit Orizaba (http://summitorizaba.com) and Servimont (http://servimont.com.mx), both with their own accommodation in Tlachichuca.

Córdoba

CÓRDOBA is a busy modern city at the centre of the area's coffee trade, built around a stunning colonial centre. Founded in 1618 by thirty Spanish families – and so also known as the "City of the Thirty Knights" – its main claim to fame is that in 1821 the last Spanish viceroy, Juan O'Donoju, signed the **Treaty of Córdoba** with General Iturbide here, formally giving Mexico independence.

The city is easy to navigate: Avenida 1 and Calle 1 intersect at the Palacio Municipal on the Plaza 21 de Mayo: avenidas run east–west, with even numbers north of the zócalo and odd numbers south. Calles run north–south, with even numbers west of the zócalo and odd numbers east.

Plaza 21 de Mayo

The signing of the Treaty of Córdoba took place in the Palacio de los Condes de Zevallos, now known as the **Portal de Zevallos**, on the **Plaza 21 de Mayo**; these days it's given over to handicraft shops and cafés, where you can sit and sample Córdoban coffee or julep, a rum and mint cocktail. The twin-towered **Catedral de la Inmaculada Concepción**, facing the Palacio Municipal across the plaza, is one of the most richly adorned religious buildings in the state – started in 1621, it contains a revered statue of the Virgin Mary to the right of the altar.

Museo de la Ciudad

C 3 between avenidas 3 and 5, half a block off the zócalo • Charge, discount for children

The exhibits in the **Museo de la Ciudad** (labelled in Spanish only) encompass some thirty centuries of local history, from Olmec and Totonac ceramics and sculpture, through Independence, to mementos of the Mexico '68 Olympics. They occupy a beautiful colonial building with gorgeous mountain views from its upper storey.

ARRIVAL AND INFORMATION — CÓRDOBA

By bus The bus terminal (for first- and second-class services) is 3km south of the centre at Privada 4 between calles 39 and 41, a short taxi ride to the zócalo (buy a ticket first), or hop on a local bus marked "Centro". For Orizaba, you'll find local buses on Av 2.

Tourist information The tourist office (daily 9am–7pm; 271 717 1700, http://cordoba.gob.mx) is in the Palacio Municipal.

ACCOMMODATION

Most of the big modern **hotels**, along with fast-food and fancier restaurants, are some way north of the centre on the old highway.

Bello C 5 #319 at Av 2; www.hotelbello.com/cordoba. A mid-market business-style hotel with parking and a coffee shop, and modern, functional rooms decked out in rather lurid lime green. All have a/c, cable TV and wi-fi, and some have nice mountain views. M$$$

Iberia Av 2 919; http://hoteliberiacordoba.com.mx. Budget hotel that's much better than the exterior and location might lead you to expect. Well-kept, traditionally decorated rooms have hot water, TV and wi-fi (plus a/c for an extra charge) and surround a pleasant internal courtyard. M$

★ **Mansur** Av 1 301, cnr of C 3; www.hotelesmansur.com. Characterful central hotel with huge communal terraces overlooking the cathedral. Rooms are comfortable and more modern than the exterior would suggest, but those at the front can be noisy. A/c, TV and wi-fi. M$$$

EATING

Los 30's Av 9 2004 between calles 20 and 22; http://crepasycarneslos30s.com. Huge and popular café in the restaurant zone near the highway. It's best known for delicious savoury crêpes, but they also serve steaks and a full Mexican-Mediterranean menu comprising tortas, tacos, pizza and pasta. M$$

Las Delicias Av 2 307 between calles 3 and 5; 271 714 9494. Large restaurant that's a welcome escape from the raucous street in front, especially in the quieter upstairs room; a good bet for breakfast or tasty inexpensive *comidas*. M$$

Mi Kasa Av 5 212-A between calles 2 and 4; 271 712 8602. For a break from Mexican food, try the sushi and other Japanese specialities at this friendly little restaurant in an area that's lively at night. Sushi roll prices vary. M$$

El Patio de la Abuela C1 208, between avenidas 2 and 4; 271 712 0606. A pretty place, with a tranquil courtyard and family photos on the wall, *El Patio* serves good-value breakfasts and traditional Mexican fare. Look out for the daily special. M$$

El Tabachin Portal de Zevallos; http://casazevallos.com. The best location in town, for an upmarket hotel restaurant serving steaks and more traditional Mexican food, though you can also just dawdle over a drink. Alongside is the rival *Cafe La Parroquia*, equally enjoyable. M$$$

Xalapa and around

The capital of the state of Veracruz, **XALAPA** is a big city, remarkably attractive despite its relative modernity and traffic-laden streets. Set in countryside of sometimes breathtaking beauty, sprawling across a hillside below the volcanic peak of the **Cofre de Perote** (4282m), it enjoys views to the snowcapped Pico de Orizaba and a warm, damp climate that encourages rich, jungly vegetation. In addition to these natural advantages, Xalapa has been promoted by its civic leaders as a **cultural centre**, with a classical and traditional music festival in June, an international jazz gathering in August and a major literary festival in September, as well as many lesser events year-round. Home, too, of the **University of Veracruz** and the exceptional **Museo de Antropología**, it's a lively place, enjoyable even if you simply hang out in one of the many cafés in the centre of town, sip the locally grown coffee and watch life pass by. For adrenaline junkies and lovers of nature there's much more, though, as Xalapa is also close to numerous rivers: as they crash down from the high sierra to the coast, these create numerous spectacular **waterfalls** and some of Mexico's finest opportunities for **whitewater rafting** and kayaking.

Parque Juárez

Xalapa's appealing colonial downtown is centred on the **Parque Juárez**, its trees filled with raucous birds at dusk. There are stunning mountain views towards the Cofre de Perote from the south side of the plaza, where the land drops away steeply. The **Palacio de Gobierno**, on the east side, has interesting murals by Mexican artist Melchor Peredo.

Agorá de la Ciudad

Parque Juárez • Free • 228 818 5730

A cultural centre built into the southern edge of the plaza, the **Agorá de la Ciudad** attracts Xalapa's contemporary arts crowd to well-curated, revolving exhibitions and events. As well as the art spaces, there's an auditorium hosting movies and concerts, usually free of charge.

Pinacoteca Diego Rivera

Herrera 5 • Free • 228 818 1819

Beneath the western edge of the Parque Juárez, the **Pinacoteca Diego Rivera** showcases some interesting temporary exhibitions in its modern galleries. Though it's named after Diego Rivera, none of his works is on display.

Museo Casa de Xalapa (MUXA)

Herrera 7 • Free

The **Museo Casa de Xalapa** (MUXA) occupies a lovely eighteenth-century colonial home in whose rooms a small, modern museum of local history (lots of interactivity, but mainly in Spanish) has been installed.

Catedral Metropolitana de la Inmaculada Concepción

Enríques, cnr Revolución, on the Parque Lerdo • Free • http://arquidiocesisdexalapa.com

From the outside, the most striking thing about Xalapa's eighteenth-century **cathedral** is that it only has one tower – the other was never completed. Inside there's a richly decorated nave, a striking Calvary at the altar and a chapel dedicated to Rafael Guízar y Valencia (1878–1938), who was canonized as **St Rafael Guízar** in 2006 – the first bishop born in the Americas to receive the honour. He is most admired for resisting the state's persecution of the Church in the 1920s and 1930s, forming a "guerrilla ministry" and later becoming the bishop of Veracruz.

Museo de Antropología

Av Xalapa, about 3km north of the centre • Charge, audio guide extra • http://uv.mx/max • Bus marked "Av Xalapa" from Camacho, on the northwest corner of the Parque Juárez, or taxi

Beyond question Xalapa's outstanding sight, the **Museo de Antropología** is a brilliant museum with arguably the best archeological collection in the country after that

6

PARKLIFE IN XALAPA

Xalapa is renowned for its **parks** and their wonderful tropical flora. A couple of fine potential picnic spots are within walking distance of the centre. The **Parque Los Tecajetes** (Tues–Sun 7am–6pm), ten minutes' walk west of the zócalo along María Ávila Camacho, is a pristine public park with lush vegetation and plenty of shaded seating areas. South of the zócalo, Herrera leads steeply down towards the **Paseo de los Lagos**, where walkways lead around a series of small, artificial lakes edged by parkland; popular with runners in the morning and strolling families later on. In the north of the city, the entrance to the woody **Parque Ecológico Macuiltépec** is close to the Anthropology Museum. At 1590m, the easily climbable Macuiltépec is the highest of the hills on which the town is built, and from its *mirador* you might catch a glimpse of the Gulf. There are panoramic views of the city even if you don't make it to the peak, and it also has a small **Museo de la Fauna** (Tues–Sun 10am–6pm; charge, discount for children) with a reptile house and aviary. Finally, on the edge of the city on the old road to Coatepec, about 3.5km from the centre, the **Jardín Botánico Francisco Clavijero** (charge) boasts an impressive collection of plants native to the state.

in Mexico City. Remarkable in both scope and quality, it makes for a wonderful introduction to the various pre-Hispanic cultures of the Gulf coast. The vast building itself is also magnificent, flowing down the hillside in a series of concrete and marble steps. Start your visit at the top of the hill, where the first halls deal with the **Olmecs**. There are several of the celebrated colossal stone heads, a vast array of other statuary and some beautiful masks; among the most impressive is the Señor de las Limas, a greenstone sculpture of a priest holding a sleeping or dead baby. Later cultures are represented mainly through their pottery – lifelike human and animal figurines especially – and there are also displays on the architecture of the major sites, including part of a reconstructed temple. Finally, with the **Totonac** and **Huastec** culture come more giant stone statues. Labels are in Spanish only, though audioguides are available in both Spanish and English.

ARRIVAL AND DEPARTURE — XALAPA

By plane El Lencero Airport sits 16km southeast of the city centre but, at the time of writing, was not operating any commercial flights.

By bus Xalapa's huge modern bus station is a couple of kilometres east of the centre on 20 de Noviembre; there are extensive facilities including ATMs, internet café and left luggage. You can get to the centre by regulated taxi, booked from a booth in the station; to catch a bus or *combi*, walk down to 20 de Noviembre and look for those marked "Centro"; going to the bus station, they're marked "CAXA" (Central de Autobuses de Xalapa).

Destinations Catemaco (3 daily; 5–6hr); Coatzacoalcos (13 daily; 6hr 30min); Mexico City (frequently, including some direct airport services; 4hr 30min); Orizaba (7 daily; 4hr); Papantla (8 daily; 4hr 20min); Veracruz (very frequently; 1hr 45min).

INFORMATION AND TOURS

Tourist information Xalapa's tourist office occupies a kiosk under the arches of the Palacio Municipal (Mon–Fri 10am–3pm; 228 820 2714).

Veraventuras Santos Degollado 81; 228 818 9779. Rafting, zipwires, abseiling, paint-balling and more from their base at the *Hotel Carrizal* near Jalcomulco. A rafting half-day trip can be arranged here, as can a 3-day, 2-night activity package. See also Jalcomulco (see page 399) and Tlapacoyan (see page 400).

ACCOMMODATION — SEE MAP PAGE 395

Casa Regia Hidalgo 12 at Canovas; 228 812 0591. This brightly decorated and friendly place has peaceful, cosy rooms with TV, constant hot water and a breakfast area. Wi-fi throughout the property. M$$

Clara Luna Ávila Camacho 42; www.hotelclaralunaxalapa.com. Comfortable four-star, international-style hotel close to the centre. Spacious rooms have a/c, wi-fi and cable TV, and there's a generous buffet breakfast included. M$$$

Hostal de la Niebla Zamora 24; http://pradodelrio.com. Excellent, immaculate hostel with internet, simple breakfasts of bread and coffee (included), TV in the common room, computer access and wi-fi, hot water and large lockers. M$

Limón Revolución 8; 228 817 2204. One of the best budget options, close to the centre, with small, very clean rooms around a courtyard embellished with fabulous ornate tiling. Rooms have TV and 24hr hot water, and there's a laundry. M$

Mesón del Alférez Sebastian Camacho 2 at Zaragoza; http://pradodelrio.com. Beautiful colonial house once belonging to Alférez Real de Xalapa, the last Spanish viceroy of Veracruz. Each room is unique and charmingly decorated, though perhaps not great value given the simple facilities (no a/c). There's an excellent restaurant (*La Candela*) with some vegetarian options. M$$

Posada del Cafeto Canovas 8; http://pradodelrio.com. Under the same management as the *Mesón del Alférez*. Rooms are set around a pretty courtyard garden; some have balconies, a couple with kitchen, all have a coffee-maker (with lovely local coffee), TV and wi-fi. As is often the case in these old buildings, rooms can be noisy. The on-site café serves breakfast (included) and has books to read. M$$

★ **Posada La Mariquinta** Alfaro 12; www.lamariquinta.com. Meticulously restored colonial hacienda with attractive, modern rooms – starting to show their age slightly – with cable TV and phone. There's a tranquil inner garden, a common room with a vast collection of books, and an English- and French-speaking owner. For extended stays, apartments are available in an adjoining concrete-and-wood extension, a fine example of modern Mexican architecture. M$$

6

EATING

SEE MAP PAGE 395

Good **food** is abundant in Xalapa. The city is home to the **jalapeño pepper**, and there's also excellent local **coffee** (mostly grown in nearby Coatepec; see page 398), consumed in great quantities in the city's numerous **traditional cafés**. Many of these can be found along Nicolás Bravo or its continuation Primo Verdad, and there are plenty of appetizing **restaurants** and good jugo and torta places in the couple of blocks between here and the zócalo.

★ **Café Cali** Callejón del Diamante 9; 228 818 1339. Justifiably popular coffee and lunch-time spot on a bustling bohemian alley. Copious and very cheap fast-food dishes with a (mostly) healthy twist. M$$

Café Chiquito Nicolás Bravo 3; http://cafechiquito.com. One of the largest and most distinctive cafés, with wooden tables set around a lovely colonial courtyard. There's a reasonable menu, mostly of sandwiches and *antojitos*, plus excellent breakfasts and *comidas*, along with the usual range of coffees and teas. M$$

★ **Café Lindo** Primo Verdad 21; 228 841 9166. Traditional café with mouthwatering sandwiches in addition to Mexican-style snack foods and buffet breakfasts and *comidas*. Lively, primarily young clientele in the large, dimly lit dining and drinking area; live music every evening from 9pm. M$$

La Casona del Beaterio Zaragoza 20; 228 818 2119, https://facebook.com/lacasonadelbeaterio. Hundreds of old photographs adorn the walls at one of the city's best restaurants, which serves up fine, reasonably priced Mexican food and breakfasts. Bow-tied waiters scurry around a series of small courtyards. Live traditional music Wed–Sat evenings. M$$

Don Justo South side of Parque Juárez, by the Agorá; http://cafeteriasdonjusto.com. The terrace, enjoying fabulous views south from the zócalo, is arguably the main attraction of this popular and busy meeting place, open since 1891. It's also an excellent modern-style café, with smoothies, frappucinos and coffees as well as panini, crêpes and cakes. M$

La Parroquia Zaragoza 18; 228 817 4436. Venerable fifty-year-old establishment best known for its breakfast menus, but whose unpretentious and busy dining room is also open for lunch and dinner. M$$

La Parroquia de Veracruz Enríquez s/n, beside the Palacio Municipal; http://laparroquiadeveracruz.com. This branch of the famous Veracruz café has overtaken its local namesake as the smartest place to be seen downtown. A few noisy tables outside face the zócalo, but most are in the chilly, glassed-in interior; *café lechero*, breakfast and a full menu. Expect to queue for breakfast at the weekend. M$$

Postodoro Primo Verdad 11; http://postodoro.com. The home-made pasta and delicious pizzas are the things to go for at this welcoming Italian restaurant, with tables in a tranquil courtyard. Good wine list too. M$$

DRINKING AND NIGHTLIFE

SEE MAP PAGE 395

Xalapa is a city of great creative energy. A number of **bars** offer live music and occasional poetry readings or theatre; downtown the place to be is the Callejón de la Perla, whose bars are packed every night. Louder **clubs** and bars tend to be further out. The giant Plaza las Américas mall on the edge of town has a good multiplex **cinema**.

La Condesa Callejón González Aparicio 4A (Callejón de la Perla); 228 298 9110. Bar-club that epitomizes the busy alleyway – a good place for an early evening beer, getting increasingly lively as the evening wears on and the dancefloor fills to house and dance music.

Cubanias Callejón González Aparicio 2 (Callejón de la

Perla); 228 211 1641. Next door to La Condesa, this Cuban-themed restaurant and bar is a great late-night spot for music, mojitos and Cuba libres.

Dejavu Ávila Camacho 33; 228 843 9060, https://facebook.com/dejavuoldies. A popular bar which fills the floor at weekends with classic rock, pop and funk from the Seventies to the Noughties – a fun, if cheesy, place to start a night out. Expect two-for-one drinks deals and football on the big screens.

Teatro del Estado Ávila Camacho at Ignacio de la Llave; 228 812 3836, https://facebook.com/TeatroDelEstado. For a more relaxed evening, the State Theatre hosts regular concerts by the Orquesta Sinfónica de Xalapa, dance performances by the Ballet Folklorico de Veracruz and plenty of other theatrical and musical events.

DIRECTORY

Laundry Try Diamante at Rojano 21-A (charge per kg), a block north of the post office.

Money and exchange There are plenty of banks and ATMs around the centre, including HSBC on Parque Juárez and Bancomer on Rafael Lucio.

Post office The main post office is on Zamora, at Diego Leño. This is also where you'll find a Western Union office.

Coatepec

COATEPEC, less than 15km south of Xalapa, is a very popular weekend outing for folk from the city. An enjoyable little town with a beautiful setting and fine colonial architecture, it's the source of much of the coffee consumed in Xalapa – the aroma is unmistakeable as you drive in – and this, along with fresh trout (*trucha*) from the river, is the speciality at the many local cafés and restaurants. In May, the **Feria del Café** celebrates the local crop, and there's also a big celebration in September to honour the local patron saint, San Jeronimo. In addition to restaurants, you'll find a number of high-class **artesanía** outlets around the zócalo, especially in the Plazuela El Zaguán, next to Finca Andrade. It's also worth wandering into the **Casa de Cultura**, on Campillo at the corner of Cuauhtemoc, a block from the zócalo, more for the beautiful, crumbling colonial building it occupies than the occasional art or photography exhibitions housed therein.

ARRIVAL AND INFORMATION — COATEPEC

By bus Buses run regularly from Xalapa to Coatepec. Most frequent are the local services from the Terminal Excelsiór (also known as Los Sauces, after the market next to it), 2km southwest of the zócalo, though there are also second-class buses from the main terminal.

Tourist information The tourist office is in the Palacio Municipal, on the zócalo (daily 9am–2pm & 4–7pm, http://somoscoatepec.com).

ACCOMMODATION AND EATING

Thanks to all the visitors from the city, there are a number of very comfortable hotels and excellent places to eat here. Locals like the riverside **restaurants** alongside the old road from Xalapa, on the edge of town.

Angela Carolina Bravo 108; 228 816 3863. It's no looker, but this whitewashed low-rise, a 15min walk southeast of the zócalo, offers basic, clean (if old-fashioned) rooms with TV, a/c and wi-fi. The walls are paper-thin – bring earplugs. M$

★**Casa Bonilla** Juárez 20, at Cuauhtémoc; http://casabonilla.mx. Charming, traditional seafood restaurant that centres on a plant-lined courtyard filled with bright, tropical songbirds. The adjacent bar is wonderfully atmospheric, with cheeky artwork and saloon doors at the entrance. In business for more than seventy years. M$$

★**Casa Real** Zamora 58; 228 816 6317. Very pretty, expansive property, with stylish, whitewashed buildings encircling a tiled courtyard. Continental breakfast included, and there's an on-site spa that has astonishing mountain views. M$$$

Finca Andrade Lerdo 5 on the zocalo; 228 816 4887. An excellent, elegant restaurant which also serves good *cafe lechero* and *pan dulce*. There's also live music in the evenings here, Fri to Sun. M$$

Mesón del Alférez Jiménez del Campillo 47, five blocks east of the plaza; http://pradodelrio.com. Imaginatively restored colonial building with rooms off a pretty internal courtyard; some have beds on a raised gallery. Fan only – a/c is rarely needed here – and wi-fi. M$$$

Posada Coatepec Hidalgo 9, cnr Aldama; 228 816 0544. The best-known hotel in Coatepec is still one of the most luxurious, if not quite as much as in its heyday. Standard rooms are bright and cheerful, but there are also vast suites, a pool and garden. Wi-fi doesn't extend to all the rooms, but they have a/c. M$$$

El Tío Yeyo Santos Degollado 4, a block south of the plaza; http://restauranteltioyeyo.com.mx. The best place in the centre to sample the local trout, served in at least thirty different guises including with tamarind and prawn or in an almond sauce. Good steaks too and hand-made tortillas. M$$$

6

Xico

XICO is a small colonial town, 9km southwest of Coatepec, whose big attraction is the spectacular **Cascada de Texolo**, to which you'll see signs on the edge of town as you enter. The falls lie 2km along a rough, cobbled road (just about driveable, or forty minutes' hot walk); beside the road along the way, coffee is grown in the shade of banana palms. If you're scared of heights, this may not be for you, as you emerge right at the top of the main 80m cascade, with only some hopelessly inadequate-looking railing to prevent you plunging over. It's a beautiful spot, though, with lots of wildlife and a couple of restaurants: the *mirador* on the far side has the best view, but it's a stiff climb up. Five minutes' walk upstream is the **Cascada la Monja**, a far smaller fall, but one where you can get very close to the bottom, and enjoy the cooling spray. Locals swim here, but it's not recommended. As a popular outing from Xalapa, Xico has a number of unexpectedly fancy restaurants. These are mostly clustered in the lower half of town towards the falls, particularly along Hidalgo, half a dozen blocks downhill from the main plaza.

ARRIVAL AND INFORMATION — XICO

By bus Local buses run frequently from Coatepec to Xico, as well as from the Xalapa bus terminals.

Tourist information Staff inside the Casa de Cultura, at Hidalgo 76, are very helpful and can provide plenty of information on Xico and places to stay in the surrounding countryside, although not much English is spoken here.

EATING

El Campanario Zaragoza 96, cnr Matamoros, near the tiny Capilla de la Santa Cruz; 228 813 0675. The food in Xico is worth making a special trip for, and *El Campanario* is arguably the best place to sample it. Local fruit, nuts and vegetables feature strongly: delicious *mole de Xico* is sweeter and fruitier than classic *mole poblano*, while *sopa xonequi* is a soup made with black beans and corn dumplings, flavoured with *xonequi*, a pungent green leaf. M$$$

Museo Ex Hacienda El Lencero

Carretera Xalapa–Veracruz Km 10 • Charge, discount for children under 10 • If you don't have transport of your own, it's best approached by taxi (15–20min from Xalapa)

The **Museo Ex Hacienda El Lencero** is a colonial hacienda that was originally granted to one of Cortes' companions, Juan Lencero, and later became the property of controversial general and president Antonio López de Santa Anna (see page 789). It has been restored and furnished in its full nineteenth-century splendour, and both the grounds, with plenty of gentle walks, and the surrounding countryside are stunning. An inviting, formal restaurant occupies part of the main building.

Jalcomulco

JALCOMULCO is the prime spot in Veracruz for **whitewater rafting** and other adventure sports including kayaking, canyoning, rappelling, zipwires, horseriding and mountain biking. The village – gradually becoming something of an eco-resort, though still catatonic midweek – is about 25km southeast of Coatepec, on the banks of the Río Antigua (also known as the Río de los Pescados). Coming from Xalapa, you descend from the highlands into a steamy and impressive valley where the river runs through a series of rapids of varying intensity.

ADVENTURE TOURISM IN JALCOMULCO

A dozen or more adventure tour **operators** have bases in and around Jalcomulco, the majority of them on the riverbank some way out of town. Most offer all-inclusive packages including accommodation, meals and activities, so there's a lot to be said for booking in advance. These are some of the best:

Aldea Ecoturismo Riverside about 3km out of town; 279 832 3751, https://facebook.com/AldeaEcoturismo. Accommodation is in villas sleeping four to six, and there's the usual broad range of activities, plus pool and *temazcal*. M$$

★ **Jalco Expediciones** 20 De Noviembre 17; http://jalcoexpediciones.com.mx. A friendly and professional operation with a base in town so you don't necessarily have to book ahead. Wide range of activities from rafting to zipwires to paintballing; activity packages vary widely in price. Accommodation arranged in local hotels.

Mexico Verde Riverside about 4km out of town; http://mexicoverde.com. One of the longest-established operators, whose "eco-resort" offers accommodation in safari-style luxury tents, a *temazcal* and spa. Three day, two night packages available. M$$$

Rodavento Natural Camino a Santa Maria #5, a five-minute walk south of the town centre; www.picocanoarodavento.com. Stylish resort combining the usual offerings – rafting, mountain biking, rappelling, and *temazcal* – with accommodation in palapa-thatched cottages set in peaceful gardens. M$$$

Viajes de Aventura Zaragoza 54, on the plaza; 22 832 2730. Local agent who can arrange everything from zipwires to inclusive rafting packages, with a choice of camping, hostel or hotel accommodation. Visit for a day's activities or stay overnight. M$$$

ARRIVAL AND DEPARTURE — JALCOMULCO

By bus Local buses run at least hourly throughout the day between Coatepec and Jalcomulco, terminating on the plaza, and there are half a dozen or so direct connections with Cardel and Xalapa.

ACCOMMODATION AND EATING

Los Alcatraces Morelos s/n, off the main road into town; http://bit.ly/LosAlcatraces. Pleasant, yellow-painted, colonial-style hotel whose rooms, all with a/c and wi-fi, are arranged around a courtyard with a small pool. M$

Los Cachanes Far bank of the river, between the two bridges; https://facebook.com/LosCachanes. With a sandy (occasionally muddy) outdoor area right beside the river, *Los Cachanes* serves up great fish and seafood, including a mean *chilpachole*. M$$$

Nachita II Madero s/n, on the river by the pedestrian puente colgante (suspension bridge); 279 832 3519. Enjoying a prime riverbank location, this is the best of several restaurants with terraces overhanging the water. Good, home-cooked Mexican food. M$$

La Pizzeria 20 de Noviembre 17, close to the road bridge; http://jalcoexpediciones.com.mx. Run by the same people as Jalco Expediciones, this appropriately named restaurant has a great atmosphere, and a simple weekday menu of pizzas, baguettes, garlic bread and fries; at weekends the menu expands to include pasta and Italian specials. M$$

Tlapacoyan

TLAPACOYAN, some 70km north of Xalapa en route to the coast at Nautla, is another centre for rafting and river adventures, bounded to the south by the Río Bobos and to the north by the Río María de la Torre. A sizeable but unspoilt and friendly place, and a centre of citrus-fruit production, Tlapacoyan is surrounded by forested hills and pre-Columbian ruins, most important of which are the massive, little-known sites of **Filo Bobos**.

ARRIVAL AND DEPARTURE — TLAPACOYAN

By bus Tlapacoyan has regular direct connections with Xalapa, Puebla and Mexico City; for first-class services to Veracruz or Papantla, you may have to change in nearby Martínez de la Torre. First- and second-class terminals are opposite each other, and pretty central, at Zaragoza and Ferrer: walk uphill on Ferrer then right at 5 de Mayo for the zócalo.

ACCOMMODATION AND EATING

Las Acamayas 5 de Mayo, cnr Heroes de Tlapacoyan, on the plaza; 225 315 0291. The fanciest restaurant in town by far, with formal service but reasonable prices and good food. The meat dishes are tasty here but the speciality is seafood, especially giant prawns, served in a variety of guises. M$$

Posada Oliver Cuauhtemoc 400 on the plaza; https://facebook.com/HOTELPOSADAO. Lovingly cared-for courtyard hotel, beautifully decorated and full of greenery, whose simple but comfortable rooms are the best in town and more importantly have good a/c – the same management also run the nearby *Plaza*, slightly cheaper, without a/c. M$$

Filo Bobos

Work is ongoing at the **Filo Bobos** archeological project, some 15km from Tlapacoyan, where you can explore two of the several pre-Hispanic sites identified along the Río Bobos valley, **El Cuajilote** and **Vega de la Peña**. Both are worth visiting as much for the beauty of their locations, the birdlife and the serenity, as for the ruins themselves. No one yet knows for certain who occupied the Filo Bobos sites. They are increasingly described as Totonac, in keeping with the style of the sculptures found there, although signs of a fertility cult suggest a **Huastec** influence, and the earliest buildings at El Cuajilote, which may date as far back as 1000 BC, are decidedly Olmec. Archeologists speculate that Filo Bobos was the centre of an as yet unknown Mesoamerican civilization, which provided an important trade link between the Gulf coast, its environs and the central valleys.

El Cuajilote

Charge • It's best to arrange a hiking or river tour from one of the camps at El Encanto (best confirmed in advance, see below) or you cantake a local bus towards Santiago/Plan de Arroyos and walk the final 5km; signed for drivers from Tlapacoyan – 15km followed by 5km on dirt roads

El Cuajilote is an impressive site, with platforms and pyramids arranged north–south around a long, rectangular plaza measuring 31,500 square metres. A spring-fed brook snakes across the middle of the plaza. The surrounding buildings (mostly dating from 600–900 AD) appear to be a series of temples dedicated to a fertility cult: a monolithic, phallic stele more than 2m tall and oriented to the stars stands in the middle of the plaza, and at Shrine A4 more than 1500 other phallic figurines were found, though none remains at the site today.

Vega de la Peña

Charge • Arrange a hiking or river tour from one of the camps at El Encanto (best confirmed in advance, see below) or drive or take a local bus to Encanto and walk the final 4km; get directions at the site for the riverside trek to Cuajilote, another 5km

Vega de la Peña covers some eight thousand square metres. There's little doubt that structures buried beneath the lush greenery here extend beyond that; some archeologists believe they may have stretched as far as Nautla. If true, this would radically alter the accepted conception of Mexican and Mesoamerican pre-Columbian history, placing the central Gulf coast in a far more prominent position than previously thought. What you see here today are small buildings, with more palatial dwellings than at El Cuajilote, and a small ball-court.

RAFTING AT TLAPACOYAN

Most of the rafting takes place near **El Encanto**, about 5km from the centre of Tlapacoyan off the Nautla road. There's a waterfall here, and spectacular river views enjoyed by a cluster of rafting camps. Good ones to try are:

Aventurec http://aventurec.com. Lots of activities including horseriding and kayaking as well as rafting. Accommodation is in large cabins, hostel dorms or camping, and can be purchased as part of a one-night package. M$$$

Filobobos Camp http://filobobos.com.mx. The largest of the operators, with a restaurant and pool plus a variety of activities in addition to rafting, including a zipwire, hiking and mountain-biking. Accommodation is in basic wooden cabins or camping. M$$

Veracruz to Papantla

Immediately north of Veracruz lie the oldest Spanish settlements in Mexico, and the sites of the Indigenous towns which became Cortes' first allies. A short stretch of toll highway takes you as far as **CARDEL**, a busy little town and handy place to change buses or visit the bank, at the junction of the coastal highway and the road up to Xalapa. La Antigua lies 2km off this road. Beyond Cardel there's very little to stop for in the long coastal stretch (about 4hr on the bus) to Papantla. At **NAUTLA**, 153km from Veracruz, you pass the largest town en route to Papantla, surrounded by coconut groves, at the heart of the so-called "**Costa Esmeralda**". There are hotels, some of them pretty fancy, trailer parks and campsites all the way up here, but most are just metres from the highway, which runs close to the shore. The grey sand is frequently desolate and windswept, and it's not really a place you'd want to stay.

La Antigua

For all its antiquity, there's not a great deal to see in **LA ANTIGUA**, site of the second Spanish settlement in Mexico (it's often incorrectly described as the first – Villa Rica is further north, see opposite). It is, however, a beautiful, cobbled tropical village, just 20km north of Veracruz on the banks of the **Río La Antigua** (or Río Huitzilapan). At weekends it makes a popular excursion for Veracruzanos, who picnic by the river and swim or take boat rides.

In the semi-ruined centre of the village stand some of the oldest surviving Spanish buildings in the country: on the plaza are the **Edificio del Cabildo**, built in 1523, which housed the first *ayuntamiento* (local government) established in Mexico, and the **Casa de Cortés**, a fairly crude stone construction, which, despite the name, was probably never lived in by Cortés and is now an atmoshperic ruin overrun by the ancient roots of strangler figs. Entry is free, and you'll likely find some kids hanging around willing to give you a tour (in Spanish) for a small donation (around M$50). Nearby is the tranquil **Ermita del Rosario**, the first Christian church built in New Spain, which also dates from the early sixteenth century, though it's been altered and restored since.

On the riverbank stands a grand old tree – the **Ceiba de la Noche Feliz** – to which it is claimed that Cortés moored his ships. A pedestrian suspension bridge crosses the river near the tree, and on this stretch of the bank are *lanchas* offering river trips and a little row of restaurants with waterside terraces, the pick of which is *Las Maravillas*.

ARRIVAL AND DEPARTURE — LA ANTIGUA

By bus Although La Antigua does see an occasional bus, you'll find it much easier and quicker to take one heading for Cardel (about every 30min from the second-class terminal in Veracruz) and get off at the tollbooths. From here it's a 20min walk up a signed road.

Cempoala

12km north of Cardel, 4km west of Hwy-180 • Charge

The first native city visited by the conquistadors, **CEMPOALA** (or Zempoala) quickly became their ally against the Aztecs. When Cortés arrived, the city, under the leadership of Chicomacatl (dubbed the "Fat Chief" by conquistador Bernal Díaz del Castillo), had been under Aztec control for little over fifty years. Its people, who numbered some 25,000 to 30,000, had already rebelled more than once and were only too happy to stop paying their tribute once they believed that the Spaniards could protect them. This they did, although the inhabitants must have begun to have second thoughts when Cortés ordered the idols of their deities to be smashed and replaced with crosses and Christian altars.

The site

The ruins, though nowhere near as dramatic as El Tajín further north, make for an absorbing detour and take no more than an hour to explore. They date mostly from the Aztec period, and although the buildings have lost their decorative facings and thatched sanctuaries, they constitute one of the most complete surviving examples of an Aztec ceremonial centre – albeit in an atypical tropical setting and on a very small scale. The double-stairway pyramids, grouped around a central plaza, must have resembled miniature versions of those at Tenochtitlán. Apart from the main, cleared site, consisting of the **Templo Mayor**, the Gran Pirámide and the Templo de las Chimeneas, there are lesser ruins scattered throughout, and around, the modern village. Look out in particular for the circular **Templo de Ehecatl** (Temple of the Wind God) on the opposite side of the main road through the village.

ARRIVAL AND DEPARTURE **CEMPOALA**

By bus There are a few direct second-class services between Cempoala and Veracruz, but it's generally quicker to go to Cardel and change there: local buses marked "Zempoala" leave from the bus station. Cardel has very frequent first-class services from both Veracruz and Xalapa, and even more second class.

By taxi or tour From Cardel there are plenty of green-and-white taxis to the site; travel agencies in Veracruz organize day trips.

Villa Rica

Around 15km north of Cardel, the sleepy village of **Villa Rica** was the first permanent Spanish settlement in New Spain. Established by Cortés in 1519, it was abandoned in 1524 for La Antigua, and only foundations remain today, close to the normally deserted beach.

Quiahuitzlán

Charge

The ruins of **Quiahuitzlán** lie some 3km inland of Villa Rica, beneath an extraordinary looming basalt outcrop known as the Peñon de Bernal. Here the first alliance between the Totonacs and the conquistadors was made, and it's an exceptionally atmospheric and little-visited spot: utterly tranquil and with incredible views over the coast. The town was built on a series of hillside terraces – most striking today are over seventy small stone tombs, in the form of miniature temples, scattered throughout the site.

Tecolutla

A growing resort that marks the northern end of the Costa Esmeralda, where the highway finally turns inland, **TECOLUTLA** is pretty much the closest beach to Mexico City – easily accessed via the toll highway to Tuxpán – and thus can be very busy on weekends and Mexican holidays, especially Semana Santa. The rest of the time it's an enjoyably laid-back beach town with bargain accommodation, and a possible alternative base for Papantla and El Tajín. With the coast on one side and the broad Río Tecolutla on the other, the town occupies a point at the river mouth, with a lighthouse at its furthest extremity – the older and more attractive development is at this end of town.

Campamento Tortuga

Beach near the end of Niños Heroes, close to the ADO • Free, donation or purchase required to release turtles • http://vidamilenaria.mx

At the **Campamento Tortuga**, right in the middle of the beach, Fernando Manzano has been rescuing and releasing sea turtles for almost forty years. It has been a hugely successful project, and releasing the baby turtles to find their way to the sea is both

6

EL BAILE DE LOS NEGRITOS

Popular at festivals across the state of Veracruz, the frenetic **Baile de los Negritos** is a Totonac dance dating back to colonial times, when African slaves were imported to work on local plantations, often living and labouring alongside *indígenas*. Stories abound as to the origin of the dance: the most popular version has it that a female slave and her child escaped from a plantation near Papantla and lived in the dense jungle with local Indigenous groups. After her child was poisoned by a snake bite, the mother, using African folk medicine, danced herself into a trance. The Totonacs around her found the spectacle highly amusing and, it is said, began to copy her in a spirit of mockery.

Good opportunities to see the dance are **Corpus Christi** (late May–June) in Papantla, or in Tlapacoyan (see page 400) at the **Feast of Santiago** (July 25) or the **Day of the Assumption** (Aug 15); it's frequently performed on a smaller scale at other village festivals in the area.

moving and fun. At the camp there are displays about turtles, and you can see the hatchlings and recovering adults. Turtles are released daily between May and November (7.30am–9am).

ARRIVAL AND DEPARTURE — TECOLUTLA

By bus There are eight daily first-class buses from Tecolutla to Papantla (1hr) and Mexico City (6hr) and very frequent second-class services to Papantla via Gutiérrez Zamora, the closest point on the highway, also accessible by local bus. Change at Gutiérrez Zamora for first-class services to Veracruz (3hr 30min), Tuxpán (2hr 30min) and elsewhere.

ACCOMMODATION AND EATING

Good seafood **restaurants** line both the beach and the riverfront (where many also offer river trips, for a flat fee per boat), while there's a concentration of budget hotels around the bus station. Beachfront properties are slightly more expensive, though out of season bargains are on offer.

Dora Emilia Hidalgo 45; 766 846 0185. A courtyard hotel with an exuberant paint-job, on the main street just beyond the plaza, the *Dora Emilia* has a small pool and simple, a/c rooms. M$

Posada La Casa de las Hamacas Rafael Murillo Vidal s/n, close to the ADO; 766 106 6406. Friendly budget place close to the Campamento Tortuga. Rooms are tiny but clean, with fans and comfy beds, and there's free wi-fi in the lobby and a small pool. M$$

Tecolutla Matamoros s/n; 766 846 0262. The original hotel here, right at the far end of town on the point by the *faro*, with slightly faded, old-fashioned rooms (not all a/c) but a fabulous position, direct access to the beach and good facilities including a large pool. M$$

Papantla and around

PAPANTLA, 227km from Veracruz, is the most attractive town on the route north, straggling over an outcrop of low, jungly hills. Even so, if it weren't for the proximity of El Tajín, few people would consider staying here. In addition to being one of the most important centres of the Mexican **vanilla** industry – the sweet, sticky odour frequently hangs over the place, and vanilla products are on sale everywhere – Papantla is also one of the last surviving strongholds of **Totonac** culture. You might see Totonacs, barefoot and in loose white robes in the markets, and can regularly witness the amazing dance-spectacle of the **Voladores de Papantla** (see opposite).

On the edge of the zócalo, the huge **Mural Cultural Totonaca** depicts the clash between modern and traditional life, with sculpted images of Totonac gods, myths and the pyramids of El Tajín alongside oil rigs and farm machinery (the tourist office has a leaflet describing this in detail). It's best appreciated in the evening, when floodlights pick out the relief and the **zócalo** itself is wildly animated, especially at weekends, when there's often live music and dancing. On the terrace above the mural stands the solid

Catedral de la Asunción, beyond which you can climb to the **Volador monument**, a giant statue affording tremendous views of the town.

ARRIVAL AND INFORMATION PAPANTLA

By bus First-class buses use the ADO terminal on Juárez, just off the main road through town; walk uphill and you'll soon be able to see the cathedral above you, about a 10min walk (or a short taxi ride). The second-class terminal is much closer to the centre on 20 de Noviembre – walk steeply uphill past the Mercado Hidalgo to reach the zócalo.

Destinations First-class services to: Mexico City (9 daily; 4–6hr); Tuxpán (10 daily; 2hr); Veracruz (5 daily; 4hr); Xalapa (9 daily; 4hr). Second class to all the above and to Poza Rica (30min); Tecolutla (1hr); and Tlapacoyan (3hr).

Tourist information There's a small tourist kiosk (Mon–Fri 9am–5pm; https://www.zonaturistica.com/en/destinations/veracruz/papantla) in the *Ayuntamiento* at Reforma 100 on the zócalo. You'll find plenty of information here, and usually an English-speaker.

6

ACCOMMODATION

Hotel Pulido Enríquez 201; 784 842 0036 This small and locally owned hotel isn't anything special but the rooms are clean, there's no extra charge for a/c and the location is near enough to everything that matters. M$$

Tajín Nuñez 104 beside the cathedral; http://hoteltajin.mx. The town's top hotel, which isn't saying a great deal. Rooms are rather musty, but clean; some have good views across the city, while others face only the corridor. There's a small pool which clients of the café can also use, and wi-fi. M$$

EATING

Papantla has an enticing spread of **local specialities** to sample, chief of which is *sacahuil* or *zacahuilt*, a giant tamale of chicken and beans, which you'll find in the markets. These are also the place to head for cheap eats: on the whole, the restaurants aren't great. There are two markets right by the zócalo: Mercado Hidalgo at the top of 20 de Noviembre, and Mercado Juárez, on the opposite (uphill) side of the *Ayuntamiento* at Reforma and 16 de Septiembre; they're basically working markets, but you can stock up here on small bottles of locally produced vanilla, and both have food stalls.

Café Catedral Below the cathedral at Nuñez and Curato, by Hotel Tajín; 784 842 5317. An ultra-traditional café serving little other than coffee and *pan dulce* (also available to take away) at old-fashioned wooden tables. M$

Café Gourmet Volantini Reforma alongside the Ayuntiamento; 784 842 6817. Upstairs, with a balcony in a corner of the zócalo, this modern-style café serves proper cappuccinos and a range of coffees and iced drinks to mainly youthful locals. M$

THE VOLADORES DE PAPANTLA

Although the full significance of the dance of the **voladores** has been lost over time, it has survived much as the earliest chroniclers reported it, largely because the Spanish thought of it as a sport rather than a pagan rite. It involves five men: a leader who provides acoustics on flute and drum, and four performers. They represent the five earthly directions – the four cardinal points and straight up, from earth to heaven. After a few preliminaries, the five climb to a small platform atop a pole, where the leader resumes playing and directs prayers for the fertility of the land in every direction. Meanwhile, the dancers tie ropes, coiled tightly around the top of the pole, to their waists and at a signal fling themselves headfirst into space. As they spiral down in increasing circles the leader continues to play, and to spin, on his platform, until the four hit the ground (hopefully landing on their feet, having righted themselves at the last minute). In all, they make thirteen revolutions each, symbolizing the 52-year cycle of the **Aztec calendar**.

At **Papantla** (performances in front of the cathedral Fri, Sat & Sun 10.30am–7pm) and **El Tajín** (regular performances outside the entrance to the ruins starting at 11am), the ritual has become primarily a tourist spectacle, as the permanent metal poles attest. In local villages there is still more ceremony attached, particularly in the selection of a sufficiently tall tree to act as the pole, and its temporary erection in the place where the dance is to be performed. Note that performances are nominally free, though if you catch one of the regular shows in Papantla or El Tajín you'll be expected to make a donation.

Plaza Pardo Enríquez 105 on the zocalo; 784 842 0059. The most popular restaurant in town is also the best. *Plaza Pardo* has an unbeatable position with a first-floor terrace overlooking the zócalo, and great food to match. A great place for breakfast or an evening beer. M$$

Sorrento Enríquez 105, on the zocalo; 784 842 0067. The view and ambience at the street-level *Sorrento* are less attractive than at its neighbour, the *Plaza Pardo*, but the food is considerably tastier and the prices marginally lower. Breakfast, daily *comida*, a wide choice of *antojitos* and meat and fish dishes available. M$$

DIRECTORY

Banks and exchange All of the major banks, where you can change travellers' cheques and find ATM machines, are on Enríquez, just off the zócalo.

El Tajín

Charge

With numerous substantial structures spread over an extensive site, **EL TAJÍN** is by far the most important and impressive archeological site on the Gulf coast. It divides broadly into two areas: **Tajín Viejo**, which centres on the amazing Pirámide de los Nichos, and **Tajín Chico**, a group of official residential buildings belonging to the city's ruling class built on an artificial terrace. The site **museum**, by the entrance, has a model of the site worth examining before you venture in, along with a collection of the more delicate stonework salvaged from the ruins, notably murals and columns, bits of pottery and statues – displays are primarily labelled in Spanish, but there are a few English explanations.

Brief history

The principal architecture at El Tajín dates from the Classic period (300–900 AD); the city declined in the early Post-Classic (900–1100 AD), and by the time of the Conquest it had been forgotten. Our knowledge comes entirely from archeological enquiries made since the accidental discovery of the site in 1785 – El Tajín remains one of the most enigmatic of all of Mexico's ancient cities. No one even knows who built it: some claim it was the Huastecs, others the Totonacs. Most archeologists prefer not to speculate too wildly, instead calling the civilization **Classic Veracruz**. You'll notice many

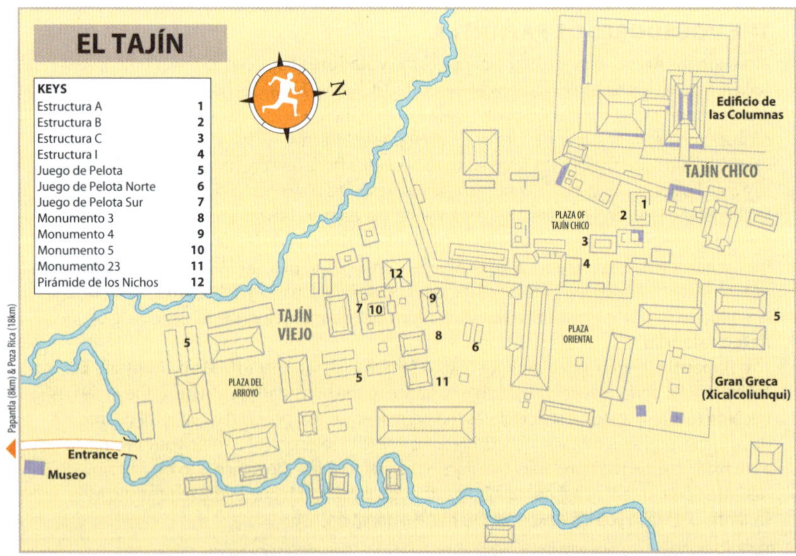

of its hallmarks at El Tajín, including niches in temple walls and complex ornamental motifs known as "scrolls". Classic Veracruz influence was widespread, and is strongly felt at Teotihuacán (see page 142), to the extent that some believe that city may have been built by Veracruzanos.

Tajín Viejo

From the site entrance, a track leads through a small group of buildings to the **Plaza del Arroyo**, the city marketplace, and into the heart of **Tajín Viejo**. Around the plaza are several **ball-courts**, the most prominent of which is the South Court, or **Juego de Pelota Sur**; it looks like a wide avenue between two small pyramids. Seventeen such courts are known here, and more possibly lie unexcavated; it's thought that the game took on a greater importance here than at any other known site. The superb bas-relief sculptures that cover the walls of the South Court include portrayals of a decapitated player, and another about to be stabbed with a ritual knife by fellow players, with Death waiting to his left. Such bas-reliefs are a constant feature of the site, adorning many of the ball-courts and buildings, with more stacked in the museum.

The unique **Pirámide de los Nichos**, one of the last to be built here, is the most famous building at El Tajín, and indeed one of the most remarkable of all Mexican ruins. It rises to a height of about 20m in six receding tiers, each face punctuated with regularly spaced niches; up the front a steep stairway climbs to a platform on which the temple originally stood. If you tally up the niches, including those hidden by the stairs and those, partly destroyed, around the base of the temple, there are 365 in all. Their exact purpose is unknown, but clearly they were more than mere decoration: theories include each holding some offering or sacrifice, one for each day of the year, or that they symbolized caves to the underworld – the dwellings of the earth god. Originally they were painted black, with the pyramid in red, to enhance the impression of depth. Niches are also present on other buildings at the site, some bearing the attributes of **Quetzalcoatl**, the plumed serpent, El Tajín's most depicted god.

Around the plaza in front of the pyramid stand all the other important buildings of Tajín Viejo. Opposite is **Monumento 3**, a similar pyramid without niches, and behind it **Monumento 23**, a strange steep-sided bulk, one of the last structures to be built here. To the right of the Pirámide de los Nichos, Monumento 2, a low temple, squats at the base of **Monumento 5**, a beautiful truncated pyramid with a high decorative pediment broken by a broad staircase; on the left, Monumento 4 is one of the oldest at El Tajín, and only partly restored.

Tajín Chico

From the back of Monumento 4 the path continues past the **Juego de Pelota Norte**, with its worn relief sculptures, onto the levelled terrace of **Tajín Chico**, home of the city's elite. From here, you get a great overview of Tajín Viejo. Only parts of the buildings survive, making a rather confusing whole. **Edificio C** and the adjoining **Edificio B** are the most impressive remains: Edificio C has stone friezes running around its three storeys, giving the illusion of niches. In this case, they were purely decorative, an effect that would have been heightened by a brightly coloured stucco finish. It also has the remains of a concrete roof – originally a huge single slab of poured cement, unique in ancient Mexico. **Edificio A** had a covered interior, and you can still see the entrance covered by a false arch of the type common in Maya buildings.

Estructura I (aka Edificio de las Pinturas) is distinguished by a palapa roof protecting its elaborate decoration, including relief carvings and delicately painted murals. Such luxurious decor suggests that this was probably the residence of some major political or religious figure. On the hill above Tajín Chico stood the **Edificio de las Columnas**, which must have dominated the entire city. El Tajín's most famous ruler, 13 Rabbit, lived here; bas-reliefs on columns recorded his exploits, and some of these are now on show in the museum.

Gran Greca

From the terrace of Tajín Chico you can walk down the stone path to the **Gran Greca** complex, also known as Xicalcoliuhqui, whose spiral walls contain two ball-courts and more pyramids. It has been only partially cleared of jungle, but you can stroll along the walled edges to get a sense of its vast size. Built towards the end of the city's life, it is regarded as a sign of growing crisis, Tajín's rulers becoming increasingly obsessed with monumental projects in order to maintain control over a disenchanted populace.

ARRIVAL AND DEPARTURE — EL TAJÍN

By bus The easiest way to get to El Tajín is from Papantla, 8km away. Local buses take around 15min and can be picked up on Septiembre 16, behind Hotel Tajín. Note that any bus to Poza Rica will pass the ruins, though you'll have to walk 500m from the main highway. After, you can flag one down to continue northwards, connecting in the ugly oil-boom city of Poza Rica. Both buses and taxis drop you off at the collection of touristy stalls and cheap restaurants that surround the entrance, where there's also plenty of parking.

By taxi Taxis run to Tajín from Papantla.

Tuxpán

TUXPÁN (or Tuxpam) offers a far preferable overnight stay to its uglier southern neighbour, Poza Rica, on the journey up the coast to Tampico (see page 436). The town is built on the north bank of the broad Río Tuxpán, where giant tugs and half-built oil rigs lend an industrial air, and where in the evening half the town comes to stroll as the traffic rushes past them.

Museo de la Amistad México-Cuba

Obregón 1 • Free • 783 834 0597 • Take one of the small boats (for a small charge) that shuttle across the river from in front of the Palacio Municipal; on the other side walk inland a couple of blocks and then turn right on Obregón: the museum is right at the end of the street where it hits the river

Occupying the house where Fidel Castro spent a year planning his revolutionary return to Cuba, the **Museo de la Amistad México-Cuba** is Tuxpán's only significant sight. From here, Castro, Che Guevara and eighty others sailed in November 1956 aboard the *Granma* yacht (designed for just twelve passengers), almost sinking on the way, and arrived in Cuba only to find Batista's forces waiting. The museum comprises just a couple of small rooms of photos of the revolutionaries plus assorted memorabilia, but the riverbank setting, modernist house and boat trip to get here add up to a worthwhile excursion.

Barra de Tuxpán

If you're craving a day on the sand, Tuxpán has some long, if mediocre, beaches at **Barra de Tuxpán**, by the river mouth some 12km east of town. **Buses** (marked "Playa") run all day along riverside Bulevar Reyes Heroles, past fishing boats and tankers, and arrive twenty minutes later at a vast stretch of grey sand. There are restaurants and changing rooms here, and palapas where you can sling a hammock.

ARRIVAL AND DEPARTURE — TUXPÁN

By bus The ADO bus terminal lies on Rodríguez near the junction with Juárez, half a block from the river and some 300m east of the Palacio Municipal. Ómnibus de México (with both first- and second-class services, principally to and from the north) is further east along riverfront Reyes Heroles, beyond the huge bridge across the river. To get to the centre from either bus station, head west along the river to the Palacio Municipal and cathedral: behind these runs Juárez, and in the four blocks from here to the Parque Reforma, Tuxpán's liveliest plaza, you'll find banks, shops and most other things you might need, including the bulk of the hotels and restaurants.

Destinations From ADO: Mexico City (32 daily; 4–6hr); Poza Rica (very frequently; 1hr); Tampico (56 daily; 3–4hr); Veracruz (17 daily; 5hr 30min); Xalapa (11 daily; 6hr).

INFORMATION AND TOURS

Tourist information The helpful, well-stocked tourist office (Mon–Fri 9am–5pm, Sat 10am–2pm; 783 834 9496;

http://tuxpanveracruz.gob.mx) is in a kiosk on the forecourt of the Palacio Municipal, at Juárez 20.

Tours A wide variety of river trips, from half an hour to a full day, is on offer. Head for the embarcadero on the riverfront a couple of blocks west of the Palacio Municipal, or contact Paseos Turísticos Negretti (783 833 4564, http://bit.ly/PaseosTurísticos), who can also arrange kayaking, fishing and diving.

ACCOMMODATION

Posada del Sol Guerrero 31; 783 835 4697. Cheerful budget hotel a few blocks north of the river, with a sunny yellow-and-blue colour scheme and old-fashioned rooms which are perfectly comfortable, if a little poky. Good location for the bus stations. M$

Reforma Juárez 25, opposite the cathedral; http://hotel-reforma.com.mx. The town's best: a traditional courtyard hotel that has been classily refurbished to provide a/c rooms with flatscreen cable TVs, wi-fi and fridges. M$$

Riviera Tuxpan Reyes Heroles 17-A; http://bestwestern.com. One of the few hotels in the centre with a river view, though by no means from all rooms. It's a *Best Western*, so comfortable and efficient (with wi-fi), if a little dull. M$$$

EATING

A line of stalls along one side of the Parque Reforma serves *licuados* and snacks, with tables set out on the square. There are plenty of food stalls in and around the **market** too – it's on the riverfront between Rodriguez and Pípila, opposite the ADO. Younger locals hang out along the river downstream of the centre, where there are numerous fast-food places.

Antonios Juárez 25, in the Hotel Reforma; http://hotel-reforma.com.mx. Excellent, somewhat formal restaurant, with linen tablecloths, good steaks and live music on Fri and Sat. There's an excellent *menu del día* for a set price. M$$

El Mejicano Morelos 49 on Parque Reforma; 783 101 0610. Brightly coloured, enjoyable, straightforward Mexican restaurant facing the plaza, with a wide choice of *antojitos*, fish and meat mains and a lunch-time buffet. M$$

Nuevo 303 Pípila 4, between Juárez and the river; 783 834 2527. One of numerous places around the market, *303* is open 24hr and busy with locals for almost all of them. In an elegant, wood-panelled dining room they serve breakfasts, hamburgers and veggie options, as well as seafood dishes such as an excellent *caldo de camarón*. M$$

Tu Casa Morelos 20; http://restaurantucasa.com. Hearty portions of classic Mexican and regional dishes (try the *filete a la Veracruzana*), in an ever-popular, slightly frantic setting with ceiling fans whirring above a bustling open kitchen. M$$

South of Veracruz

Leaving Veracruz to the south, Hwy-180 traverses a long expanse of plain, a country of broad river deltas and salty lagoons where the river port of **Tlacotalpan** oozes elegant decay. Some 150km south of Veracruz, the volcanic hills of the **Sierra Tuxtla** are home to the townships of **Santiago Tuxtla** and **San Andrés Tuxtla**. This beautiful region of rolling green hills, known as "La Suiza Veracruzana" (the Switzerland of Veracruz, plainly named by someone who'd never been to Switzerland), makes a welcome change from the flat plains, and the cooler climate is an infinite relief. The idyllic **Laguna Catemaco**, around which the last expanse of Gulf coast **rainforest** is preserved, makes a rewarding place to break the journey south, with plenty of opportunities to explore the nearby mountains and coast. Beyond the Tuxtla mountains, low, flat, dull country leads all the way to Villahermosa (see page 670).

Historically, the region's great claim to fame is that it was the birthplace of Mexico's first civilization, the **Olmecs**. Here lies the **Volcán de San Martín**, where the Olmecs

FIESTA DE LA VIRGEN DE LA CANDELARIA

For ten days starting on January 31, Tlacotalpan is inundated with thousands of visitors as it celebrates its famous **Fiesta de la Virgen de la Candelaria**. Processions, bull runs, dance and music take over the town, especially for the first three days, culminating on February 2, when the image of the Virgin processes downstream accompanied by a mass of assorted riverboats.

believed the earth to have been created; they built a replica "creation mountain" at their city, La Venta, on the border with Tabasco (see page 669). Their second major city, at **Tres Zapotes** near Santiago Tuxtla, is now little more than a mound in a maize field. For most modern Mexicans, however, this part of southern Veracruz, especially around Lago de Catemaco, is best known as the **Tierra de los Brujos** (land of the witches/wizards).

6

Tlacotalpan

TLACOTALPAN is a beautiful, languid town on the north bank of the broad Río Papaloapan. An important port and railhead in the eighteenth and nineteenth centuries, it now has a population of around eight thousand, and its elegant colonial architecture has led to its being declared a UNESCO World Heritage Site. At the weekend it can be packed with locals, who come here to eat at the riverside restaurants, fish, swim or take boat rides on the river, browse the artesanía shops and hang out in the bars and cafés on the plaza. Come on a weekday afternoon and you'll find the place all but deserted.

Among Mexicans, Tlacotalpan is known as the place where musician and composer **Agustín Lara** (1900–70), whose works have been interpreted by the likes of Pavarotti, Carreras and Domingo, spent his early childhood. Two museums and a cultural centre honour the man, but unless you're a huge fan they're not worth the admission – the true pleasure here is simply to wander the streets, admiring the architecture (many of the buildings are labelled with their history) and soaking up the steamy, tropical atmosphere. On the Plaza Zaragoza are two magnificent churches and a florid, wrought-iron bandstand; Enriquez and Miguel Chazaro, parallel streets heading west from here, are lined with magnificent colonnaded houses. A market occupies a wonderful nineteenth-century building on the waterfront, just east of the centre.

Museo Salvador Ferrando

Alegre 6, on Plaza Hidalgo • 288 884 2495 • Charge

The most enjoyable of the town's few sights is the **Museo Salvador Ferrando**. Named after one of the town's most respected painters, it's a fine old house containing an Old Curiosity Shop of paintings, antique furniture, historical artefacts and junk, around which you're given a lightning-paced tour in Spanish.

ARRIVAL AND DEPARTURE — TLACOTALPAN

By bus Tlacotalpan lies some 100km south of Veracruz, 15km inland on the winding road that heads towards Tuxtepec (and eventually Oaxaca). There are frequent buses to and from Veracruz; second-class buses drop you right in the heart of town, while the ADO terminal is a 10min walk west of the centre on the road out towards Tuxtepec.

INFORMATION

Tourist information There's a small tourist office (Mon–Fri 9am–3pm; 288 889 5838) in the Palacio Municipal, on the Plaza Zaragoza;at busy times a tourist information kiosk also operates on the waterfront Plaza Colon.

ACCOMMODATION AND EATING

Casa de la Luz Aguirre 15, 5min walk north of Plaza Zaragoza; 288 884 2331. For a 'house of light' this is actually pretty gloomy, although the place is cheerfully decked out in blue and yellow, and walls adorned with goofy-looking traditional masks. There are just two rooms here, so book ahead. Free coffee in the mornings. M$

Los Jarochos Rivera del Río, between the market and Plaza Zaragoza; 288 690 0929. A typical, good-value Tlacotalpan riverside restaurant, with tables overlooking the river. Local specialities include *jaibas a la Veracrizana*, made with local crab, and *arroz a la tumbada* – rice piled high with seafood. M$$

Posada Doña Juana Enríquez 32, at Murillo; 288 884 3480. Lovely, inviting hotel with modern rooms in an attractive orange-and-white building set around a small shaded courtyard. All have Sky TV, a/c, wi-fi and hot water, and there's free coffee in the lobby. M$$

Posada Doña Lala Carranza 11, close to river and zocalo;

288 884 2580. The fanciest place in town, comfortable if a bit stuffy, with wi-fi, small pool and a smart restaurant serving great seafood. M$$

Santiago Tuxtla

SANTIAGO TUXTLA is the smaller of the two Tuxtlas, a quiet country town which can make for a peaceful overnight break. On the zócalo a giant **Olmec head**, 3.4m high, is proudly displayed – this is the largest ever found, and unusual also for its closed eyes, scowling mouth and simplified features.

6

Museo Regional Tuxteco

Ángel Carvajal, on the south side of the plaza • Charge • 229 465 8194

The small **Museo Regional Tuxteco** boasts an Olmec head which, by contrast to that outside on the plaza, is the smallest known; it is, however, exceptionally expressive and finely worked. The other star exhibit among a plethora of Olmec sculpture and pottery is a figure, probably an altar, known as "El Negro" – visiting celebrities and locals come here to rub their thumbs over his forehead, which reputedly provides positive energy and miraculous cures.

ARRIVAL AND DEPARTURE — SANTIAGO TUXTLA

By bus Buses stop on the main road, a short walk from the zócalo. Frequent buses pass through heading for San Andrés (20min) and Catemaco (45min), or in the other direction to Veracruz (2hr 30min).

ACCOMMODATION

Gran Santiago Plaza 5 de Mayo, on the zocalo; 294 947 0300. A thoroughly incongruous, seven-storey, circular concrete construction, with business-style rooms – comfortable and efficient with wi-fi – as well as a full-size pool and coffee-shop style restaurant. M$$

Mesón de Santiago 5 de Mayo 8, in the corner of the zocalo; 294 947 1670. A lovingly converted colonial building whose elegant rooms (with a/c and wi-fi) are set around a courtyard with a small pool. M$$

EATING

Posada Colonial Veracruz-Minatitlán, at Flores Magón, 500m north of the town centre; 294 688 0868. Rather grand by local standards, this smart restaurant sits in a colonnaded building on the main road into town, and does a decent line in enchiladas, tacos, *arrachera* and all the other generic favourites. M$$

Super La Joya Juárez, at the corner of the zocalo; 294 947 0177. Supermarket and restaurant where exceptional-value, simple Mexican fare is served at tables outside. M$$

La Tamehua 16 de Septiembre; https://facebook.com/LaTamehua. Simple, plastic-chair *taquería*, popular in the evenings with locals, serving hamburgers, tortas and grilled meats as well as tasty tacos. Cash only. M$$

DIRECTORY

Money and exchange There are two ATMs at the Palacio Municipal on the zócalo, and another on the main road opposite the bus station.

San Andrés Tuxtla and around

SAN ANDRÉS TUXTLA is the administrative centre of the Tuxtlas region, a substantial town with every facility you might need. Surrounded by tobacco fields, it's also home to several **cigar factories** where you can watch *puros* being hand-rolled. One such is the **Santa Clara cigar factory** (http://santaclarapuros.com) right at the heart of town, on the highway one block from the ADO bus station. The tour is fascinating and informal, and there's very little pressure to buy.

ARRIVAL AND INFORMATION — SAN ANDRÉS TUXTLA

By bus Local buses from Catemaco or Santiago will take you right into town, but the majority drop you at the top of the hill where the highway passes by; from here, Juárez leads straight down to the zócalo, a 15min walk or a short taxi ride. Moving on, Catemaco is around 11km east, and Santiago is 13km to the west: both are easily accessible on frequent local buses that depart in front of the giant Fenix supermarket at Pino Suárez and Constitución, two blocks east of the zócalo. There are also frequent buses to Veracruz from the main terminal, but note that buses to Villahermosa tend to leave in the evening, getting you there in the early hours.

Destinations Catemaco (frequently; 30min); Coatzacoalcos (7 daily; 2hr 30min); Veracruz (frequently; 3hr).

Tourist information There's an exceptionally helpful tourist office in the Palacio Municipal (ask inside to find them; open office hours, but a booth is open outside on busy weekends).

ACCOMMODATION

Figueroa Pino Suárez 10 at Belisario Domínguez, a couple of blocks northeast of the plaza; 294 942 0257. Budget hotel with a friendly welcome and lots of information and brochures on what is happening in the region. Rooms are tiny and rather clinical, but perfectly comfortable, and have a/c and wi-fi. M$$

Hotel del Parque Madero 5 on the zócalo; http://hoteldelparque.com. Big, well-run business-style hotel with the best position in town and very well-appointed, a/c rooms with cable TV and wi-fi. M$$

Posada San Martin Juárez 304, halfway between the plaza and the bus station; 294 942 1036. Large, attractive motel-style rooms, with painted wood furniture and red-tiled floors, arranged around a peaceful garden and a small pool. M$

EATING

Grilly's Carranza 321; 294 942 1456. No prizes for guessing what's on the menu here, with a wide array of juicy steaks taking pride of place; this is also a great place to come throughout the day for a hearty breakfast or coffee and cake. M$$

Montepio Allende 8 cnr Bernardo Peña, an alley off Madero by the Hotel Isabel; https://montepiorestaurante.wixsite.com/montepio. Traditional spot open since 1950, with excellent steaks, a good wine list and a bar that welcomes women. M$$

Market 5 de Mayo west of the zócalo. Excellent market with plenty of cheap food stalls. M$

Mr. Taco Segovia Allende 79; 294 100 7810. Simple taco stand with a few outdoor seats. Very busy at lunch time and a great spot if you're looking for something quick and cheap on the go. M$

Reserva de la Biosfera Los Tuxtlas

Trips into the **Reserva de la Biosfera Los Tuxtlas**, centred on the village of **Ruíz Cortines**, which preserves the primal forest around the sacred **Volcán de San Martín**, are best organized through the tourist office in San Andrés; it's not advisable to turn up unannounced. The main sights here are the **Laguna Encantada** or Enchanted Lake, so-called because its level rises in dry weather but drops when it rains, and **Yambigapan** (294 115 7634), a campsite with a couple of basic cabins where, by arrangement, local "pre-Hispanic" food is prepared and adventurous local tours are on offer.

Salto de Eyipantla

Charge • Frequent local buses signed "El Salto" (30min) run from a stop opposite the *Hotel del Parque* in San Andrés; for drivers it's well signed off the highway between San Andrés and Catemaco

The **Salto de Eyipantla**, a powerful waterfall 50m wide and 40m high, is a popular outing from San Andrés, about 12km away. Some 244 steps lead down to the base of the falls, which are pretty spectacular despite being crowded out by touristy stalls; summer weekends can see them packed with locals.

Catemaco

Squatting on the western shore of the enchanting Lago de Catemaco, and by tradition a centre of native witchcraft, **CATEMACO** is a picturesque spot – perfect to break up a journey if you're heading south – with an impressive backdrop of volcanic mountains. The lake and nearby marshland and lagoons are a haven for wildlife, supporting large colonies of **water birds**, including herons, cormorants, wintering ospreys and dozens of other resident and migratory species. The town itself isn't particularly attractive, but there's plenty to do on and around the lake. Veracruzanos arrive in force at weekends

SHAMANISM, WITCHCRAFT AND WIZARDRY

Every March a gathering of *brujos* takes place on Cerro Mono Blanco (White Monkey Hill), just north of Catemaco town. Mexico has thousands of **witches**, warlocks, shamans, herbalists, seers, healers, psychics and fortune-tellers, whose belief system blends Catholicism with ancient rites and practices. The thirteen *brujos* of Catemaco, who call themselves "the Brothers", are acknowledged as the high priests of the trade.

These days, shamanism is big business in Catemaco. Many *brujos* have websites and toll-free numbers over which they sell long-distance spells, and in town you'll be pestered by their agents. By no means all of those claiming shamanistic powers are the real thing, so if you do want a consultation take advice from people locally, and be sure to know what you're getting and how much you'll be paying for it. The rituals can be fascinating – but they can also be theatrical flimflam, designed to empty your wallet rather than expand your consciousness.

and holidays, when the main strip can get pretty busy; at other times the place can be dead, and many of the facilities shut.

Lago de Catemaco

A **boat trip** around the lake is one of the highlights of southern Veracruz. You're unlikely to escape the attentions of the *lancha* operators as you approach the lakefront: they all offer similar ninety-minute trips to the lake's main sights and some of its beaches (pricy during peak season but a bargain when it's quiet). On the tiny **Isla de los Changos** there are stump-tailed macaques (monkeys native to Thailand), introduced here by Veracruz University in 1974 – they look bored stiff in their restricted habitat. In 1988, endangered Mexican howler monkeys were introduced to the much larger Agaltepec Island; these are far more active and aggressive. You are almost guaranteed to see a huge variety of **birds** too – herons, egrets, cormorants and shags, as well as more exotic kingfishers and ospreys.

Morelet's crocodiles, a relatively small species (up to 3m long), live in the lake too, nesting on the far bank. They're well fed and, apparently, never attack. Certainly plenty of people swim in the lake: stick to the main **beaches** and close to others if you feel uneasy. Playa Espagoya is just a short walk beyond the eastern edge of town, with Playa Hermosa and Playa Azul not much further beyond.

Iglesia de Nuestra Señora del Carmen

On the zócalo

The pretty church of **Nuestra Señora del Carmen**, with some fine stained glass, is home to a miraculous statue of the Virgin of Carmen, who is said to have appeared to a fisherman in 1714 in a narrow grotto known as El Tegal, roughly twenty minutes' walk around the lakeshore towards Playa Azulan. For Mexican Catholics the church is an important place of pilgrimage, above all around the Virgin's festival on July 15–16.

ARRIVAL AND DEPARTURE — CATEMACO

By bus The ADO first-class terminal, surely the most scenic in the country, faces the lake on the eastern edge of town, about a 5min walk from the centre. Some second-class buses also terminate at the ADO station, but most stop at the AU terminal on the main highway on the edge of town. Local buses from San Andrés Tuxtla will drop you at Lerdo and Revolución, directly inland from the ADO.

By colectivo Share-taxis to San Andrés leave from halfway up Carranza towards the main highway, near the mound known as El Cerrito. Piratas (*colectivo* pick-ups) heading to Sontecomapan and the beaches (see page 415), depart from the local bus stop at Lerdo and Revolución.

INFORMATION AND ACTIVITIES

Activities Kayaking, mountain-biking, jungle tours, shamanic spiritual cleansing, *temazcales* and more are on offer around town; some of the best activities are offered by the various lodges around the lake, especially *Nanciyaga* and *Ecobiosfera* (see page 415).

Tourist information There's a tourist office in the Palacio

6

Municipal (Mon–Fri 9am–3pm; 294 943 0625) on the main plaza, as well as a booth on the highway at the entrance to town at busy periods. http://catemaco.info is a helpful local website.

ACCOMMODATION

Hotel standards in Catemaco town are not very high, though there are some great back-to-nature eco-resorts around the lake.

IN TOWN

Los Arcos Madero 7, between the zócalo and the lake; 294 943 0003. Clean, well-run hotel with pleasant, a/c rooms with TV around an attractive pool. Some of the higher rooms have lake views. A basic Mexican breakfast is included. M$$

Juros Playa, behind Los Arcos; 294 943 0084. Central, orange-hued hotel with pleasant, modern rooms, some of which have balconies. The rooftop pool has stunning views of the lake. M$

Posada Koniapan Revolución at the lakefront, on the eastern edge of town by the ADO; http://hotelposadakoniapan.com.mx. Gated compound with a pool and wi-fi, with simple, comfortable motel-style rooms; those upstairs have glimpses of the lake. Breakfast included, served overlooking the garden. M$$

OUT OF TOWN, SEE MAP PAGE 414

Bahia Escondida On the southern lakeshore, 10km from

Catemaco; 294 109 3417. Basic eco-resort in idyllic spot with camping, dorms, private rooms and cabins; there's a communal kitchen, café-bar, limited electricity and friendly welcome. M$

Ecobiosfera Dos Amates, 10km from Catemaco on the road to Sontecomapan; http://ecobiosfera.com. Fairly basic cabañas, close to nature in a stunning hillside position overlooking the lake; camping is also an option here. They run all sorts of excellent nature and cultural tours from here, in particular into the Reserva de la Biosfera and to various waterfalls. M$

La Finca Hwy 180 km147, on the west bank of the lake about 2km from town; http://lafinca.mx. The best hotel on the lake, with stunning views from almost every room, especially upstairs, a/c and wi-fi, a lovely lakeside pool and spa treatments including massage and *temazcal*. M$$$

Hotel Prashanti Tebanca On the eastern lakeshore near Tebanca, 15km from Catemaco; https://prashanti.hotelesdeveracruzmexico.com. Fancier than average lakeshore retreat with comfortable, though still simple, rooms and cabins, and treatments including crystal therapy, shamanic cleansing and *temazcal*. There's also a beach annexe, Prashanti Playa, at La Barra (opposite). M$$$

★ **Reserva Ecológica Nanciyaga** On the eastern lakeshore, about 7km from Catemaco; http://nanciyaga.com. Simple cabañas by the lake for up to four people (shared bathroom; no TV or phone); activities (daily; open to non-guests) include *temazcal*, mud bath, shamanic cleansing, massage, guided jungle walks and kayaking. M$$$

EATING

Seafood **restaurants** abound along the lakefront, most offering the local speciality, *mojarra* (small perch from the lake), best sampled when cooked *a la tachagovi* – with a delicious hot sauce. A few more modern places, serving innovations like cappuccino and pizza, are also starting to appear. At the other end of the scale, the **market**, half a block from the zócalo on Madero, has plenty of cooked-food stalls.

Casa de los Tesoros Aldama 4 Altos, overlooking the plaza; 294 943 2910. Lovely café which is also an excellent artesanía store and a helpful source of local information, with free wi-fi. Good coffee, exotic teas and delicious omelettes, burgers, sandwiches, snacks and home-made cakes; they also have wine by the glass or bottle. M$$

La Casita Matamoros between Bravo and Melchor Ocampo, a few blocks north of the plaza (hard to find, so ask); 294 943 1026. Not the prettiest views, but the well-priced Mexican dishes and seafood here are perennially popular with locals. M$$

La Casona Aldama 6; 294 110 1150. Enchanting old building on the zócalo which has plenty for seafood- and meat-lovers, served in an attractive dining room looking out onto a verdant garden or on a balcony over the zócalo. Try the *arroz a la tumbada*, lemon-scented rice with seafood. M$$

Il Fiorentino Paseo del Malecón 11, just east of the centre; 294 943 2797. Italian restaurant serving decent pizza, calzone and pasta dishes, with a great location and upstairs terrace looking out over the lake. M$$$

La Ola Paseo del Malecón, cnr Union; 294 943 0010. Much of this popular restaurant is rather gloomy, but get a seat towards the far end of its cavernous interior and there are lovely views of the lake. The food's good to match, with all the local specialities on offer, including *mojarra, jaiba* (crab) and *tegololos* (freshwater snails). M$$

DRINKING

69 club bar Paseo del Malecón, cnr Union; 294 154 9751. In the likely event that you should fancy a break from Catemaco's slew of karaoke bars, this is just the ticket: a trendy waterfront bar next the *La Ola* restaurant.

La Panga Paseo del Malecón 21, near the centre. Catemaco's most scenic spot is this palapa-roofed bar-restaurant, which floats on the lake at the end of a rickety wooden boardwalk. A lovely place for a sunset beer or to sample some of the local delicacies.

Sontecomapan and the Costa de Oro

From Catemaco a paved road heads 18km to the coast and the small fishing village of **SONTECOMAPAN**. Here you can take a variety of *lancha* trips through the mangroves on the freshwater **Laguna de Sontecomapan**, which offers good **bird watching** possibilities. The most common trip is all the way to the mouth of the Laguna at **La Barra**, about 8km away (also accessible via a very rough road), where there's a lovely stretch of sand, usually deserted.

Beyond Sontecomapan a good road heads northwest along the coast for some 40km, before turning inland to rejoin the main highway beyond Santiago Tuxtla. It passes through the **Reserva de la Biosfera los Tuxtlas**, a nature reserve most easily visited on a tour with *Ecobiosfera* (see page 415) or from San Andrés (see page

FIESTAS IN VERACRUZ

Día de la Candelaria (Feb 2). The final day of a week-long fiesta, complete with dances, boat races and bulls let loose in the streets, in Tlacotalpan (see page 410). Colourful fiesta in Jaltipán, near Acayucan, which includes the dance of La Malinche (Cortés' interpreter and mistress, who is said to have been born here).

Carnaval (the week before Lent; variable Feb–March) is celebrated all over the region, most riotously in Veracruz (see page 380).

Congreso de Brujos (first Fri in March). Shamans, witches, wizards and healers from across Mexico attend purification rituals and celebrations in and around Catemaco (see page 412), amid a festival that attracts plenty of visitors.

Fiestas de San José (March 18–19). In Naranjos, between Tuxpán and Tampico, a fiesta with many traditional dances. In Espinal, a Totonac village on the Río Tecolutla, not far from El Tajín and Papantla, you can witness the spectacular *voladores*.

Semana Santa (Holy Week, March/April). Re-creations of the Passion are widespread in this area. You can witness them in Papantla (see page 404), where you'll also see the *voladores*; in Coatzintla, a Totonac village nearby; in Cotaxtla, between Veracruz and Córdoba; and in Otatitlán. Naolinco, a beautiful village near Xalapa, stages a mock Crucifixion on Good Friday. Also celebrations in Catemaco (see page 412) and in the port of Alvarado – a ribald Fish Fiesta following the spirit of the Veracruz Carnaval.

Feria del Cafe (two weeks during May). Coatepec (see page 398) celebrates the local crop.

Corpus Christi (variable; the Thurs after Trinity Sun). The start of a major four-day festival in Papantla (see page 404) with regular performances by the *voladores*.

Día de San Juan (June 24). Celebrated with dancing in Santiago Tuxtla (see page 411), and in Martinez de la Torre, near Tlapacoyan, where the *voladores* perform.

Día de la Virgen del Carmen (July 15–16). A massive pilgrimage to Catemaco (see page 398), accompanied by a fiesta which spills over into the following day. At the same time, Xico (see page 399) has a week-long celebration of Mary Magdalene.

Día de Santiago (July 25). Celebrated with fiestas in Santiago Tuxtla (see page 411) and Coatzintla; each lasts several days. In Tlapacoyan (see page 400) you can see the bizarre Baile de los Negritos (see page 404).

Day of Assumption (Aug 15). Widely celebrated, particularly in Tlapacoyan (see page 400), where you can see El Baile de los Negritos, and with a week-long festival in Tuxpán (see page 408) that includes dancing and the *voladores*.

Independence Day (Sept 15–16). Celebrated everywhere.

San Jeronimo (last week of Sept). Big celebrations in Coatepec (see page 398).

Fiesta de la Virgen del Rosario (Oct 7). In La Antigua (see page 402) the patroness of fishermen is honoured with processions of canoes on the river, while Alvarado, outside Veracruz, enjoys a fiesta filling the first two weeks of the month.

Día de los Muertos (Day of the Dead; Nov 2). Observed everywhere.

Dia del Niño Perdido (Dec 7). Huge candle-lit processions in Tuxpán (see page 408).

Día de la Virgen de Guadalupe (Dec 12). Widely observed, especially in Huatusco, Cotaxtla and Amatlán de los Reyes, near Córdoba.

Christmas (Dec 25). Celebrated everywhere. There's a very famous festival in Santiago Tuxtla (see page 411) that lasts until Twelfth Night (Jan 6).

411). Some of Veracruz's most alluring and least-visited **beaches** lie down dirt tracks off this road.

Montepío

At **MONTEPÍO**, 39km from Catemaco, the road finally runs right by the coast. The beach here offers warm, shallow swimming – people also swim in the nearby river –

and is lined with palapa restaurants serving seafood and *cocos fríos*. At holiday times there are *lanchas* and banana-boat rides; out of season it's often deserted.

Costa de Oro

North of Montepío, the coast is being promoted as the **Costa de Oro**, though as yet there's no real development, and only the odd isolated place to stay; there are excellent beaches at Playa Hermosa and Costa de Oro, though, and a popular dive spot at Roca Partida – the split rock.

ARRIVAL AND DEPARTURE SONTECOMAPAN AND THE COSTA DE ORO

By pirata *Colectivo* pick-ups known as *piratas* traverse the coastal road regularly; they charge a small amount from Catemaco to Sontecomapan, but it's more to Montepío; there are also very occasional second-class buses.

By boat At Sontecomapan you can hire a *lancha* to take you to La Barra, or for a tour of the mangroves and lagoon. The journey to La Barra is a set cost for the entire boat, including an hour or so at the beach; at busy periods you can get a *colectivo* ride for less.

KRYSTAL
HOTEL
Hotel Monterrey
Hotel Monterrey

The north

MONTERREY

The north

Rich in legends of the country's revolutionary past, Mexico's north has a modern history dominated by its relationship with the United States, just across the Río Bravo. Though much of the region is harsh, barren and sparsely inhabited, far less visited than the country's tourist-saturated southern states, cross-border trade – as much about the daily movement of people as goods – means it's one of the richest and most dynamic parts of Mexico. It's not all business, though. Rugged and untamed, the north is home to deserts, mountains, seedy frontier towns and modern cities, as well as a proud and hospitable people deeply rooted in ranching culture, perhaps best symbolized by folk hero Pancho Villa (see page 448).

Archeological remains are also scattered throughout the north, including ancient petroglyphs and ruined Chichimec cities, all of which are thoroughly distinct from the Mesoamerican metropolises of the south. Most notable is the site of **Paquimé**, where a maze of adobe walls once housed an extensive and highly developed desert civilization.

The north promises urban appeal too. **Durango** offers a taste of colonial grandeur comparable to Mexico's heartland, while similarly attractive **Chihuahua** boasts a wealth of nineteenth-century architecture and stylish contemporary museums. The real draw, however, is **Monterrey**. Young, energetic and cosmopolitan, this modern city offers a host of cultural and artistic diversions.

Travelling overland from the south of Mexico towards the US border, there are a couple of obvious routes, with the **central corridor** via Durango and Chihuahua ending at **Ciudad Juárez** – a sprawling border town notorious for its violent drug wars. Further east, a string of smaller, calmer crossings provides rapid (and generally safer) access to Texas. The very shortest route north follows the **Gulf coast**. Hot, steamy and uncomfortable, this route is not especially recommended, but it is the fastest from the fine beaches and archeological ruins of Veracruz (see page 436), and, travelling by bus, avoids Mexico City.

Monterrey

The third-largest city in Mexico (with over four million in the metro area), and capital of Nuevo León, **MONTERREY** is a dynamic showcase for contemporary Mexico, though the heavy industry that made its wealth has far less importance these days – the biggest steel works closed in 1986. While the vast network of factories, the traffic, urban sprawl, pollution and ostentatious wealth that characterize the city are relatively recent developments, the older parts retain an air of colonial elegance. The city's setting, too, is one of great natural beauty – ringed by jagged mountain peaks, the Cerro de la Silla, or "Saddle Mountain," dominates the landscape. The city in general rewards a day of wandering, but there are three places specifically worth going out of your way to visit – the old **Obispado** (bishop's palace), on a hill overlooking the centre, the giant **Cervecería Cuauhtémoc** to the north and the cluster of world-class museums around the **Macroplaza**.

Brief history

Spanish conquistador **Diego de Montemayor** founded Monterrey in 1596, at a spring close to the current location of the Museo de Historia. Steel production began in

PREHISTORIC STRUCTURES AT THE PAQUIMÉ RUINS

Highlights

❶ **Monterrey** Art and culture reign in this bold, modern city, where superb museums and restaurants await. See page 420

❷ **Cabrito asado** Succulent roast goat is a speciality of Mexican cowboy country, best experienced at restaurants such as *El Rey del Cabrito* in Monterrey. See page 430

❸ **Valle de Parras** Explore the rambling vineyards and haciendas of North America's oldest wine-growing region, home to some eminently quaffable Cabernet Sauvignon. See page 435

❹ **La Tierra del Cine** Travel back to the Wild West at the John Wayne film sets at Villa del Oeste and Chupaderos. See page 443

❺ **Chihuahua** Lively colonial city sprinkled with grandiose nineteenth-century mansions, including the home of Pancho Villa. See page 445

❻ **Paquimé** The enigmatic ruins at Casas Grandes are remnants of the most significant pre-Columbian culture in northern Mexico. See page 450

HIGHLIGHTS ARE MARKED ON THE MAP ON PAGE 422

1900, fuelling an economic boom that continues today, with Cemex (the world's third-largest cement company), FEMSA (Coca-Cola Latin America and owner of the OXXO convenience stores) and Banorte among the many companies based here – the business district of **San Pedro Garza García**, now Mexico's richest community, contains some of the highest skyscrapers outside Mexico City (on completion in 2017, the **Torre KOI** became the tallest in Mexico at 276m). Once known as one of the safest cities in Mexico, Monterrey's sense of calm was rattled by **Hurricane Alex** in 2010, causing severe damage costing an estimated M$16.9 billion. That same year, conflict between the Gulf Cartel and Los Zetas (see page 453), began to spread to the city for the first time, culminating in a terrifying arson attack on the Casino Royale in 2011, in which more than fifty people were killed. Things have improved dramatically since that low point, and if you take the usual precautions (especially at night) you are unlikely to have any problems.

The Macroplaza and around

At the heart of Monterrey is the **Macroplaza** (officially Plaza Zaragoza, or just the "Gran Plaza"), which was created by demolishing six blocks of the city centre. It links the intensely Modernist **Palacio Municipal**, built on stilts at the southern end of the square in 1973, to the beautiful red-stone **Palacio de Gobierno** on what used to be Plaza 5 de Mayo. The result is undeniably stunning, with numerous fountains, an abundance of striking statuary, quiet gardens and shady patios, edged by the **Catedral Metropolitana**, museums and state administration buildings. You'll also see plenty of

squawking red-crowned **Amazon parrots** in the trees here, the thriving descendants of escaped pet birds. There are frequent concerts, dances and other entertainments held in the park; in the evenings people gravitate here to stroll, and to admire the laser beam that flashes out from the top of the 70m-high slab of red concrete known as the **Faro del Comercio**, designed by the lauded Mexican architect Luis Barragán in 1984.

Plaza Hidalgo and Zona Rosa

West of the Macroplaza are the shops, offices and hotels of the **Zona Rosa**, beginning with little **Plaza Hidalgo** – a much more traditional, shady place, with old colonial buildings set around a statue of independence hero Miguel Hidalgo. Pedestrianized shopping streets fan out behind, crowded with window-gazing locals; Morelos and Juárez are the main thoroughfares.

Museo Metropolitano

Zaragoza, at Corregidora • Free • 81 8344 1971

In between Plaza Hidalgo and the Macroplaza, in the old City Hall completed in 1887, you'll find the **Museo Metropolitano** with a small exhibit introducing the city's history, from its foundation in 1596 – labels are in Spanish only, but the lovely inner courtyard is worth a look in any case. The upstairs galleries house temporary art exhibitions.

Museo de Arte Contemporáneo (MARCO)

Zuazua, at Jardón • Charge, free Wed • http://marco.org.mx

At the southern end of the Macroplaza lies the wonderful **Museo de Arte Contemporáneo**. Visitors are greeted by Juan Soriano's *La Paloma*, an immense sculpture of an obese bronze dove whose curvaceous lines stand in dramatic contrast to the angular terracotta lines of the museum building (designed in 1991 by one of Mexico's leading architects, **Ricardo Legorreta**). Inside, none of the floors and walls seems to intersect at the same angle. The vast, at times whimsical, open-plan interior centres on an atrium with a serene pool into which a pipe periodically gushes water: at the sound of the pump gurgling to life, you find yourself drawn to watch the ripple patterns subside.

Apart from a couple of monumental sculptures tucked away in courtyards, there is no permanent collection, but the standards maintained by the temporary exhibits are phenomenally high. A key factor in this is undoubtedly the bias towards Latin American (particularly Mexican) artists, who are currently producing some of the world's most innovative and inspiring works; the lithographs of Claudio Bravo, the feminist-influenced paintings of Paula Rego and Oaxacan print-maker Filemón Santiago have all featured in the past. The quality art bookshop and fancy *Restaurant Marco* (81 8262 4562) are both worth visiting (no need to pay museum admission).

Catedral Metropolitana de Nuestra Señora de Monterrey

Zuazua Sur 1100, between Abasolo and Jardón • Free • 81 1158 2281

The relatively modest eighteenth-century **Catedral Metropolitana de Nuestra Señora de Monterrey** is a beautifully maintained Baroque structure with its one highly ornate multilevel tower completed in 1899. Highlights inside include the vivid murals at the altar, completed by Durango-born artist Ángel Zárraga in the 1940s. The palatial edifice just to the north of the cathedral is the **Casino Monterrey**, a posh entertainment centre for government types and strictly off-limits.

Barrio Antiguo

The oldest part of downtown survives to the east of the Macroplaza, where the **Barrio Antiguo** is populated with painted adobe houses dating from the 1890s, schools, independent galleries and, traditionally, the city's best bars and clubs. Sadly, since

2011, drug cartel violence has seen nightlife shrink in the area, and despite the improvement in security many bars have closed permanently. The Barrio Antiguo is safe during the day and is still busy at the weekends, but check with your hotel before you go out at night.

DramaticoMx

C. de Morelos 1081 • Charge • 81 2971 2344

DramaticoMx is a small theatre and museum with an extensive events calendar, fuelled by local players. Some of the show can be a bit hit and mix but the riverside location always seems to help fill the seats.

Museo Estatal de Culturas Populares

Abasolo 1024, at Mina • Free • http://conarte.org.mx

There's usually a host of artistic goings-on at the **Museo Estatal de Culturas Populares** in the handsome Casa del Campesino (dating from 1740), where a warren of courtyards leads to small galleries showing a range of temporary art exhibitions in a variety of media. Note the bold murals smothering the entrance, created by local artist Crescenciano Garza Rivera in 1938 – the "Emiliano Zapata" auditorium to the left of the first courtyard is covered with them too.

Museo del Palacio

Zaragoza, at 5 de Mayo • Free • http://3museos.com

At the northern end of the Macroplaza, the **Museo del Palacio** occupies the Nuevo León state government building, completed in 1908 as a magnificent example of late Neoclassical style. The museum uses its surroundings to hypnotic effect: rooms are dimly lit and suffused with ambient music, with historic artefacts enhanced with video, images, computer screens and small, easily digested stories. The exhibits chart the history of Nuevo León, focusing on the themes of government and law – displays piece together the transition from colony to federal state, examine the evolving role of the governor over time, and end as a sort of shrine to Mexican democracy, covering the development of a Mexican constitution, elections and a free press. There are also rooms dedicated to the region's commercial development (think goats, sugar cane and oranges), and how transport and communications helped create modern Monterrey. The original *Galería de Gobernadores* is also preserved in gilded splendour – the state legislature held sessions here until 1985, when the new **Congreso del Estado** building further down the plaza took over (the governor of Nuevo León still maintains offices in the old building).

Museo de Historia Mexicana

Dr Coss Sur 445 • Charge, free Tues & Sun; entry is free with a Museo del Noreste ticket • http://3museos.com

The **Museo de Historia Mexicana** is another bold architectural statement with temporary and permanent displays on **Mexican national history**, with everything presented in a fairly unconventional manner. The permanent exhibits are upstairs in a vast, open-plan hall centred on the Área Tierra, a dimly lit contemplative space surrounded by faux rainforest. The rest is split into four galleries, with minimal labelling, an array of traditional costumes, interactive computer consoles and carefully selected exhibits. The highlights of the **Mexico Antiguo** section are the scale models of ancient cities such as Palenque, Monte Albán and Teotihuacán, while the **Virreinato** area covers the colonial period with a vast golden *retablo* the centrepiece (a 1960s copy of a 1670 original). The nineteenth-century and **Mexico Moderno** galleries complete the picture. This is very much an impressionistic museum – don't expect lots of dates and details – but nevertheless, if you don't read Spanish you might find the monolingual captions frustrating.

Museo del Noreste

Montemayor Sur 510 • Charge, free Tues & Sun; entry is free with a Museo de Historia Mexicana ticket • http://3museos.com

A covered walkway connects the Museo de Historia Mexicana to Monterrey's star attraction, the **Museo del Noreste**, or just MUNE. As you'd expect by now, this is not your average history museum – though it covers the **history of northeast Mexico** chronologically, from pre-colonial times through to the present, it uses a similar multimedia approach and is deeply thought-provoking. For starters, the exhibits begin with modern times and work backwards. More significantly, the "northeast" here includes the US state of Texas, and virtually every exhibit is approached through the prism of cross-border relations; the idea that the fate of both sides has been fundamentally entwined for hundreds of years makes sense, but the focus on Mexico's cultural impact on Texas, and the suggestion that it has a paramount role in its future ("by 2025 half of the Texan population will be of Mexican origin") would be viewed as highly controversial by many Americans. The museum also presents a fresh look at the much neglected Indigenous tribes of the region, takes an unusually positive view of the Díaz regime and systemically lays out the tortured history of how the current US/ Mexico border came to be. Labels are in Spanish and English.

Paseo Santa Lucía

Boats daily 10am–9.30pm, every 30min • Charge per return trip • 81 8126 8500

Just below the MUNE plaza lies one of the city's most impressive attractions, the **Paseo Santa Lucía**, a landscaped canal-side path replete with waterfalls, gardens and snack stalls that leads 2.5km east to the Parque Fundidora (see below) – it's a sweaty but tranquil thirty-minute walk, or a leisurely cruise in one of the boats that regularly plies between the two sites. Tickets are good for return trips the whole day.

Parque Fundidora

Fundidora, at Adolfo Prieto • Free • http://parquefundidora.org • **Centro de las Artes** • Free • http://conarte.org.mx • **Parque Plaza Sésamo** Agrícola Ote 3700-1 • Charge, free for children under 90cm • http://parqueplazasesamo.com • Take Metrorrey Line 1 to Parque Fundidora (the park lies south of the station, across Madero)

Just east of the centre, at the end of Paseo Santa Lucia, **Parque Fundidora** is a surreal landscape of green parkland, industrial chimneys and former steel-processing plants, which have been converted into art halls, stadiums and museums. Get a map (free) at the park entrance, from where it's another fifteen minutes to the end of the canal and boat dock, marked by a waterfall set in a giant steel cauldron. If time is short, head straight to the **Museo del Acero Horno-3**, but the **Centro de las Artes** is also worth a look, a series of three warehouses displaying temporary modern art exhibits. Toddlers will love the entertaining theme park honouring Sesame Street – **Parque Plaza Sésamo**.

Museo del Acero Horno-3

Parque Fundidora • Charge • Paseo Cima • Charge • 81 3158 6555

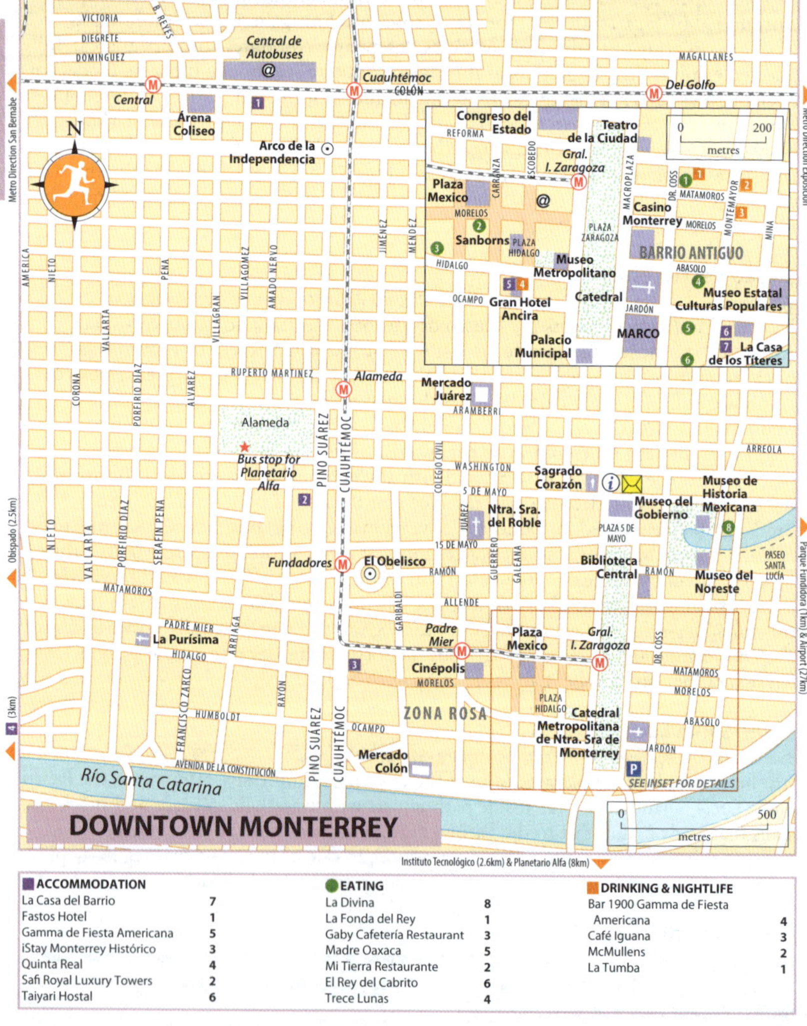

The centrepiece of the Parque Fundidora is the **Museo del Acero Horno-3**, a remarkable museum created out of the guts of a jagged steel mill. Inside are galleries tracing the history of the steel industry in Monterrey (with English labels), as well as the steel-manufacturing process itself – the highlight is the **Show del Torne**, which reproduces the dazzling (and fiery) spectacle of steel-making. You can also scale the 40m viewing platform via special iron elevators ("Paseo por la Cima"), and eat at *El Lingote* (http://ellingoterestaurante.com).

El Obispado

Fray Rafael José Verger, off Padre Mier • Take the R4 bus, alighting where it turns off Padre Mier, then continue to the top of the steps at the end of Padre Mier and turn left; it's a 10min walk in all. Return to the centre using any bus heading east on Hidalgo

The elegant and beautifully renovated **Obispado**, the old bishop's palace, tops the hill to the west of downtown Monterrey like a golden temple. Its commanding position – affording magnificent views when haze and smog allow – has made it an essential target for Monterrey's many invaders. Completed in 1787, it has served as a barracks, a military hospital and a fortress: among its more dramatic exploits, the Obispado managed to hold out for two days after the rest of the city had fallen to US general Zachary Taylor in 1846.

Museo Regional de Nuevo León

Fray Rafael José Verger s/n • Charge (free Sun) • 81 8333 9588

After so much history elsewhere in the city, you might baulk at the **Museo Regional de Nuevo León** inside the Obispado – essentially another journey through the past of Nuevo León, with an emphasis on religious and secular art, arms from the War of Independence, revolutionary pamphlets and old carriages – but the collection has an oddly appealing charm and is evocatively set in the original stone chambers with timber ceilings. Labels are in Spanish only.

Mirador Asta Bandera

Cerro del Obispado • Free • 81 8347 1533

A short, steep walk up the road behind the Obispado takes you to the top of the Cerro del Obispado and the **Mirador Asta Bandera**, a sensational viewpoint (775m) topped with a giant, 100m tall Mexican flag. Raised in 2005, the flag is the second largest in Mexico (the biggest flies in Piedras Negras on the US border, a whopping 120m tall), part of the "banderas monumentales" programme initiated by President Zedillo in 1999.

Cervecería Cuauhtémoc Moctezuma

Alfonso Reyes Nte 2202 • Tours are usually in Spanish, and you need to make a reservation if you require an English-speaking guide – reservations are recommended in any case • Free • 1hr–1hr 30min • http://heinekenmexico.com • **Jardín Cerveza** • Free

If you like beer, head out to the massive premises of **Cervecería Cuauhtémoc Moctezuma** (Cuauhtémoc Brewery), established in 1890 and just as representative of Monterrey as any of the city's more historic sites (though it became a subsidiary of Heineken in 2010). This is where they make the wonderful Bohemia, Indio and Tecate beers you'll find throughout Mexico (as well as the rather bland Carta Blanca and export-only Sol). Free guided tours of the brewery run almost hourly throughout the day from the office next to the **Jardín Cerveza** (beer garden), 1km north of the bus station. You can claim one free glass of beer (usually Carta Blanca) here, or buy the better draught beers on offer. Note that male visitors cannot wear shorts, sandals or short-sleeved shirts, and you cannot take photos.

Museo del Vidrio

Escobedo 1735 • Charge, free Sun • https://museodelvidrio.com.mx • Metrorrey Line 1 to Del Golfo station (walk two blocks west and then five blocks north up Escobedo)

For decades, glass production has been one of Monterrey's industrial strengths (for one thing, it has to provide all the beer bottles to the brewery), and to tap into the long history of Mexican glassware, pop along to the **Museo del Vidrio**. A small but select display of pieces over the centuries and a mock-up of a nineteenth-century apothecary's only act as a prelude to the attic, where modern, mostly cold-worked glass sculpture is shown to advantage; Raquel Stolarski's *Homage to Marilyn* is particularly fine.

ARRIVAL AND DEPARTURE — MONTERREY

BY PLANE

Flights arrive at Aeropuerto Internacional Mariano Escobedo (81 8345 4434), 6km or so northeast of the city, accessible by bus or taxi – taxi fares are set according to a zone system, with the centre and San Pedro Garza García charged accordingly (buy a ticket at the terminal before you exit). Heading back to the airport from the centre is a set fare also. Noreste (http://noreste.com.mx) operates buses between the airport and the Central de Autobuses every hour (daily 5am–8pm; 45min).

Aeroméxico and budget carrier Viva Aerobus make Monterrey a hub. Virtually every major destination in Mexico is fairly affordable from here if you book in advance (the list below is just a sample).

Destinations (domestic) Acapulco (4 weekly; 1hr 50min); Cancún (8 daily; 2hr 10min); Chihuahua (2 weekly; 1hr 25min); Guadalajara (5–7 daily; 1hr 25min); Los Cabos (1 daily; 1hr 50min); Mazatlán (1 daily; 1hr 25min); Mexico City (16 daily; 1hr 30min); Oaxaca (3 weekly; 1hr 50min); Puerto Vallarta (1 daily; 1hr 30min); Tampico (4 weekly; 1hr 5min); Tijuana (1 daily; 1hr 40min); Toluca (2 daily; 1hr 20min); Veracruz (1 daily; 1hr 35min).

BY BUS

Arrival Buses pull into the enormous Central de Autobuses, northwest of the centre on Colón at Amado Nervo, complete with its own shopping centre and 24hr left luggage (guardería) on the west side. To get from the bus station to the central Macroplaza, turn left on Colón to the Cuauhtémoc metro station and take Line 2, or pick up a #1, #7, #17 or #18 bus heading down Pino Suárez and get off at a suitable intersection: Ocampo, Zaragoza or Juárez, for example. You can also get just about anywhere by taxi; taxis are supposed to the use meters (insist on it).

Destinations Chihuahua (12 daily; 9–11hr); Durango (14 daily; 8–9hr); Matamoros (hourly; 4hr); Matehuala (hourly; 4–5hr); Mexico City (hourly; 11–12hr); Nuevo Laredo (every 30min; 3hr); Piedras Negras (9 daily; 5–7hr); Reynosa (every 30min; 3hr); Saltillo (hourly; 1hr 30min); San Luis Potosí (hourly; 7hr); Zacatecas (hourly; 7hr–7hr 30min).

Buses to Texas Monterrey is also a good place to pick up transport into Texas: Transportes del Norte (http://transportesdelnorte.com.mx) has direct connections with the Greyhound system in Laredo via transfers in Nuevo Laredo (every 15–30min; 3hr 10min); Turimex also runs direct to San Antonio via Laredo (6hr 30min–7hr).

INFORMATION

Tourist office There's usually someone who can speak English at the helpful tourist office in the Palacio de Gobierno on the Macroplaza, 5 de Mayo (Mon–Fri 9am–5pm, Sat & Sun 10am–6pm; 81 8152 3333, http://nuevoleon.travel).

GETTING AROUND

BY TAXI

The easiest way to get around Monterrey is by taxi, though traffic can be bad at the usual rush-hour times. Most taxis you hail in the street should use meters (the rates increase 10pm–4am) – trips anywhere in the centre will rarely break the bank. Uber (http://uber.com) is also available in Monterrey, and their rates to the airport are generally the best (outside of surge pricing).

BY METRORREY

Though limited in scope, the fastest way to get around the city – and certainly between downtown and the bus station – is to take the clean and efficient Metrorrey light rail system, which runs on two lines: Line 1 is elevated and runs east–west above Colón (you see it as soon as you emerge from the bus station); and Line 2 runs underground from Sendero in the north of the city to the Macroplaza (at the station General I. Zaragoza), connecting with Line 1 at the Cuauhtémoc stop, right by the bus station (Line 3 runs from General Anaya station on Line 2 through Barrio Antiguo). It's simple to use: tickets cost a set fee per journey and are available singly or as a multi-journey card (at a small saving) from the coin-operated ticket machines (no notes or places to change them). You can also buy rechargeable smart cards ("Tarjeta Mia" which includes an initial four trips). The system runs from around 5am until midnight.

BY BUS

The streets of Monterrey are almost solid with buses, following routes that appear incomprehensible at first

FESTIVE MONTERREY

In addition to the national and religious holidays, Monterrey has a number of exuberant local festivals.

Festibaúl Internacional de Títeres (mid-July) This one-week puppet "festibaúl" is particularly appealing to kids, with Mexican and international puppeteers holding shows in the city.

Festival Internacional de Cine de Monterrey (end of Aug) http://monterreyfilmfestival.com. The Monterrey film festival is one of Latin America's largest, showcasing the best Mexican, Latin American and international films, as well as organizing lectures and other free events.

Festival Internacional de Santa Lucía (Sept/Oct) http://festivalsantalucia.gob.mx. Massive celebration of performing arts, with international dance, music and theatre.

Festival Internacional de Danza Extremadura-Lenguaje Contemporáneo (end of Oct) http://danzaenmonterrey.com. Scintillating dance festival with a heavy emphasis on local and Mexican troupes (contemporary), as well as some international guests.

sight. The city authorities have tried to resolve the confusion by numbering all the stops (*paradas*), having the fares written on the windscreen and occasionally providing the tourist office with route plans, but it still takes a fair amount of confidence to plunge into the system. Useful MetroBús (daily 5am–midnight) routes include #1, #17 and #18, which run north–south through town and out to the northern sights – fares are fixed within the city. Transfers to the Metrorrey system are free.

BY CAR

Car rental If you fancy renting wheels to get out to the sights immediately around Monterrey, or to explore the mountains, head to the airport or the Zona Rosa where all the main agencies have offices; Hertz is at the *Sheraton*, Hidalgo 310 (999 911 8040).

ACCOMMODATION

SEE MAP PAGE 426

La Casa del Barrio Montemayor 1221; http://lacasadelbarrio.com.mx. Budget option in the heart of the Barrio Antiguo, with friendly, helpful owners who can help with all sorts of adventure tours. Dorms (four or six beds) and comfy single or double rooms, some en suite. Laundry and kitchen included, plus coffee and toast for breakfast. Dorms M$; doubles M$$

Fastos Hotel Colón Pte 956 (opposite the bus station); http://fastoshotel.mx. Comfortable, modern hotel with large rooms all featuring a/c and satellite TV, and internet access in the lobby. Perfect for those passing through on early/late buses. M$$

★ **Gamma de Fiesta Americana** Ocampo Ote 443 (enter at Hidalgo and Escobedo, on Plaza Hidalgo); http://gammahoteles.com. Built as the *Gran Hotel Ancira* in 1912 (visit the small museum in the lobby) and full of Art Nouveau elegance, including a winding marble staircase and posh restaurant replete with gilded birdcages, this old gem is still an outstanding option; now owned and operated by Fiesta Americana, it's not as modern or luxurious as the city's newer hotels, but delivers plenty of historic charm. Rooms are spacious and come with cable TV, though some are showing their age – check first. Deals on the web can make this surprisingly reasonable. M$$$

iStay Monterrey Histórico Morelos Pte 191; http://istay.com.mx. This centrally located member of the iStay chain offers top value for money; it's essentially a budget business hotel, with compact but modern rooms, flatscreen TVs, a gym, helpful staff and a small restaurant. M$$

Quinta Real Diego Rivera 500, Valle Ote, San Pedro Garza García; http://caminoreal.com. Generally regarded as Monterrey's top hotel, this opulent pile is a luxurious amalgam of modern comfort and colonial style; it's a 15min ride from downtown in the hip Valle area. The spacious suites come with marble-covered bathrooms and living room; some have balconies. M$$$$

Safi Royal Luxury Towers Pino Suárez 444; http://safihotel.com. Luxurious hotel with expansive marble floors, elegant staircases and garden. The rooms are spacious, and there's a restaurant attached. M$$$

Taiyari Hostal Montemayor 1221; https://taiyari-hostal.monterrey-hotels.com. Spotless, trendy hostel in the Barrio Antiguo, with rustic wood bed frames, cheap dorms (triple-decker bunks) and double rooms with shared bathrooms. Guests can use the TV room, kitchen and terrace. Full breakfast is extra. Dorm M$, doubles M$$

EATING

Monterrey's **restaurants** cater to hearty, meat eating *norteños*, with *cabrito al pastor* or the regional speciality *cabrito asado* (whole roast baby goat) given pride of place in window displays. In the **centre** there are dozens of places around the Macroplaza and Barrio Antiguo, all convenient for downtown hotels, but if you're prepared to drive or take taxis, the up-and-coming area known as **Zona Valle** (south of the centre in the affluent suburb of San Pedro Garza García and along Lázaro Cárdenas), and southeast Monterrey (along Garza Sada) are where you'll find the latest trendsetters and a range of international cuisines.

CENTRO, SEE MAP PAGE 426

La Divina Montemayor Sur 507; https://ladivina.mx. Conveniently located close to the history museum, this traditional cantina features rustic stonewall rooms and a menu featuring tacos, stews, pastas and more substantial grilled steaks. Mariachis serenade customers in the evenings. M$$

La Fonda del Rey Matamoros Ote 816; 81 8344 9531. Bright and cheery cantina that serves tasty and economical Mexican staples (cactus salad, spicy enchiladas) for breakfast and lunch. M$$

Gaby Cafetería Restaurant Hidalgo 369; 81 8342 0596. Popular 1950s theme diner, serving a decent mix of international favourites and local specialities. There's also a sizable onsite bakery. M$$$

Madre Oaxaca Jardón Ote 814; 81 8345 1459. The speciality of this beautiful restaurant is Oaxacan cooking, the most delicious of Mexico's regional cuisines. Check this place out, especially if you can't get down south. M$$$

Mi Tierra Restaurante Morelos Ote 640; 81 8140 5611. A fun, no fuss Mexican restaurant serving up specialities like *chile relleno* and spicy *enchiladas*. It doesn't look like much but you can't beat the price and the quality. M$$

★ **El Rey del Cabrito** Constitución Ote 817 at Dr Coss; 81 8345 3232, https://facebook.com/reydelcabrito. The best place in town for *cabrito* is this slightly otherworldly restaurant, adorned with stuffed lions, an incongruous statue of Hindu elephant god Ganesha and even Egyptian hieroglyphs. The main event is sizzling, succulent baby goat meat, and you can also try their charcoal-grilled beef – all best experienced in a group. M$$$$

Trece Lunas Abasolo 870 (next to Casa del Maiz); https://facebook.com/eltrecelunas. Hip Barrio Antiguo café serving excellent coffee, sweet and savoury crêpes, Spanish-style tortilla, club sandwiches and cannelloni salads in a space decorated with murals and graffiti. Hosts tango and yoga lessons and other artsy events. M$$

ZONA VALLE, SEE MAP PAGE 424

El Gaucho Arroyo Seco 100 (off Garza Sada); http://restauranteelgaucho.com. One of the best Valle restaurants, worth the taxi ride for the finest steaks in the city – prime slabs of Argentine beef are pricy but delicious. M$$$$

★ **Pangea** Roble 660 (Valle del Campestre), San Pedro Garza García; http://restaurantepangea.com. The place for Mexican haute cuisine in Monterrey, helmed by local celebrity chef Guillermo González Beristáin: feast on roast chicken thighs stuffed with Serrano ham and goat cheese, seared sea scallops with foie gras, or rack of lamb with creamy porcini rice. M$$$$

Tacos del Julio González 115; Río Orinoco 81, Zona Valle (San Pedro Garza García); 81 8338 2033. Popular Monterrey chain since 1993 that has spread north of the border thanks to its high-quality tacos and plates of five *taquitos* stuffed with all manner of tasty fillings; try the *volcanes*, with steak and cheese. M$$

DRINKING AND NIGHTLIFE

The traditional heart of Monterrey nightlife was the **Barrio Antiguo**, five square blocks of cobbled streets bounded by Dr Coss, Matamoros and Constitución. Since the drug cartel violence of 2011–2012 the crowds have dropped off considerably – check the latest with your hotel before going out. Alternatively, take a taxi to Zona Valle or San Pedro Garza García where the latest mega clubs and bars play host to a smart, affluent set.

CENTRO AND BARRIO ANTIGUO, SEE MAP PAGE 426

Bar 1900 Gamma de Fiesta Americana Ocampo Ote 443 (enter at Hidalgo and Escobedo, on Plaza Hidalgo); http://gammahoteles.com. Colonial-style bar with cosy booths or bar stools, wood floors and decorated with bold Art Nouveau murals – live music most nights and a decent range of bottled beers, wines and spirits.

Café Iguana Montemayor Sur 927; http://cafeiguana.com.mx. Monterrey's best rock club (though their DJs play techno and electronica most Thurs & Fri nights). Live rock bands usually perform on Sat. Entry is either free or capped at a reasonable amount.

McMullens Montemayor 843; https://facebook.com/monterrock. Not really an Irish pub, "El Mc" is a jumping bar with live bands and blend of ska, rock and indie sounds. There's usually a cover here.

La Tumba Padre Mier Ote 827; http://facebook.com/laTumba. The main draw at this large, semi-outdoor bar is live acoustic music Thurs–Sat, and jazz on Tues. Expect to hear anything from *trova* and *son* to blues and rock. Cover varies depending on who is playing.

SAN PEDRO GARZA GARCÍA AND OUTER SUBURBS, SEE MAP PAGE 424

Far West Rodeo Jardín Cerveza, Expo de Guadalupe, Juárez Ote 917; 81 8351 3030. To remind yourself that you are still in Norteño country, make for this western-themed bar and live venue, which relocated to the beer garden of the Guadalupe expo centre in 2008. Tickets for live shows vary in price, but not by much.

El Porfiriato Alemán 200 (Paseo La Fe mall), San Nicolás de los Garza; https://elporfiriato.com. A nice little spot for some communal grub with a bar menu that's geared towards sharing. The drinks are especially good here, but they can also pack a punch.

Sierra Madre Brewing Co José Vasconcelos Ote 564, San Pedro Garza García; http://smbc.com.mx. Craft beer aficionados can indulge at the first brewpub in northern Mexico, with samplers of the local brews. Great bar food (especially the nachos and mini burgers). Also has an outpost just off the Macroplaza, on Morelos.

El Tercer Tiempo Garza Sada 2660; 81 8021 9770. Located across from the Tecnológico de Monterrey University and popular with students, this congenial sports bar features big-screen TVs for live games and events (mostly Mexican soccer, but some US sports also shown).

DIRECTORY

Banks and exchange You can change money at any of the several *casas de cambio* on Ocampo between Zaragoza and Juárez. Most banks (almost all with ATMs) are on Padre Mier, downtown.

Books Sanborn's, Escobedo Sur 920, just off Morelos, sells numerous magazines, some in English.

Consulates Australia, Parque Corporativo, Equus Torre Sur, Ricardo Margain 444, San Pedro Garza García 81 8158 0791; Canada, Gómez Morín 955, Suite 404, San Pedro Garza García (Mon–Fri 8.30am–1.30pm & 2.30–5pm; 81 8378 0240); South Africa, Díaz Ordaz 200, Colonia Santa María, 81 8335 5949; US, Alfonso Reyes 150, Col. Valle Poniente, Santa Catarina (Mon–Fri 8am–2pm; 81 8047 3100, http://mx.usembassy.gov).

Emergencies 066; Ángeles Verdes (078); Cruz Roja (065); Cruz Verde (81 8371 5050); Police Federal de Caminos (81 8343 0173).

Post office In the Palacio Federal, Washington 648, at the north end of the Macroplaza.

Around Monterrey

Monterrey is surrounded by surprisingly wild and scenic countryside, though getting around the sights in the vicinity – the **Parque Ecológico Cola de Caballo**, for example – can be a hassle without your own vehicle. The exception is the colonial city of **Saltillo**, a worthwhile destination in its own right and easily reached by bus.

Parque Grutas de García

Carr García km 10 • Charge (includes cable car, museum and 45min–1hr guided tour); • https://grutasdegarcia.com • Buses run several times daily to Villa de García (1hr) from outside the Central de Autobuses, and from there you'll need to take a taxi for the remaining 9km; the round trip is 3–4hr from downtown Monterrey

From Monterrey it's a relatively easy drive to the subterranean caverns of **Parque Grutas de García** which, despite some overdevelopment, contain an impressive array of contorted stalactites, stalagmites and an underground lake. The location is also spectacular, nestled beneath the craggy peaks of the Cerro del Fraile (1080m). Visits are by regular tours only, which run through around 2km (and 600 steps) of caverns – guides only speak Spanish, but the small museum at the entrance has English labelling. Some 46km west of Monterrey near the village of **VILLA DE GARCÍA** (located 19km off Hwy-40), the caves are a popular outing from the city, especially at weekends, when hundreds of people can be found taking the ten-minute cable car to the main entrance (you can walk along a steep trail to the caverns instead to save the fee, but the height gain is around 750m).

Parque Ecológico Cola de Caballo

Carr 20 Laguna de Sánchez km 6, La Cieneguilla • Charge • 81 2285 4525 • Agree on the taxi fee for a return trip (3–4hr) before you set out to the park from downtown Monterrey

The trip to the **Parque Ecológico Cola de Caballo** (Horsetail Falls), 45km south of Monterrey on Hwy-85, is only really worthwhile after the rains, when the falls gush down a 25m cliff-face in scintillating fashion. The falls are a relatively easy 600m hike from the car park, with a carnival-like atmosphere prevailing at the weekends (bungee jumps, cheap cocktails, horseback riding and the like). The horses and horse-drawn carriages on offer are not recommended.

AN IRISHMAN IN SALTILLO

Business in Saltillo in the early twentieth century was dominated by **William Purcell** (1844–1909), a talented Irishman who left his home to seek his fortune in Texas and Mexico aged 17. When he died in San Antonio he was a millionaire, owning half a million acres of cattle ranches, cotton farms and several silver mines. In the 1890s he opened a bank in Saltillo (now a gallery, see below). You can also view the **Casa Purcell**, at Hidalgo 231, a grand English Gothic mansion built by Purcell in 1906.

Santiago

Museo Histórico de Villa de Santiago Abasolo 100, at Juárez • Free • 81 2285 0060

Set on the shores of the Presa Rodrigo Gómez (reservoir), **SANTIAGO** is heavily promoted as a Pueblo Mágico, with cobbled streets, a pretty 1745 church, the **Parroquia de Santiago Apóstol** and several handicraft stalls worth browsing – assuming the tour buses are not around. The region's history is chronicled in the small **Museo Histórico de Villa de Santiago**, in front of the church.

7

ARRIVAL AND DEPARTURE — SANTIAGO

By bus Santiago lies 35km south of Monterrey on Hwy-85. To get here by bus, take a Lineas Amarillas service from the main bus station; for Cola de Caballo you need to get off at El Cercado, just south of Santiago centre, where *camiones* wait to take you to the falls at the junction with Hwy-20.

Saltillo

Capital of the state of Coahuila, **SALTILLO** feels far more provincial than Monterrey, despite being another large city of some seven hundred thousand. Lying just 85km to the southwest, through a high desert of yucca and Joshua trees, it's infinitely quieter than Monterrey and, at 1600m above sea level in the Sierra Madre Oriental, usually feels a little cooler.

If you read Spanish you'll get a lot out of Saltillo's surprisingly good cache of museums, but if not it's still a lovely place to stroll around, admire some beautiful buildings and soak up the colonial ambience.

Plaza de Armas and around

Mercado Juárez Plaza Acuña • Free

Two contrasting, and almost adjoining, squares grace the centre of town: the old **Plaza de Armas** is formal, tranquil, illuminated at night and sometimes hosts music performances, while **Plaza Acuña**, two blocks south, is surrounded by crowded shopping streets marking the rowdy heart of the commercial city. On the south side of Plaza Acuña, **Mercado Juárez** is a good place to browse for *sarapes* and souvenirs, and grab a cheap *caldo de res* or torta.

Catedral de Santiago

Hidalgo and Juárez, Plaza de Armas • Free, donation suggested

The magnificent eighteenth-century **Catedral de Santiago** is one of the most beautiful churches in northern Mexico, with an elaborately carved churrigueresque facade and doorways, an enormous bell tower and a smaller clock tower. The spacious Neoclassical interior is relatively plain, but there are two giant gold *retablos* in the transepts, and numerous oil paintings, including an early eighteenth-century *Virgen del Carmen* by Antonio de Torres.

Museo del Palacio

Palacio del Gobierno, Hidalgo and Juárez, Plaza de Armas • Free • 844 411 8529

Set inside the former Coahuila government house, completed in 1885, the stately **Museo del Palacio** contains temporary historical displays (topics have included the 1812 Constitución of Cádiz), and a permanent exhibition on the history of Coahuila.

Galería del Instituto Coahuilense de Cultura

Juárez at Hidalgo (Plaza de Armas) • Free • 844 414 5080

On the south side of the Plaza de Armas the **Galería del Instituto Coahuilense de Cultura** often hosts diverting temporary exhibits by Coahuila artists, and also houses a decent Spanish bookshop and the best place for a coffee (and delicious pastries) in town, *Cafeteria Kala*.

Recinto del Patrimonio Cultural Universitario

Hidalgo 211 • Free • https://facebook.com/recintodelpatrimonioculturaluniversitario

Just off the north side of the Plaza de Armas is Saltillo's fanciest gallery space, the **Recinto del Patrimonio Cultural Universitario**, housed in a mansion dating back to 1680. The galleries here are tastefully presented, and though the collection of eighteenth- and nineteenth-century Mexican paintings is nothing special, there are a few quality pieces, including a couple of **Miguel Cabrera** portraits. There's also work by Jose Obregón, Ignacio Rosas and a startling triptych from Saturnino Herrán (see page 352), *La Leyenda de los Volcanos*. The **Museo del Sitio** section covers the history of the building, with a section on William Purcell (see page 432), a remarkable Irish merchant.

7

Centro Cultural Vito Alessio Robles

Hidalgo, at Aldama • Free • 844 412 8458

Saltillo's oldest streets fan out from Plaza de Armas, lined with some fine colonial houses. One historical building worth seeking out is the carefully preserved **Centro Cultural Vito Alessio Robles**, the old town hall, one block north of the plaza. The walls of the courtyard and the staircase are adorned with murals completed by Elena Huerta 1973–75, depicting the history of the town from prehistoric times to the 1950s, while temporary art exhibits take up the inner galleries. There's also the small Sala Museográfica dedicated to historian **Vito Alessio Robles** (born in Saltillo in 1879), containing mementos and personal effects (his piano, uniform, photos and the like).

Museo de la Revolución Mexicana

Hidalgo Sur 167 • Free • 844 410 4794

The illuminating **Museo de la Revolución Mexicana** is focused solely on the 1910 Mexican Revolution, a homage in part to local son and former president **Venustiano Carranza**, who was born in Coahuila in 1859 and studied in Saltillo. It's an impressive display, with touchscreens, videos, music and a variety of artefacts to highlight the key stages of the Revolution beginning with the Díaz regime – there's even a recording of the old dictator speaking. Francisco Madero gets his own section, as does Carranza (with photos of him in Saltillo), and the 1917 constitution is covered in some detail. Labelling is in Spanish only.

El Sarape de Saltillo

Hidalgo Sur 305 • 844 414 9634

Saltillo is famous for its **sarapes** (multicoloured woollen shawls), and there are several small shops where (at least on weekdays) you can watch the manufacturing process. The best is tucked at the back of the artesanía shop **El Sarape de Saltillo**. Sadly, the old ways are vanishing fast, and most now use artificial fibres and chemical dyes: many of those in the market are mass-produced in virulent clashing colours.

Museo del Sarape y Trajes Mexicanos

Allende Sur 160 • Free • 844 481 6900

This eighteenth-century former home is now the **Museo del Sarape y Trajes Mexicanos**, a celebration of the city's most famous product. It's not known why sarape production blossomed here in particular from around 1750, though it's thought that the boom in sheep farming during colonial times helped, as did the migration of Indigenous Tlaxcalan weavers from central Mexico. The main exhibition contains forty brightly dyed sarapes to highlight this history, and there's a showroom of traditional Mexican costumes from pre-Hispanic times.

Museo de las Aves de México

Bolívar 151, at Hidalgo • Charge • http://musave.org

Bird lovers should visit the **Museo de las Aves de México**, housed in what once was the Jesuit-run Colegio de San Juan, overlooking San Juan Nepomunceno church. Inside the museum you'll find five themed areas, beginning with the origins of birds and their physiology – beaks, feathers, eggs and skeletons. The birds of Mexico, from parrots to pelicans, are featured, along with a section on bird migration (the only section labelled in English) and birds from Coahuila. The main focus throughout is on a vast collection of stuffed birds, including a giant Californian condor, albatross, owls, hawks and ostrich. There's also a fun song room where the cries and tweets of various species are played.

Museo de los Presidentes Coahuilenses

Nicolás Bravo Sur 264, at Juan Antonio de la Fuente • Free • https://museopresidentes.org.mx

The compact **Museo de los Presidentes Coahuilenses** honours the five presidents of Mexico to hail from Coahuila: Venustiano Carranza (1915–20), Roque González Garza (1915), Eulalio Gutiérrez (1914–15), Francisco Madero (1911–13) and Melchor Múzquiz (1832). Each of the great men is remembered by a small exhibit containing documents, artefacts and personal effects (the first presidential sash, worn by Guadalupe Victoria, is also here), but everything is labelled in Spanish only.

Museo del Desierto

Carlos Avedrop Davila 3745, in Parque Las Maravillas • Charge, discount for children 6–12 • http://museodeldesierto.org

About 3km east of the centre, the impressive **Museo del Desierto** charts the development and history of deserts, displays a huge array of dinosaur and prehistoric animal fossils, and rare artefacts from Neolithic cultures in the region. Labelling is in Spanish only.

ARRIVAL AND INFORMATION — SALTILLO

By plane Saltillo's tiny airport (Aeropuerto Internacional Plan de Guadalupe) lies 16km northeast of the city centre and serves daily Aeroméxico flights to Mexico City (3 daily; 1hr 30min). Taxis run into the city from here.

By bus Buses (marked "Centro/Camionera" or #9) run between Saltillo's Centro de Autobuses, 3km south of the centre on Luis Echeverría, the cathedral on the Plaza de Armas and onwards a couple more stops to the Plaza Acuña, right at the heart of things (to get back, catch it on Aldama near Zaragoza). Taxis are legally required to use the meter, so insist on it.

Destinations Durango (5 daily; 6–7hr); Parras (7 daily; 2hr 30min); Mexico City (every 1–2hr; 10–12hr); Monterrey (hourly; 1hr 30min); Nuevo Laredo (every 1–2hr; 4–5hr); San Luis Potosí (hourly; 5hr); Zacatecas (hourly; 4–6hr).

Tourist information Visit La Dirección de Turismo Municipal, at Allende 124 (Mon–Fri 9am–5pm; 844 439 7195, http://saltillo.gob.mx).

ACCOMMODATION

City Express Saltillo Sur Luis Echeverría 350-A; www.marriott.com. Hard to beat for convenience if travelling by bus – this modern motel is right opposite the bus station. Rooms are standard business style, with flatscreen TVs, and breakfast is included. M$$$

★ **Hotel Colonial San Miguel** General Cepeda Sur; 844

WINES OF PARRAS

The biggest draw in the Valle de Parras is wine – most vineyards offer tours and tastings and can be visited on day trips from Parras de la Fuente.

Antigua Bodega de Perote Ramos Arizpe 131 (2km west of Parras de la Fuente); http://antiguahaciendadeperote.com. Produces fine wines as well as brandy and *sotol*, the local spirit. Runs a hotel on site (M$$$); call ahead for tours and visits.

Las Bodegas de Casa Madero Carretera 102 Paila-Parras km 18.5, Hacienda San Lorenzo (8km north of Parras de la Fuente); http://madero.com.mx. This is the largest and oldest Parras wine producer, with roots going back to the Americas' first winery, established here in 1597 by the Spaniards. You can take free 30min tours of the facilities and museum, buy and taste the wine and admire the colonial Hacienda de San Lorenzo on site.

Las Bodegas El Vesubio Madero 36, at Andrés S Viesca, Parras de la Fuente. Established by Italian Nicolás Nicolielli in 1891 in downtown Parras, this is a smaller operation. The shop is open daily.

410 3082, https://facebook.com/hotelcolonialsanmiguel. Stylish rooms set in a historic building with a small pool and courtyard, blending original wood shutters and doors with contemporary furnishings, cable TV and a/c. M$$

Hotel Urdiñola Victoria 211; http://hotelurdinola.com. If you want to savour some faded colonial splendour on a budget, check out this old gem, with its tiled open lobby dominated by a wide staircase flanked by suits of armour, and fountains trickling amid the greenery of the courtyard. Basic but adequate rooms with fans only. M$$

7

EATING

La Canasta Carranza 2485; 844 415 8050. Highly acclaimed since it opened in 1965, this restaurant serves fine international and Mexican cuisine, steaks, and their specialities, *arroz huerfano* ("orphan" rice with ham, nuts and bacon) and lemon meringue pie. M$$$

Cafeteria Kala Galería del Instituto Coahuilense de Cultura, Juárez 109 at Hidalgo (Plaza de Armas); 844 414 1781. For the best coffee, frappes, muffins and panini in town, visit this cosy café in the corner of the Cultural Institute. M$$

El Mesón Principal Carranza 4671, at Egipto; http://mesonprincipal.com. For high-quality sit-down meals, take a taxi out to *El Mesón Principal*, which specializes in sizzling *cabrito al pastor* (barbecued baby goat), and mouthwatering *fritada* (grilled steak platter). M$$$$

Panadería Mena Pan de Pulque Madero 1326; 844 412 1671. Try Saltillo's famous *pan de pulque*, bread made of wheat, egg, cinnamon and unrefined cactus juice, at this classic bakery from 1925, three long blocks west of Carranza. M$

DIRECTORY

Banks There are banks with ATMs all over the centre of town, including Banamex and HSBC, just off the plaza.

Pharmacy Try the large Farmacia Guadalajara at Victoria and Purcell, overlooking the Alameda.

Post office The post office is at Guadalupe Victoria 303.

Valle de Parras

Around 160km west of Saltillo, the **Valle de Parras** is the oldest **wine-growing** region in Mexico. Dismissed as poor quality for years, the region's Cabernet Sauvignons in particular, which account for around seventy percent of production, are finally garnering a following in international markets.

The region is anchored by the pleasant oasis town of **PARRAS DE LA FUENTE**, a good place to base yourself.

ARRIVAL AND DEPARTURE — PARRAS DE LA FUENTE

By bus Parras is around 160km from both Torreón and Saltillo in the south of Coahuila, and is served by buses from Saltillo (7 daily; 2hr 30min) and Monterrey (4 daily; 3hr).

ACCOMMODATION

Hostal el Farol Ramos Arizpe 301; http://hostalelfarol.com. The best place to stay in the town itself is this colonial beauty, with rustic furniture, antique bed frames, cable TV and free bottles of water. M$$$

The coastal route

If you're determined to travel between the Yucatán, Veracruz and the US by the shortest route, avoiding Mexico City altogether, you'll need to follow the **coastal route**. North of Tuxpán (see page 408), there's plenty of sandy beachfront, but access is difficult, beaches tend to be windswept and scrubby, and much of the area is marred by oil refineries. Several small-scale resorts have been developed here (such as **La Pesca** and the villages around **Laguna Madre**), but these tend to be popular with nearby city-dwellers and have little to offer compared with the beaches further south. It's also very, very hot.

Another issue is drug violence – **Tamaulipas**, the focus of the bloody conflict between the Gulf Cartel and Los Zetas, had become the most dangerous part of Mexico by 2012. Though things seemed to be improving, the homicide rate spiked up again in 2017 and 2018, and it remains blighted by shootings and kidnapping – the current US State Department travel warning ranks the state at Level 4, the same as countries such as Afghanistan, Iraq, Libya and Syria (see page 453).

If you have time you'd be well advised to cut inland from Tampico to **Monterrey** (see page 420), where there's plenty of metropolitan diversions and a larger choice of routes to the border.

Tampico

Some 490km north of Veracruz, on the Río Pánuco and just across the border in Tamaulipas state, **TAMPICO** is one of Mexico's busiest ports, with a population of around 860,000. It was from here that Humphrey Bogart set out to unearth *The Treasure of the Sierra Madre* in 1948, and the older parts of town still have a slightly dilapidated feel, with peeling, ramshackle clapboard houses contrasting with the affluent but characterless US mall-style development on the outskirts. However, in a bid to attract more tourists, the downtown area has been spruced up with a host of thoughtful restoration projects, and the graceful New Orleans-style cast-iron buildings add a vaguely sophisticated charm to the main plazas.

Plaza de Armas and Plaza de la Libertad

Downtown, the city's dual nature is instantly apparent. Within a hundred metres of each other are two plazas: the grandiose **Plaza de Armas** – rich and formal, it is ringed by government buildings, the impressive **Catedral Inmaculada Concepción** (built in the 1930s with money donated by American oil tycoon Edward Doheny) and the smart hotels; and the **Plaza de la Libertad**, which is raucous, rowdy – there's usually some form of music played from the bandstand each evening – and peopled by wandering vendors. Ringed by triple-decker wrought-iron verandas, it has been spruced up to form an attractive square.

Espacio Cultural Metropolitano (METRO Tampico)

Adolfo López Mateos s/n, Col Obrera • 833 126 0888 • **Museo de la Cultura Huasteca** • Charge • **Galería de Exposiciones Temporales** • Free • Walk north on Olmos from Plaza de Armas till you hit the Laguna del Carpintero, then stroll (anticlockwise) around the edge till you see it (2km); or catch a "Central Camionera" bus from Olmos and ask to get off at the Parque Metropolitano

Worth a look is the **Espacio Cultural Metropolitano** or **METRO Tampico**, home to two theatres, Teatro Metropolitano and Teatro Experimental, the highly regarded **Galería de Exposiciones Temporales**, featuring temporary art exhibits, and the **Museo de la Cultura Huasteca**, which provides an absorbing introduction to Indigenous Huastec culture through original artefacts and engaging displays. **Huastec civilization** blossomed in the Postclassic era (eleventh to fifteenth centuries), before being conquered by the Aztecs and then the Spanish – today there are over 60,000 Huastec speakers, living predominantly in the Río Pánuco region.

7

ARRIVAL AND INFORMATION — TAMPICO

By plane Arriving at Tampico's Francisco Javier Mina airport, some 15km north of the city, you'll have to take a taxi (or pay around a small fee for a *colectivo*). The most frequent connections are to Mexico City or Monterrey.

By bus Tampico's modern Terminal Central de Autobuses (guardería 6am–midnight), Bustamante 210, is in an unattractive area some 10km north of the city. To get downtown, take a bus, a rattling *colectivo* or one of the shared *perimetral* taxis. Buses back to the terminal leave from Plaza de Armas, at the corner of Olmos and Carranza.

Destinations Ciudad Victoria (hourly or better; 3hr); Matamoros (hourly; 7–8hr); Mexico City (every 1–2hr; 8hr); Monterrey (hourly; 7–8hr); Nuevo Laredo (2 daily; 10hr); San Luis Potosí (11 daily; 7hr); Veracruz (8 daily; 9hr).

Tourist information You'll find tourist information booths on both plazas, though these seem to be open quite irregularly.

ACCOMMODATION AND EATING — SEE MAP PAGE 437

7

Elite Restaurante & Helados Díaz Mirón Ote 211 (near Plaza de Armas); 833 212 0364. A quiet haven in this noisy town, *Elite* does excellent ice cream, coffee, frappucinos and good Mexican staples. Has roots in a street stall opened in 1948. M$$

Hotel Inglaterra Díaz Mirón 116; http://hinglaterra.com.mx. On the Plaza de Armas, this is one of the most comfortable and safe central options, with compact modern rooms, a restaurant and a small pool. M$$

Impala Díaz Mirón Pte 220; 833 212 0990, https://facebook.com/Hotelimpaladetampico. This aged hotel has been renovated many times over the years and remains exceptionally clean, if relatively simple; the huge buffet breakfast is included (you can sometimes get a cheaper rate if you skip breakfast). M$$

Jardín Corona Hidalgo 2405; 833 213 9383. Plush Argentine seafood and steak restaurant since 1964, worth the taxi ride for the huge plates of shrimp, crab and fresh fish, as well as fabulous *bife de chorizo*. Reckon on spending at decent amount per head for a good meal. Live Latino sounds every Fri & Sat. M$$$$

El Porvenir Hidalgo 1403, at Oaxaca; http://elporvenir.rest. Best seafood in the region since 1923 – come especially for the huge plates of prawn and crab, boiled, stuffed or spiced a variety of ways ("El Mercedes Benz" is fish fillet with shrimp in garlic sauce topped with clams). M$$$

DIRECTORY

Banks There are banks on the Plaza de Armas and all through the central area.

Post office At Madero 309, on the north side of the Plaza de la Libertad.

The central corridor

The central corridor between Mexico City, the Bajío and the US border is one of the most well-travelled and well-served routes in the country, with fast highways and numerous bus services all the way. It's worth a diversion into **Durango**, certainly the most attractive city on route, or historic **Hidalgo del Parral**. History lovers will also enjoy **Chihuahua**, the home of Pancho Villa and a relatively affluent city that has invested a lot in its heritage, museums and art. If you have time, an excursion to the ruins at **Paquimé**, near Nuevo Casas Grandes, is worth the four-hour ride from Chihuahua – and if you have a car, there are several other enticing destinations nearby.

Durango

In the 1960s John Wayne came to the beautiful colonial city of **DURANGO** to make seven Westerns (among them *Chisum* and *The War Wagon*), a tradition maintained today in studios outside the city. Although the Sierra Madre still looms on the western horizon, the country around the city itself is flat; just two low hills mark it out from the plain: the **Cerro del Mercado**, a giant lump of iron ore that testifies to the area's mineral wealth, rises squat and black to the north, while to the west a climb or cable-car ride up the **Cerro de los Remedios** provides a wonderful panorama over the whole city. Durango, with its roughly 630,000 inhabitants, sits between these two hills in the Valle del Guadiana.

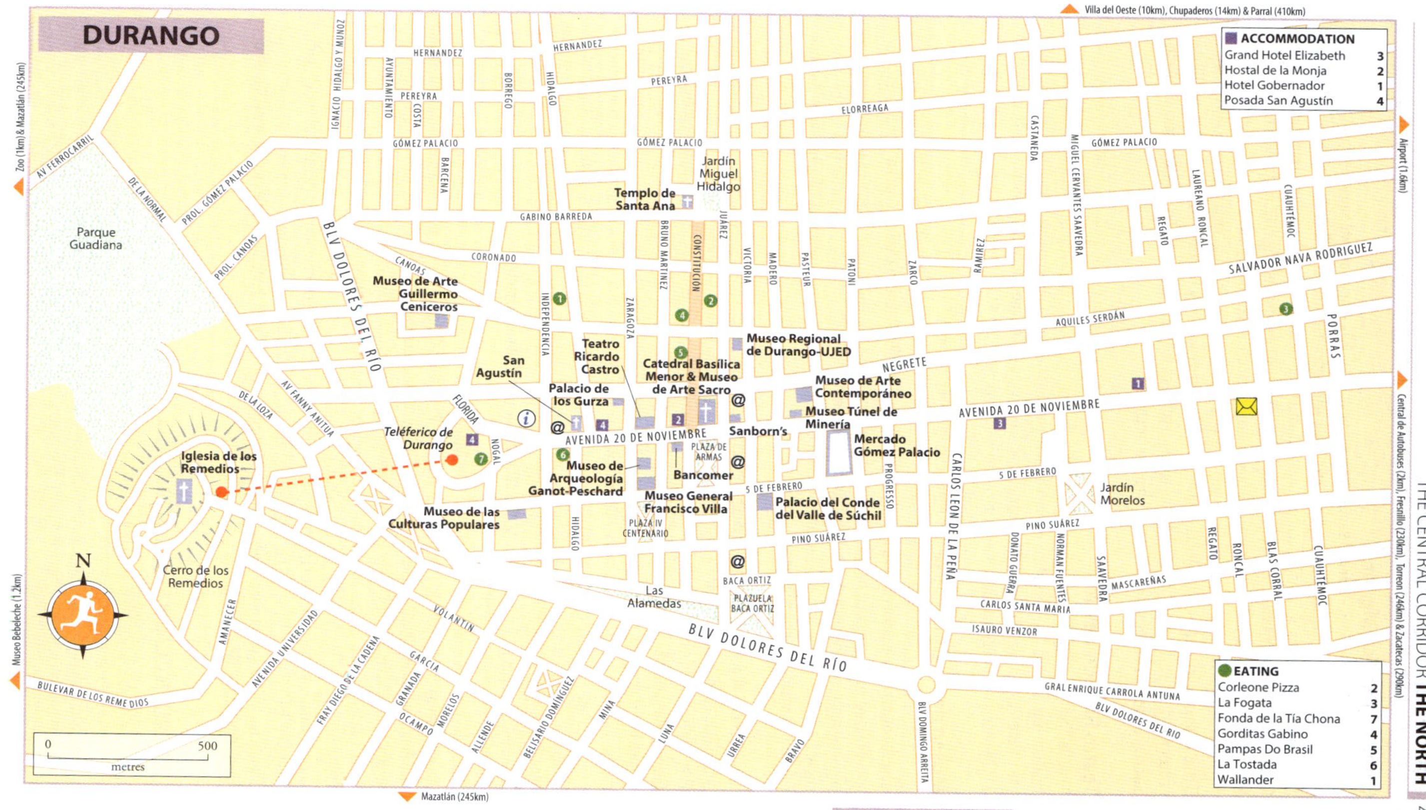
DURANGO
ACCOMMODATION
Grand Hotel Elizabeth 3
Hostal de la Monja 2
Hotel Gobernador 1
Posada San Agustín 4
EATING
Corleone Pizza 2
La Fogata 3
Fonda de la Tía Chona 7
Gorditas Gabino 4
Pampas Do Brasil 5
La Tostada 6
Wallander 1
Villa del Oeste (10km), Chupaderos (14km) & Parral (410km)
Airport (1.6km)
Central de Autobuses (2km), Fresnillo (230km), Torreon (246km) & Zacatecas (290km)
Zoo (1km) & Mazatlán (245km)
Museo Bebeleche (1.2km)
Mazatlán (245km)
Parque Guadiana
Templo de Santa Ana
Jardín Miguel Hidalgo
Museo de Arte Guillermo Ceniceros
San Agustín
Teatro Ricardo Castro
Catedral Basílica Menor & Museo de Arte Sacro
Museo Regional de Durango-UJED
Museo de Arte Contemporáneo
Museo Túnel de Minería
Palacio de los Gurza
Sanborn's
Mercado Gómez Palacio
Teleférico de Durango
Iglesia de los Remedios
Museo de Arqueología Ganot-Peschard
Bancomer
Plaza de Armas
Museo General Francisco Villa
Palacio del Conde del Valle de Súchil
Museo de las Culturas Populares
Plaza IV Centenario
Jardín Morelos
Cerro de los Remedios
Las Alamedas
Plazuela Baca Ortiz
BLV DOLORES DEL RÍO
AVENIDA 20 DE NOVIEMBRE
N
0
500
metres

Catedral Basílica Menor

Negrete Pte 601 (Plaza de Armas) • **Catedral Basílica Menor** • Free • 618 812 5077 • **Museo de Arte Sacro** • Charge • 618 119 6235

Almost all the monuments in downtown Durango are clustered in a few streets around the **Plaza de Armas** and the huge covered market nearby. On the plaza itself is the **Catedral Basílica Menor**, its two robust domed towers dwarfing the narrow facade. Dating back to 1695, it's a typical Mexican church: externally imposing, weighty and Baroque, with a magnificent setting overlooking the plaza, but the interior is a little disappointing – dim and uninspired by comparison. Much better is the opulent collection of religious art and historical artefacts within the cathedral's **Museo de Arte Sacro**; enter on Negrete, behind the cathedral.

Teatro Ricardo Castro

Bruno Martínez 220, at 20 de Noviembre • Free • 618 811 4694

Following 20 de Noviembre down from the cathedral (stretching away to the left as you face it) brings you to the grandiose Porfiriano **Teatro Ricardo Castro**, completed in 1924, with its elegant interior of marble floors and crystal chandeliers.

Museo de Historia y Arte "El Palacio de los Gurza"

Negrete Pte 901, at Zaragoza • Charge • 618 811 1720

The beautifully restored **Museo de Historia y Arte "El Palacio de los Gurza"** features innovative galleries chronicling the history of the city through ancient coins, photography, newspaper articles and contemporary art. The Porfiriana-style house mostly dates from the mid-nineteenth century, when it was owned by Antonio Gurza López, a wealthy merchant.

Museo de Arqueología Ganot-Peschard

Zaragoza 315 • Charge • 618 813 1047

For a glimpse into Durango's pre-Columbian past visit the **Museo de Arqueología Ganot-Peschard**, which has a fine display of prehistoric finds, fossils and ancient skulls (Spanish captions only), in a nineteenth-century edifice that once served as the state archives. The museum is named in honour of its founders and current directors, Jaime Ganot and Alejando Peschard, who uncovered numerous examples of pre-Hispanic cave art in the region in the 1970s.

Museo General Francisco Villa (Palacio de Zambrano)

5 de Febrero 800 • Charge • 618 811 4793

The elegant porticoed facade of the **Museo General Francisco Villa (Palacio de Zambrano)** dominates the north side of **Plaza IV Centenario**, one block west of Plaza de Armas. Originally the eighteenth-century mansion of Spanish mining magnate Juan José Zambrano, it was taken over by the local government after independence and became the governor's residence. Local artist Francisco Montoya de la Cruz decorated the stairwells and walls of the two-storey arcaded patio inside in 1950, with bold murals depicting the state's history. Exhibits chart the political and social history of the region since the Revolution, with special attention given to hero Pancho Villa (see page 448). Spanish labels only, but English-speaking guides are usually available (free).

FERIA NACIONAL DE DURANGO

Durango's month-long **festival**, held in July, celebrates the city's foundation on July 8, 1563 by Spanish explorer Francisco de Ibarra. Festivities commence several days before and run right through till the fiesta of the Virgen del Refugio on July 22 – well worth going out of your way for, though rooms are booked solid. See http://mexicoescultura.com for more information.

Museo de las Culturas Populares

5 de Febrero 1107 • Charge • 618 825 8827

A few blocks west of Plaza IV Centenario, along 5 de Febrero, lies the **Museo de las Culturas Populares**, with rooms dedicated to local, native styles of weaving, ceramics, basketware and mask making. Enthusiastic guides explain all, and there are often interesting temporary exhibitions.

Casa de Cultural Banamex (Palacio del Conde del Valle de Súchil)

5 de Febrero Ote 401, at Madero • Free • http://fomentoculturalbanamex.org

The most elaborate of Durango's Spanish-style mansions is the **Palacio del Conde del Valle de Súchil**, now reborn as the **Casa de Cultural Banamex** thanks to the Mexican banking giant. Completed in 1764 for the Conde de Súchil, former Spanish governor of Durango, its exuberantly carved columns and wealth of extravagant detail are quite undamaged by time. Inside, a series of galleries hosts temporary exhibitions from modern photography to eighteenth-century art.

7

Museo Regional de Durango-UJED

Victoria Sur 100, at Aquiles Serdán • Charge • http://museo.ujed.mx

The stately former residence of ex-Governor Francisco Gómez Palacio, completed in 1890, is now the Universidad Juárez's **Museo Regional de Durango-UJED** or "Museo del Aguacate", after the avocado (*aguacate*) trees growing in the courtyard. It contains several absorbing galleries on local archeology and history, including special sections on Tepehuana culture, and Miguel Cabrera's cycle of ten paintings depicting the life of Mary.

Museo de Arte Guillermo Ceniceros

Serdán 1225 • Charge • http://guillermoceniceros.com

The legacy of whom many describe as the last great Mexican muralist is preserved at the **Museo de Arte Guillermo Ceniceros**, a vibrant showcase for local Durango artists as well Guillermo Ceniceros himself. Ceniceros was born in Durango in 1939, and later worked with muralist David Alfaro Siqueiros. The museum displays more than fifty of his works, on the top floor of the elegant nineteenth-century mansion known as "El Sabino" (originally built for German-Mexican businessman Bruno Harzer). The ground floor houses temporary exhibitions from local and national artists.

Paseo Túnel de Minería

Plaza Juan Pablo II • Tues–Sun 11am–4pm • Charge • 618 133 0413

One of Durango's biggest crowd-pleasers is the **Paseo Túnel de Minería**, commemorating the city's mining heritage but popular mainly because of the chance to shuffle through a 280m tunnel some 8m below the streets. The tunnel – enhanced with mining exhibits – links Plaza Juan Pablo II, at the Arzobispado, with Plaza de Armas (the tunnels were originally used by clergy, not miners).

Teleférico de Durango

Calle de la Cruz, between Calvario and Florida (by the central library); Remedios station on Linda Vista by Remedios church • Charge; 50 percent discount for Paseo Túnel de Minería ticket holders • 618 813 5133

Durango's popular **Teleférico** (cable car) connects the Cerro del Calvario in the centre with the viewpoint on the **Cerro de los Remedios** some 750m away, topped with the Parroquia de Nuestra Señora de los Remedios and offering sensational panoramas of the city (both stations offer free wi-fi).

Parque Guadiana

Av de la Normal • Daily 24hr • Free • **Museo Bebeleche** Armando del Castillo Franco km 1.5 (Parque Sahuatoba) • Charge (discount for children) • 618 827 2525 • Take a bus marked "Remedios/Parque Guadiana" from outside the cathedral

Covering the northwestern flanks of the Cerro de los Remedios, 1km west of the city centre, the **Parque Guadiana** is a vast area of fragrant eucalyptus and shady willows, dotted with fountains and kids' playgrounds. Durango's pride and joy adjoins the park: the **Museo Bebeleche**, a lavish hands-on museum and learning centre. Youngsters will enjoy most of the interactive exhibits, though labels are in Spanish only.

ARRIVAL AND DEPARTURE — DURANGO

By plane Durango's small airport (Aeropuerto Internacional General Guadalupe Victoria) lies 15km northeast of the centre, served primarily by flights from Mexico City and Tijuana. Low-cost TAR Aerolineas operates flights to Guadalajara, Monterrey and Ciudad Juárez. Taxis regularly run into the centre from here.

By bus Buses arrive at the Central de Autobuses or just "La Camionera" (guardería, 7am–11pm), over 4km east of downtown at Francisco Villa 102; to get to the centre, take one of the off-white buses marked "Centro" or "ISSSTE" from in front of the station. These will drop you right at the Plaza de Armas near the cathedral. Taxis are metered.

Destinations Aguascalientes (20 daily; 6hr); Chihuahua (12 daily; 8–11hr); Ciudad Juárez (at least hourly; 12–14hr); Mazatlán (11 daily; 3–3.5hr); Mexico City (14 daily; 11–13hr); Monterrey (8 daily; 7hr); Parral (10 daily; 6hr); Zacatecas (roughly hourly; 4–5hr).

7

INFORMATION

Tourist office The main tourist office (Secretaria de Turismo) is at Florida Pte 1106 (Mon–Fri 9am–8pm, Sat 10am–6pm; 618 811 9677, http://mexico-durango.com). Information kiosks are normally open in Plaza de Armas (daily 9am–8pm) and the bus station (Mon–Sat 9am–9pm, Sun 9am–3pm).

ACCOMMODATION — SEE MAP PAGE 439

Grand Hotel Elizabeth 20 de Noviembre 204; https://facebook.com/GrandHotelElizabethDurango. Excellent hotel on the edge of the old centre, with comfy modern rooms and a rooftop terrace with views over the city, though the British theme is a little kitsch. M$$

Hostal de la Monja Constitución Sur 214; http://hostaldelamonja.com.mx. Ignoring the international chains on the outskirts, this is the most comfortable place to stay in town, a gorgeous colonial property right on the main plaza. All rooms and suites feature polished wood floors and a simple, clean style, but the cheapest rooms are small and fairly plain, given the price. M$$$

Hotel Gobernador 20 de Noviembre Ote 257; https://facebook.com/gobernadorhotel. This luxurious monolith is surrounded by verdant gardens; the spacious rooms come with marble-clad bathrooms and wall-mounted LCD TVs, and there's a pool, gym and all the business-related extras. M$$$

Posada San Agustín 20 de Noviembre Pte 906, at Hidalgo; https://facebook.com/posadasanagustindurango. Excellent mid-range option, with simple but cosy a/c rooms with cable TV, set around a courtyard in a graceful nineteenth-century building. Free wi-fi in the courtyard. M$

EATING — SEE MAP PAGE 439

Corleone Pizza Constitución Nte 114, at Serdán; 618 811 6900. One of the best Italian joints in the city, this buzzing family restaurant is best known for its pizzas and an admirable range of cocktails. M$$

La Fogata Cuauhtémoc Sur 200, at Negrete; 618 817 0347. This moderately priced, elegant restaurant is the choice of Durango's movers and shakers, serving international and Mexican food but best known for its succulent steaks. M$$$

Fonda de la Tía Chona Nogal 110; 618 811 7748. A local dinner favourite, the rustic, antique-strewn interior is often packed with *Duranguenõs*. It serves excellent traditional Durango cuisine (try their *caldillo durangueño*, beef stew) at reasonable prices. M$$

Gorditas Gabino Constitución Nte 100; 618 813 0121. Bright, clean, economical restaurant serving steaks, tacos, burritos and burgers. They do a pretty decent *enchiladas rojas* for a few pesos, and the trademark gorditas (deep-fried corn meal with sausage) are fabulous. M$

Pampas Do Brasil Constitución Sur 102, in the San Jorge hotel; 618 827 6121. Fun place to stuff yourself; the menu largely comprises Brazilian cuts of juicy grilled steak and meats, in something resembling *churrascuria*-style eating. M$$$

La Tostada Florida 1125; 618 811 4577. This pleasant, clean restaurant near the cable car is popular with the locals. It serves Mexican staples and good breakfasts too. M$$

★ **Wallander** Independencia Nte 128; www.wallander.mx. Tempting store loaded with locally made cheeses, baked goods, cookies, cakes and huge tortas for lunch. They also serve locally brewed Cerveza Duranguea craft beers. M$$

DIRECTORY

Banks There's a convenient branch of Bancomer right by the plaza at the corner of 20 de Noviembre and Constitución, in addition to several other banks nearby.

Post office Some twelve blocks east of the cathedral, at 20 de Noviembre Ote 500-B.

La Tierra del Cine

The region around Durango is heavily marketed to domestic tourists as the **La Tierra del Cine**, the "land of cinema", in honour of the vast number of **film** units that once came to the area to take advantage of its remarkably constant, clear, high-altitude light, its desert and mountain scenery. Westerns were the speciality, and although only half a dozen movies have been shot here in recent decades (Luc Besson's *Bandidas* in 2004 was the last major foreign one, though the History Channel mini-series *Texas Rising* was shot here in 2014 and plenty of Mexican movies are still made on site), you can still see the permanent sets at **Villa del Oeste** and **Chupaderos**.

Villa del Oeste

Carr Durango–Parral km 12 (Hwy-45) • Charge; show free with park entry • https://facebook.com/paseodelviejooestedgo

Villa del Oeste (officially "Parque Temático Paseo del Viejo Oeste"), 12km north of Durango, is a kind of small theme park comprising the 100m-long street of "Bandido", which looks straight out of the Wild West until you realize the saloons and shops have been refashioned into a themed restaurant, music hall and a bar and grill. During the week it's fairly quiet, but at weekends there's a kitschy but enjoyable show featuring gun-slinging cowboys and cabaret girls.

Set Cinematográfico de Chupaderos

Carr Durango–Parral km 14 (Hwy-45) • Charge • 618 112 2882

The original Durango movie set – where films were shot starting in 1954 with Robert Wagner's *White Feather* – lies 2km north of Villa del Oeste in the dusty village of **CHUPADEROS**, preserved since 2012 as the **Set Cinematográfico de Chupaderos**. Villagers had pretty much taken over the faux Wild West main street, but thanks to government funds it now offers elaborate cowboy shows by professional actors.

ARRIVAL AND DEPARTURE — LA TIERRA DEL CINE

By bus The main road between Parral and Durango (Hwy-45) runs within a few hundred metres of the movie sets, so it's easy enough to get there by bus, though flagging one down when you leave can take much longer – alternatively, you can take the special buses to both Villa del Oeste and the Set Cinematográfico de Chupaderos on Sat and Sun from Plaza de Armas in Durango (the fare includes admission), 40min before each show (returns 2hr later).

By taxi The movie sets can also be reached by taxi but be sure to agree on the fare before you set off.

Parral

PARRAL, or "Hidalgo del Parral" as it's officially known, is fixed in Mexican consciousness as the place where **Pancho Villa** (see page 448) met his demise under a spectacular hail of hot lead in 1923. The town's history goes much further than this, however, having been established in the early seventeenth century as a silver-mining centre.

Museo Francisco Villa

Gabino Barrera 13, at Juárez • Charge • 627 525 3292

The **Museo Francisco Villa**, located close to the spot where Villa's bullet-ridden vehicle came to a halt, commemorates the assassinated hero with displays of Revolution-era effects, antique weapons, a small shrine and plenty of enigmatic old photos. Every year in July, Villa's death is re-enacted here.

Mina La Prieta

Estaño 2 • Charge • 627 525 4400

The ramshackle spectre of the **Mina La Prieta**, the once great silver mine founded in 1629, overlooks Parral from a hill on the edge of town. It closed in 1975 but you can take a short tour of some of the mine workings, 40m down by elevator, left almost as they were over forty years before. At the mine head there's the **Museo Regional de Minería**, containing heaps of old mining equipment.

Palacio Alvarado

Riva Palacio 2 • Charge • 627 522 0290

Mineral profits helped build some of the town's more impressive edifices, including the **Palacio Alvarado**, an opulent 1903 mansion built for local mining magnate Don Pedro Alvarado. He was reputedly a close friend and business associate of Pancho Villa, which might explain why Villa was carried to burial in the Alvarado funerary wagon, now parked inside the building. You'll find some excellent photos that chart the town's development.

Templo de San José

Francisco Moreno Domínguez, at Plaza Principal

The town of Parral is home to several striking churches, and the **Templo de San José** on the main plaza (not to be confused with the cathedral on the Jardín Plaza de Guadalupe) is one of the oldest and most beautiful. It dates back to the 1670s, and houses the remains of the town's founder, Don Juan Rangel de Biesma.

Templo de Nuestra Señora del Rayo

Damaso Jiménez s/n, at Estanfort (just off Independencia)

Legend has it that the gorgeous plateresque **Templo de Nuestra Señora del Rayo** was constructed in the early seventeenth century by an Indigenous Mexican on the proceeds of the gold mine he had discovered and worked in secret. The authorities tortured him to death in an attempt to find the mine, but its location died with him. The venerated image of the Virgin Mary inside is said to have received a scar in 1686 thanks to a miraculous lightning strike that heralded much-needed rains (thus the name "Our Lady of Lightning").

ARRIVAL AND INFORMATION — PARRAL

By bus Parral's compact colonial heart is a 20min walk from the main bus terminal (C de Lille 5) – turn left, then left again onto Independencia – or take a taxi. There are buses almost hourly to Durango and Chihuahua, as well as frequent services to Juárez.

Destinations Chihuahua (roughly hourly; 4hr); Durango (10 daily; 5–6hr); Guachochi (6 daily; 3hr 30min).

Tourist information The Oficina de Turismo (daily 10am–3pm; 627 525 4400) is at the Mina La Prieta (see page 444).

ACCOMMODATION

Hotel Acosta Agustín Barbachano 3; 627 522 0657. Comfortable budget option and pleasantly old-fashioned, with tiled-floor rooms that overlook the city, a rooftop terrace and 1950s atmosphere. M$

Hotel Los Arcos Pedro de Lille 5; https://www.hotellosarcosparral.com.mx. For a bit more comfort, only

CANDY TOWN

No one really knows why the tradition started, but Parral is lauded all over Mexico for its old-fashioned milk sweets, addictive **dulces de leche** made with coconut, apricots, pecans, peanuts, hazelnuts and pineapples. Sample the wicked treats at ★ **Dulcería La Gota de Miel**, 20 de Noviembre 51 (627 522 1217), the shop founded in 1932 by Don Pablito, the acknowledged godfather of Parral's modern sweet industry.

a stone's throw from the bus station, this well-maintained hotel offers rooms facing a modern, plant-filled courtyard and that come with satellite TV; there's also a decent restaurant. M$$

EATING AND DRINKING

★ **Enchiladas Doña Cuca** Del Rayo 7, at Libertad (near the river); 627 143 8282. *Doña Cuca*, "de las enchiladas", is a legendary stall that opened in 1922, making its famous enchiladas exactly the same way ever since: try the *enchiladas verdes* made with *chile pasado*, or *enchiladas rojas* with *chile California*. Cash only. M$

Panificadora Parralense Ojito 13, at Del Rayo; 627 523 2110. Visit this venerable bakery to try Parral's other culinary gem, *rayadas* (bread rolls baked with a hint of anise), knocked out of its ageing brick ovens. M$

Chihuahua

7

The capital of the largest state in the republic, **CHIHUAHUA** was the favourite home of Mexican folk hero **Pancho Villa**. It's also been the scene of some crucial episodes in Mexico's history, not least the execution of **Miguel Hidalgo** (see page 446) in 1811. Today it's a sprawling, workaday city of around 900,000, but the colonial centre boasts several fine museums and is sprinkled with grandiose nineteenth-century mansions, built when silver brought wealth to the region's landowning class. This is also *vaquero* heartland, and one of the best places in the country to look for **cowboy boots**: you're spoilt for choice in the centre, especially in the blocks bounded by Calle 4, Juárez, Victoria and Ocampo. Incidentally, you're unlikely to see many of the little bug-eyed dogs here, said to have been discovered in the state in the 1850s – though in the summer months you will see over thirty multicoloured chihuahua sculptures scattered around town as part of the annual "Dog Parade".

Catedral Metropolitana

Libertad 814 (Plaza de Armas) • Free

Chihuahua's centre of activity is the teeming **Plaza de Armas**, where its fine **Catedral Metropolitana** stands opposite a wonderfully camp statue of the city's founder, Don Antonio Deza y Ulloa, in the very act of pointing to the ground, as if to say, "Right lads, we'll build it here." The Baroque, twin-towered edifice was begun in 1725 but took more than one hundred years to complete: work well worth it, though, since the interior detail is the equal of the ornate facade. Look inside for the shrine to **Pedro Maldonado** (born here in 1892), who was beaten to death by soldiers of Mexico's anti-Catholic government in 1937. Now known as San Pedro de Jesús Maldonado Lucero, he became Chihuahua's first saint in 2000. Previously located in the crypt beneath the cathedral, the **Museo de Arte Sacro** is expected to open sometime in 2020 in new purpose-built premises opposite the Teatro de la Ciudad (on Calle Ojinaga).

Museo Casa de Juárez

Juárez 321, at C 5 • Charge • 614 410 4258

Aficionados of Mexican history should visit the **Museo Casa de Juárez**, essentially a monument to **Benito Juárez** and the turbulent years of the French Intervention; forced out of Mexico City by the French, President Juárez spent three years here from 1864, when this house was the epicentre of the independent national government. Today his former offices and personal chambers have been furnished in period style, and many of his letters and personal affects are on display, including his battered horse-drawn carriage. Other rooms put the whole period in context, though you'll need to read Spanish to make the most of this.

Casa Chihuahua

Libertad 901 • Charge, free Sun • http://casachihuahua.org.mx

At the north end of pedestrianized Libertad you can't miss the **Casa Chihuahua**, the former Palacio Federal and now a thoroughly absorbing museum. Built in 1910, the current structure replaced the eighteenth-century Jesuit college and hospital where **Padre Miguel Hidalgo** and **Ignacio Allende**, the inspiration and early leaders of the Mexican War of Independence, were imprisoned in 1811, before being executed across the road (see below). Only one stone tower was preserved from the older structure, containing the **Calabozo de Hidalgo**, "Hidalgo's dungeon", where the rebels are said to have been held. Hidalgo's cell now forms the centrepiece of the lower-level **Museo**

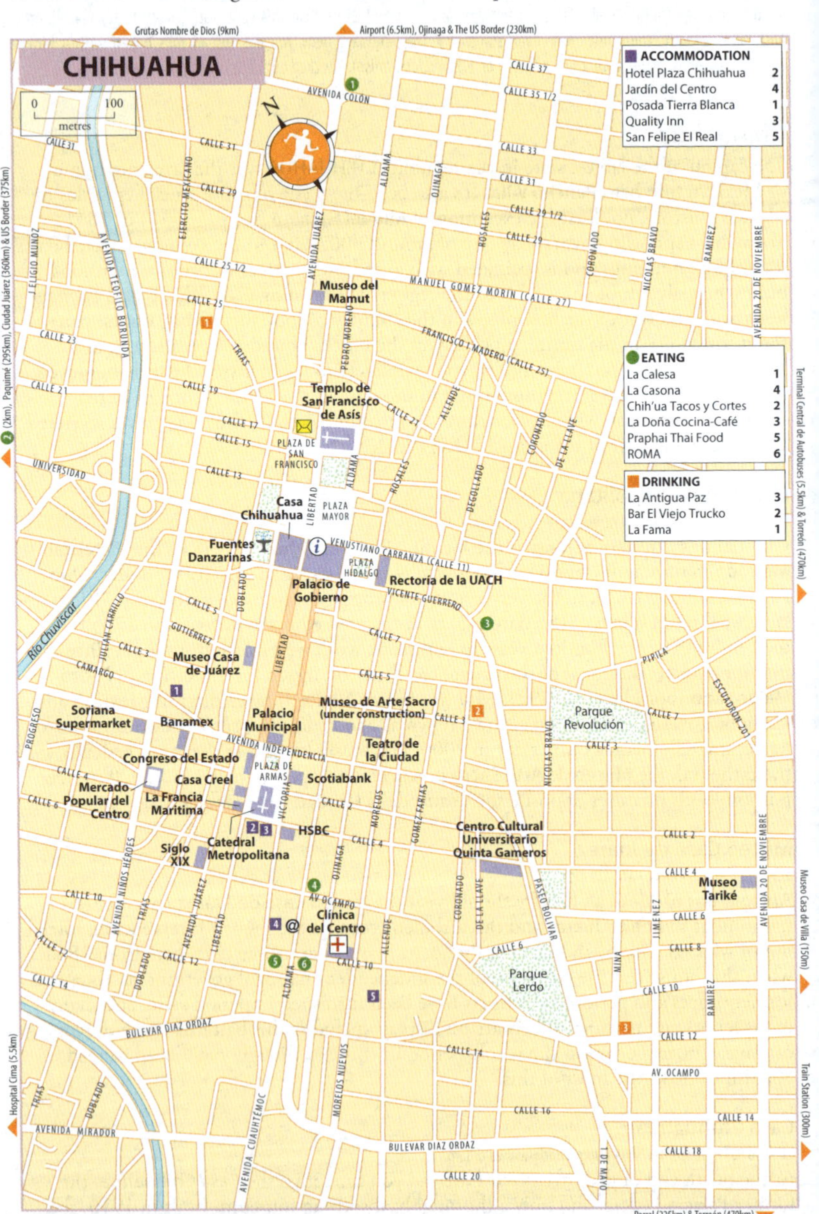

del Sitio, a series of multimedia exhibits charting the history of the building from the early Spanish missions to its rebirth as a museum. Upstairs, the **Museo Patrinomio** is an innovative series of galleries introducing the state of Chihuahua, divided thematically between deserts, plains and mountains, and featuring sections on art, history, traditional dress and popular culture: look out for the display on Hollywood star **Anthony Quinn**, who was born in the city in 1915, and enlightening sections on the Mormons and Mennonites.

Museo Galería de Armas and Museo de Hidalgo

Libertad, at Carranza • Free • 614 410 4258

Chihuahua's **Palacio de Gobierno**, completed in 1892 on the other side of the former Jesuit college, contains two small museums worth a quick peek. The **Museo Galería de Armas** houses an assortment of weapons from the Independence struggle, including the extraordinary 3m-long "Rifle de Avancarga", while the **Museo de Hidalgo** commemorates Miguel Hidalgo himself with a replica of the sacristy in Dolores where it all began (see page 789); dioramas represent the Dolores church, the Querétaro Conspiracy and the attack on Guanajuato (Spanish labels only). Beyond here the main courtyard is an enthralling space lined with bold **murals** of scenes from Mexico's colonial past painted by Aarón Piña Mora in the 1960s – Hidalgo and Allende were executed here in 1811, their severed heads sent for public display in Guanajuato. The site of the deed is marked with a small shrine, the **Altar de la Patria** ("the nation's altar") on the ground floor.

Plaza Mayor

North of the Palacio de Gobierno lies the modern expanse of **Plaza Mayor**, with its grand monument to freedom, the Ángel de la Libertad, erected in 2003. At the north end, the **Templo de San Francisco de Asís** is considered the oldest building in the city (dating from 1726), and though fairly plain inside has increased importance due to another Hidalgo connection. The attached Capilla de San Antonio is where the hero's headless torso was initially buried in 1811, before being exhumed and triumphantly entombed in Mexico City in 1823.

Museo Casa de Villa

C 10 no. 3010 • Charge • 614 416 2958 • Walk along Ocampo, or take a bus (marked "Ocampo") two blocks past the huge Iglesia del Sagrado Corazón de Jesús, then turn left along Mendez for two more blocks

Chihuahua's premier sight, the **Museo Casa de Villa**, is 2km east of the centre. This enormous mansion was built by Pancho Villa (see page 448) in the early twentieth century (though he only spent time here in 1914, when governor of the state) and inhabited, until her death in 1981, by Villa's "official" widow Doña Luz Corral (there were allegedly many others); it has now been taken over by the Mexican army. The collection is a fascinating mix of weapons, war plans and personal mementos, including the bullet-riddled Dodge in which Villa was assassinated in 1923. Look out for Villa's incredibly elaborate saddles and a grimly comical recruitment poster of 1915, urging "gringos" to head south and ride with Villa for "gold and glory". Quite apart from the campaign memories, the superbly preserved old bedrooms and bathrooms, richly decorated with florid murals and Spanish floor tiles, give an interesting insight into wealthy Mexican life in the early 1900s.

Centro Cultural Universitario Quinta Gameros

Paseo Bolivar 401, at C 4 • Charge, free Sun • http://uach.mx

The extraordinarily elaborate **Centro Cultural Universitario Quinta Gameros** was just the sort of ostentatious display of wealth that Villa and his associates were hoping to stamp out in their battle against the landed elite. The *belle époque* showcase was built for successful mine owner Don Manuel Gameros as an exact replica of a posh

7

PANCHO VILLA

Few Mexican folk heroes command so much reverence as Francisco "Pancho" Villa, the ruthless *bandito* and cattle rustler turned revolutionary, though facts about his life remain surprisingly obscure. Born in San Juan del Río, Durango, around 1878 (sources differ), to a simple peasant family, he became an outlaw while still a teenager and seems to have developed a loyal group of followers. Though he had virtually no formal education, Villa was not the average bandit; quick-witted and ambitious, in 1910 he decided to support the revolt of Francisco Madero (see page 792) against the Díaz regime. As commander of the formidable División del Norte, Villa became a key player in the **Mexican Revolution**. He became a bitter enemy of Victoriano Huerta after Madero was executed in 1913, helping to oust the dictator the following year and briefly becoming governor of Chihuahua after hard-fought victories at Chihuahua, Ciudad Juárez, Tierra Blanca and Ojinaga. When Villa fell out with the new president, Carranza, fighting continued and even spilled across the border (leading to a failed US expedition to capture the rebel). With the death of Carranza in 1920, Villa finally laid down his guns, dividing time between Hidalgo del Parral and Chihuahua. Violence continued to haunt him, however, and he was assassinated in Parral in 1923 – it was never determined who ordered the killing.

In Mexico, Villa remains a national hero, a Robin Hood-like figure who not only defeated the Mexican regime, but was also the only foreigner to attack the US (since the War of 1812) and survive. North of the border his image was enhanced by lurid US media reports – indeed, his sombrero and cartridge belts have become the stereotypical accessories of Mexican movie *banditos* ever since. Villa himself courted **Hollywood** and even starred in a film incorporating actual scenes of the Battle of Ojinaga in 1914 (portrayed by Antonio Banderas in *And Starring Pancho Villa As Himself*).

Parisian home – completed in 1910, just in time for the Revolution. The hapless Gameros fled the country and his mansion became the home of Venustiano Carranza (the Gameros family did reclaim the house in the 1920s before selling to the state in 1926). Today the house is fastidiously maintained by the Universidad Autónoma de Chihuahua, the interior sumptuously restored with magnificent Art Nouveau stained glass and ornate woodwork, and, curiously, scenes from *Little Red Riding Hood* painted on the children's bedroom wall.

Las Grutas de Nombre de Dios

Vialidad Sacramento, at Monte Albán • Charge; tours 45min–1hr • 614 200 4800

The remarkable five-million-year-old cave system known as the **Grutas de Nombre de Dios** is just fifteen minutes' ride from downtown, accessible by guided tours only. You'll be taken through seventeen caverns on a 1.3km trail studded with astonishing features such as the "Tower of Pisa" and the "Grand Canyon", a maze of crumpled rocks and dripping stalactites. Taxis charge a flat free with wait time.

ARRIVAL AND DEPARTURE — CHIHUAHUA

By plane From Chihuahua's General Roberto Fierro Villalobos International Airport (Juan Pablo II km 14; 614 420 5104), 18km southeast of the city, a fixed-fare taxi system operates – buy your voucher as you leave the terminal (around 30min to downtown). All the major car rental firms have desks at the airport, but there are no buses.

By train The Copper Canyon railway (see page 482) terminus (614 439 7200) is 2km southeast of the centre at Mendez and C 24; taxis are generally reasonable. Chepe Regional trains leave for Los Mochis at 6am Mon, Thurs & Sat (scheduled to arrive at Creel 11.47pm, Los Mochis 9.28pm).

By bus The Terminal Central de Autobuses (with guardería 9am–11pm) is 10km east of the centre, near the airport on Juan Pablo II; local buses run from right outside to and from downtown, and there are plenty of taxis, though they will insist on a base fare. Note that most buses from Creel will drop you in the centre of town (near the plaza) before heading out to the bus terminal – check when you get on.

Destinations Ciudad Juárez (hourly; 5–6hr); Creel (every

1–2hr; 4–5hr); Durango (10 daily; 10–13hr); Mexico City (every 2hr; 19–22hr); Monterrey (8 daily; 11–12hr); Nuevo Casas Grandes (12 daily; 4hr 30min); Parral (hourly; 3–5hr); Zacatecas (6 daily; 11–13hr).

INFORMATION AND SERVICES

Tourist office There's a small, helpful English-speaking tourist office (Mon–Sat 9am–5pm; 614 410 3596) on the ground floor of the Palacio de Gobierno (C Victoria entrance).

ACCOMMODATION

SEE MAP PAGE 446

★ **Hotel Plaza Chihuahua** Cuarta (4a) 204; http://hotelplazachihuahua.com. Bright, contemporary hotel with stylish rooms, flatscreen cable TV, free parking and buffet breakfast included. M$$$

Jardín del Centro Victoria 818; 614 415 1832. This old hotel has lots of character, with big colonial-style rooms set around a plant-filled courtyard. The less elegant quarters are cheaper and a great bargain. There's a decent little restaurant attached. M$$

Posada Tierra Blanca Niños Héroes 102; https://facebook.com/PosadaTierraBlancaCuu. Spacious, motel-style place right in the heart of the city, with an open-air pool, gymnasium, on-site restaurant and bar. The a/c rooms are tidy and spacious, although not nearly as tasteful as they pretend to be. M$$

Quality Inn Victoria 409; http://qualityinnchihuahua.com. You can't beat the location of this comfy business hotel, right on the main plaza; rooms are standard chain fare, but come with free continental breakfast, free airport, bus and train station transfers and cable TV. M$$$

★ **San Felipe El Real** Allende 1055; 614 437 2037. This elegant boutique hotel is set in a gorgeous 1882 adobe mansion with six suites decked out with tasteful antiques and canopy beds, centred on a blossom-smothered courtyard. M$$$

EATING

SEE MAP PAGE 446

La Calesa Juárez 3300, at Colón; www.lacalesasteakhouse.com. One of Chihuahua's fanciest restaurants, all dark wood panels, crisp linen tablecloths, sparkling wine glasses and waistcoated waiters. Northern-style steaks are the house speciality. Dine on *chiles rellenos de camarón* (chiles stuffed with prawns) or a massive plate of succulent shellfish. Bookings recommended at weekends. M$$$$

★ **La Casona** Aldama 430, at Ocampo; 614 410 0063. If you fancy a splurge make sure you visit this sumptuous restaurant, housed inside the main courtyard of the Casa de Don Luis Terrazas, completed in 1893 for one of the state's richest landowners. Feast on fine contemporary Mexican cuisine or Argentine steaks. M$$$$

★ **Chih'ua Tacos y Cortes** Universidad 2902; www.chihua.com.mx; also at Plaza Vallarta and Plaza las Haciendas. This much-loved local taquería started life in 1991 as a humble stall but has morphed into a Mexican franchise; it's worth the short taxi ride to one of its modern outlets in the city to try its huge taco plates and delicious tortas. M$$

La Doña Cocina-Café Bolivar 722, at Coronado; 614 344 9823. Modern, hip coffee shop, with contemporary international cuisine and popular Mexican breakfasts. M$$$

Praphai Thai Food Victoria 1203; 614 457 0353. Insanely popular among locals, this Thai restaurant is worth waiting in line for – especially if you're in the mood for a bit of variety during your travels. The dishes are large and well presented; better still they're a bargain too. M$$

ROMA C. Juan Aldama 1202, C. Juan Aldama 1202; 614 284 0319. Casual breakfast restaurant with generous portions and budget friendly prices. The coffee here is especially good. M$$

DRINKING

SEE MAP PAGE 446

La Antigua Paz C 12 no. 2201, at Mina; 614 410 1466. Lively cantina full of characters, with a history going back to 1910 (it's been in this location since 1922 and looks it) and still owned by the Carrejo family. Antiques and mementos line the walls, and there's often live music.

Bar El Viejo Trucko Zona Centro 31000; 614 155 7295. Fun cocktail bar with live music and plenty of tequilas to choose from.

La Fama Niños Heroes 21265, at C 25a; 614 198 8447. Popular, cozy rock pub, with great live bands Sat nights and decent drink prices – friendly local crowd.

DIRECTORY

Banks Most banks are centrally located, and nearly all have ATMs, with branches on Victoria and Libertad around the Plaza de Armas.

Hospital For emergency medical assistance, dial 066; Clínica del Centro at Ojinaga 816 (614 439 8100) or Hospital Cima, Hacienda del Valle 7120, Fracc Plazas las Haciendas (614 439 2862).

Police 066; tourist police 01800 201 5589.

Post office Libertad 1700, behind the church (Mon–Fri 8am–4.30pm, Sat 8am–noon).

Paquimé

Independencia 100, Casa Grandes • Charge • 636 692 4140

The intriguing ruins of **PAQUIMÉ** are the most significant, and certainly the most thought-provoking, remains of a sophisticated civilization in northern Mexico. Originally home to an agricultural community and comprising simple adobe houses (similar to those found in Arizona and New Mexico), it became heavily influenced by Mesoamerican, probably Toltec, culture. Whether this was the result of conquest or, more likely, trade, is uncertain, but from around 1000 to 1200 AD, Paquimé flourished. **Pyramids** and **ball-courts** were constructed, and the surrounding land was irrigated by an advanced system of **canals**. At the same time local craftsmen were trading with points both south and north, producing a wide variety of elaborate ornaments and pottery. Among the finds at the site (many of them are now in the Museum of Anthropology in Mexico City) have been cages that held exotic imported birds, whose feathers were used in making ornaments; necklaces made from turquoise, semiprecious stones and shells obtained from the Sea of Cortez; and other objects of copper, bone, jade and mother-of-pearl.

Much must have been destroyed when the site was attacked, burned and abandoned around 1340 – either by a marauding nomadic tribe, such as the Apache, or in the course of a more local rebellion. Either way, Paquimé was not inhabited again, its people leaving their already depleted trade for the greater safety of the sierras. When excavation began in the late 1950s, there were only a few low hills and banks where walls had been, but by piecing together evidence archeologists have partly reconstructed the adobe houses – the largest of which have as many as fifty interconnecting rooms around an open courtyard or **ceremonial centre**. The foundations of the houses, which were originally two or three storeys high, have been reconstructed to waist height, with an occasional standing wall giving some idea of scale.

Museo de las Culturas del Norte

Independencia 100, Casa Grandes • Free with main site entry

To appreciate fully the sophistication of the civilization that built Paquimé, visit the **Museo de las Culturas del Norte**, a beautifully laid-out, if thinly stocked, museum, architecturally designed to mimic the ruins of the defence towers that once stood on the site. Inside you'll find a large model of how Paquimé must have looked, interactive touch-screen consoles with commentary in Spanish and English and intelligent displays of artefacts. Modern examples of finds from the surrounding area – drums, dolls in native costume, ceramics and ceremonial masks – compete with Paquimé objects, notably striking pottery, often anthropomorphic vessels decorated in geometric patterns of red, black and brown on a white or cream background.

ARRIVAL AND DEPARTURE — PAQUIMÉ

By bus/taxi To reach the site you have to travel 260km south of Ciudad Juárez to Nuevo Casas Grandes. Travelling from Chihuahua is also an option, as buses for the four-hour journey depart regularly. Several informal shuttle-van companies also operate daily between Nuevo Casas Grandes and Phoenix (8hr) and Albuquerque in the US; try Transportes Quezada (US +1 623 937 9650) or Transportes Los Hispanos (US +1 505 250 4049). Once in Nuevo Casas Grandes (buses arrive outside the adjoining Estrella Blanca and Omnibus offices on Obregón), take one of the hourly yellow buses ("Casas Grandes/Col Juárez"; Mon–Sat 8am–7.30pm, Sun 8am–4.30pm) from the corner of Constitución and 16 de Septiembre to the plaza in the smaller village of Casas Grandes (about 20min), from where the site is signposted – it's a 15min walk. Taxis charge from Nuevo Casas Grandes to Casa Grandes, and straight to the museum. Destinations Chihuahua (8 daily; 4hr 30min); Ciudad Juárez (6 daily; 4hr).

MORMONS IN MEXICO

George Romney (1907–95), leading Mormon, Governor of Michigan and father of 2012 presidential contender Mitt Romney, was actually born in **Colonia Dublán**, a small Mormon colony just north of Nuevo Casas Grandes. Members of **The Church of Jesus Christ of Latter-day Saints** started coming to northern Mexico in the 1880s, many to avoid prosecution for polygamy in the US. Colonia Dublán was founded in 1889, the Romneys moving here soon after, though the Mexican Revolution forced the family to flee back to the US in 1912. There's little to see in Dublán today, but **Colonia Juárez**, established in 1886 just north of Mata Ortiz (20km southwest of Casas Grandes), remains a Mormon centre, its beautiful **Colonia Juárez Chihuahua México Temple** dedicated in 1999 on a hill above town. There's also the Academia Juárez, a Mormon-owned school founded in 1897, and the Museo de Colonia Juárez chronicling the Mormon history of the region.

7

ACCOMMODATION

CASAS GRANDES

If you leave Chihuahua very early you can visit Paquimé and continue to Ciudad Juárez and the US border in the same day, but if you need accommodation, there are a few inviting options in Casas Grandes.

★ **Las Guacamayas B&B** 20 de Noviembre 1101; 636 699 0997. Closest to the ruins, "The Macaws" offers cosy adobe rooms (in part modelled on Paquimé) and breakfast in owner Mayté Luján's artsy kitchen dining room, *La Tertulia*. M$$

Pueblo Viejo Courtyards Av Victoria 420; +1 915 261 0502. You can stay at the *Pueblo Viejo Courtyards*, run by local fixtures Spencer and Emi MacCallum: they're artfully restored adobe houses near the main plaza, adorned with local antiques (wi-fi but no TV). One of the best houses is La Casa del Nopal, with a kitchen and a dining room (big discounts available for weekly rentals. M$$$

NUEVO CASAS GRANDES

Duranzo Inn Juárez Nte 605; 636 694 0847. If you get stuck here, aim to stay at the amicable *Duranzo Inn*, with cable TV, a pool and free Wi-Fi. M$$

EATING AND DRINKING

CASAS GRANDES

Los Colorados Juárez 100 (five blocks from the plaza, in the direction of Mata Ortiz); 636 692 4343. Popular with tour groups, but still serves fabulous northern Mexican cuisine.

El Mesón del Kiote Juárez 1201, at Ojinaga (near the PEMEX station); 636 690 0698. Offers delicious local food and freshwater fish, generous margaritas and addictive guava pie.

NUEVO CASAS GRANDES

Panadería La Guadalupana Hidalgo 813 (one block behind Hotel Piñón). It's worth visiting this venerable bakery, founded over seventy years ago and serving cheap *pan dulce* baked in the traditional manner in a giant brick oven. M$

Mata Ortiz

If you've trekked out all the way to Casas Grandes, you should also check out **MATA ORTIZ**, some 27km south of Nuevo Casas Grandes, a flourishing artisanal pottery community inhabited by artists from all over the world; it's been home to **Juan Quezada**, the godfather of rustic Mata Ortiz-style pottery, and his followers since the 1970s. It's a tranquil, appealing little village of adobe houses: soak up the atmosphere and visit any galleries you like the look of – most artists will be happy to introduce their work. Some of the best include **Jorge Quintana**'s gallery at the *Adobe Inn*, just before the train tracks (for fine pottery and Oaxaca textiles); **Juan Quezada**'s original gallery across from the old train station; and **Mauro Quezada**'s gallery (from Juan Quezada's house, take the street toward the river to the end and turn right).

ARRIVAL AND DEPARTURE — MATA ORTIZ

By taxi Taxis will take you to Mata Ortiz with returns from Nuevo Casas Grandes (be prepared for a waiting fee) – it's less from Casas Grandes.

ACCOMMODATION AND EATING

Adobe Inn 31861 Nuevo Casas Grandes; 636 694 6283. If you fancy staying, Jorge Quintana actually runs this comfortable inn (known locally as "the hotel"), with fifteen spacious rooms around a leafy courtyard; it also serves delicious food to non-guests (rates include three meals), but try to give them an hour's notice. M$$$

Ciudad Juárez

Sprawling **CIUDAD JUÁREZ**, just across the border from **El Paso, Texas**, is possibly Mexico's nastiest border town. Vast, dirty and riddled with visible social problems at the best of times, its spiralling drug-gang violence led to the Mexican army being deployed to patrol its bullet-spattered streets in 2008. This followed the already notorious rape and murder of over four hundred women since 1993, "las muertas de Juárez" portrayed in the depressing Jennifer Lopez movie *Bordertown* (2007) and Roberto Bolaño's seminal novel *2666*. There's an element of paranoia to this, of course; Juárez is a city of two million people that, by and large, functions like anywhere else in Mexico, and tourists are very rarely affected by drug violence (it's also just as famous in Mexico for being the home of **Juan Gabriel**, the nation's most successful singer). The security situation has improved dramatically in recent years, but it's still a good idea to pass through Juárez as quickly as possible – you won't miss much. Travelling between the main transit points is perfectly safe during the day.

ARRIVAL AND DEPARTURE — CIUDAD JUÁREZ

BY PLANE

Arriving at the Aeropuerto Internacional Abraham González, 14km south of the border, you'll find ATMs and all the major car rental firms, including Budget (656 633 0954). Taxis into town or to the border are based on a fixed-price zone system. In addition to Aeroméxico, budget carrier Viva Aerobus operates flights to Mexico City, while Viva Aerobus also serves Monterrey, Cancún and Guadalajara.

BY BUS

The city's Terminal de Autobuses (656 613 6037) lies 5km from the centre at Flores and Borunda, and has services to both US and Mexican cities. To get to the US border from the bus terminal, take a taxi or any local bus marked "Centro" (alternatively, there are shuttle buses that run direct to the El Paso Greyhound station).

Destinations Chihuahua (at least hourly; 5hr); Durango (at least hourly; 16hr); Mexico City (every 1–2hr; 24hr); Nuevo Casas Grandes (every 1–2hr; 4hr); Monterrey (11 daily; 18hr); Parral (at least hourly; 10hr); San Luis Potosí (every 1–2hr; 20hr); Zacatecas (hourly; 16hr).

US destinations International bus services are handled by Autobuses Americanos (656 610 8529). It runs a shuttle bus (every 1–2hr) to El Paso Greyhound Bus Station (1hr), and beyond: Dallas (2 daily; 12hr 40min); Los Angeles (5 daily; 16hr 15min–17hr 35min); Phoenix (6 daily; 7hr 50min–9hr 25min).

CROSSING THE US BORDER

Two downtown toll bridges serve one-way traffic in and out of Ciudad Juárez from neighbouring El Paso, Texas. Northbound vehicles cross the Paseo del Norte Bridge from Juárez, while southbound vehicles use the Stanton St/Lerdo Bridge (tolls charged per car or per pedestrian). If you're on foot you can enter on either bridge (Paseo del Norte is best); coming back, you must use the Paseo del Norte crossing. See pages 31 and 33 for border formalities. Additionally, there are two bridges that serve two-way traffic. The Bridge of the Americas (free) lies 4km east of the city centre on the edge of the Zona Pronaf, an area of sheltered tourist development a world away from the sleazy machinations of downtown Juárez. East of here lies the Ysleta (Zaragoza) Bridge (same tolls), well connected to the main highways and good for a speedy escape. All are open 24hr.

Heading into Mexico Once across the Stanton St/Lerdo Bridge, taxis run to the main Juárez bus terminal or to the airport; alternatively, you can catch a local bus from the corner of Guerrero and Villa near the market.

Heading into the US Crossing the Paseo del Norte Bridge into El Paso dumps you onto Santa Fe, a shabby street of budget stores that seems like an extension of Juárez. It's a short walk straight along here to the *Paso del Norte* hotel

THE MEXICAN DRUG WARS

Since 2006 the escalating **Mexican drug wars** – a violent struggle between rival cartels to control the flow of narcotics into the US, and increasingly, between these gangs and the Mexican government – has put a huge dent in the nation's tourist industry. The violence has continued to make prime-time news in the US, and has led to a stream of official travel warnings to Mexico ever since, as well as fuelling support for President Trump's controversial plan to build a **border wall**, first mooted in 2016.

Mexican gangs began to take over the US cocaine trade from the Colombians in the 1990s, and were originally drawn into roughly two rival camps led by the **Gulf Cartel**, based in Matamoros, and the **Sinaloa Cartel** with its ally the **Juárez Cartel** (Gulf ally the **Tijuana Cartel** has been dramatically weakened in recent years). In 2007, however, the Juárez Cartel started a vicious turf war with the Sinaloa Cartel, for control of **Ciudad Juárez**. Drug violence and political corruption have also plagued the state of **Tamaulipas**, and to a lesser extent parts of **Veracruz**. In 2011 the attention turned to the Tamaulipas border town of **Nuevo Laredo**, and to another grisly turf war between **Los Zetas** (an especially terrifying group of former Mexican special forces soldiers) and the Gulf Cartel (until 2010 the Gulf Cartel were actually allies of the Zetas).

In 2006, **President Felipe Calderón** had ended decades of government inaction by sending federal troops to the states affected by drug violence, a policy that had led to an estimated 60,000 deaths by the end of his administration in 2012. **President Peña Nieto** changed tactics slightly, focusing on reducing violence rather than head-on conflict. Zeta leader Heriberto Lazcano was killed in 2012; top Zeta bosses the Morales brothers were arrested in 2013; and Mexico's most-wanted men, Joaquín "**El Chapo**" Guzmán (Sinaloa Cartel), Vicente Carrillo Fuentes (Juárez Cartel) and Héctor Beltrán Leyva (Beltrán Leyva Cartel) were captured in 2014 (El Chapo escaped from prison in 2015 but was recaptured and is now incarcerated and on trial in the US; his trial began in November 2018 and could continue for as long as four months). Though Nieto's polices succeeded in reducing the number of killings, the drug cartels are still very much in business; in 2014, the **Iguala** mass kidnapping of 43 students by a drug gang in collusion with local police in Guerrero horrified the nation (months later it was confirmed that all 43 had been killed); the case led to national and international protests and a string of high-profile resignations and arrests. Since then the gang wars have continued, much to the frustration and despair of ordinary Mexicans. In 2018 the US State Department warned against any travel at all to the states of **Colima, Guerrero, Michoacán, Sinaloa and Tamaulipas**, ranking them alongside nations such as Afghanistan and Syria. Incoming **President López Obrador** has said he wants to end "Mexico's militarized drug war", but a change anytime soon seems unlikely.

Despite the sensational headlines, it's important to remember that most of Mexico remains peaceful. As a visitor it is extremely unlikely you'll see any sign of drug violence and there's actually little evidence that tourists are targeted by drug gangs – headlines in the media often attribute petty crime or muggings, which can happen anywhere, to drug gangs, adding to the sense of fear. It obviously makes sense to avoid the major trouble spots, however, particularly along the US border. If driving a car from the US, check the current situation with US authorities before you go (see page 62).

(see page 454), or you can grab an El Paso taxi, which are metered. El Paso airport has cheaper connections to the rest of the US than Juárez airport, though you'll usually have to change planes in Houston or Phoenix. El Paso Greyhound Bus Station is at 200 W San Antonio St (+1 915 532 5095).

INFORMATION

Tourist office The Ciudad Juárez tourist office is inconveniently located in the Pronaf zone at Av de las Américas 2551, just across the Bridge of the Americas (Mon–Fri 9am–5pm, Sat & Sun 10am–3pm; 656 611 3174, https://facebook.com/visitajuarezmx).

ACCOMMODATION

None of the hotels in Ciudad Juárez is particularly good value and there's little point in **staying the night** – most business visitors stay in the comfortable chain motels on the outskirts of town (typically M$$$), which are little use without a car. Staying in **El Paso**, across the border, is a better idea.

Gardner Hotel 311 E Franklin St, El Paso; http://gardnerhotel.com. The most atmospheric choice in El Paso, opened in 1922 and for many years a hostel but now also sporting simple doubles adorned with antique beds and furnishings. Dorms M$; doubles M$$

Hotel Colonial Abraham Lincoln 1355, Ciudad Juárez; http://juarez.hotelescolonial.com. The best choice in Juárez close to the border is *Hotel Colonial*, in the Pronaf zone around 1km south of the Bridge of the Americas. M$$

Hotel Paso del Norte 101 South El Paso St, El Paso; http://hotelpdn.com. Built in 1912 and completely renovated in 2019, the *Paso Del Norte* is the obvious luxury option in downtown El Paso, just a short walk from the border, with plush rooms and excellent facilities. M$$$$

EATING AND DRINKING

Burritos Crisóstomo Gómez Morín 8327; http://burritocrisostomo.com. This legendary burrito mini-chain is a Juárez classic, and though locals complain that quality has gone down in recent years it still knocks out tasty and filling *mole* and *barbacoa* burritos made with *guisados* (stews) and freshly made flour tortillas. M$

Club Kentucky Juárez 629; 656 632 0208. Still the classic place for a cold Tecate in Juárez, despite struggling with mounting losses since the downturn. Open since 1920 (the bartenders look like they've been here that long), and one of numerous Mexican cantinas to claim the invention of the margarita.

DIRECTORY

Banks and exchange It's easy enough to change money at *casas de cambio* and tourist shops along Juárez and 16 de Septiembre; most banks are also on 16 de Septiembre, and you'll find ATMs at nearly all of them. Most places accept US dollars, but make sure you know the current exchange rate.

Consulate US (Mon–Fri 7.30am–1pm), Paseo de la Victoria 3650, Fracc Partido Senecú, 656 227 3000, http://mx.usembassy.gov.

Hospital For emergency medical assistance, dial 066; Star Medica, Paseo de la Victoria 4370, Partido Iglesias (656 227 5700).

Internet The public library across the border in El Paso (Mon–Thurs 10am–7pm, Fri 11am–6pm, Sat 10am–6pm, Sun noon–6pm; 915 543 5433, http://elpasolibrary.org) has free internet access. Walk north past the *Paso del Norte* hotel for about two blocks; it's at 501 N Oregon on the corner of Franklin.

Police 066.

Post office Lerdo 205, at the corner of Peña, one block south of 16 de Septiembre.

The northeast border towns

Most travellers simply pass through the **northeast border towns** on their way between Texas and Mexican cities further south – the towns on the Mexican side have traditionally attracted a steady stream of day-trippers from the US for cheap bric-a-brac shopping and tasty **snacks**, though like elsewhere this trade has been severely disrupted since 2009.

The **Río Bravo**, known to Americans as the **Río Grande**, forms the border between Texas and Mexico, a distance of more than 1500km. The country through which it flows is arid semi-desert, and the towns along the lower section of the river are heavily industrialized. This is the **maquiladora** zone, where foreign-owned assembly plants produce consumer goods, most of them for export to the US.

CROSSING THE US BORDER — NORTHEAST BORDER TOWNS

Crossing the US-Mexican border can be a time-consuming affair, especially heading into the US. Canadians and US citizens require a passport to enter the US. Everyone else needs a visa or a visa-waiver (see page 33). Whichever crossing you choose, the procedures are the same, depending on what mode of transport you choose.

By bus Crossing the border by bus can save time and money, depending on your destination, though customs checks are meticulous on both sides. Heading into Mexico, there is no US immigration check, but make sure your bus driver knows if you have a foreign passport – he'll stop at the Mexican migración office so you can complete the FMM (see page 32). After that everyone gets off the bus for a thorough Mexican customs check. Heading into the US, there are no Mexican checks, but everyone gets off the bus to walk through US immigration (passport check), before a

US Customs check of bags and the bus (which can take some time). Further into Texas there is likely to be a US Border Patrol check, where officers will check IDs and question everyone on the bus.

By car If driving into Mexico, remember to pull in at the migración office to get your Immigration Form (see page 32). You'll also need to get a temporary importation vehicle permit (for details see "Getting there", page 31). This must be dropped off on the Mexican side before heading back into the US. Cars also pay a toll crossing from either side of the Río Bravo. Heading into Mexico, customs checks are often very light, whereas the queues heading back into the US can be several hours long; a US Immigration officer will check your passport at a booth (no need to leave the car), and will direct you to park if he deems a customs check necessary. If there is even a tiny hint you are carrying anything illegal, US Customs officers will literally take your car apart and have sniffer dogs all over the seats – don't expect them to clean up afterwards. You can also expect further US Border Patrol checks as you drive further into Texas, and army checkpoints on the Mexican side.

On foot Crossing the border on foot usually means a walk over a bridge traversing the Río Bravo (for a small fee), connecting with local buses or taxis on either side. Heading into Mexico, there is no US immigration and often very casual Mexican checks – remember to stop at the migración office and ask for a "multiple migration" form or "FMM". Heading into the US, you'll have to clear US immigration (no Mexican checks), and often a full customs check of your bags.

Matamoros

Just across the Río Bravo from **Brownsville**, Texas, **MATAMOROS** is a little town with more history than the settlements strung out to its west. What began in 1774 as a cattle-ranching colony eventually became known – with the introduction of the port of Bagdad – as "La Puerta México," and in the nineteenth century Matamoros (along with Veracruz) became the main port of entry for foreign immigrants. At the turn of the nineteenth century, rail lines from both sides of the border were directed through Matamoros, and again the city found itself as the necessary link in the trade crossroads. Since the passage of **NAFTA** in 1994, Matamoros has established itself as an important point for trade, with the outskirts dominated by strip malls and factories; the **Matamoros–Brownsville Metropolitan Area** has a population of almost 1.2 million,

and when restrictions on car imports were lifted in 2005 it became the used car capital of the world. Sadly, Mexico's ongoing drug wars hit Matamoros in a big way in 2015, devastating local car businesses and tourism (a feud between **Gulf Cartel** factions, nominally based here, is blamed). Though the old centre retains some provincial charm, with a slightly run-down blend of historic buildings and cheap stores, it's not advisable to visit Matamoros until the security situation stabilizes – in 2024 violence and kidnapping was still a problem. Check the latest situation online (UK foreign office at http://gov.uk/foreign-travel-advice, or the US at http://travel.state.gov).

Plaza Hidalgo

Matamoros' busy but compact *centro histórico* is focused on spacious **Plaza Hidalgo**, dating back to the 1830s, and the humble French creole-style **Catedral de Nuestra**

THE NORTHEAST BORDER TOWNS – A ROUGH GUIDE

CIUDAD ACUÑA

The smallest of the border towns, its dusty, iconic Tex-Mex streets have proved a magnet for film-makers: Robert Rodriguez' cult Mexican thriller *El Mariachi* (1992) and its sequel, *Desperado* (1995), were shot here. Today Acuña is one of Los Zetas' primary drug smuggling gateways into the US, though it's far less violent than other towns on the border and tourists are rarely impacted. Iconic *Ma Crosby's*, a restaurant since 1925, has closed, though the *Corona Club*, the bar that opened in 1946 and featured in *Desperado*, was operating at the time of research (daily noon–2am; Hidalgo 200, 877 888 0922), with live country music at the weekends.

ARRIVAL AND DEPARTURE

Local buses shuttle between the border at Ciudad Acuña and the Texan town of Del Rio 5km across the Río Bravo, where Greyhound buses (2 daily) take 4hr 15min to reach San Antonio from the Del Rio Stripes bus stop at 1602 Veterans Blvd, on the edge of town. You can also take Amtrak's thrice-weekly Texas Eagle service from the station at 100 N Main St (trains from Chicago to Los Angeles via St Louis, Dallas, Austin, El Paso and San Antonio). Del Rio is 246km and around 2hr 45min by car from San Antonio via Rte-90. The main Acuña bus station, at the corner of Matamoros and Ocampo, is just five blocks from the border and one from the plaza.

Destinations Monterrey (4 daily; 8hr); Piedras Negras (hourly; 1hr 30min); Saltillo (8 daily; 7hr).

PIEDRAS NEGRAS

Once quaint, friendly and hassle free, Piedras Negras hit the news in 2018 when former mayor Fernando Puron and Mexican congressional candidate was killed, execution-style, in the street. The city is another drug-smuggling hub, and despite making progress against violence in recent years, the gangs clearly retain a strong presence. It's also the unlikely place where nachos, the ubiquitous Tex-Mex snack food, were "invented" in the 1940s (see page 458).

ARRIVAL AND DEPARTURE

Piedras Negras lies just across the Río Bravo from Eagle Pass, Texas. Once across the border, take a taxi to the Eagle Pass Stripes Greyhound bus stop at 2093 N Veterans Blvd on the edge of town, which has two direct departures to San Antonio daily (3hr 5min). Eagle Pass is 229km and around 2hr 50min by car from San Antonio via Rte-57 and I-35. On the Mexican side of the border, the Piedras bus station (878 782 7484) is at Allende and Galeana – a taxi shouldn't set you back too much. You'll find frequent first and second-class departures to all major points south.

Destinations Ciudad Acuña (hourly; 1hr 30min); Mexico City (3 daily; 17–18hr); Monterrey (8 daily; 5–7hr); Saltillo (12 daily; 7hr).

BY PLANE

Piedras Negras airport is 9km south of the centre, and currently serves Aeromar flights to/from Mexico City. Taxis run to the border (most hotels offer free shuttles).

NUEVO LAREDO

The giant of the eastern border towns, alive with the imagery and commercialism of the frontier – which sadly includes some of the most grisly crimes committed by drug gangs such as Los Zetas. Do not linger.

Señora del Refugio, more like a big church. Completed in 1833 with twin spires, its plain interior is best known today for its valuable reproduction of Michelangelo's *La Pietà*, carved from Carrera marble in Italy in 2005. On the south side of the plaza is the beautifully restored **Casino Matamorense**, completed in 1871 and used for special events.

Teatro de la Reforma

C 6, at Abasolo • 868 812 5120

One block north of Plaza Hidalgo on Calle 6 is the historic **Teatro de la Reforma**, originally completed in 1865. In 1992 the theatre was meticulously restored to its original style at the behest of the town mayor, and now hosts drama and ballet performances and various local entertainment.

ARRIVAL AND DEPARTURE

If you're entering or leaving Mexico on foot, you'll take Puente Internacional No. 1; there's a small toll, payable in dollars or pesos if you're heading north, but in US currency only when Mexico-bound. The bridge becomes the main drag, Av Guerrero, on the Mexican side, but drivers can also use the nearby Puente Internacional No. 2 (same tolls), and bypass downtown. Numerous Greyhound buses (610 Salinas Av) connect Laredo, Texas, with San Antonio (2hr 50min). Laredo is around 250km (157 miles) and around 2hr 20min by car from San Antonio via I-35.

BY PLANE

Nuevo Laredo's airport (Aeropuerto Internacional Quetzalcóatl) is 6km southwest of the centre (and 12km from the border crossing) and currently serves Aeroméxico flights to/from Mexico City. Taxis run from here to the border.

BY BUS

The Nueva Terminal de Autobuses (867 719 3884) at César López de Lara 3228 and Oaxaca, which is used by Autobuses del Noreste and Ómnibus de México (including Turistar Ejecutivo) is one of several bus stations along this stretch of López de Lara; shuttle buses run from a dedicated station at López de Lara 4033 to the Greyhound bus station in Laredo every 2hr (1hr 35min). Battered city buses (marked "Puente"/"Centro") run frequently between López de Lara, the border crossings and Plaza Hidalgo; it's about a 25min journey. Taxis should be a modest amount, though drivers may ask for a lot more.

Destinations Austin (14 daily; 7hr); Chicago (2 daily; 36hr); Dallas (14 daily; 9hr); Guadalajara (5 daily; 14hr); Houston (9 daily; 7hr); Mexico City (10 daily; 15hr); Monterrey (every 30min; 3hr); Saltillo (8 daily; 4–5hr); San Antonio (hourly; 4hr); San Luis Potosí (14 daily; 12hr); Tampico (2 daily; 10hr); Zacatecas (6 daily; 8hr).

REYNOSA

A very easy border crossing with excellent transport connections, though drug cartel turf wars turned especially violent here in 2015, and today it remained one of the most dangerous places on the border. Monterrey is only three hours by bus.

ARRIVAL AND DEPARTURE

Buses connect the border and the centre to the Central Camionera, on Colón southeast of downtown. Buses to the rest of Mexico include services to Matamoros (1hr) and Ciudad Victoria (4hr 30min); Tampico (7hr) and Veracruz (16hr) on the Gulf coast; and Monterrey (3hr), Mexico City (13hr) and Zacatecas (10hr).

Crossing the Hidalgo International Bridge over the Río Bravo from McAllen, Texas (you pay a toll per pedestrian or car), head straight on along Lerdo de Tejada, which soon becomes Zaragoza, to the Plaza Principal, about five blocks west, where you'll find a couple of banks with ATMs. The main bus station is at J. Guadalupe López Velarde 100, around 1.6km south of the border and 1.5km southeast of the plaza. OMEX VIP (http://omexvip.com.mx) operates buses between Reynosa bus station and the Greyhound station in McAllen (where there are 7 daily departures to San Antonio; 4hr–4hr 50min), roughly every thirty minutes between 5.30am and 8.30pm. The 9km journey takes about 1hr, including immigration. McAllen is 383km and around 3hr 40min by car from San Antonio via Rte-281 and I-37.

BY PLANE

Reynosa's airport (Aeropuerto Internacional General Lucio Blanco) is 14km southeast of the centre, and currently serves the most flights of the border towns, with regular services to Mexico City, Cancún, Guadalajara and Veracruz.

Mercado Juárez and Plaza Allende

Heading west from Teatro de la Reforma, pedestrianized **Abasolo** is the traditional shopping heart of town, with **Mercado Juárez**, between calles 9 and 10, the most interesting section – it's worth browsing the handicraft stalls inside. Two blocks south of the mercado on Calle 10, **Plaza Allende** is the scruffy, modern counterpoint to Plaza Hidalgo, surrounded by cheap stores, bus stops and a line of tacos/torta stalls on the Calle 11 (west) side.

Museo Casamata

Santos Degollado, at Guatemala • Free • 868 813 5929

If you've got an hour to kill, take a taxi to the **Museo Casamata**, which houses a collection of memorabilia from the Mexican Revolution and a selection of Huastec ceramics in a fort begun in 1844 to repel invaders from north of the border. When Zachary Taylor stormed in two years later, however, the building was still unfinished.

Museo de Arte Contemporáneo de Tamaulipas (MACT)

Constitución, at C 5 • Free • 868 813 1499

You might also check out the **Museo de Arte Contemporáneo de Tamaulipas**, an exuberant Modernist structure that shows revolving exhibitions from some of the best contemporary Mexican multimedia artists.

ARRIVAL AND DEPARTURE — MATAMOROS

TO/FROM THE US

Crossing the Puente Nuevo/Gateway International Bridge (24hr) between Matamoros and Brownsville incurs a toll: tolls per pedestrians or car. On the Mexican side local buses run frequently from the border along De Las Rosas and then Obregón to the centre and the Central de Autobuses (marked "Central"). Heading back, look for buses marked "Puente Internacional". Taxis at the border run on a fixed-rate system to the bus station and the airport.

On the US side Brownsville's Greyhound bus station (755 International Blvd) offers services to San Antonio (6 daily; 5hr 45min–6hr 45min) and Houston (4 daily; 7hr 35min–8hr 40min). Brownsville is 445km and around 4hr by car from San Antonio via Rte-77 and I-37; it's 571km and around 5hr 20min from Houston via Rte-77 and 59.

BY BUS

The Central de Autobuses (871 812 2777; restaurant and guardería 6.30am–10.30pm) is south of the centre on Canales; buses marked "Centro" will take you towards the main plazas, while taxis will try to charge you as much as possible – so be sure to fix your fare to the plaza area or the border before you set off. If you're heading to the US you can take a bus straight across the border from the Central de Autobuses: Americanos runs six daily buses (25–45min) between Matamoros and the Greyhound station in Brownsville.

THE KING OF NACHOS

Contrary to popular belief, that addictive combination of crispy tortilla chips and melted cheese – a staple snack all over the US and beyond – is not traditional Mexican food. Nachos were actually dreamt up in 1943 in **Piedras Negras** by Ignacio "Nacho" Anaya, allegedly while trying to feed a group of US army wives after hours. He was forced to cook up whatever he had left in the kitchen: essentially toasted tortillas, cheese and jalapeño peppers. The idea caught on, especially in Texas, but it wasn't until the 1970s that "nachos" became popular throughout the US (it's never had quite the same appeal in Mexico). When Anaya died in 1975 a bronze plaque in his memory was erected in Piedras Negras, and the town hosts an **International Nacho Festival** around October 21 each year. The two-day event features live music, art and a goofy attempt to make the world's biggest nacho.

Sadly, the original nacho restaurant no longer exists, and the *Moderno*, where Anaya went on to work, closed in 2010.

THE NORTH'S MAJOR FIESTAS

Carnaval (week before Lent; variable Feb–March) is at its best in the Caribbean and New Orleans-like atmosphere of Tampico – also in Ciudad Victoria and Monterrey.
Birth of Benito Juárez (March 21). Ceremonies to commemorate Juárez' birth in Matamoros.
Día de Nuestra Señora del Refugio (July 4). Marked by dancing and pilgrimages in Matamoros.
Feria de la Uva (Aug 9). Exuberant festivities in Parras, between Saltillo and Torreón.
Feria de Saltillo (around Aug 13). Saltillo begins its annual festival, featuring agricultural and art exhibitions, music and dance performances, and plenty of the local *sarapes* (shawls).
Feria de Nuevo Laredo (Sept). Major festival on the border at Nuevo Laredo.
Independence Day (Sept 16). Festivities everywhere, but the biggest are in Monterrey.
Fiesta de Amistad (late Oct). Joint week-long celebrations between the border town of Ciudad Acuña and its Texan neighbour Del Rio. Bullfights, pageants and a parade, which starts in one country and ends in the other.
Día de San Martín de Porres (Nov 3). Fiesta with native dances in Tampico.
Día de la Virgen de Guadalupe (Dec 12). Big celebrations everywhere, especially in Guadalupe de Bravos; El Palmito (Durango), between Durango and Parral; Ciudad Anahuac (Nuevo León) in the north of the state; and Abasolo, near Monterrey. Monterrey itself attracts many pilgrims at this time.

Destinations Ciudad Victoria (hourly; 4–5hr); Dallas (2 daily; 13hr); Houston (2 daily; 8hr); Mexico City (14hr); Monterrey (hourly; 4hr); Reynosa (every 45min; 2hr); San Antonio (4 daily; 6–7hr); Tampico (hourly; 7–8hr); Veracruz (5 daily; 16hr); Zacatecas (2 daily; 12hr).

ACCOMMODATION

SEE MAP PAGE 455

★ **Best Western Plaza Matamoros** Bravo 1421 and C 9; http://bestwestern.com. If you're looking for a bit of comfort in the centre, this is the best choice; it's average chain hotel fare by US standards, but it's clean and safe with an airy inner atrium, and the free breakfast is good. Restaurant, parking, and rooms with a/c and cable TV. M$$$

Ritz Matamoros 612, at C 7; http://ritzhotel.org. Comfortable hotel with slightly old-fashioned rooms, but whose rates include buffet breakfast. There's a suite available for six people, plus plenty of safe parking, cable TV, and it's cheaper at weekends. M$$

EATING

SEE MAP PAGE 455

Garcia's Obregón 82; 868 812 3929. It doesn't get more touristy than this, but it's worth coming to the *Garcia's* complex once for the archetypal border experience, literally a few metres from the bridge to scoop up as many day-trippers as possible. You can shop, eat reasonable international dishes in the restaurant (steaks, etc) and drink in the cabaret-like *Fiesta Bar* (which has live bands). M$$$$

Hidalgo Botanero González 87300; 868 124 0542. Fun restaurant and café, serving healthy (and hearty) organic fare, plus decent coffees. M$$

Mi Pueblito C 5 and Constitución, opposite MACT; 868 813 8723. Popular family restaurant in a giant faux palapa, with big Mexican breakfasts and all the classics for lunch and dinner – the bar is also a good place to grab a drink, and is best known for its stock of two hundred tequilas. M$$$

DIRECTORY

Banks and exchange Banamex is at C7 and Moreles; there are decent currency exchange facilities in the centre: head for Banorte, on Morelos at C6.

Emergencies 066; Cruz Roja 812 0044; Federal Police 817 2205; International Medical Center 811 0000.

Pharmacy Try Farmacia Guadalajara, González 609, at C7.

Post office Río Bravo 15 at C 11.

Corona
Extra

The northwest and Copper Canyon

MAZATLÁN

The northwest and Copper Canyon

Divided from Baja California by the Sea of Cortez, Mexico's northwest mainland is something of a bizarre – and initially uninviting – introduction to the country, despite containing one of the region's most alluring natural attractions. The Sierra Tarahumara is wonderfully wild, pristine and remote, concealing six dizzying chasms known collectively as the Barranca del Cobre (or Copper Canyon). Mexico's last surviving passenger train, nicknamed "El Chepe", steers a phenomenal course around its rim – one of the world's ultimate train rides. Other highlights include Álamos, once a silver-mining city and now a charming retreat for expats and artists, and El Fuerte, another colonial town rich in history.

Travelling in this part of Mexico can be incredibly rewarding, but beyond the coastal resorts you'll see very few tourists. At once fertile, wealthy and heavily Americanized, in parts it is also strikingly impoverished, drab and barren – drug violence in Sinaloa and Sonora has further weakened its appeal, though the risk to visitors is slight (see page 453). The climate's not exactly welcoming, either – summer temperatures can hit 50°C, while winter nights in the desert drop to freezing levels.

Yet it's this extraordinary desert scenery that grabs your attention, which, along with the huge cacti, makes for some archetypal Mexican landscapes, while the fierce sunshine makes the beach towns in this part of Mexico doubly enticing. North of Puerto Vallarta lies **San Blas**, a small, friendly town surrounded by steamy jungle and peaceful strips of sand, and the resort of **Mazatlán** with its wealth of beaches, bars and fine seafood restaurants. Heading towards the US border are the quieter beaches of **Bahía de Kino** and **San Carlos**, and the shrimping port and burgeoning resort of **Puerto Peñasco**.

Tepic

Some 170km north of Puerto Vallarta, the first place of any size is **TEPIC**, capital of the state of **Nayarit** and home to over three hundred thousand people. Founded by Hernán Cortés' brother, Francisco, in 1544, it's appealing enough in a quietly provincial way, but for most travellers it's no more than a convenient **stopover** along the route to Mazatlán, or a place to switch buses for **San Blas** (see page 466) and the coast.

Plenty of shops sell **Huichol artesanías** (see page 465) in Tepic, including vibrant yarn paintings and bead statues. Alternatively, you can buy them directly from Huichol artists in the **Plaza Principal**, Tepic's lush central square of fountains and gardens, overlooked by the Palacio Municipal and twin neo-Gothic towers of the Catedral de la Asunción, completed in the 1890s.

Museo Regional de Nayarit

México Nte 91, at Zapata • Charge • 311 212 1900

Worth a quick look is the small **Museo Regional de Nayarit**, housed in an adobe mansion built in 1762, south of the Plaza Principal. Inside is a small but absorbing collection of local pre-Columbian and Huichol artefacts dating back to 200 BC, and objects from the Aztatlán culture (800–1350 AD).

Museo de Los Cinco Pueblos

México Nte 105, at Zapata • Free • 311 103 9420

CHEPE TRAIN IN BARRANCA DEL COBRE

Highlights

❶ **San Blas** Tranquil backwater offering phenomenal bird watching, surfing and seafood, as well as a chance for some serious lounging on the beach. See page 466

❷ **Mexcaltitán** This intriguing island town claims to be the spiritual home of the Aztecs, a miniature Tenochtitlán ringed by waterways. See page 469

❸ **Mazatlán** Old-fashioned Mexican resort enriched by a spruced-up historic centre, horse-rides along the beach, zip lines in the jungle and fresh seafood. See page 469

❹ **The Copper Canyon railway** The journey through Chihuahua state's rugged canyons offers one of the world's most gripping train experiences. See page 482

❺ **Creel and the Sierra Tarahumara** For real adventure and a window into Mexico's past, hike or bike to the waterfalls and Rarámuri villages around Creel. See page 489

❻ **Álamos** Soak up the colonial charm in this wonderfully preserved old town, with languid plazas, enticing inns and captivating desert scenery. See page 495

❼ **Reserva de la Biósfera El Pinacate** Explore this barren, moon-like reserve, a 50km-wide volcanic field of mesmerizing craters, home to all manner of wildlife. See page 503

HIGHLIGHTS ARE MARKED ON THE MAP ON PAGE 464

Tucson
USA
El Paso
Ciudad Juárez
Sonoyta
Puerto Peñasco
San Luis Río Colorado & Tijuana
Nogales
Nogales
Douglas
Cananea
Agua Prieta
Caborca
Magdalena de Kino
Santa Ana
Benjamin Hill
Casas Grandes
Río Grande
Río Bravo
SONORA
Mazocahui
Bahía de Kino
Isla Tiburón
Hermosillo
Chihuahua
San Carlos
Guaymas
Basaseachic
Cuauhtémoc
Creel
SIERRA TARAHUMARA
Ciudad Obregón
Divisadero
Copper Canyon Railway
Navojoa
Álamos
SIERRA MADRE OCCIDENTAL
Guerrero Negro
San Ignacio
Santa Rosalía
Mulegé
SEA OF CORTEZ
Batopilas
Guachochi
Hidalgo de Parral
Zacatecas
Loreto
BAJA CALIFORNIA
El Fuerte
Los Mochis
Topolobampo
Guasave
Guamúchil
SINALOA
Culiacán
La Paz
(suspended 2018)
Tropic of Cancer
Todos Santos
Durango
PACIFIC OCEAN
San José del Cabo
Cabo San Lucas
Mazatlán
0
250
kilometres
NAYARIT
Santiago Ixcuintla
Mexcaltitán
San Blas
Tepic
Guadalajara
Puerto Vallarta
Manzanillo & Acapulco
HIGHLIGHTS
1 San Blas
2 Mexcaltitán
3 Mazatlán
4 The Copper Canyon railway
5 Creel and the Sierra Tarahumara
6 Álamos
7 Reserva de la Biósfera El Pinacate
THE NORTHWEST & COPPER CANYON

The **Museo de Los Cinco Pueblos**, housed in a former nineteenth-century hotel, contains anthropological displays, artwork, embroidery and beadwork of Nayarit's four major Indigenous groups (the Coras, Huichols, Nahua, aka "mexicaneros", and Tepehuanos), as well as aspects of mestizo culture, the fifth "pueblo", recently (and controversially) added to reflect the ethnic make-up of the whole state.

Museo Amado Nervo

Zacatecas Nte 284 • Free • 311 212 2916

The **Museo Amado Nervo** commemorates the life and works of one of Mexico's most famous poets, in the house where he was born in 1870. Inside are family photographs and some books and furniture that once belonged to Nervo. Best known for poems such as *La Raza de Bronce* (written in honour of Benito Juárez), and the heart-breaking *La Amada Inmóvil*, Nervo died in Uruguay (where he was Mexican Ambassador) in 1919.

ARRIVAL AND INFORMATION — TEPIC

By bus Tepic's Central Camionera lies a few kilometres east of the centre on Insurgentes Sur, but local buses shuttle in and out from the main road outside – to reach the centre, cross the street and catch the first bus marked "Centro". Transportes Norte de Sonora runs hourly second-class buses to San Blas (1hr 45min) and Santiago Ixcuintla (2hr) till around 7.30pm.

Destinations Guadalajara (every 30min; 3hr 30min–5hr); Mazatlán (hourly; 4hr–4hr 30min); Mexico City (3 daily; 10–11hr); Puerto Vallarta (hourly; 3–4hr); San Blas (hourly; 1–2hr)

Tourist office The main state tourism office is inconveniently located 1.5km out of the centre, near the Ex-Convento de la Cruz, at Ejército Nacional 10 (Mon–Fri 9am–2pm & 4–7pm; 311 210 0037, http://visitatepic.com), although there is a useful information kiosk on the Plaza Principal (daily 9am–7pm; 311 212 8037).

ACCOMMODATION

Fray Junípero Serra Lerdo Pte 23; http://hotelfrayjunipero.com. A comfortable choice, right on the plaza, with modern but fairly standard business-oriented rooms and amenities (LCD TVs and free parking). Breakfast is extra. M$$$

Hospedaje Tepic León Sur 36; 311 157 0097. The best deal in town, with a central location and simple but comfy rooms with balconies, TVs and fans. M$

Hotel Real de Don Juan México Sur 105, at Juárez; 311 216 1888. Dripping with historic character, this colonial

THE HUICHOL

The **Huichol**, or Wixárika, are the most intensely mystical of Mexico's Indigenous peoples. Dwelling in isolated mountain settlements around the borders of Nayarit, Jalisco, Zacatecas and Durango, they practise an extant form of **pre-Columbian shamanism**, having accepted only token elements of Spanish Catholicism.

For the Huichol, religion and ritual are central elements of daily life. The cultivation of maize, particularly, is bound up with sacred rites and esoteric meaning. **Animism** – the belief that all objects are alive and imbued with spirit – is key to their enigmatic world-view: rocks, trees, rivers and sky all have souls and there are as many gods as there are things in the world.

Peyote, a hallucinogenic cactus, is the most important and powerful god in their vast pantheon. Gathering and ingesting this plant is a major part of the ceremonial calendar, which includes an annual cross-country pilgrimage to the sacred desert around Real de Catorce to acquire supplies (see page 374). Grandfather Peyote is the teacher and guardian of the Huichol. He delivers sacred visions, heals the sick and guides the community.

Huichol artesanías are particularly striking and include vivid "**yarn paintings**" that are created by pressing lengths of yarn into wax. They represent peyote visions and are filled with vibrantly rendered snakes, birds, deer and other sacred animals, as well as gourd bowls and other ritually significant objects. Circular motifs usually symbolize peyote itself, or its flower. You can buy these paintings in Tepic and elsewhere.

8

palacio overlooking the main plaza offers comfy, old-fashioned rooms (with cable TV), a rooftop lounge and much cheaper rates online – shop around. M$$

EATING AND DRINKING

Emiliano Comida y Vino Zapata Ote 91; http://emilianorestaurant.com. For something smarter (though a portrait of Mexican Revolution hero Emiliano Zapata greets you at the entrance), this top-notch restaurant offers creative Mexican dining with regional specialities and excellent wines from all over the country. M$$$$

Lonchería Flamingos Puebla 193; 311 213 1118, https://facebook.com/LoncheriaFlamingos. Not far from the plaza, this is a great spot for no-frills Mexican food, with delicious tortas, tostadas and tacos on offer. M$

Restaurant La Sierra Hotel Sierra de Álica, México Nte 180; 311 212 0322, https://facebook.com/hotelsierradealica. This hotel restaurant is a real gem, knocking out tempting dishes such as fish *chicharrones*, steak "La Sierra" style and peanut sauce chicken. Check out the set-lunch deals. M$$$

San Blas and around

The coastal plains of Nayarit are sultry, marshy and flat, dotted with palm trees and half-submerged under lagoons teeming with wildlife. You have to travel through this to reach **SAN BLAS**, once an important port but now an enjoyably laid-back travellers' hangout. For such a small town (with around fifteen thousand inhabitants), San Blas manages to absorb its many visitors – who come mainly in winter – without feeling overrun. During the summer it's virtually deserted, but in January and February the town is a magnet for **bird watchers**, and in February the city also hosts its biggest festival in honour of San Blas (St Blaise). Do not come here without insect repellent or you will be eaten alive: legions of ferocious sand flies (*jejénes*) plague the beaches mornings and late afternoons, and the mosquitoes descend en masse at dusk.

8

Las Ruinas de la Contaduría

Cerro de la Contaduría • Charge • Take a taxi (or around 30min walking from main plaza)

Beyond lying on the pristine **beaches** to the south of San Blas, **bird watching** and taking a beguiling jungle-boat trip to **La Tovara springs**, a more focused hour can be spent at **Las Ruinas de la Contaduría**, the remains of a late eighteenth-century fort which, with the vaulted remains of a chapel, **La Iglesia de Nuestra Señora del Rosario** (1769), crown the Cerro de San Basilio near the river, 1km along Juárez towards Tepic; the ruins are said to have inspired Henry Wadsworth Longfellow's poem, *The Bells of San Blas*, though the poet never came here. From the top you get sensational views over the town to the ocean, where, according to Huichol legend, the small white island on the horizon is said to represent peyote.

La Tovara and jungle boat trips

The **lagoons and creeks** behind San Blas are unbelievably rich in **bird life** – white herons and egrets are especially prevalent. The best way to catch a glimpse is to get on one of the three-hour boat trips into the jungle, the launch negotiating channels tunnelled through dense mangrove, past sunbaking turtles. Go at dawn, before other trips have disturbed the animals; you might even glimpse a crocodile or caiman along the way. Most boats head for **La Tovara**, a cool freshwater spring that fills a beautiful clear pool perfect for swimming and pirouetting off the rope swing – if you're not put off by the presence of crocodiles, that is (the pool is enclosed and is safe, with schools of tilapia and catfish the only inhabitants). Eat at the fairly pricey palapa restaurant or bring your own picnic. Bring plenty of bug spray also.

Trips leave from the river bridge 1km inland from the main plaza along Juárez: get a group together for the best prices. Trips also run to the **Cocodrilario Kiekari**, the local crocodile farm (which you can also visit separately, on land, signposted off the main road south of San Blas).

Bahía de Matanchén

As well as the fine beaches right in town (**Playa El Borrego**, at the south end of C Cuauhtémoc) and on **Isla del Rey**, just offshore, there are others some 7km away around the **Bahía de Matanchén**, a vast, sweeping crescent lined entirely by fine soft sands. At the near end, the tiny community of **Matanchén** (famed for its locally baked **banana bread**) is the launching point for the long stretch of **Playa Las Islitas** (via dirt road), which has numerous palapa restaurants on the beach that serve up grilled fish and cold beers. At the far end of the bay lies the village **Aticama** (with basic shops and places to eat), the disappointing **Playa Los Cocos**, where erosion is steadily eating away at what was once a pristine beach, and the better **Playa La Miramar** beyond. In between, acres of sand are fragmented only by flocks of pelicans and the occasional crab. There are plenty of spots where you can camp if you have the gear and lots of repellent. The waves here, which rise offshore beyond Miramar and run in, past the point, to the depths of the bay, are in the *Guinness Book of World Records* as the longest in the world: it's very rare that they are high enough for surfers to ride them all the way in, but there's plenty of lesser **surfing** potential.

8

ARRIVAL AND DEPARTURE

By bus The bus station is on Sinaloa at Canalizo at the northeast corner of the main plaza, right in the centre of town. The majority of the buses (second-class only) serving San Blas arrive from Tepic, 65km east (last bus around 8pm). Note that Puerto Vallarta is one hour ahead of San Blas. From Mazatlán you'll need to change at Tepic or ask to get off at the "crucero de San Blas", where you can also pick up the Tepic–San Blas buses (till around 7.30pm).

Destinations Puerto Vallarta (4 daily; 3–4hr); Tepic (hourly; 1hr–1hr 30min).

INFORMATION AND ACTIVITIES

Tourist office The tourist office (Mon–Fri 9am–3pm; 323 285 0221) is located inside the Palacio Municipal on the main plaza. The best source of information, though, is http://visitsanblas.com, run by local expat Pat Cordes.

Surfing Surfboards and boogie boards can be rented at Stoner's Surf Camp (323 100 6085) at Playa El Borrego by the hour or by the day (lessons are extra). You can also stay in basic cabins here or camp. M$

GETTING AROUND

By bus The beaches of the Bahía de Matanchén can be reached by one of the buses ("El Llano") that leave around four times daily (8.30am–4.30pm) from the San Blas bus station; these go along the bay through Matanchén village (where you get off for Las Islitas); Los Cocos; and on to Santa Cruz. Coming back, just flag down the first bus. You can also take a local taxi (bargain fiercely) to Los Cocos.

ACCOMMODATION

SEE MAP PAGE 467

8

★ **Casa Roxanna Bungalows** El Rey, 1; http://casaroxanna.com. Exceptional value with immaculate rooms and good kitchenettes, all with cable TV and use of pool and laundry – the pick of the self-catering apartments in town. M$$

Garza Canela Paredes Sur 106 (follow signs from Batallón); http://garzacanela.com. Luxurious a/c rooms, pool, garden and some kitchenettes. Rates include breakfast, and the poshest restaurant in town, *El Delfín*, is on site. Significant discounts during low season. M$$$

Hotel Hacienda Flamingos Juárez 105; http://sanblas.com.mx. Hotel set in a gorgeous old mansion built in 1883 with a wonderful garden courtyard with pool and ping-pong table – the building has a lot more character than the rooms, which are sleek and classy but relatively standard. M$$$

Marina San Blas Cuauhtémoc 197; http://sanblas.com.mx. Extremely comfortable mini-resort right on the estuary, with small pool (and beach on the river), plus ten simple rooms (with terrace, bathroom, a/c, TV and free coffee). M$$$

EATING

SEE MAP PAGE 467

★ **El Delfín** Garza Canela Hotel, Paredes Sur 106; http://garzacanela.com. French gourmet dining in San Blas, with such delights as baked fish with pistachio, Serrano and parsley, shrimp with curry, coconut milk and coriander and chicken stuffed with cheddar, bacon and prunes. Chef Betty Vázquez was born in San Blas but attended Le Cordon Bleu in France. M$$$$

Restaurant La Isla Paredes 33 at Mercado (two blocks from the plaza); 311 232 4525. A must, if only to admire the astonishingly kitschy decor: draped fishing nets festooned with shell pictures, shell mobiles and shell lampshades. Moderately priced meat and great seafood. Also known as *Chief Tony's*. M$$

McDonald Restaurante Juárez 75; 323 285 0432. No relation to Ronald's place, this friendly restaurant just off the main plaza since 1952 serves excellent, good-value meals. Breakfasts are particularly tasty; you'll often find a crowd of expats here to enjoy them. M$$

DRINKING AND NIGHTLIFE

SEE MAP PAGE 467

Mike's Place Juárez 75 (above McDonald). Quiet drinking midweek but livens up on Fri and Sat with dancing, live music and anything from Latin to classic rock.

San Blas Social Club Batallón 35, on the Plaza Principal; 323 285 1235. Popular expat café, bar and erstwhile jazz club helmed by the amicable Agustin, with live music Fri and Sat and hearty pub food (specializing in steaks). Free wi-fi.

DIRECTORY

Banks and exchange The Banamex at Juárez 26 just east of the plaza has an ATM, but does not change foreign currency (including US$) and is plagued by long queues, poor rates and an occasional lack of funds. Change money before you get here.

Post office A block northeast of the bus station at Sonora and Echevarría.

Santiago Ixcuintla

Centro Cultural Huichol 20 de Noviembre 452, at Constitución • Free • 323 235 1171

North of San Blas, off Hwy-15, is **SANTIAGO IXCUINTLA**, a market town of around seventeen thousand where the only real interest lies in the **Centro Cultural Huichol**, approximately 1.5km from the central plaza towards Mexcaltitán. This cooperative venture, founded by Huichol artist Mariano Valadez to support his people and preserve their traditions, raises money by selling quality Huichol art and offering various classes you can book advance; the centre is most active between November and May.

ARRIVAL AND DEPARTURE — SANTIAGO IXCUINTLA

By bus Autotransportes Noroeste de Nayarit runs a few daily buses from Tepic (1.5hr). Buses also depart San Blas daily for Santiago at 9.30am. *Combis* to La Batanga (for Mexcaltitán; 4 daily) depart the Santiago terminal at Juarez Ote 73, one block north of the plaza (45min). Taxis run between Santiago and the dock at La Batanga.

Mexcaltitán

Museo del Origen Porfirio Díaz 1 (Plaza Principal) • Charge

North of Santiago Ixcuintla, located on a lily-strewn lagoon and supporting only a few hundred habitants (mostly shrimp farmers), is the extraordinary islet of **MEXCALTITÁN**. The "House of the Mexicans" in Náhautl, the town really does look like a very tiny version of Tenochtitlán, the Aztec capital before the Spaniards arrived. Indeed, the place is one candidate for the legendary Aztec homeland Aztlán, from which the tribe set out on their exodus to the Valley of México around 1091 AD; the small **Museo del Origen** addresses that hypothesis with a collection of archeological relics. If you're in the area around the end of June you should definitely try to visit the **island fiesta**, on June 28 and 29 (the feast days of Saints Peter and Paul), when there are canoe races on the lagoons and rivers; be sure to make a reservation.

ARRIVAL AND DEPARTURE — MEXCALTITÁN

By bus Mexcaltitán can only be reached from Santiago Ixcuintla (32km). Taxis are also an option (ask them to wait if you intend to do a day trip, usually an extra fee per hr), while *combis* (4 daily) also drop you at La Batanga; the journey takes about 45min and is followed by a 15min boat ride across the lagoon (guided boat tour options available).

EATING

La Alberca Porfirio Díaz s/n; 323 235 6027. There's a handful of inexpensive restaurants in Mexcaltitán, most specializing in seafood and, unsurprisingly, shrimp (you'll smell them long before you taste them). *La Alberca* is one of the more dependable places, with basic dishes, but opening times are always subject to change. M$$

Mazatlán

The languid resort of **MAZATLÁN** is far less dominated by tourism than Acapulco or Puerto Vallarta, its direct rivals, though hotels still flank its 30km of enticing sandy beaches, and activities such as horseriding and zip lines have enhanced its appeal in recent years. Yet Mazatlán's greatest pull remains its old-fashioned seaside resort atmosphere and the museums, cafés and galleries of its resurgent *centro histórico*, where much of its nineteenth-century core has been sensitively restored. Most tourists stay in the **Zona Dorada**, the "Golden Zone" along the beach, and penetrate the *centro histórico* only on brief forays, but the latter has far more character. Mazatlán actually peaked in the 1980s, and today much of the seafront looks decidedly tired, despite the steady flow of visitors. Local authorities have certainly made huge improvements in security in recent years, however, and since 2015 all the major cruise lines have been once again making stops here.

Brief history

Mazatlán started life as a base for smugglers and pirates in the 1700s. An official customs office was opened here in 1828, and from then on it boomed as a respectable mining port; by 1850 the population had reached 5000 (despite a devastating cholera epidemic the year before). Mazatlán had grown into one of Mexico's most important ports by 1900, as well as a major manufacturing centre: beer producer **Cerveceria del Pacífico** was established here by German immigrants in 1900, and it remains one of the nation's most popular brands. The city was hit hard by the 1910 Revolution, however, and by the 1930s the Great Depression had killed off the local economy. After World War II Mazatlán reinvented itself as a fishing port (it still boasts the biggest canneries and shrimp fisheries in Mexico) and a tourist destination. Today it has a population of around half a million, the second-largest city in Sinaloa (after Culiacán, the capital).

Plaza República

Mazatlán's **Plaza República** is very much the commercial heart of the city and the *centro histórico*, harbouring the cathedral, post office, dour modern government offices, main bank branches and travel agencies.

Catedral de la Inmaculada Concepción

Plaza República • 669 981 3352

The twin-towered **Catedral de la Inmaculada Concepción** is the only real building of note on Plaza República, completed in 1899 in an eclectic style incorporating neo-Gothic, Spanish and Romanesque elements, with a particularly grand interior and main altar.

Mercado Pino Suárez

Juárez, at Valle • https://mercadopinosuarezmazatlan.com

Take time to explore the **Mercado Pino Suárez**, two blocks north of the Plaza República, a grand Art Nouveau edifice that remains exceptionally bright and clean inside. The vast iron structure was completed in 1900, and named in honour of Mexico's vice president Pino Suárez in 1915 (who had been assassinated two years earlier). You'll find the usual meat, veg and fruit stalls here, as well as souvenirs, clothes and excellent, cheap places to eat (see page 477).

Plaza Machado

Plaza Machado, a few blocks southwest of the Plaza República, is by far the most popular of the old town squares. It's surrounded by restaurants (see page 477) and fine nineteenth-century buildings, notably the **Centro Municipal de las Artes**, and the late nineteenth-century Edifico Juárez on the north side.

Teatro Ángela Peralta

Carnaval s/n • Charge • 669 982 4446

THE MAZATLÁN MOSAICS

Opened in 2009, the ultra-modern **Mazatlán International Center**, Avenida del Delfín 6303 (http://mazatlaninternationalcenter.com), is best known for exhibitions and conferences, but it is also home to the world's largest mosaic mural. Sinaloa-born local artist Ernesto Ríos created the mesmerizing 25m-high three-dimensional ceramic mosaic dubbed "*Sea of Cortés*", which covers the whole north wall of the building and explodes with colour. The centre is studded with modern artwork inside and out, further justifying the taxi ride up here.

Adjacent to the Centro Municipal de las Artes Teatro, the Neoclassical **Teatro Ángela Peralta** opened in 1874. The theatre is named after the "Mexican Nightingale", who died in the art centre next door in 1882 (it was a hotel at the time). In addition to seeing the opulent interior there's a small museum on the second floor and temporary art exhibitions inside.

Nidart Gallery

Libertad 45, at Carnaval • 669 985 5991

Just across Libertad from Teatro Ángela Peralta, the **Nidart Gallery** is one of the most popular art and crafts stores in the city. The specialty here is beautiful, elaborate sculptures made from leather, including ornate masks created by artists Loa Molina and Rak Garcia (who opened the gallery in 1992). Nidart also displays artwork from all over Mexico.

Museo Arqueológico

Sixto Osuna 76 • Charge • 669 981 1455

The small **Museo Arqueológico**, just a couple of blocks off Plaza Machado towards Olas Altas, is notable for having English labelling – the museum charts the pre-Hispanic cultures of Sonora state, with beautifully crafted **Aztatlán pottery** (750–1200 AD) and a collection of figurines, pots and statues, ending with the **Jorobado de la Nautical**, a strange figure of a hunchback thought to have magic powers.

Museo de Arte

Carranza at Sixto Osuna • Charge • 669 981 5592

Across the street from the Museo Arqueológico is the curious little **Museo de Arte**, set around a pretty courtyard and mansion built in 1898, with a permanent collection of modern Mexican paintings and sculpture from the late 1970s, and temporary exhibits of contemporary Mexican art. Exhibits rotate, but the permanent collection includes work by Sinaloan watercolour artist Edgardo Coghlan, contemporary painter Vicente Rojo, well-known abstract artist Rufino Tamayo and Oaxacan painter and sculptor Francisco Toledo.

El Acuario Mazatlán

Av de los Deportes 111 • Charge, discount for children 3–11 • https://www.granacuario.com

The city's slightly shabby aquarium, **El Acuario Mazatlán** (just off Av del Mar halfway between the *centro histórico* and the Zona Dorada) attracts a steady stream of families and school groups for its fish tanks, sea lions and aviary (largely filled with parrots). Turtles, sharks and a variety of tropical fish (mostly but not exclusively from Mexican waters) are on show, though the labelling (Spanish only) is hit and miss. The small Museo del Mar section contains a grey-whale skeleton and various shark jaws.

El Faro de Crestón

There are scintillating **views** of Mazatlán from the top of the **Faro de Crestón**, the lighthouse at the far southern edge of the city that dates back to 1879. Taxis can take you to the foot of the hill (buses also go this far), but the only way to the top is on foot (30–45min). It's a popular hike in the mornings and late afternoons. The lighthouse

itself still works and is off limits, but there's a small glass walkway that juts out over the edge at the top for thrill seekers. The path is well-paved, free and generally well policed during the day.

The beaches

Facing the Pacific on the edge of the *centro histórico*, **Playa Olas Altas** is where Mazatlán's transformation into a resort began in the 1920s, and though the faded tiles and peeling paint of the *Belmar Hotel* (which opened in 1924) are in dire need of a makeover, *Bar Belmar* (daily 7am–10pm) is still a classic place for a sunset drink. The beach here is not the best place to swim – it's rather rocky and the waves tend to be powerful (*olas altas* means "high waves"). Indeed, this is a decent place to **surf** (though not for beginners) – you can rent boards at *Looney Bean* (see page 477). From Playa Olas Altas, the paved **malecón** runs for 10km to the Zona Dorada.

The Mirador

Following the seafront drive from Playa Olas Altas around the jagged coast under the Cerro de la Nevería brings you to the **Mirador** – an outcrop from which local daredevil youths or *clavadistas* plunge into the sea. At a little over 10m, it's nowhere near as spectacular as the high-diving in Acapulco, but is dangerous nonetheless. You'll see them performing whenever there are enough tourists to raise a collection, generally starting at 10am or 11am – especially during the summer and Semana Santa – and again in the late afternoon (around 5pm) when the tour buses roll through.

Zona Dorada

From the Mirador the malecón runs along the long sweep of **Playa Norte**, but it's worth skipping this and walking (or taking the bus) all the way to the **Zona Dorada**, where the first of the big hotels went up and the sands improve greatly. The beaches right in front of the hotels – known as **Playa Gaviotas** and **Playa Sábalo** further north – are clean

MAZATLÁN'S LONESOME TRAVELLERS

Few Mexican cities seem to celebrate their (albeit tenuous) literary connections with such pride as Mazatlán, with special plaques nailed up throughout the old town. **Herman Melville** stayed in Mazatlán for nineteen days in 1844, as a humble sailor aboard the frigate *United States*, no doubt gathering material for *Moby Dick* and his other subsequent novels. In 1951 beat poet **Allen Ginsberg** passed through, while **Anaïs Nin** stayed at the *Hotel Belmar* when she visited Mazatlán the same year. In her diary, Nin admires the "pink and turquoise houses, the green shutters". The following year **Jack Kerouac** spent a night and day drinking and dossing on the beach in Mazatlán, writing about his brief time here in *Lonesome Traveler* (1960): "At Mazatlan at dusk we stopped for awhile for a swim in our underwear in that magnificent surf..."

and sheltered by little offshore islands, while further on they're wilder and emptier. Among the dozens of artesanía markets and shopping malls here, **Seashell City Museum** (http://seashellcitymuseum.com), at Gaviotas 407 in the heart of the Zona, stands out as the kitschiest of all – a two-storey emporium of seashells (for sale) with a "museum" upstairs of rare pieces and whale bones, and an indoor goldfish pond.

Isla de la Venados

If you fancy escaping the beach vendors of the Zona Dorada for a few hours take the boat trip to the **Isla de la Venados** (Deer Island) 2km offshore, the biggest (1.8km long) and most accessible of the three islands off Mazatlán (the other two are Isla de Pájaros and Isla de Lobos). There's a small beach and tide pools for snorkelling, and kayaking and even banana boat trips are available. Any of the tour operators in the Zona Dorada will sell tickets; boats usually depart Marina El Cid at 9.30am, returning at around 4pm (tour prices include activities, food and drinks).

Playa Cerritos and Playa Bruja

If your goal is to reach a beautifully serene beach, head north to either **Playa Cerritos** or **Playa Bruja** (both accessible by bus). These are at the heart of the new mega resorts and development of **Nuevo Mazatlán**, but the beaches remain fairly free of crowds and there are plenty of restaurants and places for a post-beach drink.

Isla de la Piedra

Boat trips every 10min • Charge • Buses marked "Ferry" go to the end of Carnaval, from where it's a short walk to the *Embarcadero*

Just across the harbour from the *centro histórico* but a totally different world, the **Isla de la Piedra** (actually a long peninsula) offers a slice of rustic Mexico with a long, sandy beach excellent for swimming, backed by palapa restaurants and palm trees. Small motorboats shuttle back and forth from the **Embarcadero Playa Sur**, close to the ferry terminal in Mazatlán, to the dirt road just across from the Piedra beach. It is possible to sleep out or sling a hammock on the terrace of one of the small restaurants – ask the owners first. All the restaurants on the beach serve similar menus of fresh seafood and coconuts. Once a very basic community, the island is now included in many tour itineraries and can become crowded, especially on Sunday afternoons, when locals congregate for live music, dancing and kite flying.

ARRIVAL AND DEPARTURE — MAZATLÁN

BY PLANE

Arrival Mazatlán's General Rafael Buelna International Airport (669 982 2399) is some 20km south of town (off Hwy-15), served by a system of fixed-price vans/colectivos (running to the old town, Zona Dorada and Playa Cerritos; minimum three persons) and taxis. Note that Uber is officially not allowed to provide airport pick-ups. Taxis will charge a set fee for the journey back from the *centro histórico*. You'll find ATMs and Budget, Hertz and Europcar car rental desks at the airport, as well as free wi-fi.

Departure Useful domestic flights include the daily Los Cabos and La Paz connections from Calafia Airlines (669 984 4300), Viva Aerobus (81 8215 0150) to Monterrey and Mexico City and Volaris (01 800 122 8000) to Tijuana. There are numerous flights to the US and Canada.

Destinations (domestic) La Paz (1 daily; 1hr 30min); Los Cabos (2 daily; 1hr 30min); Mexico City (4–6 daily; 1hr 30min); Monterrey (3–4 weekly; 2hr 25min); Tijuana (2 daily; 2hr 30min).

BY BUS

Arrival The Central de Autobuses lies three blocks behind Playa Norte on José Ángel Espinoza, at Panuco. Taxis and *pulmonías* run from here to the *centro histórico* and the Zona Dorada. To save money you can take a public bus: for the *centro histórico*, turn left on Espinoza and walk one block to the main road (Av Ejercito Mexicano), and get on just about any bus heading to the right – they'll get you, by a variety of routes, to the Mercado Pino Suárez. For the Zona Dorada, walk down Espinoza in the other direction to the beach (Av de la Mar) and catch any "Sábalo" bus heading to the right.

Departure Most buses from Mazatlán are *de paso*, but with services roughly hourly north and south, you should have no problems getting a ticket. Note that with the completion of the Puente Baluarte, the new "Carretera Interoceánica" to Durango has cut travel times to the interior dramatically. There are a few direct services to Puerto Vallarta, but companies like TAP also offer more frequent services via a change in Tepic (usually the wait is 30min) – they can reserve seats all the way. For San Blas you'll need to take a bus to Tepic and change. Shop around, as prices do differ between companies like TAP and Omnibus.

Destinations Durango (12 daily; 4hr); Guadalajara (every 30min; 6–7hr); Los Mochis (every 30min; 6hr 30min); Mexico City (5–6 daily; 14–15hr); Puerto Vallarta (5–7 daily; 7hr 30min); Tepic (every 30min; 4hr); Tijuana (every 30min; 26–28hr).

BY FERRY

Baja Ferries (669 123 6600, https://www.bajaferries.com.mx) has traditionally operated a ferry between Mazatlán and La Paz (3 times a week; 12hr) in Baja California (see page 544) from the port at Playa Sur, 1km southeast of the *centro histórico*.

8

GETTING AROUND

By taxi The streets of Mazatlán are patrolled by scores of taxis (or "eco-taxis"), little open *pulmonías* (they look like souped-up golf carts but are usually modified VW Beetles) which are more expensive, and larger (and cheaper) pick-up trucks (*aurigas*). Prices depend on your negotiation skills (and technically the "zone" system). Locals tend to pay a lot less for taxi trips within the Zona Dorada and the *centro histórico*, while trips between zones cost more (expect to pay 20 percent more at night between Zona Dorada and the *centro histórico*). Locals pay a small fee per person for *aurigas*, while *pulmonías* charge around more for trips between Zona Dorada or cruise terminal and the old town. *Aurigas* can fit in a lot more people than taxis. *Pulmonías* drivers can be hired for longer tours of the city, but tend to provide a running commentary of the locale wherever you are.

By bus Smaller city buses (daily 5.30am–10.30pm; every 15min) cost a small amount, while the larger a/c (or "tourist") buses are a little more. There are two main tourist bus routes: Sábalo Centro (from the ferry terminal in the old town, along the seafront to Playa Bruja); and Sábalo Cocos (from Pino Suárez market to the bus station, then to the Zona Dorada and along the seafront).

By car There are dozens of car-rental outlets in Mazatlán, including: Budget, Camarón Sábalo 413, 669 913 2000; and Hertz, Camarón Sábalo 314, 669 913 6060.

INFORMATION

Tourist office The Sinaloa Secretaría de Turismo office is at Av del Mar 882, on the seafront (Mon–Fri 9am–5pm; 669 981 8883), with the Asociación de Hoteles, Moteles y Empresas Turísticas de Mazatlán at Av Camarón Sábalo,

HUANA COA CANOPY ADVENTURE

One of the most popular day trips from Mazatlán is to the **Huana Coa Canopy Adventure** (https://huanacoacanopy.com), a 45-minute minibus ride north in the Vinata Los Osuna, a mescal farm. Nine zip lines weave between shady huanacaxtle trees on the premises, ending with a rappel down the last one and visits to the tequila factory, founded by the Osuna family in 1876, along with free shots; the bus ride back seems much faster. Tours usually run daily, with pick-ups from Mazatlán at 9.30am and 11.30am, though if a cruise ship is in town the place tends to get swamped (they also do ATV rides and horseback riding).

Centro Comercial Las Palmas 333 (669 913 8181, http://gomazatlan.com). More helpful, however, are the blue-shirted volunteers (mostly North American expats) who man stations in the old town and are a font of local information (www.mazatlantouristaide.org).

Magazines and newspapers There are several free English-language publications worth checking out if you're here for more than just a day: *Mazatlán Interactivo* (http://mazatlaninteractivo.com) is always reliable and contains useful information about events and attractions. See also http://mazatlanlife.com.

TOURS AND ACTIVITIES

Tours and activities Any major hotel will be able to arrange tours – nature, culture or adventure – around the city and to the outlying islands or villages. Jet skis, catamarans, kayaks and boats can usually be rented on the beach with no prior arrangement.

Jah Surf School http://mazatlansurfschool.com. Excellent English-speaking instructors offering 2hr lessons (including boards). Surfboard rentals are per hour or per day.

Onca Explorations Río de la Plata 409, Gaviotas; https://facebook.com/oncaexplorations. Professional whale (Dec–Feb only) and dolphin-watching outfit with a variety of tours from kayaking and snorkelling the islands off Mazatlán and dolphin adventures to tours of Las Labradas petroglyphs, north of the city.

Turtle Tours Mazatlán; https://facebook.com/turtletoursmazatlan. Enlightening tours of the Verde-Camacho Turtle Sanctuary (40min north of the city), where you get to help release new-born olive ridley turtles into the wild (minimum four persons).

ACCOMMODATION

8

CENTRO HISTÓRICO, SEE MAP PAGE 471

Casa Lucila Hotel Boutique Olas Altas 16; https://facebook.com/hotelcasalucila. Fabulous place to stay, though expensive in high season; you get wonderful ocean views, a top-floor infinity pool and eight elegant rooms enhanced with flatscreen TVs, marble-clad bathrooms and jacuzzis. M$$$$$

★ **Hostal Mazatlán** Constitución 809; 669 688 5755. Excellent budget option in the historic centre, with a mixed six-bed dorm and several private rooms, a large rooftop terrace, a/c, dependable hot showers, shared kitchen, friendly staff and free bikes. Basic breakfast included (invariably comprising fruit and banana bread baked on the premises). M$

Hotel Posada Freeman Olas Altas 79; http://grupoposadadelrio.mx. This 1940s monolith has been given a contemporary makeover with modern, smart rooms with cable TV, a/c and free, fairly substantial buffet breakfasts – the rooftop pool is tiny but a superb place to hang out with a margarita. M$$$

★ **Hotel Tierra Marina Centro Historico** Belisario Domínguez 1502-B; 669 982 1084. This contemporary hotel is one of the best value for money picks in the centre, with a glut of good bars and restaurants within easy walking distance. The rooms aren't much to write home about, but they've got everything you need – all at a decent price. M$$

★ **Las 7 Maravillas** Las Palmas 1, at Jaboneria; http://las7maravillas.com. B&B in a wonderfully renovated 1950s villa helmed by Swiss expat Tatiana Genoud, with each room themed around a specific country such as Egypt and Cuba (and decked out with authentic handicrafts from that country) with views of the ocean, one block away. Rooms come with a/c and cable TV, plus delicious breakfasts. Adults only. M$$$

Royal Dutch Casa de Santa María Constitución 627; 669 981 4396. Charming B&B in a colonial beauty built in 1888, with friendly and helpful Dutch management. Rates include a full breakfast, coffee and tea, as well as afternoon tea and pastries. Reserve at least two weeks in advance, as they are almost always full. M$$$

La Siesta Olas Altas 11, between Ángel Flores and Escobedo; http://lasiesta.com.mx. Lovely old hotel from 1952, with private balconies and great sea views (worth the extra money); drawbacks are small rooms and noise from *El Shrimp Bucket* restaurant next door. M$$

NEAR THE BUS STATION, SEE MAP PAGE 472

Emperador Río Pánuco 236 (opposite the bus station); 669 982 6288. Convenience and the budget price are the main attractions here, though rooms are clean and comfortable enough, with cable TV and a/c. M$

Hotel Sands Arenas Av del Mar 1910; http://sandsarenas.com. Facing the beach, two blocks down from the bus station. Comfortable, US-style motel with pool, slide and sea views; good value off-season, when prices drop by over fifty percent. M$$

ZONA DORADA AND NUEVO MAZATLÁN, SEE MAP PAGE 472

★ **Funky Monkey Hostel** Cerro Boludo 112, Lomas de Mazatlán; 669 431 3421. Best budget option in the Golden Zone, a ten-minute walk from the beach but with a (tiny) outdoor pool and tranquil rooftop terrace as back-up. Offers comfy mixed dorms with a/c, a private double, free bikes, shared kitchen and decent breakfast included (fruits and

FESTIVALS AND EVENTS IN MAZATLÁN

SEMANA SANTA

Remember to book accommodation well ahead if you are planning to be here around Semana Santa, when Mexicans descend on the city for massive celebrations (or July and Aug, when families pack the hotels and beaches).

CARNIVAL

You should also plan around the boisterous carnival held here in February, which involves a massive firework display known as the Combate Naval and is one of the world's largest, dating back to the 1840s.

FIRST FRIDAY ART WALKS

The *centro histórico* has become a magnet for Mexican and international artists in recent years; you can get a taster of the scene on the First Friday Art Walks (Nov–May 4–8pm; free; http://culturamazatlan.com/es/festivales), held every first Friday of the month, when numerous galleries and artists (30 at last count) open their doors for self-guided tours (pick up maps at hotels or at the website).

pancakes). Dorms M$, double M$$

Inn Beach Hotel Mazatlán Camarón Sábalo 6291; http://theinnmazatlan.com. This classy hotel–timeshare complex oozes chic (or at least the Mazatlán equivalent thereof). Larger apartment units with kitchens and tiled floors are excellent value for families or small groups. M$$$

Motel Marley Gaviotas 226; http://travelbymexico.com/sina/marley. Just sixteen comfortable units (with cable TV and a/c) in this small-scale place with a great position right on the sand, and a pool – you won't find a place on the water for much less. M$$$

Playa Mazatlán Beach Hotel Gaviotas 202; www.hotelplayamazatlan.com. Vast 1950s beachside resort – if you want the full Mazatlán experience in the heart of the action, this is a solid choice, with a huge programme of activities and a great pool, though rooms are fairly standard three-star fare. M$$$$

8

EATING

CENTRO HISTÓRICO, SEE MAP PAGE 471

Casa Etnika Sixto Osuna 50; 669 136 0139. Lovely courtyard café and contemporary art and crafts store serving fresh Oaxaca coffee, frappés (including decadent Oreo flavour) and piña colada smoothies. Free wi-fi. M$

Jimmy's Tacos Constitución 723; 669 101 2890. A fun and fast taco joint with generous portions and seasonal fillings. This cash only spot is also a good budget friendly option. M$

Looney Bean Olas Altas 166-G; http://looneybeanmzt.com. Friendly outpost of the Californian artisan coffee chain and internet café, offering fine Americanos, espressos and cappuccinos (limited seating) – the owners are also involved in the Christian Marketplace Ministry programme in Mazatlán. Free wi-fi. M$

Mercado Pino Suárez Juárez and Valle; http://mercadopinosuarezmazatlan.com. *Jugo* (fresh juice) stalls downstairs, as well as the respected *El Tigre* seafood stall (the *ceviche* is excellent); most cafés are in the upstairs gallery overlooking Juárez, serving breakfasts and cheap *comidas* – follow the crowds as always, though *Restaurante Nancy* is usually a good bet. M$

Pastelería Panamá Juárez and Canizales, opposite the cathedral; 669 984 3266. Diner-style restaurant/cafeteria, good for breakfast. You can also take away a host of delectable pastries from the bakery and eat them on the plaza. M$$

El Shrimp Bucket Olas Altas 11, between Ángel Flores and Escobedo; 669 441 4111. One of the oldest and best-known restaurants in Mazatlán (since 1963). Now in bigger, plusher premises, it still has plenty of atmosphere and generous breakfast combos, marlin stew (they serve a famed hangover cure) and plenty of shrimps, served numerous different ways. Happy hour daily. M$$$

★ **Topolo** Constitución 629, at Juárez; 669 136 0660. Justly popular restaurant that offers slightly upmarket Mexican fare (like *poblano* peppers stuffed with cheese) and their home-made roasted tomato salsa in a tranquil courtyard, while the wine bar has a daily happy hour – also good for mango margaritas. M$$$

El Túnel Carnaval 1207, opposite the Teatro Angela Peralta; 669 668 9540. Not the best food in town these days, but still a great place for Sinaloense cuisine, patronized by locals and tourists since 1945. Great Sinaloa specialities such as *asado a la plaza*, *pozole* and home-made gorditas, but no beer (although you can bring your own) and infamously, no air-conditioning. M$$$

★ **Water's Edge** Sixto Osuna 48, at Niños Héroes; 669 136 0895, https://facebook.com/WatersEdgeBistro. Romantic seaside bistro offering fine wines, artisan beers and the best ocean views to accompany dishes such as red Thai curry prawns and tequila tagliatelle with shrimp and crème fresh. M$$$

ZONA DORADA, SEE MAP PAGE 472

Los Arcos Camarón Sábalo 1019; http://restaurantlosarcos.com. Locals flock to this relaxed modern Mexican chain restaurant, close to the beach, for some of the best seafood in the city and especially good charbroiled octopus, shrimps and fish *chicharrones*. M$$$

★ **Casa Loma** Gaviotas 104 (six blocks inland from Sábalo); 669 913 5398. For that perfect romantic – and expensive – evening, this secluded restaurant in a colonial setting has far more atmosphere than the big hotels. Reservations are recommended. M$$$$

Gus y Gus Camarón Sábalo 1730 (across from Costa De Oro hotel); 669 914 4501. Great little open-air restaurant just off the road, serving especially good chicken fajitas, shrimp *ceviche* and marlin tacos. If you like classic rock you'll love the house band, which entertains a mostly tourist crowd nightly. Cash only. M$$$

Pancho's Gaviotas 408 (enter through Las Cabañas passage); 669 914 0911. This is another tourist favourite, with an attractive wood and tile dining room, tables overlooking the beach and excellent fresh seafood – think stuffed fish fillets, coconut shrimp and frog's legs. The zesty margaritas make it ideal for sunset drinks. M$$$

PLAYA CERRITOS, SEE MAP PAGE 472

Tacos Escorpio by Henry Sábalo Cerritos (parking lot of Scorpio 5 convenience store, just north of the Mayan Palace Hotel); 669 329 6402. If you make it to the beach up here be sure to stop by this lauded taco joint, where a meal of juicy *asada* and shrimp tacos will always hit the spot (the bean soup, chips and salsa are free). Cash only. M$$

8

DRINKING AND NIGHTLIFE

CENTRO HISTÓRICO, SEE MAP PAGE 471

Café Pacífico/Vintage Retro Bar Constitución 505, on Plaza Machado; 669 910 4730. Friendly bar with a selection of beers and liquors, snacks, sandwiches and coffee – the speciality is "Pacific Sunset", a rum and grenadine-based cocktail with pineapple juice. Now adorned with large TVs showing music videos from the 1980s.

Edgar's Bar Serdán 832, at Escobedo; 669 982 7218. Dating from 1949, this venerable cantina now proclaims "Ladies welcome" in English at the door; inside it's still a slice of traditional Mazatlán, with old photos on the walls, ancient patrons, cheap beers and live music at night.

★ **Sky Room** Hotel Posada Freeman, 11/F, Olas Altas 79; www.bestwestern.com. Worth a visit for the spectacular views across the old town and lower Mazatlán, the cruise ships and islands, especially at night. Drinks are reasonable, and you'll often have the place to yourself.

ZONA DORADA, SEE MAP PAGE 472

Bar Lago Azul Costa da Oro Hotel, Camarón Sábalo 710; www.hotelcostadeoro.mx. Part coffee shop, part lounge bar, expect exceptional espresso coffee, unusual cocktails and potent margaritas.

Fiestaland Camarón Sábalo at Buelna, Zona Dorada; 669 984 1666.This bizarre, all-white castle-like structure is a conglomeration of pricey clubs, discos and bars, of which *Valentino's* is the most popular, open from 11pm.

★ **Kelly's Gasoline Alley Bar** La Laguna 500, at Garzas; 669 132 1494.This Canadian-owned bar and restaurant has garnered a loyal following, mainly due to its party atmosphere, phenomenal margaritas – try the watermelon, mint and cucumber – and the excellent live bands. The Sunday roast and fish and chips aren't bad either; and the Jell-O shots are sold for charity. Cash only.

SHOPPING

SEE MAP PAGE 472

★ **Onilikan** Gaviotas 505; https://facebook.com/Onilikan. This small micro-distillery was established by Canadian investors in 2010, using a rare copper still imported from Germany. It specializes in potent liqueurs and spirits made from local mango and agave (the name loosely translates as "liquor place" in Nahuatl).

DIRECTORY

Banks and exchange Citibank, Camarón Sábalo 424; HSBC, Camarón Sábalo 1662 (Zona Dorada) and Belizario Domínguez and Ángel Flores (*centro histórico*); and Banamex, on Juárez at Ángel Flores by the main plaza. Most places in the Zona accept US dollars though often at a poor rate, so you may want to make use of Mazatlán's numerous *casas de cambio*. Bancomer (with ATM) is at Juarez and 21 de Marzo but does not exchange cash.

Consulates Canada (consular agency only; Mon–Fri 9.30am–12.30pm), La Marina Business & Life Commercial Center, Blvd Marina, 669 913 7320; US (consular agency only; Mon–Fri 9am–1pm), Av Playa Gaviotas 202 (opposite

Hotel Playa Mazatlán) 669 916 5889.

Emergencies 911.

Hospital Balboa Hospital at Sábalo 4480 has a 24hr walk-in clinic with English-speaking doctors (669 916 5533 or 669 916 7933, https://hospitalbalboa.com.mx).

Internet In *centro histórico* try the *Looney Bean* café. You will find many internet places on Camarón Sábalo in the Zona Dorada, though most are pricey. The malecón has wi-fi, as do many restaurants.

Pharmacy Farmacia Guadalajara has branches at Ocampo 2 (daily 7am–10pm), 21 de Marzo 820 (24hr) and Aleman 1 at Carnaval (24hr), and also in the Zona Dorada at Sábalo1493 (24hr).

Police 060 for emergency assistance; tourist police 669 914 8444.

Post office Juárez and 21 de Marzo 1500, Plaza República (669 981 2121); there's another branch at the bus station.

Northern Sinaloa

Mazatlán lies at the southern end of the vast state of **Sinaloa**, a landscape of scrubby desert and jagged mountains spilling into pristine beaches along the Sea of Cortez. The main city in northern Sinaloa is **Los Mochis**, an uninteresting destination in itself, but, as the western terminus of the **Copper Canyon railway**, an important transport hub. Many train passengers prefer to head inland to **El Fuerte**, a tranquil colonial backwater some two hours east. In recent years Sinaloa has garnered a reputation as a centre of drug cartel violence, with a subsequent drop-off in tourist numbers, but despite the scary statistics the places of interest remain safe for visitors.

8

Los Mochis

The modern city of **LOS MOCHIS** is a relatively new creation by Mexican standards, its origins going back to the establishment of a utopian colony on Topolobampo Bay in 1881, led by American socialist **Albert Kimsey Owen**. The colony was abandoned in the early 1900s, and Los Mochis really owes its existence to the **Sinaloa Sugar Company**, a US-owned monolith that was established by Benjamin Johnston in the 1890s (the founder and his wife are commemorated with reverential portraits in the lobby of *Hotel Santa Anita*). The city grew up around the extensive company works, and today it's a broad-streeted, prosperous, but rather dull place of 257,000 with few attractions, notable only as a major crossing point for road, rail and ferry, and above all the western terminus of the incomparable **Copper Canyon railway** (see page 482). If you're planning to take the ferry or train you'll have little choice but to stay at least one night here – don't expect much excitement. On Sundays you can check out the chaotic but fun **tianguis** (open-air market), which takes place on Zaragoza and Cuauhtémoc south of Castro. The sweltering grid of streets that makes up central Los Mochis otherwise has no real focus, but what there is of a commercial centre is on Hidalgo and Obregón, between Allende and Leyva.

Museo Regional del Valle del Fuerte

Obregón at Rosales • Charge • 668 812 4692 • Free

Facing the town's shady Plazuela 27 de Septiembre and its humble church, **Sagrado Corazón**, the **Museo Regional del Valle del Fuerte** acts as the town's equally humble main attraction. Inside are small exhibits on the history of the area, including the local **Yoreme** culture, as well as a decent bookshop.

ARRIVAL AND DEPARTURE — LOS MOCHIS

BY PLANE

Federal del Valle del Fuerte International Airport (668 818 6870) is southwest of the centre off the Topolobampo highway at km 12.5. Taxis operate on a fixed-rate system – buy a ticket at the booth before you exit the terminal. Aeroméxico flies to Mexico City, Volaris flies to Tijuana and Guadalajara, while Aéreo Servicio Guerrero and Calafia Airlines offer useful connections across to Baja California.

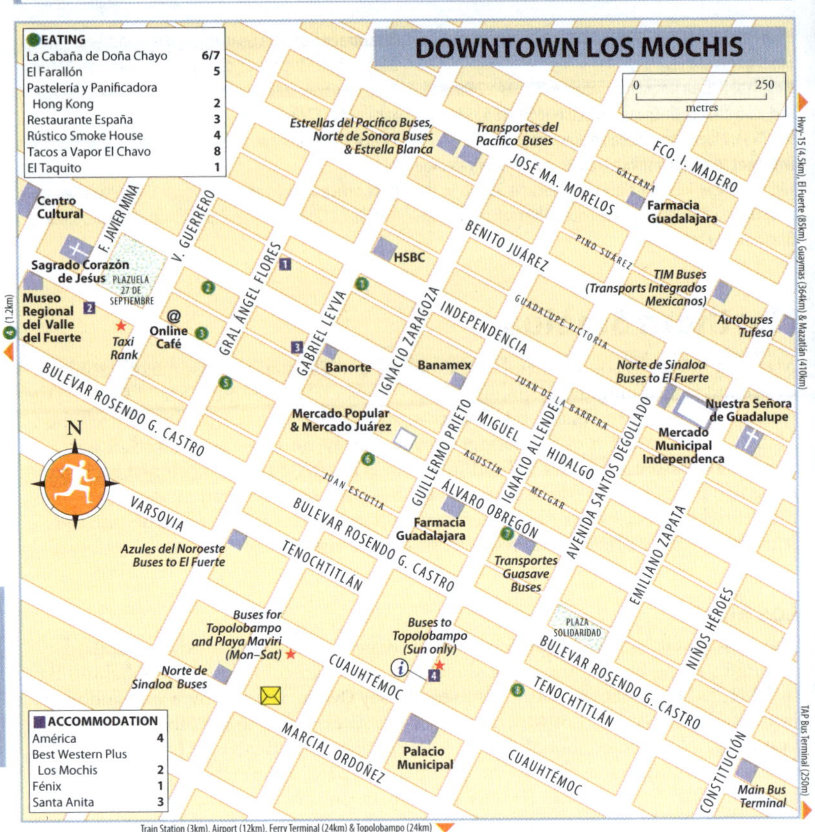

8

BY TRAIN

The train station for the Copper Canyon railway is 3km southeast of the centre; there are frequent buses during the day (allow at least one hour), but if you're aiming to catch the 6am train, take a taxi to be safe. The *Hotel Santa Anita* lays on a minibus to the station for guests through the Viajes Flamingo agency, arranged in advance.

Schedules Two trains now make the Copper Canyon run – the luxury daily Chepe Express (between Los Mochis and Creel only) and the Chepe Regional (3 days a week, but running the full route between Los Mochis and Chihuahua). Regional trains leave for Chihuahua at 6am, while the Express departs at 3.50pm. See page 484 for full details.

Tickets Fares vary considerably – note also that prices tend to increase every January. On the Express, "executive" class one-way fares should be a fixed rate to El Fuerte, and are considerably more to Creel/Divisadero. The slightly less luxurious "tourist" one-way tickets will be less to El Fuerte and Creel/Divisadero. Regional trains also have two classes: "regional tourist" fares vary to El Fuerte, Divisadero, Creel and Chihuahua. Buy an economy ticket if you want to save a lot of money – it's not as rough as travel agents make out. The ticket office at the station opens at 5am for same-day sales for both trains – this is the only way to buy the cheapest tickets. Tickets for the "regional tourist" class or any ticket on the Chepe Express can be purchased in advance.

Destinations Chihuahua (16hr); Creel express (9hr), regional (9hr 39min); El Fuerte express (1hr 55min), regional (2hr 19min).

BY BUS

The main first-class bus station, serving Elite, Futura, Transportes Chihuahuenses and Turistar, is at Castro and Constitución 302, south of the centre, while TAP has its own terminal one block further along at Castro 620, at Domínguez. Estrella del Pacifico, Norte de Sonora and Transportes del Pacifico have terminals at Morelos 337 between Zaragoza and Leyva, while first-class Tufesa is at Zapata between Juárez and Morelos. Second-class Norte de Sinaloa is at Zaragoza and Ordonez. All of these stations are within walking distance of most downtown hotels and restaurants. Taxis will charge a fixed fee from bus stations for trips around the centre.

To Álamos For Álamos, take a first-class bus to Navojoa (every hr; 2hr) and change there (see page 495).

To El Fuerte Buses to El Fuerte are shared by two companies and departing roughly every hour 5am–8.15pm (usually with a/c but no toilets): Azules del Noreste (668 812 3491) runs from the terminal at Leyva 399, at Tenochtitlán, while Norte de Sinaloa leaves from the Terminal Independencia inside the Mercado at Independencia and Degollado (Azules also stops here). Buses marked "expresso directo" will take around 1hr 15min; others will take up to 2hr.

Other destinations Guadalajara (hourly; 13–15hr); Guaymas (every 30min; 5–6hr); Hermosillo (every 30min; 6–7hr); Mazatlán (every 30min; 6–7hr); Mexico City (hourly; 19hr); Tijuana (every 30min; 19–21hr); Topolobampo (every 15min; 40min).

BY FERRY

The La Paz (see page 544) ferry arrives at the port of Topolobampo, 24km south of Los Mochis. Local buses ply back and forth, terminating at Cuauhtémoc in Los Mochis, between Zaragoza and Prieto (Mon–Sat every 30min; 40min), and Allende between Cuauhtémoc and Tenochtitlán (Sun), or you can take a taxi.

Current Baja Ferries (http://www.bajaferries.com.mx) departures for the seven-hour crossing to La Paz are Mon–Fri at midnight and Sun at 11pm (no service Sat); you can buy tickets as you board, but it's safest to purchase tickets and check the timetable in advance. The cost of a standard ticket includes a reclining seat, but it's extra for a cabin and there is a charge per car; they can be bought at the office at Plaza Encuentro, Centenario and Rosales (daily 9am–5pm; 668 818 6893), or at Topolobampo port (daily 9am–11pm; 668 862 1003).

INFORMATION

Tourist office The city tourist office (Mon–Fri 8am–5pm; 668 818 3992) is located at Allende Sur 655 (at *Hotel América*).

ACCOMMODATION

SEE MAP PAGE 480

América Allende Sur 655; https://www.losmochishotel.com/america. Cheerful, relatively cheap business hotel in the centre that offers excellent value. Rooms are clean and modern, with a simple, contemporary design. M$$

Best Western Plus Los Mochis Obregón 691; http://bestwestern.com. The town's best hotel is traditionally favoured by tour groups, offering smart but standard chain fare right on Plazuela 27 de Septiembre, 1km from the main bus station. M$$$

Fénix Flores 365; 668 812 2623. Decent budget option for an overnight stay, with modern, basic but adequate rooms, cable TV and a/c. M$

Santa Anita Leyva and Hidalgo; https://facebook.com/santaanitahotel. This is the second luxury option in town, though it's a little old-fashioned. Rooms are still comfy and very spacious, with cable TV and a mountainous breakfast buffet. There's also a rather expensive restaurant, a bar and the Viajes Flamingo travel agency (with buses laid on for the Copper Canyon train station). The hotel often fills up with tour groups in high season. M$$$

EATING

SEE MAP PAGE 480

La Cabaña de Doña Chayo Obregón 99, at Allende; 668 690 5300. This basic diner, established in the 1960s, specializes in tacos *carne asada* or tacos *moreno* (dried beef), with quesadilla versions of both; you get a lot of succulent meat for the price, but the salsas are not as fresh as on the street stalls. It also does excellent roast chicken. There's a second "Centro" branch at Zaragoza and Obregón. M$$

El Farallón Obregón 499, at Flores; https://facebook.com/elfarallonrestaurante. Founded in 1961, this is still the best restaurant in Los Mochis, with an intriguing and delicious seafood menu (fish fillet cooked in numerous ways), and *Sinaloenses* classics. M$$$

Pastelería y Panificadora Hong Kong Hidalgo 569; 668 812 2737. Not a Chinese restaurant (the name is just a gimmick) but a local bakery chain selling delicious pastries, cakes and bread (doughnuts, muffins and the "ojos de buey", bright red, coconut-sprinkled cakes). M$$

Restaurante España Obregón 525; http://espanarestaurante.com. This reliable Mexican-Spanish restaurant has international pretensions and prices to match, though the breakfast plates are good value, and it knocks out decent paella and buffets. M$$$

★ Rústico Smoke House Canuto Ibarra 601; 668 249 9999. This BBQ smoke house restaurant in Los Mochis is a good spot for meat lovers, though anything off the set menu can be quite expensive. The best thing on the main menu is the rib-eye steak. M$$$

★ Tacos a Vapor El Chavo Degollado 625; https://facebook.com/tacoselchavomxl. This venerable stall has a chequered history that goes back to the early 1960s, and remains the best place to grab cheap and tasty *tacos a vapor*, smothered in rich sauce – closes by early afternoon. M$

El Taquito Leyva 333 at Barrera, near the Hotel Santa Anita; 668 818 0900. No-frills canteen with formica tables, loud TVs and cheap Mexican food (expect burritos and other classics); though on the bland side, it's clean, safe and open 24hr. M$$

DIRECTORY

Banks and exchange There's a Banamex with an ATM at the corner of Prieto and Hidalgo.

Post office Ordoñez 226, between Zaragoza and Prieto.

The Copper Canyon

Northeast of Los Mochis, the rugged mountains of the **Sierra Tarahumara** rise from the Sinaloa coast and crumple into the southwestern part of the state of Chihuahua, encom-passing the beautiful region known as the **Copper Canyon**. Confusingly, the area actually contains six rivers and over eleven major canyons – the actual **Barranca del Cobre** usually refers to the northern valley of the Río Urique. The main gorges boast depths of more than 2000m, and if you include the whole area the Grand Canyon is tiny in comparison.

Scenically, however, it's very hard to compare this region with the great canyons of the southwestern US. Part of the difficulty is in getting a true sense of its size and beauty: though the **Copper Canyon railway** cuts across some spectacular valleys, you only get a glimpse of the actual **Barranca del Cobre** once, at **Divisadero**. The train only brushes the northern edge of the Parque Nacional Barranca del Cobre, which is hard to access: there are no well-marked hiking tracks and official campsites, and serious hikers need to devote the best part of a week to their endeavours. **Creel** makes a sensible base from which to organize further exploration.

8

Ferrocarril Chihuahua al Pacífico

The 653km, sixteen-hour train journey along the **Ferrocarril Chihuahua al Pacífico** (Copper Canyon railway, or "El Chepe" for short), which starts on the sweaty Pacific coast at Los Mochis, fights its way up to cross the Continental Divide amid the peaks of the Sierra Madre Occidental, then drifts down across the high plains of Chihuahua, is one of the world's most extraordinary rail journeys. Mesmerizing views come thick and fast as the line hangs over the vast canyons of the **Río Urique** and its tributaries, with jagged peaks smothered in dense forest, and narrow, precipitous gorges falling away on both sides.

The route

From Los Mochis (see page 479) or El Fuerte (see page 484), the start of the journey is an inauspicious grind across the humid coastal plain. As the line breaks into the mountains the train zigzags dizzily upwards for six hours, clinging to the canyon wall, rocketing across bridges and plunging into tunnels, only to find itself constantly just a few metres above the track it covered twenty minutes earlier. Eventually, you arrive at **Divisadero**, where there's a halt of fifteen minutes to marvel at the view of the Copper Canyon itself. There are a couple of expensive places to stay here and a few bare-bones cheaper ones as well, but for most people it's all too rapidly back on the train, which clanks on for an hour to **Creel**, just past the halfway stage and, at 2330m, close to the highest point of the line (note, though, that after Divisadero the scenery is far less scintillating). This is the place to stop if you seriously want to explore the **Sierra Tarahumara** and the canyons.

From Creel, the Regional train takes a further six hours to reach Chihuahua – though beautiful, it's not a truly spectacular run. There's also a regular **bus** service from Creel to Chihuahua: it's cheaper than even the economy train fare, is quicker and covers much the same ground.

INFORMATION

FERROCARRIL CHIHUAHUA AL PACÍFICO

The Copper Canyon line is operated by the Ferrocarril Chihuahua al Pacífico (CHP), from which the train derives its affectionate nickname, "El Chepe". There are two different trains: the luxurious **Chepe Express** (with two classes and free wi-fi) is a daily tourist service between Los Mochis and Creel only (with intermediate stops at El Fuerte and Divisadero only), while the **Chepe Regional**, much cheaper but still fairly comfortable, runs just three days a week between Los Mochis and Chihuahua. On this train, regional tourist class offers a/c and reserved, reclining seats – but the views are the same in the economy section, and if you'd rather squeeze up with the locals, you'll save a lot of cash and practise more Spanish in the cheapest carriages.

TICKETS

Tickets for economy seats can only be bought from the station on the morning of departure, but regional tourist or Chepe Express tickets can be booked in advance either at the station (Los Mochis: Mon–Fri 5–7am & 9am–5.30pm, Sat 5–7am & 10am–12.30pm, Sun 5–7am & 8–10am; Chihuahua: Mon–Fri 5–7am & 10am–5.30pm, Sat 5–7am & 9am–12.30pm, Sun 5–7am), from travel agents (see *Hotel Santa Anita* in Los Mochis), or from Ferrocarril

EL CHEPE TIMETABLE

The timetable for El Chepe often changes (or is affected by weather), so it's important to check in advance on the official website (http://chepe.com.mx) or with local travel agents for the latest. At the time of research two different trains were running along portions of the route. The luxury Chepe Express runs daily, but only between Los Mochis and Creel (though the Los Mochis to Creel leg is mostly in the dark); the Chepe Regional runs along the whole line between Los Mochis and Chihuahua, but only three days a week; from Chihuahua Mon, Thurs & Sat, and from Los Mochis Tues, Fri & Sun. The official times below tend to be reliable only for the Chepe Express; expect the Regional train to be up to 1 to 2 hours late by the end of the trip (and rarely, if ever, is it on time to connect with the La Paz ferry in Los Mochis).

CHEPE EXPRESS

Los Mochis	3.50pm	3.05pm
El Fuerte	5.45pm	12.55pm
Divisadero	11.20pm	7.15am
Creel	12.55am	6am

CHEPE REGIONAL

Los Mochis	6am	9.28pm
El Fuerte	8.19am	7.19pm
Bahuichivo	12.24pm	3.12pm
Divisadero	2.25pm	1.41pm
Creel	3.42pm	11.47pm
Cuauhtémoc	7.07pm	8.25am
Chihuahua	9.34pm	6am

Mexicano direct (614 439 7212, http://chepe.com.mx). Reserve early to be sure of a first-class seat, especially from May to Sept and during Semana Santa.

Prices vary dramatically depending on which train and class you take. It's advisable to break up the journey, not only to get the most out of it, but also because the trip, even travelling first class, can become very tedious either side of the dramatic central section.

Stops on route Chepe Express tickets allow stop-offs at both stations on route (El Fuerte and Divisadero), with no additional cost (you have to remain at least one night); Chepe Regional tickets allow stop-offs at three different stations, but this includes your final stop – if you want to break the journey more than twice you'll have to buy separate tickets.

FOOD AND DRINK

You'll save money by taking along your own food and drink; though technically you are not allowed to eat on any train (especially the Chepe Express), snacks are generally tolerated. It's not essential in any case; meals, snacks and drinks are available on the train (though not cheaply), and throughout the journey people stand on the platforms selling tacos, *chiles rellenos*, fresh fruit, hot coffee and whatever local produce comes to hand.

El Fuerte

Founded in the sixteenth century, **EL FUERTE** is a tranquil, verdant town of handsome colonial architecture and lush mango trees. In the 1800s it became rich from mining, and was made a city in 1906; the Revolution devastated the place and it's been a backwater ever since. In 2009 the town joined Mexico's burgeoning *Pueblos Mágicos* programme, and since then the otherwise doomed-to-decay Spanish architecture near the plaza has gradually been restored. Though several boutique hotels have opened up, thanks to low tourist numbers El Fuerte has yet to see a full-scale transformation – the commercial area along Juárez remains just as scrappy as ever, the plaza relatively tourist free and most of the restored buildings are still empty. Bizarrely, attempts to market El

Fuerte as the birthplace and childhood home of Don Diego de la Vega, aka **Zorro** – the fictional character whose adventures were set in California – seem to have worked, with nightly shows at the *Posada del Hidalgo* (see page 486).

Located 75km northeast of Los Mochis on the rail line, El Fuerte certainly makes a pleasant alternative start (or end) to the Copper Canyon train ride, and is a far more appealing place to stay than Los Mochis. Just make sure you take insect repellent – Fuerte's *bobos* (tiny two-winged insects more officially known as *Paraleucopis mexicana*) are a real pest in the spring.

The town centre is small and easy to navigate, being focused on the elegant *portales* of **Plaza de Armas**, with its grand **Palacio Municipal** (1907), the modest **Iglesia Sagrado de Corazón** (1745) and the fort (*fuerte*) itself, a short walk south (and clearly visible).

Museo Fuerte Mirador

5 de Mayo • Charge • 698 893 1501

El Fuerte grew up around a Spanish **fort** (from which it takes its name), completed in 1615 by steely conquistador Diego Martínez de Hurdaide to suppress the local tribes. Though the original has been lost, a reasonably authentic replica was completed in 2001 on its possible location, supplying commanding views of the streets and surrounding countryside. Inside, the **Museo Fuerte Mirador** contains an array of historical artefacts and old photos of the town (some by Ira Kneeland, a member of Kinsey's colony at Topolobampo), with mostly English labelling; old guns, an 1885 hearse and local Yoreme arts and crafts among them.

ARRIVAL AND DEPARTURE — EL FUERTE

8

By train The train station is a few kilometres out of town, and you'll need to arrange transport if you hope to catch the train to Chihuahua, Creel or Los Mochis – the pricier hotels should do this for you, but otherwise you should scout around for a shared taxi near the plaza or market (these also meet trains at the station). Note that there are no buses to either Creel or Chihuahua from here.

By bus Buses (1hr 30min–2hr) from Los Mochis (see page 479) arrive and depart (until 7pm) frequently at Juárez, next to the town market, near 15 de Septiembre and a short walk from Plaza de Armas.

By taxi Taxis from Los Mochis will charge around a set fare for the journey to El Fuerte, and will also negotiate return trips.

INFORMATION

Tourist information The small information kiosk on Plaza de Armas (Mon–Fri 8am–3pm; 698 893 0349), usually has maps and English-speakers if you get stuck – your hotel is likely to be more helpful, however.

THE RARÁMURI

Even when the bare mountain peaks here are snow-covered, the climate on the Copper Canyon floor is semitropical – a fact that the Indigenous **Rarámuri** (also known, incorrectly, as the Tarahumara) depend on, migrating in winter to the warmth of the deep canyons. The Rarámuri, who were driven here after the Spanish Conquest and whose population now totals some sixty thousand, live in isolated communities along the rail line and in the surrounding Sierra Tarahumara, eking out an existence from the sparse patches of cultivatable land. Although their isolation is increasingly encroached upon by commercial forestry interests, ranchers and growing numbers of travellers, they remain an independent people, close to their traditions. Despite centuries of missionary work, their religious life embraces only token aspects of Catholicism and otherwise remains true to its animist roots, their chief deities being the gods of the sun, moon and rain. Above all, the tribe is renowned for running: a common feature of local festivals is the **foot races** between villages that last at least one day and sometimes several on end, with the runners kicking a wooden ball ahead of them as they go: Norogachi is one of the best places to see this (see page 493), as is Urique, the home of the Copper Canyon Ultramarathon (see page 487).

ACCOMMODATION

Hotel La Choza 5 de Mayo 101; http://hotellachoza.com. Charming, mid-range option, with 32 a/c rooms simply decorated with tiled floors and colourful bedspreads – you get TV, a gorgeous little pool and decent restaurant on site. Free wi-fi in public areas only. M$$$

Hotel El Fuerte Monteclaros 37; www.hotelelfuerte.com.mx. A beautiful three-hundred-year-old hacienda once owned by the wealthy Ibarra family, with exquisite rooms and a jacuzzi fed by illuminated waterfalls. Loads of colour, elegance and style make this one of the best deals in town. Breakfast is extra. M$$

Posada del Hidalgo Hidalgo 101; https://facebook.com/posadadelhidalgo. First-class service is provided by a small army of staff in this grand old hotel, the former 1890 home of the Almada family and self-proclaimed birthplace of Zorro. Popular with tour groups, there are spa facilities, a restaurant, pool and plenty of quiet, leafy patios. There's also a kitsch Zorro show, nightly (included). Free wi-fi in public areas; shuttles to the station are a fixed price. M$$$

Posada Don Porfirio Juárez 104; https://facebook.com/hotelposadadonporfirio. Tranquil hotel with clean, bright a/c rooms and a shady courtyard slung with hammocks. Ask the owners for a copy of *Legends of the City*, a small booklet that tells the history of El Fuerte. M$$

★ **Torres del Fuerte** Robles 102; http://torresdelfuerte.com. Gorgeous old hotel that drips with colonial charm: lavish period rooms come with marble floors, stone sinks, rugs and Mudéjar-influenced antiques, but with modern amenities. The patio bar and gardens are a great place to relax. Free wi-fi in public areas only; breakfast is extra. M$$$

EATING AND DRINKING

Mesón del General Juárez 202 (behind the plaza); 698 893 0260. Relatively economical option serving a range of seafood (including the prized local black bass or *lobina*) and steak dishes in a charming old courtyard and mansion built in 1860, enhanced by plants and murals. Famed for being the former home of local Revolutionary hero General Don Pablo Macías Valenzuela. M$$$

8

Restaurant Diligencias Hotel La Choza, 5 de Mayo 101 (on the plaza); 698 893 1274. For a posh meal and the best bar in town head to *La Choza*, where delectable local delicacies (including the ubiquitous *lobina* and crayfish) are served in a bright, friendly dining room. M$$$$

El Supremo Rosales 108 at Constitución (one block from plaza); 698 893 0021. For no-frills, reasonably priced home-cooked fare, visit this local diner – it looks a bit dark and dingy from the outside, but the food is good. M$$

DIRECTORY

Banks You'll find a Banamex at Juárez 212 near the bus station, and Bancomer on Juárez and Constitución.

Post office The post office is at 5 de Mayo 95 (698 893 0126).

Cerocahui

The first place worth considering as a base in the mountains, travelling on the Copper Canyon railway from Los Mochis and El Fuerte, is the tiny Rarámuri *ejido* of **CEROCAHUI** (1525m), accessed from the train station at **Bahuichivo** (1600m). Very much in the formative stages of tourist development, with around nine hundred inhabitants, Cerocahui gives access to the **Urique** canyon system and a range of attractions including the mesmerizing **Cerro del Gallego** viewing point, hikes to Las Cascaditas (the "Little Waterfalls", around 3km round-trip) and the old Sangre de Cristo gold mine. There's also the Jesuit mission of **San Francisco**, founded by Juan Maria de Salvatierra in 1694, before he moved on to Loreto (see page 538).

ARRIVAL AND DEPARTURE — CEROCAHUI

By train Cerocahui is around 17km by road from Bahuichivo train station (the latter is 6hr 24min from Los Mochis). Moving on, the Chepe Regional to Divisadero (1hr 25min), Creel (3hr 15min) and Chihuahua (9hr 10min) departs Bahuichivo at 12.24pm. If you opt to stay here your hotel will arrange a pick-up from the train station.

By bus Noroeste buses from Bahuichivo to Creel (1hr 30min) via Divisadero usually depart ever two hours, but check the latest timetable with your hotel.

ACCOMMODATION

Hotel Misión Plaza del Poblado (opposite the church); 635 456 5017. Opened in 1968, this mountain lodge offers 41 spacious rooms with old-fashioned Mexican decor, tiled bathrooms and wood stoves. Rates include lodging for two and three meals per person a day (including the hotel's famed apple pie). No internet/wi-fi. M$$$

★ **Jade Hotel** Plaza del Poblado; http://pobladohoteles.com. Friendly owners Alberto (who speaks English) and Francia (who is an excellent cook) run this budget hotel, with ten well designed rooms with views over the town, and a variety of guided tours (no TV or wi-fi). Breakfast is extra. M$$

San Isidro Lodge Carr Bahuichivo–Urique km 24 (9km south from Cerocahui); 635 104 4389. Lovely and economical accommodation can be had at this lodge run by the Muñoz family, who have ties to the local Rarámuri. The cabañas are all spacious, clean and airy with private baths. The cheapest rates do not include meals, but do include transport from Bahuichivo station. Wi-fi passes are charged per 24hrs. M$$$

Wilderness Lodge at Cerocahui Carr Bahuichivo–Urique km 23 (9km south from Cerocahui); 635 199 3684. With just six rooms, this is an extremely romantic choice, a wooden lodge overlooking the gorge with Spanish colonial-style rooms and bathrooms. Breakfast included, but no internet/wi-fi. M$$$

Urique

The four-hour drive from Cerocahui to the bottom of the Barranca de Urique is stunning, and the town of **URIQUE** (485m) itself, at its conclusion, marks the start (or end) of the popular two-night, three-day trek to Batopilas (see page 491). The 1600 inhabitants of Urique – founded in 1724 and a former gold- and silver-mining town – survive today on their tropical fruit, corn, peanuts and coffee crops, though unofficially marijuana and poppy crops are likely the biggest earners. The main attractions here are the jaw-dropping views all around, though there is also an old kiln, church, cemetery and hikes to isolated Rarámuri villages such as Guadalupe Coronado. Urique is also the home of the **Copper Canyon Ultramarathon** (see page 487). Note that it's always very hot down here, with rainy season June to September.

8

ARRIVAL AND DEPARTURE — URIQUE

By bus Unless you take a hotel-arranged tour, reaching Urique usually involves hiring a car at Bahuichivo train station or driving yourself from Creel – you'll need an SUV because the road is unpaved for much of the way. Public buses do make the 54km trip down (3.5–4hr) from Bahuichivo train station; they depart after the train from Chihuahua arrives around 1.30pm, and return from Urique at 7am (arriving at Cerocahui around 10am and Bahuichivo at 11am).

ACCOMMODATION AND EATING

Urique contains several small, family-owned **restaurants** such as *Mama Tita's* that offer traditional Mexican dishes such as rice plates with re-fried beans, various meats and hand-made tortillas. There are also several shops selling basic groceries. Note that internet is very patchy in Urique and power cuts are common.

Entre Amigos http://amongamigos.com. Legendary lodge established in 1975, with lovingly maintained dorms, camping sites, shower rooms, kitchen and organic food prepared amid hummingbird gardens and spectacular views. Double rooms in the main house are also available. Shared toilets (outhouses). M$$

THE RUNNERS OF COPPER CANYON

Popularized by Chris McDougall's best-selling book *Born to Run* (2009), the Copper Canyon Ultramarathon or **Ultramaraton Caballo Blanco** was established in 2003 by extreme runner Micah True (his nickname was *Caballo Blanco*, or "White Horse"). True (who died in 2012) wanted to draw attention to the plight of the impoverished **Rarámuri** in the region, and the 80km race provided food vouchers and blankets to Rarámuri runners. In large part thanks to the book, the race became a legend in the world of ultra-running, attracting around 100 international runners each year. Traditionally held in February or March in Urique, in 2015 the race was suspended indefinitely due to concerns about drug-related gang violence in the valley. However, the local government in Urique has since stepped in to organize its own version of the race (see http://facebook.com/UMCB.URIQUE).

Divisadero

Around 50km northeast of Cerocahui lies **DIVISADERO**, where the train pauses for fifteen minutes for the mind-blowing "one-hundred-mile" view of the canyons – this is the closest you'll get to that Grand Canyon-like panorama, at least on the rail line. A slightly bizarre carnival atmosphere pervades when the train arrives, with Rarámuri children begging for change, mariachi singers serenading snack eaters, and trinket stalls lining the steps down to the *mirador* – below this are the depths of the **Barranca del Cobre** and, adjoining it, the **Barranca de Urique** and the **Barranca de Tararecua**. The platform at Divisadero is smothered in snack stalls, most of them selling variations of **gorditas** – absolutely scrumptious and crammed with a variety of home-made fillings, chiles, beans and cheeses (finish them before you reboard).

Parque de Aventura Barrancas del Cobre

Charge for basic admission and cable car journeys (every 30min; 10min each way with 20min at the *mirador*) • http://parquebarrancas.com

Divisadero is home to the Copper Canyon's most popular attraction, the government-funded **Parque de Aventura Barrancas del Cobre**. In addition to boasting spectacular views across the canyon, the "Adventure Park" features a 2.75km **cable car** (*teleférico*) that soars over a 400m ravine to the *mirador* at the Mesa de Bacajipare. Among many activities, the park also includes **Via Ferrata** (featuring rappelling, walking a wire, climbing the canyon wall and swinging bridges) plus a panoramic restaurant and seven **zip lines** (450m high, with lengths ranging from 300–1200m). The **ZipRider** (basically a zip line but with a more stable chair system to sit on) is an incredible 2.53km long and costs extra. You can walk to the park from Divisadero station via a trail along the canyon edge (2.5km), but quad bike riders will take you for a fee.

ARRIVAL AND DEPARTURE — DIVISADERO

By train The Chepe Express service runs from Los Mochis to Divisadero; on the Chepe Regional the regional tourist tickets are more expensive compared to the economy option. Moving on, express trains depart for Creel daily at 11.30pm (1hr 25min), while the Chepe Regional departs at 1.50pm for Creel (1hr 49min) and Chihuahua (7hr 44min) Tues, Fri & Sun. Express trains depart for Los Mochis daily at 7.30am (7hr 35min); the Chepe Regional departs at 1.41pm (7hr 47min) Mon, Thurs & Sat.

By bus Around nine Rápidos and Noroeste buses a day ply the 44km between Divisadero train station and Creel (1hr), the first one departing at around 7am and last one departing at about 3.30pm; at least four buses head in the other direction towards Bahuichivo. It's always worth checking the schedule for changes, though, so you don't get stuck.

ACCOMMODATION

If you decide to break your journey here, you'll find some stunning but pricey accommodation near the station, and more options 5km southwest near the Posada Barrancas station, which serves the sleepy village of Areponápuchi (aka "Arepo").

Divisadero Barrancas Ferrocarril Chihuahua al Pacífico km 622; http://hoteldivisadero.com. Steps away from Divisadero station, and perched right on the edge of the canyon, this hotel is a tour-group favourite featuring spacious rooms with wood-beam ceilings, most with spectacular views of the gorges – only some have balconies, though, so always ask when you make a reservation. Rates include three meals and a couple of walking tours; wi-fi is extra. M$$$

Hotel Mirador (Posada Barrancas) Ferrocarril Chihuahua al Pacífico km 622; https://hotelmirador.mx. Fabulous location, etched right into the canyon edge like an ancient monastery, and modern, clean rooms make this a justly popular option – each room comes with a balcony, the best feature, though there are no TVs. The set meals (included) are pretty good, usually comprising a Mexican meat dish (typically fish or pork, sometimes beef) with vegetables and rice. You'd be hard pressed to find a vegetarian or indeed vegan option though. No internet/wi-fi. M$$$$

Mansión Tarahumara Posada Barrancas; http://hotelmansiontarahumara.com. A rather surreal hotel resembling a fairy-tale castle (it's known as *El Castillo*); the Alpine-style cabins are clean and bright, but only the new rooms have the stunning canyon views. Breakfast included; full board available. Wi-fi (charged by the hour) available in public areas only. M$$$

Creel

Once nothing more than a rough-and-ready backwater, **CREEL** (2330m) has rapidly transformed into a full-blown mountain resort of ten thousand people. Indeed, Creel is yet another *Pueblo Mágico* and has seen tourism all but replace logging as its main industry; on most days (but especially Sunday) you'll be greeted by a weird juxtaposition of laid-back Western backpackers, smartly dressed locals, rich Mexican tourists in their 4WDs and ragged Rarámuri trinket sellers and their children, trying to make a buck or two. In July and August the town is invaded by Mexican tour groups – the best hotels often get completely booked up at this time. This is not to say that the town has become completely commercial; beneath the facade of development, Creel is still a rural mountain town at heart, and an ideal base from which to explore the area.

Museo de la Casa de las Artesanías

Ferrocarril 178 • Charge • 635 118 6248

There isn't much to do in Creel itself, other than enjoy the refreshing, pine-scented mountain air, though the **Museo de la Casa de las Artesanías** across the rail tracks from the plaza is certainly worth a visit. It contains displays on Rarámuri culture that give intriguing insights into their archaic philosophy, most notably with a series of black- and-white photos revealing their vivid ceremonial and religious life.

Artesanías Misión

Plaza Principal • 635 294 3811

If you're in the market for handicrafts, the Catholic mission shop **Artesanías Misión**, right on the plaza, has a host of wares including blankets, baskets, dolls, drums and violins; their products lack the vibrancy of other Mexican crafts, but make up for it with rustic charm. Profits fund the local mission hospital.

ARRIVAL AND DEPARTURE CREEL

By train Creel is 9hr from Los Mochis, 1hr 15min from Divisadero and around 5hr 20min from Chihuahua. Note that the Chepe Express only runs south to Los Mochis from here. See page 484 for full details.

By bus Two companies (Rápidos Cuauhtémoc and Autotransportes Turísticos del Noroeste) offer services to Chihuahua via Cuauhtémoc between 6.30am and 5pm, with Noroeste providing the most comfortable buses. Buses also run every two hours to Divisadero from 10.30am to 6.30pm, and usually end up at Bahuichivo. The train station and bus stops are all near the main plaza in the centre of town. The bus to Batopilas usually leaves from outside Three Amigos office at Mon–Sat at 7.30am – check the current schedule in advance and buy tickets at *Hotel Artesanías Towi* (López Mateos 41, across from Three Amigos).

Destinations Bahuichivo (5 daily; 1hr 30min); Batopilas (1 daily; 4hr); Chihuahua (every 30min; 4–5hr); Divisadero (8 daily; 1hr); Guachochi (2 daily; 3hr).

INFORMATION

Tourist information There's no official tourist office in Creel, though the small kiosk on the plaza dispenses leaflets on regional attractions. The best place to go for local information is Three Amigos (see page 492), López Mateos 46 (daily 9am–7pm). They can supply you with maps, information and advice regarding Creel and the Copper Canyon more generally.

ACCOMMODATION SEE MAP PAGE 489

Complejo Eco-Turístico Arareko Carr Creel–Guachochi km 7; 635 456 0126. If you fancy staying in more natural surroundings, this Rarámuri-run accommodation agency has an office on López Mateos and rents out the basic *Cabañas Batosarachi* and the more comfortable *Cabañas Segorachi* (minimum six people) around Lake Arareko, part of the San Ignacio de Arareko *ejido* (7km south of Creel on the Batopilas road). No internet access; cash only. M$

Hotel Ecológico Temazcal Bakusuki, at González Olivas; 635 105 9851. It's a short walk outside the centre, but this is one of the best deals in town, a family-run inn with friendly owners, well-equipped shared kitchen and clean, contemporary en-suite rooms (with under-floor heating no less), and cable TV. M$$

Hotel Los Valles Elfido Batista s/n, next to Plaza Mexicana Margarita's; http://losvallescreel.com. This efficient motel off the main drag has eight small, clean rooms with satellite TV for decent prices; one of the better bargains in town. M$

★ **The Lodge at Creel** López Mateos 61; http://thelodgeatcreel.com. Easily the best place to stay in town, run by *Best Western* and offering cabin-style rooms with spa, sauna, jacuzzi, and full restaurant and bar. The wood-trimmed, rustic huts are ample and full of amenities, including coffee-makers, purified water and telephones. M$$$

La Posada de Creel Ferrocarril s/n; 635 456 0805. This backpacker-friendly hotel (aka *Posada Santa Cruz*) behind the station offers very basic rooms and dorms, though it remains one of the cheapest places to crash; breakfast included, but don't expect much. Free wi-fi in public areas. M$

Villa Mexicana Creel Mountain Lodge López Mateos, on the edge of town; http://vmcreel.com. Creel's rustic resort offers a host of facilities including a restaurant and games room. Its accommodation ranges from comfy log cabins to more luxurious suites (rates drop drastically by 50 percent in low season), all with satellite TVs. Breakfast is extra. M$$$

8

EATING SEE MAP PAGE 489

Pizza del Rey López Mateos 15, on the plaza; 635 456 0264. This small outpost of the Chihuahua chain serves reasonable enough pizzas, but also popular ice creams in summer. Takeout or eat in the pleasant second-floor lodge-like dining area. M$$$

Restaurant Verónica López Mateos 33; 635 456 0703. Solid bet for all the usual Mexican classics; try their speciality, the "Norteño" – fried beef and vegetables topped with melted cheese. Free wi-fi. M$$

Sierra Madre The Lodge at Creel, López Mateos 61; http://thelodgeatcreel.com. This hotel restaurant is best known for its decent pizzas but also does the usual range of Mexican classics (tortilla soup is a speciality) plus a tasty apple pie. M$$$

Tío Molcas López Mateos 35; 635 456 0033. Serves Mexican food but is most popular as a bar catering primarily to travellers, with a wood fire in winter. Free wi-fi. M$$

DIRECTORY

Bank Banco Santander at López Mateos 17 has two ATMs, though it often runs out of cash.

Hospital Clínica Santa Teresita, Parroquial (635 456 0105).

Post office There's a post office in the Presidencia Seccional on the south side of the main plaza.

Sierra Tarahumara

Once in Creel, most travellers take the bus or continue on the Copper Canyon railway to Chihuahua (see page 445), but exploration of the **Sierra Tarahumara** around Creel is highly recommended. The rugged scenery is exceptionally wild and beautiful. If you're not up to strenuous activity, or have only limited time, an **organized tour** is the best way to see the canyons (though these normally require four to six people; see page 492).

San Ignacio de Arareko

Many tours from Creel take in attractions belonging to the *ejido* (a collectively owned community) of **San Ignacio de Arareko**, a Rarámuri land-owning cooperative on the edge of town. To see them independently, follow López Mateos towards the highway, take a left onto the dirt road and continue past the cemetery and uphill into the pine forest.

A few kilometres from the *ejido* entrance (admission charge), you'll encounter the eighteenth-century **Misión de San Ignacio** and a series of otherworldly rock formations, including the **Valley of the Mushrooms** (*Valle de los Hongos*) which contains surreal structures closely resembling giant toadstools, and the **Valley of the Frogs** (*Valle de las Ranas*), with its squat amphibian-like boulders. The **Valley of the Monks** (*Valle de los Monjes*) lies 5km away (there's a toll), and has tall upright stones revered by the Rarámuri as symbols of fertility. Serene **Lago de Arareko,** 7km from Creel on the main highway to Batopilas, is a beautiful spot for fishing (largemouth bass) and camping – you can stay in a cabin on the lake or rent a boat by the hour.

Recowata hot springs

The **Recowata hot springs** (admission charge) are 22km from Creel at the bottom of Tararecua Canyon, within biking or riding distance; follow the road to Divisadero for 7km and look for the turning on the left. Here you can bathe in seven different concrete pools of steamy, clean, sulphurous water. Note that the steep 3km descent to (and return from) the pools can be very strenuous, and shouldn't be undertaken by the faint of heart (or when it's wet – it's a cobblestone trail). Rarámuri quad bikers are sometimes on hand to provide rides up and down (charge each way).

8

Cascada de Cusárare

Carr Creel–Guachochi km 22 • Charge

The **Cascada de Cusárare**, 30m-high falls most impressive during the rainy season (but just a trickle in April/May), lies some 22km from Creel on the Batopilas/Guachochi road, and a forty-minute walk from the highway. You can reach the falls and village by bike, or on the daily Batopilas/Guachochi buses, though you'll have a long hike back to Creel if you don't stay overnight. Hitching is a possibility, though you should exercise the usual precautions.

Cusárare

Misión de Cusárare Donation suggested • **Museo de Loyola** Charge

The village of Cusárare itself is 3km further along the road from the Cascada de Cusárare, and contains the eighteenth-century Jesuit **Misión de Cusárare**, adorned with Rarámuri wall paintings completed in the 1970s; the mission's original art, including a set of twelve rare oil paintings by Miguel Correa (scenes from the life of Mary, painted around 1713), were painstakingly restored in the 1990s and are now housed in the **Museo de Loyola** next door.

Batopilas

If you want to get a true idea of the scale and beauty of the Sierra Tarahumara, consider a trip to isolated **BATOPILAS** (460m). Located 123km south of Creel, the town is more accessible now the **new road** has been opened, though the journey still takes at least four hours. The route rises and falls through four of the sierra's six canyons before commencing a final, convoluted descent to the floor of Batopilas canyon. Founded in 1632, the town emerged as a prosperous **silver-mining** centre, with production peaking in the nineteenth century under the auspices of the American-owned Batopilas Mining Company. After the Mexican Revolution began in 1910, the town went into a permanent decline and the population plummeted. Today Batopilas is a subtropical place with a population of about 1200 – resplendent with bougainvillea, palm and citrus trees

TOURING THE SIERRA TARAHUMARA

For tours of the Sierra Tarahumara, try Three Amigos or the more popular hotels like *Casa Margarita's*. Rates should be about the same, but it's worth shopping around. Roughly speaking, a four-hour spin through the **San Ignacio** *ejido* or a two- to three-hour trip to **Cusárare** shouldn't break the bank (with a minimum of four people); and the same can be said for a day-long trip to **Basaseachi**. Find out if food is included with your tour and if there are additional costs like museum entrance or toll fees before you set out. If you don't speak Spanish, check that your guide speaks English before parting with any money. Taxis run from Creel to Sierra Tarahumara and nearby destinations, with fees inclusive of waiting times and return trips.

El Aventurero Ecopaseos López Mateos; www.elaventurero.com.mx. A truly memorable way of exploring the canyons is on horseback, and if you want to be assured of animals that are cared for, speak to guide Norberto Padilla Rodriguez. Excellent, professional tours include a three-hour ride through the San Ignacio *ejido* (two-person minimum).

Three Amigos Canyon Expeditions López Mateos 46; http://amigos3.com. The most professional and best-equipped outfit in town. They can advise on your trip, organize a well-priced tour or rent you a well-maintained mountain bike or two-person scooter. Customers also get free internet use at the shop. See also their sister operation, Amigo Trails (http://amigotrails.com), for longer expeditions.

and strung along a single 2km road by the Río Batopilas, it's a world away from the fresh pine forests of Creel. Though it has garnered a reputation for drug cartel activity in recent years, tourists are never affected and the town was made a Pueblo Mágico in 2012.

8

Museo de Batopilas

Free

You can get a taster of the town's rich and complex past at the tiny **Museo de Batopilas**, manned by enthusiastic volunteers. The entrance looks like a mine tunnel, and inside you'll find old photos and articles from the town's glory days – estimates suggest that over three hundred mines, claims and workings have been operated in the Batopilas district since silver was first found here.

Hacienda San Miguel

Charge

Just outside Batopilas you can visit the romantic ruin of **Hacienda San Miguel**, once the opulent home of Batopilas Mining Co founder (and ex-Washington D.C. governor) **Alexander Shepherd**, who washed up here in 1880. Shepherd is a fascinating and somewhat controversial figure in the US, admired for his social reforms and essentially creating modern D.C., but eventually fired for bankrupting the city. The house itself dates back to the seventeenth century and had been used by mining magnates years before Shepherd took over the place. Abandoned in the 1920s (Shepherd had died in 1902), the hacienda has been in a state of elegant decay ever since, one tower virtually engulfed by a sprawling bougainvillea. To reach the site, walk upriver for around thirty minutes, crossing the bridge when you see the ruins.

The hikes

There are several worthwhile **hikes** here, leading from Rarámuri villages as well as to abandoned mines and waterfalls. The best of these go to the "Lost Cathedral", the eighteenth-century **Misión de San Miguel de Satevó**, 8km away in a desolate landscape of cacti and dust. A longer, three-day trek leads to the town of **Urique**, and can be organized with an operator in Creel (see page 492).

ARRIVAL AND DEPARTURE BATOPILAS

By bus Buses usually leave Creel six times a week from López Mateos (Mon–Sat 7.30am; 4hr). Return buses leave from outside the church in Batopilas at around 5am (Mon–Sat), but always check for changes in the schedule.

INFORMATION

Tourist information There is no official tourist office in Batopilas – Three Amigos in Creel can supply you with a map and other useful information, and the staff at the Museo de Batopilas run an informal information desk.

Banks There is no bank here, so bring enough cash for your stay.

ACCOMMODATION

Casa Monse Plaza Principal (Nigromante); 635 294 3712. Run by the affable Monse family for many years, with clean, cheap hostel-like rooms in a courtyard overflowing with plants and mangos just off the plaza – best of the budget options. M$

Hotel Juanita's Plaza Principal (next door to Casa Monse on Nigromante); 614 120 5652. Managed by the indomitable Juanita herself, with large, comfy rooms, a courtyard overlooking the river and many quiet enclaves in which to relax. M$

Real de Minas Donato Guerra 1 (one block south of the plaza); http://coppercanyonlodges.com. The best mid-range option, with bright, beautifully decorated rooms around a central courtyard and fountain, littered with antiques. M$$$

Riverside Lodge (two blocks north of the plaza, next to the church); http://coppercanyonlodges.com. The exquisite, blue-domed *Riverside Lodge* offers luxurious accommodation, each with claw-foot bathtubs and antique beds, and even a small library, but is only open Sept to April. M$$$$

EATING AND DRINKING

Restaurant Carolina Plaza de la Constitución 10 (south of the Plaza Principal); 649 104 8123. Does decent and affordable home-cooked Mexican staples for breakfast, and local specialities such as grilled trout. M$$

8

Guachochi and Cañon de la Sinforosa

About 170km to the south of Creel, **GUACHOCHI** is an unattractive ranching town of around twelve thousand that nonetheless provides access to the sierra's most remote and awe-inspiring locale, the **Cañon de la Sinforosa** (a further 18km south). Some of the hikes in Sinforosa are fairly hardcore – the canyon is 1830m deep and a trek along its length, for example, can take up to three weeks – while easier walks lead to stunning vantage points overlooking the valleys. There are also various hot springs and waterfalls in the region; the most spectacular is the **Cascada Rosalinda**, with an 80m drop. Rarámuri culture is thriving here, with **Norogachi**, 60km from Guachochi, one of the last remaining Rarámuri ceremonial centres, especially renowned for the vivid celebrations that occur during Semana Santa.

Museo Comunitario Norawa

Paseo de las Garzas s/n • Charge • 649 543 2145

The only real sight in Guachochi itself is the tiny **Museo Comunitario Norawa**, a sincere attempt to highlight Rarámuri history and culture (Spanish only) and to sell the work of Indigenous artisans, especially local ceramics.

ARRIVAL AND DEPARTURE — GUACHOCHI

By bus Two buses connect Creel with Guachochi daily, but there are also direct buses to Chihuahua from the Estrella Blanca bus station, located in a pink building around a kilometre from the plaza, near where you'll find the Transportes Ballezanos station, which also runs several daily services to Parral.

INFORMATION AND TOURS

Information The Modulo de Información Turistica (information kiosk) is located at the entrance to town next to the Museo Comunitario Norawa.

Tours If you'd like to hike in the Cañon de la Sinforosa you will need to hire a local guide in Guachochi or contact Cristina's Canyon Tours (668 818 8421, http://cristinascanyontours.com).

ACCOMMODATION AND EATING

Hotel Melina Domínguez 14; www.hotel-melina.com. Around half a kilometre from the plaza, you'll find *Hotel Melina*, with clean, comfortable rooms, satellite TV and an adjoining restaurant. M$$

THE MENNONITES

Towards the eastern end of the Copper Canyon rail line, the city of Cuauhtémoc contains Mexico's largest **Mennonite community** (around fifty thousand). You'll come across Mennonites throughout Chihuahua and Durango – the men in bib-and-tucker overalls and straw stetsons, as often as not trying to sell the tasty cheese that is their main produce, and the women, mostly silent, wrapped in long, nineteenth-century dresses with a headscarf. The Christian sect, founded in the sixteenth century by a Dutchman, Menno Simons, believe only in the Bible and their personal conscience: their refusal to do military service or take national oaths of loyalty has led to a long history of persecution; today there are famously large communities of Mennonites and their Amish cousins in Pennsylvania, US. The Mennonites arrived in Mexico in the 1920s from Manitoba, Canada, but among themselves they still speak a form of German, although so divergent as to be virtually unintelligible to a modern German-speaker. Note that the Mennonites of Cuauhtémoc are not as traditional as their American cousins these days – indeed, they own local banks, stores and restaurants.

Los Adobes 20 de Noviembre, at Pascual Orozco; 649 543 0629. An inviting place to try the town's speciality – fresh *trucha* (trout) from the nearby Lago Las Garzas – and plenty of other tasty regional specialities. M$$

DIRECTORY

8

Banks and exchange If you need to change money or withdraw cash, there's a branch of Scotiabank (649 543 0006) at Francisco Villa 102 (enter at Pascual Orozco and Belisario Domínguez).

Cascada de Basaseachi

The jaw-dropping 312m **Cascada de Basaseachi** (also "Basaséachic") is the second-highest waterfall in Mexico (though the highest, Piedra Volada, a day's hike from Basaseachi, only flows during the rainy season). The falls make a long but spectacularly rewarding day's excursion – about four hours' drive to the north of Creel (163km via San Pedro), followed by two hours on foot. It's best to visit in the rainy season (mid-June to Aug), when the falls are fullest (May is the driest month). There are two viewpoints; the first is above the falls beyond the otherwise sleepy village of Basaseachi itself, while the second lies on the other side of canyon, affording the best views (trails connect both viewpoints). The falls are located within the largely unexplored **Barranca de Candameña**, the widest canyon in the region, with staggering sheer rock walls.

TOURS — BASASEACHI

Tours Public transport is very limited in this region and it's best to visit via tours arranged in Creel (see page 492).

Cuauhtémoc

As the Copper Canyon railway winds its way east, the pine trees, canyons and mountains of the Sierra Tarahumara gradually give way to ranching country, centred on the town of **CUAUHTÉMOC**, 70km from Creel and 130km from Chihuahua. This is one of the chief centres for Mexican **Mennonites** (see page 494). To see Mennonite cheese being made, visit *La Quesería América* (http://queseriaamerica.com.mx) at Country Road 2-B km 7 (off Hwy-5), north of the town centre.

Museo Menonita

Álvaro Obregón (Hwy-5) km 10 • Charge • http://museomenonita.org • You'll need to take a return taxi from the Estrella Blanca bus station at C 9 and Allende

There's not much to Cuauhtémoc itself, but if the curious Mennonite connection interests you, make a trip to the **Museo Menonita**, which displays traditional artefacts (mostly farm tools) in a replica of a typical wood-frame Mennonite home and sells Mennonite crafts, jams and the famous cheese.

ARRIVAL AND DEPARTURE — CUAUHTÉMOC

By train Chepe Regional trains (see page 484) depart Cuauhtémoc for Chihuahua at 7.07pm Tues, Fri & Sun (2hr 26min); the train departs for Creel (3hr) and Los Mochis (12hr) at 8.25am Mon, Thurs & Sat.

By bus Buses regularly make the trip to Chihuahua (2hr) and Creel (2–3hr) from the Estrella Blanca terminal at C 9 and Allende and the Noroeste terminal nearby.

Sonora

North of Sinaloa, Hwy-15 slices into **Sonora**, the second-largest state in Mexico and the nation's breadbasket; note that Sonora is one hour behind Sinaloa in the summer (April–Oct). There's little to stop for on the road, though the handsome colonial town of **Álamos** is a worthy diversion, and low-key beach resorts at **San Carlos**, **Bahía de Kino** and **Puerto Peñasco** provide some relief from the scorching heat. From the coast it's a long drive through the desert to the US border at Nogales (see page 504) or the boundary with Baja California at the Colorado River – you'll also have to put your watch back an hour when you cross this state line, unless Baja California is on Daylight Saving Time (April–Oct), in which case there's no change.

8

Álamos

Another Pueblo Mágico, the enchanting town of **ÁLAMOS** offers a tranquil slice of colonial Mexico and a welcome break from the dusty cities along the main north–south highways. It's a great place to do nothing for a while: a tour of the town takes no longer than a couple of hours, and there's little else to do but soak up the languid atmosphere.

In the cooler winter months, Álamos is also a good base for exploring the fairly distinct ecosystem hereabouts; the meeting of Sonoran and Sinaloan deserts, at the foot of the

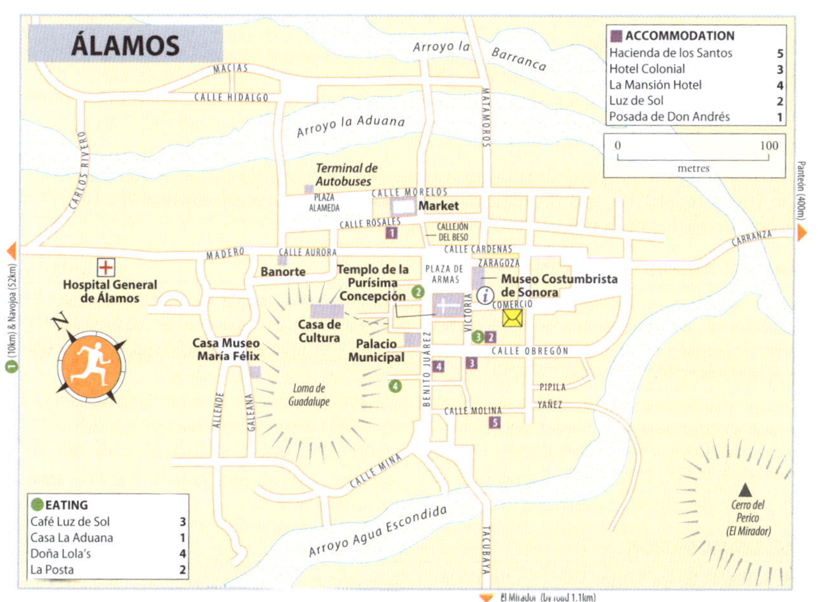

Sierra Madre Occidental, has created a home for a broad range of flora and fauna. In particular, this is a **bird watching** paradise, boasting several hundred different species.

Plaza de Armas

The historic centre of Álamos is the arcaded **Plaza de Armas** and elegant **Templo de la Purísima Concepción**, a Baroque church dating from 1786. The **Palacio Municipal**, one block from the plaza on Juárez, is an odd but striking red-brick affair from 1899, looking a bit like a fortress, but there's not much to see inside other than the stage used during the Ortiz Tirado festival (see page 497). From the plaza, the **Callejón del Beso** (Kissing Alley) isn't as narrow as the famous street in Guanajuato, but leads to the busy market (mostly fruit and meat), Plaza Alameda and the bus station.

Museo Costumbrista de Sonora

Guadalupe Victoria 1, Plaza de Armas • Charge, house tour extra • 647 428 0053

On the east side of the Plaza de Armas, the mildly diverting **Museo Costumbrista de Sonora** illustrates the town's zenith through a mock-up of La Quintera silver mine, coins from the old mint and grainy photos of moustachioed workers (all in Spanish). There's also a whole shrine-like section dedicated to acclaimed singer **Dr Alfonso Ortiz Tirado**, who was born in Álamos in 1893 – his sombrero is preserved along with photos.

The museum is also the place to join the hour-long **house tour**, which visits three of the finest homes in town. Indeed, among the most appealing aspects of Álamos are these magnificent old Andalucian-style **mansions**, brooding and shuttered from the outside, but enclosing beautiful flower-filled patios.

Casa de Cultura

Loma de Guadalupe • Free

Crowning the Loma de Guadalupe, the small hill behind the Plaza de Armas, the **Casa de Cultura** occupies **El Cárcel**, the old eighteenth-century stone jail (some tiny cells are still visible at the back). It houses temporary art exhibitions and holds events, but the main reason for the short climb is the stellar view of the town. Take the side street at the Palacio Municipal, turn right at the end and climb the steps up.

Casa Museo María Félix

Galeana 41 • Charge • https://facebook.com/HotelCasaMariaFelix

The birthplace of legendary Mexican actress María Félix has been converted into a hotel (undergoing extensive remodelling at the time of research) and a small museum, the **Casa Museo María Félix**. The museum displays personal items, portraits and artefacts discovered on the property during renovation. Félix (1914–2002) rose to stardom in the 1940s and 1950s, and is still beloved in Mexico where she is known as "La Doña" (from her character in the 1943 movie *Doña Bárbara*).

ARRIVAL AND INFORMATION — ÁLAMOS

By bus Álamos lies some 250km south of Guaymas, and 50km east of Navojoa, the nearest town on Hwy-15. Hourly buses (some a/c; no toilets) run back and forth to Álamos (6.30am–8.30pm; 1hr; 647 428 0096) from Navojoa, arriving at the tiny Terminal de Autobuses at Morelos 7 on Plaza Alameda. Most long-distance buses heading north or south along the Hwy-15 corridor stop at Navojoa; the TAP/Elite/Pacífico bus station is at Calzada de la Revolución (aka Sufragio Efectivo) and Allende (most of the other stations are around here). Buses to Álamos leave from the Albatros/TBC station at Guerrero and C No Reelección, four blocks away; from TAP walk up Allende to C No Reelección (three blocks) and turn right. Moving on from Navojoa, you can pick up a variety of *de paso* buses north or south every hour, though you won't be able to reserve tickets in advance (just turn up). Los Mochis is just two hours south.

Tourist office Victoria 5, Plaza de Armas (Mon–Fri 8am–6pm, Sat & Sun 9am–2pm; 505 662 8105, www.visitlosalamos.org).

ACCOMMODATION — SEE MAP PAGE 495

★ **Hacienda de los Santos** Molina 8; http://haciendadelossantos.com. Gorgeous colonial architecture (carved

FESTIVAL ORTIZ TIRADO

In January, everything changes in Álamos, when thousands of people descend upon the town for the week-long **Ortiz Tirado music festival**, established in 1985 in honour of the late Dr Alfonso Ortiz Tirado (born in Álamos in 1893), sometimes referred to as the "Mexican Pavarotti". The festival includes exhibitions, dance performances, workshops, lectures, musical events and concerts from Mexico's best classical musicians and singers. Accommodation is usually booked solid at this time, so reservations are a must. See http://zonaturistica.com/en/events.

out of three Spanish mansions and an eighteenth-century sugar mill), enhanced with modern amenities and antique furnishings in every room, tranquil gardens and a pool – the restaurants are also excellent (breakfast is extra). M$$$$

Hotel Colonial Obregón 4; 647 428 1371. This elegant American-owned hotel occupies a mansion built in 1875, one block from the plaza, and offers ten sumptuous rooms, all decorated with antiques and furniture from around the world. There's a restaurant and a pool (breakfast included). M$$$

La Mansión Hotel Obregón 2; 647 110 9890. This hotel is nothing much to look at from the outside but there's a lovely enough courtyard within and the rooms are well maintained. A/C included at no extra charge. M$$$

★ **Luz de Sol** Obregón 3; http://luzdelsolalamos.com. This fabulous colonial-style B&B features a small pool, en-suite rooms with a/c and delicious homemade food served in the courtyard. M$$$

Posada de Don Andrés Rosales 24; 647 428 1110, http://posadadedonandres.com. This charming hotel lies on the Alameda Central in front of the market, with great views from the clean, comfy rooms (though street noise can be an issue) and friendly owner. M$$$

EATING

SEE MAP PAGE 495

Café Luz de Sol Obregón 3; 647 428 0466. Take a break from Mexican food at this bright café (and B&B) around a courtyard, serving healthy breakfasts, salads and frappuccinos. Free wi-fi. M$$

★ **Casa La Aduana** La Aduana; 647 404 3473. If you have transport, it's worth making reservations at this isolated restaurant and inn, 3km on a dirt road off the main Álamos highway (taxis run to this spot also). Housed in a romantic adobe building dating from the 1630s, the restaurant does a superb fixed-price menu of "new Sonoran cuisine" highlighting local produce: dishes like chicken in apple, *chipotle* and cream, and *shrimps al ajillo*. M$$$

Doña Lola's Volantín, off Juárez; 647 428 1109. Popular local diner, serving excellent home-cooked Mexican classics. Connoisseurs order the *agua de cebada* (barley water), *cazuela* (beef stew) and the *molletes con carne*. M$$

La Posta Juárez 6, Plaza de Armas; 647 108 2254. Atmospheric old bar and the best spot to people-watch on the plaza. Has a pool table, big-screen TV and karaoke. M$$

DIRECTORY

Banks Banorte is the only bank with an ATM, across the Alameda at Madero 27.

Hospital Hospital General de Álamos (647 428 0225) on Madero offers fairly basic medical services.

Post office The post office (647 428 0009) is inside the Biblioteca Pública (library) on Comercio, just off Plaza de Armas.

San Carlos

Around 16km west of Guaymas, the small town of **SAN CARLOS** is gradually becoming a larger resort geared towards a mainly retired North American clientele. The main activities here are **diving** and **fishing**, though the chief attraction above the water is the scenery: the resort is dominated by the barren, jagged peaks of Cerro Tatakawi, and the scorched desert landscape makes a stunning backdrop to a series of inviting bays, beaches and cobalt-blue waters. Founded only in the 1960s, San Carlos sports a seasonal population of around seven thousand.

ARRIVAL AND GETTING AROUND

SAN CARLOS

By bus Buses (daily; every 30min 6.30am–7pm, then 8pm, 9pm & 11pm) for San Carlos leave Guaymas from C 19 by the post office, but it's easier to catch them as they head up Serdán (try the corner of C 18). It can take up to an hour to reach San Carlos.

By taxi Taxi charges vary a lot for trips in San Carlos (fix the

TRAVELLING BY CAR: THE SONORA "FREE ZONE"

If you plan to travel with a US or Canadian vehicle in Sonora north of Empalme (the area west of Hwy-15 to the coast and the border with Baja), you do not have to register and obtain a Temporary Vehicle Importation Permit (TIP); Puerto Peñasco, San Carlos, Hermosillo, Kino Bay and Guaymas are all covered. The southern end of the "free zone" is at km 98 on Hwy-15, just south of Empalme. You are still required to fill in a multiple migration form or "FMM" at the US border, but for stays of no more than three days there is no need to pay the Non-immigrant Fee. If you plan to travel beyond the Sonora "free zone", you must obtain a vehicle permit (see page 31).

price in advance), but you should be able to lock in a set fee for trips to Guaymas; from Guaymas airport (see page 500) the charge will vary (you can rent cars at the airport with Budget or Hertz).

INFORMATION AND ACTIVITIES

Tourist information The best source of information is http://whatsupsancarlos.com.

Bank CI Banco (with ATM) is at Manlio Beltrones km 9.5 (next to Pemex petrol station).

Gary's Dive Shop Manlio Beltrones km 10; 622 226 0049, http://garysdivemexico.com. Donna and Gary Goldstein run various dive trips with options including a basic two-tank dive, and cruises around Seal Island (a sea lion colony). They also have a fast broadband internet connection upstairs.

ACCOMMODATION

Posada del Desierto Bajada Comodoro 195–196, Club de Yates; 622 226 0467. This barebones budget option near the marina offers decent value, with seven clean, a/c rooms, basic kitchenettes and friendly owners – water pressure can be a problem, however. M$$

Sea of Cortez Beach Club Paseo Mar Bermejo Parcela 7; http://diamondresortsandhotels.com. There's no shortage of luxurious resorts along the shore in San Carlos, though with pool, restaurants and all the trimmings (all rooms have patios or balconies), this oceanfront Diamond Resorts property is great value. M$$$

Totonaka RV Park Manlio Beltrones km 8; http://totonakarv.com. For something a little cheaper, aim for this RV park on the right-hand side as you enter San Carlos; it also offers free wi-fi or internet usage from its office and 24 basic apartments (with cable TV), as well as RV (full hook-ups) and tent sites. M$$

EATING AND DRINKING

Blackie's Manlio Beltrones km 10.3 (next to PEMEX); 622 103 9351. Expat favourite and a good choice for dinner, with juicy steaks, seafood and the odd local dish – the signature rib-eye is a good choice here. M$$$

Charly's Rock Manlio Beltrones km 9; http://charlysrock.com. If you're in the mood for seafood, this restaurant serves enormous lobsters, all-you-can-eat fish and chips on Tues, and is also a good spot to have a margarita and watch the sun go down (the view is spectacular) – service can be hit and miss, though, so be patient. M$$$

Piccolo Manlio Beltrones km 9.5; 622 226 0503. On the main strip, this diner serves up a fine all day breakfast selection and is especially well known for the Sunday brunch. It's massively popular among locals too and the go to dish here is the enormous omelette. M$$$

Hermosillo

The thriving state capital of Sonora some 117km north of Guaymas, **HERMOSILLO** is a neat, affluent but rather odd-looking place of around 800,000, home to one of the largest Ford manufacturing plants outside the US. It's surrounded by strange rock formations and presided over, right in the centre, by the **Cerro de la Campana**, a tall outcrop crowned by radio masts and surreally illuminated at night to resemble a giant, spiral snail-shell (you can hike up or take a taxi, though sunsets can get very busy up there).

While there's little to see in the way of traditional sights, Hermosillo's laurel-lined avenues, overflowing meat markets, shops full of cowboy paraphernalia and tasty snack food make for an engaging stopover on the route north or south. Hwy-15 from

Nogales (270km to the north) comes into town as Bulevar Eusebio Kino, known as Bulevar Rosales as it runs north–south through the centre of town. Virtually everything you might want to see lies to the south near Plaza Zaragoza or Serdán, the main commercial street downtown. Note that **summers** here are fierce, with temperatures often exceeding 48 °C.

Plaza Zaragoza

Palacio de Gobierno • Free

The spacious **Plaza Zaragoza** is the venerable, shaded heart of Hermosillo and a good place to begin any wanderings around the centre. The plaza is framed by the stately **Palacio de Gobierno**, completed in 1906 and boasting a series of florid murals (painted in the 1980s) highlighting the history of Sonora, and the striking **Catedral de Nuestra Señora de la Asunción**, a grand edifice completed in 1908 but added to throughout the twentieth century.

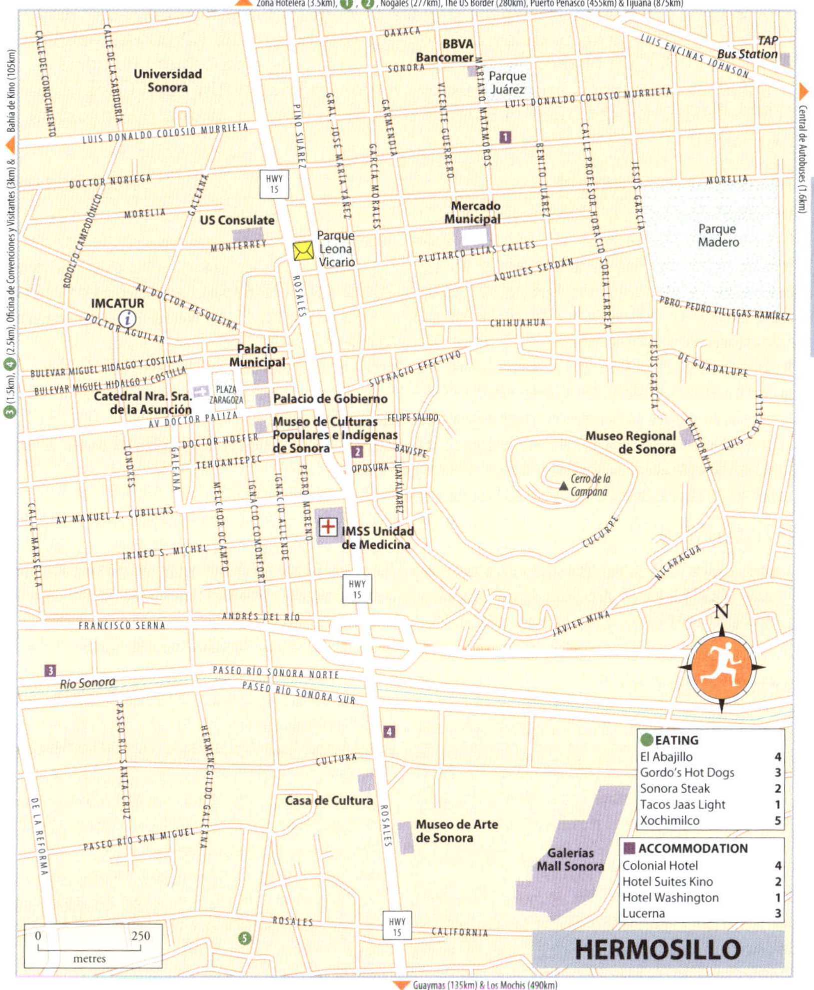

Museo Regional de Sonora

Jesús García • Charge • 662 217 2714

On the east side of the Cerro de la Campana you'll find the **Museo Regional de Sonora**, which houses exhibits charting the historical development of Sonora, from the conception of the Earth to the construction of *maquiladora* plants.

Museo de Arte de Sonora

Agustín Vildósola, at Cultura • Charge (free on Sun) • 662 254 6397

Hermosillo's most contemporary museum is the **Museo de Arte de Sonora** (MUSAS), a stylish art centre and gallery space for rotating contemporary art exhibitions. Past shows have featured Los Mochis-born artist Hugo Lugo, Gustavo Monroy and Helga Krebs, a German artist who settled in Hermosillo.

Museo de Culturas Populares e Indígenas de Sonora

Comonfort 22 • Free • 662 212 6418

Housed in a grand French-influenced mansion built for German immigrant Geo Grürinig in 1904 (who established Sonora Brewery here in the 1890s with one Dr Alberto Hoeffer, who later inherited the house), the **Museo de Culturas Populares e Indígenas de Sonora** is primarily a showcase for American artist Ethel Cook (1887–1976), whose vibrant murals based on the Indigenous peoples of Sonora fill two galleries.

ARRIVAL AND DEPARTURE — HERMOSILLO

By plane Aeropuerto Internacional General Ignacio L. Pesqueira, an important Aeroméxico hub (with flights to Mexico City, Los Angeles and numerous domestic destinations), is 10km out at Carr Bahía de Kino km 9.5. Fixed-fare taxis run most destinations in the city. *Colectivos* are a cheaper option into the centre.

By bus The Central de Autobuses is at Luís Encinas 400, 3km east of the centre. Most intercity buses passing through Hermosillo are *de paso*, and it can be very hard to get tickets. TBC (depot left of the Central de Autobuses at Encinas 354) runs local buses to Guaymas, Navojoa and, four times daily, to Álamos. First-class Tufesa is further west at Encinas 297. To get downtown from the bus station area, take a "Ruta 1" microbus, or a "Multirutas" town bus across the main road. To get back, catch a bus marked "Central Camionera" from Juárez (on east side of Jardín Juárez). Second-class buses to Bahía de Kino depart the terminal on Sonora between González and García.

Destinations Bahía de Kino (13 daily; 2hr); Guadalajara (every 30min; 21–23hr); Guaymas (every 30min; 2hr); Los Mochis (every 30min; 7–9hr); Mexico City (hourly; 29–33hr); Nogales (hourly; 3–4hr); Tijuana (every 30min; 12–14hr).

INFORMATION

Tourist office The Instituto Municipal de Cultura Arte y Turismo (IMCATUR) has an office at Dr Aguilar 33 (enter at Campodonico and Galeana in Col Centenario; 662 213 8638, https://imca.hermosillo.gob.mx), open Mon–Fri 9am–5pm. The helpful Oficina de Convenciones y Visitantes has an office at Navarrete 329, Colonia Raquet Club (Mon–Fri 9am–2pm & 4–7pm, Sat 9am–1pm; 662 285 5050, http://ocvhermosillo.com), but only really accessible if you have a car.

ACCOMMODATION

SEE MAP PAGE 499

Nearly all the cheaper **hotels** in Hermosillo are poor value, but some very pleasant mid-range places cater to business people and the wealthy *rancheros* who come here for the markets. The most expensive hotels, such as the *Fiesta Americana* and a number of motels, are almost all in the **Zona Hotelera**, 5km northeast from the centre on Kino (Hwy-15), and only practical if you have a car.

Colonial Hotel Vado del Río 9; http://hotelcolonialhermosillo.com. Plush, modern motel on the southern edge of downtown, worth the extra walk if you're not driving; includes breakfast, satellite TV, laundry, gym and even a small pool on site. M$$

Hotel Suites Kino Pino Suárez 151, just off Rosales near Plaza Zaragoza; http://hotelsuiteskino.com. Colonial-style hotel set in a nineteenth-century building with standard, motel-style rooms and all the facilities, including cable TV, coffee, parking and a pool, for low rates. M$$

Hotel Washington Noriega 68, near Guerrero; 662 213 1183. Best budget option in town: ageing but good-value rooms, excellent hot showers, a very helpful staff and free coffee in the lobby. Cash only. M$

Lucerna Paseo Río Sonora Nte 98; http://hoteleslucerna.

EL CARNAVAL DE GUAYMAS

An important shrimp-fishing port on the main Hwy-15 corridor, **GUAYMAS**, around 180km north of Navojoa, claims some proud history but has little to offer visitors. Unless you're looking for somewhere to crash for one night, it's advisable to head for nearby beaches; the resort town of **San Carlos** is just a short bus ride away (see page 497). One reason to linger in Guaymas is the annual **carnival**, held here in February since 1888 and one of Mexico's best (it begins on the Thurs before Ash Wednesday and ends at the beginning of Lent). Concerts and parades are held all over town (the main location is the Plaza de los Tres Presidentes), beginning with the traditional burning of an effigy of something or someone who has upset the public that year (Vicente Fox and George Bush have both featured in the past). Note that accommodation in town is booked months in advance for carnival.

ARRIVAL

Most bus companies have terminals on C 14 near C 12, a couple of blocks south of Serdán and within walking distance of the waterfront. Tufesa and TAP have terminals 1km west at García López 927 and 915 respectively (near C Jaiba).

By ferry Ferries from Santa Rosalía in Baja California (see page 544) arrive at the docks 2km east of the centre, easily reached on local buses along Serdán. The ferry from Guaymas to Santa Rosalía departs on Tues, Thurs and Sat at 8pm, arriving 6am the following day. Always call in advance, though, as schedules often change. You'll often get a discount on tickets on Sundays. A cabin will cost extra and there's a charge per car (one-way). The ticket office inside the terminal is open Mon–Sat 8am–3pm (622 222 0204, http://mexbound.com/mexico-ferry).

ACCOMMODATION

Armida Hotel Carr Internacional Salida al Norte s/n; 443 137 8728. If you have to stay in Guaymas, aim for this well-equipped hotel, close to the TAP and Tufesa terminals, with 124 rooms ranging from luxurious suites to economy doubles. M$$$

Hotel del Sol García López 995; 622 221 9411. Prices here are cheaper than the *Armida*, with 25 simple but adequate rooms close to the main bus terminals. M$$

EATING AND DRINKING

★ **Coctelería Doug Out** García López between calles 11 and 12; 622 222 2626. A no-frills food court offering excellent crab and various *ceviche, pulpo cocido* and other shellfish (half kilo of shrimp is a bargain here). Cash only. M$$

★ **Lonchería Doney** Serdán at C 25; 622 222 4270. A justly popular local *comedor* at the far end of Serdán, lauded for its giant *papas locas* (huge baked potatoes stuffed with meat, cheese and cream) and *tacos carne asada*. Cash only. M$$

8

com. One of the best options if Hermosillo's selection of modern hotels and motels on the outskirts appeals, with stylish rooms, consistently high standards of service and a small pool, just south of the centre. Book ahead. M$$$

EATING

SEE MAP PAGE 499

Don't leave the city without trying some of the local specialties: **hot dogs** are fabulously over the top here, wrapped in bacon and piled with all sorts of toppings – some of the best stalls are around the entrance to the Universidad de Sonora, at Luís Encinas and Rosales. Also try some of the **carne asada** – this is beef country, after all – and the **coyotas**, sweet cookies made from flour, brown sugar, molasses and milk (best sampled on the stalls along Obregón).

El Abajillo Periférico Pte 325 (Blvd Solidaridad), Col Palmar del Sol; 662 218 3555. High-quality *carne asada* with the added bonus of later opening hours and live mariachi bands. M$$$

★ **Gordo's Hot Dogs** Colosio 389, at Olivares. This place is a local institution, serving the best hot dogs in town – huge, juicy, masterpieces of bacon-wrapped dogs and ground beef in a giant bun, slathered in an array of zesty condiments. M$$

Sonora Steak Eusebio Kino 914 (Hwy-15); https://sonoragrill.com.mx. Treat yourself to Sonora's pride and joy at this classic steakhouse, where staff will show you a selection of cuts before you choose the thickness of the meat – steaks are charged by the gram. Favourite of Hermosillo's dignitaries – Sonora state governor's official residence is next door. M$$$$

★ **Tacos Jaas Light** Mariscal 23 at Gómez Farías; 662 210 0137. The place to gorge on prime *tacos de carne asada*. They have several locations, but this is the best, though it's a no-frills open-air place with plastic tables and chairs. "Light" versions, wrapped in lettuce leaves, are also available. M$

Xochimilco Obregón 51; 662 250 4052. A Hermosillo *carne asada* favourite since 1949, serving great sit-down meals and "special plates" of charcoal-broiled beef, ribs, beans and giant tortillas. M$$

DIRECTORY

Banks and exchange There are numerous *casas de cambio* and banks on Serdán, and a handy Bancomer with ATM at Matamoros and Sonora, on Jardín Juárez a block from the *Monte Carlo* hotel.

Consulate US (Mon–Fri 8am–4.30pm; 662 289 3500), Monterrey 141, between Galeana and Rosales.

Post office Monterrey 84, at Pino Suárez.

Bahía de Kino

Boasting more than 15km of pristine Sea of Cortez coastline, 110km west of Hermosillo, **BAHÍA DE KINO** is a popular weekend escape for locals and increasingly a winter resort for North American snowbirds. For good reason; the seafront is padded with many kilometres of inviting sands, the placid waters are perfect for swimming and kayaking, the offshore islets and strange rock formations make the sunsets particularly memorable and the resort remains relatively low-key – for now. There are two settlements around the bay: the old fishing village of **Kino Viejo**, a dusty collection of corrugated-iron huts culminating at the pier (**Muelle Bahía de Kino**), and the younger **Kino Nuevo** – an 8km strip of one-storey seafront houses, trailer parks and a handful of hotels and restaurants. Local operators run snorkelling and dive trips to **Isla Alcatraz** a small island just 1.4km offshore that is often smothered with nesting birds.

8

Museo Comcáac

Mar de Cortés, at Progreso • Charge • 662 242 0680

In Kino Nuevo, the modern Museo Comcáac is dedicated to the Seri (see page 502), who call themselves "Comcáac". Displays cover everything from local history and Seri language, to tribal clothing and crafts, enhanced with traditional ironwood artefacts and incredible baskets created by Seri artisans. Spanish labels only.

ARRIVAL AND INFORMATION — BAHÍA DE KINO

By bus Buses to Bahía de Kino leave Hermosillo from the small bus station on Sonora, a block and a half east of the *Monte Carlo* near Jardín Juárez, between Jesús García and González. There are about 12–13 a day – hourly from 5am to 1.30pm, then every two or three hours up to 7pm – with more at busy weekends; they take around two hours and end up in Kino Nuevo on Mar de Cortés, the main avenue. Once here you can ride these buses up and down the seafront (taxis run between Kino Viejo and Kino Nuevo).

ACCOMMODATION

Casablanca Inn Mar de Cortés 674 (Kino Nuevo); http://casablancainn.net. Justly popular family-owned guesthouse, with clean, bright rooms (a/c and satellite TV), breakfast included (the restaurant is open all) and the Palapa Bar. M$$$

Hotel Hacienda Guaymas at Manzanilla (Kino Viejo); 662 242 0590. Friendly hotel with simple but clean rooms with tiled floor set around a small courtyard and pool (the

THE SERI

The coast around Bahía de Kino is the traditional home of the **Seri** people, once semi-nomadic hunter-gatherers who have managed to hang on to their linguistic and cultural traditions. Their former home on the offshore **Isla del Tiburón** (Shark Island) was made into a wildlife refuge in the 1960s but is still administered by the tribal government. You may come across Seri hawking traditional (and not so traditional) ironwood carvings along the beach in Kino Nuevo, though their main settlement is **Punta Chueca**, 35km north – you can buy genuine crafts here, but you'll need your own wheels to reach the settlement. The **Museo Comcáac** (see page 502) gives a little more information on Seri culture.

suites are a bit more comfortable and stylish, but not much bigger). M$$$

La Playa RV & Hotel Mar de Cortés 101, at Beruit; 662 242 0273. Gorgeous Mediterranean-style resort right on the beach between old and new Kino, its rooms equipped with tiled-floor, marble-clad bathrooms, satellite TV, fridge and microwave (also offers 48 full hook-ups for RVs). M$$$

EATING AND DRINKING

Kino Bay Jorge's Restaurant Mar de Cortés and Alicantes; 662 242 0049. *Jorge's* is one of a handful of places that dish up local seafood (especially lobster) just off the beach, at the northern end of Kino Nuevo. M$$$

El Pargo Rojo Mar de Cortés 1426; 662 242 0205. Head south from *Jorge's* and you'll arrive at *El Pargo Rojo*, another popular and reputable restaurant in the middle of Kino Nuevo serving decent breakfasts and seafood dishes. M$$

Puerto Peñasco

Not long ago, **PUERTO PEÑASCO** was little more than a tiny shrimping port on the edge of the Altar desert. Since the 1990s, though, the town has exploded into a major resort for Arizona's beach-starved masses, and it is now filled with high-rise condominiums. Travel warnings and the 2009 US recession hit Puerto Peñasco hard, but now things have settled down the development is sure to continue: a new highway along the coast (reducing driving times from California) opened in 2008, and the Mar de Cortés International Airport was inaugurated one year later (though it only services charter flights and private aircraft). If you like resorts, golf or just fancy a couple of days on the beach before heading into the US, "Rocky Point" (as the expat community calls it) can be lots of fun. Note that temperatures regularly top 40°C in the summer.

Sandy Beach

From the malecón and the Old Port, the main Bulevar Juárez (Hwy-8) runs nearly parallel to the water before heading off towards Sonoyta, while the town's main attraction, **Sandy Beach**, stretches off to the northwest, an 8km strip backed by condos and resort hotels ending at **La Choya** (or Cholla Bay in English). Tides here can raise and lower sea levels by several metres, creating large numbers of tidal pools at low tide, often crammed with crabs, starfish and other marine life.

San Jorge Island

San Jorge Island, a series of iceberg-like rocks in the Sea of Cortez 45km from Puerto Peñasco, is frequented by hordes of cormorants, red-billed tropicbirds, brown pelicans and some 2500 sea lions. If they're feeling up to it, and haven't been laid low by the daytime heat, you can swim with the latter. Otherwise, there are usually numerous dolphins frolicking around. CEDO (see below) and various tour operators run trips here (6–7hr, minimum six people).

Centro Intercultural de Estudios de Desiertos y Océanos

Las Conchas, off Blv Josefa Ortiz de Domínguez • Free • http://cedo.org

If you don't have the inclination to get in the water, you can visit the **Centro Intercultural de Estudios de Desiertos y Océanos** (CEDO), in Las Conchas residential zone 4km east of the harbour, the foremost authority on local wildlife, and currently researching the harmful effects of development on regional ecology. Inside you can check out the Gran Desierto de Altar Botanical Gardens, a 20m fin whale skeleton and the Earthship Visitors' Center (which houses various ecological exhibits). CEDO also runs various expert-led **tours** of the Estero Morúa coastal wetlands by kayak (5hr), the Gran Desierto dunes (5hr; Sept–May) and the Pinacate Biosphere Reserve (6hr; Sept–May only).

Reserva de la Biósfera El Pinacate y Gran Desierto de Altar

Charge • http://elpinacate.com.mx • Museo y Centro de Visitantes Schuk Toak, 7km west of Hwy-8 km 72; 638 108 0011 • La Estación Biológica, Hwy-8 km 52, Ejido Los Norteños; 638 105 8016

The region's most impressive natural attraction, the **Reserva de la Biósfera El Pinacate y Gran Desierto de Altar**, lies north of Puerto Peñasco on Hwy-8. NASA used this otherworldly expanse of volcanic cinder cones and craters to train its astronauts for lunar landings. One of Pinacate's largest and most awe-inspiring craters, "**El Elegante**", is 1.6km wide and 250m deep and can be seen from space. Exhibits at the **Museo y Centro de Visitantes Schuk Toak** provide background, as well as displays of artefacts made by the **Tohono O'odham**, the Native American people of the Sonoran Desert. No public transport runs to the reserve, so you'll have to drive or join a tour.

ARRIVAL AND DEPARTURE — PUERTO PEÑASCO

By bus The main bus stations are located on Benito Juárez (the main road into town), around 1km from the seafront (malecón); Águila (buses to Mexicali and Tijuana) is at Constitución and Juárez, while Albatros (638 388 0888) is further up at Juárez 292; the latter runs 13 buses a day to Hermosillo, four to Nogales and two to Guaymas. Several outfits also run direct minibuses to Arizona: Head Out to Rocky Point (US+1 866 443 2368, http://headouttorockypoint.com) runs buses from Phoenix (4hr) with one-way and return prices determined by the number of people.

By car Puerto Peñasco is just 100km south of the US border and around four hours' drive from Phoenix, Arizona – most visitors drive here on Hwy-8.

INFORMATION

Oficina de Convenciones y Visitantes de Puerto Peñasco Plaza Pelícanos, Coahuila 444, between Freemont and Víctor Estrella (Mon–Fri 9am–2pm & 4–7pm; 638 388 0444, http://cometorockypoint.com) has an ample assortment of flyers and glossy brochures. See also http://puerto-penasco.com.

8

GETTING AROUND

By bus The Camioncito Urbano (city bus) offers two primary routes for a flat fee (usually Mon–Sat 6am–7pm); bus #2 runs between the Albatros bus station on Juárez down to the malecón.

By taxi One of the omnipresent white taxis (locals pay around less for a ride anywhere in town; fix the price first) should get you to wherever you need to be.

ACCOMMODATION

Peñasco del Sol Paseo las Glorias 1; http://penascodelsolhotel.com. Justly popular resort hotel, especially lively at Spring Break and holidays when this is the best place to party. The 203 handsomely furnished rooms come with plasma TVs and coffee-makers. Great deals online. M$$$$

Posada La Roca Primero de Junio 2; http://hotelposadalaroca.blogspot.com. The oldest building in town (1927); room no. 10 was frequented by Al Capone during Prohibition. A great budget option with cool quarters, free coffee and a cosy living room. M$$

Sonoran Spa Resort Camino La Choya km 3.7; http://sonoranspareservations.com. One of the best luxury lodgings in Puerto Peñasco, right on Sandy Beach with three pools and all the extras; rooms are one- to three-bedroom suites with kitchens and sea views. M$$$$

CROSSING THE US BORDER: NOGALES

Like most of the other US/Mexico border towns, **Nogales** is a fast-growing melange of cheap stores, *maquiladoras* (factories), street hustlers and rough bars. Crossing the border (24hr) into Mexico is straightforward; remember to have your tourist card stamped by *migración* if you're heading further south (see page 32). From here López Mateos (Hwy-15) leads south towards the main bus stations; buses to Mexico City run every hour (32–34hr) from the Central Camionera, just off the highway (Obregón 2562) about 5km south of the border; Omnibus and TAP are at Obregón 2036 (631 319 4154), with buses to Hermosillo every 30min (3.5hr) and six daily to Mazatlán (17hr); further south is the Tufesa terminal at Obregón 2030. If you plan to go to Puerto Peñasco, Albatros (631 319 4190) runs three daily buses from Obregón 1945 (7.30am, 11am & 3pm; 5hr). TBC buses to Álamos also run from here (1 daily). Taxis run between the border and the bus stations. Tufesa runs buses across the border, between Nogales bus station and Tucson, Arizona (2hr), and Phoenix (4hr, http://tufesa.com.mx).

EATING AND DRINKING

RESTAURANTS

Aqui Es Con Flavio Malecón Kino 10, at Primero de Junio; 638 383 5252. Unpretentious place right on the boardwalk, where most people come for the margaritas, frolicking pelicans and the views rather than the food. The seafood is not bad, though – groups should opt for the huge seafood combo. M$$$

★ **Blue Marlin** Zaragoza 11, at Primero de Junio; 638 388 6564. Fabulous family-owned seafood restaurant popular with locals, specializing in flounder, shrimp tacos and marlin (local, when they can get it fresh); try the smoked marlin, one of the town's best dishes, or the Neptune platter for two, loaded with a variety of seafood. M$$$$

La Casa del Capitán Av del Agua 1, Cerro de la Ballena; https://facebook.com/lacasadelcapitan. One of the most popular restaurants in town to view the sunset (when it's always packed), with gorgeous views across the sea. There's a full international and Mexican menu. Follow Juárez to Antonio's liquor store; from there you'll see the entrance to the path leading to the top of "Whale Hill", a 15min walk. M$$$

Friendly Dolphin Alcantar 44; 638 383 2608. Local favourite with a big seafood menu and reasonable prices a 5min walk from the seafront, enhanced with antique pictures of Mexico. Food is also served on an outdoor patio upstairs. Occasionally one of the owners will play guitar and sing to the tables. M$$$

Mary's Seafood Malecón Kino 42; 638 388 8395. Delicious and always fresh seafood on the boardwalk (with great upper deck for viewing the harbour); stand-outs include the seabass, fried shrimp and fish or beef tacos. M$

BARS AND CAFÉS

JJ's Cantina 58 Seaside Av, La Choya (Cholla Bay); 638 383 2785. A beach bar and seafood joint that does great fish, tacos and burgers, about 20min drive (12km) from the malecón. If you don't mind the expat crowd – monthly events include chile cook-offs and "Bathtub Races" – it's an excellent place to watch the sun set over the bay. Cash only. M$$

Kaffee Haus Juárez 216-B; 638 388 1065. This friendly European-style café serves rich coffee, wonderful breakfasts and addictive pastries such as apple strudel with vanilla sauce and cherry coconut cake. Incredibly popular, so be prepared to wait. M$$$

DIRECTORY

Banks There are several strung along Juárez, with ATMs; US dollars are accepted everywhere.

Post office Chiapas 1285, off Fremont (638 383 2350).

Baja California

PLAYA DE BALANDRA

9

Baja California

Graced with tantalizing desert landscapes, lush oases and rich marine life, Baja California is one of the most compelling and popular destinations in Mexico. Its human history is no less enticing, with a legacy of remote cave paintings, crumbling Spanish missions, luxury beach resorts and fabulous seafood. Yet even today, Baja maintains a palpable air of isolation from the rest of Mexico. The peninsula lies over 1300km west of Mexico City, and the sheer distances involved in traversing its length – it's over 1700km long – are not conducive to quick exploration.

One of the most magical sights in Baja is the annual **grey whale** migration from December to April; the best places to see the whales are the Laguna Ojo de Liebre, just off **Guerrero Negro**, or the lagoon near **San Ignacio**, where the town is an attraction in itself. The peninsula is also home to some of the most bewitching and thought-provoking **cave art** in the world – the Sierra de San Francisco, between Bahía de los Angeles and Loreto, was declared a World Heritage Site by UNESCO in 1993 because of its five hundred particularly vivid rock-art sites.

And all along the coast you'll find turquoise waters and white-sand **beaches**; most towns in Baja California Sur offer fantastic opportunities for diving, fishing and kayaking, but **Bahía Concepción**, **Loreto**, **La Paz** and the remote settlements on the **East Cape** are the standouts among them. In complete contrast, right at the end of the peninsula, the booming resort of **Los Cabos** offers its own special blend of boutique hotels, beach activities, top-notch restaurants and wild nightlife.

ESSENTIALS — BAJA CALIFORNIA

Baja information Visit http://bajanorte.com for information on the region, and especially for up-to-date travel regulations. Call 078 for visitor assistance 24hr a day.

Visas Coming from the US land border, note that all US and Canadian citizens, and foreigners who have a valid US visa, can travel as far as Ensenada without having to obtain a tourist card (FMM), provided the length of the stay does not exceed 72hr. Between 72hr and 7 days you'll need a card/form, but are not obliged to pay the fee. If you intend on staying for more than seven days in any region of Mexico, you are required to pay a Non-immigrant Fee (DNI) when obtaining the tourist card – if you fly in, it's included. See page 514 for crossing the border at Tijuana.

Tijuana and around

American day-trippers have been coming to **TIJUANA**, the definitive booze-soaked border town, in significant numbers since the 1950s. Visits crashed ninety percent between 2005 and 2009 thanks to escalating drug-related violence and subsequent US travel warnings (see page 453), but things are much improved since then, and the main commercial drag, **Avenida Revolución**, aka **La Revo**, has recovered some of its former colour. Indeed, police crackdowns have left central Tijuana safer than ever before, and drug violence rarely affects tourist areas.

Founded in 1889, Tijuana now has a population of almost two million, and despite its often shabby appearance, the region's duty-free status and its legion of **maquiladores** (assembly plants) have helped make it one of the richest cities in Mexico. The city has developed dynamic **arts** and **culinary** scenes, with institutions like Centro Cultural Tijuana (CECUT) emerging as a breeding ground for home-grown artistic and cultural movements. In the **Zona Río**, beyond the areas where most tourists venture, you'll find sophisticated restaurants, clubs and modern concrete and

FISH TACOS

Highlights

❶ **The Transpeninsular Highway** One of the world's great road trips, Highway 1 runs the length of Baja California for 1711km, an enchanting drive of starry nights, vast deserts and empty beaches. See page 511

❷ **Fish tacos** The seafood in this part of Mexico is always exceptional, but the real star is the humble fish taco, found all over Baja but best experienced in Ensenada. See page 522

❸ **Valle de Guadalupe** Tour the vineyards of this rapidly maturing wine area. See page 523

❹ **Whale watching at Laguna San Ignacio** Each winter migrating grey whales journey from the Arctic Circle to nurse their calves in the warm waters of this pristine inlet. See page 533

❺ **Cave art** The wild, rugged mountains of Baja California protect some of the most spellbinding prehistoric cave art in the world, best explored with a local guide. See page 536

❻ **Bahía Concepción** Camp underneath a star-filled sky, lounge on gorgeous beaches and kayak alongside dolphins in serene aquamarine waters. See page 537

❼ **La Paz** All of Baja's best qualities: great restaurants, cheap rooms, vibrant street life and outdoor adventure opportunities. See page 541

HIGHLIGHTS ARE MARKED ON THE MAP ON PAGE 510

BAJA CALIFORNIA
HIGHLIGHTS
1 The Transpeninsular Highway
2 Fish tacos
3 Valle de Guadalupe
4 Whale watching at Laguna San Ignacio
5 Cave art
6 Bahía Concepción
7 La Paz
CALIFORNIA
ARIZONA
SONORA
USA
MEXICO
BAJA CALIFORNIA
BAJA CALIFORNIA SUR
PACIFIC OCEAN
SEA OF CORTEZ
0
100
kilometres
San Diego
Tijuana
Tecate
Rosarito
Ensenada
Mexicali
Yuma
San Luis Río Colorado
Tucson
Sonoyta
Puerto Peñasco
Nogales
Cananea
Hermosillo
Guaymas
Ciudad Obregón
Navojoa
PARQUE NACIONAL CONSTITUCIÓN DE 1857
PARQUE NACIONAL SIERRA DE SAN PEDRO MÁRTIR
Picacho del Diablo
SIERRA SAN PEDRO MÁRTIR
Isla Montague
San Vicente
San Felipe
San Quintín
Puertecitos
El Rosario
Cataviña
Gonzaga
Isla Ángel de la Guarda
Chapala
PARQUE NATURAL DEL DESIERTO CENTRAL
Isla Tiburón
Punta Prieta
Bahía de los Ángeles
Isla Cedros
Bahía de Sebastian Vizcaíno
Guerrero Negro
Laguna Ojo de Liebre
Desierto de Vizcaíno
Bahía Tortugas
RESERVA DE LA BIÓSFERA EL VIZCAÍNO
San Ignacio
Santa Rosalía
SIERRA DE SAN FRANCISCO
PARQUE NATURAL DE LA LAGUNA DE SAN IGNACIO
Laguna San Ignacio
Mulegé
Bahía Concepción
La Purísima
SIERRA DE LA GIGANTA
Loreto
PARQUE NACIONAL BAHÍA DE LORETO
Isla Carmen
Ciudad Insurgentes
Ciudad Constitución
San Carlos
Bahía Magdalena
Isla San José
Isla Espiritu Santo
Isla Santa Margarita
(suspended 2018)
Topolobampo
Mazatlán
Isla Cerralvo
La Paz
Los Barriles
Todos Santos
Cabo Pulmo
San José del Cabo
Cabo San Lucas
Tropic of Cancer
HWY 1
HWY 2
HWY 3
HWY 5
HWY 8
HWY 12
HWY 15
HWY 19
8
10
15

THE TRANSPENINSULAR HIGHWAY (HWY-1)

The **Transpeninsular Highway** is one of North America's great road trips. Part of the thrill comes from the long spaces separating major towns, the narrow segments of highway that snake along precarious cliffs, and the animals and washouts that can block the road. But the biggest draw is the near-constant beauty of the desert, mountain, sea and ocean vistas and their illumination by brilliant blue skies and starry nights. The times below include necessary stops for petrol and army inspections; all cars and buses are searched at military checkpoints stationed between Tijuana and Ensenada (2); north of El Rosario; north of Guerrero Negro; north of San Ignacio; and north of La Paz.

Tijuana to Mexicali	1hr 50min	(198km)
Mexicali to San Felipe	2hr 15min	(195km)
San Felipe to Ensenada	3hr 10min	(245km)
Tijuana to Ensenada	55min	(109km)
Ensenada to San Quintín	3hr	(190km)
San Quintín to El Rosario	55min	(56km)
El Rosario to Cataviña	1hr 50min	(123km)
Cataviña to Parador Punta Prieta	1hr	(103km)
Parador Punta Prieta to Bahía de los Angeles	45min	(69km)
Parador Punta Prieta to Guerrero Negro	1hr 50min	(135km)
Guerrero Negro to San Ignacio	1hr 30min	(146km)
San Ignacio to Santa Rosalía	45min	(72km)
Santa Rosalía to Mulegé	40min	(62km)
Mulegé to Loreto	1hr 45min	(138km)
Loreto to Ciudad Insurgentes	1hr 20min	(141km)
Ciudad Insurgentes to La Paz	2hr 20min	(209km)
La Paz to Todos Santos	45min	(77km)
Todos Santos to Cabo San Lucas	55min	(77km)
Cabo San Lucas to San José del Cabo	25min	(32km)

PRACTICALITIES

Many Americans and Canadians take their cars to Baja; despite the scary headlines when it comes to drug violence along the US-Mexico border, this is generally easy and safe. If you intend to go on from Baja to mainland Mexico, you need to apply for a Temporary Importation of Vehicle Permit (see www.banjercito.com.mx/registroVehiculos and Basics page 31). Car insurance is not mandatory but is highly recommended. There are many companies along the US-Mexico border that sell Mexican car insurance by the day, week or month (most normal US insurance policies don't provide coverage for driving in Mexico). Note also that in Tijuana, tinted windows are now banned. Other nationalities can always **rent cars** on arrival – easy enough in Los Cabos or Tijuana. See relevant sections for details.

glass buildings, offering the best glimpse of Tijuana's other life – one that has more in common with San Diego than the adult-themed carnival atmosphere of La Revo. And the **food** is fabulous – Tijuana excels at tasty street snacks but also boasts some of the best restaurants in Mexico.

Zona Centro

If you're only in town to spend a few hours, you need not wander far from the stream of bars, dance clubs and souvenir stalls on **Avenida Revolución** between calles 1a and 8a, in the **Zona Centro**. With plenty of police around, the main drag is generally safe (take the usual precautions at night). The tourist offices are here, as is *Caesar's*, the landmark restaurant (see page 516), and a tacky wax museum, but you'll also see

Tijuana's "famous" **donkeys** on street corners – painted to look like zebras (seriously). Check out **Pasaje Rodríguez** (just south of Calle 3), a passage lined with murals and independent stores, for a taster of Tijuana's artsy side.

Zona Río

When the lure of cheap souvenirs and beers begins to pall, you'll do yourself a favour by heading east to the **Zona Río**; the district's backbone, Paseo de los Héroes, is Tijuana's grandest boulevard and contains the city's best restaurants, malls and cultural attractions.

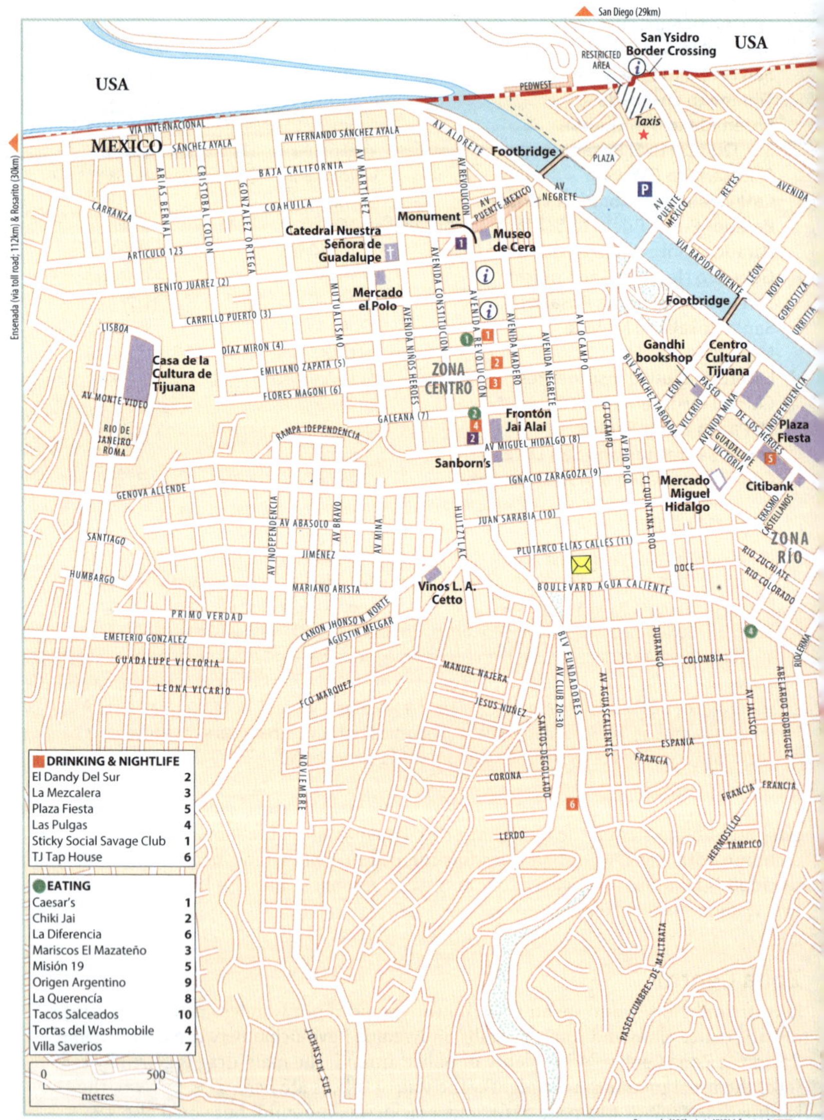

Centro Cultural Tijuana

Paseo de los Héroes 9350, at Independencia • http://cecut.gob.mx • **Museo El Cubo** Tues–Sun 10am–7pm • Charge (Sun free) • **Temporary art exhibits** Free • **IMAX theatre** Charge • **Jardín Caracol** Free

The prestigious **Centro Cultural Tijuana**, or CECUT, is home to a major performance space, temporary art exhibits and an **IMAX** movie theatre – the brown globe the cinema is housed in gives the complex its nickname, "La Bola". There's also a tranquil garden dotted with replicas of Mesoamerican sculpture, a café, the absorbing **Museo de las Californias** and **Museo El Cubo**, an imaginative gallery designed by local architect Eugenio Velásquez, which houses innovative contemporary artwork.

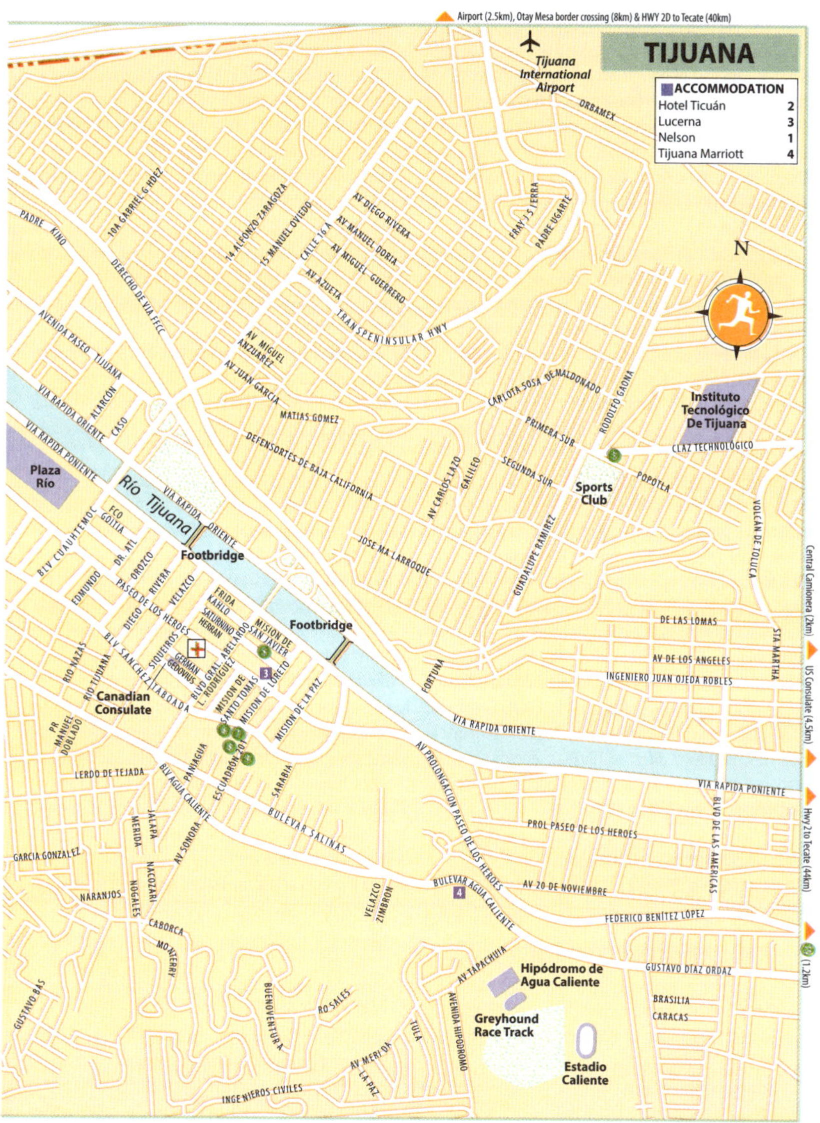

Museo de las Californias

Paseo de los Héroes 9350, at Independencia • Charge (Sun free) • http://cecut.gob.mx

By far the most rewarding part of the cultural centre is the **Museo de las Californias**, which chronicles the history of Baja California with scale models, old maps, artefacts and English labelling. The reproductions of cave paintings and Spanish missions are especially good, and there's information on Baja's now extinct Native American tribes such as the Guaycura. Aspects of the region's modern history – from the development of Tijuana and Mexicali to Chinese immigration and the Mexican Revolution – are covered in detail.

ARRIVAL AND DEPARTURE — TIJUANA

By plane The Aeropuerto Internacional de Tijuana (664 607 8200) is 6km east of downtown, next to the US border on the Carretera Aeropuerto (the airport features a pedestrian skybridge across the border; see page 514). Taxi rates are tied to a seven-zone system; most places in the Zona Centro should be a fixed rate (as should trips to the Zona Río). Alternatively, city buses pick up passengers in front of the terminal. Tijuana is a hub for Aeroméxico, which operates daily flights to/from eleven Mexican cities, and also serves as the base for low-cost Volaris; time-saving connections include flights to Hermosillo, La Paz, Los Mochis, Mazatlán, Puerto Vallarta, Los Cabos and Zacatecas, as well as the Calafia Airlines flight to Loreto.

By bus The large Central de Autobuses (664 621 2982), at Lázaro Cárdenas 15751, is north of the river and 6km east of the city centre. Local buses marked "Centro" take 30min to get to the centre of Tijuana via C 2a; taxis should all charge the same amount (get a ticket from the booth outside) but agree on the fee before you set off. You can take hourly Greyhound/Autobuses Americanos services to the US from here (San Diego; 2hr 15min; includes transfer in San Ysidro), or numerous destinations in Mexico; buses to Ensenada and Mexicali are most frequent.

Destinations Ensenada (hourly; 1hr 45min); Guadalajara (every 30min; 36hr); Guerrero Negro (3–4 daily; 12hr); La Paz (3–4 daily; 24hr); Los Mochis (every 30min; 19hr); Loreto (3–4 daily; 18hr); Mexicali (every 30min; 3hr); Mexico City (hourly; 44hr).

By taxi (rosarito) The easiest way to travel between Rosarito and Tijuana is to take a yellow taxi – which run between here and the border. Tijuana airport taxis will charge quite a lot more.

CROSSING THE US BORDER

Crossing the US-Mexico border at Tijuana is a simple but often time-consuming affair, given the volume of traffic. Allow more time heading into the US, especially during morning and evening rush hours, when the wait for cars and pedestrians can take up to 3hr. Both San Ysidro and Otay Mesa (around 8km east of San Ysidro) crossings are open 24hr. See pages 31 and 32 for more on border formalities. If you're planning to head straight out of Tijuana by bus, it makes more sense to take the hourly Greyhound service (see page 514) from the San Diego bus terminal at 120 West Broadway direct to Tijuana's long-distance bus station. If taking a flight from Tijuana airport, use the CBX skybridge (see page 515).

VIA SAN YSIDRO

On foot The San Diego Trolley connects downtown San Diego to the border at San Ysidro (45min), or you can leave your car at Border Station Parking, 4570 Camino de la Plaza (US 619 428 1422; charge) in San Ysidro. Taxis run from San Diego Airport to the border on the meter. You can just walk across the border, but remember to stop at the *migración* office and ask for a multiple migration form or "FMT" (this is accompanied by a Non-immigrant Fee), if you intend to go further than Ensenada (these are not handed out automatically – leaving the States there is no US immigration and only very casual Mexico checks for pedestrians). Take the left-hand exit for taxis (see below), or the right-hand exit if you prefer the 20min walk to La Revo; it's a fairly well-signed route via the footbridge and along C 1a to Av Revolución. It's perfectly safe during the day, but it's best to take a taxi at night.

By car If driving across the border, remember to pull in at

TIJUANA WINE TASTING

If you're not planning to visit any of Mexico's wine-growing regions, stop in at **Vinos L.A. Cetto** (http://lacetto.mx), 3km southwest of La Revo at Av Cañón Jhonson 2108. One of the largest producers in the Valle de Guadalupe (see page 523), their Tijuana outpost offers tastings (*traditionales* or *reserva* for a fee) and the chance to tour the packing area and underground cellars (free).

TIJUANA–SAN DIEGO SKYBRIDGE

A pedestrian skybridge dubbed Cross-Border Xpress or "CBX" (http://crossborderxpress.com) spans the US-Mexico border at Tijuana's airport, connecting with a passenger building on the San Diego side (2745 Otay Pacific Drive, Otay Mesa). To use the bridge you must have a CBX ticket (there's a charge each way) and an airline boarding pass for a flight either departing Tijuana Airport within 24 hours or having arrived within 2 hours. On the US side there are a variety of bus, shuttles or taxis waiting to take you into San Diego (35min) or further afield.

the *migración* office to get your Immigration Form. Once across the border, the road splits off into a series of right-hand exits to Playas de Tijuana and the scenic toll road south to Ensenada; C 3a (Carillo Puerto), which heads downtown; and Paseo de los Héroes into Zona Río. Streets are well marked – at times half a block in advance – and blue signs on lampposts identify the distance to prominent locations. If you're taking your car off the Baja Peninsula, you'll need to get a temporary importation vehicle permit at the branch of Banjercito at the border (for details, see page 31).

Entering the US Entering the US can be extremely time-consuming at Tijuana (1–3hr), and Canadians and even US citizens now require a passport to enter. Everyone else needs a visa or a visa-waiver to enter the US (crossing the land border does not require ESTA approval, but you will need to fill in an I-94W form, and pay a fee; see page 31). Coming in to the US, pedestrians now have the option of using the PedWest entry point, a short walk west of the main entry point (coming in to Mexico there's still just one entry point). From PedWest it's just a 10min walk to the San Ysidro Transit Center.

INFORMATION

Tourist offices Coming from the US, the most convenient tourist office is right at the border, at the pedestrian entry point (Mon–Sat 9am–6pm, Sun 9am–3pm; 664 683 1405). The main state-run tourist information centre is on Revolución between calles 2a and 3a (Mon–Fri 8am–8pm, Sat & Sun 9am–1pm; 664 973 0430); there's another information booth on Revolución between calles 3a and 4a (daily 9am–6pm, closed alternate Weds; 664 685 3117).

GETTING AROUND

By bus Tijuana by bus is cheap but confusing – taxis are easier to use. The system includes larger city buses (*camiones*) and smaller minibuses or old school buses (known as *calafias*), but all of them should have the final destination on the windscreen, such as "Central Camionera" – just flag them down on the street. There are no route maps, however, and you'll need to speak Spanish well to use them.

By taxi The easiest and quickest way to get around is by taxi. Cheapest are the fixed-route taxis (*los taxis de ruta*), which operate more like small minibuses. Regular cabs generally fall into two groups: the yellow *taxis amarillos*, which don't use meters and follow a fixed-rate system, and the independent *taxis libres*, which sometimes use the meter but usually set their own prices. Yellow taxis should have a set fare from the border to Zona Río or La Revo, to the airport and to the bus station (check the prices on the board at the taxi rank; you can pay in US$). Similarly, *taxis libres* will usually charge a flat fee for trips within the centre. Uber (http://uber.com), the ride-sharing service, is available in Tijuana.

By car All the major firms have desks at Tijuana airport: Budget 664 634 3303; Hertz 664 607 3950; Thrifty 664 683 8130.

ACCOMMODATION

SEE MAP PAGE 512

★ **Hotel Ticuán** 8190 C 8, at Revolución (Zona Centro); http://hotelticuan.mx. By far the best hotel in downtown Tijuana, with a convenient location just off La Revo and a 20min walk from the border. Rooms are spacious, modern and come with flatscreen TVs with cable. Friendly, English-speaking staff complete the experience. M$$$

Lucerna Paseo de los Héroes 10902 (Zona Río); http://hoteleslucerna.com. The six-storey main building and three annexes surround an outdoor pool with a mini waterfall. The best rooms, along with two restaurants and a bar, face this courtyard area. Every room has satellite TV, a balcony, coffee-maker, a/c and purified water. M$$$$

Nelson Revolución 721, at C 1a (Zona Centro); 664 685 4302. Right at the top of La Revo, this stucco palace can't be beaten for location or price, but the street noise can be relentless at times. *Nelson* is one of La Revo's oldest hotels (open since 1948), so although the rooms have a/c and cable TV with a few channels, they're otherwise quite dated and worn. M$

Tijuana Marriott Agua Caliente 11553 (Zona Río); http://

marriott.com. The former *Emporio* has been revamped as an upmarket *Marriott* with all the extras – business centre, gym and pool – though the rooms are fairly standard business hotel affairs. Free parking for guests and reasonable online discounts make this a good deal. M$$$$

EATING

SEE MAP PAGE 512

ZONA CENTRO

★**Caesar's** Revolución 1071, between C 4 and C 5; https://www.grupoplascencia.com/caesars. Legend has it that Caesar Cardini first whipped up his eponymous salad in Tijuana in 1924, and this shrine to his memory still prepares the dish tableside with raw egg and garlic, Parmesan cheese, anchovies and hearts of Romaine lettuce in an elaborate ceremony. The rest of the menu is continental-style, with pastas, steaks and the like. M$$$

Chiki Jai Galeana 1931, at Revolución; 664 685 4955. Enticing Spanish Basque *taberna*, draped with bullfighting memorabilia, fading photos of Tijuana and paintings of Don Quixote. Come here for decent tapas, paella, sangria and *vino tinto*. Open since 1947: the likes of Errol Flynn, Rita Hayworth and Ava Gardner once ate here. M$$

★**Tortas del Washmobile** Jalisco 2424, just south of Agua Caliente (fifteen blocks south of La Revo). This famous stall (with tall yellow top) was established in 1964 next to a petrol station with a car wash (still there), and serves only one thing: a mouthwatering *mesquite* grilled steak sandwich marinated in a zesty sauce (*torta carne asada*). Served on *pambaso* rolls; ask for *con todo* and you'll also get heaps of guacamole and a topping of red onions, tomatoes and salsa. Taxis should know it. M$$

ZONA RÍO

La Diferencia Sánchez Taboada 10521; http://ladiferencia.com. *Diferencia* has a more daring menu than most places in Tijuana, with tasty interpretations of Mexico's pre-Hispanic cuisine. Unfamiliar dishes like beef-tongue strips with chiles, the Aztec delicacy crêpes Cuitlacoche (an edible corn fungus) and prickly-pear salad are made more appealing within a romantic setting complete with a courtyard and fountain. M$$$

Mariscos El Mazateño Calzada Tecnológico 473 at Popotla, Fracc Tomás Aquino; https://mariscos-el-mazateo.shop. Take a taxi to this iconic *taquería* for their spicy Sinaloan-style *Taco Mazatena* (*camarón enchilado* or shrimp taco), and filling smoked marlin tacos. Tables inside, but most locals eat standing up or crouched on the sidewalk outside. Cash only. M$

★**Misión 19** Misión de San Javier 10643; http://mision19.com. Javier Plascencia's fashionable temple to "Baja Med" cuisine, all concrete, wood and floor-to-ceiling windows, features innovative menus fed by local wine and produce: think Peking duck with kumquat, sweet potato and blood orange sauce, risotto with beans and truffles and charred octopus with pistachio, *garbanzo* beans and smoky *habanero* sauce. M$$$$

Origen Argentino Escuadrón 201, no. 3151; https://origenargentino.com. Argentine grill lauded for its succulent steaks, chops and extensive wine list, as well as the city's best fries, coated in parsley and garlic. M$$$$

★**La Querencía** Escuadrón 201, no. 3110; 664 972 9935. Established in 2006 by celebrity chef Miguel Guerrero, this fancy restaurant with lacquered steel dining tables and open kitchens is one of the creators of contemporary Baja Med cuisine, a blend of traditional Mexican ingredients with Mediterranean flavours. Try the *betabel* (beet) carpaccio, oyster (*ostión*) tacos or more substantial fish of the day. M$$$$

★**Tacos Salceados** Ermita Nte 30-A; 664 608 1744. Known locally as *La Ermita*, after the street, this knocks out the best beef tacos in the city with at least fifteen spicy salsas to choose from. Chef Javier Campos Guttiérez is also known for his gourmet creations such as smoked salmon, shrimp and strawberry, or *nopal* tacos (prickly-pear cactus). Seating is available here, but it's so popular there's almost always a wait for tables. Cash only. M$

Villa Saverios Sánchez Taboada and Escuadrón 201; http://villasaverios.com. Set inside a marble, Tuscan-themed villa, this is another superb exponent of Baja Med cuisine, with such dishes as classic chicken cordon bleu and "Retro" scampi, the classic dish from the 1970s (pan-seared shrimp/crab, with garlic lemon and caper cream sauce). Situated in the heart of Tijuana's Zona Gastronómica. M$$$$

DRINKING AND NIGHTLIFE

SEE MAP PAGE 512

Traditionally, the rowdiest action in Tijuana is along **La Revo**, where numerous pubs pump out rock music and hip-hop – aim for "La Sexta" (C 6 off Revolución) for a more contemporary cluster of bars. Most locals and visitors in the know shun La Revo in favour of the clubs and bars clustered around the shopping areas of **Zona Río**. The city has also experienced a boom in **microbreweries** in recent years, with Plaza Fiesta (see below) a good place to start.

BARS

★**El Dandy Del Sur** C 6 (Flores Magón) no. 2030, between La Revo and Madero; 664 688 0052. Open since 1957 but immortalized by local techno group the Nortec Collective in 2005, this jukebox bar just off La Revo is popular with artists and plenty of locals escaping the tourist drag. The walls are decorated with mirrors and pictures of movie stars; tends to attract serious drinkers long into the early hours.

La Mezcalera C 6 no. 8267 (between Revolución and Madero); 664 688 0384. Friendly bar and restaurant that looks like a shopfront, featuring, unsurprisingly, mescal, the traditional and extremely potent Mexican spirit made from the agave plant. They usually have at least six different brands of the stuff and nine different types of crema de mescal (a blend of mescal and agave syrup).

★ **Plaza Fiesta** Paseo de los Héroes 1001. Can't decide where to go? Locals often head here without a specific place in mind, preferring to wander between the bars and clubs until they find a scene that appeals to them. In recent years local craft microbreweries have moved in, with *El Tigre* serving Lúdica Artesanal beers, *El Depa* serving Cerveza Silenus, the *Border Psycho Tasting Room* and *Bierjar The Beer Kingdom*.

★ **TJ Tap House** Fundadores 2951; 664 638 8662. Home of *Cerveza Tijuana*, the city's acclaimed microbrewery houses a congenial pub, a few minutes' south of La Revo by taxi. Decked out with dark wood panelling and hardwood floors, the pub usually offers five or six hand-crafted Czech-style lagers and a menu of decent bar food. You can look into the brewery floor through a window, but tours must be arranged in advance.

CLUBS

Las Pulgas Revolución 1127 (between C7 and C8); http://laspulgas.mx. Party central on La Revo, a massive club with several rooms pumping out banda, salsa, Latino pop and Norteño, with live bands often supplementing house DJs. Cover charge at weekends.

Sticky Social Savage Club Av. Revolución 993; 664 847 6123. This super-club-performance space is a gathering place for Tijuana's creative class, who turn up for the foam parties and late-night raves.

DIRECTORY

Banks and exchange US dollars are accepted almost everywhere in Tijuana, but you do get a slightly better return on pesos. If you're visiting no further south than Ensenada there's really no reason to change your currency – you'll lose in the exchange rate whatever savings you'd get buying in shops. If you do change it's no problem, with *casas de cambio* on virtually every corner. ATMs along Revolución dispense both dollars and pesos.

Books Sanborn's department store, at Revolución 1102 and C 8a (664 688 1433), has books and magazines, some from across the border. The Gandhi bookshop at Paseo Héroes 9111, at General M. Márquez in Zona Río (http://gandhi.com.mx), also has a good selection.

Consulates Canada, Germán Gedovius 10411, Zona Río, 664 684 0461 (Mon–Fri 9.30am–12.30pm); UK, Salinas 1500, 664 686 5320; US, Paseo de las Culturas s/n, Mesa de Otay, 664 622 7400 (Mon–Fri 9am–2pm).

Hospital Centro Medico Excel, Paseo de los Héroes 2507; 664 634 7001.

Police If you become a victim of crime, a rip-off or simply want to make a complaint, pick up any local phone and dial 078 (foreign mobiles often cannot connect with this number). Call 066 for emergencies.

Post office Negrete and C 11a (Mon–Fri 8am–4pm, Sat & Sun 9.30am–1pm), though to send international mail you're better off crossing the border.

Rosarito

To escape the hectic pace and noise of Tijuana, head for the coastal city of **ROSARITO**, about 45 minutes' drive south on the old road to Ensenada. **Beaches** in Tijuana are invariably crowded and dirty, so Rosarito's longer and sandier beach is a good alternative and provides a more restful atmosphere during the week (the water is still chilly, however). Rosarito has been hit hard by US travel warnings (even putting off US spring-breakers), though you'll see plenty of domestic tourists on the beach surfing or riding ATVs, horses and camels; visitors (and the city's fourteen thousand expats) rarely experience any trouble. As in Tijuana, US dollars are accepted virtually everywhere.

ARRIVAL AND DEPARTURE — ROSARITO

By bus If you're continuing south to Ensenada and beyond, you can try to pick up long-distance buses (at least hourly) at the *autopista* tollbooth 1km south of the tourist office, past the *Rosarito Beach Hotel*, but it's much easier to head back to Tijuana's main bus station (see page 514).

By car To get to Rosarito from Tijuana, drive south along either the toll (*cuota*) Hwy-1D or free (*libre*) Hwy-1 for 25km.

By taxi Taxis from the border charge a moderate amount. You can also take one of the cheaper *taxi de ruta* vans that leave from Madero between calles 3 and 4; to get back, try flagging down a *taxi de ruta* on Juárez, Rosarito's main street.

INFORMATION

Rosarito Convention and Visitors' Bureau Runs three tourist information booths during US holidays and special

9

LOBSTER TOWN

Once not much more than a dusty roadside settlement between Rosarito and Ensenada at Hwy-1 km 44, **Puerto Nuevo** is nowadays known the length of the peninsula for its near-fanatical devotion to the local speciality that bears its name: Puerto Nuevo-style grilled Pacific **lobster**. Found off the coast and throughout the rest of the Pacific Rim, these lobsters don't grow as large as their Atlantic counterparts (actually, they're giant langoustines more closely related to shrimps) and they don't have claws, but they're just as delicious.

Choosing where to sample the revered dish is made easy enough by the town's one-way street plan, which juts to the west from Hwy-1; almost every one of the thirty-odd restaurants here serves lobsters the same way, grilled and split in half with beans, rice and warm flour tortillas (prices vary depending on the size of the lobster). Most restaurants open 10am to 8pm on weekdays, with some open until 11pm Friday and Saturday. Cash only.

events, the most convenient of which can be found at the Centro Comercial Oceana Plaza, Local 14, Blvd Benito Juárez 907 (Mon–Fri 9am–6pm, Sat 10am–1pm; 661 612 0396, http://rosarito.org).

ACCOMMODATION

Accommodation prices are highest during Spring Break (Feb/March) and the week after Christmas, but drop considerably the rest of the year. Throughout the year it's advisable to reserve at least a week in advance if you plan on staying Fri or Sat night.

★ **Rosarito Beach Hotel** Benito Juárez 31; http://rosaritobeachhotel.com. Legendary hotel, established in 1926 and giving the city its name; it's now a mini-village with a spa, restaurants, bars, two pools, time-share apartments, a racquetball court, craft shops, liquor stores, a history museum and an internet café. Many of the rooms have ocean views but are otherwise without charm; request an older room with garden view – they've managed to retain some character. M$$$$

EATING

La Flor de Michoacan Benito Juárez 291 (Hwy-1); 661 612 1858. Founded in 1950 on the north side of town, this popular family restaurant pulls in tourists and locals for its piles of crispy *carnitas* (fried pork) served with rice, beans, guacamole and fresh tortillas. You might want to throw in a pitcher or two of strawberry margaritas when you're here. M$$

★ **Tacos Baja Junior** Carretera Libre Rosarito–Ensenada (Hwy-1) km 28.8; 661 119 7216. Another local favourite, this diner-like place stands on the main road 1.5km south of the *Rosarito Beach Hotel*. Try their *Plato Fiesta,* which comes with local fish, shrimp, calamari, octopus and tacos (enough for two people). Their trademark tacos are pretty good too; the *taco gobernador* is crammed with shrimp marinated in chiles and lemons. M$

★ **Tacos El Yaqui** La Palma 51, at Mar del Norte; 661 612

BAJA LEGENDS: HALFWAY HOUSE AND LA FONDA

Some 25km south of Rosarito, the legendary **Halfway House** (aka *Medio Camino,* "halfway" between Tijuana and Ensenada, at Hwy-1 km 53; http://mediocamino.com) opened as a cantina in 1922 on a cliff overlooking the ocean. Today the old-fashioned dining room may have changed little since the 1920s, but the menu certainly has: think quality seafood and the infamous "golden cadillac" margaritas.

A little further south, at km 59.5 in La Misión, **La Fonda Hotel** is another legendary hideaway (Eva Gabor spent her honeymoon here), established in 1962 by Eve Stocker. It was sold to Orest "Joe" Dmytriw in 1975 who sold it in turn to US expats Gary "Doc" and Shawnie Rettig in 2004. However, since then the site has been divided in two thanks to ongoing legal disagreements between Dmytriw and the Rettigs; the latter runs the newer "**Gary's La Fonda**" (https://cafedelafonda.mx) offering stellar food, sensational views and live entertainment, while Dmytriw manages the original, ageing, rustic Mexican inn ("**Dmytri's Original La Fonda Resturant**"), with easy access to the beach (one of the best **surf breaks** in Baja). Both restaurants offer the famed buffet and all-you-can drink Bloody Marys on Sunday.

1352. This small taco joint knocks out some of the best (and biggest) *carne asada* tacos on the coast. Tacos (flour tortillas only) with all the toppings are around a bargain; you can add cheese for a couple more pesos. Cash only. **M$**

DRINKING AND NIGHTLIFE

Traditionally, Rosarito's most popular bars and clubs have been contained within what's known as the Barbachano Zone, the area between Juárez (Hwy-1) and Coronado downtown. Thanks to the drop in US visitors (especially college students), things have quietened down considerably in recent years – visit *Papas and Beer* to check out the latest situation.

Papas and Beer Coronado 400, at Eucalipto; http://papasandbeer.com. College party-goers flock to this mega club, the largest on the West Coast (with a pool, mechanical bull and volleyball court thrown in). Tacos, burritos, quesadillas, nachos and fries help soak up the Corona and tequila shots. Busy Fri & Sat but often empty on weekdays.

Ensenada

Perched on the edge of the Bahía de Todos Santos, 100km south of Tijuana, the attractive port of **ENSENADA** is far calmer, cheaper and smaller than its northern rival, making for an inviting pit stop and jumping-off point for the **wineries** to the east. Like Tijuana, Ensenada is a relatively recent creation by Mexican standards, despite being officially "founded" (ie discovered by the Spanish) in 1542; nothing much happened until 1872, when gold was unearthed in nearby Real de Castillo. Ensenada was gradually developed as a port, the modern town effectively planned and developed by American investor George H. Sisson and the British-owned Mexican Land & Colonization Co in the 1880s. The town remained a backwater, however, with tourism and modern development only taking off in the 1950s. Note that US cruise excursions to Ensenada are booming, so be prepared for crowds on days that ships are in port (mainly during the summer months).

Downtown

Ensenada's downtown is centred on the parallel **Bulevar Lázaro Cárdenas** (the waterfront) and **Avenida López Mateos** (or C 1a, "La Primera"). On the latter you'll find scores of souvenir shops and outfits offering sport-fishing trips, as well as the bulk of the bars, hotels and restaurants. The six-block-long malecón, running along the waterfront parallel to Lázaro Cárdenas, is where the city's residents gather for sunset strolls and special events; the centrepiece is the **Plaza Ventana al Mar**, with its monumental Mexican flag visible all over town. In contrast, the real commercial heart of town is **Avenida Juárez**, five blocks north, where you'll find all the Mexican chain stores.

Mercado de Mariscos

Malecón, at Miramar

At the northwestern end of the malecón, the **Mercado de Mariscos** (aka Mercado Negro) contains numerous stalls selling the day's catches. The diversity of what's on display – from squirming eel and smoked fish to giant abalone – is impressive, and it's a good place to try the town's lauded **fish tacos**, which were supposedly invented in Ensenada and have been served at the market since it opened in 1958 (see page 523).

Museo Histórico Regional de Ensenada

Gastélum 56, between López Mateos (C 1) and Virgilio Uribe • Free • 646 178 3692

For a general history of the peoples and cultures of Baja California, head over to the **Museo Histórico Regional de Ensenada**, built in 1886 as a military barracks and serving as the Ensenada jail until 1986. The old cells and rooms now act as galleries chronicling the history of the building, the town and the region with rare black-and-white photos, artefacts and displays (mostly Spanish only).

9

ENSENADA

ACCOMMODATION

Casa Petri Hotel	2
Estero Beach Resort	5
Hotel Coral & Marina	6
Hotel Cortez	3
Posada El Rey Sol	1
San Nicolás Hotel & Casino	4

EATING

Bronco's	2
La Cocedora De Langosta	6
La Guerrerense	4
El Charro	3
Manzanilla	8
El Rey Sol	5
Tacos Fenix	1
Tacos Lucero	7

DRINKING & NIGHTLIFE

Bar Andaluz	4
Cervecería Wendlandt	3
Hussong's Cantina	1
Papas & Beer	2

Terminal de Autobuses
C 10A
C 9A
C 8A
C 7A
C 6A
Ryerson
Moctezuma
Obregón
Ruiz
Gastélum
Miramar
Riveroll
Alvarado
Blancarte
Castillo
Arroyo de Ensenada
Parque Revolución
Bodegas de Santo Tomás
Quinta
Cuarta
Tercera
Segunda
Avenida Juárez (C 5A)
Calimex Supermarket
C 4A
C 3A
C 2A
Macheros
Espinosa
Floresta
Guadalupe
Hidalgo
Chapultepec Hills
Avenida López Mateos (C 1A)
Museo de la Exaduana Marítima
Museo Histórico Regional
Taxi Rank
Plaza Cívica
Malecón
Bulevar Lázaro Cárdenas
Mercado de Mariscos
Plaza Ventana al Mar
Tricones
Bucaneros
Centro Cultural Riviera
Club Rotario
Centro Estatal de la Artes
Las Rocas
Museo El Caracol
Las Brisas
All Saints Bay
Cruise ship terminal
Bulevar Tte Azueta
0 300 metres
La Paz San Felipe (250km) via HWY 3
5 (12.5km), La Bufadora (36km), El Rosario (250km) & La Paz (1370km)
6, Tijuana (100km) via HWY 1 Free and Toll Roads & Valle de Guadalupe (40km) via HWY 3

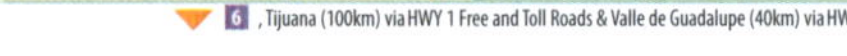

Centro Cultural Riviera de Ensenada

Lázaro Cárdenas 1421, at Club Rotario • Free • http://rivieradeensenada.com.mx • **Museo de Historia** Charge • 646 178 3692

The Riviera del Pacifico, a former casino and hotel completed in lavish Spanish Revival style in 1930, is now the bayfront **Centro Cultural Riviera de Ensenada**. You can wander through the tranquil gardens, grab a drink at *Bar Andaluz* (see page 523), or visit the absorbing **Museo de Historia** inside. Exhibition rooms here focus on prehistoric and native cultures of Baja California, the eighteenth-century Spanish missions and the ultimate decimation of the native population through disease, all via old photos, objects and labelling in Spanish and English.

Caracol (Museo de Ciencas)

Club Rotario 3 • Charge (discounts for children 6–12 and students) • https://www.caracolbc.org

The mammoth complex opposite the cultural centre is the **Caracol (Museo de Ciencas)** a fancy science museum showcasing the geology and environments of Baja – its opening was delayed for years thanks to budget shortfalls, a planned aquarium remains unfinished, and only a fraction of the space is currently being used. Nevertheless, the interactive displays that are open can be fun for kids, with one of the highlights a very realistic earthquake simulator (Spanish labels only).

Museo de la Exaduana Marítima

Ryerson 99, at Ruiz • Free • 646 178 2531

The tiny **Museo de la Exaduana Marítima** is located within a wooden Victorian building that was actually shipped over from England in 1887. Initially occupied by the American Co (developer of the city), it was taken over by Mexican Land & Colonization Co before becoming the customs house in 1922. Today it houses temporary exhibitions on the trade history of the region, such as artefacts recovered from the wrecks of Spanish galleons.

Bodegas de Santo Tomás

Miramar 666, between calles 6a and 7a • Charge for tastings • http://santo-tomas.com

Established in 1888, the **Bodegas de Santo Tomás**, one of the peninsula's largest and oldest wineries, offers tastings (of cheese and olive oil in addition to wine) and tours of its Ensenada museum and premises. You can also visit the main **vineyard** (daily 10am–5pm; call ahead) on the site of the old Santo Tomás mission. It's the only major producer not located in the Valle de Guadalupe – you'll find it off Hwy-1 at km 49 (no public transport).

The beaches

Although it enjoys an enviable position on the Pacific, Ensenada lacks good **beaches**, and to find a decent stretch of sand you'll have to head about half an hour south. As in other parts of Baja it can be difficult to get to many of the best beaches without your own transport; however, you can catch a local bus from Cárdenas (every 30min) to **San Miguel**, 11km north of downtown. Devotees claim San Miguel has the **best waves** in northern Baja and it's been a surf hot spot for years; huge swells barrel down a rocky headland here, and it's definitely not for beginners. It also gets very crowded, so arrive early. The best **beaches** for swimming and sunbathing are at **Estero**, some 10km to the south and 2km off the main road.

La Bufadora

The most popular natural attraction in the Ensenada area, **La Bufadora** ("the snorter") is actually a blowhole, where the combined action of wind, waves and an incoming tide periodically forces a huge jet of sea water up through a vent in the roof of an undersea cavern, in ideal conditions (high tide) reaching 25–30m. Even though it's more than 20km off the main road (34km from Ensenada), and accessed by a gauntlet of souvenir stands, it's definitely worth a visit (free entry). To get there, catch a local bus at Cárdenas and Macheros labelled "Maneadero" and tell the driver you want to visit La Bufadora. Where he drops you you'll be able to catch another local bus to the blowhole at the end of Punta Banda. The whole trip should take around one hour. Taxis are open to negotiation, but tend to ask for pretty sizable return fare (minimum four), including an hour at the site.

ARRIVAL AND DEPARTURE — ENSENADA

By bus The tiny Terminal de Autobuses is at C 11a and Riveroll; there's a café and ATM but not much else. To reach the bayfront, turn right out of the station and head down Riveroll – it's a long walk with luggage (over 1km). Taxis also run along this route. Getting to Tijuana is easy from here, but most of the buses to points south in Baja are *de paso* (passing through), so try to book in advance. Most buses north make for the inconvenient Tijuana central bus station, but some go direct to the airport or the US border (*frontera*) – make sure you get the right one (if you're staying near La Revo in Tijuana, get the bus to the border). Buses to Guadalajara and Mexico City are also less frequent, and you have to change in Mexicali for most other destinations.

Destinations Guerrero Negro (6 daily; 10hr); La Paz (4 daily; 22hr); Loreto (4 daily; 16hr); Mexicali (4 daily; 4hr); San Felipe (2 daily; 4hr); Tijuana (hourly; 1hr 30min).

By car You'll pay three tolls coming south from Tijuana on Hwy-1D (*cuota*). In Ensenada, Hwy-1, Hwy-1D and Hwy-3 merge into one four-lane local road that, once downtown, becomes Blvd Lázaro Cárdenas (also known as Blvd Costero) and runs along the waterfront. Entering town from the south is a bit messier. Hwy-1 enters the city as Av Reforma; to get downtown, turn left on Libramiento Sur.

BOATS, BIKES AND THE BAJA 1000

Ensenada hosts numerous events aimed squarely at the large US encampment in town, from sporting contests to food and wine festivals. The **Newport to Ensenada Yacht Race** (http://nosa.org) in April is one of the largest international regattas in the world, with yachts leaving Newport, California, on a Friday afternoon and finishing in Ensenada a day later, when the partying commences and the town gets packed. April (and September) is also when the **Rosarito–Ensenada Bike Ride** (http://rosaritoensenada.com) draws thousands of cyclists here for the scenic 80km "fun ride", while off-road racing is the focus during the **Baja 500** (June) and the **Baja 1000** (Nov).

INFORMATION AND ACTIVITIES

Tourist information The helpful Ensenada Visitor Information Centre (daily 8am–8pm; 646 178 2411, http://facebook.com/proturismoensenada) is at the Hwy-1 entrance into town at Lázaro Cárdenas 540 and Teniente Azueta, with a smaller booth in Plaza Cívica de la Patria, on Cárdenas at Macheros (daily Tues–Sun 10am–6pm; 646 178 3070). The state-run tourism centre is at the southern end of the malecón at Lázaro Cárdenas 609 and Los Rocas (Mon–Fri 8am–5pm, Sat & Sun 9am–1pm; 646 178 8578).

Whale-watching tours From mid-December to mid-April, the California grey whale migration from the Arctic to the peninsula's Pacific coast can be seen on daily whale-watching tours from Ensenada, although what you'll see is nothing compared to Baja California Sur (see pages 531 and 533). There are several tour companies in the harbour that offer half-day excursions, charged per person. See http://sergiosfishing.com.

ACCOMMODATION

SEE MAP PAGE 520

If you're hoping for somewhere to **stay** at the weekend – the best time for nightlife – book ahead or arrive early; during the week there should be no problem. Though **rates** in general are high (and higher still at weekends), you'll find cheaper places on López Mateos. The best **resorts** tend to be located a long taxi ride from the centre, and are only really practical for those with cars.

CENTRO

Casa Petri Hotel Av Adolfo López Mateos 1487; www.casapetri.com.mx. One of the best central hotels in Baja — with especially good weekend rates (if booked well in advance). M$$$

Hotel Cortez López Mateos 1089; https://bajainn.com/baja-inn-ensenada. The *Baja Inn* hotels are the northern peninsula's three-star stalwarts: rather plain, but always clean and packed with basic amenities like a/c, TV, a gym and a heated pool. M$$$

Posada El Rey Sol Blancarte 130 1119; http://posadaelreysol.com. Great boutique hotel near the centre, with nicely renovated, contemporary-style rooms with cable TV, small pool and spa plus decent breakfast included. M$$$

San Nicolás Hotel & Casino López Mateos 1536, at Guadalupe; http://snhotelcasino.com. The closest hotel to the downtown waterfront has popular packages that include meals and deals with local aquatic outfitters. Murals by a protégé of Diego Rivera adorn many of the public spaces, and there's an Olympic-size swimming pool – the general effect is of a slightly quirky, 1970s throwback. Breakfast is always good, as are the margaritas. M$$$

OUTSIDE ENSENADA

Estero Beach Resort Lupita Novelo, off Hwy-1 around 13km south of downtown; http://hotelesterobeach.com. Best-value resort in the region; some rooms are starting to show their age, but come with terracotta-tiled floors, cable TV, private patios and gardens. Most offer views across the private beach and bay. The pool, bars and restaurants are all excellent, though taxis will charge you a fair bit for rides into town. M$$$$

Hotel Coral & Marina Hwy-1 km 103, Zona Playitas 3421; http://hotelcoral.com. This luxurious option is popular with American yachties for the excellent on-site marina facilities, and is a great choice for families or for those looking for a comfortable resort; standard rooms come with breezy ocean views and all the amenities, but it will cost you to take a taxi into town. M$$$$

EATING

SEE MAP PAGE 520

Bronco's López Mateos 1525; http://broncossteaks.com. The five blocks that separate *Bronco's* from the heart of the tourist district will save you a good amount on a filet mignon. With spurs everywhere, the Wild West theme is over the top, but live bands on weekends add to the authenticity. Good-value lunch buffet Sat & Sun. M$$$

La Cocedora De Langosta La Marina; 646 178 3742. For some of the best seafood in town (without the usual tourist price hike), get in line at La Cocedora De Langosta. The queue rarely goes beyond twenty minutes and the ceviche served with mango and pickled onions is well worth it. The Bloody Marys are particularly good here too. M$$$

★ **La Guerrerense** Alvarado at López Mateos; http://laguerrerense.com. You'll see tiny mobile seafood stalls all over Ensenada, but you should definitely try this one helmed by Doña Sabina Bandera ("La Guerrerense" herself, now a minor celebrity thanks to TV chefs Anthony Bourdain and Rick Bayless). Fresh fish, shrimp, clam, sea urchin (*erizo*), mussel tostadas and crab *ceviche*, as well as sea cucumber for the more adventurous, have been served here since 1960. Go early; cash only. Try also her small restaurant (same name) around the corner at López Mateos 917. M$

El Charro López Mateos 454; 646 178 2114. Knocking out crisp rotisserie chicken since 1956 (you'll see them roasting in the window), but also serves the full roster of classic Mexican dishes. M$$$

Manzanilla Teniente Azueta 139; http://rmanzanilla.com. This outpost of celebrity chef Benito Molina next to the port features a spacious, antique bar decorated with local art and wonderful food, from posh Spanish bar snacks like fresh sardines on toast to dinners featuring specials such as *pescado en caldo* and seafood risotto. Pricey but worth it. M$$$$

El Rey Sol López Mateos 1000; http://elreysol.com. This venerable French-style seafood restaurant was opened in 1947 (by the daughter of a French engineer working in Santa Rosalía), and despite the hype remains an essential Ensenada experience. Stick with classics such as French onion soup, Caesar salad for two and clams "El Rey Sol". M$$$

★ **Tacos Fenix** Espinosa at Juárez, 646 977 1191. This three-person stand operates from a sidewalk next to the former Ferretería Fenix tyre shop, from which it derives its name. The superb fish tacos are made to order with home-made batter and angel shark, and in your hands before they have time to cool. Not to be confused with the almost as good *Tacos Mi Ranchito "Fenix"* at the corner of Espinosa and C 6. M$

Tacos Lucero Mercado Negro. The market is littered with stalls selling fish tacos, but this is one of the more dependable vendors, a small stand tucked away near the southern entrance. The fish is fresh and succulent, but the tubs of help-yourself salsas on each table really make this a stand-out option. M$

DRINKING AND NIGHTLIFE

SEE MAP PAGE 520

★ **Bar Andaluz** Centro Cultural Riviera, Lázaro Cárdenas 1421; http://rivieradeensenada.com.mx/bar-andaluz. This elegant Spanish Revival bar is one of the most appealing watering holes in Baja, with tiled floors, vivid murals, a wooden bartop and sunny courtyard. One of many claimants for "home of the margarita" (David Negrete allegedly created it here in 1948, for one Margarita King Plant).

★ **Cervecería Wendlandt** Costero 248; 646 178 2938. Like other Baja towns, Ensenada is fast developing its own craft brew scene, with local beer maker Wendlandt operating this warehouse and tap room for connoisseurs to sample its popular oatmeal stout, Vaquita Marina pale ale and excellent Perro Del Mar IPA.

Hussong's Cantina Ruiz 113; 646 178 3210. Established in 1892 by German immigrant Johann Hussong and now a tourist destination with its own line in T-shirts, *Hussong's* is still an honest bar packed with locals and gringos. The floors are covered in sawdust, the bands are *norteña* and the drink of choice is a margarita – like other bars in the area, legend has it the tequila cocktail was actually invented here in 1941 (for one Margarita Henkel).

Papas & Beer López Mateos 335 at Ruiz; http://papasandbeer.com. It's hard to ignore the ubiquitous Baja party chain, but at least it delivers; plenty of wild boozing, live music and themed party nights, especially during Spring Break.

DIRECTORY

Banks Most are on Ruiz, a few blocks north of López Mateos; with the upsurge in cruise-ship visitors, almost every business in the centre accepts US dollars.

Internet Free wireless hot spots are all over town – try the malecón – and wi-fi is offered free in many restaurants and bars.

Post office Club Rotario and Mateos.

Valle de Guadalupe

The vineyards of the **Valle de Guadalupe**, just east of Ensenada, are not quite Napa Valley standard, but the region is clearly on the right track, as illustrated by growing international acclaim and the pioneering work of French-trained winemaker Hugo d'Acosta since the 1990s. Though you can show up at the major wineries without a reservation, it is best to call **vineyards** before visiting, especially if you're coming in the warmer months (July–Sept). The villages of **San Antonio de las Minas** in the southwest and **Francisco Zarco** and **El Porvenir** in the northeast are the centres of the valley's production.

BAJA WINES: FIVE OF THE BEST

Once derided for watery grapes and poor vintage, Baja wines have gathered a loyal following since the late 1990s thanks to small-production, high-quality boutique wines. These are five of the best:

Vino de Piedra, Casa de Piedra Tones of black fruit lace this blend of Tempranillo and Cabernet Sauvignon.

Viñas de Camou, Château Camou Bordeaux-style blend of Cabernet Sauvignon, Cabernet Franc and Merlot.

Cabernet Sauvignon/Merlot, Monte Xanic Smooth, dark-red wine with a peppery aroma.

Special Reserve Chardonnay, Château Camou One of the best white wines in the valley.

Gabriel, Adobe Guadalupe Another exquisite red-wine blend (55 percent Merlot), produced by Hugo d'Acosta.

Museo de la Vid y el Vino

Hwy-3 km 81 (just outside Francisco Zarco) • Charge • https://museodelavidyelvinobc.com

Surrounded by vineyards, the beautifully designed **Museo de la Vid y el Vino** offers an impressive introduction to the region and its history of wine-making through digital media, exhibits and displays (from giant wine barrels to antique grape presses and ancient amphorae), though not much is labelled in English. The museum staff can also help arrange tours of the valley.

Museo Comunitario Ruso

Principal 276, Francisco Zarco • Charge • 646 155 2030

Only a handful of current residents of the valley claim **Russian ancestry** (see page 525), but you can get to grips with their legacy at **Museo Comunitario Ruso** in Francisco Zarco, which preserves a small collection of bits and pieces in a restored Russian home dating from 1905. The complex now contains a restaurant (*Restaurante Familia Samarin*) and a shop selling local produce and offering tastings of local wines (M$100). Ask here about the **Panteón Ruso**, the old cemetery nearby, where you'll find fifteen ageing Russian tombstones.

Château Camou

Valle de Guadalupe (from Hwy-3, follow main road into Francisco Zarco, turn north after 3km) • Tours charge • Tours (25–30min) • www.vinicola-chateaucamou.com

Two hundred acres of vineyards surround the mission-style **Château Camou**, housing a modern winery and small tasting room. From here Camou turns out thirty thousand cases of Bordeaux, Zinfandel and a dessert blend of Chardonnay, Chenin Blanc and Sauvignon Blanc. Reservations required.

Casa de Piedra

Hwy-3 km 93.5 • Tastings by appointment only • Free • 646 156 5267, http://vinoscasadepiedra.com

Casa de Piedra is a boutique producer owned by Hugo d'Acosta, producing the highly respected Vino de Piedra (red) and Piedra del Sol (white); since his first harvest in 1997, Acosta's wines have achieved cult-like celebrity.

L.A. Cetto

Hwy-3 km 73.5, Francisco Zarco • Tastings by appointment only • http://lacetto.mx

Although the Cetto family has been bottling wine in Baja California since 1928, they didn't set up their current operation, **L.A. Cetto**, until 1974; they're now the largest producer of table wines in Mexico, noted for their outstanding Nebbiolo, Petite Sirah, Cabernet Sauvignon and Zinfandel. For first-timers, Cetto offers a great introduction to the process through its free wine tours and tastings; it's also one of the few wineries to have food and a dining area.

Adobe Guadalupe

Parcela A-1 s/n, Col Rusa de Guadalupe (from Hwy-3, exit west at the sign to El Tigre, follow the dirt road 4km and turn north; proceed 6km past Vinos Bibayoff, then turn left at the stop sign adjacent to the Unidad Médica Familiar) • Charge • http://adobeguadalupe.com

Gorgeous property owned by US expats Donald and Tru Miller, doubling as an enticing bed and breakfast (see page 525) and gallery for local artist Cecilia García Amaro. Their first harvest was in 2000, with Cabernet Sauvignon, Merlot, Nebbiolo, Cabernet Franc, Tempranillo and Shiraz grown.

Viñedos Bibayoff

Rancho Toro Pintos, Valle de Guadalupe (from Hwy-3, exit west at the sign to El Tigre, follow the dirt road 4km then turn north for another 5.6km) • Tours and wine tasting by appointment only • Charge • https://bibayoff.com.mx

The only Russian-run vineyard still open to the public, **Viñedos Bibayoff** was established in 1906 and still produces five estate wines, including a Nebbiolo and Colombard. The on-site **Museo de la Familia** charts Bibayoff family history since their arrival in Mexico.

ARRIVAL AND TOURS — VALLE DE GUADALUPE

By car To reach the valley from Ensenada, leave the city along Cárdenas and follow Hwy-1 (north) through El Sauzal and exit on Hwy-3 (La Ruta del Vino) towards Tecate, just prior to the beginning of the Hwy-1D toll road north of San Miguel. The vineyards and stores begin in about 10km, near San Antonio de las Minas. With a few exceptions, the valley's vineyards are located on dirt roads that branch off a 25km stretch of the main highway. Detailed signs direct visitors how to navigate the unmarked dirt roads that link the vineyards.

Organized tours If you don't have a car you can arrange a tour from San Diego, Rosarito, Ensenada or Tijuana. Baja Viajes (http://bajaviajes.com) runs popular tours (three vineyards and Museo de la Vid y el Vino) from Tijuana, Rosarito or Ensenada. An interesting option is Valley Girl Wine Tours (646 211 3852, https://facebook.com/valleygirlwinetours), operated by Ava Carolina Perez and Shari Sisco, who give fun and illuminating bespoke tours of the area. Baja Wine Tours (664 625 1240, bajawinetours.net) offers a variety of tours from Tijuana. You can also try and negotiate a half- or full-day tour with taxi drivers in Ensenada.

ACCOMMODATION

Adobe Guadalupe Parcela A-1 s/n, Col Rusa de Guadalupe, off Hwy-3; http://adobeguadalupe.com. This romantic six-room B&B run by American ex-banker Don Miller and his wife Tru also produces wine (see page 525). Rates include breakfast for two and wine tasting (dinner and lunch are extra but wine is included), and you can ride their horses through the vineyards. M$$$$

La Villa del Valle Hwy-3 km 89; http://lavilladelvalle.com. Another gorgeous hotel managed by Brit Phil Gregory and his wife Eileen, with six stylish rooms, a complimentary glass of wine every evening at 5.30pm (from their Vena Cava winery), outdoor pool and jacuzzi. M$$$$

EATING

Laja Hwy-3 km 83, Francisco Zarco; http://laja.meitre.com. Former *Daniel* and *Four Seasons* New York chef Jair Téllez opened this prix-fixe destination (four course and eight course menus available) restaurant in 2001, and with

THE MILK DRINKERS

The **Molokans** (Russian for "milk drinkers") belonged to a religious sect that broke away from the Russian Orthodox Church in the seventeenth century (the name refers to their practice of drinking milk on fast days). During the early twentieth century, around two thousand Russian Molokans emigrated to the Los Angeles area – from here a smaller colony of five hundred, led by Moses Samaduroff, split off and settled in Mexico's Guadalupe Valley in 1905. Wine was already being made here at that time (Bodegas de Santo Tomás opened in 1888), but the Molokans – notably the Bibayoffs, who are still here – helped give the industry a boost.

9

protégé Chef Rafael Magaña now at the helm it continues to draw eager diners with its changing, seasonally influenced menu – expect dishes like sea trout (*curvina*) with roasted peppers and courgettes, and oven-roasted pig with butternut squash and beets. Reservations essential. M$$$$

South to La Paz

South of Ensenada, most travellers follow Hwy-1 as it shifts from suburban sprawl to farmland and then into curvy, hilly passes that eventually drop into the **Santo Tomás valley**. From here it's around 1375km to **La Paz**, a journey which can take twenty hours direct, or preferably several days, taking in the entrancing landscapes and small towns along the way – you'll see far fewer tourists on this stretch of the **Transpeninsular Highway** (see page 511). The alternative (if you have your own transport) is to detour via Hwy-3 and Hwy-5 to **San Felipe**, then take the rugged route along the Sea of Cortez to rejoin Hwy-1 north of Guerrero Negro.

San Felipe

When the paved road to **SAN FELIPE** was completed in 1951, the tiny village was already attracting adventurous sport fishermen for its vast schools of totoaba or **totuava** (a species now fished onto the endangered list). Now a firmly established Baja fishing legend, San Felipe is no longer a frontier town; it still pulls in the fishing crowd, but also accommodates a blend of North American retirees, RV campers, spring-breakers and **off-road motorsports** enthusiasts – thousands of kilometres of trails wind their way through the surrounding desert and folded ridges of the San Pedro Martír mountains. Indeed, San Felipe's population hits around 25,000 in the winter, including some eight thousand North American residents. If fishing and biking don't appeal, San Felipe's gorgeous **beaches** and warm, emerald waters might – it's the best place to swim in northern Baja (at high tide – see page 526).

ARRIVAL AND DEPARTURE — SAN FELIPE

By bus Buses from Mexicali (5 daily; 2hr 30min) and Tijuana (via Mexicali; 4 daily; 5–6hr) via Ensenada arrive at the bus station on Mar de Caribe (Hwy-5) south of the centre: turn left out of the bus station and right down Manzanillo to get to Av Mar de Cortés (1.2km), which runs parallel to the sea. If you're travelling on public transport, this is the end of the line – you'll need to cut back to Tijuana or Mexicali to continue south.

By car Most visitors drive to San Felipe along Hwy-5 from Mexicali and the US border (around 2hr, depending on waits at the military checkpoints en route); fill up in Mexicali because there are no petrol stations on the way. Heading further south, see page 529.

INFORMATION AND ACTIVITIES

Tourist office The tourist office, Chetumal 101 at Mar de Cortés (Mon–Thurs 10am–4pm, Fri & Sat 10am–7pm; 646 577 1865), gives out maps and information, while the best online resource is https://bajacalifornia.travel.

Condor Baja Tours 686 202 2600, http://condorbajatours.com. Professional outfit organizing guided San Felipe dirt bike tours and tours further afield.

Tony Reyes Sports Fishing US +1 714 538 8010, www.facebook.com/tonyreyesfishingtours. Fishing legend Tony Reyes pioneered six-day Midriff Islands boat trips (out to the area of the Sea of Cortez, rich in fish, aka "yellowtail alley") in the 1950s – his son now runs the business.

THE TIDES OF SAN FELIPE

The upper reaches of the Sea of Cortez experience the world's third-largest **tides** – fluctuations of 6–7m are common. You'll soon realize why tide calendars are so common in San Felipe; water that laps lazily against the beach in the morning can recede a kilometre into the hazy distance by mid-afternoon.

ACCOMMODATION

★ **Casa La Vida** Misión de Santo Tomás 2738; http://casalavida.com. Managed by friendly US expats 3km south of downtown (one block from the beach), these three spacious suites come with US cable TV and kitchens. M$$$

La Hacienda de la Langosta Roja Chetumal 125; http://sanfelipelodging.com. The "red lobster" offers 39 simple but comfy rooms in a central part of town, with a/c and satellite TV. M$$

Hotel Las Palmas Mar Baltico 1101, at Isla de Cedros; 686 577 1333. Opened in 1956, this is a place with a colourful history (the on-site restaurant is named after Sicily-born owner Alfredo Bellinghieri, the man who claims to have invented the alfredo sauce), bougainvillea-covered patios, fountains, simple but clean rooms (triples available), satellite TV and small pool. M$$$

EATING

Not surprisingly, **seafood** is the staple diet here, with San Felipe best known for its **fish tacos** and shellfish cocktails; you'll find the best stands at an area known as Plaza Maristacos at the south end of the malecón, near the *Costa Azul Hotel* (the best stall is *Mariscos La Morena*).

Baja Mar Restaurant & Taco Factory Mar de Cortés 100; 686 577 2648. Beachfront diner and sports bar serving seafood, steaks, and classic Mexican and American dishes (with free wi-fi). M$

Fat Boy's Chetumal 101, at Mar de Cortés; 686 577 4092. This expat favourite knocks out decent pizza (try the chorizo), pasta and sandwiches – they also have taco Tuesdays, TV showing US sports events and punchy 64oz margaritas. M$

Rice and Beans Mar de Cortés 262, between Acapulco and Zihuatanejo; 686 577 1770. Sit on the veranda and soak up the sea views over breakfast, good-value fresh fish (excellent fish stew), all sorts of omelettes and stellar margaritas. Free wi-fi. M$$

La Vaquita Puerto Peñasco 233 at Mar de Cortés; 686 577 2837. Local favourite serving the best seafood in town, from *chiles habaneros* stuffed with shellfish and fresh sea bass, to seafood *molcajetes* and Orly shrimps (breaded and filled with cream cheese). Mexicali craft beers served. M$$

DRINKING

★ **Barefoot Bar** Hotel El Cortéz, Mar de Cortés, at Isla de Cedros; 686 577 1055. Classic Baja bar on the sand in front of the *Cortéz*, its wood walls adorned with signed photos of famous off-road racers and sport fishermen; there's even a stained-glass window and a dartboard.

Pizzas & Beer Mar de Cortés 271; 686 516 1936. One row back from the waterfront this simple but chic bar does two things well – pizza and beer. More surprisingly, however, they also mix some pretty decent cocktails.

DIRECTORY

Banks Along Cortés there's a Bancomer (at Acapulco), and a Banamex at Chetumal 42, both with ATMs (though US$ are accepted everywhere).

Hospital There is no hospital in San Felipe; if you have an accident or get sick, there is a small Centro de Salud (medical centre) in town (686 577 1521), on Mar Bermejo Sur and Ensenada, but the closest real hospitals are in Mexicali or across the US border.

Post office Mar Blanco 187, just off Chetumal, five blocks inland.

South of San Felipe

South of San Felipe, cars and motorbikes can continue for around 200km (5–7hr) on Hwy-5 to rejoin Hwy-1 at **Chapula**, a once harrowing journey that is now much easier thanks to the gradual paving of the road. Nevertheless, conditions can change fast; diversions over rougher tracks to avoid road works are common, and in 2018 **Hurricane Rosa** washed out the highway in several places, making the journey possible by 4WD only for several months – always check the latest conditions before setting out. Fill up in San Felipe, as there's no guarantee that you'll find petrol en route. **Puertecitos**, 85km south of San Felipe, is a small US retirement community where you'll find natural hot springs on the beach, a basic restaurant (Sat & Sun only) and a PEMEX petrol station that should be open. Some 68km south of Puertecitos is the turning for the Papa Fernández store and restaurant (http://papafernandez.com), 2km east on the **Bahía San Luis Gonzaga**, one of the most alluring stretches of coast in Baja (you can also camp here). Another 4km south on Hwy-5 is the Gonzaga PEMEX petrol station, across from the Rancho Grande mini market (daily 8am–9pm). Here a dirt road leads

THE VALLEY OF GIANTS

Around 6km south of San Felipe, on the road to Puertecitos (km 14), the privately-owned **Valle de los Gigantes** makes for an intriguing half-day excursion. This section of the desert is littered with towering **cardón cacti**, some of them over 1500 years old and 15m tall. The reserve is open daily 8am–8pm; you can drive the loop road (4WD not needed, unless it has rained) for a fee, or park at the entrance and walk around for a smaller amount.

3km off Hwy-5 along the coast to *Alfonsina's* (664 648 1951, alfonsinasreservations@gmail.com; charge) on the bay, where you can stay in basic digs (a/c 8pm–8am only) and eat. From the Gonzaga PEMEX it's another 37km to isolated Coco's Corner (basic supplies), with a final 21km drive to Hwy-1.

Parque Nacional Sierra de San Pedro Martír

Sierra de San Pedro Martír • Charge • **Observatorio Astronómico Nacional** by reservation only • Free • 646 174 4580

Some 130km south of Ensenada on Hwy-1, a side road at km 141 (San Telmo) heads inland towards the magnificent **Parque Nacional Sierra de San Pedro Martír**, a tranquil alpine reserve that resembles the high sierras of California. The road winds 100km up into the mountains (the park entrance is at km 84; the road is unsurfaced but in good condition beyond here), which includes the peninsula's highest peak, **Picacho del Diablo** (3095m) – where it snows in winter. As you climb, the land becomes increasingly conifer-rich, and at the end of the road (2830m) the **Observatorio Astronómico Nacional** takes advantage of the piercingly clear air – there are mesmerizing views in every direction. The **Museo del Centro de Comunicación y Cultura** (free) near the observatory offers an introduction to the Indigenous history and ecology of the area. Numerous poorly defined trails wind through the park, but again, there's no public transport (or food and gas stations – fill up at the PEMEX station at San Telmo) and you need to be fully equipped for wilderness **camping** if you want to linger (**cabins** are also available M$$$; 646 172 3000).

ACCOMMODATION — PARQUE NACIONAL SIERRA DE SAN PEDRO MARTÍR

Rancho Meling http://ranchomeling.com. Some 50km from Hwy-1, just off the road into the Parque Nacional Sierra de San Pedro Martír, this legendary ranch dates back to 1893, was rebuilt after being destroyed during the 1911 Revolution, and now offers an authentic taste of the Old West, with comfy cabins and rooms. Swimming, biking and horseriding are the most popular activities. Meals are extra. M$$$

San Quintín

Baja's pismo clam capital, **SAN QUINTÍN** is the first town of any size south of Ensenada, and even here, though there are a couple of big hotels, most of the buildings look temporary – English colonists established the town in the 1880s, but development never really took off. Apart from a pit stop to sample the **clams**, there's no reason to stay overnight here unless you are one of the many weekend fishermen destined for the **Bahía San Quintín**, which is undeniably attractive, with five cinder-cone volcanoes as a backdrop to a series of small sandy beaches, endless fishing and superb clam digging. Daily fishing licences can be obtained from local tackle shops or from http://sportfishingbcs.gob.mx. The closest beach (**Playa Santa María**) is some 20km from town (5km off Hwy-1), and there's no public transport.

ARRIVAL AND DEPARTURE — SAN QUINTÍN

By bus Buses heading north and south stop at Lázaro Cárdenas, 5km south of San Quintín, but without your own transport there's little point in getting off here.

ACCOMMODATION AND EATING

Most of the thirty million **clams** harvested in San Quintín end up north of the border, but you can sample the smoked, oversized molluscs at numerous roadside vendors in town.

Hotel Jardines Baja Lázaro Cárdenas (signposted off Hwy-1); www.hoteljardinesbaja.com. One of the best hotels in the San Quintín area, with a variety of comfortable, modern rooms with ceiling fans, lovely gardens and a great. M$$

The Old Mill Lázaro Cárdenas, 5.5km west off Hwy-1 (via a dirt road); 616 165 6030. Converted from the ruins of the old English mill in 1951, this hotel is another Baja classic, reopening in 2012 under new management right on the waterfront; rooms have been renovated, there's hot water and everything works (mostly). The *Molino Viejo* restaurant next door (managed separately) has great food (including clams) and drinks. M$$

El Rosario

Some 60km south of San Quintín, Hwy-1 passes through **EL ROSARIO**, the original site of the first Dominican mission in Baja, founded in 1774. Not much remains of the first mission site – since dubbed **Misión de El Rosario de Arriba** – or its 1802 replacement down river, the **Misión de El Rosario de Abajo**. Since being abandoned in 1832, the remaining adobe ruins of the latter resemble little more than melted walls.

Modern El Rosario is essentially just another pit stop, comprising a petrol station, a few **motels** and a Baja culinary treasure, **Mama Espinoza's**. Beyond El Rosario, the road turns sharply inland and runs down the centre of the peninsula for some 360km to Guerrero Negro, cutting through the protected **Parque Natural del Desierto Central de Baja California**. This is where you head into Baja California proper – barren and godforsaken. For the most part the scenery is dry, brown desert, with the peninsula's low mountain spine on one side and nothing else but sand, a bizarre landscape of cactus and rocks.

ARRIVAL AND DEPARTURE — EL ROSARIO

By bus Long-distance buses will drop off and pick up passengers at the PEMEX station on demand, but moving on you won't be able to book seats in advance. Get an early start (5.30am) and pay on the first bus you see. It's about 7hr through to Tijuana (1hr to San Quintín and 3hr to Guerrero Negro).

By car If you're driving, it's absolutely essential to fill up your tank at the PEMEX station (24hr) here: there's no dependable pump until just north of the state border with Baja California Sur (320km away).

ACCOMMODATION AND EATING

★ **Baja Cactus Motel** Hwy-1 km 55 (San Quintín–Punta Prieta); 616 165 8850. http://bajacactus.com. One of the best bargains in Baja, with plush rooms (make sure you stay in the new wing at the back), satellite TV and wi-fi access. Conveniently positioned between the PEMEX station and *Mama Espinoza's*. M$$

Mama Espinoza's Hwy-1 km 56; 616 165 8770. One of the oldest restaurants on the peninsula, with roots in the 1930s – founder Doña Anita "Mama" Espinoza herself (daughter of a French engineer from Santa Rosalía) passed away at 109 years old in 2016 (there's a museum in her honour). Her famous lobster burritos are rather overpriced, but everything else – beef and pork tacos and big burritos – qualifies as the best food between here and Bahía de los Ángeles. Check out the Baja 1000 and Baja 500 memorabilia on the walls. M$$$

Bahía de los Ángeles

If you have your own transport, a worthy detour off Hwy-1 is **BAHÍA DE LOS ÁNGELES** (also known as L.A. Bay), a small community of fewer than one thousand on the Sea of Cortez. The town maintains an underdeveloped, frontier feeling, little changed from when author John Steinbeck sailed through in 1941 (researching *Log from the Sea of Cortez*), while the eponymous bay teems with sea life and is hemmed in by contorted mountains and lots of enticing beaches. Because of the difficulty getting supplies to the bay, lodging and food are more expensive than you'd expect, and there are no banks or ATMs, so make sure you have enough cash.

Museo de Naturaleza y Cultura

Bahía de los Ángeles • Free • 200 124 9101

There's little in town other than a few hotels, cafés and fishing boats; the one exception is the small bilingual **Museo de Naturaleza y Cultura**, two blocks west of the waterfront. Its location is marked by a narrow-gauge locomotive, a relic of the gold and copper mines that first attracted Europeans to the area. Mining history and that of the local *ranchero* life is well covered, along with details of sea life in the bay. The museum is closed in August and September.

Pinturas Rupestres de Valle Montevideo and Misión San Francisco Borja

About 13km west of Bahía de los Ángeles, signposts off Hwy-12 lead a further 11km along dirt roads to the precious **Pinturas Rupestres de Valle Montevideo**, still vivid (and unprotected) rock art estimated to be ten thousand years old. A drive out here can be combined with a visit to the enigmatic ruins of the **Misión San Francisco Borja**, 20km further along the same dirt road. Built by the Jesuits in 1762 (and abandoned in 1818), much of Borja remains standing. The road can be very rough – 4WD recommended but usually not essential. Allow two hours for the drive each way.

ÁPFF – Islas del Golfo de California

Reserve office • Permit charge per day • 200 124 9106

The pristine bay itself is the star attraction at Bahía de los Ángeles, rich in marine life and studded with sixteen weathered islands, part of the **Área de Protección de Flora y Fauna Islas del Golfo de California**. Visiting or camping on them requires a permit; you can obtain one from the reserve office in town, near the *Hotel Villa Vitta*, which also can advise on boat operators and fishing guides. Highlights include the colonies of **sea lions** near **Isla Coronado**, also known as "Smith Island", and the **whale sharks** that visit the area each summer (July–Oct).

Isla Ángel de la Guarda

The largest island in the Sea of Cortez, **Isla Ángel de la Guarda** dominates the bay and is the biggest focus of Bahía de los Ángeles' leisure activities; it's the best place on the northern coast for diving and kayaking trips. Though you'll find plenty of **fishing** outfits, there aren't any other speciality operators in town, and any activity you'd like to indulge in (including **swimming with whale sharks**) is typically arranged through your campsite or motel.

ARRIVAL AND INFORMATION — BAHÍA DE LOS ÁNGELES

By car Bahía de los Ángeles is about 224km from El Rosario on Hwy-1, followed by a 66km jaunt east along well-maintained Hwy-12 from the Parador Punta Prieta junction. The town has two PEMEX petrol stations, both open daily 7am–9pm. There is no public transport to Bahía de los Ángeles. Visit https://bahiadelosangeles.org for the latest information on the area.

ACCOMMODATION AND EATING

Camping is popular in Bahía de los Ángeles, with most hotels and restaurants maintaining simple sites and some free camping available along the road to Punta la Gringa, at the north end of the bay – ask in town before setting up a tent, just in case (you may have to pay a small fee). There are several cheap taco stands on the main road.

Daggett's Beach Camping & Sportfishing 664 376 5779. Between *Larry's* and the town, this local institution (the Daggetts are descended from an English sailor who jumped ship in the 1880s) is primarily an RV community, but they've reserved the beachfront for palapa-shaded plots (with barbecues) for campers and have cabins with one to three beds, a/c and hot showers. Free wi-fi. Camping M$, cabins with kitchen M$$$

Guillermo's 646 239 3714. The best place to eat a full meal or grab a cold drink is *Guillermo's*; the fish tacos and burgers are good but the beachside location and views of the offshore islands are spectacular. Basic doubles M$$$

Villa Bahía Carretera a Campo Juárez http://villabahia.com. On the way to La Gringa (5km north of town), this laid-back complex comprises 12 casitas on the beach, with each unit holding at least six people, a full kitchen, and use of an outdoor communal kitchen with grills. Free satellite wi-fi and kayaks is a nice bonus, and the whole place runs on wind and solar power. M$$$

Villa Vitta Resort http://villavitta.com. Centrally located motel with basic but clean rooms (all with a/c and satellite TV), a pool, restaurant-bar and boat ramp. The adjoining RV park and campsite has 25 spots with electrical hookups and eleven without, and showers. M$$

Guerrero Negro

Continuing south on the main highway, there's little between El Rosario and the 28th parallel, where an enormous metal monument marks the border between the states of Baja California and **Baja California Sur**; you'll have to set your watch forward an hour when you cross. **GUERRERO NEGRO**, just across the border, offers little in the way of respite from the heat and aridity that has gone before (winters, however, can find the town quite chilly). Flat and dust-blown, it was only established in the 1950s as a supply centre for Exportadora de Sal, the world's largest salt manufacturer, and is surrounded by vast saltpans and drab storage warehouses. At most times of year you'll want to do little more than grab a drink and carry straight on, especially if you don't have a car – it's a dispiriting place to navigate on foot. In January and February (and, peripherally, Dec & March–April), however, Guerrero Negro is home to one of Mexico's most extraordinary natural phenomena, the congregation of scores of **grey whales** just off the coast (see page 531).

ARRIVAL AND DEPARTURE — GUERRERO NEGRO

By plane The tiny airport is 6km north of town (taxis are available), with Aéreo Servicio Guerrero flying Cessna aircraft to/from Ensenada (Mon, Wed & Fri), Hermosillo (Thurs) and Guaymas (Tues, Thurs & Sat). Calafia Airlines also serves Hermosillo/Guaymas (Mon & Sat).

By bus The Terminal de Autobuses is on Rubio, just off Zapata at the eastern end of town near Hwy-1. Buses passing through Guerrero Negro are often full; try to buy your ticket at least a day in advance.

Destinations Ensenada (6 daily; 10hr); La Paz (3–4 daily; 11–12hr); Loreto (3–4 daily; 6.5hr); Mulegé (3–4 daily; 4–5hr); San Ignacio (3–4 daily; 2hr); Tijuana (3–4 daily; 12hr).

By taxi The taxis at the stand in front of the Mercado Tianguis supermarket on Zapata adjust their rates depending on how long you'll have to wait for a bus.

ACCOMMODATION

Los Caracoles Zapata, at Calz de la República; 615 157 1088. On the right as you travel along Zapata, this once

WHALE WATCHING FROM GUERRERO NEGRO

Whale watching is the principal reason people visit Guerrero Negro, as hordes of friendly California grey whales (up to 2000 at a time), which spend most of their lives in the icy Bering Sea around Alaska, can be observed (at remarkably close quarters) from within the nearby **Laguna Ojo de Liebre** (aka Scammon's Lagoon), thirty minutes south of town. It's a magical experience – and many visitors actually get to touch the whales, which sometimes come right up to bobbing vessels after the engines are switched off.

Organized tours (see below) begin in Guerrero, but you can also drive to the lagoon and hire a cheaper *panguero* (boat) yourself. Take Hwy-1 south for 9km and look for the sign to the **Parque Natural de la Ballena Gris**. From here it's 6km along a rough dirt road to a gate (which someone will open, but only during the whale-watching season Jan–March), and another 18km to the lagoon. Boats usually charge M$760–955 per person for 90min trips around the bay. Taxis will take you all the way there and back (they wait for you at the lagoon).

Malarrimo Eco-Tours Emiliano Zapata s/n; http://malarrimo.com. Runs 3hr whale tours (daily 8am, noon; charge), as well as eight-hour tours to the Sierra de San Francisco to see cave paintings (Oct–Dec; charge) from the hotel of the same name (see below).

Mario's Tours Hwy-1 Km 217.3; http://mariostours.com. Whale-watching trips from Mario's are a four-hour trip (8am and 11am) and include a complimentary drink or two.

stellar option needs a renovation, but still offers clean rooms, satellite TV and friendly staff, free coffee and excellent whale-watching trips. M$$

Malarrimo Zapata, at Pipila; http://malarrimo.com. Another solid option, open here since 1974, with clean rooms with TV, and RV spaces (M$) – you can also camp here (M$). Non a/c rooms M$; with a/c; M$$

TerraSal Zapata (just off Hwy-1); 615 157 0133. Relatively new hotel with clean, large rooms with a/c, TV and powerful showers, right at the entrance to town. M$

EATING

Malarrimo Zapata, at Pipila; http://malarrimo.com. This hotel contains *Scavenger's Bar* (decorated with items found on windswept Malarrimo Beach) and a restaurant with excellent seafood (halibut with crispy garlic and daily lunch specials), as well as decent breakfasts (lobster omelette). M$$$

Restaurant Mario's Hwy-1 km 217.3; http://mariostours.com. On Hwy-1, just before Zapata, is this solid rustic option for breakfast and the basics, as well as some great deals – although a dinner for two can be expensive if you opt for their steak and lobster combo. M$$$$

Santo Remedio Carballo Félix; 615 157 0750. The best restaurant in town can be hard to find, but is well worth the effort (turn right at El Morro and look for the signs), with fresh, local produce (seafood, Baja beef, fruit jams and California wines) and a menu that features everything from steaks to fish tacos. M$$$

San Ignacio

Leaving Guerrero Negro, Hwy-1 winds 142km inland for the hottest, driest stage of the journey, across the Desierto Vizcaíno. In the midst of this landscape, **SAN IGNACIO**'s appeal is immediate, even from a distance. Gone are the dust and concrete that define the peninsula, replaced by green palms and a cool breeze; it remains an oasis any desert traveller would hope for, and another excellent base for **whale-watching** and **cave-painting tours**. There are **no banks** in town and few places accept credit cards – it's best to come with a supply of cash.

Misión San Ignacio de Kadakaamán

Gilberto Valdivia Peña (Plaza Ecoturismo) • **Museo de Pinturas Rupestres de San Ignacio** May–Oct Tues–Sat 8am–6pm; Nov–April daily 8am–5pm • Free • 615 154 0222

In town, the central **Plaza Ecoturismo**, shaded by six huge Indian laurel trees, plays hosts to concerts, festivals and children's soccer games, and is dominated by the **Misión San Ignacio de Kadakaamán** (usually open during services only). This gorgeous church was constructed from lava blocks over 1m thick, dug up from Volcan las Tres Virgenes to the east. Completed in 1786, it's probably the prettiest example of colonial architecture in the whole of Baja California, and was also one of the most successful missions, operating until 1840. The left wing of the mission now houses the tiny **Museo de Pinturas Rupestres de San Ignacio**, which contains photos and cave-art exhibits, with a focus on the nearby Sierra de San Francisco (Spanish-only captions).

ARRIVAL AND DEPARTURE — SAN IGNACIO

By bus The centre of San Ignacio lies almost 3km off the main highway, where all the buses stop. Upon arrival you may be lucky enough to pick up a taxi; otherwise it's a 30min walk down the road through the palms. Getting onward tickets can be tough: buses currently depart for Guerrero Negro (2hr) and points north at 5.55am, 6.30am and 5.50pm. Buses depart for Santa Rosalía (1hr) and points south at 11.50am, 3pm and 11.35pm.

By taxi Local taxi drivers will ask for a minimum fare both for Guerrero Negro and for Santa Rosalía.

ACCOMMODATION AND EATING

Some of the best food in San Ignacio is cooked up in the taco stalls on the plaza; try the juicy *carne asada* tacos at *Taquería Lupita* or the frozen *raspado de tamarindo* at *El Capu*. Don't miss the addictive *pan de datil* (date pie) and date empanadas sold by Luz Romero from her kitchen on the edge of the plaza.

Desert Inn (on road to San Ignacio, 1.5 km off Hwy-1); 615 154 0300. The best place in town, a hacienda-style hotel set around a pool, with comfy motel chain-style rooms and TVs. Breakfast is extra. M$$$

Ignacio Springs Bed and Breakfast http://ignaciosprings.com. Camping at *Ignacio Springs Bed and Breakfast* on the northern side of Río San Ignacio is a rather bizarre but comfortable affair; the novelty here is staying in well-appointed yurts with queen-size beds, tile floors, a/c and patios; some even have their own bath. Rates include breakfast. Near the road, so can be noisy at night. M$$$

Ricardo's Rice & Beans Hwy-1, San Lino; 615 154 0283. The bus stop is actually in San Lino, a little settlement anchored by the campsite and restaurant *Ricardo's Rice & Beans*, just west of the intersection along a road parallel to the highway. There are old but clean rooms here, with hot showers, a/c and plenty of space to camp outside. The restaurant serves traditional Mexican and seafood dishes. M$$

Santa Rosalía

South of San Ignacio, Hwy-1 emerges on the east coast at **SANTA ROSALÍA**, the largest town in central Baja (with a population of around twelve thousand), and one of the most intriguing places to explore on the peninsula. Established by French miners in 1885, it has something of a transient air, and many of its buildings look strikingly un-Mexican. The streets are narrow and crowded, with the workers' houses in the

TOURS AND TRIPS FROM SAN IGNACIO

WHALE WATCHING

Although whales are most in evidence in January and February, **whale-watching** tours to the nearby **Laguna San Ignacio** (around 50km from town, on mostly paved road) are offered from December to April. If you have your own car you can cut your expenses considerably (allow 1hr to be safe). Tours arranged at the lagoon are charged per person; transport from San Ignacio to the lagoon can be arranged on the plaza.

Antonio's Ecotours 615 112 5387, http://cabanas sanignacio.com. Whale watching (2hr; lunch is extra, as is the van for travel from San Ignacio), or you can opt for a one night stay over in the simple but comfy *Cabañas San Ignacio* on the lagoon (shared toilets, hot showers, free wi-fi area), with three meals and two whale excursions included.

Ecoturismo Kuyimá Morelos 23, at Hidalgo; 615 154 0070, http://kuyima.com. Located opposite the church (daily Dec–April 8am–1pm & 3–8pm; May–Nov 9am–1pm), tour options include an all-inclusive four-day, three-night package, and for whale-watching it's an extra charge per van for day-trippers from San Ignacio. Kuyimá also offers accommodation at the lagoon, with tents and clean palapas with solar power, plus they serve food. It's possible to visit and return in one day, but it's better to stay the night as the whales are best seen in the early morning when they venture into the shallow waters. You can camp with your own equipment or rent tents.

CAVE ART

Cave-art tours from San Ignacio focus on the Sierra de San Francisco about 45km north of town, where 320 sites exist, dating back some eight thousand years; tour operators usually pass through the little town of San Francisco de la Sierra and head for the easily accessible **Cueva del Ratón**, or remoter caves such as the Cueva Pintada and Cueva de las Flechas in Cañón San Pablo, which require a minimum of two days. Ecoturismo Kuyimá (see above) offers day trips Oct–May to **Ratón** for three days, but if you want to save some cash you can arrange a mule trip yourself in San Francisco de la Sierra (see below). **Antonio's Ecotours** (see above) also offers trips to Cueva del Ratón and the more isolated La Cueva del Palmarito.

Independent tours are possible, but you must always be accompanied by a guide (*guías arrieros*) and are required to get **INAH permission**, gained in San Ignacio from the INAH office next to the church (Mon–Sat 8am–3pm; 615 154 0222); there's a park entry fee plus an extra charge for cameras, plus a mandatory guide fee (per four persons) for Ratón and for other caves (the guide will meet you at the cave). You'll then need your own transport to get there: at km 115, 45km north of San Ignacio, you'll find a signposted road heading 36km east (30km paved) to San Francisco de la Sierra, with **Cueva del Ratón** just over 2km further on (4WD normally required). The *Buenaventura Hostel* (615 156 4747; M$) in the village offers basic accommodation, meals and tour guides. For the more remote caves, once you've sorted out a guide and a mule (charged by the day), you'll be able to camp at "El Cacarizo" in the Cañón de Santa Teresa (M$), five hours hike from San Francisco de la Sierra.

valley, which feature low, angled roofs and hibiscus-flanked porches, resembling French Caribbean dwellings, and grander colonial residences for the managers lining the hill to the north.

Iglesia de Santa Bárbara

Obregón and Pedro Altamirano

The premier sight in Santa Rosalía is the **Iglesia de Santa Bárbara**, three blocks from Parque Morelos, a prefabricated iron church said to have been designed by Gustave Eiffel and exhibited in Paris before it was reassembled here in 1897. The rather austere interior is softened somewhat by vivid stained-glass windows reflecting its Art Nouveau style, though some experts now believe Eiffel was not the designer – just don't say that to the locals.

Museo El Boleo

Frances Altamirano, at Jean M.Cousteau • Free • 615 152 2999

Progress up the hill from the Iglesia de Santa Bárbara and you'll see more leftovers from the mining period, culminating with the **Museo El Boleo** at the top, housed in the old mining offices. The museum outlines the history of the mine and the town through old photos and mining curios. The area around the museum is known as the **Mesa Francés**, and contains the grandest examples of the town's French architectural legacy.

ARRIVAL AND DEPARTURE — SANTA ROSALÍA

By plane Aéreo Servicio Guerrero flies to Guaymas, Cabo San Lucas and Guerrero Negro from Santa Rosalía's tiny Palo Verde Airport, some 30km south in San Bruno; buy tickets at the office in the ferry terminal (daily 8am–1pm & 3–6pm; includes transport to airport; 615 155 1453, http://asg.com.mx).

By bus Buses use the ferry terminal parking lot to drop off and take on passengers, with around three buses a day heading north to San Ignacio (1hr) and Guerrero Negro (3hr 40min), but only a couple continuing to Tijuana (14hr); five buses head south to La Paz (8–9hr) via Loreto (3hr) and Mulegé (1hr). Taxis (615 152 0266) shuttle between the bus and ferry terminal and the hotels.

By ferry Ferries connect Santa Rosalía with Guaymas (see page 36), across the Sea of Cortez in the state of Sonora. The ferry terminal lies 2min walk south of centrally located Parque Morelos, on Hwy-1. You can rent a cabin onboard and there's a charge per vehicle. The ticket office (800 672 9053) inside the terminal is open daily 10am–7pm. Always call in advance, though, as schedules often change.

Destinations Guaymas (departs Wed & Fri 8.30am, Sun 8pm; 9hr).

By taxi If you can't wait for a bus, you should be able to negotiate a taxi to San Ignacio or Mulegé.

ACCOMMODATION

Las Casitas Hwy-1 km 195 Santa Rosalía–Loreto; 615 152 3023. A long walk uphill from downtown, but the panoramic views of the sea from its hillside perch make it worthwhile. The large, ceramic-tiled rooms have modern amenities (free wi-fi in common areas only) and large windows overlooking the water. M$$$

Hotel Francés Jean M.Cousteau 15; 615 152 2052. A charming colonial-style building on the hill to the north of town, beyond the museum. Built in 1920 (the original opened in 1886 but burnt down), rooms are basic and functional, but it's worth the price for a glimpse into Rosalía's French past. Satellite TV, with simple breakfast included. Cash only. M$$

EATING

Several inexpensive stalls are scattered along Obregón: *Super Tacos*, on Obregón just off Parque Morelos, serves tasty beef tacos, while *Tacos El Arabe*, on the south side of Parque Morelos, is noted for its similarly priced fish tacos. M$

El Muelle Plaza and Constitución; 615 152 0931. Restaurant set in an old wooden building with an outdoor patio serving decent *carne asada* and *arrachera* steaks, plus craft beers. M$$$

Panadería El Boleo Obregón 30, between calles 3 and 4; 615 152 0310. Sadly, no French restaurants remain as a reminder of the town's beginnings. This bakery dates back to 1901 and certainly looks the part, but is definitely past its prime – the cakes are fresh enough in the morning, but the bread is nothing like the real thing. M$$

Terco's Pollito Obregón on Parque Morelos; 615 152 0075. You can eat very well here, with succulent barbecue chicken and well-prepared Mexican dishes. M$$$

EL BOLEO

Legend has it that while walking in the hills around Santa Rosalía in 1868, rancher José Villavicencio chanced upon a **boleo**, a blue-green globule of rock that proved to be just a taster of a mineral vein containing more than twenty percent copper. By 1880, the wealth of the small-scale mining concessions came to the notice of the **Rothschilds**, who provided financing for the French Compagnie du Boléo (or "El Boleo") to buy mining rights and to build a massive extraction and smelting operation in 1885. Six hundred kilometres of tunnels were dug, a foundry was shipped out from Europe, and a new wharf built to transport the smelted ore north to Washington State for refining. Ships returned with lumber for the construction of a new town, laid out with houses built to a standard commensurate with their occupier's status within the company. By 1954, falling profits from the nearly spent mines forced the French to sell the pits and smelter to the Mexican government who, though the mines were eventually left idle, continued to smelt ore from the mainland until the 1990s. Starting in 2004, Canadian-listed Baja Mining Corp worked hard to reopen the mine – despite running into financing problems in 2012 (Korean Resources Corp is now the main shareholder) and damage caused by Hurricane Odile, production of copper, cobalt and zinc finally began in 2015, with the new El Boleo expected to have a minimum life of 22 years. Minera y Metalúrgica del Boleo has promised to work with local authorities to develop housing, infrastructure and utilities, and so far has created around 1000 new jobs in the area (with 65 percent local hires).

DIRECTORY

Banks Both banks are on Obregón, and have ATMs: Bancomer (at C 5) and Banamex (opposite).

Post office The post office is on Constitución at C 2.

Mulegé

Some 60km south of Santa Rosalía lies **MULEGÉ**, a rural town on the site of one of the original Jesuit missions. Like San Ignacio, it's a real oasis: tucked into a lush valley, the town sits on the north bank of the palm-fringed Río Santa Rosalía and has clung onto its small-town atmosphere, despite a growing US expat community. The calm was shattered in 2009, when **Hurricane Jimena** caused extensive damage, and again in 2014 when **Hurricane Odile** ripped up roads and demolished houses – though the town has largely recovered since then. Mulegé's streets branch eastward from Hwy-1 and surround both sides of the estuary, though the old centre and **Plaza Corona** lie on the north bank – base yourself here if you don't have a car.

The beaches

Outside of hurricane season the town makes a good base for the superb **beaches** strung out along the **Bahía Concepción** (see page 537). Yet again you'll miss out on the best of them without your own transport, but here hitching is at least a realistic (and safe) possibility – many visitors commute to the beaches daily, particularly during the high season (Nov to April).

Museo de Mulegé

Cananea • Charge • 615 153 0056

There's not a great deal to see in Mulegé itself, though the former prison has been converted into a local history museum, the **Museo de Mulegé**. Built in 1907, it was known as "prison without doors," as it allowed its inmates to work in town in the mornings and afternoons – and some were even married there. Inside you'll find information about the old mission (see below) and a handful of prehistoric artefacts (Spanish labels only). Perched on a hillside (walk up Zaragoza and follow the signs), it also offers decent views across Mulegé.

CAVE ART AROUND MULEGÉ

Other than as a springboard for the beaches to the south, the main reason to stop at Mulegé is to take one of the **cave-painting tours** out to the Sierra de Guadalupe. This range boasts the densest collection of rock art in Baja, as well as some of the most accessible at **La Trinidad** (29km west of town), requiring as little as five hours for the round trip (including 6.5km on foot). Getting a group together to cut costs shouldn't be a problem in high season, but you still need to shop around as the tours differ considerably. Expect to pay a lot less with your own transport. Overnight excursions are possible too, including a night at a 260-year-old ranch and two different cave locations. Head to *Las Casitas* (see page 536), which also acts as an informal tourist office for information on other local attractions and tours. They can connect you with Mulegé Tours, run by Salvador Castro Drew (615 153 0232) – Salvador grew up in the area and is one of the most knowledgeable local guides.

Misión de Santa Rosalía de Mulegé

For a short hike (20–30min) and stellar panoramas visit the **Misión de Santa Rosalía de Mulegé**. Founded by the Jesuits in 1705, the current building was completed sixty years later and sits atop a hill 3km on the other side of town – like most of the Baja missions, it was abandoned in 1828 after the Indigenous population died out. The church only opens for the occasional Mass, but it's still well worth the hike up for the spectacular view from above the palms. Follow Zaragoza south underneath the highway bridge and take the dirt road on the right that climbs to the mission.

ARRIVAL AND DEPARTURE — MULEGÉ

By bus The bus stop is at the junction of Hwy-1 and Martínez, a good 10min walk southwest of the town's central Plaza Corona; to get to the plaza, follow Martínez (under the *faux* city gate), taking a right fork, and finally a second right onto Zaragoza. Mulegé does not have a ticket office, so buy your onward ticket on the bus (no reservations). Around three to five buses daily pass through to Guerrero Negro (4hr 50min), via Santa Rosalía (1hr). At least five buses head south to La Paz (7hr 30min) via Loreto (2hr), with one going on to Cabo San Lucas (10hr 30min).

By car There are two PEMEX stations in and around town: one in the centre on Av Martínez at Zaragoza, and another 2.5km south of town along Hwy-1.

By taxi If you can't wait for a bus, taxis will take you to Santa Rosalía.

ACCOMMODATION

★ **Las Casitas** Madero 50; 615 153 0019. The former home of Mexican poet José Alán Gorosave (born here in 1920) is the best option in the centre (5min from the plaza). The gift shop and restaurant give way to an orchard-like yard and dribbling fountains at the back, while the charming rooms come with TVs, ceiling fans and bathroom. Free wi-fi in garden only. M$$

Clementine's Oasis Rio Baja (off Hwy-1); http://clementinesbaja.com. Excellent option near the river, with a variety of rental properties (casitas) and smaller rooms managed by expat owners who also run a B&B in Oregon. All the casitas feature modern furnishings, a/c and kitchens. Doubles M$$, Casitas M$$$

Hotel Hacienda Madero 3 (just off the plaza); 615 153 0021. One of the classic Baja hotels; the front section dates back to the 1770s and it's been a hotel since the 1950s. Rooms are fading a bit, but come with Sky TV and a/c, and the small pool, pleasant courtyard and on-site parking make this an attractive option. M$$

Serenidad Hwy-1 km 139; http://serenidad.com.mx. Just south of town on the east side of the Transpeninsular, this comfortable hotel is another stalwart from the 1960s, though it's also starting to show its age (no TV, spotty wi-fi, no hot water). Look out for the summer three-night-stay specials, and the legendary Sat-night pig roast, a tradition since 1970. Closed Sept. M$$$

EATING

Cool Scoops de Mulegé Martínez 52; 615 107 0729. No frills ice-cream shop selling delicious flavour combinations, plus every sugary topping imaginable. M$$

Los Equipales Moctezuma 7 (near Zaragoza); 615 153 0330. The best Mexican restaurant in town, offering large steaks and seafood portions on an open second-floor terrace –steaks are served complete with soup, salad and potatoes. Great bar for drinks also. M$$$

Taquitos Mulegé Plaza Corona. The best fish and shrimp tacos in town are usually available at this stall till 1pm, or until the seafood runs out; tacos are a bargain. M$

DIRECTORY

Banks Mulegé has a Bancomer with an ATM on Zaragoza between Martínez and Moctezuma.

Post office The small post office is at Zaragoza and Madero.

Bahía Concepción

There is good diving and fishing immediately around Mulegé, but the best beaches are between 10km and 50km south of town along the shore of **Bahía Concepción**, for once easily accessible from Hwy-1 – the drive down to Loreto along this stretch of road is truly spectacular. The bay ranges from 3km to 6.5km wide, is 48km long and is enclosed on three sides and dotted with islands. The blue-green waters, tranquil bays and white-sand beaches are spellbinding and relatively undeveloped – though you will at times find teams of RVs lining the waters – and it's a good place to break your journey for a day or so before travelling south. As far as **kayaking** goes, there are few places better than Bahía Concepción.

Playa Punta Arena

The best stretches of sand include windy **Playa Punta Arena**, signposted at Hwy-1 km 119 (17km south of Mulegé) and 3km along a dirt road, where there should be some basic palapa shelters to rent (no facilities) – it's popular with windsurfers and kiteboarders.

Playa Santispac

Playa Santispac (km 114; cars charged for parking/camping per night), some 5km further on from the Punta Arena turning, is right on the highway – despite the winter crowds of RVs, it has plenty of room to **camp** and enough life to make staying here longer-term a realistic option (toilets, showers, basic groceries). Stop at *Ana's* (Thurs–Tues 8am–10pm, summer 2–10pm) for cheap fish tacos and potent Bloody Marys; you can also rent **kayaks** and snorkelling gear by the day.

Posada Concepción and Playa Escondida

Posada Concepción, 2km south of Santispac on Hwy-1, shows the beginnings of Cabo-style development, and has permanent residents (mostly retirees). If you follow the rough road to the south of Posada Concepción (of Hwy-1 at km 111), you'll arrive after 1km at the rather secluded **Playa Escondida**. Few trailers can make it over the hump, so the campsite is more hospitable to tent campers. It is rustic (cold showers and outhouses) and there are no services.

Playa El Coyote and Playa El Requesón

Further south there are few facilities for anything other than camping: the popular, bone-white beaches of **Playa El Coyote** (6.5km south of Santispac) and **Playa El Requesón** (a dazzling sandbar poking into the bay, 15km south of Coyote at km 92.5; admission charge per car) are the last and the best opportunities for this (fee includes the use of palapas). Note that there's no fresh water (pit toilets only) available at either, but locals drop by in the early morning and afternoon selling everything from water to fresh shrimps.

ACCOMMODATION — BAHÍA CONCEPCIÓN

★ **Playa Frambes Lighthouse Resort** Playa Punta Arena (off Hwy-1 km 118); http://mulege.org. Gorgeous property 20km south of Mulegé, comprising three spacious, modern 2-bedroom cottages, a pool and a lighthouse (that you can also rent for the same price). All units are air-conditioned and powered by solar energy, and breakfast is included. M$$$$

Posada Concepción Hwy-1 km 112; http://posadaconcepcion.net. This gated expat community offers ten RV spots with full hookups, and comfy 2-bedroom houses for nightly, weekly or monthly rental. Comes with use of the tennis court, thermal hot springs and wi-fi; kayaks are M$100 for 2 hours. Book on airbnb.com. Houses M$$

Loreto

Another popular escape for fishing and diving enthusiasts, **LORETO** was the site of the earliest permanent settlement in the Californias. Founded in 1697 by **Juan María Salvatierra** as the first Jesuit mission to the region, Loreto served as the administrative capital of the entire California territory until a devastating hurricane struck in 1829 and La Paz took on the role. Today Loreto is booming again; much of the centre is given over to craft shops and galleries, many selling silver, while the seafront **malecón** and central **Plaza Cívica** have been spruced up in recent years. Some 8km south of town lies the largely expat community of **Nopoló (aka Villages at Loreto Bay)**, one of the most ambitious residential developments in Mexico, and the posh *Villa del Palmar* resort. Construction has provided a massive economic boost to the entire region, but critics claim that the project threatens to overwhelm the already limited water supply and Loreto's delicate natural assets: Mexico's largest marine park, **Parque Nacional Bahía de Loreto**, lies just offshore, while the weathered landscapes of the **Sierra de la Giganta** provide a stunning backdrop.

Misión de Nuestra Señora de Loreto de Conchó

Salvatierra, at Pino Suárez • Free • 613 135 0005

In downtown Loreto, Avenida Salvatierra turns into a tree-lined pedestrian mall beyond Independencia, and the few buildings of note are along this six-block-long promenade to the sea. The old mission church, the **Misión de Nuestra Señora**

de Loreto de Conchó, is still standing, though heavily restored after centuries of earthquake damage. Its basic structure – solid, squat and simple – is little changed since 1752.The inscription over the door, which translates as "The head and mother church of the missions of upper and lower California", attests to its former importance, as does the richly adorned Baroque *retablo* originally transported here from Mexico City.

Museo de las Misiones

Salvatierra, between Misioneros and Pino Suárez • Charge • 613 135 0441

Next door to the mission, in a former storage house and courtyard complex, stands the illuminating **Museo de las Misiones.** The museum chronicles the early conversion and colonization of Baja California and its eighteen original mission churches through a collection of religious art, weapons and tools dating from the seventeenth and eighteenth centuries.

Misión San Francisco Javier de Viggé-Biaundó

If you have a car, make time for the detour to the **Misión San Francisco Javier de Viggé-Biaundó**, 36km southwest of Loreto in the heart of the mountains. Established in 1699, it became the base of **Father Juan de Ugarte** two years later, one of the leading Jesuit pioneers in Baja. The current church, completed in 1758, is one of the most isolated and evocative on the peninsula (it was abandoned in 1817 after a devastating attack by Guaycura people). Mass is heard here once a month, but the church is usually open daily from around 8am to around 5pm (free entrance) – you'll find fine gilded *retablos* and a gracious statue of San Javier inside. The mission is signposted at km 118 on Hwy-1, south of Loreto, from where a paved road snakes between vast desert mountains, dry *arroyos* and massive faces of cracked rock. Taxis can be arranged for the round-trip.

Parque Nacional Bahía de Loreto

Park office Adolfo López Mateos (malecón) at Carrillo • Charge • 613 135 0477

Loreto's greatest asset is the giant body of protected waters along its eastern shore –you'll get an entrancing view of the islands from the breezy malecón. The **Parque Nacional Bahía de Loreto** was established in 1996 to protect over 2000 square kilometres of the Sea of Cortez from overfishing, and it's become another superb place for **diving** and **kayaking**. If you just want a closer look at the islands, take a tour with the Cooperativa Parque Marino, formed by 21 local fishermen (see page 540).

ARRIVAL AND DEPARTURE — LORETO

By plane Loreto International Airport is 5km south of town off Hwy-1. Calafia Airlines offers domestic flights to Guaymas, La Paz and Tijuana, while Alaska Airlines operates flights from Los Angeles. Alamo, Hertz and Europcar have car-rental counters at the entrance and have offices downtown. There are no public buses into town: yellow *colectivo* taxis wait for passengers, driving to downtown Loreto when full, and dropping off at hotels. Private taxis booked in advance with companies like Wild Loreto (see page 540) are expensive – regular taxis will charge less for trips to Loreto Bay. Ignore the timeshare hawkers in the terminal.

By bus Loreto's bus terminal is at Salvatierra and Paseo Pedro de Ugarte (613 135 0767), just in front of the baseball field. It's a hot 20min walk east along Salvatierra to the Plaza Cívica, and a further 10min in the same direction to the beach – taxis usually meet buses and charge a flat fee to anywhere in town.

Destinations (bus) Ensenada (3–4 daily; 15hr); Guerrero Negro (5 daily; 6–7hr); La Paz (8 daily; 5–6hr); Mulegé (7 daily; 2hr); San Ignacio (5 daily; 4hr); Santa Rosalía (7 daily; 3hr); Tijuana (3 daily; 18hr).

By taxi Taxis will run drive to Mulegé (90min) and you can usually negotiate the price. The taxi stand at Hidalgo near Madero serves Sitio Juárez (613 135 0915), while Sitio Loreto (613 135 0424) is usually from Juárez one block west.

INFORMATION

Tourist office The English-speaking tourist office (Mon–Fri 8am–3pm; 613 135 0411) is located in the Palacio de Gobierno at Madero and Salvatierra, on the west side of the pedestrian Plaza Cívica.

TOURING LORETO BAY

Don't leave town without exploring the pristine waters and islands (there are five, including Coronados and Del Carmen, the largest) of the Parque Nacional Bahía de Loreto.

Cooperativa Parque Marino 613 111 8813. Tours of Isla Coronados take 5hr on a boat that can take six – you'll be able to snorkel and see a sea lion colony here. Tours of Isla Danzante take 5hr – you'll see a lot more marine life here, such as sea lions, whale sharks, dolphins, manta rays and whales. Book tours at the booth on the marina (daily 5am–9pm; Adolfo López Mateos at Carrillo).

Dolphin Dive Baja Juárez between Mateos and Davis; 613 135 1914, http://dolphindivebaja.com. Runs two-tank dive trips to Isla Coronados, Isla Del Carmen and Isla Danzante that include tanks, all gear, snacks, guide, boat and park fees – they also offer snorkelling off Coronado and PADI open-water certifications (four days).

Wild Loreto Salvatierra; 613 135 1493, http://wildloreto.com. Reputable operator running tours to Coronados but also the San Javier mission and climbing at Tabor Canyon.

ACCOMMODATION

SEE MAP PAGE 538

★ **Las Cabañas de Loreto** Morelos (just off the malecón); http://lascabanasdeloreto.com. Justly popular spot (book ahead), with spotless, spacious cabaña studios (with a/c and kitchenettes), welcome fruit basket, free bikes for the ride into town, outdoor community kitchen, laundry, pool and hot tub. M$$$

★ **Coco Cabañas** Davis 92, at Constituyentes; http://hotelcococabanas.com. All eight cabañas surround a patio with a lovely sunken pool and barbecue area. The rooms have kitchens and private baths (no TVs), but the real draw here is the welcoming owners Stephen and Barrett, who can set up virtually any activity and are experts on the local area. M$$$

Iguana Inn Juárez s/n, at Davis; http://iguanainn.com. Another friendly bargain near the centre of town. The owners live in the front house, guests stay in the four spotless cabañas situated around a gurgling fountain and courtyard in the back. The relatively modern rooms, with tile floors, a/c, TV and ceiling fans, have kitchenettes and private baths. M$$$

La Mision Rosendo Robles, at the malecón; http://lamisionloreto.com. This reconstructed behemoth has retained some of its former charm (it originally opened in 1969), and is certainly the most luxurious option on the malecón. The colonial-style rooms feature marble floors and baths, hardwood furnishings, flatscreen TVs and patios or balconies overlooking the ocean. M$$$$

Posada de las Flores Salvatierra, at Madero and Plaza Cívica; 613 135 1162. Alluring boutique hotel in the centre of town, set in an old building with courtyard smothered in blossoms. The theme is eighteenth-century Mexico, with rooms decked out with antiques and a wonderful rooftop pool and bar area. M$$$$

EATING

SEE MAP PAGE 538

Finding simple Mexican **food** is no problem at the taco stands along Hidalgo or Juárez, while the best views can be found along the malecón. The best supermarket is El Pescador (daily 7am–11pm), on the corner of Salvatierra and Independencia. For a romantic drink, try the roof-top bar at the *Posada de las Flores* (see above).

Café Olé Madero, just off Plaza Cívica; 613 135 0496. Popular place under a shady palapa that does good-value breakfasts and *antojitos* like burritos and fresh fish. M$$

Los Mandiles de Santa Lucía Malecón, at Hildalgo; 613 135 1099. Fine home cooked Mexican fare and definitely a destination if you're in the mood for some comfort food, served in large portions. There's also some decent wines by the glass. M$$

★ **Mita Gourmet** Davis 13 (Plaza Cívica); 613 135 2025, https://facebook.com/restmitagourmet. Best place for a splurge in Loreto, with outdoor seating on the plaza and a menu that features fabulous salads and local fish and shrimp, cooked in a variety of ways. The clams *gratinada* (twelve clams smothered in melted mozzarella) makes a heavenly starter. M$$$

El Rey de Taco Juárez 61, near Misioneros. This takeout place (there are a few seats inside) has garnered a loyal following for its fresh battered fish tacos and tacos *carne asada*, though hours can be erratic – opens at 9am and tends to close between noon and 2pm, but days differ. M$

Sabor! Restaurant Just off Transpeninsular Highway (Hwy-1), near the turning to San Javier; 613 135 0496. Always packed, this Southwestern US and Mexican hybrid set around a small pool and garden specializes in lip-smacking wood-fired chicken, home-made breads, dishes from Jalisco and Loreto's best hamburgers. The only catch – it's on the main road just outside town, on the way to Nopoló, so you'll need to drive or take a taxi. M$$$

DIRECTORY

Banks Bancomer, just across the street from the tourist office on Plaza Cívica, have the most dependable ATMs between

Santa Rosalía and Ciudad Insurgentes, but the bank no longer exchanges foreign currency. Note that US dollars are increasingly accepted throughout town (credit cards are not accepted in most stores and restaurants, however).

Internet More spots in town are adding wi-fi internet access; just walk the streets with your device until you've picked up a signal.

Post office The post office is on Deportiva 13, just off Salvatierra on the way into town, not far from the bus terminal.

La Paz

Everyone ends up in **LA PAZ** eventually, the state capital and largest city of Baja California Sur. The outskirts may be an ugly sprawl, but the old town centre near the languid **malecón**, modernized as it is, has managed to preserve something of its sleepy provincial atmosphere. During the last week in February, La Paz livens up with its boisterous **carnival**, a plethora of colourful parades and cultural events that transform the town, while **eating** here is a real pleasure at any time. There's not much to see in the city itself, but the surrounding **beaches** are lots of fun, and a boat trip to the **Isla Espíritu Santo**, rich in marine life, should not be missed.

The malecón

The **malecón** in La Paz is one of the most attractive in Mexico; a tranquil promenade overlooking small strips of sand with ravishing views of the mountains across the bay, especially at sunset.

Museo de la Ballena

Obregón (malecón) at 16 de Septiembre • Charge (cash only) • http://museodelaballena.org

Marked by a monster 25m blue whale skeleton outside, the **Museo de la Ballena** (whale museum) reopened in these plush new premises on the malecón in 2015. Inside you'll find a large collection of whale and dolphin skeletons, educational movies and enlightening exhibits on local whales and marine life.

Centro Cultural La Paz

16 de Septiembre 120, at Domínguez • Free • 612 122 0065

One block from the malecón on 16 de Septiembre, the **Centro Cultural La Paz** is the most visible sign of the city's regeneration in recent years, housed in the artfully restored 1910 Palacio Municipal (old city hall). Inside you'll find a bookshop, courtyard café and several gallery spaces for temporary exhibitions with a Baja theme. The **Sala Codex Península** contains an absorbing display of photographs, videos and text (in English) on the history and culture of the region.

Plaza Jardín Velasco

Centro de Artes y Culturas Madero, between 5 de Mayo and Independencia • Free • 612 129 4176

The **Plaza Jardín Velasco** (aka Plaza Constitución), three blocks inland from the malecón on 5 de Mayo, stands as the city's tranquil but rather faded main square, presided over by the modest **Catedral de Nuestra Señora de la Paz** (daily 8am–10pm). Completed in 1865 near the site of the old mission established by Jesuit priest Jaime Bravo in 1720, it's plain inside by Mexican standards. On the other side of the plaza the nineteenth-century Casa de Gobierno has been converted into the **Centro de Artes y Culturas**, a small but atmospheric space for temporary local art and photography exhibitions.

Museo Regional de Antropología y Historia

Altamirano at 5 de Mayo • Charge • 612 125 6424

To get a taster of local history, visit the **Museo Regional de Antropología y Historia** (if you read Spanish – there are no English captions). The permanent exhibits begin on

9

the first floor with geology and prehistory, with some rare arrowheads dating from 1180–1280, prehistoric skulls and some reproductions of traditional Indigenous graves. The next floor features photos of Baja's mind-blowing cave paintings, while the top floor is dedicated to the development of Baja California Sur since Independence, with sections on William Walker (the US freebooter who invaded the region in 1853), the 1911 Revolution, gold, silver and copper mining in Baja, the "Loreto 70" movement and the creation of the state constitution in 1975.

The beaches

Make time for the enticing **beaches** between La Paz and the port of Pichilingue, beginning with **Playa del Tesoro** (Carr. Pichilingue km 12), and **Playa Pichilingue** itself (km 18), just beyond the ferry terminal, home to *Restaurant Playa Pichilingue* (612 122 4565), offering great seafood, and loungers for a daily fee. The most unspoiled beach is **Playa de Balandra** (km 23), a series of shallow bays, most of which are no more than waist deep (great for families and snorkelling). There are minimal vendors here and few people on weekdays – you can also rent kayaks. The biggest and busiest beach is **Playa de Tecolote** (km 24), with a real party atmosphere at the weekend – it's also the best for swimming, with views across to Isla Espíritu Santo and *El Tecolote* restaurant and bar (612 122 0672), offering seafood, drinks and boat tours.

ARRIVAL AND DEPARTURE — LA PAZ

BY PLANE

The Aeropuerto Internacional Manuel Márquez de León, Ciudad Insurgentes–La Paz Hwy-1 km 10 (612 122 2959), is 12km southwest of the city. All the major rental car companies have desks in the airport's only terminal. Transporte Terrestre (612 125 1156) has a monopoly on all transport from the airport (though other firms can take you back); taxis run to hotels on the malecón, while shared minibus (*colectivo*) are also available. As always, confirm the price before entering the taxi or shuttle. Useful budget flight connections to La Paz include Calafia Airlines flights to Los Mochis and Mazatlán, and Volaris to Tijuana.

Destinations (domestic) Guadalajara (3 daily; 1hr 30min); Guaymas (1 daily; 40min); Los Mochis (1 daily; 55min); Mazatlán (5 weekly; 1hr 50min); Mexico City (4 daily; 2hr); Tijuana (1 daily; 2hr).

BY BUS

Most buses arrive at the Terminal Turística on the malecón at C Independencia. Buses may also pull in at the Central Camionera (main bus station) at Jalisco and Héroes de la Independencia first, but don't get off here – it's around 25 blocks from the main section of the malecón. Heading south, Ecobajatours (http://ecobajatours.com) run to Cabo San Lucas and Todos Santos (6.30am, 8am & 10am), Los Barriles (7am, 9am & 11am) and Los Cabos airport (6 daily) for its minibus service; Águila run to Cabo (including San José), every 30min or so; routes "via corta" (short) go via Todos to Cabo, while "via larga" (long) go via Los Barriles and San José. Águila/ABC Services north are far less frequent – try to buy tickets in advance.

Destinations Cabo San Lucas via corta (every 30min; 2hr–2hr 30min); Ensenada (2 daily; 23hr 30min–24hr); Guerrero Negro (3 daily; 12hr–12hr 30min); Loreto (7 daily; 5hr 30min); Mexicali (1 daily; 27hr); Mulegé (5 daily; 8hr); San Ignacio (3 daily; 9hr 30min–11hr); San José del Cabo via larga (6 daily; 3hr); Santa Rosalía (5 daily; 9hr); Tijuana (2 daily; 25hr); Todos Santos (every 30min; 1hr 15min).

SEA LIONS, WHALE SHARKS AND ISLA ESPÍRITU SANTO

There are plenty of opportunities for fishing, diving and **boat trips** from La Paz, but it would be a shame to leave without visiting the azure waters of uninhabited **Isla Espíritu Santo**, a short boat ride north of the city. Protected within the **Parque Nacional Archipiélago de Espíritu Santo** (including the nearby **Los Islotes**, a small group of islands that hosts a colony of **sea lions**), snorkelling trips invariably encounter dolphins, manta rays and, depending on the time of year, fin whales and whale sharks (Nov–March) – the sea lions are a sure bet and always the most entertaining. Costs vary, but usually include lunch. See page 544 for details on specific operators.

9

BY FERRY

Baja Ferries (www.bajaferries.com.mx) connects Terminal Pichilingue, 18km north of central La Paz, with Mazatlán (see page 475) and Topolobampo (the port for Los Mochis, page 481) across the Sea of Cortez. If you have a vehicle, it's worth checking out the alternative service provided by TMC (http://ferrytmc.com), which specializes in trucks and freight but also takes cars to Mazatlán and Topolobampo. Águila minibuses run between Terminal Pichilingue and the Terminal Turística on the malecón (departing La Paz daily 7am, 8am, 9am, 10am, noon, 1.30pm, 3pm & 5pm), or take a taxi and aim to arrive at the ferry three hours in advance of the departure time.

To/from Topolobampo Ferries currently make the 7hr journey to Topolobampo Mon to Fri at 2.30pm (arriving at 8.30pm), and Sat at 11pm, arriving at 6am; ferries to La Paz depart midnight Mon–Fri and 11pm Sun. One-way tickets include the seat only; cabins and cars are extra.

To/from Mazatlán Ferry tickets for this route are around 20 percent more expensive than the Topo route.

Tickets Try to buy tickets as far ahead of time as possible, and check the website for updates to routes and schedules, as they change often and routes can close unexpectedly for months at a time. You can buy tickets with a credit card on the website, or in person at Baja Ferries downtown office at Ignacio Allende 1025 at Marcelo Rubio (Mon–Fri 8am–5pm, Sat 8am–2pm; 612 123 6600); the office at the terminal (612 125 6324) is open Mon, Wed & Fri 8am–4pm, Tues & Thurs 8am–6pm, Sat 9am–11pm and Sun 9am–5pm. Tickets can be paid for with major credit cards. Bicycles go free. Tickets for the TMC ferry must be purchased in cash or with Visa and MasterCard at its counter at Terminal Pichilingue (612 123 9226).

Car permits and FMM Car drivers should ensure they have a permit to drive on the mainland. This should have been obtained when crossing the border into Mexico (see page 31), but if not, take your vehicle and all relevant papers to the branch of Banjercito at the ferry terminal (daily 9am–2pm) a couple of days before you sail. If for some reason you've managed to get this far without having your multiple migration form or "FMM" stamped, you should also attend to that before sailing – there's an immigration office at 5 de Febrero between Forjadores and Durango (Mon–Fri 9am–5pm).

GETTING AROUND

LA PAZ

By taxi/bus Getting a taxi in La Paz is never difficult; there are stands on the malecón in front of *Hotel Perla* and *Seven Crown Hotel* and on both sides of the cathedral on the plaza. They don't use meters, but you shouldn't pay much for most trips in the city. Local buses (including the modern Ruta de La Paz buses) charge a set fare per journey, but you are unlikely to need them.

By car Renting a car is a good way to see the beaches and surrounding area, with all the major chains at the airport and along the malecón: Alamo 612 122 6262; Avis 612 122 2651; Budget 612 123 1919; Europcar 612 122 3107; Fox 800 225 4369; Hertz 612 122 0919; National 612 125 6585; and Thrifty 612 125 9696.

By bike The malecón now features a special bike lane for most of its length and renting bikes has become a popular activity for Mexican tourists. TIM Rent a Bike on the malecón (Wed–Sun 9am–9pm, Mon & Tues by reservation; 612 219 7986, http://timrentabike.com) rents various bikes by the hour or day.

THE BEACHES

By bus Águila buses to the beaches leave the Terminal Turística on the malecón daily, traversing the coast to Pichilingue ferry terminal, and on to Balandra and Tecolote. Departures are 10am, noon, 1.30pm, 3pm & 5pm and 6pm (the earlier morning departures terminate at Pichilingue). The last bus back should be at around 6pm (each bus takes around 45min, then turns around when full), but check before you leave La Paz.

INFORMATION AND TOURS

Tourist information The useful tourist office (daily Mon–Fri 9am–7pm; 612 125 6844, http://golapaz.com) is next to the Casa de Cultura at 16 de Septiembre and Domínguez. You can also visit the Got Baja? Store (612 125 5991, https://facebook.com/@gotbajastore) at Madero 1240, between Constitución and 5 de Mayo, for maps of the region.

Baja Diving & Service Obregón 1665-2 (La Paz Malecón); 612 122 1826, http://clubcantamar.com. Offers good diving and whale shark snorkelling tours, and 4-day PADI courses – they'll pick you up from town.

Baja Outdoor Activities Carr Pichilingue km 1; 612 125 5636, http://kayactivities.com. Kayak rental and multi-day kayak expeditions to nearby islands, or half day coastal tours and speedboat rides to see the sea lion colony (Oct–June). Located a 30min walk from downtown La Paz on the road to Pichilingue next to the *El Molinito* restaurant.

Cortez Club La Concha Beach Resort, Carr Pichilingue km 5; 612 121 6120, http://cortezclub.com. Runs beginner's through to divemaster courses for PADI dive certification, and two-tank dives.

Funbaja Carr Pichilingue km 6.1 (Marina Costa Baja); 612 106 7148, http://funbaja.com. Runs snorkelling and scuba-diving trips, excursions to the islands, whale watching, camping, kayaking and land tours.

ACCOMMODATION

SEE MAP PAGE 542

Bermejo Hostel & Backpackers Revolución de 1910 no. 2430, at Márquez de León; http://hostelbermejo.com. Cosy hostel a few blocks inland from the seafront, with clean dorms (with a/c), shared lounge, laundry and tranquil garden with barbecue. Basic continental breakfast included. Dorms M$

Hotel Catedral La Paz Independencia 411; http://hotelcatedrallapaz.mx. In close proximity to everything you could need, this hotel has good clean rooms and great views of the city's skyline (although a good number of the rooms face inwards and overlook the courtyard). The pool here is an added bonus. M$$$$

Lorimar Nicolás Bravo 110; 612 125 3822. This small hotel two blocks from the malecón is La Paz's best budget option, especially when you factor in the helpful desk staff. Each basic but clean room has a private bath and a/c, with the larger suites also equipped with kitchens and TVs. M$$

Peace Hostel Rangel 10, between Sonora and Sinaloa; www.peacehostelmx.com. Hip hostel a short walk south of Marina La Paz, with bunks and beds crafted from reclaimed wood, relaxed *palapa*-style common areas, shared kitchen and a choice of comfy doubles and well-maintained dorms. Dorms M$, doubles M$$

Pension California Degollado 209; 612 122 2896. The very basic but bargain *Pension California* is in an old building with a courtyard just off the main shopping street. The spare, cell-like rooms all have bath and fan, and public areas include a communal kitchen and laundry. M$

★ **Posada de Las Flores** Obregón 440; 612 125 5871. Well-designed rooms with Mexican-colonial chic decor, plush bath products and a minibar; you'll pay more here for the boutique hotel experience than it's worth, but the location on the malecón and the view from the attached second-storey restaurant are superb. Breakfast included. M$$$$

Posada Luna Sol Topete 564, between 5 de Febrero and Navarro; http://posadalunasol.com. The location, along a residential block west of the marina, is a bit removed from the action, but the rooms – with artisan-tiled private baths, flatscreen TVs and a/c – break from the cookie-cutter hotel norm and the knowledgeable staff are excellent local resources. There's also secure, on-site parking. M$$$

Seven Crown Hotel Obregón 1710; http://hotelsevencrown.com. Top location right on the malecón, with fairly simple but stylish rooms done out in minimalist furnishings and tiled floors (plus satellite TV). The fourth-floor restaurant and rooftop bar have fabulous views of the bay. Parking on site. M$$$

Yeneka Madero 1520; 612 125 4688. The quirkiest hotel on the peninsula is liberally sprinkled with folk art and eccentric furniture in the comfortable, clean rooms, some of which come with a/c and TV (can be noisy, however). You also get, laundry, complimentary coffee, continental breakfast and a free shot of tequila in the evening. M$

EATING

SEE MAP PAGE 542

Eating is a real pleasure in La Paz – the seafood, especially, is excellent. The cheapest stalls lie next to the **Mercado Francisco Madero** – look for the "Área de Comedor" facing Revolución de 1910 (at Degollado) for big plates of Mexican classics. Just inside the market itself you'll find *jugos* stalls with fresh juices. M$$

Bismark-Cito Obregón, at Hidalgo y Costilla; https://cleomgruporestaurantero.com. This enticing open-air restaurant and *taquería* since 1968 has been spruced up in recent years, with tables under a smart brick-lined palapa, waiters in white and the best lobster and tacos in town. M$

Doce Cuarenta Madero 1240, between 5 de Mayo and Constitución; http://docecuarenta.com Hip modern café dubbed "1240" (sharing a space with Got Baja?), with shaded patio, distressed wood tables and a menu that includes excellent coffee and a range of cakes, pastries and light meals such as sandwiches and quiche. M$$

La Fuente Obregón, between Agustín Arriola and Lerdo de Tejeda. Always busy thanks to the scrumptious home-made ice cream on offer, from simple but tasty vanilla to delicious chocolate chip concoctions, by the vaso (cup) or cone. Cash only. M$

J&R Ribs Costilleria 5 de Mayo, at Domínguez; http://ribsjr.com. It might seem a little out of place here in Baja, but this tiny barbecue joint on the corner knocks out authentic, mouth-watering baby back ribs or *costillas*, with sauces allegedly based on an old Montana cowboy recipe. M$$

Mc-Fisher Morelos y Pavón 965, between Revolución and Madero; 612 122 4140. Family-run, laid-back seafood joint with breakfast plates and lunch dishes of seafood pasta, marlin enchiladas, grilled shrimp and the exceptional yellowfin tuna (the most expensive option is lobster). M$$

★ **Rancho Viejo** Márquez de León 228, at Domínguez; 612 125 6633. One of the most famous taco joints in La Paz, renowned for its *arrachera* (steak) taco and roast potatoes stuffed with cheese, mushroom and marinated *al pastor*. Also serves beer, unusually for a *taquería*. Open 24hr. There is a convenient second branch on the malecón at Obregón 460-D. M$$

★ **Sorstis Restaurante** Constitución 145; 612 128 8985. Exquisite Mediterranean dishes with a flurry of Italian staples thrown in for good measure — should you be in the mood for something a little less healthy. Favourites here include the asparagus and chicken salad, and the lasagna. M$$

★ **Taquería Hermanos González** Lerdo de Tejada, at Madero; 612 412 0346. Delicious fried fish tacos, shrimp tacos and tacos *carne asada* are the essential eats at this popular stand (also known as "Super Tacos de Baja California"), accompanied by dollops of the help-yourself salsa and salads. M$

9

Las Tres Vírgenes Madero 1130; 612 123 2226. Great choice for a splurge, with a romantic courtyard and posh menu of "Baja High Cuisine" featuring fine meats, seafood, poultry and exceptional dishes such as blue crab enchiladas; expect big portions. M$$$

DRINKING AND NIGHTLIFE

SEE MAP PAGE 542

Cervecería La México Obregón 1665, between 16 de Septiembre and Callejón La Paz; 612 123 0697. Huge, trendy bar on the malecón, packed out with locals enjoying the litre mugs of frothy Tecate beer and live football on TV.

Harker Board Obregón 299, at Constitución; 612 868 5034. This paddle-board outfit by day is a popular restaurant/bar by night, serving Baja Brewing microbrews on tap, Coors, decent hamburgers and giant hot dogs, right on the waterfront.

Kinkis La Paz Carlos M. Esquerro 1620; 612 157 2440. One of several glitzy clubs along the malecón popular with a local crowd, with live Banda and Norteña as well as DJs spinning Latino pop and traditional Mexican sounds.

La Lupita Rock Café C. Francisco I. Madero 1438; 612 106 8257, https://facebook.com/lalupitarockcafe. A small but atmospheric live music bar with a focus on all things rock and roll. There's also a decent wine selection with no head bangers to worry about.

★ **Mezcaleria La Miserable** 274 Domínguez, between 5 de Mayo and Constitución; 612 129 7037. Superb little mescal bar with a friendly atmosphere and far more laid-back than the scene on the malecón. Try and nab one of the tables on the back patio.

★ **Tailhunter Restaurant & Fubar Cantina** Obregón 755; https://tailhunter.com. Justly popular joint just north of the centre, right on the malecón, with a three-storey wooden deck, sports on TV, plenty of great home-cooked food (burgers, Baja hot dogs and fish and chips) and cold beers.

DIRECTORY

Banks Most banks and ATMs are on 16 de Septiembre near the waterfront; Banamex is at Agustín Arriola and Mutualismo, while Bancomer and HSBC are on 16 de Septiembre near Mutualismo.

Books Librerías Educal (daily 10am–8pm) on 16 de Septiembre, inside the Centro Cultural, sells some English-language magazines and books, but Allende Books, at Independencia 518 (Mon–Sat 10am–6pm; 612 125 9114), has the best selection of English books, maps and guides on Mexico.

Emergencies 066; tourist police 612 122 5939; Angeles Verdes (roadside assistance) 078; Hospital Fidepaz 612 124 0400.

Laundry La Paz Lava, Mutualismo 260 at Ocampo 612 122 3112 (Mon–Sat 8am–8pm; charge per load), is just behind *Seven Crown Hotel* and the malecón.

Post office Constitución, at Revolución de 1910 (Mon–Fri 8am–5pm, Sat 8am–1pm).

Los Cabos

South of La Paz, Baja California finally runs out of land where the Pacific Ocean and the Sea of Cortez come together in spectacular fashion. The ocean and sea meet at the sister towns of **Cabo San Lucas** and **San José del Cabo**, known collectively as **Los Cabos** – easily the most exclusive parcel of land in Baja. Undeniably beautiful and home to the lion's share of the peninsula's lavish resorts, golf courses and oft-photographed beaches, the area is one of the fastest-developing regions in Mexico, supporting a sizeable North American expat population and hordes of time-share owners.

But Los Cabos is just a tiny part of the cape. Many of its most remarkable areas still require a great deal of time and preparation to access, and many travellers rent cars to drive the **loop** north of Cabo San Lucas: via the fast Hwy-19 running straight up the Pacific coast through historic **Todos Santos**; the older Transpeninsular Highway (Hwy-1) trailing north from San José del Cabo to La Paz; and the third, most exhausting, route along the **East Cape**.

ARRIVAL AND DEPARTURE

LOS CABOS

BY PLANE

Aeropuerto Internacional de Los Cabos, Hwy-1 km 43.5 (624 146 5111), lies 19km north of downtown San José del Cabo and a further 32km from Cabo San Lucas. Arrival at Los Cabos can be a rather confusing experience, thanks to the mobs of time-share salesmen that greet you in the terminals (who offer rides plus sales pitch). Terminal 1 handles domestic flights, while Terminal 2 (a 10–15min walk away) is for international flights. You'll find car rental desks and ATMs (Bancomer) in both terminals, plus *cambios*, but don't change money here – the exchange rates are always very poor. There is no official information desk at the airport.

Shared minibuses The most popular option is to take a shared minibus (or "shuttle bus") operated by Transportistas Josefinos (https://www.transportistasjosefinos.com), which runs to San José, Corridor hotels and Cabo San Lucas. You can usually pay for these on arrival (at the desks at the terminal) – several other companies allow you to book in advance, but shop around (they'll often make you pay for return trips): Cabo Transfers (US+1877 737 2226, http://cabotransfers.com), Gray Line (US+206 331 3812, http://graylineloscabos.com), Los Cabos Airport Shuttle (624 142 3238, http://loscabosairportshuttle.com), Cabo Airport Shuttle (624 146 5393, https://caboairportshuttle.net) and Trans Baja (US+1877 225 2123, http://transbaja.com). All these services drop passengers off at hotels.

By bus Ecobajatours (877 899 1122, http://ecobajatours.com) runs small buses direct from Terminal 1 to La Paz (3–3.5hr) every hour from 12.30pm to 5.30pm; the 12.30pm and 2.30pm buses travel via Los Barriles, while the others go via Cabo San Lucas and Todos Santos (stopping at bus terminals only). You can pre-book online.

Local buses By far the cheapest option are the Ruta del Desierto modern a/c buses that run every 10–20min between the Águila bus station in Cabo San Lucas and the airport at Terminal 1, and the upper level (departures) of Terminal 2 (buses stop along Lázaro Cárdenas at Puerto Paraíso Mall in Cabo San Lucas, and along Hwy-1 on the edge of San José del Cabo): from the airport it's the same fare for any destination on the route (allow 1hr for Cabo San Lucas).

Taxis Airport taxis are very expensive but there are fixed rates to San José del Cabo, Cabo San Lucas and the Corridor resorts. Buy tickets at the dedicated taxi booth before leaving the terminal (no need to pre-book).

Destinations (domestic flights) Guadalajara (3–4 daily); Loreto (Thurs, Fri, Sat); Los Mochis (1 weekly); MexicoCity (4 daily); Mazatlán (1 weekly); Monterrey (1 daily); Tijuana (2 daily); Toluca (1 daily).

BY BUS

Both San José and Cabo San Lucas have long-distance bus connections to La Paz and the rest of Baja – see individual sections for details.

GETTING AROUND

BY BUS

Travelling between Todos Santos, San José and Cabo San Lucas by bus is the cheapest option, though the bus stations are not especially convenient. See relevant sections for details.

BY CAR

Renting a car is the sensible option if you want to really explore the area and get off the beaten path. Car rental agencies have kiosks in the arrivals section of each airport terminal, and in Cabo and San José. Dec and Jan is the busiest time for rentals, when SUVs and minivans usually sell out. The fastest way from the airport to Cabo San Lucas is along the new toll road that bypasses central San José (with another extension that bypasses Cabo San Lucas on route to Todos Santos).

Car rental agencies (airport) Alamo 624 146 1900; Avis 624 146 0201; Budget 624 146 5333; Dollar 624 146 5060; Hertz 624 146 1803; National 624 146 5021; Payless 624 105 8411; Thrifty 624 142 1671. See www.carflexi.com for one-way rentals to the US border.

BY TAXI

Travelling around the area by taxi is very expensive unless you have a group (most taxis are minivans).

INFORMATION

Tourist information The Los Cabos Tourism Board, Carretera Transpeninsular Km 4.3, Plaza Providencia, Cabo San Lucas (office hours Mon–Fri 9am–5.30pm; 624 143 4777), runs the useful http://visitloscabos.travel and sponsors the quarterly *Los Cabos Magazine* (http://loscabosmagazine.com and sister site http://loscabosguide.com), a glossy monthly usually handed out for free in Cabo.

Todos Santos

The beautifully preserved old town of **TODOS SANTOS**, located just north of the **Tropic of Cancer**, marks the halfway point between Cabo San Lucas and La Paz. Close to some fabulous beaches and home to relatively affordable boutique hotels, Todos is also a great spot for **whale watching** from the shore: sit on any of the beaches in the winter months and you are bound to see several. The tiny centre is easily explored on foot and is crammed with **cafés**, **art galleries** and **studios**.

TURTLES IN TODOS SANTOS

One of the most popular activities in Todos Santos is being able to witness the release of baby turtles by **Tortugueros Las Playitas** (http://todostortugueros.org) which runs a successful sea turtle population recovery program (especially focused on the critically endangered Pacific Leatherback population). Hatchling releases (most days at sunset, Dec–March) at the "Campamento Tortuguero" (Turtle Camp) in Las Tunas Sanctuary (between calle Mangos and Camino Internacional, just north of town) are always open to the public and free – check their Facebook page for the latest updates.

Plaza Todos Santos

Palm-fringed **Plaza Todos Santos** lies in the heart of town (one block off Juárez, the main street), surrounded by the modest church (see below) and the elegant **Teatro General Manuel Márquez de León** (Mon–Fri 9am–2pm; 612 145 0225), completed in Spanish Revival style in 1944. The theatre still hosts the local film festival (http://todossantoscinefest.com; Feb–March) and art festival (Feb). In a small plaza to the right of the theatre, look for the **Sun Monument**, based on the Aztec calendar and completed in 2012 with help from the Heaven and Earth Art Project.

Misión de Nuestra Señora del Pilar de la Paz

Plaza Todos Santos • Free • 612 145 0043

The squat, pale yellow **Misión de Nuestra Señora del Pilar de la Paz** was founded in 1723 as Misión de Santa Rosa, but was destroyed in the Pericú Revolt ten years later. Re-established, the name was changed after the La Paz mission was relocated here in 1748 – like many Baja missions, it was finally closed in 1840. Despite maintaining a simple, colonial-style eighteenth-century exterior, the current church was mostly rebuilt in the 1960s – the venerated image of the Virgin inside is said to date back to 1733.

Centro Cultural Profesor Nestor Agúndez Martínez

Juárez, between Obregón and Hidalgo • Free • 612 145 0041

The **Centro Cultural Profesor Nestor Agúndez Martínez** occupies a red-brick primary school built in 1931 (some of its original murals are still extant in the entrance). Inside are modest but absorbing collections of prehistoric tools, local art and handicrafts and a room of ageing black-and-white photos – this is more interesting than it sounds, with detailed descriptions and personal stories of the photo subjects (translated into English); look for the remarkable Don Ramón Wong, who emigrated from China in 1910, and the group photo of the "captivating women of Todos Santos".

The beaches

Playa La Poza is the first of several beaches strung out between here and Cabo San Lucas, a bumpy ten-minute ride west along any unmarked dirt road; 2km south of Todos on Hwy-19, look for the signs to **Playa Punta Lobos**, a further 2.5km west. From here, beaches line the coast for 10km south, most of them prime **surfing** country (see page 549).

ARRIVAL AND INFORMATION — TODOS SANTOS

By bus With the Hwy-19 bypass completed, central Todos is now blissfully free of through traffic, though Águila buses (with the exception of express buses) still stop at the tiny bus station at the corner of Colegio Militar and Zaragoza (facing Zaragoza, turn right to reach Juárez, the main street). Buses leave every 30min–1hr for Cabo San Lucas (6.30am–11pm; 1hr–1hr 15min) and La Paz (6am–11pm; 1hr 10min–1hr 40min). Minibus taxis line up outside the bus station, but the centre is easy to explore on foot.

Websites Todos has no information centre but is well served by websites: try http://todossantos.com.

TOURS AND ACTIVITIES

Todos Santos Eco Adventures 612 145 0189, http://tosea.net. Arranges a vast range of activities, from horseriding, bird watching and nature walks through the Sierra de la Laguna Biosphere Reserve, to historical tours of the town and surf lessons.

ACCOMMODATION

California Juárez, between Morelos and Márquez de León; http://hotelcaliforniabaja.com. An evening's stay at this gem (completed in 1950) might make it worth parting with some of those pesos you've been setting aside for a rainy day. Rooms are multicultural *mestizos* of Mexican and Moorish decor. There's a pool and restaurant, as well as ocean views from the top floor, though claims that this is the inspiration behind the Eagles' famous 1970s hit have long been dismissed by Don Henley and co. M$$$

María Bonita Colegio Militar, at Hidalgo; 612 145 0855. Best of the budget hotels in town, with twelve simple but clean rooms with small bathrooms above a cosy café, though the road can be a bit noisy. M$$

★ **Hotelito** Dom Conocido s/n Rancho de la Cachora (take C Topete off Juárez); http://thehotelito.com. Fabulous boutique hotel, with a hip contemporary Mexican style, bold colours and four individual cottages set around a central courtyard. Each comes with a terrace and seating area (with hammock), and British expat owner Jenny Armit is a font of local information. M$$$

Posada La Poza Domicilio Conocido, Barrio La Poza (take Olachea off Hwy-19/Degollado, south of the centre); http://lapoza.com. This tranquil boutique is justly lauded for its high quality and extra touches: binoculars and bird guide in each room, sweat lodge, saltwater swimming pool, free kayaks, bikes, fishing gear and internet. All suites have ocean or lagoon views and smart furnishings – no TVs or phones, though (no kids under 13). M$$$$

Todos Santos Boutique Hotel Legaspi 33, between Topete and Obregón; www.hoteltodossantos.com. The most romantic historical hotel in Todos. Built in 1872 by a local sugar baron, this old hacienda contains eight elegantly decorated rooms, a lush garden patio and an enticing pool. M$$$$

EATING

Los Adobes Hidalgo 18, between Juárez and Colegio Militar; http://losadobesdetodossantos.com.mx. Expect pricey but high-quality *alta cocina* such as hearty *sopa de mariscos*, *mole poblano* and organic *chiles rellenos*, served in a serene cactus garden dining room. M$$$$

Café Santa Fe Centenario 4, on the plaza; 612 145 0340. One of the cape's best restaurants, *Santa Fe*'s Northern Italian menu showcases locally sourced ingredients (lobster ravioli) and a stellar wine list that combines vintages from the Valle de Guadalupe and abroad. Tables are set inside an 1850s hacienda or outside on the courtyard patio. M$$

Caffé Todos Santos Centenario 33, between Obregón and Topete; 612 145 0300. Decorated by local artists, this expat-run café with timbered-beam hall and back garden does fine breakfasts, coffees, hot chocolate and muffins. Lunch and dinner are several steps above deli fare. M$$

★ **La Copa Cocina** Legaspi 33, at Todos Santos Boutique Hotel; www.hoteltodossantos.com. Justly popular restaurant with an intimate courtyard, fire pit and garden. Highlights include the fresh fish tacos, seafood pastas and

SURF AND SWIM EL PESCADERO

Before heading further south consider stopping at **El Pescadero**, just 12km from Todos, a small dusty village close to some of the best surf breaks and beaches on the coast: **Playa San Pedrito**, a short walk from the village, and gorgeous **Playa Los Cerritos**, 1km south (look for the turn at km 65). Both beaches are good for swimming. **Mario's Surf School** (612 142 6156, http://mariosurfschool.com) rents surf boards by the day and offers group lessons at Playa Los Cerritos. Cabo San Lucas is another 60km south from Pescadero. Most buses stop at Pescadero, on Hwy-19 (every 30min or so in both directions), but you really need a car to make the most of the area.

ACCOMMODATION

Cerritos Surf Town Playa Los Cerritos, Hwy-19 km 65; http://cerritossurftown.com. Luxurious beachfront resort with palm-roofed, solar-powered studios and villas (with kitchens), pool and bar, and free wi-fi (no TVs). M$$$

Pescadero Surf Camp Hwy-19 km 64 (El Pescadero); http://pescaderosurf.com. Perfectly located to make the most of the beaches and the surf, this collection of cosy palapas, each with electricity, water and bathroom, also has a pool with swim-up bar and can organize surf lessons and board rentals. M$

9

ginger martinis. M$$$

La Coronela Hotel California Juárez, between Morelos and Márquez de León; http://hotelcaliforniabaja.com. Touristy but still a solid bet for Mexican food – eggs Benedict with smoked marlin and cilantro hollandaise or sea bass in tamarind sauce – and tapas on a separate menu. The bar is a great place to grab a drink or sandwich. M$$$

Miguel's Degollado (Hwy-19) and Rangel; 612 145 0814. Rustic Mexican restaurant under a palapa, popular with surfers and locals for its fish tacos and superb battered *chiles rellenos* smothered in salsa. The menu also features cheeseburgers and ice-cold margaritas. M$$

★ **Tacos George's** Colegio Militar 85, between Hidalgo and Márquez de León; 612 102 8768. No-frills street canteen with a few plastic tables selling delicious fried fresh fish tacos using home-made salsas and local tortillas. M$

DRINKING

Shut-up Frank's Degollado (Hwy-19), betweeen Rangel and Cuauhtémoc; 612 145 0707. The town's only sports bar and a popular hangout for US expats, with great burgers, draught beer, free wi-fi and some traditional Mexican food. Cash only.

DIRECTORY

Books and maps Librería El Tecolote (Oct–May Mon–Sat 10am–5pm, Sun 11am–3pm; reduced hours June–Sept; 612 145 0295) on Juárez at Hidalgo has a great selection of new and used English books, and sells detailed local maps. Free maps by Got Baja? (https://facebook.com/@gotbajastore) are available all over town.

Cabo San Lucas

Billfish capital of the world, golfing paradise, home to luxury resorts and a crazy, tequila-fuelled nightlife, **Cabo San Lucas** is hard to ignore. All around lie kilometres of gorgeous beaches set against a pristine desert hinterland, and the jagged cape which gave the town its name remains utterly entrancing – if you're looking to snorkel or dive, the allure will be even greater, with a vast range of marine life and even a friendly **sea lion** colony nearby.

True, Cabo isn't like the rest of Baja. Until the 1980s it was little more than a dusty village and tuna cannery occasionally visited by adventurous sports fishermen – Steinbeck calls it a "sad little town" in *The Log from the Sea of Cortez*. Today it can seem more like an enclave of the US than part of Mexico, with almost all aspects of civilization geared to tourism – millions of North Americans vacation here, and it's a well-established cruise port and Spring Break party town (Feb–March). Transactions are conducted in US currency and million-dollar second homes occupy the best vantage points. Yet it would be a shame for independent and budget travellers to skip Cabo – there's plenty of bargains to be had, and it's hard to resist a couple of nights of sushi, watersports or just unabashed partying.

The marina

Cabo's premier attraction is the rugged cape of **Land's End** (see page 552), though activity in the town itself is centred around the **marina** and **Puerto Paraíso** mall (http://puertoparaiso.mx), which contains over two hundred stores and restaurants, and a ten-screen multiplex cinema (Cinemex; http://cinemex.com). The marina is

WHEN TO VISIT CABO

High season here, as in the rest of Baja, is November until May, though domestic tourists also provide a mini boom July and August. January and February is the best time to see whales. Avoid Christmas and Easter (packed) and Spring Break (Feb/March) if you want to sleep; the fishing competition season in October and November can be fun but also busy. In the summer and early autumn off-season (May–June and Sept–Oct), the heat (up to 42°C) makes things less appealing (though the sea is warm; many locals swim at night). Whenever you visit, you can be assured that it rarely rains – all the fresh water comes from desalination plants.

smothered in yachts and motorboats, and ringed by a pleasant **boardwalk** lined with shops, bars and hawkers touting glass-bottomed boat trips, fishing, waterskiing, scuba diving, snorkelling, paragliding or bungee jumping. Competition is fierce, prices fluctuate daily and places come and go, so shop around. Even with all this activity, you'll see plenty of pelicans and even the odd puffer fish gliding between the boats; a sea lion even makes an appearance (invariably dubbed "Paco" by the locals). The most distinctive building along the marina is the **Pabellón Cultural de la República**, a striking contemporary structure containing a theatre and open-air performance space. Next to it is the **Flea Market El Arroyo**, a lane of covered stalls selling cheap souvenirs, crafts and clothes.

Cabo Adventures

Paseo de la Marina Lote 7-A • 888 526 2238, http://cabo-adventures.com

Towards the southern end of the marina boardwalk, **Cabo Adventures** offers a variety of interactive dolphin packages; the Dolphin Encounter is a twenty-minute swim and play experience with bottlenose dolphins, while other packages offer more time in the water. You can also be a "trainer for a day" for an additional fee.

Museo de Cabo San Lucas

Cabo San Lucas and Lázaro Cárdenas (on Plaza Amelia Wilkes) • Charge • 624 105 0661

Facing sleepy Plaza Amelia Wilkes, the **Museo de Cabo San Lucas** occupies the old town primary school (where Baja educational pioneer Amelia Wilkes Ceseña once taught). Inside there are small rooms displaying fossils from the Sierra de la Laguna (there's also a huge whale skeleton outside), the skeleton of an ancient Pericú woman and galleries on the history, geology and biology of Cabo. Tiny **Parroquia de San Lucas**, just down Avenida Cabo San Lucas, dates back to 1746, a mission established by Jesuit priest Nicolás Tamaral. English and Spanish labels.

Playa El Médano

To the east of the marina is **Playa El Médano**, Cabo's swimming-safe beach – and the place to party. The middle section is a mass of beach bars (see page 555), vendors, booming music, jet skis, parasailing and sunbathers. **Sea Sports in Cabo** (624 155 0051, https://seasportsincabo.my.canva.site) is one of several outfits organizing activities. It's a fun scene, but it's also easy to escape the crowds – the main beach is over 3km long, and mostly deserted at either end. Note that you can walk to the southern end of the beach by following the marina boardwalk to the end.

Playa del Amor (Lovers' Beach)

The small wedge of sand near the tip of the peninsula is known as **Playa del Amor** (Lovers' Beach). The only way to reach it safely is via water taxi or tour boat from the marina or Playa El Médano: the cheapest return trip includes two hours on the beach. You can swim at Playa del Amor, but the beach on the Pacific side of the point – **Playa Divorcio** – is for looking only; the **riptide** will finish off any swimmers.

A steep cliff blocks the Divorcio section from similarly precarious **Playa Solmar** (staff from *Grand Solmar* will try and prevent you from swimming here also, though plenty of hardy surfers ignore the danger). From Del Amor it's possible to swim in the direction of the marina to **Pelican Rock**, where the underwater shelf is home to shoals of tropical fish.

Land's End and El Arco

El Arco, the huge rock arch at Finisterra or **Land's End** itself, not far from Del Amor –where the Sea of Cortez meets the Pacific – is an extraordinary place, with a clear division between the shallow turquoise seawater on the east and the profound blue of the ocean out to the west; a colony of **sea lions** lives on the surrounding rocks. When it's low tide, you can walk right up to the arch from Del Amor, otherwise you'll need to take a boat trip or kayak to get close.

ARRIVAL AND DEPARTURE — CABO SAN LUCAS

By plane Aeropuerto Internacional de Los Cabos lies 43km north of Cabo San Lucas (see page 546). Don't confuse this with the grandly titled Cabo San Lucas International Airport, a small airfield 7km northwest of central Cabo with turboprop flights operated by Calafia Airlines to La Paz, Los Mochis, Mazatlán and Puerto Vallarta. Taxis run into the centre.

By bus Águila buses arrive at the Terminal Central Águila at Hidalgo and Reforma (624 143 5020), 2km from downtown Cabo; taxis run from thr terminal into town, but you might have to flag them down. Local buses trundle past the terminal frequently – any marked "Centro" or "Muelle" should get you to the marina (you can also flag down the air-conditioned Ruta del Desierto buses here, which will drop you on Lázaro Cárdenas, near the marina).

To La Paz the fastest route is "via corta" ("short route"; 2hr 30min) through Pescadero (45min) and Todos Santos, rather than "via larga" ("long route"; 4hr 15min) through San José

and Los Barriles (2hr 15min). Destinations further north in Baja are served far less frequently – one daily direct bus goes as far as Santa Rosalía via Loreto and Mulegé. For points further north (including Tijuana and Mexicali) you'll have more choice in La Paz. Ecobajatours minibuses run direct to Los Cabos airport (45min) at 9.15am, 10.45am, & 12.45pm.
Destinations La Paz via larga (7 daily, every 2hr 5.15am–5.15pm; 3–4hr); La Paz via corta (hourly; 2hr 30min); Loreto (3 daily; 8–9hr); Mulegé (1 daily; 10hr 30min); San José del Cabo (roughly hourly; 30–45min); Santa Rosalía (1 daily; 12hr 15min); Todos Santos (15 daily; 1hr 5min).
Local buses Ruta del Desierto buses run up and down the Corridor between Cabo and San José (daily 4am–11pm; every 10–20min; buses continue all the way to Los Cabos airport) – flag them down on Vicario or at the bus stop on Lázaro Cárdenas (just outside Puerto Paraíso mall). Allow 30–40min to San José. Cabo Baja buses run the same route and are a little cheaper, but not as comfortable.

GETTING AROUND

By bus *Colectivo* buses trundle up and down Blvd Marina every few minutes from the Navy base at the southern end ("Muelle"), towards the bus station via Morelos, El Faro Viejo and Hidalgo (they come down Leona Vicario in the other direction).
By taxi Taxis will try to charge US dollar rates if they can, which are always higher. Trips to Los Cabos airport will set you back the most. If you have a group, rates tend to be better (taxis are usually mini-vans).
Car rental Avis 624 143 4606; Budget 624 143 4190; Hertz 624 146 5088; National 624 143 1414; and Thrifty 624 146 5030. All are located relatively close to each other on Lázaro Cárdenas in the centre (with branches at the airport).

INFORMATION AND ACTIVITIES

INFORMATION

Tourist information Cabo has no official tourist office; the dozens of booths labelled "Tourist Information", while staffed by friendly locals, are really just places dishing out maps, drink coupons and information on tours.

TOUR OPERATORS

Andromeda Divers Playa El Médano; 624 143 8232, http://scubadivecabo.com. Offers local one-tank dives, two tanks, PADI scuba diver courses fand open-water diver courses.
Cabo Adventures Blvd Paseo de la Marina Lote 7-A; 322 226 8413, http://cabo-adventures.com. In addition to its dolphin encounters on Cabo marina (see page 550), it runs zip line tours into the Boca de Sierra Biosphere, camel safaris, snorkelling trips and flyboarding (where you lift into the air above the water).
Cabo Expeditions Blvd Marina (Plaza de la Danza); 624 143 2700, https://caboexpeditions.com.mx. Offers swimming with whale sharks, family-friendly submarine rides, parasailing, kayaking, snorkelling tours, Snuba and Cabo by mountain bike tours.
Cabo Sky Tours 624 144 1294, https://caboskytours.com. Variety of sensational aerial tours (10–60min) with pilot Ernesto Magaña on ultralights (motorized handgliders).

CABO BOAT TRIPS

Buccaneer Queen http://buccaneerloscabos.com. Faithful reproduction of a Spanish galleon (aka pirate ship) that offers family-friendly cruises in local waters.
Cabo EcoTours (EcoCat) 624 157 4685, http://caboecotours.com. Snorkelling trips on the biggest catamaran in Cabo – good for families.
Cabo Escape 624 105 0177, http://caboescapetours.com. This catamaran is the preferred option for the party crowd – on the sundown cruise the main deck transforms into bar and club, with sounds booming across the water long after the boat docks.
CaboRey 624 143 8260, http://caborey.com. Popular sunset and margarita cruises (2hr 30min) with Las Vegas-style Mexican-Argentine floor show on a huge catamaran – it seems a lot less cheesy after a few cocktails. Offers whale watching Dec–March.

ACCOMMODATION

SEE MAP PAGE 551

Most of the resorts occupy the prime real estate immediately around the marina, while downtown has a small selection of budget **accommodation**. The resorts to the east of the marina empty out onto the active Playa El Médano; those to the west have the beautiful but unswimmable Playa Solmar at their doors. Note that airbnb (http://airbnb.com) now offers hundreds of properties in and around Cabo.
Bahia Hotel & Beach Club El Pescador s/n; http://bahiacabo.com. Funky boutique just behind Playa El Médano, with plush modern rooms featuring contemporary Mexican decor and the lauded *La Esquina* restaurant on site. M$$$$
★ **Bajas Cactus Hostel** Lázaro Cárdenas, between Ocampo and Matamoros; 624 178 2102. Excellent budget option and the only hostel in the centre of town, with brightly painted private rooms (shared bathrooms) and shared dorms, all with a/c and cable TV. Rates include breakfast. Dorms M$; doubles M$$
★ **Bungalows Hotel** Libertad, near Herrera; http://thebungalowshotel.com. Perennial favourite and one of the hotels in Cabo; even the smallest rooms are cosy

9

SAND FALLS AND NEPTUNE'S FINGER

Dive trips are big business in Cabo. Experienced **divers** shouldn't miss the rim of a marine canyon at a site known as Anegada, off Playa del Amor, where unusual conditions at 30m create the "**Sand Falls**" (famously discovered by Jacques Cousteau in the 1970s), with streams of sand starting their 2000m fall to the canyon bottom. Nearby, **Neptune's Finger** is a rock pile smothered in sea sponges, gorgonias and sea fans.

suites, the location is perfect (just far enough from the madness), the breakfasts are incredible, and the staff are super-helpful. M$$$$

Casa Bella Boutique Hotel Hidalgo 10 (Plaza Amelia Wilkes); http://casabellahotel.com. This handsome hacienda-style property is definitely worth a splurge, with large, clean rooms, beautiful, blossom-strewn courtyard, small pool and friendly owners in the older part of town. No TVs but breakfast included. M$$$$

Mar de Cortez Lázaro Cárdenas, between Guerrero and Matamoros; http://mardecortez.com. Colonial-style decor in a lovely planted setting with a mix of older and modern, larger rooms around a pool; some have terraces and all have a/c. Also has a good restaurant, free wi-fi and free parking. Closed Sept. M$$$

Los Milagros Matamoros 116; http://losmilagros.com.mx. Tasteful, studio-like rooms, a small pool and a sun deck make this a real find, just a few blocks from the action. Reservations recommended. M$$$

★ **Norman Diego's The Mexican Inn** 16 de Septiembre and Abasolo; http://themexicaninn.com. The dirt road just outside the door gives a false impression of the comfort at this small B&B. Coffee and *postres* are served around the courtyard's fountain every morning and Mexican tile work, queen-size beds, a/c and TVs adorn the rooms. M$$$

Tesoro Los Cabos Marina s/n; https://tesororesorts.com/en. Best all-round location if you're aiming to be in the heart of the action, with large, comfy rooms in the giant adobe-like palatial property overlooking the marina and a fabulous pool deck; the junior suites are much bigger than the standards, some with kitchens. M$$$

EATING

SEE MAP PAGE 551

Bar Esquina El Pescador 1; http://bahiacabo.com. This Alhambra-themed restaurant (think Moorish lamps and tiles) with lovely veranda specializes in Mexican-influenced Mediterranean flavours, using locally grown, organic produce and seafood; highlights include the short rib, blue cheese pizza and a decadent sticky toffee pudding. The attached coffee shop sells decent espresso and muffins. M$$$

Captain Tony's Marina 8–6 (near the Tesoro); http://piscesgroupcabo.com/captain-tonys. Right on the water, knocking out special beer-battered fish tacos and freshly cooked catch of the day (they'll also cook yours for you). The wood-smoked pizzas are also pretty good. M$$$$

Latitude 22+ Roadhouse Hwy-1 km 4.5 (next to Costco); 624 143 1516. Classic old Baja bar and diner, despite the incongruous location, draped with fishing memorabilia and offering a menu of slow-roasted prime rib, Philly cheese steak, burgers and pastas. M$$

★ **Mama's Royal Café** Hidalgo at Zapata; 624 143 4290. Best known for its amazing breakfasts, especially the French toast and two-dozen *huevos* choices, this gringo staple is now open for lunch (sandwiches and Mexican dishes with huge salsa bar), but remains a lot cheaper and better than most of what Cabo has to offer. M$$

Maro Shrimp House Hidalgo at Zapata; 624 264 0868. Revived incarnation of the famed *Shrimp House* (now operated by Maro, one of the ex-employees) serving shrimp special sauce, fresh boiled shrimp by the kilo or half kilo, lobster and some Mexican plates, home-made ice cream and the famous Bulldog cocktail (comprising tequila, lemonade and beer). M$$$

Mi Casa Cabo San Lucas (Plaza Amelia Wilkes), at Lázaro Cárdenas; http://micasarestaurantcabo.com. This old Cabo joint has new Cabo prices in its otherwise low-key open-air restaurant decorated with handmade lanterns. The pan-Mexican menu features carnitas de Michoacán (pork), chicken in Oaxacan *mole* and Sonoran beef. M$$$

Nick-San Plaza de la Danza, Blvd Marina Lote 10 Local 2; http://nicksan.com. Plenty of restaurants in Baja will sell you raw fish without knowing what they're doing with it – *Nik-San* is the exception (helmed by Ángel Carbajal and Masayuki Niikura). In addition to the extensive selection of locally caught sushi and sashimi, the Indonesian-inspired lobster soup is especially tasty. M$$$$

★ **Roasted Grill & Bar** Pescador 2342; http://roastedcabo.com. This small but chic flame grill restaurant has a good number of weekly specials and a fair few innovative dishes too. It's a little on the pricey side, but if you're looking for ambiance and good food it's worth it. M$$$$

Tacos Gardenias Paseo de La Marina 3; http://tacosgardenias.com. This justly popular taco restaurant, with an open-front, no-frills interior, has been knocking out tasty fish and shrimp tacos and shrimp molcajete (with salsa, onion and cheese) since 1980. M$

Taquería El Paisa Lazaro Vicario, at Alikan; 624 144 4046. This legendary taco spot offers flame-grilled steak or pork tacos topped with blackened onions making a delicious, cheap meal. You'll see several imitators with similar names all over town, but this is the original. M$

DRINKING AND NIGHTLIFE

SEE MAP PAGE 551

Baja Brewing Co Marina Boardwalk, at Puerto Paraíso Mall; http://bajabrewingcompany.com. Baja Sur's original microbrewery comes to Cabo, serving pints such as Baja Blond and Peyote Pale Ale with live music Thurs–Sat nights after 8pm. Plenty of pub food available. There's another branch on the rooftop terrace of the Cabo Villas Beach Resort on Playa Médano.

Billygan's Island Playa Médano (Paseo del Pescador); 624 139 7373. The smallest of the three central beach bar-restaurants that caters to partygoers all day, famed for its house cocktail simply dubbed "Billygan's". Breakfast, lunch and dinner are served right on the sand, and tropical drinks

THE CORRIDOR'S BEST BEACHES

The distinction between Cabo San Lucas and San José del Cabo blurs further each year as new resorts are erected along the 33km Corredor Turístico (aka Hwy-1), or just the **Corridor**, separating the two towns. As a general rule, Sea of Cortez beaches may be swimmable and Pacific beaches never are, but before you **swim** or **surf** anywhere in Los Cabos, ask a local and read any posted signs. Obey any **signs** warning you off wet sand and note that beaches deemed safe one season may not be safe year-round – summer especially can be hazardous.

The good news is that every beach is free and open to the public, though getting to and from them can be a hassle without your own car. With the exception of Playa El Médano in Cabo San Lucas and Palmilla in San José, you can't comfortably reach any of the beaches on foot unless you're staying at one of the adjacent resorts. If you've got your own transport you can turn off Hwy-1 at any of the beaches and park in the sand; **local buses** (see page 553) run up and down the highway every twenty to thirty minutes between around 5am and 10pm daily (just flag them down). There are no toilets or lifeguards at the beaches, and if you want shade, food or drink, bring your own. All distances below are measured east from Cabo San Lucas towards San José del Cabo, 33km away.

Barco Varado, km 9. The remains of a Japanese trawler that sank in 1966 lie offshore here, making diving the main focus of this beach, though it's also a popular surfing spot. Take the marked dirt access road off the highway; mind the rocks on your way down.

Bahía Santa María, km 13. You can scuba and snorkel on rock reefs (rays and turtles hang out here) at both ends of this horseshoe cove, and go swimming at the protected beach in the middle. There's a secure parking lot ten minutes' walk from the beach (signposted from the highway).

Bahía Chileno, km 14.5. There are toilets here (the only beach that has them) and a dive shop that rents watersports equipment (nothing with a motor, though), making Chileno one of the easiest beaches to enjoy. Definitely the best family beach; excellent for swimming, diving and snorkelling, or just relaxing along the well-packed sand – it's also one of the few beaches with shady palm trees. Look for the signs to "Chileno Beach Club". It's popular, so go early.

Playa Palmilla, km 27. Good, safe 1.5km-long beach used by San José hotel residents needing escape from the strong riptide closer to home. Point and reef breaks when surf's up. Popular for standup paddle boarding. Access the beach by following signs to *One & Only Palmilla* and taking the only dirt-road cut-off to the left, about 2km from Hwy-1.

Playa Acapulquito, km 28. AKA Old Man's, this is a top surfing beach for beginners, blurring into Costa Azul. Also home to super-cool Cabo Surf.

Costa Azul, km 28.5. The region's best surfing beach is known for the Zippers and La Roca breaks during the summer (look out for rocks at low tide). Board rentals available at the car park. Swimming is possible during the late winter and early spring, but ask at *Zippers* beach restaurant (daily 11am–10.30pm; 624 172 6162) before you dip in.

are poured and consumed nonstop.

Cabo Wabo Vicente Guerrero, between Lázaro Cárdenas and Madero; http://cabowabocantina.com. Rocker Sammy Hagar (of *Van Halen* fame) opened his boisterous club in 1990 (marked by the landmark mini-lighthouse). It's still a good place to hear live music – and if you're going here over a US public holiday, perhaps you can catch Sammy himself on stage. The bar also makes a popular tequila of the same name (used on its tequila shrimp and in the signature Red Rocker cocktails), and a sensational lobster burrito.

Cachet Beach Club Playa Médano (Paseo del Pescador); http://corazoncabo.com/dining/corazon-beach-club. The first beach bar on the Médano strip heading east is a relatively new edition (part of Cabo Villas Beach Resort), with shaded loungers and beach chairs serviced by a crew of cocktail-carrying staff. You get a chair with a towel and umbrella with the entry fee (or free if you buy at set amount of food and drink).

Giggling Marlin Marina s/n, at Matamoros; http://gigglingmarlin.com. A Cabo institution, drawing an older set than other places on the strip. Mostly a place to drink and dance to Latin standards: chances of getting out without hearing *La Bamba* are slim.

Mango Deck Playa Médano (Paseo del Pescador); http://mangodeckcabo.com. Sprawling complex and one of the hottest spots on the beach (especially during Spring Break, Feb–April), where local celebrity "Big Johnson" dispenses tequila shots. Bikini contests, staff shows and wet T-shirts – you get the idea. Excellent buffet and live music.

La Pintada Lázaro Cárdenas s/n, at 20 de Noviembre; http://lapintada.mx. Cabo's only microbrewery occupies large, wood-beamed premises on the otherwise uninspiring main drag; try beers such as Premium Lager and Chocolate Stout on tap, served with tasty olive and cheese breads (free), with a large range of bottled beers and an excellent happy hour. Decent but pricey food cooked up on a wood-fired grill.

El Squid Roe Lázaro Cárdenas s/n, at Zaragoza; http://elsquidroe.com. If you just want to go nuts, this Cabo three-storey classic should be your first stop; a wild party atmosphere where table dancing is allowed. There's a full dinner menu of Tex-Mex dishes alongside cocktails such as the yard-long margarita.

DIRECTORY

Banks and exchange Reliable ATMs at Bancomer on Lázaro Cárdenas at Hidalgo; ATMs also line the marina boardwalk. Note that since almost every business in Cabo accepts US dollars, most banks have stopped exchanging dollars into pesos (they might change other currencies, but if you need to change money, try one of the town's several *casas de cambio*; there's one by *Giggling Marlin*, which offers decent rates until 11pm). Don't change money at the airport; it has the worst rates. Note that if you do use US dollars to pay for things quoted in pesos, expect a very poor exchange rate.

Consulates Canada at Plaza San Lucas, Carretera Transpeninsular km 0.5, Local 82 Col El Tezal, 624 142 4262; US at Tiendas de Palmilla, Carretera Transpeninsular km 27.5, San José del Cabo, 624 143 3566.

Emergencies 066; Green Angels highway help 074; Police 624 143 3997 or 624 142 0361; Federal police 088.

Hospital AMC American Medical Center (624 143 4911, http://amchospitals.com) is open 24hr at Lázaro Cárdenas 911 (entrance on Paseo de la Marina).

Internet You can pick up free wi-fi all over town, and most restaurants and bars now offer free wi-fi in Cabo San Lucas.

Post office On Lázaro Cárdenas, at Camino Real (Mon–Fri 8am–7pm, Sat 9am–3.30pm).

Visa extension Migración office is at Lázaro Cárdenas 1625 (to the right of Europcar). Mon–Fri 9am–4pm.

San José del Cabo

SAN JOSÉ DEL CABO, 33km northeast of Cabo San Lucas, is the older and more sedate of the two towns – if Cabo's nightlife and beach activities have little appeal, stay here instead. Founded as a mission in 1730 by Jesuits, it was abandoned after the Pericú revolt just four years later. A mix of ex-pirates, lapsed missionaries and drop-out miners began to repopulate the town in the early nineteenth century and turned the area into a small port and an agricultural centre. Although frequently referred to as colonial, no traces remain of San José's first settlement, and none of the buildings dates further back than the late 1880s.

Plaza Mijares

Though increasingly hemmed in by shops and resorts, sleepy **Plaza Mijares** and **Bulevar Mijares** (which now leads to the modern **Zona Hotelera** about 1km seaward) are still more or less unspoiled, though there's little to do beyond browsing the numerous high-end shops, art galleries and restaurants that line the streets and shady courtyards, aimed squarely at well-heeled tourists. Dubbed the **Art District**, this part of town has been given a tasteful makeover in recent years (see Art Walk page 558).

The plaza's twin-towered church, **La Misión de San José del Cabo Añuití**, was built in 1932 on roughly the site of the original Jesuit foundation; though it isn't much to look at from the outside (note the tile mural on the facade depicting the murder of Father Tamaral by the Pericú), the interior offers a tranquil and cool respite from the afternoon heat. On the other side of the plaza near the giant Mexican flag, the **Jardín de los Cabeños Ilustres** proudly displays statues of the region's famous sons, including

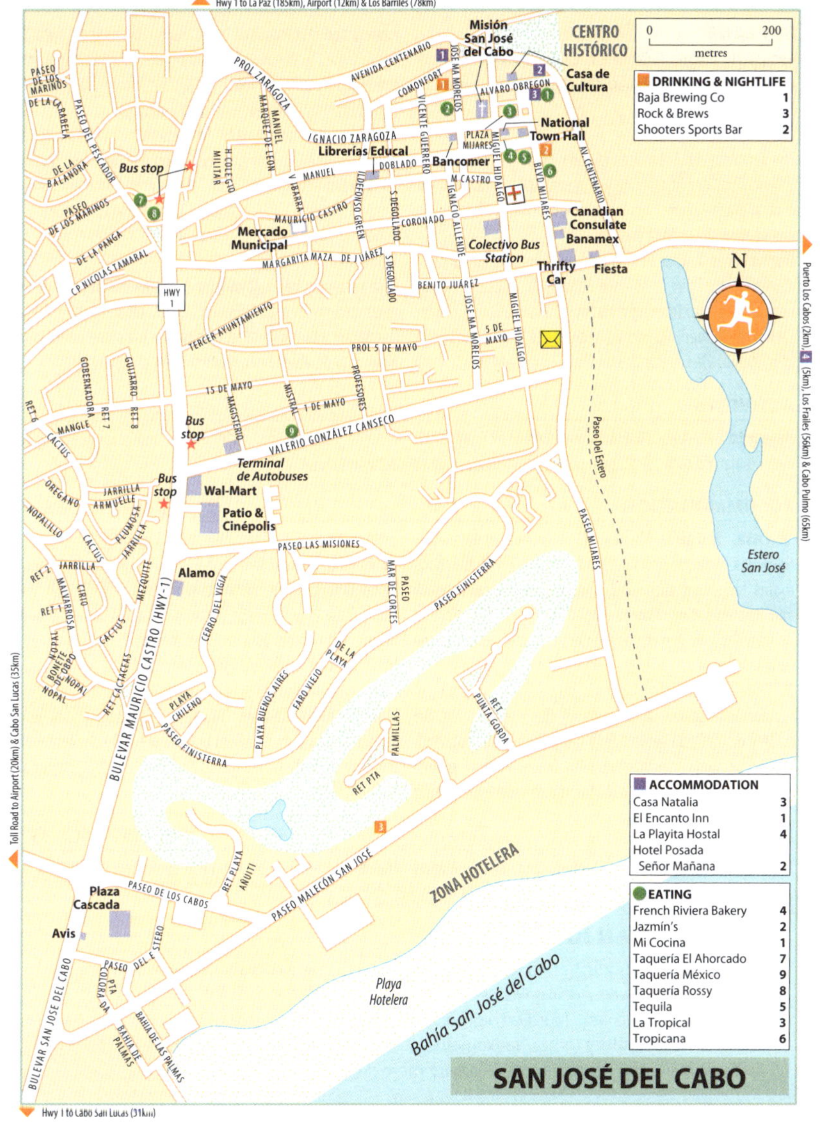

9

Antonio Mijares (local hero of the Mexican-American War), though non-Mexicans will have a hard time recognizing any of them.

Mercado Municipal

Between Coronado and Castro, at Ibarra

The modest town market, the **Mercado Municipal**, is a short walk from the plaza, a relatively small indoor setup with souvenir stalls, crafts, textiles and fresh veg and meat sellers. Next door is a covered annexe crammed with cheap *loncherías*.

ARRIVAL AND DEPARTURE — SAN JOSÉ DEL CABO

BY PLANE

Aeropuerto Internacional de Los Cabos lies 19km north of downtown San José del Cabo (see page 546).

BY BUS

The Terminal de Autobuses (Águila; 624 130 7339) is on Valerio González just off Hwy-1, a long, hot walk from the central Plaza Mijares. Taxis (usually waiting) will take you anywhere in town for a flat fee.

Departures Águila runs buses to Cabo San Lucas (30–45min) every hour or so 4am–10pm; the route to La Paz (3hr–3hr 20min) from here on Hwy-19 via Cabo (and Todos Santos) is dubbed "via corta" ("short route"). Buses to La Paz (3hr 30min) via Los Barriles on Hwy-1 are "via larga" ("long route") and less frequent (6am, 8am, 10am, 1pm, 4pm & 6pm). Buses to various places along the Baja Peninsula are much less frequent; Loreto (3 daily; 9hr 30min) and Mulegé (1 daily; 11hr 20min) are also on the network.

Local buses Modern Ruta del Desierto a/c buses run up and down the Corridor between Cabo and San José (every 10–20min) – flag them down at the marked bus stops on Hwy-1 (Mauricio Castro). Allow 30–40min to Cabo.

BY TAXI

Each company has its own stand; there's one on the main plaza at Zaragoza and Hidalgo, while most of the others line Mijares, but they all tend to charge the same rates. Your hotel may be able to negotiate slightly cheaper prices.

ACTIVITIES

Bajawild Hwy-1 km 28, Plaza Costa Azul 5; 624 148 2222, http://bajawild.com. Arranges snorkelling and kayaking tours to Cabo Pulmo, surfing tours and a range of other activities.

ACCOMMODATION — SEE MAP PAGE 557

★ **Casa Natalia** Mijares 4; http://casanatalia.com. Gorgeous boutique hotel right on the plaza, with luxurious rooms festooned with bold, contemporary local artwork and sporting tiny, flower-draped terraces. Breakfast is delivered to your terrace, and there's a shuttle service to the beach. M$$$$

El Encanto Inn Morelos 133; http://elencantoinn.com. Comfortable option, just north of the plaza in the art gallery district and set inside two separate buildings, both with courtyards overflowing with blossoms and plants. Hacienda-style rooms have charm, though some are ageing a little; the pool is a great place to relax. M$$$

La Playita Hostal Rincon del Datilillo, La Playita; http://laplayitahostal.com. Backpacker-friendly hostel, out on tranquil La Playita beach (5km from town). Offers 6-bed dorms, with access to a small shared kitchen, plus cheap, basic doubles with a/c (some with private bathrooms). Dorm M$, doubles M$$

Hotel Posada Señor Mañana Obregón 1; http://senormanana.com. Excellent budget option in the centre of town, with clean, comfy rooms and a wonderful communal kitchen. M$$

EATING — SEE MAP PAGE 557

French Riviera Bakery Manuel Doblado, at Miguel Hidalgo; 624 105 2624. People keep coming to this trendy,

ART WALK, SAN JOSÉ

Get an insider's introduction to San José 's art galleries at the **Art Walk**, Thursdays 5–9pm (Nov–June only), when local galleries open their doors with special events and the odd glass of wine. There were fourteen high-quality galleries here at last count, among them the **Frank Arnold Gallery** (http://frankarnoldart.com), Comonfort 1137, home of the respected Californian artist. See http://artcabo.com for more details.

contemporary café for coffee, French pastries, cakes and both savoury and sweet crêpes – you can also buy baguettes and other freshly baked delights to take out. Free wi-fi. M$$$

Jazmín's Morelos, between Zaragoza and Obregón; http://jazminsrestaurant.com. The best-value traditional Mexican food in town, in a pretty dining room decorated with brightly coloured *papel picado* (paper art) and Pancho Villa memorabilia. Also has excellent breakfasts, *and* perhaps the best *chilaquiles* on the cape. M$$$$

★ **Mi Cocina** Mijares 4, inside Casa Natalia; http://casanatalia.com/cuisine. The torch-lit atmosphere is captivating, and chef Loïc Tenoux's French-influenced Mexican dishes are inspired. Charred *poblano* chiles stuffed with lamb share the menu with Baja fish and chips and seafood risotto. M$$$$

Taquería El Ahorcado Pescadores and Marinos; 624 152 3989. AKA "Tacos the Hangman", this popular local stall serves juicy roasted meat, Pibil pork, quesadillas and, for the adventurous, beef tongue and even brain tacos. Walk to the end of Doblado, cross Hwy-1 and take the first right (on Pescador). M$

Taquería México Valerio González, at Maestros (not far from bus station); 624 105 2171. Diner with thatched palapa roof, popular as much as for its *pozole*, stuffed potatoes, fresh juices and burritos as for its beloved tacos *arrachera* and *pastor*. Try also the *taco de gobernador* (shrimp taco covered with cheese). M$$

Taquería Rossy Hwy-1 km 33 (opposite Manuel Doblado); 624 142 6755. This small restaurant on the west side of Hwy-1 is the lunch spot of choice for budget travellers seeking fish tacos – worth the 20min walk from the plaza (you can also take a bus). Battered pieces of fillets, marlin, dorado and *carne asada* tacos are the mainstay here. M$

Tequila Manuel Doblado 1011, between Mijares and Hidalgo; 624 142 1155. The top choice in town for Mexican *alta cocina*, with a gorgeous courtyard, garden dining area and attentive waiting staff. Cigar fans should check out the walk-in humidor. M$$$$

★ **La Tropical** Plaza Mijares; 624 175 7858. Simple hole-in-the-wall selling mouth-watering ice "paletas" (lollies/popsicles) in a huge array of tropical fruit flavours (guava, pineapple, tamarind) as well as ice cream on sticks. M$

Tropicana Mijares 38; 624 142 1580. A colonial-style restaurant with an attractive tiled, palapa-covered sitting area on the main drag that's a popular choice for meals or afternoon drinks. Serves excellent breakfasts and usual Tex-Mex fare, often with dancers providing entertainment in the evenings. M$$$

DRINKING AND NIGHTLIFE

SEE MAP PAGE 557

Baja Brewing Co Morelos 1277, between Obregón and Comonfort; http://bajabrewingcompany.com. Baja Sur's best microbrewery – founded by three guys from Colorado – serves its fresh beers in an open, wood-covered bar. Excellent happy hour and there's live music Thurs–Sat.

Rock & Brews Plaza el Pescador, Paseo Malecón; http://rockandbrews.com. The US rock-themed franchise, owned by KISS band members, opened here in 2013, delivering its trademarked live shows (from local bands), music videos, American comfort food and decent selection of craft beers.

Shooters Sports Bar Doblado, at Mijares; 624 146 9900. Rooftop bar with views over the town and the plaza. Also does decent bar food like chicken wings and quesadillas.

DIRECTORY

Banks ATMs at Bancomer, on Zaragoza and Morelos, and Banamex, at Mijares and Coronado.

Books Librerías Educal (449 994 1009), Doblado at Idelfonso Green.

Emergencies Police 624 143 3997 or 624 142 0361; IMSS Hospital 624 143 1594.

Pharmacy Numerous around the plaza and several on Mijares (most close for lunch).

Post office On Mijares, on the way to the hotel zone from the beach (Mon–Fri 9am–6pm).

The East Cape

The **East Cape** region features 120km of wild coastline, littered with stunningly beautiful **beaches**, especially around **Cabo Pulmo**. There is only a handful of towns and villages, with far less development than Cabo San Lucas and San José del Cabo, though thanks to a major influx of North American "snowbirds", US dollars are also widely accepted here, and English is often spoken.

Cabo Pulmo

The best of the East Cape is protected within **Cabo Pulmo National Marine Park** (https://cabopulmonationalpark.com), with pristine beaches and a rare hard coral reef just offshore. The area is anchored by the off-the-grid village of **CABO PULMO**, which has a population of around 250, basic facilities (only solar power), no

9

paragliders and no jet skis. The beach here is rocky with strong riptides, but just fifteen minutes' drive south on a bumpy gravel road is **Playa Los Arbolites** (entry charge), a gorgeous privately owned beach with palapas, toilets and showers, and decent snorkelling. About five minutes further south by car is **Playa Los Frailes** (free, no facilities), a picturesque cove with sensational snorkelling – it can be like swimming in a fish tank, with rays and turtles also gliding around. There's also a **sea lion colony** about 1km further along the shore, accessed by boat, kayak or by a combination of wading and swimming (strong swimmers only). Rent snorkelling gear back in Cabo Pulmo.

ARRIVAL AND DEPARTURE — CABO PULMO

By car/taxi There is no public transport to Cabo Pulmo. Driving, it's best to take Hwy-1 towards Los Barriles from San José, and turn off (right) where the signs says "Cabo Riveria" or "Cabo Pulmo" at km 93, before a long bridge. After the own of La Ribera the surfaced road runs out and the last 30min is via bumpy gravel and sand track (if it's not raining heavily, normal cars can make it). Allow 2hr from Cabo San Lucas.

ACTIVITIES

Cabo Pulmo Dive Center Cabo Pulmo Beach Resort; 624 141 0726, http://cabopulmo.com. Offers a host of dive trips and PADI courses.

ACCOMMODATION AND EATING

Baja Bungalows http://bajabungalows.com. Huge range of affordable rooms and vacation rentals, from small bungalows to more luxurious suites and casitas (some with full kitchen), all a 3min walk from the beach (bring shampoo). Solar-powered electricity and free but slow wi-fi is available. M$$$

El Caballero Cabo Pulmo 624 113 9129. Best place to eat Mexican food around here, and the most dependable hours, with outdoor seating under palapas and the obligatory blaring TV. Also has a bar and sells groceries. M$$$

Cabo Pulmo Beach Resort http://cabopulmo.com. Rustic palm-thatched bungalows just off the beach, with kitchens, solar power and a/c in the three deluxe casitas. Doubles as the Cabo Pulmo Dive Center. M$$$

Los Barriles

The largest and most accessible resort town on the East Cape is **LOS BARRILES**, a **sportfishing** and **windsurfing** centre some 66km north of Los Cabos airport on Hwy-1 (beyond the turning to Cabo Pulmo). Though it gets busy in the winter, it retains a fairly laid-back scene, with low-key development along the shore. Calle Los Barriles runs down from the highway to Calle 20 de Noviembre, the main beach access road and where most of the hotels, restaurants and ATV rental shops are located. The wind, best in winter, is brilliant for experienced windsurfers (less so for beginners) and makes this a regular venue for international competitions.

ARRIVAL AND DEPARTURE — LOS BARRILES

By bus The "via larga" Águila buses between Cabo San Lucas/San José and La Paz (2hr) drop you at the intersection of the highway and Calle Los Barriles, from where there's a half-kilometre walk down to Calle 20 de Noviembre. Moving on, just flag them down at the same junction.

ACTIVITIES

Vela Baja Playa del Sol Hotel, Los Barriles; https://vanwormerresorts.com. The best place to rent equipment or take windsurfing lessons, operating out of the *Playa del Sol* hotel on the beach. Nov–March only.

ACCOMMODATION

East Cape RV Resort http://eastcaperv.com. Prettiest RV park on the cape, not far from the beach in the heart of town; has a pool and hot tub, with wi-fi is extra. M$$

Hotel Los Barriles 20 de Noviembre, north of C Los Barriles; http://losbarrileshotel.com. You'll find simple, clean and good-value lodgings at this congenial hotel, with a pool, plenty of boats for rent and all sorts of activities on offer. M$$$

Hotel Palmas de Cortez http://vanwormerresorts.com. This plush, landmark resort dates back to 1959, right in the heart of Los Barriles, and can arrange a plethora of activities and outings for you. You can also get package deals that include all meals. M$$$$

EATING

The choice of restaurants in Los Barriles increases every year, from no-frills *taquerías* and cafés to burger joints and gourmet restaurants, most lining 20 de Noviembre.

Caleb's Cafe C. 20 de Noviembre; 612 141 0531. Small café and diner in the heart of the main drag, offering grilled fish sandwiches, fish and shrimp tacos, burgers and breakfasts ranging from oatmeal to big plates of eggs. M$$

Tío Pablo's C. 20 de Noviembre; 612 141 0340. This US-expat-run restaurant with a mammoth menu of delicious burgers, fish, and especially good pizzas, remains a dependable choice. M$$$

Oaxaca

CHURCH OF SANTO DOMINGO DE GUZMÁN

Oaxaca

The state of Oaxaca is one of the most enticing destinations in Mexico. The state capital, cosmopolitan yet utterly Mexican, encapsulates much of what the region has to offer. Here and in the surrounding countryside Indigenous traditions are powerful; nowhere else in the country are the markets so infused with colour, the fiestas so exuberant, or the old languages still so widely spoken. There are traditions in the villages that long predate the Spanish Conquest; yet the city can also offer sophisticated modern dining, great places to stay and wild nightlife. The landscape, too, represents a fundamental break, as the barren deserts of the north are replaced by thickly forested hillsides, or in low-lying areas by swamp and jungle. On the Pacific coast, Puerto Escondido and Huatulco are established resorts with very different characters, while Puerto Ángel and its surrounds offer a more back-to-basics beach experience.

If you've come from Mexico City or the north, the physical differences of the region are compounded by its relative lack of development. Industry is virtually nonexistent, and while the city of Oaxaca and a few coastal hot spots have thrived on tourism, the rest of the state is woefully underdeveloped – the "Mexican economic miracle" has yet to reach the south. Indeed, the region witnessed considerable **political disturbance** in the early years of the twenty-first century, though for the moment the protests seem to have been subdued.

The city of **Oaxaca** is the region's prime destination, close enough to Mexico City to attract large numbers of tourists to its fine crafts stores, markets, seemingly constant fiestas, cobbled, gallery-lined walkways and excellent restaurants. The church of Santo Domingo here is one of the region's – and the whole of Latin America's – most magnificent examples of **Baroque** architecture, fusing Spanish and native influences to spectacular effect. And it's just one of many. Nearby, the Zapotec and Mixtec sites at **Monte Albán**, **Yagul** and **Mitla** are less well known than their ancient contemporaries in central and eastern Mexico, but every bit as important and impressive. All this is set among spectacular mountain scenery where the Sierra Madre del Sur meets the Sierra Madre de Oaxaca, the continuation of Mexico's central volcanic belt.

On the coast, west of the mountains, lie some of the emptiest and best **Pacific beaches** in Mexico. The resorts of **Puerto Escondido** and **Huatulco** are now firmly on the map, though Escondido still has the flavour of the surfer hangout in which it has its origins, while Huatulco, conceived and purpose-built as an environmentally conscious resort, can still boast some wonderful and relatively empty sands. Between the two, around **Puerto Ángel**, are several tranquil beach villages with a distinct "alternative" vibe.

Oaxaca

The city of **OAXACA** sprawls across a grand expanse of deep-set valley, 1600m above sea level. Its colour, folklore, Indigenous markets and magnificent colonial centre make it one of the country's most rewarding destinations even though, with a population of over 250,000, it is well on its way to becoming an industrial city. Many streets are choked and noisy and a thin veil of smog often enshrouds the valley – yet in the **colonial centre** the city's provincial charm is hardly affected and just about everything can be reached on foot. Simply being in Oaxaca, wandering through its streets and

MAZUNTE

Highlights

1 Oaxaca Indigenous traditions fuse with colonial grandeur in one of Mexico's most hypnotic cities. See page 564

2 Oaxacan food The rich *moles*, potent mescals and aromatic dishes of this exquisite regional cuisine are best experienced in Oaxaca city. See page 579

3 Monte Albán A potent symbol of Zapotec power, these ruins were once an astounding ancient city with a population of over twenty thousand. See page 581

4 Teotitlán del Valle Experience the rich artisan traditions of Oaxaca's Valles Centrales while shopping for iconic *tapetes* (rugs). See page 586

5 Mitla The ancient Zapotec ceremonial centre with sublime greca stonework is considered to be without peer in Mexico. See page 588

6 Benito Juárez Get away from it all in this quaint village named after Oaxaca's most famous son, where you can hike in gorgeous mountain surroundings. See page 594

7 Puerto Escondido Ride the Mexican pipeline – or just watch – at this world-famous surfing spot. See page 597

8 Mazunte See the queens of the sea, female Golfina turtles, in this tranquil oceanside town, or take a trip to the local crocodile lagoon. See page 610

HIGHLIGHTS ARE MARKED ON THE MAP ON PAGE 566

PUEBLA
Mexico City (460km)
Orizaba (313km)
Córdoba (337km)
Izúcar de Matamoros
Tehuacán
Acatlán de Osorio
Lake Miguel Alemán
Teotitlán del Camino
SIERRA MADRE DE OAXACA
Huajuapan de León
Coixtlahuaca
Santiago Apoala
Tejupan
Teposcolula
Yanhuitlan
Nochixtlán
San Martín Huamelulpan
MIXTECA
PARQUE NACIONAL BENITO JUÁREZ
Ixtlán de Juárez
Tlaxiaco
Etla
Benito Juárez
Oaxaca
Monte Albán
San Antonio Arrajola
San Bartolo Coyotepec
Zaachila
Dainzú
Teotitlán del Valle
Lambityeco
Tlacolula
Santa Ana del Valle
San Martín Tilcajete
Santo Tomás Jalieza
Ocotlán
VALLE DE OAXACA
Ejutla
Acapulco (745km)
SIERRA MADRE DEL SUR
Pinotepa Nacional
San José del Pacifico
Río Grande
Lagunas de Chacahua
Laguna Manialtepec
Puerto Escondido
Pochutla
Mazunte
San Augustinillo
Zipolite
Puerto Ángel
PACIFIC OCEAN
HWY 190
HWY 150
HWY 125
HWY 135D
HWY 131
HWY 175
HWY 145
HWY 200
HWY 175D
HIGHLIGHTS
1 Oaxaca
2 Oaxacan food
3 Monte Albán
4 Teotitlán del Valle
5 Mitla
6 Benito Juárez
7 Puerto Escondido
8 Mazunte

OAXACA
N
GULF OF MEXICO
Tlacotalpan
HWY 175
Tuxtla
Sontecomapan
S. Andrés Tuxtla
Catemaco
HWY 180
Villahermosa (600km)
Coatzacoalcos
Tuxtepec
Minatitlán
Acayucan
HWY 185
ISTHMUS
OF
TEHUANTEPEC
Tuxtla Gutiérrez (541km) & San Cristóbal (599km)
SIERRA NORTE
Matías Romero
HWY 185
HWY 190D
HWY 190
HWY 185D
HWY 190
Guiengola
Juchitan
Tehuantepec
Tapachula (677km)
HWY 200
Salina Cruz
Paredón
Puerto Arista (475km)
Gulf of Tehuantepec
uatulco
0
50
kilometres

absorbing its life, is an experience, especially if you happen to catch the city during a **fiesta** (they happen all the time – the most important are listed on page 618). The city is an important **artistic** centre, too, with several state-run and private galleries, craft and jewellery masterclasses and regular exhibitions.

Among the highlights of any visit are the **Museo de las Culturas** and the **Museo Tamayo**, the **markets** (craft shopping in Oaxaca ranks with the best in the country) and the churches of **Santo Domingo** and **La Soledad**, along with the nearby archeological sites of **Monte Albán** and **Mitla**.

Brief history

Once central to the **Mixtec** and **Zapotec** civilizations, Oaxaca had a limited role during the early years of the Spanish Conquest. **Cortés**, attracted by the area's natural beauty, created the title of Marqués del Valle de Oaxaca, and until the Revolution his descendants held vast estates hereabouts. For practical purposes, though, the area was of little interest to the Spaniards, with no mineral wealth and, due to the rugged mountain terrain, no great agricultural value (though coffee was grown). This meant that the **Indigenous** population was largely left to get on with life and did not have to deal with much outside influence beyond the interference of a proselytizing Church.

Nevertheless, by 1796 Oaxaca had become the third-largest city in Nueva España, thanks to the export of cochineal and, later, textile manufacturing. In the nineteenth century it produced two of Mexico's most influential statesmen: **Benito Juárez** (see page 572) is commemorated everywhere in Oaxaca, a privilege not shared by **Porfirio Díaz** (see page 791), the second most famous *Oaxaqueño*, whose dictatorship most people have chosen to forget. Thereafter Oaxaca was something of a political backwater until autumn 2006, when it made international headlines as striking teachers occupied the city's main plaza and clashed with riot police in a dispute that began over wages and mushroomed into protests over corruption and political cronyism; the city is perfectly safe for tourists, but occasional protests and demos rumble on to this day.

Around Plaza de la Constitución

Plaza de la Constitución, along with the adjoining **Alameda de León**, is Oaxaca's kaleidoscopic central reference point. Closed to traffic and surrounded by *portales* (arcades) sheltering languid cafés, the twin plazas offer some of the best free entertainment in the city – displays of music, song and dance, political speeches and protest marches, all overseen by a steady stream of beggars, hawkers, business people, tourists and locals. On Sundays and many weekday evenings you'll find a band playing in the centre, or else a performance or exhibition opposite the cathedral.

Museo del Palacio

Plaza de la Constitución, entry on Flores Magón • Free

Also known as the Government Palace (Palacio de Gobierno), this Neoclassical style local seat of government also plays hosts to a variety of travelling art exhibits. The building is an attraction in itself with fine murals on the stairwells depicting the history of the state, and a high-tech tented roof over the courtyard. The exhibition space, when occupied, can be a bit hit or miss, however the enthusiastic staff almost make up for it. Continuing on from the permanent exhibits that preceded the current set up, the displays follow a theme of biodiversity and the environment. Also, approximately three to four times a year, artwork from local competition winning school children is exhibited front and centre.

Catedral de la Asunción

Alameda de León • Free

Begun in 1553, the **Catedral de la Asunción** wasn't completed until the eighteenth century, thanks to several earthquakes. Since then it's been repeatedly pillaged and restored; as a result, despite a fine Baroque facade, it's far from the most exciting of Oaxaca's churches. It is impressively large though, with a heavy *coro* (choir) blocking the aisle in the heart of the church and a ring of chapels dedicated to various saints surrounding the nave. These days, most of the services are held in the Capilla del Señor del Rayo, centred on a Calvary embellished with gold votives, at the far end of the nave near the altar.

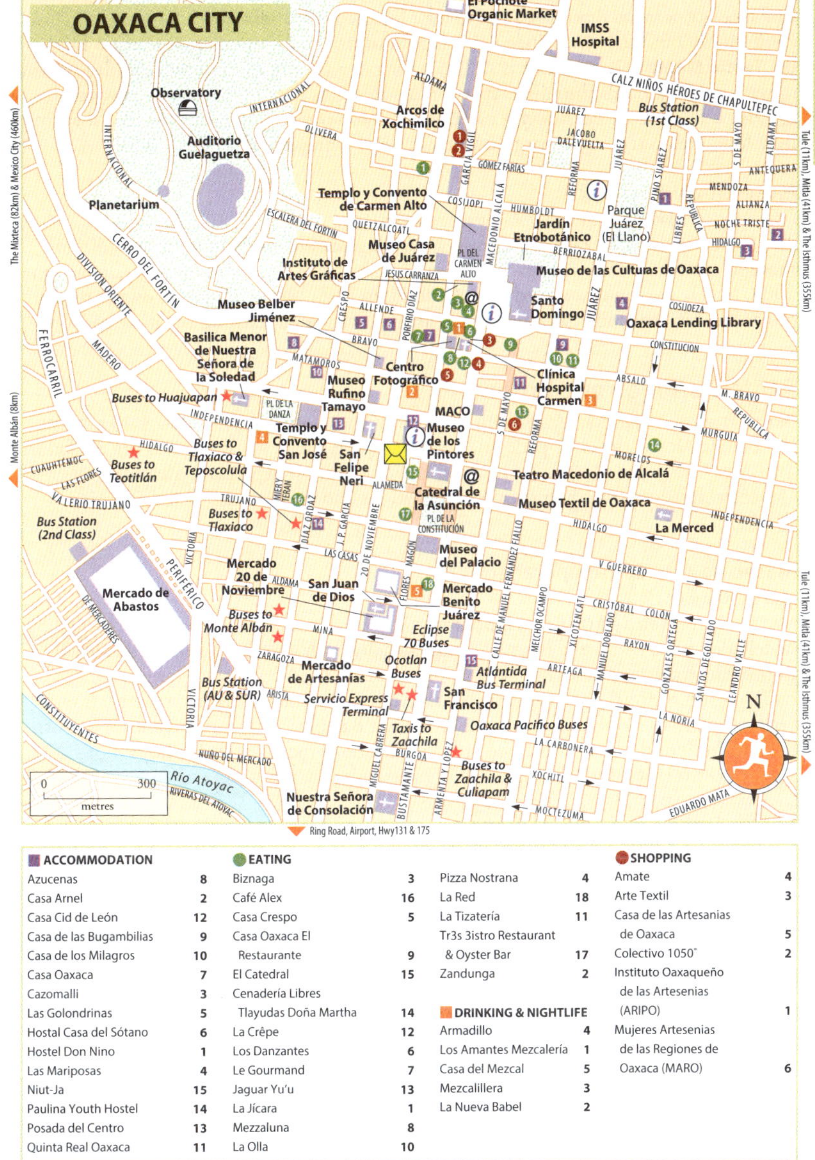

Museo de los Pintores Oaxaqueños

Independencia 607, cnr García Vigil • Charge • 951 516 5645

Just across from the cathedral, the **Museo de los Pintores Oaxaqueños** occupies a beautifully renovated sixteenth-century mansion, in which it hosts temporary exhibitions of modern Oaxacan painters. The quality is usually high, and often the contemporary works are contrasted with those of earlier regional artists.

Teatro Macedonio de Alcalá

Independencia 900, cnr Armenta y López • show tickets for purchase • http://facebook.com/teatromacedonioalcala

Built in 1909 in the French style fashionable during the dictatorship of Porfirio Díaz, the **Teatro Macedonio de Alcalá** is still operating as a theatre and concert hall. It's typical of the grandiose public buildings that sprang up across Mexico in the early twentieth century – behind the *belle époque* exterior, the interior (try going to a show, or sneaking in before one, to see it) is a magnificent swathe of white marble and red plush.

Museo Textil de Oaxaca

Hidalgo 917 • Free, donations requested • http://museotextildeoaxaca.org

The **Museo Textil de Oaxaca** is a showcase for the state's high-quality textile traditions, though it also has temporary exhibitions of textiles from all over the world. Opened in 2008, largely via funds supplied by Alfredo Harp Helú, the ex-Banamex owner turned philanthropist, the museum occupies an artfully renovated sixteenth-century convent.

Santo Domingo and around

North from the Plaza de la Constitución, Valdivieso crosses Independencia to become **Macedonio Alcalá**, the city's pedestrianized shopping street, known also as the Andador Turistico. This is the place to come for the best, and most expensive, Mexican and Oaxacan crafts: exquisitely intricate silver designs and finely executed, imaginative textiles.

Museo de Arte Contemporáneo

Alcalá 202 • Charge • 951 501 1104

MACO, the **Museo de Arte Contemporáneo**, is housed in a seventeenth-century building widely described as Cortés' house, though actually built after his death. Refurbished to provide expansive, modern galleries, the museum hosts temporary exhibits of national and regional contemporary art that can include anything from internationally celebrated artists like Frank Auerbach or Francis Bacon, through collections of Zapotec folk art and political caricatures, to video installations focusing on the impact of Mexican immigration to the US.

Centro Fotográfico Alvarez Bravo

Bravo 116 • Free • www.cfmab.com.mx

The **Centro Fotográfico Alvarez Bravo**, established by painter Francisco Toledo, has seven galleries with permanent and temporary exhibitions of historical and contemporary photographs, plus an excellent reference library.

Santo Domingo de Guzmán

Alcalá s/n • Free

The church of **Santo Domingo de Guzmán** is one of the real highlights of Oaxaca. Consecrated in 1611, this elaborately carved and decorated extravaganza is one of the finest examples of Mexican Baroque anywhere, its external walls (10m thick in some places) solid and earthquake-proof, the interior extraordinarily rich. Parts were damaged during the Reform Wars and the Revolution – especially the chapels, pressed into service as stables – but most of the interior was restored during the 1950s.

The church drips with gold leaf throughout, beautifully set off, especially, by the afternoon light. Highlights include the great gilded main altarpiece and, on the underside of the raised choir above you as you enter, the family tree of Felix de Guzmán, father of St Dominic (the founder of the Dominican Order), in the form of a vine with leafy branches and tendrils, busts of leading Dominicans and a figure of the Virgin right at the top. Looking back from the altar, you can appreciate the relief scenes high on the walls and the biblical events depicted in the barrel roof and the ceiling of the choir, a vision of the heavenly hierarchy with gilded angels swirling in rings around God. The adjoining **Capilla de la Virgen del Rosario** (completed in 1720) is also richly painted and carved: the Virgin takes pride of place in another stunning altarpiece, all the more startlingly intense in such a relatively small space. No sightseeing during Mass.

Museo de las Culturas de Oaxaca

Alcalá s/n • Charge, audio guide extra • 951 516 2991

Next to the church of Santo Domingo, the old Convento de Santo Domingo has been restored to house the absorbing **Museo de las Culturas de Oaxaca**. Construction of the vast *convento* began in 1572, and the church held its first Mass in 1608; from then until 1812 it was occupied by Dominican friars. During the Revolution, the building served as barracks for the Mexican army; the damage inflicted during this period wasn't restored until the 1990s, when the exhibits were installed.

The museum traces the history of Oaxaca in an expansive and elaborately executed labyrinth of galleries that hold displays covering everything from the pre-Hispanic period through to the present day. The archeological finds defy hyperbole, especially the true highlight here: sala 3, dedicated to the magnificent **Mixtec jewellery** discovered in Tomb 7 at Monte Albán (see page 584), including a couple of superb gold masks and armbands. This lavish treasure trove constitutes a substantial proportion of all known pre-Hispanic gold, since anything the conquistadors found they melted down. The museum also owns smaller gold pieces, as well as objects in a wide variety of precious materials – mother-of-pearl, obsidian, turquoise, amber and jade among them. The final galleries, in typically idealistic style, are dedicated to the pluralism of modern Mexico; an enlightening video shows members of each of the state's fifteen Indigenous peoples speaking their own language. Signage throughout is in Spanish only, so the audio guide may be a worthwhile investment.

Jardín Etnobotánico

Entry at cnr of Reforma and Constitución • Guided visits only, charge • http://jardinoaxaca.mx

If you visit the Museo de las Culturas de Oaxaca you'll catch tantalizing views of the mountains as well as another hidden artistic masterpiece – the cactus garden, or **Jardín Etnobotánico**. Beyond the garden's sensual appeal – it's not just an ornate collection of cacti, orchids and plumeria (frangipani), but an oasis of calm in the heart of the city – the tours are also extremely illuminating. The grounds preserve species native to Oaxaca and provide information on plants and insects, such as the *cochinilla* that dwells inside certain varieties of cactus and secretes a substance that is used to produce natural dyes for textiles.

Instituto de Artes Gráficas

Alcalá 507 • Free • www.iago.com.mx

The **Instituto de Artes Gráficas** is one of the many cultural centres in Oaxaca state sponsored by painter Francisco Toledo. Above all there's a fabulous art library, open to the community and always busy with students, with plenty of material in English on art, archeology and literature. The institute also houses an inexpensive café in its shady courtyard and hosts temporary exhibitions and evening music recitals.

Museo Casa de Juárez

García Vigil 609 • Charge • 951 516 1860

10

BENITO JUÁREZ

Benito Juárez ranks among Mexico's greatest national heroes. He was the towering figure of nineteenth-century Mexican politics, and his maxim – *"El respeto al derecho ajeno es la paz"* ("Respect for the rights of others is peace") – has long been a rallying cry for liberals. A **Zapotec**, he strove against nineteenth-century social prejudices and, through four terms as president, successfully reformed many of the worst remnants of Spanish colonialism, earning a reputation for honesty and fair dealing.

Juárez was born in **San Pablo Guelatao** in 1806. His parents died when he was 3, and he grew up speaking only Zapotec; at the age of 12 he was adopted by priests and moved to **Oaxaca**, where he began to study for the priesthood. Turning his talents to law, he provided his legal services to impoverished villagers free of charge, and by 1831 had earned a seat on Oaxaca's municipal council, lending his voice to a disenfranchised people. Juárez rose through the ranks of the city council to become **state governor** from 1847 to 1852, on a liberal ticket geared towards improving education and releasing the country from the economic and social stranglehold of the Church and the aristocracy. In 1853, the election of a conservative government under Santa Anna forced him into eighteen months of exile in the US.

Liberal victory in 1855 enabled Juárez to return to Mexico as minister of justice and give his name to a law abolishing special courts for the military and clergy. His support was instrumental in passing the **Ley Lerdo**, which effectively nationalized the Church's huge holdings, and bills legalizing civil marriage and guaranteeing religious freedom. In 1858, President Ignacio Comonfort was ousted by conservatives enraged by these reforms, and Juárez, as **the head of the Supreme Court**, had a legal claim to the presidency. However, he lacked the military might to hold Mexico City and retired to Veracruz, returning three years later, victorious in the War of Reform, as constitutionally elected **president**. Stymied in his attempts to reduce the power of the Church by an intractable Congress and empty coffers, Juárez suspended all national debt repayments for two years from July 1861. To protect their investments, the British, Spanish and French sent their armies in, but when it became apparent that Napoleon III had designs on the control of Mexico, the others pulled out, leaving France to install Habsburg **Archduke Maximilian** (see page 791) as puppet emperor. Juárez fled again, this time to Paso del Norte (now Ciudad Juárez) on the US border, until by 1867 he was able to return to the capital and to round up his army and execute the hapless Maximilian.

Juárez was returned as president in the 1867 elections but alienated much of his support through attempts to use Congress to amend the constitution. Nevertheless, he secured another term in the 1870 elections, spending two more years trying unsuccessfully to maintain peace before dying of a heart attack in 1872.

The **Museo Casa de Juárez**, opposite the fortress-like Templo y Convento de Carmen Alto, now mostly government offices, is where Oaxaca's most famous son, **Benito Juárez** (see page 572), lived between 1818 and 1828. The house belonged to bookbinder Antonio Salanueva, who virtually adopted the young Benito after hiring him, providing him with a crucial leg-up in Mexican society. The renovated house contains a small collection of Juárez' possessions along with seminal historical documents. Wander through the kitchen, bedroom and dining area exhibits to get an idea of what life must have been like for the middle class in early nineteenth-century Oaxaca, though nothing is original to the house.

Arcos de Xochimilco

Four blocks north of Carmen Alto and the Casa Juárez, shadowing García Vigil, the **Arcos de Xochimilco** are remnants of the eighteenth-century aqueduct of San Felipe. The surrounding streets – increasingly gentrified and home to boutique B&Bs – make a pleasant place to stroll in relative peace, with multicoloured, low-slung, colonial-style houses surrounded by crumbling walls draped in bougainvillea, hole-in-the-wall taco joints, snoozing dogs, street lanterns and giant cacti.

El Pochote organic market

Santo Tomas Xochimilco church, north of Niños Héroes

Tucked away in a churchyard, this small **organic market** features both produce and food stalls, with everything from onions or fresh goat's cheese to Italian pastries and handmade tacos. There are some great drinks stalls, too, with juice, local coffee and traditional Mexican chocolate all on offer, as well as traditional medicines and artesanías. The market is open Fri-Sun, 8am–3pm.

West of the centre

West of the plaza, the streets rapidly become busier and more traffic-choked, the shops and businesses less focused on visitors. In this direction lies one of Oaxaca's finest churches, along with a couple of interesting small museums.

Basílica Menor de Nuestra Señora de la Soledad

Jardín Socrates, between Independencia and Morelos about five blocks west of the Alameda • Free • **Museum** Free, donation requested

The **Basílica Menor de Nuestra Señora de la Soledad**, built between 1682 and 1690, is one of Mexico's most important religious sites. It contains one of the most revered monuments in the country, a statue of the Virgen de la Soledad, Oaxaca's patron saint since 1909. The story goes that in 1620, a statue of the Virgin was mysteriously found in the backpack of a mule en route to Guatemala; some versions claim that Mary herself miraculously appeared. The basilica was constructed in her honour around the rock where this miracle is supposed to have happened (now in an iron cage on your right as you enter the church), though its wedding-cake facade is more recent. Inside, the sumptuous decoration includes a diamond-encrusted crown adorning the statue of the Virgin (a replica, since the original was stolen in the 1980s).

The church is set on a small plaza surrounded by other buildings associated with the Virgin's followers. It's a peaceful spot to watch *Oaxaqueño* life unfold over an ice cream or sorbet, both of which are sold in a beguiling variety of flavours at a cluster of stands – try *tuna* (prickly pear) and mescal in combination. The adjoining **Plaza de la Danza** is the setting of outdoor concerts, *folklórico* performances and specialist craft markets. At the back of the church courtyard the small **Museo Religioso de la Soledad** is devoted to the Virgin's followers. It's a bizarre jumble of junk and treasure – native costumes displayed on permed-blonde 1950s mannequins, *ex voto* paintings giving thanks for miracles and cures – among which the junk is generally far more interesting.

Templo de San Felipe Neri

Independencia, cnr Tinoco y Palacios • Free

The church of **San Felipe Neri** is mostly Baroque, with a richly decorated proliferation of statues on its plateresque facade. It's the interior decor, though, that really makes it interesting. The church was completed in 1773 and later used as barracks during the Revolution. By the 1920s it badly needed to be repainted, which it was – in an incongruous Art Nouveau style. The building's other claim to fame is that it's the church in which Benito Juárez and Margarita Maza were married in 1843.

Museo Rufino Tamayo

Morelos 503 • Charge • http://rufinotamayo.org.mx

A private collection of pre-Hispanic artefacts gathered by the *Oaxaqueño* abstract artist Rufino Tamayo (1899–1991), the **Museo Rufino Tamayo** is set in an attractive house that dates from 1902. The displays include some truly beautiful items, especially pottery and carvings, from all over Mexico; rather than try to explain the archeological significance of its contents, the collection is deliberately laid out as an art museum, with the focus on aesthetic form. Aztec, Maya and western Indigenous cultures all feature strongly, though there's surprisingly little that is Mixtec or Zapotec.

Museo Belber Jiménez

Matamoros 307 • Charge • 951 514 5095

The galleries of the **Museo Belber Jiménez** display the private collection of renowned jeweller Francisco Jiménez and wife Ellen Belber, a treasure trove that includes some magnificent gold Mixtec jewellery, colonial chains and necklaces and a fine collection of twentieth-century silver work by some of Mexico's great masters, including American expats Frederick Davis and William Spratling. There's also a selection of Oaxacan folk art, from rugs and traditional clothing to pottery and lacquer chests. Pride of place goes to the necklace given to Frida Kahlo by Diego Rivera in 1937, engraved with the word "Amor", and a woollen Mexican flag, presented to President Díaz on a visit to Oaxaca. There's also a great, if expensive, shop with high-quality crafts and jewellery including the likes of silver-chased saddles and traditional masks.

South of the Plaza de la Constitución

The **markets** are the main reason most travellers venture south of the plaza. Traditionally, **Saturday** is market day and, although nowadays the markets operate daily, it's still the day to come if you want to see the old-style *tianguis* at its best. *Indígenas* flood in from the villages in a bewildering variety of costumes, and Mixtec and Zapotec dialects replace Spanish as the *lingua franca*.

Mercado Benito Juárez

Occupying the block bordered by Las Casas, Flores Magón, Aldama and 20 de Noviembre

Just one block south of the plaza, the **Mercado Benito Juárez** has something of everything: raw meat, fruit, clothes and bag stalls rub shoulders with some of the best budget places to eat in town. There are also plenty of stalls more obviously focused on tourists: mescal, local cheese and *mole* are the products of choice.

Mercado 20 de Noviembre

Occupying the block bordered by Aldama, Flores Magón, Mina and 20 de Noviembre

The **Mercado 20 de Noviembre** is essentially a giant food court, a cacophony of sights, smells and tastes. Indigenous women wander labyrinthine corridors amid plumes of incense, inviting you to try curious Oaxacan dishes such as *chapulines* (crunchy baked grasshoppers) and *chicharrones* (crispy pork fat). An excellent place to eat, the market is lined with *comedores* serving inexpensive food, such as *chiles rellenos* and tamales. You'll also find the best **mescal** and **chocolate** stores in the surrounding streets (see pages 574 and 580).

MOLE AND CHOCOLATE

Calle Mina, south of the Mercado 20 de Noviembre, is lined with **spice** vendors selling plump bags of the chile-and-chocolate powder that makes up most Oaxacan **moles**. Cinnamon-flavoured **chocolate powder** is also available, for cooking or making into drinking chocolate. One of the best places in this area to try a mug of hot chocolate, laced with almond, cinnamon, sugar or chile and served with *pan dulce*, is *Mayordomo* (http://chocolatemayordomo.com.mx), the Willy Wonka of Oaxaca; the main branch is at the corner of Mina and 20 de Noviembre. You can also buy pure cacao by the kilo and all sorts of chocolate products. Nearby *La Soledad* at Mina 212 (http://chocolatedeoaxaca.com.mx) has a row of old bean-crushing machines and is drenched in the overpowering aroma of sweet cacao – chocolate addicts beware.

Mercado de Artesanías

20 de Noviembre, between Mina and Zaragoza

The **Mercado de Artesanías** is the place for village handicrafts, though again there's also plenty of fresh produce and flowers as well as the infamous *chapulines* (toasted grasshoppers). While many of the goods here are low in price, be warned that it's very touristy – you're harassed far more by the vendors than elsewhere and you may have to bargain fiercely to get your price. Quality is often poor, too, so always check carefully before you buy; *sarapes*, in particular, are often machine made from chemically dyed artificial fibres. You can tell real wool by plucking out a thread – artificial fibres are long, thin and shiny, woollen threads short, rough and curly. There are numerous shops around town that will give you a good idea of the potential **quality** of items you can buy in the market; see page 580 for a few of the best.

Mercado de Abastos

Periférico by the second-class bus station

Biggest, busiest and arguably best of Oaxaca's markets is the sprawling **Mercado de Abastos**. This is where the serious business of buying and selling everyday goods happens; it's the place to go for fruit, vegetables, meat, herbs, spices and all manner of household goods, from traditional cooking pots to wooden utensils and furniture – you could easily spend a couple of hours lost in here, and they certainly wouldn't be wasted.

ARRIVAL AND DEPARTURE — OAXACA

BY PLANE

Oaxaca's airport (Aeropuerto Internacional Xoxocotlán), around 7km south of the city, mainly serves Mexico City; for most other destinations you'll need to change there. Transportación Terrestre Aeropuerto (951 511 5453) operates shared and private taxis; buy your ticket at the desk. They can also bring you back to the airport; call, or visit their office at Alameda de León 1-G, opposite the cathedral (Mon–Sat 10am–2pm). Note that there are no private taxis *from* the airport, only rides headed to it. Between them Aeroméxico (http://aeromexico.com) and VivaAerobus (http://vivaaerobus.com) operate seven to ten direct daily flights to Mexico City, with onward national and international connections; fares increase dramatically during Mexican holiday times. VivaAerobus also flies twice a week to Monterrey, Volaris (http://volaris.mx) five times weekly to Tijuana, and United (http://united.com) three times a week to Houston. Aerotucán (951 502 0840, https://aerotaxisdemexico.com) has a daily flight to Puerto Escondido in a small plane and has in the past also offered flights to Huatulco – it only takes 30min, but the fare is well over ten times the cost of a bus or van.

BY BUS

Bus stations Oaxaca has two main bus stations. The first-class terminal is at Calzada Niños Héroes de Chapultepec 1036, uphill from and northeast of the centre; from here your best bet is to find a taxi. The second-class terminal is west of the centre, off the Periférico by the Mercado de Abastos. AU and Sur second-class buses (north and west towards Mexico City and Puebla especially) stop further round the Periférico; from here cross the road. For the Pacific coast, virtually all the first-class buses take a huge detour along Hwy-190 via Salina Cruz, an 11–13hr marathon. It's much faster to take a direct minivan over the mountains (see below).

Ticketbus offices There are downtown Ticketbus offices at Valdivieso 106, half a block from the plaza, and 20 de Noviembre 103, between Hidalgo and Independencia (daily 8am–8pm; http://ticketbus.com.mx).

Destinations Mexico City (very frequently; 6hr 30min); Pochutla (3 daily; 9hr); Puebla (frequently; 4hr 30min); Puerto Escondido (3 daily; 10hr 30min); San Cristóbal de las Casas (3 daily; 11hr); Tehuantepec (at least hourly; 4hr 30min); Veracruz (5 daily; 7hr); Villahermosa (3 daily; 12hr).

BY MINIVAN AND COLECTIVO

Much the quickest way from Oaxaca to the coast is by minivan, though the direct route across the mountains can be cramped and stomach-churning (for the steadiest ride, aim for a seat close to the front). Most of the operators can be found close to the markets, south of the plaza; in the same area, particularly around the church and park of San Francisco, close to the junction of Armenta y López and La Noria, and also outside the Mercado de Abastos, you'll find terminals for *colectivo* taxis to virtually any village in central Oaxaca.

Destinations Of the minivan operators Eclipse 70 (Armenta y López 504, 951 516 1068) runs to Pochutla (for Puerto Ángel and around) almost hourly from 3.30am to 11.15pm; Atlántida (La Noria 621 at Armenta y López; 951 514 7077) has eleven daily departures to Pochutla; Servicio Express

(Arista 116 and Cabrera; 951 516 4059) has around twenty departures to Puerto Escondido every day. It's about five hours to Pochutla, six to Puerto Escondido, and fares are much the same everywhere.

GETTING AROUND

10

By bus The bus routes are byzantine, and even if you manage to hop on the right one, the traffic is so slow that you could usually have strolled to your destination in half the time.

By car Alamo, 5 de Mayo 203 (951 514 8534, http://alamo.com.mx), generally seem to have the best car rental deals; Europcar are nearby at Matamoros 101 (951 516 9305, http://europcar.com.mx). Both have desks at the airport and their best prices online. You can also try locally based Only Rent a Car (951 514 0255, http://onlyrentacar.com) at 5 de Mayo 215.

By taxi Taxis can usually be found on Independencia at García Vígil opposite the cathedral, or flagged down anywhere. Cabs are not metered, so fix your price first. Note that fares go up at night.

By bike For bike rental try Bicicletas Pedro Martínez, hidden away inside Mesón la Brisa at Aldama 418 (951 514 5935, http://bicicletaspedromartinez.com), or Zona Bici, Garcia Vigil 406 (951 516 0953). Rentals are by the hour or the day. See also tours, below.

On foot Walking is by far the best way to get around central Oaxaca.

INFORMATION

Tourist information The best places for tourist information are the booths at Independencia 607, inside the entrance of the Museo de los Pintores (Tues–Sun 10am–5pm) and on the plaza in front of Santo Domingo, off Alcalá (Mon–Sat 10am–5pm, Sun 10am–3pm). Staff at both are helpful and can supply maps and other handouts. You'll also find maps and leaflets at the state tourism office, Juárez 703, in the Teatro Juárez (daily 8am–8pm; 951 502 1200, http://oaxaca.travel), and the municipal tourist office at Matamoros 102 (daily 8am–8pm; 951 514 1461, https://casadelaciudad.org), though the latter is primarily an admin centre and you'll have to walk inside to find someone to speak to.

Oaxaca Lending Library The Oaxaca Lending Library, at Pino Suárez 519 (Mon–Fri 10am–2pm & 4–7pm, Sat 10am–1pm; 951 518 7077, http://oaxlibrary.org), is a hub of local expat activity, with lectures, meetings and books to borrow or buy, a café and a bulletin board packed with info about what's on locally. There is a small membership fee to take out books.

Newspapers There are plenty of free publications on offer in cafés and tourist offices; the free monthly English-language newspaper, the *Oaxaca Times* (http://oaxacatimes.com), carries topical features, events listings and apartment rentals (handy for those taking courses). The Spanish-language newspaper *Noticias* (http://nvinoticias.com) also has rental ads, and can be bought from newspaper vendors around the plaza.

Websites You can find more on Oaxaca, including accommodation listings and language courses, online at http://oaxaca-mio.com.

TOURS

Scores of operators throughout the centre offer half-day trips to **Monte Albán** and day tours of the villages of the surrounding valleys. Operators include Turismo El Convento de Oaxaca, 5 de Mayo 300 in the *Quinta Real* hotel (http://oaxacatours.mx), Monte Alban Tours, Alcalá 206-F (951 226 2896, http://montealbantours.com), and Descubre Oaxaca, Independencia 709 (951 514 5806).

Adventure and ecotours Expediciones Sierra Norte, Bravo 210-A (951 514 8271, http://sierranorte.org.mx), lead one- to five-day treks around the Pueblos Mancomunados in the Sierra Norte; with everything on offer from horse riding and mountain biking, to good old fashioned hiking and birdwatching tours. Rancho Buenavista, based in San Pedro Ixtlahuaca just outside town (901 228 2951, https://hotelranchobuenavista.com), organizes more adventurous hiking, mountain-biking and rock-climbing expeditions.

Bike tours Bicicletas Pedro Martínez (see page 576) runs brilliant bike tours, from half a day round the valley to a four-day off-road trip to Puerto Escondido; some of the adventure operators above also offer mountain biking.

Horseriding Horseback Mexico, Murguía 403 (951 199 7026, http://horsebackmexico.com), offers anything from two-hour to five-day trips.

ACTIVITIES

Cookery courses Cookery classes are booming in Oaxaca. *Casa Crespo* restaurant, Allende 107 (see page 578; 951 688 1799, https://casacrespo.com), offers four-hour sessions that include shopping and sampling the produce (Tues–Sat 10am, Sun 11am). El Sabor Zapoteco (951 524 4658, http://cookingclasseselsaborzapoteco.blogspot.com) is also excellent. It's run out of Teotitlán del Valle, and the fee includes transportation and a market tour. Seasons of My Heart cooking school, in Rancho Aurora on the northern fringes of town (951 508 0469, http://seasonsofmyheart.com), has a huge variety of courses and culinary tours, from half a day to a full week.

Charity and volunteering The Oaxaca Street Children Grassroots project (Centro de Esperanza Infantil) aims to bring a brighter future to Oaxaca's neediest children. You can contribute to their food and medical programme, or volunteer with them in Oaxaca by contacting the centre at Crespo 308 (951 501 1069, http://oaxacastreetchildren.org). Fundación En Vía, based at the Instituto Cultural Oaxaca, Juárez 909 (951 515 2424, http://envia.org), provides interest-free microfinance loans to local women, as well as offering free English-language classes and promoting ecotourism. They run fascinating half-day tours to local villages to meet the women they finance (all proceeds used for loans) and are in need of volunteer English teachers and tour leaders.

Spanish courses Some of the most popular language classes are offered by Amigos del Sol, Calzada San Felipe del Agua 322, meeting at Pino Suárez 802 at Llano park (951 196 8039, http://amigosdelsolspanishschool.com); the teachers are very friendly and student ability is properly assessed by tests on arrival. Similar services are offered at the small-scale Becari Language School, Plaza San Cristóbal, M. Bravo 210 (951 514 6076, http://becari.com.mx). Other good schools include Instituto Cultural Oaxaca, Juárez 909 (951 515 3404, http://icomexico.com); and Oaxaca Spanish Magic, Berriozábal 200 (951 516 7316, http://oaxacaspanishmagic.com).

Temazcal, massage, yoga Traditional *temazcal* sauna and massage are offered in a peaceful garden on the outskirts of town through *Casa de las Bugambilias,* Reforma 402 (951 516 1165, http://lasbugambilias.com; reserve at least a day in advance). Casa del Ángel, Jacobo Dalevuelta 200, between Reforma and Juárez near the Parque Juárez (951 222 9678, http://casadelangel.com.mx), is a yoga centre and café offering a variety of activities and therapies; Sat Nam Yoga y Masajes, Callejón Boca del Monte 121 between Tinoco y Palacios and Crespo (951 178 9950), offers yoga, massage, reiki and more.

ACCOMMODATION

SEE MAP PAGE 569

Oaxaca's cheaper **hotels** tend to be **south of Independencia**, especially around the markets where some are none too salubrious. Most of the newer and more upscale hotels can be found in the touristy zone near the **Plaza de la Constitución** and **north of Independencia**. In general, only the priciest places have a/c, though it's rarely a necessity here. **Rates** drop by ten to thirty percent outside the Christmas, Semana Santa, July and August high seasons.

PLAZA DE LA CONSTITUCIÓN AND SOUTH

Niut-Ja Armenta y López 609; 951 501 1623. Old-style, inexpensive courtyard hotel that's been revamped with some cute, artsy furnishings by its friendly young owners; the inward-facing rooms are quieter at the back. M$$

Paulina Youth Hostel Trujano 321; http://paulinayouthhostel.mxhotel.site. Large, efficiently run hostel which is immaculately clean and white. There are separate, large dorm rooms for men and women, clean bathrooms and some dorm-like private rooms, as well as a rooftop lounge and a small garden with fountains, but little atmosphere. Good breakfast included, but the location, on a harried street corner, isn't great. M$

Posada del Centro Independencia 403; https://posadadelcentro.mx. Very friendly travellers' place with the feel of a hostel – communal areas, lots of information, wi-fi throughout – though in fact all rooms are private (some trebles and quads). They're set around a tiled courtyard; en-suite ones at the back are tranquil, shared bath ones nearer the front can have traffic noise. Shared bath M$, en suite M$$

NORTH OF INDEPENDENCIA

Azucenas M. Aranda 203, at Matamoros; http://hotelazucenas.com. Pleasant colonial house in a quiet corner of town, with only the squeals from the school playground opposite to disturb your peace. The ten comfortable rooms come with a spread of welcoming extras: morning coffee in your room, buffet breakfast, self-serve rooftop bar (with lovely views) and wi-fi. M$$

Casa Arnel Aldama 404; http://casaarnel.com.mx. A popular, family-run place with reasonably priced rooms (with or without bath – sizes vary) around a leafy courtyard. There's a rooftop bar, where breakfast (additional cost) is served, laundry, wi-fi and a library; they also offer tours in Oaxaca and outlying areas. Newer rooms and apartments lie across the street. M$$

Casa Cid de León Morelos 602; https://hotelcasaciddeleon.com.mx. With just four suites, all beautifully and idiosyncratically restored by owner, poet and artist-in-residence Leticia Rodríguez, this is one of Mexico's most memorable hotels. Each spacious room is crammed with antiques, books and trinkets – a regal, timeless aura pervades every artfully conceived nook and cranny. There is a lovely terrace where breakfast is served, and the staff are charming and efficient. Rates are halved midweek and halved again in low season. M$$$$

★ **Casa de las Bugambilias** Reforma 402; http://lasbugambilias.com. Peaceful and central colonial B&B with nine very individual rooms, each tastefully decorated with work by local artists. Some are a little small, but all are extremely comfortable, with some kind of outdoor area or balcony; upstairs rooms have a/c. Delicious breakfast included, and if they're full they may have rooms at sister B&B *El Secreto*. M$$$

Casa de los Milagros Matamoros 500; 951 516 1165. Justifiably a favourite, this small, family-run, colonial hotel has just three immaculate, individually styled rooms in a dream home setting. There's a beautiful communal kitchen,

10

a dining room and a patio – the Ángeles room even has its own "waterfall". M$$$

★ **Casa Oaxaca** García Vigil 407; http://casaoaxaca.com.mx. If you are going to splurge, *Casa Oaxaca*, the personal favourite of Gabriel García Marquéz, is the place. Seven tastefully serene, spacious rooms are set around a pristine white courtyard with a tiled pool. With an emphasis on intimacy and tranquillity, the service is faultless – there's even a small library – and Oaxacan artistry is woven through every detail. Delicious breakfast included. M$$$$

Cazomalli Salto 104, cnr Aldama; 951 513 3513. Quaint little posada hidden away in an untouristy corner. The comfy rooms have carved and painted wooden furniture, and there's a gorgeous rooftop breakfast area. M$$$

★ **Las Golondrinas** Tinoco y Palacios 411; http://lasgolondrinasoaxaca.com. Simple but comfortable pristine rooms in an old colonial house, set around a series of flower-filled patios. Very tranquil with a distinctly local flavour. M$$

Hostal Casa del Sótano Tinoco y Palacios 414; http://guelaguetzaoaxaca.com. Classily modernized colonial mansion with pretty, brightly painted rooms with folk-art flourishes, all with a/c. Some are very small, though. There's an inviting terrace café, with views, where a basic breakfast (included) is served. M$$

★ **Hostel Don Nino** Pino Suárez 804 on Parque Juárez; https://hoteldonnino.com. Stylish, well-run hotel and hostel with excellent facilities including laundry, well-equipped kitchens, wi-fi, computer terminals and several seating areas with flatscreen TVs. Airy, well set-up three-bed dorms, plus private rooms better than at many downtown hotels; good breakfast included. M$$

Las Mariposas Pino Suárez 517; http://hotellasmariposas.com. Delightful colonial-style hotel with helpful staff and spacious rooms, some with kitchenettes and all with private bathrooms, clustered around a vibrant courtyard complete with flowers and fish-filled fountains. Very popular with long-stay Spanish students. Light breakfast and wi-fi included. M$

Quinta Real Oaxaca 5 de Mayo 300; http://quintareal.com. Oaxaca's priciest hotel (lowest off-season prices start around M$3270 a night), in the beautifully converted sixteenth-century Ex-Convento de Santa Catalina. Candles light the way through flower-filled courtyards to characterful, if medievally dimensioned, rooms. If a night's stay is beyond your budget, a lingering coffee or cocktail in the courtyard is a worthy substitute. M$$$$

EATING

SEE MAP PAGE 569

The food in Oaxaca is sensational. The cheapest places to eat are in the **markets**, especially the Mercado 20 de Noviembre (see page 574), the Mercado de Abastos (see page 575) and El Pochote organic market (see page 573). You'll also find a medley of **street stalls** dotted around the **plaza** and the surrounding streets, and on García Vigil near Carmen Alto, that serve filling staples such as *elote* (corn on the cob), tamales and *flautas* (deep-fried, rolled tortillas filled with mozzarella-like string cheese or meat). The Plaza and Alameda are also ringed by **cafés** and restaurants where you can sit outside – irresistible as ever and not as expensive as you might fear, though the food is rarely up to much – and there are plenty of simple places for everyday meals in the streets round about. Oaxaca also provides plenty of options for **vegetarians**, while at the pricier end, colonial-style and contemporary upscale restaurants offer nouvelle Mexican dishes using local herbs and produce. Virtually all the travellers' cafés and many restaurants offer free **wi-fi**.

PLAZA DE LA CONSTITUCIÓN AND SOUTH

★ **Café Alex** Díaz Ordaz 218, at Trujano; 951 501 2030. Popular with locals and travellers, this boisterous Mexican-style diner offers excellent breakfast menus ranging from omelettes, yogurt and hot cakes to refried beans, *huevos rancheros* and fresh-fruit *licuados* – it also opens early by Oaxaca standards. M$$

La Red Las Casas 101, cnr Bustamante; 951 514 8840. A bustling, no-frills seafood joint that looks a bit like a fast-food place, serving generous portions of fish (fillet and whole), soups, prawn cocktails, *ceviche* and octopus. Little atmosphere but plenty of flavour. M$$

Tr3s 3istro Restaurant & Oyster Bar Portal Las Flores 3; http://tr3s3istro.com. An innovative, albeit touristy, spot where they can do just about anything with veggies and oysters. If you only try one thing here, make sure it's the mushroom cakes. M$$$

NORTH OF INDEPENDENCIA

Biznaga García Vigil 512; 951 516 1800. Elegant place popular with expats set in a lemon-walled courtyard festooned with artwork. A chalk-board outlines the daily menu, which ranges from wholesome salads and soups to *pastor*-style (tomato, oil, cilantro) fish and chicken *milanesa* filled with cheese. Service can be slow – sip an excellent margarita or Belgian beer while you wait. The lunch-time menu includes mescal and coffee. M$$$

Casa Crespo Allende 107; http://casacrespo.com. High-concept restaurant where chef Oscar Carrizosa runs cookery courses (see page 576) and creates elaborate modern versions of traditional Oaxacan dishes. Choose from starters such as *memelitas* with cheese, agave worms and grasshoppers, chile stuffed with shrimp or lentil soup with plantain, pineapple and bacon, and mains like fish in a pumpkin seed *mole*, or turkey in *mole amarillo*, using rare varieties of chile. There's a wine list and chocolatería to match. M$$$

Casa Oaxaca El Restaurante Constitución 104-A; http://casaoaxacaelrestaurante.com. The contemporary Oaxacan

LAND OF THE SEVEN MOLES – OAXACAN CUISINE

Oaxaca is known as the "land of the seven *moles*" after its most famous sauces: *mole negro* or *Oaxaqueño* (the most popular, made with chocolate, giving a distinct roasted flavour), *amarillo*, *coloradito*, *mancha manteles*, *chichilo*, *rojo* and *verde*. *Moles* are typically served with chicken or enchiladas, but you don't have to go to one of the smart restaurants serving contemporary Oaxacan cuisine to sample them: *mole negro* is often better from street or market vendors. Other specialities include **tamales**, worth trying in any form, and **chapulines**, crunchy seasoned grasshoppers. **Tlayudas**, giant crisp tortillas dressed with beans and a mild Oaxacan string cheese called **quesillo**, are staples of cafés and street stands after dark.

The place to go for exceptional home-made **ice cream** is the plaza in front of the church of La Soledad, full of rival vendors and tables where you can sit and gorge yourself while watching the world go by. Flavours are innumerable and often bizarre, including *elote* (corn), *queso*, *leche quemada* (burnt milk; even worse than it sounds), *sorbete* (cinnamon-flavoured sherbet) and exotic fruits like *mamey*, *guanabana* and *tuna* (prickly pear; a virulent purple that tastes wonderful). There are also more ordinary varieties like chocolate, strawberry and coconut. At the opposite end of town, you can sample many of these flavours at Museo de las Nieves, Alcalá 706, just up from Santo Domingo.

restaurant of the *Casa Oaxaca* hotel proved so popular that it outgrew its origins and had to move out. It still serves some of the best food in town, with starters like ricotta-stuffed squash blossoms with honey and *epazote* or fish quesadillas, and mains ranging from turkey in *mole negro* to vanilla-scented sautéed shrimp or crispy suckling pig with *mole verde*. The gourmet menu comes in traditional or contemporary versions. You'll need to book. M$$$$

El Catedral García Vigil 105; www.restaurantecatedral.com.mx. Gorgeous, long-established fine-dining favourite, with tables topped by white linens and pale blue walls lit with chandeliers. There's a wonderful Sunday buffet brunch, but El Catedral is mainly favoured for dinner, with distinguished takes on Oaxacan cuisine like *mole* and contemporary dishes like roast beef seasoned with cinnamon and tamalito bean. M$$$$

★ **Cenadería Libres Tlayudas Doña Martha** Libres 212. Incredibly popular late-night snack stop, cooking up tasty *tlayudas* (stodgy, plate-sized tortillas chargrilled and stuffed with meat, cheese and beans) to queues of hungry clubbers and taxi drivers. They're cooked over charcoal in the street, though there are tables inside in case you want to sit down to eat: you may have a long wait in the early hours. M$$

La Crêpe Alcalá 307, upstairs; https://lacrepeoaxaca.cafe. There may not be much Oaxacan flavour to the food, but it's popular with locals, always lively and enjoys a great setting overlooking Alcalá. Vast range of sweet and savoury crêpes, from squash and cheese to nutella and banana, and baguettes, as well as fruit salads, ice creams and a range of excellent salads. Good dessert stop-off when the music draws the pre-party crowd. M$$

Los Danzantes Alcalá 403; https://losdanzantesoaxaca.com.mx. Fancy restaurant in the unlikely setting of the interior of the Plaza Comercial – in an inner courtyard where the stark modern decor is offset by ponds and water features. Good cocktails – try the mescal margarita (they produce their own excellent line of the liquor) – and imaginative dishes like mango- and mint-infused octopus, shrimp *ceviche*, barbecue chicken strips tossed with fried cactus and Oaxacan chocolate soufflé. Prices are steep by local standards but the lunch-time *comida* on Wed & Fri is more affordable. M$$$$

Le Gourmand Porfirio Díaz 410; www.voraz.xyz/gourmand. Superb little New York-style deli (of all things), with home-made pickles, craft beer and ham that's cured in house. The "reuben" sandwich (with corned beef) is excellent, while bagels with all the fixings are a good deal. M$$

Jaguar Yu'u Murguía 202; 951 466 2400. Friendly modern café with good beverages and inexpensive snack food – sandwiches, baguettes, French toast, eggs, salads – and a daily *menu del día*. M$$

La Jícara Porfirio Díaz 1105; www.librespaciolajicara.com. Arty, sunny little café, filled with potted plants and bright flowers, that's set in a bookstore and community meeting centre. Lunch dishes includes soup and a salad. It's far from the centre, but great if you're near the Arcos de Xochimilco (see page 572). M$$

Mezzaluna Alcalá 403; 951 516 8195. A local favourite for all things authentically Italian, Mezzaluna is the best spot in town for a wood fired pizza. Enjoy a slice on the terrace and take in the panorama; perfect for people watching. A whole pizza with all the trimmings is pretty good value here. M$$$

La Olla Reforma 402; http://laolla.com.mx. Quaint, relaxed café/gallery with a reliable breakfast menu featuring Oaxacan specialities, enchiladas and *chilaquiles* as well as more wholesome choices. At lunch time there's a *comida* and a full menu with mains at a fixed price; an easy

10

MESCAL

Mescal (or mezcal) is the *Oaxaqueño* drink of choice, sold everywhere in bottles that usually have a dead *gusano* worm (actually a type of caterpillar) in the bottom. Tradition has it that the creature lives on the cactus-like maguey plant and is there to prove that the ingredients are genuine, although these days most of the worms are farm raised. You don't have to eat the worm, though few people are in any state to notice what they're ingesting by the time they reach the bottom of the bottle. Like tequila (which is technically a type of mescal), mescal is made from the sugary heart of the agave plant, which is baked, pulverized and then distilled. Many of the best **mescal stores** can be found around the Mercado 20 de Noviembre where you can taste before you commit to buying; good brands include Los Amantes (also has a great shop, see above), Los Danzantes (also a restaurant, see above), Mezcal Amores and Alipús.

Several towns produce mescal, but the original is **Santiago Matatlán**, 45km from Oaxaca City near Mitla (see page 590). **Mescal tours** are advertised everywhere; one of the best guides is Canadian expat Alvin Starkman, owner of the *Casa Machaya* B&B (951 132 8203). Alternatively, ask after Ulises Torrentera at Los Amantes (see above).

introduction to Oaxacan cuisine. M$$$

Pizza Nostrana Alcalá 501, cnr Allende; 951 514 0778. Another top spot in town for pizza and well-executed pasta dishes with a vegetarian slant. The intimate, old-fashioned atmosphere and location close to Santo Domingo lend a romantic, relaxed vibe. M$$$

La Tizatería Reforma 402; 951 516 6668. A popular bar and grill house, with a decent selection of steaks and organic fresh veggie sides. The bar is also worthwhile, with a good range of professionally mixed (albeit potent) cocktails. M$$$

★ **Zandunga** Garcia Vigil; www.zandungasabor.com. Colourful, dynamic dinner spot with a stylish clientele but an unfussy, welcoming vibe. The food is affordable and beautifully presented: splurge on oven-roasted chicken with salsa or stay within your budget and order an excellent *platano tamale*. Great mescal list, too. M$$$

DRINKING AND NIGHTLIFE

SEE MAP PAGE 569

If you're not content to sit around the plaza over a coffee or a beer or to while away a balmy night to the accompaniment of mariachi or brass bands, sample some of Oaxaca's handful of decent bars and clubs. Most open daily 7pm to 3am, though clubs won't get busy till after midnight and usually close between Sun and Wed. The **folk dances** at the Quinta Real Oaxaca (entry fee includes buffet; see page 578) will at least give you a taster of the famous *guelaguetza* festival if you can't attend the real thing. Also, if you drink and dance a little too much, there are handy (but pricy) hotel rooms upstairs, where you can sleep it off, and rest your feet.

Armadillo Mier y Terán 103. A chilled spot with cheap beer, middle shelf mescal and a good jukebox, this is a good pick if you want a quiet night out; somewhere you can hold a conversation without shouting to be heard.

Los Amantes Mezcalería Ignacio Allende 107; https://losamantes.com. Mixing chilled DJ vibes with high-end mescal and extravagant cocktails, this spot has an infectious, positive energy; guaranteed to put a smile on your face.

Casa del Mezcal Flores Magón 209; https://www.facebook.com/casadelmezcal. Classic Mexican cantina in the market district, open since 1935, with cheap shots of mescal and a fairly liberal attitude to female patrons (though it's generally frequented by men). Pounding music and a Maya mystic theme, with murals and a carved wooden bar.

Mezcalillera Murguía 403a; 951 514 1757. Set in a charming colonial house, *Mezcalillera* has a mescal and cocktail menu, longer than your arm. Earlier in the evening, it can be a little touristy, but come 10pm, there's live music and a fair few more locals around – making this more of an authentic Oxaca experience. Be prepared to pay a cover charge.

La Nueva Babel Porfirio Díaz 224. Loungey wine bar with a Mexican kitsch theme, featuring live folk music, salsa (*son Cubano*) and poetry readings, most nights from 10pm (free). Opens as a café during the day, serving breakfast, coffee and snacks.

SHOPPING

SEE MAP PAGE 569

If it's **crafts and artesanías** you're after, you'll find dozens of high-quality shops on and around Alcalá. It's substantially cheaper, and a great deal more fun, to buy in the markets (see page 574), or even better in the villages in which the goods originate: even if that's what you intend to do, however, it's well worth checking the quality and price of the goods in the shops first.

Amate Alcalá 307; 951 516 6960. An excellent selection of new and secondhand English-language books, primarily about Mexico (including literature, travel, archeology and cooking), and magazines.

Arte Textil Alcalá 403-2; 951 526 9361. Gorgeous, pricey textiles to covet or gift. Plush scarves, table runners, button downs and more.

Casa de las Artesanias de Oaxaca Matamoros 105; http://casadelasartesanias.mx. A big commercial store with high-quality goods and plenty of them, from fabrics to tin, ceramics to *alebrijes*; many similar places in the vicinity.

Colectivo 1050° Rufino Tamayo 800; http://1050grados.com. Forged from traditional practices but shaped into contemporary styles, the pottery at this superb collective – which is devoted to preserving Oaxaca's craft and artisan culture – is well worth carting home in your suitcase.

Instituto Oaxaqueño de las Artesanías (ARIPO) García Vigil 809; 951 514 1354. State-run store that feels as much like a gallery as a shop; quality and fair prices to producers are assured.

Mujeres Artesanías de las Regiones de Oaxaca (MARO) 5 de Mayo 204; 951 516 0670. Craft shop run by an association of local women to promote their own crafts. There's nothing very fancy but there's a lot to choose from, all very fairly priced; a great place for inexpensive souvenirs.

DIRECTORY

Banks and exchange *Casas de cambio* litter the town centre and all the major banks can be found within a few blocks of the plaza. Close to the cathedral there's Santander at García Vigil, cnr Independencia, Banorte at García Vigil 103, between Morelos and Independencia, Bancomer at García Vigil and Morelos, and Banamex at Morelos and Porfirio Díaz. South of the plaza, HSBC is at Armenta y López and Guerrero, and there's another Banamex at Armenta y López and Hidalgo.

Consulates Canada, Pino Suárez 700, office 11B (951 513 3777); US, Alcalá 407, Office 20 (951 514 3054).

Emergencies Dial 060. For roadside assistance, call the Angeles Verdes on 078 or 951 516 9597.

Hospitals Aurelio Valdivieso, Porfirio Díaz 400 (951 515 1300). Clínica Hospital Carmen at Abasolo 215 (951 516 2612) has 24hr walk-in service and usually has English-speakers on hand. The vast IMSS Hospital is at Porfirio Díaz 141, north of the centre (951 515 6021).

Internet Internet cafés are abundant; most have copy and printing services, and some have long-distance call booths. Open latest is Café Internet, upstairs in the *Hostel Alcala* at Valdivieso 120 and Independencia – it closes most nights at 11pm; Inter@ctive at Alcalá 503, across from Santo Domingo, has phone services too.

Laundry Service-wash launderettes and dry cleaners are plentiful, including: Lavandería Santa Maria, Bravo 407 cnr Tinoco y Palacios (charge by the kg); Tintorería Antequera, Murguía 408.

Post office Alameda de León 2 at Independencia.

Monte Albán

Charge

The extraordinary city of **MONTE ALBÁN** is one of the world's great archeological treasures, legacy of the advanced Zapotec culture that dominated this part of Mexico well over a thousand years ago. Founded around 500 BC, most of the city was abandoned by 950 AD, though the Mixtecs later used it as a magnificent burial site. The main structures were cleared and restored in the 1930s; today it's the great flattened mountain top (750m by 250m), the scale of the monuments and the views over the valley that impress more than any individual aspect of the site. Sombre, grey and formal as it all appears now, in its heyday, with its roofs and sanctuaries intact, the whole place would have been brilliantly polychromed. Late afternoon, as the sun sinks into the valley, is the best time to see it.

There's a car park, restaurant and souvenir shop by the entrance, and a small **museum** in the same complex: the collection is tiny, but there are some important finds on display, including the carvings of the "dancers" (see page 583), intricate sculptures, ceramics and some gruesome mutilated skulls, presumably victims of the Zapotecs.

Brief history

It seems almost madness to have tried to build a city here, so far from the obvious livelihood of the valleys and without any natural water supply (in the dry season water was carried up and stored in vast urns). Yet that may have been the Zapotecs' point – to demonstrate their mastery of nature. By waging war on potential rivals, the new city soon came to dominate an area that extended well beyond the main valley – the peculiar *danzante* figures ("dancers") carved in stone that you can see at the ruins today are widely considered to be depictions of prisoners captured in battle.

By 200 AD, the population had expanded to such a degree that the Zapotecs endeavoured to level the Monte Albán spur completely to create more space, essentially forming a massive plateau. The resulting engineering project boggles the mind: without the aid of the wheel or beasts of burden, millions of tonnes of earth were shifted to build a vast, flat terrace on which the Zapotecs constructed colossal pyramids, astronomical observatories and palaces. What you see today is only the very centre of the city – its religious and political heart. On the terraced hillsides below lived a bustling population of between twenty-five thousand and thirty thousand craftsmen, priests, administrators and warriors, all of whom, presumably, were supported by tribute from the valleys. It's small wonder that so top-heavy a society was easily destabilized. That said, there is still much speculation as to why the site was ultimately abandoned.

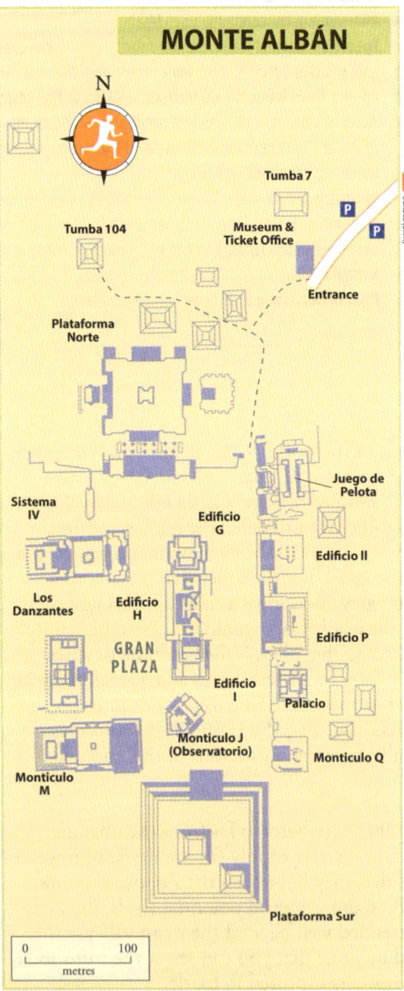

Plataforma Norte

The **Plataforma Norte**, straight ahead as you enter the site at its northeast corner, may have been the most important of all the temples at Monte Albán, although now the ceremonial buildings that line its sides are largely ruined. What survives is a broad stairway leading up from the Gran Plaza to a platform enclosing a square patio with an altar at its heart. This ceremonial centre was constructed between 400 and 750 AD, when Monte Albán was at its zenith. At the top of the stairs are the remains of a double row of six broad columns, which would originally have supported a roof to form a colonnade, dividing this plaza from the main one.

The Gran Plaza

The main path takes you south along the eastern side of the Plataforma Norte to the **Gran Plaza**, the vast, ceremonial focus of the city, surrounded by all its major buildings. As you enter you'll pass the **Juego de Pelota** (ball-court), a simple I-shaped space with no apparent goals or target rings, obviously an early example. The ball-game was used as a means to solve conflict – it is believed that the losing team was sacrificed to the gods. Otherwise, the platforms on the east side of the plaza are relatively late constructions, dating from around 500 AD onwards. Facing them from the middle of the plaza is a long tripartite building (**Edificios G**, **H** and

I) that must have played an important role in any rites celebrated here. The central section has broad staircases by which it can be approached from east or west – the lower end temples have smaller stairways facing north and south. From here a complex of tunnels runs under the site to several of the other temples, presumably to allow the priests to emerge suddenly and miraculously in any one of them. You can see the remains of several of these tunnels among the buildings on the east side.

Monticulo J

South of the central block, **Monticulo J**, known as the observatory, stands alone in the centre of the plaza, its arrow-shaped design marking it out from its surroundings. Although the building's orientation – at 45 degrees to everything else – is almost certainly for astronomical reasons, there's no evidence that this was actually an observatory; more likely it was built (around 250 AD, but on the site of an earlier structure) to celebrate a victory in battle. The carvings and hieroglyphics on the back of the building apparently represent a list of towns captured by the Zapotecs; indeed, much of the imagery at Monte Albán points to a highly militaristic society. In the vaulted passage that runs through the heart of the building, several more panels carved in relief show *danzante* figures – these, often upside down or on their sides and in no particular order, may have been reused from an earlier building.

Plataforma Sur

The southern end of the Gran Plaza is dominated by its tallest structure, the unrestored **Plataforma Sur**, a vast square pyramid offering the best overview of the site, as well as fine panoramas of the surrounding countryside.

Monticulo M and Sistema IV

On the western side of the Gran Plaza, **Monticulo M** and **Sistema IV** are the best-preserved buildings on the site. Each consists of a rectangular platform reached by a stairway from the plaza.

Los Danzantes

The gallery and building of **Los Danzantes**, between Monticulo M and Sistema IV, are the most interesting features of Monte Albán. A low wall extending from Monticulo M to the base of the Danzantes building forms the **gallery**, originally faced all along with blocks carved in relief of "dancers". Among the oldest (dating from around 500 BC) and most puzzling features of the site, only a few of these *danzantes* remain – the originals are now preserved in the museum and what you see here are replicas. The significance of the nude male figures is disputed: many of them seem to have been cut open and may represent sacrificial victims or prisoners; another suggestion is that the entire wall was a sort of medical textbook, or that the figures are dancers, ball-players or acrobats. Whatever the truth, they show clear **Olmec** influence, and many of them have been pressed into use in later buildings throughout the site.

The outer buildings

Several lesser buildings surround the main plaza, and although they're not particularly interesting, many contain tombs in which rich treasures were discovered (as indeed did some of the main structures themselves).

Tumba 104

Tumba 104, reached by a small path behind the Plataforma Norte or from the site's main entrance, is the best preserved tomb at Monte Albán. Its vaulted burial chamber, one of several in the immediate vicinity, still preserves excellent remains of murals; polychrome frescoes vividly revealing the mystical symbolism of the Zapotec gods.

Tumba 7

Tumba 7, where the important collection of Mixtec jewellery now in the Museo de las Culturas de Oaxaca (see page 571) was found, lies a few hundred metres down the main road from the site entrance. Built underneath a small temple, it was originally constructed by the Zapotecs towards the end of Monte Albán's heyday, but was later emptied by the Mixtecs, who buried one of their own chiefs here along with his magnificent burial trove.

ARRIVAL AND DEPARTURE — MONTE ALBÁN

10

By minibus Monte Albán is 9km southwest of Oaxaca, up a steeply switchbacking road. The most reliable company to make the Monte Albán run with is Lescas (951 516 0666) at the *Hotel Rivera del Ángel*, Mina 518. Based out of C Mina, they offer return tickets and sometimes negotiate on price if you bring enough friends. There are hourly departures (every 30min high season and weekends) from 8.30am to 3.30pm, returning between noon and 5pm – you'll be allocated a fixed return time, giving three hours at the site, but it's OK to take a different bus back if there's space.

By taxi For a group of four people, it costs much the same to go by taxi as it does by minibus, though you may have to wait for a return ride.

On foot Walking back to Oaxaca is a realistic option: more than two hours, but downhill almost all the way – get a guard or one of the kids selling "genuine antiquities" to show you the path. The route is an eye-opening experience, veering through slum dwellings that are a far cry from the comforts of much of the city below.

The Zapotec and Mixtec heartland

The region around Oaxaca can be divided into two parts: the **Valles Centrales**, comprising three valleys which radiate from the state capital to the south and east, towards Mitla, Ocotlán and Zaachila (collectively the Valle de Oaxaca); and the **Mixteca**, which extends northwest towards Puebla and arcs down to the Pacific coast via Tlaxiaco and Pinotepa Nacional. The Valles Centrales include the state's most famous and frequented archeological centres, craft villages and colourful markets, while the Mixteca, rich in ruined Dominican convents and ancient towns and villages, is less visited but well worth exploring.

This area saw the development of some of the most highly advanced civilizations in pre-Hispanic Mexico, most notably the Zapotecs and Mixtecs. Their craft skills – particularly Mixtec weaving, pottery and metalworking – were unrivalled, and the architecture and planning of their cities rank among ancient Mexico's greatest achievements. Traditional ways of life and Indigenous languages are still vigorously preserved by Mixtec and Zapotec descendants in villages today.

GETTING AROUND — THE ZAPOTEC AND MIXTEC HEARTLAND

By bus/colectivo Every village in the region will have a bus service from the second-class terminal in Oaxaca; for the smaller places this may be very occasional, however, or involve a walk from the highway. In addition, *colectivo* taxis run throughout the Valles Centrales, and to bigger places further afield; their termini are in the streets around the markets in Oaxaca, in particular Bustamante, La Noria and Zaragoza around the church of San Francisco; they leave when full. While it's easy enough to get to a village, it's much harder to connect between them – you may have to walk back to the highway to flag down onward transport, or use taxis for short hops between villages.

By car Car rental is as pricey here as anywhere in the country, but if you are planning extensive exploration of the valleys it may prove worthwhile, allowing you to trade a week of waiting for buses for a couple of days of independence; see page 576 for agents. Note that poor signposting can be frustrating, and that getting in and out of Oaxaca can be a nightmare.

Brief history

The Valles Centrales are the cradle of some of the earliest civilizations in Mexico. The story begins with the **Zapotecs**, who founded their first city – now called San José Mogoté, and little more than a collection of mounds, a few kilometres north of the state capital – some time before 1000 BC. As the city grew in wealth, trading with Pacific coastal communities,

STAYING IN LOCAL COMMUNITIES AROUND OAXACA

Indigenous communities in the mountains and valleys of Oaxaca have been developing their ecotourism potential since the 1990s, when a cabins programme was established. These small, self-contained *cabañas ecoturísticas* were designed to bring income to the villages while minimizing the disruptive effects of tourism. These days many villages organize **tours** (hiking, coffee farms, biking, adventure sports and agrotourism) and some sort of "community lodging", from **homestays** to simple but comfy **cabins**, usually arranged through a local Comité de Ecoturismo. Either type of accommodation makes a convenient and economical base for exploring the villages and archeological sites of Oaxaca state. Many communities have particular **handicraft traditions**, such as carpet-weaving, wickerwork or pottery; others have museums devoted to local archeological finds and the life of the villagers.

The best place for information and reservations – ideally made a few days in advance, especially for the more accessible sites – is Oaxaca's state tourist office at Juárez 703 (see page 576); be warned that individual staff may know little about this, that their information may be out of date, and that even where they do make a reservation it may take a while to seek out the key locally when you arrive. The lending library (see page 576) is another great resource for rentals. For the Sierra Norte and the Pueblos Mancomunados contact Expediciones Sierra Norte (see page 576), which coordinates all the local community programmes in that area. For Ixtlán contact Ecoturixtlán (see page 594) directly.

Cabins are usually inexpensive, but this varies according to how many people are sharing; they generally have bedroom(s), fully equipped kitchen and outside shower and toilets (which can also be used by people camping in the grounds). Camping is also available.

its inhabitants turned their eyes to the stars, and by 500 BC they had invented the first Mexican calendar and were using hieroglyphic writing. At this time, San José, together with smaller villages in the area, established a new administrative capital at Monte Albán, a vantage point on a mountain spur overlooking the principal Oaxaca valley (see page 581). Just like Teotihuacán, Monte Albán mysteriously began to implode from about 700 AD, and the Zapotec influence across the Valles Centrales waned. Only Yagul and Mitla, two smaller cities in the principal valley, expanded after this date, though they never reached the imperial glory of Monte Albán. As the Zapotecs disappeared, the gap they left behind was slowly filled by the **Mixtecs**, pre-Hispanic Mexico's finest craftsmen, who expanded into the southern valleys from the north to occupy the Zapotecs' magnificent cities. Influenced by the Zapotec sculptors' abstract motifs on the walls at Mitla, the Mixtecs concentrated their artistic skills on metalwork and pottery, examples of which can be seen in the state capital's museums. By the fifteenth century, the Mixtecs had become the favoured artisans to Mexico's greatest empire, their conquerors, the **Aztecs**; Bernal Díaz recounts that Moctezuma ate only from plates fashioned by Mixtec craftsmen.

Valle de Tlacolula

Hwy-190 provides access to the alluring villages of the **Valle de Tlacolula**, slicing some 45km east of Oaxaca towards **Mitla** (see page 588), before cutting south to Tehuantepec and the coast. The route is well served by *colectivos* and buses from the second-class terminal (every 30min or so), making day trips possible, even without a car. Check with the tourist office, or see the page 587, for which village has a market on the day you're going. If you want to explore the valley further it's a good idea to stay in one of the villages, some of which have self-catering facilities (see page 585).

Santa María del Tule

SANTA MARÍA DEL TULE (or simply El Tule), 13km east of Oaxaca, is famous for just one thing, the giant **Árbol del Tule** in the centre of town. This mighty tree, said to be at least

1500 years old (some say two thousand), is a good 36m round (the signboard claims a girth of 58m, but this is disputed by most experts), 42m in height, and weighs in around 500 tonnes. There's a small fee to go right into the churchyard where the tree stands (daily 8am–8pm), but you can get pretty close even without paying. The notice board gives all the vital statistics, though some of these are rather dubious: suffice to say that it must be one of the oldest living (and flourishing) objects on earth, and that it's a rare Montezuma cypress (*Taxodium mucronatum*), the national tree of Mexico. Local environmentalists claim that the Tule tree – along with other cypresses nearby – is threatened by development that has led to falling water levels; the site was added to UNESCO's World Heritage Tentative List in 2001, but more than 20-years later, has yet to be nominated.

Locals and tourists flock to visit the tree, and nearby there's a tacky souvenir market and a Mercado de Antojitos (food market), plus a string of restaurants along the main road.

ARRIVAL AND DEPARTURE — SANTA MARÍA DEL TULE

By bus Buses depart from Oaxaca's second-class bus station every 30min; you can save a great deal of time by flagging one down on Niños Héroes near the junction with Blv Eduardo Vasconcelos, one block east of Oaxaca's baseball stadium (look for "Tule").

Dainzú

Charge

The main allure of the ancient Zapotec site of **Dainzú** resides in its raw appeal, with few tourists or imposing facilities to detract from soulful contemplation. Just over 20km from Oaxaca on Hwy-190, Dainzú, established around 700–600 BC, stands partially excavated in a harsh landscape of cactus-covered hills around 1km south of the main road. The chief structure, **Edificio A**, is a large, rambling hillside construction set around a courtyard, with elements from several epochs. Along the far side of its base a series of *danzante* figures can be made out, similar to those at Monte Albán except that these clearly represent ball-players. Nearby is the **ball-court**, only one side of which has been reconstructed. **Edificio B** is another large and complex platform structure; its most striking feature is a tomb whose entrance is carved in the form of a jaguar.

Teotitlán del Valle

TEOTITLÁN DEL VALLE, 4km north of Hwy-190, is the most famous weaving town in Oaxaca. The rugs are the product of a cottage industry that seems to involve almost every family in town; along the road as you approach and all over the village you'll see bold-patterned and brightly coloured **rugs** and **sarapes**, some following traditional designs from Mitla, others more modern, including many based on the work of Dutch graphic artist M.C. Escher.

Even if you're not buying, poke your head into one of the compounds with rugs hanging outside. There's little hard-sell, and most weavers will be more than happy to provide a demonstration of pre-Hispanic weaving and dying techniques; traditional dyes use natural substances including indigo, pomegranate and cochineal, the latter made from a substance secreted by the cochineal beetle that, when dried, creates an inimitable blood-red colour. There's a small **Mercado de Artesanías** on the main plaza with a decent range of rugs, but quality and prices are generally better if you go direct to the producers.

Templo de la Virgen de la Natividad

On the plaza

The ancient local church, the **Templo de la Virgen de la Natividad**, is beautifully frescoed and decorated. Worship here is a fusion of Catholic and Indigenous ritual, and in the courtyard that blend finds physical expression in the incorporation of material from the Zapotec temple that once stood here, with Mitla-style decoration. Around the back of the church you can see more substantial remains of this temple, whose base stands about 2m high.

MARKET DAYS IN THE VILLAGES AROUND OAXACA

Despite Oaxaca's many craft stores, if it's quality you're after, or if you intend to buy in quantity, visiting the villages in which the goods originate is usually a far better, cheaper bet. Each has a different speciality (rugs in Teotitlán del Valle, or black pottery in San Bartolo Coyotepec, for example), and many have their own market each week. In the villages you'll be able to see the craftspeople in action and you may be able to have your own design made up, while a village market is an experience in itself.

Monday Miahuatlán: mescal, bread, leather. Ixtlán de Juárez: flowers, produce.
Tuesday Santa María Atzompa: pottery.
Wednesday Etla: cheese, flowers.
Thursday Zaachila: livestock, meat, nuts. Ejutla: mescal, embroidered blouses.
Friday Ocotlán: flowers, meat, pottery, textiles. San Bartolo Coyotepec: pottery.
Saturday Oaxaca: everything. Tlaxiaco: leather goods, blankets, *aguardiente* (the local firewater), baskets.
Sunday Tlacolula: mescal, ceramics, rugs, crafts.

Museo Comunitario Balaa Xtee Guech Gulal

On the plaza • Free, donation suggested

The stated aim of the absorbing **Museo Comunitario Balaa Xtee Guech Gulal** is "to know what we were, and understand what we are". As such, the small collection covers everything from pre-Hispanic life and artefacts to information about present-day culture and carpet-weaving in the area.

ARRIVAL AND DEPARTURE — TEOTITLÁN DEL VALLE

By bus Direct buses run hourly throughout the day from the second-class bus station in Oaxaca. Alternatively, take any bus or *colectivo* along the highway; at the junction, *colectivo* taxis wait to cover the short run into the village.

ACCOMMODATION AND EATING

El Descanso Juárez 51, cnr Hidalgo; 951 524 4152. An incongruous, hard-to-miss modern building in the centre of town houses a craft shop, carpet workshop and restaurant – they also have bungalows to rent on the edge of town. Food is simple but good, especially the *moles*. M$$

Tlamanalli Juárez 39; 951 524 4006. A favourite with locals as well as tour groups, *Tlamanalli* serves delicious local classics such as squash-blossom soup and stewed chicken; the menu changes daily. M$$$

Lambityeco

Charge

Right beside the highway, the small Zapotec site of **Lambityeco**, prettily planted with agave and cactus, is easy to get to on any passing bus; you can see the whole thing in twenty minutes, but it's worth it for the exceptional carvings and stucco-work. Just two buildings of the two hundred or so that have been identified have been excavated, along with some outbuildings that include an original *temazcal*. The smaller building at the back is the **Templo de Cocijo**, extensively decorated with masks of Cocijo, Zapotec god of rain and thunder, in the form of a stylised jaguar; two stunningly preserved versions flank the tiny central patio. The larger **Palacio de los Racoqui** is thought to have been the home of several generations of an important family – perhaps the city's rulers. There are some superb friezes, including those on the lintels of two tombs, excavated where they had been buried deep inside the building, with remarkable portraits of the individuals buried there.

Tlacolula

Buses leave frequently for Tlacolula from Oaxaca's second-class bus station, and there are plenty of *colectivo* taxis too

TLACOLULA is a large and rather scruffy village, worth visiting above all on a Sunday, when it hosts one of the most important **markets** in the valley (see page 587). The one sight is a sixteenth-century church, the **Parroquia de la Virgen de la Asunción**, whose interior is as ornate as Oaxaca's Santo Domingo, though less skilfully crafted. In the adjoining Capilla del Señor de Tlacolula, some gory carvings of martyrs include a decapitated St Paul.

Santa Ana del Valle

Take a taxi or local bus (usually every 10min) from the highway junction in Tlacolula or hike the 4km into Santa Ana

SANTA ANA DEL VALLE, 5km north of Tlacolula, is a tiny, very quiet and very traditional village with a fine selection of locally produced **rugs**. You'll see them for sale everywhere. There's a tranquil and well-managed **homestay programme** (see page 585) in case you want to stay; the local **baker** makes delicious bread and there's a shop where you can buy basic **provisions**. A three-hour walk, outlined on a board outside the community museum, will take you to Iki ya'a, a hilltop Zapotec site with fine views.

Museo Shan-Dany

On the plaza • Charge • 951 562 1705

The **Museo Shan-Dany** was the first community museum established in Mexico. Its name is Zapotec for "foot of the hill" – that is, the foot of the hill on which Iki ya'a stands – and it marks the exact spot where a couple of **tombs** were discovered in the 1950s, though they were only excavated more recently. Probably contemporary with Dainzú and Monte Albán, the Zapotec site here boasted some fine glyphs. Excavations have also been carried out beneath what are now basketball courts outside, and the pots and stones recovered there are also proudly displayed. Other exhibits (labelled in Spanish only) feature local folklore, dances, crafts and the weaving industry, and there's extensive coverage of the bloody fighting that took place here during the Revolution.

Yagul

Charge

One of the least-visited archeological sites in the region, **Yagul** lies to the north of the highway at about the 35km mark – a signposted twenty-minute walk (or 1.5km drive). The large site spreads expansively across a superb defensive position, and although occupied by the Zapotecs from a fairly early date, its main features are from later on (around 900–1200 AD, after the fall of Monte Albán) and demonstrate **Mixtec** influence. On the lowest level is the **Patio de la Triple Tumba**, where the remains of four temples surround an altar and the entry to the **Triple Tomb**, whose three funereal chambers show characteristically Mixtec decoration. Immediately above the patio, you'll see a large and elegantly simple ball-court, the largest known after Chichén Itzá. Higher up, the maze-like **Palacio de los Seis Patios**, probably a residential complex, features six small courtyards surrounded by rooms and narrow passages. From here a good path leads up to a viewpoint on a mesa-like crag, with superb views over the surrounding valleys.

Mitla

Charge

The town of **MITLA** ("Place of the Dead") is a dusty and none too attractive place, which you'd visit only to see the stunning Mixtec **site** at the upper edge of town. It may not have the grandiose scale and setting of Monte Albán, but Mitla is magnificently decorated with elaborate stone mosaics that are among the finest in Mexico. You'll see these superlative bas-reliefs and geometric designs at their best if you arrive towards closing time, when the low sun throws the patterns into sharp, shadowed relief, and the bulk of the visitors have left.

Brief history

Mitla reached its apogee during the post-Classic period, when Monte Albán was in decline. Construction at the site continued until the late fifteenth century, at which point it was finally conquered by the Aztecs. The abstract designs on the buildings seem to echo patterns on surviving **Mixtec** manuscripts, and have long been viewed as purely Mixtec in style. But more recent opinion is that the buildings were constructed by **Zapotecs** and that the city was a ceremonial centre occupied by the most important Zapotec high priest. This Uija-Tao, or "great seer", was described by Alonso Canesco, a fifteenth-century Spaniard, as being "rather like our Pope", and his presence here would have made Mitla a kind of Vatican City.

Grupo de las Columnas

The **Grupo de las Columnas** is the best preserved and most impressive of the five main complexes that make up Mitla, and the obvious place to head for from the entrance. The first large courtyard is flanked by constructions on three sides – its central **Templo de las Columnas** is magnificent, precision-engineered and quite overpowering in effect. Climbing the broad stairway and through one of three entrances in its great facade, you come to the **Salón de las Columnas**, named after the six monolithic, tapered columns of volcanic stone that supported its roof. A low, narrow passageway leads from here to a small inner patio, the **Patio de las Grecas**, lined with some of the most intricately assembled of the geometric mosaics; each of the fourteen different designs here is considered representative of the universe and the gods. Four dark rooms that open off the patio continue the mosaic theme. It is in these rooms that the Uija-Tao would have lived: if the latest theory is correct, the Zapotec architects converted the inner room of the traditional Mesoamerican temple, in which priests usually lived, into a kind of exquisitely decorated "papal flat" arranged around a private courtyard.

The second courtyard of the Columns group, adjoining the southwestern corner of the first, is similar in design though less impressive in execution. Known as the **Patio de las Tumbas**, it contains two cross-shaped tombs, long since plundered by grave-robbers. In one, the roof is supported by the **Columna de la Muerte**; legend has it that if you embrace this, the gap left between your hands tells you how long you have left to live, hand-widths being translated into years remaining (mercifully, you can no longer hug the column to test this myth).

Grupo de la Iglesia

The **Grupo de la Iglesia** is so called because the Spaniards built a church over, and from, much of it in 1590: the Templo de San Pablo Apóstol. Two of its three original courtyards survive, however, and in the smaller one the mosaic decoration bears traces of the original paint, indicating that the patterns were once picked out in white from a dark-red background.

Lesser buildings

Three other groups of buildings, which have weathered the years less well, complete the site. All of them are now in the midst of the modern town, fenced off from the surrounding houses: the **Grupo de los Adobes** can be found where you see a chapel atop a pyramid; the **Grupo del Arroyo** is near Los Adobes; and the **Grupo del Sur** lies right beside the road to the main site.

ARRIVAL AND DEPARTURE — MITLA

By bus/mototaxi/on foot Second-class buses run from Oaxaca to Mitla (1hr 30min) about every 15min throughout the day. If you don't fancy the 10–15min walk through town up to the ruins, a tricycle mototaxi will get you up there, or you can take a *colectivo*.

ACCOMMODATION AND EATING

Despite all the tourists, Mitla has little to offer on the food front, and few places to stay. There's one decent hotel-restaurant, but otherwise you're best off eating at one of the stalls or small *comedores* in the tacky market close to the site entrance.

Hotel Don Cenobio Juárez 3, just off the main plaza;

http://hoteldoncenobio.com. With a cheery blue-and-yellow paint job and individual, elaborately carved and painted wooden furniture in each room, the *Don Cenobio* does its best to brighten up drab Mitla. The better rooms look inward, onto a courtyard where there's a small pool. The restaurant serves all day, from breakfast through to evening, with a rather pricey *menu turistico* at midday. M$$

Santiago Matatlán

10

Mescal producers, from one-man artisan distilleries to large factory operations, and shops selling their products dot the countryside around Mitla. The small town of **SANTIAGO MATATLÁN**, on Hwy-190 just 8km beyond Mitla, is the traditional centre of the industry; here you can visit the ateliers in which the drink is made, enjoy free samples from the town stores and eat the maguey plant itself. Be warned that a few samples of home-made mescal can wreak havoc with your senses.

ARRIVAL AND DEPARTURE — SANTIAGO MATATLÁN

By bus/colectivo/tour Being right on the highway, Santiago Matatlán sees plenty of second-class buses from Oaxaca. However, given the fact that some of the more interesting producers are out of town, and the state you may be in, it's much easier to take a mescal tour from Oaxaca (see page 580); many will also visit Mitla and Hierve el Agua, or other villages. *Colectivos* are also available, and charge a little more than the buses.

Hierve el Agua

Charge • 951 502 1200

Hierve el Agua, some 25km east of Mitla, much of it on rough dirt road, is the site of a spectacular calcified rock formation that resembles a bubbling **waterfall**. As water with a very high mineral concentration bubbles out of the ground, it becomes petrified over the vertiginous cliff-tops; the resultant stalactites are a beautiful sight and the panoramas from above the pools, where there are several stalls serving tacos and other snacks, are jaw-dropping. Sadly, tourism here threatens to be more destructive than in the rest of the valley: the area can barely support the volume of visitors it receives and disputes between local villagers over how to split the proceeds sometimes close the road to the site.

ARRIVAL AND DEPARTURE — HIERVE EL AGUA

By car/colectivo/tour Though you could drive (expect 30min of dirt road) or get a *colectivo* from Mitla, the tricky access makes it far easier to visit Hierve El Agua as part of an organized day trip (see page 576); most will also take in Mitla and Teotitlán del Valle, and probably a mescal distillery.

Valle de Zimatlán-Ocotlán

The **Valle de Zimatlán-Ocotlán**, almost due south of Oaxaca, doesn't have the same concentration of interesting sites as the Valle de Tlacolula, but some of the region's finest artesanía comes from these villages. You can travel around the area reasonably easily by **public transport**, or **cycling** on rented bikes from Oaxaca isn't as arduous as it might sound, especially if you are careful about the midday heat. Two major roads run in this direction: Hwy-175, the route to Pochutla and Puerto Ángel, via San Bartolo Coyotepec and Ocotlán, and Hwy-131 which eventually reaches the Pacific at Puerto Escondido, via Zaachila. With your own transport, it's easy to combine the two routes in a loop.

San Bartolo Coyotepec

Thirteen kilometres south of Oaxaca on Hwy-175, **SAN BARTOLO COYOTEPEC** is an otherwise dreary town famed for the shiny black pottery, **barro negro**, which can be found in crafts shops all around Oaxaca state, but is only made here. In 1934, one **Doña Rosa** developed a technique for adding the unique lustre to the previously ordinary pottery made in San Bartolo. The pottery may now be too weak to carry mescal to market on the back of a mule, as it did for centuries, but Doña Rosa's invention has yielded a new, purely ornamental incarnation that draws thousands of tourists every year. Her workshop (see below) still sells some of the finest quality pieces, though prices are lower elsewhere and in the little market in the centre of town, where they're prepared to haggle.

Alfarería Doña Rosa

Juárez 24 • 951 551 0011

Although Doña Rosa died in the 1980s, her family still runs the biggest *alfarería* (workshop) in town, an unashamedly touristy showroom with pieces ranging from beautifully simple amphorae to ghastly clocks. To find Doña Rosa from the highway, look for the street signed *alfarerías*.

Museo Estatal de Arte Popular de Oaxaca

Independencia on the south side of the plaza • 951 551 0036

The modern **Museo Estatal de Arte Popular de Oaxaca** contains an impressive display of Oaxacan folk art. There's high-quality black pottery, of course, but also interesting, often quirky, examples of all sorts of other arts and crafts from papier mâché to *alebrijes*, and a good shop too.

ARRIVAL AND DEPARTURE — SAN BARTOLO COYOTEPEC

By bus/colectivo/minibus There are plenty of second-class buses along Hwy-175 that will drop you in San Bartolo, but the best way to get here is by *colectivo* from the Mercado de Abastos in Oaxaca, or minibus run by Automorsa (cnr Miguel Cabrera and Zaragoza) or Oaxaca Pacifico (Armenta y López 121).

San Martín Tilcajete

SAN MARTÍN TILCAJETE is a sleepy town, a short distance off the highway 27km from Oaxaca. The main street is lined with workshops in which the bright copal-wood figurines known as *alebrijes* are carved, painted and polished. They come in all manner of designs, from Day of the Dead skeletons to whimsical creatures, and although not as famous as those from Arrazola (see page 592), there are still plenty of attractive examples.

ARRIVAL AND DEPARTURE — SAN MARTÍN TILCAJETE

By colectivo/bus *Colectivo* taxis are the most regular form of transport between Oaxaca and San Martín. The Oaxaca terminus is at Arista 107 between Cabrera and Bustamente.

EATING

Azucena Zapoteca Hwy 175 km 23.5, at the San Martín Tilcajete junction; https://azucenazapoteca.com. Big roadside restaurant serving up much better than expected local food at competitive prices, as far as possible home-made from local ingredients. It also has an excellent craft shop. **M$$**

Santo Tomás Jalieza

In the tiny village of **SANTO TOMÁS JALIEZA**, the women specialize in weaving cotton on backstrap looms. An all-women's cooperative market in the centre of town sells thick woven cotton tablecloths and placemats, bags, backpacks, clothing and belts at fixed (though generally reasonable) prices.

ARRIVAL AND DEPARTURE — SANTO TOMÁS JALIEZA

By colectivo *Colectivos* for Santo Tomás depart from outside the Mercado de Abastos in Oaxaca; second-class buses will drop you at the highway junction, just five minutes' walk to the market.

Ocotlán

The substantial regional centre of **OCOTLÁN**, a little over 32km from Oaxaca, is known as the birthplace of celebrated Oaxacan artist **Rodolfo Morales** (1925–2001) and for the extraordinary **clay figures** crafted here by the Aguilar sisters. The adjacent workshops of

Josefina, Guillermina, Irene and Concepción, each of whom produces slightly different items in the distinctive Aguilar style originated by their mother, are on the main road into town, just past the huge *Hotel Real Ocotlán*. You can find examples of their work in Oaxaca, but a trip out here allows you to see the full range, from grotesque to amusing to religious, including figures of animals, men and buxom women at work and play, and even Nativity scenes (apparently no subject matter is off-limits), gaudily decorated in polka dots or geometric patterns. Josefina's work is especially off-the-wall and prices are very reasonable for really elaborate work. Ocotlán's Friday **market** is one of the finest in the region.

Ex-Convento de Santo Domingo de Guzmán

Zaragoza and Amador, on the zócalo • Charge

The **Ex-Convento de Santo Domingo de Guzmán** is a magnificent church and monastery that was restored to much of its former glory with money from Rodolfo Morales; appropriately the paintwork and frescoes are particularly fine. Upstairs, part of the complex has been transformed into a gallery, with works by Morales himself (including his final painting, in which he foresees his death) and some brilliant examples of the Aguilar sisters' work.

ARRIVAL AND DEPARTURE — OCOTLÁN

By colectivo/bus/minivan *Colectivo* taxis depart from outside the Mercado de Abastos in Oaxaca and there are second-class buses from the nearby terminal; in addition, Automorsa (cnr Miguel Cabrera and Zaragoza) and Oaxaca Pacifico (Armenta y López 121) run regular minivans.

San Antonio Arrazola

SAN ANTONIO ARRAZOLA, 8km southeast of Oaxaca, 5km west of Hwy-131, is the home of the local woodcarvers and painters who produce many of the delightful boldly patterned *alebrijes*, animals made from copal wood, that you'll see for sale in Oaxaca and all over Mexico. The man responsible for transforming this local craft into an art form was Manuel Jiménez (1919–2005), still revered locally. Following on the heels of his success, entrepreneurial townspeople have created a thriving cottage industry that produces a fantastical profusion of spiky figures and polka-dot, hooped or expressionist styles, most very reasonably priced. Carvers from other villages are catching on to the popularity, but few, if any, are better than in Arrazola, where almost every home seems to contain a workshop.

ARRIVAL AND DEPARTURE — SAN ANTONIO ARRAZOLA

By colectivo/bus/bike *Colectivos* for San Antonio depart from outside the Mercado de Abastos in Oaxaca; second-class buses run from the nearby terminal. It's an easy cycle, too.

Cuilapam de Guerrero

Ex-Convento de Santiago Apóstol • Charge

The village of **CUILAPAM**, 14km southeast from Oaxaca, is something of a place of pilgrimage for Mexicans, as it was here that revolutionary hero **Vicente Guerrero** was executed by firing squad in 1831. The place is entirely dominated by the vast, turreted hulk of the Dominican **Ex-Convento de Santiago Apóstol** where he was held captive and where the execution took place. Though in poor condition and with virtually no signage, it's an impressive place to wander around, with a Renaissance twin-aisled nave and largely intact vaulting; behind is the atmospheric monastery cloister, full of dark corners and hidden stairways.

ARRIVAL AND DEPARTURE — CUILAPAM DE GUERRERO

By colectivo/minibus *Colectivos* for Cuilapam can be found in Oaxaca on Bustamante, south of the markets near the church of San Francisco. Autotransportes Añasa at Bustamante 606 has minibus services.

Zaachila

ZAACHILA's Thursday **livestock market**, a huge affair that seems to take over half the town, is a thoroughly entertaining spectacle that attracts plenty of tours and visitors. At weekends a few locals visit; the rest of the time it's very quiet indeed. The one local sight is a small **zona arqueológica** (daily 9am–6pm; charge, free on Sun) on the little hill behind the main plaza. A substantial Zapotec town is thought to have flourished here from 1200 to 1521, though it was taken over by the Mixtecs towards the end of this period; it was one of the few such cities still inhabited when the Spanish arrived. Only one small pyramid has been excavated – there are far larger unexcavated mounds alongside – from which you can climb down into two opened tombs dating from the early sixteenth century. One of them, the tomb of Lord 9-Flower, probably a Mixtec priest, is lavishly decorated, with stone-carved owls guarding the entrance and two marvellous glyphs showing 9-Flower himself: richly dressed with a large headdress, carrying a bag of copal incense. A collection of treasures was buried with him, comparable to that discovered in Tomb 7 at Monte Albán and including gold, jewels, jade and turquoise masks; there are photos of these in the little site museum.

10

ARRIVAL AND DEPARTURE — ZAACHILA

By colectivo/minibus *Colectivos* for Zaachila can be found in Oaxaca outside the Mercado de Abastos and on Bustamante, south of the markets near the church of San Francisco. Autotransportes Añasa (Bustamante 606) has minibus services.

EATING

La Capilla Km 14 on the main road, on the edge of town; 951 528 6115. A huge, open-air restaurant with a theatrical open kitchen and communal seating for hundreds, as well as more private tables under palapas dotted around the grounds. Most fun when it's busy, either on Thursday with market visitors and tour groups, or at weekends with locals; at these times mariachis and other musicians wander among the diners. The traditional Oaxacan food can tend towards mass-catering, but is generally good, if a little pricier than average. **M$$$$**

The Sierra Norte

North of the Oaxaca valleys the wild ranges of the **Sierra Norte** stretch for over 100km, a pristine world of pine forests, mist-cloaked mountains and rustic Zapotec villages.

The Pueblos Mancomunados

The **Pueblos Mancomunados** (literally "joint villages") occupy the southern edge of the Sierra. The landscape here is spectacular and the **biodiversity** phenomenal, with birdlife, butterflies and mammals, including ocelot, puma and jaguar – some sections of the pine forest have been classified by the World Wide Fund for Nature (WWF) as among the richest and most varied on earth. It's a rewarding place to spend a few days, enjoying nature and getting first-hand experience of rural Oaxacan life.

The hills are laced with more than 100km of signposted rural **footpaths and country roads**, suitable for hikers and mountain-bikers of all abilities, and almost every community offers simple accommodation, local guides and a roster of activities. The paths have been used for centuries by local people accustomed to sharing resources with surrounding communities, and the villages are an impressive example of social organization, with eight small towns perched on common land. One of the most enchanting hikes is along the 15km high-altitude footpath between the isolated villages of Latuvi and San Miguel Amatlán, which passes though mystical cloud forest and is believed to be part of a larger pre-Columbian route that connected the Zapotec cities in the Valles Centrales with the Gulf of Mexico – you can still see the remains of an old road along the trail (tours usually take two days to hike this route).

Benito Juárez

Perched on a ridge overlooking the Oaxaca valleys (18km north of Teotitlán) and surrounded by pine trees, the little village of **BENITO JUÁREZ** is the gateway to the Pueblos Mancomunados. Known for its spectacular sunsets – in clear weather you can see all the way to Mexico's highest mountain, Pico de Orizaba – Benito Juárez makes a good base for exploration. There's a river where you can **fish** for trout, and plenty of walking and other activities are on offer.

INFORMATION AND TOURS — THE PUEBLOS MANCOMUNADOS

Tourist information office If you prefer to travel independently, the small tourist information office (Mon–Sat 9am–5pm; 951 545 9994) in Benito Juárez, next to the town square, is extremely helpful. It has excellent maps which show the varying demands of each trek, and rents out reliable mountain bikes, but only with a Spanish-speaking guide (charge per day, plus an access fee). They can also help out with accommodation, and other activities such as horse riding.

Tours Don't expect one afternoon to be enough time to see this area; a visit requires forward planning and at least a couple of days to be worthwhile. Although you can travel independently, accommodation and food are best organized in advance: much the easiest, most efficient and lowest impact way to go is through one of the tour operators in Oaxaca (see page 576). Tierraventura and Expediciones Sierra Norte organize trips with guides, transport, accommodation and meals.

Ixtlán de Juárez

IXTLÁN DE JUÁREZ, a pretty Zapotec village near San Pablo Guelatao (the birthplace of Benito Juárez), 61km north of Oaxaca, is in an area of great natural beauty, and its cloud forests and pine and oak woodlands are claimed to be home to five hundred bird varieties and six thousand species of plants. Ixtlán is accessible by direct bus from Oaxaca's second-class station (2 daily), Cuenca first-class bus or by *colectivo* (all around 2hr).

ACCOMMODATION AND TOURS — IXTLÁN DE JUÁREZ

Ecoturixtlán 16 de Septiembre, at the cnr of Revolución; 951 553 6075. Locally run *Ecoturixtlán* organize tours of all the local beauty spots (Mirador del Cerro Cuachirindo, the Grutas del Arco, the Cascada del Mesofilo and the gentle woodlands of the Bosque Mesofilo), as well as the eighteenth-century village church, the Templo Santo Tomàs Apòstol. They also rent thirteen basic but comfy cabañas in the forest bordering the village, run the best local *comedor*, arrange a host of bird watching tours, rent bikes and offer ziplining, horse riding and rappelling. Cabañas M$$

The Mixteca

Oaxaca's **Mixteca** region is not at first an obvious tourist destination: the pre-Hispanic sites here are far less spectacular than those in the Valles Centrales and there are no artisan centres to compare with Teotitlán or Arrazola. However, the colonial buildings are widely regarded as some of the country's most important, there's stunning mountain scenery and the low number of visitors means that you are likely to have vast crumbling monasteries and Mixtec ruins to yourself; the main appeal is their

CAPILLAS ABIERTAS

Among the most striking features of the monasteries of the Mixteca Baja are their **capillas abiertas**. These graceful open-air chapels, found only in the New World, look like unfinished, roofless churches, or cathedrals chopped in half. They face out onto huge open areas where the idea was that mass conversions of and services for Indigenous people, too numerous for the church to accommodate, would take place. They are designed for congregations of thousands; the very same people whose prodigious labour produced these vast churches in the first place. Sadly, even by the time they were first completed, those populations had been decimated by disease and the demands of the Spanish overlords; the *capillas* became vast white elephants, testament to a vanished population.

aching, faded glory and the spine-tingling sense that you're witnessing a scene that has remained relatively unchanged since before Cortés.

Broadly the region divides into two – the barren hills of the **Mixteca Baja** and the mountainous, pine-clad **Mixteca Alta**. Toll Hwy-135D, one of the country's best roads, cuts through the Baja's deforested hillsides en route from Oaxaca to Mexico City. The Mixteca Alta lies off to the south, where Hwy-125 climbs into and through the sierra before eventually descending to the Pacific coast. The **Mixteca Baja**'s highlights are three vast **Dominican monasteries** – Yanhuitlán, Teposcolula and Coixtlahuaca – imposing relics of Mexico's imperial past. All three have been expertly restored and can easily be visited as a day trip from Oaxaca if you have your own transport; it's less easy if you're relying on public transport, though still possible.

Santo Domingo Yanhuitlán

Templo y Ex-Convento de Santo Domingo • Charge

The first of the great Dominican establishments northwest of Oaxaca is the **Templo y Ex-Convento de Santo Domingo** at **SANTO DOMINGO YANHUITLÁN**. There was an important Mixtec city here before the Conquest, and the church, built on an enormous pre-Hispanic platform overlooking the village, was no doubt intended to remind the Mixtecs of the supremacy of the new religion. The permanent seat of the diocese of the Mixteca during the sixteenth century, the church is massive, dominating the countryside for many kilometres around, with a vaulted ceiling soaring 27m above you as you enter. The main altarpiece, dating to 1570, is the work of the Spanish artist Andrés de la Concha.

ARRIVAL AND DEPARTURE — SANTO DOMINGO YANHUITLÁN

By bus There are services from Oaxaca's second-class bus station (1hr 30min), or Autotransportes de Tlaxiaco buses pass through every 45min. Their Oaxaca base is on Díaz Ordaz between Trujano and Las Casas.

By car Yanhuitlán is on Hwy-190, not far from the Nochixtlán junction of Hwy-135D.

Teposcolula

Charge

TEPOSCOLULA is close to the start of Hwy-125, the road that heads up to the Mixteca Alta. Here the **Ex-Convento de San Pedro y San Pablo** has one of the finest *capillas abiertas* in the Americas, completed in the 1560s. The church itself is every bit as gargantuan as the others, though its position at the heart of a reasonable-sized town perhaps makes it seem a little smaller. Notice the extraordinary scallop-shell roof of one of the chapels and, in the otherwise relatively plain interior, a huge gilded *retablo*. In the cloister are some sixteenth-century paintings, but it's the outdoor chapel that really impresses; newly restored with pristine stonework and a gilded and painted ceiling, it faces a vast field where the congregation would have gathered.

ARRIVAL AND DEPARTURE — TEPOSCOLULA

By bus There are services from Oaxaca's second-class bus station (2hr), or Autotransportes de Tlaxiaco buses pass through every 30min en route to Tlaxiaco. Their Oaxaca base is on Díaz Ordaz between Trujano and Las Casas.

Coixtlahuaca

Ex-Convento de San Juan Bautista • Free

COIXTLAHUACA lies just 2km east of Hwy-135D at the Coixtlahuaca exit. The small village is entirely dominated by the **Ex-Convento de San Juan Bautista**, dating from 1576 and one of the best preserved of the region's colonial structures. Newly restored to pristine perfection, it's of a size to match any European cathedral, with an elaborately carved facade and, inside, a beautiful painted ceiling and a magnificent, ceiling-height churrigueresque altarpiece. In the garden cloister there's a display on the church's restoration, and on the opposite side of the church a fine *capilla abierta*.

ARRIVAL AND DEPARTURE COIXTLAHUACA

By bus/taxi Second-class Sur buses from Oaxaca drop off at Coixtlahuaca en route to Puebla and Mexico City. If you want to head on towards Teposcolula or Yanhuitlán, there is an occasional local bus across to Tejupan, on Hwy-190, or you can get there by taxi. Alternatively, head back south to Nochixtlán and connect there.

Santiago Apoala

10

The rural village of **SANTIAGO APOALA** is tucked into a captivating high valley about 98km north from Oaxaca. It's a wild place, ideally located for hiking, biking and other outdoor activities involving the nearby rivers, lagoons and falls; it's hard to get to, but that ensures its continued unspoilt isolation. You're strongly advised to use a guide to explore the region, where most trails are poorly marked. Among the highlights are the **Picturas Repuestas**, five-thousand-year-old glyphs considered to be the oldest example of Mixtec art, and the hike following the Apoala River to the 60m **Cola de Serpiente** waterfall – you can swim in the pool at the bottom.

ARRIVAL AND TOURS SANTIAGO APOALA

By bus The best way to reach Apoala is on a tour; alternatively, take a second-class bus or *colectivo* from Oaxaca to Nochixtlán, where a taxi or microbus (Wed & Sat 1pm, Sun noon, but check beforehand if possible) can make the remaining climb into the mountains.

By car From Nochixtlán, easily accessed on Hwy-135D, it's a further 40km to Apoala, almost all on rough dirt road.

Comité de Turismo de Santiago Apoala Pino Suárez, cnr Independencia; 561 504 2660. The village ecotourism cooperative can arrange meals, accommodation, expeditions and guides and provide general information; it offers basic cabañas and campsites. They also rent bikes by the day. Tierraventura (see page 594) organize tours from Oaxaca, which is certainly the easiest way to come.

San Martín Huamelulpan

Museo Comunitario Hitalulu • Charge • http://museoscomunitarios.org/huamelulpam • Tlaxiaco-bound buses (see below) will drop you at the turn-off. From there you'll have to walk, hitch or hope to find a taxi for the last couple of kilometres into town

SAN MARTÍN HUAMELULPAN lies high in the pine forests of the **Mixteca Alta**, 2km up a side road off Hwy-125. This tiny mountain village has an extensive and mostly unexplored Mixtec archeological site, with two large plazas cut out of a hill, a ball-court and some temple complexes. Some of the sculptures found here have been embedded in the walls of the eighteenth-century colonial church; other artefacts from the ruins are displayed in the small **Museo Comunitario Hitalulu**, which also has information about Indigenous medicines, still used by traditional healers in the local community. The surrounding countryside is picturesque, with deer and coyotes in the woodland, and a variety of unusual plants.

Tlaxiaco

TLAXIACO is traditionally the economic heart of the Mixteca; a big place, with an important **Saturday market** that attracts Indigenous people from across the region – many of them in traditional dress. The town is also famed for its *pulque*, the lightly fermented drink made from cactus, best savoured at the market stalls. An attractive town square and nearby good-value hotels could serve as a base for exploring the countryside and the Mixtec and Triqui villages nearby.

ARRIVAL AND DEPARTURE TLAXIACO

By minivan/bus Autotransportes de Tlaxiaco minivans run every 30min (3hr) from their Oaxaca terminus on Díaz Ordaz between Trujano and Las Casas. There are also OCC first-class and Sur and Autobuses Fletes y Pasajes second-class buses. Many of these continue to Pinotepa Nacional (5–6 daily; 5hr), where you can change for Puerto Escondido and the Pacific coast.

ACCOMMODATION AND EATING

Hotel del Portal Plaza Constitución 2; 953 552 0154. This colonial mansion on the main plaza, directly opposite the market, could hardly be better located. The rooms are a little old-fashioned, but comfortable enough, especially if you get one of the pricier ones in the old building. The restaurant in the hotel courtyard is much fancier (and pricier) than you'd expect, with flowers on the table and unusual local specialities such as beef ribs with *memelitas* (bean-filled parcels) and *nopalitos* (cactus leaves) served on a sizzling plate, or *molcajete*, a stone bowl of hot stewed meat and vegetables. Food M$$, accommodation M$$$

San José del Pacífico

The 240km journey south from Oaxaca to Pochutla and the Pacific coast via Hwy-175 is dramatic, passing through mountainous forests and descending into tropical lowlands. Around three hours' drive in this direction, perched on the side of a pine-smothered mountain with wonderful views, though often enveloped in plumes of mist, lies **SAN JOSÉ DEL PACÍFICO**. It's a great, restful place to break the journey, or to stay for a day or two if you want to enjoy the forest trails and cool mountain air (winter nights can get very chilly) before descending to the tropical lowlands of the coast. It is also known for its **mushrooms**, both culinary and hallucinogenic, and it's the latter that draw the majority of the town's visitors, many of whom make the short trip from Zipolite (see page 609), just two hours away. Mushroom season coincides with the rains, from about July to October, but they're sold preserved in honey during the rest of the year. Be warned that the mushrooms are illegal, and penalties potentially severe.

ARRIVAL AND DEPARTURE — SAN JOSÉ DEL PACÍFICO

By minivan Any minivan on the direct route between Oaxaca and Pochutla can drop you in San José del Pacífico; see page 608 for details.

ACCOMMODATION AND EATING

Cabañas/Hotel La Puesta On the main road; http://sanjosedelpacifico.com. The simple wooden cabañas here offer the best accommodation in town, with incredible views over the valley. Try to get one of the cabañas furthest from the restaurant so that you get a clear view. There's also a good restaurant serving *comidas*, *dulces* and mescal. M$$

Rayito del Sol Main road in the centre of the village; 951 572 0111. Pleasant café and restaurant which also serves as an information centre and has cabañas. Excellent quesadillas – try the version with squash blossom – and hot chocolate to fight off the chills. M$$$

Puerto Escondido and around

Though no longer the tranquil hangout it was thirty years ago, **PUERTO ESCONDIDO** ("Hidden Port") remains an irresistible draw. With direct flights from the capital, kilometres of sandy beaches and an international surf reputation as home of the "**Mexican Pipeline**", Escondido has firmly established itself as a destination. For all the crowds, though, the place has managed to retain a languid, laid-back air; small-scale, casual and uninhibited, there is still the hint of the village it once was, and it's a world away from resorts such as Cancún. This is most evident in the early morning, when fishermen return to Playa Principal, their boats laden with marlin and red snapper. While there is a tremendous number of **hotels** to choose from, the majority tend to

SAFETY IN PUERTO ESCONDIDO

Despite Puerto Escondido's laid-back atmosphere, there has in the past been a problem with **muggings**, especially in La Punta and above all walking between Zicatela and town late at night. Bright new lighting has been installed in many places – try to avoid dimly lit areas and isolated beaches at night, and stick to the main road if walking back to town; better still, flag down a taxi. Take normal, sensible precautions, however, and you shouldn't have any problems.

be small and basic, catering to long-stay travellers. Most of the visitors are young, with **surfing** high on their agendas.

10

Broadly speaking, Escondido can be divided into four areas. **Puerto Escondido** itself sprawls across a hill behind the bay, divided by Hwy-200 into a busy Mexican town inland, where few visitors venture except to catch a bus or visit the bank, and the tourist zone behind Playa Principal. Here the central section of the main thoroughfare, Avenida Pérez Gasga, is known as El Adoquín – Spanish for "paving stone". Closed to traffic at 6pm, it's packed with shops, bars and restaurants. Most surfers, however, hang out not in Escondido itself but in **Zicatela**, barely 1km to the east, behind the chief surf beach, Playa Zicatela. Where once stood just a few weather-beaten huts, there's now a thriving community with dozens of hotels and increasingly sophisticated restaurants and bars. Non-surfers and surf groupies have also latched on, and Zicatela is arguably now a bigger destination than Escondido town.

For those seeking the alternative vibe that Zicatela once had, the action has moved down to **La Punta**, 3km away at the far end of Playa Zicatela. Here the sand streets, wooden shacks, camping and cabañas (though not necessarily the prices) recall a simpler

era. In the other direction, west of the centre, the rapidly developing neighbourhood of **Rinconada**, with access to the calmer beaches at Puerto Ángelito and Carrizalillo, is quieter and more family oriented, with a number of lovely boutique hotels.

Zicatela hosts a huge **surf tournament** in November, and lesser ones throughout the year. The sea is warm pretty much year-round, and the summer rainy season can leave the town oppressively humid, with a vacant, lacklustre air, but this doesn't deter the hard-core surfers.

The beaches

Apart from **shopping** for international surf designs, beachwear and crafts, Escondido offers little beyond the standard **beach activities**: swimming, surfing, eating, drinking and watching beautiful sunsets, though there is a growing number of places offering classes in everything from salsa to cookery, as well as plenty of Spanish language schools.

The choice of sandy **beaches**, even within a couple of kilometres of town, is impressive. Note that wherever you are, the surf should be treated with respect – the

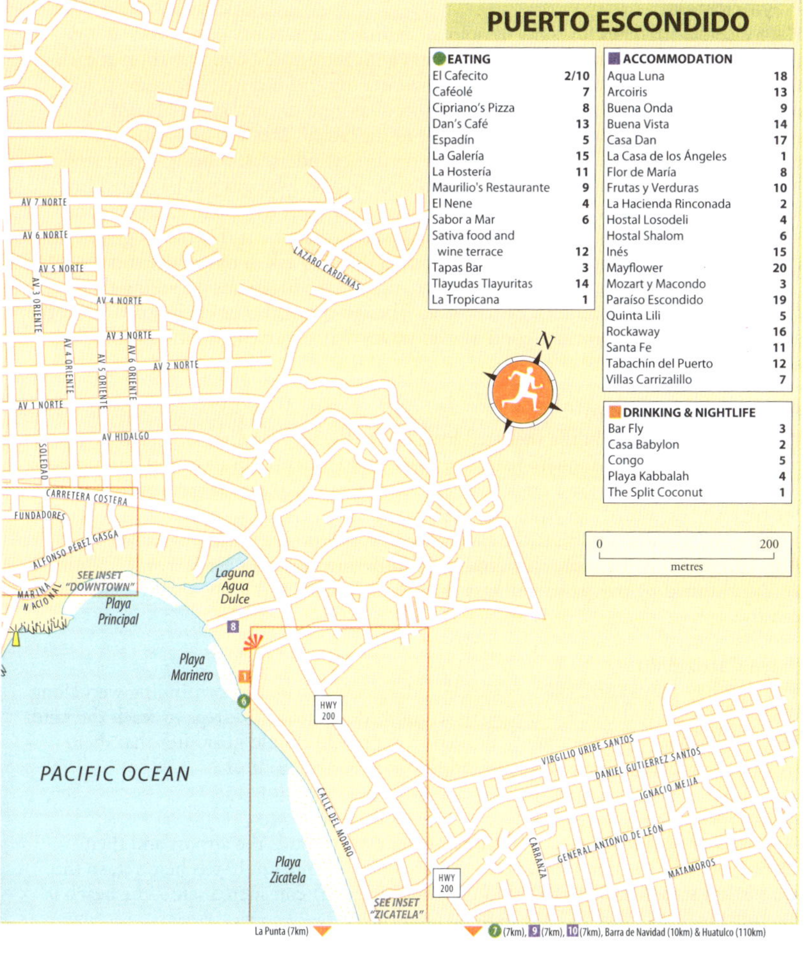

waters along Zicatela, especially, have a lethal **undertow**. There are **lifeguards** on all the main beaches, so respect their advice.

Playa Principal

The town beach, **Playa Principal**, stretches out directly in front of town, just a step or two from the Adoquín. Frequented primarily by Mexican families, it makes for a lovely stroll after dinner, but, thanks to the number of people and the constant comings and goings of *lanchas* and fishing boats, is perhaps not the best place to swim. Come here if you want to catch a boat ride to another beach, or out to see the turtles.

Playa Marinero

Immediately east of Playa Principal, beyond the **Laguna Agua Dulce** (most of the year you can walk straight across; in wet season you may have to go round via the bridge on the main road), **Playa Marinero** is quieter and sometimes graced with gentle waves – it's a good place to bodyboard. At the far end, the rocky outcrop of El Morro divides Marinero from Zicatela.

Playa Zicatela

Playa Zicatela stretches for some 4km in all, with beach bars and palapa restaurants scattered pretty much the whole way, though with the greatest concentration at each end, at Zicatela and La Punta. One of the world's top surf beaches, Zicatela ("place of big thorns") regularly receives beach breaks of around 4m and can maintain the surf swell for days on end. This is the home of the fabled "**Mexican pipeline**" – so-called because the breaking waves curl into perfect cylinders, permitting expert surfers momentarily to ride inside the tubes. Surfboards and bodyboards can be rented from a number of places along the beach and in town, but take advice and consider your strength and fitness before venturing into the water when the surf is running (you can check wave reports online at one of the internet cafés, or ask in one of the surf shops): occasionally even experienced surfers drown, despite the lifeguards patrolling the beach. La Punta generally has a much easier break. Though it can also be exceptional when the swell is up, it usually provides good, slower waves that are excellent for longboarding and for learners.

Bahía Puerto Ángelito

There are two beaches in the sheltered little bay of Puerto Ángelito, separated by a rocky outcrop; **Puerto Ángelito** itself and **Manzanillo**. They're about twenty minutes' walk from town, either by a track that leads to the left off Pérez Gasga, or direct from the highway on a road signed to Puerto Ángelito.

The water is calm and blue, the sand powdery, but both beaches, especially Ángelito which is the more sheltered and family-oriented, get very crowded. Both are surrounded by palapa restaurants with shady tables, and loungers their customers can use.

Playa Carrizalillo

The next bay, **Playa Carrizalillo**, is a spellbinding cove reached by continuing west along the same track. At the end you have to scramble down over 170 steps to reach the sand; this, and the fact that boats aren't allowed to approach, should guarantee that there won't be too many other people around. It's well worth the effort.

Playa Bacocho

Playa Bacocho is further out, following the highway towards the airport and then cutting through the hotel zone. There aren't a great number of hotels here yet, so the sand is still somewhat secluded, though swimming isn't considered safe – the beach is pounded by heavy surf and has a **strong undertow**.

Punta Colorada

Punta Colorada, a little-visited, clean beach around the point at the far end of Bacocho, is perfect for bodyboarding; you'll get tubes, and left and right breaks up to 2m high – it tends to be shallow, though.

ARRIVAL AND DEPARTURE — PUERTO ESCONDIDO

By plane Puerto Escondido's airport (954 582 0977), 3km north of town, sees only a couple of flights a day and has almost no facilities. Shared taxis run into the centre; if you really want to save money, walk out to the main highway and flag down a *colectivo*. VivaAerobus (http://vivaaerobus.com) flies three times a week to Mexico City. Aerotucán (954 582 3461, https://aerotaxisdemexico.com) has daily flights to Oaxaca.

By bus Puerto Escondido has two main bus stations. The smart, modern OCC/ADO terminal is right by El Crucero, the junction where the main road between the town and the tourist zone crosses the Carretera Costera (Hwy-200). From El Crucero it's a 5min walk down to the Adoquín and about 20min to Zicatela; taxis run to the latter. The second-class Terminal Turistica is on Av Oaxaca, way out on the inland edge of the modern town. Taxis run from here to downtown and to Zicatela. Heading for Oaxaca, only second-class buses take the direct route over the mountains; the first-class ones take a huge loop round via the Isthmus, so you're better off travelling by van (see below); for Mexico City you'll save several hours taking the route via Acapulco (Turistar or Estrella Blanca from the Terminal Turistica), rather than ADO via Oaxaca.

Destinations Acapulco (6 daily 2nd class; 8hr); Huatulco (hourly 1st and 2nd class; 2hr 30min); Mexico City (3 daily 1st class, 3 2nd class; 18hr); Oaxaca (3 daily 1st class; 11hr; 2 daily 2nd class; 8hr); Pochutla (hourly 1st and 2nd class; 1hr 30min); San Cristóbal de las Casas (2 night buses daily, 1st class; 14hr); Tehuantepec (9 daily 1st class, 6 daily 2nd class; 4hr).

By minivan Much the quickest way to Oaxaca is by minivan, though the direct route across the mountains can be cramped and stomach-churning (aim for a seat near the front). The most frequent and convenient service is with Servicio Express, based at the *Hotel Luz del Angel* on 1 Nte, cnr Av Oaxaca (954 582 0122; 7hr), with around fifteen departures every day; Villa del Mar, with fewer departures, is nearby on Hidalgo, just off Oaxaca (954 132 6182); others depart from the second-class bus station.

GETTING AROUND

By boat Take a *lancha* from Playa Principal to the nearby beaches; you can arrange a pick-up at an agreed time. The same boats offer a cheaper group rate for a full tour of the coast, beaches and local turtles.

By car For car rental, try Viajes Dimar (see page 603) or Los Tres Reyes (954 582 3335).

By taxi Taxis around town operate on a fixed-rate system (check at the tourist booth for the latest rates). Popular routes include the run between downtown and Bacocho, and to Zicatela. You can flag them down anywhere.

INFORMATION

Tourist information booth By far the best source of information on Puerto Escondido is the booth (Mon–Fri 10am–2pm & 4–6pm, Sat 10am–2pm; 954 582 1186) manned by the enthusiastic Gina Machorro at the western end of the Adoquín – she can help with accommodation and tours and is a font of knowledge on the whole region.

Tourist office The main official tourist office (Mon–Fri 9am–2pm & 4–7pm; 954 582 0175) is on Hwy-200 at the western edge of town, near the turn-off to the hotel zone (near Playa Bacocho).

ACCOMMODATION — SEE MAP PAGE 598

Finding somewhere to stay in Puerto Escondido shouldn't be a problem, except over Christmas, Easter and during the major surfing contests, when **prices** can rise considerably. Hotel quality is generally much lower than in Oaxaca City. Many of the hotels in town are particularly depressing; Zicatela (where most places have pools, since the sea is almost always too rough for swimming) is mostly better, while there are a few very good (but expensive) alternatives in Rinconada. Unless stated, they all have **wi-fi**. If you have a large group or intend to stay for a week or longer, consider an apartment or **villa rental**; simple studios or apartments can be rented by the week and you can get a fairly luxurious beachside property here. For ideas, inquire at the information booth on arrival (see above).

PUERTO TOWN, PLAYA PRINCIPAL AND PLAYA MARINERO

★ **Flor de María** 1a Entrada a Playa Marinero; http://mexonline.com/flordemaria.htm. With a perfect location at the entry to Playa Marinero, within easy reach of Zicatela and the Adoquín, and offering great-value, laid-back comfort, this is a traveller favourite. Fan-cooled, well-kept rooms are individually decorated; some have balconies. There's a rooftop terrace with small pool and fine views, plus a restaurant (high season only) and bar. M$$$

Mayflower Andador Libertad s/n, up a flight of steps from the Adoquín; 954 147 8973. Travellers love or hate this well-known place overlooking the Adoquín. Double rooms and dormitories, a bar, a communal kitchen and ample common areas foster a long-term, sociable traveller vibe – but this is definitely what the locals call "gringolandia". Some upper rooms have little balconies where you can glimpse the Pacific. Wi-fi in common areas only. Dorms and private rooms available. M$$

Paraíso Escondido Unión 10; http://hotelpe.com. One of the longest-established hotels in the area, on the hill above the Adoquín, with stellar views and lush gardens. Tidy rooms all have balconies and are artistically decorated with kitsch mirrors, tiles and sculptures; top-floor suites have great views. There is also a central pool, bar and restaurant area. Can be a real bargain in low season. M$$

ZICATELA

Aqua Luna Vista Hermosa s/n; http://hotelaqualuna.com. Hidden away in the backstreets, this smart, minimalist hotel's rooms range from spartan simplicity to a fully equipped luxury apartment – it's as close to a boutique hotel as you'll get in Zicatela, though still with a distinctly surfie atmosphere. Hospitably run by an Australian-Mexican couple who are knowledgeable about the area, it makes a very pleasant base. There's the added allure of a swimming pool, bar with wide-screen TV and pool table, and rooftop terrace with hot tub. Five-day minimum stay in high season. Adults only. Fan room M$$, deluxe apartment M$$$

Arcoiris C del Morro s/n; http://hotelarcoirismexico.com. Rambling, yellow-painted complex with rooms on several levels; one of the better-value options if you want to be at the heart of the Zicatela surfing action. Big choice of rooms, some with fans, some a/c (for an extra charge), some with kitchenettes and large balconies with great views, along with luxuriant gardens, a secluded pool and a restaurant with glimpses of the ocean. M$$

Buena Vista C del Morro s/n; 954 582 1474. Zicatela favourite, beloved for its great views of the surf (its elevated setting offers a great perspective on the beach, just out front), but also for its friendliness and affordability. M$$

★ **Casa Dan** Jacaranda 14; http://hotelcasadan.com. Very cool place with lots of character, a short walk behind the beach. A variety of rooms is available, each with a kitchen, terrace, great views and artfully decorated bathrooms. Larger rooms are very spacious and cost-effective for groups or families; there's also a book exchange and great café (see page 604). Cabaña M$$$, room M$$

Inés C del Morro s/n; http://hotelines.com. Excellent, sprawling place that seems to have something for everyone, from simple cabañas for four to a luxurious honeymoon suite. German-run, *Inés* has plentiful facilities for this price range, including pool, a sauna and spa, hammocks and a good dive centre. Cabaña M$$, a/c room M$$$

Rockaway C del Morro s/n; https://rockawayzicatela.com. Long-standing Zicatela haunt that recently received a souped-up redesign. Bright white rooms are clustered around a courtyard with two small swimming pools, and there's a gym (rare in these parts) and small shopping centre. M$$$

Santa Fe C del Morro s/n; http://hotelsantafe.com.mx. Much the most traditional-feeling and elegant hotel in Zicatela, a beautiful, colonial-style place with waxed, red-tile floors and a range of a/c rooms with tiled bathrooms, cable TV and little balconies. There are two pools, a couple of bungalows with kitchens, and a terrace bar and restaurant overlooking the beach. M$$$

★ **Tabachín del Puerto** C del Moro s/n; http://hotel tabachin.com. Hidden away behind the *Hotel Santa Fe*, this cluster of six quirky studios, some with large, breezy balconies, is crammed with books, knick-knacks and vases that add to its comforting appeal. Substantial (and largely organic) breakfasts are included. M$$$

LA PUNTA

Buena Onda Av Alejandro Cárdenas s/n, right on the beach, 1.5 blocks from the end of the road; 954 582 1663. Cabañas as they should be, right on the beach surrounded by sand and palm trees, with cement floor, fan, bed and mosquito net, but little else. There's a communal sitting area, umbrellas and loungers on the beach and a couple of rooms and a dorm, though these are cramped and stuffy. Dorm and cabañas available. M$

Frutas y Verduras Av Alejandro Cárdenas s/n; 954 123 0473, http://frutasyverdurasmexico.org. Rooms, camping and cabañas in a collection of palapa-roofed wooden structures. There's an observation tower, terrace with jacuzzi, communal kitchen, bar and a café-restaurant serving local produce; basic accommodation but great atmosphere. Camping and cabaña M$, room M$$

RINCONADA

La Casa de los Ángeles Zaachila 9; https://hotelboutique puertoescondido.com. Tranquil, luxurious boutique hotel away from the action for non-surfing Escondido visitors; there are six one-bedroom suites, with kitchen, living room and terrace, hot tub and tiny outdoor gym in the garden, and rooftop palapa with telescope and barbecue. M$$$

La Hacienda Rinconada Cuilapan 15; www.hotel suiteshacienda.mx. Thanks to their gracious French owner, the six very comfortable, spacious bedrooms with kitchenettes and a/c ooze home-spun style. Outside, a colonial theme prevails, with flower-filled patios and a swimming pool surrounded by tropical foliage. A 5min walk from Playa Carrizalillo, it's not cheap, but one of the better places if you are inclined to splurge. M$$$$

Hostal Losodeli 2 Nte, just off Carre Costera; http://losodeli.com. Friendly, locally run place with simple

ADVENTURE AND ACTIVITIES IN PUERTO ESCONDIDO

Activities and ecotourism adventures are big business in Puerto Escondido; lagoon trips, cycling, camping, rock climbing, bird watching and tours of hot springs and coffee plantations are all on offer. You can also head out onto the water in search of turtles, dolphins and even whales, or seek personal development by learning to surf, to dive, to speak Spanish or simply to unwind with yoga or massage.

TOUR AGENCIES

Viajes Dimar Pérez Gasga 905-B, Adoquín and Del Morro in Zicatela (at the Bungalows Puerta del Sol); 954 129 4450, https://facebook.com/dimarmexico. Helpful travel agency that can arrange almost any of the activities below, as well as tours, plane and bus tickets, and car rental.

SURFING

Central Surf Del Morro s/n at Bungalows Acuario, Zicatela; 954 111 9718. Lessons, gear rental and a shop selling surfwear.

Oasis Surf Juárez, Rinconada; 954 582 1445, http://tomzap.com/SurfFactory.html. Board manufacturer and a big surf school.

ECOTOURISM

Hidden Voyages Ecotours Based at Viajes Dimar (see page 603); 519 326 5193, http://peleewings.ca. Bird watching trips led by Canadian ornithologist Michael Malone to Laguna Manialtepec and to a coffee ranch in the hills. Dec 15–March 25 only.

Lalo Ecotours Based in the village of Las Negras, Laguna Manialtepec; 954 588 9164, http://lalo-ecotours.com. A variety of boat, kayak and hiking tours to and around Laguna Manialtepec (see page 606), also evening tours to see the phosphorescence in the water. They also offer bird watching tours, plus horse riding tours to the Atotonilco hot springs.

FISHING AND BOAT TRIPS

Omar Sportfishing Playa Puerto Ángelito; 954 559 4406, http://tomzap.com/omar.html. Captain Omar Ramírez goes after marlin and sailfish for an hourly fee. Also dolphin and whale-watching tours.

MASSAGE, YOGA AND HEALING

Manos Curativas Las Brisas, Zicatela; 954 101 3525. Yoga, massage, aromatherapy and much more – including surf lessons!

Temazcalli Infraganti, cnr Temazcalli, inland off Hwy-200 past Zicatela; http://temazcalli.com. A range of therapies and treatments, from massages to *temazcal*.

SPANISH COURSES

Experiencia Andador Revolucion, off Adoquín; 213 701 6093, http://experiencia.com. With a great base in a former hotel just off the Adoquín, Experiencia can offer excellent on-site accommodation, as well as homestays, volunteering programmes and other activities.

Oasis Language School Juárez, Rinconada; 954 582 1445, http://spanishandsurflessonsmexico.com. Private and group lessons, which can be combined with homestays or apartment rentals, or surf courses.

but well-set-up six-person dorms and private rooms. Communal area with cable TV, pool, hammocks, surf classes and bike rental. M$

Hostal Shalom Juárez 4082; 954 582 3234, https://facebook.com/HostalShalomPuertoEscondido. The good news about the *Shalom* is that it has spacious grounds where you can camp, a great position just a short walk from Puerto Ángelito, a pool, communal areas with a party atmosphere, and boards and bikes to rent. The less good news is the dorm room accommodations, which are hot and cramped. Wi-fi in café only. M$

Mozart y Macondo Tortugas 77; www.hotelmozartymacondo.com. Suburban house whose lovingly tended rooms are full of art (available to buy). There's a two-bedroom penthouse with a kitchen, and in the garden, which is the German owner's pride and joy, a breakfast area and outdoor kitchen. Carrizalillo beach is an easy walk, and guests have rights to use a nearby hotel's beach club. M$$

★ **Quinta Lili** Cangrejos 104; http://quintalili.mx. Delightful place, close to the beach, with neat, spacious rooms, LCD TVs, fans and balconies with sea views, all set in a whimsical beach house, half-palapa, half-Moorish palace. Small pool, roof terrace with jacuzzi, excellent breakfasts and helpful hosts. M$$

Villas Carrizalillo Carrizalillo 125; http://villascarrizalillo.com. In a peaceful spot above the namesake beach, these discreet, spacious, individually designed villas with kitchens and stunning views are perfect for young couples and families who want a few home comforts away from the party scene. There is a great restaurant enjoying the best of the views, pool, book exchange, and bike, bodyboard and surfboard rental. M$$$$

EATING

SEE MAP PAGE 598

It doesn't cost much to eat well in Escondido. Many of the restaurants and cafés are laid-back, low-key affairs open to cool breezes. The **seafood** is always fresh, and you can vary your diet with **vegetarian** food, excellent bread and cakes, and **international** food including Swiss, Japanese, German and Italian. For cheap snacks, it's worth strolling into the old town to the **Mercado Juárez** and the taco stalls along Oaxaca, and you can buy self-catering provisions at the Super Che supermarket near El Crucero. In Zicatela especially, plenty of restaurants double as bars as the sun goes down.

PUERTO TOWN, PLAYA PRINCIPAL AND PLAYA MARINERO

La Galería Adoquín; 954 582 4079. One of the best Italian joints in town, with platters of home-made tortellini, spaghetti, ravioli and gnocchi as well as delicious salads and an array of pizzas, all served in a polished setting with art displayed on the walls and exposed brick. M$$$$

Sabor a Mar Eastern end of Playa Marinero; 954 102 7090. Right at the end of the beach, this relaxed open-air place serves some of the best seafood in town – including fish fillets, octopus and a huge prawn cocktail. M$$$

Tlayudas Tlayuritas Av. Alfonso Pérez Gasga; 951 145 8472. If you've never had *tlayuda* before, this is the perfect spot to try it. The restaurant serves nothing but this traditional Oaxacan cuisine; think fried tortillas with various toppings to choose from. M$$

La Tropicana 2 Nte, just west of Av Oaxaca; 954 154 0547. Escape "gringolandia" with a stroll into town for some of the best *tacos al pastor* on the coast – add quesillo for the full special; also tortas and beans. M$$

ZICATELA

El Cafecito Del Morro s/n; https://facebook.com/ElCafecito PuertoEscondido. Justifiably long-standing favourite, best known for its substantial breakfasts, served in an open-air palapa, including the vast Gran Slams aimed at starving surfers (in various combinations of pancakes, French toast, bacon and eggs). Prices are steeper than they seem as coffee and juice are not included; there are also freshly baked pastries from their own *panadería*. The lunch-time menu has an international flavour, with burgers, croissants, whole-grain sandwiches and burritos. Tasty, simple seafood dishes and other filling Mexican staples feature in the evening. M$$$$

Cipriano's Pizza Del Morro s/n; 954 134 6546. Thin, crispy, cheesy pizzas, cooked in a wood-fired stone oven and served at romantic tables wedged into the sand. There's also a full Mexican menu. M$$$$

Dan's Café Jacaranda 14; 954 104 2640. The restaurant at *Casa Dan* (see page 602) serves arguably the best, and best value, breakfast in Escondido. Great coffee and French toast, healthy *licuados*, and an interesting, mixed crowd. Or come at lunch time for the legendary fish tacos and cold beer. M$$

La Hostería Del Morro s/n; 954 582 0005. A huge and busy Italian-themed place with wood-oven pizzas and everything from hearty breakfasts to imaginative Italian and nouvelle Mexican dishes, served with flair and a decent wine selection. M$$$$

Maurilio's Restaurante Del Morro s/n, on the beach opposite Rockaway; 954 101 6087. Sometimes slow service, but the beachfront setting and great seafood make it worth the wait; the brunch menus is a big hit here. M$$$

Sativa food and wine terrace Del Morro s/n; https://sativapuerto.com. Chic bar-restaurant with an East Asian theme, reflected in dishes like prawns *sativa* (with coconut, mango and *chipotle*) or seafood curry; also salads and cocktails. M$$$$

LA PUNTA

Caféolé Av Alejandro Cárdenas s/n; 954 103 8533. The café at *Frutas y Verduras* (see page 598) serves delicious, mostly organic, local produce – crêpes, omelettes and fruit and vegetable salads as well as home-made yogurt and cakes. M$$

RINCONADA

El Cafecito Juárez, between Focas and Mantarrayas; https://facebook.com/ElCafecitoPuertoEscondido. Another branch of the Zicatela institution (see left). M$$$

★ **Espadín** Villas Carrizalillo, Carrizalillo 125; http://espadinrestaurante.com. Fine dining in a posh palapa restaurant, with mesmerizing views of the bay – try to get a table on the edge of the terrace. The modern Mexican menu features the likes of *dorado* with pumpkin seeds, sweet mango *mahi mahi ceviche*, chicken in *mole negro* and spicy shrimp tacos. Also breakfast. M$$$$

El Nene Juárez 14; https://facebook.com/Restaurant ElNene. Simple but great Mexican restaurant with a few pavement tables, serves tasty tacos, *hamburguesas*, natural juices and the special, chile con carne. Also mains like Cajun chicken and the best margaritas in town. M$$$

Tapas Bar Juárez, between Pargos and Focas; 954 582 308. Authentic, Spanish-run tapas bar with delicious, reasonably priced tapas (such as the *camarones al ajillo*) as well as main dishes. M$$$

DRINKING AND NIGHTLIFE

SEE MAP PAGE 598

Puerto Escondido's busiest **nightlife** scene is in Zicatela, where many of the restaurants morph into bars as the evening progresses – a couple of the longest-established bar/clubs are just off the Adoquín, though, and many of the hostels have a pretty wild party scene of their own in high season.

Bar Fly Del Morro s/n, Zicatela, upstairs from La Hostería. This eclectic lounge with a balcony overlooking the beach plays good Latin and international music and has comfy cushions for you to lie on while you sip a frosty cocktail.

★ **Casa Babylon** Del Morro s/n, Zicatela, next door to the Hotel Arcoiris; 954 582 0875. Arty, friendly, late-night bar with board games, mellow music, great mojitos and a useful reference library with travel books.

Congo Adoquín. Raucous, African-themed club right in the heart of town; the narrow space around the tiled bar only adds to the atmosphere, and there's a miniature terrace out back. Live salsa on Wed.

Playa Kabbalah Del Morro s/n, Zicatela; http://playakabbalah.com. Cool bar-restaurant on Playa Zicatela, with the accent firmly on drinking and dancing rather than eating. Plenty of themed parties, plus Ladies' nights which include a free cocktail.

The Split Coconut Eastern end of Playa Marinero; 954 582 0736. Favourite expat bar (also known locally as *Brad's Split Coconut*) serving mouth-watering barbecue and burgers, with live music on Sun, good wi-fi, satellite TV showing major sports events and daily happy hours. The July 4 celebrations are big here.

10

DIRECTORY

Banks and exchange Inside the ADO is an ATM for Scotiabank, and there are three ATMS at the Super Che. Most banks are in town, though, including HSBC on 1 Nte just off Carr Costera (near the ADO), Bancomer at 3 Nte and 2 Pte, and Banorte on Hidalgo, just off Oaxaca.

Laundry Excellent laundry service (charge per kg) at Lava-Max, Pérez Gasga 405, just below Union (near *Hotel Paraíso Escondido*).

Police 066 or their booth at the eastern end of the Adoquín 954 582 0721.

Post office In the old town at Oaxaca and 7A Nte.

Around Puerto Escondido

All but the most hardcore surfers and sun-worshippers are going to feel the need to explore after a few days relaxing on the beach. There's a wide range of activities on offer through agencies in town (see page 603), many involving trips out of the city, but there are also some you can do yourself. Most obviously, these involve visiting the nearby **lagoons**, and heading out on a boat to enjoy the wildlife.

Barra de Navidad

Barra de Navidad is immediately east of Puerto Escondido, where the **Laguna Las Naranjas** at the mouth of the Río Colotepec reaches the sea. The deserted beach across the lagoon is a haven for **birdlife**, while the lagoon itself has **crocodiles** and much else to see. In the village, Galo's **Iguanario** (open daylight hours – just go in and call out; small donation) is an extraordinary place set up to preserve rare iguanas. The ramshackle complex now has several hundred of them, along with half a dozen crocodiles, snakes, birds and tortoises. Locals can take you on a 45-minute walking tour around the lagoon (the price varies), where information boards describing local wildlife have been set up; or take a *lancha* from La Ballena (see below).

ARRIVAL AND TOURS — BARRA DE NAVIDAD

By colectivo Barra de Navidad is 10min east of Puerto Escondido, off Hwy-200. Drivers should turn right immediately after the bridge that crosses the river. *Colectivos* marked "Barra" can be flagged down on the highway near El Crucero in Escondido, or behind Zicatela – more information at the tourist booth on the Adoquín (see page 601). Beyond the village of Barra the dirt road splits, the left fork leading towards the mouth of the lagoon and *La Ballena* (about 1700m), the right one to Don Juan (1km); either is walkable.

Tours At *La Ballena* restaurant, you can organize a *lancha* (charged per person; it's also customary to tip) to take you round the lagoon.

EATING

La Ballena At the mouth of the lagoon. *La Ballena* is a community project named after the vertebrae of a stranded grey whale that are displayed here. It's a very basic place consisting of benches and an open-air kitchen, most of which is destroyed every rainy season. M$$

La Huerta de Don Juan y Doña Lola 954 588 3269. Local families descend at the weekend to enjoy home-cooked fish and shellfish under a huge palapa with plastic tables and chairs, set in the midst of lush coconut palms; they also have a riverside area. M$$$

10

Laguna Manialtepec

Laguna Manialtepec, about 15km west of Puerto Escondido at km 124 on Hwy-200 to Acapulco, is cut off from the sea most of the year, forming a freshwater lake extraordinarily rich in **birdlife**. You can easily spot fifty-odd species (there are said to be 360 in total), including parrots, hawks, falcons, ospreys, kingfishers and ibises; there are also crocodiles in the water. You'll see far more if you arrive very early, around 7am, or at sunset. At night, boat tours glide over plankton that glows, as if by magic, with phosphorescence.

ARRIVAL AND TOURS — LAGUNA MANIALTEPEC

Tours The most convenient way to visit is to take an organized tour through one of the travel agencies in Puerto Escondido (see page 603). La Flor del Pacifico (954 588 9164), on the shore right in the village, is the local base for Lalo Ecotours (see page 603) and offers *lancha* trips. *La Puesta del Sol* (954 132 8294), on the lagoon 1km before the village of Las Negras, is a friendly and well-organized restaurant right on the water; they offer *lancha* trips (charged per boat) and kayak rental by the hour.

By taxi/colectivo You can also visit independently, and if you have a group of three or more you'll save some money this way in a taxi to the lagoon. A Río Grande-bound *colectivo*, from 2 Nte and 3 Pte, is even more affordable.

Parque Nacional Lagunas de Chacahua

The **Parque Nacional Lagunas de Chacahua**, 75km west of Puerto Escondido, is an expansive and lush national park incorporating some 370,000 acres of mangroves, sand dunes and forests teeming with birdlife, turtles and crocodiles. To visit independently – a great back-to-nature experience – you'll need a couple of days at the very least.

The village of **CHACAHUA**, on the shore of the lagoon close to the magnificent ocean beach, is interesting in itself, with a small Afro-Mexican population and basic **cabañas** to rent by the water; there's also space to camp and a row of outdoor seafood restaurants where you could hang a hammock. There's good surf on the beaches and occasionally even in the lagoon; currents can be strong, though, so check where it's safe to swim.

ARRIVAL AND DEPARTURE — LAGUNAS DE CHACAHUA

Tours The easy way to visit Chacahua is with a tour (see page 603), though a day trip may only whet your appetite. A two-hour boat tour of the lagoon will is charged per boat. For more information check https://visitingmexico.com/lagunas-de-chacahua-national-park.

By taxi To get here independently from Escondido you could negotiate a cab to take you all the way to the crossing point, a 2min boat ride from Chacahua. But the taxi can be expensive and the road is often impassable.

By colectivo/boat *Colectivos* (every 20min) run from 2 Nte and 3 Pte to Río Grande, 50km west of Puerto Escondido on Hwy-200; then change to one of the frequent minibuses to the port of Zapotalito. From here you can take a *lancha* to Chacahua (fixed fee for a group). *Colectivo* boats are also an option.

Puerto Ángel and around

Some 65km from Puerto Escondido, at the junction of Hwy-175 from Oaxaca and coastal Hwy-200, the oppressive, shabby city of **Pochutla** is the service hub for a string of beach towns and resorts that unfurl east towards the Isthmus of Tehuantepec. **Puerto Ángel**, now firmly on the tourist radar, is a fishing village that draws budget travellers with its unpretentious, low-key vibe and picturesque setting. Seven kilometres west, the beautiful beach of **Zipolite** has gained a reputation for its liberal-minded, European-hippy vibe, while north over the headland, attractive **San Agustinillo** has a more restrained feel. Further west, **Mazunte** is the main nesting site for Golfina turtles. Rapidly developing, it has something of the feel of a junior Zipolite.

Puerto Ángel

Though it's well established as a tourist destination, **PUERTO ÁNGEL** goes about its business as a small, down-at-heel fishing port with minimum fuss. Everything remains resolutely low-key – you may very well find pigs and chickens mingling with the visitors on the streets – and locals fish off the huge concrete dock, catching yellowtail tuna and other gamefish with a simple rod and line. Though it has a gorgeous setting – around a sheltered bay ringed by mountains – the beaches are less than pristine. Small hotels, rooms and simple places to sling a hammock, however, are abundant, with some of the most promising on the road between the main village and the Playa del Panteón. If you're on a tight budget Puerto Ángel can be a fun place to spend a few days, meandering and sampling the superb local **seafood**.

The beaches

Puerto Ángel has two beaches: **Playa Principal** is right in front of the town, and **Playa del Panteón** is opposite, beyond a rocky promontory. Panteón is the cleaner of the two, reached by a steep road or a path around the base of the cliffs. Here there is some interesting snorkelling around the rocks, as well as a profusion of tenacious hawkers. By afternoon it's in the shade, so most people wander round to the town beach. With just a little more effort you can visit one of the far better beaches either side of Puerto Ángel. To the west is the more primitive **Zipolite** (see page 609), while to the east, about fifteen minutes' walk up the Pochutla road and then down a heavily rutted track to the right, is tranquil **Estacahuite**. Here you'll find three tiny, sandy coves divided by outcrops of rock. The rocks are close in, so you can't swim far, but there's wonderful **snorkelling** (beware of sharp coral and undercurrents) and rarely more than a handful of other people around.

There are other lovely beaches near Estacahuite, including idyllic **Playa del Boquilla**, where you'll find the *Hotel Bahía de la Luna* and a **restaurant**, accessible by boat from Puerto Ángel. Boquilla is signposted from the main road to Pochutla, but it's inadvisable to drive down here, as the 7km road is in a terrible state. A better idea is to arrange a boat trip in advance to both beaches, turtle-spotting along the way. You'll see plenty of **boat trips** offered, or there's **scuba diving** with Azul Profundo (958 584 3109), based at the *Hotel Cordelia* in Playa del Panteón.

ARRIVAL AND INFORMATION — PUERTO ÁNGEL

By pasajeras/colectivos *Pasajeras* and *colectivos* from Pochutla drop off at the junction of Vasconcelos and Uribe, the continuation of the main road into town (there's also a taxi stand here). There are occasional *colectivos* on towards Zipolite, as well as private taxis.

Tourist information The tourist information booth is located at the pier entrance on Uribe (Mon–Fri 10am–noon & 4–8pm, Sat & Sun 10am–noon, but erratic).

ACCOMMODATION

Bahía de la Luna Playa la Boquilla; http://bahiadelaluna.com. An escape for couples happy to do without creature comforts, this jungle retreat close to beautiful Boquilla beach (wonderful snorkelling) is hard to beat. Bungalows for two to five people cling to the hillside, and a restaurant-café on the beach serves fresh fish. It also offers holistic therapy treatments, personal development workshops and yoga, and sea kayaks and scuba gear are available to rent. Taxis run from here into town. M$$$

★ **Buena Vista** La Buena Compañia s/n, a short walk along the footpath north from Uribe, next to the Arroye River; http://labuenavista.mx. High above town and set back from the main road, *Buena Vista* has accommodation arranged over three floors, with an ocean view from the top-floor restaurant terrace and a rooftop swimming pool. The quiet rooms may not be well equipped – not even hot water – but the Robinson Crusoe ambience is part of the appeal. M$$

La Cabaña Playa del Panteón; http://lacabanapuertoangel.com. Just metres from the beach, *La Cabaña* has spotlessly clean rooms with bathrooms, small fridge, cable TV and fans (some with a/c). There's free coffee and tea in the mornings, a tiny pool and a rooftop terrace and restaurant with spectacular views. M$$

Casa de Huéspedes Gundí y Tomas Uribe 2; 958 584 3068. One of the best budget options in the village, this jungle-clad guesthouse has simple if rather worn rooms with fans, mosquito nets and random folksy flourishes. The atmosphere is very friendly – travellers exchange tales in the open-fronted lounge area and Gundí's sons, who now run the place, offer surf lessons as well as bike and motorbike rental. The restaurant serves very good food, especially the bountiful breakfasts. M$

Puesta del Sol Uribe s/n; 958 584 3315, https://facebook.com/puesta.delsol.524. A great low-priced option. Not much in the way of a view, but spotless, spacious rooms (hot water for a few pesos more) around a garden with hammocks, laundry, internet access, library, satellite TV and communal space lined with photos. M$

Soraya Vasconcelos s/n; 958 584 3009. A bland but efficient choice, right in the centre of town overlooking the pier. There is little character to this modern hotel – rooms are basic with frilly bedspreads, fan (some with a/c and terrace) and private bath – but it is clean and spacious and the staff are very helpful. Good sea views from the restaurant, and from a couple of the rooms. M$$

EATING

Beto's Uribe s/n, on the outskirts of town on the way to Zipolite. High-quality seafood at very good prices served in an unassuming, low-key setting. It becomes a lively spot for drinks later on in the evening. M$$

Buena Vista La Buena Compañia s/n; www.labuenavista.mx. Romantic hotel-restaurant serving a reliable menu of Mexican and Italian classics in a lovely floral setting overlooking the bay; they also serve breakfast. Reservations recommended in high season. M$$$

Maca Uribe s/n at the bottom of the pier, no phone. Palapa-roofed open terrace beside the beach, serving good Mexican food and excellent seafood cocktails. The real attraction is the upstairs bar, though, a great place to watch the sun go down. M$$

El Rincón del Mar Precariously balanced on the cliff between playas Principal and Panteón; 958 113 4024. Boasting windy views of the ocean, this locally renowned restaurant serves the best fish and seafood in the area. The thick, seared loins of tuna are mouthwatering, and the nightly specials menu features imaginative renditions of the daily catch – bonita, lobster, shrimp, snapper – all invariably delicious. M$$$

Villa Serena Florencia Uribe s/n. At its namesake hotel, this is a popular place with European and American travellers, serving hearty Italian staples such as antipasto, pasta bolognese, *arrabiata* and marinara, as well as large, leafy salads, pizzas and traditional Mexican dishes. M$$$$

DIRECTORY

Banks and exchange There's a Bancomer ATM (not one hundred percent reliable) on Uribe opposite the pier. Banco Azteca on Uribe is more a pawn shop than a bank, but it does change money (at poor rates) and has a branch of Western Union.

Internet Gel@Net, Vasconcelos 3 (just off Uribe), is a handy internet café.

Laundry Lavandería El Ángel (charge per kg) is on Vasconcelos high above town.

Post office The post office is on Av Principal, the main road into the centre.

Pochutla

Anyone visiting Puerto Ángel and the other beach communities along the coast almost inevitably comes through **POCHUTLA**, a scruffy city on Hwy-175, 2km north of Hwy-200. Apart from catching a bus or changing money – there are no banks at the beaches beyond Puerto Ángel – there's no reason to spend time here.

ARRIVAL AND DEPARTURE — POCHUTLA

By bus The bus stations – second-class Estrella Blanca (958 584 0380) and first-class OCC (ADO; 958 584 0274) – are close to each other on Lázaro Cárdenas, the main street which runs through the centre of town.

Destinations Huatulco (7 daily 1st class, 3 daily 2nd class; 1hr); Oaxaca (3 daily 1st class via the Isthmus, 2 daily 2nd class; 7–9hr); Mexico City (2 daily 1st class, 2 daily 2nd class; 16hr); Puerto Escondido (hourly 1st and 2nd class; 1hr 30min); San Cristóbal (2 daily 1st class; 11hr).

By minivan The quickest and most convenient route to Oaxaca is with the many minivans that head directly there on Hwy-175, rather than the very long way round via the isthmus that most buses take. Several operators have offices on Cárdenas in the same block as the bus stations. Oaxaca Pacífico (958 584 0349) has three daily departures; Eclipse at Cárdenas 85 (958 584 0840) and Atlantida in the nearby *Hotel Santa Cruz* (958 584 0116) each run vans hourly from around 4am to 10pm. For Huatulco, Transportes Rapidos de Pochutla, in the same block, have rattly vans every 15min throughout the day.

By colectivo/pasajera "*Pasajeras*" (covered pick-up trucks) and *colectivo* taxis head frequently to Puerto Ángel, Zipolite and Mazunte; they may be waiting for passengers at the bus station, or you could just flag one down as they head along Cárdenas. Fares are rarely expensive, although if you want to go further than Puerto Ángel, over to Playa del Panteón for example, make this clear as you set out or you'll be charged an outrageous amount for the last part of the journey.

ACCOMMODATION

Posada San Jose Constitución, a block from the second-class bus station; 958 584 9170. Acceptable, inexpensive hotel if you find yourself stranded here, with rooms around a large courtyard and an often drained pool; they claim cable TV and wi-fi too, but the claims may be as empty as the pool. M$$

Zipolite

While some people rave about Puerto Ángel for its laid-back lifestyle, others are ecstatic about **ZIPOLITE**, 3km north along the road. Certainly there can be few places in Mexico better for doing absolutely nothing. Everything here revolves around the beach, first discovered by hippies in the 1970s, allegedly looking for a spot to witness an eclipse. Even today the travellers' grapevine is alive with tales of widely available hallucinogens, low living costs and a liberal approach to **nudity** – rumours that are largely well founded, much to the chagrin of the locals. Certainly, nude bathing, predominantly at the western end of the beach, is sanctioned by the local military; keep cover handy for trips to the restaurants. As for drugs, grass, mushrooms and acid are just as illegal as – though more prevalent than – anywhere else in Mexico; unscrupulous dealers are not above setting people up. **Theft**, particularly along the beachfront at night, can be a problem, but seems in no way to detract from the lure of a few days of complete abandon. The village behind the main beach has a laundry and a few small shops with internet access, beach gear and other bare necessities; for anything else you'll have to head to **Pochutla**.

The beach

The origin of the name "Zipolite" is uncertain – one theory is that it comes from the Náhuatl word meaning "beach of the dead", hence the constant references to it as the "playa de los muertos". The **beach** itself is magnificent, long and gently curving, pounded by heavy surf with a **riptide** that requires some caution – drownings are depressingly common (although there are lifeguards, as well as flags denoting danger levels up and down the beach). It is divided into three segments: Roca Blanca (aka Playa Shambala) towards the western end, Playa Zipolite or simply Centro in the middle and Playa del Amor at the eastern end nearest Puerto Ángel. Palapa huts line all three, catering to visitors' basic accommodation and dining needs.

ARRIVAL AND ACTIVITIES — ZIPOLITE

By colectivo/pasajera *Colectivos* and *pasajeras* connect Zipolite with Pochutla via Mazunte and San Agustinillo every 20min or so, much less often via Puerto Ángel; there are also plenty of private taxis.

Boat trips All the palapas along the beachfront advertise boat trips out to sea, where you can snorkel and sometimes spot turtles, dolphins and, if you're really lucky, whales on their way up to Baja California. Scuba diving is on offer, but the reef isn't particularly impressive here.

Yoga The Solstice Yoga Center (http://solstice-mexico.com) based at *La Loma Linda* (see below) runs regular classes, as well as five-day programmes, including meals and accommodation.

ACCOMMODATION

Accommodation is abundant and inexpensive, but mostly pretty makeshift. At the beachfront places **hammocks** (there's a charge) are strung from every rafter, but it can be worth getting a room if only to have a safe place to store your gear. Most feature shared bathrooms (cold water only), mosquito nets and a working fan if you're lucky.

El Alquimista Playa Shambala; http://elalquimistahotel.mx. Fourteen cosy palapas right on the beach and one of the best restaurants in town (see page 610), as well as bonfire parties at night. The artfully designed cabañas have private bathroom, hammocks, terrace and fan. Wi-fi. M$$$

Castillo Oasis C del Amor 97; 958 106 1763, http://castillooasis.com. At the far eastern end of Zipolite beach (near Playa del Amor), with five clean, beautifully designed rooms in a leafy green oasis; all come with hammocks, and a couple have bathrooms. Wi-fi throughout. M$

★ **Lo Cósmico** Playa Shambala; http://locosmico.com. One of Zipolite's best options, this idyllic hotel lies at the western end of the beach. It has beautiful cabañas, some sleeping up to six people, with views of the coast, a secluded beach out front and a restaurant serving delicious crêpes. Hammocks are also available, on a special "hammock terrace". M$$

10

★ **La Loma Linda** On the hillside overlooking Playa Zipolite; http://lalomalinda.com. Six colourful, thoughtfully designed cabañas, all with hammocks, fans, fridges, stellar views and tiled bathrooms; also a yoga centre (see page 609). M$$

A Nice Place on the Beach Playa Shambala; http://aniceplaceonthebeach.weebly.com. Eight very simple but appropriately named rooms, right next to the beach, with fans, some with private bath. There's a popular bar, too. M$

Nude Playa Zipolite; http://nudezipolite.com. To the horror of some, perhaps, a vision of what Zipolite might become – elegant, modern, two-storey, white concrete cabañas on the beach, some with a/c. There's a pool, "sky-lounge" bar and wi-fi. As the name suggests, this spot is clothing optional. M$$$

Posada México Playa Shambala; http://posadamexico.com. Among the most popular places on the beach: the ten cosy rooms (some in cute two-storey palapas) equipped with double beds, hammocks, safes and mosquito nets are a real bargain, and there's excellent Italian food and cocktails, all right on the sand. M$$

Sebastian de los Milagros Eastern end of Playa Zipolite; www.sebastiandelosmilagros.com. Friendly, LGBTQ+ friendly option with space to lock luggage as well as a small pool, communal areas with a bar, and wi-fi throughout. M$$

★ **Shambhala** Playa Shambala; http://shambhalavision.com. This long-established and slightly eccentric meditation retreat is tucked away up the side of a hill by a rocky outcrop. It boasts beautiful vistas and shares *Lo Cósmico's* beach area, with some shabby and some nicer, new, private-bath cabañas; also dorm room and a terrace for hammocks. The area at the top of the hill behind the cabins is a meditation spot and a great place to watch the sun rise (or set) over the bay. No alcohol permitted. Dorm M$, cabaña M$$

EATING

Zipolite is a great place for cheap, fresh food, with most of the popular **restaurants** located along the western beachfront.

3 Diciembre A block inland from the main street in the village; 958 584 3157. Best known for its tasty pizzas, *3 Diciembre* also serves vegetarian Mexican dishes, *pozole* and home-made cheesecake. M$$$

★ **El Alquimista** Playa Shambala; https://elalquimistahotel.mx. Extensive menu of international and Mexican food, with excellent seafood, chicken, steak and wood-oven pizza, plus good coffee. What really draws the crowds, though, especially in the evenings, is the chilled-out music and the cocktails from the bar. M$$$$

Memo's Cafe Main road in the village, above Café Zipol. Breezy upstairs terrace where they serve juices, teas, coffee, smoothies, frappuccinos, ice cream and cake, and there's free wi-fi. M$$

DRINKING AND NIGHTLIFE

La Puesta Cnr of the main road down to Playa Zipolite. This cheesy but popular open-air disco is the heart of local nightlife, with occasional live bands and a party every night; doesn't get lively till midnight.

San Agustinillo

Rounding the headland north of Zipolite you come to **SAN AGUSTINILLO**, another fine beach graced with good surfing waves. Fast developing, it has a more restrained vibe than Zipolite, with some charming and upmarket places to stay and eat. The sand is backed by restaurants, which offer space for a hammock or small rooms for rent in addition to reasonably priced, fresh seafood. *Colectivos* and *pasajeras* pass frequently along the main road, heading in one direction to Zipolite, in the other to Mazunte and Pochutla.

ACCOMMODATION AND EATING — SAN AGUSTINILLO

Cabañas Punta Placer On the beach; http://puntaplacer.com. Four luxurious beach-side cabins containing eight circular rooms: gorgeous all-white spaces with drape beds, bathrooms and tranquil terraces, plus fridge and wi-fi. The owners run a variety of boat trips and inland tours. M$$$

★ **Posada La Termita** On the seafront; http://posadalatermita.com. Four rooms, all en suite with fan and mosquito nets; the bonus here is the restaurant, with specialities from Argentina and Italy, including mouthwatering pizza. M$$$

Un Sueño On the beach; 958 113 8749, https://facebook.com/unsuenocabanasdelpacifico. Twelve stylish, breezy cabañas with private bath at the east end of the beach. Their restaurant, *Un Secreto*, is one of the best in town, with a Mexican-Mediterranean menu. M$$$

Mazunte

Though it has grown in recent years, the tiny village of **MAZUNTE** remains a languid, laid-back place with a dazzling beach. It's more peaceful than Zipolite, and lacking the party vibe, though still very much with an alternative feel. The surf is less powerful here, and at the western end of the beach, beyond the rocky outcrop, there's a smaller bay where the waves are even gentler and it's safer to swim. The village's name is derived from the Náhuatl word "maxonteita", which means "please come and spawn", a reference to the **Golfina turtles** that come here to breed. Mazunte was the site of a turtle industry and abattoir that, at its most gruesome, supposedly slaughtered three thousand of the creatures a day. In 1990, the Mexican government bowed to international pressure and effectively banned the industry overnight, removing in one fell swoop the livelihood of the villagers, who then turned to slash-and-burn agriculture. Since then, Mazunte has been declared a reserve, and more sustainable, long-term ecotourism programmes have been encouraged.

Centro Mexicano de la Tortuga

Main road at the east end of the village • Charge • Guided tours in Spanish every 15min • http://centromexicanodelatortuga.org

The government-funded **Centro Mexicano de la Tortuga** is one of the programmes set up to create a new economy for Mazunte. It features an aquarium with some particularly large turtles and a turtle research centre; well worth the visit, especially as proceeds go towards the conservation of this majestic species.

Cosméticos Naturales

Main road through the village • http://cosmeticosmazunte.com

Cosméticos Naturales, a cooperative of local families set up with help from companies such as The Body Shop, is another venture aiming to create a new sustainable economy. It produces and sells prettily packaged beauty products made from local ingredients and organic produce.

Punta Cometa

Don't leave Mazunte without following the trail next to the *Balamjuyuc* (see page 611), which runs past the remains of some unmarked **ruins** to **Punta Cometa**, a thirty-minute walk. This entrancing park on top of the rocky headland next to Mazunte beach is the southernmost point in Oaxaca, and has mesmerizing views at sunset. The "jacuzzi", a rocky pool that fills with foamy surf as the waves rush in, can be accessed by scrambling down the rocks at the south end of the headland – it makes a good photo but it's not safe to go in.

Playa Ventanilla

Administered by the village cooperative http://laventanilla.com.mx • Charge • **Boat rides** extra

The lagoon at **Playa Ventanilla**, some 2km west of Mazunte, is home to around four hundred crocodiles, as well as a rich profusion of birdlife. You can test your heart rate by going out on the water in a shallow boat to navigate among the scaly inhabitants.

ARRIVAL AND DEPARTURE — MAZUNTE

By colectivo/pasajera *Colectivos* and *pasajeras* pass frequently along the main road, heading in one direction to San Agustinillo and Zipolite, in the other to Pochutla. If you're coming from Puerto Escondido you can save time and money by getting dropped off at San Antonio, a cluster of just a few houses and a restaurant, where you can flag down a *playera* or take a private taxi for the final 5km to Mazunte.

ACCOMMODATION

The palapas on the beach have **cabañas** and hammock space, along with **restaurants** serving basic breakfasts, seafood and pasta. If you are equipped and feel so inclined, you can also pitch your tent right on the beach (free).

★ **Alta Mira** Up the hill above the west end of town; http://altamiramazunte.com. Smart bungalows with tiled bathrooms and jaw-dropping views from the terrace restaurant. The solar power is intermittent, but that adds to the alluring atmosphere in the evening, when candles provide the only illumination. M$$

Cabañas Balamjuyuc Up the hill at the west end of the beach; https://www.balamjuyucmazunte.com. Friendly place with impressive views of the ocean and five comfy, brightly coloured, shared-bath cabañas of varying sizes. Also has a restaurant, massage, boat trips, hammock space and fully equipped tents to rent. Cash only. Hammock M$,

10

tent M$, cabaña M$$

★**Casa Pan de Miel** On the hill overlooking town; https://casapandemiel.mx. Five luxurious modern a/c suites overlooking the beach (adults only), with satellite TV, bathroom, kitchenette and wi-fi. Small pool and stellar views included. M$$$$

El Copal C de Panteón s/n, above Playa Mermejita, near Punta Cometa; http://elcopal.com.mx. Gorgeous cluster of four palapas surrounded by palms and terraces, blending modern amenities (free wi-fi) with an ecofriendly ethos (candles at night, cold water, dry toilets and recycling). Closed Oct. M$$$

Posada Arigalan Between San Agustinillo and Mazunte; http://arigalan.com. One of the best places in the area, with stunning views from its modern but charming rooms; all have private baths (most with hot water) and fan; three "suites" have a/c, king-size beds and plunge pools; there are also cabañas. Cabaña M$$$, room M$$$$

Posada del Arquitecto At the western end of the sandy stretch, past the rocks at the second small bay; http://posadadelarquitecto.com. Eco-conscious cabañas with private bath close to the area's best swimming, with great views, café-bar, wi-fi and hammocks. Hammock M$, cabaña M$$

Posada Ziga East end of the beach, near the turtle centre; 958 583 9295, http://posadaziga.com. Congenial option with a range of rooms with private bathroom and wi-fi, and services ranging from fan and mosquito net to a/c and Sky TV. There are glorious sea views from the patio restaurant, which serves decent Mexican and international food. M$$

EATING

La Dolce Vita On the main road; 958 584 3464. An excellent Italian-run restaurant (they also have rooms), *La Dolce Vita* offers delicious wood-oven pizza, pastas with seafood and occasional movies in the evenings. Probably the priciest place in town, but also the best. M$$$$

La Empanada Main road at western end of town; 554 345 3556. Popular travellers' hangout with an international menu that ranges from sushi and stir-fry to pizza and salads – also hearty sandwiches on home-made bread and blended juices (try the delicious cucumber and lemon). M$$

Tania Main road at western end of town; 958 115 9886. The gregarious *Tania* offers good-value meals along with tourist information; the menu includes plenty of vegetarian choices alongside the usual *carnes* and *mariscos*. M$$$

Huatulco

At **HUATULCO**, some 35km from Puerto Ángel, the government began developing the latest of Mexico's purpose-built resorts in the 1980s, on a series of then-deserted bays and beaches. The intention was to construct an environmentally conscious international destination, but growth has been slower than expected, and international visitors in the minority. A safe, sanitized, manicured resort with a beautiful setting, Huatulco is certainly not at first sight the place for budget or independent travellers keen to experience the real Mexico. Nonetheless, Mexico has a way of subverting the best-laid plans, and the town of La Crucecita has its earthy side, with plenty of reasonably priced accommodation, food and drink, while the further-flung beaches, a couple protected within a national park and entirely undeveloped, are magnificent. If lying on the sand, snorkelling and tripping off to coffee plantations and attractive coves are your priorities, you could do much worse.

La Crucecita

LA CRUCECITA is the main service centre for the resort area. Though designed to house the ten thousand locals needed to support and staff the bayside hotels, it has become a tourist centre in its own right. You won't find much to see beyond the **Parque Central** and the modern **Parroquia de Nuestra Señora de Guadalupe** (which houses a 20m mural of the Virgin of Guadalupe, said to be the world's largest), but in its thirty years of existence, Crucecita has matured well to become a friendly, functional place. You'll find the best of the budget accommodation here, along with plenty of cheap places to eat, lively bars and tacky tourist shops.

Santa Cruz Huatulco and the beaches

Just 2km from La Crucecita, **SANTA CRUZ HUATULCO** was conceived as the token "Mexican village", something it patently fails to be. In fact, it feels more like the

Mexican section at Epcot Centre, dressed up with a marina, handicraft stalls, a few relatively inexpensive seafood restaurants and a handful of condos. Santa Cruz's **harbour**, though, is the local transport hub and its huge pier the docking point for visiting cruise ships. From here, fishing and diving trips can be organized, or you can catch one of the *lanchas* that ply the coast to the beaches and more remote bays. **Playa Santa Cruz** itself is small and overcrowded, though it does have some excellent seafood restaurants on the sand.

Playa La Entrega

Just around the bay from Santa Cruz (2.5km by road), **Playa La Entrega** is a lovely white-sand beach with trees for shade. Easy access means it's always pretty busy, predominantly with Mexican families who congregate at the numerous palapas serving fresh seafood.

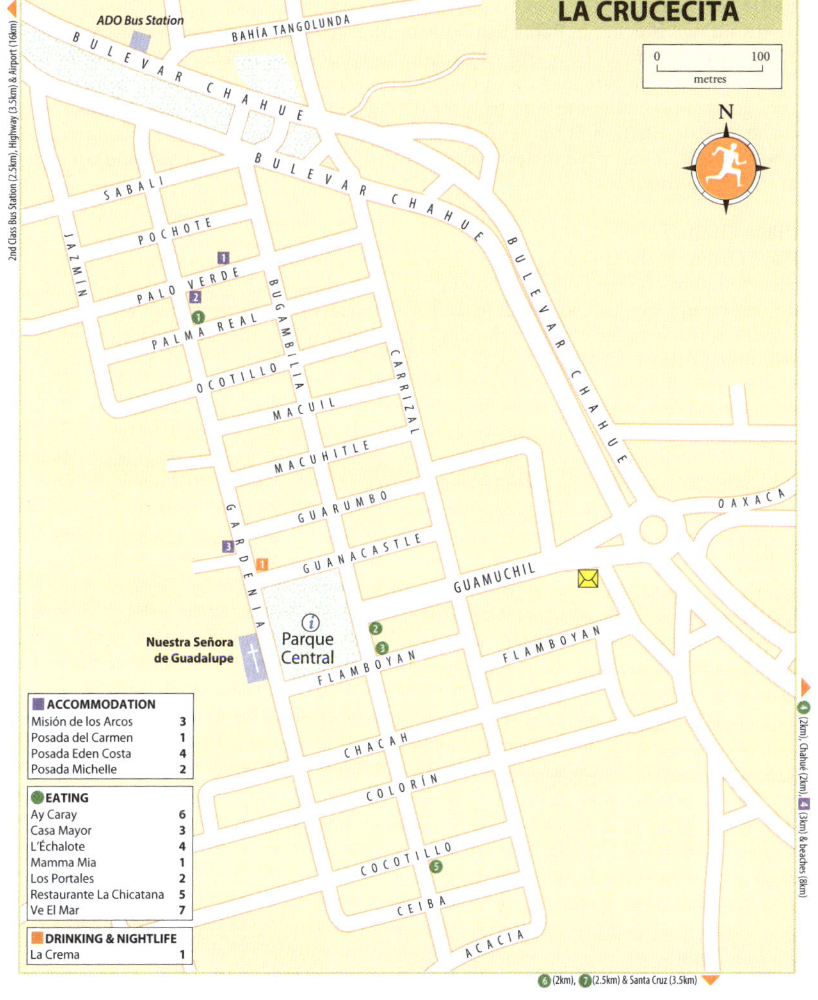

10

Playa Maguey

A steep flight of sixty-odd steps leads down from the road to **Playa Maguey**, in the next bay west from La Entrega. Its tranquil, green-blue waters curve around jungly headlands in a sheltered bay that at quiet times feels very isolated indeed. Quiet times are rare, though, as this is another beach that can be reached by road and hence gets busy. Snorkel gear and kayaks can be rented from the restaurants and shops behind the beach, and they also offer fun tours in tiny, glass-bottomed rowing boats (M$140, including use of snorkel gear).

Playa Cacaluta

West of Bahía Maguey, the pristine sand dunes of **Playa Cacaluta** (and its neighbour Chachacual) are protected in a national park, and accessible only by boat. Cacaluta is where much of the movie *Y Tu Mamá También* was filmed, and it really is almost as magical as it appears there; at least if not too many boats are visiting.

Bahía San Agustín

There are two beaches in **Bahía San Agustín**, the westernmost extremity of Huatulco. San Agustín itself can be reached by road, though it's over 30km from Crucecita, the second half on dirt track. It's popular with Mexican holidaymakers, and has very good snorkelling, offshore reefs for diving and plenty of amenities. **La India** is the final destination of many of the boat trips from town; glorious and entirely undeveloped, it can nevertheless seem crowded when too many *lanchas* end up here at the same time.

Playa Chahué

Playa Chahué is the closest beach to Crucecita, directly south of the town. There are plenty of hotels on the boulevard behind, a couple of beach clubs (with pools) right on the water, a marina and very fine sand. Despite all this it's little visited, probably because waves breaking right on the shore, combined with a powerful undertow, make swimming tricky.

HUATULCO BAYS AND BEACHES

Bahía Tangolunda

East from Chahué and Crucecita, **Bahía Tangolunda** is by far the most developed resort area, with the vast majority of Huatulco's luxury hotels along with chichi homes and an eighteen-hole golf course. The beach is fine but almost impossible to access unless you are a guest at one of the hotels, and in the restaurants you will pay upscale New York or London prices.

Bahía Conejos

The next bay east from Tangolunda, Conejos, marks the eastern edge of Huatulco. Much of the area inland has been taken over by residential development, with road access barred by security guards. However, on the far side, 500m beyond *Secrets* resort, you'll find a mosquito-ridden path through the forest that leads to **Playa Conejos** itself, a stunning crescent of sand sheltered by a thumb of land. At one end is the resort; the rest is often virtually empty, with a seasonal shack-restaurant and a few fishing boats drawn up.

ARRIVAL AND DEPARTURE — HUATULCO

BY PLANE

From Huatulco's airport, some 16km west of La Crucecita, *colectivos* offer a fixed rate of to any of the main resort centres within Huatulco (buy a ticket at the booth in the terminal); private airport taxis charge set fees to La Crucecita, Puerto Ángel and Puerto Escondido, though you'll pay less than half if you walk 500m out of the terminal towards the highway and the waiting cars of Sitio Agua JE El Zapote (958 589 3337, http://taxihuatulco.com). As for flights, there are numerous charters serving Canada and regional Mexican airports, but scheduled services only to Mexico City (at least three daily) with Aeroméxico (http://aeromexico.com), Magni Charters (http://magnicharters.com) and VivaAerobus (http://vivaaerobus.com), and to Houston, Texas (one a week), with United (http://united.com). Aerotucan (https://aerotaxisdemexico.com) offers daily flights to Oaxaca.

BY BUS

There are two bus terminals on the northern edge of La Crucecita: OCC, ADO, AU and Sur services arrive at the busy terminal on Blv Chahué at Rizcalillo; most second-class buses, including Estrella Blanca, Turistar and Transportes Rapidos de Pochutla (vans to Pochutla every 15min), have a station further out, off Blv Chahué on Av Carpinteros. For Oaxaca, it's generally quicker to go to Pochutla and catch a minibus on the direct mountain route; most buses take a long detour via the isthmus. For Mexico City, services via Acapulco, from the second-class station, are generally much quicker. From the OCC you can walk to the centre; from the second-class terminal, cross Blv Chahué and go nine blocks down Gardenia to the plaza. If you're heading straight for the beaches, take a taxi; rates are fixed and should be displayed for trips to Santa Cruz, Chahué and Tangolunda.

Destinations Acapulco (4 daily 2nd class; 10hr); Juchitán (8 daily 1st class, 6 daily 2nd class; 4hr); Mexico City (4 daily 1st class, 3 daily 2nd class; 16hr); Oaxaca (4 daily 1st class; 9hr; 2 daily 2nd class; 7hr); Pochutla (hourly 1st class, every 15min 2nd class; 1hr); Puerto Escondido (hourly 1st and 2nd class; 2hr 30min); San Cristóbal (2 night buses daily, 1st class; 11hr); Tehuantepec (8 daily 1st class, 6 daily 2nd class; 3hr 30min).

GETTING AROUND

By boat From the harbour at Santa Cruz you can charter a *lancha* to any of the beaches; the same boats offer sport fishing, charged by the hour. Also from here are tours of the seven bays with stops for swimming and snorkelling; expect to pay more for the faster catamaran.

By taxi Taxis around town operate on a fixed-rate system, with the fares displayed at all the major taxi ranks.

INFORMATION AND ACTIVITIES

Tourist information There's a helpful tourist information kiosk (Mon–Fri 9am–2pm & 4–7pm, Sat 9am–1pm) in the Parque Central in La Crucecita.

Adventure tours Booths on the Parque Central in La Crucecita and agents in most hotels offer a huge variety of adventures, from trips to the Cascada de Copalitilla to half-day quad-bike or horseriding tours, rafting or zipwires, along with gentler activities including massage and *temazcal*. Explora Mexico (958 587 2058) offers more challenging rafting day trips, as well as early-morning bird watching.

Scuba diving Hurricane Divers (based at Xpert & Professional Travel at Plaza Coyula 11, behind Banamex on Santa Cruz beach 958 587 1107, http://hurricanedivers.com) are a professional outfit offering dive trips throughout the area, along with PADI and DAN certification.

ACCOMMODATION

Budget accommodation is mostly in **La Crucecita**; the fancier resorts and hotels, at **Tangolunda** and **Playa Conejos**, are almost invariably better value if booked as part of a holiday package. Outside the high season (Dec, Semana Santa, July & Aug) prices can drop by up to fifty percent.

LA CRUCECITA AND PLAYA CHAHUÉ, SEE MAP PAGE 613

Misión de los Arcos Gardenia 902; http://misiondelosarcos.website. Friendly, Mexican/American-run colonial-style hotel just off the plaza, with bright, airy rooms with cable TV and a/c. There is a decent restaurant, free internet and discounted access to a beach club at Chahué. M$$

Posada del Carmen Palo Verde 307; 958 587 0593. Decent budget choice close to the heart of things, with good-sized rooms equipped with cable TV, fan and wi-fi. Not as fancy as it appears from outside. M$

Posada Eden Costa Zapoteco 27, at Chahué, just off Blv Juárez; http://edencosta.com. Lovely mid-range option just one block from Playa Chahué, with ten rooms and four large suites, all with terraces leading out to the pool; wi-fi and continental breakfast included. Excellent on-site restaurant (see below). M$$

Posada Michelle Gardenia 1301, at Palo Verde; 958 587 0535. Friendly hotel with a range of very cheap singles and doubles, all with TV and wi-fi, some with a/c; some are tiny, so check rooms first. A good place to arrange tours. M$$$

TANGOLUNDA AND PLAYA CONEJOS

Agua Azul La Villa Residencial Conejos; http://bbaguaazul.com. For a slice of tranquillity close to the beach, check out this Canadian-run B&B overlooking the bay. The ambience is welcoming and sociable, the hosts knowledgeable, and excellent breakfasts are served in a communal palapa dining room/lounge area. Adults only. M$$$$

★ **Dreams Huatulco Resort & Spa** Juárez 4; www.hyattinclusivecollection.com. Best value of all the major resorts, with excellent deals online, great service and a huge roster of amenities. Modern, stylish rooms overlook the bay and come with satellite TVs and a balcony. M$$$$

Quinta Real Juárez 2; 958 581 0428, http://caminoreal.com. Unabashed luxury in an exotic whitewashed property embellished with Moorish domes and curves, just off the beach. With lavish suites, a private beach club, posh restaurants and a colony of torpid iguanas in the nearby palms, you are unlikely to venture much further. M$$$$

★ **Villas Fa-Sol Huatulco** Residencial Conejos; www.villasfasol.com. An intelligent choice for groups, a gorgeous apartment complex close to the beach. All rooms have fabulous views of the sunset and coast. M$$$

EATING

SEE MAP PAGE 613

Ay Caray Playa Maguey; 958 121 5584. Everyone loves this laid-back place right on the sand, overseen by the indomitable Alfredo. Especially good for fresh fish and fish tacos – fishermen can also take their catch to be cooked on site – it's also a great spot to while away the afternoon over a beer. M$$

Casa Mayor Bugambilia 601, cnr Flamboyan on the plaza, La Crucecita; http://cafecasamayor.com. Café-bar on a first-floor terrace overlooking the plaza; a chilled-out spot with live music many evenings, serving coffees, baguettes, *antojitos*, hamburgers, omelettes and the like by day, cocktails at night. Fast wi-fi too. M$$$

★ **L'Échalote** Posada Eden Costa, Zapoteco 27 at Chahué, just off Blv Juárez; https://edencosta.com. Exceptional restaurant featuring an eclectic menu that blends Asian, Mexican and European traditions, everything from Vietnamese dishes to Spanish classics and fabulous fondue (the owners hail from Switzerland and Laos). M$$$$

★ **Mamma Mia** Gardenia, cnr Palma Real, La Crucecita; 958 589 0220. Excellent pizzeria that's almost always packed with locals. In addition to good pizzas, cooked in a wood-fired oven, they have pasta, authentic Italian specials like baked rabbit with polenta and mushrooms, and a lunch-time *comida*. M$$$

Los Portales Bugambilia 603, on the plaza, La Crucecita; http://losportaleshuatulco.com. Arguably the best of a number of simple Mexican restaurants on the east side of the plaza, open from breakfast (try the loade plates full of crispy hash browns with eggs and bacon) through to the early hours, with inexpensive *antojitos*, addictive nachos and cold beer plus the fancier likes of fajitas or rib-eye steak. M$$$

Restaurante La Chicatana Bugambilia 203, La Crucecita; https://facebook.com/RestauranteLaChicatana. This spot is more about the ambience, the view and the a/c than the food, but everything on the menu is perfectly palatable, and the cocktails are well above par. It's reasonably priced for this part of town too. M$$$

Ve El Mar Playa Santa Cruz, close to the pier; 958 587 0364. It's hard to find sand on Playa Santa Cruz not taken over by restaurant tables, so best to give in, have a drink, and enjoy the crowds, the music and the vendors. An extra plus of this waterside restaurant is that the fish and seafood are fresh, the cocktails zippy. There's everything here from plain fish or prawn dishes to specialities like seafood kebabs, pineapple scooped out and filled with dorado, or sweet Pacific lobster for. There's even wi-fi. M$$$$

DRINKING AND NIGHTLIFE SEE MAP PAGE 613

La Crema Gardenia 311, La Crucecita; 958 587 0702. Quirky, crowded bar overlooking the plaza with a diverse clientele, lively rock music and tasty pizza (try the Crema Special), baked potatoes and nachos.

DIRECTORY

Banks and exchange There are plenty of banks around the centre, including HSBC at the junction of Blv Chahué and Bugambilias, and Banamex at Carrizal, cnr Guamucil opposite the Plaza El Madero mall; there are also branches of Banamex and Bancomer in Santa Cruz, on the main road just past the beach, and an ATM in the OCC bus station.

Post office Blv Chahué 100, on the eastern edge of La Crucecita.

The Isthmus of Tehuantepec

The **Isthmus of Tehuantepec**, where the Pacific and the Atlantic are just 210km apart and the land never rises to more than 250m above sea level, is the narrowest strip of land in Mexico. It's a hot and steamy region, with a fascinating and unique cultural identity. The people are descendants of various Indigenous groups, principally Zapotec. Historically, the Zapotec *indígenas*, especially those in the south, have been a **matriarchal** society. Though you'll still find women dominating trade in the markets (they are renowned for their tenacious, even aggressive, sales skills) while the men work in the fields, this is a tradition that is dying faster than most others in macho Mexico. Nevertheless, some elements remain: the women exude pride, many dressed in ornate hand-woven dresses and draped with gold jewellery; it's still the mother who gives away her child at a wedding (and occasionally still the eldest daughter who inherits land); and on feast days the women prove their dominance by climbing to the rooftops and throwing fruit down on the men in the *Tirada de Frutas*.

The best reason to stop in this region is if there's a **fiesta** going on, as they're among the most exciting in the country. Otherwise, you can go straight across – from Oaxaca to **Tuxtla Gutiérrez** or **San Cristóbal** in Chiapas – in a single, very long, day. Most first-class buses bypass the grimy port town of Salina Cruz, dominated by a giant oil refinery; better places to stop are Tehuantepec itself, around 250km from Oaxaca City, or nearby Juchitán.

Tehuantepec

The modest town of **TEHUANTEPEC** visibly preserves many of the isthmus's local traditions, has some of the **best fiestas** in the region and is generally a pleasant place to stop, with several inexpensive hotels. In the evening, the central plaza comes alive, with singing birds and people strolling and eating food from the stalls set up by the townswomen, some of whom still proudly wear the traditional flower-embroidered *huipil* and floor-length velvet skirt of the Zapotec. Perhaps because the town is so concentrated – a walk of ten blocks in any direction will take you out into the countryside – it's extraordinarily noisy; the din of passing buses is redoubled by the flatbed motor tricycles (*motos*) that locals use as taxis. There's a very busy **market**, just off the main plaza, which sells fruit, herbs, bread, flowers and other local produce.

Santo Domingo Cosijopí

Callejón Cosijopí, off Hidalgo • Free

Tehuantepec's one real sight is the Dominican **church** and Ex-Convento of Rey Cosijopí. The church is an unusual double building, with a more modern Neoclassical edifice alongside the traditional conquistador-style church; the two are joined internally. The original church and monastery were founded in 1544 by Cosijopí, the last Zapotec ruler here, who formed an alliance with the Spanish against his Aztec and Mixtec rivals, and converted to Catholicism. The remains of the monastery now house the **Casa de la Cultura**, where temporary exhibitions and cultural events are held;

restored in the 1980s, it has been quietly rotting ever since, though you can still make out remains of murals on the wall. It has a separate entrance; to get there head out of the church and take the first three right turns.

The ruins of Guiengola

15km north of Tehuantepec • Free, though the caretaker may ask for a small fee

The hilltop fortress of **Guiengola** was a Zapotec stronghold, and in 1496 its defenders successfully fought off an Aztec attempt to gain control of the area, which was never fully incorporated into their empire. It continued to be a centre of resistance during the early years of the Conquest and was a focus of Indigenous revolt against Spanish rule throughout the sixteenth and seventeenth centuries.

At the site you'll see remains of pyramids and a ball-court, but the most striking feature is the massive **defensive wall**. By definition, Guiengola's superb location makes it somewhat inaccessible and it's probably best to take a **taxi**, though **buses** to Oaxaca do pass the turn-off to the site, 8km from Tehuantepec on Hwy-190 (look out for the "Ruinas Guiengola" sign). From here it's a hot, 7km walk uphill.

FIESTAS IN OAXACA

New Year's Day (Jan 1). Celebrated everywhere, but particularly good in Oaxaca and Mitla.

Día de San Sebastián (Jan 20). Big in Tehuantepec.

Día de la Candelaria (Feb 2). Colourful Indigenous celebrations in Santa María del Tule.

Carnaval (the week before Lent; variable Feb–March). At its most frenzied in the big cities – especially Oaxaca – but also celebrated in hundreds of villages in the area.

Día de San Isidro (May 15). Peasant celebrations everywhere – famous and picturesque fiestas in Juchitán.

Día de San Juan (June 24). Falls in the midst of festivities (June 22–26) in Tehuantepec.

Fiesta de la Preciosa Sangre de Cristo (first Wed in July). Teotitlán del Valle, near Oaxaca, holds a festival with traditional dances and religious processions.

Guelaguetza (last two Mon in July). In Oaxaca, a mixture of traditional dancing and rites on the Cerro del Fortín. Highly popular; tickets for the good seats are sold at the tourist office.

Fiestas (Aug 13–16). Spectacular festivities in Juchitán (Vela de Agosto) and Tehuantepec (Fiesta del Barrio de Santa María Relatoca).

Fiesta de San Bartolomé (Aug 24). In San Bartolo Coyotepec, near Oaxaca.

Blessing of the Animals (Aug 31). In Oaxaca locals bring their beasts to the church of La Merced to be blessed.

Fiesta del Señor de la Natividad (Sept 8). In Teotitlán del Valle.

Independence Day (Sept 16). Celebrated everywhere.

Feria del Árbol (second Mon in Oct). Based around the famous tree in Santa María del Tule.

Día de los Muertos (Day of the Dead; Nov 2). Observed everywhere, with particularly strong traditions in Xoxocotlán and in Atzompa.

Día de la Inmaculada Concepción (Dec 8). Observed widely. There are traditional dances in Juquilla, not far from Puerto Escondido, and Zacatepec, on the road inland from Pinotepa Nacional.

Fiesta de la Virgen de la Soledad (Dec 18). Celebrations in Oaxaca in honour of the patroness of the state – expect fireworks, processions and music.

Fiesta de los Rabanos (Radish Festival; Dec 23). There's an exhibition of statues and scenes sculpted from radishes in Oaxaca.

Christmas Eve (Dec 24). In Oaxaca there's music, fireworks and processions before midnight Mass. *Buñuelos* – crisp pancakes that you eat before smashing the plate on which they are served – are dished up at street stalls.

Juchitán

JUCHITÁN, 28km east of Tehuantepec, is a dusty commercial centre clogged with traffic and somewhat lacking in tourist infrastructure. Despite this, the city has a rich cultural life, offering glimpses into the matriarchal society the region is known for, and frequent **fiestas**, also known as **velas**, where women dress in colourful *traje* and men in formal wear for all-night marathons of music and dancing. These take place throughout the year, and in May seem to be almost daily. The residents are also known for strong political views, socialist leanings and a relatively tolerant attitude towards homosexuality; it's one of the few places in Mexico where gay men live openly, sometimes even attending *velas* in drag.

Casa de la Cultura

Belisario Domínguez cnr Colón • Free • 971 711 4598

The **Casa de la Cultura**, beside the church of San Vicente Ferrer (which has a fine gilded altarpiece), was funded by Juchitán-born artist Francisco Toledo. Set around a courtyard whose low, wooden *portales* have a northern feel to them, it has an archeological display with pre-Hispanic stone carvings and pottery, some fine historical paintings and a roster of interesting events and temporary exhibitions.

ARRIVAL AND INFORMATION — ISTHMUS OF TEHUANTEPEC

By bus A constant stream of buses connects Tehuantepec and Juchitán. Though services in both places are broadly the same, few buses originate in Tehuantepec; if you can't find the connection you need there, it may be easier to head for the busier hub of Juchitán. In Tehuantepec buses stop at the OCC terminal at the northern edge of town on Hwy-185, a short moto or taxi ride from the centre (or less than 1km walk, but that's taxing in the steamy climate). The main bus station in Juchitán is on 16 de Septiembre (which passes right through the heart of town) where it meets the highway; shared taxis to the centre wait outside and charge per person.

Destinations Acapulco (3 daily; 12hr); Coatzacoalcos (every 30min; 3hr); Mexico City (8 daily; 11hr); Oaxaca (hourly; 4hr 30min); Puerto Escondido (5 daily; 4hr); Tuxtla Gutiérrez (4 daily; 5hr); Veracruz (2 daily; 7hr 30min); Villahermosa (6 daily; 7hr).

ACCOMMODATION

TEHUANTEPEC

Hostel Emilia Ocampo 8, one block south of the plaza; 971 715 0008. *Emilia* is much the most pleasant place to stay, with simple rooms with cable TV and wi-fi and a very helpful owner keen to promote local tourism through, for example, gastronomic tours of the isthmus. Fan M$, a/c M$$

JUCHITÁN

Hotel Central Efraín R. Gómez 30; http://hotelcentral.com.mx. A relatively new addition to the accommodation options in Juchitán, *Hotel Central* has clean and simple rooms, for a fair price, with a/c as standard - not fans. The staff are also great at arranging trips and tours to all the local attractions. M$$$

EATING AND DRINKING

Good **places to eat** are thin on the ground, especially in Tehuantepec. As ever, the best cheap eats are at market stalls. In Tehuantepec try the Mercado de Jesús on the west side of the plaza, or the steaming taco carts lining the east side of the square; and be sure to try some of the **corn bread** that local women hawk to everyone arriving on the bus. In Juchitán there are stalls set up under the *portales* of the Palacio Municipal, on the plaza.

TEHUANTEPEC

Cafetería Yizu Juárez 10, in courtyard of Hotel Donají; 971 715 0064. Decent coffee, *licuados* and "*smudys*" drinks, plus breakfast and a good menu of snacks and light meals; late-night (by local standards) hangout for fashionable young *Tehuantepecos*. M$$

JUCHITÁN

Internacional 16 de Septiembre 25; 971 711 2071. Coffee-shop-style place with blissfully effective a/c, good breakfasts and a substantial *menu del día*; also baguettes, sandwiches and *antojitos*. M$$$

OXXO Juárez 12; 818 320 2020. An unexpectedly elegant restaurant with leather chairs and dark-wood furnishings occupying a naturally cool internal courtyard. The food, from breakfast to dinner, is good, with an emphasis on fish and seafood (try the *Ensalada Casa Grande*, with prawn and pineapple or the fish dishes). They also have a tiny art cinema out back. M$$$$

Chiapas and Tabasco

SAN CRISTÓBAL DE LAS CASAS

Chiapas and Tabasco

Chiapas and Tabasco are very different states – the former mountainous, the latter covered by steamy lowlands – but are grouped together here because many travellers pass through both of them en route to the Yucatán. Endowed with a stunning variety of cultures, landscapes and wildlife, Chiapas has much to tempt visitors, but the biggest draw is how many Indigenous traditions survive intact, as well as how much pristine wilderness exists. The state of Tabasco, by contrast, is less aesthetically attractive than its neighbour, and its rural areas see almost no tourists. But its capital, Villahermosa, is a transit hub, and archeology buffs know the region as the heartland of the Olmecs, Mexico's earliest developed civilization.

Chiapas was administered by the Spanish as part of Guatemala until 1824, when it seceded to join newly independent Mexico. The state is now second only to Oaxaca in Indigenous population: about 25 percent of its five million plus people are thought to be *indígenas*, of some fourteen ethnic groups, most of Maya origin. Tuxtla Gutiérrez is the capital, but travellers usually head straight for the colonial town of **San Cristóbal de las Casas**, tucked among the mountains in the centre of the state and surrounded by strongholds of **Tzotzil** and **Tzeltal** Maya culture. Ancient customs and religious practices carry on in these villages, yet as picturesque as life here may sometimes seem, villagers often live at the barest subsistence level, with their lands and livelihoods in precarious balance. These troubles helped fuel the 1994 **Zapatista rebellion** (see page 625), and although that conflict has long subsided, many of the core issues concerning land use remain unresolved. Now illegal immigration is the bigger issue, and a heavy **military** presence focuses more on the Guatemalan border and the eastern half of the state.

In Tabasco, **Villahermosa** is the vibrant, modern capital, with a wealth of parks and museums, the best of which is **Parque La Venta**, where the original massive Olmec heads are on display. In the extreme southwest, bordered by Veracruz and Chiapas, a section of Tabasco reaches into the Sierra de Chiapas up to 1000m high. Here, in a region almost never visited by outsiders, you can splash in pristine rivers in **Tapijulapa** and explore the astonishing ruins of **Malpasito**, a city of the mysterious **Zoque** culture.

Chiapas

The state of **CHIAPAS** rises from the Pacific coastal plain to the peaks of two ranges, the Sierra Madre de Chiapas and Los Altos de Chiapas. The **climate**, like the land, varies

THE 2017 CHIAPAS EARTHQUAKE

On **September 7, 2017**, an 8.2-magnitude earthquake struck just off the coast of Chiapas. It was the most powerful quake in Mexico in centuries, producing tsunamis, causing massive tremors across the country, damaging over 41,000 homes and claiming the lives of at least 98 people (including 16 in Chiapas and four in Tabasco). Twelve days later, a second earthquake hit Puebla, which although less powerful, claimed around 370 lives.
Restoration efforts started up soon after the Chiapas quake, but you may well come across evidence of the earthquake on your travels across the two states.

MURAL DEPICTING A WAR SCENE, BONAMPAK

Highlights

❶ **Cañón del Sumidero** Enjoy a boat ride through this spectacular gorge, with jungle-covered cliffs soaring 1000m up. See page 638

❷ **San Cristóbal de las Casas** An enchanting colonial city in Chiapas, surrounded by villages rich in Indigenous culture. See page 639

❸ **Iglesia de San Juan Bautista** Witness extraordinary displays of religious faith in this haunting church in the highlands village of San Juan Chamula. See page 647

❹ **Parque Nacional Lagos de Montebello** An isolated corner of Chiapas where the mountain lakes change colour in the sunlight. See page 653

❺ **Palenque** Visit the evocative ruins of one of the greatest Maya cities, then bathe in the refreshing cascades outside the town. See page 657

❻ **Bonampak** Over one thousand years old, the vivid murals here provide a startling insight into ancient Maya culture. See page 664

❼ **Yaxchilán** Perhaps the most magical of the Chiapas ruins, set deep in the forest, a boat ride away from civilization. See page 668

❽ **Parque La Venta** See the massive, Olmec-carved stone heads salvaged from the site of La Venta and now in a pretty park in Villahermosa. See page 672

HIGHLIGHTS ARE MARKED ON THE MAP ON PAGE 624

enormously. The coastal areas can be hot and muggy, while in highland towns like San Cristóbal de las Casas, nights can call for a jumper, even in August.

Chiapas has the greatest **biological diversity** in North America. Its forests are home to howler monkeys, red macaws and jaguars. Most visitors will likely see these animals only at the **zoo** in **Tuxtla Gutiérrez**, but you can venture into the heart of the huge **Montes Azules Biosphere Reserve**, a section of the largest remaining rainforest in North America. From Ocosingo you can make forays into its heart, **Laguna Miramar**, a truly isolated wilderness destination. There's also **cloud forest** in the south of the state, protected in **El Triunfo Biosphere Reserve.** From the pretty colonial town of Comitán de Domínguez, the isolated Frontier Highway runs along the Guatemala border and past the beautiful lakes and hills of the **Parque Nacional Lagos de Montebello**.

On the east side of the mountains, at the edge of the Yucatán plain, the Classic-period Maya city of **Palenque** is one of Mexico's finest ancient sites. The limestone hills

THE LEGACY OF THE ZAPATISTA REBELLION

On **January 1, 1994**, the day that the North American Free Trade Agreement (**NAFTA**) came into effect, several thousand lightly armed rebels calling themselves **Zapatistas** (after early twentieth-century revolutionary Emiliano Zapata) occupied San Cristóbal de las Casas, the former state capital and Chiapas' major tourist destination. The Zapatistas declared themselves staunchly anti-globalization, as well as opposed to local efforts by paramilitary groups to force Indigenous people off the land. When the Mexican army recovered from its shock, it launched a violent counterattack, but international solidarity with the rebels soon forced the Mexican government to call a halt.

A ceasefire was agreed in 1995, and negotiations have continued over the years, as yet to conclude in a peace treaty. But eventually the issue of Indigenous rights spread beyond the state's borders, with large-scale disturbances in Oaxaca in 2006 making Chiapas seem relatively peaceful.

More than twenty years on, the word "Chiapas" is still synonymous with violent revolution, but while the Zapatistas remain nominally "at war" with the Mexican government, the struggle is now largely ideological. The organization still runs its own municipalities, "caracoles", on land seized from large landowners, and is largely left alone by the government.

Tourists have always visited Chiapas with few problems other than delays due to army (and occasional Zapatista) checkpoints. The government is hostile to foreign Zapatista sympathizers, however, as their presence is considered an illegal influence on Mexican politics – so showing obvious Zapatista support in Chiapas can potentially lead to deportation.

in this area are pierced by exquisite waterfalls. Palenque is the best starting point for a trip down the **Usumacinta valley**, to visit the remote ruins of **Bonampak** and **Yaxchilán**, where you can cross to Guatemala by boat. This remote eastern half of Chiapas is also the home of the **Lacandón Maya**, who retreated into the forest when the Spaniards arrived, and shunned all outside contact until some fifty years ago.

On a safety note: illegal roadblocks and car-jackings are not uncommon in Chiapas, so it is best to travel during the day – particularly if you are driving – and to use toll roads wherever possible.

The Chiapas coast

Running parallel to the coast about 20km inland, Hwy-200 provides a fast route from the Oaxaca border to Tapachula. If you're heading straight for Guatemala, this is the road to take. It traverses the steamy coastal plain of the Soconusco, once a separate province within Guatemala, but forced into union with Mexico by Santa Anna in 1842 and promptly absorbed by Chiapas. From the highway, the 2400m peaks of the Sierra Madre de Chiapas, little-visited mountains penetrated by roads only at their eastern and western extremities, are always in view. If you have your own vehicle you can explore some of the side roads leading from Hwy-200, either up into the mountains, where heavy rains give rise to dozens of rivers and waterfalls, or down to near-deserted beaches. Note, however, that the highway is two lanes each direction, often out of sight of each other; don't pull back onto the road going the wrong way – you must use the signed U-turn points.

This is a fertile agricultural area, mainly given over to coffee and bananas. Tapachula, the "capital" of the Soconusco plain, is cut off from the rest of Chiapas by the mountains, but has frequent connections to the southern border crossings into Guatemala. From Tapachula you can also take a relaxing trip up through coffee plantations to the delightful little town of Unión Juárez, the base for expeditions to Volcán Tacaná, the highest peak in Chiapas.

CHIAPAS ON A PLATE

While the **cuisine** of Chiapas is not as famous as that of neighbouring Oaxaca, you can still eat very well while visiting the state. Dishes to look out for include *pepita con tasajo* (sliced beef marinated in chilli and herbs), tamales flavoured with local herbs like *hoja santa* and *chipilín*, pork in a *pipian* (pumpkin seed) sauce, and (in the coastal regions) dried shrimps in a tomato sauce. The city of San Cristóbal de las Casas is known for its Spanish-style cured hams and sausages, while the area around Ocosingo produces a good range of artisanal cheeses, and Chiapa de Corzo is famous for its suckling pig dishes. In terms of drinks, as well as excellent coffee from the state's highland regions, there are some more unusual beverages to sample, such as *tazcalate* (a blend of toasted corn, chocolate and cinnamon) and *pozol* (a sugary corn and chocolate drink).

Tonalá

The gateway to the main beach resorts of Chiapas, the market town of **TONALÁ** is 39km from the Oaxaca state border and just off Hwy-200. It has all the basic services but not much to see. Tonalá means, quite aptly, "hot place" in Náhuatl, and you're better off pressing on to the coast, where the beachside accommodation can be more appealing.

Everything you need in Tonalá is either on the *parque central* (main plaza) – where you can start your day with a bowl of chilled *pozole* – or within a couple of blocks of it (the market is to the south, at Matamoros). The main feature of the park is the **Estela de Tlaloc**, a large, standing stone carved by the Olmecs, depicting the rain god Tlaloc and showing the influence of Teotihuacán. The 1794 **Templo de San Francisco de Asís**, a couple of blocks northeast of the plaza, merits a quick peek for its pretty pink facade, ceiling murals and impressive gold *retablo*.

ARRIVAL AND DEPARTURE — TONALÁ

By bus All the bus companies terminate along Hidalgo, the town's main street: the main first-class companies (ADO/OCC), plus second-class Rápidos del Sur, pull in about 500m west of the plaza; all other second-class services, to the east. Taxis run to the centre from here.

Destinations ADO/OCC have first-class departures to Oaxaca (1 daily at 11.30pm; 9hr 30min); Mexico City (6 daily; 13-17hr); Tapachula (roughly hourly; 3–4hr); and Tuxtla Gutiérrez (roughly hourly; 2hr–2hr 30min). Rápidos del Sur runs to Tapachula via all the towns on the coast highway (every 40min or so; 4hr–4hr 30min).

ACCOMMODATION AND EATING

Galilea East side of the plaza; 966 663 0239. *Galilea* is well located in an attractive old building, and has basic rooms with ancient a/c units and TVs, as well as private parking. It also has a restaurant, the *Colonial*, overlooking the plaza and serving well-prepared Mexican standards. M$

Hotel Tonala Hidalgo 172; 966 663 0480. Situated just east of the bus station, the Hotel Tonala is a most convenient spot to stay in Tonalá, especially if you have to catch an early bus. It offers good value for money, with large, clean, comfortable en-suite rooms with TVs and a/c. Food M$$, accommodation M$$

El Tizón Hidalgo 61; 966 102 5641. On the west side of the plaza, overlooking all the action, where the typical Mexican dishes nod to the bounty of the Pacific (only a 20min drive away): try the rich seafood soup. M$$

Puerto Arista and around

Not far from the border with Oaxaca, the first point of interest is **PUERTO ARISTA**, the only place on the Chiapas coast that even remotely resembles a resort town. Although this slightly run-down village may not be everyone's idea of a perfect beach hangout, Puerto Arista, with its kilometres of grey sand, wheeling frigate birds and crashing waves, does offer a chance to escape the unrelenting heat of the inland towns. Unless you arrive in the summer, at Christmas or during Semana Santa, it has a bit of a ghost-town feel, but it's a handy place to stop if you've been doing some hard travelling. The road from Tonalá dead-ends at Puerto Arista's only street, Avenida Matamoros, which locals call "el bulevar"; a landmark lighthouse, and most of the hotels, are just north. Walk a couple of kilometres northwest or southeast and you'll be on a deserted shoreline. While the waves are refreshing, be aware of the potentially dangerous **riptides** that sweep along the coast – never get out of your depth.

Boca del Cielo

You can easily get transport from Puerto Arista (or direct from Tonalá) to **Boca del Cielo**, a cluster of houses and fishing boats 15km down the coast on the landward side of Laguna La Joya, where you can board a *lancha* and speed across to a beautiful beach. It's best at high tide, when the water comes right up to the restaurants, and at sunset. That said, without your own transport you'll need to head back well before 7pm, as it's almost impossible to find a taxi after dark. Some of the palapa restaurants will let you sling a hammock for a small fee, though be prepared for mosquitoes. The beaches along this stretch of coast are used by **turtles** for nesting: in October, the turtles lay their eggs in the sand; the next year, in June and July, the hatchlings struggle out to the sea.

ARRIVAL AND DEPARTURE — PUERTO ARISTA AND AROUND

By colectivo and combi In Tonalá, orange shared taxis (on Matamoros, between 5 de Mayo and 20 de Marzo) leave when full for Puerto Arista (22km south; 30min) and Boca del Cielo (37km; around 45min). *Combis* depart one block away on Juárez between 5 de Mayo and 20 de Marzo.

By taxi Green-striped city taxis are available here for the Puerto Arista–Tonalá journey.

ACCOMMODATION AND EATING

There are many **hotels** in Puerto Arista but generally few customers: you could try to bargain with a couple of the places listed here – and you could always **camp** on the beach for free (though this, of course, is not without risk). For food, a selection of beachfront *palapa* **restaurants** near the lighthouse serve seafood, but only five or six are ever open at once; we recommend one below, but if it's closed, you can expect similar prices and menus from the others. At night, stalls sell inexpensive tacos along the main street, and there are a couple of basic restaurants for *antojitos* on the main road near the lighthouse.

José's Camping and Cabañas 1km south of Puerto Arista's main intersection and inland one block; 961 330 2458. Canadian-born José's place is the friendliest in Puerto Arista and great for budget travellers, with sturdy thatched bungalows, campsites with electricity and a flower-filled patio with hammocks and a pool. Some cabins have (clean) shared bathrooms. M$

Lizeth 300m north of Puerto Arista's main intersection, across from the lighthouse; 994 600 9038. The most convenient place to stay in town, with a bright yellow exterior, cramped but clean rooms and a pool. Even though the balconies don't face the beach, you can hear and smell the surf. Rooms have either fans or a/c. M$

Madre Sal 30km south of Puerto Arista; http://elmadresal.com. Just off a quiet stretch of beach, by a mangrove-fringed lagoon, this ecotourism venture is a great place to get away from it all. Staff offer wildlife-watching boat trips (sea turtles hatch on the sand here), accommodation is in rustic cabins sleeping up to four people each, and there's a seafood restaurant. Note: there's only limited electricity and no wi-fi. M$$

Otavento 4A Poniente 1, on the beach; 994 600 9137. One of Puerto Arista's many palapa-roofed beachfront places, with tables so close to the surf you're better going barefoot. The seafood *cockteles* are huge. M$$

Playa Palo Blanco

20km south of the transit town of Pijijiapan • A *combi* from terminal in Pijijiapan (where second-class buses from Tuxtla Gutiérrez, Tapachula and Tonalá all stop), two blocks south and one east from the bus station

Around Pijijiapan, 75km from Tonalá, a series of dirt roads leads to unspoiled beaches and lagoons with opportunities for fishing, swimming or merely relaxing in the sun. The best of these is **Playa Palo Blanco**. Similar to Boca del Cielo, it's reached by launch across a narrow lagoon. Like most beaches, on Sundays, it's busy with families, who come for lunches under the large palapas between the towering palms, but during the rest of the week the incredibly broad stretch of brown sand can be deserted.

Tapachula

Some 150km northeast of Tonalá by road, in the shadow of the 4060m Volcán Tacaná, lies the busy commercial city of **TAPACHULA**. Just 16km from Guatemala, it's a border city as well as the capital of the Soconusco region, with a lively cultural mix comprising immigrants from Central America as well as small German and Chinese communities. The Germans were invited to settle here by the Mexican government in the 1880s to boost the economy, establishing the state's coffee industry and leaving a legacy of fine haciendas nearby. The Chinese initially came to work on the railway, in part because the rebellious locals refused to do so; the most visible sign of their community today is the high proportion of Chinese restaurants in the city centre.

While the surrounding countryside offers some worthwhile diversions, there's not much to see in the city itself. As always, the centre of activity is the **plaza (Parque Hidalgo)**, a pleasant place to while away an evening listening to the marimba bands. Look out for vendors selling *jocotes*, so-called hog plums – they look like giant olives and are pickled in rum.

Museo Arqueológico del Soconusco

8a Av Nte 24, between 1a and 3a Pte • Charge • 962 626 4173

The main attraction in Tapachula is the **Museo Arqueológico del Soconusco**, in the former Palacio Municipal, a gold-trimmed colonial gem on the west side of the plaza. It has displays of prehistoric and Olmec finds and a decent collection of artefacts from Izapa and other local sites (explanations in Spanish only).

ARRIVAL AND DEPARTURE — TAPACHULA

BY PLANE

Tapachula's airport (962 626 4189), 18km south of the city, is served by regular flights to Mexico City (4 daily; 2hr), operated by Aeroméxico (http://aeromexico.com) and

TAPACHULA ORIENTATION

The town's **layout** is a little confusing: although the streets are organized in the regular numbered grid common in Chiapas, the main plaza, Parque Hidalgo, is actually three blocks west and one block north of where Calle Central meets Avenida Central.

Volaris (http://volaris.com). *Colectivos* run to town; buy a ticket at the Transportes Terrestre booth just outside the arrivals hall. If you are in a group, it's cheaper to take a taxi.

BY BUS

All the main bus stations are north of the city centre. The terminals of the various second-class companies are within walking distance of the plaza, while the first-class terminal is further out. All buses to Comitán and San Cristóbal are *via altos* and head over the mountains. All first-class and most second-class buses to Tuxtla are *via costa*, meaning they travel up the coast through Tonalá.

First-class buses OCC/ADO services (and some of the better second-class services) leave from the terminal at 17a C Ote between 1a Av and 3a Av Nte. Taxis run to the centre; walking takes 20min or so.

Destinations Comitán (5 daily; 6hr 45min–7hr 15min); Mexico City (8 daily; 16hr 30min–21hr); Oaxaca (1 daily at 7.15pm; 13hr 15min); San Cristóbal (7 daily; 7hr 40min–9hr 20min); Tonalá (roughly hourly; 3–4hr); Tuxtla Gutiérrez (roughly hourly; 5hr 15min–6hr); Villahermosa (3 daily at 12.30pm, 5pm & 6.30pm; 12hr).

Second-class buses The main second-class bus operators are TRF, at the corner of 16a Av Nte and 3a C Pte, and AEXA, opposite.

BY COMBI AND TAXI

The main *combi* terminals lie along 5a C Pte beyond the market, between 12a Av and 14a Av Nte. Unión y Progreso runs frequent services to Cacahoatán (every 20min or so; 30min) for Unión Juárez, as well as to the Talismán Bridge (every 5min; 30min) for Izapa and the Guatemalan border. Next door and opposite, respectively, Omnibus de Tapachula and Costeños de Chiapas run frequent buses to Ciudad Hidalgo (45min). On the opposite side of the plaza, Gen Paulino Navarro also offers regular *combis* to Ciudad Hidalgo (every 10–15min; 45min) from 7a C Ote and Av Central Nte. Shared taxis to Ciudad Hidalgo leave from 7a C Pte, between 2a Av and 4a Av Nte.

TO GUATEMALA

By bus Three first-class companies offer direct services to Guatemala City (around 6–8hr): Trans Galgos (3 daily at 6am, 12.15am, 11.45pm; 962 625 4588), Linea Dorada (1 daily at 3pm) and Tica Bus (1 daily at 7am; 962 626 2880, http://ticabus.com); the latter two are a bit cheaper, though the buses aren't as nice. All run from the ADO/OCC terminal; buy tickets from a kiosk in the arrivals hall. At the border crossing at Talismán, you'll have to get off the bus for Mexican immigration, walk across the bridge, pass through Guatemalan immigration and then re-board.

Guatemalan consulate C Central Ote 42, at the junction with 5a Av Nte (Mon–Fri 10am–3pm & 4–6pm; 962 626 1525). Even if you don't need a visa, come here for free maps, leaflets and other information.

11

INFORMATION

City tourist office On the plaza in the former Palacio Municipal (Mon–Fri 8am–4pm; 962 628 7725).

Regional tourist office 2km east of the centre in Plaza Kamico on the main road to the border (Mon–Fri 8am–8pm, Sat 8am–2pm; 962 625 5409, www.turismochiapas.gob.mx).

ACCOMMODATION

SEE MAP PAGE 628

★ **Casona Maya Mexicana** 8a Av Sur 19; http://casonamaya.com. A historic and beautifully decorated hotel arranged around a flower-laden courtyard. Its en suites are tastefully adorned with art and antiques, and there's also a pool and a charming restaurant with tables in the leafy courtyard garden. M$$$

Fénix 4a Av Nte 19; http://fenix.com.mx. The best-value budget hotel in the city centre, offering large rooms with either fan or a/c (the latter are substantially nicer and roughly double the price), and decent bathrooms. There's a cooling fountain in the courtyard plus leafy gardens complete with parrots. The place is surprisingly tranquil given the downtown location. M$

Galerias Hotel & Arts 4a Av Nte 21; 962 642 7590. A solid mid-range choice, with clean, comfortable and decidedly beige en suites – all come with a/c and TVs – a decent location, and a certain artistic flair. There's also a good bar on site. M$$$

Hotel & Suites Mo Sak 4 Av Norte 97, between 13 and 15 west; 962 626 6787. A solid, lower mid-range hotel, with spacious though rather bare rooms, each with a modern bathroom, a/c and TV. If you want a kitchenette, opt for one of the king-size rooms. M$$

EATING

SEE MAP PAGE 628

Stalls around the plaza sell local food, while 1a C Pte is lined with inexpensive **restaurants**, most with breakfast options and a comida corrida. As usual, there are budget places to eat and some *panaderías* around the market, beginning with the row of **juice bars** on 10a Av Nte, just west of the plaza. The row of restaurants on the south side of the plaza, under the *portales*, is a good place for drinks, while the city's liveliest clubs are clustered in the Zonas Discotecas, 2km east on C Central Ote.

★ **Pan Malo** 7a Av Sur 53; 962 210 7598. The pick of the downtown bakeries, *Pan Malo* also serves up excellent espressos, lattes and more made from Chiapas-grown beans, which you can drink in or take away, plus tasty sandwiches, cakes and snacks. M$

La Parrilla 8a Av Nte 14, just south of the plaza; 962 118 1428. Offers South American-style grills as well as a delicious *taquiza mixta*, with five mouthwatering types of *supertacos*, all served in a fast-food-style diner. M$$

DIRECTORY

Banks and exchange The main banks are one block east of the plaza, with HSBC at 1a C Pte and 2a Av Nte, but for changing cash you'll get much quicker service from Cambio de Divisas, 2a Av Nte 9, between C Central and 1a C Pte (962 625 1315); you can also get Guatemalan quetzales here.

Internet There are plenty of internet cafés around the city centre.

Post office The post office is a long way southeast of the plaza at 1a C Ote between 7a Av Nte and 9a Av Nte.

11

North of Tapachula

The foothills north of Tapachula are studded with coffee plantations, established as far back as the late nineteenth century. Many of the old haciendas have been well maintained, some even by the original German families, and are an idyllic sight, tucked amid the dense forest. The peak of Volcán Tacaná, the highest in Chiapas, looms over all.

Ruta del Café

West of Tapachula • Driving from Tapachula, follow 8a C north out of town and follow signs • Taxis run to this location

This winding road north and west of Tapachula passes a large number of impressive old haciendas built by German coffee barons in the late nineteenth and early twentieth centuries – several are open for various tours and activities, and some provide (rather lavish) accommodation. It's a pretty but slow drive of about 40km on narrow, unpaved roads through *pequeña Alemania* – the distance and isolation make it best for an overnight trip or longer, rather than a day outing. And you'll need your own transport or a taxi to get up here – or you can arrange a tour with transport through Finca Hamburgo (see next page), which has an office in Tapachula (on 9a Av Ote at 11a C Nte). Established in 1888 and still run by the same German-Mexican family, it also manages nearby Finca La Chiripa, where there are hiking trails and other outdoor activities.

ACCOMMODATION AND EATING

RUTA DEL CAFÉ

Finca Hamburgo End of the Ruta del Café; http://fincahamburgo.com. This grand chalet could be in the Alps – but the view down the forested mountain slope is pure Chiapas. The wood-panelled cabins here are luxurious, and the restaurant has a bit of German flair – *spätzle* (small noodles) with a chile kick, for instance. M$$$

Volcán Tacaná and around

For those travelling by bus, the route northeast of Tapachula up to **Volcán Tacaná** provides a more accessible taste of the area's coffee culture, similar to the Ruta del Café (see page 630) but more manageable as a day outing; the tours and lodging are also a bit more budget friendly. The road climbs up the lush green valley of the Río Suchiate, which forms the border with Guatemala. The bananas and cacao give way to coffee, and you begin to enjoy good views of two majestic **volcanoes**: Tacaná, at 4092m, the highest peak in Chiapas; and the 4220m peak of Tajumulco, the highest mountain in Guatemala (and indeed Central America).

Casa Braun

35km from Tapachula • Charge • 962 627 0050

As you climb into the foothills of Volcán Tacaná, the first town of interest is **Santo Domingo**, home to the wonderfully restored **Casa Braun**, a three-storey coffee-plantation house from the 1920s. Set in beautiful gardens, with balconies all around, it was the home of Enrique Braun Hansen, whose German origins are reflected in the building's architectural style – early North American meets Alpine hotel, with Art Nouveau interiors. Now part of a community-based tourism project, the house includes a restaurant, a swimming pool at the back and a coffee museum (same hours) with displays and photos charting the area's history.

Unión Juárez

Another 9km up the road, and 51km from Tapachula, the last substantial settlement on the road is **Unión Juárez**, one of the last remaining areas for the Mam people in Mexico (most of this Maya group now lives in Guatemala). Perched at 1100m on the flank of Volcán Tacaná, the community is the starting point for some of the finest hiking in southern Chiapas, passing scores of waterfalls. With a guide, you can reach the summit, where a monument symbolizes the kinship between Mexico and Guatemala. The best time to climb is the dry season between November and March, particularly December and January.

11

ARRIVAL AND TOURS — VOLCÁN TACANÁ AND AROUND

By bus and combi From Tapachula, take a *combi* or second-class bus to Cacahoatán (30min); bring your passport, as security checks are common near the border. From Cacahoatán, frequent buses leave from the station across the street from the Unión y Progreso terminal for both Santo Domingo (around 30min) and Unión Juárez (around 45min). Shared taxis, which are slightly faster, also wait here. Returning, buses leave Unión Juárez every 15min till 8pm; the last bus from Cacahoatán to Tapachula leaves around 9pm.

ACCOMMODATION AND EATING

SANTO DOMINGO

Hotel Santo Domingo Opposite the entrance to Casa Braun (see page 631), around 100m along the street and just off the main road; 962 627 0060. A good-value place to stay, whose ten en suites – with comfortable beds – are set around a patio garden. There's also an economical restaurant. Get off the bus at the lower end of the village, near the plaza, and you should be able to follow the signs for the "Centro Turístico" – the house is around 200m from the main road. M$

UNIÓN JUÁREZ

Colonial Campestre Hidalgo 1; 962 647 2237. The economical rooms and suites here are comfortable and spacious, with private bathrooms and TV. The owner knows his coffee, having written a book about its history in the area, and his son, guide Fernando, runs hikes in the surrounding mountains. M$

Izapa

14km east of Tapachula Free, but the gatekeepers at each section appreciate small donations • Take any bus or *combi* to the Talismán border and ask the driver to drop you off at the signposted site

The road to the border passes straight through the archeological site of **Izapa**, an important, if little-visited, group of ruins. Besides being easy to get to, the site is large – with more than eighty temple mounds – and significant for its evidence of both the Olmec and Maya cultures. Izapa culture is seen as a transitional stage between the Olmecs and the Classic Maya period. Many of the best carved monuments have been removed to museums, but you can still see early versions of the rain god Chac and other gods, many in rather sad-looking huts surrounded by barbed wire. From its founding before 1250 BC, Izapa flourished up to and throughout the Maya pre-Classic period, until around 300 AD; most of what remains is from the later part of this period, perhaps around 200 AD.

The **northern side** of the site (left of the road as you head to the border) is the most interesting. There's a ball-court and several steles, which, though not Olmec in origin, are carved in a recognizable Olmec style. The **southern side** (Grupo A and B) is down a track about 1km back along the main road towards Tapachula. These sections are more overgrown, but you can spot altars with animal carvings – frogs, snakes and jaguars – and several unexcavated mounds.

The Guatemalan border: Talismán Bridge and Ciudad Hidalgo

Both of these southern crossing points are easy places to enter Guatemala. **Talismán Bridge** is closer to Tapachula (16km) and better for onward connections if travelling by bus, especially to Quetzaltenango and the Western Highlands. With only a few grubby hotels and unappealing *comedores*, however, the village of Talismán is not a place to linger; El Carmen, on the Guatemalan side, isn't much better.

South of Talismán Bridge, and 37km from Tapachula, the border town of **Ciudad Hidalgo** is a very busy road crossing, but useful only if you're aiming for the beaches along the Carretera al Pacifica (Pacific Highway) or the ruins at Abaj Takalik near Retalhuleu (connected to Hidalgo's Guatemalan neighbour **Tecún Umán** with regular buses).

11

ARRIVAL AND DEPARTURE — TALISMÁN BRIDGE AND CIUDAD HIDALGO

TO GUATEMALA

The two major crossings at Talismán Bridge and Ciudad Hidalgo (both are officially open 24hr, though it's generally easier to cross during the day) are usually hassle free, but things can be less predictable at several minor points of entry: Frontera Corozal, Ciudad Cuauhtémoc and El Carmen Xhan, in Chiapas, as well as El Ceibo in Tabasco. The soliciting of illegal fees sometimes still occurs at these crossings, but requesting a receipt is often a sufficient response to get them to waive the fee.

Money and exchange Changing money is best done in Tapachula, where rates are more favourable and you can check the official exchange rate beforehand.

Time Note that Mexico observes daylight-saving time, but Guatemala does not, which means that, in summer, Guatemala is one hour behind Mexico.

VIA TALISMÁN BRIDGE

To Guatemala City Buses (every 1–2hr; 5–6hr) are usually waiting, but these typically travel along the Carretera al Pacifica via Tecún Umán (closer to Ciudad Hidalgo). The faster option is one of the international bus services from Tapachula direct to Guatemala City (see page 629).

To Quetzaltenango and the Western Highlands Take a shared taxi to Malacatán or Coatepeque and continue from there.

To Mexico Travelling into Mexico, you'll be given a tourist card at immigration; *combis* head to Tapachula, and first-class buses go from Tapachula onwards. You may have your passport checked along Hwy-200.

VIA CIUDAD HIDALGO

To Guatemala Plenty of willing locals offer to pedal you across the Puente Rodolfo Robles to Umán in Guatemala, but it's an easy walk. You have to pay a small fee to cross the bridge.

To Mexico The ADO/OCC terminal is one block from immigration, where you can pick up shuttles to Tapachula every 15min (30–45min).

Tuxtla Gutiérrez and around

This city is the main gateway from central Mexico and a major transport hub. As home to over half a million, the modern, crowded capital of Chiapas does its best to deny most of the state's attraction and tradition (if you prefer a more rural setting, press on to Chiapa de Corzo or San Cristóbal de las Casas). A couple of **museums** can fill your time if you do stay here, and the city is the best base for a drive along the cliff-tops and *miradores* of the **Cañón del Sumidero** (see page 638).

The plaza and around

Museo de la Ciudad • Free

11

The **plaza**, known as the Plaza Cívica, is an expanse of ostentatious marble, fountains and a statue of General Joaquín Miguel Gutiérrez Canales (1796–1838), former governor of Chiapas and campaigner for *indígena* rights. West along Avenida Central Poniente, at 2a Calle Poniente Sur, is the **Museo de la Ciudad** (961 612 5508), with an absorbing collection of photos and items documenting the city's history, notably its role in the Mexican revolution.

Catedral de San Marcos

Av Central • Free

Just opposite the plaza, the whitewashed **Catedral de San Marcos** was established in the sixteenth century. Its bell tower is one of the leading local entertainments: every hour a mechanical procession of the twelve apostles goes through a complicated routine accompanied by a carillon of 48 bells.

Museo del Café

2a C Ote Nte 236, just east of the plaza • Charge • 961 611 1478, https://facebook.com/museodelcafedechiapas

In an old colonial house with a shady courtyard, this museum tells the story of coffee production in Chiapas, and Mexico generally, since its introduction as a commercial crop 160 years ago. Exhibits cover the Ruta del Café near Tapachula, plus early cultivation and processing methods – as contrasted with contemporary sustainable methods.

Parque de la Marimba

C Central Pte between 8a C Pte and 9a C Pte • **Museo de la Marimba** Charge, free Sun • 961 111 3980

Unlike in many Mexican cities, the central plaza is not the true social centre. **Parque de la Marimba** is where evening crowds gather, often for live music, as well as to lounge in the various modern cafés around the perimeter. Real fans of marimba can visit the **Museo de la Marimba** on the corner, which highlights the history of the musical genre (displays in Spanish only).

Parque Madero

About 1km northeast of the centre • **Museo Botánico** Free • **Museo Regional de Chiapas** Tues–Sun 9am–5pm • Charge • **Museo de Paleontología** Charge

About 1km northeast of the centre, **Parque Madero** is another place where locals go to stroll in the late afternoon and evening. A promenade leads off 5a Avenida Norte Oriente, first passing the pleasant (and free to enter, being part of the park) **Jardín Botánico** and the less interesting **Museo Botánico** opposite, and on to the **Museo Regional de Chiapas**, which details the history of pre-Hispanic Chiapas and the results of the Conquest.

The highlights are the intricately carved human fencers from the ruins of Chiapa de Corzo. At the end of the promenade is the city theatre and next to it the **Museo de Paleontología**, which displays local fossils, amber and the skeleton of a sabre-tooth tiger.

Zoológico Miguel Álvarez del Toro (ZOOMAT)

1a C Ote Sur, Francisco I Madero, 5km south of the centre • Charge • Bus #60, marked "Cerro Hueco" or "Zoológico", departs 1a C Ote Sur between Av 6a Sur and 7a Av Sur Ote, but can take up to 45min • https://www.zoomat.chiapas.gob.mx

If you're interested in local wildlife, it's worth heading out to the so-called **ZOOMAT (Zoológico Miguel Álvarez del Toro)**. It claims to have every species native to Chiapas, and as far as zoos go, it's not bad, with good-sized cages, natural vegetation and freshwater streams. A number of animals, including *guaqueques negros* (agoutis) – rodents about the size of a domestic cat – and large birds such as currasows and chachalacas, roam the zoo grounds. The *vivario* contains a vast collection of snakes, insects and spiders.

ARRIVAL AND DEPARTURE — TUXTLA GUTIÉRREZ

BY PLANE

Tuxtla's airport, Aeropuerto Ángel Albino Corzo, is inconveniently located 27km south of the city. All the major car rental companies and top-end hotels have desks in the arrivals hall, but there is nowhere to change money. There is a Bancomer ATM tucked away in the departures hall upstairs, but this is often out of order. There's no bus to the city; buy taxi tickets at the desk in the arrivals hall (Tuxtla and Chiapa de Corzo; both 35–45min). For San Cristóbal de las Casas, an ADO/OCC bus runs four times daily (1hr).

Destinations Mexico City (6–10 daily; 1hr 40min).

Airlines AeroMéxico, Belisario Dominguez 302, Plaza Bonampak (961 121 4379, http://aeromexico.com).

BY BUS

First-class buses The large ADO/OCC station is on 5a Av Nte Pte, in the Plaza del Sol mall on the northwest side of the city. Taxis run to the centre from the station. First-class buses to Villahermosa travel via the Puente Chiapas, which looks less direct but is much faster than going over the mountains. There is a TicketBus office on 2a C Pte Nte at 2a Av Pte Nte, to spare you the trip out to the station.

Destinations Cancún (4 daily; 18hr 15min–21hr); Ciudad Cuauhtémoc, for Guatemala (2 daily at 10.15am & 4.15pm; 4hr 45min); Comitán, for Lagos de Montebello or the Guatemalan border (roughly hourly; 3hr 10min); Mérida (6 daily; 13hr 50min–16hr; Mexico City (9 daily; 12–14hr); Oaxaca (4 daily; 10hr); Palenque (8 daily; 7hr–7hr 30min); San Cristóbal (roughly hourly; 1hr 10min); Tapachula (roughly hourly; 5hr 15min–6hr); Tonalá (roughly hourly; 2hr–2hr 30min); Villahermosa (roughly hourly; 4hr 20min–5hr 20min).

Second-class buses and colectivos The main second-class terminal, the Central Camionera de Sur, is on 10a Av Sur Ote at 15a C Ote Sur. Autotransportes Tuxtla Gutiérrez (ATG) is the main company, serving San Cristóbal, Oaxaca, Villahermosa, Mérida, Palenque and Cancún. Scores of smaller companies and *colectivos* pull in here. *Colectivos* for Bochil and San Cristóbal depart from the 9a Av side. The most frequent service to San Cristóbal is with Omnibus, from a dedicated station on 4a Av Sur Oriente at 15a C Oriente Sur. For Chiapa de Corzo (30min), *colectivos* leave from the southeast corner of 1a Av Sur Ote at 5a C Ote Sur. Taxis run to the centre from the Central Camionera.

BY CAR

For the ascent by car into the hills from Tonalá and the coast highway, a short toll highway outside Arriaga bypasses about 20km of pretty but almost comically winding road.

11

GETTING AROUND

Car rental Hertz is at Belisario Domínguez 1195, in the *Camino Real* hotel (961 617 7777, http://hertzmexico.com), as well as at the airport. Europcar (961 121 4922, http://europcar.com.mx) also has a central location, at Belisario Dominguez 2075, near the Walmart.

INFORMATION

Municipal tourist office at the Museo de la Marimba, Av Central Pte at 9a C (Mon–Fri 9am–8pm, Sat 9am–2pm; 961 612 5511). Also maintains kiosks on the plaza and at Parque Madero (both daily 10am–6pm).

Chiapas state tourist office Torre Chiapas, on Paso Limón (daily 8am–4pm; 961 617 0550). Located a good way east in a high-rise. Security is tight, and parking near impossible, but if you need an English-speaker, it's worth a phone call.

ACCOMMODATION

SEE MAP PAGE 633

Tuxtla has a reasonable selection of **places to stay**, with plenty of budget options, but they're a bit characterless, and if you arrive late in the day in busy seasons (especially Aug), you'll have to hunt for a room. Most of the low-cost hotels are on or around 2a C Nte Ote, while the city's smartest hotels – generally bland but reliable international chains like Marriott, Hilton and Holiday Inn – are concentrated 3–4km west of the centre along Belisario Domínguez, convenient only if you have a car.

Casablanca 2a Av Nte Ote 251; 961 611 0142. One of the better budget options, the Casablanca has brightly painted rooms – the cheaper ones have fans, while the more expensive ones come with a/c and TVs – facing an inner palm-fringed garden. There's luggage storage as well. M$

Fernando 2a Av Nte Ote 515; 961 613 1740. The best value of the options just east of the plaza, the Fernando is a modern hotel with some large, comfortable rooms, wooden furniture and TVs. Parking spaces are across the street. M$

Hostal Tres Central C Central Nte 393; 961 139 7439, https://facebook.com/TresCentral. Easily the best bet for backpackers in the city centre, this hostel has good dorms and private rooms (with shared or private bathrooms), a TV lounge, laundry facilities, and a terrace café. M$

Real Avenida Av Central Pte 1230; 961 612 2347. Adequate, though rather overpriced, mid-range hotel with clean rooms, each boasting flatscreen TVs, phones and wi-fi.

It is a relatively long walk into the centre (though it is close to the Parque de la Marimba). M$$

Regional San Marcos 2a C Ote Sur 176, at 1a Av Sur Ote; 961 613 1887. Located near the cathedral, the *Regional* is a decent option for those on a budget who want a bit of privacy. The rooms are small, but there's a/c, plus a decent restaurant and bar. M$

EATING

SEE MAP PAGE 633

The centre of Tuxtla has dozens of reasonably appetizing **restaurants**, and you need never wander more than a block or so either side of Av Central to find something in every price range, including juice bars and bakeries. The very **cheapest** places are in the Mercado Díaz Ordáz, C Central Sur, between 3a and 4a Av Sur Oriente; there's also a string of pleasant, inexpensive lunch operations on 1a Av Nte, just west of C Central, with set menus. Most popular for socializing and people-watching are the terrace restaurants under the arches on **Plaza San Marcos** behind the cathedral, and, for a younger scene, the cafés and bars around **Parque de la Marimba**.

11

Café Avenida Av Central Pte 230. An old-school Mexican coffee shop where they grind their own beans and elderly men sip black coffee to a background of mariachi music and unhurried waiters. M$

Las Canteras 2a Av Nte Ote, at 1a C Pte; 961 611 4310. An open, airy restaurant serving traditional but refined *chiapaneco* cookery, often accompanied by live marimba music – don't expect a quiet meal here. There's a good-value set lunch here. M$$

La Gran Muralla 2a Av Nte Pte 334; 961 613 0899. "The Great Wall" is a passable Cantonese restaurant, for anyone needing a break from Mexican food: the range of dishes is so vast, it seems to want to be Tuxtla's Chinatown all by itself. M$$

Naturalissimo 6a C Pte Nte 124, just off Av Central Pte; 961 614 5343. A bright vegetarian chain restaurant that's inexpensive, clean and modern. There's a daily two-course set lunch, a well-stocked salad bar, and a la carte dishes that include an Indian-spiced lentil burger. M$$

★ **Las Pichanchas** Av Central Ote 837, east of the plaza between calles 7 and 8 Ote; http://restaurantelaspichanchas.com. A bit touristy, but a great place for dinner, with marimba all evening, folk dancing and decent *chiapaneco* food all dished up in a two-storey house with a courtyard. Try the *platón de botana regional* (a selection of local cheese, sausage and more). M$$

DIRECTORY

Banks There are plenty of banks along Av Central, with a branch of HSBC right on the plaza (C Central Nte 137).

Post office The main post office is at 1a Av Nte Ote, near the Plaza Cívica.

Chiapa de Corzo and around

An elegant town of about seventy thousand, **CHIAPA DE CORZO** overlooks the **Río Grijalva**. As it's barely twenty minutes east of Tuxtla (and an easy taxi ride from the airport), it makes a scenic alternative to the big city. It's best known as the starting point for boat rides through the **Cañón del Sumidero** (see page 638), and has quite a tourist scene during Mexican holiday times. The first Spanish city in Chiapas, it was officially founded in 1528, though it had already been an important centre in pre-Classic times. A stele found here bears the oldest **Long Count date** yet discovered, corresponding to December 7, 36 BC. The ruins that remain are on private land behind the Nestlé plant, at the far end of 21 de Octubre on the edge of town (see page 637).

Fuente Colonial

Plaza Ángel Albino Corzo

The most striking feature of Chiapa de Corzo is the elaborate sixteenth-century fountain that dominates the central Plaza Ángel Albino Corzo. Built of brick in the Mudéjar style, in the shape of the Spanish crown, **Fuente Colonial** is one of the most impressive surviving early colonial monuments in Mexico. It has become a state symbol – you may recognize it from Chiapas licence plates. Just behind the fountain, the huge tree bursting from its confines is **La Pochota**, a national monument to the suffering of the *indígenas* under Spanish rule, said to have been standing here when the town was founded.

Casa Museo Ángel Albino Corzo

Northwest side of the plaza • Free • 961 149 9228

This museum is the former residence of the national reformer for whom the town was named. Housing an interesting jumble of period furniture and historical artefacts, it features two cannons used in the so-called Pastry War against France in 1838 (explanations in Spanish only).

Templo de Santo Domingo de Guzmán and Centro Cultural

South of the plaza • Free • 961 616 0005 • https://facebook.com/parroquiasdguzmanchiapa

On the southern side of the plaza, *portales* (arcades) house a series of reasonably priced handicraft stores, which continue south along 5 de Febrero towards the river and the *embarcadero*. Behind the arcades is the lovely **Templo de Santo Domingo de Guzmán** and ex-convent, with a tall nave and timbered ceiling. Forming part of the complex, behind the main entrance to the church, is the **Centro Cultural**, an ambitious project that is gradually converting the old convent into a series of tasteful galleries and art studios. Upstairs on the first floor, the **Museo de Laca** (same hours) recounts the history of lacquer-making in Mexico, from pre-Hispanic times to the present, featuring various lacquered objects from gourds to pots and chests.

Chiapa de Corzo ruins

3km northeast of Chiapa de Corzo plaza • Charge • Take any microbus heading east, and get off at the junction with Hidalgo and follow the signs, walking 15min to an unmarked gate; it's also possible to walk from the plaza, passing the sixteenth-century church ruin of San Sebastián • 961 613 4554

On an ancient trade route high above the Río Grijalva lie the ruins of **Chiapa de Corzo.** Having begun as a farming settlement in the early pre-Classic period (1400–850 BC), it was, by the late pre-Classic period (450 BC–250 AD), the largest centre of population in the region. The ruins are still being excavated and aren't immediately impressive. Although it is the longest continually occupied site in Chiapas, comprising some two hundred structures, what you see today are mainly low pyramids, walls and courtyards, sitting on private property split among several owners and sliced in two by the Panamerican Highway (Hwy-190).

ARRIVAL AND DEPARTURE — CHIAPA DE CORZO

By bus Long-distance buses from Tuxtla typically stop only on the main highway (about 4km north of town) on request. At peak times, you may find a *colectivo* waiting; otherwise you'll need to walk or take a private taxi to the centre.

By combi Shared vans and *colectivos* to Chiapa del Corzo from Tuxtla (southeast corner of 1a Av Sur Ote at 5a C Ote Sur) enter the town along Av Cuauhtémoc, north of the plaza, terminating near the Nestlé plant – get off at C Mexicanidad, or where the driver says "parque", and turn right for the plaza. Heading back to Tuxtla, pick them up along the top of the plaza (Av 21 de Octubre).

By taxi If you want to carry on to San Cristóbal, the only option is to hire a taxi. This is also an option to get from Chiapa de Corzo or central Tuxtla to Tuxtla airport. For a shorter commute, Chiapa de Corzo is a decent alternative place to stay the night before a flight.

ACCOMMODATION AND EATING

For **food**, don't miss the vendors near the **market** (southeast of the plaza), who specialize in *cochito horneado*, chile-roasted pork in a rich broth. Several **restaurants** specialize in *chiapaneco* cuisine, though they tend to be a little overpriced. The *embarcadero* along the river is a pretty spot for a drink, though nothing differentiates the somewhat pricey seafood restaurants here, and most start to wind down early.

Los Ángeles Julian Grajales 2, southeast corner of the plaza; http://hotel-chiapas.com. The courtyard may double as a car park, but the small rooms here are comfortable, with quiet a/c systems. The ones on the upper floor are larger, most with nice views of the plaza. M$

El Campanario Coronel Urbina 5, behind the municipal building east of the plaza; 961 616 0390, https://facebook.com/elcampanariochiapadecorzo. The best dining choice in town, though there's not a great deal of competition and prices are a little steep. *El Campanario* has an inviting garden and courtyard, colourful flags hanging from the ceilings, and a menu filled with regional fare. M$$$

La Ceiba Domingo Ruíz 300, three blocks west of the plaza; http://laceibahotel.com. Probably the smartest hotel option in Chiapa de Corzo, La Ceiba has several floors enclosing a tranquil palm-filled garden, small pool and caged parrots. Rooms are simple but comfortable, with a/c and TVs. M$$

Cañón del Sumidero

10km north of Chiapa de Corzo • From the plaza in Tuxtla, Autobús Panorámico (Sat & Sun 9am & 1pm; 3hr 30min; minimum five passengers) runs a bus along the canyon rim; for boats, see page 638

On the highway east from Chiapa de Corzo towards San Cristóbal, you catch occasional glimpses of the Río Grijalva and the lower reaches of one of Mexico's deepest canyons, with walls up to 1000m high in some places. Its rock walls are sprinkled with patches of bright green vegetation and odd rock formations, and carved out with shallow caves. A drive along the rim passes *miradores* (lookout points) that are unnervingly close to the edge – the most dramatic is at Las Coyotas. A boat ride up the river from Chiapa de Corzo (see page 638) is just as awe-inspiring, snaking through the whole gorge up to the Chicoasén Dam, which forms a lake at the northern end. Along the way are several waterfalls, including the remarkable El Árbol de Navidad, where calcareous formations covered in algae resemble a Christmas tree. Crocodiles and spider monkeys can often be spotted, along with pelicans, egrets and cormorants.

The one drawback to the water-level view from the boat is the undeniable amount of rubbish in the water that collects along the stagnant edges of the canyons. It's periodically rounded up and disposed of, but it's particularly bad during the rainy season, when the water is highest. But this shouldn't deter you from seeing the greatest geological wonder in Chiapas.

Bochil and Simojovel

Just beyond Chiapa de Corzo, Hwy-195 cuts off to the north. It's an inconvenient route, as there's no continuous bus service, but for those with time and inclination, it's a part of mountainous Chiapas that's well off the tourist track. The road climbs through mountains wreathed in cloud to **BOCHIL**, some 60km from Tuxtla and a centre for the **Tzotzil Maya**.

From there, another 40km up, **SIMOJOVEL** is at the head of a spectacular valley. The pretty town is the source of most of the amber you'll find sold in local markets, and plenty of shops sell it, often for a bit less than elsewhere in the state.

ARRIVAL AND ACCOMMODATION — BOCHIL AND SIMOJOVEL

By bus and combi Second-class buses run from Tuxtla over the mountains to Pichucalco in southern Tabasco, passing through Bochil on the way. From Pichucalco, you can catch another eastbound for Teapa. From Bochil, *combis* run regularly up to Simojovel.

Posada San Pedro 1a C Pte Nte, a block from the plaza, Bochil; 919 653 0062. One of a couple of simple places to stay, *Posada San Pedro* has a collection of basic rooms set out around a courtyard; to find it, head for Banamex at the top of the plaza and turn right. M$

El Triunfo Biosphere Reserve

Cradled within the slopes of the Sierra Madre de Chiapas, on the northern edge of the Soconusco, this dense cloud forest is a refuge for hundreds of species of birds, including the rare quetzal, the great currasow and the azure-rumped tanager, as well as (very

CHIAPA DE CORZO BOAT TOURS

In Chiapa de Corzo, several companies offer **boat trips** down the canyon, all for around the same price (8am–5pm; charge per person). The first office you reach is Turística de Grijalva (961 600 6402), on the west side of the plaza. Or you can head straight south down the street to the *embarcadero*, where other companies operate. During Mexican vacation times, boats fill with the requisite ten people almost immediately, and it doesn't matter where you buy your ticket. In slower times, it's best to show up early and go from company to company to see which boat is closest to full. Tours last a couple of hours.

THE CHURCH IN THE WATER

In October 2015 locals living near the Nezahualcóyotl reservoir in the far west of Chiapas reported a ghostly sight: the ruins of a sunken sixteenth-century church had emerged from the waters, which had plunged by 25m during a drought. The Temple of Santiago – also known as the Temple of Quechula – was submerged in 1966, when the Río Grijalva was dammed to generate hydroelectric power, creating a reservoir spanning almost 1000 sq km. The church had lost its roof, but its 10m walls, arches, columns and hall were all in remarkably good shape. It was built in 1564 by a group of Dominican friars led by Bartolomé de las Casas, who later became the first Bishop of Chiapas and – after initially supporting colonial policies – a fierce critic of the Spanish subjugation of Mexico's Indigenous peoples. A town subsequently emerged around the Temple of Santiago, but in the 1770s a plague hit the region, and it was largely abandoned. The church, which last emerged from the waters during a drought in 2002, became something of a tourist attraction, with enterprising fishermen offering tourists impromptu boat trips out to the ruin before the water levels rose again.

hard-to-spot) pumas, jaguars and Geoffroy's spider monkeys. Very few people come this way, so it's best to contact the reserve organization several weeks in advance to make arrangements. The jumping-off point is the town of **JALTENANGO**, also known as **Ángel Albino Corzo**, ringed with coffee plantations.

ARRIVAL AND DEPARTURE — EL TRIUNFO BIOSPHERE RESERVE

By bus Buses to Jaltenango leave Tuxtla several times a day (3–4hr) from the Cuxtepeques y Anexas station at C 10 Ote Nte and Av 3 Nte Ote.

By tour Based in Tuxtla, the Fondo de Conservación El Triunfo (961 125 1122, http://fondoeltriunfo.org), at San Cristóbal 8, 3km northwest of the Plaza Cívica, is responsible for tourism. It runs four-day packages that include transport from Tuxtla, lodging at the simple *Campamento El Triunfo* in the mountains, a guide at the coffee *fincas* and in the wilderness, and porters.

San Cristóbal de las Casas and around

The unofficial capital of highland Chiapas, **SAN CRISTÓBAL** – or Jovel, as many locals call it – is a major stop on the travel circuit. But the city, a clutch of tile-roofed houses huddled together in the bowl of a valley, has held up to tourism well. The modern edges don't make a good first impression, but the centre has none of this unchecked development: pedestrianized central streets foster a low-key social scene, with a cosmopolitan mélange of small bars and restaurants that thrive on a certain degree of leftist-revolutionary cachet. It's also a great base for studying at one of the numerous Spanish-language schools.

San Cristóbal is also a prime base for exploring highland Chiapas, perhaps the most scenic part of Mexico. The densely forested mountains give way to dramatic gorges, jungle valleys flush with orchids, vividly coloured birds and raucous monkeys. In addition, the area's relative isolation has allowed the **Indigenous population** to carry on with their lives little affected by Catholicism and modern commercialism – and this includes clothing and craft traditions as brilliantly coloured and rich as the wildlife (though older people in particular maintain a traditional aversion to photography – be sure to ask permission first, and respect the answer). Villages to the west of San Cristóbal are generally **Tzotzil**-speaking, and those to the east speak **Tzeltal**, but each village has developed its own identity in terms of costume, crafts and linguistics. Some simple words are given on page 643.

Just 75km from Tuxtla, up the fast toll highway that breaks through the clouds into pine forests, San Cristóbal is almost 1700m higher, at 2100m. Even in August, the evenings are chilly – be prepared.

Brief history

San Cristóbal was designed as a Spanish stronghold against what was an often-hostile Indigenous population – the attack here by Zapatista rebels in January 1994 (see page 625, for more on the Zapatistas) was only the latest in a long series of uprisings.

The colonial era

It took the Spaniards, led by conquistador Diego de Mazariegos, four years to pacify the area enough to establish a town here in 1528. The so-called Villareal de Chiapa de los Españoles was more widely known as Villaviciosa (Evil City) for the oppressive exploitation exercised by its colonists. In 1544, Bartolomé de las Casas was appointed bishop, and he promptly took an energetic stance in defence of the native population, playing a similar role to that of Bishop Vasco de Quiroga in Pátzcuaro (see page 283). His name is still held in something close to reverence by the local population. Throughout the colonial era, San Cristóbal was the capital of Chiapas (at that time part of Guatemala), but lost this status in 1892 as a result of its continued reluctance to accept the union with Mexico.

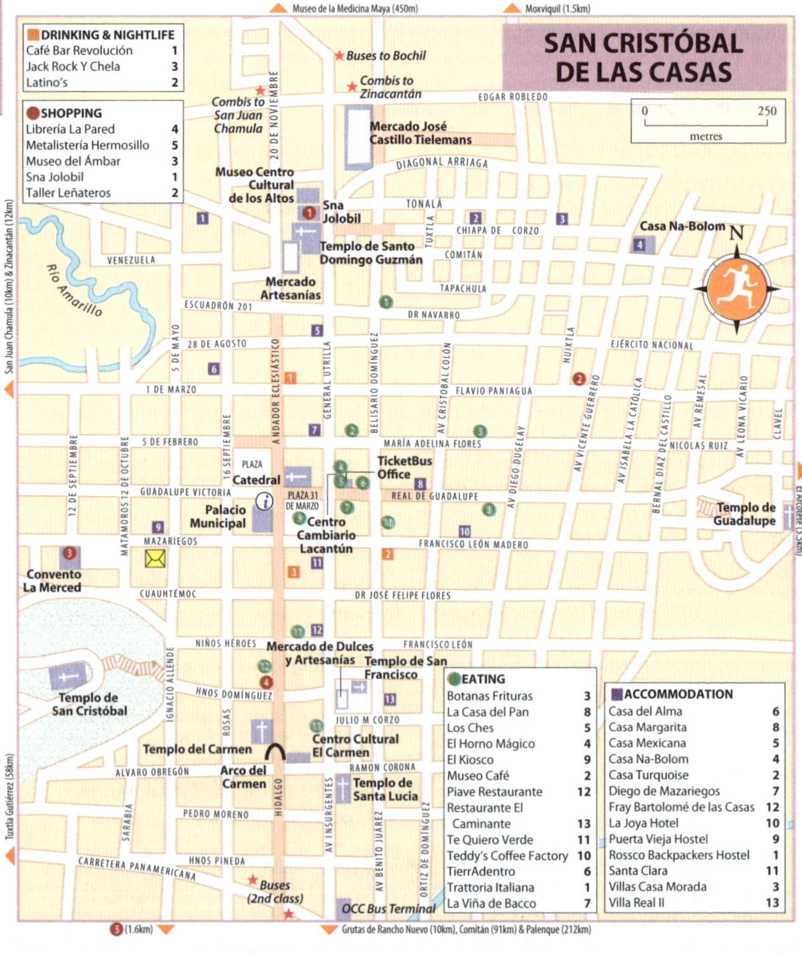

San Cristóbal de las Casas today

Independent as the Indigenous groups are, economic and social status in the mountains around the city lags far behind the rest of Mexico. This is in part due to the long duration of the *encomienda* system of forced labour, which remained in place here long after the end of Spanish colonialism. Many small villages still operate at the barest subsistence level. It's worth noting that many Indigenous communities and some local transport operators refuse to observe the **time change** in summer, preferring *la hora vieja* – the old time, or, as some savvy marketers have dubbed it, "Zapatista time".

Thankfully most of the city's historic buildings escaped major damage during the September 2017 earthquake (see page 622) that rocked Chiapas.

Plaza 31 de Marzo

Usually referred to simply as *el parque*, this plaza is the heart of the city, encircled by a cluster of attractive colonial mansions and the sixteenth-century **cathedral**, which boasts an ornate, pale orange facade, impressive *artesanado* ceiling and grand *retablo*. The finest of the mansions is **La Casa de las Sirenas**, now home to the *Hotel Santa Clara*, which is said to have been built by the conquistador Andrés de la Tovilla in the mid-sixteenth century and has a very elaborate doorway around the corner on Insurgentes. In the middle of the plaza there's a bandstand and a café.

11

Andador Eclesiástico and around

Cutting through the centre is the **Andador Eclesiástico**, a pedestrianized thoroughfare that connects the Templo del Carmen, 300m south of the plaza (on Hidalgo), to Santo Domingo, 400m to the north (on 20 de Noviembre). It's lined with touristy shops, restaurants, cafés and ice-cream parlours. The **Templo del Carmen** stands opposite the Arco del Carmen, which spans the road, and once served as the gateway to the city. Built in 1677, it shows a slight Mudéjar (Moorish) influence. The church is not particularly inspiring architecturally, but on the other side of the arch, the **Centro Cultural El Carmen** (daily 8am–8pm; free) contains a couple of galleries of contemporary painting and craftwork around gardens filled with traditional Maya plants. Considering the amount of artistic activity in and around San Cristóbal, these sights are pretty disappointing, partly due to a serious fire in 1993 that destroyed much of the city's artwork.

Templo de Santo Domingo Guzmán

20 de Noviembre, at Real de Mexicanos • Free • 967 678 1399

This church is the most intrinsically interesting in San Cristóbal. Constructed between 1547 and 1551, its lovely pinkish Baroque stucco facade combines Oaxacan and Guatemalan styles. Inside, it's gilded everywhere, with a wonderfully ornate pulpit – if you see it in the evening, by the light of candles, you might well believe it's solid gold.

Museo Centro Cultural de los Altos

20 de Noviembre, at Real de Mexicanos, next to the Templo de Santo Domingo Guzmán • Charge • 967 678 2806

Adjacent to the Templo de Santo Domingo, in the old convent space (look for it just to the left of the convent's main entrance, beyond Sna Jolobil; see page 646), the **Museo Centro Cultural de los Altos** has recently reopened after refurbishment. The exhibits tell the story of the city, with vivid portrayals of how the Indigenous people fared under colonial rule.

Mercado José Castillo Tielemans

General Utrilla north of the Templo Santo Domingo

San Cristóbal's daily market is an absorbing place, largely because its chaos and the crowds in its souk-like lanes contrast with the rather manicured centre, where Indigenous people in traditional dress can seem a bit like part of the scenic background. Here, though, commerce is the important thing, and every villager in town for the day participates – arguing over prices of fried ants, selecting the best live chickens, picking through piles of dried fish. The market is far bigger than it first appears, with sections for housewares and clothing in a network of narrow covered alleys.

Casa Na-Bolom

Vicente Guerrero 33 • **Museum** Charge, extra with a tour; tickets available from gift shop opposite in Jardín de Jaguar • **Library** Free • http://nabolom.org

Behind Templo de Santo Domingo Guzmán, Chiapa de Corzo leads east towards the **Casa Na-Bolom**, an ethnographic museum also housing one of the best hotels in San Cristóbal and a **library** of anthropological texts. This was the home of Danish explorer and anthropologist Frans Blom, who died in 1963, and his Swiss wife, Gertrude, an anthropologist and photographer who died in 1993. Today it's renowned as a centre for the study of the region's Indigenous cultures, particularly of the isolated Lacandón Maya. The centre is overseen by the Asociación Cultural Na-Bolom, which arranges some small-scale volunteer cultural and agricultural projects, though you'll need to speak Spanish to participate (see the hotel review on page 644 for contact info).

Jardín de Jaguar

Located across the road from the main complex, the gift shop-cum-ticket office in the **Jardín de Jaguar** contains a few exhibits and information boards about the various ethnic groups in Chiapas. In one corner is a replica of a traditional highlands house, made with wooden walls covered with mud and a roof thatched with grass.

The museum

The main museum occupies rooms set around a series of beautiful courtyards – it's not particularly large, and a guided tour can be illuminating, if you're able to time your visit for one. The museum exhibits discoveries from the site of **Moxviquil** (see page 642) and explains the history and culture of the Chiapas highlands and the Lacandón forest. There's also a collection of items belonging to Frans Blom, including the detailed maps for which he is known. After the tour, you can watch a film (mainly in English) about the life of the Bloms and the ecology, culture and politics of Chiapas.

Museo de la Medicina Maya

General Utrilla, 500m north of the centre • Charge • 967 678 5438

This museum is an absorbing journey through the world of Maya medicine, complete with medicinal plants growing in the gardens and a herbal pharmacy on site to dispense remedies. You'll learn more than you ever thought to ask about Maya midwifery, and it's a great place to visit before heading out to the church at San Juan Chamula, as it explains a lot of the rituals you might see performed there.

The churches of Guadalupe and San Cristóbal

On either side of town, two churches perch on hilltop sites: **Templo de Guadalupe** to the east and **Templo de San Cristóbal** to the west. Neither offers a great deal architecturally, but the climbs are worth it for the views – San Cristóbal, especially, is at the top of a dauntingly long and steep flight of steps. It's best not to climb up to either of these relatively isolated spots after dark; there have been reports of women being harassed at San Cristóbal church.

Moxviquil

1.5km north of San Cristóbal centre via Av Yajalón • **Reserve** Charge • **Greenhouse** Free • https://iesdhs.edu.mx • Follow Av Yajalón north to the ring road (about 30min), then bear left; you will see a sign marked Reserva Ecológica; taxis run to this location

USEFUL WORDS IN TZOTZIL AND TZELTAL

	Tzotzil	Tzeltal
To ask permission	Chíkhelav	Ya shka shan
Hello	Kúshee	Bish chee
Goodbye	Batkun	Bónish
Please	Avokoluk	Há wokolook
Thank you	Kalaval	Wókolawal
Sorry/Excuse me	Tsik bunjoomul	Pasbón
Yes	Chabal	Heech
No	Moo yuk	Ho'o

The completely deserted and ruined Maya ceremonial site of **Moxviquil** is part of a small forest reserve on the northern edge of town that makes a pleasant excursion of a few hours on foot – it's a great opportunity to explore outside town without joining a tour or getting on a bus. If you're particularly interested in the ruins, study the plans at the Casa Na-Bolom (see page 642) before you go, so you'll be able to see the logic behind the piles of rough limestone. From the entrance, a clearly marked loop trail covers about 3km in the forest, climbing fairly steeply. The ruins, such as they are, are reached via a faint spur trail (to the left if you're walking clockwise around the trail) that leads to a ridge, then a flat hilltop.

If you're alert during your hike, you may see wild orchids along the trail. And if you miss them, you can still see them at Orquídeas Moxviquil, the reserve's lovely orchid greenhouse and botanic gardens, at the base of the hill near the entrance. They preserve some very rare species from around Chiapas.

11

ARRIVAL AND DEPARTURE — SAN CRISTÓBAL DE LAS CASAS

BY BUS

First-class buses For destinations in the state and throughout the Yucatán, buses arrive at and leave from the ADO/OCC terminal, on the Carretera Panamericana (Hwy-190) on the southern edge of town (taxis run from here to the city centre). For the centre, turn right and head seven blocks north on Insurgentes to the plaza. South across the highway, AEXA runs buses to similar destinations. You can also buy first-class tickets from the TicketBus office (Mon–Sat 7.30am–10pm, Sun 9am–5pm; 967 678 0921) in the centre at Real de Guadalupe 14. For Villahermosa, it's usually easier to get any bus to Tuxtla and change there. Buses to the Yucatán coast go via Chetumal, where you can catch connections to Belize.

Destinations Cancún (17hr–22hr 20min) via Chetumal (3 daily at noon, 2.30pm & 5pm; around 12hr); Ciudad Cuauhtémoc, for Guatemala (2 daily at 11.30am & 5.30pm; 3hr 30min); Comitán (roughly hourly; around 2hr); Mérida (around 17hr) via Campeche (2 daily at 6pm & 7pm; around 10hr); Mexico City (5 daily; 13hr 45min–15hr 20min); Oaxaca (4 daily at 10.15am, 6.10pm, 8pm & 10.45pm; 11hr–11hr 20min); Palenque (8 daily; 8–9hr); Tapachula (7 daily; 7hr 40min–9hr 20min); Tuxtla Gutiérrez (roughly hourly; 1hr 10min); Villahermosa (5 daily; 6hr 20min–6hr 50min).

Second-class buses Most stop along Hwy-190 to either side of the OCC first-class terminal, and AEXA, across the highway, runs some second-class services as well. The exception is the service for Bochil – these buses are just north of the market area.

To Guatemala Travel agency Chincultik, Real de Guadalupe 34 (967 678 0957), runs a daily bus to Guatemala City.

BY COMBI

Shared vans are a good alternative for nearby destinations such as Tuxtla Gutiérrez and Comitán – they tout for customers outside the bus stations on the main highway.

BY CAR

The toll highway runs to/from Tuxtla Gutiérrez.

GETTING AROUND

By bike & moped An enjoyable way to get out to the surrounding villages is on a bike or motorbike. Los Pingüinos, Ecuador 4B (967 126 6379, https://facebook.com/jesusjoelpalmamolina), and Croozy, Belisario Domínguez 7 (967 683 2223), have bikes for daily rentals. The former offers tours, while the latter also has scooters and motorbikes for rent; note that they don't come with insurance, so if you get into an accident, you'll have to cover the costs.

By taxi Taxis run within the centre and should be inexpensive.

INFORMATION

State tourist office In the Palacio Municipal (Mon–Fri 8am–8pm, Sat 9am–8pm, Sun 9am–2pm; 967 678 1467, https://www.sancristobal.gob.mx). Offers free city maps, up-to-date lists of hotels, bus schedules and event information, though little English is spoken.

Municipal tourist office Next door to the state tourist office (daily 8am–8pm; 967 678 0665), and likewise has few English-speakers.

TOURS AND ACTIVITIES

Day tours San Cristóbal has dozens of agencies, most doing the same four standard tours: San Juan Chamula and San Lorenzo de Zinacantán; the Cañón del Sumidero; Lagos de Montebello; and Palenque and Agua Azul. Some will also arrange tours further afield to Bonampak and Yaxchilán. Nichim Tours, Hermanos Domínguez 5-A (967 678 3520, http://chiapastoursyexpediciones.com), has a broader range of tours than most; Explora, 1 de Marzo 30 (967 674 6660), specializes in trips to the Lacandón forest (see page 665), including rafting, kayaking and caving expeditions. Alex and Raul Tours (967 678 3741, www.alexyraulmashitos.com) run good-value, culturally sensitive tours to Chamula and Zinacantán; tours leave daily at 9.30am, returning at 2–2.30pm; meet at the wooden cross in front of the cathedral.

Horse riding Casa Utrilla (967 100 9611) runs trips to Chamula, leaving daily from the Chilam Balam bookstore, General Utrilla 3, at 9am & 12.30pm. If you phone ahead, they'll pick you up from your hotel.

ACCOMMODATION

SEE MAP PAGE 640

Vast numbers of visitors and competition for business mean that San Cristóbal has some very good-value **hotels**. There are a few reliable places around the ADO/OCC terminal, but walking up Insurgentes to the plaza, you'll pass more establishments in all price ranges. Most of the best **budget options** are found in the streets east of the plaza, particularly along Real de Guadalupe and around. An ever-larger proportion of hotels here call themselves "**posadas**", and most live up to the convivial ambience this is presumably meant to convey, but it's always worth seeing your room before you pay. Even the most basic places now have hot water, though not necessarily all of the time. Nights can be pleasantly cool in summer, but cold in winter, so make sure there are enough blankets. For **longer stays**, check out the many notice boards in the bus stations, language schools and popular cafés, where you'll find rooms and even whole houses for rent.

HOTELS AND GUESTHOUSES

Casa del Alma Av 16 de Septiembre 24; http://casadelalma.mx. Hard-to-beat boutique hotel with a city centre location, distinguished en suites with balconies/terraces, plant- and flower-filled communal areas, in-house spa, and excellent restaurant. M$$$$

Casa Margarita Real de Guadalupe 34; http://hotelcasamargarita.mx. Justifiably popular guesthouse with comfortable rooms set around a patio. The location couldn't be more central (though this does mean that rooms at the front can be a bit noisy). It has a slightly smarter, sister hotel, *Parador Margarita*, at Flores 39. M$$

Casa Mexicana 28 de Agosto 1; http://hotelcasamexicana.com. Charming converted colonial-era townhouse with spacious, wood-beamed en suites set around a lush, jungle-like garden and terrace. There's a sauna, a restaurant-bar, small gallery and a craft shop. A fine choice all round. M$$$

★ **Casa Na-Bolom** Vicente Guerrero 33; http://nabolom.org. Offers very comfortable rooms with fireplaces and private bathrooms around courtyards, as well as lovely private cottages in the tranquil gardens. All are decorated with textiles, artefacts and photos taken by the scholars who founded the place (see page 642). Rates include breakfast (with organic produce from the garden) and entry to the museum. M$$$

Casa Turquoise Chiapa de Corzo 40; 967 286 0266. If you prefer a bed and breakfast to a hotel, then Casa Turquoise will prove to be a good fit. The rooms are spacious, light, airy and replete with plants. There's also a good sized communal kitchen, if you like prefer to cook your own meals, and the ever helpful host is always on hand. M$$

Diego de Mazariegos 5 de Febrero 1; http://diegodemazariegos.com. San Cristóbal's most polished colonial hotel, set in two buildings on either side of General Utrilla. Spacious rooms – all featuring a fireplace, antique furniture and beautifully tiled bathrooms – are arranged around attractive courtyards. Book ahead, as it's often busy with tour groups. M$$$

Fray Bartolomé de las Casas Niños Héroes 2, at Insurgentes; 967 678 0932, http://facebook.com/hotelfraybartolome. Split into two sections, *Fray Bartolomé de las Casas* has a charming older wing, arranged around a pretty courtyard with a central fountain. The newer section, however, is far less appealing. M$

La Joya Hotel Madero 43A; http://lajoyahotelsancristobal.com. Swish boutique hotel, bang in the centre of town, with five elegant suites decked out with working fireplaces, antiques and pieces of art; three of them have private balconies or terraces. Two-night minimum stay. Book well in advance. M$$$$

Santa Clara Insurgentes 1, at the corner of the plaza; 967 678 1140. The spacious, plant-filled patio and lobby of this colonial mansion are adorned with period artefacts, though the rooms are a bit worn. Its heated pool is a treat, though, and discounts are often available if you pay in cash. The hotel couldn't be more central, but this does mean noise is an issue. M$$$

Villas Casa Morada Diego Dugelay 45; http://casamorada.com.mx. A top-end hotel with artfully decorated, well-equipped en suites (good advanced deals available via the website), as well as a good restaurant-bar serving Mexican and Italian dishes (room service is available), and a garden area to relax in. M$$$

Villa Real II Benito Juárez 24; 967 678 2930. Comfortable, well-furnished, carpeted rooms all with private bathrooms, TV and access to parking. Sister hotel *Villa Real I*, down the road at Juárez 8, is in a category cheaper, and much less pleasant. M$$

HOSTELS AND CAMPING

Puerta Vieja Hostel Diego de Mazariegos 23; http://puertaviejahostel.com. Smart, well-run hostel with a 12-bed women-only dorm, a 16-bed mixed dorm and private rooms (some en suite) sleeping up to four people, all set around a pleasant courtyard. There's a restaurant-bar, weekly film nights, yoga sessions, and even free cocktails nights. M$

★ **Rossco Backpackers Hostel** Real de Mexicanos 16; www.hostelworld.com. One of the best hostels in Chiapas, with enthusiastic English-speaking owners, clean, renovated dorms (4- to 14-beds; there's a separate one for women) and private rooms. There are also free breakfasts, lockers, TV lounger and common room, daily use of a gym, Spanish lessons and a cosy campfire in the garden most evenings. Dorms M$; doubles M$$

11

EATING

SEE MAP PAGE 640

San Cristóbal has no lack of places to eat, with a huge variety of economical **restaurants** in the streets immediately east of the plaza, especially on Madero. Where the city really shines, however, is in lively, more international places with a bohemian feel and enticing menus with plenty of **vegetarian** options; in addition to the establishments listed here, several of the boutique hotels have good restaurants, notably *Casa del Alma* (see page 644) A battery of sweet-sellers regularly sets up under the *portales* on the west side of the plaza, and a much smaller, more locally used plaza north on Belisario Domínguez often has snack carts and stands selling clove-spiked *ponche*, a warm pineapple drink that's great on a chilly night.

CAFÉS, CHEAP EATS AND SNACKS

La Casa del Pan Real de Guadalupe 55; www.lacasadelpannj.com. A superb range of reasonably priced vegetarian (and vegan) food and baked goods, made with local, organic ingredients. Breakfast/brunch options are particularly good, and there's also a hearty buffet. It's popular with expat development workers, and there's often live music or film screenings at night. M$$

El Horno Mágico General Utrilla 7, just north of the plaza; 967 147 2870. The facade of "the Magic Oven" may be Maya, but the goods inside testify to baking skills honed in France. There's a wonderful selection of baguettes, croissants, pains au chocolat and other pastries, as well as a few sandwiches. There's another branch in Tuxtla. M$

El Kiosco In the plaza; 961 631 5154. In a great location under the bandstand, where you can enjoy a coffee or alcoholic drink at the outdoor tables and watch the world go by; there's often live music and dancing in the evening. M$

Museo Café María Adelina Flores 10; 967 678 7876. Attached to a small coffee museum (entry charge), where beautiful illustrations depict the history of the coffee trade in Mexico, this café serves delicious coffee and some of the best *chocolate con leche* in town. Also for sale are organic beans from a cooperative of local coffee producers (one of which you can visit – ask at the museum for information). M$

Teddy's Coffee Factory Belisario Domínguez 1; 967 272 1881. Superior café with a cool, modern interior and an extensive range of coffees, including several hard-to-find preparations (such as a Viennese-style *Einspänner*). Authentic Korean and Japanese food is also on offer. M$$

RESTAURANTS

Botanas Frituras Periférico Oriente 10; 967 678 7851. Popular Brazilian joint with a short but sweet menu with the focus firmly (and somwehat bizarrely) on toast, alongside some very hearty accompaniments. Serving everything from steak to soup, *Botanas Frituras* is certainly different, but enjoyable all the same. M$$

Los Ches Real de Guadalupe 12; 967 631 6386. Welcoming little Argentine *parrilla* (steakhouse) with images of national heroes on the walls – Maradona, Messi, Gardel, Pope Francis – and succulent steaks and empanadas, served with a tangy *chimichurri* dressing. M$$$

Piave Restaurante Hidalgo 11; 967 678 2749. This popular, Italian run restaurant has a solely organic food focus and serves all your standard pizzas, and pastas. There's also a good fish dish selection and an impressively large dessert menu. Be warned however, this is an immensely popular spot with locals so be sure to reserve a table well in advance. M$$$$

Restaurante El Caminante Insurgentes 45; http://caminantelascasas.com. This spot does a hearty and affordable all day breakfast, with a particular focus on inventive omelettes. There are no bells and whistles here, so what you see is what you get, but that also means it's a great budget friendly option. Beyond the breakfast, the enchiladas and plantains are good here. M$$

Te Quiero Verde Niños Héroes 5; www.tqverde.mx. Economical vegetarian restaurant with an eclectic menu: soups and salads, pasta dishes and (vaguely) Indian-style curries, vegan brownies and fresh juices. M$$

TierrAdentro Real de Guadalupe 24; 967 674 6766. Set around a large courtyard with leather chairs, this meeting place and cultural centre has everything from coffee to waffles, pizzas to quesadillas. The Zapatista sympathies are evident from the quotes from various revolutionaries on the walls and place mats. M$$$$

Trattoria Italiana Dr Navarro 10; http://trattoriaitaliana.com.mx. Authentic, Italian-run restaurant serving delicious home-made pasta (the gnocchi is particularly good) with a range of sauces, which the chef is happy to customize to your taste. M$$$

★ **La Viña de Bacco** Real de Guadalupe 7; 967 631 6565. A snug little tapas bar that looks straight out of Spain – but there's a big selection of Mexican (and international) wines by the glass, as well as platters of locally made cheeses, sausages and ham, sandwiches and tapas. You get a free bite-size *botana* with each glass. Arrive early to snare one of the few tables on the pavement. M$$$$

11

DRINKING AND NIGHTLIFE

SEE MAP PAGE 640

The major bar strips are on Real de Guadalupe and the pedestrianized street north of the plaza, but there are many smaller bar-cafés on quieter blocks throughout the centre, many with a mellow candlelit atmosphere. On a practical note, this is a rare city in Mexico where there's good wine to drink, as well as beer. Many of the cafés and bars host **live music** in the evenings, usually salsa or Latin pop, and only rarely impose a cover charge. *Madre Tierra* (see page 645) also has a bar and live music upstairs.

Café Bar Revolución 20 de Noviembre and Flavio Paniagua; 967 678 6664, https://facebook.com/elrevomx. Zapatista chic is the style at this bar on the pedestrian street. Beers and decent bar food pervade. Happy hour is a generous daily affair and there's live music most nights.

Jack Rock Y Chela Hidalgo, at Mazariegos; 967 272 1417. Fun, dimly lit sports bar with a good mix of locals and travellers. Unless there's an exceptionally big match on, there's no cover charge.

Latino's Madero, at Juárez; 967 678 9927, http://facebook.com/latinossc. Boisterous bar and *discoteca* playing a variety of live and recorded music, from salsa and reggae to jazz and rock, though weekends favour cumbia and merengue. Cover charges are reasonable.

SHOPPING

SEE MAP PAGE 640

San Cristóbal is a destination for textile collectors, as every village in the area specializes in a distinctive style of weaving, embroidery and more. If you see something you like (here or in any village), you should buy it, as there's no guarantee you'll see it again in the next town. The plaza in front of Santo Domingo church, filled with **craft stalls**, is often the best place to buy souvenirs, and the **Mercado de Dulces y Artesanías** on Insurgentes is another worthwhile place to look, although traders here are less willing to bargain.

Librería La Pared Hidalgo 13-B; 967 145 3151, https://facebook.com/LibreriaEscritorioSc. A great bookshop, with one of the largest selection of new and secondhand books in English in the region; you can rent, trade or buy. Photos are also for sale.

Metalistería Hermosillo Jardinera 12, about 2km southwest of the centre; 967 105 1617. Pick up delicate handcrafted door knockers, locks or a traditional ornate cross for perching on your roof as a house blessing at this renowned metalworker's workshop.

Museo del Ámbar Convento de la Merced off Diego de Mazariegos; https://museodelambardechiapas.org.mx. Learn about amber at the museum adjoining this exquisite shop. Even if you don't buy here, you'll be educated for future purchases. Several other shops in town have adopted the same name; don't be deceived.

Sna Jolobil 20 de Noviembre; 967 678 2646. The former convento adjacent to Santo Domingo church has been converted into a craft cooperative that sells textiles and other village products. The quality is generally of a high standard, though the prices are fixed.

Taller Leñateros Flavio Paniagua 54; http://tallerlenateros.com. One of the more fascinating craft shops, where you can see the process of making paper by hand from banana leaves, cornstalks and bamboo, and coloured with natural dyes. The finished sheets become beautiful cards and notebooks.

DIRECTORY

Banks and exchange Several banks (with ATMs) are on or near the plaza; most will exchange dollars and give cash advances (generally mornings only). HSBC is at Mazariegos 6. You'll get much quicker exchange, however, at good rates from *casa de cambio* Centro Cambiario Lacantún at Real de Guadalupe 12-A; it changes most major currencies and usually has Guatemalan quetzales.

Immigration office 2km west of the centre, at the junction of the Carretera Panamericana and Diagonal Centenario (Mon–Fri 9am–3pm; 967 678 7910).

Internet It's scarcely possible to walk a block in the centre without coming across an internet café.

Laundry There are numerous laundries around the centre, most charging by the kg.

Post office Ignacio Allende, between Diego Mazariegos and Cuauhtémoc. In addition, most hotels have Mexipost boxes, and many of the larger ones sell stamps.

Spanish courses Instituto de Lenguas Jovel, Madero 45 (967 678 4069, http://institutojovel.com) is a good institution and can arrange accommodation with local families.

Grutas de Rancho Nuevo

10km southeast of San Cristóbal, off the main road to Comitán • Charge • Second-class buses to Comitán stop on request; by bike, it's about a 50min ride, uphill most of the way from San Cristóbal; the spot is well signed • 967 136 0995

Some organized outings from San Cristóbal go to this enormous cavern extending deep into a mountain – but it's easy enough to go on your own as well. There's an average restaurant here for refreshment, and you can hire horses. Although the cave system is quite extensive, only 400m of pathway is open to the public.

11

El Arcotete

3.5km east of San Cristóbal • Follow Real de Guadalupe out of town, past the Guadalupe church, where it becomes the road to Tenejapa; about 3.5km past the church, El Arcotete is down a signed track to the right

Another popular trip from San Cristóbal, good for a few hours or so, is to **El Arcotete**, a natural limestone arch above a clean and gently flowing river. It's a nice destination if you just want to stroll out of town (or ride a bike) and see a bit of the surrounding hills. On a warm day you'll be tempted to swim, but be aware that the river, coming from below ground, is extremely chilly.

San Juan Chamula

Usually referred to as just **Chamula**, this is the closest Indigenous village to San Cristóbal (10km), as well as the most frequently visited. It has a population of fifteen thousand or so, and more than ninety thousand in the surrounding municipality – despite the fact that thousands of residents have been cast out in recent decades for converting to Protestant faiths (these so-called *expulsados* create many of the crafts sold in San Cristóbal proper).

Chamula and the surrounding Indigenous communities are essentially self-governing, and have their own schools, police force, and a small prison with two cells that are semi-open so as to expose the criminals to "public shame". Over the centuries, the village has been far more resistant to change than neighbouring Zinacantán, putting up fierce resistance to the Spaniards from 1524 to 1528, then acting as the centre of a rebellion described as the second "Caste War" from 1867 to 1870, inspired by the uprising in the Yucatán.

In keeping with the very traditional atmosphere in the village, photography is generally not appreciated, and it is explicitly banned inside the church.

Iglesia de San Juan Bautista

North side of the Plaza Principal • Charge for access to both the church and the museum • Buy tickets from the tourist office in the Palacio Municipal, on the east side of the plaza

This two-hundred-year-old church, painted a festive turquoise, is the epicentre of Tzotzil Maya religion in the area, and one of the most intensely sacred spots in Mexico. A visit can be a humbling and moving experience. The interior is glorious, the floor covered with pine needles and the light of a thousand candles casts an eerie glow. Lining the walls are statues of the saints adorned with offerings of clothes, food and

KINTA JIMULTIK IN SAN JUAN CHAMULA

During the annual Kinta Jimultik, the **carnival** (five days in Feb/March), representatives of all the villages in the area around San Cristóbal attend in traditional dress, marching in circles around Iglesia de San Juan Bautista and up to strategically placed crosses on the hillsides for the first four days. On the final day, which coincides with the last of the five ill-fated days of the Maya calendar, purification rites and fire-walking ceremonies take place in the plaza.

mirrors (thought to aid communication with the laity), while above the altar, San Juan, patron saint of the village, takes pride of place. The customs practised inside the church incorporate aspects of Christian and Maya beliefs – each villager prays by clearing an area of pine needles and arranging a "message" in candles, and rituals frequently involve tearful chanting, singing, an array of fizzy drinks – locals believe expelling gas through burping helps to release evil spirits – and *posh*, a sugar-cane alcohol. Eggs, bones and live chickens – which are sacrificed in the church and later eaten or buried – are also used in these ceremonies.

There are no priests, Masses or marriages here, only baptisms, and the church is open 24 hours (though tourists are welcome only during daylight). It plays a central role in healing ceremonies.

Admission to the church also grants entry to the **Museo Etnográfico**, behind the Palacio Municipal. Rooms display artefacts of village life, musical instruments and costumes from Chamula and other villages.

San Lorenzo de Zinacantán

An easy 7km walk from San Juan Chamula (and 12km west of San Cristóbal), this village is more open than its neighbour. The locals here have embraced flowers as an export crop, and the steep hillsides are dotted with greenhouses. Traditional practices have not completely disappeared, and are on impressive display during fiestas. Some older men still wear the rose-pink and blue-green ponchos with silver threads (called *pok 'ul*), decorated with tassels and embroidered flowers, and the same colours and designs feature in the women's costumes. Tours include a visit to a typical house, where you'll see the family altar, women weaving beautiful table mats decorated with large

VISITING CHAMULA AND ZINACANTÁN

Almost everyone who stays in San Cristóbal visits the Tzotzil Maya villages of **San Juan Chamula** and **San Lorenzo de Zinacantán**. Both places have retained much of their unique cultural identity, including a religion that is a blend of traditional animist belief and Catholicism. The church at Chamula, in particular, is one of the most moving sights in Mexico.

It's hard not to feel a sense of intrusion in these settings, where you may be a spectator at some intense religious ritual. Though an organized tour (very easy to arrange in San Cristóbal) can feel a little rushed and contrived, paradoxically it may make you feel like less of a gate-crasher – your presence in the church is made a bit more "official", and the guides can explain some of the rituals. Tours generally depart around 9.30am, visit both villages and return to San Cristóbal around 2pm (there is little difference between companies; see page 644).

If you do come on your own, you'll feel less conspicuous in busy tourist times (Aug primarily), when there's more of a Mexican tourist crowd, and a festive atmosphere. Inexpensive *combis* leave frequently for Chamula, Zinacantán and other villages from Edgar Robledo, just north of the market in San Cristóbal. There are no *combis* between Chamula and Zinacantán.

embroidered flowers and the house fire where tortillas are prepared. You might also be invited to taste *posh*, the local spirit, made from sugar cane and sometimes flavoured with fruit or cinnamon.

Zinacantán also has a museum, the **Museo Ik'al Ojov** ("Our Great Lord"), which has displays of costumes from different social groups and a tableau of a house interior (donation requested). The museum is a short walk downhill from the main plaza (follow the signs) and the **Iglesia de San Lorenzo** (where no photography is permitted, not even in the churchyard).

Independent visitors must pay a small fee at the kiosk at the entrance to the village; this includes entrance to the church, and you will almost certainly pick up a few small children who want to lead you to craft shops. It's worth going because some also serve delicious handmade tortillas to hungry shoppers.

Comitán de Domínguez and around

The fourth-largest city in Chiapas, **COMITÁN** is 88km from San Cristóbal, southeast along the Panamerican Highway through scintillating scenery. Strategically poised on a rocky hillside, the city is surrounded by rolling farms and wild countryside in which orchids bloom. Once past the scrappier outskirts, the city has an elegant colonial core and a small but absorbing market, as well as a mellow timetable, with many businesses still observing an afternoon siesta. Travellers often pause here before heading for the border with Guatemala or deeper into the wild at the Lagos de Montebello or the Lacandón forest.

Once a major Maya population centre (the ruins of Bonampak and Yaxchilán, and even Palenque, are not far, as the parrot flies), Comitán was originally known as Balún Canán ("Nine Stars", or "Guardians"), but was renamed Comitán ("Place of Potters" in Náhuatl) when it came under Aztec control. At 1560m, it's not as high as San Cristóbal but can still be more refreshing than the sweltering lowlands; make sure your hotel has blankets.

The plaza

Centro Cultural Rosario Castellanos • Free • 963 632 0624

Comitán's spacious, manicured **plaza** is arranged on several levels around a central bandstand. The whitewashed **Palacio Municipal** dominates the north side, while the seventeenth-century **Templo de Santo Domingo**, with its partially exposed Neoclassical stone facade, is to the east. Inside is a spacious nave, timbered ceiling and marble-covered altar. On the plaza's southeast corner, the **Centro Cultural Rosario Castellanos**, named after the respected poet and author who grew up nearby, has a pretty courtyard featuring a mural depicting the city's history.

Museo de Arqueología

1a C Sur Ote, at 2a Av Ote Nte • Free • 963 632 5760

Just east of the plaza, the splendid little **Museo de Arqueología** offers a chronology of local Maya sites through displays of jewellery and pottery, as well as some unsettling tooth necklaces and children's skulls deliberately deformed for ceremonial purposes.

Casa Museo Belisario Domínguez

Av Central Sur • Charge • 963 632 1300

One block south of the plaza, the most evocative of the city's museums is the former home of the local doctor and politician who was assassinated in 1913 for his outspoken opposition to Huerta's usurpation of the presidency. Though it's packed with memorabilia (including a solemn display of the famous anti-Huerta speech that precipitated his murder), it's hard to appreciate unless you understand Spanish. Most interesting is the pharmacy, its shelves lined with diverse lotions and potions, where Domínguez would administer free treatment to the poor.

Museo de Arte Hermíla Domínguez de Castellanos

Av Central Sur at 3a C Sur • Charge • 963 632 2082

Named after the wife of Belisario Domínguez (see page 650 for the Casa Museo Belisario Domínguez), this museum houses a vibrant collection of largely modern artworks by Mexican artists; several canvases by Oaxacan painter Rufino Tamayo are displayed in one room.

Templo de San José

3a Av Sur, west of Av Central • Free

This twin-towered construction, skirted with white and gold and featuring a blend of Gothic and Baroque architecture, is the most unusual of the churches in the city. Its interior is particularly attractive, with tiled floors and stained-glass windows.

Iglesia de San Caralampio

1a Av Nte Pte, two blocks east of the plaza • Free

Also worth seeking out is this Neoclassical construction from 1852, with its elaborately painted stucco facade. It is dedicated to a martyr who became an object of devotion after cholera and smallpox epidemics decimated the town in the nineteenth century. A fiesta in his name is celebrated in mid-February. Alongside the plaza at the front, Comitán's cold, potable mountain-spring water gushes from a row of fountainheads.

11

ARRIVAL AND DEPARTURE — COMITÁN DE DOMÍNGUEZ

By bus Buses stop along the Panamerican Highway (known as Bulevar Dr Belisario Domínguez), the wide commercial strip through town; only ADO/OCC has a terminal, between 7a and 8a Av Sur, while all others just pull in at the roadside nearby. To walk to the centre, cross the road, turn left and walk about three blocks to 1a C Sur Pte, then turn right and walk seven blocks to the plaza. A booth in the ADO/OCC terminal will call a taxi if required. Note that if you're headed to Ciudad Cuauhtémoc on the border, it's typically cheaper and more convenient to take a *combi*, rather than a bus.

First-class destinations Ciudad Cuauhtémoc (3 daily at 1.40pm, 7.30pm & 7.50pm; 1hr 30min); Mexico City (3 daily at 2.30pm, 6.30pm & 8.30pm; 15hr 30min–16hr 20min); Tapachula (5 daily; 6hr 45min–7hr 15min); Tuxtla Gutiérrez (3hr 10min) via San Cristóbal (roughly hourly; around 2hr).

Second-class destinations Lagos de Montebello, including Laguna Bosque Azul (every 30min–1hr; 1hr), Tziscao, Maravillas and Ixcán (every 30min; 1hr 30min–2hr); Palenque via Benemérito and San Javier (7hr), for Bonampak (roughly hourly; 10hr).

By combi Transportes Cuxtepeques runs *combis* to Tuxtla Gutiérrez via Amatenango del Valle (5am–9pm; 1hr) and San Cristóbal from Domínguez at 2a C Nte Pte. Transportes Francisco Sarabia, at 3a Av Pte Sur 10 (between C Central Pte and 1a C Sur Pte), runs an hourly *combi* service from its ramshackle terminal to Tenam Puente (every 30min; 20min). For the Lagos de Montebello and the Frontier Highway, take one of the frequent *combis* run by Transportes Lagos de Montebello from its terminal at 2a Av Pte Sur 23, between 2a and 3a C Sur Pte. For Ciudad Cuauhtémoc, take the Alfa y Omega *combi* from Domínguez opposite 1a C Sur Pte. Transportes Tzobol runs to Amatitlán (3hr; for boats to Laguna Miramar) from its small terminal 3km from the centre along 4a Av Pte Sur, near 13a C Sur Pte, from 4am to 2pm.

INFORMATION AND TOURS

Tourist information The helpful state tourist office is on 1a Av Nte, between 2a C and 3a C (daily 8am–8pm; 963 632 4047). The municipal tourist office is at Av Central Nte 27, between 2a and 3a (Mon–Fri 8am–4pm, Sat 9am–2pm).

Tours Viajes Tenam, Pasaje Morales 11 (963 632 1654, http://agenciadeviajestenam.exodus.mx), can arrange domestic and international flights, as well as organize day trips to local attractions such as El Chiflón.

ACCOMMODATION — SEE MAP PAGE 650

Hotel del Virrey Av Central Nte 13; 963 632 1811. A pretty, flower-filled courtyard and a friendly staff give this attractive colonial-style hotel a welcoming feel. The rooms are bright and clean, with attached bathrooms and TVs. There's also a laundry service. M$

Hotel Nak'an Secreto Maya 1a Av Ote Nte 29; http://nakan.mx. A reliable, modern mid-range choice, *Hotel Nak'an Secreto Maya* has comfortable, if not particularly stylish en-suite rooms, welcoming staff, and a decent restaurant, as well as bike rental. M$$$

Internacional Av Central Sur 16; 963 632 0110. Smart, modern hotel with a stylish edge. It's calm and cool past the wrought-iron doors. Carpeted rooms aren't large – and bathrooms are quite small – but the roomy upper lobby and communal terrace provide welcome space for relaxing. There's also a restaurant, *Girasoles*. M$$$

Posada Casa Lupita 3a C Sur Ote 22; http://posadacasalupita.weebly.com. A converted home run by a friendly family, the *Lupita* has just five rooms, in various configurations, with clean bathrooms (some shared) wedged in odd corners. There's also a nice front patio covered in bougainvillea. M$

Posada El Castellano 3a C Nte Pte 12; 963 632 3347. Despite a recent renovation, *Posada El Castellano* still has an old-fashioned style, with an attractive courtyard with a fountain, reasonable en-suite rooms, and a decent on-site restaurant. M$$

EATING

SEE MAP PAGE 650

Most of the best **places to eat** in Comitán are on the plaza. In the evening, for example, look for the local snack of a *cascara preparada*, a spicy vegetarian mix on a puffed rectangular tortilla the size of a roofing tile; there's usually a vendor in front of the cultural centre on the southeast corner of the plaza. The **market**, one block east of the plaza, is filled with fruit stands and ringed with some very good *comedores*. It's beautiful in its own right, with golden light casting a sepia-tone glow over the stacks of herbs and chiles in its narrow aisles.

11

Acuario Av Central 9, northwest corner of plaza; 963 106 3729. Good-value Mexican food served in clean surroundings, including tables out under the arches. Highlights include typical breakfasts like *chilaquiles* with eggs in a mild, vinegary green-chile sauce. M$$

Los Portales del León 3a Av Ote Nte, opposite the Iglesia de San Caralampio; 963 632 8238. This smart cantina and grill is great for evening meals (which range from steak tartare to sea bass in a lobster sauce), as well as watching the plaza action and listening to the marimba bands. M$$$

Sabores de Comitán 8A C Sur Pte 2; https://facebook.com/saboresdecomitan. A cheerful little cafe-restaurant specialising in local snacks such as *pan compuesto*, a tasty roll packed with pork or chicken, refried beans, chiles and tangy pickles. M$

Ta Bonitio Av Central 5; http://facebook.com/tabonitio.mx. One of the best restaurants in town, *Ta Bonitio* has a wide-ranging menu that features dishes like plantain-stuffed chicken breast and succulent 12-hour-cooked pork ribs. M$$$

DRINKING

Comitán is dotted with a number of lively **bars**, which go in and out of fashion with remarkable regularity – ask around to find out the latest hotspot. If you're in the mood for a **drink**, be sure to try *comiteco*, a rich local spirit made from agave (as tequila is) and flavoured with fruits. Most restaurants and bars serve it, even if it's not on the menu. You can buy excellent-quality bottles at Comiteco Nueve Estrellas (http://facebook.com/comiteco.nueveestrellas) on 1a Av Pte Sur near 2a C Sur Pte. **Free entertainment** comes in the form of live marimba, usually played in the plaza Thurs and Sun from 7pm.

DIRECTORY

Banks and exchange Bancomer, on the plaza, is useful for currency exchange and dollar cash advances, and also has an ATM. HSBC is at 2a C Sur Pte 7, just down from the plaza.

Consulate Guatemala, inside the complex Barrio de Guadalupe at 1a C Sur Pte 35, three blocks west of the plaza (Mon–Fri 9am–5pm; 963 632 0491).

Internet There are plenty of cyber cafés on and around the plaza.

Post office One and a half blocks south of the plaza on Av Central Sur.

El Chiflón

40km southwest of Comitán • Charge • https://visitchiapas.com • From Comitán, take a Rápidos de la Angostura *combi* (every 30min, 5am–6pm) from Blv Domínguez at 1a C Sur Pte

A 120m-high waterfall is the attraction at **Centro Ecoturístico Cascadas El Chiflón**, not far from the village of Tzimol. It's a popular day outing from Comitán, as well as from San Cristóbal de las Casas. Trails run along the river, past smaller cascades with pale blue mineral-rich waters, and there's a zipline, too. Tour operators sometimes also call the place Cascadas Velo de Novia, or Bridal Veil Falls – this is the official name of the park entrance and ecotourism centre, with similar facilities, on the west side of the river, when you come from San Cristóbal.

ACCOMMODATION

EL CHIFLÓN

Cabañas El Chiflón 963 112 8716, https://facebook.com/CascadaselChiflon. The ecotourism group offers a dozen lovely en-suite rooms, each furnished with hand-carved wood and opening onto a long front porch ideal for watching the falls and the forest. A very good deal. M$$

Tenam Puente

14km south of Comitán, 5km off the main road • Charge • Combis run frequently from Comitán until about 6pm, from 3a Av Sur Pte, near 1a Sur Pte • 961 612 8360

This site, uncovered by Frans Blom in 1925, marks a settlement that was at its peak from 600 to 900 AD and finally abandoned around 1200 AD. The most important group of ruins, the acropolis, has three ball-courts and a 20m-high pyramid that affords magnificent views of the Comitán valley. To get to it, keep climbing the stone terraces until you reach the highest point. A path leads up past the guard's hut and into a meadow with a huge stone terrace.

Ciudad Cuauhtémoc

80km south of Comitán

A visit to the Lagos de Montebello (see page 653)is a good introduction to the landscapes of Guatemala, but if you want to see the real thing up close, it's only another 60km or so from the junction at La Trinitaria (served by plenty of passing buses) to the Mexican border post at **Ciudad Cuauhtémoc**. It's not a city at all – just a cluster of houses, the immigration post, a restaurant and the ADO/OCC bus station; standards at the hotels here are low, so you're better off staying in Comitán, El Chiflón or around Parque Nacional Lagos de Montebello.

ARRIVAL AND DEPARTURE — CIUDAD CUAUHTÉMOC

To Guatemala The Guatemalan border post is at La Mesilla, a 3km taxi ride away. As always, it's best to cross in daylight – you may not be able to get your passport stamped after 8pm. Officials at La Mesilla were once notorious for exacting illegal charges from tourists, though things are much improved. Buses to Huehuetenango (hourly; 2hr) and Quetzaltenango (hourly; 3hr 30min) wait just over the border. The money-changers will give you reasonable rates for dollars, but not as good for pesos.

To Mexico Getting into Mexico is easy: the Mexican tourist card (see page 31) will be issued free, and vans or buses will be waiting to take you to Comitán (1hr 30min).

Chinkultic

At km 31 on the Frontier Highway, at the end of a 2km track • Charge • Second-class buses from Comitán to Lagos de Montebello pass the turn

Southeast of Comitán, off the road to Lagos de Montebello, a track leads north to these Classic-period Maya ruins. Only a small portion of the site has been cleared and restored, but the setting is dramatic – worth a stop if you're travelling by car, or staying near the lakes farther down the road.

Climb the first large mound as you enter the site, and you're rewarded with a view of a small lake, with fields of maize beyond and forested mountain ridges in the background. Birds, butterflies and dragonflies abound, and small lizards dart at every step.

A ball-court and several steles have been uncovered, but the highlight is undoubtedly the view from the top of the tallest structure, **El Mirador**. Set on top of a steep hill, with rugged cliffs dropping straight down to a *cenote*, the temple occupies a commanding position; peaceful now, this was clearly an important hub in ancient times.

Parque Nacional Lagos de Montebello

50km southeast of Comitán, via the Panamerican Highway to the Frontier Highway • Charge

Fifty kilometres southeast of Comitán, along the border with Guatemala, this national park is beautiful wooded country studded with more than fifty lakes, sixteen of them very large, and many edged with small restaurants providing local food and basic cabañas. The combination of forest and water is reminiscent of Scotland or Maine, with kilometres of hiking potential. For the less energetic, roadside viewpoints provide glimpses of various pools, lent different tints by natural mineral deposits and the angle of the sun. The lakes themselves are actually a series of *cenotes* (sinkholes) formed by the erosion of limestone over millions of years.

You could see quite a bit of the park in a long day trip – buses cover the route all day, with the last bus leaving the park entrance around nightfall. But to really enjoy the wilderness, and to visit the small but spectacular nearby ruins of Chinkultic (see page 653) as well, you're better off staying in or near the park.

Laguna Bosque Azul

The most easily accessible hike is at **Laguna Bosque Azul**, just past the park entrance on a 3km spur from the main highway. Most *combis* and buses come this way. This route passes a park ticket booth, then dead-ends at the lake car park. From here, you can take the dirt track a few hundred metres further to a fork. The left-hand path, signposted "Gruta San Rafael del Arco", heads into the jungle through an exquisitely forested gorge and eventually to a massive limestone arch over a river and, at the end, a cave in the cliff-face.

Laguna Tziscao

11

The main Frontier Highway continues deeper into the park and passes turnings for several other lakes, including **Laguna Tziscao**, 9km along. There's another park ticket booth here, and you can swim and take a tour on a wooden *balsa* (raft).

ARRIVAL AND DEPARTURE — PARQUE NACIONAL LAGOS DE MONTEBELLO

By bus Second-class buses leave Comitán (roughly every 30min; 45min–1hr) for either Laguna Bosque Azul or Tziscao. Buses headed for destinations further along the Frontier Highway also pass Laguna Tziscao, among others, and will stop on request. The last bus back to Comitán leaves the park entrance around 7.30pm, but from Laguna Tziscao, the last passes at around 5pm.

By combi Transportes Lagos de Montebello depart when full from a terminal at 2a Av Pte Sur 23, between 2a and 3a C Sur Pte.

By car The main route through the park is the Carretera Fronteriza (Frontier Highway; Hwy-307), which splits from the Panamerican Highway 16km outside Comitán, at La Trinitaria. Past the park, the paved road roughly follows the Guatemalan border and runs all the way to Palenque. There are often army checkpoints – you may be asked for your passport at any time. The soldiers are invariably polite, but make sure your tourist card is valid.

ACCOMMODATION

★ **Museo Parador y Hotel Santa María** 22km from the La Trinitaria junction, then 1.3km south on a dirt track; 963 251 5028. The most comfortable of several hotels and guesthouses along the road to the park. A former hacienda, it's a lovely place, furnished with antiques and oil paintings and steeped in colonial history. There's hot water and electricity but rooms are also lit with oil lamps. A small museum (charge) in the grounds is filled with religious paintings and other ecclesiastical art from the seventeenth century. M$$$

El Pino Felíz North side of Frontier Hwy near km 32; 963 131 8548. Also known as *Doña María's*, this joint has very basic rooms in wooden cabins set in a farmyard with animals ranging just outside. Baths and showers are shared (opt for the front section, to avoid always-tricky electric showerheads). The engaging hosts serve home-cooked meals. Buses and *combis* will stop right outside. M$

The Frontier Highway east

The main road continues beyond the Lagos de Montebello and through mountains with spectacular views, rushing rivers and precipitous ridgelines on its way along the Guatemalan border and north to Palenque. The largest settlement – which is not saying much – along the road is **Las Maravillas de Tenejapa**, a pretty village about two hours from Lake Tziscao.

If you drive the Frontier Highway, it's best to do it during daylight hours – there are army checkpoints and Zapatista outposts to contend with, and a chance of robberies. Benemérito, at least three hours from the Lagos de Montebello, is the closest town on the route with rudimentary services like restaurants (we can't recommend the hotels), and the only one with a Pemex station. It's possible to reach Palenque in the same day, if you leave on a very early bus, but you would have no time to stop at Bonampak and Yaxchilán. You could conceivably stay the night near either of these ruins (see pages 664 and 668), then tour them the next day, but an early start is still essential, to be sure taxis are still running from where the bus will drop you on the highway.

ACCOMMODATION — FRONTIER HIGHWAY

Ara Macao Las Guacamayas Ejido Reforma Agraria, north off the highway 20km east of Flor de Café; http://lasguacamayas.org.mx. This remote ecotourism operation is run by the village of Ejido Reforma Agraria. Tidy cabins (ranging from basic huts to comfortable en suites), a restaurant and a camping area are set amid chicken runs and pastures, against a dense wall of jungle that teems with wildlife, including endangered red macaws; guides can lead you on kayak trips down the Río Lacantún, or on nature hikes. Double M$$; camping M$

Ocosingo and around

With its streets lined with single-storey, red-tiled houses and the air thick with the scent of wood smoke, this mountain town midway between San Cristóbal and Palenque makes a good place to escape the tourist crowds. Like the other villages winding up Hwy-186 to their mountain perches, **OCOSINGO** has stayed close to its rural roots, with farmers in cowboy hats in from their ranches and local women selling *maíz* from great bubbling vats. Central to town life is the **plaza**, surrounded by *portales*, a big old country church on the east side and the modern *ayuntamiento* opposite. Ocosingo is historically something of a flash point for civil unrest in Mexico and there are often outpourings of this in the surrounding area, particularly on the road between the town and Palenque. It is important to check the latest security situation before travelling here.

11

ARRIVAL AND DEPARTURE — OCOSINGO

By bus At the time of writing, there were no buses to/from Ocosingo because of unrest in the surrounding area.

By combi *Combis* still stop on the main road, near the ADO/OCC terminal. Services down the road to Palenque or San Cristóbal end around 7.30pm.

By car Because of the ongoing unrest, we do not advise driving to Ocosingo.

ACCOMMODATION

Central Av Central at C Central, north side of plaza; 919 673 0024. The neat-and-tidy rooms at Central are nicely furnished, with tiled floors and clean bathrooms. All have optional a/c for an additional charge; the upper rooms are the best bets, as they come with fans as well. M$$

EATING

In the **market**, traditionally dressed Indigenous women sell fruit and vegetables and locally produced cheeses, including the round and waxy *queso de bola* and the creamy and delicious *queso botanero*. To get there turn right at the church for one block, then left along C 2 Sur Ote for another four. Several other budget **places to eat** are on the square.

El Desván South side of the plaza; 919 673 0117. This low-key joint serves simple but good Mexican fare, as well as pizzas. The upstairs terrace is a great perch for welcome breezes and people-watching from the late afternoon onwards. M$$$

Restaurante y Cafe Espresso Av Central Ote 23, just across from the plaza; 919 673 0930. This place has pavement tables and a menu in English. The Mexican favourites (such as chicken in *mole*) aren't the same quality as in bigger towns, but the coffees are good and the prices fair. M$$

DIRECTORY

Banks and exchange There are a couple of ATMs, one at Banamex on the plaza, and another at Banco Santander opposite *Hospedaje Esmeralda* on C Central Nte.

Internet Cyber cafés include Compu Centro, near the plaza on C Central Nte.

Toniná

14km east of Ocosingo • **Museum and ruins** Charge • *Combis* marked "Predio/Ruinas" leave from the market area

This Classic-period Maya site is large and impressive, especially for its massive, seven-layered central complex. Yet, as most people are rushing on to Palenque or San Cristóbal, it sees few visitors. At its height, **Toniná** was a great regional power: the city defeated Palenque and captured its ruler in 699 AD, and from then until after 900 AD, when it became the last of the great Maya centres to fall victim to whatever disaster led to them all being abandoned, it was probably the greatest power in the Usumacinta basin. It's also the place where the latest **Long Count date**, corresponding to 909 AD, was recorded, and, like all the major Maya centres, it was abandoned not long after.

The museum

At the site entrance is a good **museum**, with a helpful model of the site, as well as drawings of some of the relief carvings still in place in the buildings. It also displays some of the more fragile sculptures from the site, many of which are images of bound prisoners and of decapitation – a bit unnerving when packed together in the gallery space.

The ruins

The **ruins** themselves, a five-minute walk from the entrance (passing a small café selling locally grown macadamia nuts and coffee), are virtually all one enormous building, the **Acrópolis**, a series of seven artificial terraces built into the hillside and incorporating dozens of temples and other buildings. This is the "house of stone" that gave the site its Tzeltal name. A torch is useful to explore the labyrinthine interiors and internal staircases.

Of the remaining stucco reliefs, the finest is the enormous (16m x 4m) **Mural de las Cuatro Eras**, on the sixth platform. This remarkably well-preserved stucco codex tells the story of Maya cosmology by following the eras of the world as they were created and destroyed. The worlds are depicted as decapitated heads surrounded by flowers. A grinning, skeletal Lord of Death presents a particularly graphic image as he grasps a skinned human head. At the summit is the **Templo del Espejo Humeante** (Temple of the Smoking Mirror), built around 840 AD, and a great vantage point across the valley.

Laguna Miramar

A much more remote excursion from Ocosingo is this pristine lake in the heart of the Lacandón forest. It's part of the enchanting **Montes Azules Biosphere Reserve**, the largest surviving area of rainforest in North America. The high-canopy forest is home to abundant wildlife, including howler and spider monkeys, tapirs and jaguars, and there are rivers and caves to explore. An island in the lake has traces of a fortress, a Maya stronghold until it was finally conquered in 1559. It's best to avoid the rainy season (June–Oct).

When you arrive in Emiliano Zapata, the *ejido* near the lake's western edge that manages ecotourism here, ask for the *comisario* or *presidente*. Either will be able to organize practicalities, charged per day: expect to pay for a guide and the use of canoe. From the village, it's a 9km hike to the lake. There's an additional charge per person to camp or sleep in hammocks in lakeside palapas. There are a few shops and simple cafeterías in San Quintín, but supplies in Emiliano Zapata are limited, so it's best to bring your own food.

ARRIVAL AND DEPARTURE — LAGUNA MIRAMAR

You can visit Miramar on your own or on an organized tour (see page 658). To travel independently takes some time and effort.

BY PLANE

Servicios Aéreos de San Cristóbal (963 632 4662) makes the trip from Ocosingo, Comitán or Palenque in a light plane, with room for four to five people. If you can't fill a plane, it's still worth contacting the airline as they may be able to add you to another group and/or fly one way.

BY TRUCK AND COMBI

Most transport stops at the town (and army base) of San Quintín; from there, you need to catch a lift or walk the 2km to Emiliano Zapata.

From Ocosingo Trucks known as *tres toneladas* leave from behind the market on 3a C Sur Ote (9am–noon), running to San Quintín, the town/army base on the highway, 2km from Emiliano Zapata. It's a bone-rattling 6–7hr to cover 130km.

From Comitán First take a frequent *combi* to the small town of Las Margaritas, 16km northwest, then pick up a truck to San Quintín, about 3–4hr away. This route passes through La Realidad, a celebrated Zapatista stronghold, and may lead to extra hassle at military checkpoints in the area – check with the Comitán tourist office before trying this.

BY BOAT

A far more exciting alternative is to come by river from the village of Amatitlán, about 15km due south of the lake. Here you can arrange a boat (3hr) to take you up the winding Río Jataté to Emiliano Zapata, where you may be asked to pay another "entrance" fee, per boat. To get to Amatitlán from Comitán, take a Transportes Tzobol *combi* (roughly 4am–2pm); the terminal is 3km south of the centre on 4a Av Pte Sur, near 13a C Sur Pte.

Palenque and around

Set in thick jungle buzzing with insects, the ancient Maya **ruins of Palenque** are one of Mexico's finest Maya sites: less crowded than Chichén Itzá, larger than Uxmal, and with the most spectacular setting. It is a relatively small site – you can see everything in a morning – but a fascinating one, strongly linked to the lost cities of Guatemala while displaying a distinctive style.

Nine kilometres east of the ruins, the rather helter-skelter **town of Palenque** functions as the base for exploring the ruins and the waterfalls in the nearby hills. With every facility a visitor might need, it's lively enough, but it has no real intrinsic appeal. As there are a number of excellent campsites, cabañas and hotels near the ruins, you may prefer not to stay in town at all.

11

ARRIVAL AND INFORMATION — PALENQUE AND AROUND

BY PLANE

Palenque's small airport (916 345 1692) is 5km northwest of town. The taxi fee to/from town is open to negotiation. Flight operators and schedules vary without warning, so be sure to call ahead. The airport in Villahermosa (see page 673), 150km away, has a much better range of connections; ADO runs hourly buses from Villahermosa airport to Palenque.

BY BUS

Travelling on any long-distance bus (except for Lagos de Montebello vehicles), you'll arrive in Palenque town at one

TOURS AROUND PALENQUE

Touts offer a huge variety of **tours** to local attractions in the vicinity of Palenque, above all the waterfalls at Agua Azul and Misol-Há and the ruins of Bonampak and Yaxchilán. There are also trips to Tikal in Guatemala or to Toniná, and adventure tours, including kayaking and horseriding. Prices vary according to season (and even time of day, if there's one seat left to fill) and what you visit; popular itineraries include the waterfalls, and day trips to Bonampak and Yaxchilán. Be sure to check what's included – entrance fees, meals and English-speaking guides most importantly. One of the more reliable agents is Viajes Na Chan Kan (916 345 2154, chiapastour@hotmail.com or viajes.nachankan@hotmail.com), on Hidalgo at Jiménez; most hotels can also arrange tours.

of two nearby terminals in the west of the town, just off the main highway. Both stations have lockers if you want to leave your stuff while you head for the ruins. At the time of writing, there were some security issues in the region around Palenque, notably on the road to Ocosingo (see page 655): ask around for the latest and, to be on the safe side, aim to travel during the day, rather than at night.

First class The first-class ADO/OCC terminal is near the traffic circle at the intersection of Juárez and Pakalna. It's worth buying your onward ticket as soon as you know when you're leaving, because buses, particularly the first-class services, often run full.

Destinations Campeche (5 daily; 5hr 15min–5hr 50min); Cancún (4 daily at 6pm, 9.10pm, 9.45pm & 11.40pm; around 13hr); Emiliano Zapata (4 daily at 8am, 6pm, 8.45pm & 9.45pm; 50min), for Tenosique and Guatemala; Mérida (5 daily; 7hr 40min–8hr 40min); Mexico City (1 daily at 6.30pm; 14hr 50min); Oaxaca (1 daily at 5.30pm; 16hr); San Cristóbal (8 daily; 8–9hr); Tuxtla Gutiérrez (8 daily; 7hr–7hr 30min); Villahermosa (roughly hourly; around 2hr 30min); Villahermosa airport (roughly hourly; 2hr 10min).

Second class Auto Cardeso, Expreso Azul and others run to Cancún, Tuxtla and Villahermosa from a terminal on Juárez, a short walk from the ADO terminal. For closer destinations, Transportes Comitán Lagos de Montebello, on Velasco Suárez, just past the market, and Transportes Río Chancalá, on 5 de Mayo, run along the Frontier Highway, beginning at 3.40am. All go to Bonampak (3hr) and the turn-off (*crucero*) for Frontera Corozal (for Yaxchilán; 3hr 30min). Montebello's early-morning departures continue all the way to Comitán via Benemérito and the Lagos de Montebello. Transportes de Chamoán, on the west side of the traffic circle by the statue of the Maya head, runs regular minivans to Frontera itself; these cost a bit more, but you don't have to pay for a taxi into town.

Tourist office In the Plaza de Artesanías on Juárez at the corner of Abasolo, a block below the main plaza (Mon–Sat 9am–8pm, Sun 9am–1pm; 916 345 0356). The staff are very friendly, but the information they provide isn't always accurate. There's also a booth on the east side of the plaza (same hours). You'll generally get better information from local tour operators or at your hotel.

GETTING AROUND

By taxi/combi A taxi from the ADO/OCC bus station to the hotels on the road to the ruins should be a flat fee, but during daylight hours, it's just as easy to flag down one of the many *combis* headed for the ruins (see page 663). In town, taxis wait on the northeast corner of the plaza. They run to Agua Azul, Bonampak, Frontera, Ocosingo, Palenque ruins and around town (you can negotiate for them to wait for you while you look around).

ACCOMMODATION

Palenque has plenty of hotels on the rather noisy streets leading from the bus stations to the plaza, especially Hidalgo and 20 de Noviembre. A quieter option is the pleasant area called **La Cañada**, named for the ravine that divides it from the town centre. With brick-paved streets and soft lighting, it feels a little like a chic subdivision. It's set in a swathe of trees (the many birds and monkeys can make quite a racket) and is only a short walk from the action. Most hotels here are more upmarket, but there's one very good budget option. High season in the Palenque area is Mexican vacation periods – July, Aug, Christmas and Semana Santa; outside that time, rates can drop significantly.

IN TOWN, SEE MAP PAGE 657

Hotel Canek 20 de Noviembre 43; 916 690 5279. *Hotel Canek* is good value, and the friendly staff look after solo travellers like family. Dorm beds can be rented singly in peak times, and double rooms are huge, especially the third-floor "penthouse" with a grand view. Some have a/c, are en suite and have a street-side balcony. Meals, luggage storage and tours all available. M$

Maya Rue C Aldama, between Juárez and 5 de Mayo; 916 345 0743. The sharpest option in central Palenque: a standard urban low-rise hotel, done up with modern furnishings and oversize photographs of old Mexico. The lobby doubles as a chic coffee shop. The style compensates for the small a/c rooms and the lack of a pool or private parking. M$$

LA CAÑADA, SEE MAP PAGE 657

Casa Janaab Palenque 2a Avenida Nte; www.casajanaab.com. Welcoming hostel with ample communal areas: a nice kitchen, games, TV, and a restaurant. Accommodation includes dorms, and doubles/twins with shared or private bathrooms. Dorms M$; Doubles M$$

Hotel Maya Tulipanes Cañada 6; http://mayatulipanes.com. A solid mid-range choice, *Hotel Maya Tulipanes* has comfortable and spacious en suites with tiled floors and plenty of space, as well as an outdoor pool, a restaurant and even a karaoke bar. M$$$

Xibalba Merle Green at Hidalgo; 916 103 1482. Pretty, white rooms are accented with green and brown, giving a vaguely natural feel, even if they're not very large. Staff are friendly, and there's a restaurant, roof terrace and helpful travel agency. The only off note is the occasional waft of diesel from the Pemex station across the ravine. M$$

OUTSIDE TOWN

For more isolation, opt for the places lining the road to the ruins or south of the town, covering every category from luxury hotel to campsite – though the latter are becoming fewer.

Chan Kah Village Resort 3km west of town, on the left; http://chan-kah.com.mx. This tranquil resort, built in a patch of jungle either side of the Río Michol, has some 90 rooms and cabins (all are large, fully fitted and well spaced). The highlight is undoubtedly the stunning *cenote*-inspired swimming pool, which is shaded by coconut palms. There's also a breezy restaurant-bar on a terrace overlooking the pool, games room, and a spa. M$$$

Margarita and Ed's El Panchán, 5.1km west of town on the left, just before the park entrance; http://margaritaandedcabanas.blogspot.mx. Located in a large swathe of forested land known as El Panchán, which contains a number of separate lodging operations, divided by screens of trees and sharing a couple of restaurants and other facilities, *Margarita and Ed's* is the best of the bunch, with thatched cabins or conventional double rooms with a/c. M$

Mayabell 6km west of town and inside the park, just before the museum; http://mayabell.mx. A favourite with backpackers and adventure-tour groups, this camping spot and trailer park has something for everyone: palapa shelters for hammocks, vehicle pads with electricity and water, and very comfortable private cabañas with hot water. The shared showers have hot water, and there's also a *temazcal* (traditional sweat lodge), spa, laundry and decent freshwater swimming pool (with occasional fish), plus frequent live music in the restaurant. M$

★ **Quinta Chanabnal** 2.2km west of town, on the right; http://quintachanabnal.com. A stunning luxury hotel with vast, ochre-toned rooms – all suites – furnished in purpose-built hardwood furniture and antique Guatemalan fabrics in a fusion of European, Far Eastern and Mexican styles. The Italian owner is an expert in Maya iconography, and modern Maya glyphs throughout the complex tell his story and that of the hotel. There's a pool, a restaurant and a small lake alive with birdlife. It's great value for the quality. M$$$$

Winíka Alterra 5km southeast of town, on the road to the Agua Azul waterfall; http://winika.mx. This lodge has a vaguely back-to-nature vibe, with nicely furnished cottages, well-tended grounds, an infinity pool, and restaurant-bar. The main drawback is the location – it's only really suitable if you have your own vehicle. M$$$

EATING

Food in Palenque town is fairly basic, and most restaurants serve up similar dishes, often just pasta and pizza, to customers who've really only come for the ruins. There are also several places along the road to the site – some of which cater mainly to tour groups – including a couple in *El Panchán*. In town, bargains can be found among the set menus posted on boards outside most restaurants. **Av Juárez** also has several budget options between the bus stations and the plaza, while **Hidalgo** has more Mexican-style food. The restaurants in the La Cañada hotels are well worth a look.

IN TOWN, SEE MAP PAGE 657

★ **Café de Yara** Hidalgo 66, at Abasolo; 916 345 0269. Charming café delivering proper coffee (hot, cold and alcoholic varieties are available), various breakfast options, and good-value set meals. In high season, there's often live music on Fri and Sat evenings. M$$

Tropitacos Juárez 49, between Allende and Abasolo; 916 345 0204. This fast food-style joint, with two branches, diagonally opposite each other, delivers the goods at economical prices. Stick to the Mexican dishes: the tacos are the highlights, though there are also some hearty main meals. M$$

LA CAÑADA, SEE MAP PAGE 657

Cafe Jade Hidalgo 1; http://facebook.com/cafejadechiapas. Part of *Hostal Yaxkin* (see page 659), this all-day venue is a popular spot, despite the slightly steep prices. The menu boasts breakfast options, salads, pasta dishes and burgers, as well as good coffee and cakes. M$$

★ **El Huachinango Felíz** Merle Green, at Hidalgo; 916 129 8231. A split-level restaurant in La Cañada that serves great fish and shrimp baked in banana leaves, among other seafood. Prices are reasonable, portions are generous and the setting is pretty and quiet – a nice break from restaurants in town. Good cocktails too. M$$

Maya Cañada Merle Green, at Hidalgo; 916 345 0780. Smarter than average restaurant in a peaceful La Cañada location: the selection of regional specialities and the fresh fish dishes are well worth a try. M$$$

ON THE ROAD TO THE RUINS

Don Mucho El Panchán, 5.1km from town; 916 112 8338. The social centre of *El Panchán*, serving tasty Mexican and Italian food in the evening, with live music nightly from 8pm. Great for breakfast or a leisurely lunch after visiting the ruins, though it can be a victim of its own success – so packed with tour groups that it can be hard to find a table. Happy hour daily. M$$

DIRECTORY

Banks and exchange Several banks along Juárez have ATMs. There's also an ATM at the ADO/OCC terminal.

Internet Most hotels here have computers for guests and wi-fi, and internet cafés are plentiful.

Laundry Several in town, including La Gota Azul, on Independencia between 20 de Noviembre and Corregidora.

Post office On Independencia, a block from the plaza.

11

The ruins of Palenque

9km west of Palenque town • Last entry 4.30pm • Ruins charge, with tickets also sold at museum after 9am; additional one-off national park entry fee for an additional charge; guides extra (for groups of up to 7; prices negotiable)

The ruins of Palenque are located in the **Parque Nacional de Palenque**, the border of which is just after *El Panchán*. The main road first passes a well-stocked artesanía shop, a café and the site museum. You can enter at the gate across the road, hiking up to the main part of the site via the waterfalls trail, but most people will press on to the main site entrance, at the top of the hill another 2km up a winding road. Near this main entrance, there's a small café and numerous souvenir stalls selling drinks, as well as toilets and some expensive lockers.

The ruins themselves bear a closer resemblance to the Maya sites of Guatemala than to those of the Yucatán, but ultimately the style here is unique – the **towered palace** and **pyramid tomb** are like nothing else, as is the abundance of reliefs and inscriptions. The setting, too, is remarkable. Surrounded by jungle-covered hills, Palenque is right at the edge of the great Yucatán plain – climb to the top of any of the structures and you look out over an endless stretch of low, pale-green flatland. If you arrive early enough in the day, the mist still clings to the treetops and the howler monkeys are roaring off in the greenery.

Brief history

Founded around 100 BC as a farming village, it was four hundred years before Palenque began to flourish, during the Classic period (300–900 AD). Towards the end of this time the city ruled over a large part of modern-day Chiapas and Tabasco, but its peak, when the population is thought to have numbered some one hundred thousand, came during a relatively short period in the seventh century, under two rulers: **Hanab Pakal** (**Jaguar Shield**) and **Chan Bahlum** (**Jaguar Serpent**). Almost everything you can see (and that's only a tiny, central part of the original city) dates from this era.

The museum

Palenque's excellent **museum**, on the road 1.5km from the site entrance, will give you a good idea of the scale of Palenque, and a look at some of its treasures. Many of the glyphs and carved relief panels found at the site are on display, as are examples of the giant ceramic incense-burners in the form of gods or mythological creatures. An intricate model of El Palacio reveals how it would have appeared in the Classic period – with the tops of the buildings adorned with roof combs.

The back wing is devoted to a replica of Pakal's sarcophagus lid from the Templo de las Inscripciones – entrance is restricted to small groups, every half hour or so. One of the most renowned iconographic monuments in the Maya world, the engraved sarcophagus lid depicts Pakal at the moment of his death, falling into Xibalba, the underworld, symbolized by a monster's jaws. Above the dead king rises the **Wakah Kan** – the World Tree and the centre of the universe – with **Itzam-Yé**, the Celestial Bird, perched on top representing the heavens. So that the deified king buried here should not be cut off from the world of the living, a psychoduct – a hollow tube in the form of a snake – runs up the side of the staircase, from the tomb to the temple.

Site entrance

As you enter the site, **El Palacio**, with its extraordinary watchtower, stands ahead of you. The path, however, leads to the right, past a row of smaller structures – one of them, the so-called **Tumba de la Reina Roja** ("Tomb of the Red Queen"), is open inside, and you can climb in to see a sarcophagus still in place.

Templo de las Inscripciones

The enormous **Templo de las Inscripciones** is an eight-step pyramid, 26m high, built up against a thickly overgrown hillside. You are not permitted to climb the pyramid, so you have to imagine the sanctuary on top, filled with stone panels carved with

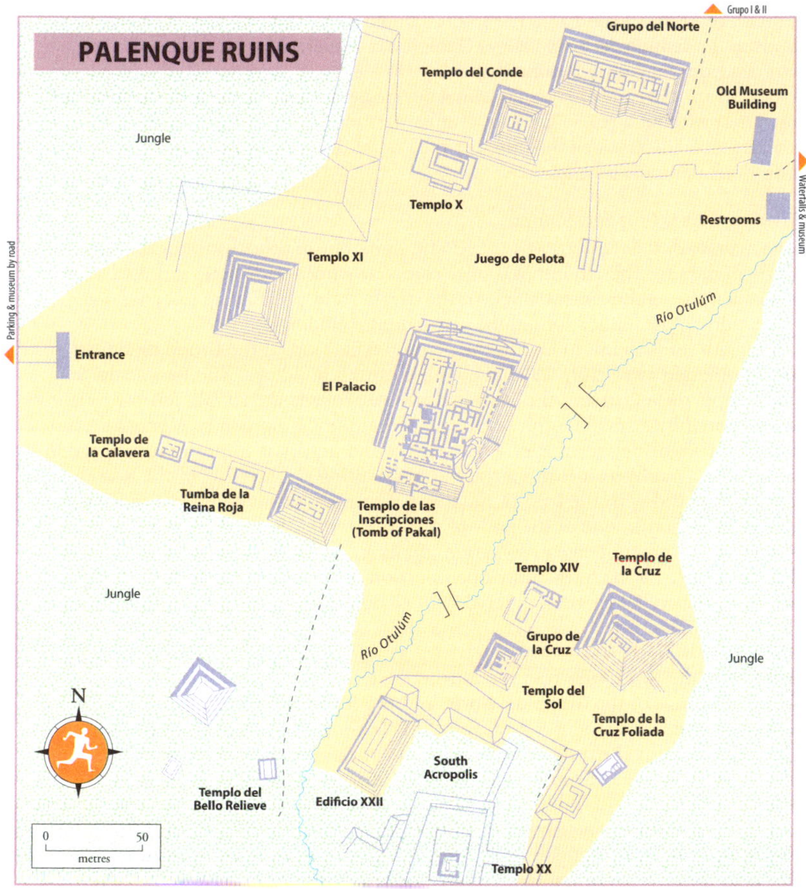

hieroglyphic inscriptions relating to Palenque's dynastic history. Deep inside the pyramid is the **tomb of Hanab Pakal**, or Pakal the Great (615–683 AD). Discovered in 1952, this was the first such pyramid burial found in the Americas, and is still the most important.

In 2015 a Mexican archeologist deciphered a hieroglyphic on the tomb as "The House of the Nine Sharpened Spears". Some of the smaller objects found – the skeleton and the jade death mask – are on display at the Museo Nacional de Antropología in Mexico City (see page 97), but the massive, intricately carved stone **sarcophagus** is still inside; a reproduction is in the site museum (see above).

El Palacio and around

The centrepiece of the site, **El Palacio**, is in fact a complex of buildings constructed at different times to form a rambling administrative and residential block. Its square **tower** is unique, and no one knows exactly what its purpose was – perhaps a lookout post or an astronomical observatory. Throughout you'll find delicately executed **relief carvings**, the most remarkable of which are the giant human figures on stone panels in the grassy courtyard, depicting rulers of defeated cities in poses of humiliation. An arcade overlooking the courtyard held a portrait gallery of Palenque's rulers, though many of these have been removed.

South of El Palacio and adjacent to the Templo de las Inscripciones, a small path leads to the **Templo del Bello Relieve** (**Templo del Jaguar**). More temples are being wrested from the jungle beyond, but the paths are closed, and though the path leads eventually to the *ejido* of Naranjo, you won't be permitted to pass much further into the forest without a guide. Even so, clambering around here, it's easy to believe you're walking over unexcavated buildings, as the ground is very rocky and some of the stones don't look naturally formed.

The Grupo de la Cruz and around

The main path then leads across the Río Otulúm, one of several streams that cascade through the site. The Otulúm was once completely lined with stone and used as an aqueduct; the reinforcement also kept the stream from overflowing its banks and undermining the foundations of the surrounding buildings.

The path leads uphill to end in the plaza of what's called the **Grupo de la Cruz**, oddly oriented away from Palenque's more central buildings. The **Templo del Sol**, the **Templo de la Cruz** and the **Templo de la Cruz Foliada** are all tall, narrow pyramids surmounted by a small temple with an elaborate stone roofcomb. All contain carved panels representing sacred rites – the cross found here is as important an image in Maya iconography as it is in Christian, representing the meeting of the heavens and the underworld with the land of the living. On the right-hand side of the Templo de la Cruz, God L, one of the gods of the underworld, is depicted smoking tobacco – the oldest known image of someone smoking. A small path next to the Templo de la Cruz Foliada leads to the only open portion of the South Acropolis, a building with a replica relief carving, covered with elaborate glyphs and a triumphant king.

The Grupo del Norte and around

Following the Río Otulúm to the northern edge of the cleared site, you reach the lesser buildings of the **Grupo del Norte** and the **Juego de Pelota** (ball-court), on lower ground across a grassy area from El Palacio. Beyond them, two **paths** lead downhill towards the museum. One goes down some perilous stairs behind Grupo del Norte, leading to **Grupo I** and **Grupo II**, intricate complexes of interconnected rooms. The other path follows the stream as it cascades through the forest and flows over beautiful limestone curtains and terraces into a series of gorgeous pools (no swimming allowed, though). The paths join again just after a suspension bridge crossing the river; eventually the route emerges on the main road opposite the museum. If you don't want to exit here, and want to make a loop, it's best to go down via Grupo I and II – the steeper route – then make your way back up by the other, somewhat easier, trail.

ARRIVAL AND DEPARTURE — RUINS OF PALENQUE

By combi Two *combi* services, Transportes Chambalú and Transportes Pakal, run frequently (at least every 15min, 6am–6pm) from their terminals near Juárez in town, and will stop anywhere along the road to the ruins – also useful if you're staying at one of the hotels or campsites near the ruins. After 6pm, you'll either have to walk or take a taxi.

By car There's very limited parking space at the main entrance at the top of the hill. Even if you have your own car, you may still prefer to take a *combi*, as this enables you to exit on the downhill side of the site by the museum, and spare yourself having to hike back up to your vehicle.

Misol-Há

18km from Palenque • Charge • Second-class buses between Ocosingo and Palenque stop at the turn on request; it's a 10min walk to the falls

These smaller falls along the road to Ocosingo are a much easier day trip from Palenque than Agua Azul (see page 658) if travelling by public transport, and in many ways they're far more pleasant, with none of the slapdash development present at its celebrated neighbour. A 25m waterfall provides a stunning backdrop to a pool that's safe for swimming, and a fern-lined trail leads along a ledge behind the cascade – refreshing from the spray and mist even if you don't go for a dip. It's an easy 1.5km walk downhill from the road.

Organized tours often combine a visit here with Agua Azul (the bigger attraction) and Agua Clara. These latter falls are even less visited than **Misol-Há**, but aren't remarkable enough to merit a trip on your own, so we don't include them here. Also consider Welib-Ja, on the Frontier Highway (see page 664).

ACCOMMODATION AND EATING — MISOL-HÁ

Misol-Há Cabañas http://misol-ha.com. The good-value accommodation here is a pleasant way to break up the journey if you're coming from Ocosingo by car, or if you just want to relax in the woods. Each beautiful wooden cabaña has a private bathroom and electricity, and some also have kitchens. Advance reservations are recommended, especially during Mexican holidays. M$$

Restaurante Misol-Ha At Misol-Há waterfalls; http://misol-ha.com. Though it's often catering to large tour groups, this place nonetheless cranks out decent local cuisine. The freshwater-fish *empapeladas*, baked in foil, are winners, with lime, tomatoes, onions, rice and handmade tortillas. M$$

Agua Azul

Midway between Ocosingo and Palenque, 4km north from the main road • Charge • *Combis* between Ocosingo and Palenque stop at the turn on request; it's a 45min walk down to the falls, or a short taxi ride, if one's waiting

These impressive waterfalls are worth a visit, though as a popular stop-off on the day-trip circuit, they are sometimes inundated with tourists. The main cascades lie near the car park, with several smaller but equally appealing rapids stretching for 1km up the river. The whole area is certainly picturesque, though the river near the lower falls is lined with rows of souvenir stalls and snack vendors. You could ask for lodging at the Module de Información near the car park but the cabins at **Agua Azul** are not as nice as the ones at Misol-Há (see page 663). Adjust your expectations accordingly, and it still makes for a pleasant trip.

If it's safe to walk upstream (it may not be in the rainy season), you'll come across a perilous-looking bridge over the river and eventually reach an impressive gorge where the **Río Shumulhá** explodes out of the jungle-covered mountain. At the right time of year, the river is alive with butterflies. Swimming isn't advisable: people drown here every year, and though a few signs warn of **dangerous currents**, they don't begin to mark all the perilous spots. Although you may want to get as far from the tourist scrum as possible, keep in mind that violent attacks have occurred here in the past (allegedly due to village rivalries over tourism operations). A heavy federal police guard has proved a deterrent, but you're always safer with other people nearby.

The Usumacinta valley and the Frontier Highway

The Carretera Fronteriza (**Frontier Highway**) heads south from Palenque into the Lacandón forest and the Río Usumacinta, passing the two great Maya sites of **Bonampak** and **Yaxchilán**. The remote highway, which was paved only in 2000, to help delineate the border with Guatemala, has a reputation as a dangerous place. Although tourist convoys are no longer required, it's still not advisable to drive the road after dark: there is a risk of robbery, a lot of wildlife, and few people to help you if you break down, have an accident or encounter any trouble. Army checkpoints are common, so make sure you have your passport. If you don't visit with a group, try to pick up an information sheet on the Lacandón community from **Casa Na-Bolom** in San Cristóbal (see page 642). For a description of the road past Benemérito, see page 654.

GETTING AROUND — THE USUMACINTA VALLEY

By organized tour The easiest option, arranged in Palenque (see page 658). Day- or overnight-trips are options – if you stay overnight, it will be with accommodation at the Lacandón Maya community of Lacanjá Chansayab. Going with a group guarantees a place to stay and meals, both of which are harder to arrange independently.

By combi Travelling on your own, with a *combi* from Palenque, is possible, but it's tricky to visit both sites in one day. But you do benefit from arriving at the remote sites relatively alone, and it's substantially cheaper, although the final cost will depend on finding people to share the boat from the settlement of Frontera Corozal to Yaxchilán.

By car There is a Pemex station at Chancalá, where the Frontier Highway meets Hwy-353, and another in Benemérito, past Yaxchilán.

To Guatemala You can get a boat a short distance upstream from Frontera Corozal to Bethél across the border (see page 629).

Welib-Ja

30km southeast of Palenque, on the Frontier Highway • Charge • All Frontier Highway *combis* (see page 654) pass here – ask to be let off at the cascadas; start looking for a ride back by 4.30pm or so – flag down standard *combi* vans as well as pick-up trucks

These beautiful waterfalls see fewer visitors than Agua Azul or Misol-Há, and because they're only 500m from the road they're also easier to reach by public transport. A forest path leads alongside the river and down to the base of a towering split cascade, close enough for the mist to spray over you. There are a few palapas for picnicking in the shade, as well as a protected kids' swimming area, upstream from the falls.

ACCOMMODATION — WELIB-JA

A few breeze-block rooms, managed by the local *ejido*, are available for overnight stays. There's no phone, but usually two or three staff members present. They have very basic rooms with shared toilets (you can pay extra for en suite); the price includes access to the waterfalls. Note that walls separating rooms do not reach all the way to the top of the pitched palapa roof, making "private" a relative term.

Bonampak

Just outside the Montes Azules Biosphere Reserve, 2.5km from Lacanjá Chansayab village • Charge for the INAH, with an additional fee for the local community

Relatively small compared with other ruined Maya cities, **Bonampak** is unique due to its fascinating **murals**, evocative memorials to a lost civilization. Bonampak's actual buildings, most from the eighth century, are small and not the most spectacular, but the murals definitely make it worth the visit – there is very little like them elsewhere in the Maya world, and even in their decayed state, the colours are vivid and the imagery memorable.

THE LACANDÓN

You may already have encountered the impressively wild-looking **Lacandón Maya**, dressed in simple white robes and selling exquisite (and apparently effective) bows and arrows at Palenque. Until recently, they were the most isolated of all the Indigenous groups. The ancestors of today's Lacandón are believed to have migrated to Chiapas from the Petén region of Guatemala during the eighteenth century. Prior to that the Spanish had enslaved, killed or relocated the original inhabitants of the forest.

The Lacandón refer to themselves as "Hach Winik" (true people). Appearances notwithstanding, some Lacandón families are (or have been) quite wealthy, having sold timber rights in the jungle, though most of the timber money has now gone. This change has led to a division in their society, and most live in one of two main communities: **Lacanjá Chansayab**, near Bonampak, a village predominantly made up of evangelical Protestants, some of whom are keenly developing low-impact tourist facilities (see page 666); and **Nahá**, where a small group still attempts to live a traditional life, and where it is possible to arrange stays in local homes. The best source of information on the Lacandón in Chiapas is Casa Na-Bolom in San Cristóbal de las Casas (see page 642), where you can find a manuscript of *Last Lords of Palenque*, by Victor Perera and Robert Bruce. *Hach Winik*, by Didier Boremanse, is an excellent recent study of Lacandón life and history.

Bonampak lies in the small biosphere reserve controlled by the Lacandón on the fringe of the much larger Montes Azules Biosphere Reserve. The site is quite isolated, and the only facilities are toilets and a couple of huts selling crisps and carved-wood souvenirs. The nearest settlement is the village of Lacanjá Chansayab, about 2.5km away – basic cabañas, rented by the Lacandón people, are available here (see page 665).

Brief history

The outside world first heard of Bonampak, meaning "painted walls", in 1946, when Charles Frey, an American who'd dodged the draft by heading to the Mexican forest during World War II, was shown the site (but apparently not the murals) by the Lacandón who still worshipped at the ancient temples. The first non-Maya actually to see these murals – astonishing examples of Classic Maya art – was the American photographer Giles Healey, who arrived shortly after Frey's visit, sparking a long and bitter dispute over exactly who was responsible for their discovery.

La Gran Plaza

After crossing an airstrip, you are at the northwest corner of the central plaza, 110m long and bounded by low walls that mark the edges of a former palace. In the centre of the plaza **Stele 1** shows a larger-than-life **Chaan Muan II**, the last king of Bonampak, dressed for battle – at 6m, it is one of the tallest steles in the Maya world. You'll encounter other images of him throughout the site.

The Acrópolis

Ahead of the Gran Plaza, atop several steep flights of steps, lies the **Acrópolis**. On the lower steps, more well-preserved steles show Chaan Muan with his wife, Lady Rabbit, preparing himself for blood-letting and apparently about to sacrifice a prisoner. From the highest point of the acropolis there's an impressive sense that you're surrounded by primeval forest – the Selva Lacandona – with just a small cleared space in front of you.

Edificio de las Pinturas

The highlight is the modest-looking **Edificio de las Pinturas**, halfway up the steps of the acropolis. Inside, in three separate chambers and on the temple walls and roof, the **Bonampak murals** depict vivid scenes of haughty Maya lords, splendidly attired in jaguar-skin robes and quetzal-plume headdresses, and equally well-dressed ladies; and bound prisoners, one with his fingernails ripped out, spurting blood. Dating to around 790 AD, these paintings show the Bonampak elite at the height of their power: unknown to them, the collapse of the Classic Maya civilization was imminent. Some details were never finished, and Bonampak was abandoned shortly after the scenes were painted.

Though you can't enter the rooms fully, the vantage point inside the doorway is more than adequate to absorb what's inside. No more than three people are permitted to enter at any one time and queues are possible, but you shouldn't have to wait long. Having said that, time and early cleaning attempts have clearly taken their toll on the murals, and apart from a few beautifully restored sections, it takes some concentration and imagination to work out what you're looking at.

The murals

In **Room 1**, an infant wrapped in white cloth (the heir apparent?) is presented to assembled nobility under the supervision of the lord of Yaxchilán, while musicians play drums, pipes and trumpets in the background. **Room 2** contains a vivid, even gruesome, exhibition of power over Bonampak's enemies: tortured prisoners lie on temple steps, while above them lords in jaguar robes are indifferent to their agony. A severed head rolls down the stairs and Chaan Muan II grasps a prisoner (who appears to be pleading for mercy) by the hair – clearly about to deal him the same fate. **Room 3** shows the price paid for victory: Chaan Muan's wife, **Lady Rabbit**, prepares to prick her tongue to let blood fall onto a paper in a pot in front of her. The smoke from burning the blood-soaked paper will carry messages to ancestor-gods. Other gorgeously dressed figures, their senses probably heightened by hallucinogenic drugs, dance on the temple steps.

ARRIVAL AND ACTIVITIES — BONAMPAK

By combi and taxi Take a *combi* from Palenque to San Javier (about 3hr and 132km from Palenque) on the highway, where there's a large palapa on the right side of the road. Taxis are usually waiting to take you to the site-transport parking area, about 3km off the highway, or to the village of Lacanjá Chansayab. From the parking area you can access the ruins only in Lacandón-run *combi* vans. Alternatively, rent a bike to ride up to the ruins, though the business is set up another 250m past the parking area for the *combis*, and the *combi* drivers may tell you that the bikes don't exist. Note that private cars are not allowed into the Lacandón forest; you must park in the same area where taxis stop and board one of the Lacandón-run *combis*.

Hiking The cabañas operations in Lacanjá Chansayab can arrange guided walks in the forest. Top destinations are the Cascada Ya Toch Kusam, a glimmering waterfall, and the remote Lacanhá ruins. The hikes are great in the dry season (Jan to late April), but be prepared for mud at other times.

ACCOMMODATION AND EATING — LACANJÁ CHANSAYAB

Finding **accommodation** is easiest if you have a particular spot in mind – Lacanjá Chansayab is too spread out to walk around comparing options. The prices are all roughly the same – the differences come in the upkeep of the facilities. None of the ten or so operations has a phone, but there's little chance you'll wind up with nowhere to sleep.

Camping Margarito At the combi car park. The easiest, if not the best-kept, option for spending a night in the area, this place has a few simple cabins and room for tents, and also runs a restaurant with a simple menu of soups, stews and fried chicken (M$$). Prices are per person. Cabins M$

Cueva del Tejón On the road to Lacanjá Chansayab; cuevatejon@hotmail.com. The first place you reach en route to the village, after leaving the *combi* car park, is set by a broad section of the river. It has large concrete cabañas – with four beds in two rooms, bathrooms and power. M$

Río Lacanjá 1km beyond the village, at the end of the road to the left of the main junction; http://ecochiapas.com. By far the most organized place, but booking is essential through Explora in San Cristóbal (the number listed here). It has a big restaurant (serving stews, tamales, tacos, fajitas and the like) and a good range of rooms, from basic options with shared facilities to private cabañas with their own bathroom and riverside terrace. It also has a tiny waterfall and swimming hole, and a 45min jungle nature walk on a well-signed path (charge for non-guests). M$$$$

Tucan Verde On the road to Lacanjá Chansayab; http://tucanverde.com. The second place along the road between the car park and the village, Tucan Verde is run by a very sweet family. It offers riverside camping, but its cabins are, sadly, a bit dilapidated now. M$

Frontera Corozal

Fifteen kilometres beyond San Javier (the drop-off point for Bonampak) is the turn for the border village that's the gateway to **Yaxchilán**, one of the most enigmatic Maya ruins in Mexico. The ancient city can only be approached from the village by boat along the Río Usumacinta. There's not much in Frontera Corozal itself, but it is nonetheless more developed than Lacanjá Chansayab; staying here is more comfortable and a bit easier to organize, but doesn't offer the same cultural experience as the Lacandón settlement.

On the edge of town, a kiosk collects a "conservation fee" per person. While *combis* usually bypass the main road in to pass the unremarkable centre of the village (a couple of scrappy **plazas** and a market about 400m south from the main paved road and 300m back from the river), visitors' first destination is the *embarcadero* on the banks of the Usumacinta, where you catch the boats to Yaxchilán. There's a Mexican **immigration post** (for border procedures see page 31) 200m back along the main road coming in.

11

Community museum

Opposite the immigration post • Charge

Frontera Corozal's community **museum** showcases the history of the settlement, founded only in 1976, and the relationships between the Chol, Lacandón and Tzeltal people, local archeology (there are a few large steles) and flora and fauna. Its restaurant also has one of the few telephones in the village.

ARRIVAL AND DEPARTURE — FRONTERA COROZAL

By combi and taxi A few *combis* from Palenque go into the village, but the majority drop you on the highway at the turn-off to Frontera (the *crucero de Corozal*); it's marked by a *comedor* and shop selling basic supplies. From here you can pick up a taxi for for the ride 15km down the road to town.

TO GUATEMALA

Entering Guatemala from this small town is relatively easy, with plenty of *lanchas* between Frontera Corozal and Bethél, a boat ride away upstream (30min, plus any time spent waiting for the boat to fill up). There's a Mexican immigration post 200m back along the main road into Frontera: if you're crossing permanently to Guatemala, you should surrender your tourist card here; if you're coming back, hold on to it. Guatemalan immigration procedures can be completed in Bethél, from where buses normally depart for Flores (noon and 5pm; 5hr), mostly along dirt roads. The bus can, if you wish, be prearranged through travel agents in Palenque.

TOURS

Escudo Jaguar On the riverbank south of the boat dock; 00502 5353 5637 (Guatemala number). Arranges boat trips downstream from Yaxchilán to the impressive ruins of Piedras Negras on the Guatemalan bank (same day or overnight for one to five people). There are rapids above the site, meaning you may well have to get out and walk along the bank at times. It's a beautiful journey, though, and well worth making if you have the time.

Siyaj Chan 00502 5047 5908 (Guatemala number), http://siyajchan.blogspot.com. Leads hiking trips to Gruta Tzolkin, a cave deep in the forest (6hr).

ACCOMMODATION AND EATING

Corazón Lacandón en la Selva Main road into Frontera Corozal, 200m past turn for embarcadero, north side of street; 502 2448 2106 (Guatemala number). A palapa-roofed, open-air operation big enough to accommodate Yaxchilán tour groups, but still informal enough to have chickens pecking around the side yard. It serves commendable Mexican foods, such as tender *pollo en mole*, and cold beer. M$$

Escudo Jaguar On the riverbank south of the boat dock; 961 423 1788. The longest-established place in the area, with clean-enough concrete-block rooms and somewhat nicer cabañas arrayed in a compound just above the water. They're the top choice for every tour group and can fill up early. There's also a restaurant. Camping and doubles M$; cabañas M$$.

Nueva Alianza One block back from the river, north of

the boat dock; http://hotelnuevaalianza.org. Not as ideally situated as *Escudo Jaguar*, as it's bounded by private homes, and farther from the water, but it can be cheaper, with big group rooms in wood cabañas and camping space. Its private cabañas are better, and many are in an area kept intentionally dark at night. Cabañas M$$; camping M$

Yaxchilán

Guides through INAH office; only a few speak English; during July, Aug, Christmas and Easter, they wait at the site itself; guides and *lanchas* can also be arranged through the *Escudo Jaguar* hotel and tour operator Siyaj Chan (see page 667) • Charge for the INAH, additional fee for the local community; buy your ticket in Frontera Corozal, at the INAH office by the museum; guides cost extra • 961 612 2824

A larger and more dramatic site than Bonampak, **Yaxchilán** was an important Classic-period centre. From around 680 to 760 AD, the city's most famous kings, Escudo Jaguar (Shield Jaguar) and his son Pájaro Jaguar IV (Bird Jaguar), led a campaign of conquest that extended Yaxchilán's sphere of influence over the other Usumacinta centres and made possible alliances with Tikal and Palenque. The buildings occupy a natural terrace above the river, with others climbing steep hills behind – a superb natural setting.

Not so many people make the trip here, which involves a ride in a narrow *lancha* with a tin roof for shade, down the broad, fast-flowing river with Mexico on one bank, Guatemala on the other. At the site, it's easy to be alone in the forest with nothing but moaning howler monkeys around you. Giant trees keep the place shady, but nonetheless the jungle heat can be palpable – bring plenty of water, as there are no services at the ruins.

Pequeña Acrópolis

From the site entrance, the main path leads straight ahead to the Gran Plaza, but if you have the energy for climbing, it's more rewarding to explore the wilder parts of the site first. Follow the branching path to the right that leads up the hillside to the **Pequeña Acrópolis**, a set of thirteen buildings. A lintel on the most prominent ruin, known as **Edificio 42**, depicts Escudo Jaguar with one of his warriors.

Templos del Sur

Walk behind Edificio 42 to find another narrow trail down through the jungle, over several unrestored mounds, until you reach a fork: to the right, the path climbs steeply once again until it reaches, in about ten minutes, Edificios 39 to 41, also called the **Templos del Sur**, 90m above the river level – buildings that probably had some kind of astronomical significance. High above the main forest, this is also a good spot to look for canopy-dwelling birds like parrots, though the trees also obscure any view.

El Palacio

Retrace your steps back to the main path, and continue on until it emerges at the back of **Edificio 33**, the most famous building at the site, also known as **El Palacio**. It overlooks the main plaza from a high terrace. The lintels here are superbly preserved, and inside one of the portals is a headless statue of Pájaro Jaguar IV. In ancient times the building was a political court; more recently, it served as a religious site for the Lacandón Maya.

Gran Plaza

Descending 40m down the stairs in front of the Palacio brings you to the long **Gran Plaza**. Turn back to look up at the Palacio: with the sun shining through the building's roofcomb and tree roots cascading down the stairs, this is what you imagine a pyramid lost in the jungle should look like, especially if you've been brought up on Tintin.

To your left, just above the level of the plaza, **Edificio 23** has a few patches of coloured stucco around its doorframes – just one patch of many well-preserved paintings and relief carvings on the lintels of buildings surrounding the long green lawn. Some of the very best works were removed in the nineteenth century and are now in the British Museum in London, but the number and quality of the remaining panels are unequalled at any other Maya site in Mexico. Many of these depict rulers performing rituals.

This can also be seen on **Stele 1**, right in the middle of the plaza, near the base of the staircase. It depicts Pájaro Jaguar IV in a particularly eye-watering blood-letting ceremony, ritually perforating his penis. **Stele 3**, originally sited at Edificio 41, has survived several attempts to remove it from the site and now lies at the west side of the plaza, where it shows the transfer of power from Escudo Jaguar to Pájaro Jaguar IV.

El Laberinto

Heading back to the entrance, be sure to pass through **El Laberinto** (The Labyrinth) at the plaza's northeast corner, the most complex building on the site, where you can walk down through dim passages out onto the main path.

ARRIVAL AND DEPARTURE — YAXCHILÁN

By boat A number of companies offer services. Most are based at the *embarcadero* on the riverfront at Frontera Corozal, the easiest place to find other travellers to share a boat. Return fares vary with group size (30min, though the return leg can take up to 1hr). To allow enough time at the site, the latest you should get on a *lancha* is 2pm. If you're headed back to Palenque or Lacanjá Chansayab the same day, you'll have to go much earlier, as the last buses and *combis* leave from in front of the *embarcadero* at 4pm. The earliest you can leave for the site in the morning is 8am, when the INAH office opens.

Tabasco

Few visitors view the state of **Tabasco** as more than a transit corridor for Palenque. Crossed by numerous slow-moving tropical rivers on their way to the Gulf, the low-lying, humid region is the homeland of the ancient **Olmec**, **Maya** and **Zoque** cultures. You can see the legendary Olmec stone heads in a beautifully done exhibition in state capital **Villahermosa**, a city otherwise often maligned for its concrete and chaos, yet boasting a historic, lively and pedestrian-friendly downtown.

Hwy-180 runs close to Tabasco's **coast**, alternating between estuaries and sand bars, salt marshes and lagoons. Though the sands are a bit insect-ridden, and the views often marred by the offshore oil industry, they do have the virtue of being frequented only by locals, if at all. Much of inland Tabasco is very flat, consisting of the flood plains of a dozen or so major rivers. **Boat trips** along the Grijalva and the Usumacinta are the best way to glimpse remote ruins and abundant birdlife. You can also travel by river into the Petén in **Guatemala**, from the far eastern corner of the state.

In the far south of the state, the foothills of the **Sierra Puana** offer a retreat from the heat and humidity. Waterfalls spill down from the mountains, and a few small spas (*balnearios*) have developed. Village tracks provide some great **hiking trails** too.

Brief history

Throughout the Maya period, Tabasco was a natural crossroads, its great rivers important trade routes to the interior. But its local Maya communities were relatively unorganized, and when **Hernán Cortés** landed at the mouth of the Río Grijalva in 1519, he easily defeated the Chontal Maya. But the town he founded, Santa María de la Victoria, was beset first by attacks by Indigenous groups and then by pirates, eventually forcing a move to the present site and a change of name to "Villahermosa de San Juan Bautista" in 1596.

Nineteenth and early twentieth centuries

For most of the colonial period, swampy Tabasco remained a relative backwater. **Independence** did little to improve matters, as local leaders fought among themselves,

A TASTE OF TABASCO

The **food** of Tabasco state relies heavily on seafood and tropical fruits such as pineapple and passion fruit, which are both cultivated here, along with coffee and cacao. A freshwater fish, the skinny *pejelagarto*, is particularly prized: the green-fleshed, pike-like fish is usually barbecued and served with chile, lime and a salsa of deadly, caper-size chiles. Other typical dishes to look out for include smoked oysters, coconut tortillas, banana bread, and chirmol, a rich *mole* sauce flavoured with pumpkin seeds and local herbs that works particularly well with fish. In terms of drinks, hot (or cold) chocolate and *iliztle*, a sugar-cane alcohol flavoured with pear or peach, are popular. But note that **Tabasco Sauce** isn't actually a speciality: although Tabasco peppers are named after the state, they don't grow here, and the celebrated condiment is in fact an American product made from peppers grown in Louisiana.

and it took the **French invasion** of 1862 to bring some form of unity, though Tabasco offered fierce resistance to this foreign intrusion. The industrialization of the country under dictator Porfirio Díaz passed Tabasco by, and even after the **Revolution** it was still a poor state, dependent on cacao and bananas. Though **Tomás Garrido Canabal**, Tabasco's socialist governor in the 1920s and 1930s, is still respected as a reformer whose laws regarding workers' rights and women's suffrage were decades ahead of the rest of the country, his period in office was also marked by intense **anticlericalism**. Priests were killed or driven out (a process vividly brought to life in Graham Greene's *The Power and the Glory*; he covers the aftermath in *The Lawless Roads*), all the churches were closed, and many, including the cathedral in Villahermosa, torn down.

The oil boom

The region's **oil**, discovered in the 1930s but not fully exploited until the 1970s, provided the impetus to bring Tabasco into the modern world, enabling capital to be invested in the agricultural sector and Villahermosa to be transformed into the cultural centre it is today.

Villahermosa

Huge, hot, noisy and brash as only a Mexican city can be, **VILLAHERMOSA** – or "Beautiful Town" – could at first sight hardly be less appropriately named. For travellers in this area, though, it's something of an inevitability, as a junction of road and bus routes. But it's also a distinct place, and it can grow on you. Quite apart from the sudden vistas of the Río Grijalva's broad sweep, there are attractive plazas, quiet old streets, impressive ultramodern buildings and several art galleries and museums.

Most sights are in or around the pedestrianized downtown core (called the Zona Luz), though some tourist services are 2km or so northwest, in the modern commercial centre called Tabasco 2000. Between the two areas are the spires of a half-built Gothic cathedral, begun in 1973 – a fine symbol of the city's new-old aesthetic.

Zona Luz

The oldest part of Villahermosa can be found downtown, where vestiges of the nineteenth-century city survive on streets busy with shoppers and commerce. Many of the main shopping blocks are pedestrianized, and the buildings along them are gradually being cleaned up and restored.

Parque Juárez

Madero at Zaragoza • **Centro Cultural de Villahermosa** Free

At the northern end of the Zona Luz, this park is bustling in the evenings, as crowds swirl around watching the street entertainers. Facing the plaza on the east side, the futuristic glass **Centro Cultural de Villahermosa** presents changing exhibitions of art, photography and costume, as well as film screenings and concerts – stroll by and check out the schedule.

La Casa Siempreviva and around

Sáenz, at Lerdo de Tejada

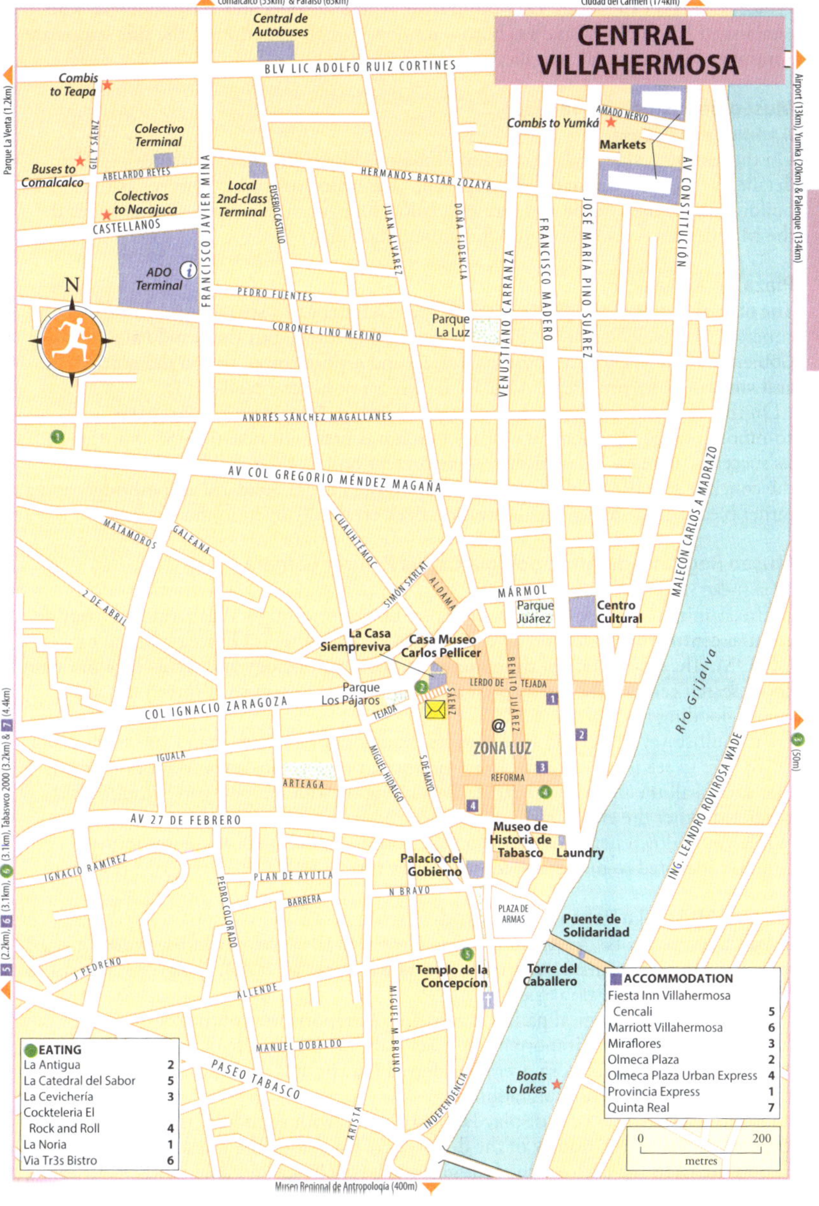

West of the Parque Juárez, the distinctive pink and purple paint on this old mansion immediately catches the eye. One of the few fully restored houses from the early twentieth century, it has beautiful tiled floors and arched stained-glass windows. It's usually open as a gallery with a small café, and is the anchor for a bit of an arts scene in the surrounding blocks.

At the end of Lerdo de Tejada, steps lead up to a small park where budgies sing in a large cage. Around the corner on Sáenz, also look for the Casa Museo Carlos Pellicer Cámara (Tues–Sun 9am–5pm; free), where the poet and anthropologist who established Parque La Venta was born – it's now a small museum. In the side streets are a number of other small art galleries.

Museo de Historia de Tabasco

27 de Febrero, at Juárez • Charge

On the southern side of the Zona Luz, Tabasco's history museum provides a quirky, detailed account of the state's development. The main attraction, however, is the 1915 building itself, tiled inside and out with colourful patterns from all over Europe and the Middle East – each room is different and dazzling.

Plaza de Armas

The official centre of the city, a patch of green adjacent to a sprawling expanse of concrete, is actually less lively than the area farther north. But the grand **Palacio del Gobierno**, with its classical columns, turrets and a clock tower, sits on the north edge, and you can poke your head inside to see any art or history exhibitions.

On the south side of the park lies the pretty, white **Templo de la Concepción** – commonly called "La Conchita". The church was first built here in 1799, but this and its successor were each demolished – the present building dates only from 1945. Off the concrete side of the plaza, steps lead up to the Puente Solidaridad footbridge, and a rather bleak square tower, its observation deck erratically open to the public.

Museo Regional de Antropología Carlos Pellicer Cámara

Av Carlos Pellicer 511, on the river • Charge • 993 312 6344

A fifteen-minute walk south from the Zona Luz brings you to Villahermosa's riverside cultural centre, the Centro de Investigaciones de las Culturas Olmeca y Maya, or CICOM. The centrepiece of the complex is this anthropology and archeology museum and research centre, renovated and reconfigured over the course of three years after record flooding in 2007.

The multistorey exhibition space houses thousands of artefacts grand and small. Come down here to see four fragments from the ancient hieroglyph-laden Maya monument that caused all the upset about 2012. Depending on which expert you consulted, they predicted either the end of civilization or the onset of a new era in human progress. While you're down here, you can also check out the other small museums in the complex (devoted to music and contemporary art), as well as the very good restaurant.

Parque-Museo La Venta and around

Blv Adolfo Ruíz Cortínes (Hwy-180), 2km northwest of the centre • Charge; sound-and-light show extra; buy tickets and enter at a second gate, about 250m southwest along Paseo Tabasco • Look for *combis* on Madero marked "Tabasco 2000", "Circuito 1", "Parque Linda Vista" or "Fracc Carrizal"; taxis also run to and from this spot • 993 312 7947

A visit to this archeological park and museum 2km northwest of the centre could easily fill half a day. The most important artefacts from the Olmec site of La Venta, some 120km west of Villahermosa, were transferred here in the late 1950s, when they were threatened by Pemex oil explorations.

Just inside the entrance, a display familiarizes you with what little is known about the Olmecs, as well as the history of the discovery of La Venta. The most significant and famous items in the park are the four gigantic **basalt heads**, notable for their African-

OLMEC CULTURE

Relatively little is known about the **Olmec culture**, referred to by many archeologists as the mother culture of Mesoamerica. Its legacy, which includes the Long Count calendar, glyphic writing, a rain deity and probably also the concept of zero and the ball-game, influenced all subsequent civilizations in ancient Mexico. The name Olmec comes from Nahautl (the language of the Aztecs) word "Olmecatl", meaning "rubber people"; this is a reference to the Olmecs practice of extracting latex from trees growing in the region and mixing it with the sap of local vines to produce rubber.

The fact that the Olmecs developed and flourished in the unpromising environment of the Gulf coast swamps 3200 years ago only adds to their mystery. After emerging around 1200 BC, and eventually spanning across northern Central America and much of central Mexico, the civilization began to decline around 400 BC, and over the subsequent thousand years the plains were gradually absorbed by the great Maya cities to the east, an influence most notable at **Comalcalco** (see page 679).

looking features. They're also extraordinary because the material from which they were hewn does not occur locally in the region, so they must have been imported from what is now Veracruz, Oaxaca or Guatemala. Additionally, there's a whole series of other Olmec stone sculptures.

To conjure a jungle setting, monkeys, agoutis (large rodents) and coatis (members of the racoon family) wander around freely, while crocodiles, jaguars and other animals from the region are displayed in sizeable enclosures. At night, there's a rather good **sound-and-light show** that involves strolling from monument to monument, dramatically illuminated amid the shadowy trees. Parque La Venta is actually set on the edge of the much larger Parque Tomás Garrido Canabal, stretching along the shore of an extensive lake, the **Laguna de Ilusiones**. There are walking trails here and boats to rent, or you can climb the Mirador de los Águilas, a tower in the middle of the lake.

Museo de Historia Natural

Blv Adolfo Ruíz Cortínes • Charge • 913 314 2175

Opposite the La Venta entrance, this small museum is a nice counterpoint to the archeology, as it focuses on the living heritage of Tabasco. Displays cover the state's geography, geology, animals and plants, focusing on the interaction between humans and the environment.

Yumká

Ranchería Las Barrancas, 14km from the centre, near the airport • Charge • http://yumka.gob.mx • *Combis* leave regularly from along Amado Nervo behind the market at the top end of Constitución, and a shuttle bus (charge) departs from Ruíz Cortines, west of Parque La Venta, on weekends at 9am, 10.30am, noon and 1.30pm; taxis are also available

You probably didn't come to Mexico to see hippos, but this safari park is well managed and fun on weekends, when it's popular with local families. It covers more than six square kilometres, so after a guided walking tour of the Tabasco jungle, complete with monkeys, you board a train for a tour round paddocks representing the savannahs of Africa and Asia – elephants, rhinos, giraffes and antelopes are rarely displayed in Mexico and almost never in such spacious surroundings. After a stop at the restaurant, you can take a boat tour of the lagoon, where, in addition to hippos, there are good bird watching opportunities.

ARRIVAL AND DEPARTURE — VILLAHERMOSA

BY PLANE

Aeropuerto Carlos A. Rovirosa (993 356 0157) is about 13km east of the centre on the main road towards Escárcega and Palenque. No buses run to the centre of Villahermosa, though ADO does have hourly buses to Palenque.

Destinations Cancún (5 weekly; 1hr 30min); Guadalajara (6 weekly; 2hr); Mexico City (7-12 daily; 1hr 30min).

Airlines Aeroméxico, Carlos Pellicer Cámara 511, 993 139 4541, http://aeromexico.com; VivaAerobus, Plaza Farole, 818 215 0150, http://vivaaerobus.com.

BY BUS

The bus stations are pretty close to each other northwest of the Zona Luz. Most buses into Chiapas travel via Puente Chiapas, which seems circuitous but knocks several hours off the journey. For San Cristóbal de las Casas, it's often easier to change at either Tuxtla or Palenque.

First-class buses The first-class station, with service from ADO, OCC and TRT, is a modern building on Javier Mina. The front of the station deals with services originating here; tickets for *de paso* services are sold in a separate complex behind, to the west. There's luggage storage and an information booth, usually unstaffed. *Combis* ply the road outside, but to get to the Zona Luz requires changing buses at the market – it's less hassle (and less confusing) to take a taxi or walk (about 20min). To get to the terminal from the centre, catch a *combi* from the malecón heading for "Chedraui".

11

Destinations Campeche (17 daily; 6hr 10min–7hr 30min); Cancún (17 daily; 12hr 30–15hr); Chetumal (6 daily; 8–9hr); Emiliano Zapata (roughly hourly; 2hr); Frontera (roughly hourly; 1hr 10min); Mérida (roughly every 2hr; 8hr-10min-9hr); Mexico City (every 1-2hr; 11hr 50min-13hr); Palenque (roughly hourly; around 2hr 30min); San Andrés Tuxtla (4 daily at 3.25am, 3.50pm, 11am & 7.55pm; 5hr 20min–7hr 25min); San Cristóbal de las Casas (5 daily; 6hr 20min–6hr 50min); Tapachula (3 daily at 4.05am, 9am & 6.15pm; 10hr 30min); Tenosique (roughly hourly; 3hr 10min); Tuxtla Gutiérrez (roughly hourly; 4hr 20min–5hr 20min); Veracruz (roughly hourly; 7hr–10hr 30min).

Second-class buses The main second-class terminal, the Central de Autobuses, is on Ruíz Cortines, just a few minutes farther from the centre than the ADO; you'll have to walk or take a taxi.

Destinations Tacotalpa and Coatzacoalcos, for La Venta (every 30min; 2hr 30min); Teapa (every 30min; 1hr); Tenosique (10 daily; 5hr).

Other terminals There's another, more dilapidated, second-class terminal for relatively local buses near the ADO, off Eusebio Castillo near Zozaya, with frequent buses to Emiliano Zapata, Frontera and Paraíso, as well as Palenque and Escárcega. Several companies run buses to Comalcalco, the best of which is Comalli Bus, on Gil y Sáenz above Abelardo Reyes, not far from the ADO (4.45am–10pm; 1hr).

BY COMBI AND COLECTIVO

On Gil y Sáenz, *combis* run to Nacajuca (for Cupilco; 30min), and, just around the corner, pale yellow *colectivos* go from Castellanos, just east of Gil y Sáenz. Just to the north, off Ruíz Cortines, La Sultana runs a comfortable service to Teapa (every 30min, 5am–10.30pm). *Colectivos* are usually faster than buses or *combis*, and not that much more expensive. The terminal for many other destinations is just north of the ADO on Abelardo Reyes. The shared taxis leave when full for Palenque, Paraíso, Frontera and Tacotalpa. You won't have to wait long, at least in the morning.

GETTING AROUND

By taxi Villahermosa's humidity might make you consider taking taxis more frequently – rates are generally a flat fee within most of the city.

By bus The local bus system comprises a confusing jumble of *combi* minivans, with the Mercado Pino Suárez acting as the main hub.

INFORMATION AND TOURS

Tourist information Despite the growth in visitor numbers in recent years, there's no handy tourist office in Villahermosa. Booths at the airport, history museum, Parque La Venta and ADO bus station can only offer leaflets, and the main state and federal office on Av de los Ríos, south of Paseo Tabasco in Tabasco 2000 (Mon–Fri 9am–3pm; 993 310 9700 ext 5238, http://visitetabasco.com), is too far away from the centre to be of much use.

Travel agents There's no shortage of travel agencies in the Zona Luz. Creatur, Paseo Tabasco 1404, on the right just beyond Ruíz Cortines (993 310 9900, http://creaturviajes.com), is one of the best in the region, with multilingual staff.

Boat tours On the east bank of the river, across the Puente de Solidaridad, more casual pleasure boats gather at weekends.

ACCOMMODATION

SEE MAP PAGE 671

Budget hotels in Villahermosa are not great value; most are on Madero or Lerdo de Tejada, close to the heart of things – though none is particularly praiseworthy. A few of the top-end hotels, on the other hand, are actually keenly priced compared with more touristy cities, but a steady stream of Pemex employees can keep the rooms full. These pricier places are located in the Tabasco 2000 district, about 2km west of the centre along Paseo Tabasco.

Fiesta Inn Villahermosa Cencali Paseo Tabasco, at Juárez; http://fiestainn.com. The best-value spot in the Tabasco 2000 area. Set in quiet, luxuriant gardens on the shore of a lagoon, the *Cencali* has an inviting pool, comfortable, well-furnished rooms with a/c and suites with beautiful, tiled bathrooms; upstairs rooms have balconies. Parque La Venta is a 1km walk. M$$$

Marriott Villahermosa Paseo Tabasco 1407; http://marriott.com. One of the newer top-end hotels in the Tabasco 2000 area, the Marriott won't win any prizes for character, but it's very comfortable, well staffed and often good value, especially at weekends. M$$$

Miraflores Reforma 304; http://hotelmiraflores.com. This solid mid-range hotel has spick-and-span en-suite rooms with nice balconies, as well as pleasant staff, a lobby bar and cafe, and parking for guests. M$$

Olmeca Plaza Madero 418; http://hotelolmecaplaza.com. A slick hotel with contemporary en-suites, a bar and restaurant, a great location and a swimming pool. Walk-in rates are a bit steep, but the receptionists can often be persuaded to offer a discount. M$$

Olmeca Plaza Urban Express Aldama 404; https://olmecaplazaexpress.com. Probably the pick of the budget options, though its prices are a bit higher than many of its rivals, it's worth stretching your budget. Rooms are modern and clean, if a little stark. M$

Provincia Express Lerdo de Tejada 303; 993 314 5377. Reasonably clean and welcoming small-chain option near the malecón, with smallish rooms and bracing a/c. Ask for a room on an upper floor and east side, to get a balcony with a view of bustling Madero and the river. M$

Quinta Real Paseo de la Choca 1402; http://caminoreal.com. The best of the city's luxury hotels, in grand mansion style, with vast rooms and two pools. It's 5km west from the centre, but right by the city's outer ring road, making it easily accessible for drivers, yet not too far from Parque La Venta. M$$$

11

EATING

SEE MAP PAGE 671

The Zona Luz boasts mostly **fast food and cafés** – with a couple of exceptions noted below. On Aldama north of Lerdo de Tejada are half a dozen taco joints. As ever, the **market** – here, a vast, tidy two-storey complex trimmed with white wrought-iron trellises – is good for fruit, bread and inexpensive tacos. It is several blocks north of the Zona Luz on Constitución.

CAFÉS, CHEAP EATS AND SNACKS

La Antigua Lerdo de Tejada 608, on the steps by Casa de la Siempreviva; 993 186 2474. A pleasant café for good coffee, smoothies and sandwiches, plus more substantial food including decent pasta dishes. There's often live music in the evening. M$$$

La Catedral del Sabor Independencia 204, adjacent to the Templo de la Concepción; 993 312 9549. Cool down with a refreshing *horchata de coco* – a Tabasco speciality – at this little pavement stand, which dates back over 40 years. There's also a selection of ice creams and lollies. M$

Cockteleria El Rock and Roll Reforma 307; 993 514 3009. A bustling place with excellent seafood cocktails, *ceviche* and fish in a variety of sauces. Sadly, the rock jukebox has given way to videos on flatscreen TVs. There's slightly quieter seating upstairs. M$$

RESTAURANTS

La Cevichería Francisco José Hernández Mandujano 114; http://lacevicheriatabasco.com. On the west side of the river, this busy, brightly coloured joint draws a steady stream of locals (and increasing number of travellers) thanks to its top-notch, artfully presented dishes. Alongside the super-fresh *ceviches*, the shrimp tostadas and the tuna *carnitas* tacos are real hits. M$$$

La Noria Gregorio Méndez Magaña 1008; 993 314 1659. Comfortable a/c restaurant serving inexpensive Lebanese and Middle Eastern dishes like kebabs, pilafs and hummus, dishes that are rare elsewhere in the state. M$$$

Via Tr3s Bistro Via 3, Local 14–17, La Hacienda, Tabasco 2000; 993 146 5602. If you're staying in the Tabasco 2000 area and want to avoid US-style fast food, this Mexican bistro is a good alternative, with a multinational menu and a focus on healthy eating. M$$

DIRECTORY

Banks and exchange Branches of all major banks, with ATMS, are at the airport and in the centre, on Madero or Juárez.

Internet One of the most centrally located is Ciber, at Aldama 526A.

Laundry Lavandería Yaveyire, corner Madero 27 de Febrero.

Post office The main post office is in the Zona Luz at Sáenz.

South of Villahermosa

South of Tabasco's capital, the foothills of the Sierra de Chiapas are heavy with banana plantations, while higher up, thick forest remains and the roadside pools and wetlands are as wild as ever. The highlights of this region include numerous **caves and grottoes**, as well as several accessible spas, created by tectonic activity, in the main town of **Teapa**. From here, you can catch a series of second-class buses over the mountains, a good slow route into Chiapas.

Teapa

Fifty-nine kilometres to the south of Villahermosa, the small, friendly town of **TEAPA** is a lovely base for visiting nearby caves and hot-spring spas. The springs are sulphuric but soothing, and popular at weekends; during the week, they're often empty. We recommend one popular hotel built around them – it's also open to day visitors.

Río Puyacatengo

Walk or take the bus for Tacotalpa; taxis also available

There's swimming in the Río Teapa in town, but it's better on this larger river, 3km east. Follow signs for *balnearios* just off the road to the right of the bridge, where big natural pools form in the river and several restaurants serve food.

Grutas del Coconá

4km northeast of Teapa • Charge; guided tour extra • Green-and-white *colectivos* run from next to the plaza in Teapa; or walk, in about 45min: from Méndez, head for the Pemex station and turn right, following the sign – when you get near the forested hills, bear left where the road divides and cross over the rail track

Eight chambers of these spectacular caves are open to tourists, as is a small museum displaying pre-Hispanic artefacts found inside. A stroll through takes about 45 minutes. The caves are surprisingly humid, and lined with oddly shaped stalactites and stalagmites.

ARRIVAL AND DEPARTURE — TEAPA

By bus Second-class buses (every 30min; 1hr) run from Villahermosa's Central de Autobuses. They pull in at the market near the edge of town. To get to the centre, walk a couple of blocks down the hill and turn left at the green clock onto Méndez, which takes you to the plaza.

ACCOMMODATION

Los Azufrés 8km west of Teapa on Hwy-195 to Tuxtla Gutiérrez; 993 315 1048; second-class buses toward Pichucalco stop here. This spa hotel, open to day visitors, has a huge pool and a restaurant serving local specialities, including *pejelagarto*. It also offers guided walks, bike rental and fishing. Some of the Cabins have private thermal pools. Cabins M$$$

Quintero Eduardo Rosario Bastar 108, Teapa; 932 322 8329. One block away from easy swimming in the river shallows. The simple rooms have cool brick floors, a/c and TV. The restaurant-bar serves regional *antojitos* and cocktails. M$$

Tapijulapa

To escape the humidity of the lowlands, head up the valley of the Río Oxolotán to the Sierra Puana, Tabasco's "hill country". This is an extraordinarily picturesque area, with quiet colonial towns set in beautiful, wooded valleys, and a turquoise river laden with sulphur. The main destination is **TAPIJULAPA**, a beautiful, whitewashed village with narrow cobbled streets that could, at first glance, be mistaken for a mountain town in Spain. Dubbed a Pueblo Mágico by the federal government, it's celebrated for wicker craftspeople, who have workshops all over town, and it's the starting point for a beautiful natural park. From the edge of the village, the main street, López Portillo, leads downhill to a pretty little **plaza**. At weekends, local women serve exceptionally delicious tamales and other inexpensive food in the large civic building. There were no reliable hotels at the time of research – it's best to plan on a day trip only, though you'll need to make a fairly early start.

ARRIVAL AND DEPARTURE — TAPIJULAPA

By bus From Teapa, take a bus to Tacotalpa from the OCC terminal on Méndez (roughly every 30min; 20min), then switch for another to Tapijulapa (hourly; 45min). The last bus back to Teapa (with connections to Villahermosa) leaves at 7pm.

Parque Natural Villa Luz

Free

You probably won't make it far in Tapijulapa before you're accosted by kids offering to take you to **boats** for this natural park with its spa pools, cascades and caves. The park's outstanding feature – not least for its powerful aroma – is the stream running through it, which owes its cloudy blue-white colour to dissolved minerals, especially sulphur. Where it meets the Río Oxolotán, it breaks into dozens of cascades and semicircular pools. Thousands of butterflies settle on the riverbanks, taking nourishment from dissolved minerals, and jungle trees and creepers grow wherever they find a foothold – a truly primeval sight.

Casa Museo Tomás Garrido Canabal

1.5km outside town • Charge

From the boat dock, well-signed trails (no need for a guide) lead 1.5km to the waterfalls, passing the country retreat of Canabal, the controversial former governor of Tabasco. It contains a few of his personal effects, as well as Zoque artefacts and handicrafts from the area.

Cuevas de las Sardinas Ciegas

Another path leads to the **Cuevas de las Sardinas Ciegas** – the caves of "blind sardines", sightless fish with translucent scales that have adapted to the cave's sulphur-rich waters. The gases in the cave are so powerful that it's impossible to breathe inside, but you can peer into their precipitous entrances. In Maya cosmology the openings are believed to lead to the underworld (Xibalba). During Semana Santa, the local people catch the fish and dedicate them to the rain god, Chac. Beyond the caves are a couple of *albercas*, stream-fed **swimming pools** said to have therapeutic properties.

ARRIVAL AND DEPARTURE — PARQUE NATURAL VILLA LUZ

By boat A couple of companies offer boats from Tapijulapa: plan for a 2hr waiting time. The better-established operation is past the plaza: follow López Portillo till it dead-ends then turn right to the river.

On foot It's an easy 3km (35min) walk from Tapijulapa: cross the river on the suspension bridge (to the right before you reach the plaza), head left on the concrete path, across the football field, then follow the track over the hill, keeping close to the main river.

By car The main entrance is on the main highway toward Oxolotán, a few km past the turn for Tapijulapa.

West of Villahermosa

The main attractions west of the city is a series of isolated ruins, the most famous being the Olmec site at **La Venta**, although, with the best pieces now residing in Villahermosa, the site itself is a bit empty. The little-known ancient Zoque people also flourished in this area, and the ruins at **Malpasito** reflect that unique culture.

La Venta

This small town on the border between Tabasco and Veracruz, 128km from Villahermosa, would be of little interest were it not for the nearby **archeological ruins**. The town is served by a steady stream of **buses** from Villahermosa and Coatzalcoalcos, so there's no need or real reason to stay.

The ruins

Charge • Buses from Villahermosa (roughly every 30min 5am–9pm; 2hr 30min)

This ancient city, the name of which remains unknown, was occupied by the Olmecs between 1200 and 400 BC and is regarded as their most important centre. Most of the finest pieces found here, including the famous **basalt heads**, were transferred to Villahermosa's Parque La Venta (see page 672) in 1957 and 1958. The **museum** at the entrance to La Venta itself (800m north of the bus station) has a model of the grounds, as well as glass cases with rather confusing displays of unlabelled pottery.

The site itself retains some replicas of the sculptures and heads now displayed in Villahermosa, and a few weathered steles and monuments, but the highlight is the huge grass-covered mound, about 30m high, clearly a pyramid, with fluted sides believed to represent the ravines on the flanks of a sacred volcano. The climb up is worth the effort for the views and the breeze. Paths below take you through the jungle – fascinating for its plants and butterflies, but haunted by ferocious mosquitoes.

Malpasito and around

100km southwest of Villahermosa • Charge • To reach the area by car, exit the toll highway immediately north of the Puente Chiapas; signs point to Las Flores and Malpasito village off Hwy-187

Some 100km southwest of Villahermosa, between the borders of Veracruz and Chiapas, a narrow triangle of Tabasco thrusts into mountains known as the **Sierra Huimanguillo.** These rugged peaks are not that high, only up to 1000m, but in order to appreciate them fully, you'll need to do some hiking: not only to canyons and waterfalls, but also to the ruins of **MALPASITO**, with their astonishing **petroglyphs**.

A car, however, is necessary. Although you can get to Malpasito by bus, it arrives too late to hike up to the ruins themselves, and there is no reliable overnight accommodation in the village (though you could, in a pinch, ask in the village for Guillermo Pérez, who sometimes rents rooms).

As you're in the area, you can cool off at the **Cascadas Las Pavas**, a beautiful series of waterfalls that are set in a tranquil spot down a path through dense flowering trees, and often surrounded by butterflies. To get there from Malpasito, backtrack along the road to town, and bear left at the fork.

The archeological site

The post-Classic **Zoque** ruins are overshadowed by jagged, jungle-covered mountains, the highest point in Tabasco. Though the ruins bear a certain resemblance to Palenque, the Zoque were not a Maya group – one of the few facts known about them. On the way into the site you pass terraces and grass-covered mounds, eventually arriving at the unique **ball-court**. At the top of the stone terraces forming the south side of the court, a flight of steps leads down to a narrow room, with stone benches lining either side. Beyond this, and separate from the chamber, is a square pit more than 2m deep and 1.5m wide. This room may have been used by the ball-players to make a spectacular entrance as they emerged onto the top of the ball-court.

But the most amazing features of this site are its **petroglyphs**. More than three hundred have been discovered so far: animals, birds, houses and more, etched into the rock. One large boulder is covered in enigmatic flat-topped triangles surmounted by a square or rectangle, and shown above what look like ladders or steps – stylized houses or launching platforms for the chariots of the gods, depending on your viewpoint.

North to the coast

The journey from Villahermosa along **the coast**, either west to Veracruz or east to Campeche, is beautiful. The road hugs the shore, and it's never hard to find deserted beaches and lagoons. Attractive as the coastal route is, it's undeniably slow, and almost no tourists travel it, preferring the inland route to the Yucatán in order to stop by Palenque on the way. But travellers with extra time will be well rewarded by spending a day north of Villahermosa, at the ruins of **Comalcalco**. The road winds through Tabasco's **cacao plantations**, with a few minor diversions along the way.

Cupilco

Thirty kilometres out of Villahermosa, the main road passes through **CUPILCO**, notable for its roadside church, the **Templo de la Virgen de la Asunción**. Decorated in gold and blue with floral patterns, it's a beautiful example of the distinctive *tabasqueño* approach to sacred spaces.

Hacienda la Luz

In the area around Comalcalco several **cacao haciendas** have opened their doors to visitors. The first you pass, 2km before Comalcalco, is Hacienda la Luz (933 337 1122, http://haciendalaluz.mx; tours Tues–Sun 9am, 11am, 1pm & 3pm), which makes an interesting diversion if you've got your own car – and there are plenty of chocolates on offer, if you have a sweet tooth.

Comalcalco

58km northwest of Villahermosa • Charge, including museum

The Classic-period site of **COMALCALCO** is an easy, very worthwhile trip from the city. The westernmost Maya site, Comalcalco was occupied around the same time as Palenque (250–900 AD), with which it shares some features, and it may have been ruled by some of the same kings.

The area's lack of building stone forced the Chontal Maya to adopt a distinctive form of construction: kiln-fired brick. As if the bricks themselves were not sufficient to mark this site as different, the builders added mystery to technology: each brick was stamped or moulded with a geometric or representational design before firing, with the design deliberately placed facing inwards, so that it could not be seen in the finished building. Many of these astonishing designs are on display in a museum; there are also restrooms and a small café at the site.

The museum

The labels here are in Spanish only, but the marvellous work on the bricks speaks for itself. Animals depicted include crocodiles, turtles, frogs, lizards, dogs and mice, while those portraying the sculpted faces of rulers display an advanced level of artistic development. One of the most amazing figures is of a skeleton that appears to be leaping out at you from the surface of the brick.

The abundant clay that provided such a versatile medium for architects and artists here also formed the basis for many more mundane artefacts. Comalcalco means "place of the *comales*" – fired clay griddles for cooking tortillas – and these and other clay vessels have been excavated in great numbers. Some of the largest jars were used as **funerary urns** and several are on display here, including one with an intact skeleton.

The site

Though there are dozens of buildings at Comalcalco, only ten or so of the larger ones have been restored. Because the brickwork is so fragile, you're not allowed to enter or climb on many of them, but you can follow a path up to Structure 3 and around the Palacio.

Entering the site, you first come to **Temple I**, the main structure of the **North Plaza Cluster**, a tiered pyramid with a massive central stairway. Originally, the whole building (like all of the structures here) would have been covered with stucco made from oyster shells, sculpted into masks and reliefs of rulers and deities, and brightly painted. Only a few of these features remain – the exposed ones protected from further erosion by shelters, while others have deliberately been left buried.

Facing Temple I at the opposite end of the site is the **Gran Acrópolis**, a complex of buildings, some still being excavated, raised above the plaza. Here you can climb up to **El Palacio** for some excellent close-up views of the brickwork, including a series of massive brick piers and arches that once formed an enormous double corbelled vault,

80m long and over 8m wide – one of the largest enclosed spaces the Maya ever built. There's a fine stucco mask of Kinich Ahau, the Maya sun god, on **Templo VI**, and at the side of **Temple V** a small, corbel-arched room contains stucco reliefs of nine, richly dressed, half-life-size figures apparently in conversation or even argument – they may represent the **Lords of Xibalba**, the Maya underworld.

ARRIVAL AND DEPARTURE — COMALCALCO

By bus Comalli Bus in Villahermosa (see page 674) has services to the town of Comalcalco, on the west side of the highway (where you'll be dropped off at or near the ADO terminal) about 3km south of the ruins. There are plenty of buses back to Villahermosa (look for TRT buses, which take the fast route via Cárdenas, every 45min, or Allegro and Comalli buses, which go via Cupilco) or on to Paraíso (20min), running along the highway. From town, you can then flag down any second-class bus heading north to the ruins; ask the driver for "ruinas", or get off after 5min, when you see the sign on the right. The ruins are 1km from the highway, down a long straight paved road.

By combi From Comalcalco town, green *combis*, found outside the ADO terminal, ply the route to the ruins; some go all the way to the site, but others will drop you on the highway, 1km away.

By taxi Taxis run betweem Comalcalco and the ruins.

The north coast

Passing through areas of wetland teeming with wildlife, the little-travelled **north coast** road is a treat. Mangroves and lagoons are covered with flocks of feeding water birds, and if you look hard enough you may spot the odd crocodile. However, the beaches themselves are a bit disappointing: the sand is grey-brown and, though generally clean, you've always got the oil refinery in sight to the east. There are few hotels along this stretch, but plenty of spaces for **camping** – if you can stand the swarms of mosquitoes and sandflies.

Paraíso

A weekend escape for Villahermosa residents, **PARAÍSO**, 75km away on the banks of the Río Seco, is a sleepy place, with some beaches nearby – pleasant enough if you need to wind down, and a better place to spend the night than Frontera, 77km east on the way to Campeche. The nearest beach, **Playa Limón**, where locals go for picnics on weekends, is a short *combi* or taxi ride north of Paraíso.

ARRIVAL AND GETTING AROUND — PARAÍSO

By bus Paraíso's ADO bus station is 1km south of the centre along Benito Juárez, the main road. Turn right out of the station and keep walking: eventually you'll see the town's most distinctive monument – the twin-towered colonial church – across the river up ahead. There's a daily first-class bus to Villahermosa (5pm; on the return leg the bus departs Villahermosa at 9.18am; 1hr 45min–2hr 5min). The main second-class station, with departures for points along the coast, is north of the centre and well served by *combis*; to make the 15min walk, turn south (left) and aim for the church towers.

By combi Playa Limón is a 20min ride north of Paraíso.

By taxi Taxis run to and from the beaches.

ACCOMMODATION AND EATING

El Llenador 86600 Centro, north side of the plaza; 933 166 6301. This restaurant has an extensive menu of Mexican and international fusion foods, all at mid-range prices. The location is the main attraction and the portions are plentiful. M$$

Sabina Melchor Ocampo 115, east side of the plaza; http://hotelsabinaparaiso.com. The *Sabina* offers clean, bright a/c en-suite rooms with TVs. Aim for one on the second floor, where the terraces and big windows are more open to the occasional ocean-scented breezes. M$

Puerto Ceiba and the coast road east

Ten kilometres east of Paraíso, the road passes through **PUERTO CEIBA** on the shores of the **Laguna de Mecoacán**. There's a *parador turístico* here offering boat trips (for up to fourteen people) and a restaurant serving regional dishes and fish straight out of the

FIESTAS IN CHIAPAS AND TABASCO

The states of Chiapas and Tabasco are extremely rich in festivals. Local tourist offices should have more information on what's happening.

New Year's Day (Jan 1). San Andrés Chamula and San Juan Chamula, both near San Cristóbal, have civil ceremonies to install a new government for the year.

Día de San Sebastián (Jan 20). In Chiapa de Corzo, a large fiesta with traditional dances (including the masked *parachicos*) lasts several days, with a re-enactment on Jan 21 of a naval battle on the Río Grijalva.

Día de la Candelaria (Feb 2). Colourful celebrations at Ocosingo.

Fiesta de San Caralampio (Feb 11–20). In Comitán, celebrated with a parade to San Caralampio church, where elaborate offerings are made and dances held in the plaza outside.

Carnaval (the week before Lent; variable Feb & March). Celebrated in hundreds of villages throughout the area, but at its most frenzied in the big cities, especially Villahermosa.

Anniversary of the foundation of Chiapa de Corzo (March 1). Town fair with kiddie rides, live music and more.

Semana Santa (Holy Week). Widely observed. There are particularly big ceremonies in San Cristóbal de las Casas. Ciudad Hidalgo, at the border near Tapachula, has a major week-long market.

Feria de San Cristóbal de las Casas (April 1–7). Festival in San Cristóbal de las Casas celebrating the town's foundation.

Feria de Villahermosa (second half of April). Villahermosa hosts its annual festival, with agricultural and industrial exhibits and the election of the queen of the flowers.

Día de San Pedro (April 29). Celebrated in several villages around San Cristóbal, including Amatenango del Valle and Zinacantán.

Día de la Santa Cruz (May 3). Celebrated in San Juan Chamula and in Teapa, between Villahermosa and San Cristóbal.

Día de San Isidro (May 15). Peasant celebrations everywhere – famous and picturesque fiestas in Huistán, near San Cristóbal. There's a four-day nautical marathon from Tenosique to Villahermosa, when craft from all over the country race down 600km of the Río Usumacinta.

Día de San Antonio (June 13). Celebrated in Simojovel, near San Cristóbal, and Cárdenas (Tabasco), west of Villahermosa.

Día de San Juan (June 24). The culmination of several days' celebration in San Juan Chamula.

Día de San Cristóbal (July 17). Celebrated enthusiastically in San Cristóbal de las Casas and in nearby villages such as Tenejapa and Amatenango del Valle.

Día de Santiago (July 25). Provokes widespread celebrations, especially in San Cristóbal de las Casas.

Fiesta de Santo Domingo de Guzmán (last week of July, first week of Aug). Comitán's fair, with concerts, rodeos and more.

Fiesta de San Lorenzo (Sun nearest Aug 10). Celebrated in Zinacantán, with much music and dancing.

Día de Santa Rosa (Aug 30). Celebrated in San Juan Chamula, when the locals don traditional garb and play Tzotzil harps and instruments outside the church.

Independence Day (Sept 14–16). In Chiapas, independence celebrations are preceded by those in honour of the state's annexation to Mexico.

Día de la Virgen del Rosario (first Sun in Oct). Celebrated in San Juan Chamula and Zinacantán with Tzotzil folk music and dances. There's also a special craft market.

Día de los Muertos (Day of the Dead; Nov 1–2). The most captivating celebration of the Day of the Dead in Chiapas takes place in Comitán, where the cemeteries overflow with flowers and ornate altars.

Día de la Virgen de Guadalupe (Dec 12). An important day throughout Mexico. There are particularly good fiestas in Tuxtla Gutiérrez and San Cristóbal de las Casas.

Feria and cheese expo (Dec 17–22). Held in Pijijiapan, on the coast highway to Tapachula.

lake. The road then crosses **Laguna Santa** to the east, and there are turn-offs for several decent beaches before it meets Hwy-180, 50km or so north of Villahermosa. The first beach is **Playa Azúl**, where you can rent boats and jet skis. **Playa Pico de Oro**, 6km or so further on, is more tranquil. If you're travelling light you could easily camp at any of these and get back to the main road in the morning.

East to the Usumacinta and Guatemala

East of Villahermosa, Hwy-186 cuts across northern Chiapas before swinging north into Campeche to Francisco Escárcega, then east again as the only road across the base of the Yucatán Peninsula. At Catazajá, in Chiapas, 110km from Villahermosa, is the junction for **Palenque**. If you've already been there and want to see Tikal in Guatemala's Petén, you can go via **Tenosique** and **La Palma**, although it's quicker and cheaper to go from Frontera Corozal (see page 667); however, if you go this way, through this odd, seldom-visited side of Tabasco, you could stop at the nearby ruins of **Pomoná**. You'll pass through the town of **Emiliano Zapata** on the way, though there's little reason to stop unless you're coming from Palenque, in which case you'll probably need to change buses here.

Tenosique

Around 220km southeast of Villahermosa, on the banks of the now placid Río Usumacinta, is the town of **TENOSIQUE**. Streets are numbered according to the Yucatán system, with even numbers running north–south, and odd numbers running east–west. Between the main street, Calle 26 (also called Pino Suárez), which leads up to the plaza, and Calle 28, you'll find pretty much everything you need.

There's not a lot to do in Tenosique. Its main claim to fame is as the birthplace of Mexican national hero Pino Suárez (September 8, 1869). His former house is on Calle 26; it's now painted blue and white, as it's the offices of Telcel.

ARRIVAL AND DEPARTURE — TENOSIQUE

By bus Buses arrive at a small terminal close to the highway, 2.5km out of town. Inexpensive *colectivos* and shared taxis run frequently to the centre; get off when you see a large white church with red trim on the right. There are regular buses to/from Villahermosa (every 30min–1hr; 3hr 10min–3hr 30min). For the Yucatán, it's generally best to get one of the frequent buses to Emiliano Zapata (10–12 daily; 1hr–1hr 30min) and change there.

TO GUATEMALA

It's more convenient to enter Guatemala at the heavily policed border crossing of **El Ceibo**, 60km southeast of Tenosique, rather than the town of La Palma, cutting travel time to Flores to around 6hr in total. Buses leave Tenosique (hourly 6am–5pm; 1hr) behind the market on the corner of C 45 and C 16, and take an hour to reach the border. From there, you can pick up a minibus to cross the new bridge to El Naranjo in Guatemala. At least eight daily buses leave for Flores (3hr). Be sure to get your passport stamped by both Mexican and Guatemalan immigration before you leave, as there is no office on the Guatemala side. There are a number of rather desperate hotels and *comedores* on El Naranjo's main road.

ACCOMMODATION AND EATING

Most of the restaurants in the centre are unimpressive and cheap, and have similar menus. A row of *comedores* lines the front of the market, off the northwest corner of the plaza. If you are going to Guatemala, stock up on provisions here.

Hacienda Tabasqueña C 26 no. 512; https://facebook.com/hotelhaciendatenosique. If you do have to stay the night in Tenosique, this is probably the best option, though it certainly doesn't live up to its grandiose name. It has reasonable en-suite rooms, some of which come with a/c, plus a small café. M$$

DIRECTORY

Banks The banks in Tenosique aren't interested in changing money, but Bancomer on the plaza has an ATM; for Guatemalan quetzales ask around in the shops on C 28.

Pomoná

30km west of Tenosique on Hwy-203, then 4km east • Charge • Taxis to here run from Tenosique or Emiliano Zapata; *colectivos* also run from either town along Hwy-203, leaving you to walk the final 4km

Although this site, located in rolling countryside with views of forested hills to the south, makes a pleasant diversion, a visit is really only for the dedicated. The restored structures date from the Late Classic period; the site's largest building is a stepped pyramid with six levels. **Pomoná** was a subject of the much larger city of Piedras Negras in Guatemala, further up the valley of the Usumacinta. The small **museum** houses some interesting carved panels and steles, made even more mysterious by the omission of any explanations as to what you're seeing.

Moral-Reforma

45km north of Tenosique, near Cascadas de Reforma • Free • Take a *colectivo* from Tenosique to Cascadas de Reforma, then walk 2km (some drivers may take you all the way if you ask)

Excavations at this site since 2009 have uncovered an amazing collection of stucco decoration, steles and masks. The most fragile and significant pieces are now at the archeology museum in Villahermosa (see page 673) for study and preservation, but the work has also led to the opening of two previously buried temples, with many others waiting to be rediscovered.

The Yucatán

PYRAMID OF THE MAGICIAN, UXMAL

The Yucatán

Until the 1960s, when proper road and rail links were finally completed, the Yucatán Peninsula – the states of Campeche, Yucatán and Quintana Roo – had more contact with Europe, Cuba and the US than with central Mexico. Today, the region remains distinct, with traditional Maya life alongside massive tourist attractions such as the great ruins of Chichén Itzá and the mega-resort of Cancún. Once the province of Maya rebels and palm-plantation owners, the Caribbean coast is now known as the Riviera Maya, which includes the tourist hotspots of Playa del Carmen and Tulum. But away from these big centres, especially in the south, where settlements are sparsely scattered in dense forest, there's still a distinct pioneering feel.

In northern Yucatán state, the landscape is relatively spare: shallow, rocky earth gives rise to stunted trees, and underground springs known as *cenotes* (see page 708) are the only source of water. Campeche state, by contrast, boasts a huge area of **tropical forest**, the Calakmul Biosphere Reserve. The entire coastline is perfect for spotting **wildlife** – notably turtles at the Sian Ka'an Biosphere Reserve in Quintana Roo and flocks of flamingos at Celestún and Río Lagartos in Yucatán. Along the Caribbean coast, magnificent offshore **coral growth** forms part of the world's second-largest barrier reef.

There's really only one main route around the Yucatán Peninsula; the variation comes in where you break the journey or make side trips. Whether you come from Palenque or along the coast from Villahermosa, you'll find yourself on Hwy-180, which heads up to **Campeche** then veers away from the **Gulf Coast** towards **Mérida** and east to **Valladolid** and the Caribbean coast. Near Mérida are both the excellent craft town of **Izamal** and the **Ruta Puuc**, which includes major Maya sites such as Uxmal and **Chichén Itzá**, as well as a trove of smaller, less-visited ruins. Past these, you can push on to the Caribbean beaches.

The stretch of coast between **Cancún** and **Tulum**, known as the Riviera Maya and including **Playa del Carmen** and **Isla Cozumel**, is one of Mexico's most heavily touristed areas. South of Tulum, the **Sian Ka'an Biosphere Reserve**, encompassing mangroves thick with birdlife and coral reefs offshore, briefly slows the march of progress. The coast south of the biosphere – dubbed the **Costa Maya** – is on its own development trajectory, but it's still your best bet for hammock camping. The vast, beautiful **Laguna de Bacalar** is a crystal-clear lake that's rich in wildlife and an affordable alternative to the beaches. **Chetumal**, the state capital and a duty-free border town, is chiefly important as a gateway to and from Belize.

The road across the south of the peninsula is much less travelled. It passes through jungle territory dotted with ruins, collectively known as the **Río Bec sites**. The star is the enormous site of Calakmul, deep in the forest reserve near the Guatemalan border. From the top of its main pyramid, the tallest in the Maya world, the forest stretches to the horizon like a green sea.

Brief history

The Yucatán Peninsula is the longest continuously settled part of Mexico, with evidence of **Maya** inhabitants as early as 2500 BC. The Maya were at their cultural peak during the **Classic period** (300–900 AD), during which time they used solar, lunar and astral cycles to develop their complex and highly accurate calendar; they also had an elaborate mathematical and hieroglyphic system. Five hundred years before the Renaissance, moreover, the Maya had developed a sophisticated perspective in art. In the early ninth

CAMPECHE

Highlights

1. **Campeche** This lovely walled city with narrow streets, pastel-coloured houses and public artworks is kept immaculate by its proud citizens. See page 690

2. **Mérida** Although the "White City" is the largest on the peninsula it retains a tranquil charm. See page 697

3. **Ruta Puuc** See the distinctive sculpture at the Maya sites in this area, and stay in one of the quiet towns nearby. See page 709

4. **Izamal** The best place in the Yucatán to buy craftwork and meet artisans, this little town east of Mérida is also studded with ruined pyramids. See page 718

5. **Chichén Itzá** Visit the best-known of the Maya sites, with its vertiginous temple, Chac-mool figures and dramatic, snail-shaped observatory. See page 719

6. **Cozumel** The reefs around this island, just off the coast from Playa del Carmen, are some of the best places in the world for snorkelling and scuba diving. See page 750

7. **Tulum** The longest, finest white-sand beach on the Caribbean coast, with turquoise water and candlelit cabañas near ancient ruins, as well as the Sian Ka'an Biosphere Reserve just to the south. See page 758

HIGHLIGHTS ARE MARKED ON THE MAP ON PAGE 688

century AD, southern lowland cities (Tikal, in Guatemala, and Calakmul, among others) were abandoned, and northern cities such as Chichén Itzá grew. These in turn collapsed around 1200 AD, to be succeeded by Mayapán and a confederacy of other cities that probably included Tulum and Cozumel.

After the Conquest

By the time the Spanish arrived, the Maya had splintered into tribalism – although still with cities and long-distance sea trade that awed the conquistadors. The

Yucatán Peninsula proved the hardest area of the country to pacify, with the Maya resisting slavery and debt peonage through constant armed rebellion.

The latter half of the nineteenth century saw the **Caste Wars**, when the Maya briefly gained control of the entire peninsula. The guerrilla fighters were eventually pushed back into the wilds of southern Quintana Roo, and held out until the early twentieth century, ending their struggle with conciliation from the Mexican government. It was one of the most successful fights against colonialism in the New World.

SAFETY IN THE YUCATÁN

Drug cartel-related violence has increased in the Yucatán in recent years. There have been several fatal shootings in Playa del Carmen – including one at a music festival in 2017 in which five people were killed – and Cancún. In February 2018, a bomb exploded on a Playa del Carmen-Cozumel ferry, injuring more than 20 passengers. Two weeks later an undetonated device was discovered on another ferry plying the same route. The local authorities have since stepped up security, with an increased police presence in the major tourist areas. But it is important to check the latest safety advice (see page 62), remain vigilant and follow local advice.

The Yucatán today

Today, the Maya still live in the Yucatán, in many cases remarkably true to their old traditions and lifestyle. The culture and language remain a strong source of pride that sets this area apart from central Mexico.

On February 1, 2015, the state of Quintana Roo, which includes Cancún, changed time zones, swapping Central Standard Time for Eastern Standard Time. The aim was to boost tourism by creating longer, lighter evenings.

Campeche and around

Capital of the state that bears its name, beautiful **Campeche** is one of Mexico's finest colonial cities, but draws reasonably few tourists. At its heart, relatively intact, lies a historic port town still surrounded by hefty defensive **walls and fortresses**; within them, interspersed with the occasional grand Baroque church, are elegant eighteenth- and nineteenth-century houses painted in pastel shades and neatly restored. Nonetheless, the place, a UNESCO World Heritage Site, doesn't feel like an outdoor museum, with appliance stores and internet cafés occupying many of the shopfronts. Around the old **centre** are the trappings of a modern city that is once again becoming wealthy, while the **seafront**, built on reclaimed land, provides a thoroughly modern vista. Though the city is far less lively than Mérida, its immaculately preserved and tranquil streets compare favourably, and *campechanos* live up to their reputation as some of the most gracious people in Mexico.

Beyond the archeological museum in the Fuerte de San Miguel – a "must-see" – and the market, which lies just outside the wall by the Puerta de Tierra, you don't really need to venture into the modern city. Instead, one of the greatest pleasures to be had in Campeche comes from simply wandering around the old town in the early evening and on Sundays, when the central Plaza de la Independencia (which locals call the *parque principal*, or just *parque*) is closed to cars for a mellow party.

Brief history

In 1517, a crew of Spanish explorers under Francisco Hernández landed outside the Maya town of Ah Kin Pech, only to beat a hasty retreat on seeing the forces lined up to greet them. Not until 1540 did second-generation conquistador **Francisco de Montejo the Younger** found the modern town. Until the nineteenth century, Campeche was the peninsula's chief port, exporting mainly **logwood** (source of a red dye known as hematein) from local forests. It was an irresistible target for **pirates** until locals prevailed upon the Spanish authorities to fortify the city: construction of the walls, with eight massive bulwarks (*baluartes*), began in 1686 after a particularly brutal massacre. Although large sections of the walls have been replaced by a ring road, two major sections still survive, along with seven of the eight *baluartes*.

La Catedral de Nuestra Señora de la Concepción

Plaza de la Independencia • Free, but a donation is expected

The city's most central landmark is **La Catedral de Nuestra Señora de la Concepción**, on the north side of the plaza. Founded in 1540, it's one of the oldest churches on the peninsula. The bulk of the construction, though, took place much later, and what you see now is a wedding-cake Baroque structure. Look in the adjacent museum (accessed via the cathedral) for a seventeenth-century statue of Christ, interred in a dark wood and silver catafalque, among other relics.

Centro Cultural Casa Seis

Plaza de la Independencia • Charge • 981 816 1782

On the southwest side of the plaza, this cultural centre and small museum has an elegant permanent display of Baroque interiors. It also hosts art shows and performances, including musical *serenatas* most Thursdays. There's also a souvenir shop.

Museo de la Arquitectura Maya

Plaza de la Independencia • Charge • Free sound-and-light show Thurs–Sun 8pm (30min) • 981 816 9136

On the seaward side of the plaza, the Baluarte de la Soledad, just south of the public library, houses a collection of columns, steles and other stone details helpfully arranged by regional style – Chenes, Puuc and more. Keep an eye out for the recently returned Calakmul jade mask. Many of the carved stone pieces are accompanied by a sketch outline of the decoration – this helps train your eye to see the details. You can also climb up onto the top of the city walls.

El Palacio Centro Cultural

Plaza de la Independencia • Free • Free sound-and-light show Thurs–Sat 8pm (25min) • 981 816 7741

Opened in 2014, **El Palacio Centro Cultural** will excite most history buffs. This modern museum charts the history of the city through interesting multimedia displays and wide-ranging exhibits, from eighteenth- and nineteenth-century costumes to replica Spanish galleons. Mostly in Spanish, but there are some displays in English.

Baluarte de San Carlos

C 8 at C 65 • Charge • 981 816 9111

From the plaza, heading southwest along the line of the wall brings you to this bulwark with cannons on the battlemented roof and, underneath, the beginnings of a network of ancient tunnels that runs under much of the town. Sealed off now, the tunnels provided refuge for the populace during pirate raids, and before that were probably used by the Maya. The *baluarte* houses Campeche's **Museo de la Ciudad**, a tiny but rather lovely collection of local memorabilia that includes models of ships, with Spanish commentary.

12

Puerta de Tierra

C 18 at C 59 • **Ramparts and museum** Charge • **Sound-and-light show** Thurs–Sun 8pm (1hr) • Charge

The second remaining chunk of city wall is on the landward side, hence the name **Puerta de Tierra**. It hosts a surprisingly dynamic and enjoyable **sound-and-light show** four times a week, starting from the Puerta de Tierra and walking along the wall in the company of the "soldiers" guarding it.

Just north along the wall, at the Baluarte de San Francisco, you can climb the ramparts and walk along the top of the walls and look over the old town on the one side and the newer, less preserved city on the other, typified by the market and the Alameda Francisco de Paula Toro, the Havana-inspired promenade next to it. Downstairs in the bulwark is a piracy museum, though it has very few physical objects, save some blunderbusses, cutlasses and crossbows: it's probably appealing for pirate obsessives only.

Fuerte de San Miguel and the Museo Arqueológico

Av Escénica, 4km south of the centre • Charge • Take a taxi or city bus marked "Lerma" or "Playa Bonita" along the coast road), though once you get off you'll still have a stiff climb uphill to reach the fort

On a steep hill on the southwest side of town, about 4km from the centre, the **Fuerte de San Miguel** houses Campeche's impressive archeological museum. Plaques are in Spanish only, but the beautiful relics from all over the peninsula speak for themselves. Maya artefacts from Edzná and Jaina make up much of the collection; highlights include delicate Jaina figurines, fine sculpture and pre-Hispanic gold. But the best part is the treasure from the tombs at Calakmul, including the first mummified body to be found in Mesoamerica, unearthed in 1995. The jade death masks are mesmerizing. Enjoy the view over the ramparts, too.

Fuerte de San José

C 5 at Francisco Morazán, 3.5km north of the centre • Charge • Take a taxi or buses marked "Morelos" or "Bellavista", starting from in front of the market

On the north side of the city, directly uphill from the *paradores de cockteleros* (see page 694), the **Fuerte de San José** faces down a giant statue of Benito Juárez on the neighbouring hill. Its museum contains armaments, scale models of the city and ships and sundry items salvaged from shipwrecks, such as centuries-old Dutch gin bottles (signage is in Spanish only). Although this museum is not as compelling as the other fort's, the view north to the green swathe of protected marshland is striking.

ARRIVAL AND DEPARTURE — CAMPECHE

BY PLANE

The airport is about 10km southeast of town and there's a dedicated taxi stand. There are daily flights (3 daily; 2hr) to Mexico City on Aeroméxico (http://aeromexico.com).

BY BUS

Campeche has two main bus stations, one each for first- and second-class services, as well as a separate terminus for local and rural buses.

ADO station The first-class station, called "El ADO", has ADO, OCC and some ATS services. It's about 2km from the centre on Av Central. Taxis line up outside, as do buses and *colectivos* (look for "Mercado" or "Centro"). To get back, look for "Av Central or "ADO" buses.

Destinations Cancún (9 daily; 7hr–7hr 40min); Chetumal (1 daily at 2pm; 6hr 45min) via Xpujil (4hr 30min); Ciudad del Carmen (roughly hourly; 2hr 55min–3hr 40min); Escárcega (6 daily; 2hr 10min); Mérida (every 30–45min; around 2hr 30min); Playa del Carmen (2 daily at 10.45pm & 11.45pm; 8hr 35min); Veracruz (2 daily at 8.15pm & 10.40pm; 12hr–14hr 15min); Villahermosa (every 1–2 hours; 6hr–7hr 10min).

Second-class station The second-class terminal, with Sur and some ATS buses, is 600m northeast of the centre on Gobernadores, serving towns on Hwy-180. Walk west on Gobernadores or cross the street and take a city bus marked "Centro" or "Mercado". All head to the market, just outside the city wall on the landward side. To get back, look for "Universidad" or "Terminal Sur" buses.

Destinations Hecelchakán (every 15–30min; 45min); Francisco Escárcega (roughly hourly; 1hr 30min); Hopelchén (roughly hourly; 1hr); Iturbide (around 10 daily; 1hr 15min); Uxmal and Santa Elena (5 daily; 2hr).

Sur Terminal A small ticket office on Av República handles Sur buses going along the coast to the south (Champotón, Seybaplaya, etc). Independent local buses stop out front, for various surrounding villages. Buses to Pich, the town nearest to Edzná, leave from here until 11.30am.

BY COLECTIVO

Colectivos for towns north and east depart from Gobernadores near the second-class station – you'll pass the marked stops where taxis wait to fill up.

12

GETTING AROUND

By taxi Within the city, taxis are inexpensive but not always plentiful. Look for them at taxi stands around the centre or call 981 816 2363, 981 816 2359 or 981 816 2355.

Bike rental Buena Ventura (981 811 9191 ext 405), on 16 de Septiembre in the *Best Western Del Mar* car park and KankabiOK Tours (see below), rent cruisers with baskets (around M$30/hr) and lead tours around town.

Car rental Europcar, at the airport (981 823 4083, http://europcar.com.mx).

INFORMATION AND TOURS

State tourist office Plaza Moch Couoh on 16 de Septiembre opposite the Palacio Legislativo (daily 8am–4pm & 6–9pm; 981 127 3300 or 1 800 900 2267, http://campeche.travel). Helpful, and there's usually someone who speaks English. It has a list of guides (speaking various languages) who lead tours of the city and archeological zones, though you might be expected to provide transport; try to make reservations a day ahead.

Campeche Tours 16 de Septiembre, in Hotel Baluartes; 981 816 3911, https://facebook.com/ToursEnCampeche. This agency runs a range of trips, including kayaking and fishing excursions.

City tourist office On the plaza, opposite the cathedral (daily 8am–8pm; 981 816 1782). More convenient but less equipped than the state tourist office. Smaller information booths are at the bus stations, in the Baluarte de San Pedro and in the Casa Seis.

City tours For a concise overview of the city try the *tranvía* tour, with commentary in Spanish and English, which departs from the main plaza (hourly 9am–2pm & 5–8pm), taking a pleasant tour around neighbourhoods beyond the walls.

KankabiOK Tours C 59 no. 3-A, between C 8 and C 10; 981 811 2792, http://kankabiok.com.mx. Small agency running excursions to Edzná and Calakmul, as well as nearby *cenotes* and beaches.

ACCOMMODATION

SEE MAP PAGE 691

Campeche's **hotels** are only just beginning to match tourist demand – there is an increasing number to choose from, and a couple of them are outstanding. The few decent budget options are within a few blocks of the Plaza Principal; some top-end choices are just outside the old city walls. In any case, avoid rooms overlooking the street, as Campeche's narrow lanes tend to amplify noise.

Casa Don Gustavo C 59 no. 4, between C 8 and C 10; http://casadongustavo.com. Stately, high-end boutique hotel with thoughtfully designed, romantic en suites – some with four-poster beds – set around a central patio. There's also a small pool and an excellent restaurant. M$$$$

Castelmar C 61 no. 2-A, between C 8 and C 10; 981 811 1204. Based in a former army barracks that dates back to 1800, this charming, colonial-style place has old floor tiles, a large courtyard and soaring ceilings. Modern touches include a small pool, a/c and satellite TV. M$$$

López C 12 no. 189, between C 61 and C 63; http://hotellopezcampeche.com.mx. A nicely renovated hotel catering mainly to Mexican business travellers (hence the free newspaper in the morning); modern a/c rooms are in a pretty Deco-era building with open halls (though the bathrooms can be a bit musty). There's a small pool. M$$

Maya Campeche C 57 no. 40, between C 14 and C 16; http://mayacampechehotel.com. This small place just up from the plaza has fifteen fairly spacious rooms. Two floors open onto a slender courtyard, with a narrow shaded walkway above. All rooms have a/c, and regular promos can bring prices down by a good amount. M$$

★ **Puerta Campeche** C 59 no. 61, between C 16 and C 18; https://www.ihg.com. Located just inside the Puerta de Tierra, Campeche's finest hotel occupies the shell of a colonial home and warehouse. The pool winds through crumbling walls and is overlooked by a breezy terrace, a great spot for an evening drink. M$$$$

Rest & Recreation C 57, between C 12 and C 14; 981 120 6268. A justifiably popular hostel with a mix of dorms and private rooms – all with a/c. It's good value, considering the quality. Dorms M$, doubles M$$

12

EATING

SEE MAP PAGE 691

Campeche is well known for good food, and restaurants abound. **Seafood**, available almost everywhere, is a good bet. For breakfast, the cafés along C 8 near the government offices offer everything from tacos to fresh juices and pastries. Later in the day, the café in the centre of the plaza serves good coffee and ice cream. Campeche's **market**, just east of the walled city, is surrounded by *comedores* offering cheap and tasty lunches. Another local favourite is the stretch of *paradores de cockteleros* on the malecón – these seafood-vending kiosks are open until around 4pm. At **night**, people snack at Portales de San Martín, just north of the walls between C 10 and C 12. Bars aren't open late, but stop by the rooftop bar at the *Puerta Campeche* hotel (Fri & Sat only) for the view.

CAFÉS, CHEAP EATS AND SNACKS

Café Frappísimo C 8 s/n; www.frappisimo.mx. A modern, a/c coffee shop, just off the square, with well-made cappuccinos, lattes, frappuccinos and the like, plus tempting cakes, cookies and filled baguettes. There are also magazines, newspapers and books to flick through. M$

Chocolates de la Mora Corner of C 59 and 10; 981 817 5658. The speciality at this delightful café is drinking chocolate spiked with cinnamon and almond, served hot or iced. There's also a good range of cakes, pastries, sandwiches and snacks, as well as home-made chocolates. M$$

Luz de Luna C 59 no. 6, between C 10 and C 12; 981 100 8556. A quirky restaurant-gallery, *Luz de Luna* offers a generous variety of Mexican favourites – from *ceviche* to fajitas. Breakfasts are particularly good and plentiful, including cinnamon-scented *cafe de olla*. M$$$

La Parroquia C 55 no. 8, between C 10 and C 12; 981 816 2530, https://facebook.com/LaParroquiaCam. High ceilings echo with the clink of dishes at this big open-front diner. Staff can be inconsistent, as can the food, but it's inexpensive and convenient. M$$

RESTAURANTS

El Bastión C 57, on the plaza; http://elbastion.mx. The best place to eat with a plaza view (you can compare it with the old-photo wallpaper inside), though the traditional *campechano* menu isn't quite as good as others. M$$$

Casa Vieja C 10 no. 319, on the plaza; 981 811 8016, https://facebook.com/casaviejadelrio. A Cuban-owned restaurant with well-appointed balcony overlooking the main square. Food is a bit international-bland, but it's a great spot for a rum cocktail or cold beer. M$$

Marganzo C 8 no. 267, between C 57 and C 59; 981 811 3899. Touristy but still pleasant and not as expensive as it looks. The varied menu includes tasty crab quesadillas and generous *botanas* (bite-size snacks). M$$$

La Palapa Resurgimiento, 2.5km south along the malecón from the city centre; http://lapalapadeltiofito.com. A good destination for a malecón stroll, this large bar-restaurant is right on the water. It has big seafood plates, but you can also make a meal from the delicious *botanas* served with every drink. M$$$

★ **La Pigua** Alemán 179-A; 981 160 1684, https://facebook.com/lapiguacam. Follow C 8 north to find one of the city's most legendary restaurants, a pretty, rather elegant spot with exceptionally delicious seafood, such as creamy shrimp soup and fresh fillets with garlic and herbs. Reserve for dinner. M$$$$

DIRECTORY

American Express In the VI-PS travel agency, C 59 between Ruíz Cortines and 16 de Septiembre behind the *Best Western Del Mar* (981 811 1010).

Banks and exchange HSBC, C 10 at C 55, is just off the main square and has an ATM.

Internet There are internet cafés on virtually every street in the centre of Campeche.

Laundry The most central is La Antigua at C 57, between 12 and 14.

Post office 16 de Septiembre near C 53.

Edzná and the Chenes sites

Some 50km from Campeche lie the ruins of **Edzná**, surprisingly large and richly decorated, yet relatively little known to tourists. Beyond Edzná, you'll need a car to follow Hwy-261 towards the town of Hopelchén and the so-called **Chenes sites**: the ruins of Hochob and Dzibilnocac (completists can also ask for directions to El Tabasqueño and Santa Rosa Xtampak as well). They share a similar style of architecture, with colonnaded facades and monster-mouth doorways, evolved from the Río Bec further south.

Edzná

12

45km southeast of Campeche • Charge • **Sound-and-light show** Charge

At the height of its power, between 250 BC and 150 AD, **Edzná** was a large city, on the main route between the Maya communities of the highlands and the coast. The ruins show evidence of a complex drainage and irrigation system that probably supported a large agricultural project and more than a thousand people. Its architecture features elements of Río Bec, Classic Maya and Puuc design. The sound-and-light show is surprisingly good, and involves tramping around the site (make sure you wear insect repellent) rather than just sitting in a seat.

Templo de los Cinco Pisos

The most important structure is a stepped palace-pyramid more than 30m high. Unusually, each of the five storeys contains chambered "palace" rooms. While both solid temple pyramids and multi-storey "apartment" complexes are relatively common, it's rare to see the two combined in one building. At the front, a steep monumental staircase leads to a three-room temple, topped by a roofcomb. It's a hot climb, but the view takes in the dense greenery and the hills that mark this side of the peninsula.

As you look out over two plazas, the further of which must have been capable of holding tens of thousands of people, it is easy to imagine the power that the high priest or king commanded. Beyond lie the unexcavated remains of other large pyramids, and behind them, the vast flat expanse of the Yucatán plain. Inside the west-facing temple, a stele of the god of maize was illuminated by the sun twice a year, on the dates for the planting and harvesting of the crop.

The lesser buildings

Lesser buildings surround the ceremonial precinct. The **Nohochná** (Casa Grande, or Big House), a palace on the northwest side, is some 55m long and contains a room used as a *temazcal* (traditional sauna), with stone benches and hearths over which water could be boiled. Over in the **Pequeña Acrópolis**, the **Templo de los Mascarones** contains two eerie masks representing the sun god, rising on the east (left-hand) side and setting on the west.

Dzibilnocac

1km east of Iturbide • Free

Dzibilnocac is a small site, and an easy stop if you're in a car (note that many road signs for Iturbide refer to the town as Vicente Guerrero). By bus, it's feasible, but you may feel it was not quite worth the trouble. The buildings here show the ultra-decorative facades typical of the Chenes style – its restored western temple pyramid is quite pretty.

Hochob

15km southwest of Dzibalchén (follow signs to Chencoh) • Charge

Hochob features an amazing three-room temple (low and fairly small, as are most Chenes buildings), with a facade richly carved with stylized snakes and masks. The central chamber is surmounted by a crumbling roofcomb, and its decoration, with fangs, eyes and ears, creates the effect of a huge face, with the doorway as a gaping mouth.

Grutas de X'tacumbilxuna'an

3km south of Bolonchén • Charge

Near Bolonchén, you'll see signs for these **caves**. Though deep and rather dramatically lit, the area you actually visit is limited, and as a result, the attraction feels a bit overpriced. But if you happen to be driving by, it's a brief scenic stop.

12

ARRIVAL AND DEPARTURE — EDZNÁ AND THE CHENES SITES

By bus For Edzná, Autobuses Ejidales services (30–40min) leave from in front of the Sur terminal in Campeche daily a few times in the morning, until about 11.30am, but the last bus returns at 3.45pm (confirm with the driver). For Dzibilnocac, the only other site really accessible by bus, take a second-class service from Campeche to Iturbide (8–9 daily, 7.45am–5.35pm; 1hr 15min), from where it's a 1km walk.

By combi For Edzná, *combis* for Pich, a village 20km past the ruins, depart from in front of the Campeche market. To get back, you'll need to ask the driver to collect you at the site, or walk to Pich; go as early in the day as possible.

By car If you're driving to the Río Bec from Campeche, you can continue south from Hochob to Xpujil – it's a good back route that avoids a lot of the truck traffic that plagues Hwy-186.

By tour Organized tours from Campeche (see page 693) cover Edzná and a couple of smaller sites, and are less rushed than visiting independently on public transport.

ACCOMMODATION AND EATING

Hacienda Uayamón Carretera Uayamon–Edzná km 20, Uayamón; https://www.ihg.com. Off the fast road to Edzná, this hotel, part of the IHG group, was founded as a cattle ranch in the sixteenth century and later became one of the largest henequen (a type of agave used for rope-making) haciendas in the country. In addition to the luxurious rooms, many with private terrace and plunge pool, another attraction is the exuberant birdlife plus beasties like armadillos and coatis. The hacienda's restaurant is a good option for a romantic meal, or just an excuse to poke around the grounds. Call ahead for a dinner reservation. M$$$$

Hwy-180 to Mérida

From Campeche north to Mérida, first-class buses take **Hwy-180**, which was once the colonial Camino Real ("Royal Road"). While the highway bypasses most of the towns along the way, second-class buses from Campeche and Mérida stop at almost all of them, and two signposted detours are especially worthwhile if you're driving. The area is a nice slice of semi-rural Maya life, with *triciclo* taxis running alongside cars, and many women wearing traditional embroidered *huipiles*.

Museo Arqueológico del Camino Real

Main plaza, Hecelchakán • Charge • http://inah.gob.mx • Second-class buses (every 30min–1hr; around 1hr 15min) run frequently from Campeche and Mérida

Located in the town of Hecelchakán, about 80km from Campeche, this small archeology **museum** is notable for its collection of Jaina figurines, beautifully detailed clay portraits of Maya people unearthed on the Isla de Jaina, just off the coast due west of here (and unfortunately not open to visitors). Typically just 10–20cm tall, the figures have been a key to research on the everyday life of ancient Maya people: what they wore, how they altered their appearance, what they did for entertainment. The figures were placed in the graves of the people they depicted, often held in their hands or laid on their chests.

Becal

Off Hwy-180, 35km north of Hecelchakán • Second-class buses run frequently from Campeche and Mérida (see page 693)

The town of **BECAL** is synonymous with the ubiquitous Yucatecan *jipi*, or "Panama" hat (the original Panama hats actually came from Ecuador). Shops throughout town sell them, and it's interesting to see a village so consumed with a single cottage industry – a fountain made of concrete hats even graces the town square.

If you pull over, you're likely to be approached by a friendly local who will take you to a nearby hat shop, and perhaps stop at one of the town's many *cuevas*, the cool, damp cellars in which the villagers traditionally make and store the hats to keep them soft and flexible. As for the hats themselves, the best (which can be crumpled into a ball and spring back to shape) are hard to come by even here at the source; shops offer cheap and mid-range options, depending on the fineness of the fibres and tightness of the weave.

Mérida

Nicknamed "La Ciudad Blanca" after its white limestone buildings (now covered in peeling layers of gem-coloured paint), the capital of Yucatán state is in every sense the leading city of the peninsula. Within its historic core, though, **MÉRIDA** retains a sense of small-town graciousness coupled with an extremely lively and sometimes avant-garde cultural scene. It draws thousands of visitors, both Mexican and foreign, and has seen a rash of expat investment over the last fifteen years. Yet even as the buzz increases, the city retains its grace and manners. Every street in the centre boasts a well-maintained colonial church or museum, and the plazas throng with locals enjoying free music and other attractions. Not only can you live well here, but it's a great base for excursions to the surrounding Maya sites of Uxmal and Chichén Itzá.

Brief history

Founded in 1542, Mérida is built over, and partly from, the ruins of a Maya city known as **Tihó** or Ichcansihó. Its fortune grew as the capital for exporting **henequen**, the rope fibre that was Yucatán's "green gold".

Trade was interrupted in the spring of 1849, when, early in the Maya uprising that became known as the **Caste Wars**, rebel armies laid siege to Mérida. They were within a hair's breadth of capturing the city, when, legend has it, the Maya peasant fighters left the siege to plant corn. The Yucatecan elite quickly arranged a deal with the central Mexican government ceding the peninsula's independence in exchange for support against future Maya rebellions.

Mérida became an extraordinarily wealthy city, much of it poured into grandiose mansions along Paseo de Montejo. Then the henequen industry all but died around World War II, when nylon became the rope-making material of choice. But Mérida remains elegant, prosperous and intellectual, a vibrant mix of Maya, *mestizos*, Lebanese (who emigrated here in the early twentieth century) and more recent transplants from Mexico City and abroad.

Plaza Grande

Any exploration of Mérida begins naturally in this plaza, officially called the **Plaza de la Independencia**, and the largest in the city, at the intersection of calles 60, 61, 62 and 63. It's the hub of city life, particularly in the evenings, when couples meet on park benches and trios of *trovadores* wait to be hired for serenades.

Catedral de San Ildefonso

C 60 on the Plaza de la Independencia • Free

Built in the second half of the sixteenth century, Mérida's largest **church** is in a rather severe style that veered away from earlier, more ornate Spanish styles. The building was heavily looted during the Mexican Revolution in the early twentieth century, though in a chapel to the left of the main altar, people still venerate the Cristo de las Ampollas

12

(Christ of the Blisters), a crucifix carved from a tree in the village of Ichmul that burned for a whole night without showing the least sign of damage. Later, in 1645, the parish church at Ichmul burned down, and the crucifix survived, though blackened and blistered.

It is entirely likely that the original crucifix was also destroyed in the looting of 1915, but whether the existing statue is a reproduction is irrelevant – it remains the focal point of a local fiesta from mid-September to mid-October, when each day a different professional group, or *gremio* (taxi drivers, bakers and so on), pays its respects at the church, then parades on the plaza.

MACAY

Pasaje de la Revolución, off C 60 on the Plaza de la Independencia • Free • http://macay.org

Beside the cathedral, the former bishop's palace has been converted into shops, offices and the Museo de Arte Contemporáneo Ateneo de Yucatán (**MACAY**), which has the best modern art collection in southern Mexico, with permanent displays featuring the work of internationally acclaimed Yucatecan painters Fernando Castro Pacheco, Gabriel Ramírez Aznar and Fernando García Ponce.

Museo Casa Montejo

C 63 on the Plaza de la Independencia • Free guided tours (1hr) • 999 253 6732

Francisco de Montejo was the first conquistador to attempt to bring the peninsula under the control of Spain, in 1527. He failed, but his son secured the north of the peninsula in the 1540s. The father built this **palace** in 1549; it's now a Banamex office. Visitors can see the lavishly restored wood-panelled dining room, off the back right corner of the Moorish-feeling courtyard. Above a staid doorway of Classical columns, the facade is decorated in the manically ornate plateresque style (probably the first instance of it in the New World), with conquistadors depicted trampling savages underfoot.

12

Palacio Municipal

C 62 on the Plaza de la Independencia • Free

Facing the cathedral, Mérida's **city hall** (*ayuntamiento*) is another impressive piece of sixteenth-century design, with a beautiful clock tower and a large painting upstairs that depicts the *mestizaje*, the birth of the first mixed-blood Mexican.

Palacio de Gobierno

C 61 on the Plaza de la Independencia • Free

Completing the square, the nineteenth-century state government building is a must-see. On the ground floor and in the large front room upstairs, enormous, aggressively modernist murals by Fernando Castro Pacheco cover the walls. They powerfully depict the violent history of the Yucatán and the trials of its Indigenous people.

North of the Plaza Grande

Most of the remaining monuments in Mérida lie north of the plaza, along the main commercial streets of Calle 60 and Paseo de Montejo. Calle 60 is a parade of historically significant buildings, and Paseo de Montejo is lined with the magnificent mansions of the henequen-rich grandees who strove to outdo one another around the end of the nineteenth century.

Museo del Arte Popular de Yucatán

C 50-A at C 57 • Charge • 999 928 5263

This is a small but flawless collection of Mexican **craftwork**, worth a detour if you have time and interest in the subject. It's set in an old house, with a sense of humour about the bathrooms. The small but well-stocked gift shop is a good place for souvenir hunting.

Museo de la Canción Yucateca

C 57 between C 48 and C 50 • Charge, free Sun • http://museodelacancionyucateca.com

Behind the former monastery of La Mejorada, this pleasantly old-fashioned **museum** details the development of the Yucatán's traditional, painfully romantic *trova* music. It traces the diverse influences, from pre-Columbian traditions to Afro-Cuban styles, and shows off many of the classic stars. Its gift shop has plenty of CDs.

Museo de Antropología Yucatán (Palacio Cantón)

C 43 at Paseo de Montejo • Charge • http://inah.gob.mx • 30min walk from the plaza

The former site of the city's museum of Maya culture (now at the Gran Museo del Mundo Maya, see below) reopened in 2012 after renovation. As well as anthropological and other exhibits, the **museum** is worth a visit for the building itself, a Beaux Arts palace, trimmed in wrought iron and marble. It was built at the beginning of the twentieth century by Francisco Cantón Rosado, the railway tycoon, state governor and general who was a key supporter of dictator Porfirio Díaz.

Gran Museo del Mundo Maya

C 60 Norte, 9.5km north of the centre, just inside the ring road • Charge • **Sound-and-light show** Free • http://granmuseodelmundomaya.com.mx

Opened in 2012 to great fanfare, the **Gran Museo del Mundo Maya** brings to life the world of the Maya, from origins to the present day, through hundreds of archeological, anthropological, ethnological and historical exhibits. The main draw is the free sound-and-light spectacle (this was suspended at the time of research; check the website for the latest), an immersive audio-video art installation that covers Maya history and culture in grand terms. There are plenty of activities for children as well.

South of the Plaza Grande

Heading south of the Plaza Grande, Mérida becomes somewhat scruffier, with the streets getting a bit more jammed with traffic and commerce, especially around the massive public market, the Mercado Lucas de Gálvez, close to which is a good museum.

Mercado Lucas de Gálvez

C 67 at C 56 • Free

Mérida's main **market** is in two vast joined halls, plus a clutch of stalls around the periphery, with more than two thousand vendors plying their trades. It's a wild scrum of consumer goods, from freshly hacked-up beef to hand-tooled leather belts to numerous varieties of bananas. Arrive before noon to see the most bountiful foodstuffs; **craft shops** (many in a separate wing on C 56-A at C 65) are open all day.

Museo de la Ciudad

C 56 between C 65 and C 65-A • Free • http://facebook.com/museodelaciudaddemerida

A nice touch of culture on the edge of the market, the grand city **museum** occupies the beautiful old central post office. The exhibits trace city history from ancient Maya times through the henequen boom. The text is in Spanish and English. There's also a gallery of local contemporary art.

ARRIVAL AND DEPARTURE — MÉRIDA

BY PLANE

Mérida's Manuel Crecencio Rejón airport (999 940 6090, https://themeridaairport.com) is 7km southwest of the centre. It has a tourist office (daily 8am–8pm), post office,

long-distance phones and car-rental desks. Taxis run to and from the city centre. You could also take bus #79 ("Aviación"), which goes to Parque San Juan, but the stop is a very long walk from the terminal, and it runs infrequently.
Destinations Guadalajara on Volaris (2 daily; 1hr 35min); Mexico City on Aeromexico, VivaAerobus and Volaris (19 daily; 2hr).

BY BUS

Mérida has two major bus stations, both on the southwest side of town, plus several smaller stations and stopping points, just about all of which are south of the plaza. In theory, they all deal with different companies and destinations, but in practice, there's a bit of overlap. In addition to the larger stations below, AutoProgreso (C 62 between C 65 and C 67) serves Progreso and nearby Dzibilchaltún, while AutoCentro (C 65 at C 48) runs an additional service to Izamal, and the only service to the ruins of Aké.

TERMINAL CAME

Located on C 70 between C 69 and C 71, for express ADO, ADO GL, ADO Platino and OCC. You'll likely arrive here if you're coming directly from Cancún, Campeche or Chichén Itzá. City buses don't head to the main plaza. Taxis are available or it's a 20min walk.
Destinations Campeche (every 30min–1hr; 2hr 30min); Cancún (every 30min–1hr; 4hr 15min); Chetumal (4 daily at 7.30am, 1pm, 6pm & 11pm; 5hr 30min–6hr); Escárcega (5 daily; 4hr 40min); Mexico City (6 daily; 20–22hr); Palenque (4 daily at 8.30am, 8.40pm, 10pm & 11.45pm; 8–9hr); Playa del Carmen (every 30min–1hr; 4hr 5min–5hr 25min); Tulum (5 daily; 4hr); Valladolid (every 30min–1hr; 2hr 15min); Villahermosa (every 30min–1hr; 8hr–9hr 5min).

TERMINAL TAME

Officially the Terminal de Segunda Clase, the TAME is across the street from the CAME, on C 69 between C 68 and C 70. ATS, Clase Europea, Mayab, Sur, TRT and some Oriente buses leave from here. Coming from Campeche, you may arrive here. There's luggage storage (at a window outside, facing the CAME entrance). City buses don't head to the main plaza. You can take a taxi or it's a 20min walk.
Destinations Campeche via Maxcanú, Hecelchakán and Becal (every 30–45min; 2hr 30min); Cancún via Valladolid (roughly hourly; 4–6hr); Cancún via Felipe Carrillo Puerto (12 daily; 5–8hr); Chetumal (7–8 daily; 6hr); Chiquilá, for Holbox (1 daily at 10.30pm; 5–6hr); Escárcega (3 daily at 11am, 1.10pm & 3.40pm; 6hr); Felipe Carrillo Puerto (11 daily; 2hr 30min); Hopelchén via Santa Elena and Uxmal (6–7 daily; 2hr 30min); Oxkutzcab via Ticul (roughly hourly; 2hr); Playa del Carmen (hourly; 5–7hr); Tulum (10 daily; 5–7hr).

FIESTA AMERICANA

Some deluxe buses (ADO, ADO GL and Platino) arrive at a car park on C 60 at Colón, just west of the Fiesta Americana, north of the centre. Take a taxi from here or walk one block east and flag down a southbound city bus.
Destinations Cancún (8 daily; 4hr–4hr 35min); Cancún airport (3 daily at 6.15am, 9.15am & noon; 4hr); Villahermosa (2 daily at 9.30pm & 11pm; 9hr 15min).

NORESTE TERMINAL

On C 67 at C 50. Second-class buses (LUS, Noreste and Oriente) from here serve the coast and small interior towns.
Destinations Cancún via Chichén Itzá and Valladolid (roughly hourly; 4hr); Cuzamá (7 daily; 1hr 30min); Izamal (roughly hourly; 1hr); Maní via Acancéh and Tecoh (10 daily; 2hr); Río Lagartos (1 daily at 5.30pm; 4hr); San Crisanto (3 daily at 7am, 10.15am & 6.30pm; 1hr 45min); San Felipe (1 daily at 5.30pm; 6hr 30min); Tizimín (6 daily; 3–4hr); Tulum via Cobá (1 daily at 5.20am; 8hr).

BY COLECTIVO

Minivans often provide a more frequent service to destinations an hour or two outside the city, and to smaller villages. These, as well as small buses to Dzibilchaltún, Oxkutzcab and Ticul, congregate on Parque San Juan (C 62 at C 69). For Progreso, *colectivos* leave from the east side of C 60 between C 65 and C 67.

GETTING AROUND

By bus The city-bus system is convoluted, but in general, northbound buses run up C 56. For Paseo de Montejo, look for #17 on C 59 between C 56 and C 58, or #18 on C 56 at C 59. You can flag buses down at any corner; fares are posted on the doors.

By taxi Taxis can be hailed all around town and from ranks at Parque Hidalgo, the post office and Parque San Juan. The ones at ranks charge according to a zone system – with fees cheaper around the centre and more expensive in the outskirts. Cars roving the streets (signed "Radio Taxi") use meters, and are often cheaper.

Bike rental On Sun mornings for the Bici-Ruta (see page 704), bicycles are available for rent on the plaza; the rest of the week, contact Bicimaya Matriz, on C 65 between C 54 and C 56 (999 924 6562, https://bicimaya.com; rent by the hour or the day).

Car rental Family-run Mexico Rent a Car, at C 57A between C 58 and C 60, has good rates with insurance (999 923 3637, http://mexico-rent-acar.com). International agencies have offices in a strip on C 60 between C 55 and C 57, in the *Fiesta Americana* and at the airport.

INFORMATION AND TOURS

INFORMATION

Tourist office Teatro Peón Contreras, C 60 at C 57-A (daily 8am–8pm; 999 925 5186, http://merida.gob.mx/turismo). Mérida's main tourist office is usually staffed with at least one English-speaker. Pick up a copy of the helpful *Yucatán Today* (http://yucatantoday.com), in English and Spanish. Other tourist information booths are in the Palacio de Gobierno on the Plaza de la Independencia (daily 8am–8pm), the TAME bus station (Mon–Sat 8am–8pm, Sat–Sun 8am–2pm) and on Paseo de Montejo (daily 8am–8pm) at Colón, just south of the *Fiesta Americana* hotel. Info kiosks staffed with tourist police (999 942 0060) are set up at the plaza.

Websites The website Yucatan Living (http://yucatanliving.com) is an excellent resource, posting a weekly events calendar and commenting on local bars, restaurants and news.

CITY TOURS

Bus tours An open-sided bus tour goes further afield than you'd walk. It departs from Parque de Santa Lucía (daily 9am–8pm; 999 920 7636, http://turibus.com.mx).

Horse-drawn carriages *Calesas* run a 45min trip around the centre and up Paseo de Montejo.

Walking and cookery tours Mérida's tourism bureau gives a free walking tour (Mon–Sat at 9.30am); reserve at the office in the Palacio de Gobierno (see above). Guru Walk (https://www.guruwalk.com/p918-merida) also offers free English-language walking tours during the high season. Chef David Sterling (http://los-dos.com; 8hr) offers a range of cookery classes and food-related tours.

TOUR OPERATORS

Adventures Mexico C 10 no. 374-C, Pedregales de Tanlum; 999 925 1700, http://adventures-mexico.com. Does a good range of day trips to attractions around the city, as well as cookery classes and cantina tours.

Red de Ecoturismo de Yucatán 999 926 7756, http://redecoturismoyucatan.blogspot.mx. A network of community eco-adventure projects, offering activities like bike trips and camping excursions.

ACCOMMODATION

SEE MAP PAGE 698

Although Mérida can get crowded at peak times, you should always be able to find a good, reasonably priced **hotel**

YUCATECAN CUISINE

Though it varies across the peninsula, **food** in the Yucatán has a few unifying elements, most based on **traditional Maya combinations** and accented with many earthy **spices**. Little of the food is hot, but go easy on the *salsa de chile habanero* that most restaurants have on the table. It's also called *xnipek*, Maya for "dog's nose", because the fiery chile induces a clammy sweat. The most popular dishes are:

Puchero A mutable stew that often includes chicken, beef, pork, squash, cabbage and sweet potato in a broth seasoned with cinnamon and allspice, all garnished with radish, coriander and Seville orange.

Poc-chuc A combination of pork with tomatoes, onions and spices, widely considered the region's signature dish.

Sopa de lima Chicken broth with fragrant local citrus and tortilla chips, and the most popular appetizer or evening snack.

Pollo or cochinita pibil Chicken or suckling pig wrapped in banana leaves and cooked in a *pib*, a pit in the ground, the shredded meat then utilized in many other snacks.

Papadzules Tacos filled with hard-boiled eggs and covered in a very rich red and green pumpkin-seed sauce.

Pavo en relleno negro Turkey in a black, burnt-chile sauce.

Salbutes Crisp corn tortillas topped with shredded turkey, pickled onions, avocado and radish, ubiquitous at dinner time.

Panuchos The same as *salbutes*, with an added dab of beans.

Chaya A spinach-like green that's reputed to cure everything that ails you, often blended into a drink with pineapple.

Huevos motuleños A sweet-savoury mix of fried eggs and beans on a crisp tortilla, topped with mild salsa, ham, cheese, peas and fried banana slices.

room. Unless you have a very early bus to catch, there's not much point in staying in the grimier area near the **main bus stations**, nor in the generic top-end hotels along **Paseo de Montejo**. The best options are all within a few blocks of the central plaza – which is still just a long walk or a short cab ride from the furthest transport and sights. In addition to the usual hotels, Mérida has a glut of good **B&Bs** and smaller inns in converted colonial homes.

HOTELS

Casa Lucía C 60 no. 474, between C 53 and C 55; http://casalucia.com.mx. Located opposite the park of the same name, close to the action, this smart, slightly prim hotel provides attractive mid-range rooms – featuring nice touches like wrought iron bed frames – set around an appealing pool. M$$$

Dolores Alba C 63 no. 464, between C 52 and C 54; http://doloresalba.com. Popular, clean mid-range place situated around two courtyards (one colonial style, and one sporting a dazzling array of mirror glass) and a large swimming pool. With parking, laundry facilities and more, you get a lot for your money, but it is on the scruffier side of the plaza. M$$

Eclipse C 57 no. 491, between C 58 and C 60; http://hoteleclipsemerida.com.mx. Suffering from colonial overload? This hip-and-modern hotel has spare white rooms, each with a different theme suggested with fabric accents and accessories (a lava lamp, a Warhol print, etc). A glittery-tile pool sits in the centre, and there's a small café. A/c and flatscreen TVs are part of the package. M$$$$

Hacienda Xcanatun 12km north of Mérida on the road to Progreso; www.angsana.com/es/mexico/hacienda-xcanatun. The closest hacienda to the city, this elegant eighteenth-century plantation house sits on lush grounds. Some of the luxurious suites have baths hewn from local rock. There's also a full spa and an excellent restaurant. M$$$$

Hotel Eclipse de Merida C 57 no. 491, at C 57; 999 923 1600. This dated but reliable hotel is good for a few nights if you're on a budget and don't mind a bit of maintenance noise during the daytime. There's also good internet access here and some deep tissue massage level water pressure. M$$

★ **Julamis** C 53 at C 54; http://hoteljulamis.com. Owned (and decorated) by two Cuban artists, *Julamis* is a great opportunity to stay in a colonial house for barely more than far less-inspiring budget hotels. The six rooms and one suite all have a/c, and mix modern furnishings with soaring ceilings and old tiled floors. Perks include free beers in the in-room fridges and a plunge pool on the roof. M$$$

★ **Luz en Yucatán** C 55 no. 499, between C 58 and C 60; http://luzenyucatan.com. Delightful rambling place with fifteen rooms to suit every traveller: studios, kitchenettes, private terraces or patios (and even a whole house just down the street). Pool, kitchen, and owners who were once tour guides, so well attuned to guests' needs. The rooms are dynamically priced depending on whether you class yourself as "exceedingly", "moderately" or "not at all" financially successful. M$$$

Mucuy C 57 no. 481, between C 56 and C 58; www.mucuyhotel.com. Quiet and well run, with kind staff, good-value rooms, a small pool and wi-fi in the lobby (but not, generally, in most rooms). Housekeeping isn't always as diligent as it should be, but overall it's tidy and the best of the non-hostel budget spots. A/c is extra. M$$

B&BS, GUESTHOUSES AND HOSTELS

★ **Casa Ana** C 52 no. 469, between C 51 and C 53; 999 924 0005. Charming little B&B with just four simple a/c rooms, each one sparklingly clean and comfortable (the four-bed Pitahaya option is a great choice for families and groups). There's also a small pool and a pleasant garden. M$$$

★ **Merida Santiago** C 74-A no. 499, between C 57 and C 59-A; http://hotelmeridasantiago.com. This colourful colonial home with six bright rooms is farther west than other options, but worth the walk for whirlpool tubs and plush beds, great breakfasts, a big pool, spa treatments, and a helpful Mexican-Dutch couple as hosts. M$$$$

Nómadas C 62 no. 433, at C 51; http://hostelche.com.mx. Mérida's longest-established hostel is a smooth operation, with both mixed and single-sex dorms, space for hammocks or tent camping, and fan-only private rooms, some of which are en suite. There's even a pool, and (generally free) activities and entertainment almost nightly M$

12

EATING

SEE MAP PAGE 698

Good **restaurants** are plentiful in the centre of Mérida, though the best (and some of the least expensive) are often open only for lunch. At dinner, many restaurants cater largely to foreigners and are a bit overpriced; locals tend to frequent the **snack stalls** on Plaza Santa Ana (C 60 at C 47) and Parque de Santiago (C 59 between C 70 and C 72) for *panuchos*, *salbutes* and *sopa de lima*. There are also pavement cafés on **Parque Hidalgo**, along C 60 between C 61 and C 59, and a good juice bar on the southwest corner of the plaza.

CAFÉS, CHEAP EATS AND SNACKS

Bistro Cultural C 66 at C 41; 999 221 9756, https://facebook.com/Bistro.Cultuural. Off the beaten track, but well worth the walk, this delightful French-run joint has a tranquil garden, murals on the walls, and a small, economical menu: daily specials from Europe, Mexico and further afield, plus cooling frappés and desserts like *tarte tatin*. They sometimes put on live music in the evenings. M$$

Café Crème C 41 at C 60; 999 192 9565. Another French-run place, this café and patisserie with a shady patio garden

MÉRIDA'S FREE ENTERTAINMENT

The historic centre hosts a party nearly every night of the week, all free and attended largely by locals. Many films and concerts happen at the **Centro Olimpo de Cultura**, on the northwest corner of the plaza. In addition, these are the recurring events:

Mon *Jarana* folk dances, in or in front of the Palacio Municipal on the west side of the main plaza. 9pm.

Tues Big band music, heavy on the mambo, Parque de Santiago (C 72 at C 59); *trova* at the Centro Olimpo. 8.30pm.

Wed Concert at the Centro Olimpo. 9pm.

Thurs Serenata Yucateca, traditional *trova* music, Parque Santa Lucía; classical music at the Centro Olimpo. 9pm.

Sat Noche Mexicana, music from all over Mexico, at the start of Paseo Montejo, Calle 56-A; jazz, salsa and more on the Plaza de la Independencia. 8pm.

Sun Car-free centre: in the morning (8am–noon), bicycles take over the streets for the Bici-Ruta (http://merida.gob.mx/biciruta); in the afternoon and evening, the plaza is filled with music, dancing, food stalls and more. There's also an all-day flea market in the Parque Santa Lucía.

has a tempting range of pastries, plus sandwiches, quiches and salads, as well as set meals and top-notch coffee. M$$

Dulcería y Sorbetería El Colón C 61 on the central plaza; 999 927 6443. A slice of old-town Mérida, with a refreshing range of fruit sorbets (from coconut to watermelon), black-and-white photos on the walls, and efficient waiters dressed in salmon-pink shirts. There's another branch on Paseo de Montejo between C 39 and C 41, near Palacio Cantón. M$

12

La Habana C 62 at C 59; 999 928 6502. Mérida's older bohemian intellectual crowd doesn't come around this coffee shop so much since the national smoking ban went into effect. But the black-and-beige-clad waiters still dish out Mexican-style diner food, and there are economical daily meal deals. It also roasts its own coffee. M$$

Manjar Blanco C 47 no. 496, between C 58 and C 60; 999 547 6237, https://facebook.com/elmanjarblanco. Excellent little café serving traditional Yucatecan cuisine (see page 702) at fair prices: try the tasty *poc-chuc* or the *cochinita pibil*. The only downside is that it's not open later. M$$

★ **La Reina Itzalana** Parque de Santiago, C 59 between C 70 and C 72; 999 928 5796, https://facebook.com/Lareinaitzalanasantiago. This and several other basic restaurants around the same park are some of the few places near the centre to get a casual, super-cheap dinner of *panuchos, salbutes* and *sopa de lima*. They're packed with local families in the evenings. M$$

RESTAURANTS

Amaro C 59 no. 507, between C 60 and C 62; 999 271 4368, https://facebook.com/restauranteamaromerida. Set in a lovely tree-shaded courtyard with a fountain and a romantic guitarist Wed–Sat. A little overpriced, but interesting veggie options, such as *crepas de chaya* (see page 702), are novelties for non-meat-eaters tired of quesadillas. M$$$$

★ **La Chaya Maya** C 62 at C 57; http://lachayamaya.com. A simple, sparkling-clean restaurant with a thorough menu of Yucatecan specialities – including *pavo en relleno negro*, *poc-chuc* and *panuchos* (see page 702) – with handmade tortillas and lots of *chaya*, pumpkin seeds and other earthy flavours. M$$

★ **El Marlin Azul** C 62, between C 57 and C 59; 999 2278 8169. Long-standing local favourite for seafood, including great fish tacos and perfect fresh *ceviche*. If there's no space in the main restaurant (under a blue awning), try the separate, smarter dining room next door to the north. M$$

Rosas y Xocolate Paseo de Montejo 480, at C 41; http://rosasandxocolate.com. This hip hotel restaurant is a double treat: excellent creative Mexican food (don't miss the crispy-fried octopus) plus eye candy in the form of the upper-crust *meridano* crowd. Toothsome desserts and regular live jazz performances, too. M$$$

El Trapiche C 62, between C 59 and C 61; 999 928 1231. Just off the plaza, this basic, budget-friendly Yucatecan restaurant is open all day and serves everything from fresh juices for breakfast to *poc-chuc* for dinner. M$$

DRINKING AND NIGHTLIFE

SEE MAP PAGE 698

For drinks beyond the hotel bars, there are of course hard-drinking men-only **cantinas** (all over the city, including a couple on C 62, just south of the plaza), plus traditional **family bars** (*bares familiares*; look for signs saying "*100% familiar*"). These are a more mixed affair, with, yes, sometimes even kids. They're open only till about 6pm, serving beer accompanied by *botanas* – small-plate snacks delivered with each round – and often live music.

Pancho's C 59, between C 60 and C 62; 999 834 5301. A steak restaurant with a pricey haute Mexican menu, this sprawling space is better as a bar, with tasty mojitos and margaritas. Hit the happy hour for the best deals.

Piedra de Agua C 60 no. 498, between C 59 and C 61, in the hotel of the same name; http://piedradeagua.com. Not a big party scene, but insiders know they can hide away in this courtyard bar and drink and talk late. The illuminated spires of the Iglesia Santa Lucia tower just beyond the ivy-covered walls.

La Pócima C 57 no. 482B; 999 828 9248. Advertised for the tapas but frequented by those in the know for the bar, this little hole in the wall is always a safe bet for a good night out. Most things here are also gentle on the wallet, making this a good spot if you're sticking to a budget.

La Quilla C 69, between C 44 and C 46; http://laquilla.blogspot.com. This artist-friendly café is officially an afternoon hangout but on irregular evenings (and occasional Sun afternoons) it hosts bands, DJs and films (cover charge) and stays open much later. Check the schedule, but either way, it's still a nice place for a beer.

ENTERTAINMENT

In addition to the options below, there is free music in the various **plazas** every night (see page 704). Or you can opt for a personal serenade at the central plaza from trios of *trovadores*, in their white shirts and trousers – for a tip.

Centro Cultural Universitario C 60 at C 57; http://cultura.unam.mx. The Universidad de Yucatán's Ballet Folklórico puts on a colourful performance of traditional Mexican and Maya ceremonies every Fri night. It's touristy but still low-key and inexpensive.

Teatro Peón Contreras C 60 at C 57; 999 923 1333. Check the calendar at the city's grand old theatre, where events range from visiting pop musicians to the Yucatán symphony orchestra (the group plays alternating Fri & Sun Oct–April).

SHOPPING

SEE MAP PAGE 698

In addition to hammocks, other good buys in Mérida include **clothing**, in particular men's *guayabera* shirts, which both Cubans and *meridanos* claim to have invented; Panama hats, known here as *jipis*; and embroidered *huipiles*, plus the traditional lace under-layer and checked *rebozo* shawl. Mérida's distinctive *trova* **music** is available in many gift shops on CD; it's especially cheap at the weekly serenade on Parque Santa Lucía, where vendors sell remastered classics or newer songs in the same vein. For all **crafts**, prices (and quality) in the main market are not great, unless you're an unusually skilled and determined haggler.

Casa de Artesanías C 63 two blocks west of the central plaza, in the Casa de la Cultura; 999 928 6676. This government-sponsored shop sells consistently high-quality crafts, including delicate silver filigree jewellery, at fixed prices. The clothing options are somewhat limited, however.

Librería Dante C 62 no. 502, on the central plaza; http://libreriadante.com.mx. This bookshop (one of several branches around town) has predominantly Spanish-language stock, but also sells some guidebooks and maps, as well as its own line of field guides.

La Poblana C 65 no. 492, near C 60; http://hamacaslapoblana.com. More a warehouse than a shop, this place has hundreds of hammocks stacked against every wall, sold by weight; a high-quality, dense-weave *doble* weighs about 1.5kg.

12

DIRECTORY

Banks and exchange Most banks are around C 65 between C 60 and C 64, have ATMs and are open 9am–4pm. The most centrally located is Banamex, in the entrance to the Museo Casa de Montejo on the south side of the plaza; it also has an ATM.

Consulates Opening hours are limited, so phone ahead. Belize, C 58 no. 450, at C 35, 999 928 6152; Cuba, C 42 no. 200, between C 1 E and C 1 D, Fracc Campestre 999 944 4216; US, C 60 no. 338-K, between C 29 and C 31, Colonía Alcala Martín 999 942 5700.

Hospitals Mérida is the Yucatán's centre for medical care. Clinica de Mérida hospital, Itzáes 242 at Colón (999 942 1800, http://clinicademerida.mx), is accustomed to dealing with foreigners.

Internet Internet cafés dot every street in central Mérida, and especially C 61 west of the plaza. There's free wi-fi in most of the city's parks.

Laundry Lavandería La Fe, C 64 between C 55 and C 57, offers an inexpensive service.

Post office C 53 between C 52 and C 54 (Mon–Fri 8am–4.30pm, Sat 9am–1pm). For packages, try Mayan Mail shipping service, C 58 between C 57 and C 59.

Gulf Coast

A wide, fast road (Hwy-261) connects Mérida with the **GULF COAST** to the north, first passing the ancient Maya complex of **Dzibilchaltún**, then arriving after 36km in the port of **Progreso**, on which *meridanos* descend en masse in summer. Due west of Mérida, the little village of **Celestún** offers a very different coastal experience from Progreso, being surrounded by a large nature reserve. In fact, most people hit the beach only after taking a boat tour around a long inlet that's home to a massive flamingo colony.

Dzibilchaltún

20km north of Mérida, east off Hwy-261 • Museo del Pueblo • Charge; guides are extra for up to six people • *Combis* for Chablecal leave from Mérida's Parque San Juan (C 62 at C 69) and stop near the ruins; leaving, you can walk or hitch a ride to Hwy-261, where you can flag down a Progreso- or Mérida-bound bus or *combi*

The archeological importance of the ruins of the ancient city of **Dzibilchaltún** is hardly reflected in what you actually see. What it lacks in grandiosity, though, it makes up for in the small yet excellent **Museo del Pueblo Maya**, which examines the persistence of Maya culture until modern times, with exhibits on traditional crafts and religion. There's also a very pretty **cenote**, in which you can swim, and the area is part of an **eco-archeological park**, where birders can spot the rough-winged swallow and the Yucatán woodpecker. Allow about two hours to see everything.

The place was settled from 1000 BC right through to the Conquest, the longest continuous occupation of any known site. More than eight thousand structures have been mapped, but unfortunately little has survived, in particular because the ready-dressed stones were a handy building material, used in local towns and in the Mérida–Progreso road. There is very little signage at the site, so it's worth hiring a **guide** at the main entrance.

Templo de las Siete Muñecas

From the museum at the entrance, a meandering nature trail leads to the so-called Temple of the Seven Dolls. The temple was originally a simple square pyramid, subsequently built over with a more complex structure. Later still, a passageway was cut through to the original building and seven deformed clay figurines (dolls) were buried, with a tube through which their spirits were meant to commune with the priests. The structure is remarkable for being the only known Maya temple to have windows, and for having a tower in place of the usual roofcomb. On the **equinoxes**, the sun shines straight through the tower doors, in a display of ancient astronomical savvy that draws a crowd of tourists.

Cenote Xlacah

One of the ancient causeways that linked the city's major points runs straight from the temple to another cluster of ruins. The centre of the grassy field is dominated by the shell of a Franciscan chapel. A little further west, **Cenote Xlacah** not only provided the ancient city with water, but also held ritual importance for the Maya. More than six thousand offerings – including human remains – have been discovered in its deeper end. It's also home to several types of fish, including the Yucatán tetra, a type of sardine found only in the peninsula.

Progreso

First impressions of **PROGRESO** – a working port with a 6km-long concrete pier – can be uninspiring, especially at the end of a summer weekend when crowds of day-trippers have pulled out, leaving beer bottles and food wrappers in their wake. But if you're craving a beach, the long, broad one here makes a pleasant enough day out from Mérida. If you're here in the winter, the beach will be empty, except perhaps for a few intrepid tourists from one of the cruise ships that dock here occasionally. The towns of **Yucalpetén**, **Chelem** and **Chuburná** – respectively fifteen, twenty and thirty minutes from Progreso – are much quieter, especially in the low season. Further west, though, the road is impassable, and it's not worth making a detour back to the coast at **Sisal**, Mérida's chief port in colonial times – it's now practically deserted.

Progreso itself is a small place, and it's not difficult to find your way around. Calle 80 is the main street, running north–south and dead-ending at the beach. Here you'll find the market (the fruit and veg vendors are usually shut by 2pm), along with a few banks with ATMs, and a couple of internet cafés.

ARRIVAL AND INFORMATION — PROGRESO

By bus Frequent departures from Mérida's AutoProgreso depot (see page 701), arriving in Progreso's station on C 29 at C 82, four blocks south of the water. Returning to Mérida, you can catch the bus, or a *combi*, from C 80 at C 31 near the post office, on the north side of Progreso's Parque Central. Leaving on summer Sunday evenings, with the rest of the weekend crowds, you'll have a very long wait for a seat.

Tourist information The tourist office is in the Casa de la Cultura on C 80 at C 27 (Mon–Fri 8am–2pm, Sat 8am–1pm; 969 935 0104), but it has only a free map and a few leaflets.

ACCOMMODATION AND EATING

Hotels in town range from very seedy to somewhat overpriced, but Progreso is a popular family destination, so many have large rooms ideal for groups. The high season is July, Aug and Semana Santa; outside of that, prices drop considerably. You can also often find good house-rental deals for this stretch of coast on http://vrbo.com and similar sites. For cheap comidas corridas, the town's small market, on C 80 at C 27, has several good stalls; also try the area around the plaza at C 80 and C 31.

Eladio's Malecón at C 80; http://eladios.com.mx. A lively, fairly slick bar-restaurant on the beach, where you can easily make a meal of the tasty *botanas* that come free with beers. M$$$

Playa Linda C 76, between 19 and 21; 969 220 8318. Located right on the seafront, a few steps away from the beach, this whitewashed hotel has bright rooms and larger suites with balconies and kitchenettes; all types of rooms have TVs and a/c. M$$

East of Progreso

It's best to have a car to explore this direction, as the pleasures come more from poking along the ever-narrowing road rather than heading for a particular destination. Chicxulub Puerto is notorious as the spot where a meteor crashed some 65 million years ago, one of the most significant events in the history of the earth (see page 708); there's now a very good seafood restaurant. Alongside Hwy-27 at the Uaymitún inlet (around km 15), there's a free viewing platform (*mirador turístico*) for spotting flocks of flamingos; go in late afternoon, but before the 6pm closing time (7pm in summer). The road continues to **Telchac Puerto**, a laid-back seaside village popular in the summer with escapees from Mérida, then another 9km to **San Crisanto**, where a village organization leads **mangrove tours**. In the village of Santa Clara, the beach is tranquil and the seafood fresh.

Finally, at the end of the coast road is **Bocas de Dzilam**, a state nature reserve in the Parque Natural San Felipe comprising freshwater springs on the seabed. The water's minerals nourish turtles, tortoises, crocodiles and dozens of bird species.

ARRIVAL AND TOURS — EAST OF PROGRESO

By bus Buses from Progreso do come out this way, but infrequently. You can get a more direct bus to Dzilam de Bravo from Mérida from the Noreste terminal (4 daily at 5am, 7.15am, 2pm & 8pm; 1hr 30min).

San Crisanto cooperative Just south of the crossroad, San Crisanto; 991 105 3710, http://sancrisanto.org. The village leads trips through the mangroves in small rowing boats (charge per person; 1hr 30min) – great for birding, and you end at a *cenote* for a swim. Look for the office south of the main road, near the baseball field.

Sayachuleb cooperative One block east from the north edge of the square, Dzilam de Bravo; 999 141 2532. Runs tours (for up to five people; 5hr) to the Bocas de Dzilam.

ACCOMMODATION AND EATING

You can easily cover this area as a day drive; if you get stuck overnight, the hotel options are limited. On the other hand, you can eat quite well and inexpensively out this way.

Moctezuma Off the northeast corner of the plaza in Chicxulub Puerto; 969 934 0403. Also known as *"Los Barriles"*, a reference to the giant wood barrels that form

CHICXULUB AND CENOTES

Some 65 million years ago the Chicxulub asteroid struck the Yucatán Peninsula – near the town of the same name (see page 707) – an event that is considered to have contributed to the extinction of the dinosaurs. The strike also caused large sections of the region's limestone bedrock to collapse, in turn forming thousands of *cenotes* (sinkholes).

The region's network of *cenotes* – which are generally filled with fresh water – was crucial for the Maya civilization that dominated the Yucatán Peninsula before the arrival of the Spanish conquistadors in the 1500s. These flooded subterranean chambers were vital sources of potable water in an area short on rivers and lakes, and towns, villages and ceremonial sites often sprung up around them. They were also considered sacred gateways to the Maya underworld, known as Xibalba ("the place of fear"). At Cenote Sagrado at Chichén Itzá (see page 722), for example, the Maya threw statues, pottery, incense, textiles, jade, gold and human sacrifices into the water as offerings to the gods of the underworld. The few human sacrifices who survived the ordeal, incidentally, were considered to have spoken with the gods, and have developed prophetic powers.

Today the region's *cenotes* – some of them have been turned into theme parks, others remain blissfully undeveloped – are perhaps the most memorable places for a swim, snorkel or dive in the Yucatán. Two of the most spectacular are Cenote X'Keken and Cenote Samula (see page 726), just outside the city of Valladolid.

its front entrance, this long-running seafood restaurant is a traditional favourite for a lazy lunch of fried fish and other delights. M$$

San Crisanto Cooperative Just south of the crossroad, San Crisanto; http://sancrisanto.wordpress.com. The same group that runs mangrove tours in this town (see above) also rents out large, clean and fairly basic cabañas that can sleep up to six people (just about). M$$

Celestún

Were it not for its amazing flamingo-filled lagoon, **Celestún,** 93km west of Mérida, would be little more than a one-boat fishing village. It's literally the end of the road, dead-straight for most of the drive through the forest, until you emerge and cross a bridge to the end of a sandbar on the northwest coast of the peninsula. The town has grown a tiny bit in the twenty-first century (with an ATM and a petrol station, finally), but still has a castaway feel; it's busy only on occasional Sundays and during Mexican holidays.

The beach is wide, and the sea is cloudy yet clean – but it's the birds in the 600-square-kilometre Ría Celestún Biosphere Reserve here that are the real draw. A typical boat tour takes in the flamingos, most numerous from November to May, when blue-winged teal and shovellers also migrate. Dedicated birders can hire a skilled guide, or, if you are looking for something more active, there is the option to bike and canoe through the mangroves.

ARRIVAL AND DEPARTURE — CELESTÚN

By bus Departures from Mérida's Noreste terminal (12–13 daily; 2hr).

By car If you're driving from Mérida and don't want to backtrack, take the small road south via Chunchucmil; it makes a nice loop.

ACCOMMODATION AND EATING

For inexpensive home cooking, visit one of the *loncherías* by the small market (just off the inland side of the plaza). There's also a bakery on the plaza, and a bar-restaurant that's open in the evening; the seafood places on the beach are generally open for lunch only.

Casa Raquelita C 12 no. 1-a; 999 346 9712. Good if you want to settle in for a while, this restored house, 1km north of town on the beach road, has four rooms with a shared kitchen. Fishing trips, bikes and kayaks are all available, as are discounted weekly accommodation rates. M$$$

Manglares de Dzinitún 1km south of the main highway, just west of the parador turístico; 999 645 4310. This bare-bones ecotourism place has a solar-powered cabaña and camping space (they'll supply the tent). It's a great wild location next to the mangroves, but pack some DEET-heavy insect spray. M$

María del Carmen C 12 no. 111, at C 15; 999 995 6321. An adequate choice for accommodation on the beach, *María del Carmen* has rooms with balconies overlooking the water; a/c costs a little extra. Very popular during Mexican holiday times, so you'll need to book ahead. M$$

La Palapa C 12; 988 154 4470. Of several seafood restaurants along the beach, this one is the biggest and unfortunately the priciest, but it's also generally more reliable than others in the centre. M$$$

Xixim 10km north of town; http://hotelxixim.com. Operating primarily on wind and solar power, this remote and lovely eco-resort has stylish cabañas with outdoor showers, plus a good restaurant. The real treat, though, is the utterly wild beach. A number of tours are on offer. M$$$

South and east of Mérida

South of Mérida are two scenic routes, steeped in Maya and colonial history: both are best experienced in a car, though you can get to a couple of major attractions by bus. East of the city, by car or bus, lies the *pueblo mágico* ("magic village" – an official Mexican government designation) of Izamal, which is exceptionally scenic and rich in tradition. Taken as a whole, this area represents the essence of Maya rural life, the heart of the Yucatán, in dozens of villages linked by narrow roads through dense forest. Life is slower here, often conducted by bicycle – stay alert while driving.

Ruta Puuc

About 80km south of Mérida in the Puuc hills lies a group of important and well-restored archeological sites, linked along a road commonly called the **Ruta Puuc**. The chief attraction is **Uxmal**, second only to Chichén Itzá in tourist appeal, as well as in its size and historical significance. From Uxmal, Hwy-261 continues on to the lesser site of **Kabáh**; shortly after that, bearing east on a smaller side road, you pass **Sayil** and **Labná**. From Labná you can continue to the farming town of **Oxkutzcab**, on the road between Muna and Felipe Carrillo Puerto, and head back to Mérida via **Ticul** and Muna. Or you can follow the longer **Ruta de los Conventos** (see page 716) back.

The distinctive **Puuc sites** clearly evolved from themes in the Río Bec and Chenes regions: you'll see the same gaping monster mouths and facades decorated in mosaic-like Xs and checkerboards. In both cases, though, the techniques reflect a new strategy of **mass production** – the mask-covered front of the Codz Poop at Kabáh, for instance, is dotted with hundreds of consistently round carved eyes. A new core-and-veneer style of construction, rather than stone blocks stacked with mortar, yielded sounder buildings with a smoother appearance.

Uxmal

Hwy-261 • Charge • **Sound-and-light show** Charge • **Guides** charge per group

Meaning "thrice-built", the UNESCO World Heritage Site of **Uxmal** (pronounced OOSH-mal) represents the finest achievement of the Puuc-region Maya culture before it fell into its ultimate decline near 1000 AD. Its spectacular buildings are encrusted all over with elaborate, and sometimes grisly, decoration. Uxmal is

TRANSPORT ON THE RUTA PUUC

Because the sites on the Ruta Puuc are far apart, and on a road poorly served by buses, it's best to rent a car in Mérida. You can drive through in a day, but if you spend the night mid-route, you can explore the key sites and take in the Ruta de Conventos as well. Scores of Mérida travel agencies offer Puuc-route **trips** that include meals and a guide.

potentially more rewarding than a visit to Chichén Itzá, as the crowds can be a bit lighter, the decorative detail is fascinating, and you can still climb one of the pyramids. If you arrive close to opening time (the drive from Mérida takes about an hour), you can see the major buildings in a couple of hours and leave before the buses start rolling in. There's a pay car park at the entrance to the site, where the visitor centre includes a small museum, bookshop with guides to the site, crafts store, snack bar and ATM.

The main restored buildings are set out on a roughly north–south axis in a large cleared site; the alignment of individual buildings often has astrological significance. As in all Maya sites in the Yucatán, the face of **Chac**, the rain god, is everywhere. Chac must have been more crucial in this region than almost anywhere, for Uxmal and the other Puuc sites have no *cenotes* or other natural sources of water, relying instead on *chultunob*, jug-shaped underground cisterns, to collect and store rainwater (most have been filled in, to prevent mosquitoes breeding, but Kabáh has an extant one).

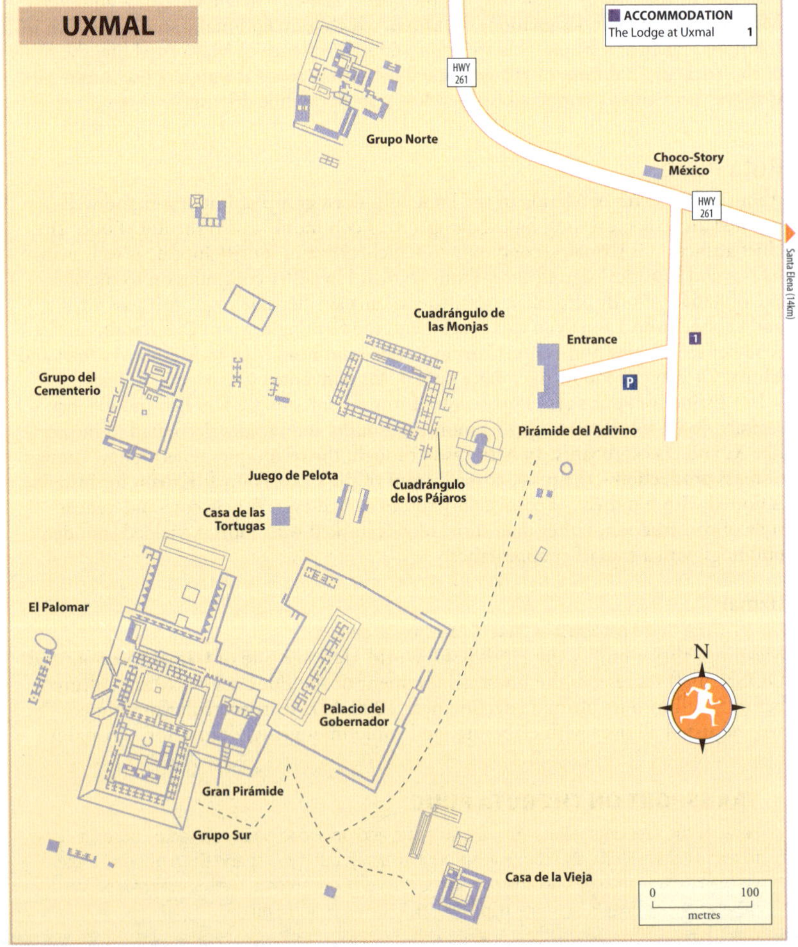

Brief history

Little is known of the city's history, but the chief monuments, which marked its peaks of power and population, were erected around 900 AD. Sometime after that, the city began to decline, and by 1200 Uxmal and the other Puuc sites, together with Chichén Itzá, were all but abandoned. Political infighting, ecological problems and loss of trade with Tula, near Mexico City, may have played a part. Later, the **Xiu dynasty** settled at Uxmal, making it one of the central pillars of the League of Mayapán (see page 716), but a 1441 rebellion put an end to centralized Maya authority.

Pirámide del Adivino

Entering the site, you first see the most remarkable of all Mexican pyramids, the so-called **Pyramid of the Magician**, soaring at a startling angle from its uniquely oval base. The legend of the pyramid's creation tells that an old sorceress, who lived in a hut where the pyramid now stands, hatched a dwarf son from an egg and encouraged him to challenge the king to a series of tests – all of which the dwarf won, thanks to a little magic. Finally the king challenged him to build a pyramid overnight. The dwarf succeeded, and became ruler of Uxmal.

Archeological evidence is a bit less magical, showing at least five stages of construction – six if you count the modern restoration, which may not correspond to any of its earlier incarnations. At the base of the rear (east) stairway, a tunnel reveals **Templo III**, one of the earlier levels. Walk around to the west face of the pyramid into the **Cuadrángulo de los Pájaros** (named for the macaws that stud the roofline of the building on the west side) to admire the even steeper stairway that runs down either side of a second, earlier sanctuary in a different style. Known as the **Edificio Chenes** (or Templo IV), as it reflects the architecture of the Chenes region (see page 695), the building's entire front forms a giant mask of Chac. At the bottom of the west face, divided by the stairway, is the very first stage of construction.

Cuadrángulo de las Monjas

Behind the pyramid, the **Nunnery Quadrangle** is a beautiful complex enclosing a plaza. The Spanish gave it this name, but it wasn't a convent; theories range from a military academy to a sort of earthly paradise, where intended sacrificial victims would spend their final months in debauchery. The four buildings, probably constructed between 895 and 906 AD, are each set on a slightly different level, possibly representing the four main levels of the Maya universe. The facade of each is decorated with complex reliefs, and the quadrangle itself is a slightly irregular shape, apparently to align with Venus.

Maya architectural skills are at their finest here, as the false vaults of the interiors are taken about as wide as they can go without collapsing (wooden crossbeams provided further support), and the frontages are slightly bowed in order to maintain a proper horizontal perspective. The **north building**, probably also the oldest, has a strip of plain stone facade (from which doors lead into vaulted chambers) surmounted by a slightly raised panel of mosaics, featuring geometric patterns and human and animal figures, with representations of Maya huts above the doorways. The **west building**, which has been heavily reconstructed, boasts even more varied themes, and the whole of its ornamentation is surrounded by a coiling, feathered rattlesnake with the face of a warrior emerging from its jaws. The **east building** mirrors the west one in its proportions; its snake decorations, however, run in long horizontal bars.

An arched passageway through the middle of the **south building**, the lowest of the four, is directly aligned with the **ball-court** (ham-fistedly rebuilt with cement) outside.

Casa de las Tortugas

Today a path leads between the ruined side walls of the ball-court and up onto the levelled terrace on which stands the **Casa de las Tortugas** (House of the Turtles).

This very simple, elegant building, named after the stone turtles carved around the cornice, demonstrates another constant theme of Puuc architecture: stone facades carved to resemble rows of narrow columns. These, marked with bands of masonry, probably represent the Maya huts still in use today, with walls of bamboo or saplings lashed together.

Palacio del Gobernador

Adjacent to the Casa de las Tortugas, the **Governor's Palace** marks the finest achievement at Uxmal. Arriving at the then virtually unknown site in June 1840, explorer and writer John L. Stephens did not doubt its significance. "If it stood this day on its grand artificial terrace in Hyde Park or the Garden of the Tuileries," he wrote, "it would form a new order…not unworthy to stand side by side with the remains of the Egyptian, Grecian and Roman art."

The palace faces east, away from the buildings around it, probably for astronomical reasons – its central doorway aligns with the column of the altar outside and the point where Venus rises. The use of light and shade on the long, low facade lends a remarkable harmony, as do the strong diagonals that run through its broad band of mosaic decorations. Close up, the mosaic features masks of Chac alternating with grid-and-key patterns and highly stylized snakes. The patterns vary in depth, lending a fascinating texture to the facade.

Grupo Sur

Behind the palace, you can climb the rebuilt staircase of the **Gran Pirámide** to see the temple on top, decorated with macaws and more masks of Chac – some of these have even smaller carved faces set inside their mouths. **El Palomar** was originally part of a quadrangle like that of the Nunnery, but the only building to retain any form is this, topped with the great latticed roofcomb that gives it its name: it looks somewhat like a dovecote.

Beyond, the scrub forest is the perfect place to spot some of the Yucatán's more distinctive birds, such as the turquoise-browed motmot with its pendulum-like tail, particularly along the path that runs off the south side of the Palacio del Gobernador. The trail leads to an odd display of small **stone phalluses**, protected by a thatch roof – collected from all over the site, they're evidence of a fertility cult centred on Uxmal (they're also worked into the back of the building on the west side of the Nunnery Quadrangle).

ARRIVAL AND DEPARTURE — UXMAL

By bus Buses (5 daily; 1hr) run direct from Mérida, and any bus heading down the main road towards Hopelchén will drop you a short walk from the entrance. Note that no buses run back to Mérida after the hour-long sound-and-light show.

ACCOMMODATION AND EATING — SEE MAP PAGE 710

Several **hotels** are close to the site, but none in the budget category. All are subject to sudden arrivals of huge tour groups, which can make the quality of service and food erratic, but you may be able to negotiate a good deal when they're not full. A short drive away, however, are good budget options in Santa Elena (see page 713), as well as the ultra-deluxe *Hacienda Temozón* (see page 713).

The Lodge at Uxmal Adjacent to the Uxmal site entrance; http://mayaland.com. Spacious and filled with greenery, if a bit overpriced. Its breezy restaurant and bar, *La Palapa*, is a convenient spot for a cool drink. The same management runs *Hacienda Uxmal*, on the highway opposite the turn to the site; the rooms have more colonial grandeur, for similar rates. M$$$$

Choco-Story México (Ecomuseo del Cacao)

Ruta Puuc, a 5min walk north of Uxmal • Charge • http://choco-storymexico.com

Choco-Story México (also known as **Ecomuseo del Cacao**) produces and celebrates the main ingredient in quality chocolate. The Belgian owner, who also operates chocolate shops in Mérida, is working with a Maya collective to re-establish cacao production in the region. The museum explores the sacred significance of the cacao bean to the Maya and shows sustainable production methods. And don't miss the tastings, of course, of chocolate in both liquid and solid forms.

Santa Elena

16km south of Uxmal, and just 7km from Kabáh, **SANTA ELENA** is worth visiting mainly for the magnificent view from its large hilltop **church**, visible for many kilometres around. Beside the church is a morbidly interesting small **museum** (daily 8am–6pm; free) with displays on local funerary practices, including the two-hundred-year-old mummified remains of four children discovered under the church floor in 1980. Just outside town, where Hwy-261 bypasses the centre, are several exceptionally pleasant places to stay; buses can drop you next to them on request.

ACCOMMODATION AND EATING — SANTA ELENA

El Chac Mool Hwy-261; 997 107 1784. The only restaurant not affiliated with a hotel around the ruins, *El Chac Mool* does decent local food, cheaper than the other options, although it closes a bit early. M$$

Flycatcher Inn Off Hwy-261 by the Santa Elena turn; 997 978 5350. The first accommodation you reach when coming from Uxmal, a B&B with seven rooms and a separate guest cottage, all decorated with local craftwork and furnished with comfy beds. It's about a 5min walk south from the main square, or buses from Mérida will drop you on the highway very nearby. M$$$

★ **Nueva Altía** Off Hwy-261, just south of Santa Elena turn; http://nuevaaltia.com. Just a five-minute ride from Santa Elena, but with the feel of a rural retreat, *Nueva Altía* boasts bright and airy en suites, a curvy pool, friendly staff and plenty of birdlife in the surrounding grounds. M$$$

★ **The Pickled Onion** Hwy-261, east of the Santa Elena turn; https://thepickledonionuxmal.com. British expat Valerie Pickle rents a handful of Maya-style cabañas in all sizes, with bigger ones great for families. There's also a large pool. Her restaurant (mains M$$$) has a mostly international menu but also does excellent versions of local dishes; picnic lunches and children's meals are available. M$$$

12

Ticul

Located 80km south of Mérida on Hwy-184, **TICUL** is another good base for exploring the Puuc region, though not especially scenic. Historically an important centre of Maya shamanism, it's also a shoe-manufacturing town, full of shops stocked with wildly impractical sparkly sandals. It's well served by **buses** to and from Mérida and with services to Cancún and the east coast. The centre of town is around the junction

HACIENDA HOPPING

Along the Ruta Puuc are numerous ruined henequen plantations, in various states of repair. *Yaxcopoil* and *Ochil* lie right beside the road, so it's easy enough to be dropped here if travelling by bus, and flag down the next bus or *colectivo* to continue to Uxmal or Mérida (though check the schedule before you leave, as buses aren't terribly frequent).

Hacienda Ochil 40km south of Mérida, just west of Hwy-261; 999 924 7465. This attractively refurbished hacienda operates as a good Yucatecan restaurant, a small museum and some excellent handicraft workshops, plus a small land-art work in a *cenote* by James Turrell. The entry fee is waived if you're eating at the restaurant. M$$$

Hacienda Temozón 35km south of Mérida, about 8km east off Hwy-261; www.ihg.com. One of the peninsula's best hotels – lavish rooms, a swish restaurant with an international menu, an opulent spa and a delightful swimming pool. Breakfast is not too expensive, so if you're doing the route by car, it can be a treat to start your day here. M$$$$

Hacienda Yaxcopoil On the edge of Yaxcopoil village; http://yaxcopoil.com. One of the closest haciendas to Mérida, and also one of the most dramatic. At its height, it employed four hundred people, but now the main house stands in a state of picturesque disrepair – peeling walls, sagging ceilings, rooms full of mildewed tablecloths and faded pictures. It also has wonderful (and less decrepit) accommodation in an adjacent guesthouse: a huge, high-ceilinged room with two double beds, as well as a stand-alone casita. A restaurant on the grounds serves delicious Yucatecan dishes, and tours (charge) are offered, if you're not staying. M$$$

of calles 25 and 26, with a large plaza to either side, plus a massive church and several hotels; the market, locally noted for great tortas at night, is to the west on Calle 23 between calles 28 and 30.

ARRIVAL AND DEPARTURE — TICUL

By bus Buses from Mérida and elsewhere use a station directly behind the church at the corner of C 24 and C 25-A. Destinations Caribbean coast via Felipe Carrillo Puerto (16–17 daily; 4hr 20min); Chetumal (6 daily; 6hr).

By colectivo *Colectivos* for Mérida, as well as Santa Elena, Oxkutzcab and surrounding villages, set off when they're full from various points in the immediate vicinity of the bus station: for Mérida near the corner of C 24 and C 25, other destinations mainly from C 25-A alongside the church.

ACCOMMODATION

Plaza C 23 no. 201, between C 26 and C 26-A; http://hotelplazayucatan.com. The smartest option in town, *Hotel Plaza* has all the amenities, if no particular style. As you'd expect, the en-suite rooms all come with TVs, telephones and a/c. There's a decent restaurant, and staff can organize guides and tours. M$$

Posada Jardín C 27 no. 216, between C 28 and C 30; 999 114 4443. For a little greenery, head away from the centre to *Posada Jardín,* which has four excellent-value cabins with separate sleeping and sitting areas, set in a bright garden with a small, sometimes murky, pool. All rooms have fridges, but a/c and breakfast cost extra. M$$

EATING

La Carmelita C 23 at C 26; 997 972 0515. In the centre of town, just off the plaza, this casual restaurant serves up an inexpensive set meal, as well as other à la carte dishes: the seafood options are particularly good. M$$

Kabáh

Hwy-261 east of Uxmal • Charge

This site lies on both sides of the highway some 25km from Uxmal. Much of Kabáh ("Mighty Hand") remains unexcavated, but the one great building, the **Codz Poop**, or Palace of Masks, lies not far off the highway. The facade of this amazing structure is covered all over, in ludicrous profusion, with goggle-eyed, trunk-nosed masks of Chac – to get into the doorways, you need to tread over the mask's noses. Even in its present state, with most of the curved noses broken off, this remains one of the strangest and most striking of all Maya buildings, decorated so obsessively, intricately and repetitively that it seems the product of an insane mind. At the front of the building is a rare working *chultun* (cistern), with a concave stone floor gathering water into the underground chamber.

On the other side of the road is an unusual circular **pyramid** – now simply a green conical mound that, once you spot it, is so large you can't believe you missed it. Just beyond, a sort of triumphal arch marks the point where an ancient 30km causeway, or *sacbé*, from Uxmal, entered the city.

Sayil

Ruta Puuc, 5km east of the junction with Hwy-261 • Charge

A sober, restrained contrast to the excesses of Kabáh, **Sayil** was once one of the most densely populated areas in the Puuc region, home to an estimated seventeen thousand people from 700 AD to 1000 AD. It is dominated by one major structure, the 80m-long **Gran Palacio** (Great Palace), built with three storeys, each smaller than the one below. Although several large masks of Chac adorn a frieze around the top of the middle level, the decoration mostly takes the form of stone pillaring that mimics the look of bamboo poles – seen more extensively here than at any other Puuc site. The interiors of the middle level, too, are lighter and airier than usual, thanks to the use of broad openings, their lintels supported on fat columns.

Few other structures have been cleared, and those that have been are widely scattered in the forest – a walk to these remote spots is a long, hot one, but it gives you a better sense of the scale of the old city, as well as a chance to view wildlife such as hummingbirds. From the Gran Palacio a path leads through the forest to the small temple of **El Mirador**, and in the other direction to a stele, carved with a phallic figure and now protected under a thatched roof. The path (in fact, a former ceremonial *sacbé*) carries on to the **Palacio Sur**, a large, little-restored structure with another characteristic bamboo facade.

Xlapak

Ruta Puuc km 10 • Free

The minor road continues from Sayil past the smallest and least-visited of the Puuc sites. If you have the time, stop to see the one restored building, a small, elegant palace with huge Chac masks above its doorways and geometric patterns on the facades.

Labná

Ruta Puuc, 3km east of Xlapak • Charge

This ancient city was historically far smaller and less important than Sayil, but it is in many ways a more impressive site. There has been more excavation here, so the main buildings can all be seen as part of a harmonious whole. The **Palacio**, near the entrance, bears traces of sculptures including the inevitable Chac, and a crocodile-snake figure with a human face emerging from its mouth – thought to symbolize a god emerging from the jaws of the underworld. Remnants of a *sacbé* lead from here to the **Arco de Labná**. Originally part of a complex linking two great squares, like the Nunnery at Uxmal, it now stands alone, richly decorated on both sides: on the east with geometric patterns, on the west (the back) with these and niches in the form of Maya huts or temples. Nearby is **El Mirador**, a barely restored temple mound topped by the well-preserved remains of a tall roofcomb. An inner passageway at one time led to the site's principal temple.

Grutas de Loltún

Ruta Puuc, south of the junction with Hwy-18 • Tours daily • Charge • From Oxkutzcab, take a *colectivo* or truck from C 51 next to the market; getting back may require a wait, as trucks are full of workers and produce; you can also taje a taxi here from town

Located just before you reach Oxkutzcab on the road from Labná, these are the most impressive **caves** in the Yucatán. The compulsory ninety-minute tour (for which you can request an English-speaking guide) concentrates on strange rock formations and patterns in giant stalactites and stalagmites. At the entrance, a huge bas-relief Maya warrior guards the opening to the underworld, and throughout are traces of ancient paintings and carvings on the walls. The surrounding jungle is visible through the collapsed floor of the last gallery, and 10m-long tree roots find an anchor on the cavern floor.
Note: guides here are prone to demanding exorbitant tips from foreign tourists: despite what they say, don't be bullied into paying more than what you think is fair.

Oxkutzcab

From Labná, you can head back to Mérida on the fast Hwy-18 (look for signs just north of the Grutas de Loltún), or you can stop off in the village of **OXKUTZCAB**, at the heart of Yucatán's citrus orchards. If you visit early in the morning, you'll see its huge daily **market** at the centre of town, at the junction of calles 50 and 51.

ARRIVAL AND DEPARTURE — OXKUTZCAB

By bus Buses to Mérida via Ticul (roughly hourly; 2hr) depart from the Noreste bus station at the corner of C 56 and C 51.

By colectivo Shared vans come and go from beside the market on C 51.

ACCOMMODATION

★ **Hotel Puuc** C 55 at C 44, on the way out of town towards Labná; https://hotelpuuc.com.mx. The best accommodation option in town, with a sand-coloured, fortress-like exterior, *Hotel Puuc* is a good-value place, with bright, clean rooms (a/c costs extra) and a pool. The only drawback is the less than central location, which is awkward if you don't have your own wheels. M$$

Ruta de los Conventos

From Mérida by car, the easiest route out is C 69 east to the *periférico* (ring road), then following signs to Mayapán. This takes you to Hwy-18, with the towns all well signposted and only a short way from the new road. Second-class buses to Maní stop at all the smaller towns en route, and can be flagged down on the highway

The "Convent Route" – Hwy-18 from Oxcutzcab to Mérida – is a natural extension of the Ruta Puuc, or an easy day outing from Mérida on its own. Every town along the route has an immense fortress church, but the historic highlights are **Maní** and the late Maya site of **Mayapán**. The **churches** date mainly from the seventeenth century or even earlier, as the Spanish were trying to establish their control. They were built so huge partly to impress, as a sign of the domination of Christianity over traditional gods, and partly as fortresses and places of refuge in times of trouble.

Maní

12km north of Oxkutzcab • Regular buses from Mérida's Noreste terminal (C 67 at C 50) until about 8pm

This small town was founded by the Xiu after they abandoned Uxmal, and it was the largest city encountered by the Spanish in the Yucatán, though almost no trace now survives. Avoiding a major confrontation, Maní's ruler, Ah Kukum Xiu, converted to Christianity and became an ally of the Spanish. In 1548 one of the earliest and largest **Franciscan monasteries** in the Yucatán was founded here. This still stands, surrounded now by Maya huts, and just about the only evidence of Maní's past glories is the ancient stones used in its construction and in walls around the town. In front of the church, in 1562, Bishop Diego de Landa held his infamous auto-da-fé, in which he burned the city's records (because they "contained nothing in which there was not to be seen the superstitions and lies of the devil"), destroying virtually all original Maya literature.

Mayapán

Hwy-18, halfway between Maní and Mérida • Charge • Buses from the Noreste terminal to Maní (see page 715) stop at the ruins on request

The ruins of the most powerful city in the Yucatán from the thirteenth to the fifteenth centuries sit right beside the road. It was a huge population centre by the standards of the day, with some fifteen thousand people living on a site covering five square kilometres, in which traces of more than four thousand buildings have been found.

What can be seen today is less than grand – the buildings were crude and small by Maya standards, at best poor copies of what had gone before, and only a few have been restored (a visit doesn't take long). The Mayapán society was initially dismissed as decadent and failing, but a case can be made for the fact that it was merely a changing one. As the priests no longer dominated here, what grew instead was a more genuinely urban society: highly militaristic, no doubt, but also far more centralized and more reliant on trade than previous Maya culture.

Brief history

According to Maya chronicles, Mayapán, Chichén Itzá and Uxmal formed the **League of Mayapán**, which exercised control over the entire peninsula from around 987 to 1185. It broke up when Mayapán's **Cocom** dynasty attacked the already declining Chichén Itzá and took control of the peninsula. The archeological evidence, however, suggests Mayapán was not founded until 1263, after the fall of Chichén Itzá.

Either way, hegemony was maintained until 1441, when Ah Xupan, a Xiu leader from Uxmal, overthrew the Cocom and destroyed their city. But this led to factionalism, which aided the Spanish Conquest considerably.

Acancéh

Maya pyramid Charge

A mix of Maya, modern and colonial architecture, the town of Acancéh (pronounced "ah-kan-KAY") encapsulates Yucatecan history. At the central plaza, beside the sixteenth-century church, is a large Maya pyramid plus two smaller ones, all surrounded by everyday life. At the top of the large pyramid are four huge stucco masks, some of the finest of their kind.

The ancient Maya Palacio de los Estucos is about four blocks away, behind the market (get directions from the booth at the main pyramid). The stucco decoration on the long, low building is far from complete, but there are plenty of easily identifiable figures, animals and glyphs.

Los Tres Cenotes

Village of Chunkanán, south of Cuzamá • Charge per *truk* (up to 4 passengers; the last one departs around 3.30pm) • LUS buses (15 daily; 1hr 30min) and minibuses (2hr) depart from Mérida's Noreste terminal and Parque San Juan respectively for Cuzamá; from here take a *triciclo* to Chunkanán; *combis* also run from Acancéh

The trip to three cavernous **cenotes** is less a detour off the convent route than a separate day outing, as it typically takes at least six hours, including the drive from the main highway to the village of Chunkanán, followed by a 45-minute ride on a *truk* (or *carrito*), a rickety, horse-drawn carriage down old narrow-gauge rail lines. But the reward is great scenery, refreshing swims and a taste of bygone hacienda history. You'll want to bring swimming gear, towels and perhaps a picnic, as locals do on weekends.

The process of hiring a *truk* is slightly complicated by a business rivalry. Coming from Cuzamá, east of Acancéh, you first reach a large parking area off the right side of the road, signed as Los Tres Cenotes. This is an upstart organization, run by people from Cuzamá and greatly resented by the people of Chunkanán – another 2km south on a narrow road – who have no other income in their village. If you press on less than 1km down the road, you will find the original operation, in front of a multi-storey palapa restaurant. If you're in a taxi or *triciclo* from Cuzamá, you'll inevitably get steered to the first, Cuzamá-run *truk* stop; if you want to go to Chunkanán without raising a fuss, you can always say you're headed for the restaurant.

12

ACCOMMODATION AND EATING — RUTA DE LOS CONVENTOS

★ **El Dzapakal** Main road, Chunkanán; 999 564 2435. *El Dzapakal* is a superb restaurant serving hearty Yucatecan food (avoid the so-so international dishes), beautifully presented and very reasonably priced. M$$

El Príncipe Tutul-Xiu C 26 between C 25 and C 27, Maní; 999 929 7721. Méridans often come down to Maní on day trips to dine at this festive palapa-roofed restaurant that has been serving Yucatecan standards for more than thirty years. It can be an absolute zoo on Sundays, but the food is always delicious. There are other branches in Mérida and Oxkutzcab. M$$

Sac-Nicté Chunkanán; 999 923 7598. An authentically Maya-style compound (which can accommodate up to six people), where one small palapa hut houses two hammocks (with mosquito nets), another has a toilet and bathtub, and another has a kitchen and extra hammock. At the back is a pool, and there are good-value weekly rates too. M$$$

Aké

Midway between Izamal and Mérida on the back road via Cacalchén • Daily 8am–5pm • Charge • From Mérida or Izamal AutoCentro buses pass the ruins (6 daily; 45min); last bus to Mérida is around 8pm, but confirm before setting off; by car turn south in Euan, or take the direct road from Hwy-180, opposite Tahmek

On the scenic, slow route from Mérida, dense with Maya towns, these **ruins** are partially integrated into an inhabited village and working henequen plantation. Aké was probably in alliance with the old city of Izamal, as it is linked by one of the peninsula's largest *sacbeob* (Maya roads). The most impressive building is the **Edificio de las Pilastras**, a large platform topped with more than twenty stone pillars. The Maya rubble intermingles with San Lorenzo de Aké, a fine neo-French henequen **hacienda** from the late nineteenth century. You're welcome to wander through the antique-looking machinery to see the fibre-making process.

Izamal

This excellent regional crafts centre is easy enough to visit from Mérida on a day trip, but don't leave before sunset, when the place takes on a perfect golden glow, thanks to the striking ochre-yellow that covers all of the buildings. If you prefer the country to the city, **Izamal** can also be a good alternative to Mérida as a base for sightseeing. In this case, though, it's nice to have a car, as Izamal is served only by second-class buses.

Convento de San Antonio de Padua

Central plaza • **Convent** Free • **Sound-and-light show** Charge • **Museum** Charge

In 1552 Fray Diego de Landa (later responsible for a vicious Inquisition and auto-da-fé in Maní) lopped the top off a pyramid and began building this grand convent, which now anchors Izamal's two adjacent main plazas. The porticoed atrium occupies some 24,000 square metres. When the complex was completed in 1561, de Landa consecrated it with one of two statues of the Virgin that he had brought from Guatemala.

Several years later, when church leaders from Valladolid attempted to claim the statue, it is said to have become impossibly heavy, and they were forced to leave it in Izamal. A cult developed and she is now the official patroness of the Yucatán; on a visit to the town in 1993, Pope John Paul II gave her a silver crown. During the **fiesta** dedicated to the Virgin on December 8, penitents climb the monastery's staircase on their knees, and worshippers sing in the church for the entire night before.

The statue is on view in the *camarín*, a chapel around the back of the main altar. Next to the chapel, the **Museo Santuario de Nuestra Señora** shows many elaborate gowns that have clothed the statue. In the evenings, a **sound-and-light show** is projected on the front facade of the main church.

Kinich Kakmó

C 27 between C 28 and C 26 • Free

Izamal was formerly an important religious centre for the Maya, where they worshipped **Itzamná**, mythical founder of the ancient city and one of the gods of creation, at a series of huge pyramid-temples. Most of these are now no more than low mounds in the surrounding country, but several survive in the town itself, and are fascinating to see right in the middle of the residential grid; some businesses on the plaza have pyramids literally in their backyards. Kinich Kakmó is the largest pile, dedicated to the sun god and now partly restored. It's just a couple of blocks north of the two adjacent central plazas.

A CRAFT TOUR OF IZAMAL

A free map, available from most hotels and businesses, identifies the workshops of wood-carvers, papier-mâché artists and other artisans around Izamal – they're all well marked and easily reached by bike, available from the craft museum. Be sure to visit Don Esteban, on Calle 26 at Calle 45, whose jewellery made from henequen spines is striking and modern, and whose effusive character is memorable. Agustín Colli, on Calle 19 between calles 24 and 26, makes double-weave hammocks that are positively luxurious (and well worth the price tag).

For a broader selection of craftwork, visit Hecho a Mano (988 954 0109, http://facebook.com/Hechoamanomexicanfolkart) on the south side of the convent plaza. This particularly good craft and folk-art shop is stocked with everything from Mexican wrestling masks to Huichol yarn paintings from Nayarit, as well as excellent photography by the owner; note that the hours (daily 9am–2pm) can be erratic.

Centro Cultural y Artesanal

C 31 on the plaza • Charge • 988 954 1020

This museum showcases choice pieces of craftwork from all over Mexico, with a wing devoted to Yucatecan specialities. It houses a nice shop, a small café (peek behind to see some pyramid remnants) and a quiet, perfumed back room where you can get a foot massage.

ARRIVAL AND INFORMATION — IZAMAL

By bus All buses arrive at a small station one block west of the main plaza. For Mérida-bound services, Oriente is preferable to Centro because you arrive closer to the town centre.

Destinations Cancún (roughly hourly; 4hr; slightly faster Oriente service 3 daily, via Tizimín); Valladolid (roughly hourly; 1hr); Mérida (every 30–45min; 1hr 30min–2hr).

By car From Mérida, it's easiest to go via Tixkokob or Motul. Coming from the west on Hwy-180 *libre*, go to Kantunil then turn north by following signs for the *cuota* to Cancún, then make an awkward U-turn. From the westbound *cuota*, look for a direct right turn off the highway immediately before km 68. If you miss the turn (easy to do), you can continue to Hoctún, then backtrack.

Tourist office North plaza (daily 9am–9pm; 988 954 0009).

GETTING AROUND

By horse-drawn carriage Horse-drawn carriages lined up around the plaza will take you for a pleasant *paseo* around the town (20min).

By bike Rent a bicycle from the Centro Cultural y Artesanal on the plaza.

ACCOMMODATION

Macan Ché B&B C 22, between C 33 and C 35; http://macanche.com. This B&B has an assortment of comfortable cottages (a/c costs extra) tucked among rambling gardens taking up nearly a whole block east of the plaza; rates include breakfast, and other meals are available as well. M$$$

Rinconada del Convento C 33 no. 294, at C 28; http://grupoizamal.com. On the south side of the convent, *Rinconada* has eleven a/c rooms with shiny tile floors, mission-style furniture and plenty of natural light through large windows and patio doors. There's a pool in a tiered garden-courtyard. M$$$

San Miguel Arcangel C 31-A no. 308, between C 30 and C 30-A, on the plaza; http://sanmiguelhotel.com.mx. An airy two-storey hotel just across from the convent. Rooms are clean and bright and have a/c, while the upper ones along the front have balconies (for an additional fee) that afford close-up views of the plaza action. For less noise, ask for a room off the courtyard, where you'll have a view of one of Izamal's ruined pyramids. Communal facilities include a hot tub. M$$

EATING

Los Arcos C 28, on the north plaza; 988 954 0662. Of the handful of evening snack operations under the *portales* that edge the north plaza, this one's notable for its breakfast options, enormous tortas and delicious fresh fruit drinks. M$

Kinich C 27, between C 28 and C30; http://restaurantekinich.com. This palapa-roofed place is a good traditional restaurant, even if it is a top tour-group destination. Women pat tortillas by hand, and the Yucatecan dishes like *sopa de lima* and *poc-chuc* are reasonably priced. M$$$

El Toro C 33 no. 303-G, at C 30; 988 954 1169. Just south of the convent, this small family-owned place is open for dinner, with a hearty Yucatecan menu of dishes like *chaya* tamales and *queso relleno*. M$$

DIRECTORY

Banks and exchange On the north plaza, C 31 at C 28, you'll find a Banorte bank with ATM; there's another ATM at the Super Willy's grocery, just off the main plaza.

Internet An internet café is on C 32 just south of the bus station.

Laundry A laundry is on C 30 two blocks north of the north plaza.

Post office On the main plaza.

12

Chichén Itzá and around

The most famous, the most extensively restored and by far the most visited of all Maya sites, **Chichén Itzá** lies conveniently along the main highway from Mérida to Cancún, a little more than 200km from the Caribbean coast. To do the ruins justice and to see them when they're not entirely thronged with tourists, an overnight stop is well worth considering – either at the site itself or, less extravagantly, in the rather dreary village of **Pisté**, about 3km west. The village exists almost entirely to provide visitors with accommodation so they can get an early start. Larger **Valladolid**, to the east, is a better option as a base, as it's both convenient and inexpensive, and has some general city life.

12

The ruins

Hwy-180 *libre*, just east of Pisté • Charge (comprising two tickets for two separate site management bodies) • **Sound-and-light-show** (in Spanish) Charge • **Guide** (2hr) charge • **Horseriding trips** are bookable at *Hotel Mayaland*

The main entry to the site is on the west side. A huge visitor centre houses a museum, restaurant, ATM and shops selling souvenirs, film, maps and guides. You can also get in at the smaller eastern gate by the *Hotel Mayaland*. Either way, you'll want to go in at opening time, as tour buses from Cancún and Mérida start arriving around 10.30am. Allow about three hours to see the site, and if crowds are light, start with the iconic buildings in the Itzá-era Chichén Nuevo (New Chichén) on the north side, then retreat to the Terminal Classic (Chichén Viejo) to the south, where fewer visitors go.

Brief history

Though in most minds Chichén Itzá represents the Maya, it is in fact the site's divergence from Maya tradition that makes it archeologically intriguing. Experts are fairly certain that the city was established around 300 AD, and began to flourish in the Terminal Classic period (between 800 and 925 AD). The rest of its history, however, and the roots of the **Itzá clan** that consolidated power in the peninsula here after 925 AD, remain in dispute. Much of the evidence at the site – an emphasis on human sacrifice, the presence of a huge ball-court and the glorification of military activity – points to a strong influence from central Mexico. For decades researchers guessed this was the result of the city's defeat by the Toltecs, a theory reinforced by the resemblance of the Templo de los Guerreros to the colonnade at Tula, near Mexico City, along with Toltec-style pottery remains and numerous depictions of the Toltec god-king, the feathered serpent Quetzalcoatl (Kukulcán to the Maya).

12

Work since the 1980s, however, supports a theory that the Itzá people were not Toltec invaders, but fellow Maya who had migrated from the south, which would explain why their subjects referred to them in texts as "foreigners". The Toltec artefacts, this view holds, arrived in central Yucatán via the Itzás' chief trading partners, the **Chontal Maya**, who maintained allegiances with Toltecs of central Mexico and Oaxaca.

Chichén Nuevo

The main path leads directly to **El Castillo** (also called the Pyramid of Kukulcán), the structure that sits alone in the centre of a great grassy plaza. It is a simple, relatively unadorned square building, with a monumental stairway ascending each face (though only two are restored), rising in nine receding terraces to a temple at the top. The simplicity is deceptive, however, as the building is in fact the **Maya calendar** rendered in stone: each staircase has 91 steps, which, added to the single step at the main entrance to the temple, amounts to 365; other numbers relevant to the calendar recur throughout the construction. Most remarkably, near sunset on the spring and autumn equinoxes, the great serpents' heads at the foot of the main staircase are joined to their tails (at the top of the building) by an undulating body of shadow – an event that lasts just a few hours and draws spectators, and awed worshippers, by the thousands. The effect is re-created nightly in the sound-and-light show.

Inside El Castillo, where visitors cannot enter, an earlier pyramid survives almost intact, and in the temple's inner sanctuary, archeologists discovered one of the greatest treasures at the site: an altar, or perhaps a throne, in the form of a jaguar, painted bright red and inset with jade "spots" and eyes.

The "Toltec" plaza

El Castillo marks one edge of a **plaza** that formed the focus of Chichén Nuevo, and in addition to a *sacbé* leading to **Cenote Sagrado**, all its most important buildings are here, many displaying a strong Toltec influence in their structure and decoration. The **Templo de los Guerreros** (Temple of the Warriors), lined on two sides by the **Grupo**

de las Mil Columnas (Group of the Thousand Columns), forms the eastern edge of the plaza. These are the structures that most recall the great Toltec site of Tula, both in design and in detail – in particular the colonnaded courtyard (which would have been roofed with some form of thatch) and the use of Atlantean columns representing battle-dressed warriors, their arms raised above their heads.

The temple is richly decorated on its north and south sides with carvings and sculptures of jaguars and eagles devouring human hearts, feathered serpents, warriors and, the one undeniably Maya feature, masks of the rain god Chac, with his curling snout. On top (now visible only at a distance, as you can no longer climb the structure) are two superb examples of figures called **Chac-mools**, once thought to be introduced by the Toltecs: offerings were placed on the stomachs of these reclining figures, which are thought to represent either the messengers who would take the sacrifice to the gods or perhaps the divinities themselves.

The "thousand" columns alongside originally formed a square, on the far side of which is the building known as the **Mercado**, although there's no evidence that this actually was a marketplace. Near here, too, is a small, dilapidated ball-court.

North of El Castillo is the **Plataforma de Venus**, a raised block with a stairway up each side guarded by feathered serpents. Here, rites associated with Quetzalcoatl when he took the form of Venus, the morning star, would have been carried out. Slightly smaller, but otherwise identical in design, the adjacent **Plataforma de Águilas y Jaguares** features reliefs of eagles and jaguars holding human hearts. Human sacrifices may have been carried out here, judging by the proximity of a third platform, the **Tzompantli**, where victims' heads likely hung on display. This is carved on every side with grotesque grinning stone skulls.

Gran Juego de Pelota

Chichén Itzá's ball-court, on the west side of the plaza, is the largest known in existence, with walls some 90m long. Its design is a capital "I" surrounded by temples, with the goals, or target rings, halfway along each side. Along the bottom of each side runs a sloping **panel** decorated with scenes of the game. Although the rules and full significance of the game remain a mystery, it was clearly not a Saturday-afternoon kick-about in the park; for more on the game's significance, see page 582.

On the panel, the players are shown proceeding from either side towards a central circle, the symbol of death. One player, just right of the centre (whether it's the winning or losing captain is up for debate), has been decapitated, while another holds his head and a ritual knife. Along the top runs the stone body of a snake, whose heads stick out at either end. The court is subject to a whispering-gallery effect, which enables you to be heard clearly at the far end of the court, and to hear what's going on there.

Templo de los Jaguares

This temple overlooks the playing area from the east side. At the bottom – effectively the outer wall of the ball-court – is a little portico supported by two pillars, between which a stone jaguar stands sentinel. The outer wall panels, the left and the right of the interior space, are carved with the images of Pawahtuns, the gods who supported the sky and who are thought to be the patrons of the Itzá people. Inside are some worn but elaborate relief carvings of the Itzá ancestors inserted in the Maya creation myth – a powerful demonstration of their entitlement to rule.

Cenote Sagrado

The city's largest *cenote* lies at the end of the *sacbé* that leads about 300m off the north side of the plaza. It's an almost perfectly round hole in the limestone bedrock, some 60m in diameter and more than 30m deep, the bottom third full of water. It was thanks to this natural well (and perhaps another in the southern half of the site) that the city could survive at all, and it gives Chichén Itzá its name (literally "at the edge of the well of the Itzá"). The well was regarded as a portal to the underworld, called Xibalba, and the Maya threw in offerings such as statues, jade and engraved metal discs (a few of them gold), as well as human sacrifices – all of them boys, recent research has shown. The Maya thought that any boy who managed to survive the ordeal had communed with the gods.

Chichén Viejo

The **southern half of the site** is the most sacred part for contemporary Maya, though the buildings here are not in such good condition. They were built for the most part prior to 925 AD, in the architectural styles used in the Puuc and Chenes regions.

El Osario

A path leads from the south side of El Castillo to the major structures, passing first the pyramid **El Osario** (the Ossuary; also called the High Priest's Grave), the only building in this section that shows Toltec-style detail. Externally it is very similar to El Castillo, but inside a series of **tombs** was discovered. A shaft, first explored at the end of the nineteenth century, drops down from the top through five crypts, in each of which was found a skeleton and a trap door leading to the next. The fifth is at ground level, but here too was a trap door, and steps cut through the rock to a sixth chamber that opens onto a huge underground cavern: the burial place of the high priest.

El Caracol

Follow the main path and you arrive at **El Caracol** (the Snail, for its shape; also called the Observatory), a circular, domed tower standing on two rectangular platforms and looking remarkably like a modern-day observatory. The roof has slits aligned with various points of astronomical significance. Four doors at the cardinal points lead into the tower and a circular chamber. A spiral staircase leads to the upper level, where observations were made.

Las Monjas

Immediately to the south of El Caracol, the so-called **Monjas** (Nunnery) palace complex shows several stages of construction. Part of the facade was blasted away in the nineteenth century, but it is nonetheless a building of grand proportions. Its **annexe**, on the east end, has an elaborate facade in the Chenes style, covered in small heads of Chac that combine to make one giant mask, with the door as a mouth. By contrast, **La Iglesia**, a small building standing beside the convent, is a clear demonstration of Puuc design, its low band of unadorned masonry around the bottom surmounted by an elaborate mosaic frieze and roofcomb. Masks of Chac again predominate, but above the doorway are also figures of the four mythological creatures that held up the sky – a snail, a turtle, an armadillo and a crab.

Beyond Las Monjas

A path leads, in about ten minutes, to a further group of ruins that are among the oldest on the site, although they are unrestored; this is a good area for bird watching, with few people around to disturb the wildlife. Just east of Las Monjas is the **Akab Dzib**, a relatively plain block of palace rooms that takes its name ("Obscure Writings") from undeciphered hieroglyphs found inside. Red palm prints – frequently found in Maya buildings – adorn the walls of some of the chambers. Backtrack along the main path to the building opposite El Osario, the **Plataforma de las Tumbas**, a funerary structure topped with small columns; behind it is a jungle path that heads back to the main east–west road via the site's other water source, Cenote Xtoloc.

Grutas de Balankanché

Hwy-180, 1.6km east of the *Dolores Alba* hotel (see page 724) • **Tours** (in English) Daily • Charge • Second-class buses and *colectivos* between Valladolid and Mérida can drop you at *las grutas*; you can also take a taxi here from Pisté

These damp caverns are a refreshingly cool way to pass an hour. They were reopened in 1959, when a sealed passageway was discovered, revealing a path to an underground altar to Chac, the rain god. Tours with taped commentary lead past an underground pool, stalagmites and stalactites to a huge rock formation that resembles a *ceiba*, the Maya tree of life. Around its base lie many of the original Maya offerings, such as clay pots in the shapes of gods' faces.

Cenote Yokdzonot

Hwy-180, 14km west of Pisté • Charge • Any of the second-class buses along Hwy-180 *libre* stop on request at the town plaza; the *cenote* is about 350m south; if you take a taxi you should factor in some waiting time

The village of Yokdzonot is known for its well-kept *cenote*. It has excellent facilities, with good showers and toilets, plus a restaurant and camping facilities. Life jackets and snorkel gear are available, and you can take a bike tour to another nearby *cenote*.

ARRIVAL AND DEPARTURE — CHICHÉN ITZÁ AND AROUND

Arriving at Chichén Itzá, Hwy-180 *libre* curves around the site to the north, making an arc that merges with the site access road (the original highway straight through) at both ends.

12

THE RUINS

By bus First-class buses from all the peninsula's major towns and cities stop in the site parking lot.

Destinations Cancún (8–9 daily; 4hr); Playa del Carmen (2 daily at 7.35am & 4.30pm; 3hr 20min–3hr 50min); Tulum (2 daily at 7.35am & 2.45pm; 2hr 20min–2hr 50min), with the first bus stopping at Cobá (2hr 10min); Valladolid (roughly hourly; 40min-1hr).

PISTÉ

By bus There are two bus stations, one at each end of town. You can buy tickets for any service at either station, but first-class buses stop only at the east end.

Destinations All destinations are the same as at the ruins, plus Mérida on second class (12–14 daily; 3hr).

ACCOMMODATION AND EATING

Visitors to Chichén Itzá have a choice of staying in more expensive **hotels** immediately **east of the ruins** (all but one are on the short east-side access road off Hwy-180 *libre*, signposted "Zona Hotelera"), or cheaper ones along the main street in the town of **Pisté**, west of the site. In Pisté, most hotels are on the main road, between the village and the ruins, so it's easy to shop around – though quality can be low and occupancy high. Though the town is short on good places to eat, there is a row of *loncherías* at the west end of town, facing the plaza – they serve comida corrida, and are also open in the evenings, with lighter meals.

NEAR THE RUINS, SEE MAP PAGE 720

Dolores Alba Hwy-180 libre km 122, 2km east of Chichén Itzá east entrance; http://doloresalba.com. The best-value hotel near the ruins, with clean, colourful rooms (though rather tiny, spare bathrooms), a good restaurant and two swimming pools. Transport is provided to the site, but not back. The restaurant is good and affordable, and diners can use the pool. Across the road, you may notice the appealing-looking Parque Ikkil, but it is a massive package-tour-with-buffet juggernaut, not really even worth entering for its *cenote*. M$$

★ **Hacienda Chichén** Off Hwy-180 libre, near the east entrance to the ruins; http://haciendachichen.com. Of the two luxury choices at the ruins (*Mayaland* is the other), this place has a more old-colonial, Mexican feel: the hacienda it is based on dates back to 1523. Some rooms are in cottages that housed Carnegie Institution archeologists in the 1920s. There's also a spa. M$$$$

Villa Arqueológica Chichén Itzá Off Hwy-180 libre, near the east entrance to the ruins; https://www.villaschichen.com. Not as lavish as its neighbours, but comfortable enough, and handy for the site. The snug, thick-walled rooms (each with a double bed and a single bed) and suites are set round a patio enclosing a pool and cocktail bar. M$$$

PISTÉ

Hacienda Xaybe´h D´ Camara C 15-A no. 42; 985 851 0000. One of the more welcoming places in Pisté, this oh so green themed restaurant (think bright neon tablecloths) serves up simple but tasty food, with no pretense and a decent price tag. M$$

Posada Olalde On C 6, off Hwy-180 libre; turn south across from Posada Carrousel; 985 851 0086. This is one of the quieter spots in town, as it's off the main road. Palapa-roofed cabañas with fans crowd the tiny yard behind the main house, but they're a fresher alternative to the tired rooms in the older complex behind. M$

Valladolid and around

Yucatán state's second city, **VALLADOLID** is around 40km east of Chichén Itzá, still close enough to beat the crowds to the site on an early bus, and of interest in its own right. Although it took a severe bashing in the nineteenth-century Caste Wars, it has retained a strong colonial feel and exudes the unpretentious attitude of a rural capital, catering to the farmers and ranchers who live nearby, and the village women who come here to sell their hand-embroidered *huipiles* and other crafts. It's also an excellent place to eat, with traditional Yucatecan food still flourishing.

The heart of the city is the *parque principal*, the main plaza at the intersection of calles 39 and 40, where the two white towers of the eighteenth-century Catedral de San Gervasio rise gracefully over the south side. It's the place to be at dusk, when the curving love seats are filled with chatting couples and the bubbling fountain, topped with a statue of a woman in a traditional Yucatecan *huipil*, is lit from below. During the day, you can walk upstairs in the city hall (*ayuntamiento*; on the southeast corner) to see murals and photos of Valladolid's history, including a wall of portraits of city leaders.

Casa de los Venados

C 40 no. 204, just off the plaza • **Tours** Daily (in English and Spanish) • Charge • 985 856 2289

This private home, a beautifully renovated seventeenth-century mansion, contains a truly dazzling collection (over 3000-strong) of modern Mexican folk art, shown by house-proud owners, an American couple, who are delighted to answer questions. Pre-arrange a visit by email, ideally, or drop by at 10am, the default tour time. The entry fee supports local charities.

Iglesia de San Bernardino de Siena

Parque de San Bernardino, 1km southwest of the plaza via C 41-A • **Church** Free • **Museum** Charge

Franciscan missionaries began work on this sturdy **church** shortly after the Spanish established Valladolid as an outpost in 1545. In 1848 Maya rebels sacked it; despite this, a fine Baroque altarpiece from the eighteenth century remains, as do some striking seventeenth-century paintings on the side walls.

The monastery on the north side is now a museum, where you can see weapons that were dredged up from the on-site *cenote*, and other relics from the revolution. You can also see the beautiful structure that houses the water wheel over the *cenote*, and the sprawling gardens where the self-sufficient monks grew their own food.

Cenote Zací

On the block formed by C 34, C 36, C 37 and C 39 • Charge

This *cenote* was the water source for the former Maya stronghold of Zací ("white hawk"), from where the fierce Cupul clan fought against the first conquistadors. Broad stairs lead down into a huge cavern where the air is cool, and light reflects off the green water. It's also home to lots of catfish. Swimming is permitted, but not encouraged – there are no changing rooms, though you could tidy up in the open-air restaurant at the top, so long as you order something.

Cenotes X'keken and Samula

7km west of Valladolid on Hwy-180 *libre* • **Cenote X'keken** Charge • **Cenote Samula** Charge • *Colectivos* run to the village of Dzitnup from outside the *María Guadalupe* hotel on C 44 (see page 727); or cycle on a paved bike path starting from C 49 west of San Bernardino; or take a taxi

Perhaps the most photogenic swimming hole in the Yucatán, the remarkable **Cenote X'keken** is also called Dzitnup like the nearby village. Visitors descend through a tunnel into a huge vaulted cave, where a nearly circular pool of crystal-clear turquoise water glows under a shaft of light from an opening in the ceiling. A swim in the ice-cold water is an invigorating experience. A short walk away, in the same complex, at the even more impressive (thanks to spooky natural lighting) **Cenote Samula**, the roots of a huge tree stretch down towards the pool. Facilities include changing rooms, souvenir stalls, life jackets (to rent) and a restaurant. Not to be missed.

ARRIVAL AND DEPARTURE — VALLADOLID

By bus Valladolid's main bus station is on C 39 at C 46, a block and a half west of the main plaza. Additionally, AutoCentro buses serve Izamal (15 daily; 1hr) from the old Oriente terminal west of the centre, C 37 at C 54.

Destinations Cancún (1–2 hourly; 2hr 15min–4hr 20min); Chichén Itzá (roughly hourly; 40min); Izamal (2 daily at 12.45pm & 3.50pm; 3hr); Mérida (roughly hourly; 2hr 15min), plus numerous second-class services; Playa del Carmen (roughly hourly; 2hr 30min–3hr 10min); Tizimín (4 daily at 8.50am, 12.25pm, 7.25pm & 9.30pm; 50min–1hr); Tulum via Cobá (roughly hourly; 1hr 40min–2hr 10min).

By colectivo Shared vans and taxis are convenient for nearby towns and sights, such as Tizimín, Ek-Balam and Dzitnup. Most depart from marked points along C 44 just west of the plaza, though the Ek-Balam service seems to shift around. For Chichén Itzá, Servicio Plus vans leave from

C 39 between C 44 and C 46; these can be faster than buses in the morning, and much cheaper. They also serve X'keken and Samula, with departures at 8am from the same spot.

GETTING AROUND

By bike With its small scale and light traffic, Valladolid is a good place to get around by bike; you can also reach nearby *cenotes* via bike paths. Rent from MexiGO Tours, which offers a self-guided bike tour (see below).

INFORMATION AND TOURS

Tourist office On the southeast corner of the main plaza, by the *ayuntamiento* (Mon–Fri 9am–9pm, Sat 9am–8pm, Sun 9am–7pm; 985 856 2529). It has plenty of information, including free maps, but is erratically staffed.

Tours MexiGO Tours (C 43 no. 204-C, between C 40 and C 42; 985 856 0777, http://mexigotours.com) runs trips to Río Lagartos and other nearby attractions, as well as bike trips (self-guided is an option) to local houses and *cenotes*.

ACCOMMODATION

SEE MAP PAGE 725

Valladolid's budget hotels are good, and higher-end places are excellent value. Also note that the *Genesis Retreat* (see page 729) is less than half an hour away.

La Aurora C 42 at C 35; http://hotellaaurora.com. Great mix of old colonial style and new features: sparkling rooms around a central courtyard and pool but retaining the building's old tile floors. For quiet, though, request a room away from the street, where traffic noise hammers off the stone pavements. M$$

★ **La Candelaria** Parque la Candelaria, C 35 between C 44 and C 42; http://hostelvalladolidyucatan.com. The excellent local hostel, facing one of the city's loveliest squares, has colourful and spotless dorms and private rooms, plus a garden, laundry facilities, an outdoor kitchen and low-cost bike rental. M$

★ **Casa Hamaca** C 49 no. 202-A, at C 40 on the southwest corner of Parque San Juan; 800 696 7666. Set in a garden packed with fruit trees, this charming B&B has eight expansive rooms in a big two-storey building. There's also a pool, and the expert owner can arrange massages, spa treatments and nature tours. M$$$

María Guadalupe C 44 no. 198, between C 39 and C 41; 985 856 2068. A solid, reasonably priced hotel, *María Guadalupe* has well-kept rooms featuring private baths and optional a/c in a small two-storey 1960s building. *Colectivos* for *cenotes* X'keken and Samula leave from outside. M$$

El Mesón del Marqués C 39 no. 203, on the main plaza; https://www.mesondelmarques.com. Lovely hotel that started in a mansion, then expanded into neighbouring buildings. It's where most tour groups stay, but the quality is high. It has a wonderful palm-fringed pool, and one of the best restaurants in town (see page 727). M$$$

Zací C 44 no. 191, between C 37 and C 39; 985 856 2167. A pleasant, modern, three-storey hotel with a quiet courtyard and pool, all of which make it exceptionally good value. The big rooms have a fan, or – for a few dollars more – a/c and TV. M$$

EATING

SEE MAP PAGE 725

Whatever your budget, you'll eat well in Valladolid – all of the restaurants recommended here could be considered "author picks". The city market, the Mercado Municipal, is on C 32 between C 35 and C 37 and ringed with snack stands. For nightlife, there's not much beyond people-watching on the plaza, where there's usually some live music on Sun.

El Bazar Northeast corner of the main plaza; 958 856 2634. A sort of semi-open-air food court with an excellent selection of inexpensive, busy *loncherías* and pizzerias. M$$

★ **Casa Italia** Parque Candelaria, C 35 no. 202-J, between C 42 and C 44; http://casaitalia.uzimenu.com. Sweet, family-owned Italian restaurant that's both delicious and inexpensive. It draws local families as well as tourists, and there are seats outside on the city's prettiest small plaza. M$$

Conato 1910 C 40, between C 45 and C 47; 985 111 5533, http://facebook.com/conato.valladolid. A few rooms in an old house, furnished with antique oddities and vinyl booths. The food is eclectic, beautifully presented and home-made, and includes a few sweets such as a rich coconut pudding. It's a family place, but still has a special atmosphere. M$$$

Hostería El Marqués C 39 no. 203, in El Mesón del Marqués; https://www.mesondelmarques.com. Valladolid's best (and quite reasonably priced) restaurant is set in an interior courtyard on the main plaza. Don't be put off if you see it packed with a tour group – the excellent menu features Yucatecan classics such as *sopa de lima* and *poc-chuc*, along with city specialities like *escabeche de Valladolid* (chicken in a spicy vinegar broth). M$$$

★ **Restaurante la terraza Covarrubias** C 39 no. 201, between C 46 and C 48; 985 105 3561. A fast but fun restaurant serving popular Mexican dishes and a smattering of American offerings. The core of the menu is Yucatecan, alongside the likes of burgers and fries. M$

Zací C 36, between C 37 and C 39; 985 856 0721. The restaurant at the *cenote* of the same name is reasonably priced and features some hearty regional food, such as ultra-smoky *longaniza* sausage, and handmade tortillas. The setting is cool and shady. M$$

DIRECTORY

Banks and exchange There are numerous banks in the city centre. Bancomer, next door to the post office on the plaza, changes travellers' cheques and has an ATM.

Internet There are several internet cafés in the centre, including the Ladatel *caseta* on the plaza.

Laundry Lavanderia Daniela at C 41-A, on the way to the Iglesia de San Bernardino de Siena.

Post office On the plaza, C 40 near the corner of C 39.

North of Valladolid

From Valladolid, most traffic heads straight east to the Caribbean beaches. The north, however, is less explored and makes a nice detour for wildlife: flamingo colonies at Río Lagartos are the main draw. You can also visit the small but flawless Maya site of Ek-Balam.

Ek-Balam

20km north of Valladolid, then 7km east • Charge; given the rich detail at the site, it's worth hiring a guide for a small group; Juan Canul, who has worked on many excavations, is recommended (ask for him at the ticket desk); he speaks Spanish and English

Notable for the high quality and unique details of its fantastically preserved stucco sculpture, **Ek-Balam** is nonetheless rarely crowded. The compact site, enclosed by a series of defensive walls, is really only the ceremonial centre; the entire city, which was occupied from the pre-Classic period through to the Spanish Conquest, spreads out over a very wide area, punctuated by *sacbeob* leading out in all directions.

The entrance is along one of these ancient roads, leading through a freestanding four-sided arch. Beyond are two identical temples, called **Las Gemelas** (the Twins), and a long **ball-court**.

12

El Acrópolis

The principal building, on the far side of the plaza, is the massive **Acrópolis**, the stones along its 200m-long base adorned with bas-reliefs. Thatched awnings at the top protect the site's finest treasure, an elaborate stucco frieze fully uncovered only recently; 85 percent of what you see is original plaster from the ninth century that didn't even require retouching once the dirt was brushed away.

A staircase leads up the centre of the building. On the first level, two doorways flanking the steps display near-matching designs of twisted serpents and tongues; in the right-hand carving, the snake's tongue is emblazoned with a glyph thought to represent the city. Just below the summit, a **Chenes-style doorway** in the form of a giant gaping mouth is studded with protruding teeth. This is the **entrance to the tomb** of Ukit-Kan-Lek-Tok, Ek-Balam's king in the mid-ninth century. The lower jaw forms the floor, while skulls, lilies, fish and other symbols of the underworld carved below reinforce its function as a tomb gateway. Back on the ground, in the plaza, an exceptionally well-preserved **stele** depicts a king receiving the objects of power from Ukit-Kan-Lek-Tok, who is the smaller seated figure at the top of the stele.

Cenote Xcanché

Charge • 985 113 4511

In the parking area at the Ek-Balam site, you'll find someone selling tickets to a seemingly bottomless pool that's a 2km walk from the ruins. You can rent a bike to ride there, and try other activities such as rappelling and kayaking at the *cenote*. There's a small restaurant too.

ARRIVAL AND DEPARTURE — EK-BALAM

By colectivo The village and ruins are easily reached from Valladolid in a *colectivo*, departing from C 44 just west of the plaza.

By taxi A round-trip taxi from Valladolid is moderately expensive given the waiting time that's included.

ACCOMMODATION AND EATING

★ **Genesis Retreat** East of the village plaza; http://genesisecooasis.com. Not far from the ruins, this beautiful ecolodge has a big garden and a bio-filtered pool. Guests can take tours around the village and in the nearby forest. The vegetarian café makes a great stop after the ruins, with organic, local produce. Some taxi drivers may attempt to take you to another, less savoury, lodge around the corner – *Genesis* has a doghouse labelled "Concierge" out front. En-suite rooms cost extra; the treehouse-style "Birdhouse" room is a fun option for children. Phone connections are patchy in this area, so email ahead. M$$$

Tizimín

Travelling by bus from Valladolid north to Río Lagartos, you have to transfer in **TIZIMÍN**, the unofficial capital of Yucatán's cattle country, 51km from Valladolid. It's pleasant enough, but travellers rarely come this way, even though it is a handy transport hub for northeastern Yucatán (you can go straight from here to Mérida or Cancún, for instance). One seasonal draw is the Feria de los Tres Reyes, which takes place during Epiphany in early January. The fair's festivities draw both Catholic pilgrims and cowboys (who show off their barbecue skills). The rest of the year, it's worth arranging your schedule to pass through Tizimín at lunch time, for a meal at one of the region's best restaurants.

ARRIVAL AND DEPARTURE — TIZIMÍN

By bus Two bus stations are around the corner from each other at C 46 and C 47, about a 10min walk northeast of the main plaza.

Destinations Cancún (6 daily; 4hr–4hr 10min); Chiquilá for Holbox (3 daily at 7.30am, 1.30pm & 4.30pm; 3hr); Mérida (5 daily; 3hr); Río Lagartos (12 daily; 1hr–2hr); San Felipe (7 daily; 1hr–1hr 30min).

12

ACCOMMODATION AND EATING

Hotel San Carlos C 54 no. 407, between C 51 and C 53; 886 863 2094. There's no real reason to stay the night in Tizimín, but if you do want to, *Hotel San Carlos* is one of the better options in town, with tidy en-suite rooms with a/c and TVs. M$

★ **Tres Reyes** C 52 at C 53; 986 115 0596. A great restaurant with hand-patted, chewy tortillas, black-as-ink beans and succulent meats – the soul of Yucatecan cooking. It's on the plaza, a 10min walk from the two bus stations. M$$

Río Lagartos

This village 100km north of Valladolid is set on a small spit, surrounded on three sides by water and protected from the open sea by a barrier island. The resulting shallow inlet is inhabited much of the year by tens of thousands of **pink flamingos**, among nearly four hundred bird species in the **Río Lagartos Biosphere Reserve**. Though there's not much in the town itself, the flamingos alone make a visit worthwhile; the best time of year to see them is the spring nesting season, from April to July. There are no banks or ATMs in town, so make sure you bring enough cash with you.

ARRIVAL AND DEPARTURE — RÍO LAGARTOS

By bus The station is on C 19 just east of the main north–south street through town. There's a return service from

FLAMINGO TOURS IN RÍO LAGARTOS

As soon as you arrive at the bus station or get out of your car, you'll be approached about boat tours to see the flamingos. Several experienced **guides** operate in town: try Río Lagartos Adventures (986 111 9286, http://riolagartosexpeditions.com) at the *Ria Maya* restaurant and guesthouse (see page 730), on the waterfront. Their **boats** visit the many feeding sites; a three-hour sunset tour or a "deluxe tour" also includes a "spa treatment" at some mud flats and a swim. The agency also offers fishing, birding, photography and after-dark crocodile trips for the more adventurous.

Tizimín (10–12 daily; 1–2hr), but the last bus back there (for connections to Mérida or Cancún) departs around 5.15pm.

By combi Ask around the bus station area for shared taxis – they often depart at more convenient times.

ACCOMMODATION

Ria Maya C 19 no. 134; 986 100 8390, http://riolagartosnaturetours.com. A 5min walk from the waterfront, this small-scale guesthouse-restaurant is run by the people behind Río Lagartos Adventures (see page 729); the rooms are comfortable and come with a/c, TVs and a light breakfast in the morning. M$$$

Hotel Villa de Pescadores End of C 14, on the waterfront; http://hotelvilladepescadores.com. An appealing hotel, right on the water, with spick and span rooms with a/c and TVs; some have tiny balconies with views over the inlet. There's a restaurant onsite, and staff can arrange tours. M$$$

San Felipe

If it's beaches you're after, head to this tidy town, where an offshore spit is lined with white sand. The town, which is also a popular destination for sport-fishing, is 12km west of Río Lagartos; many of the buses from Tizimín to Río Lagartos come out here as well.

The beach

Boats (charge per person) depart from the east end of the malecón, where you can also buy tickets for various bird watching and nature tours

At Mexican holiday times – notably July, August and Semana Santa – the beach is crowded; the rest of the year, though, it's quite deserted, and you can set up camp here. If you do, be sure to bring protection against mosquitoes.

ARRIVAL AND DEPARTURE SAN FELIPE

By bus From Tizimín, there are several daily buses (7 daily; 20min) to San Felipe; the last one back leaves around 5.45pm.

ACCOMMODATION

San Felipe de Jesús C 9, between C 14 and C 16; 998 734 8202, https://facebook.com/HotelSanFelipeDeJesus. San Felipe's one hotel is average at best (nearby Río Lagartos has better options; see page 730), but it has a decent restaurant and the views across the water are undoubtedly beautiful. M$$

Isla Holbox

Near the northeastern corner of the Yucatán, **HOLBOX** (pronounced "ol-BOSH") has just one small sand-street village of about two thousand people, wooden houses and virtually no cars. It's technically not an island, but a very long peninsula – but you still must cross by ferry from the village of Chiquilá. The gulf waters here do not have the same glittering clarity as the Caribbean (nor the vibrant reefs), but they're warm and clean, and Isla Holbox is rapidly becoming the trendiest coastal destination in the region.

Development is of course marching on, but fishing remains the main industry and much of the area remains wild and harbours all manner of birds, including flamingos. From May to mid-September, visitors come to see the huge and rare whale sharks (see page 730) that congregate just off the cape; on the hour-long boat ride to see and swim with them, you may also see dolphins, rays and flying fish.

ACTIVITIES ON ISLA HOLBOX

For whale sharks, every hotel and guesthouse can arrange the trip. The price is typically the same with every company (the charge per person includes lunch and snorkel gear; 5–6hr), but may change from season to season. For **fishing**, try *Posada Mawimbi* (see page 731), which runs a three-hour trip; it also runs **diving** and **snorkelling** excursions – though there is not so much to see underwater here – as well as kayaking. Kitesurfing lessons/equipment rental and horseriding trips are available at *Casa las Tortugas* (see page 731).

One spot of trouble in paradise: truly fearsome mosquitoes during the wet season. And after the bustle of whale-shark season, the island basically shuts down for the rest of September and October – it can feel a bit dreary at this time.

ARRIVAL AND DEPARTURE — ISLA HOLBOX

By bus There are daily buses from Cancún to Chiquilá (7.50am, 9.40am, 10.30am & 12.50pm; returning 7.45am, 12.40pm, 1.45pm, 2.15pm & 3.15pm; 3hr 30min–4hr). There are also services from Playa del Carmen (5 daily; 2hr 10min–2hr 50min), Mérida (2 daily at 6.45am & 7.15am; 5hr–5hr 30min), Tulum (1 daily at 8.10am; 3hr 25min) and Valladolid (1 daily at 9.55am; 3hr). Services do fluctuate a bit, and drop off in the winter: stay up to date at http://the.holboxeno.com.

By car Turn north off Hwy-180 *libre* (there's no exit off the toll highway) at the tiny town of El Ideal. Secure parking is available near the ferry pier in Chiquilá (set the price before you leave).

By ferry There are numerous ferries (roughly hourly, though fewer during the winter; 15–30min). If you're with a group or arrive between departures, you might want to hire a private boat. But don't miss the last ferry: Chiquilá is not a place to get stranded. There's a restaurant, basic hotel, store and petrol station, but little else.

GETTING AROUND

For orientation, you'll usually receive a map on the ferry, though street names are seldom used.

By pedicab When you arrive, you'll be greeted by *triciclo* or golf-cart taxis, which can spare you the 10min trek to the plaza, straight ahead from the ferry dock; check the maximum charge to the very furthest hotels.

By golf cart The popular alternative to cars, which are rare. They're available to rent from several outlets near the *parque*.

By bike You can also get around by bike, from many of the same golf-cart-rental agencies, though they aren't always maintained very well.

12

ACCOMMODATION

Small-scale hotel development stretches east of town for a couple of kilometres. In early summer and before Christmas, rates for some of the upmarket rooms can fall by almost half; July and August, however, can be priced nearly as high as Christmas and Easter weeks. The beachfront hotels are all mid-range to luxury, but there are a few decent cheaper options away from the water. Locals have successfully contested plans for large-scale resorts in the past, but pressure from hoteliers remains.

Casa Barbara Tiburón Ballena, between the pier and the plaza; http://hotelcasabarbara.mx. You're away from the beach here (about a 10min walk), but also away from the town hubbub. The a/c rooms are clean and spacious and set along a deep courtyard with a pool. M$$$

Casa Takywara off Coldwell, west of the plaza; http://casatakywara.com. A bit of a hike west, but right on the beach and away from party noise. The Colombian owner uses the hotel income to fund her pet project, the island's only animal refuge (injured pelicans, stray raccoons, even a crocodile have a home here – securely fenced and away from guests). There are six rooms in total, including one cabaña on the water; all have kitchenettes. M$$$$

Casa las Tortugas On the beach two blocks east of the plaza; http://holboxcasalastortugas.com. Italian-run *Casa las Tortugas* has a great little collection of round, two-storey, a/c cabañas, beautifully decorated and tucked among dense greenery. There's a spa, and staff can organize yoga, horseriding and kiteboarding, among other activities. There's also an excellent restaurant-bar. Minimum three-night stay. M$$$$

Ida y Vuelta Escobedo, east of the plaza, behind Xaloc; https://holbox-hostal.hotelesislaholbox.com. A friendly hostel just a couple of blocks off the beach, with screened shelters for tents or hammocks, a mixed dorm, and a range of simple cabañas. The Swiss-Italian owner also has a tour company that can arrange fishing, snorkelling and of course whale-shark trips. Dorms, camping (per person) and hammock (per person) M$; cabaña M$$

Posada Mawimbi On the beach two blocks east of the plaza; https://mawimbi.com. *Posada Mawimbi* has a similar set-up to *Casa las Tortugas* in terms of layout, but the rates are slightly lower. All rooms have a/c, but if you like a breeze it's worth paying extra for an upstairs room with a balcony. M$$$$

★ **Tribu** Coldwell, three blocks west of the plaza; http://tribuhostel.com. One of the best hostels in the Yucatán, located just a half-block from the beach, and notable for its extremely helpful staff and back to basics, natural aesthetic. The complex, which includes a big kitchen, a bar and a movie room, was mostly hand-built by the owners. Tidy and simple private rooms might even convert non-hostel fans. Minimum two-night stay. Dorms M$; doubles M$$

EATING

Dining options on Holbox generally consist of Mexican, Italian and seafood, though the range of choices is expanding. Restaurants are all very casual, and this can extend to opening hours as well – they vary greatly depending on the season.

Buena Vista Juárez at Coldwell; 984 875 2102. A very simple family-run fish restaurant, half a block back from the beach, *Buena Vista* specializes in seafood. Fried whole fish – plucked straight from the water that day – is the thing to order. M$$$

La Cabane Charal, close to the beach; 998 258 7370. This open-air restaurant is a great way to start a day in paradise, with ample breakfasts, hearty lunch offerings and very good cocktails come the evening. M$$

★ **La Combi Holbox** West side of the plaza; 984 177 9775. Proper pub food buut with some creative (and tasty) local twists. There's also live music each night and some pretty good cocktails to boot. M$$

Empanadas La Conquista Coldwell at Tiburón Ballena, one block north off the northwest corner of the plaza. This screened-in wooden hut is a typical local place, and one of the best places to eat if you're on a tight budget – you'd be hard-pushed to spend much on a meal. There are great empanadas and daily seafood specials. M$$

DRINKING AND NIGHTLIFE

Don't expect much in the way of nightlife on Holbox; locals generally lounge around on the plaza.

Angeles y Diablitos Porfirio Díaz, on the main square; 984 203 1813. As well as a good selection of craft beers – try a bottle of Cerveza Artesanal Pescadores' IPA, brewed in Puerto Moreles – "*Angels and Devils*" makes its own ice cream.

Alma Bar Paseo Kuka, Km1; 984 131 9303, https://facebook.com/almabarholbox. Perched above *Hotel Villas Tiburón*, this rooftop pool bar is an ideal spot for a sunset cocktail. Sample one of the flavoured mojitos – the passion fruit and coco cream La Tigre is particularly good – and lounge in a hammock over the pool.

DIRECTORY

12

Services On the modest main square, called the *parque*, you'll find a post office, money-exchange desk and a trio of (unreliable) ATMs – always bring extra cash. Internet access is also a bit patchy.

Websites http://holboxisland.com, http://the.holboxeno.com, http://holboxguide.com and http://en-holbox.com are all useful, and http://ipaffestival.com has info on the International Public Art Festival, which is held in April.

Cancún and around

Independent travellers often find the glitz of Mexico's mammoth resort city, **CANCÚN**, off-putting and its beachfront pleasures brash and expensive. Certainly, for anyone who has been out in the rest of the Yucatán or is eager to get there, all the concrete can be a downer. But a night spent here on the way in or out doesn't have to be wasted, so long as you appreciate the city as an energetic, successful frontier experiment, rather than lament its lack of history. A closer look reveals hidden beach bars and inexpensive taco stands frequented by *cancunenses* who are friendly and proud of their city's prosperity.

Brief history

If nothing else, Cancún is proof of the government's remarkable ability to get things done in a hurry – so long as the will exists. In the late 1960s, the Mexican government decided to develop a new resort area to diversify the economy. Computers crunched weather data, and surveyors scouted the country's natural attractions to

PRICES ON THE CARIBBEAN COAST

Because Cancún, Cozumel and other destinations along Quintana Roo's coast (including Isla Holbox) cater largely to foreign tourists, local businesses often quote prices in US dollars, and peg them to the exchange rate. In this guide we list prices in pesos, except when a business quotes a price solely in US dollars. For easier comparison, the peso equivalent at the time of research follows in brackets (for hotels) or after a forward slash – it's meant as a guideline only.

identify a 25km-long barrier island just off the northern Caribbean coast as the ideal combination of beautiful beaches, sparse population and accessible position. Construction began in 1970, and when the first hotel opened in 1974, it relied on a generator for electricity and trucked-in water.

Cancún today

In the twenty-first century, the city has struggled to shed its reputation for tacky fun (Spring Break happens only a month a year, after all), but it has successfully courted Mexican tourists. It faced a serious crisis after Hurricane Wilma severely eroded the beach in 2005, but restoration schemes finally seem to have taken hold.

The security situation in Cancún has worsened in recent years, and despite an increased police presence, it is important to keep abreast of the latest situation, follow local advice and remain vigilant.

Downtown Cancún

There's little in the way of sights in **downtown Cancún**, though it is a pleasant place to stroll in the evenings. Both the sociable **Parque de las Palapas** and **mercados 23 and 28** are good places to browse for a souvenir or get something to eat.

Parque de las Palapas

This large "park" – really, a large concrete **plaza** – at the heart of Cancún's downtown is the city's social centre. It's liveliest on Sundays, when the bandstand hosts some kind of music or entertainment, and most evenings, families come here to socialize. Craft stands are set up on one side, and on the other is a row of excellent food stalls, open every night. Smaller parks in the neighbourhood host craft or art shows.

Markets

For a sense of the city's hum away from the tourist trade, head for **Mercado 23**, north of the bus station off Avenida Tulum at Cedro. The market is a small maze of stalls with the flavour of a village market, complete with butchers, herbalists and vegetable sellers. The bigger **Mercado 28**, west on Avenida Sunyaxchén, was formerly the main general market, but now stocks primarily tourist tat; its restaurants are quite good, though.

Zona Hotelera

Most visitors head straight for the overdeveloped *zona hotelera* and its myriad resorts, restaurants, bars and **beaches**. Each of the latter is popular with a different crowd: among the best are **Playa Las Perlas**, **Playa Caracol** and **Playa Delfines**.

Beaches

Paseo Kukulcán

The public beaches on the north coast of the *zona hotelera* face a bay, so the water is calm and often shallow. Playa Las Perlas (km 2.5) is small and has a playground for kids and palapas for shade. Playa Tortugas (km 6) has several good bars and more casual restaurants, while Playa Caracol (km 8.5) is the prettiest of the bay beaches, with plenty of palm trees; official entrance is by the Xcaret bus stop, but it's easier to walk through *Kinha Villas* hotel (which has a nice simple bar).

On the east coast, the beaches have more surf and occasionally dangerous currents. Delfines (km 17.5) is by far the most scenic because it doesn't have hotels behind it, and even when it's packed with locals at weekends, there's still plenty of room.

El Rey

Paseo Kukulcán km 18 • Charge

CANCÚN ORIENTATION

The city has two separate parts: the *centro* (downtown) on the mainland and the *zona hotelera*, or hotel zone, a narrow barrier island shaped like a "7" that holds a long strip of hotels, malls, restaurants and other tourist facilities. The island is connected to the mainland at each end by causeways enclosing a huge lagoon. Paseo Kukulcán runs the length of *zona hotelera*, from the airport up to Punta Cancún (where the road splits around the convention centre and a warren of bars) and back onto the mainland. Street addresses in the beach zone are all kilometre markers on Paseo Kukulcán. The count starts on the north end, near downtown. It's not an exact science: two sets of markers exist, and are out of sync by about half a kilometre, so addresses are guidelines at best.

12

This small **Maya ruin** overlooks the Nichupté Lagoon. It's the largest Maya site in Cancún, though that's not saying a lot. The buildings are on the small side, built during the empire's decline in the late Post-Classic period, contemporary with those on Cozumel and at Tulum. There's very little information available to explain them, but the area is peaceful and good for spotting birds and iguanas.

Museo Maya de Cancún

Paseo Kukulcán km 16.5 • Charge • 998 885 3844

This long-overdue **museum** provides a rare dose of culture in Cancún. The space displays hundreds of small finds from ruins along the coast like Tulum, including Maya jewellery, burial masks, weapons, ceramics and the 10,000-year-old La Mujer de las Palmas ("The Woman of the Palms"), whose remains were found in a *cenote* in 2002.

UNDERWATER ART

Cancún may not have any museums on land, but under the waves are more than four hundred sculptures. This underwater sculpture park, the **Museo Subacuático de Arte** (MUSA;, http://musamexico.org), is the work of English artist Jason deCaires Taylor. The concrete casts are largely based on real Mexicans, and some create surreal scenarios, such as a bureaucrat's office on the sea floor. The aim of the ever-expanding museum is to draw visitors away from stressed reefs, while also giving coral a new place to grow. The first works were installed in 2009 and today the figures are sprouting colourful buds, and attract other sea life.

A few of the works are in shallow water (4–10m), so snorkellers can drift above them. But the MUSA is really better visited as a **dive excursion** (see page 737): with a full scuba kit, you can submerge and look the strikingly realistic portraits in the eye. There are also glass-bottom boat trips (see the website for more info).

It also hosts occasional travelling shows from the national archeology trove in Mexico City. The site also contains the modest San Miguelito ruins (entry included in the museum admission fee), which include a small pyramid.

ARRIVAL AND DEPARTURE — CANCÚN

BY PLANE

Charter flights from Europe and South America, along with direct scheduled flights from dozens of cities in Mexico, the Caribbean and North and Central America, land at Cancún International Airport (http://cancun-airport.com), 20km south of the centre. Most international flights arrive at terminal 3; domestic flights and some charter flights come into terminal 2; terminal 1 is mainly served by charter and low-cost flights. The terminals have currency exchange desks and ATMs.

Buses run from the terminals (every 30min; 25min) to the bus station downtown; look for the ADO desk after customs. There are also buses directly to Playa del Carmen (every 45min; 1hr), stopping at Puerto Morelos on request. Transfer/shuttle services like Yellow Transfers (998 193 1742) will take you to any part of the *zona hotelera* for a fixed price (book online or buy tickets at the respective desks outside customs). Taxis will take you to anywhere in the *zona hotelera* or downtown.

Destinations Aguascalientes (1–2 weekly; 2hr 40min); Bogotá (4 daily; 3hr 25min; Guadalajara (up to 10 daily; 2hr 45min); Havana (4 daily; 1hr 20min); León (5 weekly; 2hr 35min); Mexico City (around 40 daily; 2hr 30min); Monterrey (8–10 daily; 2hr 25min); Panama City (6 daily; 2hr 35min); Puebla (2 daily; 2hr 15min); San Salvador (2 daily; 1hr 35min); Veracruz (1–3 daily; 1hr 45min); Villahermosa (5 weekly; 1hr 30min).

BY BUS

Arriving by bus, you'll pull in at the city's main station at the corner of Tulum and Uxmal downtown; it has luggage storage (daily 6am–9.30pm). The bus to Playa del Carmen and Puerto Morelos has its own lane and ticket desk. You can walk to most downtown hotels, or take a city bus to *zona hotelera* options.

Destinations Campeche (9 daily; 7hr–7hr 40min; Chetumal (every 30min–1hr; 5hr 30min–7hr) and second class (roughly hourly; 7hr); Chiquilá, for Holbox (5–6 daily; fewer in the winter; 3hr 30min–4hr); Izamal on second class only (12–14 daily; 4hr); Mahahual (1 daily at 4.45pm, plus more in summer; 5hr); Mérida (every 30min–1hr; 4hr 15min); Palenque (4 daily at 3.45pm, 5.45pm, 8.10pm & 8.30pm; around 13hr); Tizimín (1 daily at 9.30am; 3hr); Playa del Carmen via Puerto Morelos (every 15min; 1hr); Tulum (every 30min–1hr; around 2hr 30min); Valladolid (1–2 hourly; 2hr 15min–4hr 20min); Villahermosa (17 daily; 12hr 45min–15hr 10min).

BY CAR

Heading west by car to Valladolid, Chichén Itzá and Mérida, you have a choice between the speed-bump-filled free road (*libre*) or the fast toll highway (*cuota*). From the bus station, drive north on Tulum about 1km, then turn left onto López Portillo; after a few kilometres you can get on the toll road. There's another entrance to the *cuota* only off Hwy-307, 1.5km south of the airport. You pay in advance, at the booths on the highway, for the sections you intend to travel along.

Car rental International groups at the airport, most hotels and various locations downtown. A local option is Speed Car Rental, Uxmal 22 (998 845 1373).

BY COLECTIVO

Often more efficient (and slightly cheaper) than the bus,

these shared vans run between Cancún and Playa del Carmen whenever they're full (a matter of minutes at peak times). The most comfortable, run by Playa Express, depart from the bus station parking lot. Across Av Tulum are other, slightly more cramped, vans, to either Puerto Morelos or Playa del Carmen.

GETTING AROUND

By bus To get to and around the *zona hotelera*, city buses marked "R-1 – Hoteles" run along Tulum every few minutes; several others run from different parts of downtown, all likewise marked "Hoteles". For the ferry to Isla Mujeres, buses marked "Juárez" run north on Tulum, but these are not so frequent, so look for *colectivos* as well. For rentals contact Benotto (https://tienda.benotto.com); book in advance and they'll deliver your wheels to your hotel.

By car A car isn't necessary within the city, but it's not a liability either, as parking is not too difficult.

By colectivo You'll need these shared minivans for getting to Gran Puerto (for the Isla Mujeres ferry) from the bus station. They're marked "Pto Juárez" or "Punta Sam" and stop in front of the *McDonald's* on Tulum.

By taxi Taxis are plentiful and can be hailed almost anywhere. Fares are based on a zone system, and you should agree on the fare before getting in. Big hotels have sample rates posted, which reflect a small surcharge to what you'd pay from the street.

By bike Numerous places rent out bikes; not quite all of the *zona hotelera* has a proper bike lane or pavement, though, so proceed with caution.

INFORMATION AND TOURS

Tourist information The FONATUR tourist office (998 884 0610, http://fonatur.mx Mon–Fri 9am–3pm & 4.30–6pm) is at the corner of Náder and Cobá, 1km south of the bus station. Kiosks advertising "tourist info" are usually selling timeshares or excursions.

Tours Most hotels in the *zona hotelera* have in-house agencies that can arrange standard day trips to the chief Maya sites. For more variety, EcoColors (Camarón 32, SM 27, north and west of Mercado 28; 998 884 3667, http://ecotravelmexico.com), runs single- and multi-day kayaking, birding, whale- and shark-watching or cycling tours.

12

WATERSPORTS IN CANCÚN

SNORKELLING

Most **snorkelling** in Cancún is at Punta Nizuc, at the far southern point of the peninsula, but its coral has been damaged by crowds – you're much better off making the short trip down the coast to the great reef at Puerto Morelos. In Cancún, operators spice up the ho-hum local snorkelling with a so-called jungle tour, which entails riding two-passenger speedboats through lagoon mangroves, then out to the reef. A trip can be arranged at most hotels and many marinas along the lagoon.

Another popular snorkelling trip, only in the summer, is to see the whale sharks near Isla Holbox (see page 730). It's a long boat ride, but well worth it. Trips are cheaper from Isla Mujeres (see page 742), but you can arrange through your Cancún hotel for a surcharge.

DIVING

Other reefs off Cancún's coast make good beginner **diving**, with easy access and little current, as does the Museo Subacuático de Arte (see page 736). Contact Manta Divers (Paseo Kukulcán km 16; 998 849 4050, http://mantadivers.com); open-water certifications are available here

KITEBOARDING

Ikarus (984 803 3490, http://kiteboardmexico.com), based in Playa del Carmen (see page 746), gives classes on a remote beach north of Cancún.

SURFING

360 Surf School (998 241 6443, http://360surfschoolcancun.com) offers private and group classes, with a guarantee you'll be able to stand on the board; equipment is also available to rent. Sign up at the office on Paseo Kukulcán km 9.5 in the *zona hotelera*.

ACCOMMODATION

Cancún has a dizzying number of hotels. **Downtown**, on or near Av Tulum, holds the only hope of a true budget room, as hostels have proliferated. In the **zona hotelera**, you can stay on the lagoon side for less than in the glittering beachfront palaces – but on the beach, last-minute or low-season online deals can be impressive. Try "opaque" booking sites like http://hotwire.com, where you reserve without knowing the name of the hotel – you're on safe ground with most four- and five-star properties.

HOTELS

DOWNTOWN, SEE MAP PAGE 733

Alux Uxmal 21; https://www.hotelalux.com. *Alux* has unremarkable but perfectly functional rooms: although they are a bit dim, they do come with a/c and TVs. The hotel's main appeal is the short walk to the bus station. M$$

Ibis Cancún Centro Tulum s/n at Nichupte; http://ibis.accor.com. This sizeable outpost of the international chain is a good-value, if unexciting, choice: clean, comfortable rooms (with a/c and TVs), professional staff, and a reasonable on-site restaurant. M$$

International Suites Gladiolas 16; http://cancuninternationalsuites.com. This hotel eschews the glitz generally associated with Cancún, opting instead for a modest, understated style. Its beige en suites are clean, comfortable and good value, and the downtown location is convenient for transport connections and restaurants. M$$$

El Rey del Caribe Uxmal 24 at Nader; http://elreydelcaribe.com. Sunny yellow rooms with kitchenettes, plus a pool, spa services and generous breakfast at this casual hotel that feels like it should be on a beach in Tulum. One of the few places in Cancún with a real ecofriendly sensibility. M$$$

ZONA HOTELERA, SEE MAP PAGE 735

★ **Beachscape Kinha Villas** Paseo Kukulcán km 8.5; http://beachscape.com.mx. No frills, but in the best possible way: big, clean rooms with two double beds, as well as family-friendly suites. Every room has a terrace or balcony, and the beach is deep and palm-shaded – the best on the bay side. The handy location is within walking distance of Punta Cancún. M$$$

Le Blanc Spa Resort Paseo Kukulcán km 12; http://cancun.leblancsparesorts.com. Although the main building is something of a monolith, this well-run, modern luxury resort delivers the goods: elegant en suites, on point service, great swimming pools, and variety of great places to eat and drink. Rates are all inclusive. M$$$$

Kempinkski Hotel Retorno del Rey 36, near Paseo Kukulcán km 14; https://www.kempinski.com. The last word in luxury in Cancún: all chandeliers, oil paintings, and deep carpeting, plus impeccable service. While high-season rates are predictably high, this former *Ritz-Carlton* is a great example of Cancún's off-season value, when prices can drop dramatically. M$$$$

Sina Suites Quetzal 33; https://www.sinahotels.com. Personable staff preside over comfy rooms and suites with TVs and quiet a/c systems; the suites have either one or two bedrooms, a sofa bed in the living room and a full kitchen and dining room. There's a huge pool, and the sundeck overlooks the lagoon. M$$$

HOSTELS

DOWNTOWN, SEE MAP PAGE 733

Hostel Quetzal Orquideas 10; 998 883 9821. Styles itself as the "wildest party hostel" in town, so you'll either love it or hate it. The dorms and private rooms aren't bad at all, and there is an array of activities on offer, from barbecues to drinking games by the pool. Rates include breakfast and dinner. Dorms M$; doubles M$$

Mundo Joven Uxmal 25; http://mundojovenhostels.com. Cancún's official Hostelling International hostel is nicely designed, and its all-white decor looks crisp, not dingy. There's a/c everywhere, and both single-sex and mixed dorms, as well as private rooms. The hot tub on the roof says it all, though – this is a party place, for better or worse. Dorms M$; doubles M$$

ZONA HOTELERA, SEE MAP PAGE 735

Mayapan Paseo Kukulcán km 8.5, west end of Plaza Maya Fair; 998 883 3227. The only hostel in the *zona hotelera*, with a great central location. However, there are a few drawbacks: rather pricey private rooms, no common hangout space and a weird setting in a spooky wing of an abandoned mall. Dorms M$; doubles M$$

EATING

In downtown Cancún, the most popular eating places line Tulum and its side streets. For **budget food**, follow the locals for lunch at the downtown markets: **Mercado 23** and **Mercado 28** (see page 734). At night, excellent food stalls at **Parque de las Palapas** serve open-face *huaraches* and quesadillas with an array of toppings; they're open until about 11pm. Many of the restaurants in the **zona hotelera** are a rip-off, but the exceptions recommended here are solidly delicious.

CAFÉS, CHEAP EATS AND SNACKS

DOWNTOWN, SEE MAP PAGE 733

100% Natural Sunyaxchén Mza 6; www.100natural.com.

Largely vegetarian and decidedly wholesome, with veggie burgers and granola, as well as fresh-tasting Mexican dishes. Breakfasts are especially nice, with lots of interesting juice combos. M$$

Los Bisquets Obregón Nader 9; http://bisquetsobregon.com. Part of a national chain, this bustling diner serves *café con leche*, Mexican pastries and a range of cooked breakfasts in the morning, plus a selection of light lunches. M$$

Pescaditos Yaxchilán at Gladiolas; 998 884 0305. A bit of the beach downtown: light reggae vibe, with fantastic lightly battered fish and shrimp, deadly shrimp-stuffed *chiles rellenos*, and good *ceviches*. M$$$

Ty-Coz Tulum, behind Comercial Mexicana; 998 884 6060. This French sandwich shop is a treat. The specialities are stacked baguettes, but *Ty-Coz* is also good for breakfast, with buttery pastries and strong coffee. There are a few other "Express" branches in and around the *zona hotelera*, including at km 9, near the Chedraui supermarket. M$$

ZONA HOTELERA, SEE MAP PAGE 735

★ **El Fish Fritanga** Paseo Kukulcán km 12.5 http://elfishfritanga.com. Hidden behind a *Domino's*, this lagoon-side seafood specialist is inexpensive, laid-back and frequented by residents – there's even a bit of beach, so you can stick your feet in the sand while you eat. The menu ranges from *ceviche* to lobster tails in a garlic butter sauce. M$$$

The Surfin Burrito Paseo Kukulcán km 8; http://facebook.com/TheSurfinBurrito. This hidden gem, on a nondescript parade of shops and eateries, serves up Californian-style burritos, plus tacos, fajitas, chips and dip, well-mixed margaritas, and cold beer. Delivery available. M$$

Sushi Go Paseo Kukulcán km 8; http://sushigo.com.mx. Close to *The Surfin Burrito*, this is a good, low-key spot for fresh sushi, as well as rice and noodle dishes, tempura, *teppanyaki* and soups. There are a couple of other branches in town, and they will also deliver to your hotel. M$$

RESTAURANTS

DOWNTOWN, SEE MAP PAGE 733

Checándole Xpuhil 6; 998 884 5099. A buzzing, popular restaurant that has been around since the earliest days, with a breezy terrace and a selection of satisfying and fresh-tasting Mexican classics like enchiladas. M$$

★ **Mora Mora** Av Palenque 10; http://facebook.com/moramoracocinaurbanaygaleriadearte. Tucked away behind a wall of graffiti, this unmarked hip restaurant-bar-gallery's wide-ranging menu features inventive pizzas, pasta, burgers, and more all cooked and served with a flourish. Live music most nights. Reservations recommended. M$$

El Rincon de los Antojos Av Kabah, between Holbox and Nizuc; https://facebook.com/ElRinconDeLosAntojos. A local joint with an international reputation, thanks to its appearances in US newspapers and TV shows. It specialises in delicious snacks like *gorditas* (fried tortilla pockets packed with shredded pork belly) and pambazos (compressed sandwiches dipped in a pepper sauce and stuffed with goodies). M$$

ZONA HOTELERA, SEE MAP PAGE 735

★ **La Buena Barra** Paseo Kukulcán km 12.5; https://labuenabarra.mx/cancun. A cool seafront joint just south of *El Fish Fritanga* that serves steaks, with all the trimmings, at decent prices. M$$$$

MB Paseo Kukulcán km 12.5, in Live Aqua; http://liveaqua.com. No sea view, but one of Cancún's best hotel restaurants. Miami chef Michelle Bernstein mixes Latin, Spanish and even Asian flavours in a stylish but not-too-formal atmosphere. There's a small but good wine list, too. M$$$$

Río Nizuc Off Paseo Kukulcán near km 22. Few tourists find this seafood spot tucked amid the mangroves at the south end of the hotel zone. *Ceviche* and *tikin-xic* fish are popular with locals, who crowd in at weekends. Look for the turn just west of Puente Nizúc. M$$

12

DRINKING AND NIGHTLIFE

Cancún's goal is to entertain millions of visitors each year, with the **zona hotelera**'s array of huge dance clubs, theme bars and top-volume everything (most clustered around Punta Cancún and rolling from about 10pm till the wee hours). **Downtown** offers a mellower scene: people often dance on weekend evenings at the Parque de las Palapas to traditional Mexican music, and the stretch of Yaxchilán north of Sunyaxchén is a popular local nightlife area, with terrace restaurant-bars and karaoke open till 3am or 4am, all punctuated by roving *trovadores*.

BARS, CLUBS AND LIVE MUSIC

DOWNTOWN, SEE MAP PAGE 733

El Camarote Uxmal 26, in the Plaza Kokai hotel; 998 193 3170. Ignore the sports bar outside; in the small theatre inside, *El Camarote*, Yucatecan crooners perform romantic classics for an older crowd. Cover charge.

ZONA HOTELERA, SEE MAP PAGE 735

Bulldog Paseo Kukulcán km 9.5, south end of Krystal hotel; http://bulldogcafe.com. A mega-club in Punta Cancún, notable because, outside of high Spring Break season, it's frequented more by local kids, with hip-hop and *rock en español* on the speakers, and the occasional touring band.

Coco Bongo Paseo Kukulcán km 9.5, in the Forum by the Sea shopping centre; http://cocobongo.com. *Coco Bongo* remains the epitome of the Cancún nightclub experience, and what the other mega-clubs imitate. The night warms up with a floor show involving acrobats, impersonators of everyone from the Beatles to Lady Gaga and roving candid cameras showcasing the best dancers. The music, once it really gets started, is of the broadest, most crowd-pleasing variety. Entry fee includes cover and open bar.

Señor Frog's Paseo Kukulcán km 9.5; http://senorfrogs.com. Practically synonymous with Cancún, *Frog's* is the first stop off the plane for the Spring Break hordes – think foam parties, karaoke nights, and so on. Pop in for live reggae or just as an anthropological experience. Definitely don't go for the food.

DIRECTORY

Banks and exchange Most banks are along Tulum between Uxmal and Cobá and in the biggest shopping malls – Kukulcán, Plaza Caracol – in the *zona hotelera*. The HSBC, Tulum 192, stays open until 7pm on weekdays.

Consulates Canada, Centro Empresarial, Paseo Kukulcán km 12, 998 883 3360; Cuba, Pecari 17 SM 20, 998 884 3423; South Africa, Granada 30, SM 2A; 998 884 9513; UK, Paseo Kukulcán km 13.5, at the *Royal Sands*, 998 881 0184; US, Torre La Europea, Paseo Kukulcán km 13, Torre La Europea, 998 883 0272.

Hospital The largest hospital close to the *zona hotelera* is AmeriMed, on Bonampak at Nichupté, behind Plaza las Américas (998 881 3400 or 881 3434 for emergencies, http://amerimedcancun.com).

Internet Immediately across from the bus station and northwest on Uxmal are several internet cafés; some are *casetas* as well. In the *zona hotelera*, web access is significantly more expensive, but every hotel, and virtually every bar and restaurant, offers free wi-fi.

Laundry Lavandería Las Palmas, on Uxmal just west of the bus station (open daily). In the *zona hotelera*, try Lumi Express at Paseo Kukulcán km 9.5 (closed Sun), next to The Surfin Burrito.

Post office Sunyaxchén at Xel-Ha.

Isla Mujeres

12

Just a few kilometres off the coast of Mexico, in the startlingly clear Caribbean, little **ISLA MUJERES** is substantially mellower than Cancún, drawing people for long stays despite (or because of) the lack of tourist attractions. The 8km-long patch of land is now substantially built up – it's no desert island – yet retains a certain air of bohemian languor in its narrow streets lined with colourful wooden houses. It's a respite for anyone who has been travelling across Mexico, as well as a pleasant place to start your trip in Mexico (the whole trip from Cancún airport takes under two hours).

The attractions are simple: beach and sea – plus the fun of zipping around the island, on the lone perimeter road, by bike, moped or golf cart, to more sea, more beaches and the tiny Maya temple that the conquistadors chanced upon, once full of female figures, which gave the place its name.

Playa Norte

Northern end of the island • Free

The most popular **beach**, just five minutes' walk from the town plaza, is **Playa Norte** – curving up and around the northern tip of the island, but protected from the open sea by a promontory on which stands a large resort. Aim to be under the palms here by late

ISLA MUJERES BEACH CLUBS

Aside from the broad expanse of Playa Norte, the island has a few other stretches of sand with lounge chairs and restaurants – they're not dramatically more beautiful than Playa Norte, but they are a very good excuse for a golf-cart outing and a nice lunch.

Capitán Dulche Southwest coast; http://capitandulche.mx. This sprawling place has beautiful grounds and good food (though it's fairly pricey). There's a small maritime museum, open occasionally for guided tours (charge), and intriguing art scattered around. M$$$

Garrafón de Castilla Southern end of the island; 998 259 4573. This basic beach club adjacent to Garrafón Park is set around a small, protected bay where you can spot a few colourful fish. There's not a lot of actual sandy beach, but different levels and areas for lounging. Food is reasonably priced, after an entry fee. M$$

Playa Lancheros Mid-island, just south of the roundabout; 998 894 1250. This small, palm-fringed beach is virtually deserted except at lunch time, when the good, very simple restaurant fires up the grill for *tikin-xic* fish. It's been in operation for decades and is one of the best places to sample this Maya beach classic. M$$

afternoon, as it's one of the few places along Mexico's east coast where you can enjoy a glowing sunset over the water. After dark, the palapa-roofed bars become the island's mellow nightlife centre.

Hacienda Mundaca

Mid-island, at the roundabout • Charge

About halfway down the length of the island lurk the barely visible remains of the **Hacienda Mundaca**, to which scores of romantic pirate legends are attached. Only

one small house has been pieced together, with a few photos of old-time Isla Mujeres inside. There's also a somewhat random display of a traditional Maya hut. The best spot is the suitably gothic-feeling garden at the back of the property – where insect repellent is a must. In front of the entrance, outside the hacienda grounds (so no need to pay hacienda admission), the island's cultural directorate manages a few galleries with photos of the island, local art projects, crafts (sometimes including someone demonstrating hammock-weaving) and more.

Turtle Farm

Sac Bajo road • Charge • 998 888 0705

Heading north from the mid-island roundabout, the road up the Sac Bajo Peninsula leads to a government-run **turtle farm** and research centre, which breeds endangered sea turtles for release in the wild. It also rescues threatened nests and keeps them buried in the sand on the grounds until they hatch. The entrance fee helps fund the preservation project.

Garrafón Park

Southwestern tip of the island • Charge, depending on what package of activities you go for – discounts available via the website • http://garrafon.com

The longest stretch of reef on Isla Mujeres is mostly dead, and now enclosed in **Garrafón Park**, a slick operation with a zipline, kayaking, the chance to swim with dolphins, and other mild thrills. But it's grossly overpriced and usually crowded with day-trippers from Cancún. The penny-pinchers' alternative is *Garrafón de Castilla* beach club next door (see page 740); better, though, to go on a trip with the *lancheros* (see page 740).

Templo de Ixchel

Southern tip of the island • Charge

In an area known as Punta Sur, the **Templo de Ixchel** isn't much of a **ruin** (the fertility figures the Spaniards spotted here have been removed), and the walk to it has been tarted up with some now-rusty modern sculptures, to justify the admission price. But it is situated on low rocky cliffs where the waves crash dramatically. As the

ACTIVITIES ON ISLA MUJERES

There are several **dive shops** on the island – recommended is Enrique's Unique Dives (Medina 1, by the Pemex station; 998 145 3594), which offers a range of trips, including some to the MUSA (see page 736), as well as the "Cave of the Sleeping Sharks", where tiger, bull, grey reef, lemon and nurse sharks are regularly encountered. You can also take **snorkelling** trips with a couple of *lancheros* cooperatives, which are set up on the piers, and last two hours.

The *lancheros* also offer tours to see the **whale sharks** that gather off the coast from (roughly) mid-May to mid-September (a trip more commonly taken from Isla Holbox; see page 730). While every shop touts the trip, only a small number of boats have the permit. Boats usually leave at 7.30–8am, and the trip to the sharks takes a couple of hours; there's lunch and reef snorkelling on the way back.

If it's not whale-shark season, the next-best outing is to the bird sanctuary of **Isla Contoy**, 30km north. Designated a national park in 1961, the small island is home to some 150 bird species, including large colonies of pelicans, cormorants and frigates. You can go with the *lancheros* cooperative, or with Captain Tony García (Matamoros 7; 998 877 0229, captaintony@hotmail.com); both come highly recommended by island regulars. Tours last from 9am till 3pm or so and include a basic breakfast, grilled fish for lunch, soft drinks and snorkel.

easternmost point of Mexico, it's where islanders come on New Year's Day to watch the sun rise.

ARRIVAL AND DEPARTURE

ISLA MUJERES

By passenger ferry Passenger ferries arrive at Isla Mujeres town at two adjacent piers; the car ferry comes in further south. From the piers, it's about a 20min walk to the opposite side of the island and the most distant hotels. Ultramar (http://ultramarferry.com) runs passenger ferries from Cancún to Isla Mujeres. Its boats leave from the terminal in Puerto Juárez, on Av López Portillo (every 30min, 5am–11.30pm; 20min). Some boats also run from Playa Tortugas in the *zona hotelera*.

Transport to the ferry In Cancún, buses ("R-1 – Pto Juárez") that go this far north are not common; also look for *combis* (marked "*Juárez*"), which stop in front of the *McDonald's* on Tulum, across from the bus station. Taxis run from the bus station to the *zona hotelera*.

By car ferry There's also a car ferry (charge per car with one driver, additional fee per extra person; 4–7 daily; 45min), but you don't need a vehicle, as the island is quite small and has plenty of bicycles and mopeds for rent. The boat leaves from Punta Sam, 6km north of Puerto Juárez.

GETTING AROUND

By bus Every 30min from Rueda Medina in the main town down to the southern end of the island.

By moped or golf cart The best way of getting around the small island is by moped or golf cart. Virtually every other shop rents out both forms of transport for approximately the same rates.

By taxi Rates are posted at the stand between the ferry piers, and vary between the main town and the south end of the island.

By bike Many places rent out bikes. You should be in decent shape to make a full island loop – there are a couple of hills, and usually a headwind coming back north.

12

INFORMATION

Tourist office On Medina just northwest of the passenger ferry piers (Mon–Fri 8am–8pm, Sat & Sun 9am–2pm; 998 877 0307). You can pick up leaflets and maps.

ACCOMMODATION

SEE MAP PAGE 741

Isla Mujeres has a few solid budget places to stay, though they fill up quickly in the high season – advance reservations are recommended. Most of the reasonably priced options are on the northwestern edge of the island; some of the less expensive waterfront views are on the northeastern side, where the sea is generally too rough for swimming.

HOTELS AND SELF-CATERING

Carmelina Guerrero 4; 998 877 0006. The rooms at this motel-style budget operation, trimmed in lavender paint, are a steal, considering they have a/c and a fridge. However, the singles can be dismally small. M$

Casa Sirena Hidalgo between Bravo and Allende; http://casasirenamexico.com. Very nicely redone home that has kept some old details, such as tiled floors, and added modern bathrooms and a breezy roof terrace. Breakfasts are lavish, happy hour on the roof deck is legendary and there are even two small pools. Three-night minimum stay in winter, two in summer; advance reservations required. M$$$$

Francis Arlene Guerrero 7, at Abasolo; 998 877 0310. A small family-owned hotel with well-tended courtyards, a big roof terrace and clean, brightly painted – if rather twee – rooms with plenty of comforts (though a/c is an additional cost). M$$$

El Marcianito Abasolo 10; 988 877 0111. This budget hotel is a good-value option: the simple but clean rooms come with fans and well-maintained private bathrooms; the breezier, a/c ones on the upper floors cost more. M$$

Na Balam Zazil Ha 118; http://nabalam.com. Overlooking Playa Norte, *Na Balam* is a good, upper mid-range all-rounder: spacious rooms and suites, a lush garden, spa facilities, pool, hot tub, restaurant-bar, and an on-site yoga school (see page 744). M$$$$

Nautibeach Condos Playa Norte; http://nautibeach.com. A good option for families or groups, *Nautibeach* has enormous two-bedroom apartments, each with a balcony or veranda, in a modest, well-maintained complex facing the beach. M$$$$

★ **La Sirenita** Hidalgo 3, at Bravo; https://sirenitaisla.com. The five rooms at this stylish hotel get booked up fast. All have one bed, plus a separate living room with a daybed. The minimalist-cool wood furniture here is made on the island. M$$$

HOSTELS

Poc-Na Matamoros at Carlos Lazo; http://playapocnatulum.com. This compound sleeps 150, but it's split into many smaller rooms that feel a bit cosier. Facilities can be less than spotless and there's no guest kitchen, but it opens directly onto a broad beach (great for camping) on the windy side. There's an on-site dive centre. M$

EATING

SEE MAP PAGE 741

The area along and around Hidalgo between Morelos and Abasolo is lined with **restaurants** and **bars**. For inexpensive, basic Mexican food and great fruit salads, head for the few **loncherías** on Guerrero between Mateos and Matamoros, opposite *Las Palmas* hotel. In the adjoining public market, you can get inexpensive juices and produce. There's a supermarket on the plaza.

★ **Barlito** Marina Paraiso Hotel, Rueda Medina, around 1.5km south of the centre; 998 877 0253. Huge and mouth-watering bagels, hot sandwiches and panini are the speciality at this café-restaurant. Good breakfast options are available too, including home-made cinnamon buns packed with almonds and raisins. M$$

La Cazuela M&J Abasolo at Guerrero; http://lacazuelamj.com. This casual café serves inexpensive (mostly Mexican) breakfasts. Its speciality is egg dishes baked in small casseroles (*cazuelas*). Big glasses of green *chaya* juice are another healthy option. M$$

Cocktelería Picus Rueda Medina, just north of the ferry piers. One of several similar joints, this small beachfront hut with plastic chairs in the sand serves fresh and inexpensive *ceviche* and shrimp cocktails. M$$$

12

La Lomita Juárez 25-B, two blocks southeast of the plaza; 998 939 2331. Locals line up for a helping of the chef-owner's daily special, anything from bean soup and *chiles rellenos* to pan-fried fish with salsa verde. Hearty home cooking that's worth the hike up the small hill two blocks south of the plaza. M$$$

El Poc-Chuc Abasolo at Juárez; 998 214 4469. This bargain *lonchería* with red vinyl tablecloths and a giant mural of Chichén Itzá is handily also open for dinner (although not all of the big meals are available at night). Fish soup and crispy *panuchos* are two reliable offerings. M$$

Polo's Mango Cafe Payo Obispo, 2.8km south of the ferry terminal; 998 274 0118, https://facebook.com/mangocafeisla. With breakfast options like coconut French toast and stuffed poblano peppers and lunch ones like jerk chicken tacos and barbecued pork empanadas, this cafe is well worth the journey from the centre of town. M$$$

Romano Restaurante Hidalgo, between Mateos and Matamoros; 998 413 5029. There's a great range of pizzas, pastas and salads at *Romano Restaurante*: If you're struggling to choose, go for the signature lasagne. M$$$

El Varadero West coast, adjacent to Puerto Isla Mujeres; 998 877 1600. This super-casual Cuban restaurant, drawing a predominantly local crowd, is nestled among palm trees a little way out of town. Garlicky pork and refreshing mojitos are the specialities. M$$

DIRECTORY

Banks and exchange HSBC, on Rueda Medina opposite the ferry docks, has an ATM; Banamex is on Morelos at Juárez.

Internet There are numerous internet cafés in the centre of town.

Laundry The cheapest laundry is Lavandería Mis Dos Angelitos, Guerrero at Mateos (closed Sun).

Post office Guerrero at Mateos.

Yoga Vastu School of Yoga (http://vastuyoga.com) offers daily yoga classes at the *Na Balam* hotel (see page 743).

Puerto Morelos

The quietest town in the Riviera Maya, **PUERTO MORELOS**, is actually the closest to Cancún, just fifteen minutes from the airport by taxi or bus. With a working fishing fleet, it's unpretentious and calm, drawing visitors for long stays – but although it's not ritzy, even the cheapest hotels might be over budget for some. The **Mesoamerican Barrier Reef** begins here, just 600m offshore, and it's in very good shape due to efforts of the townspeople to protect it. It's a great, uncrowded place to get your scuba certification.

There are two parts to PoMo, as it is sometimes referred to: the beach town 2km from Hwy-307, with a small traditional plaza and church; and the rapidly growing *zona urbana* (or *colonia*) on the inland side of the highway. Most visitors will spend all their time in the beach town.

Ixchel Jungle Market

C 2, *zona urbana* • http://mayaecho.com

If you're in town on a Sunday, don't miss the **Ixchel Jungle Market**, where an Indigenous women's cooperative sells their wares, which include great food as well as handicrafts. There's also a dance performance (starting at 11.30am). It's a touristy event, but all low-pressure, local-run fun, and a good excuse to explore the inland side of town. The same group of women runs a very affordable spa in the same spot year-round.

CENOTES NEAR PUERTO MORELOS

The so-called Ruta de los Cenotes is a road that runs inland from Puerto Morelos, passing several swimming holes and **caves** (all open daily 10am–5pm). Look for the turn inland just south of the main Puerto Morelos intersection, marked by a large cement arch. The price of round trip taxis from Puerto Morelos depends on waiting time. Dive shops in Puerto Morelos (see page 745) also run snorkelling and diving trips out here.

Several spots are for group tours from Cancún, but a couple are open for independent travellers. The best is **Cenote Las Mojarras** (998 109 7753), at km 12.5, a big open pool with a zipline. Entry fees can be lower if you're only staying a couple of hours, but with nature trails, lunch cooked over a wood fire and an enthusiastic manager who knows everything about the local plants, you can spend all day here.

Several kilometres further is **Siete Bocas** (charge), a water-filled cave with seven points of entry, best for divers, as there's not much natural light. At km 17.5, **Verde Lucero** (charge) is a pretty, rustic-feeling pool with only basic facilities – some bathrooms and basic snacks.

Jardín Botánico Dr Alfredo Barrera Marín

East side Hwy-307, south of town • Charge • http://facebook.com/JBPuertoMorelos

These rambling **botanical gardens** provide a good overview of the Yucatán's flora. A 3km path leads through medicinal plants, ferns, palms, some tumbledown Maya ruins and a mock-up *chiclero* camp, where you can see how the sap of the *zapote* (sapodilla) tree is tapped before being used in the production of gum.

12

ARRIVAL AND GETTING AROUND — PUERTO MORELOS

By bus Buses between Cancún and Playa del Carmen stop on Hwy-307 at the town's main intersection on request (every 15min; 30min). They also leave directly from Cancún's airport (every 45min; 30min). Taxis wait on the east side of the highway to take you the 2km into the beach town. If you're leaving on the airport bus, buy your ticket at least one day in advance, to make sure the bus stops and has a seat for you. If you're just hopping to central Cancún or Playa del Carmen, it's easier to flag down a *colectivo* van.

By bus Contact Tequila Bike Rental (998 305 9253) in advance and they'll deliver your wheels to your hotel.

TOURS AND ACTIVITIES

Cooking classes The Little Mexican Cooking School, on Rojo Gómez two blocks north of the plaza (998 251 8060, http://thelittlemexicancookingschool.com), runs half-day cooking classes in a sunny kitchen with an enthusiastic Mexican-Canadian chef. The school also has a small shop that sells cooking tools and locally produced foods.

Diving Long-established Diving Puerto Morelos OMDelfin just east of Jardín Botánico (998 354 2556, https://omdelfin.com) offers certification courses and one and two-tank dives, as well as diving tours to inland *cenotes*.

Snorkelling You can go with Diving Puerto Morelos, or with any of the boats at the two piers in town. Note that a couple of booths on the plaza are actually selling timeshares, but might try to reel you in by offering a snorkelling trip. Regardless, although you could swim to the reef, regulations require you to go with a guide.

Day tours Ecab Explorer (998 871 0257, https://facebook.com/ecabexplorer) runs day trips to Chichén Itzá, Tulum, Cobá, Ek-Balam, and more.

ACCOMMODATION

Most people stay in rental properties – Alma Libre bookshop (see page 746) has nice ones – so the hotel scene is fairly limited.

Amar Inn On the seafront, 500m north of the main plaza; http://amarinn.mx. This bohemian, family-run hotel just off the beach has seven large rooms and three cabañas (fan only); some have high ceilings, loft beds and kitchenettes. A delicious Mexican breakfast is included. M$$$

Casa Cacahuate C 2 in the zona urbana; http://mayaecho.com. With two spacious guestrooms, the "Peanut House" is a great chance to be in the forest in relative comfort, as well as to interact with the non-touristy side of Puerto Morelos. It's also a handy place for solo travellers to get acclimatized, under the wing of hostess Sandra Dayton, a long-time Mexico resident (who also runs the Ixchel Jungle Market; see page 744). Jungle walks and birdwatching trips can be arranged, too. M$$$

Dreams Riviera Cancun Resort & Spa On the beach,

5km north of town; www.hyattinclusivecollection.com. Located a 40min walk from town (turn near the entrance to the Crococun zoo), this is a little slice of resort heaven, with a private beach and all the luxuries you could want for. M$$$$

Hacienda Morelos Rafael E. Melgar; http://haciendamorelos.com. With one of the best views of the water in these parts, the Hacienda Morelos hotel has got it where it counts. You'll find sturdy, albeit dated, furniture throughout and eighties era bathrooms that are so clean, they look near enough brand new. Also, and most importantly during the summer months, the a/c here rarely gives out. M$$

★ **Hotel el Moro** Rojo Gómez 17, just north of the plaza; http://casaelmoro.com. This appealing hotel has sunny, spacious rooms with a/c, plus suites with kitchenettes. There's also a pretty little garden, a small pool, and a great restaurant. M$$$

EATING

For a town of its size, Puerto Morelos has a disproportionately large number of great **places to eat**, offering a mix of local cuisine and flavours brought in by various expats. Most places are on the plaza, where everyone seems to convene at night. Also look out for informal eateries run out of people's front yards.

Café d'Amancia Southwest corner of the plaza; https://cafeamancia.com. Come here for deadly strong coffee and a breakfast bagel or lunch-time sandwich, plus a great vantage point for watching the action on the square. M$$

La Casa del Pescador North side of the plaza; 984 320 5163. This restaurant, run by the fishermen's cooperative (located up the green spiral staircase), is simple and great value – a good place for lunch, or for dinner, when *La Playita* is shut M$$$

Al Chimichurri Rojo Gómez, south of the plaza; http://chimipuerto.com. If you've overdosed on seafood, follow the smell of sizzling steak to this expert Uruguayan restaurant, where you can stock up on prime cuts of beef, house-made pasta dishes, and *dulce de leche* crêpes. It also serves breakfast and lunch at an adjacent café. Service, however, can be slow. M$$$

★ **La Playita** Melgar, half a block north of the plaza. This casual spot on the beach is where the town fishermen kick back and enjoy the fresh catch of the day, sold by the kilo and perfectly fried. A whole *pescado frito* for two and a few beers is a good choice here. M$$$$

Siempre Sano Av Niños Héroes; 998 321 3549. If you're after some healthy vegetarian/vegan fare, head to *Siempre Sano*, where you'll get a hearty main (for example a chunky stew) and salad, plus a cup of soup, dessert and a soft drink for a good deal. M$$

12

SHOPPING

Alma Libre On the plaza, south side; http://almalibrebookstore.com. Probably Mexico's most extensive secondhand English-language bookshop, the Canadian-run *Alma Libre* has some twenty thousand volumes to choose from, including many on the area's natural and archeological attractions. They also stock some good-quality souvenirs.

Hunab-Ku Artesanía Two blocks south of the plaza on Rojo Gómez. Reasonably priced craftwork in a little "Maya mini-mall" where you can often see the artisans at work. As a bonus, crocodiles hang out in the swamp just behind.

DIRECTORY

Banks and exchange A few ATMs are scattered around the plaza, but there is no actual bank. Avoid the generic machines not run by a specific bank, as their fees are extortionate. A couple of *cambios* can be found on the plaza.

Internet There is an internet café on the southwest corner of the plaza, next to the Oxxo shop. There's free wi-fi around the plaza.

Playa del Carmen and around

Once a soporific fishing village where travellers camped out en route to Isla Cozumel, **PLAYA DEL CARMEN** (often called simply "Playa") is now a hot spot with pretensions of being the next Miami Beach – and, from a local perspective, a goldmine of employment in construction. Mexico City's elite pop in, as do day-trippers from Cancún and passengers from cruise ships docked on Cozumel. As a result, the town's main centre of activity, Avenida 5 (also called **La Quinta**), a long, pedestrianized strip one block back from the sea, is often packed to capacity with tourists rapidly emptying their wallets in pavement cafés, souvenir outlets and designer-clothes shops.

Nonetheless, the low-rise development and numerous European-owned businesses make it seem, at least on the quieter north side, relatively cosmopolitan and calm

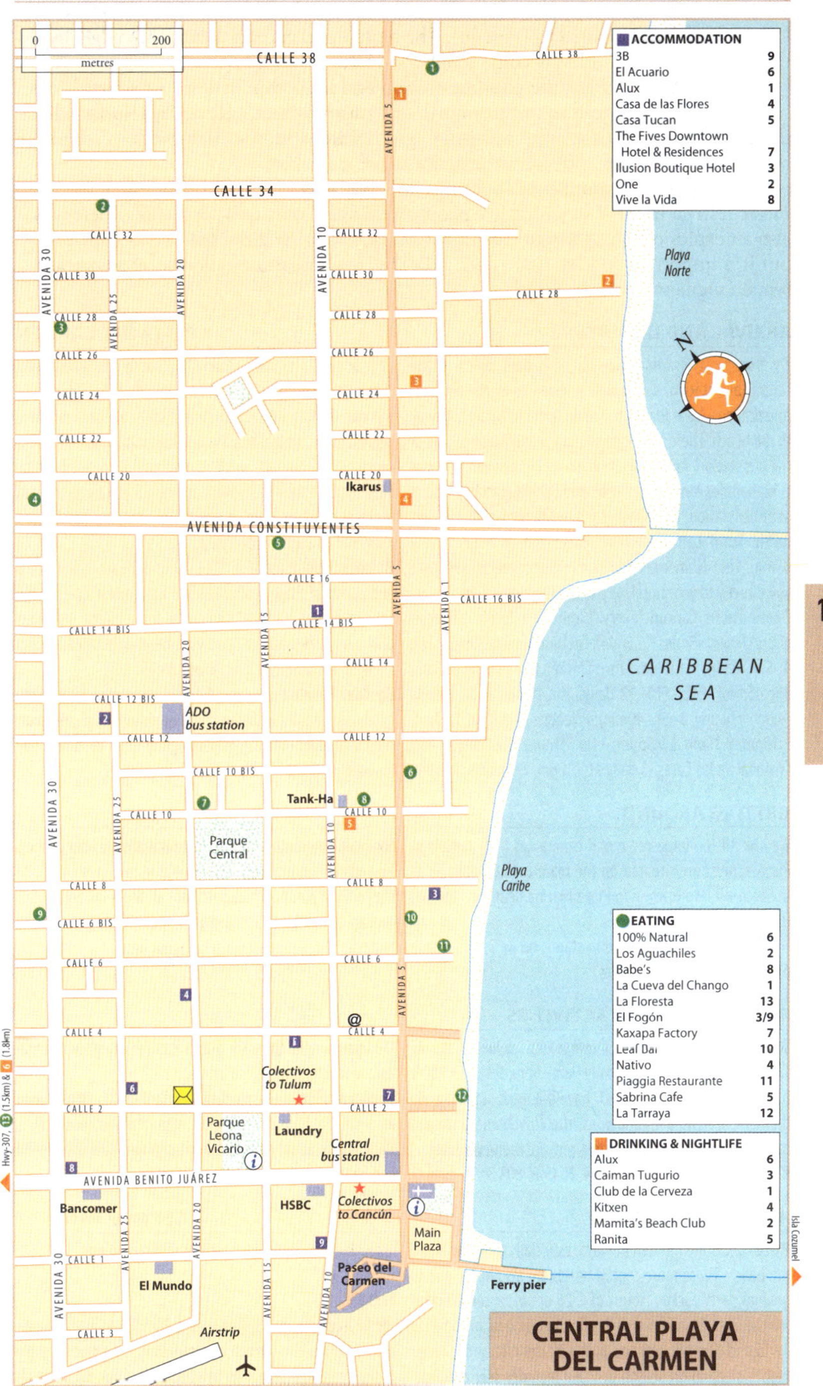
CENTRAL PLAYA DEL CARMEN
ACCOMMODATION
3B 9
El Acuario 6
Alux 1
Casa de las Flores 4
Casa Tucan 5
The Fives Downtown Hotel & Residences 7
Ilusion Boutique Hotel 3
One 2
Vive la Vida 8
EATING
100% Natural 6
Los Aguachiles 2
Babe's 8
La Cueva del Chango 1
La Floresta 13
El Fogón 3/9
Kaxapa Factory 7
Leaf Dai 10
Nativo 4
Piaggia Restaurante 11
Sabrina Cafe 5
La Tarraya 12
DRINKING & NIGHTLIFE
Alux 6
Caiman Tugurio 3
Club de la Cerveza 1
Kitxen 4
Mamita's Beach Club 2
Ranita 5
0 200
metres
CALLE 38
CALLE 34
CALLE 32
CALLE 30
CALLE 28
CALLE 26
CALLE 24
CALLE 22
CALLE 20
AVENIDA CONSTITUYENTES
CALLE 16
CALLE 16 BIS
CALLE 14 BIS
CALLE 14
CALLE 12 BIS
CALLE 12
CALLE 10 BIS
CALLE 10
CALLE 8
CALLE 6 BIS
CALLE 6
CALLE 4
CALLE 2
AVENIDA BENITO JUÁREZ
CALLE 1
CALLE 3
AVENIDA 30
AVENIDA 25
AVENIDA 20
AVENIDA 15
AVENIDA 10
AVENIDA 5
AVENIDA 1
Ikarus
ADO bus station
Tank-Ha
Parque Central
Playa Norte
Playa Caribe
CARIBBEAN SEA
Colectivos to Tulum
Laundry
Parque Leona Vicario
Central bus station
Bancomer
HSBC
Colectivos to Cancún
Main Plaza
Paseo del Carmen
El Mundo
Airstrip
Ferry pier
Isla Cozumel
Hwy-307, 13 (1.5km) & 6 (1.8km)
12

(certainly when compared to Cancún). The **nightlife** in particular has a hip edge, but as the town has grown, it has become tougher on budget travellers.

Playa's **main beach** has suffered some erosion and looks thin in some stretches. More serious beach-goers head to the area north of Constituyentes, called **Playa Norte**, where the deep, silky sand drops into waist-high green water with mid-size swells. A couple of beach clubs (see page 750) form the major social scene here.

There have been a number of shootings in Playa in recent years, including one at a music festival in 2017 in which five people were killed outside a nightclub. There was also an explosion on a ferry to Cozumel (see page 752). Security has been stepped up, but it is important to keep up to date with the latest situation, follow local advice and remain vigilant.

ARRIVAL AND DEPARTURE — PLAYA DEL CARMEN

By bus Most visitors arrive on short-haul buses at the central bus station, sometimes referred to as the *terminal turística*, on Av 5 at Juárez, the main street from the highway to the beach. There are luggage storage facilities upstairs at the bus station. Another station, on Av 20 between C 12 and C 12, handles longer-haul trips on ADO; you can buy tickets at either station. From both, taxis run to the hotels furthest north. From Cancún airport, buses run to Playa (every 45min; 1hr). Numerous private minibus operators will take you directly to your hotel, or you can take a taxi.

Destinations Cancún (every 15min; 1hr 15min); Cancún airport (every 45min; 1hr 5min); Chetumal (every 30min–1hr; 4–5hr 20min) via Tulum (1hr); Chichén Itzá (1 daily at 8am; 3hr 45min); Cobá (10–12 daily; 1hr 45min–2hr); Mérida (roughly hourly; 3–5hr 40min); Palenque (4 daily at 5.10pm, 7.10pm, 9.30pm & 9.55pm; 11hr 35min–11hr 55min); San Cristóbal de las Casas (3 daily at 5.10pm, 7.10pm & 9.55pm; 19hr 50min–21hr); Valladolid (1–2 hourly; 2hr 40min–3hr 20min); Villahermosa (9 daily; 12hr 15min–14hr 10min).

By car Driving into or through Playa can be a bit of a chore, due to the traffic. Easing things slightly is an express overpass on Hwy-307 with several well-signed off-ramps onto Playa's major east–west arteries. If you need to head north or south in town, it can make sense to head toward Hwy-307 and use the overpass.

By colectivo To reach smaller towns or beaches just north and south of Playa, *colectivos* are the easiest option: the Cancún service departs frequently from Juárez just west of the main bus station, and vans heading south to Tulum leave from C 2 between Av 10 and Av 15.

By taxi Private taxis can take you anywhere you need to go along the coast – they're more expensive than *colectivos*, but far cheaper than any tour company, even when you pay for waiting time.

GETTING AROUND

By car All the large car-rental companies have outlets in Playa – most are situated on the main coastal highway at the turn-off into town or in Plaza Marina near the Cozumel ferry pier at C 1 Sur.

By taxi You can hire taxis from stands on Av 5, or flag one down on the trafficked streets.

By bike The central area of town is walkable, but as Av 5 extends ever northward, it can be nice to ride a bicycle to the farthest points; a bike path runs along Av 10. For rentals contact Holabike (http://holabike.com); book in advance and they'll deliver your wheels to your hotel.

INFORMATION AND ACTIVITIES

Tourist information Tourist info kiosks, on Juárez near Av 15 and on the main plaza (daily 9am–5pm; 984 873 2804, turismo@solidaridad.gob.mx), have bilingual staff who do their best to answer any enquiries. http://rivieramaya.mx and http://everythingplayadelcarmen.com are useful websites.

Kiteboarding Ikarus, Av 5 at C 20 (984 803 3490, http://kiteboardmexico.com; 3hr group lesson); equipment rental and advanced tuition also available.

Scuba diving and snorkelling Tank-Ha, C 10 between Av 5 and Av 10 (984 873 0302, http://tankha.com), offers PADI certification courses, one- and two-tank dives and snorkelling trips.

ACCOMMODATION — SEE MAP PAGE 747

Hotel prices are inflated in Playa, especially along Av 5 and the beach. These more central hotels are also noisy, due to general party ruckus (south of C 26 or so) or construction (on the ever-expanding north side). Heading inland a bit, to Av 15 and beyond, gets you both a better rate and a better night's sleep. High season in Playa includes July and Aug, when Europeans come, as well as mid-Dec to April.

HOTELS

★ **El Acuario** Av 25, between C 2 and C 4; http://hotel-acuario-playa-del-carmen.micasaonline.es. A great example of the deals you can get by heading away from the beach, *El*

Acuario has a dozen big rooms, all with a terrace or balcony, and kitchenette, plus a bigger suite, clustered around a central pool and garden (which also features a tortoise enclosure). Nice touches include free coffee and beach towels, plus a book exchange. Good online offers. M$$$

Alux C 14, between Av 10 and Av 15; http://hotelaluxplaya.com. *Alux* is a little frumpy, like its downtown Cancún counterpart (see page 738), and marketing is not its strong suit, with a barely legible sign out front. But on the whole it's a good deal; rooms have a/c and the more expensive options have kitchenettes. M$$$

Casa de las Flores Av 20, between C 4 and C 6; http://hotelcasadelasflores.com.mx. A charming place to stay, with spacious and stylish en-suite rooms overlooking the lush garden (all have a/c; rooms with TVs and fridges cost extra). There's a nice pool, and bikes are available to rent. M$$$

Casa Tucan C 4, between Av 10 and Av 15; http://casatucan.de. A Playa institution, retaining a hippy atmosphere. Rooms can be a bit dark and musty – and you'll either love the elaborate murals or hate them. But with perks like laundry service, a big swimming pool, and great coffee at the restaurant, it's hard to beat the price. Rooms come with fans or a/c and there are also larger studios. Book ahead. Doubles M$$; studios M$$$

The Fives Downtown Hotel & Residences 10 Avenida Nte.; http://www.thefiveshotels.com/resorts/the-fives-downtown. Convenient for the bus station and the colectivo stands, the Fives Downtown Hotel & Residences adds a nice amount of luxury to this part of Central Playa del Carmen. The roof terrace and deluxe pool certainly add to the appeal and with so many good restaurants within easy walking distance, you'd be hard pushed to make a misstep during a stay here. M$$$

Illusion Boutique Hotel Av 5 at C 8; 984 544 2701. On a prime corner on La Quinta, this hotel has a picture-perfect courtyard and a pool with a swim up bar. The little balconies here are also fun for people-watching. M$$$

One Av 25, between C 12 and C 12 bis; http://onehoteles.com. This large, rather generic business traveller-style chain hotel is near the long-distance bus depot. Ordinarily it wouldn't be worth recommending, but in Playa del Carmen, it represents a rare spot of mid-range value. M$$$

HOSTELS

3B Av 10 at C 1; http://hostel3b.com. A self-described "party hostel", *3B* has a rooftop bar (named *SOS Lounge* and often hosting international DJs), modern kitchen, positively chic bathrooms and furniture, and professional staff. Despite its "boutique" aspirations, it's still very much a hostel, convenient for buses, *colectivos* and the Cozumel ferry. Dorms M$; doubles M$$

Vive la Vida C 2, between Av 25 and Av 30; 984 109 2457. A rare good hostel in Playa, this one is clean, well designed and well managed by an enthusiastic young staff. There's a pool in the smallish courtyard, and a well-stocked communal kitchen. M$

EATING

SEE MAP PAGE 747

Playa del Carmen is heaving with **restaurants** of every kind, and even the traditional Mexican places stay open late. **Av 5** is lined with tables – but if you're on a **budget** you'll need to search out where locals go: try the taco carts on Juárez close to the beach (breakfast and lunch only), stalls on Av 10 at C 6 (open at night) and various restaurants on Av 30. There's a **supermarket** on Av 30 at C 20, and the smaller DAC store, half a block north, has great produce. One warning: the turnover in restaurants in Playa is so high as to make a guidebook writer despair – half these places may have closed by the time you go; the good news is that new places will have opened.

CAFÉS, CHEAP EATS AND SNACKS

100% Natural Av 5, between C 10 and C 12; http://100natural.com. This link in a mini-chain serves fresh, healthy versions of Mexican food (lots of it vegetarian), fresh fruit juices and great breakfasts. A good alternative to *La Cueva del Chango* (see below), in a more central location. M$$

★ **Los Aguachiles** C 34 at Av 25; 998 168 1604. An array of salsas arrives at your table along with the menu at this open-air seafood-snack place, and the challenge is not ordering too many dishes as an excuse to use them all. Even a simple *aguachido* (a tostada piled high with fish, cabbage and herbs) is a substantial snack here. M$$

★ **La Cueva del Chango** C 38, between Av 5 and the beach; http://lacuevadelchango.com. This garden restaurant is a local favourite, especially for long, late breakfasts. The menu includes tasty empanadas and crêpes, house-roasted coffee, and inventive main meals like sesame-crusted tuna steaks. M$$$

★ **La Floresta** West side of Hwy-307, just north of Av Juárez; 984 266 6483. This big palapa next to the highway is a road-tripper's delight, serving overstuffed *tacos de camarón*, the perfect marriage of battered shrimp, mayo and chunky tomato salsa. Should you need variety, seafood cocktails and *ceviches* are available, too. M$

Nativo Av 30, between Constituyentes and C 20; 984 147 8489. Delicious fresh-fruit smoothies and Mexican food like tortas and tacos, across the street from the similarly excellent DAC market. M$$

Sabrina Cafe Constituyentes, between Av 10 and 15; 984 204 1206, http://facebook.com/SabrinaPlayadelCarmen. An Italian-style café serving fine coffee, pastries, sandwiches, pasta and pizza. It's also a good spot for gelato, especially if you come during the happy hour. M$$

RESTAURANTS

Babe's C 10, between Av 5 and Av 10; https://babesnoodlesandbar.com.mx. This cheerful, Swedish-owned pan-Asian restaurant – which also serves a fine Cuban mojito – typifies Playa's international hodgepodge. Dishes like pad thai and chicken teriyaki come in huge portions. M$$

El Fogón Av 30 at C 6 bis; 984 803 0885. Follow your nose to the meat-covered grill at this basic, brightly lit taco joint that's generally mobbed with locals. No booze is served, but you can wash down all the meat with a big selection of *aguas frescas*. There's another branch on Av 30 near C 28. M$$

Kaxapa Factory C 10, between Av 15 and 20; 984 169 5699. A great Venezuelan restaurant specialising in *arepas*, cornbread pockets packed with delicious fillings like shredded beef and Manchego cheese. You can also get empanadas and *kaxapas*, corn hot cakes folded over cheese, meat, and the like. M$$

★ **Leaf Bar** Av 5, between C 6 and C 8; 984 879 3331. Tucked inside the Jardín del Marieta, amid art galleries, this modest little veggie restauarant serves delicious and inventive fresh salads, using all organic produce. M$$$

Piaggia Restaurante C 6 at Av 5; 984 179 8471. Seafood, steaks and pasta rule the roost at this high-end, beachfront restauarant. Be sure to get a reservation well in advance for this especially indulgent spot. M$$$$

La Tarraya On the beach at C 2; 999 543 0160, https://facebook.com/tarrayaplaya. This local institution has been open for more than thirty years, well before Playa was a gleam in a developer's eye. It still serves standard beach food like *ceviche* and *pescado frito* with plenty of cold beer. M$$

DRINKING AND NIGHTLIFE

SEE MAP PAGE 747

At night, La Quinta becomes one long street party, and you can find any sort of music in the array of bars, though most people will wind up around the lively intersection with C 12. If you're looking for a mellower atmosphere, head north of C 16, even as far up as C 40. Happy-hour specials can ease you into the night without depleting funds too rapidly.

12

BARS AND CLUBS

Alux Juárez, 400m west of Hwy-307; http://aluxrestaurant.com. It's expensive and a trek from the main drag (tell the cab driver "ah-LOOSH"), but how often do you get to party in a technicolor-lit cave? Opens early for drinks, followed by dinner (way overpriced, but fine); a DJ or a floor show of belly dancers and jazz musicians gets started around 10pm. Usually no cover charge.

Caiman Tugurio C 24, between Av 5 and Av 10; 984 803 5250. A welcome change of pace from the often brash Playa bar scene, *Caiman* is a low-key joint with a friendly crowd of locals and expats.

Club de la Cerveza Av 5, between C 34 & 38; https://www.clubdelacerveza.mx. There are circa 100 beers on offer at this bar, with plenty of craft options from around Mexico (and beyond). If you're struggling with all the choice, go for one of the draft ales, Mundo Maya or Akumal.

Kitxen Av 5, between Av Constituyentes and C 20; 984 894 7292. This cool bar-restaurant is owned by a member of legendary Mexican rock group Los Jaguares, so live bands often accompany good bar-snack food and drinks.

Ranita C 10, between Av 5 and Av 10; 984 873 0389, https://facebook.com/bar.ranita. A crew of regulars – mostly expats – hang out around the horseshoe-shaped bar. Unless there's a live band wedged into the small space, it's a mellow scene and a welcome break from other high-volume places.

BEACH CLUBS

Mamita's Beach Club C 28 at the beach; http://mamitasbeachclub.com. Of the two clubs at Playa Norte (*Kool* is the other), this one is marginally nicer and has better food. It has plenty of room to spread out and a hip but not overbearing party atmosphere. Chairs and umbrellas are for rent, or you can spread a towel at the water's edge and still get waiter service for drinks; there's also a champagne bar and a pricey steak restaurant.

DIRECTORY

Banks and exchange HSBC, Juárez between Av 10 and Av 15; Bancomer, Juárez between Av 25 and Av 30. Both have ATMs.

Consulates Canada, Av 10 at C 1, Plaza Paraíso, 984 803 2411; US, C 1 Sur between Av 15 and Av 20, 984 873 0303.

Internet The streets off Av 5 hold numerous internet cafés; La Tabería on C 4 between Av 5 and Av 10 doubles as a *caseta*.

Laundry Lavanderías are scattered every other block on the side streets. Try Gigalav, on C 2 between Av 10 and Av 15 (daily 8am–9pm; charge per kg).

Post office Av 20 at C 2 (Mon–Fri 8am–2pm); geared to dealing with tourists.

Isla Cozumel

A 40km-long island directly off the coast from Playa del Carmen, **ISLA COZUMEL** is known to package tourists as a cruise-ship port: nearly every day, up to ten liners, each

ISLA COZUMEL
ACCOMMODATION
Hotel B Cozumel 1
Blue Angel Resort 2
Ventanas al Mar 3
Punta Molas
Punta Norte
Isla de la Pasión
San Gervasio
Carretera Costera Norte
SEE "CENTRAL SAN MIGUEL" MAP
Playa del Carmen
Puerto Calica
Punta Langosta
San Miguel
International pier
Puerta Maya
Carretera Transversal
Mezcalito's
CARIBBEAN SEA
Carretera Costera Poniente
Paradise Reef
Playa Dzul-Ha
Punta Morena
Coconuts
Chen Río
PARQUE CHANKANAAB
Playa San Martín
Carretera Costera Oriente
Tormentos Reef
El Cedral
Playa Bonita
Alberto's
Playa Palancar
Carretera Costera Sur
Palancar Reef
FARO CELARAIN ECO PARK
Templo El Caracol
Colombia Reef
Punta Celarain
PARQUE MARINO NACIONAL ARRECIFES DE COZUMEL
Punta Sur Reef
0 4
kilometres
N

REEF ETIQUETTE

Coral reefs are among the richest and most complex ecosystems on earth, but they are also very fragile. The colonies grow at a rate of only around 5cm per year, so they must be treated with care and respect if they are not to be damaged beyond repair. Follow these **simple rules** – and advise your guide to do so as well – while you are snorkelling, diving or in a boat.

Use only biodegradable sunscreen in reef areas; oils in standard formulas stifle coral growth.

Never touch or stand on corals, as the living polyps are easily damaged. Also avoid disturbing the sand around them, as it can smother them.

Don't remove anything from the reef.

Don't anchor boats on the reef; use permanently secured buoys instead.

Check where you are allowed to go fishing.

Review your diving skills before you head out.

In addition to these guidelines, it is well worth visiting the Sustainable Travel International website (http://sustainabletravel.org), which has further advice and information on the Mesoamerican Reef Tourism Initiative (aka MARTI).

with several thousand passengers, dock at one of the island's three dedicated piers, all just south of the only town, **San Miguel**. But Cozumel's other major attraction provides the perfect escape from the crowds: the reefs that dazzled Jacques Cousteau in the early 1960s are some of the finest in this hemisphere. Even if you don't dive, there's a certain appeal in wandering the relaxed inland blocks of San Miguel, away from the piers, spotting Maya ruins and birds (the Maya called the island cuzamil – "land of the swallows") in the dense forests and being the only person on the windswept eastern beaches.

In early 2018, there was an explosion on a Playa del Carmen-Cozumel ferry that injured more than 20 passengers; an unexploded device was found on another ferry weeks later. Security has since been stepped up, but it is important to stay vigilant.

San Miguel

Along the malecón (Av Rafael Melgar), downtown **SAN MIGUEL** caters to cruise-shippers with restaurants, souvenir shops, tour agencies and jewellery stores. There are typically fewer boats in port at weekends, and on Sunday evenings, *cozumeleños* come out to the main plaza for live music.

Museo de la Isla de Cozumel

Av Melgar between Av 4 and Av 6 • Charge • 987 872 0093

This attractive museum has small displays of the flora, fauna and marine life of the island, as well as a good collection of Maya artefacts, vintage diving suits, and old photos. It occasionally hosts live music and theatre events – ask at the tourist office to find out what's on when you're on the island – and has an atmospheric restaurant (see page 756).

The southwest coast

Aside from a small public beach on the north side of San Miguel (at C 16) and a small strip north of town, all the beach action is south of town on the Carretera Costera Poniente. Beach clubs typically charge about a little above average for beers, and seafood mains; you're expected to buy a nominal amount.

Parque Chankanaab

Southwest coast, 8km south of San Miguel • Charge • http://cozumelparks.com

Tourists are usually steered right to the **Parque Chankanaab**. It's a lovely lagoon, but overdeveloped, with mini-golf, dolphin pens, botanical gardens and kayak tours. You'll probably want to skip it unless you have kids, who will like the calm water.

El Cedral

A large arch on the inland side of the road at km 17.5 marks the turn for the village of **El Cedral**, founded in 1847 and now primarily a vacation spot for San Miguel's better-off residents. There's no reason to drive up except in late April and early May, when the village hosts the ten-day-long Fiesta de la Santa Cruz, a huge fair with bullfights, prize-winning livestock and dancing.

Alberto's

Southwest coast, km 17.5 • http://albertosrestaurants.com

Immediately opposite the turn for El Cedral, this is the most rustic of the **beach clubs** on the west coast, with a great beach and snorkelling. There's nothing but a small, very good restaurant, boasting fish fresh-caught with its own boats (lobster is a particular specialty). Snorkel and glass-bottom boat trips to the best reefs run from here. The boat ride is shorter (and cheaper) from Playa Palancar (see page 754), but Alberto's is a

12

more appealing club. Note that there are a couple of other Alberto's (part of the same chain) around the island, so make sure you go to the right one.

Playa Palancar

Southwest coast, km 19 • Snorkel tours available • 987 118 5154

The last **beach** on the western shore is pretty, centred around a restaurant that serves good *tikin-xic*, and there's a dive shop where you can arrange a boat ride (2hr) out to Palancar Gardens just offshore. With parasailing, wave-runners and kayaks on offer, it's good for active beach-goers; others might find it a bit noisy.

Faro Celarain Eco Park

Southern tip of the island • **Museum of Navigation** (same ticket) • Charge • http://cozumelparks.com

The southernmost point of the island is a protected reserve for diverse wildlife, the **Faro Celarain Eco Park** (also called Punta Sur Eco Beach Park). The site contains several lovely beaches, where you can hang out in a hammock, take a kayak tour around the lagoon or snorkel out and possibly spot some hawksbill turtles. This is also a prime spot for **bird watching**, as the mangroves host both migratory and endemic species, including the widespread Cozumel vireo and the Cozumel thrasher, once thought to be extinct. On the way in, you pass the tiny **Templo El Caracol**, which may have been built by the Maya as a lighthouse, though it's awfully squat. When the wind is right, it whistles through the shells embedded in its walls. You can climb to the top of the Punta Celarain **lighthouse** for amazing views over the coast, or visit the adjacent **museum of navigation** in the former lightkeeper's house.

12

Within the park, a bus transports visitors between various sites (or you can rent bicycles), including viewing towers over a network of lagoons and a beach restaurant serving good fried fish.

San Gervasio

6km north of the Carretera Transversal • Charge

Midway across the island, **San Gervasio** is the only excavated Maya site on Cozumel (the main ancient city, part of a major sea-trade network in the pre-Conquest era, was covered by a US air base, now the airport). With several small temples connected by *sacbeob*, or long white roads, it was one of the many independent city-states that survived the fall of Chichén Itzá, flourishing between 1200 AD and 1650 AD. It was also one of the most important Mesoamerican centres of pilgrimage for Ixchel, the goddess of fertility and weaving – though it's not particularly impressive now. As part of a larger nature reserve, however, the site is worth a visit for the numerous birds and butterflies you can spot early in the morning or late in the day.

The east coast

Cozumel's rugged, windy eastern shore remains undeveloped because it faces the open sea and is usually too rough for swimming. The Carretera Costera Oriente runs 20km south to Punta Sur, passing many tantalizing empty **beaches** (swim only where you see others, and be wary of currents) and the occasional beach hut serving margaritas, but only until sundown because there's no electricity. Punta Morena occasionally draws surfers, and the beach at Chen Río has two protected coves where you can swim or snorkel, plus a very good restaurant (*El Galeón*). Playa San Martín, just south, is usually best for swimming.

ARRIVAL AND DEPARTURE — ISLA COZUMEL

By plane From the airport, where there's an ATM, a *combi* van service makes the short trip into town. Destinations include Cancún (on Mayair; 3–5 daily; 20min).

By bus You can buy tickets for onward mainland travel at the ADO office on Av 10 at C 2.

By passenger ferry The passenger ferry dock is in the centre of San Miguel, with the plaza directly across the street. Two passenger ferry companies, Winjet (formerly

Mexico Waterjets; http://winjet.mx) and Ultramar (http://ultramarferry.com), depart from the pier at C 1 Sur in Playa del Carmen, for San Miguel in Cozumel (roughly hourly, 6am–11pm). The price is the same and the boats are roughly equivalent as well, so just pick whichever is departing soonest – and buy only a one-way ticket, so you have the same freedom on the return trip. Returning to Playa, the ferries depart Cozumel hourly (5am–10pm), though this can change according to the season.

In early 2018, there was also an explosion on a Playa del Carmen-Cozumel ferry that injured more than 20 passengers; an unexploded device was found on another ferry weeks later. Security has been stepped up, but it is important to stay vigilant.

By car ferry Transbordadores del Caribe (987 872 7688, http://transcaribe.net) operates a car ferry (Mon–Sat 4 daily, Sun 2 daily; 1hr 15min) to Cozumel from Puerto Calica (also called Punta Venado), 7km south of Playa del Carmen. Prices are per car, including passengers. If you opt not to take your car, the closest parking to the ferry terminal in Playa del Carmen is the secure car park behind the main bus station.

GETTING AROUND

By bus Buses run around town, but the only one you might use is the hourly one to the beaches and hotels just north and south of town. Look for the northbound bus on Av 10; the southbound, on Av 15. But note that the majority that go by are for other routes within San Miguel. To get outside town, you'll have to book a tour, take a taxi or rent a vehicle.

By car Numerous local *rentadoras* in the town centre have similar prices and haggling often doesn't get you much; you can often do better booking with a chain online.

By taxi If you have substantial luggage, you'll want a taxi for any hotel east of Av 10. They're plentiful and operate on a zone system.

By bike Cycling is only really feasible in town and to the beaches to the north or south as far as Parque Chankanaab, where there's a separate track. Sombrero Rentals (987 857 0085, http://sombrerorentals.com) has well-maintained mountain bikes and beach cruisers; they'll deliver to your hotel, and also offer a range of guided tours

By moped Fun on a clear day, but opt for a car if there's any sign of rain. In addition to the discomfort, roads are very slick when wet. Sombrero Rentals (see above) has them.

INFORMATION

Tourist office The island tourist office (Mon–Sat 9am–5pm; 987 872 7585) is in the complex on the east side of the plaza, up the escalators.

Website http://www.cozumeltravelandtours.com is a useful source of information.

ACCOMMODATION

The **hotels** in Cozumel are divided into two categories: resorts (most all-inclusive) strung out along the coast on

UNDERWATER IN COZUMEL

DIVING

Some of the top **dive spots** are Colombia Deep and Punta Sur, directly south from the marshes on the southern tip, but the latter has strong currents. There are dozens of **dive shops** in town – Deep Blue (Salas at Av 10; 987 872 5653, http://deepbluecozumel.com) is one of the best, offering tailor-made small-group tours and a two-tank dives. For certification courses, Caribbean Divers (Av 5 at C 3; 987 876 1426, http://facebook.com/cozumeldivingcenter) comes recommended, as does Blue Magic Scuba (C 4 no. 71; 987 872 6143, http://bluemagicscuba.com).

SNORKELLING

As soon as you get off the ferry, you'll be offered trips. Short tours (1–2hr) go to nearby reefs such as Villa Blanca, which are fine but not spectacular. The best destinations are Palancar Shallows and Colombia Shallows; they're off the southwest coast, so better visited from Playa Palancar's beach club (see page 754) or via a dive centre like Deep Blue. There's also **walk-in snorkelling** – the good sites closest to San Miguel are Villa Blanca Shallows (Carretera Sur km 3.5), near the *Sunset Grill*, and Paradise Shallows – turn off near Carretera Sur km 5, then turn right at the marina.

either side of San Miguel, and more affordable places in the town centre – though none of these, even the lone **hostel**, is very cheap. Along the beach, the hotels to the north require a taxi ride into town, while a few to the south are within walking distance from the action. At the town hotels, sea views are overrated, as they usually come with traffic noise from the malecón (San Miguel's seaside promenade) below.

SAN MIGUEL, SEE MAP PAGE 753

Amaranto C 5 no. 321, between Av 15 and Av 20; www.amaranto-bedandbreakfast.com. Winding staircases and curving walls distinguish these three fanciful stucco palapas and two apartments stacked in a tile-trimmed tower. Rooms – all with fridge and microwave, most with a/c – are clustered around a cosy courtyard and small pool. M$$

Las Anclas Av 5 Sur 325; http://hotelvillalasanclas.com. A cluster of two-storey suites with kitchenettes; each sleeps up to four, with a queen-size bed upstairs and two day-beds downstairs (though the latter are best for kids). A lush central garden makes the place feel homely. M$$$

La Casona Real Juárez at Av 25; http://casonarealcozumel.com. So long as you love orange and yellow (the wall colours of choice) and you can forgive exposed and questionably joined pipes in the bathrooms, you'll appreciate the excellent value at this modern hotel with a/c and a courtyard pool. M$$$

12

Flamingo C 6, between Melgar and Av 5; http://hotelflamingo.com. Popular with the scuba set, with a roof terrace and a bar (noise alert: occasional live salsa bands). "Courtyard" rooms aren't as breezy as the larger "superior" ones, but all have a nice modern style, and the full inclusive breakfast is very good. M$$$

Hostelito Av 10 no. 42, between Juárez and C 2; 987 878 5356. A fine hostel, with six-bed dorms (including one with a/c) and private a/c rooms, as well as a convenient location, a small book exchange, a roof terrace and luggage storage. Dorms M$; doubles M$$

Pepita Av 15 Sur 120, at C 1 Sur; http://hotelpepitacozumel.com. One of the oldest hotels in town, and also one of the best kept, with clean, simple tiled-floor rooms with a/c, fridges and TVs. Amenities include a pretty courtyard and free coffee in the morning. M$$

Tamarindo B&B C 4 no. 421, between Av 20 and Av 25; http://tamarindobedandbreakfast.com. At this French-owned B&B/hostel, rooms have cosy nooks and whimsical touches. A full breakfast is included, and the owner's excellent cooking and island expertise put guests at ease. As well as a good range of private rooms, there's also a well-kept palapa-roofed dorm. Dorms M$; doubles M$$

OUTSIDE SAN MIGUEL, SEE MAP PAGE 751

Hotel B Cozumel Carretera Playa San juan, 2.6km north of town; http://hotelbcozumel.com. A slick boutique hotel, ideal for turning off and tuning out. Right on the seafront (though lacking a sandy beach), in a tranquil location, it offers swish en suites, yoga and spa treatments, and a fine restaurant-bar. M$$$

Blue Angel Resort Carretera Costera Sur km 2.2; http://blueangelresort.com. Close to town, and with an excellent dive shop and shallow-dive training both in the pool and right off the hotel's small beach. All rooms have sea views and private balconies. M$$$

Ventanas al Mar On the east coast, 5km south of Mezcalito's beach bar and the intersection with the Carretera Transversal; http://ventanasalmarcozumel.com. This hotel – the only one on the east coast – runs entirely on wind power. The giant rooms and the two-storey suites, which sleep four, have basic kitchenettes, as well as terraces overlooking the crashing surf. Bring groceries if you plan to stay a while. M$$$

EATING

SEE MAP PAGE 753

A good number of San Miguel's **restaurants** are pasta-and-steak tourist traps catering to a dull palate, but tucked in the backstreets are a surprising number of small family-run operations. The cheapest snacks of all can be had through the afternoon at the city market, on Salas between Av 20 and Av 25.

CAFÉS, CHEAP EATS AND SNACKS

Chilangos Av 30, between C 3 and Morelos; 987 869 7960. At this tiny family-operated place, design your own quesadilla or *huarache* by pointing at the ingredients on display in a small glass case – lots of veggies, among other things. Then the masters behind the counter assemble a great, reasonably priced meal. M$$

Corazón Contento C 2 at Av 10; 987 872 0838. At this very welcoming operation near the plaza, the coffee is atypically strong and delicious, and the breakfasts – which range from fruit salads to French toast – are good value. M$$

Nacho Crazy Boy Av 20, between C 1 and Juárez. The eponymous Nacho operates a battery of blenders and squeezers in front of his house, to create inexpensive and delicious juice drinks. Opening hours can be a bit erratic. M$$

Panadería la Cozumeleña C 3 at Av 10; 987 872 0189. Stop by this sweet-smelling bakery (entrance on C 3) to pick up a pastry to go, or, for a more leisurely light breakfast, settle in at the adjacent coffee shop, a neighbourhood hangout (entrance on the corner). M$

Restaurant del Museo Melgar, between C 4 and C 6, at the Museo de la Isla de Cozumel; 987 120 2255. Enjoy a quiet breakfast, lunch or dinner on the balcony of the museum with a view of the sea. The food – from *huevos rancheros* to club sandwiches, fajitas to ceviche – is fresh and filling. M$$$

RESTAURANTS

La Candela Av 5 at C 6 Nte; 987 878 4471. Home-cooked breakfast and lunch, with a half-Cuban twist (black beans and rice, mojitos). The "fish Candela" (in a tomatillo cream sauce) is just one of many tasty house dishes. Nice breezy terrace seating at the back. M$$$

Casa Denis C 1, between Av 5 and Av 10; https://facebook.com/Casadeniscozumel. A little wood-frame house, this is the best bet for eating near the plaza, even if some of the bigger meals can be a little bland. Best to stick with a beer and some snacks and watch the action from your pavement table. M$$

★ **Le Chef** Av 5 at C 5 Sur; http://lechefcozumel.com. A charming little spot (also known as *Le Bistrot*) where the chef-owner devises new specials every day, such as tapas, pizzas and creative sandwiches (the lobster and bacon combo is the house speciality). M$$$

Conchita del Caribe Av 65, between C 13 and C 15; 987 869 1218. This locally famous informal seafood spot is worth the cab ride deep into town. The generous portions of *ceviche* are particularly good, and on Sundays you can get paella. M$$

New Especias C 3 Sur at Av 5; http://facebook.com/NewEspecias. A good-value restaurant specializing in Italian food, from bruschetta and gnocchi to thin-crust pizzas, seafood and steaks. The menu also features a few more unusual dishes, such as lion fish (an invasive species that threatens Cozumel's reefs) fillets with capers, olives and fresh tomato. M$$$$

Rock'n Java Melgar 602, between C 7 and Quintana Roo (C 11); http://rocknjavacozumel.com. At this American-owned seafront diner, sandwiches, salads, and veggie chile are balanced out by hearty burgers, baked potatoes slathered with cheese, bacon and sour cream, and fantastically rich and delicious desserts (like key lime pie). M$$$

DRINKING AND NIGHTLIFE

SEE MAP PAGE 753

Cerveceria Punta Sur Av 10 229; http://cerveceriapuntasur.com. Pizza might have put this place on the map but the IPA menu and the cocktail list have kept it there. With a near mind blowing selection to choose from, this friendly, local watering hole is the kind of place where you might run into your diving instructor, or tour guide during their off-hours.

Tiki-Tok Melgar, between C 2 and C 4; 987 872 5704. This second-floor bar doles out the umbrella drinks, and the party gets started earlier than most, as this is one of the few bars in town with a sunset view over the water. There's live salsa music (dance classes Fri night) later on.

DIRECTORY

Banks and exchange HSBC is on Av 5 at C 1 Sur.

Internet Scarce in the centre of town, but more numerous around the public market.

Medical care Hyperbaric chamber and clinic on C 5 between Melgar and Av 5 (987 872 5050, http://cozumelhyperbaricchamber.com). 24hr Centro de Salud, on Av 20 at C 11 (987 872 0140). Most doctors are accustomed to dealing with English-speaking patients and those with diving-related issues.

Post office Melgar at C 7 Sur.

South to Tulum

Much of the seafront **south of Playa del Carmen** has been developed into resorts or condominium villages, and their access gates line the east side of Hwy-307, leaving little or no access to the sea for non-guests. There are just a couple of good beach spots, but on the inland side, you'll find some good **cenotes**.

Xcaret

6km south of Playa del Carmen • Charge (a bit cheaper if you book online) • http://xcaret.com • Second-class buses stop on request; dedicated ADO buses from Playa del Carmen run 3 times daily (8.30, 9.30am & 9.50am; returning 5.40pm, 9.45pm & 9.55pm; 30–40min); you can also take a taxi here from Playa

The attraction you see billboards for everywhere is actually a surprisingly pleasant theme park: **Xcaret** offers all the Yucatán's attractions in one handy place, with a museum, a tropical aquarium, a "Maya village", a beach, some small authentic ruins, pools and more than a kilometre of subterranean rivers down which you can swim, snorkel or float. Neighbouring Xplor (http://xplor.travel) is dedicated to ziplines and other outdoor adventure – but it's very expensive for what it is.

Río Secreto

6km south of Playa del Carmen, opposite Xcaret • Tours daily • Charge • http://riosecretomexico.com • Second-class buses stop on request; taxis will take you here from Playa del Carmen

This tour through a water-filled cave is a slick operation, but an undeniably cool one. You don a wetsuit to clamber over rocks and swim through sparkling-clear rivers, and the only light comes from your own headlamp. It's a good adventure, but still doable for kids or not-so-strong swimmers. It's also a good activity for a rainy day.

Parque Xel-Há

Hwy-307, 13km north of Tulum • **Park** Charge (a bit cheaper if you book online) including all food and drink • http://xelha.com • **Ruins** • Charge

Despite a sky-high entrance fee and a theme-park feel, this **natural water park** is a highlight of this coast, especially if you have children. If you spend a full day, it can seem pretty good value. Built around a system of lagoons, inlets and caves, it's a beautiful place with rope swings, snorkelling, cliff jumping and a lazy tube float. Across the highway, not to be confused with the water park, is a set of small **Maya ruins** with some notable paintings of birds, and miniature temples like those at Tulum.

Hidden Treasures

Hwy-307, 14km north of Tulum • **Tours** Daily • Snorkelling and diving; charge • **Dos Ojos** Charge • 984 877 8535

Formerly known as Hidden Worlds, this park area encompasses some exceptionally beautiful *cenotes* and caverns. Guided group snorkelling and diving trips run several times a day. You can also visit glimmering **Dos Ojos** *cenote* on your own, for a fee paid at a separate entrance just to the north on Hwy-307, though it is also a popular place to dive.

AROUND TULUM

Cenotes, Cobá (44km) & Valladolid (99km)
Playa del Carmen (59km) & Cancún (126km)
Felipe Carrillo Puerto (97km) & Chetumal (250km)
Punta Allen (44km) & Sian Ka'an Biosphere Reserve (68km)
Kitesurfing Extreme Control
Tulum ruins
SEE "TULUM RUINS" MAP
HWY 307
Acuatic Tulum
SEE "TULUM TOWN" MAP
El Paraiso Beach Club
CARIBBEAN SEA
Cenote
0 1 kilometre

EATING	
Arca	7
El Capitán	2
Cetli	1
Hartwood	6
Mateo's	3
Qué Fresco	4
El Tábano	5

ACCOMMODATION	
Dos Ceibas	5
Hostal Chalupa	1
Nueva Vida de Ramiro	4
Teetotum	2
Zamas	3

DRINKING & NIGHTLIFE	
Mezzanine	1
La Zebra	2

Tulum and around

To visitors, **TULUM** can mean several things. First, it's one of the most picturesque of all the ancient Maya sites, poised on 15m-high cliffs above the impossibly turquoise Caribbean. Tulum also refers to a stretch of broad, white beach, dotted with lodging options that range from bare-bones to ultra-swank; many of them, as well as many super-casual beach bars, still show their backpacker-friendly roots in style, if not in price. Finally, it's a booming town (often called **Tulum Pueblo** to distinguish it from the beach) that has evolved from roadside waystation to real population centre, where visitors can arrange tours into the Sian Ka'an Biosphere Reserve (see page 765), among other things.

Long considered the hippest coastal destination in the region – a title Isla Holbox is now vying for (see page 730) – Tulum is rapidly developing:

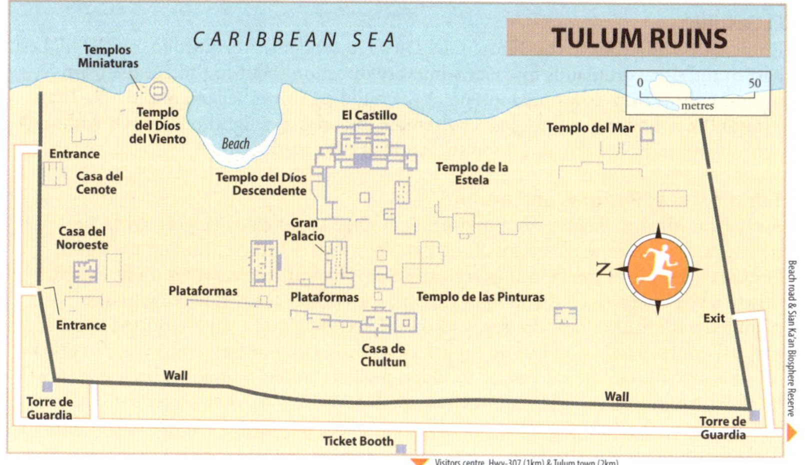

there's even a *Starbucks* now. The area also hit the headlines in 2016, when some 16 beachfront hotels and restaurants were forcibly seized in a controversial land dispute, amid allegations of political corruption. Some of the owners have since regained their properties and legal battles are ongoing. Despite all this, it remains a wonderful place to visit.

12

Tulum ruins

Hwy-307 • Charge • Parking on the main highway; tickets sold at the site entrance, about 1km east; a shuttle (charge) runs between the parking area and the ruins; you can also approach from the south, parking at the dead-end of the beach road and walking in

On a sunny day, with the turquoise sea glittering behind the weather-beaten grey stones, your first glimpse of the **Tulum ruins** can be breathtaking, despite the small scale of its buildings, all clustered in a compact mass. When the Spaniards first set eyes on the place in 1518, they considered it as large and beautiful as Seville. They were, perhaps, misled by their dreams of El Dorado and the brightly painted facades of the buildings, for architecturally Tulum is no match for the great Maya cities. Mostly built after 1200, the structures seem a bit haphazard because walls flare outward and doorways taper in – not the effect of time, but an intentional design, and one echoed in other post-Classic sites along the coast like El Rey in Cancún and San Gervasio on Cozumel.

The site itself takes only an hour or so to see, though you may want to allow time to **swim** at the tiny, perfect beach that punctuates the cliffs (see page 760). Arrive in the early morning or late afternoon to avoid the worst crowds. You walk in through a breach in the wall that surrounded the city on three sides; the fourth faced the sea. The first building past the entrance is the **Casa del Noroeste**, one of the many small-scale buildings which typify the site, with their slanty walls and narrow windows. Closer to the sea sits the **Casa del Cenote**, a square structure straddling what was once a water-filled cave, the source of life for the settlement. On the bluff above and to the right are the **Templos Miniaturas**, several small-scale temples, complete with tiny lintels and mouldings, which were probably used as shrines.

Templo del Díos Descendente

Skirt the small beach to reach the **Templo del Díos Descendente**. The small, upside-down winged figure depicted above the temple's narrow entrance appears all over the city, but in only a handful of places elsewhere in the Maya world. It may represent the setting sun, or the bee god, as honey was one of the Maya's most important exports.

El Castillo

Immediately adjacent to the Templo del Díos Descendente, the **Castillo**, on the highest part of the site, commands fine views in every direction – but to protect the worn stones, visitors may now only look up at the building from the base of the hill. The pyramid may have served not just as a temple, but also as a lighthouse. Even without a light, it would have been an important landmark for mariners.

Templo de las Pinturas and around

Away from the sea, a cluster of buildings is arranged on a city-like grid, with the chief structures set on stone platforms along parallel streets. Of these, the **Templo de las Pinturas** (Temple of the Paintings) is intriguing: the intricate carvings on its exterior slowly reveal themselves as you look closely. The corners form glowering masks trimmed with feather headdresses, and the "descending god" can be spotted in one niche. Unfortunately, you can no longer view this section of the temple, as it's closed off (it is actually on the *exterior* of an older, smaller temple, which has been preserved by the surrounding gallery), but one remarkable scene, created at a later date than the others, shows the rain god Chac seated on a four-legged animal – likely inspired by the conquistadors on horseback.

The best view of the whole site is from the cliff edges to the south of the Castillo. A small trail leads along the edge, delivering a great perspective on the sea and the ruins, then loops down through the greenery.

Tulum beach

Tulum town is generally empty of visitors by day because they've all decamped to the **beach**, the longest, most impeccable stretch of sand outside Cancún. The easiest access is at one of the beach clubs, where you pay for lounge chairs and drinks; far south, especially in the **biosphere reserve**, there's easier free access. The most popular clubs are walking distance from the ruins, making it easy to sightsee, then grab lunch and a spot in the sun. *El Paraiso Beach Club*, about 500m south of the ruins' back entrance, has a generous stretch of sand, often with bands, beach soccer and volleyball. The designated public beach close to the ruins is Playa Maya, a little south of El Paraiso; local fishermen's co-ops here offer snorkel tours and fishing trips. And just south of that is *El Mariachi Beach Club*, which is more of a locals' hangout.

ARRIVAL AND DEPARTURE — TULUM

By plane Airport shuttle Tucan Kin (984 134 7535, http://tucankin.com) runs both from, and to, Cancún airport, dropping at all hotels; a private vehicle and a shared service are available.

By bus The bus station is near the southern end of Tulum Pueblo; during the high season it's worth booking your seat in advance.

Destinations Cancún (every 30min–1hr; 2hr 20min–3hr);

TULUM ORIENTATION

Coming into the Tulum area on **Hwy-307** from the north, you arrive first at the well-marked pedestrian and bus entrances to the **ruins** – the site itself is on the water, 1km east. There's a long-haul bus stop here, so you don't have to double back from town.

Another kilometre or so south is a traffic light marking the main intersection. A left turn here leads, in about 3km, to the **beach**, where accommodation is strung along a narrow but paved road running north–south along the water. To the north (left from the junction) are a few hotels, the better publicly accessible beaches and, after 2km, a back entrance to the ruins. To the south (right from the junction), hotels dot 7km of road, up to the border of the Sian Ka'an Biosphere Reserve.

Back on Hwy-307 (here called **Av Tulum**), the centre of town is just a little further south.

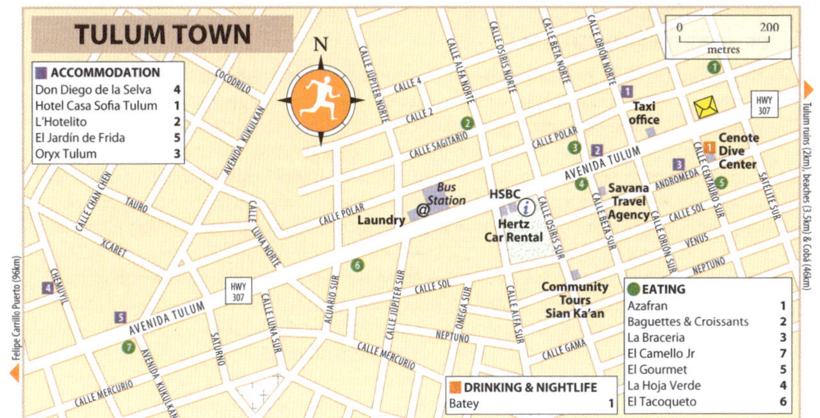

Chetumal via Felipe Carrillo Puerto and Bacalar (roughly hourly; 3hr 15min–4hr 10min); Chichén Itzá (2 daily at 9.05am & 2.45pm; 2hr 40min); Cobá (10 daily; 40min–1hr); Mahahual (1 daily at 6.50pm; 3hr); Mérida (10 daily; 3hr 55min–4hr 20min); Playa del Carmen (every 30min or so; 1hr); San Cristóbal de las Casas (2 daily at 6.15pm & 8.15pm; 18hr 50min–20hr); Palenque (three daily at 6.15pm, 8.15pm & 10.30pm; 10hr 30min-11hr); Valladolid (roughly hourly; 1hr 40min–2hr 10min).

By colectivo *Colectivos* gather almost next door to the bus station. Passenger vans run very frequently to Playa del Carmen and every hour or so to Felipe Carrillo Puerto, stopping anywhere in between on request.

GETTING AROUND

By car To rent a car for a day outing, try Hertz (http://hertz.com) on Av Tulum.

By taxi The main taxi office is on the west side of Av Tulum between Centauro and Orión; most prices are shown on a board outside. Tulum's taxi drivers have a reputation for denying the existence of hotels that don't pay them commission; if you have planned on a particular hotel, insist on being taken there.

By bike Many hostels and hotels offer bikes to rent (or even free for guests), as do most travel agencies. Alternatively, contact Ola Bike Tulum (https://www.olabiketulum.com) in advance and they'll deliver your wheels to your hotel.

INFORMATION, TOURS AND ACTIVITIES

INFORMATION

Tourist information Info kiosk with erratic hours on Av Tulum at Osiris, just north of HSBC.

TOUR OPERATORS

Community Tours Sian Ka'an Osiris and Sol de Oriente; 984 871 2202, http://siankaantours.org. The best tours of Sian Ka'an Biosphere Reserve, run by Centro Ecológico Sian Ka'an. Birding, sunset (with cheese and wine), kayaking and fishing are among the trips on offer.

Savana Travel Agency Av Tulum Oriente 10; 984 871 2091, https://www.savana.mx. A full-service travel agency for flights and car rental, as well as local birdwatching, kayaking and other tours.

ACTIVITIES

Diving Reefs off the coast are fine but not lush – *cenote* diving is the real attraction in this area. Acuatic Tulum are reliable operators, just off Hwy-307 on the road to the beach (984 871 2508, http://acuatictulum.com).

Kitesurfing and paddle-boarding Extreme Control at Caleta Tankha, north of the ruins (984 745 4555, http://extremecontrol.net).

ACCOMMODATION

SEE MAPS PAGES 758 AND 761

Basic sand-floor cabañas **on the beach** made Tulum famous with hippy backpackers, but they're in short supply now, as more comfortable (and much more expensive) places have sprung up. In fact, you may want to stay in **town** if you arrive late, have a limited amount of time (and money) or just prefer hot water round-the-clock: most hotels on the **beach road** have power only in the evenings (though this is changing), drawing on solar

CENOTES NEAR TULUM

The area north and west of Tulum has one of the largest concentrations of **cenotes** on the peninsula, including **Ox Bel Ha**, which at almost 170km is the longest water-filled cave system in the world. Many of these freshwater sinkholes are accessible from Hwy-307 or off the road to Cobá. Some, like Hidden Treasures (see page 758), have been developed as adventure centres, and the guides and marked trails at these places can help put first-time visitors at ease in dark water and tight spaces. But it's also worth visiting one of the less developed alternatives, such as **Gran Cenote**, 4km up the road to Cobá from Tulum (8am–4.45pm; charge), where the only service is snorkel-gear and life-jacket rental. Either way, you can float above stalagmites and other rock formations – all the fun of cave exploration, with none of the scrabbling around. Zacil-Há, 4km further (charge), is a local hangout and a great beginner pool, as you can see the sandy bottom.

Divers must have open-water certification for **cavern diving** (in which you explore within the reach of daylight), but **cave diving** (in which you venture into closed passageways and halls) requires rigorous training. One of the best cave-diving specialists in the area is Aquatech Divers at *Villas de Rosa* (984 875 9020, http://cenotes.com) at Aventuras beach.

Local development may threaten *cenotes* in the long run, but clumsy visitors can do more damage in the short term. All the same rules for reef preservation (see page 752) apply here; and be very careful climbing in and out of the water – use the paths and ladders provided.

12

panels, windmills and (less ecofriendly) diesel generators. Depending on your point of view, the candle-lit ambience is rustic charm or expensive primitivism, and the thatched palapa roofs on cabañas can be a liability in the rain. As in Playa del Carmen, most hotels also charge high-season rates in the European holiday period of July and Aug. Addresses for the beach hotels are given in terms of distance from the junction with the highway access road.

HOTELS, B&BS AND CABAÑAS

ON THE BEACH

Dos Ceibas 5.5km south of the junction; http://dosceibas.com. Colourful, spacious cabañas in front of a turtle-hatching beach. Solar power and recycling mean that *Dos Ceibas'* "eco" label is more convincing than most; yoga and meditation classes offered. The cheapest cabaña has a bathroom outside. M$$$

Nueva Vida de Ramiro 4.5km south of the junction; http://tulumnv.com. Peaceful, quirky eco-hotel powered entirely by wind turbines. Attractive wood cabins on stilts and cement cabins with big tiled bathrooms are built over and around untamed greenery. The restaurant serves tasty seafood. With several suites and whole houses, it's a good choice for families and groups. M$$$$

Zamas 1.3km south of the junction; http://zamas.com. Enormous, comfortable rooms and bathrooms, some right on one of the prettiest stretches of beach in Tulum. Hot water and electricity are plentiful, but the style remains bohemian. Good restaurant (see page 763) too. M$$$$

IN TOWN

Don Diego de la Selva West side of Hwy-307, south of town; http://casadondiegotulum.com.mx. French-owned hideaway just out of town, with a pool, tranquil garden, Gallic-influenced restaurant and big, white rooms with terraces; choice of fan or a/c. Guests can use facilities at beachfront sister hotel, *Don Diego de la Playa* (which is also recommended). M$$$

L'Hotelito West side of Av Tulum between Beta and Orión; 984 136 1240. Good-value Italian-run hotel with palapa roofs and a garden courtyard, quiet despite its location in the middle of town. Rooms have an old-fashioned, comfy feel: upstairs with high ceilings and fans or a/c. M$$

★ **Oryx Tulum** Calle Luna Nte 2; 984 259 2993. This simple but clean hotel has tranquil rooms set around a small courtyard, with welcoming and helpful staff. This is a good budget option, not too far from the thick of it. M$$

Teetotum On the road to the beach, 200m from Hwy-307; http://hotelteetotum.com. Four sharply designed rooms with iPod docks, a/c and mod furniture – though it's overpriced, and housekeeping, and service in general, needs sharpening up. There's a plunge pool and a café-bar, and the location on the road to the beach hits a sweet spot: quiet, but walking distance to town and an easy bike ride (on free bicycles) to the water. M$$$$

HOSTELS

IN TOWN

Hostal Chalupa On the road to the beach, 50m from Hwy-307; http://hostalchalupa.mxhotel.site/en. Excellent hostel with rooftop bar and small pool; dorm beds are in four- or five-bed dorms, all a/c and en suite. Two private rooms, sleeping up to four people, are available too. Dorms M$; doubles M$$

Hotel Casa Sofia Tulum Calle Orión Nte, just south of the bus station; 984 872 2526. A convenient budget hotel in town with basic but large rooms — all en-suite. Breakfast is only served here during high season. M$$

El Jardín de Frida East side of Hwy-307 at the south edge of town; 984 871 2816. Billing itself as an "Eco-Cultural Poshtel" inspired by Frida Khalo, *El Jardín* aims to stand out from the crowd. Mural-filled rooms and dorms are set around a luxuriant garden, and there's a cafe-restaurant, book exchange and communal kitchen. Dorms M$; doubles M$$

EATING

SEE MAPS PAGES 758 AND 761

Tulum has a burgeoning dining scene – world-renowned, multi-Michelin-starred restaurant *Noma* even hosted a pop-up here in 2017. Because the accommodation is spread over 10km and the town is so far from the beach, almost every hotel has its own restaurant and bar. Guests tend to stick to their own hotels, but a few **places to eat** along the beach road merit a special trip. In town, a number of inexpensive **cafés** serve comida corrida and rotisserie chicken, and there's an increasing number of cheerful, mid-range places run by European expats.

CAFÉS, CHEAP EATS AND SNACKS

IN TOWN

Azafran Av Satelite Nte, near corner with C 2 Pte; 984 207 3866. If you've had a heavy night, this is the place to start your recovery: the "hangover breakfast" (featuring sausages, bacon, rye toast, mashed potato and scrambled eggs) is legendary in these parts. If you want a less calorific option, go for a bagel, crepe or fruit salad. Great coffee, too. M$$

Baguettes & Croissants Sagitario Pte at Alfa; 987 247 2581. Good-value bakery café, a short walk off the main drag, serving sandwiches and filled baguettes, cakes, pastries, light meals and decent coffee. Useful for picnics or bus journeys. M$

La Braceria North side of Av Tulum between Orión and Beta; 984 745 1438. A busy steak restaurant with some imposing decor and super size portions. M$$$

El Camello Jr East side of Hwy-307 at the south edge of town; 984 871 2036, http://facebook.com/RestauranteElCamelloJr. Unpretentious, plastic-table-and-chair place, but the crowds will tell you the seafood is excellent and cheap – from the *ceviche* to whole fried fish. M$$

El Gourmet Centauro Sur, between Andromeda and Sol; 984 146 9989. An Italian deli serving excellent salads, sandwiches and panini, plus smoothies. Perfect if you need a picnic lunch for the beach or a day trip, though you can also eat in. M$

La Hoja Verde Beta, just off Av Tulum; 984 177 8638. This vegetarian/vegan restaurant offers a pleasing change of pace, with tasty ratatouille, falafel, quinoa risotto and curries, plus great juices and smoothies. M$$

El Tacoqueto East side of Av Tulum at C Acuario. A dependable *lonchería* with gut-busting daily specials (feel free to poke your head in the kitchen to see what looks good), or delicious hot-off-the-grill tacos for even less. M$$

RESTAURANTS

IN TOWN

El Capitán On the road to the beach, 200m from Hwy-307; 984 164 5812. Vast portions of high-quality, keenly-priced fish, seafood and Mexican classics are served up at this friendly restaurant: the *ceviche* is particularly good. The mosquitos, however, are ferocious, so bring repellent. M$$$

★ **Cetli** Carretera Tulum-Coba km 2.5; 984 108 0681, https://facebook.com/cetlitulum. Chef-owner Claudia trained in Mexico City's premier culinary academy; at her casual restaurant, try refined versions of Mexican classics, such as chicken stuffed with *chaya* (similar to spinach) with a cactus fruit jelly. The restaurant has moved from its original location and is now 3km north of the town centre. M$$$

ON THE BEACH

Arca 4.2km south of the junction, on the beach road; http://arcatulum.com. Hyper-creative dishes made from locally sourced ingredients are served in an elegant jungle setting. Dishes include grilled octopus *al pastor*, suckling pig roulade, and roast pepper tartare with cured egg yolk; whatever you go for, don't miss the wonderful house-made sourdough. M$$$$

Hartwood 7.6km south of the junction, on the beach road; http://hartwoodtulum.com. The menu at this jungle-side restaurant, run by a New Yorker who aims to have a zero-carbon impact, changes daily, uses local (and often unusual) produce, and is cooked entirely on a wood fire. Expect modern, international dishes like slow-braised pork ribs, tangy lime tart and cinnamon-spiked plantains. M$$$$

Mateo's 1.3km south of the junction, on the beach road across from Zamas; 984 168 5524, https://facebook.com/MateosTulum. Very popular Tex-Mex-style roadside diner with burgers, tacos, fajitas, coconut shrimp and the like. Service may be slow, as almost everything is cooked on a single oil-drum barbecue. M$$$

Qué Fresco 1.2km south of the junction, on the beach road, at Zamas; http://zamas.com. Very popular mid-range restaurant with fresh salads, pastas, pizzas, and some of the healthier Mexican dishes. Its beachside setting makes it a great way to start the day, too. M$$$

El Tábano 2.3km south of the junction, inland side of the beach road; 984 182 9661 As an open-air operation in an area without utilities, every day at this creative Mexican place starts with spanking-fresh seafood and produce – nothing from the freezer here. The setting means mosquitoes, though, so bring repellent. M$$$

DRINKING AND NIGHTLIFE

SEE MAPS PAGES 758 AND 761

You'll have to ask around about nightlife as there's no single place where people reliably congregate, though *El Paraiso Beach Club* often has a party around the full moon.

IN TOWN

Batey Centauro, just off Tulum. An old VW Beetle out front has been converted into a sugar-cane press at this hip bar, which specializes in mojitos (try the ginger flavour) and is a great spot for a sundowner. There's often live music and DJs, and a selection of tapas is on offer.

ON THE BEACH

Mezzanine 800m north of the junction, on the beach road; http://mezzaninetulum.com. This cool bar-lounge does excellent cocktails and Thai food; it's the only place on the beach where you can regularly find a dance scene in high season, every Fri. (Annoyingly, though, non-guests can't rent loungers/umbrellas.)

La Zebra 4.6km south of the junction, on the beach road; http://lazebratulum.com. Live music from Thursday right through the weekend, with a Sun salsa party that draws both tourists and residents, starting with free classes at 6pm (coinciding with happy hour). There's a huge selection of tequilas and cocktails, and the restaurant's Mexican food is good as well.

DIRECTORY

12

Banks and exchange HSBC, with an ATM, is in the middle of town, on the east side of Tulum between Osiris and Alfa; there are other ATMs at the bus station and nearby on the west side of Av Tulum.

Internet Plenty of places offer internet access, and most hotels have wi-fi. Reliable downtown places include Riviera Movil, just south of the ADO.

Laundry Several in town, including Lavandería Cheemil-Po, Av Tulum, just south of the bus station.

Post office West side of Av Tulum between Satélite and Centauro.

Cobá

45km northwest of Tulum • Charge

A wide highway cuts through the jungle inland from Tulum, leading to the ancient city of **COBÁ** (and the tiny Maya village next to it). It's a fascinating and increasingly popular site. The clusters of buildings are spread out over several kilometres, so the area can absorb lots of visitors without feeling crowded, and you can ramble through the forest in peace, looking out for toucans, egrets, coatis and myriad tropical butterflies, including the giant iridescent blue morpho. A visit here requires at least a couple of hours; renting a **bicycle** just inside the site entrance is highly recommended. Although the ruins aren't as well restored as those at Tulum, their scale is more impressive, and the dense greenery and wildlife make a good counterpoint to the coast.

Ceramic studies indicate that the city was occupied from about 100 AD up until the arrival of the Spaniards – the site is even mentioned in the *Chilam Balam* of Chumayel, a book of Maya prophecy and lore written down in the eighteenth century, well after the city was abandoned. The city's zenith was in the Late Classic, around 800 AD, when its wealth grew from links with the cities of **Petén**, in lowland Mexico and Guatemala. These cities influenced Cobá's architecture and use of steles, typically seen only in the southern Maya regions. Cobá also prospered later through its connections with coastal cities such as Tulum, and several structures reflect the style found at those sites.

Nohoch Mul

The centrepiece of the site is the giant pyramid **Nohoch Mul**, taller than El Castillo at Chichén Itzá and, in its narrow and precipitous stairway, resembling the pyramid at Tikal in Guatemala; at the top, a small temple, similar to structures at Tulum, dates from around 1200. The view takes in nearby lakes, as well as the jungle stretching uninterrupted to the horizon.

Grupo Macanxoc

If you're feeling intrepid, head 1km down a shady *sacbé* to **Grupo Macanxoc**, a cluster of some twenty steles, most carved during the seventh century AD. Stele 1 shows part of the Maya creation myth and the oldest date recorded in the Maya Long Count calendar system, which tracks the days since the moment of creation. Other steles depict a high number of women, suggesting that Cobá may have had female rulers.

Cobá cenotes

6km south of Cobá • Charge • Buy tickets and arrange a taxi at the entrance to the Cobá parking area; by car, buy tickets at the first *cenote*

After visiting the ruins, or as a separate excursion, you can make a trip to a group of **cenotes** outside the village of Cobá. The first you reach, Choo-Ha, is the least good for swimming, though its stalactites are impressive. The second, Tankah-Ha, is the most spectacular, a grand subterranean dome. Multún-Ha is deeper, and no natural light penetrates.

ARRIVAL AND DEPARTURE — COBÁ

By bus Numerous buses (10 daily; 40min–1hr) run to Cobá from Tulum. Confusingly, there are generally fewer buses heading in the opposite direction.

By taxi Taxis from Tulum run to and from Cobá.

ACCOMMODATION AND EATING

Hotelito Sac-bé On the south side of the main street through the village; 984 206 7140. Leagues better than the other budget options in town, *Hotelito Sac-bé* has a handful of clean rooms offering various amenities (some have a/c). The restaurant here serves an excellent, generous inclusive breakfast. M$$$

La Pirámide Facing the lake; 984 173 7470. The best of the big restaurants that ring the parking lot by the site entrance, this is a casual, open-sided place dishing up all the usual Yucatecan specialities. M$$$

12

Reserva de Monos Arañas de Punta Laguna

Highway to Nuevo X-Can, 18km northeast of Cobá roundabout • Charge, plus extra for a guide for a group of up to ten people • No buses come this way; arrange a taxi or tour in Tulum

This small forest reserve protects one of the northernmost populations of **spider monkeys**. From the entrance kiosk, you're required to hike with a guide to where the monkeys usually congregate. There's no guarantee you'll see them, but they're at their liveliest in the morning and after about 3.30pm. You can also rent canoes at the lake here.

Sian Ka'an Biosphere Reserve

SIAN KA'AN means "the place where the sky is born" in Maya, which seems appropriate when you experience the sunrise in this beautiful part of the peninsula. Created by presidential decree in 1986 and made a UNESCO World Heritage Site in 1987, the biosphere reserve is a sparsely populated region sprawling along the coast south of Tulum. One of the largest protected areas in Mexico, it covers 1.3 million acres. Most of the thousand or so permanent residents are fishermen and subsistence farmers gathered in the village of **Punta Allen**. Most visitors enter at the north border, from Tulum, on day trips; only a few hardier travellers press on to Punta Allen and stay for a stretch.

The reserve contains all three of the principal ecosystems found in the Yucatán Peninsula and the Caribbean: the area is approximately one-third **tropical forest**, one-third fresh- and saltwater **marshes** and **mangroves**, and one-third **marine** environment, including a section of the Mesoamerican Barrier Reef. All five species of Mexican

TOURING THE SIAN KA'AN BIOSPHERE

You can enter the biosphere unaccompanied (daily sunrise–sunset; charge), on the road south from Tulum's beach hotels, but you will benefit far more from an organized tour, easily arranged in Tulum. One of the best operators is **Community Tours Sian Ka'an** (984 871 2202, http://siankaantours.org), part of a non-profit group called Centro Ecológico de Sian Ka'an (CESIAK), which funds its research and educational programmes with a few tours. One heads off by day through the ancient Maya canals that crisscross the marshy areas here, while another is a late-afternoon excursion that takes in sunset inside the reserve. Half-day kayaking and fly-fishing excursions are available too, as are trips looking at the process behind making traditional Maya-style chewing gum. These are great trips around the fringes of the reserve's vast open spaces, with excellent opportunities for bird watching. You can reserve a spot at the office in Tulum (see page 761).

If you really want to go it alone, you can stop and swim at deserted beaches almost anywhere along the way, and there's a visitor centre about 9km inside the reserve where you can rent kayaks, follow nature trails and arrange boat trips around the lagoons.

In Punta Allen, hotels can arrange fishing tours, as can the local tourism co-op; book at the office signed "tourist info", beside the beach as you enter the village. The co-op can also arrange nature tours of the Sian Ka'an lagoons.

12

wild cat, including jaguars, live in the forest, along with spider and howler monkeys, tapir and deer. More than three hundred species of **birds** have been recorded. The Caribbean beaches provide nesting grounds for four endangered **marine turtle** species, while extremely rare West Indian **manatees** have been seen in the inlets. Morelet's and mangrove **crocodiles** lurk in the lagoons.

Punta Allen

Right at the tip of a narrow spit of land, with a lighthouse guarding the northern entrance to the **Bahía de la Ascensión**, the remote fishing village of **PUNTA ALLEN** is not the kind of place you stumble across by accident – it really is the end of the road, with no mobile signal, no ATMs and limited internet access. Bonefish and tarpon in the bay are a draw for active travellers; layabouts come for hammock-lounging. The beach isn't great for swimming, though, as there's lots of sea grass, and, depending on the currents, a bit of rubbish.

Chunyaxché

Hwy-307, 20km south of Tulum • Charge; boardwalk charge; 2hr boat tours, charge • Second-class buses or *colectivos* from Tulum to Chetumal stop on request; it's easier to return to Tulum than to continue south, as *colectivos* are often full

The little-visited ruins of **Chunyaxché** – also known as **Muyil**, for the nearby village – lie on the north border of the Sian Ka'an Biosphere. Despite the size of the site – probably the largest on the Quintana Roo coast – and its proximity to Hwy-307, you're likely to have the place to yourself, as few people travel further south than Tulum.

Muyil was occupied from the pre-Classic period until after the arrival of the Spanish, after which its people probably fell victim to European diseases. Most of the buildings you see today date from the post-Classic period, between 1200 and 1500. The tops of the tallest structures, just visible from the road, rise 17m from the forest floor. There are more than one hundred mounds and temples, none of them completely clear of vegetation, and it's easy to wander around and find buildings buried in the jungle, but climbing them is forbidden.

The centre of the site is connected by a *sacbé* to the small **Muyil lagoon** 500m away. This is joined to the large Chunyaxché lagoon and ultimately to the sea at **Boca Paila** by an amazing **canalized river** – the route used by ancient Maya traders. Wildlife scatters as you follow the boardwalk that leads through the mangroves to the lagoon. At the end of the path, you might find someone offering a boat tour down the canals and past less-explored Maya sites – but it's not a reliable way to enter the reserve.

ARRIVAL AND DEPARTURE — SIAN KA'AN BIOSPHERE RESERVE

By car The road south from Tulum has helped maintain Punta Allen's special quality: it's famously rutted and flooded – and often impassable – in the rainy season, and can still be slow going during the dry months, typically requiring at least 3hr for the 50km drive. Think twice about coming down here in a rental car, especially if there's any chance of rain; even if you can get through, you may be trapped if there's a storm. There are perpetual rumours the road will be paved, but this is unlikely due to reserve regulations. There's an alternative, very bumpy route from the highway south of Chunyaxché (see page 766) and in to Vigia Chico, where you can catch the launch that meets the Punta Allen *colectivo*.

By colectivo A *colectivo* (daily at 2pm; around 3hr) runs from next to the taxi syndicate in Tulum (call 984 879 8040 in the morning to reserve a seat). Another goes from Felipe Carrillo Puerto (see page 767; daily at 6am; around 3hr) via an even more bone-rattling route to Vigia Chico (also called El Playón), where launches cross the bay to the village. From Punta Allen, the *colectivo* for Tulum leaves at 6am, and the launch for the Carrillo Puerto service goes at 7am (reserve your seat beforehand at Tienda Caamal).

ACCOMMODATION AND EATING

Although there are many enticing stretches of sand along the road from Tulum, biosphere regulations prohibit camping to control erosion – which is not to say it's not done, unfortunately. All hotels in the area have their own restaurants, and independent restaurants are very few. A truck travels the peninsula on Wed and Sat, selling fresh items you can't get in the Punta Allen tiendas; it arrives in the afternoon or evening, depending on road conditions.

Posada Sirena Northern end, Punta Allen; 984 877 8521. Entering Punta Allen from the north, past the naval station on the right and beached boats on the left, the first and cheapest of the accommodation options is the bohemian *Posada Sirena*, with four cabañas and an owner with tales to tell. M$$

Serenidad Shardon Southern end, Punta Allen; http://shardon.com. *Serenidad Shardon* has the most comfortable beach houses, as well as space for camping (which is permitted in the grounds here) with the option of renting tents and all the gear inside, all with access to showers and a communal kitchen. M$

12

Tulum to Chetumal

The road from Tulum to Chetumal skirts the Sian Ka'an Biosphere Reserve and heads into the Maya heartland, past the ruins of Chunyaxché and on to **Felipe Carrillo Puerto**, the capital of Maya resistance. Closer to Chetumal is **Laguna de Bacalar**, as scenic as any Caribbean beach.

Felipe Carrillo Puerto

The slow-paced agricultural town of **FELIPE CARRILLO PUERTO** doesn't look like much on the surface, and few people make a special trip here, except perhaps to catch a *colectivo* to Punta Allen (as an alternative to the one from Tulum). But if you're driving, it's an interesting short stop, being an important cultural and spiritual centre for the modern Maya, following its role as capital of the independent "Zona Maya" during the nineteenth-century Caste Wars (when it was called **Chan Santa Cruz**). In the 1850s, rebels from the north gathered forces here and took guidance and inspiration from a miraculous talking cross that told them to fight on against their oppressors.

You can still visit the **Santuario de la Cruz Parlante**, built on the site of the talking cross (its remnants have been moved to a smaller town nearby). To reach it, turn west off the main street (C 70 or Av Juárez) at the Pemex; the complex is at Calle 62. Back on the plaza, the Franciscan-style **Iglesia de Balam Na** was in fact built by the rebel Maya as a temple – using the slave labour of captured white fighters, no less; it was consecrated as a Catholic church only in 1948.

ARRIVAL AND INFORMATION — FELIPE CARRILLO PUERTO

By bus The station is on the plaza at the corner of C 65 and C 66, a couple of blocks west of the highway. Buses between Tulum and Chetumal stop here, as do buses from Mérida via Ticul.

By colectivo *Colectivos* from Tulum (1hr) stop on Hwy-307 at C 73, one block north of the main traffic circle, and a few blocks northeast of the plaza. The *colectivo* to Punta Allen (2 daily at 9am & 3pm; 3hr) leaves from the first block east out of the main traffic circle.

Tourist information The small tourist office, on C 70 at C 59 (Mon–Fri 9am–4pm; 983 267 1452), has information on surrounding Maya villages. Or stop in at Xiimbal Tours, on the plaza at C 65 (983 834 1073).

ACCOMMODATION AND EATING

Hotel Turquesa Maya On the main road, at C 56; https://facebook.com/hotelturquesamaya. If you need to stay a night, this is the best option in town, a solid mid-range hotel that does the simple things well: comfy, well-equipped en suites, a good restaurant, and efficient staff. M$$

Costa Maya and Bacalar

The beaches that line the 250km of coast between the southern edge of the Sian Ka'an reserve and the Belizean border may not be as picture-perfect as those in Tulum – they're often shaded with pines, not palms – but they are beautiful in their sheer emptiness. Despite development pressure in the form of a cruise-ship pier, the **COSTA MAYA**, as the area is known, still has a very end-of-the-world feel. The two towns in the area, **Mahahual** and the smaller **Xcalak**, were hit hard by Hurricane Dean in 2007. Mahahual was rebuilt, but Xcalak is still quite battered. Beachcombers typically stay around Mahahual; divers and anglers head south to Xcalak.

12

Inland from the coast is the surprise respite of **Laguna de Bacalar**, every bit as clear and beautiful as the Caribbean and harbouring its own special wildlife. Like the Costa Maya, its shores are a respite from development up the coast.

Mahahual

Puerto Costa Maya, where the cruise ships dock, is out of sight north of **MAHAHUAL** (60km east of Hwy-307), but its influence is felt on cruise-ship days, when the village springs to life with souvenir stands and jet-ski rentals along the slick seafront promenade, an extremely miniature version of Playa del Carmen. It's a surreal juxtaposition with the rest of the ramshackle town. To avoid any crowds and capture the real Robinson Crusoe vibe, just head down the bumpy dirt beach road south of town.

ARRIVAL AND INFORMATION — MAHAHUAL

By bus Mahahual is linked to Cancún (2 daily at 10.30am & 5.30pm; 5hr 15min) and Chetumal (2 daily at 2.30pm & 7.30pm; 2hr–2hr 30min) by daily buses. Additional buses may run at weekends and peak Mexican holiday times. Given the limited direct services, consider taking a bus to Limones (2 daily at 6.30am & 3.30pm, returning at 7.15am & 5.45pm;

DIVING ON THE COSTA MAYA

The **Banco Chinchorro**, declared a biosphere reserve in 2003, lies 35km off the coast. The lush coral atoll, littered with shipwrecks, is the main draw for divers visiting the Costa Maya, and it can be reached from either Mahahual or Xcalak – though not all shops have a licence to visit. Dreamtime Dive Centre, about a kilometre south of town on the coast road (983 124 0235, http://dreamtimediving.com; single-tank dives and full-day trips availble), is a reliable place with regular trips; Gypsea Divers, on the malecón at Nacional beach club (983 130 3714, http://gypseadivers.com; diving and snorkelling), also comes highly recommended.

In Xcalak, Diving XTC (983 831 0461, http://xtcdivecenter.com) has a Chinchorro licence. The reefs closer to the shore here are lovely too; it also runs snorkelling and fishing trips, and offers open-water certification courses.

55min), at the junction on Hwy-307, then a taxi to the coast.
By car There's a Pemex station on the main road just outside Mahahual, the only fuel locally. Be prepared for a roadblock and thorough car inspection on the main road leaving Mahahual.
By taxi You can get a taxi from Limones, but the price will depend on your bargaining skills and final destination. In Mahahual, local taxis hang out at the corner of Sierra, just beyond the bus station.
Money It's wise to bring plenty of cash: there are at least three ATMs (at V@mos internet, the Pemex station and *Hotel Luna de Plata*), but they are frequently out of order.

ACCOMMODATION

We give addresses for places in town below, though the only street signs are on the malecón; Huachinango is the main street south through town. Virtually everything is here or on the malecón. Many places have higher rates at weekends, when it's a popular escape for Chetumal residents.

Almaplena Eco Resort and Beach Club Coast road south at km 12.5; http://almaplenabeachresort.com. At the higher end of lodging options, but done right, with a commitment to the "eco" in its name and sparkling rooms with handmade Argentine furniture and tapestries from Chiapas. To avoid the long haul on the rutted beach road, take the paved inland road toward Xcalak, then cut toward the coast road and turn north. M$$$

Balamku Coast road south at km 5.5; 983 839 5332. Serious ecofriendly outlook, recycling grey water, generating solar power and keeping natural landscaping around its attractive white stucco, thatch-roofed cottages. Wi-fi access and kayaks are included. M$$$

Las Cabañas del Doctor Coast road immediately south of town; http://lascabanasdeldoctor.com. Across the road from the beach and in easy walking distance of the centre, this place has economical rooms and bungalows (with private bathrooms). Kayaks and snorkelling gear are available to rent. Doubles M$$$; bungalows M$$

Cabañas Kohun Coast road south at km 7; 983 700 2820. A good budget option with a handful of clean and roomy palapa-roofed cabañas (each with a shady terrace and hammock) so close to the surf you're nearly in the Caribbean. Kayaks and bikes are available to rent. M$$

★ **Maya Luna** Coast road south at km 4.5; https://facebook.com/Hotel.Restaurant.Maya.Luna. Idyllic bungalows right on the beach (no a/c, but breezy enough), with private roof terraces for stargazing, plus a couple of smaller apartments. The restaurant serves Dutch/Indonesian/Mexican fusion food, and rates include an excellent breakfast. Primarily solar-powered. M$$$

★ **Mayan Beach Garden** Placer, on the coast 20km north of Mahahual; http://mayanbeachgarden.com. A real getaway: a beautiful spot on a relatively empty beach, with lovely, well-equipped palapa-roof rooms. Some units have kitchens and a/c. Use of kayaks and snorkel gear is included; excellent meals are available too. M$$$

Posada Pachamama Huachinango between Martillo and Coronado; http://posadapachamama.com. Run by friendly Italian owners, *Posada Pachamama* has a selection of very comfortable rooms with a/c (though no real views), a café, and access to the beach club next door. Staff can organize tours and activities. M$$$

12

EATING

Lilo Smoothie Bar Malecón between Sierra and Chema; 984 133 7738. This sand-floored, palapa-roofed place is the best in town for simple smoothies, or wraps, both made with all organic ingredients. M$

★ **Travel in'** Coast road south at km 6; 983 110 9496. A popular meeting place for the local expat community with great food from an eclectic menu (like shrimp curry and pork *shawarma*), home-made pitta bread and frequent theme nights – tapas on Wed, for example, and regular fondue sessions. There's also an attached guesthouse. M$$

Xcalak

It's hard to believe **Xcalak** was once the largest town in Quintana Roo: today it's a desolate village that still hasn't recovered from being flattened by a hurricane. Forty kilometres south of Mahahual, it can only be reached by a paved but potholed road that runs inland. The main reason to visit is its superb **snorkelling**, **diving** and **fishing**; it has no real beaches. Phone service remains patchy, so some companies conduct much of their business by email; see the website http://xcalak.info for more information.

ARRIVAL AND DEPARTURE — XCALAK

By bus Caribe buses depart Chetumal daily (around 6am and 4pm; 5hr). Return journeys from Xcalak go at around 5am and 2pm; schedules are prone to change, so check before setting off. From anywhere on Hwy-307, you can connect with the Caribe bus at the town of Limones (around 7.30am and 5.30pm), where most first-class services on the main highway should stop.
By car Xcalak is 40km south of Mahahual, but the coast

road is impassable. You must take a narrow road, paved but potholed, that turns south off the highway just before you reach Mahahual. The only petrol station is in Mahahual.

ACCOMMODATION AND EATING

Costa de Cocos Coast road north of town; http://costadecocos.com. A long-established, laid-back fly-fishing and diving centre with its own boats and dive instructor, plus good snorkelling off the dock. Accommodation is in old-fashioned wooden cabañas and there's also a popular restaurant. M$$$

Tierra Maya North of town; 983 839 8012. This welcoming guesthouse is a short drive north of town, and unlike other places around Xcalak, it has a bit of a sandy beach. All the rooms have fans, and most face the water. There's a good restaurant, too. M$$$

Laguna de Bacalar

Inland from the Costa Maya and some 35km north of Chetumal, the gorgeous **Laguna de Bacalar** stretches along the east side of Hwy-307. If you haven't checked a map, it's easy to mistake it for the Caribbean, glinting through the trees in flashes of colour from palest aqua to deep indigo. About 45km long and 1km wide, it's the second largest lake in Mexico (after Laguna de Chapala, south of Guadalajara), but still attracts only a small number of Mexican tourists and a small expat community with a bent for ecology and yoga. The birdlife here is exceptionally vibrant.

The small town on the edge of the lake, **BACALAR**, was once a key point on the pre-Columbian trade route, and unexcavated **Maya remains** surround the lake. The *Chilam Balam* of Chumayel, one of the Maya's sacred books, mentions it as the first settlement of the Itzá, the tribe that occupied Chichén Itzá.

12

Museo de San Felipe

Bacalar plaza • Charge

Bacalar's juicy history is detailed in this small but interesting **museum**, set in a restored fort built by the Spanish in 1730 for protection against pirates from what's now Belize, and later used as a Maya stronghold in the Caste Wars. The fort is just off the plaza, the centre of Bacalar town, about 1.2km from the highway, where the bus stops.

Balneario Municipal

Lakeshore just downhill from the Fuerte de San Felipe, Bacalar • Charge

The liveliest and most scenic of the **swimming** spots on the lake, this town-run "beach" has changing rooms, a reasonably priced restaurant and other facilities. The water is shallow, with a white-sand bottom – easy for kids to frolic in.

Cenote Azul

Southern end of the lake, a few kilometres south of Bacalar on the lakeshore drive • Charge • Take a taxi from Bacalar

A distinct attraction from the lake itself, this "bottomless" *cenote* is an enormous inky-blue hole in the ground, with invigorating cold water. Around the edge is a restaurant that features live musicians at weekends, when it's a destination for Mexican families – this is the only time the place is busy with swimmers and dive-bombing teens.

ARRIVAL, INFORMATION AND TOURS — LAGUNA DE BACALAR

By bus Second-class buses (every 1–3 hours; 30–40min) northbound from Chetumal stop at Av 5, off the plaza; southbound services stop on Av 7, a block uphill. Some first-class buses will drop you off on the highway.

Information http://bacalarmosaico.com is a useful website.

Tours Active Nature (983 120 5742, http://activenature.aventours.de), based at *Villas Ecotucan*, does 2hr jungle walks, birdwatching or lake trips in kayaks, as well as multi-day kayak camping trips.

ACCOMMODATION

Casita Carolina In Bacalar, south of the fort on the lakeshore drive; https://facebook.com/casitacarolina

bacalarmx. A pleasant guesthouse with seven rooms as well as accommodation in two parked RV trailers (named "Boler" and "Scamp") in a spacious back garden that stretches almost to the shore. There's a pool, and kayaks are available to rent. M$$

Laguna Azul At the northern tip of the lake; 744 469 6000. A remote location, but wonderfully welcoming, with a great little restaurant and bar. Choose from sturdy en-suite cabañas, camping spaces or RV sites, and rent a kayak to explore the lake. M$

Laguna Bacalar South of Bacalar, on the lake; http://lagunabacalarhotel.com. Kitsch and comfortable, this old-style Mexican resort is decorated with seashell-encrusted countertops and plaster pillars galore. There's a pool that's also open to anyone dining at the restaurant. M$$$

Villas Ecotucan Hwy-307, 5km north of Bacalar; http://ecotucan.com. Large cabañas on attractively landscaped grounds between the lake and acres of untouched forest. You can also visit just for a swim and to climb the observation tower; there's a small fee to use both. *Colectivos* and second-class buses can drop you on the highway near the entrance. M$$$

EATING AND DRINKING

Orizaba Av 7, one block off the northwest corner of the plaza, Bacalar; 983 834 2069. This popular, low-key place has a loyal local following. It serves up satisfying but inexpensive Mexican classics, as well as a good-value daily set meal. M$$

Chetumal and around

If you're heading south to Belize, you can't avoid the capital of Quintana Roo, **CHETUMAL**, 1.5km from the border. The neighbouring country's influence is reflected in everything from people's quirky English names to the clapboard houses. Many of these old wooden cottages were wiped out by Hurricane Janet in 1955, however, and Chetumal was rebuilt in concrete. The city is bustling but largely oblivious to tourists, which can be refreshing after the hedonism of the Riviera Maya. But you must have a particular love for border towns to appreciate the place as a destination. It does make a decent one-day stop for resting and restocking, as everything (except car rental) is relatively cheap. Nightlife is pretty tame, but on weekend evenings the plaza by the malecón has food stalls, and residents flock to the bar-restaurants strung along the seafront east of here.

12

Museo de la Cultura Maya

Niños Héroes at the northern edge of the centre • Charge • 983 832 6838

Architecturally spectacular, this **museum** is in desperate need of refurbishment, as many of its interactive features only work sporadically. Nonetheless, the full-scale replica of the mural-filled room at Bonampak is great, especially if you'll be headed to those Chiapas ruins. An auditorium, meanwhile, hosts film screenings and free modern art displays. On the street in front, the *Alegoría del Mestizaje* sculpture is one of the most striking depictions of the popular theme of the intermingling of Spanish and Indigenous cultures, showing modern Mexico born of a conquistador and a Maya woman.

Museo de la Ciudad

Niños Héroes at Chapultepec • Charge

If you have a nostalgic streak, the city museum, with its romantic memorabilia of Chetumal's swashbuckling days, is a better use of your sightseeing time than the Maya museum. It's next to the **Centro Cultural de las Bellas Artes**, a striking 1936 neo-Maya-style compound, where there's usually live music on weekend evenings.

Maqueta Payo Obispo

C 22 de Enero near Av Reforma • Free

A Caribbean house contains this scale model of Chetumal as it looked in the 1920s, hand-carved by a resident with the perfectly *chetumaleño* name of Luís Reinhardt McLiberty. The small adjacent **museum** tells the story of the lighthouse barge *Chetumal*, with which the Mexican army helped establish the town and the country's border with British Honduras.

ARRIVAL AND DEPARTURE — CHETUMAL

By plane The airport, with services to Mexico City (2hr 15min), is 2km west of town.

By bus Chetumal's main bus station is on the north side of town, a short taxi ride from the centre. A bus ticket office in town, on Belice at Colón, handles long-haul services. A few second-class buses, including Mayab services to Cancún, actually depart from the dusty yard adjacent to this office – it's worth checking here for service before heading out to the main station.

Destinations Cancún (every 30min or so; 5hr 20min–6hr 25min), most via Tulum (3hr 5min–3hr 50min) and Playa del Carmen (4hr 10min–5hr); Escárcega (8 daily; 4hr) via Xpujil (2hr), for the Río Bec; Mahahual (2 daily at 10am & 10.10am, with additional services in Aug; 2hr); Mérida (5 daily first class; 6hr) and second-class Clase Europea and Mayab (around 10 daily; 6hr 30min); San Cristóbal de las Casas (3 daily at 2.35am, 10.05pm & 11.55pm; 15hr 10min–16hr 10min), via Palenque (7hr); Villahermosa (7 daily; 8hr 20min–9hr 10min).

By car Continental (983 832 2411, http://continentalcar.com), in the lobby of the *Capital Plaza Hotel* (see page 773), or Europcar, Niños Héroes 129, opposite *Los Cocos* (983 833 9959), and at the airport (983 107 9008, http://europcar.com.mx).

By combi The Terminal de Combis on Hidalgo at Primo de Verdad. Services include Bacalar (every 30min; 45min) and Nicolás Bravo (4 daily; 1hr 15min), for the nearest Río Bec sites.

TO BELIZE

Entry requirements Citizens of the UK, US, Canada, Australia and New Zealand do not need a visa to enter Belize. If you are planning to return to Mexico, make sure to keep your tourist card, or you will have to purchase another.

By bus Buses run frequently between Chetumal and Corozal (1hr), the closest town across the border. You must get off the bus and walk over the bridge at Subteniente López, 8km west of Chetumal. The cheapest, very rattle-trap buses leave from the mercado nuevo, 1km north of the centre on Calzada Veracruz (roughly 4am–5pm; more frequently in the morning). A few of these continue to Orange Walk (2hr 30min) and Belize City (5hr). First-class services – a bit more comfortable – run by Linea Dorada, San Juan and Premier Lines depart from the main bus station (5 daily; 3hr to Belize City), as do at least two buses a day to Flores in Guatemala (for Tikal, via Belize), one or more in the early morning (around 6am) and another at lunch time (around 12.45pm).

By water taxi From the *Muelle Fiscal* on the downtown waterfront, Water Jets International (+501 226 2194 in Belize, http://sanpedrowatertaxi.com) runs services (daily 3pm) to San Pedro on Ambergris Caye and Caye Caulker, as does San Pedro Belize Express (983 839 2324, http://belizewatertaxi.com; daily at 3.30pm). Buy tickets at the dock, from travel agents in town or via the companies' websites.

By car Cars rented in Mexico cannot generally be driven into Belize.

12

INFORMATION AND TOURS

Tourist information The main tourist office, on 5 de Mayo at Carmen Ochoa de Merino (Mon–Fri 9am–5pm; 983 832 2031), is friendly enough but not particularly knowledgeable. There are also information kiosks at the bus station and on the malecón at Hidalgo.

ACCOMMODATION

SEE MAP PAGE 772

Arges Lázaro Cardenas 212, between Niños Héroes and Juárez; http://hotelarges.com. The Lebanese-Yucatecan owner of this place is determined to make this blocky, Soviet-inspired hotel more appealing, with big, cleanish rooms at reasonable prices, a pool and free parking. **M$$**

Capital Plaza Hotel Niños Héroes 171; 800 712 1717. A centrally located, mid-range hotel, *Capital Plaza* has comfortable (if bland) en suites, plus numerous facilities including a restaurant, a swimming pool, a gym, car rental (Continental; see page 773) and an in-house travel agency. **M$$$**

Los Cocos Niños Héroes 134; http://hotelloscocos.com.mx. The pick of the downtown deluxe hotels with large, comfortable rooms (the "premier" category is worth the upgrade), a pool and a sprawling terrace bar and restaurant. Also has some very pleasant suites. **M$$$**

Juliet Efraín Aguilar 171; http://hoteljulietchetumal.com.mx. On a pedestrian walkway just off Niños Héroes, close to the old market, *Hotel Juliet* has clean all-white rooms with TVs, and fans or a/c. Bland, but comfortable enough. **M$$**

Ucúm Gandhi 167; 983 832 0711. One of the better deals in town, though it looks unpromising from the motel-like front section (where a few bargain rooms are a good price, but dim and noisy). Rooms in the back building, however, by the huge pool, are brighter and quieter, and have a choice of a/c or fan. **M$**

EATING

SEE MAP PAGE 772

The intersection of Niños Héroes and Obregón has the highest concentration of **restaurants**, while the stalls at the "old market", south of the Museo de la Cultura Maya, have good, inexpensive lunches.

Las Arracheras de Don José Blv Bahía, between Cozumel and Josefa Ortíz; 983 832 8895. The speciality of this sprawling terrace restaurant, very popular on weekend nights, is meat tacos of every kind, served with an array of fresh salsas. You can also get good-value steaks, stuffed baked potatoes and pastas. **M$$**

El Emporio Merino, just east of Reforma; 983 285 4373, https://facebook.com/EmporioChetumal. An excellent

Uruguayan restaurant in a historic wooden house – steaks are served with lashings of garlicky *chimichurri*, the empanadas make a tasty starter (for those with big appetites), and there's a good selection of South American wines. Follow the smell of grilled meat. M$$$$

Marisquería Mi Viejo Av Belice 166; 983 833 5342. This *bar familiar*, with a crooner onstage backed by a tired keyboard player, may not seem promising at first glance. But the food is a lot livelier: try the *sopa de mariscos*, which brims with purple squid tentacles and shrimp, or the *ceviche*. M$$$

Los Milagros Zaragoza, between Niños Héroes and 5 de Mayo; 983 832 4433. Enjoy a tasty, inexpensive breakfast at this little pavement café, busy day and night, with a real air of a locals-in-the-know hangout. M$$

Pantoja Gandhi at Av 16 de Septiembre; 983 832 3957. With a good comida corrida and hearty dishes like *mondongo* (tripe), *chilaquiles* and hefty tortas, this is a popular spot for a morning or midday meal. M$$

DIRECTORY

Banks and exchange Banks with ATMs cluster at the junction of Juárez and Obregón.

Consulates Belize, Genova 369 (Mon–Fri 9am–noon; 983 285 3511).

Internet Plenty of options, including Arba, with branches in the old market and opposite, on Aguilar.

Post office Plutarco Elias calles at 5 de Mayo.

Calderitas

Frequent buses depart Chetumal from Cristóbal Colón west of Niños Héroes, behind the Museo de la Cultura Maya, but do not go on to Oxtankah

12

At weekends, Chetumal descends en masse on the small seaside resort of **Calderitas**, just 6km north around the bay. You can hire a boat at *El Rincón de las Tortugas* bar (983 834 4220) for various day outings: to the beaches on the nearby empty island of Tamalcab; a tour around the bay to look for manatees (around 3hr); or to several other nature spots.

Oxtankah

7km north of Calderitas • Charge • Taxi from Chetumal

Established in the Classic period (200–600 AD), the ancient city of **Oxtankah** is more interesting for its recent history. It's allegedly the site of the first *mestizaje*, where

VISITING THE RÍO BEC SITES

The typical strategy for visiting this string of ruins is to spend the night in **Xpujil**, hire an early-morning taxi to visit **Calakmul** and **Balamkú**, and return to Xpujil to see the ruins in town in the late afternoon. You can then take a late bus to Chetumal or Campeche. If you have the time, though, it will be a more rewarding and relaxing visit if you take at least two days and allow yourself to see more. Renting a car in Campeche or Chetumal affords the most flexibility, but taking **taxis** can cost about the same amount, leaving you the option of continuing on a loop route rather than returning your car.

Using Xpujil as a base, taxis can be arranged through the hotels, though you'll usually get a slightly better rate if you deal directly with the drivers gathered at the crossroads in town. Rates vary depending on both the number of people and your bargaining skills; the most popular destinations include Calakmul, Balamkú, Kohunlich, Dzibanché, Chicanná, Becán and Xpujil.

If you're not in a hurry, it's also possible to start off sightseeing from Chetumal by taking a *combi* to the town of **Nicolás Bravo**, hiring a taxi from there to visit Dzibanché and Kohunlich, and then flagging down a second-class bus to Xpujil.

Alternatively, there are organized **tours** to Calakmul from Campeche (see page 693); if your Spanish is up to it, go with the experienced (but not very bilingual) team at Servidores Turísticos de Calakmul (983 871 6064), which runs the unofficial tourist office in Xpujil and a campsite in the biosphere reserve. Tours may costs more, but a good guide can really make the area come alive, as many of the sites have little or no signage.

shipwrecked conquistador Gonzalo Guerrero married into a Maya family and fathered mixed-race children – the origin story of modern Yucatán, and Mexico. What remains are the ruins of several buildings around two squares, with an architectural style similar to that of the Petén region in Guatemala, and a chapel built by the Spanish. It's a peaceful wooded place, with trees and other flora neatly labelled.

Río Bec sites

West of Chetumal, along the border with Guatemala, lie the little-visited but dramatic **RÍO BEC** sites, many tucked in dense jungle that harbours diverse birds and beasts, especially in the Calakmul Biosphere Reserve, around the ruins of the same name. The area was once heavily populated by lowland Maya, and linked with the site of Tikal in Guatemala. The largest ruins here, with their long, low buildings, dramatic towers (really elongated, stylized pyramids) and intricate carvings, are easily as impressive as Chichén Itzá, heightened by the jungle setting. The area is accessible either from Campeche or from Chetumal, and you'll need to have a car or hire a taxi to see many of these sites – but this means you'll see few other tourists.

The largest town in the area is **Francisco Escárcega** (usually just called Escárcega), far to the west in Campeche state. It's a major bus hub, but somewhat dusty and unwelcoming, so most visitors to the sites use the much smaller village of **Xpujil**, on the border of Campeche and Quintana Roo, as a base for visiting the area. It's a one-street town straddling Hwy-186, with basic hotels and restaurants, as well as taxi drivers prepared to shuttle visitors around. If you're in your own car, note that there's a gas station just east of town.

Xpujil

Hwy-186 in Xpujil, 250m west of the bus station • Charge

The most accessible of the Río Bec sites, **Xpuhil** is also the smallest. Dating from between 500 and 750 AD, it is in excellent condition, and it has three striking ersatz pyramids, which have almost vertical and purely decorative stairways.

Becán

Off Hwy-186, 6km west of Xpujil then 500m north • Charge

Unique among Maya sites, the city of **Becán** is entirely surrounded by a dry moat, 16m wide and 5m deep. Along with the wall on its edge, it forms one of the oldest known defensive systems in Mexico. This has led some to believe that Becán, rather than present-day Flores in Guatemala, was the site of Tayasal, an early capital of the Itzá, who later ruled at Chichén Itzá. First occupied in 600 BC, Becán reached its peak between 600 and 1000 AD. Unlike the sites in northern Yucatán, many of the buildings here seem to have been residential rather than ceremonial. In fact, the tightly packed structures – with rooms stacked up and linked by internal staircases – create a strong sense of urbanism, akin to modern apartment blocks.

Chicanná

Off Hwy-186, 2km west of Becán and just south • Charge

The buildings at **Chicanná** are the precursors of the Chenes style, with their elaborate decoration and repetitive masks of Chac. The gaping, square-carved doorway at the impressive Structure II gives the site its name ("House of the Serpent Mouth"). The rest of the building is covered in smaller masks of hook-nosed Chac, made up of intricately carved mosaic pieces of limestone, many still painted with red stucco, in a style that was developed in this area and the adjacent Chenes cities, then picked up and refined by later builders in the Puuc region to the north.

Balamkú

Off Hwy-186, 5km west of the turn-off to Calakmul • Charge

This main draw at **Balamkú** is the elaborate, beautifully preserved 17m-long stucco frieze. It's inside the site's central palace; ask the caretaker to let you in. The embellished wall, crawling with toads, crocodiles and jaguars, seems to undulate in the dim light, and the rolling eyes of the red-painted monster masks, though smaller than those at Kohunlich (see page 777), are perhaps more alarming here.

Hormiguero

22km south of Xpujil • Free • Take a taxi and negotiate the waiting time

The small site of **Hormiguero** is accessible only by a bumpy, forty-minute ride, and a visit takes the same amount of time. But the decoration and the wild jungle setting make it a particularly transporting one. Excellently preserved carved monster mouths from the Late Classic era adorn the two excavated buildings, which are topped with impossibly steep towers. Keep your eyes on the forest floor here as you explore – Hormiguero has its name ("anthill") for good reason.

Río Bec

Off Hwy-186, 10km east of Xpujil and south of the *ejido* of 20 de Noviembre

The scattered buildings of the city of **Río Bec** are usually closed to visitors, though some years it opens for a few months in the spring. If you do visit, you will see the most extreme example of the Río Bec false-pyramid style: as at Xpujil, the "steps" on the twin towers were never meant to be climbed – the risers actually angle outward. Ask at the tourist office in Xpujil about arranging an expedition on horseback.

Calakmul

Off Hwy-186, down a signposted road midway between Escárcega and Xpujil • Charge, plus an extra fee to enter the reserve

The ruined Maya city of **Calakmul** is one of the best places for contemplating the culture's architectural legacy. The complex is only partially restored and a long drive south of Hwy-186, but its location in the heart of the jungle and its sheer size are awe-inspiring. Probably the biggest archeological area in Mesoamerica, Calakmul has nearly seven thousand buildings in the central area alone and more steles and pyramids than any other site; the great pyramid here is the largest Maya construction in existence, with a base covering almost five acres.

The view of the rainforest from the top is stunning, and on a clear day you can even glimpse the tip of the Danta pyramid at El Mirador in Guatemala. Arrive early (the gate to the biosphere on Hwy-186 opens at 7am) to look for **wildlife** such as wild turkeys, peccaries, toucans and jaguars. Even if you don't spot anything, you'll likely hear booming howler monkeys and raucous frogs. Plan to spend about four hours exploring the site – longer if you're a Maya-phile. Bring snacks and water, as there's no vending at the ruins.

Brief history

During the Classic period, the city had a population of about two hundred thousand and was the regional capital. A *sacbé* (Maya road) running between Calakmul and El Mirador (another leads on to Tikal) confirms that these cities were in regular communication. Calakmul reached its zenith between 500 and 850 AD but, along with most other cities in the area, it was abandoned by about 900 AD. Excavations begun in the 1980s have so far uncovered only a fraction of the buildings, the rest being earthen mounds. Some of Calakmul's treasures are on display in the archeological museum at Campeche (see page 692), including two hauntingly beautiful jade masks. Another mask was found in a tomb in the main pyramid in 1998.

Kohunlich

Off Hwy-186, about 60km west of Chetumal, then 9km south from the village of Francisco Villa • Charge

If you stop for only one ancient site in the Río Bec area, make it **Kohunlich**. The ruins, seldom visited by anyone other than enormous butterflies and wild parrots, are beautifully situated, peering out above the treetops. The buildings date from the late pre-Classic to the Classic periods (100–900 AD) and the majority are in the Río Bec architectural style. Foliage has reclaimed most of them, except for the **Templo de los Mascarones**, which is named after the five 2m-high stucco masks that decorate its facade. Disturbing enough now, these wide-eyed, open-mouthed images of the sun god, Kinich Ahau, once stared out from a background of smooth, bright-red-painted stucco. Also look for an elite residential area called the **27 Escalones**, worth the detour to see the great views over the jungle canopy from the cliff edge on which it is built (prime real estate was just as valuable 1400 years ago, it seems).

12

Kinichná and Dzibanché

North off Hwy-186 81km west of Chetumal • Charge

Set in a drier area sparsely populated with trees, these two neighbouring ruins are on a smaller scale than Kohunlich but still merit a visit. **Kinichná**'s hulking pyramid, built in metre-high stones layer upon layer by successive leaders, barely clears the trees, but you can look over the surrounding terrain (and spot a glimpse of the rather squat **Dzibanché**), now broken into farmland.

ARRIVAL AND DEPARTURE — RÍO BEC SITES

BY BUS

XPUJIL

From the bus stop in Xpujil, ADO (2 daily) and Mayab (4 daily) buses run to Chetumal, plus at least four more second-class services, a couple of which continue all the way to Cancún. To Escárcega, there are around fourteen departures, many continuing to Villahermosa. Second-class buses run north out of town, past the Chenes sites towards Hopelchén; most continue to Campeche, though some head to Mérida via the Ruta Puuc.

ESCÁRCEGA

The ADO first-class bus station is at the west end of town, at the junction of Hwy-261 and Hwy-186; from there, it's 1.5km to the east end and the Sur second-class bus station, which you might use for more frequent services to Xpuhil (you can buy tickets for all services at ADO).

Destinations from ADO Campeche (8 daily; 2hr); Chetumal (9 daily; 3hr 45min–4hr 30min); Mérida (7 daily; 4hr 40min); Palenque (5 daily;3hr 10min–3hr 40min); San Cristóbal de las Casas (3 daily; 11hr 25min–12hr 30min); Xpujil (5 daily; 2hr 5min).

BY CAR

If you're driving from Mérida or Campeche, the back route via Hopelchén and Hwy-269, arriving in Xpujil from the north, is a good road, narrow but usually empty. Expect a police checkpoint at the border between Yucatán and Campeche states.

INFORMATION AND TOURS

Tourist information At the east end of Xpujil, about 2km from the crossroads, ecotourism group Servidores Turísticos Calakmul runs an unofficial info office (Tues–Sun 9am–1pm & 4–7.30pm; 983 871 6064). The group can also arrange day tours and ecotourism activities, such as camping and hiking, though staff primarily speak Spanish.

FIESTAS IN THE YUCATÁN

A highlight of village festivals in the area is the massive bullrings, elaborate hand-built structures made entirely of saplings. Expect plenty of fireworks and *jaranas*, one of the traditional Maya dances. Carnaval, the week before Lent, is colourfully celebrated in Mérida and on Cozumel and Isla Mujeres. For events in smaller villages, ask at the Yucatán state tourism office in Mérida, which maintains a full list, or check the weekly events bulletin at http://yucatanliving.com, which often mentions nearby fiestas.

Fiesta de los Tres Reyes (Jan 1–6). In the cattle town of Tizimín (Yucatán); expect steak.

Día de la Candelaria (Feb 2). Candlemas: candlelight processions at Tecoh and Kantunil (Yucatán). The week prior is a fiesta in Valladolid (Yucatán).

Equinox (March 21). Huge gathering for the serpent shadow at Chichén Itzá.

Semana Santa (Holy Week, beginning Palm Sunday, variable March–April). Passion plays in Mérida, Acanceh and Maní (Yucatán).

Fiestas de Santa Cruz (end of April). Two-week fair in Cozumel's El Cedral (Quintana Roo), ending on or near May 3.

Fiesta de la Cruz Parlante (May 12–18). Chancah Veracruz (Quintana Roo), near Felipe Carrillo Puerto, celebrates the Talking Cross of the Caste Wars.

Feria del Jipi (May 20). In Becal (Campeche), celebration of the Panama hat.

Torneo de Pesca (last weekend in May). Fishing tournament and party in Puerto Morelos.

Día de la Chispa (June 4). In Valladolid (Yucatán), re-enactment of the battle that sparked the 1910 Revolution.

Fiesta de San Pedro y San Pablo (June 26–30). On Cozumel and in Panaba (Yucatán).

Fiesta de Nuestra Señora del Carmen (July 15–30). Ciudad del Carmen (Campeche) and Motul (Yucatán).

Chac ceremony (dates variable). In Edzná (Yucatán), to encourage the spring rains.

Feria (Aug 10–16). Town celebration in Oxcutzcab (Yucatán).

Feria de San Román (Sept 14–30). Campeche's city festival.

Gremios (mid-Sept to mid-Oct). Pilgrimages and processions to Mérida's main church.

Equinox (Sept 21). Another serpent spectacle at Chichén Itzá (see March).

Día de San Miguel (Sept 29). Cozumel's main town festival.

El Cristo de Sitilpech (Oct 18–28). The miraculous Black Christ is paraded from Sitilpech (Yucatán) to neighbouring Izamal, where there's ten days of celebration.

Feria del Estado de Yucatán (first three weeks of Nov). At fairgrounds south of Mérida.

Feria de Motul (Nov 4–11). Festival in Motul (Yucatán) with bullfights.

Día de la Inmaculada Concepcíon (Dec 8). Widely celebrated, especially in Izamal, where crowds gather to sing the entire night before.

Día de la Virgen de Guadalupe (Dec 12). Celebrated everywhere; roads are filled in the days prior with church groups running relays.

Christmas Fiesta (Dec 25–Jan 6). In Temax (Yucatán), featuring the procession of Las Pastorelas, in which images of the Holy Family are carried from house to house.

ACCOMMODATION AND EATING

XPUJIL

Calakmul About 500m west of the bus station, Xpuhil; 983 871 6029. Of the two main places to stay in Xpujil (the other is the *Mirador Maya*, another 500m west), this one is marginally preferable, with tidy and comfortable cabins with decent a/c and TVs. The perfectly functional restaurant stays open a little later than most things in town and is good for simple snacks and drinks. M$

CHICANNÁ

Chicanná Ecovillage Resort Hwy-186, across the highway from the Chicanná site; 981 811 9192, http://chicannaecovillageresort.com. The most comfortable rooms (in cute thatched-roof bungalows) in the area – though the "eco" label isn't really accurate. If you're breaking a sweat sightseeing, you can also stop by here for a drink at the restaurant and a dip in the pool. It also has great access to local nature trails. M$$

CALAKMUL

Rio Bec Dreams Hwy-186 km 142, west of Calakmul turn; http://riobecdreams.com. A smaller lodging option, as well as a great travellers' resource: the owners are archeology buffs who can advise on the latest site openings and arrange good tours. The restaurant, with its varied (non-Mexican) menu, is open to all. Rooms include en-suite cabañas (quieter, as they're away from the road) or wood "jungalows" on stilts with shared toilets. M$$$

Yaax' Che Calakmul reserve road km 7; www.ecoturismocalakmul.com.mx. Servidores Turísticos Calakmul, an excellent ecotourism organization, maintains this campsite with basic cabañas and space for tents. It also rents gear and will point you to nature trails within the reserve. You can try stopping in for a meal, but as the kitchen uses all local products, it may not have provisions on hand in slow seasons. M$

KOHUNLICH

Explorean Km 6.5, a 40min drive from Chetumal; http://explorean.com. The most luxurious hotel in the region, by some distance, *Explorean* provides accommodation in delightful bungalows, plus a well-equipped spa and a lovely pool. A wide range of tours is on offer, and rates are all-inclusive. M$$$$

ESCÁRCEGA

Hotel Real Primaveras C 55 s/n; https://facebook.com/real.primaveras. If you're stuck overnight in Escárcega, this is a good mid-range choice. All the en suites here are bright and well equipped (a/c, TVs, etc), and there's a café and small terrace. M$$

La Teja Southwest across the traffic circle from the ADO station; 982 824 0635. For a bite to eat in Escárcega, this is one of the nicer options, and convenient for the bus station. All the usual Mexican and Yucatecan dishes are on offer, with fresh juices too. M$$

HERNÁN CORTÉS ENTERING CHOLULA

Contexts

History

The modern, independent nation of Mexico has existed since 1821, yet its people are descended from civilizations that date back thousands of years. Our knowledge of these peoples is largely taken from histories recorded long after the events or from archeological conjecture, as the Spanish did their best to erase all traces of the extraordinary societies that preceded them.

Early civilizations

The first signs of settled habitation in Mexico – the cultivation of corn, followed by the emergence of crude pottery, stone tools and even some trade – come from the **Archaic** period, around 8000 to 2000 BC. The first established civilization did not appear until the **pre-Classic** or **Formative** era (2000 BC to 250 AD) with the rise of the Olmecs.

The Olmecs (1500–400 BC)

Still the least understood of all the ancient societies, the **Olmecs** thrived in the low-lying coastal jungles of Tabasco and Veracruz. Many of their political, cultural, artistic and architectural innovations can be observed in later Mesoamerican cultures (including **ritual blood-letting** and the **ball game**, and possibly even writing and the Long Count calendar). What you see of them in the museums today is a magnificent artistic style, exemplified in their sculpture and famous colossal basalt heads. These, with their puzzling "baby-faced" features, were carved from monolithic blocks and somehow transported over 90km from the quarries to their final settings – proof in itself of a hierarchical society commanding a sizeable workforce. By the end of the pre-Classic period, the Olmec civilization was already in decline – **La Venta**, the most important cultural centre, seems to have been abandoned around 400 BC, and the other towns followed over the next few hundred years.

Classic civilizations

As the Olmec weakened, new civilizations grew in strength and numbers, establishing cities throughout central Mexico. These sites, such as **Monte Albán** (500 BC–750 AD) near Oaxaca, were obviously influenced by the earlier Olmec. To the north, in the Valley of México, **Tlatilco** (1200–200 BC) hoarded Olmec objects, suggesting significant contact with Monte Albán – at least through trade. Meanwhile, there were hints of bigger things to come: **Cuicuilco** (700 BC–150 AD, now in the capital's suburbs) was an important city until it was buried by a volcanic eruption around the beginning of the first century AD; at the same time, the first major buildings of the city of Teotihuacán were being constructed.

Teotihuacán (100 BC–600 AD)

Teotihuacán, the first truly urban Mesoamerican society, dominated central Mexico at the beginning of the **Classic** period (250–900 AD). Its architectural and religious

8000–2000 BC	2000 BC–250 AD	250–900 AD
Archaic period.	Pre-Classic period. Rise and dominance of the Olmecs.	Classic period. Teotihuacán dominates central Mexico. Maya cities flourish in the highlands of Guatemala and Honduras, as well as the Mexican Yucatán.

THE WORLD TREE – PRE-COLUMBIAN BELIEF

The great **Mesoamerican civilizations** comprised some of the purest theocracies the world has known. Every aspect of life was a part of a cosmic interplay between the material world and the dreamlike spirit world, home to a pantheon of gods and the souls of dead ancestors. The priests and kings who governed Mesoamerica had privileged access to this realm, communicating with its denizens while in a state of trance, predicting the effect of the spiritual on the material from the motion of the stars, and maintaining the balance between the two worlds, thus avoiding misfortune or disaster. Every part of life was sacred, as were the days of the week and the cardinal points with their associated deities and spiritual properties. Every event, from the planting of crops to the waging of war, had to occur at the correct spiritual time.

One stele at the Olmec site of La Venta depicts what is thought to be the first representation of the **World Tree**, a symbol of the "axis mundi" at the centre of the Mesoamerican universe: its roots in the earth, its branches in the heavens, linking the underworld with the earth and sky. In contemporary Mexico, Day of the Dead celebrations have their roots in this shamanic conception of the universe, as do the rituals of modern Mexican witchcraft. The best modern examples, though, are the belief systems of the tribes of northern Mexico, such as the Yaqui (whose shamanic traditions have been immortalized by Carlos Castaneda) or the Huichol.

influences reached as far south as the Maya heartland of Guatemala. Even today, the ruins of the city, with the great Pyramids of the Sun and Moon, are an impressive testimony to the civilization's strength. Very little is known about Teotihuacán (even the name was coined later by the Aztecs – it means "the place where men became gods"), but what is certain is that the city's period of dominance ended between 500 and 600 AD, and that within a century it had been abandoned altogether. Mysteriously, several societies throughout Mesoamerica, particularly the Maya, seem to have been disrupted at around the same time.

Other important centres grew up on the Gulf coast at **El Tajín** (600–1200 AD), part of the **Classic Veracruz culture**, and in the **Zapotec** areas around Monte Albán – but were followed by rapid decline. There are numerous theories to account for this, but none is entirely convincing, although the fall of Teotihuacán must have affected its trading partners throughout Mexico. In all likelihood, once started, the disasters – probably provoked by some sort of agricultural failure or ecological disaster – led to a loss of faith in rulers and perhaps even rebellion, and had a knock-on effect.

The Maya

The best known and most romanticized of the classic civilizations is the **Maya**, in part because of the wealth of architectural remains and carvings they left behind in ancient cities throughout modern Mexico, Guatemala and Honduras. The great Maya centres to the south survived longer than Teotihuacán, but by around 800 AD had also been abandoned in what has become one of history's greatest unsolved mysteries. In the Yucatán the Maya fared rather better, their cities revived from about 900 by an injection of ideas from central Mexico and, archeologists now propose, new leaders from the south. The famous structures at **Chichén Itzá** mostly date from this later phase, around 900 to 1100 AD.

900–1520 AD	1325	1519	1521
Post-Classic period. The Toltecs make their capital at Tula.	Foundation of the Aztec capital of Tenochtitlán.	Cortés lands in present-day Veracruz.	Tenochtitlán falls to the Spanish and their Tlaxcalan allies; Cortés personally tortures and kills Cuauhtémoc, the last emperor, in 1525.

THE LONG COUNT CALENDAR

The Mesoamericans believed that the relationship between the spirit and material worlds was recorded in the stars. For both the Maya and Aztecs, the stars were embodiments of gods and the constellations re-enactments of cosmic events. This preoccupation led to the invention of the **calendar**, probably by the Zapotecs of Monte Albán around 600 BC. By the time of the Classic Maya (250–900 AD), a 260-day calendar had become the fundamental map of the relationship between the spirit and material worlds, and the highest tool of prediction and divination outside the trance state itself. Every number and day had its own significance; each of the twenty day names was connected with a specific god and a particular direction, passing in a continuous anticlockwise path from one day to the next until a cycle of time was completed. This calendar was used alongside a 365-day calendar, roughly matching the solar year, but lacking the leap days necessary to give it real accuracy. This was divided into eighteen groups of twenty days plus an unlucky additional five days. Each twenty-day grouping and each solar year also had a supernatural patron. When the two calendars were set in motion and were running concurrently, it took exactly 52 years for the cycle to repeat. In addition to these two calendars, the pre-Classic Maya developed what is known as the **Long Count**, recording the total number of days elapsed since a mythological date when the first great cycle began (August 11, 3114 BC, to be exact). For Mesoamerican civilizations, the ending of one cycle and the beginning of another heralded apocalypse and, afterwards, a new age and a reassertion of the ordered world from the disordered and demonic; one symbol of this new age was the construction of new temples over the old every 52 years. The Maya Long Count ended on **December 23, 2012**; many believed that this date would herald the end of the world.

The post-Classic era and the Toltecs

The start of the **post-Classic** era (900–1520 AD) saw the beginning of a series of invasions from the north that must have exacerbated any existing problems. Wandering tribes would arrive in the fertile Valley of México, like what they saw, build a city adopting many of the styles and religions of their predecessors in the area, enjoy a brief period of dominance and be subdued in turn by a new wave of invaders, or **Chichimeca**. All such marauding tribes were known as Chichimea, which implies barbarian (even if many of them were at least semi-civilized before they arrived), and all claimed to have set out on their journeys from the legendary seven caves of Chicomoztoc. Of the many people who founded cities in the valley in this bellicose era, two names stand out – the Toltecs and the Aztecs.

The **Toltec** people, who dominated the central valleys around 950–1150 AD, were among the first to arrive – indeed, some say that it was a direct attack by them that destroyed Teotihuacán. Later, they assumed a mythical significance for the Aztecs, who regarded them as the founders of every art and science and claimed direct descent from Toltec blood. In fact, it appears that the Toltecs borrowed most of their ideas from Teotihuacán.

Nevertheless, there were developments under the Toltecs. In particular, the cult of **Quetzalcoatl** assumed new importance: at **Tula**, the Toltec capital, the god is depicted everywhere, perhaps embodied as a king or dynasty of kings, and it was from here that he was driven out by the evil god Texcatlipoca. (The prediction of his return was

1524	1546	1550–90	1551–1687	1683
The first Franciscan monks arrive.	The Spanish discover silver in the Zacatecas region.	The Chichimeca War.	Spanish conquest of the Yucatán.	Jesuit priest Eusebio Kino founds Misión San Bruno in Baja California.

later to have fatal consequences for the Aztecs.) The structure of Toltec society was at least as militaristic as it was religious, and human sacrifice was practised on a far larger scale than had previously been recorded.

The Aztecs (1325–1521 AD)

When the **Aztecs** arrived in central Mexico around the end of the twelfth century they found numerous small city-states, with none in a position of dominance. They spent some years scavenging and raiding until about 1325 – when legend has it that they saw the prophesied sign (an eagle perched on a cactus devouring a snake) telling them to build their own city.

The new city, **Tenochtitlán**, was to become the heart of the most formidable of all Mexican empires, but its birth was not easy. The chosen setting, an island in a lake (now Mexico City), was hardly promising, and the city was at first a subject of its neighbours. The Aztecs overcame the lack of arable land by growing crops on floating reed islands that they fashioned in the lake. This agricultural success led to self-sufficiency and a burgeoning population. They became the most powerful civilization in the valley, and around 1428 formed the so-called Triple Alliance with neighbouring Texcoco and Tlacopán, establishing the **Aztec empire**. The empire's achievements were remarkable – in less than a hundred years the Aztecs came to control and to demand labour tribute and taxes from the whole of central and southern Mexico. Tenochtitlán grew huge – the invading Spanish could not believe its size and grandeur – but even as it expanded, the gods continued to demand more war: to suppress rebellious subjects, and to capture fresh victims for the constant rituals of human sacrifice.

Meanwhile, other societies had continued much as they had before the Aztec rise. In present-day Oaxaca, the Zapotecs were subjected to invasions by **Mixtecs** from the mountains. By war and alliance the Mixtecs came eventually to dominate this region – developing the trades of the potter and goldsmith as never before – and fell to the Aztecs only in the last years before the Spanish Conquest. In the Yucatán, the **Maya** were never conquered, but their civilization was in decline and any form of central authority had broken down into city-states. Nevertheless, they carried on trade all around the coasts, and Christopher Columbus himself (though he never got to Mexico) encountered a heavily laden boat of Maya traders, plying the sea between Honduras and the Yucatán. On the Gulf coast Aztec supremacy was total by the time the Spanish arrived, but they were still struggling to subdue the west.

The Spanish Conquest

Perhaps the most driven, ruthless and most spectacularly successful conquistador of all time, **Hernán Cortés** (1485–1547) was born in Medellín, Spain, to a family of lower nobility. He arrived in the New World in 1504, a colonist in Hispaniola, but soon earned his military stripes as a soldier in Cuba; it was from the latter that he launched the expedition that landed on the Mexican coast near modern Veracruz in the spring of 1519. With him were just 550 men, a few horses, dogs and a cannon; yet less than three years later the Spaniards had defeated the Aztecs and effectively established control over most of Mexico. Several factors enabled them to do so. First was Cortés

1697	1767	1810	1815
Juan María Salvatierra founds the Loreto Jesuit mission in Baja.	The Jesuits are expelled from Mexico.	Hidalgo proclaims Mexican Independence with the Grito de Dolores. He is executed in 1811.	Rebel leader José María Morelos is executed.

THE GODS RETURN?

The legend goes that a great Toltec prince **Topiltzin Quetzalcoatl**, renowned for his wisdom and holiness and founder of the great city of Tula, decided to make an end to human sacrifice and attempted to convince the inhabitants of Tula to give it up. He was unsuccessful, however, as the shamanic god, Tezcatlipoca, tricked the Toltecs and forced Topiltzin Quetzalcoatl into exile. Topiltzin Quetzalcoatl built a raft and left "for the east" from the Gulf coast, promising to return one day to banish false rulers and reinstate a higher order, where human sacrifice would play no part. It is a well-known irony that Cortés landed on the Gulf coast, whence Topiltzin Quetzalcoatl was said to have left, at the time predicted for his return. But did this really lead to the fall of the Aztec empire? Probably not – most modern scholars claim that the story of Moctezuma believing Cortés to be the returning Quetzalcoatl actually developed after the Spanish Conquest.

himself: he burned the expedition's boats within days of their arrival, so that there was literally no turning back. In addition, his men had little to lose and much to gain, and their metal weapons and armour were greatly superior to anything the Aztecs had (although many Spaniards adopted Aztec-style padded cotton, which was warmer, lighter and almost as protective). Their gunpowder and cannon could also wreak havoc on opposing armies, both physically and psychologically. The horses and attack dogs, too, terrified the Aztecs. None of these, though, in the end counted a fraction as much as Cortés' ability to form alliances with tribes who were chaffing under Aztec subjugation and whose numbers eventually swelled his armies tenfold.

Moctezuma

Moctezuma, the Aztec leader, could certainly have destroyed the Spanish before they left their first camp, since his spies had brought news of their arrival almost immediately. Instead he sent a delegation bearing gifts of gold and jewels, which he hoped would persuade them to leave in peace. This served only to inflame the greed of the Spanish. By all accounts Moctezuma was a morose, moody and indecisive man, but his failure to act against Cortés had deeper roots: he was heavily influenced by religious omens, and the arrival of Cortés coincided with the predicted date for the return of **Quetzalcoatl**. The invaders were fair-skinned and bearded, as was Quetzalcoatl, and they had come from the east, where the deity had vanished (though we'll never really know what Moctezuma really believed; see page 785). Although he put obstacles in their way, even persuading his allies to fight them, when the Spanish finally reached Tenochtitlán in November 1519, Moctezuma welcomed them as his guests. They promptly repaid his hospitality by taking him prisoner within his own palace.

The Pánfilo de Narváez expedition

This first phase of the Conquest, during which Spanish troops skirmished with a number of other Indigenous people and made allies of many – most significantly the **Tlaxcalans** – lasted for about a year. In April 1520 news came of a second Spanish expedition, led by **Pánfilo de Narváez** (1478–1528), who was under orders from the governor of Cuba to capture Cortés and take him back (Cortés' mission had always been unofficial, and many others hoped to seize the wealth of Mexico for themselves).

1821	**1824**	**1833**	**1836**
Independence is achieved; Agustin de Iturbide declares himself emperor.	Iturbide is executed; the Mexican republic is founded under President Guadalupe Victoria	Santa Anna becomes president.	Texas declares independence following the battles of the Alamo and San Jacinto.

THE DESTRUCTION OF NATIVE MEXICO

When the Spaniards arrived, the **native population** of central Mexico was at least 25 million; by the beginning of the nineteenth century the total population of Nueva España was just six million, and at most half of these were Indigenous. Some had been killed in battle, a few as a result of ill-treatment or simply from being left without homes or land to live on, but the vast majority died as a result of **successive epidemics** of European diseases (mainly smallpox, influenza and hepatitis) to which the New World had no natural immunity. The few survivors found the burden of labour placed on them ever-increasing as their numbers dwindled – for certainly no European came to Mexico to do manual work – and became more and more like slaves. Today the government counts just under ten million Mexicans as Indigenous (around ten percent of the population), mostly living in the central and southern states. They remain some of the poorest people in the country.

Again, though, Cortés proved the more decisive commander – he marched back east, surprised Narváez by night, took him prisoner and persuaded most of his troops to switch allegiance.

Noche Triste

Meanwhile, the Spaniards left behind in Tenochtitlán had finally provoked their hosts beyond endurance by killing a group of Aztec priests during a religious ceremony, and were under siege in their quarters. Cortés, with his reinforcements, fought his way back into the city on June 24, only to find himself trapped as well. On June 27, Moctezuma (still a prisoner) was killed – stoned to death by his own people while attempting to appeal for peace according to the Spanish, though rumour has it that he was garrotted by Cortés himself. Finally Cortés decided to break out on the night of June 30 – still commemorated as **Noche Triste** – when the Spanish lost over half their number on the causeways across the lake. Most of them were so weighed down with gold and booty that they were barely able to move, let alone swim in the places where the bridges had been destroyed.

The fall of Tenochtitlán

Once more, though, the Aztecs failed to follow up their advantage, and the Spanish survivors managed to reach their allies in Tlaxcala, where they regrouped. The final assault on Tenochtitlán began in January 1521, with more supplies and fresh troops, tens of thousands of whom were Tlaxcalans and other Indigenous people. The city, besieged, was also ravaged by an epidemic of smallpox, among whose victims was Moctezuma's successor, Cuitláhuac. The Aztecs held out for several more months under **Cuauhtémoc** – in Mexican eyes the only hero of this long episode – but on August 13, 1521, Tenochtitlán finally fell to the Spanish. Although much of the country remained to be pacified, the defeat of the Aztec capital made it inevitable that it would be.

Spanish colonial rule (1521–1810)

By dint of his success, Cortés was appointed governor of this new territory, although in practice he was watched over by minders from Spain and never had much real

1846	1848	1852–55	1858–61
The Mexican-American War begins.	In the Treaty of Guadalupe Hidalgo half of Mexico's territory is ceded to US.	Santa Anna returns to power.	The Reform Wars between liberals under Benito Juárez and Church-backed conservatives.

freedom of action (he was to die a wealthy but embittered man back in Spain in 1547). In 1535 **Nueva España** (New Spain) was formally established. There followed nearly three centuries of direct Spanish rule, under a succession of 61 viceroys responsible to the Spanish king. By the end of the sixteenth century the entire country had effectively been subjugated, its boundaries stretched by exploration from Panama to the western states of the current US (although the area from Guatemala south, including the Mexican state of Chiapas, was administered by the Audiencia of Guatemala from 1543).

The first tasks, in the Spanish mind, were reconstruction, pacification and conversion. At first there was quite remarkable progress: hundreds of towns were laid out according to a plan drawn up in Spain, with a plaza surrounded by a grid of streets. Thousands of churches were built (by 1800, the count reached twelve thousand), often in areas that had been sacred to the Indigenous people, or on top of their pyramids; mass conversions were the order of the day. In a sense the Indigenous peoples were used to all this – the Aztecs and their predecessors had behaved in a similar manner – but they had never experienced a slavery like that which was to follow.

The Church, which at first championed Indigenous rights and attempted to record native legends and histories and educate the children, grew more and more concerned with money. Any attempt to treat the Indigenous people as human was, in any case, violently opposed by Spanish landowners, to whom they were rather less than machines (in fact, cheaper than machinery, and therefore more expendable). By the end of the colonial era, the Church owned more than half of all the land and wealth in the country, yet most native villages would be lucky to see a priest once a year.

In a sense Mexico was a wealthy nation – certainly the richest of the Spanish colonies – but its riches were confined to the local elite and the nobility in Spain. No local trade or agriculture that would compete with Spain was allowed, so the cultivation of vines or the production of silk was banned; heavy taxes on other products – coffee, sugar, tobacco, cochineal, silver and other metals – went directly to Spain or to still poorer colonies. Since the Flota de Indias (the Spanish treasure fleet) sailed between Veracruz and Spain just once a year and was even then subject to the vagaries of piracy, this was a considerable handicap.

Even among the wealthy Spanish-descended landowners there was growing **resentment**, fuelled by the status of those among them born in Mexico: only *peninsulares* or "**gachupines**", Spaniards born in Spain, could hold high office in the government or Church. Of the six million people in Mexico in 1800, only forty thousand were *gachupines* – the rest were **criollos** (creoles, born in Mexico of Spanish blood) who were generally educated, wealthy and aristocratic, and **mestizos** (of mixed race) who dominated the lower ranks of the Church, army and civil service, or lived as anything from shopkeepers and small ranchers to bandits and beggars.

The struggle for independence

By the beginning of the nineteenth century Spain's status as a world power was in severe decline. At the same time, new political ideas were transforming the world; although the works of such political philosophers as Rousseau, Voltaire and Paine were banned in Mexico, the opening of the ports in 1796 made it inevitable that their ideas would spread. Literary societies set up to discuss these books quickly became centres of **political dissent**.

1861	1861–67	1863	1867
Juárez is triumphant, and suspends payment of foreign debt. France, Spain and Britain send naval expeditions.	France invades Mexico.	The French take Mexico City, and Maximilian becomes emperor.	Juárez defeats Maximilian, and restores the Republic.

The spark, though, came when the French invaded Spain in 1808, and Napoleon placed his brother Joseph on the throne. Colonies throughout Latin America refused to recognize the Bonaparte regime. In Mexico, the *gachupine* rulers proclaimed their loyalty to Ferdinand VII (the deposed king) and hoped to carry on much as before, but creole discontent was not so easily assuaged. The literary societies continued to meet, and from one, in Querétaro, emerged the first leaders of the Independence movement: **Father Miguel Hidalgo y Costilla** (1753–1811), a creole priest, and **Ignacio Allende** (1769–1811), a disaffected junior army officer.

The Grito de Dolores

When their plans for a coup were discovered, the conspirators were forced into premature action, with Hidalgo issuing the famous *Grito de Dolores* (culminating in the rallying cry, *Méxicanos, viva México!*) from his parish church in Dolores on September 16, 1810 – the day is still celebrated as **Independence Day**. The mob of Indigenous people and *mestizos* who gathered behind the banner swiftly took the towns of San Miguel, Guanajuato and others to the north of the capital, but their behaviour – seizing land and property, slaughtering the Spaniards – horrified the wealthy creoles who had initially supported them. In spring 1811, Hidalgo's army, huge but undisciplined, moved on the capital, but at the crucial moment Hidalgo threw away a clear chance to overpower the royalist army. Instead he chose to retreat, and his forces broke up as quickly as they had assembled. Within months, Hidalgo, Allende and the other ringleaders had been captured and executed.

The rise and fall of José María Morelos

By this time most creoles had rejoined the ranks of the royalists. However, many *mestizos* and much of the Indigenous population remained in a state of revolt, with a new leader in the *mestizo* priest **José María Morelos** (1765–1815). Morelos was not only a far better tactician than Hidalgo – instituting a highly successful series of guerrilla campaigns – he was also a genuine radical. By 1813 he controlled virtually the entire country, with the exception of the capital and the route from there to Veracruz, and at the **Congress of Chilpancingo** he declared the abolition of slavery and the equality of the races. The royalists, however, fought back with a series of crushing victories. Morelos was executed in 1815, and his forces, led by **Vicente Guerrero** (1782–1831), were reduced to carrying out the occasional minor raid.

Independence

Ironically, it was the introduction of liberal reforms in Spain, of just the type feared by the Mexican ruling classes, which finally brought about **Mexican Independence**. Worried that such reforms might spread across the Atlantic, many creoles pre-empted a true revolution by assuming a "revolutionary" guise themselves. In 1820, **Agustín de Iturbide** (1783–1824), a royalist general but himself a *mestizo*, threw in his lot with Guerrero; in 1821, he proposed the **Iguala Plan** to the Spanish authorities, who were hardly in a position to fight, and Mexico was granted independence. With self-determination, though, came none of the changes which had been fought over for so long – the Church retained its power, and one set of rulers had simply been changed for another, local, set.

1876

Porfirio Díaz accedes to power.

1882

Influential writer and thinker José Vasconcelos is born in Oaxaca.

1886

Diego Rivera is born in Guanajuato.

1910

Francisco Madero stands for election, sparking the Revolution.

THE PASTRY WAR

One of the most bizarre episodes in Mexican history began in 1838, when a French pastry chef claimed that his *patisserie* in Mexico City had been looted during the lawless disorder of the previous decade. With an eye on huge debts owed to France by Mexico, French king Louis Philippe happily followed up the claim; when compensation was not forthcoming the French invaded **Veracruz**. The "**Pastry War**" lasted about four months, during which Santa Anna lost a leg, and ended with President Bustamante promising to pay the French 600,000 pesos.

The first republic

In 1822, Iturbide proclaimed himself emperor; a year later, deserted by many of his former allies, he was forced to abdicate and go into exile, and a year after that, attempting to return to the country, he was arrested and executed by firing squad. In 1824 the country was officially proclaimed the **United Mexican States**, a **federal republic**.

It was the first of many such events in a century which must rank among the most confused – and disastrous – in any nation's history. Not only had Independence brought no real social change, it had left the new nation with virtually no chance of successful government: the power of the Church and of the army was far greater than that of the supposed rulers; there was no basis on which to create a viable economy; and if the state hadn't already been bankrupted by the Independence struggle, it was to be cleaned out time and again by the demands of war and internal disruption. There were no fewer than 56 governments in the next forty years. In what approaches farce, the name of former Spanish soldier **General Antonio López de Santa Anna** (1794–1876) stands out as the most bizarre figure of all – the man became president or dictator on eleven separate occasions and masterminded the loss of more than half of Mexico's territory.

The era of Santa Anna

Under the auspices of the 1824 constitution the country was divided into thirteen states and **Guadalupe Victoria** (1786–1843), a former guerrilla general, elected its first president. He lasted three years, something of a record. In 1829, the Spanish attempted a rather half-hearted **invasion**, easily defeated, after which they accepted the fact of Mexican independence. In 1833, Santa Anna was elected president (officially) for the first time, the fifth man to hold the post thus far.

In 1836, a rather more serious chain of events was set in motion when Texas (Mexican territory but largely inhabited by migrants from the US) declared its independence. Santa Anna commanded a punitive expedition that besieged **the Alamo** in the famous incident in which Jim Bowie and Davy Crockett, along with 150 other defenders, lost their lives. Santa Anna himself, though, was promptly defeated and captured at the subsequent battle of **San Jacinto**, and rather than face execution he signed a paper accepting **Texan independence**.

Mexican-American War (1846–48)

In 1845, the **US annexed Texas**, and although the Mexicans at first hoped to negotiate a settlement, the redefinition of Texas to include most of Arizona, New Mexico and California made yet another war almost inevitable. In 1846, clashes between Mexican

1911	1913	1917	1919–20
Madero wins the election; Díaz flees into exile.	Madero is murdered; Huerta becomes president.	Mexican Constitution adopted; Carranza becomes president.	Zapata and Carranza are assassinated.

troops and US cavalry in these western zones led to the declaration of the **Mexican-American War**. Following defeats for the Mexicans at Palo Alto and Resaca, three small US armies invaded from the north. At the same time General Winfield Scott took Veracruz after a long bombardment, and commenced his march on the capital. Santa Anna was roundly defeated several times, and in September 1847, after legendary resistance by the Niños Héroes (cadets at the military academy), Mexico City itself was captured. In 1848, by the **Treaty of Guadalupe Hidalgo**, the US paid $15 million for Texas, New Mexico, Arizona and California, along with parts of Colorado and Utah; in 1854, the present borders were established when Santa Anna sold a further strip down to the Río Grande for $10 million under the **Gadsden Purchase**.

La Reforma

Mexico finally saw the back of Santa Anna when, in 1855, he left for exile (he would return to die in Mexico in 1876), but the country's troubles were by no means at an end. A new generation had grown up, knowing only an independent Mexico in permanent turmoil and espousing once more the liberal ideals of Morelos. Above all, this generation saw its enemy as **the Church**: immense, self-serving and far wealthier than any legitimate government, it had further sullied its reputation by refusing to provide funds for the American war. Its position enshrined in the constitution, it was an extraordinarily reactionary institution, bleeding the peasantry for the most basic of sacraments (few could afford official marriage, or burial) and failing to provide the few services with which it was charged. All education was in Church schools, which for 95 percent of the population meant no education at all.

The rise of Benito Juárez

Benito Juárez (1806–72), a Zapotec Indigenous person from Oaxaca who had been adopted and educated by a priest and trained as a lawyer, led this liberal movement (La Reforma) through several years of civil war. When the **liberals** first came to power following Santa Anna's exile they began relatively mild attempts at **reform**: permitting secular education, liberating the press, attempting to distance the Church from government and instituting a new democratic constitution. The Church responded by threatening to excommunicate anyone cooperating with the government. In 1858, there was a conservative coup leading to the **War of Reform** for the next three years, **internal strife** on an unprecedented scale. With each new battle the liberals proclaimed more drastic reforms, churches were sacked and priests shot, while the conservatives responded by executing anyone suspected of liberal tendencies. In 1861, Juárez emerged triumphant, at least temporarily. Church property was confiscated, monasteries closed, weddings and burials became civil affairs and set fees were established for the services of a priest. It wasn't until 1867 that most of these **Reform Laws** were fully enacted, but the conservatives had one more card to play.

The French Intervention (1861–67)

At the end of the civil war, with the government bankrupt, Juárez had suspended payment of all foreign debts, and in 1861 a joint British, Spanish and French expedition occupied Veracruz to demand compensation. It rapidly became clear,

1920	1923	1924–28	1926–29
Álvaro Obregón becomes president.	Pancho Villa is assassinated.	The presidency of Plutarco Elías Calles.	The Cristero War.

however, that the French were after more than mere financial recompense. Britain and Spain withdrew their forces, and Napoleon III ordered his troops to advance on Mexico City. Supported by Mexican conservatives, the aim was to place **Maximilian** (1832–67), a Habsburg archduke, on the throne as emperor.

Despite a major defeat at **Puebla** on May 5, 1862 (now the **Cinco de Mayo** holiday), the French sent for reinforcements and occupied Mexico City in 1863. The new emperor arrived the following year. In many ways, Maximilian was a pathetic figure. He came to Mexico with almost no knowledge of its internal feuds (having gleaned most of his information from a book on court etiquette), and expecting a victorious welcome. A liberal at heart – he refused to repeal any of Juárez' reforms – he promptly lost the support of even the small group of conservatives who had initially welcomed him. While his good intentions seem undeniable, few believe that he would have been capable of putting them into practice even in the best of circumstances. And these were hardly ideal times. With Union victory in the **US Civil War**, the authorities there threw their weight behind Juárez, providing him with arms and threatening to invade unless the French withdrew (on the basis of the Monroe doctrine: America for the Americans). Napoleon III, already worried by the growing power of Bismarck's Prussia back home, had little choice but to comply. After 1866 Maximilian's position was hopeless. He stayed at the head of his vastly outnumbered troops to the end – May 15, 1867 – when he was defeated and captured at **Querétaro**. A month later, he faced the firing squad.

The restoration of the Republic

Juárez reassumed power in 1867, managing this time to ride through the worst of the inevitable bankruptcy. The first steps towards **economic reconstruction** were taken, with the completion of a railway from Veracruz to the capital, encouragement of industry and the development of a public education programme. Juárez died in office in 1872, having been re-elected in 1871, and was succeeded by his vice-president, **Sebastián Lerdo de Tejada** (1823–89), who continued on the same road, though with few new ideas.

The Porfiriato (1876–1910)

Tejada was neither particularly popular nor spectacularly successful, but he did see out his term of office. However, there were several **revolts** during his rule and a number of plots against him, the most serious of them led by a new radical liberal, **Porfirio Díaz** (1830–1915). Díaz had been a notably able military officer under Juárez, but in 1876, despite the re-election of Tejada, he assumed the presidency himself then consolidated power to effectively become **dictator** for the next 34 years. At first his platform was a radical one – including full implementation of the Reform Laws and a decree of no re-election to any political office – but this was soon dropped in favour of a brutal policy of **modernization**. Díaz did actually stand down at the end of his first term in 1880, but he continued to rule through a puppet president, Manuel González, and in 1884 resumed the presidency for an unbroken stretch until 1911.

In many ways the **achievements** of his dictatorship were remarkable: some 16,000km of railway were built, industry boomed, telephones and telegraph were installed and major towns, reached at last by reasonable roads, entered the modern era. In the countryside, Díaz established a police force – the notorious *rurales* – which

1929	**1934–40**	**1935**
The PRI is founded (initially known as the PRD or Party of the Democratic Revolution).	Lázaro Cárdenas becomes president.	Diego Rivera completes his mural cycle at the National Palace.

stamped out much of the banditry that had plagued the nation. Almost every city in Mexico seems to have a grandiose theatre and elegant public buildings from this era. But the costs were high: rapid development was achieved basically by handing over the country to **foreign investors**, who owned the majority of the oil, mining rights, railways and other natural resources. At the same time, there was a policy of massive land expropriation, in which formerly communal village holdings were handed over to foreigners or simply grabbed by corrupt officials.

Agriculture, meanwhile, was ignored entirely. The owners of vast haciendas could make more than enough money by relying on the forced labour of a landless peasantry, and had no interest in efficiency or production for domestic consumption. By 1900 the whole of Mexico was owned by some three to four percent of its population. Without land of their own, peasants had no choice but to work on haciendas or in forests, where their serfdom was ensured by wages so low that they were permanently in debt to their employers. The rich became very rich indeed, while the poor had lower incomes and fewer prospects than they had a century earlier. The press was censored, education strictly controlled and **corruption** rife.

The Mexican Revolution (1910–21)

By the onset of the **twentieth century**, Díaz was old and beginning to lose his grip on reality. While he had every intention of continuing in power until his death, a real middle-class opposition began to develop, concerned above all by the racist policies of their government (which favoured foreign investors above native ones) and by the lack of opportunity for themselves – the young educated classes.

Phase 1: Francisco Madero

In 1910 **Francisco Madero** (1873–1913) stood against Díaz in the presidential election. The dictator responded by imprisoning his opponent and declaring himself victor. Madero, however, escaped to Texas, where he proclaimed himself president, and called on the nation to support him.

This was an entirely opportunist move, for at the time there were no revolutionary forces, but several small bands immediately took up arms. Most important were those in the northern state of Chihuahua, where **Pancho Villa** (see page 448) and **Pascual Orozco** (1882–1915) won several minor battles, and in the southwest, where **Emiliano Zapata** (see page 794) began to arm Indigenous guerrilla forces. In May 1911, Orozco captured the major border town of Ciudad Juárez, and his success was rapidly followed by a string of Revolutionary victories. By the end of the month, hoping to preserve the system, if not his own role in it, Porfirio Díaz had fled into exile (he died in Paris in 1915). On October 2, 1911, Madero was formally declared president. He freed the press, encouraged the formation of unions and introduced genuine **democracy**, but failed to do anything about the condition of the peasantry or the redistribution of land.

Phase 2: Victoriano Huerta

Madero was immediately faced by a more dangerous enemy: US business interests. **Henry Lane Wilson**, US ambassador, began openly plotting with **Victoriano Huerta** (1850–1916), a government general, and **Felix Díaz**, a nephew of the dictator, who was held in prison.

1938	1940	1942–45	1943
Oil companies are nationalized into PEMEX.	Leon Trotsky is murdered in Mexico City.	Mexico sides with the Allies in World War II.	Football (soccer) becomes professional sport in Mexico.

Fighting broke out between supporters of Díaz and those of Madero, while Huerta refused to commit his troops to either side. When he did, in 1913, it was to proclaim himself president. Madero was shot in suspicious circumstances (few doubt an assassination sanctioned by Huerta), and opponents on the right, including Díaz, were either imprisoned or exiled. The new government was promptly recognized by the US and most other foreign powers, but not by Madero's former supporters within the country.

Phase 3: Constitution versus Convention

Villa and Zapata immediately took up arms against Huerta, and in the north Villa was joined by **Alvaro Obregón** (1880–1928), governor of Sonora, and **Venustiano Carranza** (1859–1920), governor of Coahuila. Carranza was appointed head of the **Constitutionalist** forces, though he was always to be deeply suspicious of Villa, despite Villa's constant protestations of loyalty. At first the Revolutionaries made little headway – Carranza couldn't even control his own state – although Obregón and Villa did enjoy some success raiding south from Chihuahua and Sonora. Almost immediately the new US president, **Woodrow Wilson**, withdrew his support from Huerta and, infuriated by his refusal to resign, began supplying arms to the Revolution.

In 1914, the Constitutionalists began to move south, and in April of that year **US troops occupied Veracruz** in their support (though neither side was exactly happy about the foreign presence). Huerta, now cut off from almost every source of money or supplies, fled the country in July (he was to die in a US jail), and in August Obregón occupied the capital, proclaiming Carranza president.

Renewed fighting broke out straight away, this time between Carranza and Obregón, the Constitutionalists, on one side, and the rest of the Revolutionary leaders on the other, the so-called **Conventionalists** whose sole point of agreement was that Carranza should not lead them. The three years of fighting that followed were the most bitter and chaotic yet, with petty chiefs in every part of the country proclaiming provisional governments, joining each other in factions and then splitting again, and the entire country in a state of anarchy. Each army issued its own money, and each forced any men it came across to join it. It is estimated that about nine hundred thousand people were killed between 1910 and 1921, out of a population of fifteen million.

Gradually, however, Obregón and Carranza gained ground – Obregón defeated Villa several times in 1915, and Villa withdrew to carry out raids into the US, in the hopes of provoking an invasion (which he nearly did: US troops led by General "Black Jack" Pershing pursued him across the border but were never able to catch up, and withdrew following defeat in a skirmish with Carranza's troops). Zapata, meanwhile, had some conspicuous successes – and occupied Mexico City for much of 1915 – but his troops tended to disappear back to their villages after each victory. In 1919, he was tricked into a meeting with one of Carranza's generals and assassinated. Villa retired to a hacienda in his home state and was murdered in 1923.

The Mexican Constitution of 1917

Meanwhile, Carranza continued to claim the presidency, and in 1917 he set up a constitutional **congress** to ratify his position. The document it produced – the present **Mexican Constitution** – included most of the Revolutionary demands, among them workers' rights, a mandatory eight-hour working day, national ownership of all

1954

Women are given the right to vote in Mexico. Painter Frida Kahlo dies.

1968

Mexico City hosts the Olympic Games; the Tlatelolco massacre takes place.

1970

Mexico hosts the World Cup; it hosts a second time in 1986.

¡TIERRA Y LIBERTAD!

Emiliano Zapata (1879–1919), born into a peasant family in Morelos, was perhaps the one true revolutionary in the whole long conflict of the Mexican Revolution. In 1911 he fell out with Madero over land reform, supporting instead the radical Plan de Ayala which called for massive land redistribution. He fought bitterly against Huerta, but tried to stay neutral during the Villa/Carranza conflict that followed; Carranza's general Pablo González eventually attacked Zapata's stronghold in the south, ambushing and killing the rebel leader in 1919. Zapata's battle cry of "**¡Tierra y libertad!**" ("Land and liberty!") and his insistence that "it is better to die on your feet than live on your knees" still make him a revered figure among the campesinos – and revolutionaries of the namesake EZLN – of the present day.

mineral rights and the distribution of large landholdings and formerly communal properties to the peasantry. Carranza was formally elected in May 1917 and proceeded to make no attempt to carry out any of its stipulations, certainly not with regard to land rights.

Final phase: the end of Revolution

In 1920, Carranza was forced to step down by Obregón, and was shot while attempting to reach Veracruz (though some suggest he killed himself). The inauguration of Obregón as President is generally regarded as the end of the core period of Revolution.

Obregón, at least, was well intentioned – but his efforts at land reform were again stymied by fear of US reaction: in return for American support, he agreed not to expropriate land. In 1924, **Plutarco Elías Calles** (1877–1945) succeeded him and initiated some real progress towards the ideals of the Revolutionary constitution. Large public-works schemes began – roads, irrigation systems, village schools – and about eight million acres of land were given back to the villages as communal holdings. At the same time, Calles instituted a policy of virulent **anticlericalism**, closing churches and monasteries and forcing priests to flee the country or go underground.

These moves provoked the last throes of a backlash, as the **Cristero War** (1926–29) in defence of the Church, a bitter conflict that claimed some ninety thousand lives. Isolated incidents of vicious banditry and occasional full-scale warfare continued until 1935, eventually burning themselves out as the stability of the new regime became obvious, and religious controls were relaxed. In 1928, Obregón was re-elected, but was assassinated three weeks later in protest at the breach of the "no reelección" clause of the constitution. He was followed by **Portes Gil**, **Ortíz Rubio** and then **Abelardo Rodríguez**, who were all controlled behind the scenes by Calles and his political allies, who steered national politics to the right in the bleak years of the 1930s Depression.

The road to modern Mexico

By 1934 Mexico enjoyed a limited degree of peace. A new culture had emerged – most boldly reflected in the great murals of **Diego Rivera** and **José Clemente Orozco** that began to adorn public buildings throughout the country – in which native heroes like Hidalgo, Morelos, Juárez and Madero replaced European ideals.

1985	1990	1992
The Mexico City earthquake kills at least ten thousand people.	Octavio Paz becomes the first Mexican to win the Nobel Prize for Literature.	NAFTA comes into force; Zapatista uprising in Chiapas; Mexican peso crisis (aka the "Tequila crisis") caused by the sudden devaluation of the currency.

THE TLATELOLCO MASSACRE

Embarrassed by protests of around ten thousand pro-democracy students in Mexico City, just days before Mexico was to host the Olympic Games of 1968, the PRI government ordered a heavy-handed crackdown that soon got out of control; in the chaos that followed at least forty students were killed – exact numbers are still disputed (estimates range from thirty to three hundred). Indeed, the **Tlatelolco massacre** remains a controversial issue, with former President Luis Echeverria arrested on charges of genocide in 2006 (the case was dismissed in 2009).

The government of Lázaro Cárdenas (1934–40)

With the election of **Lázaro Cárdenas** (1895–1970) in 1934, such doubts were finally laid to rest. As the spokesman of a younger generation, Cárdenas expelled Calles and his supporters from the country, simultaneously renaming the broad-based party that Calles had set up the **PRI** (Party of the Institutional Revolution); it was to stay in power for the rest of the century. Cárdenas set about an unprecedented programme of reform, redistributing land on a huge scale (170,000 square kilometres during his six-year term), creating peasant and worker organizations to represent their interests at national level and incorporating them into the governing party. He also relaxed controls on the Church to appease internal and international opposition.

In 1938, Cárdenas nationalized the **oil companies**, an act which has proved one of the most significant in shaping modern Mexico and bringing about its industrialization. For a time it seemed as if yet more foreign intervention might follow, but a boycott of Mexican oil by the major consumers crumbled with the onset of **World War II**, and was followed by a massive influx of money and a huge boost for Mexican industry as a result of the war. By the time he stood down in 1940, Cárdenas could claim to be the first president in modern Mexican history to have served his full six-year term in peace, and to have handed over to his successor without trouble.

PRI rule and the Mexican Economic Miracle (1940–70)

Over the next thirty years or so, massive oil income continued to stimulate industry, and the PRI maintained a masterly control of all aspects of public life. Though it was an accepted fact that governments would line their own pockets first – a practice which allegedly reached its height under **José López Portillo** (1976–82) – the unrelenting populism of the PRI, its massive powers of patronage and, above all, its highly visible and undoubted progress maintained it in power with amazingly little dissent.

This is not to say there were no problems. The year 1959 saw the repression of a national railway strike during which ten thousand workers lost their jobs and their leaders were jailed, and in **1968**, hundreds of students were massacred in Mexico City (see page 116). The PRI was still very much in control, though, and snuffed out these movements by the mid-1970s.

Economic crisis (1970–94)

By the 1980s the PRI was losing its populist touch. The years between 1970 and 1982, later dubbed the "**Docena Trágica**" (tragic dozen), saw rapid growth based on booming oil prices. But this growth was accompanied by inflation and devaluation of the

1995	1998	2006
The Colima-Jalisco earthquake kills at least 49 people.	PAN candidate Vicente Fox Quesada is elected president; the end of PRI hegemony.	Felipe Calderón, controversially elected president, institutes a fierce campaign against the drug cartels.

peso; vast sums were misappropriated, corruption flourished as never before, and by 1982 Mexico had run up a foreign debt of almost US$100 billion, borrowed against future oil earnings. When the 1980s bubble burst and the price of oil collapsed, the government of **Miguel de la Madrid** (1982–88) found itself faced with an unprecedented economic crisis on a national and international scale. A US-educated financier, he adopted **austerity measures** imposed by the World Bank that produced massive unemployment and drastically reduced standards of living (the average wage-earner lost fifty percent of his or her purchasing power).

The movement against the PRI was accelerated in 1985, when a huge **earthquake** (8.1 on the Richter scale) hit the capital. The quake revealed widespread corruption – many of the buildings that collapsed were government-owned and turned out to have been constructed using inferior materials. The country became increasingly polarized: in the relatively wealthy, US-influenced north, the right-wing **PAN** (National Action Party) won a string of minor elections, while in the south opposition was far more radical and left-wing: a socialist/peasant alliance held power for a while in Juchitán (Oaxaca) before being ousted by strong-arm tactics.

In this climate, the **1988 election** was tainted by allegations of fraud. Predictably, the PRI candidate, **Carlos Salinas de Gortari**, was declared the comfortable winner. It is widely believed, however, that **Cuauhtémoc Cárdenas**, son of the much-loved Lázaro, actually gained the majority of the votes, having split from the PRI and succeeded in uniting the Mexican left for the first time since the Revolution.

By 1993, nearly forty million Mexicans were living below the official **poverty** line (about half the population), while 24 were listed in the Forbes list of the five hundred wealthiest men in the world, most grown rich on privatized utilities. To boost foreign investment, Salinas expanded the "**maquiladora**" programme, which allowed foreign companies to set up assembly plants along the US-Mexican border while enjoying substantial tax concessions. He also pushed through the North American Free Trade Agreement (**NAFTA**; **TLC** in Spanish) in 1994, which created a free market between Canada, the US and Mexico. None of this was popular, especially among those on the left, but perhaps the most important change from a domestic point of view was the amendment of Article 27 of the constitution. This article had been written to protect communal village landholdings, known as **ejidos**; under Salinas, their status shifted from state property to private property, allowing them to be sold.

The Chiapas uprising (1994–97)

On New Year's Day 1994, NAFTA took effect and at the same time an armed guerrilla movement known as the **Zapatista Army of National Liberation** (EZLN) took control of San Cristóbal de las Casas and four other municipalities in the state of Chiapas. The guerrillas were mainly Indigenous villagers, and their action took the country almost entirely by surprise; they demanded an end to the feudal system of land tenure in Chiapas, free elections, the repeal of NAFTA and the restoration of Article 27 of the constitution. The government reacted with a predictable use of force, committing numerous human-rights abuses along the way, including the bombing of civilians and the torture and murder of prisoners, particularly in the town of Ocosingo.

In the subsequent **negotiations** the main spokesman for the Zapatistas was **Subcomandante Marcos**. The balaclava-clad, pipe-smoking guerrilla became a cult

2009	2009	2010
Calderón sends five thousand troops to patrol Ciudad Juárez as a result of the drug wars.	The Swine Flu (H1N1) epidemic hits Mexico; 398 people die.	Carlos Slim Helú, born in Mexico City, becomes richest man in the world (worth US$71 billion).

hero, his speeches and communiqués full of literary allusions and passionate rhetoric (he was later exposed as, allegedly, Rafael Guillén, a philosophy professor from Mexico City, though this did little to dent his popularity). Negotiations ended in March, when an accord was drawn together.

In June 1994, the EZLN finally rejected the accord, and in July a leftist candidate for the governorship of Chiapas, **Amado Avendaño Figueroa**, met with a suspicious "accident" when a truck with no numberplates collided with his car, killing three passengers; Avendaño lost an eye. In national elections in August the PRI triumphed, helped by an electorate that had been shaken by the uprising. **Ernesto Zedillo** was declared president in what appeared a relatively clean election, the party also sweeping up most senate and governorship posts that were on offer.

In **Chiapas**, however, where the PRI also claimed to have won the governorship, Avendaño declared himself "rebel governor" after denouncing the elections as fraudulent. By this point Chiapas was essentially in a state of **civil war**. Ranchers and landowners organized paramilitary **death squads** to counter a mobilized peasantry. Land seizures and roadblocks were met with assassinations and intimidation, and a build-up of federal troops in the state only made things worse. On January 8, 1995, Zedillo attended the swearing-in of the PRI governor of Chiapas. Ten days later, the EZLN deployed its forces, breaking the army cordon surrounding its positions and moving into 38 municipalities (it had previously been confined to four). The government briefly launched an offensive against the EZLN, resulting in thousands of peasants, terrified by the army and by right-wing landowners' paramilitary groups, becoming internal refugees.

New negotiations eventually resulted in the **San Andrés Accords on Rights and Indigenous Cultures** (named after the village near San Cristóbal where the talks took place), signed in February 1996. The accords guaranteed Indigenous representation in national and state legislatures, but to this day they have not been fully implemented. For a while relations between the Zapatistas and the government hit a new low, while the remorseless increase of the military presence on the Zapatistas' perimeter appeared to give the paramilitary groups even greater freedom to operate. This culminated in the December 1997 **Acteal Massacre**: 45 displaced Tzotzil Indigenous people, 36 of them women and children, were murdered at a prayer meeting by forces linked to PRI officials.

Mexico today

Despite the crisis in Chiapas, Mexico's **political reforms** continued, with limits on campaign spending and the establishment of a federal electoral body in 1996 – the economy started to grow again that year (after another financial collapse, the "Tequila Crisis" of 1994), and has continued to expand ever since. But the biggest change of all came on July 2, 2000, when **Vicente Fox Quesada**, the PAN candidate, was voted in as president. It was a landmark event: not only was he the first opposition candidate ever to have been democratically placed in power, it was also the first peaceful transition between opposing governments since Independence. Most remarkably, though, it was the end of seven decades of PRI rule – the world's longest-lasting one-party dynasty, surpassing even the Soviet Communist party.

2012

Enrique Peña Nieto wins the presidency, heralding the return to power for the PRI. Writer Carlos Fuentes dies.

2014

Hurricane Odile devastates Baja California.

In spite of his political shortcomings, Fox for the most part retained his popularity, and set the stage well for the July 2006 election – which, in many ways, was even more crucial than the previous one, as it would either prove the PAN victory a fluke or help consolidate the party's power.

President Felipe Calderón (2006–12)

In 2006 PAN candidate **Felipe Calderón Hinojosa** replaced Fox as president after one of the most controversial elections in modern Mexican history. Calderón won by the slimmest of margins (0.56 percent or 233,831 votes), and his opponent, PRD-candidate **Andrés Manuel López Obrador** (the popular leftist former mayor of Mexico City) never really accepted the result, even when the Federal Electoral Tribunal ruled that his accusations of vote tampering were not sufficient to call a new vote count. The numbers told the story of a divided Mexico – every state north of the capital (for the most part, the wealthier part of the country) supported Calderón, while Obrador took all of the poorer, southern states with large Indigenous populations. The only exception in the south was Yucatán state, not coincidentally home to a substantial upper class.

Despite relative stability and continuing economic growth, the nation continued to face huge **challenges**. The outbreak of **swine flu** in 2009 did nothing to help tourism or the country's international image, while Mexico's relationship with the US, if better than it sometimes has been, remained problematic – the 592km **border fence** proposed by President Bush in 2006 was a rather brutal symbol of how intractable the debate over **illegal immigration** had become (Calderón passed a bill actually decriminalizing undocumented immigration into Mexico in 2008). On the plus side, Calderón's move towards **universal healthcare** coverage was one of his most popular policies, and he continued expanding the highway network and building new universities.

The Mexican drug war

Drugs, however, have dominated the headlines. Calderón was determined to face the problem head-on, and committed 45,000 army personnel, as well as five thousand *federales*, to what can only be described as a war against the cartels that control the transportation of cocaine, heroin, ecstasy and marijuana through Mexico into the US (see page 453). Assessing Calderón's success is difficult and highly controversial; many drug lords were killed or imprisoned, and security in some cities certainly improved. On the other hand, the biggest players remain very much in business and the steady stream of gruesome murders continues. Critics argue that the Calderón campaign simply intensified the violence, jeopardizing foreign investment and tourism in Mexico.

The 2012 Presidential election: the return of the PRI

In a typically dramatic 2012 Presidential election, the PRD candidate was once again Andrés Manuel López Obrador, with PAN nominee Josefina Vázquez Mota hoping to become the first female president of Mexico. Yet both were trumped by **Enrique Peña Nieto**, the enigmatic former PRI governor of the State of Mexico who collected 39.1 percent of the vote (Obrador came second with 32.43 percent). Unsurprisingly, Obrador once again demanded a full recount, and once again he was disappointed. With accusations of PRI voter fraud widespread, protests continued throughout the summer of 2012, but Nieto officially assumed office in December.

2014

"El Chapo" Guzmán, Sinaloa Cartel leader and Mexico's most-wanted man, is captured; he escapes in 2015 is recaptured in 2016 and then extradited to the USA the following year to stand trial which commenced in November 2018.

2017

Two powerful earthquakes kill hundreds across the country.

The Peña Nieto presidency (2012–18)

Nieto initially had some success in reducing drug cartel violence; Zeta leader Heriberto Lazcano was killed in 2012; top Zeta bosses the Morales brothers were arrested in 2013; and Mexico's most-wanted man, **Joaquín "El Chapo" Guzmán** (Sinaloa Cartel), plus Vicente Carrillo Fuentes (Juárez Cartel) and Héctor Beltrán Leyva (Beltrán Leyva Cartel) were captured in 2014. But the **Iguala mass kidnapping** of September 2014, when 43 students from Ayotzinapa were abducted and later murdered by a drug gang in collusion with local police in Guerrero horrified the nation; the case led to national and international protests and a string of high-profile resignations and arrests; the perpetrators, however, have still not been brought to justice. And in 2015, after barely a year in Mexico's top prison, **El Chapo escaped** yet again; he was recaptured the following year, and in 2017 was extradited to the USA to stand trial which commenced in November 2018.

Despite these setbacks Mexico's economy continued to grow under Nieto, with huge investments in the car manufacturing industry, low inflation and interest rates and an increase in GDP. Huge inequalities of wealth remained, however, particularly between the north and south, and between urban and rural populations.

The 2018 election: a swing to the left

Nieto's final years in office proved increasingly difficult. Tensions with the USA were severely strained by the 2016 election of Donald Trump, with his bitter anti-Mexico rhetoric and demands for a border wall. In September 2017, two devastating earthquakes struck within a fortnight – the first, measuring 8.2, was the most powerful in centuries – killing over 400 people. Drug-fuelled violence soared across the country: there were more than 29,000 murders in 2017, the highest number in decades, according to official figures. And the country continued to plummet down the press freedom table: at least 11 journalists were killed in 2017, followed by a further six in the first half of 2018, according to Reporters Without Borders.

With Nieto constitutionally barred from running again for the presidency in 2018, the initiative was seized by **Obrador**, who vowed to tackle corruption, reduce poverty and rein in the so-called "war on drugs". He won a landslide victory and a six year term, gaining over 53 percent of the vote (his nearest rival, PAN's Ricardo Anaya, only managed 22 percent). Obrador's election promised a break with the past and there has been some progress on the election promises that were made, however with the country's problems so deeply entrenched, many election promises fell short or didn't materialize at all.

The 2024 election: Mexico's first female president

In June 2024, Claudia Sheinbaum (the former mayor of Mexico City) was elected as Mexico's first ever female president. As this edition went to print, her term was still in its formative stages, however, Sheinbaum has already made headlines for her tough stance against president elect Trump, and his threats of trade tariff. Many fear a swift return to the days of extreme tension with the USA, as seen during Nieto's term, however this path forward remains to be seen.

2018

As violence soars, left-winger Andrés Manuel López Obrador wins landslide victory in the presidential election – securing a six-year term in the process.

2020

The Covid-19 pandemic, and measures taken to contain it, causes an economic downturn in Mexico.

2024

Claudia Sheinbaum is elected as Mexico's first female president.

Environment and wildlife

Mexico is one of the world's most biologically diverse countries, with the second-highest number of mammal species for its size (about five hundred), more than a thousand species of birds, at least thirty thousand species of higher plants (including half of the world's pines) and more reptile species (seven hundred) than anywhere else on the globe. Many of these are endemic, and this diversity, combined with the country's vast size (1,960,000 square kilometres) and tremendous range of natural environments, makes Mexico an ideal location for the visiting naturalist, irrespective of expertise.

Unfortunately, much of Mexico's natural beauty is under threat either from direct hunting or from the indirect effects of **deforestation** and **commercialization**. Not only is it extremely irresponsible to buy, even as souvenirs, items that involve wild animals in their production, but it is also generally **illegal** to bring them back to the UK or the US. This applies specifically to: tortoiseshell; black coral; various species of butterfly, mussels and snails; stuffed baby crocodiles; cat skins; and turtle shells. Trade in living animals, including tortoises, iguanas and parrots (often sold as nestlings), is also illegal, as is the uprooting of cacti.

Mexican flora

The influence of long-term **deforestation** for charcoal or slash-and-burn agriculture has substantially denuded large areas of Mexico. Today the northern mountains contain tracts of conifer, cedar and oak, especially around Durango, where the largest **pine forest** reserves are found. At lower altitudes, grass-covered **savannahs** are interrupted by the occasional palm or palmetto tree, and the riverbanks are graced with poplar and willow. **Tropical rainforests**, which border the Gulf of Mexico, form a band that extends southwards from Tampico across the base of the Yucatán Peninsula and northern Oaxaca. They contain mahogany, cedar, rosewood, ebony and logwood. **Seasonal tropical forest** and **dry scrub** cover the remaining areas of the Gulf coast and the lowlands of the Pacific coast. One particularly notable tree is a single **ahuehuete** (Montezuma cypress) in the state of Oaxaca, which measures 36m around; it's alleged to be at least 1200 years old. Extensive **mangrove forests** once lined much of the Gulf coast and the Caribbean, and grew along sheltered reaches of the Pacific shore, but tourism along the coasts has eaten away at the swamps – a short-sighted move, as runoff from the trees' root systems nourishes the coral reefs that draw tourists.

The tropical forests provide supplies of both **chocolate** (from the cacao trees of Chiapas) and **vanilla**. Also harvested are **chicle**, from the latex of the **sapodilla** tree, used in the preparation of chewing gum, and **wild rubber** and **sarsaparilla**. The pharmaceutical industry makes use of **digitalis** from wild **foxgloves** and various **barks** used in the preparation of purges and disinfectants. One medicinal plant unique to Mexico is **Discorea composita**, which is harvested in Veracruz, Oaxaca, Tabasco and Chiapas, and is used in the preparation of a vegetable hormone that forms an essential ingredient of the contraceptive pill.

The deserts

The flatter lands of the north, the north Pacific and portions of central Mexico are characterized by dry scrub and grassland – better known as the **Sonoran** and **Chihuahuan deserts**, though they are hardly the empty sands that the term "desert" conjures. The most conspicuous vegetation here is the **cactus**. Various species adorn these flatlands: the **saguaro** is a giant, tree-like growth which can exceed 15m in height, whereas the columns of the **cereus** cactus stand in lines, not dissimilar to fence posts, and can reach 8m. Another notable variety is the **prickly pear** (*nopal*), which produces a fruit (*tuna*) that can be eaten raw or used in the production of sweets. Other harvested varieties include the pulpy-leaved **maguey cactus** (a member of the agave family), whose fermented juice forms the basis of tequila, mescal and *pulque*, and **henequen** (another agave), which was once grown extensively on the Yucatán Peninsula and used in the production of rope. The temperate grasslands are composed primarily of clumped bunch grass and wiry, unpalatable **curly mesquite**. Low-lying shrubs found among these grassy expanses include spindly ocotillo, **creosote** bush and palm-like **yucca**, with **mesquite** and **acacia bushes** in the more sheltered, damper areas.

Flowers

Flowers are commonplace throughout Mexico and form an integral part of day-to-day life. Once, **frangipani** and **magnolia** were considered to be of such value that they were reserved for the Aztec nobility. Today the blue blossoms of **jacaranda** trees and purple and red **bougainvillea** still adorn the walls of cities and towns during the spring and summer. Even the harsh arid deserts of the north are carpeted with wild flowers during the brief spring that follows the occasional rains; the cacti blooms are particularly vivid. Many of these floral species are Indigenous to Mexico, including **cosmos**, **snapdragons**, **marigolds** and **dahlias**. In the wetter areas, several species of **wild orchid** are endemic, while more than eight hundred other species have been classified from the forests of Chiapas alone.

Insects

Insect life is abundant throughout Mexico, but numbers and diversity reach their peak in the tropical rainforests. For the most part, insect life makes itself known through the variety of bites and sores incurred while wandering through these areas: **mosquitoes** are a particular pest, with malaria still a risk in some areas. Openings in the tree canopy also attract a variety of colourful **butterflies**, **gnats** and **locusts**. The **garrapata** is a particularly tenacious tick found everywhere livestock exists, and readily attaches itself to human hosts. A range of **scorpions**, whose sting can vary from extremely painful to definitively lethal, is found throughout the country.

In the forests, long columns of **leafcutter ants** crisscross the floor in their search for tasty bits of fungus on tree bark, and surrounding tree trunks provide ideal shelter for large nests of **termites**. Carnivorous **army ants** also sweep through in waves, devouring grasshoppers and other pests but leaving greenery untouched. One species of ant, local to Tlaxcala, provides for seasonal labour twice each year: first, during the egg stage, when it is harvested for a highly prized form of caviar, and secondly during the grub stage, when it is an equally loved food source. The most spectacular insect migration can be seen in winter in eastern Michoacán, where thousands of **monarch butterflies** hatch from their larval forms en masse, providing a blaze of colour and movement (see page 298).

Fish, reptiles and amphibians

The diversity of Mexican inland and coastal habitats has enabled large numbers of both marine and freshwater species to survive. Among the freshwater species, **rainbow** and **brook trout**, **silversides** and **catfish** are particularly abundant (as are European **carp** in certain areas, where it has been introduced). The most highly regarded is a species of **whitefish** found in Laguna de Chapala and Lago de Pátzcuaro.

Offshore, Mexican waters contain over one hundred marine species of significance, including varieties of tropical and temperate climates, coastal and deep waters, surface and ground feeders and sedentary and migratory lifestyles. Among the most prevalent are **goliath grouper** (which can grow up to 5m), **swordfish**, **snapper**, **king mackerel**,

snook, **tuna**, **mullet** and **anchovy**. **Shrimp**, **crayfish** and **spiny lobster** are also important commercial species. The marine fishing grounds on the Pacific coast are at their best off the coast of Baja California, where the warmer southern waters merge with subarctic currents from the north. Similarly, deep ocean beds and coastal irregularities provide rewarding fishing in the waters of the Campeche bank in the Gulf of Mexico.

The lower river courses that flow through the southern forests are frequented by **iguanas**, **crocodiles** and their close relative, the **caiman**. **Lizards** range from tiny nocturnal lizards along the Gulf coast to **tropical iguanas**, which can reach up to 2m in length. **Marine turtles**, including the loggerhead, green, hawksbill and leatherback, are still found on both the Atlantic and Pacific coasts, though several species are endangered. Hunting of both adults and eggs is now illegal, and a number of official and unofficial turtle sanctuaries have been established, with positive results. Several kinds of **rattlesnake** are common in the deserts of northern Mexico, and further south the rainforests hold a substantial variety of other snakes, including the **boa constrictor**, **fer-de-lance**, **bushmaster** and the small **coral snake**. Amphibian life includes salamanders, several types of **frog** and one marine toad that measures up to 20cm in length.

Birds

More than five hundred species of tropical birds live in the rainforests and cloud forests of southern Mexico alone. Among these are resplendent **macaws**, **parrots** and **parakeets**, which make a colourful display as they fly among the dense tree canopy. The cereal-eating habits of the parrot family have not endeared them to local farmers, and for this reason (and their continuing capture for sale as pets) their numbers have been seriously depleted in recent times. Big-billed **toucans** perch on lower branches and a few larger game birds, such as **curassow**, **crested guan**, **chachalaca** and **ocellated turkey**, can be seen on the ground, amid the dense vegetation.

Particularly rare are the brilliantly coloured **trogons**, including the dazzling **quetzal**, which inhabits the cloud forests of the Sierra Madre de Chiapas (in El Triunfo Reserve). The ancient Maya coveted its long, emerald-green tail feathers, which were used in priestly headdresses; its current status is severely endangered. The drier tropical deciduous forests of northern Yucatán to the east, the Pacific coastal lowlands and the interior lowlands provide an ideal habitat for several predatory birds including **owls** and **hawks**. The most familiar large birds of Mexico, however, are the carrion-eating **black** and **turkey vultures** – locally *zopilote* – often seen soaring in large groups. The Yucatán is also one of the last remaining strongholds of the small **Mexican eagle**, which features in the country's national symbol.

Large numbers of coastal lagoons provide both feeding and breeding grounds for a wide variety of aquatic birds – some of them winter visitors from the north – including **ducks**, **herons** and **grebes**. Foremost among these are the substantial flocks of graceful **flamingos** which can be seen at selected sites along the western and northern coasts of the Yucatán Peninsula. In the north of Mexico, where the harsher and drier environment is less attractive, outlying towns and villages form a sanctuary for a variety of **doves** and **pigeons**, and the areas with denser cover have small numbers of **quail** and **pheasant**. Any water feature in these drier zones, as well as wetland areas further south, provides attractive migration stopover sites for North American species, including **warblers**, **wildfowl** and **waders**.

Mammals

Zoologists divide the animals of the Americas into two categories: the **Nearctic** region of the mid-latitudes, in which the native animals are of North American affinity, and the **Neotropical** region of the lower latitudes, in which the fauna is linked to that of South America. The Isthmus of Tehuantepec marks the border between these two regions, serving as a barrier to many larger mammalian species.

The Nearctic region is predominantly composed of open steppe and desert areas and higher-altitude oak and pine forests. Relatively few large mammals inhabit the highland forests, although one widespread species is the **white-tailed deer**, which is still hunted as a source of food. The northern parts of the Sierra Madre Occidental mark the southernmost extent of several typically North American mammals, such as **mountain sheep** and **black** and **brown bears**, though the latter are near extinction. Bears live in the Cumbres de Monterrey National Park, and wild horned **sheep** can be seen at the San Pedro Mártir National Park in Baja California. Other mammals include **deer**, **puma**, **lynx**, **marten**, **grey fox**, **mule sheep**, **porcupine**, **skunk**, **badger**, **rabbit** and **squirrel**. A large array of smaller **rodents**, and their natural predators, the **coyote** and the **kit fox**, are also widespread throughout the forests. Nowadays the extensive grassland plains are frequented only by sporadic herds of white-tailed deer; the days of the pronghorn and even the bison have long passed under the burden of overhunting. Within the desert scrub, the **peccary** is still widely hunted, and rodents, as ever, are in abundance, forming an ample food supply for the resident **bobcats**, **ocelots** and even the occasional **jaguar** – more commonly associated with the country's jungle regions, but also at home in the drier areas and known to roam across the US–Mexico border.

Baja California forms an outstanding wildlife sanctuary for marine mammals, harbouring nearly forty percent of the world's species. Isla Guadalupe is one of the few remaining breeding sites of the endangered **elephant seal**, and the only known mating and nursery sites of the **grey whale** are around Guerrero Negro.

Although some southern species (notably the opossum and armadillo) have succeeded in breaching the Tehuantepec line, and now thrive in northern Mexico and the southern US, on the whole the **Neotropical** region holds a very different collection of mammals. The relationship between these species and the lush vegetation of the tropical rainforest and the highland cloud forests is particularly apparent. Many species are arboreal, living in the tree canopies: these include **spider** and **howler monkeys**, **opossums**, **tropical squirrels**, the racoon-like **coati** and the gentle **kinkajou**.

Because of the paucity of grass on the shaded forest floors, ground-dwelling mammals are relatively scarce. The largest is the **tapir**, a distant relative of the horse, with a prehensile snout, and usually found near water. Two species of **peccary**, a type of wild

GREY WHALE MIGRATION AND BREEDING

Each year the **grey whale migration** attracts an estimated 250,000 visitors to Baja California. The whales' **migratory route** runs the length of the Pacific seaboard, from Baja to the Bering Sea and back; this is a round trip of some 20,000km – the longest recorded migration undertaken by any mammal. The whales spend the summer months feeding on the abundant krill in the Arctic and building up body reserves for the long journey south to the breeding lagoons. The migration begins as the days shorten and the pack ice thickens, with the majority of the whales arriving in January and February, though they can be observed here from December to April.

Nowadays human interest in the whales is purely voyeuristic, though times have not always been so peaceful; less than 150 years ago, the secret breeding grounds of the whales were discovered by **Charles Melville Scammon**. The Laguna Ojo de Liebre (renamed in recent times after the infamous whaler) was rapidly emptied of almost all of these magnificent beasts, and it wasn't until the establishment of **Scammon's Bay** as the world's first whale sanctuary in 1972 that their numbers began to rebound. The population in the area is currently estimated at about twenty thousand – a dramatic recovery in a relatively short time span. The protected area now includes nearby San Ignacio Lagoon, forming an all-embracing national park, the **Biosfera El Vizcaíno**. San Ignacio Lagoon presents a daunting entrance of pounding surf and treacherous shoals, but inside its calmer waters flatten and spread inland for 15km towards the distant volcanic peaks of the Santa Clara mountains. Accessible points for land-based observation lie further north in the Parque Natural de Ballena Gris ("Grey Whale Natural Park").

pig, wander the forest floors seeking their preferred foods (roots, palm nuts and even snakes), and there's also the smaller **brocket deer**. The **agouti** and the spotted **cavy** are large rodents living along the streams and riverbanks. These are hunted by large cats, including the **jaguar**, **puma** and **ocelot**.

The drier tropical and subtropical forests of northern Yucatán, the Pacific coastal lowlands and the interior basins produce a more varied ground cover of shrubs and grasses, which supply food for the **white-tailed deer** and abundant small rodents, including the spiny tree **rat** and the **paca**, which in turn provide food for a variety of predators such as the **coyote**, **margay** and **jaguarundi**. Other large mammals which can still be found in small numbers are **anteaters**, **opossums** and **armadillos**. The reefs and lagoons which run along the Quintana Roo coast have small colonies of the **manatee**, or sea cow, a docile creature which feeds on sea grass.

Wildlife sites

It would be almost impossible to compile a comprehensive list of sites of wildlife interest in Mexico, particularly as so much can be seen all over the country. The following is a selection of some of the outstanding areas, particularly ones that are easily accessible or close to major tourist centres. The few zoos that exist in Mexico are generally depressing places, but there is one outstanding exception – the conservation-oriented **Zoológico Miguel Álvarez de Toro** in Tuxtla Gutiérrez (see page 634).

Baja California

The peninsula of **Baja California** is a unique part of the Mexican landmass. Its coastline provides sanctuary for a wide variety of marine mammals, including the major wildlife attraction of the area, the migratory **grey whale**. The lagoons where these whales gather can also offer views of other whales, including blue, humpback, fin, minke, sperm and orca (killer whales). Dolphins, sea lions and a variety of sea birds (pelicans, ospreys, plovers and sanderlings) inhabit the lagoons too. The sparse vegetation provides roosting sites for jaegers (skuas) and peregrines, and coyotes may occasionally be seen wandering the shores.

Offshore, several small islands with protected status have been colonized by highly diverse animal communities. Furthest north is the island of **Todos Santos**, where the sandy beaches, festooned with the remnants of shellfish, are used as occasional sunning spots by the resident harbour seals. The atmosphere is ripe with an uncommon blend of guano, kelp and Californian sagebrush. The Pacific swell frequently disturbs the resting cormorants, which bask in the hot sunshine, and the skies are filled with wheeling western gulls.

Further south lies the island of **San Benito**, just northeast of the much larger Isla Cedros. San Benito provides ideal nesting grounds for migrating ospreys, which travel south from the US. The hillsides are covered by tall agave (century plants) whose brief, once-in-a-lifetime blooms add an attractive splash of colour to the slopes. These towering succulents produce a broad rosette of golden florets, which are a welcome supply of nectar for resident hummingbirds, and ravens soar above, searching for carrion. Along with Isla Cedros and the distant **Isla Guadalupe** (now a biological reserve), the island also provides a winter home to thousands of elephant seals, now happily recovering after years of overhunting. The large adult males arrive in December, and the pebbly coves are soon crammed with the noisy and chaotic colony of mothers, calves and bachelor bulls, all ruled by one dominant bull (or beach master) which can weigh up to two tonnes. The males make a terrifying spectacle as, with necks raised and heads thrown back, they echo their noisy threats to any would-be rivals.

The interior of the peninsula also has several areas of wildlife interest, many of which are now protected as nature reserves. Most significant are the national parks of the **Sierra San Pedro Mártir** and the **Desierto Central**. Here the chaparral-covered hills cede to Jeffrey pine forests and high meadows, interspersed with granite *picachos* (peaks) and volcanic mesas. The **Parque Nacional Constitución de 1857** is another green oasis in the arid lowlands, where the coniferous woodlands form a picturesque border to the central **Laguna Hanson**. These sierras are renowned for the numerous palm-filled canyons which cut deep into the eastern escarpment; they make spectacular hiking areas with their miniature waterfalls, ancient petroglyphs, caves, hot springs and groves of fan palms.

Durango

Durango lies within a dry, hilly area where the intermittent oak and pine woodland is surrounded by large expanses of low-lying scrub. These areas are frequented by large numbers of birds, whose presence is an extension of their North American range. Typical species include red-tailed hawk, American kestrel and mockingbird. The denser, wooded areas provide the necessary cover for several more secretive varieties such as Mexican jay, acorn woodpecker, hepatic grosbeak and the diminutive Mexican chickadee. This is also an occasional haunt of the mountain lion (or puma) and the coyote. In the dry scrub, scorpions abound. Other nearby sites worthy of investigation include **El Salto** and **El Palmito**.

The Teacapán estuary

South of Mazatlán on the Pacific coast, the **Teacapán estuary** is an extensive area of sands with marshy margins: ideal feeding grounds for a variety of waders and wildfowl, including marbled godwit, greater yellowlegs and willet. Large numbers of herons and egrets feed in the shallow waters (including little green and Louisiana heron and snowy and cattle egret), while further out to sea passage birds include laughing gull, gull-billed tern and olivaceous cormorant. Most spectacular of all are the magnificent, aptly named frigate birds, which make a dramatic sight as they skim over the water's surface in their search for fish, with their long wings (sometimes more than 2m across), forked tails and hooked bills.

The rocks offshore provide a breeding site for both brown- and blue-footed boobies, and the pools at the northern end of the town, behind the large hotels, have some interesting water birds, including jacana, ruddy duck and canvasback.

San Blas

Immediately around **San Blas** are lagoons with wildlife very similar to that found in the estuary near Mazatlán; boat tours from San Blas take you out to see herons and egrets, with the possibility of seeing a caiman being the big attraction. Deeper in the wetlands the landscape forms areas of thicker scrub and at higher altitudes dense forest. In the lower-lying scrub, it is possible to see the purplish-backed jay, Gila woodpecker and tropical kingbird, while the skies above have the patrolling white-tailed kite. At higher altitudes, birdlife includes the San Blas jay, white-crowned parrot and cinnamon hummingbird. The town provides sufficient scraps for scavengers such as black and grey hawks and various rodents.

Veracruz and the Gulf coast

The eastern coastline of Mexico has attractions of its own, and none is more rewarding than the final remaining tract of rainforest on the Mexican **Gulf coast**, southeast of **Veracruz**. The vegetation is lush, the tended citrus orchards yielding to rolling tropical forest, with its dense growth of ficus, mango and banana trees and the occasional coconut palm. These trees provide cover for a colourful underlying carpet, including orchids, lemon trees, camellias, fragrant cuatismilla and gardenias. The roadsides are lined with banks of hibiscus, oleander and the pretty, white-flowered shrub known locally as *cruz de Malta*. At the centre of the whole area, **Lago de Catemaco** is outstandingly beautiful.

The surrounding forest has suffered much in recent times, and many of the larger mammals that once resided in this region are no longer to be found. One sanctuary which remains amid this destruction is the ecological research station of **Los Tuxtlas**. Although the institute's holding is fairly small, it adjoins a much larger state-owned reserve of some

25,000 acres on the flank of the **San Martín volcano**. Despite problems of poaching and woodcutting, the area has the last remaining populations of brocket deer, black howler monkey, ocelot, jaguarundi, kinkajou and coati. It also boasts 92 species of reptile, fifty amphibians, thousands of insects and over three hundred species of birds. With patience, it is possible to see such outstanding avian varieties as the keel-billed toucan, black-shouldered kite, gold-crowned warbler, red-throated ant tanager, plain-breasted brush finch, red-lored parrot, ivory-billed woodpecker and the magnificent white hawk.

The Chiapas uplands and Palenque

In the **Chiapas uplands**, the absence of climatic moderation and coastal breezes creates dense, lush vegetation that makes it truly worthy of the name of tropical rainforest. The **Sierra Madre de Chiapas** is of particular interest, particularly the Pacific slopes at altitudes between 1500m and 2500m, as these are the last sanctuary of the endangered horned guan and azure-rumped tanager, and even the quetzal. **El Triunfo Reserve**, at 1800m in the very southeastern corner of the country, less than 50km from the Guatemalan border, makes an excellent base camp for exploration of the area. The cloud forest here is dense, and the tall epiphyte-laden trees grow in profusion on the slopes and in the valleys, in the humid conditions which occur after the morning fogs have risen (generally by early afternoon).

Another area of interest in eastern Chiapas is the **Parque Nacional Lagos de Montebello**, where more determined bird watchers may be rewarded with views of the azure-hooded jay and the barred parakeet. Human encroachment has substantially reduced the population of large mammals in the area, but small numbers of howler monkey, tapir and jaguar (known locally as *el tigre*) are a reminder of bygone days. Another speciality of the region is a vivid and diminutive tree frog, whose precise camouflage ensures that it is more often heard than seen.

At the archeological site of **Palenque** you're back among the tourists (and the howler monkeys), but the birding is unrivalled, and local species include the chestnut-headed oropendola, scaled ant pitta, white-whiskered puffbird, slaty-tailed trogon and masked tanager. In the area of marshland around the nearby **Río Usumacinta**, pinnated bittern, everglade kite and the rare lesser yellow-headed vulture have all been recorded.

The Yucatán Peninsula

The vegetation of the **Yucatán Peninsula** is influenced by its low relief and the ameliorating effects of its extensive coastline, which bring regular and fairly reliable rain along with year-round high temperatures. In the north it's predominantly dry scrub and bush, although large areas have been cleared for the cultivation of crops such as citrus fruits and henequen. To the south is lusher tropical and subtropical forest, where the effects of agriculture are less obvious and the dense forest of acacia, albizia, gumbo limbo and *ceiba* is in parts almost impenetrable. These form an ideal shelter for scattered populations of both white-tailed and brocket deer.

WILDLIFE AT CHICHÉN ITZÁ

When visiting the famed Maya site at **Chichén Itzá**, save a little time at the end of the day for an exploration of the forested areas which lie to the south of the "Nunnery". The drier climate and lower altitude in this part of the peninsula encourage a sparser vegetation, where the oaks and pines are less obvious. The colours among the greenness come from a variety of splendid flowers, such as the multicoloured bougainvillea, the aromatic frangipani and the blue and mauve blooms of the jacaranda tree. Occasional splashes are added by the red bracts of the poinsettia and the brilliant yellows of golden cups. The resident birds appear oblivious to the tourists, and in the quieter areas to the south and southwest of the main site, the abundant birdlife includes the plain chachalaca, ferruginous pygmy owl, cinnamon hummingbird, turquoise-browed motmot and numerous brilliant vireos, orioles and tanagers.

SIAN KA'AN BIOSPHERE RESERVE

The real highlight of the Yucatán Peninsula's protected areas is the magnificent **Sian Ka'an Biosphere Reserve**, which includes coral reef, mangroves, fresh- and salt-water wetlands and littoral forest – possibly the widest range of flora and fauna in Mexico. See page 765 for more.

The **birdlife** on the peninsula is particularly outstanding. The abundant and spectacular birds which fill the treetops include squirrel cuckoo, citreoline trogon and Aztec parakeet, while circling in the skies above are the resident birds of prey such as the bat falcon, snail kite and the ever-present black and turkey vultures (these can be distinguished, even at great heights, as the wings of the latter are clearly divided into two bands – the darker primaries and the lighter secondaries being quite distinct). It is also possible to see all three species of Mexican toucan: collared aracari, emerald toucanet and the spectacular keel-billed. The denser areas of forest also hold small remnants of the original black howler and spider monkey populations.

The village of **Cobá** borders a lake with extensive reed margins along its eastern edge, which attracts a variety of water birds. Typical visitors, either migratory or resident, include the grebe, the elusive spotted rail, ruddy crake, northern jacana and the occasional anhinga – a cormorant-like bird which captures fish by spearing them with its dagger-like bill. The reed beds provide cover for several more-secretive species, including mangrove vireo, ringed kingfisher and blue-winged warbler, as well as several varieties of hirundine such as mangrove swallow and grey-breasted martin. The lake is also home to a variety of turtles and large numbers of Morelet's crocodiles.

Cancún, Cozumel and the Caribbean coast

Even the mega-resort of **Cancún** has wildlife-spotting possibilities: the lagoons that line the outskirts have a variety of birds (such as great-tailed grackle and melodious blackbird). These wetlands form an ideal breeding ground for a number of brilliantly coloured dragonflies and damselflies.

More importantly, the longest **barrier reef** in the Americas begins just south of the city, off the coast of **Puerto Morelos**, where the scuba diving and snorkelling are stunning. Formed by the limey skeletons of dozens of species of coral, the reefs show spectacular diversity, with varieties such as star, lettuce, gorgonian, elkhorn and staghorn. The reefs provide food and shelter for more than four hundred species of fish, including several varieties of parrotfish, butterfly fish, beau gregories, rock beauties and porkfish; the blaze of colour is unforgettable. The coral also provides protection for other residents including spiny lobster, sea urchins, crabs and tentacled anemones.

Natural parks and nature reserves worthy of special mention include **Celestún**, on the west coast, and **Río Lagartos**, to the north. Both have spectacular flocks of migratory flamingos, which winter here in the milder climate. The **Isla Contoy** bird sanctuary off the northeastern tip of the peninsula is a worthwhile and popular day trip from Cancún, and **Isla Holbox**, off the north coast, is the closest point to an annual gathering of more than one hundred whale sharks. The largest **botanic garden** in Mexico is near Puerto Morelos.

Playa del Carmen is frequented by various wetland species including American wigeon, and the ferry trip to **Cozumel** island produces sightings of sea birds such as royal and Caspian terns, black skimmer, frigate birds and Mexican sheartails. On Cozumel, the most rewarding sites are a couple of kilometres inland on the main road that runs across the island. The sparse woodland and hedgerows provide shelter for many typical endemics, such as Caribbean dove, lesser nighthawk, Yucatán and Cozumel vireo, the splendid bananaquit and a variety of tanagers. Elusive species which require more patient exploration (best through the mangroves which lie 3km north of **San Miguel** along the coast road) are the mangrove cuckoo, yellow-lored parrot, Caribbean ealania and Yucatán flycatcher. Cozumel, though, is better known for its **coral reefs**.

Music

Mexico has an enormous and vibrant music scene which made world headlines in the 1950s when the **golden age** of cinema immortalized songs like "*Bésame Mucho*" and artists like **Pedro Infante**. While Cuban and Brazilian music rode the crest of the world music boom in the late 1980s, however, Mexico largely missed out – with notable exceptions like Lila Downs and Los de Abajo.

Son

Son is the music of the Mexican fiesta, the heart of a rural culture that stubbornly survives throughout the country. *Son* is where the story of Mexican music begins: the style that celebrated independence from Spain at the beginning of the nineteenth century and is still, today, a source of regional pride and identity. Although *son* survives on the margins of urban culture, more adventurous rock groups like **Café Tacuba** and divas like **Eugenia León** and **Lila Downs** have taken versions of this music to the big stage.

Like much of Latin American music, *son* is the bastard child of Indigenous, Spanish and African parents. It is what musicologists call a "super-genre", meaning that there are eight or nine different styles of *son* that vary from region to region. In general, this is the music of country dances that begin at dusk – at the end of a celebration for a saint's day or a wedding – and last through the night. It is music to be enjoyed rather than listened to passively; the public adds a line of percussion with their **zapateado** foot-stamp dancing, and the musicians respond to their calls and comments with verses that are improvised on the spot. *Son* is played mainly by string bands but in some regions – especially in Indigenous towns and villages – also by brass bands of twenty or thirty musicians. The different styles of *son* feature *copla* verses that are witty, sexual, poetic and proud.

Son Jaliscience and mariachi

Probably best known outside Mexico are the **sones** from Jalisco, the west-coast state that is the home of the **mariachi**. The latter became nationally and internationally popular in the 1950s, a time when regional music was recorded by major labels. A few of these treasures can be found in markets, although the original country sound – played on a couple of violins and guitars and sometimes a harp – almost disappeared when Rubén Fuentes rewrote the **son jaliscience** repertoire for radio and cinema, introducing slick violin sections, trumpets and the portable bass known as the *guitarrón*. These groups, made up of twelve or even sixteen musicians, spectacularly dressed in tight trousers and large hats, played their show-business versions of the traditional repertoire ("*Son de la Negra*" and "*El Cihualteco*" are two classics) as well as a simpler accompaniment for the *ranchera* stars of the day. To hear the original *son jalisciense*, look out for Vol l of *The Anthology of Mexican Sones* and also for the CD by **Mariachi Reyes del Aserradero**, a post-Fuentes group that is still very much in touch with local tastes.

The stars of big-time mariachi music are **Vicente Fernández** and, for the past twenty years or so, his son **Alejandro**, a mega-star who has taken the music so far down the commercial path that all that is really left are the lines of silver buckles down the trouser legs and some of the instrumentation. Look out too for **Aida Cuevas** (the "Queen of Ranchera') and younger stars **Pedro Fernández** and **Pepe Aguilar**; television has stripped away the original intensity of the music but the singing is still spectacular and the mariachi will always be a strong symbol of the Mexican passion to party.

Every year there is an enormous **mariachi congress** in Guadalajara (capital of Jalisco) where hundreds of bands gather from all over Mexico and the world – especially from Japan and the US, where there are countless mariachis of different genders and musical

INDIGENOUS SON

Although *son* is basically *mestizo* music, several **Indigenous cultures** play *sones* to accompany their ritual dances. These are generally purely instrumental and are slower and more melancholy than those from other regions. Exceptions are the *sones* from Purépecha and Zapotec communities which are beautiful, bilingual songs that have been widely covered by urban stars. **Sones abajeños** are the frenetic party music of the Purépecha of Michoacán, played on guitars, violins and a double bass. Between the *abajeños*, the same musicians sing the hauntingly beautiful *pirecua* love songs, with words exclusively in Purépecha. Outstanding Purépecha *son* bands include **Atardecer** (Sunset), from the lake village of Jarácuaro, and **Erandi** (Dawn). This region is probably more famous for the dances that accompany the local *sones*; there is the athletic "Dance of the Old Men" and the slow, incredibly beautiful dances of the *cúrpites* in which small, subtle steps are taken by elaborately costumed dancers. There is nothing folkloric about this tradition, which remains an important part of Purépecha fiestas. In the southern state of Oaxaca, the vibrant Zapotec culture has produced some of the country's great love songs and inspired mainstream Mexican romantic singers along the way. Sung in both Zapotec and Spanish, the **sones istmeños**, from the Tehuantepec Isthmus, are played to a slower, more melancholy 3/4 rhythm and boast some great solo passages on the *requinto* guitar. These *sones* can be accompanied by small guitar bands or by brass bands made up of at least eighteen musicians. Again, this is the music of fiestas and, to some extent, of cantinas.

abilities. Many Mexican towns and cities still have a central square where the mariachis meet to offer their music on a nightly basis. Most famous of these is **Plaza Garibaldi** in Mexico City, where hundreds of musicians serenade young girls and old ladies under the stars while hustlers bring in business for the many bars and food stalls that line the plaza. Mexicans come here at all hours of the day and night to hire bands for private parties; this is the real business for the mariachis since it is much better paid than playing to tourists.

Son Jarocho

After the *sones* from Jalisco, **son jarocho** from Veracruz is probably the best-known style. Many Jarocho musicians like **Andrés Huesca**, **Nicolás Sosa** and **Lino Chávez** tasted the big time in Mexico City before returning to the main square of Veracruz. Today, there is a new interest in *son jarocho*, especially in the country style from the south of the state, where there are some three hundred bands – many of them including fifth- or sixth-generation country musicians – playing a fairly traditional repertoire at local fiestas and on the national and international circuit.

The story of this huge revival of interest in *son jarocho* goes back to 1977 when a young *jarocho* from Tres Zapotes, a small town in southern Veracruz, emigrated to Mexico City and asked himself why the *peña* folk-clubs were full of urban musicians in ponchos playing Bolivian and Chilean music. Where was Mexican music and specifically the *son jarocho* that he had danced to as a child? **Gilberto Gutiérrez** formed a band called **Mono Blanco**, recording with some of the most outstanding musicians from southern Veracruz, setting up workshops, making records and giving countless concerts all over Mexico and the US and to some extent in Europe as well. His younger brother Ramón formed his own band, **Son de Madera**, also enormously successful on the roots circuit, and this helped to revive the *fandango* tradition of dancing within the same communities that had originally produced the music. Today, there is a huge following for *son jarocho* in Mexico City and musicians are fusing it with new and old styles so that now it's common to hear a *jarocho* band opening for a rock band or featuring in a programme of classical music.

Further north, in the port of Veracruz, the style of *son jarocho* that had made it to the big screen in the 1950s is still alive and kicking, although the worldwide success of

ON RECORD

Mexican music is widely available online: try Amazon or Smithsonian Folkways (http://folkways.si.edu). A small selection from this enormous world of musical styles includes the following:

COMPILATIONS

★ **Anthology of Mexican Sones** (Discos Corasón, Mexico). The definitive survey of Mexican traditional music, featuring wonderful recordings of rural bands. Excellent accompanying notes plus lyrics.

Beso Asesino (Discos Corasón, Mexico). Traditional *trova* from the Yucatán and from Santiago de Cuba. An excellent celebration of the shared roots of the *bolero*.

Mexico – Fiestas of Chiapas & Oaxaca (Nonesuch Explorer, US). Recordings from village festivities in southern Mexico. Marimba *conjuntos*, brass bands, some eccentric ensembles and great fireworks on the opening track.

The Rough Guide to the Music of Mexico (World Music Network, UK). This set examines a wide variety of both traditional and contemporary music, including *rancheras*, *corridos*, *boleros*, indie rock and various stylistic fusions.

La Tortuga (Discos Corasón, Mexico). A heartfelt collection of the Zapotec *sones istmeños* from southwest Oaxaca; this repertoire has been successfully mined by urban artists but here it is in the original form.

SONES AND MARIACHI

★ **Los Camperos de Valles** *La Pasión*. The definitive CD by the definitive Huastecan *son* band and the last recording by violinist Heliodoro Copado who was the inspiration for the current generation of *soneros*.

Conjunto Alma Jarocha *Sones Jarochos*. First in a series of regional Mexican releases, featuring *sones* from Veracruz with harps and *jarana* guitars.

Juan Reynoso *El Paganini de la Tierra Caliente*. A cult recording in Mexico which led the great country violinist to gain national and international fame. Other records followed, but this is considered the best.

Mariachi Coculense de Cirilo Marmolejo *Mexico's Pioneer Mariachis Vol 1*. Wonderful archive recordings from the 1920s and 1930s of one of the seminal groups.

Mariachi Reyes del Aserradero *Sones from Jalisco*. An excellent mariachi band from Jalisco state play the original *sones* from the region where mariachi was born.

Mariachi Vargas *20 Exitos*. Highly polished, big-band style mariachi from Silvestre Vargas (died in 1985), who managed to stay at the top of his field for over fifty years.

★ **Mono Blanco** *El Mundo se va a Acabar*. The most ambitious record from the band that led the revival of *son jarocho* in Mexico; although less traditional than their usual style, this is stunning.

RANCHERA AND NORTEÑO

Banda del Recodo *Nuestra Historia*. This enormously popular collective releases hit CDs rather than classics, so possibly the best introduction is this 2003 release that brings together material from their long history.

★ **Chavela Vargas** *Noche Bohemia*. There was a flood of CDs after Chavela's return to the music scene in the late 1980s (she died in 2012), but nothing rivals this early recording with the legendary guitarist, Antonio Bribiesca.

★ **Flaco Jiménez** *Ay Te Dejo en San Antonio y Más*. The best of Flaco's many recordings; he's a huge name in the Tex-Mex world north of the border.

José Alfredo Jiménez *Homenaje a José Alfredo Jiménez*. Jiménez was the king of *ranchera* and an icon in Mexico: his classic repertoire of songs tells of the perfidy of women and the healing qualities of tequila. He may have created some of the worst clichés about machismo, but his music is irresistible.

Linda Ronstadt *Canciones de Mi Padre* and *Más Canciones*. *Ranchera* classics sung very convincingly by the Mexican-American vocalist, accompanied by Mariachi Vargas.
Los Lobos *La Pistola y El Corazón*. The East LA band's brilliant 1988 tribute to their Mexican roots, with David Hidalgo pumping the accordion on their blend of *conjunto* and rock and roll.
Los Tigres del Norte *Corridos Prohibidos*. A collection of *corridos* about Mexican low life and heroism from one of the best *norteño* groups.

TROPICAL AND MÚSICA ROMÁNTICA

★ **Agustín Lara** *Agustín Lara*. The legendary *bolero* singer and composer of classics such as "*Rival*" and "*Noche de Ronda*". There are countless recordings by him and the myriad of artists who have dedicated covers of his *boleros* to him (including Plácido Domingo and Pedro Vargas).
Armando Manzanero *20 Éxitos Originales*. A key figure for Cuban artists like Omara Portuondo, this Yucatecan pianist modernized the *bolero* and, now in his 80s, is still a huge figure who moves comfortably between the commercial and the alternative. Various artists (Tania Libertad and Alejandro Sanz are just two) queue up to sing duets with him. His voice isn't great but his songs are classics and this is a typical, very polished, selection of re-mastered classics.
Guty Cárdenas *100 Años del Ruiseñor Yucateco*. A collection of *trova yucateca* and other genres in the voice and guitar of a man who was an enormous star in the early years of recorded sound but who was assassinated in 1932. The tracks have been masterfully restored and are accompanied by a documentary.
Sonora Dinamita *Mi Cucu*. Mexican *cumbia* performed by a breakaway group of artists who took the name of the Colombian originals. Their lyrics, full of double entendres, are performed with a zest that has brought huge success in Mexico.
Toña La Negra *Antología*. A well-kept secret outside Mexico – where she was an enormous star in the 1950s – this *bolero* singer from Veracruz reveals how close Mexico is to Cuba (and vice versa). She died in 1982.

ROCK AND POP

★ **Café Tacuba** *Re*. The second album in a long list of successes from a band that was at the top of the Mexican rock scene for more than twenty years, this is a highly recommended classic; try also *Cuatro Caminos* and *Sino*.
Eugenia León *Pasional*. One of the best releases by this great singer who has been much more successful on stage than on record. This 2007 album celebrates the mature voice of a woman who has a powerful, emotional presence and has been at the top of the loosely named "Latin American song" tradition for over 25 years.
Julieta Venegas *Sí*. The 2003 record that firmly established Julieta as a major figure on the pop-rock scene. There is something very attractive about her funky innocence which saves her from a closer association with mainstream pop. Her 2007 release *Limón y Sal* won the Grammy for best Latin pop album.
★ **Lila Downs** *La Sandunga*. Not the most recent but an excellent album by this singer, who presents Mexican *sones* and *boleros* to a wider audience.
★ **Maná** *Drama y Luz*. Considered the pioneers of the "Rock en Espanol" movement, this album garnered the old-timers a justly deserved Latin Grammy in 2011.
Molotov *¿Dónde Jugarán las Niñas?* This aggressive, political hip-hop album was banned in Mexico for obscenity (and possible use of an underage model on its cover). Needless to say, it was a mammoth hit, and the band's "*Gimme Tha Power*" perfectly captures a moment in Mexican youth culture. Their songs about migrant workers, corruption and minibus drivers are contemporary classics.
Nortec Collective *Tijuana Sessions Vol 3*. More so than Vol 1 (which errs on the side of generic techno), this album shows off the funky potential of remixing blaring Mexican horns for the dancefloor.

the late harpist **Graciana Silva**, "La Negra Graciana" (she died in 2013), has not been repeated by other bands. Graciana's style, like that of Nicolás Sosa and the legendary Lino Chávez, was faster than the *jaranero* style of the southern bands, and there was more African influence in the mix, whereas the *jaranero* bands (others include **Los Utrera** and **Los Cojolites**) reveal a gentle melancholy, associated with a more Indigenous culture.

For *son jarocho* fans the *jaranero* festival held on February 2 in Tlacotalpan (see page 409) is a must: a huge fiesta dedicated to the Virgin of the Candelaria with a stage for *jaraneros* on which professional, amateur, local and foreign musicians have an open microphone in a party atmosphere.

Son Huasteco

A third style that is less well known internationally, but which has a very passionate following in Mexico, is **son huasteco**, from the Huasteca region in central and northern Mexico. The line-up, in contrast with the two previous styles, is always the same: a violin, a *huapanguera* guitar and the smaller, higher pitched *jarana* guitar. These three instruments, aided by the falsetto voice of at least one of the trio, creates a music that is surprisingly complete and which has a capacity to move audiences from a frightening melancholy, through to humour and to great joy. For the past twenty years at least, the most important trio has been **Los Camperos de Valles**, led by the singer **Marcos Hernández** whose falsetto can be heard on Vol III of the *Anthology of Sones* CD set, in a recording that was made just before he formed Los Camperos. "*El San Lorenzo*", played by Los Camperos Huastecos, features Marcos' angelic falsetto as it sounded when he was 17. Today – over forty years later – it is still worth taking a ten-hour bus journey from Mexico City to Ciudad Valles to hear Marcos, accompanied by Gregorio Solano on *jarana* and the outstanding violin of newcomer Camilo Ramírez.

Son huasteco is enjoying a huge revival which is almost completely driven by local tastes. There are hundreds of trios playing in the states of Hidalgo, Tamaulipas and San Luis Potosí, as well as many more who have emigrated to Mexico City. They have recorded countless CDs, some of which have local DJ-style introductions with synthesizers and extra-echo, but, when the intro fades out, you are left with a perfect performance of the violin and two guitars playing the old repertoire. Apart from Los Camperos, look out for CDs by **Real Hidalguense** or the other classic trio **Armonía Huasteca**. There are many events in Mexico City and all over the Huasteca where it's possible to dance all night long to the *son* of different trios, but these are not usually announced beyond the local community so it can be hard to identify them. In February and April there are big local **festivals** in San Joaquín de los Minerales which are highly recommended. For the less adventurous, the Museo de Culturas Populares in Mexico City sometimes presents good trios from all over the Huasteca.

Other sones

Seldom heard in the city but enormously popular back home in the villages of the Sierra Gorda, the **arribeño style** is the most poetic form of *son*. Here, the *trovador* – who seems to be the natural successor of the medieval troubadour – is a country poet, often with no formal education, who composes verses about local heroes, the planets, the earth and the continuing struggles for land. Usually two *trovadores*, both playing the *huapanguera* guitar and each accompanied by two violins and the small *vihuela* guitar, confront each other on makeshift wooden platforms that are erected on two sides of the village square. The poets enter into musical combat, improvising verses which are interspersed with *zapateado* dancing. Each year on December 31, the greatest living *trovador*, **Guillermo Velázquez**, organizes a festival in his village, paying homage to the old musicians before starting a *topada* musical combat that lasts all night. Guillermo is an outstanding musician with a sharp wit that he uses to satirize the political situation and, in the sense of bringing a political message to deep-roots traditional music, he is unique in Mexico.

Based in the Mexican west, in the Tierra Caliente (hot lands) of the Río Balsas basin, the **son guerrerense** has a tradition of exceptional violinists, exemplified by **Juan Reynoso**, who died in 2007 at the age of 95. Reynoso became the unwitting guru of a generation of Mexico City and US musicians who would travel to Guerrero and sit at his feet, learning to play his own compositions as well as the traditional repertoire. As an old man, Reynoso toured the West Coast of the United States, participating in fiddlers' festivals. In his own region he is remembered by the name given to him by a local poet: "The Paganini of the Hotlands".

Further west, in a region where the heat is so intense that it's known as "Hell's Waiting Room", **sones de arpa grande** (*sones* of the big harp) are one of Mexico's best-kept musical secrets. These bands – made up of a big harp, one or two violins and two guitars – don't thrive as they used to, but great harpists, like **Juan Pérez Morfín** and his band **Alma de Apatzingán**, can still be tracked down in the region. In the brothels of Apatzingán and in the region's country fairs, the sound boxes of the big harps are beaten in counter-rhythm by one of the band members or by a fan who pays for the privilege. The harpist, meanwhile, must hold onto the melody with *jananeo* vocals that can sound something like a shout from the soul. Concerts are often organized by stable-owners who pride themselves on their **dancing horses**: *conjunto* music is also popular in this region, but the horses only dance to the big harp music, and they do so on wooden platforms, beating out the rhythm and counter-rhythm with their hooves.

Tropical

Mexico has had a very close musical relationship with Cuba and Colombia since the earliest days of the recording industry, and music that is born in one of the three countries tends to have a rebirth in another. It was in Mexico that **Damasio Pérez Prado** "discovered" the **mambo**; Cuban chanteuse **Celia Cruz** lived here, as did **Bienvenido Granda**, **Beny Moré**, **Rubén González**, **Enrique Jorrín** and **Miguel Matamoros** among others. All the different styles of upbeat and romantic music that these gods produced tend to be known in Mexico as **música tropical** and they are still much consumed, although the younger generation prefer **reggaetón**: a Latin (mainly Puerto Rican) version of hip-hop blaring from bars and radio all over the country.

Trova yucateca, a local style from the Yucatán, was present at the birth of the **bolero** in Santiago de Cuba and this romantic repertoire has a long history of coming and going between the two countries. This is hardly surprising, since Mérida, the sleepy capital of Yucatán state, is geographically (and in some ways culturally) closer to Havana than to Mexico City. In the 1950s, trios like **Los Panchos** took the Cuban *bolero* and the Yucatecan *trova* and established the formula of a *requinto* guitar, two Spanish guitars and the harmony of three voices.

Such trios were enormously popular throughout the second half of the twentieth century and, although they are few and far between in Mexico City today, at least ten trios gather every night in the main square of Mérida to offer their local repertoire, performed in the style of Los Panchos, while in the theatres and clubs, there is a series of excellent groups that are fusing *trova* with Cuban *son* and other styles. **Yahal Kaab** offers an almost perfect contemporary fusion of the Yucatán and Cuba while the younger, more commercial group **Los Juglares** have a spectacular energy and stage presence. For people who (understandably) fall in love with the music, look for CDs by the grandfather of this style, **Guty Cárdenas**, who died in 1932 at the age of 27 but whose magic is still very much alive. **Armando Manzanero** was a *trovador* who emigrated to Mexico City in the 1970s and developed a new *bolero* style which has made him a favourite, not just in Mexico but all over Latin America and especially in Cuba.

Danzón and cumbia

Like the *bolero*, **danzón** is originally Cuban, but the Mexican version, which is always instrumental and more formal than the original, filled oversized dance halls in Mexico City for more than half a century. It is still danced under the stars in the main square of Veracruz and behind the Ciudadela market in Mexico City: bastions of elderly couples who are masters of elegance and style and who won't let their age get in the way of a subtle sensuality that is irresistible.

It is a similar story with the **cumbia**, a commercial style that was born in Colombia and became enormously popular in Mexico in the 1970s, when **Sonora Dinamita** came, saw and conquered, and then fractured into several different groups, each with the same name.

Norteño

From Mexico's northern border came **norteño**, known in the US as **Tejano** or just Tex-Mex, traditional music that broke into the mainstream and became enormously popular in the early 1990s. This achievement is associated, above all, with **Los Tigres del Norte**, a band who had a mammoth hit with their 1988 Grammy winner "*Gracias América sin Fronteras*". *Norteño*, the preferred style for accompanying the *corrido* ballads that are also played on the Pacific coast and in Morelos in central Mexico, has a history that long predates its commercial breakthrough. The late 1920s were the golden age of the **corrido**, when songs of the recent Revolution were recorded in San Antonio, Texas, and distributed on both sides of the border. The accordion, which had arrived with German immigrants in the late nineteenth century, was introduced into the originally guitar-based groups by **Narciso Martínez** and **Santiago Jiménez** (father of the famous Flaco) in the 1930s, and the sound that they developed became the essence of *corrido* ensembles on both sides of the border.

Along with the **accordion** came the polka, and by the 1950s this had blended with the traditional duet-singing of northern Mexico and with salon dances like the waltz, mazurka and the *chotis* (the central European *schottische* that travelled to Spain and France before arriving in northern Mexico) to produce the definitive *norteño* style. The accordion pepped up the songs with lead runs and flourishes between the verses, but the *conjuntos norteños* needed to round out their sound to keep up with the big bands and so added bass and rolling drums – the basis of today's **conjuntos**.

The *corrido* ballads tell of anti-heroes: small-time drug runners, illegal immigrants, a thief with one blond eyebrow who defied the law. *Norteño* reflects the mood of a country that generally considers the government to be big-time thieves and hence has a certain respect for everyday people with the courage to stand up to a crooked system. Groups like Los Tigres del Norte and **Los Cadetes del Norte** take stories from the local papers and convert them into ballads that usually begin "Voy a cantarles un corrido" ("I'm going to sing you a *corrido*") before launching into a gruesome tale sung in a deadpan style as if it were nothing to go to a local dance and get yourself killed.

Los Tigres are still the superstars of *norteño*, on both sides of the border. Quite early in their career, the band modified the traditional line-up by adding a sax and mixed the familiar rhythms with *cumbias*; however, their nasal singing style and the combination of instruments identifies the music very clearly as *norteño*. The likes of **Ramón Ayala** continue to play the *norteño* repertoire and **Los Tucanes de Tijuana** get themselves into trouble with their narco-*corridos*, but most of the original bands have moved into the *conjunto* mould, playing romantic music as well as upbeat songs that combine elements of *música tropical* and *norteño*. Today the lines are very blurred between *conjuntos*, *norteño*, *banda* and a new favourite: the **duranguense**, which has its own, very popular dance and a range of artists such as **El As de la Sierra**, **K-Paz de la Sierra** and **AK7**, whose names confirm their origins in the narco-dominated mountain towns of the north.

The Banda boom

The enormous success of Los Tigres del Norte and their updated *norteño* sound resulted in a phenomenon that changed the face of Mexican music in the mid-1990s: **banda** music. This is a fusion of the *norteño* style with the brass bands that have played at village fiestas all over the country for the last century. There are now hundreds of *bandas* in Mexico – ranging in size from eight to twenty musicians – all playing brass and percussion, with just an occasional guitar. Their repertoire includes *norteño* polkas, *ranchera* ballads, *cumbia*, merengue and salsa. The most exciting of these groups is a fiery orchestra from Mazatlán, the **Banda El Recodo**. This is not a new band; indeed, its former leader, **Don Cruz Lizárraga**, had been in the business for half a century, starting out in a traditional *tambora* marching band (the *tambora* is the huge, carried side drum). However, Don Cruz had always had an eye for musical fashions, adapting his material to merengue, *ranchera* or whatever anyone wanted to hear. His great *banda* hit was a version of Cuban bandleader Beny Moré's classic "*La Culebra*". Other big-name bands include **Banda Limón** and the extravagant **Banda Cuisillos** that have been known to dress up in feathers and perform a neo-Aztec ritual before launching into the *banda* repertoire.

The *banda* boom dominated the national airwaves in the 1990s, and the genre remains incredibly popular. Outside the big cities, it is still the *bandas* that fill the stadiums and village halls, and it's their names you'll see painted in enormous multicoloured letters on patches of white wall along the roads. The craze brought with it a series of new dances, too, particularly the *quebradita* – a gymnastic, very intimate combination of *lambada*, polka and even a little bit of swing and hip-hop, which is danced with particular skill in points north of Guadalajara. Despite its enormous following outside the capital, *banda* music is considered very unsophisticated by the urban elite. It exists as a parallel musical culture that has created its own aesthetics in terms of the slightly off-the-note vocal style developed by singers like Mazatlán-based **Julio Preciado**, cultivating the image of the Mexican macho in tight leather pants and a black cowboy hat with lines of ladies screaming at their feet.

Divas and Música Ranchera

Don't expect **women** in Mexico to take the macho culture sitting down. There is a very long and glorious tradition of female **divas** who share less in terms of their musical styles and more in terms of their fierce independence, and the confidence to take on different influences and make them their own.

A forerunner who has inspired many of the later divas was **Lucha Reyes**, the remarkable singer of the **ranchera** repertoire which took the bucolic, upbeat *sones* and – in the flood of nostalgia that accompanied the growth of the cities in the 1940s – converted them into a sad lament for a lost way of life in which the woman was always the downfall and tequila the remedy. It was a man, **José Alfredo Jimenez**, who converted this music – so much more simple than the complex *sones* – into an art form. He composed songs like "*El Rey*" in which he sings of a man who has no money, no throne, nobody to maintain him and yet, despite that, he continues to be the king.

A close friend of José Alfredo's, **Chavela Vargas** was a remarkable figure in the 1950s. In a conservative, Catholic culture, she was proud to be gay, and she sang José Alfredo's songs in bars and nightclubs, changing the words so that she could lament and celebrate the love of a woman. Chavela retired early but, after giving up alcohol, she returned to professional life in the late 1980s and was serenaded by Pedro Almodovar, among others. She played at the Olympia in Paris, recording with the elite of Spanish superstars, and then returned to Mexico, the home she had adopted after leaving Costa Rica as a young girl. At the age of 90 Chavela recorded one final album,*Por mi Culpa*!, before passing away in 2012.

One composer favoured by Chavela was **Agustín Lara**, "El Flaco de Oro", who fused the spirit of *ranchera* music with the Cuban *bolero*, creating a style that remains enormously popular in Mexico and all over Latin America, where it coexists alongside the Cuban *boleros*. "*El rival*", "*Amor de mis amores*" and "*Mujer*" are among the many classics that have survived for more than fifty years. Each generation of mainstream Mexican artists reinvents Lara for its own glory, and the countless CDs dedicated to his memory now include several recorded by flamenco singers from Andalucía.

Possibly the greatest contemporary diva is **Eugenia León**, who typifies the style with an exquisite voice that brought her fame first as a protest singer in the 1970s, later singing *ranchera boleros, norteño* and songs that were composed especially for her by writers like the late Marcial Alejandro. Despite her repute and more than thirty years at the top, she remains remarkably natural and is a generous artist who now spends much of her time promoting the talents of other musicians through her TV interviews and documentaries.

Mexican pop and "Latin Alternative"

Latin pop music has traditionally been dominated by Colombian, Puerto Rican and American Latino performers, but Mexico has its own extremely influential scene. Since the 1990s the biggest name has been **Thalía**, the singer/dancer/actress and "Queen of Latin Pop" from Mexico City who has sold over 40 million records – she's also one of only a few Mexican artists to have recorded albums in English (the eponymous *Thalía* in 2003). Thalía's contemporary, singer **Paulina Rubio** has been almost as successful (with over 20 million records sold) and has also recorded in English (*Border Girl* in 2002) – both stars have millions of fans across the US border. Similarly iconic singers include rock-pop superstar **Alejandra Guzmán**, **Ana Gabriel** (another performer who often switches genres) and **Gloria Trevi**, who lives across the border in McAllen, Texas. On the men's side is crooner **Luis Miguel** (actually born in Puerto Rico) and **Marco Antonio Solís**, a multi-Grammy award winner, both dominating charts since the 1990s. Younger stars include Madrid-born **Belinda Peregrín**, the "Princess of Latin Pop", whose debut album *Belinda* (2003) was a massive hit. Her most recent release, *Catarsis* (2013), reached number two on the US Latin pop chart.

Lila Downs, who enjoys tremendous success both in Mexico and beyond, has remained largely apart from mainstream pop, using her admirable voice to project her own versions of music from Veracruz; *boleros*, *ranchera* classics in the style of Lucha Reyes and, more recently, a repertoire that is very much her own (sometimes dubbed "**Latin Alternative**"). The daughter of a US filmmaker and a Mixtec mother from Oaxaca, she has carved an important place for herself on both sides of the border. With her neo-Frida Kahlo image, Lila has a tremendous stage presence and she was confirmed as a major international artist with her performance at the 2003 Oscar ceremonies.

In the wake of Lila come **Julieta Venegas** from Tijuana, whose platinum-selling albums are favourites on the pop-rock circuit, but whose natural style and quirky innocence separate her from media-born artists, and two new names who have a fierce independence that distinguishes them from the mainstream. **Ximena Sariñana** and **Natalia Lafourcade** are both younger, feisty singers who move in and out of the pop-rock world, according to their different moods.

Rock en Español

One reason that traditional forms such as *son* flourished in Mexico is that the country was closed to **rock** music until the late 1980s, when the government finally lifted import regulations and laws banning rock concerts. These had been in place since the 1971 Arándaro festival, dubbed the "Mexican Woodstock", scandalized the nation and effectively drove the country's rock music culture underground. When the borders opened in 1990, international rock music flooded the local market and Mexican rock began to flourish. The boom began in Mexico City, with middle-class rockers like **Los Caifanes** playing to middle-class audiences who knew about the outside scene because they, or their parents, travelled regularly to Europe and the US. Ironically, the Caifanes' massive hit was a 1988 cover of a traditional Cuban *son*, "*La Negra Tomasa*", which appealed to a public that understood *son* and salsa better than the British punk referenced in other songs. A little later, the eclectic **Café Tacuba** began to reach a bigger audience, with an interest, to some extent, in exploring Mexican roots and reinterpreting Mexican *son* in their own way. Then came **Maldita Vecindad** from Mexico City and **Maná**, from Guadalajara, and Mexican rock – now rather slickly produced – entered the superstar level.

In the late 1990s, the scene began to splinter into subcultures. The industrial town of Monterrey, home to a prestigious university and a lot of English-speaking, US-oriented youth, was a seemingly bottomless well of talent that drew comparisons to Seattle in the grunge years. Funky mix-masters **Plastilina Mosh**, ska band **El Gran Silencio** and **Control Machete**'s hip-hop went from here to Latin MTV. In Tijuana, meanwhile, **Nortec Collective** helped create an international club scene with its remixes of classic *norteño* sounds with techno beats. In Mexico City **ska** became immensely popular alongside **hip-hop**, with excellent bands such as **Molotov** making piercing social commentary in their songs about politics, corruption and what it feels like to live on the wrong side of the US border.

The music section was originally written by Mary Farquharson. Mary is co-founder of Discos Corason (http://corason.com) and was one of the original founders of World Circuit. She has lived in Mexico since 1987.

Books

Mexico has attracted more than its fair share of famous foreign writers, and has inspired a vast literature and several classics. Until very recently, however, Mexican writers had received little attention outside the country. Books with a ★ symbol are highly recommended.

IMPRESSIONS OF MEXICO

Jeff Biggers *In the Sierra Madre*. Biggers juxtaposes the history of the Copper Canyon region – with all its Indigenous tribes and foreign treasure-hunters – with his present-day experiences living there amid the Rarámuri, the drug-runners and other colourful characters. Really lively story-telling from someone with an obvious love of the place.

Tony Cohan *Mexican Days: Journeys into the Heart of Mexico*. Cohan, an American novelist, relocated to San Miguel de Allende in the 1980s; this is a travelogue of his explorations into small towns after some twenty years in Mexico – a perspective that's both respectful and informed.

Carl Franz, Lorena Havens and Steve Rogers *The People's Guide to Mexico*. Not a guidebook as such: more a series of anecdotes and words of advice for staying out of trouble and heading off the beaten track. Perennially popular with old hippies of all ages (2012 saw the publication of the fourteenth edition), and deservedly so.

Richard Grant *God's Middle Finger: Into the Lawless Heart of the Sierra Madre* (published in the UK as *Bandit Roads: Into the Lawless Heart of Mexico*). A British journalist's adventures as he finds himself caught up in the north-east's drug wars post-2000 and barely escapes with his life; a thoroughly entertaining read.

★ **Graham Greene** *The Lawless Roads*. In the late 1930s Greene was sent to Mexico to investigate the effects of the persecution of the Catholic Church. The result (see also his novel, page 819) was this classic account of his travels in a very bizarre era of modern Mexican history.

★ **John Harrison** *1519: A Journey to the End of Time*. This 2015 book retraces the footsteps of Hernán Cortés, blending history, travelogue and accounts of the author's battle with cancer. A beautifully written, moving and evocative work. Highly recommended.

D.H. Lawrence *Mornings in Mexico*. A very slim volume, half of which is devoted to the Hopi Indigenous people of New Mexico, this is an uncharacteristically cheerful account of Lawrence's stay in southern Mexico, and beautifully written – although his characterizations of native culture will likely strike modern readers as condescending.

John Lloyd Stephens *Incidents of Travel in Central America, Chiapas, and Yucatán*. Stephens was a classic nineteenth-century traveller. Acting as American ambassador to Central America, he indulged his own enthusiasm for archeology. His journals, full of superb Victorian pomposity punctuated with sudden waves of enthusiasm, make great reading, especially as companions to the great Maya ruins, many of which he helped uncover. The best editions include the fantastic original illustrations by Frederick Catherwood; you won't have trouble finding inexpensive paperback versions in Mexico, and it's available for free on Kindle.

John Steinbeck *Log from the Sea of Cortez*. The record of Steinbeck's jaunt around Baja California by boat in 1940, part travelogue, part marine-life guide; you'll find it far more amusing than Steinbeck's often bleak novels.

John Kenneth Turner *Barbarous Mexico*. Turner was a journalist, and this account of his travels through nineteenth-century Mexico exposing the conditions of workers in the plantations of the Yucatán, serialized in US newspapers, did much to discredit the regime of Porfirio Díaz.

Ronald Wright *Time Among the Maya*. A vivid and sympathetic account of travels from Belize through Guatemala, Chiapas and Yucatán in the 1990s, meeting the Maya of today and exploring their obsession with time. The level of detail makes this a complex read – best for readers with a specific interest in ancient Maya culture.

MEXICAN FICTION

Mariano Azuela *The Underdogs*. The first novel of the Revolution (finished in 1915), *The Underdogs* is told through the eyes of a group of peasants who form a semi-regular Revolutionary armed band; it relates their escapades, progress and eventual betrayal and massacre. Initially fighting for land and liberty, they end up caught in an uncontrollable cycle of violence and descend into brutal nihilism.

Carmen Boullosa *The Miracle Worker*. One of Mexico's best contemporary writers, Boullosa focuses on traditional Mexican themes, often borrowing characters from history or myth. *The Miracle Worker* explores Mexican attitudes to Catholicism through the eyes of a messianic healer and her followers. The story can be seen as a parable about the Mexican political system, where ordinary Mexicans petition a distant government for favours, which are granted or refused in seemingly arbitrary decisions. You may be able to find Boullosa's novel *Leaving Tabasco* (2002) more readily; it's not as strong a work, but an interesting vision of small-town life (and trauma) through the eyes of a child.

María Amparo Escandón *Gonzalez & Daughter Trucking Co*. A story within a story, told with gusto by an inmate at a women's prison in Mexicali – borderline pulp, with cliffhangers and campy drama, but heartwarming and funny in its treatment of loyalty and freedom. Escandón's earlier work, *Esperanza's Box of Saints*, is a charming, quick-read tale of female emancipation.

★ **Laura Esquivel** *Like Water for Chocolate*. Adapted to film, Esquivel's novel proved a huge hit in Mexico and abroad. The book is even better: funny, sexy, sentimental (schmaltzy, even), it deals with the star-crossed romance of Tita, whose lover marries her sister. Using the magic of the kitchen, she sets out to seduce him back. The book is written in monthly episodes, each of which is prefaced with a traditional Mexican recipe. The author's 2006 novel, *Malinche*, is not nearly as successful, but presents a sympathetic version of Cortés' courtesan and translator, whose name is synonymous with "traitor" in Mexico.

★ **Carlos Fuentes** *The Death of Artemio Cruz* and *The Old Gringo*. Fuentes is by far the best-known Mexican writer outside Mexico, influenced by Mariano Azuela and Juan Rulfo, and an early exponent of magical realism. In *The Death of Artemio Cruz*, the hero, a rich and powerful man on his deathbed, looks back over his life and loves, from an idealist youth in the Revolution through disillusion to corruption and power. *The Old Gringo* takes place during the Revolution, imagining that vanished American writer Ambrose Bierce has joined Pancho Villa's army; it's shorter, but no less carefully crafted. These are the classics, but Fuentes was a prolific writer and you'll find plenty of others if these pique your interest.

Mónica Lavín (ed) *Points of Departure*. A collection of short stories from some of the country's most respected contemporary writers – the selection is a little uneven, but it may be interesting and refreshing to read stories that *don't* involve magical realism.

★ **Octavio Paz** (ed) *Mexican Poetry*. Edited by Paz (perhaps the leading man of letters of Mexico's post-Revolutionary era) and translated by Samuel Beckett, this is as good a taste as you could hope for of modern Mexican poets. Some of Paz's own poetry is also available in translation.

Elena Poniatowska *Here's to You, Jesúsa!* One of Mexico's best-known essayists and journalists lightly fictionalizes the life story of her cleaning lady to create a lively "autobiography" covering her marriage, involvement in the Revolution and the postwar period. Some of Poniatowska's other excellent works available in English include *Massacre in Mexico*, a collage of testimonies of those present at the 1968 massacre of students in Tlatelolco, and *Tinisima*, a portrait of Communist organizer and photographer Tina Modotti.

Juan Rulfo *Pedro Páramo*. First published in 1955, this is widely regarded as the greatest Mexican novel of the twentieth century and a precursor of magical realism. The living and spirit worlds mesh when, at the behest of his dying mother, the narrator visits the deserted village haunted by the memory of his brutal father, Pedro Páramo. Dark, but ultimately very rewarding. Rulfo's short-story collection, *The Burning Plain and Other Stories*, was rated by Gabriel García Márquez as the best in Latin America.

Ignacio Solares *Yankee Invasion*. An account of the 1847 US capture of Mexico City from the perspective of an ageing journalist, looking back at his youthful involvement. A sometimes uneasy mix of romance, psychology and history, but ultimately an enjoyable read. Solares is one of Mexico's leading men of letters.

FOREIGN FICTION

There are hundreds of novels by non-Mexicans set in Mexico, all too many in the sex-and-shopping genre. Apart from those below, others to look out for include a whole clutch of modern Americans, especially **Jack Kerouac**'s *Desolation Angels* and several of Richard Brautigan's novels. And of course there's **Carlos Castaneda**'s *Don Juan* series – a search for enlightenment through *peyote*.

Roberto Bolaño *The Savage Detectives*. The late Chilean author grew up partly in Mexico and his sprawling idiosyncratic, Borges-esque book follows the adventures of Arturo Belano (who bears striking similarity to Bolaño himself) in search of a 1920s Mexican poet.

Graham Greene *The Power and the Glory*. Inspired by his investigative travels, this story of a doomed whisky priest, on the run from the authorities, makes a great yarn and a wonderful movie.

D.H. Lawrence *The Plumed Serpent*. One of Lawrence's own favourites, the novel reflects his intense dislike of the country that followed on from the brief honeymoon period of *Mornings in Mexico* (see page 818). Fans of his heavy spiritualism will love it.

Haniel Long *The Marvellous Adventure of Cabeza de Vaca*. Two short stories in one volume – the first the account of a shipwrecked conquistador's journey across the new continent, the second the thoughts and hopes of Malinche, Cortés' interpreter.

★ **Malcolm Lowry** *Under the Volcano*. A classic since its publication, Lowry's account of the last day in the life of the British consul in Cuernavaca – passed in a mescal-induced haze – is totally brilliant. His *Dark as the Grave Wherein My Friend Is Laid* is also based on his Mexican experiences.

★ **B. Traven** various works. In the 1920s and 1930s, the mysterious Traven – whose true identity is itself the subject of a series of books – wrote a series of compelling novels set in Mexico. Among the best-known are *Treasure of the Sierra Madre* (later a film starring Humphrey Bogart) and *The Death Ship*, but of more interest if you're travelling are such works as *The Bridge in the Jungle* and the other six books in the *Jungle* series: *Government*, *The Carreta*, *March to the Monteria*, *Trozas*, *The Rebellion of the Hanged* and *General* *from the Jungle*. These latter all deal with the state of the peasantry and the growth of revolutionary feeling in the last years of the Díaz dictatorship.

HISTORY

Bartolome de Las Casas *A Short Account of the Destruction of the Indies*. The counterpoint to Díaz and Cortés, with Las Casas leaving no doubt that the conquest of Mexico was a bloody, gruesome affair.

Inga Clendinnen *Ambivalent Conquests: Maya and Spaniard in Yucatán 1517 to 1570*. A product of meticulous research that documents the methods and consequences of the Spanish Conquest of the Yucatán. The ambivalence in the title reflects doubts about the effectiveness of the Conquest in subjugating the Maya, and the book provides insights into the rebellions that followed: more than three hundred years later, the Maya rose in revolt during the Caste Wars, and almost succeeded in driving out their white overlords. Later editions also comment briefly on the 1994 Chiapas uprising.

Hernán Cortés *Letters from Mexico*. The thoughts and impressions of the conquistador, at first hand. Less exciting than Díaz, though.

★ **Bernal Díaz** *The Conquest of New Spain*. This abridged version is still the best available of Díaz's classic *Historia Verdadera de la Conquista de la Nueva España*. Díaz, having been on two earlier expeditions to Mexico, accompanied Cortés throughout his campaign of conquest, and this magnificent eyewitness account makes compelling reading.

Adolfo Gilly *The Mexican Revolution*. Considered the classic work on the Revolution, this was written in Mexico City's notorious Lecumberri jail (Gilly was later granted an absolute pardon). Heavy-going and highly theoretical, though.

John Mason Hart *Empire & Revolution: The Americans in Mexico since the Civil War*. A fascinating study of the relationship between the US and Mexico, and in particular US imperialist aspirations and involvement in Mexican financial affairs. Hart's *Revolutionary Mexico* is a detailed history of the Mexican Revolution following the same theme of US involvement. Both are serious works of history, heavy-going in parts.

Enrique Krauze *Mexico: Biography of Power*. First published in Spanish, this sprawling history covers most of the nineteenth and twentieth centuries – the biography format makes it very readable, and easier to dip into if you can't weather all 896 pages. Street names and public holidays will make a lot more sense, at the very least.

Greg Niemann *Baja Legends*. Essential reading for travellers to Baja California, a detailed compendium of all the crazy characters, historical events and places that make it such a magical destination.

★ **Richard and Rosalind Perry** *Maya Missions*. One in a series of expertly written guides to the sometimes overlooked treasures of Mexico's colonial religious architecture. *More Maya Missions* covers Chiapas. Both are illustrated by the authors' simple but beautiful drawings. These specialist offerings, ideal for travellers who want more information than most guidebooks can provide, are not widely available, though you can sometimes find them in tourist bookshops in the areas they cover (and online).

John Reed *Insurgent Mexico*. This collection of his reportage of the Mexican Revolution was put together by Reed himself. He spent several months in 1913 and 1914 with various generals of the Revolution – especially Villa – and the book contains great descriptions of them, their men and the mood of the times.

★ **Nelson Reed** *The Caste War of the Yucatan*. Reed's book is the authority on this tumultuous and defining era in Yucatán history, with great detail on the Talking Cross movement. A must-read for anyone intrigued by this period.

★ **Jasper Ridley** *Maximilian & Juárez*. This comprehensive, highly readable account of one of "the great tragicomedies of the nineteenth century" charts the attempt by Napoleon III to establish Archduke Maximilian as the emperor of Mexico. The colourful narrative brings to life an unmitigated political disaster with huge consequences, including the execution of Maximilian, the insanity of his wife Carlota and the emergence of the US as a world power.

Hugh Thomas *Conquest: Montezuma, Cortés, and the Fall of Old Mexico* (published in the UK as *The Conquest of Mexico*). A brilliant narrative history of the Conquest by the British historian previously best known for his history of the Spanish Civil War. A massive work of real scholarship and importance – much of the archive material was unearthed only in the 1980s and 1990s – but also humorous and readable, with appendices on everything from Aztec beliefs, history and genealogy to Cortés' wives and lovers.

ANCIENT MEXICO

Warwick Bray *Everyday Life of the Aztecs*. An informative volume about Aztec warfare, music, games, folklore, religious ritual, social organization, economic and political systems and agricultural practice. Although the book is now showing its age, and some of its conclusions are a bit dubious, its attractive comprehensiveness more than makes up for this. An excellent general introduction.

Inga Clendinnen *Aztecs: An Interpretation*. A social history of the Aztec empire that seeks to explain the importance – and acceptance – of human sacrifice and other rituals. Fascinating, though best to know something about the Aztecs before you start.

Michael D. Coe *The Maya*. The best available general introduction to the Maya: concise, clear and comprehensive. Coe has also written several weightier, academic volumes. His *Breaking the Maya Code*, a history of the decipherment of the Maya glyphs, owes much to the fact that Coe was present at many of the most important meetings leading to the breakthrough that demonstrated how the glyphs actually did reproduce Maya speech. It is a beautifully written, ripping yarn, though the attacks on Eric Thompson become a bit wearisome. In *Mexico: From the Olmecs to the Aztecs*, co-authored with Rex Koontz, he introduces Mexico's other early cultures.

★ **Nigel Davies** *The Ancient Kingdoms of Mexico*. Although no single text covers all the ancient cultures, this comes pretty close, covering the central areas from the Olmecs through Teotihuacán and the Toltecs to the Aztec empire. An excellent mix of historical, archeological, social and artistic information, but it doesn't cover the Maya. Davies is also the author of several more-detailed academic works on the Aztecs and Toltecs, including *The Aztecs, A History*.

Munro S. Edmonson (trans.) *Heaven Born Merida and Its Destiny: The Book of Chilam Balam of Chumayel*. The *Chilam Balam* is a recollection of Maya history and myth, compiled by the Maya over centuries; this version was written in Maya in Latin script in the eighteenth century. Although the style is not easy, it's one of the few keys into the Maya view of the world.

Diego de Landa *Yucatán Before and After the Conquest*. A translation by William Gates of the work written in 1566 as *Relación de las Cosas de Yucatán*. De Landa's destruction of almost all original Maya books as "works of the devil" leaves his own account as the chief source on Maya life and society in the immediate post-Conquest period. Written during his imprisonment in Spain on charges of cruelty to the Indigenous people, the book provides a fascinating wealth of detail. Various other translations are widely available in Mexico.

Simon Martin and Nikolai Grube *Chronicle of the Maya Kings and Queens*. A more graphic approach to Maya history, replete with photo illustrations, timelines, hieroglyphics and the like, making the complex dynasties a little easier to grasp.

★ **Mary Ellen Miller and Karl Taube** *An Illustrated Dictionary of the Gods and Symbols of Ancient Mexico and the Maya*. A superb modern reference on ancient Mesoamerica, written by two leading scholars. Taube's *Aztec and Maya Myths* is perfect as a short, accessible introduction to Mesoamerican mythology.

Chris Morton and Ceri Louise Thomas *The Mystery of the Crystal Skulls*. Intriguing, if somewhat sensationalist, investigation into an ancient legend that tells of a number of life-size crystal skulls said to contain vital information about the destiny of mankind. Following the discovery that such a skull actually exists, film-makers Morton and Thomas set off on a journey through Mexico and Central America, meeting experts in Maya culture, archeologists and modern-day shamans and reaching their own conclusions.

Linda Schele, David Freidel et al. *A Forest of Kings: The Untold Story of the Ancient Maya*. The authors, at the forefront of the "new archeology", have been personally responsible for decoding many Maya glyphs, revolutionizing and popularizing this field. Although their populist writing style is controversial, it has also inspired a devoted following. They have shown that, far from being governed by peaceful astronomer-priests, the ancient Maya were ruled by hereditary kings, lived in populous, aggressive city-states and engaged in a continuous entanglement of alliances and war. The story continues in *The Blood of Kings*, by Linda Schele and Mary Ellen Miller.

Robert Sharer *The Ancient Maya*. The classic, comprehensive (and weighty) account of Maya civilization, now in its sixth edition. Required reading for archeologists, it also provides a fascinating reference for the non-expert.

Popol Vuh The Quiché Maya bible, a fascinating creation myth, is available in two main translations (many others can also be found): the classic version by Dennis Tedlock is arguably still the most readable; Allen J Christenson's two-volume approach gives a literal translation as well. The Maya obsession with time can be well appreciated here, where dates are recorded with painstaking precision.

Ptolemy Tompkins *This Tree Grows Out of Hell*. An interesting attempt to piece together the mystery of Mesoamerican religion, synthesizing and making readable many of the late twentieth-century findings in the area. The latter half of the book is a thoroughly unconvincing apology for the brutality of the Aztecs.

Richard F. Townsend *The Aztecs*. Companion in the series to Coe's *Maya* book (see page 821), this attempts to be an introduction to all aspects of Aztec history and culture, but if you haven't done some prior reading, the details of names and battles may be overwhelming. That said, it's a comprehensive reference, updated in a third edition (2009).

SOCIETY, POLITICS AND CULTURE

Taisha Abelar *The Sorcerer's Crossing*. The extraordinary true story of an American woman who joins an all-female group of sorcerers in Mexico and undergoes a rigorous physical and mental training process, designed to enable her to breach the limits of ordinary perception.

★ **Jorge G. Castaneda** *Manana Forever? Mexico and the Mexicans*. Fabulous exposé of Mexican culture by a former foreign minister, tackling the thorny issue of why Mexico's soccer team has fared so poorly, as well as meatier subjects such as Mexico's relationship with the US.

Clare Ferguson *Flavours of Mexico*. All the classics are here: tortillas, enchiladas, empanadas, *flautas* and tamales, along with party-food suggestions and a few vegetarian recipes. A colourful and straightforward cookbook that will inspire you to keep feasting on Mexican cuisine once back home.

Hayden Herrera *Frida: A Biography of Frida Kahlo*. This mesmerizing biography brings to life a woman of extreme magnetism and originality. Starting with her childhood in Mexico City, the account describes the crippling accident she had as a teenager that left her in chronic pain, her tempestuous marriage to Diego Rivera and the various men with whom she had affairs, including, most notoriously, Leon Trotsky. The book contains numerous colour reproductions of her paintings.

Diana Kennedy *From My Mexican Kitchen: Techniques and Ingredients*. Kennedy was a pioneer in bringing the multifaceted cuisine of Mexico to the attention of Americans, when she published her first cookbook in 1972. This book is a good starting point for anyone new to Mexican cooking. Her many other titles are good too: look out for *My Mexico: A Culinary Odyssey with More Than 300 Recipes*, which has a great travelogue element.

Patrick Marnham *Dreaming with His Eyes Open: A Life of Diego Rivera*. A gripping account of the extraordinary life of the great Mexican muralist in which truths are revealed and myths are unravelled.

Christopher McDougall *Born to Run: The Hidden Tribe, the Ultra-runners, and the Greatest Race the World Has Never Seen*. If you're a runner, this is a must read. Among other stories, McDougall details the incredible long-distance running culture of the Tarahumara people in Chihuahua state.

★ **Susanna Palazuelos** *Mexico: The Beautiful Cookbook*. Recipes from Mexico's most popular celebrity chef, the Acapulco-based Palazuelos, translated into English. Blends the traditional with contemporary, as well as more unusual regional dishes from all over the country.

Octavio Paz *The Labyrinth of Solitude*. An acclaimed series of philosophical essays exploring the social and political state of modern Mexico. Paz, who died in 1998, won the Nobel Prize for literature in 1990 and was universally regarded as the country's leading poet and philosopher (see page 819).

★ **John Ross** *Rebellion from the Roots*. A fascinating early account of the build-up to and first months of the 1994 Zapatista rebellion, and still the definitive book on the subject. Ross's reporting style provides a detailed and informative background, showing the uprising was no surprise to the Mexican army. His *Zapatistas: Making Another World Possible: Chronicles of Resistance 2000–2006* updated the ongoing saga.

WILDLIFE AND ENVIRONMENT

★ **Les Beletsky** *Travellers' Wildlife Guides Southern Mexico*. An excellent, if rather bulky, field guide, with colour plates of not just birds but also reptiles and mammals found through the Yucatán, Oaxaca and Chiapas.

★ **Steve Howell and Sophie Webb** *A Guide to the Birds of Mexico and Northern Central America*. A tremendous work, the result of years of research, this is the definitive book on the region's birds. Essential for all serious birders, though a bit hefty to use in the field. Howell's *Where to Watch Birds in Mexico* details more than a hundred sites.

Paul Humann and Ned DeLoach *Snorkeling Guide to Marine Life: Florida, Caribbean, Bahamas*. A handy, spiral-bound field guide to corals, fish, plants and other underwater life off the Caribbean coast. The same authors have individual titles on *Reef Fish Identification*, *Reef Creature Identification* and *Reef Coral Identification* for the same area, and a separate *Reef Fish Identification* title for the Pacific coast.

Victoria Schlesinger *Animals and Plants of the Ancient Maya: A Guide*. Examines the cultural significance of more than a hundred species in the ancient Maya world.

Language

Once you get into it, Spanish is a straightforward language, and in Mexico people are eager to understand and to help even the most faltering attempt. English is widely spoken, especially in heavily visited areas, but you'll get a far better reception if you at least try to communicate with people in their own tongue. You'll be helped by the fact that Mexicans speak relatively slowly, at least compared with Spaniards.

Rules of pronunciation

Relative to English, the rules of pronunciation are clear-cut and, once you get to know them, strictly observed. Unless there's an accent, words ending in d, l, r and z are stressed on the last syllable, all others on the second last. All vowels are pure and short.

A is between the A sound of "back" and that of "father".
E as in "get"
I as in "police"
O as in "hot"
U as in "rule"
C is spoken like S before E and I, hard otherwise: cerca is pronounced "SER-ka".
G is a guttural H sound (a little softer than the ch in "loch") before E or I, a hard G elsewhere: gigante becomes "hi-GAN-te".
H is always silent.
J is the same sound as a guttural G: jamón is pronounced "ham-ON".
LL sounds like an English Y: tortilla is pronounced "tor-TEE-ya".
N is as in English unless it has a tilde (accent) over it, when it becomes NY: mañana sounds like "ma-NYA-na".
QU is pronounced like an English K.
R is rolled; RR, doubly so.
V sounds more like B, vino becoming "BEE-no".
X has an S sound before consonants; between vowels in place names, it has an H sound, like México ("MEH-hee-ko") or Oaxaca ("wa-HA-ka"). In many place names from Indigenous languages, the X is pronounced as S – as in Xochimilco ("so-chee-MIL-co"); in Maya, however, X sounds like SH – Xel-Ha is pronounced "shel-ha".
Z is the same as a soft C, so cerveza becomes "ser-VAY-sa".

Useful words and phrases

Although we've listed a few essential words and phrases here, if you're travelling for any length of time some kind of dictionary or phrasebook is obviously a worthwhile investment: the *Rough Guide to Mexican Spanish* is the best practical guide, correct and colloquial, and will have you speaking the language faster than any other phrasebook. One of the best small Latin American Spanish dictionaries is the University of Chicago version (Pocket Books), widely available in Mexico, although the Langenscheidt pocket dictionary is also handy because its yellow plastic cover holds up well. If you're using an older dictionary, bear in mind that CH, LL and Ñ are traditionally counted as separate letters and are listed after the Cs, Ls and Ns respectively; most current dictionaries, however, follow more familiar alphabetizing procedures, though Ñ retains its own section.

BASICS

Yes, No Sí, No
Open, Closed Abierto/a, Cerrado/a
Please, Thank you Por favor, Gracias
Push, Pull Empujar, Tirar
Where?, When? ¿Dónde?, ¿Cuándo?
With, Without Con, Sin
What?, How much? ¿Qué?, ¿Cuánto?
Good, Bad Buen(o)/a, Mal(o)/a
Here, There Aquí or Acá, Allí or Allá
Big, Small Gran(de), Pequeño/a
This, That Éste, Eso
More, Less Más, Menos
Cheap, Expensive Barato/a, Caro/a
Today, Tomorrow Hoy, Mañana

Yesterday Ayer

Now, Later Ahora, Más tarde

GREETINGS AND PLEASANTRIES

Hello, Goodbye ¡Hola!, Adiós
Good morning Buenos días
Good afternoon/night Buenas tardes/noches
How do you do? ¿Qué tal?
See you later Hasta luego
Sorry Lo siento/disculpeme
Excuse me Con permiso/perdón
How are you? ¿Cómo está (usted)?
Not at all/You're welcome De nada/por nada
I (don't) understand (No) Entiendo
Do you speak English? ¿Habla (usted) inglés?
I (don't) speak Spanish (No) Hablo español
What (did you say)? ¿Mande?
My name is... Me llamo...
What's your name? ¿Cómo se llama usted?
I am English Soy inglés(a)
...American* ...americano(a)
...Australian ...australiano(a)
...Canadian ...canadiense(a)
...Irish ...irlandés(a)
...Scottish ...escosés(a)
...Welsh ...galés(a)
...New Zealander ...neozelandés(a)

*Mexicans are from the Americas too, so describing yourself as American can occasionally cause offence. Another option is "estadounidense" (or, more simply, "de Los Estados Unidos", from the United States) if you are a US American.

NEEDS: HOTELS, TRANSPORT AND DIRECTIONS

I want... Quiero...
I'd like...please Quisiera...por favor
Do you know...? ¿Sabe...?
I don't know No sé
There is... (¿)Hay...(?)
(Is there...?)
Give me... Deme...
(one like that) (uno así)
Do you have...? ¿Tiene...?
...the time ...la hora
...a room ...un cuarto
...with two beds/ ...con dos camas/
...double bed ...cama matrimonial
It's for one person Es para una persona
(two people) (dos personas)
...for one night ...para una noche
(one week) (una semana)
It's fine, how much is it? ¿Está bien, cuánto es?
It's too expensive Es demasiado caro
Don't you have anything cheaper? ¿No tiene algo más Barato?
Can one...? ¿Se puede...?
...camp (near) here? ¿...acampar (cerca de) aquí?
Is there a hotel nearby? ¿Hay un hotel cerca de aquí?
How do I get to...? ¿Por dónde se va a...?
Left, right, straight on Izquierda, derecha, derecho
This way, that way Por acá, por allá
Where is...? ¿Dónde está...?
...the bus station ...la camionera central
...the nearest bank ...el banco más cercano
...the ATM ...el cajero automático
...the post office ...el correo (la oficina de correos)
...the toilet ...el baño/sanitario
Where does the bus to...leave from? ¿De dónde sale el autobús para...?
Is this the train for Chihuahua? ¿Es éste el tren para Chihuahua?
I'd like a (return) ticket to... Quisiera un boleto (de ida y egund) para...
What time does it (arrive in...)? leave ¿A qué hora sale (llega en...)?
What is there to eat? ¿Qué hay para comer?
What's that? ¿Qué es eso?
What's this called in Spanish? ¿Cómo se llama éste en español?

NUMBERS AND DAYS

1 un/uno/una
2 dos
3 tres
4 cuatro
5 cinco
6 seis
7 siete
8 ocho
9 nueve
10 diez
11 once
12 doce
13 trece
14 catorce
15 quince
16 dieciséis
17 diecisiete
20 veinte
21 veintiuno
30 treinta

40 cuarenta
50 cincuenta
60 sesenta
70 setenta
80 ochenta
90 noventa
100 cien(to)
101 ciento uno
200 doscientos
500 quinientos
700 setecientos
1000 mil
2000 dos mil
first primero/a
second egundo/a
third tercero/a
fifth quinto/a
tenth decimo/a
Monday Lunes
Tuesday Martes
Wednesday Miércoles
Thursday Jueves
Friday Viernes
Saturday Sábado
Sunday Domingo

Food and drink terms

ON THE TABLE

Azúcar Sugar
Cuchara Spoon
Cuchillo Knife
Cuenta Bill/check
Mantequilla Butter
Pan Bread
Pimienta Pepper
Queso Cheese
Sal Salt
Salsa Sauce
Servilleta Napkin
Tenedor Fork

COOKING TERMS

A la parilla Grilled over charcoal
A la plancha Grilled on a hot plate
A la tampiqueña Strips of grilled meat served with guacamole
A la veracruzana Stewed with tomatoes, onions, olives and chile
Al horno/horneado Baked
Asado/a Broiled
Barbacoa/pibil Wrapped in banana leaves and steamed/ baked in a pit
Con mole In a thick, rich sauce of chiles, nuts, spices and chocolate
Empanizado/a Breaded
En mojo de ajo Fried with slow-cooked garlic
Frito Fried
Poco hecho/a Rare/medium/ **punto/bien cocido** well done

BREAKFAST

Huevos… Eggs...
…a la Mexicana ...scrambled with tomato, onion and chile
…con jamón ...with ham
…con tocino ...with bacon
…motuleños ...fried, served on a tortilla with beans, ham and cheese
…rancheros ...fried, on a tortilla, smothered in a red chile sauce
…revueltos ...scrambled
…tibios ...lightly boiled
Pan dulce Pastries

SOUPS (SOPAS) AND STARTERS

Caldo Broth (with bits in)
Ceviche Raw fish pieces, marinated in lime juice
Entremeses Hors d'oeuvres
Sopa… Soup...
…de fideos …with noodles
…de lentejas …with lentils
…de verduras …with vegetables

TORTILLA AND CORN DISHES (ANTOJITOS)

Burritos Wheat-flour tortillas, rolled and filled
Chilaquiles Tortilla chips stewed with meat and tomato sauce

Enchiladas Rolled-up tacos, covered in chile sauce and baked
Enchiladas suizas As above, with green chile and cheese
Flautas Small, filled, fried tortillas
Gorditas Small, fat, stuffed corn tortillas
Machaca Shredded dried meat scrambled with eggs
Molletes Split roll with beans and melted cheese
Quesadillas Toasted or fried tortillas topped with cheese
Queso fundido Melted cheese, served with tortillas and salsa
Sincronizadas Tortillas with melted cheese and ham
Sopes Bite-size tostadas
Tacos Soft corn tortillas with filling
Tacos al pastor With spicy pork
Tacos dorados Deep-fried tacos
Tamales Corn husk or banana- leaf packets of steamed corn-meal dough with a savoury or sweet filling
Tlacoyo Fat tortilla stuffed with beans
Torta Filled bread roll, often toasted like a panino
Tostadas Flat crisp tortillas piled with meat and salad

FISH AND SEAFOOD (PESCADOS Y MARISCOS)

Anchoas Anchovies
Atún Tuna
Cabrilla/Corvina Sea bass
Calamares Squid
Camarones Prawns
Cangrejo Crab
Caracol Conch
Filete entero Whole, filleted fish
Huachinango Red snapper
Langosta Rock lobster
Merluza Hake
Ostión Oyster
Pez espada Swordfish
Pulpo Octopus
Robalo Bass
Sardinas Sardines
Trucha Trout

MEAT (CARNE) AND POULTRY (AVES)

Alambre Kebab
Albóndigas Meatballs
Arrachera Skirt steak
Barbacoa Barbecued meat
Bistec Steak
Cabrito Kid
Carne (de res) Beef
Carne adobado Barbecued/spicily stewed meat
Carnitas Pork cooked with garlic until crispy
Cerdo Pork
Chivo Goat
Chorizo Spicy sausage
Chuleta Chop (usually pork)
Conejo Rabbit
Cordero Lamb
Costilla Rib
Filete Tenderloin/fillet
Guisado Stew
Hígado Liver
Lomo Loin (of pork)
Milanesa Breaded escalope
Pato Duck
Pavo/Guajolote Turkey
Pechuga Breast
Pierna Leg
Pollo Chicken
Salchicha Sausage
Salpicón Shredded meat with vinegar
Ternera Veal
Tripa/Callos Tripe
Venado Venison

VEGETABLES (VERDURAS)

Aguacate Avocado
Betabel Beetroot (often as a juice)
Calabacita Courgette (zucchini)
Calabaza Squash
Cebolla Onion
Champiñones/hongos Mushrooms
Chícharos Peas
Col Cabbage
Elote Corn on the cob
Espárragos Asparagus
Espinacas Spinach
Flor de calabaza Squash blossoms
Frijoles Beans
Huitlacoche Corn fungus, "Mexican truffles"
Jitomate Tomato
Lechuga Lettuce
Lentejas Lentils
Nopales Prickly pear fronds
Papas Potatoes
Pepino Cucumber
Rajas Strips of mild green poblano pepper
Zanahoria Carrot

FRUITS (FRUTA) AND JUICE (JUGO)

Albaricoque/chabacano Apricot
Cherimoya Custard apple (sweetsop)
Ciruela Plum
Coco Coconut
Durazno Peach
Frambuesa Raspberry
Fresa Strawberry
Guanábana Soursop
Guayaba Guava
Higo Fig
Limón Lime
Mamey Large fruit with sweet pink flesh
Melón Melon
Naranja Orange
Papaya Papaya
Piña Pineapple
Pitahaya Dragonfruit, a type of cactus fruit
Plátano Banana/plantain
Sandía Watermelon
Toronja Grapefruit
Tuna Prickly pear fruit
Uva Grape
Zapote Sapodilla, fruit of the chicle tree

SWEETS (DULCES)

Ate Quince paste
Cajeta… Caramel confection often served with...
…crepas ...pancakes
…churros ...cinnamon fritters
Ensalada de frutas Fruit salad
Flan Crème caramel
Helado Ice cream
Nieve Sorbet

Glossary

Ahorita diminutive of ahora (now) meaning "right now" – but seldom applied as literally as a visitor might expect.
Alameda city park or promenade; large plaza.
Ayuntamiento town hall/government.
Aztec the empire that dominated the central valleys of Mexico from the thirteenth century until defeated by Cortés.
Barrio area within a town or city; suburb.
Camino blanco unpaved rural road, so called because it is paved with limestone gravel.
Camioneta small truck or van.
Cantina bar, traditionally men-only, but increasingly open to women.
Cenote underground water source in the Yucatán, a natural sinkhole in the limestone surface.
Chac Maya god of rain.
Chac-mool recumbent statue, possibly a sacrificial figure or messenger to the gods.
Comal large, round flat plate made of clay or metal used for cooking tortillas.
Comedor cheap restaurant, literally dining room; also called a cocina económica.
Convento either convent or monastery.
CTM central union organization.
Cuauhtémoc the last Aztec leader, commander of the final resistance to Cortés, and a national hero.
Descompuesto out of order.
Don/Doña courtesy titles (sir/madam), mostly used in letters or for professional people or the boss.
Ejido communal farmland.
Enramadas palapa-covered restaurants.
EPR Ejército Popular Revolucionario, the Popular Revolutionary Army. Guerrilla group, not allied to the Zapatistas; their first appearance was in Guerrero in 1996.
EZLN Ejército Zapatista de Liberación Nacional, the Zapatista Army of National Liberation.
Feria fair (market).
Finca ranch or plantation.
FONART government agency to promote crafts.
Fonda simple restaurant or boarding house.
FONATUR government tourism agency.
Fray Spanish word for friar.
Gringo not necessarily insulting, though it does imply North American – said to come from invading US troops, either because they wore green coats or because they sang "Green grow the rushes oh!..."
Guayabera embroidered Cuban-style shirt, usually for men.
Güera/o blonde – very frequently used description of Westerners, especially shouted after women in the street; again, not usually intended as an insult.
Hacendado plantation owner.
Hacienda plantation estate or the big house on it.
Henequen a variety of agave cactus grown mainly in Yucatán, the fibres of which are used to make rope.
Huipil Maya women's embroidered white smock dress or blouse, worn over a white petticoat, usually with a small checkered scarf.
Huitzilopochtli Aztec god of war.
I.V.A. fifteen percent value-added tax (VAT).
Kukulkán Maya name for Quetzalcoatl, the plumed serpent god.
Ladino as applied to people, means Spanish-influenced; determined entirely by clothing (and culture) rather than physical race.
Licenciado a common title, literally meaning "graduate" or "licensed"; abbreviated Lic.
Malecón seafront promenade.
Malinche Cortés' interpreter and mistress, a symbol of treachery.
Mariachi quintessentially Mexican music, with lots of brass and sentimental lyrics.
Marimba xylophone-like musical instrument, also used of the bands based around it; derives from northern Mexico.
Maya people who inhabited Honduras, Belize, Guatemala and southeastern Mexico from earliest times, and still do.
Mestizo mixed ethnic background.
Metate flat stone for grinding corn; used with a mano, a grinding stone.
Milpa a small subsistence farm plot, usually tended with slash-and-burn agricultural practices.
Mirador lookout point.
Mixtec people from the mountains of Oaxaca.
Moctezuma Montezuma, the leader of the Aztec empire when the Spanish arrived in Mexico.
Muelle jetty or dock.
NAFTA the North American Free Trade Agreement including Mexico, the US and Canada; see also TLC below.
Nahuatl ancient Aztec language, still the most common after Spanish.
Norteño literally northern – style of food and music.
Palacio mansion, but not necessarily royal.
Palacio de Gobierno headquarters of state/federal authorities.
Palacio municipal headquarters of local government.
Palapa palm thatch. Used to describe any thatched/palm-roofed hut.
Palenque cockpit (for cockfights).
PAN Partido de Acción Nacional (National Action Party), conservative party that first took power in 2000.

Paseo a broad avenue, but also the ritual evening walk around the plaza.

PEMEX the Mexican national oil company.

Planta baja ground floor – abbreviated PB in lifts.

Porfiriato the three decades of Porfirio Díaz's dictatorship.

PRD Partido Revolucionario Democrático (Party of the Democratic Revolution), the left-wing opposition formed and led by Cuauhtémoc Cárdenas.

PRI Partido Revolucionario Institucional (Party of the Institutional Revolution), the ruling party for eighty years, until the PAN upset in 2000.

PT Partido del Trabajo (Workers' Party), small party but with opposition seats in Congress.

PVEM Partido Verde Ecologista de México (Green Party), small opposition party.

Quetzalcoatl the plumed serpent, most powerful, enigmatic and widespread of all ancient Mexican gods.

Romería procession.

Sacbé ancient Maya road, paved with limestone; plural sacbeob.

Stele freestanding carved monument; plural steles.

Tenochtitlán the Aztec capital, on the site of Mexico City.

Teotihuacán ancient city north of the capital – the first major urban power of central Mexico.

Tianguis Nahuatl word for market, still used of particularly varied marketplaces.

Tlaloc Toltec/Aztec rain god.

TLC Tratado de Libre Comercio, the Spanish name for NAFTA (see above).

Toltec tribe which controlled central Mexico between Teotihuacán and the Aztecs.

Tope speed-bump or other barrier on rural roads for slowing traffic.

Trova romantic Yucatecan song style popular in the early twentieth century, still played by trovadores.

Tula the Toltec capital.

Tzompantli Aztec skull rack or "wall of skulls".

Virreinal from the period of the Spanish viceroys – ie colonial.

Wetback derogatory term for illegal Mexican (or any Hispanic) in the US; mojado ("wet") is the Spanish slang term, without the negative connotations.

Zapotec tribe which controlled the Oaxaca region to about 700 AD.

Zócalo the main plaza of any town.

Small print and index

A ROUGH GUIDE TO ROUGH GUIDES

Published in 1982, the first Rough Guide – to Greece – was a student scheme that became a publishing phenomenon. Mark Ellingham, a recent graduate in English from Bristol University, had been travelling in Greece the previous summer and couldn't find the right guidebook. With a small group of friends he wrote his own guide, combining a contemporary, journalistic style with a thoroughly practical approach to travellers' needs.

The immediate success of the book spawned a series that rapidly covered dozens of destinations. And, in addition to impecunious backpackers, Rough Guides soon acquired a much broader readership that relished the guides' wit and inquisitiveness as much as their enthusiastic, critical approach and value-for-money ethos. These days, Rough Guides include recommendations from budget to luxury and cover more than 120 destinations around the globe, from Amsterdam to Zanzibar, all regularly updated by our team of roaming writers.

Browse all our latest guides, read inspirational features and book your trip at **roughguides.com**.

Rough Guide credits
Editor: Beth Williams
Cartography: Carte
Picture Editor: Piotr Kala
Picture Manager: Tom Smyth
Layout: Pradeep Thapliyal
Publishing Technology Manager: Rebeka Davies
Production Operations Manager: Katie Bennett
Head of Publishing: Sarah Clark

Publishing information
Thirteenth edition 2025

Distribution
UK, Ireland and Europe
Apa Publications (UK) Ltd; mail@roughguides.com
United States and Canada
Two Rivers; ips@ingramcontent.com
Australia and New Zealand
Woodslane; info@woodslane.com.au
Worldwide
Apa Publications (UK) Ltd; mail@roughguides.com

Special Sales, Content Licensing and CoPublishing
Rough Guides can be purchased in bulk quantities at discounted prices. We can create special editions, personalized jackets and corporate imprints tailored to your needs. mail@roughguides.com.

roughguides.com

EU Representative
LOGOS EUROPE, 9 rue Nicolas Poussin, 17000, LA ROCHELLE, France; Contact@logoseurope.eu; +33 (0) 667937378

Printed by Elma Basim in Turkey

ISBN: 9781835292365

This book was produced using **Typefi** automated publishing software.

A catalogue record for this book is available from the British Library.

Help us update
We've gone to a lot of effort to ensure that this edition of **The Rough Guide to Mexico** is accurate and up-to-date. However, things change – places get "discovered", transport routes are altered, restaurants and hotels raise prices or lower standards, and businesses cease trading. If you feel we've got it wrong or left something out, we'd like to know, and if you can direct us to the web address, so much the better.

Please send your comments with the subject line "**Rough Guide Mexico Update**" to mail@roughguides.com. We'll send a copy of the next edition (or any other Rough Guide if you prefer) for the very best emails.

Acknowledgements

Robert Savage: Thank you to Alex Carrillo for your continued help on the ground, for this and previous editions of the guide. Thanks also to my editor Beth Williams and to my husband, Mohamed Bounaim.

ABOUT THE AUTHOR
Robert Savage is a Yorkshire-born travel writer who lives in St Petersburg, Florida. He was inspired to pursue a career in travel writing at Durham University, under the tutelage of Chancellor Bill Bryson. Robert has covered Mexico for Rough Guides since 2018, has contributed to the Guardian, Le Monde and Der Spiegal, and has written more than twenty guidebooks, a number of which are housed in the permanent collections of the British Library, and Oxford and Cambridge University libraries. When he's not on the road chasing a commission with his beloved dogs Rufus and Harper, you'll find him in London catching up with the British Guild of Travel Writers.

Photo credits

(Key: T-top; C-centre; B-bottom; L-left; R-right)

All images **iStock** and **Shutterstock**

Cover: Iglesia De Santa Lucia Church in San Cristobal de las Casas, Chiapas **Ayumi Yamashita/iStock**

Index

A

B

C

D

H

I

J

K

L

M

N

O

P

Q

R

S

T

V

Z

Map symbols

The symbols below are used on maps throughout the book

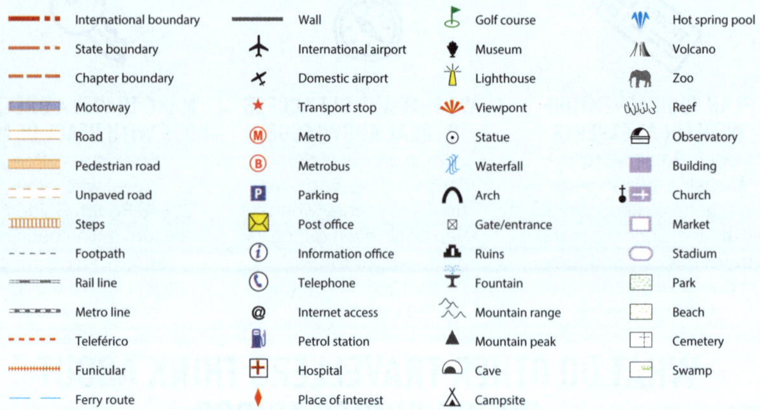

Listings key

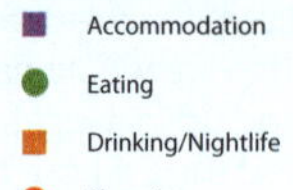

Samsonite